Who's Who
in the
People's Republic
of China

中华人民
共和国
人名录

Who's Who in the People's Republic of China

by Wolfgang Bartke

M. E. SHARPE INC. PUBLISHER
Armonk, New York

 A PUBLICATION OF THE INSTITUTE OF ASIAN AFFAIRS IN HAMBURG

A publication of the Institute of Asian Affairs, Hamburg

The Institute of Asian Affairs pursues and promotes research on contemporary Asian affairs. It cooperates with other Institutes of regional studies in Hamburg which together form the Foundation German Overseas Institute.

Opinions expressed in the publications of the Institute of Asian Affairs are the authors'. They do not necessarily reflect those of the Institute.

Research work on this book was financially supported by the Deutsche Forschungsgemeinschaft, Bonn.

English translation by Franciscus Verellen

Library of Congress Cataloging in Publication Data

Bartke, Wolfgang.
   Who's Who in the People's Republic of China.

   Title also in Chinese: Chung-hua jen min kung ho kuo jen ming lu.
   "A Publication of the Institute of Asian Affairs, Hamburg."
   1. China—History—1949–1976—Biography.
2. China—History—1976–   —Biography. 3. China—Biography.
I. Title. II. Title: Chung-hua jen min kung ho kuo jen ming lu.
DS778.A1B33   920'.051   80-27599
ISBN: 0-87332-183-9

Contents

Preface

One difficulty in compiling this *Who's Who in the People's Republic of China* stems from China's reluctance to disclose biographical data. After 1962 and until very recently, even the most important new appointments and dismissals were for the most part not officially announced. Only lists of new members of organizations are published at the end of Party and National People's Congresses, while in 1975 not even the names of the deputies to the Fourth National People's Congress were revealed. Although a better press coverage resulted from the opening of China in mid-1978, the extent to which secrecy prevails is made clear by the fact that even the name of Chairman Hua Guofeng's wife is not publicly known.

A systematic recording of personnel data requires a daily scanning of the Chinese press for references to personalities and their relevant posts, a laborious process, but the only one available to the observer of the Chinese leadership structure collecting biographical data. The compiler of these biographies started his systematic recording of these data in 1958. During the following two decades a personnel file containing 54,000 names and a file of 6,500 organizations developed. Since on the average about 1,000 data are recorded each month, the complete file contains a quarter of a million individual data. The information presented in this volume covering events after 1958 is based on these files. He drew primarily from the daily Chinese press, using such sources as *Renmin ribao*, Xinhua News Agency dispatches, and reports from the Summary of World Broadcasts of the BBC. Unofficial sources, such as the extensive Red Guard publications of the Cultural Revolution period, were not used. Pre-1958 information, including data on the pre-1949 period, based on PRC sources, was collected in Taiwan archives during two research visits and, in addition, drawn extensively from the publications of the Biographical Service of the Union Research Institute in Hong Kong.

Pre-1949 information is presented as a continuous text at the beginning of individual biographies in order to distinguish it clearly from the official post-October 1949 data, which are arranged chronologically by year and month.

Who's Who in the People's Republic of China is intended as a reference guide to the current active leadership of China. Within this limitation, clearly defined groups of cadres were included, and these are listed in the "Standards for Inclusion" on page xi. Cadres already deceased or who have disappeared were excluded, but in deference to the dramatic changes, human and political, that have occurred in China over the last several years (the deaths of Mao Zedong, Zhou Enlai, and Zhu De all in 1976, for example), a small number of biographies of deceased or purged leaders whose political significance reaches into the present is included in the section "Biographies of Important Deceased and Purged Cadres."

Military ranks were abolished in the hierarchy of the People's Liberation Army in 1965. Insofar as they are available, however, they have been included in the biographies because they continue to provide information on the structure of the military leadership.

Certain inaccuracies are inherent in an extensive reliance on the daily Chinese press. Thus, for example, cadres disappear from the press for reasons unknown. A rule of thumb, derived from more than twenty years of observing the structure of the Chinese leadership, suggests that a leading cadre may be considered purged if he or she has not publicly appeared for one year. Consequently, most of the biographies in this volume are of those cadres who have been mentioned in the press since August 1978.

In this connection it is worth noting that the writing of *Who's Who in the People's Republic of China* was begun in 1975. At that time, Mao Zedong and Zhou Enlai were alive, and the country's personnel policy was determined by the now reviled "Gang of Four." As the compilation of the *Who's Who* centered on predetermined leadership groups, 1,030 biographies had to be deleted in the course of time as a result of extensive purges. By and large they were replaced by reactivated cadres who had held ranking posts before the Cultural Revolution.

The present *Who's Who in the People's Republic of*

China is the first to include photographs. The majority of these photos have been taken from the Chinese press. Even though their quality in many instances falls short of normal standards for reproduction, it was felt that a bad photo is better than none at all.

To render the biographies more readable, certain cumbersome terms were abbreviated. For example, the *All-China* Federation of Trade Unions is referred to as "Federation of Trade Unions." Since the book deals with China, it seemed permissible to dispense with "All-China" in this and other instances.

For all those who are not yet acquainted with the *pinyin* transcription, a list of all names alphabetized in the Wade-Giles transcription has been included on pages 717-729.

Throughout the book only a few abbreviations have been used, and they are recorded in the "List of Abbreviations" on page xii. Other terms occurring several times in a biography have been written out on their first occurrence, with their abbreviations used in subsequent occurrences.

There are three types of references introducing new posts obtained by a cadre:
1. Government officials, such as ministers, ambassadors, etc., and military officers are *appointed*;
2. Party cadres and cadres of mass organizations and of the provincial administrations are *elected* (the higher cadres always after approval by the central leadership);
3. *Identified* indicates that a cadre was first recognized as holding the post at the given date, although his or her actual appointment or election may have occurred some time previously.

In order to keep individual biographies within manageable proportions, some categories of activities, particularly those pertaining to domestic affairs, were not included. For instance, the signing of a trade agreement with a foreign trade delegation visiting Beijing by one of the vice-ministers of foreign trade is a routine activity not meriting a separate entry; another example is the visit of the secretary of the Yunnan Province CP to Sichuan Province, again an activity which does not significantly contribute to our information on the rank or career of the cadre in question.

Each biography is preceded by a list of posts held as of March 1980, when work on biographies in this volume was completed. They are arranged in the following order: Party, Government, National

People's Congress, Military (including the ranks abolished in 1965), Provincial Administration, Mass Organizations, and Others. This enables the reader to size up at a glance the present influence of a cadre.

It should be noted that publications by personalities treated in this book are only mentioned if they appeared in the official source material used and that Chinese characters for about twenty-four names were not obtainable.

The sustained value of this reference work is of course restricted by the constant shifting of personalities characteristic, to various extents, of the leadership of all countries. China had a relatively stable leadership from the foundation of the People's Republic in 1949 until the beginning of the Cultural Revolution in 1966. The Cultural Revolution was a phase of extreme instability. Between 1966 and 1968 two thirds of the former elite were purged; many additional military leaders were purged in the wake of the Lin Biao affair in 1971. The period from 1973 on saw essentially a process of rehabilitation of those cadres who disappeared during the Cultural Revolution. This process temporarily came to a halt after the death of Zhou Enlai in January 1976 but was revived with the purge of the so-called "Gang of Four" and its supporters. As a result, roughly three quarters of those two thirds of all cadres who had been purged during the Cultural Revolution had been rehabilitated as of this writing: The majority had returned to office, while some were awaiting their reappointments. On the whole, the process of rehabilitation may, with the exception of a few latecomers, be considered completed. The period of personnel change was in any case succeeded in 1979 by a renewed phase of stability, comparable to the period of 1949 to 1966. This situation may be assumed to last at least as long as the present leadership with Hua Guofeng, Deng Xiaoping, Ye Jianying, and Li Xiannian remains in control. Although the Twelfth Party Congress and the Sixth National People's Congress will add a number of corrective alterations, they are not expected to bring any significant changes.

On 29 February 1980, Xinhua reported, "The Fifth Plenary Session of the Eleventh Central Committee of the CCP decided to approve the resignations of Comrades Wang Dongxing, Ji Dengkui, Wu De, and Chen Xilian and decided to remove and proposed to remove them from their leading Party and state posts." Following this report I put these four cadres into the section of "Biographies of Important Deceased and Purged Cadres." Subsequent developments proved this to be a mistake. At the memorial meeting for Liu Shaoqi on 17 May 1980, all of them were named as members of the CCP

Central Committee. "Leading Party posts" obviously means the Politburo, which in reality, of course, is the only leading body, in the sense of a decision-making organ, in the People's Republic of China.

As of March 1980, twenty-seven of the twenty-nine provinces and municipalities with provincial status had already elected their new provincial governments; only Jilin Province and Tianjin Municipality had not done so at the time. Therefore, the leading cadres included in the biographies for those two bodies are still the ones of their respective revolutionary committees. It was not until April and June 1980, respectively, that Jilin Province and Tianjin Municipality elected their people's governments, too. Therefore, the Appendix, "The Organization of the People's Republic of China," work on which extended to August 1980, contains the data for the newly elected provincial leadership.

In August 1980, after work on the Appendix in this volume was completed, the Third Session of the Fifth National People's Congress was convened in Beijing. *Beijing Review* of September 15, 1980 (No. 37), reported the leadership changes as follows:

> —Chairman Hua Guofeng of the C.P.C. Central Committee will no longer hold the post of Premier of the State Council;

> —Zhao Ziyang is now Premier of the State Council;

> —Deng Xiaoping, Li Xiannian, Chen Yun, Xu Xiangqian and Wang Zhen who are advanced in age will no longer hold the posts of Vice-Premiers of the State Council;

> —Wang Renzhong, who has taken up an important post in the Party, also will give up his Vice-Premiership;

> —Chen Yonggui was relieved of his post as Vice-Premier upon his own request;

> —The session decided on the appointment of Yang Jingren, Zhang Aiping and Huang Hua as Vice-Premiers of the State Council;

> —The session approved the resignation of Nie Rongzhen, Liu Bocheng, Zhang Dingcheng, Cai Chang and Zhou Jianren as Vice-Chairmen of the Standing Committee of the Fifth National People's Congress, and elected Peng Chong, Xi Zhongxun, Su Yu, Yang Shangkun and Bainqen Erdini Qoigyi Gyaincain as additional Vice-Chairmen of the Standing Committee of the National People's Congress.

I am grateful to all those who have lent their indispensable help in completing this book: Mechthild Warmbier carried the burden of typing the manuscript. She has been particularly conscientious and patient in modifying the Chinese names to the new *pinyin* transliteration and adding numerous revisions to the earlier version of the manuscript. A debt is also owed to Waldtraut Jarke, Anneliese Kalweit, Gudrun Hanke, Maike Engel, and Manfred Saller. I would also like to thank Professor Klaus Mehnert for his friendly support. Last but not least, my thanks go to Franciscus Verellen who translated the biographies into English and to Douglas Merwin of M.E. Sharpe, Inc. for his numerous suggestions and painstaking efforts in the final stages of preparation of this volume.

Wolfgang Bartke
Fischerhude, August 1980

Standards for inclusion

The officials holding the posts listed below are included in this volume. A separate section (pp. 571-593) contains "Biographies of Important Deceased and Purged Cadres."

Central Level

CCP	Politburo	Members, Alternative Members
	Central Committee	Members, Alternative Members
	Secretariat	General Secretary, Members
	Departments	Directors, Deputy Directors
	Military Commission	All Cadres
	Party School	President, Vice-presidents
Government	State Council	Premier, Vice-premiers
	Commissions	Ministers, Vice-ministers
	Ministries	Ministers, Vice-ministers
	Foreign Ministry, Departments	Directors, Deputy Directors
	Embassies	Ambassadors
	Others State Organs	Directors, Deputy Directors

National People's Congress — Chairman, Vice-chairmen, Members, Standing Committee

Supreme People's Court — President, Vice-presidents

Supreme People's Procuratorate — Chief Procurator, Deputy Chief Procurators

Chinese People's Political Consultative Conference — Chairman, Vice-chairmen

Military, General Staff — Chief of Staff, Deputy Chiefs of Staff

	Departments	Director, Deputy Directors
	Services	Commanders, Deputy Commanders
	Military Schools	Commandants, Deputy Commandants

Mass Organizations

	Noncommunist Parties	Chairmen, Vice-chairmen
	Political Organizations	Chairmen, Vice-chairmen

Sports Organizations — Presidents, Vice-presidents

Scientific and Other Organizations — Presidents, Vice-presidents

Below Central Level

Military Regions — Commanders, Deputy Commanders, 1st Political Commissars

Military Districts — Commanders, 1st Political Commissars

Provinces	CCP	1st Secretaries, Secretaries
	Administration	Governor, Vice-governors

The Science Apparatus

Academy of Sciences		President, Vice-presidents
	Institutes	Directors, Deputy Directors
Academy of Social Sciences		President, Vice-presidents
	Institutes	Directors, Deputy Directors
Other Central Academies		Presidents, Vice-presidents
	Institutes	Directors, Deputy Directors
Universities		Presidents, Vice-presidents
Institutes		Directors, Deputy Directors
Colleges		Directors, Deputy Directors

List of abbreviations and a note on romanization

CCP	Chinese Communist Party	NCNA	New China News Agency
CP	Communist Party	NPC	National People's Congress
CPPCC	Chinese People's Political	PLA	People's Liberation Army
	Consultative Conference	PRC	People's Republic of China
GMRB	Guangming Ribao (Guangming Daily)	RMRB	Renmin Ribao (People's Daily)
HQ	Hong Qi (Red Flag)	XNA	Xinhua News Agency
KMT	Kuomintang		

The *pinyin* system of romanization, which was officially introduced in the People's Republic of China on January 1, 1979, for transcribing Chinese names in foreign-language publications, is used throughout this book. Thus, for example, Peking is now Beijing and Canton is Guangzhou. Exceptions are the Chinese names of individuals, institutions, and places outside the People's Republic of China— Chiang Kai-shek, Kuomintang, and Hong Kong for

example. Geographical names are always presented in their *pinyin* form, e.g., Huang He instead of Yellow River and Chang Jiang instead of Yangtse River.

For those more familiar with the Wade-Giles system of romanization, a Wade-Giles/Pinyin Conversion Table appears in the Appendix, and the Wade-Giles transcription appears in parentheses after the *pinyin* version in each of the biographical entries.

中华人民
共和国
人名录

Biographies

Amudong Niyazi (Hamdinnyas) 阿木冬尼牙致

Posts held

CCP
Member of the Commission for Inspecting Discipline under the CCP Central Committee
Member of the Standing Committee, Xinjiang Autonomous Region CP
1st secretary, Ürümqi Municipality CP

Government
Member of the State Nationalities Affairs Commission

NPC
Vice-chairman of the NPC Nationalities Committee

Provincial Administration
Vice-chairman of the People's Government of Xinjiang Autonomous Region

1973,	May	Identified as a cadre in Xinjiang
1977,	Aug	Identified as 1st secretary, Ürümqi Municipality CP
1978,	Feb	Elected vice-chairman of the Revolutionary Committee of Xinjiang (until Aug 1979)
	May	Appointed vice-chairman of the Preparatory Committee for the 10th Congress of the Communist Youth League
	Jun	Identified as member of the Standing Committee, Xinjiang Autonomous Region CP
	Dec	Appointed member of the Commission for Inspecting Discipline under the CCP Central Committee
1979,	May	Appointed member of the State Nationalities Affairs Commission
	Sep	Elected vice-chairman of the People's Government, Xinjiang Autonomous Region; head of a youth and students delegation to Pakistan
	Oct	Identified as vice-chairman of the NPC Nationalities Committee

An Faqian (An Fa-ch'ien) 安法乾

Posts held

Government
Vice-minister of commerce

An is a native of Pingyuan Province. Toward the end of the revolutionary period he worked in the People's Government of Shanxi-Chahar-Shandong-Henan Border Region.

1950,	Jul	Appointed council member of the Pingyuan Provincial People's Government
1954,	Jul	Identified as member of the Federation of Supply and Marketing Cooperatives
1957,	Sep	Appointed assistant minister of food industry
1960,	Sep	Appointed vice-minister of food industry
1967		Disappears during Cultural Revolution
1976,	May	First appearance after the Cultural Revolution; identified as vice-minister of commerce

An Gang (An Kang) 安岗

Posts held

CCP
Deputy editor-in-chief of RMRB

Others
Director of the Institute of Journalism, Academy of Social Sciences

1953		Identified as a correspondent of RMRB
1960,	Mar	Identified as secretary of the Journalists Association (until Cultural Revolution)
	Jun	Identified as deputy editor-in-chief of RMRB (until Cultural Revolution)
1976,	Jan	First appearance after the Cultural Revolution
	May	Identified as holding his previous post as deputy editor-in-chief of RMRB
1979,	Jul	Identified as director of the Institute of Journalism, Academy of Social Sciences

An Pingsheng (An P'ing-sheng) 安平生

Posts held

CCP
Member of the CCP 11th Central Committee
1st CP secretary, Yunnan Province

NPC
Deputy for Yunnan Province to the 5th NPC

Provincial Administration
Chairman of the People's Congress, Yunnan Province

1953,	Nov	Identified as deputy director, Rural Work Department, South China Office of the CCP Central Committee, and as secretary-general of the Guangdong People's Government
1954,	Aug	Elected deputy for Guangdong Province to the 1st NPC
1955,	Dec	Identified as director, Office of Agriculture, Forestry and Water Conservancy, Guangdong Provincial Administration
1956,	Jul	Identified as director, Rural Work Department, Guangdong CP (until Feb 1958)
	Aug	Identified as vice-governor of Guangdong (until Jul 1961)
1960,	Apr	Identified as member, CP Guangdong Standing Committee
1961,	Jul	Identified as CP secretary and vice-chairman of Guangxi Autonomous Region
1967,	Jan	An's removal from his office as CP secretary of the Autonomous Region as reported by Radio Guangxi is not confirmed by Beijing
1968,	Aug	On establishment of the Autonomous Region's Revolutionary Committee, An is elected vice-chairman (until Jan 1976)
1971,	Feb	On reestablishment of the CP Secretariat of Guangxi Autonomous Region, An is elected deputy secretary (until Aug 1973)
1973,	Aug	Elected to first term as member of the

Central Committee by the 10th CCP Congress. Identified as CP secretary of Guangxi Autonomous Region (until Dec 1975)

1973, Dec Identified as leading member of the Sino-Vietnamese Friendship Association

1975, Dec Identified as 1st CP secretary of Guangxi Autonomous Region (until Jan 1977)

1976, Mar Identified as chairman, Revolutionary Committee of Guangxi Autonomous Region (until Jan 1977)

Apr Identified as 1st political commissar, Guangxi Military District (until Jan 1977)

1977, Feb 1st CP secretary, chairman of Yunnan Province Revolutionary Committee (until Dec 1979), 1st political commissar (until Feb 1979) and 1st CP secretary of Kunming Military District (until Jan 1979), and 1st political commissar of Yunnan Military District

1978, Feb Elected deputy for Yunnan Province to the 5th NPC

1979, May Head of an agricultural delegation to Japan

Dec Elected chairman of the People's Congress of Yunnan Province

An Qiyuan (An Ch'i-yüan)   安启元

Posts held

Government
Deputy director of the State Seismological Bureau

1977, Oct Identified as deputy director of the State Seismological Bureau

1978, Jul Head of a seismological delegation to Japan

An Shiwei (An Shih-wei)   安士伟

Posts held

Others
Member of the Standing Committee of the 5th CPPCC
Akhun of the Dongsi Mosque in Beijing

1959, Feb Identified as imam of a mosque in Beijing (until Cultural Revolution)

1975, Sep First appearance after the Cultural Revolution

1978, Mar Elected a member of the Standing Committee of the 5th CPPCC

1979, Oct Head of Chinese Moslems pilgrimage to Mecca

An Zhiwen (An Chih-wen)   安志文

Posts held

Provincial Administration
Vice-chairman of the Revolutionary Committee of Jilin Province

An was born in 1919 in Shanxi Province.

1950 Identified as deputy director of the Research Office in the Northeast China Bureau of the CCP Central Committee

Apr Member of the Cultural and Educational Committee of the Northeast China People's Government (until Nov 1952) and deputy director of the Industry Department of the Northeast China Government (until Nov 1952)

1952, Nov Appointed member of the State Planning Commission (until Oct 1954)

1954, Nov Identified as vice-chairman of the State Construction Commission (until Feb 1958)

1958, Sep Appointed vice-chairman of the State Planning Commission (until Cultural Revolution)

1959, Apr Elected member of the Standing Committee of the 3rd CPPCC

1977, Dec First appearance after the Cultural Revolution: Elected vice-chairman of the Revolutionary Committee of Jilin Province

1978, Oct Deputy head of a machine building delegation to Romania, Yugoslavia, Italy, Switzerland, the Federal Republic of Germany (head: Zhou Zijian)

An Zhiyuan (An Chih-yüan)   安致远

Posts held

Government
Former first permanent representative of the PRC Permanent Mission to the UN in Geneva

1963, Sep Identified as deputy director of the International Transport Office at the Ministry of Railways (until 1964)

1965, Mar Identified as secretary of the Chinese embassy in the USSR (until Aug 1971)

1971, Nov Member of the Chinese delegation to the UN General Assembly

1972, Jan Standing PRC representative at the UN (until May 1972)

Aug Identified as director of the Department for International Organizations and Conferences, Treaties and Laws at the Ministry of Foreign Affairs (until 1975)

1973, Mar Leader of the Chinese delegation to the Economic Commission for Asia and the Far East (ECAFE) session in Tokyo

1974, Sep Member of the Chinese delegation to the 29th UN General Assembly

1975, Oct Identified as first permanent representative of the PRC Permanent Mission to the UN in Geneva (until Feb 1980)

1976, Jul Head of the Chinese delegation to the 61st session of the UN Economic and Social Council in Abidjan, Ivory Coast

1977, Mar Head of the Chinese delegation to the UN "Common fund for integrated commodity program" Conference in Geneva

Jun Head of the Chinese delegation to the 24th UN Development Program (UNDP) Conference in Geneva

1978, Mar Head of the Chinese delegation to the UN Law of the Sea Conference

Nov Member of the Chinese delegation to the UN Conference on Common Fund

1979,   Sep Head of the Chinese delegation to the UN Conference on Prohibitions or Restrictions of the Use of Certain Conventional Weapons

An Ziwen (An Tzu-wen)　　安子文

Posts held

CCP
Member of the CCP 11th Central Committee
Vice-president of the Party School under the CCP Central Committee

NPC
Deputy for Peking Municipality to the 5th NPC
Vice-chairman of the Legal Commission under the Standing Committee, 5th NPC

An was born in Hunan Province in 1909. After studying in the USSR he was the personal secretary of Mao Zedong in the mid-30s. During the Anti-Japanese War he was secretary-general of the Headquarters of the 8th Route Army. In 1942 he was identified as a cadre of Shanyin (Daiyue) CP, Shanxi Province. In 1946 An became head of the Organization Department of the CCP Central Committee, a post he soon relinquished to Ren Bishi. He then continued to serve as deputy director of the department. In September 1949 he attended the 1st Congress of the CPPCC as a delegate for the CCP.

1949,   Oct Elected council member of the newly established Sino-Soviet Friendship Association
         Dec Appointed member of the People's Control Commission of the Government Administration Council (until Jan 1951)
1950,   Sep Appointed minister of personnel (until Oct 1954)
         Oct Appointed acting director of the Organization Department of the CCP Central Committee following the death of Ren Bishi (until Aug 1952)
1952,   Aug Appointed deputy director of the Labor

Employment Committee

1953,   Feb Appointed member of the Committee for Drafting the Election Law
1954,   Apr Appointed acting director of the Organization Department of the CCP Central Committee following the purge of Rao Shushi (until Nov 1957)
         Dec Delegate representing the CCP at the 2nd Congress of the CPPCC
1956,   Sep Elected member of the CCP Central Committee by the 8th Party Congress
1957,   Nov Appointed director of the Organization Department of the CCP Central Committee
1958,   May Member of a CCP delegation led by Dong Biwu 7th Congress of the CP Bulgaria
         Jun Member of the same delegation attending the 11th Congress of the CP Czechoslovakia
         Jul Member of the same delegation attending the 5th Congress of the Socialist Unity Party of Germany (SED) in the German Democratic Republic
1959,   Apr Delegate representing the CCP at the 3rd Congress of the CPPCC
         Dec An publishes an article in the ideological journal HQ on "People's Communes and the CCP"
1964,   Sep An publishes an article in the journal HQ on "The Training of Revolutionary Successors"
1965,   Jan Elected member of the Standing Committee of the CPPCC
1967,   Sep Denounced as a counterrevolutionary revisionist and purged
1978,   Dec First appearance after the Cultural Revolution
1979,   Feb Appointed vice-chairman of the Legal Commission under the NPC Standing Committee
         May By-elected deputy for Peking Municipality to the 5th NPC; identified as vice-president and deputy secretary of the Party School under the CCP Central Committee
         Jun Vice-chairman of the Draft Laws Committee, 2nd Session of the 5th NPC
         Sep By-elected member of the CCP by the 4th Plenary Session of the 11th Central Committee

Ba-dai (Pa Tai) 巴 岱

Posts held

NPC
Deputy for Xinjiang Autonomous Region to the 5th NPC

Provincial Administration
Vice-chairman of the People's Government of Xinjiang Autonomous Region

Ba-dai belongs to the Mongolian minority.

1964, Apr Identified as chairman of Bayingolin Autonomous Zhou in Xinjiang

1978, Feb Elected vice-chairman of the Revolutionary Committee of Xinjiang Autonomous Region (until Aug 1979) and deputy for this autonomous region to the 5th NPC

1979, Jul Appointed member of the National Games Organization Committee

Sep Elected vice-chairman of the People's Government of Xinjiang Autonomous Region

Ba Jin (Pa Chin) 巴 金

Posts held

NPC
Member of the Standing Committee of the 5th NPC
Deputy for Shanghai Municipality to the 5th NPC

Others
Vice-chairman of the Federation of Literary and Art Circles
Member of the Executive Committee of the Welfare Institute
1st vice-chairman of the Writers' Association

Ba was born in 1904 under the name Li Yaotang as the son of a landlord in Chengdu, Sichuan Province. He completed his school education in 1925 at a middle school affiliated with Southeastern University and subsequently attended the Foreign Language School in Chengdu. In 1926 he continued his studies in France. There he changed his name to Ba Jin, composed of the first syllable of Bakunin and the last syllable of Kropotkin, two anarchist writers whom he admired. In 1928 he returned to Chengdu as editor of the fortnightly Ban Yue. At the end of that year he went to Shanghai as a writer and translator. He visited Japan in 1934. In 1935 he became chief editor of the Shanghai Cultural Life Publishing House. In the following year he joined the China Literary Work Society organized by Lu Xun. In 1937 he was co-editor with Mao Dun of the Shouting Weekly and Bonfire Weekly. During the following years he was engaged in literary work in Kunming, Chongqing, and Guilin. In July 1949 he was elected a member of the Standing Committee of the Association of Literary Workers, as well as member of the Federation of Literary and Art Circles. In September of that year he took part in the 1st CPPCC which elected him a member.

1950, Oct Appointed member of the Cultural and Educational Commission of the Government Administration Council (until Sep 1954)

Nov Ba attends the 2nd World Peace Congress in Warsaw

1952, Apr Head of a delegation of literary workers to North Korea

1953, Feb Elected vice-chairman of the Union of Chinese Writers

1954, Aug Elected deputy for Sichuan Province to the 1st NPC (reelected in 1958 to the 2nd NPC)

1955, May Ba directs the anti-Hu Feng campaign in East China

1957, May Identified as chief editor of Renmin Wenxue (People's Literature) (until 1958)

Oct Member of a delegation to the 40th anniversary celebrations of the October Revolution in Moscow

1958, Jul Elected member of the National Committee of the Committee for World Peace

Sep Identified as chairman of the Shanghai Branch of the Union of Writers

Oct Deputy head of a delegation to the Afro-Asian Writers Conference in Tashkent

1959, Jul Identified as vice-chairman of the Shanghai Branch, Sino-Soviet Friendship Association

Oct Identified as council member of the Sino-German Friendship Association

1960, Aug Identified as vice-chairman of the Federation of Literary and Art Circles

1961, Mar Member of a delegation of literary workers to Japan

Nov Identified as chief editor of Shanghai Wenxue (Shanghai Literature) monthly

1962, Jul Head of a delegation to the 8th World Conference against Atomic Bombs in Japan

1963, Nov Head of a delegation of literary workers to Japan

1964, Sep Elected deputy for Shanghai Municipality to the 3rd NPC

1968, Feb Branded as a counterrevolutionary and purged

1977, Jul First appearance after the Cultural Revolution

1978, Feb Elected deputy for Shanghai Municipality to the 5th NPC

Mar Elected member of the Standing Committee of the 5th NPC

Jun Identified as vice-chairman of the Federation of Literary and Art Circles and as member of the Executive Committee of the Welfare Institute

1979, Apr Head of a writers' delegation to France; identified as vice-chairman of the Writers' Association

Jun Member of the Committee to Examine Proposals at the 2nd Session of the 5th NPC

Aug Identified as chairman of the Shanghai Branch, Writers' Association

Nov Elected 1st vice-chairman of the Writers' Association

Publications

1928	Miewang	(Extinction)
	Fuchou	(Revenge)
	Guangming	(Brightness)
	Dianyi	(Electric Chair)

1930	Siqu De Taiyang (The Dead Sun)
1931	Xin Sheng (New Life)
	Jia (The Family)
1932-33	Aiqing De Sanbuqu (Trilogy of Love) consisting of:
	Yu (Rain; 1932)
	Wu (Fog; 1933)
	Dian (Lightning; 1933)
1932	Hai De Meng (Dream of the Sea)
	Dream and Drunkenness
1933	Xue (Snow)
1936	The History of the Nihilist Movement
1937	Chun (Spring)
1940	Qiu (Autumn)
1938-43	Huo (Fire; a trilogy)
	Fathers and Sons (translated from Turgenev)
	Virgin Land (translated from Turgenev)
1944	Qi Yuan (The Garden of Rest)
1945	Han Ye (Cold Nights)
1950	Festival Day of Warsaw
1953	Living Among Heroes
1962	Three Comrades

Ba-tu-ba-gen (Pa·t'u·pa·ken) 巴图巴根

Posts held

NPC
Deputy for Inner Mongolia Autonomous Region to the 5th NPC

Provincial Administration
Vice-chairman of the People's Government of Inner Mongolia Autonomous Region

Ba-tu-ba-gen belongs to the Mongol minority.

1961,	Mar	Identified as 1st secretary of the Bayannur League CP
1966,	Aug	Identified as 1st secretary of Hohhot Municipality CP
1978,	Feb	First appearance after the Cultural Revolution: Elected deputy for the Inner Mongolia Autonomous Region to the 5th NPC
1979,	Jun	Member of the Committee to Examine Proposals at the 2nd Session of the 5th NPC
	Dec	Elected vice-chairman of the People's Government of Inner Mongolia Autonomous Region

Ba Yikai (Pa Yi-k'ai) 巴一恺

Posts held

NPC
Member of the Standing Committee of the 5th NPC
Deputy for Jiangsu Province to the 5th NPC

| 1978, | Feb | Elected deputy for Jiangsu Province to the 5th NPC |
| | Mar | Elected member of the Standing Committee of the 5th NPC |

Bai Chengming (Pai Ch'eng-ming) 白成铭

Posts held

CCP
Member of the Standing Committee of Xinjiang Autonomous Region CP

Provincial Administration
Vice-chairman of the People's Government of Xinjiang Autonomous Region

1978,	Feb	Elected vice-chairman of the Revolutionary Committee of Xinjiang Autonomous Region (until Aug 1979)
1979,	Apr	Identified as member of the Standing Committee of Xinjiang Autonomous Region CP
	Aug	Identified as director of Xinjiang Autonomous Regional Economic Committee
	Sep	Elected vice-chairman of the People's Government of Xinjiang Autonomous Region

Bai Dongcai (Pai Tung-ts'ai) 白栋材

Posts held

CCP
Member of the CCP 11th Central Committee
Secretary of Jiangxi Province CP

Provincial Administration
Governor of Jiangxi Province

Before the foundation of PR China Bai was a Party cadre in Manchuria. In June 1949 he was secretary of Nanchang District CP and political commissar of Nanchang Military District in Jiangxi Province.

1951		Identified as member of the Jiangxi Section, CPPCC
1952		Identified as director of the Party School in Nanchang District
1953		Elected member of the CP Committee, and council member of the People's Government of Jiangxi Province
1955,	Jan	Identified as secretary of Nanchang District CP, Jiangxi Province (until Nov 1956)
	Feb	Elected member of the People's Government of Jiangxi Province
1956,	Nov	Identified as secretary of Jiangxi Province CP (until Cultural Revolution)
1958,	Jun	Elected deputy for Jiangxi Province to the 2nd NPC (reelected in 1964 to the 3rd NPC)
1960,	Feb	Appointed chancellor of the Industrial Work University of Jiangxi Province (until Cultural Revolution)
1966		Branded as a capitalist-roader during the Cultural Revolution and disappears
1970,	May	First appearance after the Cultural Revolution: Identified as vice-chairman of the Revolutionary Committee of Jiangxi Province
	Dec	Elected deputy secretary of the new CP Secretariat of Jiangxi Province (until Apr 1973)

1973, Apr Identified as secretary of Jiangxi Province CP

Aug Elected alternate member of the CCP Central Committee by the 10th Party Congress

1977, Aug Elected member of the CCP Central Committee by the 11th Party Congress

1978, Feb Elected vice-chairman of the Revolutionary Committee of Jiangxi Province (until Dec 1979)

1979, Dec Elected governor of the Revolutionary Committee of Jiangxi Province

---

Bai Hua (Pai Hua) 白　桦

<u>Posts held</u>

CCP
Director of the Propaganda Department, Tianjin Municipal CP

Provincial Administration
Vice-chairman of the Revolutionary Committee of Tianjin Municipality

1958, Oct Identified as deputy director of the Propaganda Department of Tianjin Municipality CP

1977, Dec Elected vice-chairman of the Revolutionary Committee of Tianjin Municipality

1979, Jul Appointed member of the National Games Organizing Committee

Aug Identified as director of the Propaganda Department of Tianjin Municipal CP

Bai Jiefu (Pai Chieh-fu) 白介夫

<u>Posts held</u>

CCP
Member of the Standing Committee, Beijing Municipality CP

NPC
Deputy for Beijing Municipality to the 5th NPC

Provincial Administration
Vice-mayor of Beijing Municipality

1972, Oct Identified as member of the Scientific and Technical Association; deputy head of a scientific delegation to Great Britain

1978, Feb Elected deputy for Beijing Municipality to the 5th NPC

May Identified as vice-chairman of the Revolutionary Committee of Beijing Municipality (until Dec 1979)

Sep Identified as a member of the Standing Committee, Beijing Municipality CP

Oct Member of a friendship delegation to Japan

1979, Jul Appointed member of the National Games Organizing Committee

Sep Head of a Beijing Municipal friendship delegation to Belgium and Austria

Dec Elected vice-mayor of Beijing Municipality

Bai Jinian (Pai Chi-nien) 百纪年

<u>Posts held</u>

Provincial Administration
Vice-governor of Shaanxi Province

1957, May Identified as a member of the Central Committee of the Communist Youth League

1979, Dec Elected vice-governor of Shaanxi Province

Bai Qian (Pai Ch'ien) 白　潜

<u>Posts held</u>

CCP
Secretary of Liaoning Province CP

1959, Mar Identified as a member of the General Office under the Department for Finance and Trade, CCP Central Committee

1963, Jun Identified as secretary of Liaoning Province CP (until Cultural Revolution); head of a Liaoning Province friendship delegation to Pyongyang, North Korea, to take part in celebrations of the 15th anniversary of Korea's liberation

1968, May On the foundation of the Revolutionary Committee of Liaoning Province elected vice-chairman (until 1973?)

1971, Jul Head of a Liaoning Province friendship delegation to North Korea

Dec Identified as a member of the Standing Committee, Liaoning Province CP (until 1973?)

1974, Jan Bai disappears until 1979

1979, Sep Elected secretary of Liaoning Province CP

Bai Rubing (Pai Ju-ping) 白如冰

<u>Posts held</u>

CCP
Member of the CCP 11th Central Committee
1st secretary of Shandong Province CP

NPC
Deputy for Shandong Province to the 5th NPC
1st political commissar of Jinan Military Region

Bai was born in 1906 in Shaanxi Province. In 1932 he belonged to a communist underground group in his native province. In 1942 he served in the administration of the Shaanxi-Gansu-Ningxia Border Regional Government.

1949, Dec Appointed member of the Northwest China Military and Administrative Council

1950, Mar Identified as vice-chairman of the Financial and Economic Committee of Northwest China Military and Administrative Council (until Jan 1953)

1953, Jan Bai retains his former posts after the reorganization of the Northwest China Military and Administrative Council into the Northwest China Administrative Council (until Jul 1954)

1954, Jul Appointed council member of the Federation of Supply and Marketing Cooperatives (until Mar 1957)

Nov Appointed director of the Trade Bureau (until Jul 1958)

1957, Dec Elected chairman of the Federation of Trade Cooperatives

1958, Mar Appointed director of the Trade Bureau in the Ministry of Light Industry (until Jul 1958)

Jul Identified as secretary of Shandong Province CP

Nov Elected vice-governor of Shandong Province (until Dec 1963)

1961, Jan By-elected deputy for Shandong Province to the 2nd NPC (reelected in 1964 to the 3rd NPC)

1963, Dec Elected governor of Shandong Province (until Cultural Revolution)

1967 Together with Tan Qilong Bai is relieved of all posts as a capitalist-roader during the Cultural Revolution

1970, Nov First appearance after the Cultural Revolution

1971, Feb Identified as vice-chairman of the Revolutionary Committee of Shandong Province (until Aug 1975)

Apr Elected secretary of the CP Secretariat of Shandong Province after the Cultural Revolution

1973, Aug Elected to first term as member of the CCP Central Committee by the 10th Party Congress

1974, Jan Identified as 1st political commissar of Jinan Military Region; identified as 2nd secretary of Shandong Province CP (until Apr 1975)

1975, Apr Identified as 1st secretary of Shandong Province CP

Aug Identified as chairman of the Revolutionary Committee of Shandong Province (until Dec 1979)

1978, Feb Elected deputy for Shandong Province to the 5th NPC

Bai Shouyi (Pai Shou-yi, Djamal al-Din)

Posts held

白寿彝

Government
Member of the State Nationalities Affairs Commission

NPC
Member of the Standing Committee of the 5th NPC
Vice-chairman of the NPC Nationalities Committee
Deputy for Beijing Municipality to the 5th NPC

Others
Cadre of the Islamic Society
Director of the History Department of Beijing Teachers University

Bai belongs to the Hui minority.

1963 Identified as director of the History Department of Beijing Teachers University; identified as vice-chairman of the Sino-Afghanistan Friendship Association; as vice-chairman of the Islamic Society

1964 Elected deputy for Henan Province to the 3rd NPC

Aug Article in China Reconstructs: "The Heritage of the Chinese Moslems"

1966 Disappears during the Cultural Revolution

1975, Jan First appearance after the Cultural Revolution: Elected member of the Standing Committee of the 4th NPC (confirmed in Mar 1978 by the 5th NPC)

1976, Mar Identified as a cadre in the Islamic Society

Nov Member of an NPC delegation to Iran and Kuwait

Dec Identified as professor of History at Beijing Teachers University

1978, Feb Elected deputy for Beijing Municipality to the 5th NPC

Sep Identified as director of the History Department of Beijing Teachers University

1979, May Appointed member of the State Nationalities Affairs Commission

Jun Member of the Draft Laws Committee at the 2nd Session of the 5th NPC

Oct Identified as vice-chairman of the NPC Nationalities Committee

Bai Xiangguo (Pai Hsiang-kuo) 白相国

Posts held

Military
Deputy director of the Logistics Department, General Staff of the PLA

1958 Identified as political commissar of the 123rd Division, 41st Army

1963 Trained at the Political Academy of the PLA

1966 Identified as political commissar of the 41st Army

1968, Mar Elected chairman of the Revolutionary Committee of Shantou Special District, Guangdong Province

1969, Jan Identified as military leader in Guangzhou Military Region

Apr Identified as vice-chairman of the Revolutionary Committee of Guangdong Province

1970, Apr Identified as a cadre in the Ministry of Foreign Trade

Dec Identified as minister of foreign trade (until Oct 1973)

1971, Jan Head of a trade delegation to Sri Lanka

Feb Head of a trade delegation to Romania

	Jul	Member of a Party and government delegation led by Li Xiannian to North Korea on the 10th anniversary of the Sino-Korean Friendship Pact
	Sep	Head of a government delegation to France
	Oct	Head of a trade delegation to Algeria and Italy
1972,	Mar	Head of a trade delegation to Egypt
	May	Head of a government delegation to Sudan
	Jun	Head of a trade delegation to Pakistan
	Aug	Head of a trade delegation to Canada, Chile, and Peru
	Nov	Head of a trade delegation to Hungary, Yugoslavia, and Romania
	Dec	Head of a trade delegation to Sri Lanka and Burma
1973,	Jan	Head of a trade delegation to the Netherlands and Great Britain
1974,	Feb	Identified as deputy director of the PLA Logistics Department

Bai is married to Yang Yang.

Bai Xiangyin (Pai Hsiang-yin)　白向银

Posts held

Government
Vice-minister of the Capital Construction Commission

NPC
Deputy for Shaanxi Province to the 5th NPC

1953,	Jun	Identified as deputy director of the 1st Bureau in the Ministry of Foreign Trade (until Sep 1956)
1955,	Nov	Deputy head of a trade delegation to the USSR
1956,	Jun	Deputy head of a trade delegation to North Vietnam
	Oct	Appointed assistant minister in the Ministry of Foreign Trade (until Jan 1961)
1961,	Jan	Appointed vice-minister of foreign trade (until Nov 1965)
1963,	Mar	Head of a trade delegation to the People's Republic of Mongolia
1965,	Nov	Appointed minister of construction materials (until Dec 1974)
1972,	Jun	Head of a government delegation to Poland
1977,	Jul	Identified as vice-minister of the Capital Construction Commission
1978,	Feb	Elected deputy for Shaanxi Province to the 5th NPC
	May	Deputy head of a capital construction delegation to Japan

Bai Zhimin (Pai Chih-min)　白治民

Posts held

CCP
Secretary of Fujian Province CP
1st deputy director of the Party School of Fujian

In 1941 Bai served in the Shaanxi-Gansu-Ningxia Border Regional Government.

1953,	Dec	Identified as director of the Rural Work Department, Northwest Bureau of the CCP Central Committee
1954,	Jan	Identified as member of the Land Reform Committee of the Northwest Administrative Council
1956,	Mar	Identified as deputy secretary of Shaanxi Province CP
	Apr	Identified as secretary of Shaanxi Province CP
1965,	Mar	Identified as alternate secretary, Northwest Bureau of the CCP Central Committee
1967		Disappears during the Cultural Revolution
1978,	Jan	First appearance after the Cultural Revolution: Elected vice-chairman of the Revolutionary Committee of Fujian Province (until Dec 1979)
	Mar	Identified as member of the Standing Committee of Fujian Province CP (until Oct 1978)
	Jun	Identified as 1st deputy director of the Party School of Fujian
	Nov	Identified as secretary of Fujian Province CP

Banqen Erdeni Qoigyi Gyancan
(Panchen Erdeni Chhoekyi-Gyaltsan)

班禅额
尔德尼

Posts held

Others
Vice-chairman of the Standing Committee of the 5th CPPCC

Banqen Erdeni was born in November 1937 as the son of a peasant in Xunhua County, Qinghai Province. In 1941 the Banqen Kampo Lijia confirmed him as the 9th incarnation of Banqen and brought him to Gumbum (Ta-drh) monastery, the biggest in Qinghai. In 1943 he succeeded to the throne as 10th reincarnation of the 1st Banqen Lama. After the occupation of Qinghai by the Communists in 1949, Banqen Erdeni was assured of Communist support against the Dalai Lama.

1950,	Jan	The Banqen Lama sends a telegram to Mao Zedong and Zhu De asking for the "liberation" of Tibet
1951,	Apr	First meeting with Mao Zedong in Beijing
	Oct	Elected member of the National Committee of the CPPCC
1952,	Apr	The Banqen Lama arrives in Lhasa after the occupation of Tibet by Chinese troops
	Jun	The Council of the Banqen Lama is established in Xigaze
1953,	May	Elected honorary chairman of the Buddhist League at its founding session
1954,	Sep	Elected deputy for Tibet to the NPC (until Dec 1964)
	Oct	Elected member of the Standing Committee of the NPC (until Dec 1964)
	Dec	Elected member of the Standing Committee of the CPPCC and council member of the Sino-Soviet Friendship Association

1956, Apr Appointed 1st chairman of the Preparatory Committee for the establishment of Tibet Autonomous Region (PCTAR)

Nov Visit to India to the celebrations of the 2,500th birthday of Buddha

1959, Mar Appointed acting chairman of the PCTAR after the escape of the Dalai Lama to India (probably until Dec 1964)

1961, Sep Appointed chairman of the Election Committee for the Tibetan People's Congress

Oct Speech at the Standing Committee Session of the NPC in Beijing on the economic development of Tibet

1962, May Present at the May Day celebrations in Beijing

1964 At a Buddhist meeting the Banqen Lama denounces China's Tibet policy and openly speaks out in support of the Dalai Lama

1965, Jan Reelected member of the Standing Committee of the CPPCC

Sep Identified as member of the Standing Committee of Tibet Section, CPPCC

1967 Believed to have spent part of the Cultural Revolution in a labor camp

1978, Feb First appearance after the Cultural Revolution

Mar Elected member of the Standing Committee of the 5th CPPCC (until Jun 1979)

1979, Jul Elected vice-chairman of the 5th CPPCC

Bao Houchang (Pao Hou-ch'ang) 包厚昌

Posts held

CCP
Secretary of Jiangsu Province CP

Bao was born in Jiangyin, Jiangsu Province. In 1940 he led a company under the New 4th Army. In 1942 he was magistrate of Jiangyin County. In 1945 he was made commander of the Advance Unit of the 6th Division under the New 4th Army. In 1949 he became chairman of the Wuxi Municipal Federation of Trade Unions.

1950, Sep Identified as vice-mayor of Wuxi

1956, Jan Identified as secretary of Wuxi CP

1957, Oct Identified as 1st secretary of Wuxi CP (until Feb 1963)

Dec Elected member of the 8th Executive Committee of the Federation of Trade Unions

1960, May Identified as alternate secretary of Jiangsu Province CP (until Jan 1968)

1962, Jun Identified as vice-governor of Jiangsu Province

1968, Jan Denounced as a capitalist-roader

1979, May First appearance after the Cultural Revolution

Oct Identified as secretary of Jiangsu Province CP

Bao Xianzhi (Pao Hsien-chih) 鮑先志

Posts held

Military
Lieutenant-general

Others
Member of the Standing Committee of the 5th CPPCC

Bao served in the 4th Front Army during the Long March. In 1938 he worked in the Political Department of a brigade of the 129th Division, 8th Route Army. In 1947 he was deputy political commissar of the 3rd Column, Shanxi-Hebei-Shandong Field Army, and in 1949 political commissar of the 2nd Army, 2nd Field Army.

1952 Identified as member of the East Sichuan Administrative Office

1958, Aug Identified as lieutenant-general and as director of the Political Department of Nanjing Military Region

1965, Jan Identified as deputy political commissar

1967 Disappears during the Cultural Revolution

1974, Jan First appearance after the Cultural Revolution: Named as cadre of Jinan Military Region (subsequently disappears again until 1977)

1978, Mar Elected member of the Standing Committee of the 5th CPPCC

Bariltai (Pao·jih·lo·t'ai) (f) 宝日勒岱

Posts held

CCP
Member of the CCP 11th Central Committee
Secretary of Inner Mongolia Autonomous Region CP

NPC
Member of the Standing Committee of the 5th NPC
Deputy for Inner Mongolia Autonomous Region to the 5th NPC

Provincial Administration
Vice-chairman of the People's Congress of Inner Mongolia Autonomous Region

Bariltai belongs to the Mongolian minority; she was born in 1937 as the daughter of poor shepherds. At the age of nine she began tending livestock in the service of cattle owners.

1958 Identified as secretary of the Communist Youth League of Buertu Brigade in Wushenchao People's Commune, Wushen Banner, Inner Mongolia Autonomous Region. In this capacity she organized 60 youths to exterminate a poisonous plant growing in the grass savanna which until then had been a sacred plant to the Mongolians

1966, May Identified as vice-chairman of the Federation of Poor Shepherds in Inner Mongolia Autonomous Region and as secretary, CP of Buertu Brigade; article in RMRB: "Destroy the Poisonous Weeds of Society"

1967, Nov Elected member of the newly established Revolutionary Committee of Inner Mongolia Autonomous Region

1969, Apr Elected to first term as member of the CCP Central Committee by the 9th Party Congress

1970,	May	Article in the ideological journal <u>HQ</u>: "Build the Grasslands into the Fatherland's Great Wall of Steel"
1974,	Jul	Identified as member of the Standing Committee of Inner Mongolia CP (until May 1975)
	Dec	Identified as vice-chairman of the Revolutionary Committee of Inner Mongolia (until Dec 1979)
1975,	Jan	Elected vice-chairman, Standing Committee of the NPC
	May	Identified as secretary of Inner Mongolia CP
1977,	May	Member of an NPC delegation led by Seypidin to Romania
1978,	Feb	Elected deputy for Inner Mongolia Autonomous Region to the 5th NPC
1979,	Dec	Elected vice-chairman of the People's Congress of Inner Mongolia Autonomous Region

Basang (Pa·sang) (f)

<u>Posts held</u>

CCP
Member of the CCP 11th Central Committee
Secretary of Tibet Autonomous Region CP

NPC
Member of the Standing Committee of the 5th NPC
Deputy for Tibet Autonomous Region to the 5th NPC

Provincial Administration
Vice-chairman of the People's Government of Tibet Autonomous Region

Mass Organization
Chairman of the Women's Federation of Tibet Autonomous Region

Others
Chairman of the Revolutionary Committee of Langxian County, Tibet Autonomous Region

Basang belongs to the Tibetan minority; she was born in 1938 as the daughter of slaves. After the death of her mother in 1947 she served the landlord of Chika as a slave.

1956		Basang escapes service to join a unit of the PLA
1957		Sent to study at Tibetan Minorities Institute
1959		Basang joins the CCP
1966,	May	Article in <u>RMRB</u>: "The People with Mao Zedong Thought Are a Truly Iron Armored Wall"
1968,	Sep	Elected vice-chairman of the newly established Revolutionary Committee of Tibet Autonomous Region (until Aug 1979)
1971,	Aug	Elected secretary of the new CP Secretariat after the Cultural Revolution
1973,	Jul	Elected chairman of the Women's Federation of Tibet

	Aug	Elected member of the CCP Central Committee by the 10th Party Congress (confirmed in 1977 by the 11th Congress)
1974,	Nov	Identified as chairman of the Revolutionary Committee of Langxian County
1975,	Jan	Elected vice-chairman of the Standing Committee of the 4th NPC (confirmed in 1978 by the 5th NPC); head of a women's delegation to Japan
1978,	Feb	Elected deputy for Tibet Autonomous Region to the 5th NPC
1979,	Jun	Member of the Budget Committee at the 2nd Session of the 5th NPC
	Aug	Elected vice-chairman of the People's Government of Tibet Autonomous Region

Bei Shizhang (Pei Shih-chang) 贝时璋

<u>Posts held</u>

NPC
Member of the Standing Committee of the 5th NPC
Deputy for Tianjin Municipality to the 5th NPC

Others
Director of the Biophysics Institute of the Academy of Sciences

Bei was born in 1903. He studied biology in Germany and got his doctor's degree at Tübingen University. In May 1949 he was elected a member of the Preparatory Committee for the National Assembly of Scientific Workers.

1950,	Jun	Appointed director of the Institute of Experimental Biology of the Academy of Sciences
1954,	Aug	Elected deputy for Shanghai Municipality to the 1st NPC
1957,	Jun	Appointed member of the Scientific Planning Commission under the State Council
	Oct	Appointed director of the Beijing Institute of Experimental Biology
	Nov	Member of a scientific and technical delegation to the USSR
1958,	Nov	Elected deputy for Zhejiang Province to the 2nd NPC (reelected in 1964 to the 3rd NPC)
1959,	Apr	Elected member of the Standing Committee of the 3rd CPPCC
	Jul	Identified as vice-chairman of the Editorial Board of <u>Kexue Jilu</u> (Science Report), a publication of the Academy of Sciences
1961,	Apr	Identified as director of the Biophysics Institute of the Academy of Sciences
1965,	Jan	Elected member of the Standing Committee of the 3rd NPC
1970,	Feb	Member of the Chinese government delegation to Nepal to attend the wedding ceremonies for the Crown Prince
1972,	Oct	Head of a scientific delegation to Great Britain
1973,	May	Board member of the Science and Technology Association

1975,	Jan	Confirmed as member of the Standing Committee by the 4th NPC (again in Mar 1978 by the 5th NPC)
	Nov	Head of a delegation of scientists to Austria and Italy
1978,	Feb	Elected deputy for Tianjin Municipality to the 5th NPC
1979,	Jan	Identified as member of the Biology Department of the Academy of Sciences

Bi Jichang (Pi Chi-ch'ang) 毕际昌

Posts held

Provincial Administration
Vice-governor of Fujian Province

| 1978, | Jan | Elected vice-chairman of the Revolutionary Committee of Fujian Province (until Dec 1979) |
| 1979, | Dec | Elected vice-governor of Fujian Province |

Bi Jilong (Pi Chi-lung) 毕季龙

Posts held

Government
Deputy director of the Department for International Organizations and Conferences, Agreements and Laws of the Ministry of Foreign Affairs
UN under secretary-general

1961,	Jun	Identified as information officer of the Chinese delegation to the Laos Conference in Geneva
1964,	Aug	Identified as deputy director of the Information Department of the Ministry of Foreign Affairs
1966		Disappears during the Cultural Revolution
1972,	Sep	First appearance after the Cultural Revolution: Member of the Chinese delegation to the 27th UN General Assembly
1973,	Jun	Member of a delegation to the UN Environmental Protection Conference in Geneva
1974,	Aug	Identified as deputy director of the Department for International Organizations and Conferences, Agreements and Laws of the Ministry of Foreign Affairs
	Nov	Member of a delegation to the Food and Agriculture Organization Conference in Rome
1975,	Mar	Head of a delegation to the 3rd UN Law of the Sea Conference
	Sep	Member of a delegation to the 30th UN General Assembly
1978,	Sep	Representative of the delegation to the 33rd UN General Assembly
1979,	Apr	Appointed UN under secretary-general

Biken (Pi·k'en) (f) 毕肯

Posts held

NPC
Member of the Standing Committee of the 5th NPC
Deputy for Xinjiang Autonomous Region to the 5th NPC

| 1978, | Feb | Elected deputy for Xinjiang Autonomous Region to the 5th NPC |
| | Mar | Elected member of the Standing Committee fo the 5th NPC |

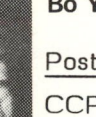

Bo Yibo (Po Yi-po) 薄一波

Posts held

CCP
Member of the CCP 11th Central Committee

Government
Vice-premier
Member of the State Financial and Economic Commission
Minister of the State Machine Building Industry Commission

NPC
Deputy for Beijing Municipality to the 5th NPC

Others
Honorary president of the Finance Society

Bo Yibo was born in 1908 in Dingxiang, Shanxi Province. After attending elementary school in Taiyuan he received schooling in Beijing. He studied at various universities but did not sit for examinations. Still as a student of Beijing University he joined the CCP in 1925 and became an active member of various student organizations. In 1932, having organized an uprising, he was arrested and sentenced to protracted imprisonment for agitation; he was released after more than three years. At the beginning of the Anti-Japanese War Bo returned to his native province of Shanxi where he founded the National Salvation Sacrifice League together with Liang Huazheng, an organization with military and political aims which presented itself as anti-Japanese but also had strong pro-communist leanings. Under Bo's leadership this league quickly grew into an influential organization in Shanxi comprising more than 100,000 members. In 1936 Bo liberated General Wang Ruofei who was held a prisoner by the warlord of Shanxi. Having organized numerous sacrifice commandos against the Japanese, Bo decided to move his forces to Southeast Shanxi following the Japanese occupation of the provincial capital Taiyuan. There his influence continued to spread as he built up his armored units and he was eventually appointed director of the Administrative Office of Southeast Shanxi. In 1939 Bo turned with a strong force against the then governor of Shanxi, Yan Xishan. Although this operation was not a complete success, Bo increased his military strength. In 1945 he was elected a member of the CCP Central Committee. At the beginning of the Civil War Bo served as political commissar in North China Military Region, later as vice-chairman of the People's Government of North China.

1949,   Oct   Appointed member of the Central People's Government Council, member of the Government Administration Council, vice-chairman of the Financial and Economic Affairs Committee, and minister of finance (until Sep 1953)

1952,   Nov   Appointed member of the State Planning Commission (until Oct 1954)

1954,   Sep   Elected deputy for Tianjin Municipality to the 1st NPC (until Mar 1959)

         Oct   Appointed vice-chairman of the State Planning Commission and director of the 3rd Staff Office under the State Council (abolished in 1959)

1956,   May   Appointed chairman of the Economy Commission

         Sep   Elected alternate member of the CCP Politburo by the 8th Party Congress

         Oct   Appointed vice-premier

1959,   Mar   Elected deputy for Hebei Province to the 2nd NPC (until Dec 1964)

         Sep   Appointed deputy director of the Staff Office of Industry and Communications (until Apr 1960)

1960,   May   Head of a Party delegation to Poland

1961,   Apr   Appointed director of the Staff Office of Industry and Communications

1964,   Oct   Elected deputy for Shanxi Province to the 3rd NPC

1966,   Jun   Branded as a counterrevolutionary revisionist and purged

1978,   Dec   First appearance after the Cultural Revolution

1979,   May   By-elected deputy for Beijing to the 5th NPC

         Jul   Appointed vice-premier and member of the State Financial and Economic Commission

         Sep   By-elected member of the CCP 11th Central Committee

1980,   Jan   Elected honorary president, Finance Society

         Feb   Appointed minister of the State Machine Building Industry Commission

Bo is married to Hu Ming.

Bu Chunzi (Pak Chun Za) (f)   朴春子

Posts held

NPC
Member of the Standing Committee of the 5th NPC
Deputy for Jilin Province to the 5th NPC

The name suggests that Bu belongs to the Korean minority and probably lives in Yanbian Autonomous Zhou.

1975,   Jan   Elected member of the Standing Committee of the 4th NPC (reelected in 1978 to the 5th NPC)

1978,   Feb   Elected deputy for Jilin Province to the 5th NPC

Bu Guxiang (Pu Ku-hsiang)   卜谷香

Posts held

CCP
Alternate member of the CCP 11th Central Committee

1973,   Aug   Elected to first term as alternate member of the CCP Central Committee by the 10th Party Congress

         Sep   Present at a session of the Women's Congress of Hunan Province

1976,   Jan   Participant at the Dazhai Symposium in Hunan

1977,   Oct   Identified as deputy secretary, CP of Jiangnan Machinery Plant in Xiangtan, Hunan Province

Bu He (Pu Ho)   布赫

Posts held

CCP
Member of the Standing Committee of Inner Mongolia Autonomous Region CP
1st secretary of Hohhot Municipality CP

Government
Vice-minister of the State Nationalities Affairs Commission

Bu belongs to the Mongolian minority.

1956,   Jun   By-elected deputy for Inner Mongolia Autonomous Region to the 1st NPC

1961,   Jul   Identified as deputy director of the Inner Mongolia Culture Office and as secretary-general of the Inner Mongolia Section, Sino-Soviet Friendship Association

1978,   Dec   Identified as member of the Inner Mongolia Autonomous Region CP's Standing Committee and as director of that CP's Propaganda Department (until May 1979)

1979,   May   Identified as vice-minister of the State Nationalities Affairs Commission

         Sep   Identified as member of the Standing Committee of Inner Mongolia Autonomous Region CP and as 1st secretary of Hohhot Municipality CP

Bu Ming (Pu Ming)   卜明

Posts held

Government
President of the Bank of China
General manager of the Bank of China

1961,   Sep   Identified as deputy director of the Economic Planning Committee of Zhejiang Province

1973,   Nov   Deputy head of a delegation to the 3rd Session of the Standing Committee, UN Industrial Development Forum in Vienna

1974,   Nov   Head of a delegation to the 5th Session of the Standing Committee, UN Industrial Development Forum in Vienna

1975,	Mar	Deputy head of a delegation to the UN Industrial Development Organization (UNIDO) Conference in Lima
	Jun	Identified as director of a department in the Ministry of Economic Relations with Foreign Countries
1976,	Jan	Identified as deputy director of the Bank of China
	Mar	Head of a banking delegation to Canada and Mexico
	Sep	Identified as vice-president of the People's Bank of China
1977,	May	Head of a Bank of China delegation to Switzerland, Federal Republic of Germany, Great Britain, Belgium
	Dec	Identified as general manager of the Bank of China
1978,	Mar	Deputy head of a economic delegation to Japan
1979,	May	Head of a banking delegation to Japan
	Oct	Identified as president of the Bank of China; head of a banking delegation to North Korea
	Dec	Head of a Bank of China delegation to Pakistan

Bu Tongxiu (Pu T'ung-hsiu)   浦通修

Posts held

Government
Vice-minister of education

| 1977, | Dec | Identified as a cadre of the State Council |
| 1978, | Jan | Identified as vice-minister of education |

Burhan Xahidi (Burhan Shahidi) 包尔汉

Posts held

Others
Member of the Standing Committee of the 5th CPPCC
Chairman of the Islamic Association

Burhan belongs to the Uighur minority. He was born in 1894 in Aksu, Xinjiang. After graduating from university in Russia he went to Germany in 1912 where he continued his studies in economics at Berlin University until he obtained a doctorate in 1916. Until 1936 he held various positions in the Provincial Government of Xinjiang, e.g. head of the Alien Residents Affairs Department in 1928. From 1937 to 1938 he was consul of the Chinese Nationalist Government in Chaisan, USSR. After his return in 1938 to Xinjiang he was accused of being a German spy by the then provincial governor Sheng Shicai and imprisoned until 1944. After his release he was immediately installed in a number of public offices, such as deputy director of the Civil Affairs Department in the Provincial Government and special commissioner for the 1st Administrative District of Xinjiang. In 1946 he was appointed vice-governor and in 1948 governor of Xinjiang. When the Communist forces entered Xinjiang in autumn 1949 he changed to the Communist side and was appointed chairman of the Provisional Provincial Government of Xinjiang.

1950,	Jan	As a result of an administrative reorganization, appointed chairman of the People's Government of Xinjiang
	Mar	Appointed chairman of the People's Court of Xinjiang; member of the Northwest China Military and Administrative Council and member of its Nationalities Committee (until Jan 1953)
1951,	Nov	Elected member of the CPPCC
1952,	Sep	Member of the Chinese delegation to the World Peace Council Session, Asia-Pacific Section
1953,	Jan	The Northwest China Military and Administrative Council is transformed into the Northwest China Administrative Council; Burhan is confirmed in his posts of March 1950 (until Dec 1954)
	Feb	Elected a member of the Standing Committee of the CPPCC
	May	Elected chairman of the newly established Muslim Society
1954,	Apr	Appointed chairman of the Preparatory Committee for the establishment of Xinjiang Autonomous Region (until Sep 1955)
	Sep	Elected deputy for Xinjiang to the 1st NPC and vice-chairman of the Nationalities Commission
	Dec	Elected vice chairman of the Chinese People's Political Consultative Conference (until Jan 1965)
1955,	Jun	Appointed a member of the Department of Philosophy and Social Sciences of the Academy of Sciences; elected chairman of the Sino-Indonesian Friendship Association; member of the Chinese delegation to the World Peace Council Session in Helsinki of which he is elected a council member
	Jul	Elected council member of the Institute of Foreign Affairs
	Sep	Elected a member of the People's Government of the newly established Xinjiang Autonomous Region
1956,	Feb	Elected vice-chairman of the Study Committee of the CPPCC and a member of the Afro-Asian Solidarity Committee
	Nov	Elected chairman of the Sino-Egyptian Friendship Association (renamed China-UAR-Friendship Association in 1958). Elected vice-chairman of the Committee for Assistance to Egypt
1957,	May	Head of the Chinese delegation to the World Peace Council Session in Colombo
	Jun	Appointed a member of the Scientific Planning Commission under the State Council
	Sep	Elected a council member of the Sino-Syrian Friendship Association
	Dec	Deputy head of the Chinese delegation to the Afro-Asian Solidarity Conference in Cairo
1958,	Jan	Member of the Chinese delegation to the mourning ceremonies for Petru Groza in Bucharest

Feb Head of a delegation to Egypt

Mar Appointed a member of the Commission for Cultural Relations; member of the Chinese delegation to the Session of the World Peace Council in New Delhi

Jul Elected vice-chairman of the Afro-Asian Solidarity Committee; appointed director of Xinjiang College; elected vice-chairman of the Peace Council (until Jun 1965); deputy head of the Chinese delegation to the International Disarmament Conference in Stockholm

1959, Feb Member of the Chinese delegation to the World Peace Council Session in Moscow

Mar Head of a cultural delegation to Iraq

May Elected permanent vice-chairman of the CPPCC; member of the Chinese delegation to the World Peace Council Session in Stockholm

1960, Apr Appointed vice-chairman of the newly established Sino-African Friendship Association

Jul Chinese delegate at the Enlarged Session of the Standing Committee, World Peace Council in Stockholm

1961, Jan Head of the Chinese delegation to the Afro-Asian Solidarity Conference in Cairo

Nov Burhan accompanies the Panchen Lama on a tour of Xinjiang

Dec Delegate at the Council Session of the Afro-Asian Solidarity Organization in Stockholm

1962, Jan Elected chairman of the Xinjiang Autonomous Region Section, CPPCC

Apr Appointed vice-chairman of the Asian-African Society

May The Beijing Experimental Theater performs a play based on Burhan's novel, Immortal Spark

1966 Disappears during the Cultural Revolution

1978, Feb First appearance after the Cultural Revolution

Mar Elected member of the Standing Committee of the 5th CPPCC

1979, Dec Identified as chairman of the Islamic Association

Burhan is married to Lashida.

Cai Banghua (Ts'ai Pang-hua) 蔡邦华

<u>Posts held</u>

Others
Deputy director of the Institute of Zoology, Academy of Sciences

1959,	Mar	Elected deputy for Shandong Province to the 2nd NPC (reelected in 1964 to the 3rd NPC)
	Aug	Identified as entomologist
1963		Identified as vice-president of the Plant Protection Society
1964		Identified as deputy director of the Institute of Entomology, Academy of Sciences
1978,	Feb	Member of the Presidium of the 5th CPPCC
	Oct	Identified as deputy director of the Institute of Zoology, Academy of Sciences

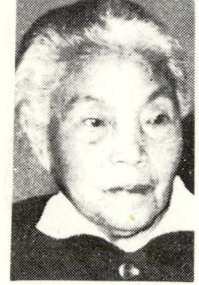

Cai Chang (Ts'ai Ch'ang) (f) 蔡 畅

<u>Posts held</u>

CCP
Member of the CCP 11th Central Committee

NPC
Vice-chairman of the 5th NPC
Deputy for Hunan Province to the 5th NPC

Mass Organization
Honorary president of the National Women's Federation

Cai was born in 1900 in Xiangxiang County, Hunan Province. Her father, an impoverished landlord, had held a position in the Jiangnan Arsenal in Shanghai which had been set up by Zeng Guofan, a Qing-dynasty state official and a remote relative of Cai Chang's mother. After her father's death she completed her school education at Zhounan Girls School. One of the teachers at this school was Xu Deli who at the same time taught Mao Zedong at Changsha 1st Teachers College. Her mother was an open-minded woman who took a close interest in Cai's development and that of her brother's, Cai Hesen, who was executed in 1931 in Guangzhou as a communist. She held an open house which became a meeting place for her children's political friends, one of whom was Mao Zedong. At the age of fifteen, Cai had already become a teacher. In 1919 she joined the New People's Study Society founded by Mao Zedong. Shortly afterwards she belonged to a group of Chinese worker-students being sent to France. There she was involved in setting up the French branch of the CCP in 1921. One year later she married Li Fuchun. After her return to China in 1924, preceded by a brief stay in Moscow, she became head of the Women's Work Department of the CCP Central Committee. Together with her brother Cai Hesen she helped to organize the strikes in Guangzhou and Hong Kong during the following year. During the Northern Expedition in late 1926-early 1927 she was engaged in propaganda work in the General Political Department of the Expeditionary Corps. In March 1927 she followed the troops to Wuhan where she organized a women's corps. After the rift between the CCP and the KMT she continued to work underground in Wuhan. In 1928 she participated in the 6th CCP Congress held in Moscow and was elected a member of its Central Committee. Taking part in the Long March of 1934-35, her health suffered to the extent that she had to leave for medical treatment in the USSR. After the outbreak of the Anti-Japanese War she returned to China to work for several years in the Organization Department of the CCP Central Committee. The 7th CCP Congress in 1945 reelected Cai as the only woman to its Central Committee. In 1948 she was elected a member of the Executive Committee and director of the Women's Work Department, Federation of Trade Unions. At the same time she was elected vice-chairman of the World Federation of Democratic Women. In March of the following year she became head of the Democratic Women's Federation. In September she took part in the CPPCC.

1949,	Oct	Appointed member of the People's Government Council (until Sep 1954)
	Dec	Elected board member of the Sino-Soviet Friendship Association (until Dec 1954) and of the Peace Council
1953,	Mar	Member of the Chinese delegation to the funeral of Stalin
	Jun	Delegate at the meeting of the World Federation of Democratic Women in Copenhagen
1954,	Oct	Elected deputy for Hunan Province to the 1st NPC and member, Standing Committee of the NPC (confirmed in 1959 and 1965 for the 2nd and 3rd NPCs)
1956,	Sep	Reelected member of the CCP Central Committee by the 8th Party Congress
	Oct	Identified as 1st secretary, Women's Work Department of the CCP Central Committee
1969,	Apr	Reelected member of the CCP Central Committee by the 9th Party Congress (confirmed in 1973 and 1977 by the 10th and 11th Party Congresses)
1972,	Apr	Last mention as chairman of the Women's Federation
1975,	Jan	Elected vice-chairman by the 4th NPC (confirmed in Mar 1978 by the 5th NPC)
1978,	Feb	Elected deputy for Hunan Province to the 5th NPC
	Sep	Elected honorary president of the Women's Federation

Cai Fenglan (Ts'ai Feng-lan) (f)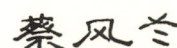

<u>Posts held</u>

CCP
Alternate member of the CCP 11th Central Committee

Provincial Administration
Vice-chairman of the Standing Committee of the People's Government, Qinghai Province

1977,	Aug	Elected alternate member of the CCP Central Committee by the 11th Party Congress
	Dec	Elected vice-chairman of the Revolutionary Committee of Qinghai Province (until Aug 1979)

1979, Sep Elected vice-chairman of the Standing Committee of the People's Government, Qinghai Province

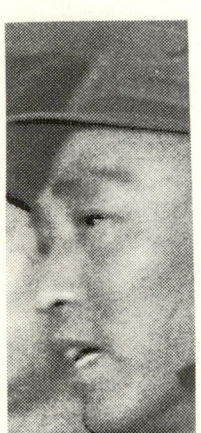

Cai Xiao (Ts'ai Hsiao)   蔡 哨

Posts held

CCP
Member of the CCP 11th Central Committee
Cadre of the United Front Work Department, CCP Central Committee

Others
Member of the Standing Committee and deputy secretary-general of the 5th CPPCC
Chairman of the Council of the General Office, Taiwan Democratic Self-government League

Cai was born in 1920 in Taiwan. He has served for many years in the PLA. In 1949, he was director of the Taiwan Cadres' Training Corps.

1973, Aug Elected to first term as member of the CCP Central Committee by the 10th Party Congress
1975, Dec Identified as a cadre of the United Front Work Department, CCP Central Committee
1976, Jun Identified as director of the Taiwan Provincial Sports Liaison Office; no later mention in this post
1978, Mar Elected member of the Standing Committee of the 5th CPPCC
       May Identified as deputy secretary-general of the 5th CPPCC; deputy head of a goodwill delegation to Yugoslavia
1979, Oct Elected chairman of the Council of the General Office, Taiwan Democratic Self-government League
       Dec Deputy head of a CPPCC delegation to Romania

Cai Ziwei (Ts'ai Tzu-wei)   蔡子伟

Posts held

Government
Vice-minister of agriculture

In 1938 Cai worked in the Department of Construction of the Shaanxi-Gansu-Ningxia Border Region.

1950, Mar Identified as deputy director of the Agriculture and Forestry Bureau, Northwest Military and Administrative Council (until Jul 1952)
1952, Jul Identified as director of that Bureau (until Dec 1954)
1954, Oct Appointed vice-minister of agriculture (until Mar 1967)
1959, Jan Identified as a member of the Committee for Promoting International Trade
1964, Sep Elected deputy for Shaanxi Province to the 3rd NPC

       Nov Identified as acting chairman of the Sino-Bulgarian Committee on Scientific and Technological Cooperation
1967, Mar Denounced as a capitalist-roader and purged
1979, Sep First appearance after the Cultural Revolution: Identified as vice-minister of agriculture

Cai Zuquan (Ts'ai Tsu-ch'üan)   蔡祖泉

Posts held

Others
Vice-president of the Light Industry Society
Director of the Research Laboratory for Electric Lighting Sources, Fudan University, Shanghai

Cai was born in 1925. He had only three years of formal schooling. Before 1949 he was a glass-blower.

1961-1965   Cai makes dozens of new types of electric lighting appliances, including the xenon arc lamp
1966, Jul Chinese delegate to the International Physics Colloquium in Beijing
1978, Mar Identified as director of the Research Laboratory for Electric Lighting Sources, Fudan University, Shanghai
       Jun Identified as chairman of the Shanghai Branch, Scientific and Technical Association
1979, Dec Elected vice-president of the Light Industry Society

Caidan Zhuoma
(Ts'ai-tan Cho-ma, Tsaidan Choma) (f)

Posts held   才旦卓玛

NPC
Member of the Standing Committee of the 5th NPC
Deputy for Tibet Autonomous Region to the 5th NPC

1963, Aug Caidan is a singer at a guest performance of a singing and dancing troupe in the USSR
1978, Feb Elected deputy for Tibet Autonomous Region to the 5th NPC
       Mar Elected member of the Standing Committee of the 5th NPC

Cao Chi (Ts'ao Ch'ih)   曹痴

Posts held

Government
Ambassador to Cyprus

1949, Oct Identified as secretary of Changsha Municipality CP

1955,   Feb   Identified as member of the People's
               Council of Hunan Province
         Sep   Identified as mayor of Changsha
1957,   Jul   Identified as 1st secretary of Changsha
               Municipality CP
1960,   Jan   Identified as director of the United Front
               Work Department of Hunan Province CP
1966,   Jan   Appointed ambassador to Iraq (until
               about 1967)
1967,   Jan   Cao heads a government delegation to
               Kuwait
1972,   Sep   Appointed ambassador to Nepal (until
               Nov 1977)
1978,   Mar   Appointed ambassador to Cyprus

Cao-da-nuo-fu (Ts'ao·ta·no·fu)   曹达诺夫

Posts held

CCP
Member of the Standing Committee of
Xinjiang Autonomous Region CP

NPC
Deputy for the PLA to the 5th NPC

Military
Major-general
Deputy political commissar of Xinjiang
Military Region

Cao belongs to the Uighur minority; he was born in 1920
(1922?). In the early 1940s he served as political officer
in the East Turkistan People's Army which was supported
by the Soviets. In autumn 1944 he took part in the Yining
Uprising under Ahomaiti. In February 1945 he became
political commissar of the East Turkistan People's Army,
and shortly afterwards deputy political commissar of
Xinjiang National Army. With the latter army he occupied
Dihua (today Ürümqi) in August 1945.

1950   Identified as deputy political commissar
               of the 5th Army and of Yining Military
               Subdistrict
1955,   Sep   Conferred the order "Liberation,"
               1st class; identified as major-general and
               as deputy director of the Political Depart-
               ment of Xinjiang Military Region
1965,   Aug   Identified as deputy political commissar
               of Xinjiang Military Region
1970,   Jun   Identified as member of the Standing
               Committee, Revolutionary Committee of
               Xinjiang (no later mention in this post)
1976,   Jun   Identified as member of the Standing
               Committee of Xinjiang CP
1977,   Jul   Identified as director of the Physical
               Culture and Sports Commission of Xin-
               jiang
1978,   Feb   Elected deputy for the PLA to the
               5th NPC

Cao Guanghua (Ts'ao Kuang-hua)   曹广化

Posts held

Others
Member of the Standing Committee of the
5th CPPCC

1965?   Identified as procurator of the Military
               Procuracy under the PLA General Politi-
               cal Department
1975,   Aug   Member of a delegation of PLA veterans
               to Algeria
1978,   Mar   Elected member of the Standing Commit-
               tee of the 5th CPPCC

Cao Juru (Ts'ao Chü-ju)   曹菊如

Posts held

NPC
Member of the Standing Committee of the
5th NPC
Deputy for Anhui Province to the 5th NPC

During the final phase of the Revolutionary War Cao
reportedly collaborated with the Communists in his capacity as director-general of the Northeast Bank.

1949,   Oct   Appointed member of the Financial and
               Economic Committee of the Government
               Administration Council; concurrently dep-
               uty director of the Central Financial and
               Economic Planning Bureau
1950,   Mar   Appointed director of the Public Shares
               Department of the Bank of China
         May   Appointed director of the Public Shares
               Department of the Bank of Communica-
               tions
1953,   Sep   Appointed vice-president of the People's
               Bank (until 1954)
1954,   Dec   Identified as standing member, Board of
               Directors of the People's Bank
1955-1957   Cao negotiates various agreements on
               international payments with Vietnam and
               Korea
1958,   May   Identified as president of the Bank of
               China (until 1963)
         Jul   Elected deputy for Qinghai Province to
               the 2nd NPC (until 1964)
1959,   Jul   Head of a People's Bank delegation to
               North Vietnam
1962,   Jun   Head of a delegation to Austria
1966   Disappears during the Cultural Revolution
1972,   Dec   First appearance after the Cultural Revo-
               lution: Identified as member of the Stand-
               ing Committee of the 4th CPPCC (un-
               til 1977)
1978,   Feb   Elected deputy for Anhui Province to the
               5th NPC
         Mar   Elected member of the Standing Commit-
               tee of the 5th NPC
1979,   Jun   Member of the Budget Committee at the
               2nd Session of the 5th NPC

Cao Keqiang (Ts'ao K'e-ch'iang)   曹克强

Posts held

Government
Ambassador to Sweden

1957,   Dec   Identified as counselor at the embassy in
               North Korea (until Dec 1960)

1961,	Feb	Identified as deputy director of the 2nd Asia Department of the Ministry of Foreign Affairs (until about Jan 1970)
1963,	Sep	Cao accompanies Chinese Head of State Liu Shaoqi to North Korea
1965,	Jun	Appointed advisor to the Chinese delegation to the planned 2nd Afro-Asian Solidarity Conference in Algiers (the conference was canceled)
1970,	Apr	Identified as deputy director of the Asia Department of the Ministry of Foreign Affairs (until Sep 1972); Cao accompanies Zhou Enlai to North Korea
1971,	Mar	Member of a Chinese Party and government delegation to Vietnam
1972,	Sep	Identified as deputy director of the West Asia and North Africa Department of the Ministry of Foreign Affairs
	Nov	Identified as director of the West Asia and North Africa Department of the Ministry of Foreign Affairs
1974,	Aug	Appointed ambassador to Syria (until 1978?)
1979,	Oct	Appointed ambassador to Sweden

Cao Lihuai (Ts'ao Li-huai) 曹里怀

Posts held

CCP
Member of the CCP 11th Central Committee

Military
Lieutenant-general
Deputy commander, PLA Air Force
3rd secretary, CP Secretariat of the PLA Airforce

Cao was born in 1907 in Hunan Province. He graduated from the 5th course at Whampoa Military Academy. In 1927 he took part in the Autumn Harvest Uprising in Hunan. From 1930 to 1933 he rose from regiment commander to the rank of division commander. In the following year he was made chief of staff of the 1st Division, 1st Front Army. In 1934-35 he took part in the Long March. He subsequently attended a course at the Anti-Japan Military and Political Academy. In 1939 he was chief of staff of the Garrison Corps of Yan'an. After the Japanese capitulation in 1945 he was appointed commander of Jilin-Heilongjiang Military District, followed by his appointment in 1947 as commander of the 1st Division, Northeast Democratic Joint Army. In the following year he commanded North Jilin Military District. In 1949 he was made commander of the 47th Army, 4th Field Army. Together with the units under Liu Yalou, Cao occupied Guizhou and Sichuan Provinces in the summer of that year.

1950,	Mar	Appointed council member of the People's Government of Hunan Province
1951,	Apr	Service in the Korean War as commander of the 47th Army
1954,	Jun	Identified as commander of the Air Force in Central-South China Military Region
1955,	Sep	Promoted to rank of lieutenant-general; appointed commander of the Air Force in Guangzhou Military Region

1956,	Oct	Identified as deputy commander of the PLA Air Force with the rank of lieutenant-general
1964		Following the escalation of the war in Vietnam, Cao is assigned tasks in connection with PLA military assistance
	Sep	Elected deputy for the PLA to the 3rd NPC
1969,	Apr	Elected to first term as member of the CCP Central Committee by the 9th Party Congress
1971,	Aug	Head of a military delegation to Albania and Romania
1973,	Jan	Deputy head of a military delegation to Pakistan
1975,	Feb	Deputy head of a military delegation to PR Vietnam
1977,	Jun	Identified as 3rd secretary, CP Secretariat of the PLA Air Force
	Sep	Member of a military delegation to France and Romania
1979,	Oct	Deputy head of a friendship delegation, led by Zhang Caiqian, to Pakistan

Cao Siming (Ts'ao Szu-ming) 曹思明

Posts held

CCP
Alternate member of the CCP 11th Central Committee

Military
Deputy political commissar, General Logistics Department of the PLA

1971,	May	Elected secretary of the newly established CP Secretariat of Xinjiang Autonomous Region (until Jul 1973)
	Sep	Identified as political commissar of Xinjiang Military Region (until 1975)
1973,	Jul	Identified as 3rd secretary of Xinjiang CP and as vice-chairman of the Revolutionary Committee of Xinjiang (until 1975)
1975,	Sep	Identified as deputy political commissar, General Logistics Department of the PLA
1977,	Aug	Elected alternate member of the CCP Central Committee by the 11th Party Congress

Cao Weilian (Ts'ao Wei-lien) 曹维廉

Posts held

Government
Vice-minister of the 1st Ministry of Machine Building

Others
Vice-president of the Quality Control Association

1958,	Jun	Identified as deputy director of the 8th Bureau under the 1st Ministry of Machine Building
1979,	Aug	Elected vice-president of the Quality Control Association
	Dec	Identified as vice-minister of the 1st Ministry of Machine Building

Cao Wenju (Ts'ao Wen-chü)   曹文举

Posts held

CCP
Member of the Standing Committee, Hunan Province CP

Provincial Administration
Vice-governor of Hunan Province
Director of the Finance and Commerce Office, People's Government of Hunan Province

1978,	Jun	Identified as a member of the Standing Committee, Hunan Province CP, and as director of the Finance and Commerce Office, People's Government of Hunan Province
1979,	Dec	Elected vice-governor of Hunan Province

Cao Yiou (Ts'ao Yi-ou) (f)   曹轶欧

Posts held

CCP
Member of the CCP 11th Central Committee

NPC
Member of the Standing Committee of the 5th NPC
Deputy for Beijing Municipality to the 5th NPC

Cao is the widow of Kang Sheng, who at one time had been active in the Higher Party School.

1950		Identified as council member of the People's Government of Shandong Province and as deputy director of the Organization Department of Shandong Province CP
1959,	Mar	Elected deputy for Jiangsu Province to the 2nd NPC (until Dec 1964)
1964,	Oct	Elected deputy for Hebei Province to the 3rd NPC
1967,	Oct	Referred to as a cadre of a department of the CCP Central Committee
1969,	Apr	Elected to first term as member of the CCP Central Committee by the 9th Party Congress
1975,	Jan	Elected member of the Standing Committee by the 4th NPC (confirmed in Mar 1978 by the 5th NPC)
1978,	Feb	Elected deputy for Beijing Municipality to the 5th NPC
	Mar	Cao disappears; probably purged

Cao Youmin (Ts'ao Yu-min)   曹有民

Posts held

Provincial Administration
Vice-chairman of the People's Congress of Gansu Province

1977,	Dec	Elected vice-chairman of the Revolutionary Committee of Gansu Province (until Dec 1979)
1979,	Dec	Elected vice-chairman of the People's Congress of Gansu Province

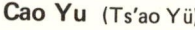 **Cao Yu** (Ts'ao Yü)

Posts held

NPC
Member of the Standing Committee of the 5th NPC
Deputy for Beijing Municipality to the 5th NPC

Others
Chairman of the Dramatists' Association
Director of the Beijing People's Art Theater

Cao was born in 1910 in Qianjiang, Hubei Province. He graduated from Qinghua University in 1931 and subsequently worked as a teacher at the National Dramatic Institute. In 1936 he was awarded the Dagong Bao Literary Prize for his drama Thunder and Storm. In 1937 he was one of the cofounders of the China Dramatic Society. From 1939 he taught at Sichuan National Dramatic School. In 1946 he and Lao She were invited to lecture on Chinese drama in the U.S.A. In 1948 he returned to Hong Kong. In March 1949 he attended the World Peace Council Session in Prague as a delegate, in July the Drama Association elected him a member of its Standing Committee; in addition, he was appointed deputy director of the Editorial Board, Federation of Literary and Art Circles, and member of that federation (until Cultural Revolution). In September 1949 he represented the Federation of Democratic Youth as a delegate at the 1st CPPCC.

1949,	Oct	Elected member of the Executive Council, Sino-Soviet Friendship Association (until 1954)
	Nov	Member of a delegation to Moscow for the anniversary of the October Revolution
	Dec	Appointed deputy director of the Central Drama Institute under the Ministry of Culture
1952,	May	Identified as council member of the Sino-Burmese Friendship Association
1953,	May	Identified as director of the Beijing People's Art Theater (until 1955)
	Oct	Identified as council member of the Union of Chinese Writers
1954,	May	Identified as council member of the Association for Cultural Relations with Foreign Countries (until Cultural Revolution)
	Aug	Elected deputy for Hubei Province to the 1st NPC (reelected to the 2nd and 3rd NPCs in 1958 and 1964)
1955,	Feb	Identified as vice-chairman of the Beijing Literary and Art Association (until Cultural Revolution)
1956,	May	Identified as director of the Beijing People's Art and Drama Institute
	Jul	Cao joins the CCP
	Aug	Member of the delegation to the World Conference against Atomic Bombs in Japan
	Dec	Elected secretary of the Union of Chinese Writers
1958,	Oct	Identified as vice-chairman of the Sino-PR Mongolian Friendship Association
1960,	Mar	Identified as council member of the Sino-Latin-American Friendship Association

Aug   Identified as vice-chairman of the Dramatists' Association

1961,   Sep   Identified as president of the People's
Academy of Dramatic Arts

1966,   Dec   Publicly denounced as a counterrevolutionary

1975,   Jan   First appearance after the Cultural Revolution: Referred to as deputy to the
4th NPC

1978,   Feb   Elected deputy for Beijing Municipality to
the 5th NPC

Mar   Elected member of the Standing Committee of the 5th NPC

Dec   Identified as vice-president of the Union
of Drama Workers

1979,   May   Identified as director of the Beijing People's Art Theater

Sep   Head of a writers delegation to Switzerland

Nov   Elected chairman of the Dramatists' Association

Publications

1934   Leiyu (Thunder and Storm)
1935   Richu (Sunrise)
1940   Shuibian (Metamorphosis)
        Beijing Ren (Beijing Man)
1941   Jia (The Family)
        The Bridge
        Meditation
1948   Film: A Sunny Day
1956   Minglan De Tian (Brilliant Sky)
        Gou Jian Restores the State

Cen Guorong (Ts'en Kuo-jung)   岑国荣

Posts held

CCP
Alternate member of the CCP 11th Cen-
tral Committee
Member of the Standing Committee of
Guangxi Autonomous Region CP

Mass Organization
Chairman of the Trade Unions of Guangxi
Autonomous Region

At the age of twelve Cen started to work in the service of
a landlord in Guangxi Province.

1950   Cen joins the PLA
1955   Cen joins the CCP
circa 1958   After discharge from the army, Cen works
at the Liuzhou Iron and Steel Complex in
Guangxi Province

1969,   Apr   Elected alternate member of the CCP
Central Committee by the 9th Party Congress (until Aug 1973)

1973,   Jun   Elected member of the Trade Union of
Guangxi Autonomous Region

Aug   Elected member of the CCP Central
Committee by the 10th Party Congress
(until Aug 1977)

1975,   Nov   Identified as member of the Standing
Committee of Guangxi CP

1976,   Jan   Identified as director of the Political
Department of Industry and Communica-
tions of Guangxi CP (until fall of 1976?)

1977,   Aug   Demoted from member to alternate member of the CCP Central Committee by the
11th Party Congress

Chai Chengwen (Ch'ai Ch'eng-wen)

Posts held   柴成文

Government
Director, Foreign Affairs Bureau in the
Ministry of National Defense

Military
Major-general

Chai was born about 1910 in Hebei Province.

1951   PRC delegate to the peace negotiations at
Panmunjong where his good English was
noted

1953,   Oct   Member of the Chinese delegation to the
cease fire negotiations at Panmunjong.
Referred to as major-general. Conferred
the North Korean orders of "Freedom and
Independence," 1st class, and "National
Flag," 2nd class

1955,   May   Ambassador to Denmark (until May 1956)
1962-1965   Various activities in Beijing
1969,   Sep   Visit of condolence to the Vietnamese
embassy on the death of Ho Chi-minh

Oct   Deputy leader of the Chinese delegation
at the Sino-Soviet border negotiations in
Beijing

1970,   Aug   Director, Foreign Affairs Bureau in the
Ministry of Defense

1973,   Jul   Member of a military delegation to Albania

1976,   Sep   Member of a military delegation to Mexico

1977,   Oct   Delegate representing the Ministry of
Defense at the Army Day celebrations in
Rwanda

1978,   Jun   Member of a military delegation to Yugoslavia (head: Yang Yong)

Chai Shufan (Ch'ai Shu-fan)   柴树藩

Posts held

Government
Minister of the 6th Ministry of Machine
Building

In 1927 Chai studied at the Sun Yat-sen University in
Moscow.

1954,   Oct   Appointed member of the State Planning
Commission (until Jun 1957)

1957,   Jun   Appointed vice-chairman of the State
Planning Commission (until Sep 1959)

1958,   Oct   Appointed vice-chairman, Capital Construction Commission (until Jan 1961)

1961,   Jan   Appointed vice-chairman, State Planning
Commission (until about 1967)

1965,   Feb   Identified as vice-chairman, State Economic Commission (until about 1967)

1973,   Feb   Identified as vice-minister of foreign
trade (until Feb 1978)

Jul   Head of a trade delegation to the USSR

1974,   Jun   Head of the Chinese delegation to the UN Law of the Sea Conference in Venezuela
       Jul   Head of a trade delegation to Cuba
       Sep   Head of a trade delegation to Syria and Kuwait
       Nov   Head of a goodwill delegation to France to inaugurate the direct air link Beijing Paris
1975,   Jun   Head of a government delegation to Cologne opening a China exhibition to the public
1976,   Dec   Head of a trade delegation to Sri Lanka
1977,   Apr   Head of a trade delegation to Afghanistan
       May   Head of an exhibition delegation to Japan
       Aug   Head of a trade delegation to Australia and New Zealand
1978,   Mar   Appointed minister of the 6th Ministry of Machine Building

Chai is married to Chen Xin.

Chai Zemin (Ch'ai Tse-min)　　柴泽民

Posts held

Government
Ambassador to the U.S.A.

Chai was born in 1915 in Wenxi, Shanxi Province. During 1937-1945 Chai served as deputy commander of South Hebei Military District and head of the Political Department of Shanyin (Daiyue) Military District. He was identified as CP secretary of Shanyin District in 1948.

1949,   Nov   Identified as CP secretary of the Beijing Suburban Work Committee
1950,   Dec   Identified as deputy secretary-general, Beijing Municipal People's Government and member of the Financial and Economic Committee, Beijing Municipal People's Government
1951,   Mar   Identified as chairman, Beijing Peasants' Association
1952,   Mar   Identified as president, Suburban Branch of Beijing People's Court
       Aug   Elected council member, Beijing Municipal People's Government
1954,   May   Identified as council member, Association for Cultural Relations with Foreign Countries
       Aug   Identified as chairman, Beijing Municipal Sports Committee (until Mar 1958)
1955,   Jul   Identified as council member, Institute of Foreign Affairs
       Sep   Identified as secretary-general, Beijing Municipal People's Council (until Oct 1957)
1956,   Aug   Deputy leader of a sports delegation to the USSR
1959,   Sep   Identified as director, Communications Department, Beijing Municipality CP
1961,   May   Appointed ambassador to Hungary (until Jul 1964)
1964,   Aug   Appointed ambassador to Guinea (until about 1967)
1970,   Jun   Appointed ambassador to Egypt (until Sep 1974)

1976,   May   Appointed ambassador to Thailand (until May 1978)
1978,   May   Appointed chief of the Liaison Office in the U.S.A.
1979,   Mar   Appointed ambassador to the U.S.A.

Chai is married to Li Youfeng.

Chang Xincun (Ch'ang Hsin-ts'un)　张新村

Posts held

CCP
Secretary of Liaoning Province CP

1978,   Nov   Identified as deputy secretary of Liaoning Province CP
1979,   Sep   Elected secretary of Liaoning Province CP

Chang Yanqing (Ch'ang Yen-ch'ing)　常彦卿

Posts held

Others
Vice-president and managing director of the Bank of China
Director of the Board of Directors, China International Trust and Investment Corporation

1959,   Jan   Identified as director of the Bureau for Industrial Equipment, Ministry of Foreign Trade
1960,   May   Member of a government delegation to the People's Republic of Mongolia (head: Zhou Enlai)
1961,   May   Appointed deputy director of the Staff Office for Economic Relations with Foreign Countries
1964,   Oct   Appointed member of the State Commission for Economic Relations with Foreign Countries
1966,   Jun   Chang disappears
1979,   Jul   First appearance after the Cultural Revolution: Identified as managing director of the Bank of China
       Oct   Appointed director of the Board of Directors, China International Trust and Investment Corporation; identified as vice-president of the Bank of China

Chen Aie (Ch'en Ai-o) (f)　　陈爱娥

Posts held

CCP
Alternate member of the CCP 11th Central Committee

Chen became known as a textile worker in Hubei Province.

1969,   Apr   Member of the presidium of the 9th CCP Party Congress
1977,   Aug   Elected alternate member of the CCP Central Committee by the 11th Party Congress

Chen Beichen (Ch'en Pei-ch'en) 陈北辰

Posts held

Provincial Administration
Vice-governor of Liaoning Province

1962, Jan   Identified as director of the United Front Work Department, Liaoning Province CP

1964, Jul   Identified as vice-chairman of the CPPCC, Liaoning Branch

1979, Sep   First appearance after the Cultural Revolution: Identified as vice-chairman of the Revolutionary Committee of Liaoning Province (until Jan 1980)

1980, Feb   Elected vice-governor of Liaoning Province

Chen Bingyu (Ch'en Ping-yü) 陈炳宇

Posts held

Provincial Administration
Vice-chairman of the Inner Mongolia People's Government

Chen belongs to the Mongol minority. He studied at Tumd Primary School.

1960, May   Identified as secretary of the Hohhot Municipality CP (until Cultural Revolution)

Jun   Identified as vice-mayor of Hohhot Municipality (until Cultural Revolution)

1965, Jan   Identified as acting director of the Organization Department, Inner Mongolia CP

1966, Sep   Denounced as a revisionist and purged

1979, Dec   First appearance after the Cultural Revolution: Elected vice-chairman of the Inner Mongolia People's Government

Chen Chu (Ch'en Ch'u) 陈楚

Posts held

Government
Permanent representative of the PRC to the UN

1949   Identified as deputy director of the Changjiang Ribao (Changjiang Daily) in Wuhan

1950, Mar   Appointed member of the Land Reform Committee in the Central-South China Military and Administrative Council

1952   Identified as deputy director of the Propaganda Department, Central-South China Bureau of the CCP Central Committee

1953, Jul   Appointed secretary-general of the Cultural and Educational Committee in the Central-South China Administrative Council

1955, Apr   Appointed director of the Soviet and East European Affairs Department in the Ministry of Foreign Affairs (until Dec 1955)

May   Advisor to a delegation led by Marshall Peng Dehuai and taking part as observer at the Warsaw Conference on Peace and Security in Europe

1956, Jan   Appointed counselor at the embassy in Moscow (until Jan 1959)

1964, Sep   Appointed director of the Department of West Asian and North African Affairs in the Ministry of Foreign Affairs (until Dec 1965)

1965, Mar   Accompanies Premier Zhou Enlai to Algeria

1966, Jan   Appointed ambassador to Ghana (until diplomatic relations were severed in Oct 1966)

1970, Aug   Reactivated after the Cultural Revolution

1971, Apr   Identified as director of the Information Department in the Ministry of Foreign Affairs

Nov   Appointed as one of the three representatives in the Chinese delegation to the 26th General Assembly of the UN

1972, Nov   Appointed as one of the three representatives of the Chinese delegation to the 27th General Assembly of the UN

1973, Mar   Appointed ambassador to Japan (until Dec 1976)

1977, May   Identified as permanent representative of the PRC to the UN

Chen Cisheng (Ch'en Tz'u-sheng) 陈此生

Posts held

NPC
Member of the Standing Committee of the 5th NPC
Deputy for Guangxi Autonomous Region to the 5th NPC

Others
Member of the Standing Committee of the 5th CPPCC
Vice-chairman of the Central Committee, Revolutionary Committee of the KMT

Chen was born in 1902 in Gui County, Guangxi Province. His father was a wellknown botanist. After graduating from the Shanghai Fudan University, Chen lectured at the middle school of History and Geography attached to the Sun Yat-sen University in Guangzhou. In 1928 he joined the KMT. After continuing his studies in Japan he served as a secretary under the head of the Education Department in the administration of his native province, Li Renren, and subsequently held various posts in the fields of culture and education in Guangxi. From 1945 to 1949 he lectured at Tate College in Hong Kong where in 1948 he was a signatory of a pro-Communist petition. In September 1949 he was invited by the Communists to attend the 1st CPPCC in Beijing.

1949, Oct   Appointed member of the Cultural and Educational Committee in the Central Government Council (until 1954)

Nov   Elected member of the Revolutionary Committee of the KMT

Dec   Appointed member of the Central-South China Military and Administrative Council

1950-1953   Various administrative offices, mainly in his native province of Guangxi

1954, Aug   Elected deputy for Guangxi Province to the 1st NPC (reelected to the 2nd and 3rd NPCs)

1955,	Feb	Elected vice-governor of Guangxi (until Mar 1958)
1957,	Nov	Identified as chief editor of the newspaper GMRB (until ?)
1959,	Apr	Elected member of the Standing Committee of the 3rd CPPCC (reelected in 1964 to the 4th and in 1978 to the 5th CPPCC)
	May	Elected deputy secretary-general of the NPC (reelected in 1965)
	Aug	Member of a government delegation visiting the PR Mongolia
1971,	Jun	Reactivated after 4 years of absence
1975,	Jan	Elected member of the Standing Committee of the 4th NPC (confirmed by the 5th NPC in 1978)
1978,	Feb	Elected deputy for Guangxi Autonomous Region to the 5th NPC
1979,	Jun	Member of the Budget and of Draft Laws Committee, 2nd Session of the 5th NPC
	Oct	Elected vice-chairman of the Central Committee, Revolutionary Committee of the KMT

Chen Daisun (Ch'en Tai-sun)　　陈岱孙

Posts held

Others
President of the Society of Foreign Economic Theories

1960,	Jan	Identified as a professor of Beijing University
1973,	Apr	Newly identified as a professor of Beijing University after the Cultural Revolution
1979,	Nov	Elected president of the Society of Foreign Economic Theories

Chen Dong (Ch'en Tung)　　陈　东

Posts held

Government
Ambassador to the German Democratic Republic

1963,	Apr	Identified as counselor at the embassy in the USSR (until Mar 1965)
1965,	Aug	Identified as consul-general in Gdansk (Poland)
1969,	Feb	Identified as chargé d'affaires in Poland
1972,	Aug	Appointed ambassador to Iceland (until Oct 1977)
1978,	Mar	Appointed ambassador to the German Democratic Republic

Chen Feng (Ch'en Feng)　　陈　风

Posts held

Government
Ambassador to Iceland

Chen served towards the end of the revolutionary period as a deputy political commissar in a division of the 4th Field Army.

1954,	Apr	Identified as CP secretary of Nanning Municipality
	Jun	Elected mayor of Nanning
1955,	May	Identified as 1st CP secretary of Nanning
1965,	Jul	Appointed ambassador to Afghanistan (until approximately 1966)
1972,	Apr	Appointed ambassador to Burundi (until Nov 1977)
1978,	Mar	Appointed ambassador to Iceland

Chen Fuhan (Ch'en Fu-han)　　陈福汉

Posts held

CCP
Member of the CCP 11th Central Committee

NPC
Deputy for Beijing Municipality to the 5th NPC

Mass Organization
Vice-chairman of the Railway Workers Union

Provincial Administration
Member of the Standing Committee, Beijing Municipality

Chen became known as chief locomotive driver of the "Mao Zedong Locomotive," breaking many records.

1977,	Aug	Elected member of the CCP Central Committee by the 11th Party Congress
1978,	Feb	Elected deputy for Beijing Municipality to the 5th NPC
	Nov	Elected vice-chairman of the Railway Workers Union
1979,	Mar	Identified as member of the Revolutionary Committee, Beijing Municipality
	Jun	Member of the Budget Committee, 2nd Session of the 5th NPC

Chen Guang (Ch'en Kuang)　　陈　光

Posts held

Provincial Government
Vice-chairman of the Revolutionary Committee of Jiangsu Province

Chen was born in 1900 in Yizhang, Hunan Province. In 1927 he took part as personal attendant in the Hunan Uprising. He then commanded a company on Jinggangshan. In 1932 he became commander of the 2nd Division of the 1st Front Army and one year later commander of the "Young Communist International Division." During the Long March he again commanded the 2nd Division of the 1st Front Army. In 1936 he took a course at the Academy of the Red Army and was subsequently given a regiment of the 1st Front Army. In 1937 he was commander of the 343rd Brigade of the 115th Division under Lin Biao in the 8th Route Army. When Lin was wounded in 1939 Chen became acting commander of the 115th Division. Shortly after, he led the "East Column" of this division to Shandong. In 1944 he operated in the area of Jiangsu Province. In 1945 he was made deputy commander of the

Military Region of Jilin-Changchun. About 1947 he became commander of Harbin Garrison. His appointment as deputy chief of staff of the Northeast Field Army followed in 1948. He retained this post after the army was renamed 4th Field Army in the following year. In August 1949 he became deputy chief of staff of Central-South China Military Region.

1950,	Jul	Identified as deputy commander of Guangdong Military District and as council member of the People's Government of Guangdong Province (until 1952)
1952,	Nov	Identified as council member of the People's Government of Jiangsu Province (until 1955)
1956,	Jun	Elected deputy for Jiangsu Province to the 1st NPC (confirmed in 1959 by the 2nd NPC)
	Jul	Identified as secretary of Jiangsu Province CP (until Dec 1962)
1962,	Dec	Elected (demoted) member of the Standing Committee of Jiangsu Province CP
1968,	Mar	Branded "the Chinese Khruschev's agent in Jiangsu" and purged
1977,	Dec	First appearance after the Cultural Revolution: Elected vice-chairman of the Revolutionary Committee of Jiangsu Province

Chen Guodong (Ch'en Kuo-tung) 陈国栋

Posts held

CCP
1st secretary of Shanghai Municipality CP

Chen was born in 1911 in Jiangxi Province.

1949,	Oct	Appointed director of the Finance Department, East China Military and Administrative Council
1952,	Aug	Appointed vice-minister of finance (until Sep 1953)
1953,	Sep	Appointed vice-minister of food (until 1966)
1965,	Jan	Elected member of the Standing Committee of the 4th CPPCC (until Feb 1978)
1967		Disappears during the Cultural Revolution
1973,	May	First appearance after the Cultural Revolution
1975,	May	Identified as a government cadre
1977,	Aug	Elected member of the CCP Central Committee by the 11th Party Congress
1978,	Mar	Appointed director of the Federation of Supply and Marketing Cooperatives (until Jun 1979)
	Aug	Advisor to an agricultural delegation to Romania, the Federal Republic of Germany, and France
1979,	Jun	Appointed minister of food (until Jan 1980)
	Jul	Appointed member of the State Financial and Economic Commission (until Jan 1980)
1980,	Feb	Identified as 2nd secretary of Shanghai Municipality CP
	Mar	Identified as 1st Secretary of Shanghai Municipality CP

Chen Hanbo (Ch'en Han-po) 陈翰伯

Posts held

Government
Acting director of the State Publication Administration Bureau

Others
Chairman of the Publishers' Association

1949,	Dec	Identified as vice-president of Beijing Information School
1962,	Apr	Elected council member of the China-Africa Society
1964,	Dec	Appointed authorized head of the Applications Evaluation Committee of the 4th CPPCC
1966,	Nov	Branded as an anti-Party element
1973,	Sep	First appearance after the Cultural Revolution: Identified as a cadre of the State Publication Administration Bureau
1978,	Aug	Identified as acting director of the State Publication Administration Bureau
1979,	Dec	Elected chairman of the Publishers' Association

Chen Hansheng (Ch'en Han-sheng) 陈翰笙

Posts held

President of the Central Asian Culture Research Society

Chen was born in 1897 in Jiangsu Province. He studied in Great Britain, the U.S.A., Germany, and the USSR. In 1927 he worked at the Institute of Social Sciences, Academia Sinica, on problems of Chinese agricultural economies. In 1928 he joined the CCP in Moscow. During World War II he worked for British intelligence in India. After the war he lectured at the University of Washington, U.S.A. He returned to China in 1949 and became professor of history at Beijing University.

1949,	Dec	Identified as deputy director of the Institute of Foreign Affairs
1951,	Sep	Member of a cultural delegation to India and Burma (delegation leader: Ding Xilin)
1952,	Mar	Elected vice-chairman of the Economic Research Society
	Apr	Member of a delegation to the International Economic Conference in Moscow
	May	Identified as vice-president of the Sino-Indian Friendship Association
	Jul	Member of a delegation to the 3rd Conference of the World Peace Council in East Berlin
1954,	May	Elected member of the Standing Committee of the Association for Cultural Relations with Foreign Countries (until Cultural Revolution)
	Aug	Elected deputy for Hebei Province to the 1st NPC (reelected to the 2nd and 3rd NPCs in 1958 and 1964)
1955,	Mar	Member of a delegation to the Asian Countries' Conference in New Delhi
	Jun	Appointed member of the Department of Philosophy and Social Sciences of the Academy of Sciences; member of a dele-

gation to the World Peace Conference in Helsinki, Finland

1956, Dec Accompanies Song Qingling to India, Burma, and Pakistan

Feb Appointed member and secretary-general of the Afro-Asian Solidarity Committee

Mar Member of a delegation to attend the World Peace Council's Conference on Disarmament and Prohibition of Nuclear Weapons in Sweden

Nov Member of an NPC delegation to the USSR and East European countries; appointed deputy director of the Research Institute of International Relations, Academy of Sciences

1967, Jun Denounced as a follower of Liu Shaoqi and purged

1977, Dec First appearance after the Cultural Revolution

1979, Nov Identified as president of the Central Asian Culture Research Society

Publications

1927 <u>Human History</u>
1929 <u>Difference Among Mu Peasants and Landlords in Heilongjiang Valley</u>
1933 <u>Land Problems of Modern China</u>
1934 <u>The Relationship of Production and Productivity in the Rural Areas of Kuangtung</u> (published in the U.S.A.)
1937 <u>The Landlords and the Peasants of China</u>
1939? <u>The Monopoly and Civil War</u>

Chen Huangmei (Ch'en Huang-mei) 陈荒煤

Posts held

Others
Deputy director of the Institute of Literature, Academy of Social Sciences
Vice-chairman of the Writers' Union

In July 1947 Chen was elected member of the 1st National Committee of the Federation of Literary and Art Circles (reelected to the 2nd and 3rd National Committees in 1953 and 1960). In September 1949 he was a delegate to the 1st CPPCC.

1950, Jan Identified as deputy director of the Propaganda Section, Political Department of the 4th Field Army

Mar Identified as deputy director of the Cultural Department of the Central-South Military and Administrative Committee

1953, Aug Identified as deputy director of the Film Bureau under the Ministry of Culture (until Oct 1959)

Sep Identified as council member of the Writers' Union

1954, May Identified as council member of the Association for Cultural Relations with Foreign Countries

1959, Oct Identified as acting director of the Film Bureau under the Ministry of Culture (until Dec 1961)

1960, Feb Identified as a member of the Editorial Board of <u>Wenxue Zazhi</u> (Literary Gazette) and <u>Dianying Yishu</u> (Cinema Art)

Jul Head of a film delegation to the International Film Festival in Prague

Aug Identified as council member of the Movie Artists' Union

1961, Dec Identified as director of the Film Bureau under the Ministry of Culture

1963, Sep Appointed vice-minister of culture (until Jul 1965)

1964, Sep Elected deputy for Hubei Province to the 3rd NPC

1966, Jun Denounced as a bourgeois element in film circles and purged

1979, Oct First appearance after the Cultural Revolution: Identified as deputy director of the Institute of Literature, Academy of Social Sciences

Dec Identified as vice-chairman of the Writers' Union

Chen Jianfei (Ch'en Chien-fei) 陈剑飞

Posts held

CCP
Secretary of Heilongjiang Province CP

NPC
Deputy for Heilongjiang Province to the 5th NPC

Provincial Administration
Vice-governor of Heilongjiang Province

Chen was born in Liaoning Province.

1950, Apr Appointed council member of the People's Government of Xinjiang Province and director of its Industry Department

1954, Dec Appointed member of the Construction Committee for State Operated Friendship Farms

1955, Jan Identified as member of the People's Government of Heilongjiang Province

1956, Dec Elected vice-governor of Heilongjiang Province (until Jan 1967)

1959, Jun Identified as deputy head of the Sino-Soviet Joint Survey Team for the Heilongjiang (Amur) River Basin

1966, Feb Identified as member of the Standing Committee of Heilongjiang Province CP

1967 Disappears during the Cultural Revolution

1973, Mar First appearance after the Cultural Revolution: Identified as member of the Standing Committee of Heilongjiang Province CP (until 1977)

1976, Mar Identified as member of the Standing Committee, Revolutionary Committee of Heilongjiang Province (until 1977)

1977, Dec Elected vice-chairman of the Revolutionary Committee of Heilongjiang Province (until Dec 1979)

1978, Feb Identified as secretary of Heilongjiang Province CP; elected deputy for Heilongjiang Province to the 5th NPC

1979, Dec Elected vice-governor of Heilongjiang Province

Chen Jie (Ch'en Chieh) 陈 洁

Posts held

Government
Vice-minister of foreign trade

1964,	Jul	Identified as deputy director of the Political Department of the Ministry of Commerce (until approximately 1966)
1970,	Aug	Identified as a government cadre
1971,	Sep	Identified as vice-minister of foreign trade
1972		Head of trade delegations to Afghanistan, Iran, German Democratic Republic (GDR), Hungary, Kuwait, Bulgaria, Nepal, Brazil, New Zealand, Zambia, Tanzania, Madagascar, CSSR
1975		Head of trade delegations to Hungary, PR Mongolia, Ghana, the USSR, Pakistan, GDR
1976		Head of trade delegations to Bulgaria, North Korea, Yugoslavia, Egypt
1977		Head of trade delegations to Hungary, CSSR, Poland, PR Mongolia, the USSR
1978,	May	Head of a trade delegation to Kenya and Uganda
	Aug	Member of the Party and government delegation, led by Hua Guofeng, to Romania, Yugoslavia, Iran
	Sep	Head of a trade delegation to Algeria, Congo (Brazzaville), Mali, Mauritania
	Dec	Head of a trade delegation to Kampuchea
1979,	Jan	Member of a government delegation, led by Li Xiannian to Tanzania, Mozambique, Zambia, Zaire, and Pakistan
	Apr	Head of a trade delegation to Pakistan
	Jun	Head of trade delegations to Argentina, Peru, and Chile
	Aug	Head of a trade delegation to the USSR
	Sep	Head of trade delegations to Mauritius and Madagascar
	Oct	Head of a trade delegation to Iraq
	Nov	Head of a trade delegation to Egypt
	Dec	Head of a trade delegation to Yugoslavia

Chen is married to Shao Yi.

Chen Jingbo (Ch'en Ching-po) 陈竞波

Posts held

Provincial Administration
Vice-chairman of the Standing Committee, Tibet Autonomous Regional People's Congress

1958,	May	Identified as secretary of the Youth Work Department of Tibet CP
1959,	May	Identified as deputy secretary-general of the Preparatory Committee for Tibet Autonomous Region
1965,	Sep	Identified as member of the People's Council of Tibet Autonomous Region
1966,	Feb	Identified as secretary-general of the People's Council of Tibet Autonomous Region; subsequently disappears
1979,	Aug	Elected vice-chairman of the Standing Committee of Tibet Autonomous Regional People's Congress

Chen Jinhua (Ch'en Chin-hua) 陈锦华

Posts held

CCP
Deputy secretary of Shanghai Municipality CP

Provincial Administration
Vice-mayor of Shanghai Municipality

1977,	Dec	Elected vice-chairman of the Revolutionary Committee of Shanghai Municipality (until Dec 1979)
1979,	May	Identified as deputy secretary of Shanghai Municipality CP
	Dec	Elected vice-mayor of Shanghai Municipality

Chen Kang (Ch'en K'ang) 陈 康

Posts held

Military
Lieutenant-general
Deputy commander of Lanzhou Military Region

Chen was born in 1911 in Hubei Province. In 1935 he led a battalion under the 4th Front Army. In 1937 he became commander of the 772nd Regiment of the 386th Brigade, 129th Division under the 8th Route Army.

1950		Identified as deputy commander of a PLA Army
	Aug	Identified as council member of the People's Government of Yunnan Province
1956,	Aug	Identified as deputy commander of Kunming Military Region (until 1975)
1958,	Apr	Identified as lieutenant-general
1963,	May	Identified as commander of Kunming Garrison
1968,	Aug	Elected vice-chairman of the Revolutionary Committee of Yunnan Province (until 1975?)
1969,	Apr	Elected member of the CCP Central Committee by the 9th Party Congress (reelected to the 10th Central Committee in 1973)
1971,	Mar	Elected secretary of Yunnan Province CP (until 1975?)
1976,	Jan	Chen disappears until Sep 1979
1979,	Sep	Identified as deputy commander of Lanzhou Military Region

Chen Kehan (Ch'en K'e-han) 陈克寒

Posts held

Provincial Administration
Vice-chairman of the People's Congress of Beijing Municipality

Chen joined the CCP in 1929 while studying at Daxia University in Shanghai. Two years later he was chairman of the Shanghai Students' Association. In 1936 he went to Yan'an to study at the Anti-Japan Military and Political Academy. The following year he served in the 8th Route

Army. In 1939 he became editor of the North China edition of NCNA. In 1948 he was identified as director of the Propaganda Department in the Central Plains Bureau under the CCP Central Committee. In May 1949 he was elected member of the Federation of Democratic Youth. In September that year he was a delegate representing journalists at the 1st CPPCC.

1949,	Oct	Appointed director of the Press Administration, Government Administrative Council (until Nov 1954)
1952,	Apr	Identified as deputy director of the Publications Administration, Government Administrative Council (until Nov 1954)
1954,	Aug	Elected deputy for Jiangsu Province to the 1st NPC
	Nov	Appointed vice-minister of culture (until Sep 1963)
1959,	May	Identified as secretary of Beijing Municipality CP (until Cultural Revolution)
	Jun	Identified as a member of the Commission for Cultural Relations with Foreign Countries
1962,	Mar	Identified as council member of the Sino-Czechoslovakian Friendship Association
1966		Denounced as an accomplice of Peng Zhen and purged
1975,	Sep	First appearance after the Cultural Revolution
1979,	Dec	Elected vice-chairman of the People's Congress of Beijing Municipality

Chen Ketian (Ch'en K'e-t'ien)　陈克天

Posts held

NPC
Deputy for Jiangsu Province to the 5th NPC

Provincial Administration
Vice-governor of Jiangsu Province

1977,	Dec	Elected vice-chairman of the Revolutionary Committee of Jiangsu Province (until Dec 1979)
1978,	Feb	Elected deputy for Jiangsu Province to the 5th NPC
1979,	Dec	Elected vice-governor of Jiangsu Province

Chen Kunti (Ch'en K'un-t'i) (f)　陈坤惕

Posts held

Others
President of the Nurses' Association

1963		Identified as president of the Nurses' Association
1966		Disappears during the Cultural Revolution
1978,	Jun	First appearance after the Cultural Revolution: Identified on her former post as president of the Nurses' Association

Chen Lei (Ch'en Lei)　陈雷

Posts held

CCP
Secretary of Heilongjiang Province CP

NPC
Deputy for Heilongjiang Province to the 5th NPC

Provincial Administration
Vice-governor of Heilongjiang Province

In 1946 Chen commanded the Heilongjiang Independent Army.

1950,	May	Identified as council member of the People's Government of Heilongjiang Province and as secretary-general of Heilongjiang Province CP
1954,	Aug	Elected deputy for Heilongjiang Province to the 1st NPC
1958,	Sep	Elected vice-governor of Heilongjiang Province
1959,	Dec	Identified as director of the Industry Department of Heilongjiang Province CP
1964,	Mar	Identified as alternate secretary of Heilongjiang Province CP
1967		Disappears during the Cultural Revolution
1977,	Dec	First appearance after the Cultural Revolution: Elected vice-chairman of the Revolutionary Committee of Heilongjiang Province (until Dec 1979)
1978,	Feb	Elected deputy for Heilongjiang Province to the 5th NPC; identified as secretary of Heilongjiang Province CP
	Oct	Member of a friendship delegation to Japan
1979,	Dec	Elected vice-governor of Heilongjiang Province

Chen Liemin (Ch'en Lieh-min)　陈烈民

Posts held

CCP
Secretary of Heilongjiang Province CP
Secretary, CP of Daqing Oil Field

Government
Vice-minister of petroleum industry

NPC
Deputy for Heilongjiang Province to the 5th NPC

Others
Chairman, Daqing Oil Field Revolutionary Committee

1978,	Feb	Elected deputy for Heilongjiang Province to the 5th NPC
	Aug	Identified as vice-minister of petroleum industry; secretary of Heilongjiang Province CP and secretary, CP of Daqing Oil Field

1979,   Jun   Identified as chairman of the Daqing Oil-
                Field Revolutionary Committee; member
                of the Budget Committee, 2nd Session of
                the 5th NPC

Chen Manyuan (Ch'en Man-yüan) 陈漫远

Posts held

Military
Leading cadre of the Central Leadership

Chen was born in 1907 in Mengshan, Guangxi Province, as
the son of a wealthy landlord. Due to differences with his
father, all financial support was stopped while he was still
a student at Wuzhou Middle School. Chen then joined the
Jiangxi Soviet where he studied at the Red Army College
in Ruijin. After completing his studies he took part in the
Long March. During the Anti-Japanese War he initially
served as regiment commander of the 8th Route Army and
later as division commander of the New 4th Army. After
the Anti-Japanese War he was appointed deputy commander of an army corps of the 4th Field Army based in
Manchuria. In September 1949 Chen represented the PLA
as a delegate at the CPPCC which elected him a member
of its National Committee (until 1954).

1949,   Nov   Appointed chairman of the Guilin Military
                Control Commission
         Dec   Appointed vice-chairman of the People's
                Government of Guangxi Province (until
                Feb 1955); appointed member of the Cen-
                tral-South China Military and Administra-
                tive Council (reorganized in Jan 1953)
1950,   Jan   Identified as member of the Standing
                Committee of South China Subbureau,
                Central-South China Bureau of the CCP
                Central Committee
1952,   Oct   Identified as political commissar of
                Guangxi Military Region
1953,   Jan   Appointed member of the Central-South
                China Administrative Council (abolished
                in Oct 1954)
         May   Identified as 2nd secretary of Guangxi
                Province CP
1954,   Jan   Appointed acting chairman of the People's
                Government of Guangxi Province
         Aug   Elected deputy for Guangxi Province to
                the 1st NPC (until Mar 1959)
1956,   Sep   Elected alternate member of the CCP
                Central Committee
1960,   Feb   Identified as chancelor of Beijing Agricul-
                tural University (until Jun 1964)
1964,   Jan   Appointed vice-minister of state farms
                and land reclamation
         Oct   Elected deputy for Sichuan Province to
                the 3rd NPC
1968,   Apr   Branded as a capitalist-roader
1974,   Sep   First appearance after the Cultural Revo-
                lution
1977,   Oct   Identified as a leading military cadre

Chen Ming (Ch'en Ming) 陈 明

Posts held

Provincial Administration
Vice-governor of Hubei Province

1959,   Jun   Identified as deputy director of the
                3rd Office, Ministry of Foreign Trade
         Oct   Head of a banking delegation to South
                America
1960,   Nov   Identified as deputy director of the
                2nd Office, Ministry of Foreign Trade
         Dec   Identified as director of the 3rd Office,
                Ministry of Foreign Trade
1961,   May   Advisor of the Chinese delegation to the
                Laos Conference in Geneva
1964,   Apr   Identified as commercial counselor in the
                embassy in Paris
1966,   Jan   Chen disappears
1980,   Jan   Elected vice-governor of Hubei Province

Chen Mingyi (Ch'en Ming-yi) 陈明义

Posts held

Military
Major-general
Deputy commander of Chengdu Military
Region

Provincial Administration
Member of the Revolutionary Committee
of Sichuan Province

In 1937 Chen was a staff officer in the Headquarters of
the 4th Front Army.

1954,   Nov   Identified as commander of the Headquar-
                ters for the Construction of the Xikang
                Road
1955,   Feb   Identified as commander of the Logistics
                Forces in Tibet Military Region
         Jun   Identified as deputy commander of Tibet
                Military Region (until 1970)
1957,   May   Identified as major-general
1964,   Oct   Elected deputy for Tibet Military Region
                to the 3rd NPC
1965,   Sep   Appointed member of the People's Council
                of Tibet Autonomous Region (until 1975)
         Nov   Identified as chairman of the Physical
                Culture and Sports Commission under the
                People's Council of Tibet
1968,   Sep   Elected vice-chairman of the newly estab-
                lished Revolutionary Committee of Tibet
                Autonomous Region (until 1975)
1971,   Aug   Elected CP secretary of the newly estab-
                lished Party Secretariat in Tibet; identi-
                fied concurrently as commander of Tibet
                Military District (the status of Tibet
                Military Region had recently been reduced
                to Military District) (both posts until
                about 1975)
1977,   Dec   Elected member of the Revolutionary
                Committee of Sichuan Province
1978,   Apr   Identified as deputy commander of
                Chengdu Military Region

Chen Muhua (Ch'en Mu-hua) (f) 陈慕华

<u>Posts held</u>

CCP
Alternate member, Politburo of the CCP 11th Central Committee
Member of the CCP 11th Central Committee

Government
Vice-premier
Minister of economic relations with foreign countries
Vice-chairman of the Central Patriotic Health Campaign Committee
Director of the Birth Planning Leading Group under the State Council

NPC
Deputy for Zhejiang Province to the 5th NPC

1962,	Jul	Identified as deputy director of the Bureau of Integrated Industrial Equipment, General Liaison Office of Economic Relations with Foreign Countries
1964,	Jun	The General Liaison Office of Economic Relations with Foreign Countries is made a commission under the State Council. Chen retains her post as deputy director of the bureau (until Dec 1970)
1965,	Jun	Appointed advisor to the Chinese delegation to the proposed 2nd Afro-Asian Conference in Algiers (the conference was canceled at the last minute)
	Sep	Mrs Chen accompanies the minister of foreign affairs Chen Yi to Pakistan, Syria, Algeria, Mali, and Guinea
1969,	Sep	Present at the negotiations between the prime ministers of China and Congo (Brazzaville)
1970,	Jun–Dec	Present in Beijing during negotiations with government delegations from Somalia, Sudan, Tanzania, Zambia, South Yemen, Pakistan, and Mali
	Dec	The Commission of Economic Relations with Foreign Countries is reorganized into the ministry of the same name; Chen is appointed vice-minister in the new ministry (until Jan 1977)
1972,	Jan	Deputy head of a government delegation to Zambia
1973,	Aug	Elected to first term as member of the CCP Central Committee by the 10th Party Congress
1975,	Mar	Chen heads the Chinese delegation to the UN Industrial Development Organization (UNIDO) Conference in Lima
1977,	Jan	Identified as minister of economic relations with foreign countries
	Aug	Elected alternate member of the Politburo by the 11th CCP Congress
1978,	Feb	Elected deputy for Zhejiang Province to the 5th NPC
	Mar	Appointed vice-premier
	Apr	Chen heads a Party and government delegation to Romania; appointed vice-chairman of the Central Patriotic Health Campaign Committee
	May	Member of a Party delegation to North Korea, led by Hua Guofeng
	Jul	Appointed director of the Birth Planning Leading Group under the State Council; Head of a government delegation to Somalia, Gabon, and Cameroun
1979,	Mar	Head of a government delegation to Australia, New Zealand, Fiji, and Western Samoa
	Aug	Chen publishes an article in <u>RMRB</u> of 11 Aug on control on population growth

Chen Peimin (Ch'en P'ei-min) 陈培民

<u>Posts held</u>

Government
Vice-minister of the Physical Culture and Sports Commission

| 1977, | Mar | Identified as vice-minister of the Physical Culture and Sports Commission |
| 1979, | Jul | Appointed member of the National Games Organizing Committee |

Chen Peng (Ch'en P'eng) 陈鹏

<u>Posts held</u>

CCP
Secretary of Beijing Municipality CP

1955,	Jul	Identified as deputy secretary of Beijing Municipality CP (until May 1957)
1957,	May	Identified as secretary of Beijing Municipality CP (until Cultural Revolution)
1963		Identified as alternate member of the Control Commission of the CCP Central Committee
1966		Disappears during the Cultural Revolution
1979,	Feb	First appearance after the Cultural Revolution
	May	Identified a secretary of Beijing Municipality CP

Chen Pixian (Ch'en P'i-hsien) 陈丕显

<u>Posts held</u>

CCP
Member of the CCP 11th Central Committee
1st secretary of Hubei Province CP

NPC
Deputy for Hubei Province to the 5th NPC

Military
Political commissar of Wuhan Military Region
1st political commissar of Hubei Military District

Provincial Administration
Chairman of the People's Congress Hubei Province

Chen was born in 1911 in Fuzhou, Fujian Province. In 1935 he was active as a cadre in the Communist Youth League in Jiangxi Province and was given the task by Chen Yi to set up a guerrilla base near Xiaofen. In 1936 he became a member of the CCP Committee for South Jiangxi. He was appointed secretary of Suzhong CP in 1937. In April 1949 the New Democratic Youth League elected him member of its Central Committee (until Jun 1953).

1949,	Oct	Identified as CP secretary of the Southern Jiangsu District Committee (until Dec 1952)
	Dec	Identified as political commissar of Southern Jiangsu Military Region (until Dec 1952); appointed member of the East China Military and Administrative Council (until Dec 1952)
1952,	Aug	Identified as 4th secretary of the East China Bureau, CCP Central Committee (until Sep 1954)
	Nov	Identified as 4th secretary, CP of Shanghai Municipality (until Oct 1954)
	Dec	Appointed member of the East China Administrative Council (until Aug 1954)
1954,	Oct	Identified as secretary, CP of Shanghai Municipality (until approximately Nov 1965)
1955,	Feb	Elected member of the People's Council of Shanghai
1956,	Sep	Elected alternate member of the CCP Central Committee by the 8th Party Congress
1957,	Nov	Elected vice-chairman, Shanghai Section of the Sino-Soviet Friendship Association
1958,	Nov	Identified as chairman of the Shanghai Section, CPPCC
1960,	Jun	Identified as political commissar of Shanghai Garrison
1961,	Apr	Head of a delegation to the May Day celebrations in Leningrad
1964,	Apr	Identified as secretary of the East China Bureau of the CCP Central Committee
1965,	Nov	Identified as 1st secretary, CP of Shanghai Municipality
1966		Chen turns against the leftest labor movement
1967		Chen undergoes self-criticism. In December a struggle and criticism demonstration against him is broadcast by television
1968		Two further struggle and criticism demonstrations against him are televised in January and March, followed by his disappearance
1977,	May	First appearance after the Cultural Revolution: Identified as CP secretary and chairman of the Revolutionary Committee of Yunnan Province (until Aug 1977)
	Aug	Elected member of the CCP Central Committee by the 11th Party Congress, identified as 2nd CP secretary, and 1st vice-chairman of the Revolutionary Committee, of Hubei Province (latter positions until Jul 1978)
1978,	Feb	Elected deputy for Hubei Province to the 5th NPC
	Aug	Identified as 1st secretary of Hubei CP
	Oct	Identified as chairman of Hubei Revolutionary Committee (until Dec 1979); depu-

ty leader of a Party workers' delegation to Romania and Yugoslavia

1979,	Jun	Identified as political commissar of Wuhan Military Region
	Aug	Head of a Hubei provincial delegation to the U.S.A.; identified as 1st political commissar of Hubei Military District
1980,	Jan	Elected chairman of the People's Congress of Hubei Province

Chen Puru (Ch'en P'u-ju) 陈璞如

Posts held

CCP
Member of the CCP 11th Central Committee
Secretary of Liaoning Province CP

Provincial Administration
Governor of Liaoning Province

1949,	Nov	Appointed chairman of the Zunyi Military Control Commission in Guizhou Province
1950,	Jul	Identified as director of the Industry and Commerce Department in the Guizhou People's Government
1955,	Feb	Identified as director of the Trade Department in the Guizhou People's Government
1956,	Jun	Elected member of the Standing Committee, Guizhou Province CP
1957		Identified as vice-governor of Guizhou Province
1960,	Apr	Elected alternate member of the Guizhou CP Secretariat
1966,	Sep	Identified as secretary of Guizhou CP
1968		Chen is publicly denounced at least four times as a deviationist and disappears
1977,	Mar	First appearance after the Cultural Revolution: Identified as CP secretary, and vice-chairman of the Revolutionary Committee, of Liaoning Province (until Jan 1980)
	Aug	Elected member of the CCP Central Committee by the 11th Party Congress
1978,	May	Member of an economic delegation to Great Britain and France, led by Gu Ming
1980,	Jan	Elected governor of Liaoning Province

Chen Qihan (Ch'en Ch'i-han) 陈奇涵

Posts held

CCP
Member of the CCP 11th Central Committee

Military
Colonel-general

Chen was born in 1898 in Pingjiang in Jiangxi Province. He received his military training at the Whampoa Military Academy and took part in the Northern Expedition of 1926 as chief of staff of the units commanded by Ye Ting. In

1927 he was an instructor in the training corps of the 3rd Army in the National Revolutionary Army. In July of the same year he participated in the Nanchang Uprising. In 1935 he commanded a unit of the 15th Army Corps led by Xu Haidong.   After Nanchang had been taken by Communist forces in June 1949 Chen became vice-chairman of the Nanchang Military Control Commission and was appointed commander of Jiangxi Military Region (until September 1954).

1950,	Jan	Appointed member of the Central-South China Military and Administrative Council (until Jan 1953)
	Mar	Identified as member of the People's Government of Jiangxi Province (until Sep 1954)
1954,	Aug	Elected deputy for Jiangxi Province to the 1st NPC (until Mar 1959)
	Sep	Appointed member of the National Defense Council (until approximately 1967)
1956,	Sep	Elected alternate member of the CCP Central Committee (until Apr 1969)
1957,	Apr	Appointed vice-president of the Supreme People's Court (until Cultural Revolution)
1959,	Apr	Elected member of the CPPCC
1963		Identified as member of the Central Control Commission of the CCP Central Committee
	Jul	Identified as colonel-general
1964,	Oct	Elected deputy for the Public Security Forces to the 3rd NPC
1965,	Jan	Elected member of the Standing Committee of the 3rd NPC (confirmed in this post by the 4th NPC in January 1975 but not by the 5th in 1978)
1969,	Apr	Elected to first term as member of the CCP Central Committee by the 9th Party Congress
Remark		Chen is believed to hold the post of president of the Military Court

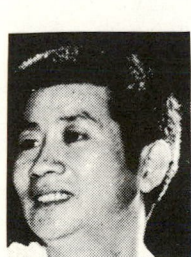

Chen Renfu (Ch'en Jen-fu)   陈仁甫

<u>Posts held</u>

CCP
Alternate member of the CCP 11th Central Committee

Others
Assistant researcher at the Shanghai Computer Techniques Research Institute

1977,	Aug	Elected alternate member of the CCP Central Committee by the 11th Party Congress
1978,	Mar	Identified as assistant researcher at the Shanghai Computer Techniques Research Institute

Chen Ruiting (Ch'en Jui-t'ing)   陈锐霆

<u>Posts held</u>

Military
Major-general

Others
Member of the Standing Committee of the 5th NPC

1956,	Oct	Identified as major-general; member of a delegation to Yugoslavia
1967,	Jul	Present at PLA ceremonies in Beijing
1972,	Mar	Identified as a cadre in the State Council
1978,	Mar	Elected member of the Standing Committee of the 5th CPPCC

Chen Rulong (Ch'en Ju-lung)   陈如龙

<u>Posts held</u>

Government
Vice-minister of finance

1954		Identified as director of the Finance Bureau, Northwest Administrative Council
	Nov	Identified as director of the General Office of the Ministry of Finance (until 1959)
1959,	Apr	Appointed assistant minister of finance (until Nov 1960)
1960,	Nov	Appointed vice-minister of finance (until Dec 1964)
1964,	Oct	Appointed director of the Central College of Finance and Currency (until Cultural Revolution)
1979,	May	First appearance after the Cultural Revolution: Identified as vice-minister of finance

Chen Shaozhong (Ch'en Shao-chung)

<u>Posts held</u>

Government
Vice-minister of the 3rd Ministry of Machine Building

1979,	Feb	Identified as vice-minister of the 3rd Ministry of Machine Building

Chen Shuliang (Ch'en Shu-liang)   陈叔亮

<u>Posts held</u>

Government
Ambassador to Romania

1952,	May	Identified as deputy director of the Asia Department in the Ministry of Foreign Affairs
	Oct	Identified as counselor at the embassy in Indonesia (until Sep 1955)
1955,	Sep	Identified as deputy director of the Asia Department in the Ministry of Foreign Affairs (until Jan 1959)
1959,	Jan	Identified as deputy director of the Foreign Trade Bureau of the Planning Commission and as director of the 2nd Asia Department in the Ministry of Foreign Affairs (until Feb 1962)

1960,   May   Member of a government delegation under
               Zhou Enlai to Cambodia

         Dec   Identified as council member of the Sino-
               Cambodian Friendship Association

1961,   May   Advisor to the Chinese delegation at the
               Laos Conference in Geneva

1962,   Feb   Appointed ambassador to Cambodia (until
               Cultural Revolution)

1967   Disappears during the Cultural Revolution

1979,   Jan   First appearance after the Cultural Revo-
               lution: Appointed ambassador to Romania

Chen is married to Kang Daisha.

Chen Shuzi (Ch'en Shu-tzu)

Posts held

Others
Executive director, China International
Trust and Investment Corporation
Vice-president of the People's Bank of
China

1979,   Oct   Appointed executive director, China In-
               ternational Trust and Investment Corpora-
               tion; identified as vice-president of the
               People's Bank of China

Chen Tie (Ch'en T'ieh)   陈   铁

Posts held

Military
Lieutenant-general

Provincial Administration
Vice-governor of Guizhou Province

Chang was born in 1900 in Cunyi, Guizhou Province. He
graduated from the Whampoa Military Academy. He
served in the KMT to become commander of the 14th Army and concurrently deputy commander of the Northeast
Bandit-Suppression Headquarters in 1948. The following
year he went over to the Communists. In September 1949
he was a specially invited delegate to the 1st CPPCC.

1950,   Jul   Identified as a member of the Southwest
               Military and Administrative Council and
               as director of its Department for Agricul-
               ture and Forestry

1953,   Jan   Appointed member of the Southwest Ad-
               ministrative Council

1955,   Feb   Identified as vice-chairman of the Gui-
               zhou Branch of the CPPCC

1956,   Feb   Elected member of the 3rd Central Com-
               mittee of the KMT Revolutionary Com-
               mittee (confirmed for the 4th Central
               Committee in 1958)

1959,   Apr   Appointed member of the National De-
               fense Council

1962,   Nov   Identified as director of the Department
               for Agriculture and Forestry, People's
               Government of Guizhou Province

1963,   Dec   Elected vice-governor of Guizhou Prov-
               ince

1964,   Oct   Elected deputy for Guizhou Province to
               the 3rd NPC

1967   Chen disappears

1980,   Jan   First appearance after the Cultural Revo-
               lution: Elected vice-governor of Guizhou
               Province

Chen Weida (Ch'en Wei-ta)   陈伟达

Posts held

CCP
Member of the CCP 11th Central Committee
1st secretary of Tianjin Municipality CP

Provincial Administration
Chairman of Tianjin Municipality Revolutionary Committee

1956   Identified as member of the Standing
               Committee of Zhejiang CP

1957,   Dec   Elected vice-governor of Zhejiang Prov-
               ince (until Sep 1964)

1960,   May   Identified as secretary of Zhejiang Prov-
               ince CP

1968,   Mar   Accused by Chen Boda as "a person in
               Zhejiang, who wanted to reverse the
               verdict on the 1967 adverse February cur-
               rent." Disappeared after accusation

1973,   Jul   First appearance after the Cultural Revo-
               lution: Identified as deputy CP secretary
               and vice-chairman of the Revolutionary
               Committee of Zhejiang

1977,   Jun   Identified as secretary of Zhejiang CP
               (until Sep 1978)

         Aug   Elected Cental Committee member by the
               11th CCP Congress

1978,   Oct   Identified as 1st secretary of Tianjin Mu-
               nicipality CP and as chairman of Tianjin
               Revolutionary Committee

Chen is married to Xu Wanhua.

Chen Weiji (Ch'en Wei-chi)   陈维稷

Posts held

Government
Vice-minister of textile industry

Others
Member of the Standing Committee of the
5th CPPCC
President of the Society of Textile Engineering

Chen was born in 1906 in Qingyang County, Anhui Province. He studied and received a doctorate at Leeds
University in England. He returned to China in 1928 and
took up a position as engineer at the Yisheng Wool
Weaving and Dyeing Mill in Shanghai. During the mid-
1930s he lectured successively at Beijing University and at
Jinan (Guangzhou) and Fudan Universities in Shanghai. In
September 1949 Chen took part in the CPPCC as a
delegate representing the Democratic Construction Association. During this period he was chief engineer of the
Textile Reconstruction Company.

1949,	Oct	Appointed vice-minister of textile industry
1952,	Apr	Delegate at the International Economic Conference in Moscow
	May	Elected member at the foundation of the Council for Promotion of International Trade
1953,	Oct	Elected member of the Standing Committee, Federation of Industry and Commerce
1954,	Feb	Elected chairman of the Textile Engineering Society at its foundation
	Dec	Appointed member of the National Committee of the CPPCC
1957,	Apr	Member of a trade delegation to Morocco
1965,	Jan	Elected member of the Standing Committee of the CPPCC (until Cultural Revolution)
	Mar	Head of a delegation to North Vietnam to inaugurate the "8th March" Textile Factory built with Chinese aid
	Oct	Head of the Chinese section of the Sino-Albanian Committee for Scientific and Technical Cooperation
1966,	Nov	Head of the Chinese delegation for Scientific and Technical Cooperation to Albania
1970,	May	Reactivated after 2 years of absence
	Sep	Identified as vice-minister of light industry (until 1977)
1971,	Feb	Member of a delegation to the trade fair in Cairo
1973,	Nov	Head of a scientific and technical delegation to Albania
1975,	Sep	Chairman of the Chinese section of the Sino-Albanian Committee for Scientific and Technical Cooperation
1978,	Mar	Elected member of the Standing Committee of the 5th CPPCC
	Apr	Identified as vice-minister of textile industry
	Jul	Identified as president of the Society of Textile Engineering

Chen Xianrui (Ch'en Hsien-jui) 陈先瑞

Posts held
CCP
Alternate member of the CCP 11th Central Committee

Military
Lieutenant-general
Political commissar of Chengdu Military Region

In 1947 Chen served as political commissar of the 12th Brigade operating in Shanyin (Daiyue) Military District. In 1949 he was political commissar of the 19th Army Corps.

1949,	Dec	Identified as council member, People's Government of Shaanxi Province
1959,	Apr	Elected member of the Standing Committee, 3rd CPPCC (confirmed in this post in 1964 by the 4th Conference)

1963		Identified as alternate member of the Central Control Commission of the CCP Central Committee
1964,	Nov	Identified as lieutenant-general and deputy political commissar of Beijing Military Region
1965,	Mar	Identified as high-ranking military leader in Beijing Military Region
1967,	Aug	Identified as deputy political commissar of Peking Military Region (until 1977?)
1969,	Apr	Elected member of the CCP Central Committee by the 9th Party Congress (confirmed in this post in 1973 by the 10th Congress)
1970,	Oct	Deputy head of a friendship delegation to North Korea on the occasion of the 20th anniversary of the entry of the Chinese People's Volunteers into the Korean War (head of the delegation: Zeng Siyu; in Korea, Chen is awarded the order of "National Flag," 1st class
1972,	Oct	Identified as political commissar of Beijing Military Region
1975,	Jan	Member of the presidium of the 4th NPC
1977,	Aug	Devoted by the 11th CCP Congress to the position of alternate member of the Central Committee
	Nov	Identified as political commissar of Chengdu Military Region

Chen Xiaoshun (Ch'en Hsiao-shun) 陈孝顺

Posts held
NPC
Member of the Standing Committee of the 5th NPC
Deputy for Shandong Province to the 5th NPC

1978,	Feb	Elected deputy for Shandong Province to the 5th NPC
	Mar	Elected member of the Standing Committee of the 5th NPC

Chen Xinggang (Ch'en Hsing-kang) 陈行庸

Posts held
CCP
Deputy secretary of Guizhou Province CP

Provincial Administration
Vice-chairman of the Revolutionary Committee of Guizhou Province

1974,	Feb	Identified as member of the Standing Committee of Guizhou CP
1975,	Mar	Identified as member of the Standing Committee, Revolutionary Committee of Guizhou (until Apr 1978)
	Aug	Identified as vice-chairman of the Revolutionary Committee of Guizhou Province
1978,	Apr	Elected deputy secretary of Guizhou Province CP

Chen Xinren (Ch'en Hsin-jen) 陈莘仁

Posts held

Government
Ambassador to the Philippines

Chen was born in 1915 in Guangdong Province.

1949,	Aug	Director of the Education Department and of the Propaganda Department of Fujian Province (until Nov 1952)
1950,	Mar	Member of the Cultural and Educational Committee in the East China Military and Administrative Council (until Dec 1952)
1952,	Nov	Vice-chairman of the People's Government of Fujian Province (until Nov 1954)
	Dec	Member of the Cultural and Educational Committee in the East China Administrative Council (until Aug 1954)
1954,	Nov	Appointed ambassador to Finland (until Jan 1959)
1958,	Jul	Elected deputy for Sichuan Province to the NPC (reelected in Oct 1964)
1959,	Jan	Appointed director of the Institute of International Relations which is associated with the Ministry of Foreign Affairs
1961,	Nov	After the Institute of International Relations is renamed Institute of Diplomacy, Chen becomes deputy director (until ?)
1972,	Mar	Appointed ambassador to Iran (until Nov 1974)
1975,	Jan	Appointed ambassador to the Netherlands (until Jul 1978)
1978,	Oct	Appointed ambassador to the Philippines

Chen is married to Xiao Zhi.

Chen Xiyu (Ch'en Hsi-yü) 陈希愈

Posts held

Government
Vice-minister of finance
Vice-president of the People's Bank
Vice-president of the Bank of China

NPC
Deputy for Shanxi Province to the 5th NPC

Others
President of the Finance Society

1950		Identified as member of the Financial and Economic Committee in the Central-South China Military and Administrative Council (until 1953)
1951		Identified as director of the People's Bank for Central-South China (1953)
1953,	Sep	Identified as vice-president of the People's Bank of China (until 1960)
1973,	Jun	Identified as vice-minister of finance
	Oct	Identified as president of the People's Bank (until Mar 1978)
1975,	Jul-Aug	Chen heads a banking delegation to Somalia, Tanzania, and Zambia
1978,	Feb	Elected deputy for Shanxi Province to the 5th NPC

	May	Identified as vice-president of the People's Bank; Chen heads a banking delegation to Japan
	Oct	Identified as vice-president of the Bank of China
1979,	Dec	Elected president of the Finance Society

Chen Xizhong (Ch'en Hsi-chung) 陈希仲

Posts held

NPC
Deputy for Fujian Province to the 5th NPC

Provincial Administration
Vice-chairman, People's Congress of Fujian Province

Others
Director of the Board of Directors, China International Trust and Investment Corporation
Chairman of the Fujian Provincial Federation of Industrialists and Businessmen

1962,	Sep	Identified as a member of the Fujian People's Council
1964,	Jan	Identified as chairman of the Fujian Branch of the China Democratic National Construction Commission
1978,	Feb	Elected deputy for Fujian Province to the 5th NPC
1979,	Oct	Appointed director of the Board of Directors, China International Trust and Investment Corporation; identified as chairman of the Fujian Provincial Federation of Industrialists and Businessmen
	Dec	Elected vice-chairman of the People's Congress of Fujian Province

Chen Yangshan (Ch'en Yang-shan)

Posts held

NPC 陈养山
Deputy for Ningxia Autonomous Region to the 5th NPC

Others
Deputy chief-procurator of the Supreme People's Procuracy
Member of the Standing Committee of the 5th CPPCC

Chen is a native of Zhejiang Province. In 1925 he took part in the "May 30th Movement" in Shanghai.

1949,	Nov	Identified as director of the Public Security Bureau, People's Government of Xi'an Municipality
1951,	May	Identified as director of the Public Security Bureau, People's Government of Nanjing Municipality
1953,	Jan	Identified as director of the Propaganda Department, North China Bureau of the CCP Central Committee and as vice-chairman of the Political and Legal Com-

mittee of the North China Administrative Council (until Sep 1954)

1954,	Oct	Appointed vice-minister of justice (until Apr 1959)
1962,	Nov	Appointed vice-president of a branch of the Institute of Foreign Affairs
1967		Disappears during the Cultural Revolution
1978,	Feb	First appearance after the Cultural Revolution: Elected deputy for Ningxia Autonomous Region to the 5th NPC
1979,	Feb	Appointed deputy chief-procurator of the Supreme People's Procuracy
	Mar	By-elected member of the Standing Committee of the 5th CPPCC

Chen Yeping (Ch'en Yeh-p'ing)　陈野萍

Posts held

CCP
Deputy director of the Organization Department, CCP Central Committee

1952,	May	Identified as member of the People's Control Committee of the Southwest Administrative Committee (until Sep 1954)
1955,	Jul	Identified as vice-president of the North Jiangsu College of Agriculture
1963,	Jul	Identified as a cadre of a department of the CCP Central Committee
1967,	Mar	Branded as a counterrevolutionary revisionist
1978,	Feb	First appearance after the Cultural Revolution
	Aug	Identified as deputy director of the Organization Department, CCP Central Committee

Chen Yisong (Ch'en Yi-sung)　陈逸松

Posts held

NPC
Member of the Standing Committee of the 5th NPC
Deputy for Taiwan Province to the 5th NPC

Chang was born in Yilan County, Taiwan Province, in 1907. He returned to China in 1973.

1975,	Jan	Elected member of the Standing Committee of the 4th NPC (confirmed by the 5th NPC in 1978)
1978,	Feb	Elected deputy for Taiwan Province to the 5th NPC
1979,	Jun	Member of the Draft Laws Committee, 2nd Session of the 5th NPC

Chen Yonggui (Ch'en Yung-kuei)

Posts held　　　　陈永贵

CCP
Member of the Politburo of the CCP
Member of the CCP 11th Central Committee
Secretary of Shanxi Province CP

Government
Vice-premier

NPC
Deputy for Shanxi Province to the 5th NPC

Chen was born in 1913 in Xiyang, Shanxi Province, as the son of a very poor land laborer. When he was 11 years old his family moved to Dazhai where he eked out an existence as an employed land laborer from this time until the Communist take-over.

1950		Shortly after the land reform, Chen set up a mutual-aid organization comprising a number of poor peasants
1953		During the establishment of agricultural cooperatives, Chen is criticized because of his own initiatives as a "supporter of utopian agrarian socialism"
1963,	Aug	Chen is identified as CP secretary of the Production Brigade of Dazhai People's Commune in Xiyang County, Shanxi Province (until 1973)
1973		Workers of Dazhai People's Commune succeed after years of very hard work in transforming the previously infertile area of Dazhai into productive land. This is made possible mainly by transporting water over a distance of many kilometres, by terracing the mountains, and by levelling large uneven areas. Because of this enormous achievement, Dazhai is made a national example of "self-reliance"
1964,	Feb	Mao Zedong issues the slogan "In Agriculture learn from Dazhai!" This happened at the time when the Party apparatus sought, under the influence of Liu Shaoqi, to belittle the methods and successes of Dazhai
	Oct	Chen is elected deputy for Shanxi Province to the NPC
1965,	Jun	Chen is identified as council member in the Chinese Committee for World Peace (the national organization of the World Peace Council)
1966,	Sep	Member of a friendship delegation to Albania
1967		During the Cultural Revolution Chen comes under renewed attack. He nevertheless succeeds in making a considerable contribution to the establishment of a Revolutionary Committee for Shanxi Province with the help of Red Guards from Beijing and other rebel organizations and by mediating between the conflicting parties
	Mar	With the establishment of the Shanxi Revolutionary Committee Chen is elected vice-chairman (reelected to this post in Dec 1977; until Dec 1979)
1968		The Chinese government reissues the slogan "Learn from Dazhai" with the effect of boosting Chen's prestige
1969,	Apr	Elected to first term as member of the CCP Central Committee by the 9th Party Congress
1971,	Feb	Elected 1st secretary of Xiyang County CP, Shanxi Province (until approxi-

mately 1972)

Apr With the reestablishment of the Party Secretariat in Shanxi Province after the Cultural Revolution, Chen is elected secretary (confirmed in this position in April 1978)

1973 Chen visits a number of Chinese provinces to propagate Dazhai work methods

Aug Elected member of the Politburo of the CCP by the 10th Party Congress

1974 Further travels throughout China to propagate Dazhai. In Dazhai itself Chen demonstrates methods developed there to foreign and Chinese delegations

1975, Jan Appointed vice-premier (confirmed by the 5th NPC in Mar 1978)

Apr Head of a friendship delegation to Mexico

1977, Dec Head of a friendship delegation to Cambodia

1978, Feb Elected deputy for Shanxi Province to the 5th NPC

Although Chen Yonggui only learned to read and to write at the age of 43, he is the author of many influential articles. The following are the most important:

1965, Jan "Self-Reliance Is a Magic Weapon," HQ

1966, May 13th "We Are Peasants of the New Type, Instructed by Mao Zedong and Determined to Destroy the Black Shop of the 3 Family Village," RMRB

Oct 2nd "We Must Lead the People's Communes as the Universities of Mao Zedong Thought," RMRB

1967, Jan "Only by Revolutionizing the Ideology, Can Production Be Developed on a Large Scale," HQ

May 5th "Finish with the Arch Enemies of the Poor and Lower Middle Peasants," RMRB

Aug "Be Determined to Defend the Proletarian Revolutionary Line of Chairman Mao," HQ

6th "Dazhai Marches Forward Through the Struggle Against the Chinese Khrushchevs," RMRB

1968, Feb 26th "Take a Firm Revolutionary Stand, Work for the Spring Harvest, and Make Another Meritorious Contribution," RMRB

May 17th "Armed with Mao Zedong Thought One Can Remain Calm in the Storm of Class Struggle," New China News Agency (NCNA)

Sep 4th "Be the Most Reliable Ally of the Working Class," RMRB

Nov 21st "Study and Use Creatively Mao Zedong Thought and Achieve a Bumper Harvest Even in Spite of Natural Catastrophies," NCNA

Nov 31st "Faithfully Follow the Great Leader Chairman Mao and Enter the Year 1969 Victoriously," NCNA

1973, Feb "On the study of Scientific Agricultural Methods," HQ

1977, Oct "On Farmland Capital Construction," HQ

Chen Yonglin (Ch'en Yung-lin) 陈 永 林

Posts held

CCP
Alternate member of the CCP 11th Central Committee

1977, Aug Elected alternate member of the CCP Central Committee by the 11th Party Congress

Dec Elected vice-chairman of Gansu Revolutionary Committee (until Dec 1979)

Chen Yongxiang (Ch'en Yung-hsiang)

陈永祥

Posts held

NPC
Member of the Standing Committee of the 5th NPC
Deputy for Beijing Municipality to the 5th NPC

1975, Jan Identified as member of the presidium of the 4th NPC

1976, Sep Identified as secretary, CP of the Xujiawu Production Brigade in Pinggu County

1978, Feb Elected deputy for Beijing Municipality to the 5th NPC

Mar Elected member of the Standing Committee of the 5th NPC

Chen Yu (Ch'en Yü) 陈 宇

Posts held

Mass Organizations
Vice-chairman of the Federation of Trade Unions

Chen was born in 1916. In 1945 he was an alternate member of the Executive Council of the World Federation of Trade Unions.

1953, May Elected member of the Executive Council of the Federation of Trade Unions

Sep Member of a delegation to the 3rd Congress of the World Federation of Trade Unions in Vienna

1954, May Elected council member of the Association for Cultural Relations with Foreign Countries

1957, Jul Delegate to the 9th Congress of the Federation of Japanese Trade Unions (entry refused by the Japanese authorities)

1958, Jul Elected member of the Afro-Asian Solidarity Committee (until Jun 1965) and member of the Standing Committee of the Peace Council

1959, Feb Identified as director of the International Liaison Department, Federation of Trade Union

1960, Mar Elected council member of the Sino-Latin American Friendship Association

Jun Delegate at the 11th Congress of the World Federation of Trade Unions in Beijing

	Aug	Delegate at the 6th Conference against Atomic Bombs in Hiroshima
1961,	Jan	Delegate at the 22nd Session of the Executive Council, World Federation of Trade Unions in East Berlin
1964,	Apr	Delegate at the 27th Session of the Executive Council, World Federation of Trade Unions in Sofia
	Jul	Delegate at a congress of the Federation of Japanese Trade Unions
	Oct	Head of a trade union delegation to Algeria
	Nov	Head of a trade union delegation to Congo (Brazzaville)
1965,	May	Deputy head of a trade union delegation to North Vietnam
1966,	Apr	Identified as secretary of the Federation of Trade Unions; subsequently disappears
1978,	Mar	First appearance after the Cultural Revolution: Identified as vice-chairman of the Federation of Trade Unions (confirmed by the Trade Union Congress in October 1978)
	Nov	Head of a trade union delegation to Yugoslavia
1979,	Oct	Head of a trade union delegation to Japan

Chen Yuanfang (Ch'en Yüan-fang) 陈元方

Posts held

CCP
Secretary of Shaanxi Province CP

Provincial Administration
Vice-chairman of the Shaanxi Provincial Revolutionary Committee

1979,	Jan	Identified as secretary of Shaanxi Province CP
	Aug	Identified as vice-chairman of the Shaanxi Revolutionary Committee

Chen Yubao (Ch'en Yü-pao) 陈玉宝

Posts held

CCP
Alternate member of the CCP 11th Central Committee

1973,	Aug	Elected to first term as alternate member of the CCP Central Committee by the 10th Party Congress
1975,	Feb	Chen is identified at a conference in Fujian Province

Chen Yun (Ch'en Yün) 陈云

Posts held

CCP
Vice-chairman of the CCP
Member of the Standing Committee of the Politburo of the CCP 11th Central Committee
Member of the Politburo of the CCP 11th Central Committee

Member of the CCP 11th Central Committee
1st secretary of the CCP Central Committee Commission for Inspecting Discipline

Government
Vice-premier
Chairman of the State Financial and Economic Commission

NPC
Vice-chairman, Standing Committee of the 5th NPC
Deputy for Shanghai to the 5th NPC

Chen Yun was born in Shanghai in 1905, under the name of Liao Chengyun. Little is known about his background. Probably Chen received only a short and incomplete school education. He was trained as a typesetter with the well-known Shanghai Publishers, Commercial Press. After moving to Shanghai in about 1921, Chen was active in the trade union movement and in that city joined Liu Shaoqi. In the course of the year 1925 he joined the CCP. In the same year he was together with Liu Shaoqi one of the leading initiators of the historic anti-Japanese "May 30th Movement." After the rift between KMT and CCP in 1927 Chen possibly went to the USSR but soon returned to China and joined the Jiangxi Soviet. There he was active in the Organization Department of the CCP Central Committee organizing industrial workers and craftsmen. During the 5th Plenary Session of the 6th CC in January 1934, Chen Yun was elected member of the CCP Central Committee. In October of the same year he joined the main Communist forces from Jiangxi on the Long March. In January 1935 he was a participant at the Party Conference in Zunyi, Guizhou Province, which discussed problems of the tactical retreat. Chen Yun may be assumed to have supported Mao Zedong's tactical views during this conference because at the time he was a member of the Revolutionary Military Council headed by Mao. Following the Communist forces' legendary crossing of the Dadu river, a tributary of the upper Chang Jiang, Chen left for a second visit to the USSR where he remained for two years. There he attended the 7th Comintern Congress during July-August 1935 in Moscow as a member of the Chinese delegation. He returned to China in 1937 together with Chen Shaoyu and Kang Sheng. On their return from the USSR they passed Xinjiang where Chen stayed until 1937. There he worked with Soviet economic officials and technicians whose presence at the time had been encouraged by Sheng Shicai. In 1938 Chen Yun joined the newly established Communist base in Shaanxi Province and in the same year became head of the Organization Department in the CCP Central Committee and in the following year head of the Central Committee's Rural Work Department. He held this post until 1943. Also in 1939 Chen Yun published his first theoretical article "On the Treatment of Cadres," one of the most important documents for the so-called Zhengfeng (rectification) movement initiated by Mao Zedong in 1942 in order to strenghten the cadres' Party discipline. In the period until 1939 Chen also gained a high reputation for his lectures on Party policy and the history of the Party at the "Anti-Japan Military and Political Academy," the "North Shaanxi School," the "Marx-Lenin Institute," and at the Party School. In 1940 he was elected a member of the Politburo; during the same year he became involved in economics when he was made chairman of the Financial and Economic Committee for the Shaanxi-Gansu-Ningxia Border Region, an office he held until 1945. His reputation as an economics expert was based on his outstanding achievements in the economic development of this area which considerably contributed to the strengthing of the communist position in North China. In 1943 Chen Yun is again referred to as director of the Organization Department, a post he had probably left when he became head of the Rural Work Department in the Central Committee. In his capacity as head of the Organization Department he was together with Li Fuchun responsible for the training of young cadres. After the end of the Anti-Japanese War in 1945, Chen Yun belonged together with Gao Gang, Li Fuchun, Lin Biao, and Peng Zhen to the group of cadres sent by Mao Zedong to Manchuria. In 1946 he was appointed secretary of the Northeast Bureau of the CCP Central Committee, an office he held until 1949, as well as chairman of the Financial and Economic Affairs Committee in the Northeast China Administrative Council. Following the occupation of Shenyang (Mukden) by Lin Biao's troops, Chen Yun in November 1948 became the leading Party cadre in the city, one of the first significant cities under communist control. Still in 1948 Chen Yun was elected chairman (until May 1953) by the 6th Congress of Chinese Trade Unions meeting in Harbin. In early 1949 Chen Yun was called to Beijing where the communist headquarters had been moved; his responsibilities in Manchuria were transferred to Gao Gang.

1949,	Oct	Appointed member of the Central People's Government Council, and vice-premier (until about 1972). Minister of heavy industry and chairman of the Financial and Economic Affairs Committee in the Government Administration Council
1952		Identified as member of the State Planning Commission (until 1954)
	Oct	Together with Zhou Enlai, Chen Yun conducts negotiations in Moscow on the return of the Manchurian railway and of the Soviet naval base at Lüda to China
1954,	Aug	Elected deputy for Shanghai Municipality to the 1st NPC
1955,	Apr	Acting premier during Zhou Enlai's absence (attending the Bandung Conference)
1956,	Sep	Elected member of the Standing Committee of the Politburo and vice-chairman of the CCP Central Committee by the 8th Party Congress (until Apr 1969)
1958,	May	Head of a delegation attending various economic and military conferences in East Europe as observers
	Oct	Appointed chairman of the Capital Construction Commission (abolished in December 1963)
1959,	Mar	Chen publishes an article on economic problems in the ideological journal HQ
1969,	Apr	Reelected member of the CCP Central Committee by the 9th Party Congress (but not of the Politburo); reelected by the 10th and 11th Party Congresses
1975,	Jan	Elected vice-chairman, Standing Committee of the 4th NPC (reelected Mar 1978 by the 5th NPC)
1978,	Feb	Elected deputy of Shanghai to the 5th NPC
	Dec	The 3rd Plenum of the 11th Central Committee elects Chen member of the Politburo and its Standing Committee, vice-chairman of the CCP and 1st secretary of the CCP Central Committee Commission for Inspecting Discipline.
1979,	Jul	Elected vice-premier; appointed chairman of the State Financial and Economic Commission

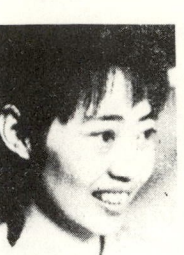

Chen Yuniang (Ch'en Yü-niang) (f)

陈玉娘

Posts held

NPC
Member of the Standing Committee of the 5th NPC
Deputy for Tianjin Municipality to the 5th NPC

Chen was women's singles badminton champion at the 7th Asian Games.

1974,	Sep	Identified as a cadre in the State Council
1975,	Jan	Elected member of the Standing Committee of the 4th NPC (confirmed by the 5th NPC in Mar 1978)
1978,	Feb	Elected deputy of Tianjin Municipality to the 5th NPC; deputy leader of a badminton delegation to the Hong Kong session of the World Badminton Federation
	Nov	Deputy head of a badminton group to Mexico
1979,	Jul	Appointed member of the National Games Organizing Committee

Chen Zaidao (Ch'en Tsai-tao)

陈再道

Posts held

CCP
Member of the CCP 11th Central Committee

NPC
Member of the Standing Committee of the 5th NPC
Deputy for the PLA to the 5th NPC

Military
Colonel-general
Commander of the Railway Corps of the PLA

Chen was born in 1908 in Macheng, Hubei Province. In 1927 he helped organize communist uprisings in his native province. In 1929 he joined the units under Xu Xiangqian operating in the Henan-Hubei-Anhui Border Region. When these troops were posted to Sichuan Province in 1932, he was given the command of a battalion in the 10th Division. Already two years later he commanded the 4th Army. After the outbreak of the Anti-Japanese War and the reorganization of the Red Army into the 8th Route Army, the units under Chen were integrated into the 129th Division commanded by Liu Bocheng. During the following years he operated mostly independently with his units in the Hebei-Shandong-Henan Area. In March 1949 he was appointed commander of Henan Military Region. In September of the same year he participated in the 1st CPPCC.

1950,	Jan	Elected member of the Central-South China Military and Administrative Council (until Jan 1953)
	Nov	Identified as commander of the 16th Corps, 4th Field Army
1954,	Oct	Identified as member of the National Defense Council and as commander of Wuhan Military Region
1955,	Sep	Made lieutenant-general; conferred the orders of "1st August," "Independence and Freedom," and "Liberation," all 1st class
1958,	Apr	Identified as colonel-general
	Jul	Elected deputy for the PLA to the NPC
1967,	Jun	Organizes the "Million Heroic Troops" (Unit 8201) which are used against the Red Guards of Wuhan, thus creating the historic "Wuhan Incident"
	Jul	Ordered to appear in front of an enlarged meeting of the CCP Central Committee in Beijing to answer charges
	Dec	Following further charges Chen disappears
1973,	Mar	First appearance after the Cultural Revolution: Identified as highranking military officer in Fuzhou Military Region
1978,	Feb	Elected deputy for the PLA to the 5th NPC
	Mar	Elected member of the Standing Committee of the 5th NPC
	Jul	Identified as commander of the PLA Railway Corps
	Dec	The Third Plenum of the CCP's 11th Central Committee elects Chen member of the Central Committee

Chen Zhaoyuan (Ch'en Chao-yüan)

陈肇源

Posts held

Government
Former ambassador to India

1954,	Nov	Identified as attaché at the embassy in Sweden (until Jun 1958)
1959,	Oct	Identified as deputy director of the International Department in the Ministry of Foreign Affairs (until 1962)
1963,	Apr	Identified as chargé d'affaires in India (until Apr 1970)
1971,	Mar	Appointed ambassador to Burma (until May 1973)
1973,	Sep	Appointed ambassador to Spain (until Jul 1976)
1976,	Sep	Appointed ambassador to India (until 1978?)

Chen Zhengxiang (Ch'en Cheng-hsiang)

陈正湘

Posts held

Military
Lieutenant-general

Others
Member of the Standing Committee of the 5th CPPCC

In 1935 Chen commanded a battalion which made a significant contribution in the crossing of the Dadu River. In 1939 Chen commanded a regiment in Shanxi-Chahar-Hebei Military Region and subsequently until 1946 a column in the same Military Region. He then disappeared.

1959,	Apr	Delegate at the 3rd CPPCC (again in 1964 at the 4th CPPCC)
1960,	Aug	Identified as lieutenant-general
1968,	Aug	Identified as a military cadre in Beijing Military Region
1978,	Mar	Elected member of the Standing Committee of the 5th CPPCC

Chen Zhifang (Ch'en Chih-fang) 陈志方

Posts held

Government
Former ambassador to Vietnam

1949,	Oct	Identified as acting secretary-general of Guangzhou People's Government
1951,	Jun	Appointed secretary-general of the Financial and Economic Committee of the Guangzhou People's Government
1954,	Jul	Appointed chairman of the Credentials Committee of the Guangzhou People's Government
1955,	Jan	Elected deputy mayor of Guangzhou (until Apr 1956)
1956,	Oct	Appointed ambassador to Syria (until Feb 1958)
1958,	Aug	Appointed ambassador to Iraq (until Sep 1960)
1962,	Jun	Appointed director of the College of Diplomacy (until Jun 1964)
1964,	Apr	Appointed ambassador to Uganda (until approximately 1966)
1970,	Dec	Appointed ambassador to Switzerland (until Aug 1975)
1972,	Jul	PRC representative at the UN Seabed Conference in Geneva
1977,	Sep	Appointed ambassador to Vietnam (until 1977?)

Chen is married to Wang Jing.

Chen Zonglie (Ch'en Tsung-lieh) 陈宗烈

Posts held

Provincial Administration
Vice-mayor of Shanghai Municipality

1960,	Aug	Identified as 1st secretary of Yancheng District CP, Jiangsu Province
1979,	May	Identified as vice-chairman of the Revolutionary Committee of Shanghai Municipality (until Dec 1979); deputy head of an agricultural delegation to Japan
	Dec	Elected vice-mayor of Shanghai Municipality

Chen Zuolin (Ch'en Tso-lin) 陈作霖

Posts held

CCP
Alternate member of the CCP 11th Central Committee
Secretary of Zhejiang Province CP

Provincial Administration
Vice-governor of Zhejiang Province

1976, Nov Identified as deputy secretary of Zhejiang Province CP
1977, Jun Identified as secretary of Zhejiang Province CP
Aug Elected alternate member of the CCP Central Committee by the 11th Party Congress
Dec Elected vice-chairman of the Zhejiang Revolutionary Committee (until Dec 1979)
1978, Sep Chen heads an agricultural delegation to Japan
1979, Dec Elected vice-governor of Zhejiang Province

Cheng Fangwu (Ch'eng Fang-wu) 成仿吾

Posts held

NPC
Deputy for Shandong Province to the 5th NPC

Others
Member of the Standing Committee of the 5th CPPCC
President of the China People's University
Honorary president of the Education Society

Cheng was born in 1888 in Xinhua County, Hunan Province. In 1913 he went to Japan and studied chemistry at the Okayama Prefectural No. 6 Higher School. He later studied together with Guo Moruo and others at Tokyo Imperial University. Having returned to China in 1922 he successively co-edited two literary journals together with Guo. In 1926 he joined the Northern Expedition. In 1927 he traveled via Japan, the USSR, and Germany to France where he edited the Communist journal Chi Guang. In 1931 he returned to China and went to the Hubei-Henan-Anhui Soviet District and two years later to the Jiangxi Soviet District. In 1934-35 he took part in the Long March. He was then given various lecturerships: principal of the Northern Shaanxi Public School (1937-38), president of the North China Associated University (1939), president of the Shanxi-Chahar-Hopei Associated University (1944), vice-president of the North China University (1948-50). In September 1949 he took part in the 1st CPPCC as a delegate representing educational workers. The conference elected him a member of its National Committee.

1949, Oct Elected council member of the Sino-Soviet Friendship Association (until Dec 1954), member of the Peace Council (until Oct 1950), council member of the Association for Reforming Chinese Written Language (until Feb 1952)

1950, Mar Appointed vice president of the People's University (until Sep 1952)
1952, Oct Appointed president of the Northeast Normal University in Changchun (until Dec 1961)
1954, Sep Elected deputy for Guangxi Province to the 1st NPC (confirmed in 1959 by the 2nd NPC)
1955, Jul Member of a delegation to the 1st World Conference against Atomic Bombs in Hiroshima
1956, May Elected member of the China Asian Solidarity Committee (until May 1958)
1961, Dec Appointed president of Shandong University (until Cultural Revolution)
1964, Sep Elected deputy for Shandong Province to the 3rd NPC
1967 Disappears during the Cultural Revolution
1974, Sep First appearance after the Cultural Revolution
1976, Apr Identified as advisor at the Party School of the CCP Central Committee
1978, Feb Elected deputy for Shandong Province to the 5th NPC
Mar Elected member of the Standing Committee of the 5th CPPCC
1979, Jan Identified as president of the China People's University
Apr Elected honorary president of the Education Society
Jun Member of the Committee to Examine Proposals, 2nd Session of the 5th NPC

Cheng Fei (Ch'eng Fei) 程 飞

Posts held

Government
Vice-minister for economic relations with foreign countries

1972, Jul Identified as director of a department in the Ministry of Economic Relations with Foreign Countries
1973, May Member of a government delegation to Sri Lanka
1976, May Member of a government delegation to Sudan
1977, Feb Identified as vice-minister for economic relations with foreign countries
1979, Jan Member of a government delegation, led by Li Xiannian, to Tanzania, Mozambique, Zambia, Zaire, and Pakistan

Cheng Guanghua (Ch'eng Kuang-hua) 程尤华

Posts held

CCP
Member of the Standing Committee of Anhui Province CP

NPC
Deputy for Anhui Province to the 5th NPC

Provincial Administration
Vice-governor of Anhui Province

1959,   Apr   Identified as deputy director of the Political and Legal Department of Anhui Province CP
1978,   Jan   Elected vice-chairman of the Revolutionary Committee of Anhui Province (until Dec 1979)
          Feb   Elected deputy for Anhui Province to the 5th NPC
          Sep   Identified as member of the Standing Committee of Anhui Province CP
1979,   Dec   Elected vice-governor of Anhui Province

Cheng Hao (Ch'eng Hao)   程　浩

Posts held

Provincial Administration
Vice-chairman of the People's Government, Ningxia Autonomous Region

1980,   Jan   Elected vice-chairman of the People's Government, Ningxia Autonomous Region

Cheng Jun (Ch'eng Chün)   成　钧

Posts held

NPC
Deputy for the PLA to the 5th NPC

Military
Lieutenant-general
Deputy commander, Air Force of the PLA

In 1932 Cheng commanded a regiment in the 1st Front Army. After the Long March he attended an Air Force training school in the USSR from 1936 until 1937. In 1941 he was commander of the 5th Brigade, 2nd Division, in the New 4th Army. In 1946 he commanded the 2nd Corps in Central China Military Region and, one year later, the 7th Corps. He has been identified as commander of the 25th Army Corps, 3rd Field Army, at the beginning of 1949. In May of the same year he was made deputy commander of the 10th Army and deputy commander of Fujian Military District.

1950   Identified as council member of the People's Government of Fujian Province
1951   Appointed commander of the Defense Forces, East China Military Region
1954   Appointed commander of the Air Defense Forces of the PLA
1955,   Sep   Promoted to the rank of lieutenant-general; awarded the order "Liberation," 1st class
1958,   Jan   Member of a military delegation to India; identified as deputy commander of the PLA Air Force
1959,   Mar   Elected deputy for the PLA to the 2nd NPC (reelected to the 3rd NPC in 1964)
          May   Cheng is in charge of the PLA sports competitions
1967   At the height of the Cultural Revolution Cheng is attacked as a supporter of He Long and relieved of his posts

1973,   May   First appearance after the Cultural Revolution: Referred to in his previous post as deputy commander of the Air Force
1978,   Feb   Elected deputy for the PLA to the 5th NPC

Cheng Shaohui (Ch'eng Shao-hui)

Posts held   程　绍迴

Others
President of the Veterinary Society

In the thirties Cheng was professor of veterinary science at the National Central University.

1949,   Dec   Identified as director of the Animal Husbandry and Veterinary Bureau, Ministry of Agriculture
1952,   Apr   Went to North Korea as a member of the Investigation Group on U.S. Imperialist Biological Warfare
1957,   Jul   Identified as vice-president of the Academy of Agricultural Science
1958,   Mar   Elected deputy for Sichuan Province to the 2nd NPC (reelected in Sep 1964 to the 3rd NPC)
1962,   Nov   Elected vice-president of the Husbandry and Veterinary Society
1966   Cheng disappears
1979,   Aug   First appearance after the Cultural Revolution: Elected president of the Veterinary Society

Cheng Shaojiong (Ch'eng Shao-chiung)

Posts held

Others
Vice-president, Academy of Agricultural Sciences
Vice-president, Society of Agronomy

1959,   Mar   Elected deputy for Sichuan Province to the 2nd NPC (reelected to the 3rd NPC in Oct 1964)
1963   Identified as vice-president of the Academy of Animal Husbandry and Veterinary Medicine
1978,   Aug   Identified as vice-president of the Academy of Agricultural Sciences and as vice-president of the Society of Agronomy
1979,   Jun   By-elected member of the 5th CPPCC

Cheng Shicai (Ch'eng Shih-ts'ai)   程　世才

Posts held

Military
Lieutenant-general
Deputy commander of the PLA Armored Forces

NPC
Member of the Standing Committee of the 5th NPC
Deputy for the PLA to the 5th NPC

Cheng is a native of Hubei Province. In 1933 he temporarily commanded the 30th Army of the 4th Red Front Army. At the beginning of the Long March he was operating in Sichuan. In 1935 he joined the main forces of the Red Army near Maoergai. In 1936 Cheng was identified as commander of the 30th Red Army. Towards the end of that year he was surrounded with his troops in the Qilian Mountains by Kuomintang forces but managed to escape to Xinjiang. In the following year Cheng returned to Yan'an. During the Anti-Japanese War he was chief of staff of the army commanded by Xiao Ke which was operating in the Shanxi-Chahar-Hebei Border Area. During this period he distinguished himself by his contribution to the militia system. In 1946 Cheng was identified as commander of Liaodong Military Region. During the following year he took part in the defense of Linjiang near the North Korean border against the forces of the KMT.

1954,	Sep	Appointed deputy commander of the Public Security Forces
1955,	Sep	Conferred the order "1st August," "Independence and Freedom," and "Liberation," all 1st class; appointed lieutenant-general
1958,	Aug	Identified as deputy commander of Shenyang Military Region
1963,	Aug	Identified as deputy commander of the Armored Forces
1966		Disappears during the Cultural Revolution
1974,	Sep	First appearance after the Cultural Revolution
1978,	Feb	Elected deputy for the PLA to the 5th NPC
	Mar	Elected member of the Standing Committee of the 5th NPC
	Jun	Identified as deputy commander of the PLA Armored Forces

Cheng Tan (Ch'eng T'an)　　程　坦

Posts held

Others
Member of the Standing Committee of the 5th CPPCC

Cheng was born in 1911 in Hunan Province. In 1949 he was director of the Peasants Department of the People's Government of Hubei Province.

1950,	Sep	Identified as deputy director of the Rural Reform Committee of Hubei People's Government
1953,	Dec	Identified as 2nd secretary of Hubei Province CP
1955,	Aug	Appointed vice-minister of supervision (until this ministry was abolished in Apr 1959)
1959,	Sep	Identified as deputy director of the Communications Work Department in the CCP Central Committee
1961,	Jul	Appointed vice-minister of internal affairs (until Cultural Revolution)
1965,	Jan	Elected member of the Standing Committee of the 4th CPPCC
1967		Disappears during the Cultural Revolution
1973,	Oct	First appearance after the Cultural Revolution: Referred to in his previous post as

member of the Standing Committee of the 4th CPPCC

1978,	Mar	Elected member of the Standing Committee of the 5th CPPCC

Cheng Wang (Ch'eng Wang)　　程　望

Posts held

Government
Vice-minister of communications

1958,	Jun	Identified as deputy director, Bureau of Shipbuilding in the 1st Ministry of Machine Building
1977,	Oct	Identified as council member of the Society of Shipbuilding Engineers; member of a shipping delegation to Japan
1978,	Nov	Identified as vice-minister of communications; head of a shipping delegation to Denmark

Cheng Xingling (Ch'eng Hsing-ling)　　程星龄

Posts held

Provincial Administration
Vice-governor of Hunan Province

1958		Identified as vice-governor of Hunan Province
1962		Cheng disappears
1979,	Dec	First appearance thereafter: Elected vice-governor of Hunan Province

Cheng Yitai (Ch'eng Yi-t'ai)　　程义太

Posts held

CCP
Alternate member of the CCP 11th Central Committee

1977,	Aug	Elected alternate member of the CCP Central Committee by the 11th Party Congress
	Dec	Elected vice-chairman of the Revolutionary Committee of Liaoning Province (until Jan 1980)

Cheng Yuanxing (Ch'eng Yüan-hsing)　　程远行

Posts held

Government
Deputy director of the West Asia and North Africa Department in the Ministry of Foreign Affairs

1972,	Sep	Adviser to the Chinese delegation to the 27th General Assembly of the UN
1974,	Apr	Member of the Chinese delegation to the Special Session of the UN General Assembly

Sep Identified as deputy director of the West Asia and North Africa Department in the Ministry of Foreign Affairs

1975, Apr Member of a government delegation headed by Li Xiannian to Iran

1977, Oct Member of a government delegation to the Arab Republic of Yemen

1978, Jul Member of a government delegation headed by Song Zhenming to Iraq

Cheng Zihua (Ch'eng Tzu-hua) 程子华

Posts held

CCP
Member of the CCP 11th Central Committee

Government
Minister for civil affairs

NPC
Deputy for Shanxi Province to the 5th NPC

Cheng was born in 1906 in Xia County, Shanxi Province, of a family belonging to the gentry. He received his school education at Taiyuan Normal School. In 1926 he attended a course at the Wuhan branch of the Whampoa Military Academy. In the following year he took part as a soldier of the Training Corps in the Guangzhou (Canton) uprising, after the failure of which he first fled to the Hailufeng Soviet. Later he commanded small military units under the KMT general Yue Weijun. With parts of the 15th Independent Brigade under General Yue he changed over to the Communists in 1929 and joined the Jiangxi Soviet. In 1931 he became commander of a regiment in the Red Army and in 1932 of the 41st Division in the Red Army. In 1933 he attended a course at the School of the Red Army in Ruijin. At the beginning of the Long March he commanded the 25th Red Army but soon fell ill and had to be transported on a stretcher over long distances. After the end of the March he was made political commissar of the 15th Army Corps. During the Anti-Japanese War Cheng held the post of political commissar successively in Central Hebei Military Region and in the Shanxi-Chahar-Hebei Border Region. The 7th CCP Congress elected Cheng alternate member of the Central Committee in 1945 (until Sep 1956). After the occupation of Shanxi Province by Communist forces in April 1949 Cheng was appointed chairman of the People's Government of Shanxi as well as commander and political commissar of the Shanxi Military Region (all posts until the end of 1950).

1950, Jul Elected vice-chairman of the Federation of Cooperatives (until Jul 1954)

Oct Appointed member of the Finance and Commerce Committee in the Government Administration Council and director of the Central Administration Bureau of Cooperative Enterprises in the same council (until Sep 1952)

1953, Aug Head of a delegation of the Federation of Cooperatives to the USSR

Sep Elected deputy for Shandong Province to the 1st NPC (until Mar 1959)

Oct Elected member of the Standing Committee of the NPC

1954, Jul Elected chairman of the Federation of Supply and Marketing Cooperatives (probably until 1963)

1956, Sep Elected member of the CCP Central Committee by the 8th Party Congress

1957, Jun Member of the CCP delegation to the Socialist Unity Party of Germany (SED) Congress in East Berlin (German Democratic Republic)

1958, Feb Identified as director of the 5th Office in the State Council (until Sep 1959)

1958, Sep Appointed minister of commerce (probably until Apr 1962)

1959, Sep Appointed director of the Office of Finance and Trade in the State Council (until Dec 1961)

1961, Mar Appointed vice-chairman of the Planning Commission

1964, Oct Elected deputy for Shanxi Province to the 3rd NPC

1965, Jan Appointed member of the National Defense Council

1966, Jul Appointed secretary of the Southwest Bureau of the CCP Central Committee

1967 Disappears during the Cultural Revolution

1977, May First appearance after the Cultural Revolution

Aug Elected member of the CCP Central Committee by the 11th Party Congress

1978, Feb Elected deputy for Shanxi Province to the 5th NPC

Mar Appointed minister for civil affairs

Chi Biqing (Ch'ih Pi-ch'ing) 池必卿

Posts held

CCP
Member of the CCP 11th Central Committee
2nd secretary, Guizhou Province CP

In 1947 Chi worked in the Shanxi-Hebei-Shandong-Henan Border Region. In 1948 he was director in the Propaganda Department of Taihang District CP.

1950, Jun Identified as secretary, Yuci District CP, Shanxi

1954, Apr Identified as member of the Standing Committee of Shanxi Province CP

1956, Jul Elected 1st secretary, Taiyuan Municipality CP (until May 1957)

1957, May Elected secretary of Shanxi Province CP

1963, Jul Identified as secretary of the North China Bureau in the CCP Central Committee

1967, Apr Chi is denounced as a counterrevolutionary revisionist and supporter of Peng Zhen and disappears

1970, Jun Identified as vice-chairman of the Revolutionary Committee of Tianjin Municipality. Renewed disappearance shortly afterwards

1976, May First appearance after six years of absence: Identified as 2nd CP secretary, and vice-chairman of the Revolutionary Committee, of Inner Mongolia Autonomous Region (until May 1978)

1977,	Aug	Elected member of the CCP Central Committee by the 11th Party Congress
1978,	Jun	Identified as 2nd secretary of Guizhou Province CP
	Oct	Identified as vice-chairman of the Revolutionary Committee of Guizhou Province

Chi Haotian (Ch'ih Hao-t'ien)　迟浩田

Posts held

Military
Major
Deputy chief of PLA General Staff

1958,	Sep	Identified as major of a unit in Nanjing Military Region
1959,	Mar	Elected deputy for the PLA to the 2nd NPC (reelected in 1964 to the 3rd NPC)
1974,	Sep	First appearance after the Cultural Revolution
1975,	Dec	Identified as deputy political commissar of Beijing Military Region
1977,	Mar	Identified as deputy editor-in-chief of RMRB
	Nov	Identified as deputy chief of PLA General Staff
1978,	Jun	Deputy head of a military goodwill delegation to Congo (Brazzaville) and Zaire

Chilin Wandan (Ch'i-lin Wang-tan)　七林旺丹

Posts held

CCP
Alternate member of the CCP 11th Central Committee
Deputy secretary of Yunnan Province CP
CP secretary of Xinlian Production Brigade in Zhongdian County

Mass Organization
Chairman of the Peasants Federation of Yunnan Province

Others
Chairman of the Revolutionary Committee of Dongwan People's Commune in Zhongdian County

Chilin was born about 1935 in the village of Xinlian, Zhongdian County, Yunnan Province. His family were Tibetan serfs. At the age of seven Chilin was himself made a serf. In spring 1951 he ran away from his slave-owner and joined a unit of the PLA where he served as a courier. But he soon returned to his native village to organize a group of former slaves into an auxiliary militia. This militia supported the local PLA Force in fighting Tibetan rebels during the spring of 1952. In 1957 Chilin was wounded in an armed uprising of Tibetan rebels while trying to obtain support for a surrounded PLA unit.

1960		Chilin takes part in the National Militia Congress in Beijing After his return he is elected secretary of the CP in his native village Xinlian

1966		During the early phase of the Cultural Revolution Chilin is declared an anti-Party element and exposed to strong criticism
1967,	Mar	Chilin is rehabilitated after the PLA sends a group to support the Left in his home area
1968,	Aug	With the establishment of the Revolutionary Committee for Yunnan Province, Chilin is elected a member. Concurrently, he is identified as chairman of the Revolutionary Committee of Dongwang People's Commune
	Nov	Identified as vice-chairman of the Autonomous Zhou of the Tibetan Diqing in Yunnan Province
1969,	Apr	Elected to first term as alternate member of the CCP Central Committee by the 9th Party Congress
1970,	Jan	Identified as CP secretary of Xinlian Production Brigade, Zhongdian County
	May	Chilin is called "Eagle of the Snow Mountains" in an article in the Chinese monthly China Reconstructs
1973,	Feb	Identified as member of the Standing Committee of Yunnan Province CP (until Oct 1973)
	Oct	Identified as deputy secretary of Yunnan Province CP
1974,	Nov	Head of a friendship delegation to North Vietnam
1976,	Jul	Identified as chairman of the Peasants' Federation of Yunnan Province
	Oct	At his own request Chilin is transferred to Zhongdian County in the Autonomous Zhou Diqing to set up an agricultural mass organization on the model of Dazhai
1977,	Dec	Chilin disappears; probably purged

Chou Youwen (Ch'ou Yu-wen)　仇友文

Posts held

CCP
Member of the Standing Committee of Liaoning Province CP

Government
Member of the Birth Planning Leading Group under the State Council

In 1948 Chou was head of the Rehe-Liaoning middle school. In the following year he was elected vice-chairman of the People's Government of Liaoxi Province (this province was abolished as an administrative unit in 1951).

1954,	Aug	Identified as vice-chairman of the People's Government of Liaoning Province (until Feb 1955)
1955,	Feb	Appointed vice-governor of Liaoning Province (until Cultural Revolution)
1960,	Oct	Identified as member of the Standing Committee of Liaoning Province CP (until Jul 1966)
1964,	Sep	Elected deputy for Liaoning Province to the 3rd NPC
1966,	Jul	Identified as alternate member, Secretariat of Laioning Province CP (until Cultural Revolution)

1973,   Jun   Rehabilitated after the Cultural Revolution: Identified as member of the Standing
Committee of Liaoning Province CP

         Sep   Identified as vice-chairman of the Revolu-
tionary Committee of Liaoning Province
(until Nov 1977)

1978,   Jul   Identified as member of the Birth Planning Leading Group under the State Coun-
cil

Chu Jiang (Ch'u Chiang)   储 江

Posts held

CCP
Member of the CCP 11th Central Committee
Secretary of Jiangsu Province CP
1st secretary of Nanjing Municipality CP

Others
Chairman of the Revolutionary Committee of Nanjing Municipality

Chu was born in 1917 in Jiangsu Province.

1965   Identified as 1st CP secretary of Suzhou
Region

1976,   May   Identified as member of the Standing
Committee of Jiangsu Province CP and as
secretary of Nanjing Municipality CP

1977,   Mar   Identified as chairman of the Revolutionary Committee of Nanjing Municipality

         Aug   Elected member of the CCP Central
Committee by the 11th Party Congress

         Dec   Elected secretary of Jiangsu Province CP

1978,   Sep   Elected 1st secretary of Nanjing Municipality CP

Chu Tunan (Ch'u T'u-nan)   楚图南

Posts held

NPC
Member of the Standing Committee of the
5th NPC

Others
Member of the Standing Committee of the
5th CPPCC
Vice-chairman of the Association for
Friendship with Foreign Countries
Vice-chairman of the China Democratic
League

Chu was born in February 1899 in Wenshan, Yunnan
Province.   He studied history and geography in Beijing.
During this period he joined a circle studying Marxism.
After graduation he became a middle school teacher in
Yunnan in 1923. In 1928 he escaped persecution because of
his procommunist leanings by fleeing to Harbin. There he
was soon arrested, however, and imprisoned until 1931.
After his release he taught at several schools in Beijing,
Shandong, Henan, and Shanghai. After the outbreak of the
Anti-Japanese War he became head of the Literature and
History Department at Yunnan University in 1937. In 1945
Chu joined the Democratic League. After Beijing was

occupied by the communists Chu moved to the capital. In
September he took part in the 1st CPPCC which elected
him member of its National Committee.

1949,   Oct   Appointed council member of the Sino-
Soviet Friendship Association (until Dec
1954)

1950,   Jul   Appointed member of the Southwest China Military and Administrative Council
and chairman of the Cultural and Educational Committee of the Military and
Administrative Council (until Jan 1953)

1952,   Nov   Appointed chairman of the Committee for
the Elimination of Illiteracy under the
Government Administration Council (until
Oct 1954)

1953,   Jan   Confirmed in his previous posts after the
above council is reorganized into the
Southwest China Administrative Council

1954,   May   Appointed chairman of the Association for
Cultural Relations with Foreign Countries
(renamed Association for Cultural Relations and Friendship with Foreign Countries in Apr 1966) (until Cultural Revolution)

         Jun   Delegate at the Disarmament Conference
in Stockholm

         Aug   Elected deputy for Yunnan Province to
the 1st NPC

1955,   Jun   Delegate to the World Peace Council
Conference in Helsinki

         Sep   Head of a dance troop which performed in
several Western European countries

1957,   Dec   Delegate at the Afro-Asian Solidarity
Conference in Cairo

1958,   Mar   Appointed vice-chairman of the Commission for Cultural Relations with Foreign
Countries (until Cultural Revolution)

         Jul   Elected member of the Standing Commit-
tee of the Peace Council (until 1965)

1959,   May   Delegate at a special session of the World
Peace Council in Stockholm

1960,   Jan   Head of a cultural delegation to Burma

         Mar   Appointed chairman of the Sino-Latin
American Friendship Association (until
Cultural Revolution)

1961,   Apr   Head of a friendship delegation to Cuba

         Nov   Head of a friendship delegation to Japan

1962,   Apr   Appointed vice-chairman of the Afro-
Asian Society (until Cultural Revolution)

1963,   Oct   Head of an acrobatic troop visiting Pakistan

         Dec   Head of an acrobatic troop visiting Burma

1965,   Jan   Elected member of the Standing Committee of the CPPCC (confirmed in this post
in Jan 1975)

1972,   Jan   Reactivated after the Cultural Revolution

1973,   Apr   Deputy head of a delegation of the Sino-
Japanese Friendship Association to Japan

1975,   Sep   Identified as advisor to the Sino-Japanese
Friendship Association; head of a friend-
ship delegation to Japan

1978,   Mar   Elected member of the Standing Committee of the 5th NPC and member of the
Standing Committee of the 5th CPPCC

         Sep   Identified as vice-chairman of the Associ-
ation for Friendship with Foreign Coun-
tries

Nov Head of a friendship delegation to Great Britain, Belgium, and France

1979, Jan Identified as vice chairman of the China Democratic League (reelected Oct 1979)

Jun Member of the Credentials Committee, 2nd Session of the 5th NPC

Cirenlamu (Tz'u·jen·la·mu) (f) 次仁拉姆

Posts held

NPC
Deputy for Tibet Autonomous Region to the 5th NPC

Provincial Administration
Vice-chairman of the Standing Committee, Tibet Autonomous Regional People's Congress

1965, Jul Identified as member of the Tibet Autonomous Regional People's Congress; subsequently disappears

1974, Nov First appearance after the Cultural Revolution

1978, Feb Elected deputy for Tibet Autonomous Region to the 5th NPC

1979, Aug Elected vice-chairman of the Standing Committee, Tibet Autonomous Regional People's Congress

Cui Guanghua (Ts'ui Kuang-hua) 崔光华

Posts held

Provincial Administration
Vice-governor of Henan Province

1979, Sep Elected vice-governor of Henan Province

Cui Jian (Ts'ui Chien) 崔健

Posts held

Government
Ambassador to Tunisia

1972, May Identified as director of the West Asia and Africa Department of the Ministry of Foreign Affairs; member of a government delegation to Sudan

Aug Appointed ambassador to South Yemen (until May 1977)

1977, Aug Appointed ambassador to Tunisia

Cui Ping (Ts'ui P'ing) 崔萍

Posts held

Others
Managing director of the Bank of China
Vice-president of the Bank of China

1971, Oct Member of a banking delegation to Romania

1973, May Identified as deputy managing director of the Bank of China

1978, May Identified as managing director of the Bank of China

1979, Oct Identified as vice-chairman of the Board of Directors of the Bank of China

Nov Identified as vice-president of the Bank of China

Cui Qun (Ts'ui Ch'ün) 崔群

Posts held

Government
Vice-minister of foreign trade

1960, May Identified as economic plenipotentiary of PR China in North Vietnam (until May 1963)

1963, Sep Identified as director of the Technical Import and Export Corporation (until Cultural Revolution)

1964, Jul Cui conducts negotiations in Beijing with a delegation of petroleum technology consultants from the Federal Republic of Germany

1977, Aug Reactivated after the Cultural Revolution

Dec Identified as vice-minister of foreign trade

1979, Jan Head of a trade delegation to Czechoslovakia, Hungary, and Poland

Oct Member of a government delegation, led by Hua Guofeng, to France, the Federal Republic of Germany, Great Britain, and Italy

Cui Yanxu (Ts'ui Yen-hsü) 崔延绪

Posts held

Government
Managing director of the Bank of China
Vice-president of the Bank of China

1979, Mar Identified as managing director of the Bank of China

Oct Identified as vice-president of the Bank of China

Cui Yueli (Ts'ui Yüeh-li) 崔月犁

Posts held

Government
Vice-minister of public health

Others
Vice-chairman of the Committee for the Protection of Children
President of the Society for Physicians and Pharmacists Practicing Traditional Chinese Medicine

Cui was born in 1920 in Hebei Province. During the 1940s he was engaged in underground activities in the Beijing area which included the supply of medical equipment to the Communists.

1949,   Oct   Identified as council member of the Beijing Branch, Sino-Soviet Friendship Association

1950,   Oct   Identified as deputy secretary-general of the Chinese Committee for World Peace (until 1958)

1956,   Feb   Identified as deputy director of the United Front Work Department of Beijing Municipality CP

1957,   May   Identified as director of the United Front Work Department of Beijing Municipality CP

1959,   Aug   Identified as director of the Department of Public Health and Physical Culture of Beijing Municipality CP

1964,   Jul   Member of a delegation to the World Conference against Atomic Bombs in Japan

        Sep   Elected deputy mayor of Beijing (until Cultural Revolution)

1965,   Aug   Identified as member of the Standing Committee of Beijing Municipality CP

1967,   May   Branded as a counterrevolutionary revisionist

1975,   Oct   First appearance after the Cultural Revolution

1978,   Jul   Identified as vice-minister of public health

1979,   Apr   Identified as vice-chairman of the Committee for the Protection of Children

        May   Elected president of the Society for Physicians and Pharmacists Practicing Traditional Medicine

        Jul   Member of the National Games Organizing Committee

Dai Guangqian (Tai Kuang-ch'ien) 戴光前

Posts held

CCP
Member of the CCP 11th Central Committee

1977,	Aug	Elected member of the CCP Central Committee by the 11th Party Congress
	Sep	Identified as a cadre in Guangdong

Dai Peizhen (Tai P'ei-chen) 戴佩震

Posts held

Government
Deputy director of the Africa Department of the Ministry of Foreign Affairs

1972,	May	Identified as chargé d'affaires ad interim in Senegal (until 1975)
1978,	May	Identified as deputy director of the Africa Department in the Ministry of Foreign Affairs

Dai Ping (Tai P'ing) 戴 平

Posts held

Deputy director of the Protocol Department of the Ministry of Foreign Affairs

Dai was born in 1932.

1951,	Aug	Identified as consul at the Consulate General in Calcutta
1958,	Dec	Identified as deputy director of the Protocol Department of the Ministry of Foreign Affairs
1959,	Jul	Identified as 1st secretary at the embassy in Indonesia
1963,	Apr	Identified as deputy director of the Protocol Department of the Ministry of Foreign Affairs
1967		Disappears during the Cultural Revolution
1978,	Jul	First appearance after the Cultural Revolution: Referred to in his former post as deputy director of the Protocol Department in the Ministry of Foreign Affairs
	Nov	Member of a government delegation led by Deng Xiaoping to Singapore

Dai Suli (Tai Su-li) 戴苏里

Posts held

CCP
Alternate member of the CCP 11th Central Committee
Secretary of Henan Province CP
Deputy director of the Henan Party School

Provincial Administration
Vice-governor of Henan Province

1960,	Mar	Identified as member of the Standing Committee, and as secretary-general of the CP, of Henan Province (until 1965)
1965,	Aug	Identified as alternate member of the Secretariat of Henan Province CP
1966,	Sep	Appointed head of the Cultural Revolutionary Group of Henan Province CP
1968,	Mar	Elected member of the Standing Committee, Revolutionary Committee of Henan Province
	May	Denounced by Red Guards as "chameleon and little reptile who crept into the Revolutionary Committee"; subsequently disappears
1971,	Aug	Again referred to as member of the Standing Committee, Revolutionary Committee of Henan Province (until May 1973)
1972,	Jul	Identified as member of the Standing Committee of Henan Province CP (until Apr 1973)
1974,	Apr	Identified as secretary of Henan Province CP
	May	Identified as vice-chairman of the Revolutionary Committee of Henan Province (until Sep 1979)
1977,	Aug	Elected alternate member of the CCP Central Committee by the 11th Party Congress
	Oct	Identified as secretary of Henan Province CP
	Dec	Identified as deputy director of the Henan Party School
1979,	Sep	Elected vice-governor of Henan Province

Dai Weiran (Tai Wei-jan) 戴为然

Posts held

CCP
1st deputy director of the Party School of Jiangsu Province

NPC
Deputy for Jiangsu Province to the 5th NPC

Provincial Administration
Vice-chairman of the People's Congress of Jiangsu Province

1973,	Mar	Identified as acting director, Propaganda Department of Jiangsu Province CP
1977,	Oct	Identified as director, Propaganda Department of Jiangsu Province CP, and as 1st deputy director of the Party School of Jiangsu Province
	Dec	Elected vice-chairman of the Revolutionary Committee of Jiangsu Province (until Dec 1979)
1978,	Feb	Elected deputy for Jiangsu Province to the 5th NPC
1979,	Dec	Elected vice-chairman of the People's Congress of Jiangsu Province

Dao Dongting (Tao Tung-t'ing)　刀栋庭

Posts held

Others
Member of the Standing Committee of the
5th CPPCC

1978,　Mar　Elected member of the Standing Committee of the 5th CPPCC
1979,　Jun　Identified as a Yunnan Province cadre

Dao Guodong (Tao Kuo-tung)　刀国栋

Posts held

CCP
Member of the Standing Committee of
Yunnan Province CP

Government
Member of the State Nationalities Affairs
Commission

Provincial Administration
Vice-governor of Yunnan Province

Dao belongs to the Dai minority.

1977,　Dec　Elected vice-chairman of the Revolutionary Committee of Yunnan Province (until
Dec 1979)
1978,　Jan　Identified as member of the Standing
Committee of Yunnan Province CP
1979,　May　Appointed member of the State Nationalities Affairs Commission
　　　　Dec　Elected vice-governor of of Yunnan Province

Deng Chumin (Teng Ch'u-min)　邓初民

Posts held

NPC
Member of the Standing Committee of the
5th NPC
Deputy for Shanxi Province to the
5th NPC

Others
Vice-chairman of the Central Committee,
China Democratic League

Deng was born in 1888 in Shishou, Hubei Province. He
studied at Waseda University in Japan. After a period of
journalistic work he joined the Wuhan Government in
1926. He left for Japan following the rift between the
KMT and the communists in 1926. After his return he was
appointed to various lectureships at the Sun Yat-sen
University in Guangzhou and the Guilin Teachers College.
During the Anti-Japanese War he worked again as a
journalist in Chongqing. In 1947 he went to Hong Kong to
lecture at Tate College. During the same year he joined
the China Democratic League and the Revolutionary
Committee of the KMT which both elected him a member
of the Central Committees. As a delegate representing
social science workers he took part in the 1st CPPCC in
September 1949 in Peking.

1949,　Oct　Appointed member of the Political and
Legislative Council of the Central Government Council; elected member of the
Peace Council and member of the Executive Council of the Sino-Soviet Friendship
Association (until Dec 1954)
　　　　Dec　Appointed chancellor of Shanxi University
1951,　Dec　Appointed member of the North China
Administrative Council (until Sep 1954)
1953　　　　Identified as board member of the Society
of Political Science and Law
1954,　Aug　Elected deputy for Shanxi Province to the
1st NPC (reelected in 1958 and 1964 to
the 2nd and 3rd NPCs)
　　　　Nov　Elected vice-chairman of the People's
Government of Shanxi (until Feb 1955)
1955,　Feb　Elected member of the Standing Committee by the 2nd CPPCC; elected vice-
governor of Shanxi Province (until
Dec 1958)
1956,　Mar　Elected member of the Central Committee, Revolutionary Committee of the
KMT, and member of the Central Committee of the China Democratic League
　　　　Jun　Elected member of the Standing Committee of the 1st NPC (reelected in 1959 and
1965 to the 2nd and 3rd NPCs)
1958,　Dec　Elected vice-chairman of the China Democratic League
1959,　Apr　Reelected member of the Standing Committee by the 2nd CPPCC (again confirmed in this post in 1965 by the
3rd CPPCC)
1975,　Jan　Reelected member of the Standing Committee by the 4th NPC (again confirmed
in Mar 1978 by the 5th NPC)
1978,　Feb　Elected deputy for Shanxi Province to the
5th NPC
1979,　Oct　Elected vice-chairman of the Central
Committee of the China Democratic
League

Publications

Treatises on Political Science
Reader for Chinese Social History
Talks on Political Problems of China
Treatises on the History of Social Evolu-
tion

Deng Diantao (Teng Tien-t'ao)　邓典桃

Posts held

NPC
Member of the Standing Committee of the
5th NPC
Deputy for Jiangxi Province to the
5th NPC

1958,　Apr　Identified as deputy director, Administrative Office of the CCP Central Commit-
tee (until Cultural Revolution)
1964,　Oct　Elected deputy for Jiangxi Province to the
3rd NPC
1967,　Apr　Branded as a "three-anti"-element and
purged

1973,	May	First appearance after the Cultural Revolution
1977,	Oct	Identified as a cadre of a department of the CCP Central Committee
1978,	Feb	Elected deputy for Jiangxi Province to the 5th NPC
	Mar	Elected member of the Standing Committee of the 5th NPC
1979,	Jun	Member of the Budget Committee at the 2nd Session of the 5th NPC

Deng Guozhong (Teng Kuo-chung) 邓国忠

Posts held

Provincial Administration
Vice-governor of Shaanxi Province

1979,	Dec	Elected vice-governor of Shaanxi Province

Deng Hua (Teng Hua) 邓华

Posts held

CCP
Alternate member of the CCP 11th Central Committee

Military
Colonel-general

Others
Deputy director of the Office of Production and Construction of Sichuan Province

Deng was born in 1900 in Guiyang County, Hunan Province. He attended elementary school. In 1927 he was political instructor of a company of the 5th Army commanded by Peng Dehuai. In that year he also joined the CCP. In the late 1920s he moved to the Communist base on Jinggangshan, and in 1934-35 he took part in the Long March. During the Anti-Japanese War he was troop commander and political commissar of various units and regions in North China. In 1947 he commanded the 7th Column of Northeast Field Army, in 1948 he was deputy commander of a corps (of the 15th Army?). In early 1949 he was made commander of the 15th Corps, 4th Field Army.

1949,	Oct	Appointed deputy commander of South China Military Region and of Guangdong Military Region as well as commander of Guangzhou Garrison following the occupation of Guangzhou (all posts until mid 1951)
1950,	Feb	Appointed member of the Central-South China Military and Administrative Council and member of the People's Government of Guangdong Province (both posts until mid 1951)
	Apr	Appointed chairman of the Hainan Military Control Commission following the occupation of Hainan Island (until mid 1951)
1951,	Jan	Appointed chairman of Hainan Military and Administrative Council (until mid 1951)
	Jun?	Transferred to Korea as deputy commander of the Chinese People's Volunteers
	Oct	Elected member of the CPPCC (until Dec 1954)
1953,	Feb	Conferred the highest order of North Korea
1954,	Sep	Appointed commander of the Chinese People's Volunteers in Korea
	Oct	Recalled from Korea; elected deputy for the Chinese People's Volunteers in Korea to the 1st NPC (until Mar 1959); appointed member of the National Defense Council (probably until Apr 1959)
	Nov	Appointed commander of Shenyang Military Region (probably until Oct 1959)
1955,	May	Acting chairman of the Sino-Soviet Military Commission supervising the transfer of Lüshun-Dalian (Port Arthur) to Chinese sovereignty
	Sep	Promoted to rank of colonel-general
1956,	Sep	Elected member of the CCP Central Committee by the 8th Party Congress (until Apr 1969)
	Oct	Head of a military delegation to Yugoslavia and Bulgaria
1960,	May	Identified as vice-governor of Sichuan Province (until Cultural Revolution)
1969,	Apr	Elected alternate member of the CCP Central Committee by the 9th Party Congress (confirmed in 1973 and 1977 by the 10th and 11th Congresses)
1974,	Sep	Identified as deputy director of the Production and Construction Office of Sichuan Province
1979,	Oct	Coauthor (together with Li Zhimin and Hong Xuezhi) of an article in Jiefangjün Bao (Liberation Army) on 25th October, "Heroism Shines Forever, Internationalism Inspires All People - Cherishing the Memory of Comrade Peng Dehuai"

Deng Jiatai (Teng Chia-t'ai) 邓家太

Posts held

NPC
Deputy for the PLA to the 5th NPC

Military
Major-general
Deputy commander of the PLA Armored Forces

1958,	Oct	Identified as PLA major-general
1975,	Oct	Identified as military leader in Nanjing Military Region
1976,	Apr	Identified as chief of staff of the Nanjing Military Region
1978,	Feb	Elected deputy for the PLA to the 5th NPC
	Aug	Identified as deputy commander of the PLA Armored Forces

Deng Liqun (Teng Li-ch'ün)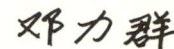

<u>Posts held</u>

NPC
Deputy for Shanghai Municipality to the 5th NPC

Others
Vice-president of the Academy of Social Sciences

Deng was born in Hunan Province.

1949,	Dec	Identified as council member of the People's Government of Xinjiang
1950,	Jan	Identified as chairman of the Cultural and Educational Committee of Xinjiang People's Government
1951,	Sep	Identified as member of the Cultural and Educational Committee of the Northwest Military and Administrative Council
1960,	May	Identified as editor of <u>HQ</u>
1964,	Jul	Identified as deputy chief editor of <u>HQ</u>
	Oct	Elected deputy for Xinjiang Autonomous Region to the 3rd NPC
1958,	Jun	Branded as a counterrevolutionary revisionist and purged
1975,	Sep	First appearance after the Cultural Revolution
	Dec	Identified as a cadre of the State Council
1978,	Feb	Elected deputy for Shanghai Municipality to the 5th NPC; appointed vice-president of the Academy of Social Sciences
	Oct	Advisor to an economic delegation to Japan
1979,	Jun	Member of the Committee to Examine Proposals at the 2nd Session of the 5th NPC
	Nov	Deputy head of a delegation to the U.S.A. to study industrial management and business administration (leader: Yuan Baohua)

Deng Xiaoping (Teng Hsiao-p'ing)

<u>Posts held</u>

CCP
Vice-chairman of the CCP 11th Central Committee
Member of the Standing Committee of the CCP Politburo
Member of the CCP Politburo
Member of the CCP 11th Central Committee
Vice-chairman, Military Council of the CCP Central Committee

Government
Vice premier

NPC
Deputy for the PLA to the 5th NPC

Military
Chief of PLA General Staff

Others
Chairman of the CPPCC

Deng was born in 1904 in Guang'an, Sichuan Province, as eldest son of a landowner. He attended middle school and subsequently took part in a preparatory course for candidates to be selected for studies in France as worker-students. He began his studies in early 1920 probably at the University of Lyon. In 1922 he joined the Chinese Socialist Youth League of which a branch had been established in France by Wang Ruofei. During the following year he helped to edit a Chinese youth journal. He joined the CCP in 1924. Later Deng told Edgar Snow that he had not studied in France at all but worked as a laborer. Before his return to China, he studied for several months in Moscow in 1926.

Back in China, Deng's first post was instructor at the Political Department of the Xi'an Military and Political Academy which the warlord Feng Yuxiang had established after a prolonged stay in Moscow. Following the rift between the KMT and the CCP in 1927, the KMT General Feng had all Communist cadres removed from the Xi'an Academy. Deng subsequently went to Shanghai to work in the CCP Central Organization for the following two years. As part of the program to mobilize the rural areas, Deng was sent to Guangxi Province in mid-1929 to help organize the 7th Red Army. He was appointed political commissar for this army. In late 1930 he served as chief of staff of the 3rd Corps (commander: Peng Dehuai), 1st Front Army. In 1931 he was posted to the CCP Central Organization headed by Mao Zedong in Ruijin where he was assigned the editorship of a Red Army journal. In early 1933 Deng was criticized as a follower of Luo Ming; Luo was accused of having developed defeatist theories in the following KMT attacks on the Communist bases. This criticism notwithstanding, Deng was given a lectureship on the history of the Communist Party at the Red Army Academy in Ruijin only a few months later.

During the Long March of 1934-35 Deng probably served as director of the Political Department of the 1st Front Army. When the outbreak of the Anti-Japanese War in 1937 led to the reorganization of the communist forces into the 8th Route Army, Deng was appointed political commissar of the 129th Division commanded by Liu Bocheng and operating in the Taihang Mountains in the Shanxi-Hebei Border Area throughout the following years. In 1945 he was elected a member of the CCP Central Committee by the 7th Party Congress. After the Anti-Japanese War Deng was appointed political commissar of the Shanxi-Hebei-Shandong-Henan Field Army. This army, later reorganized to form the 2nd Field Army, defeated the KMT Armored Forces in the Chang Jiang region after the Huai-Hai Battles of spring 1949.

In September 1949 Deng represented the 2nd Field Army as delegate at the CPPCC which elected him a member of its National Committee.

1949,	Oct	Appointed member of the Central People's Government Council and of the Revolutionary Military Council (until Sep 1954)
1950,	Jul	Having pushed forward into Southwest China and destroyed the last remnants of the KMT forces, the 2nd Field Army's Regional Command is proclaimed as the Southwest China Military and Administrative Council with Deng as vice-chairman (until Jan 1953)
1951,	Feb	Deng reports to the Government Adminis-

tration Council in Beijing on the situation in Southwest China

1952,	Aug	Appointed vice premier (until Cultural Revolution)
	Nov	Appointed member of the State Planning Commission (until 1954)
1953,	Jan	With the reorganization of the Southwest China Military and Administrative Council to form the Southwest China Administrative Council, Deng is confirmed as vice-chairman (until 1954)
	Feb	Elected vice-chairman of the CPPCC
	Sep	Appointed minister of finance (until Jun 1954) and chairman of the Financial and Economic Affairs Committee under the Central Administration Council (until Sep 1954)
until 1954		Deng plays a decisive role in the drafting of the constitution of the PRC and in the preparations for the election of the 1st NPC
1954,	May	Identified as secretary-general of the CCP Central Committee, in this capacity responsible for the Central Committee departments
	Sep	Elected one of the 15 vice-chairmen of the National Defense Council by the 1st NPC (until Cultural Revolution)
	Dec	Elected member of the Standing Committee of the CPPCC (until Apr 1959)
1955,	Mar	At a CCP national conference Deng reads the report condemning the "Anti-Party Block" under Gao Gang and Rao Shushi
	Apr	Elected member of the Politburo by the 5th Plenary Session of the 7th Central Committee
1956,	Feb	Member of a CCP delegation led by Zhu De to take part in the 20th CPSU Congress in Moscow
	Sep	At the 8th CCP Congress, Deng reads the report on the new Party statutes. He is confirmed by the Congress as member of the Politburo in which he takes the 6th place after Mao Zedong, Liu Shaoqi, Zhou Enlai, Zhu De, and Chen Yun. In addition, he is elected a member of the Standing Committee of the Politburo as well as secretary general of the CCP Central Committee.
1957,	Sep	At the 3rd Plenary Session of the 8th Central Committee Deng reads the report on the rectification campaign following the condemnation of prominent critics during the "One Hundred Flowers Campaign" as rightist deviationist
	Nov	Member of a CCP delegation led by Mao Zedong to the 40th anniversary celebrations of the October Revolution in Moscow; present at the Moscow summit meeting of leading cadres of 12 communist nations and 64 communist parties which set the stage for the Sino-Soviet conflict
1958,	May	At the 2nd Plenary Session of the 8th Central Committee Deng reads the report on the Moscow summit meeting of communist parties in November 1957
	Jul	Elected deputy for Sichuan Province to the 2nd NPC (until Dec 1964)
1959,	Oct	Article in RMRB of 2 October defending the people's commune movement; the article had been published by Pravda on the day before
1960,	Nov	Deputy head of a delegation led by Liu Shaoqi to the Moscow conference of 81 communist parties which first openly witnessed the controversy between Beijing and Moscow
1961,	Jan	At the 9th Plenary Session of the 8th Central Committee Deng reads the report on the Moscow conference of November 1960
	Sep	Head of a CCP delegation to attend the 4th Congress of the Korean Workers Party
1963,	Jul	Head of a CCP delegation to Moscow comprising Peng Zhen, Kang Sheng, Yang Shangkun, Liu Ningyi, Wu Xiuquan, and Pan Zili. The following "ideological talks," led on the Moscow side by M.A. Suslow, resulted in the open rift between Beijing and Moscow, the major points of contention being national liberation movements, "just" wars, and international communist policy
1963,	Dec-1964, Feb	Acting premier in the absence of Zhou Enlai on visits to Africa, the Mid-East, and Asia
1964,	Sep	Elected deputy for Beijing Municipality to the 3rd NPC
1965,	Jul	Head of a CCP delegation to the 4th Congress of the Romanian Workers Party
1966,	Oct	On 23 October Deng is forced to undergo self-criticism on the charge of following the bourgeois-reactionary line of Liu Shaoqi. In his self-criticism Deng declared: "I absolutely support the instructions of Chairman Mao Zedong and Comrade Lin Biao... Liu Shaoqi and I represent the capitalist, reactionary line in the Cultural Revolution. My thoughts and deeds are not directed by the thoughts of Mao Zedong. My alienation from the masses denies me the right to carry out the tasks assigned to me by the Central Committee ..."
	Dec	Last appearance on 14 December

During the Cultural Revolution Deng is never explicitly criticized by name in the official press; he is merely referred to as "Number 2" or "the other capitalist-roader" (beside Liu Shaoqi). The major accusations behind the political downfall of Deng Xiaoping were listed by the Red Guard publications Red Flag Struggle and The East Is Red as follows:

1. Unauthorized actions as secretary general of the Party
2. Condemnation of the personality cult with resulting damage to the position of Mao Zedong
3. Insult to Mao Zedong Thought at a Party conference in 1961
4. Propagation of the slogan: as long as the cat catches mice it doesn't matter if it is a white cat or a black cat - with reference to agricultural policy
5. Advocacy of a system of academic degrees and titles (1963)

6.   Weakening of the Party leadership by the "60 articles on higher education" (1961)
7.   Rejection of Mao Zedong's educational theory combining studies with manual labor
8.   Rejection of criticism in the field of culture
9.   Suppression of revolutionary students at Beijing University
10.   Suppression of the mass movement during the Cultural Revolution by the dispatch of "work groups"

His children were also drawn into the criticism of Deng Xiaoping by being required to testify against him.

An important consideration in the fall of Deng during the Cultural Revolution was his low opinion of Jiang Qing's efforts to revolutionize the Beijing Opera. He was absent at the first performance of "Red Lantern" in 1964; from 1965 he was never present at theater performances conscientiously attended by his colleagues in the Politburo. However, criticism of Deng Xiaoping during the Cultural Revolution was comparatively moderate. It rather depicted him as an independent personality with the courage of nonconformist behavior.

1973,	Apr	First appearance after the Cultural Revolution: Referred to as vice premier
	Aug	Elected member of the CCP Central Committee by the 10th Party Congress
1974,	Jan	Identified as member of the Politburo of the CCP Central Committee
	Apr	Head of the Chinese delegation to the UN Special Session of Problems of Raw Materials and Development; speech at the Plenary Session of 10 April
1975,	Jan	Elected vice-chairman and member of the Standing Committee, Politburo of the CCP Central Committee, by the 2nd Plenary Session of the 10th Central Committee
	May	Head of a government delegation to France
1976,	Apr	On 7 April Deng is again relieved of all posts, retaining only his CCP membership. He is criticized throughout the period until November 1976, two months after the death of Mao and one month after the purge of the Gang of Four
1977,	Jul	First appearance since his second downfall on 22 July: Officially named in his present posts
1978,	Jan	Head of a government delegation to Burma and Nepal
	Feb	Elected deputy for the PLA to the 5th NPC
	Mar	Elected chairman of the 5th CPPCC
	Sep	Head of a Party and government delegation to North Korea
	Oct	Head of a government delegation to Japan
	Nov	Head of a government delegation to Thailand, Malaysia, and Singapore
1979,	Jan	Head of a government delegation to the U.S.A. and Japan

Deng is married to Zhuo Lin. There are reportedly two sons from this marriage who studied at Beijing University in 1961.

Deng Yingchao (Teng Ying-ch'ao) (f)

邓颖超

Posts held

CCP
Member of the Politburo, CCP 11th Central Committee
Member of the CCP 11th Central Committee
2nd secretary of the CCP Central Committee's Commission for Inspecting Discipline

NPC
Vice-chairman of the Standing Committee of the NPC

Others
Honorary president of the Women's Federation
Vice-chairman of the Committee for the Protection of Children

Deng was born in 1904 in Xingyang, Henan Province (according to different sources in Nanning, Guangxi Province, or Kuanshancun, Hebei Province). Her father was an impoverished landlord who had been an army officer during the latter phase of the Qing dynasty. After his death, when Deng was still a child, her mother supported the family as a teacher and governess. Deng received her school education in Beijing and Tianjin. As a student at Tianjin Normal School she joined the Wake Up Society founded by Zhou Enlai and was a leading participant in the May 4th Movement in 1919. Together with Zhou Enlai and others she helped in 1920 to establish a society devoted to the study of new ideas. In the same year she went to France with a group of worker-students, where she helped to set up the French branch of the CCP during the following year. In 1924 she returned to China and was married to Zhou Enlai one year later. In 1926 she was elected an alternate member of the Central Executive Council of the KMT. After the rift between KMT and CCP she hid in Shanghai. In 1928 she participated with Zhou Enlai in the 6th CCP Congress in Moscow. In 1933 she joined the Jiangxi Soviet. Having contracted pulmonary tuberculosis shortly afterwards she had to be carried on a stretcher during the Long March in 1934-35. Deng was identified as director of the Women's Work Department of the CCP Central Committee in 1937. She was in Beijing when it was occupied by the Japanese that year. Helped by the American journalist Edgar Snow she managed to escape from the capital and the Japanese. After the KMT and the CCP had agreed on a new united front she was sent to Hankou (today: Wuhan) in 1938 to work in the communist liaison post with the KMT. In 1939 she went to the USSR for medical treatment. In 1941 she was one of the CCP representatives elected members of the Political Council of the Nationalist Government. In 1945 she was elected an alternate member of the Central Committee by the 7th CCP Congress. After the Anti-Japanese War she and her husband were delegates at the Political Consultative Conference trying to mediate between the KMT and the CCP. After the failure of these negotiations she returned to Yan'an at the end of 1946. In 1947 she was elected a board member of the International Women's Association and in April 1949, vice-chairman of the Federation of Democratic Women. In September of the same year she took part in the CPPCC which elected her a member of its Standing Committee (until Dec 1954).

1949,	Oct	Appointed member of the Committee of Political and Legal Affairs in the Government Administration Council (until Oct 1954)
	Dec	Elected board member of the Sino-Soviet Friendship Association (until Dec 1954)
1950,	Oct	Elected member of the Standing Committee, Peace Council (until Jul 1958)
1951,	Dec	Delegate to the International Federation of Democratic Women Conference in Moscow
1954,	Aug	Elected delegate for Henan Provice to the 1st NPC (reelected in 1958 and 1964 to the 2nd and 3rd NPC)
	Sep	Elected member of the Standing Committee of the NPC (confirmed in this post in 1959 and 1965 by the 2nd and 3rd National NPC)
1955		Identified as honorary chairman, Society of Nurses
1956,	Sep	Elected member of the CCP Central Committee by the 8th Party Congress
1957,	Jun	Identified as 2nd secretary, Women's Work Department of the CCP Central Committee
	Sep	Elected vice-chairman, Women's Federation (last mentioned in this post in April 1972)
1961,	Mar	Head of a women's delegation to North Vietnam
1969,	Apr	Confirmed as member of the Central Committee by the 9th Party Congress
1973,	Aug	Confirmed as member of the Central Committee by the 10th Party Congress
1974-1975		On several occasions during Zhou Enlai's illness his wife receives foreign delegations invited by Zhou
1975,	Jan	Confirmed as member of the Standing Committee by the 4th NPC
1976,	Dec	Appointed vice-chairman, Standing Committee of the NPC
1977,	Feb	Deng visits Burma at the invitation of President Ne Win
	Apr	Deng visits Sri Lanka at the invitation of Mrs. Bandaranaike
	Aug	Confirmed as member of the CCP Central Committee by the 11th Party Congress
	Nov	Head of a friendship delegation to Iran
1978,	Jan	Head of a government delegation to Kampuchea
	Jun	Appointed vice-chairman of the Committee for the Protection of Children
	Sep	Elected honorary president of the Women's Federation
	Dec	Elected member of the Politburo of the CCP Central Committee
		Appointed 2nd secretary of the CCP Central Committee's Commission for Inspecting Discipline
1979,	Apr	Head of an NPC delegation to Japan
	May	Head of a delegation to North Korea

Deng Yue (Teng Yüeh) 邓岳

<u>Posts held</u>

NPC
Deputy for the PLA to the 5th NPC

Military
Deputy commander of Nanjing Military Region

In 1937 Deng served as regiment commander in the 115th Division, 8th Route Army. In 1947 he commanded a division of the Northeast Joint Democratic Army. In 1949 he became commander of the 118th Division, 4th Field Army.

1950		Deng serves in the Korean War as commander of the 118th Division
1953		Identified as deputy commander of the 40th Army
1956?		Training at the PLA Military Academy
1958		Identified as commander of the 40th Army
1972,	Nov	Identified as deputy commander of Shenyang Military Region (until 1977)
1978,	Jan	Identified as deputy commander of Nanjing Military Region
	Feb	Elected deputy for the PLA to the 5th NPC

Deng Zhaoxiang (Teng Chao-hsiang) 邓兆祥

<u>Posts held</u>

NPC
Deputy for the PLA to the 5th NPC

Military
Rear admiral
Deputy commander of the North China Sea Fleet, PLA Navy

Deng was born in 1902 in Gaoyao, Guangdong Province. At the age of fourteen he entered a naval school set up by the Northern Warlords. In 1925 he attended Whampoa Military Academy and subsequently Yantai Naval Academy as well as the Nanjing Naval Torpedo School. He was then appointed captain of the Naval Vessels "Sea Eagle" and "Changzhi." In 1946 he was sent to Great Britain to take over a cruiser presented to China by the British Government. In England he visited the British Royal Naval Academy. He returned to China in 1948 with the warship which had been renamed "Chongqing." In February 1949 he went over to the Communists with his ship. As a delegate representing the Navy he took part in the 1st CPPCC in September of that year. In the same month he was appointed commandant of the Northeast People's Naval Academy.

1953,	Jan	Appointed member of the Northeast Administrative Council
1954,	Aug	Elected deputy for Lüshun-Dalian (Port Arthur) Municipality to the 3rd NPC
	Sep	Appointed member of the National Defense Council
1955,	Sep	Confirmed as rear admiral and awarded the order of "Liberation," 1st class
1956,	Mar	Identified as deputy chief of staff of the Qingdao Naval Base
1958,	Dec	Elected deputy for Liaoning Province to the 2nd NPC (reelected in 1964 to the 3rd NPC)
1962,	Sep	Identified as deputy commander of the North China Sea Fleet
1966		Deng disappears
1975,	Jan	First appearance after the Cultural Revolution

1977,	Jun	Identified as military leader of the North China Sea Fleet
1978,	Feb	Elected deputy for the PLA to the 5th NPC
	Nov	Identified on his previous post as deputy commander of the North China Sea Fleet

Di Jingxiang (Ti Ching-hsiang) 狄井薌

Posts held

Provincial Administration
Vice-chairman of the People's Congress of Shanghai Municipality

1960,	Apr	Identified as vice-mayor of Jinan Municipality
1963,	Nov	Identified as deputy secretary-general of the People's Council of Shandong Province
1979,	Sep	Identified as vice-chairman of the Revolutionary Committee of Shanghai Municipality (until Dec 1979)
	Oct	Head of a Shanghai goodwill delegation to Japan
	Dec	Elected vice-chairman of the People's Congress of Shanghai Municipality

Di Ququ (Ti Ch'ü-ch'ü)

Posts held

Government
Vice-minister of petroleum industry

1979,	Feb	Identified as vice-minister of petroleum industry and as responsible cadre of Daqing Oil Field

Ding Changhua (Ting Ch'ang-hua) (f) 丁长华

Posts held

CCP
Alternate member of the CCP 11th Central Committee

NPC
Deputy for Jiangxi Province to the 5th NPC

Mass Organization
Vice-chairman of the Women's Federation of Jiangxi Province

1964,	Jul	Elected member, Central Committee of the Communist Youth League
	Sep	Elected deputy for Jiangxi Province to the 3rd NPC
1965,	May	Identified as head of the "Rocket" Production Group of Xuwan People's Commune in Jinxi County, Jiangxi Province
1973,	Sep	Elected vice-chairman of the Women's Federation of Jiangxi Province
1977,	Aug	Elected alternate member of the CCP Central Committee by the 11th Party Congress
1978,	Feb	Elected deputy for Jiangxi Province to the 5th NPC

Ding Guangxun (Ting Kuang-hsün) 丁光训

Posts held

NPC
Deputy for Jiangsu Province to the 5th NPC

Others
Member of the Standing Committee of the 5th CPPCC
Vice-chairman of the 3rd Committee for Patriotic Movement of Christianity in China
Director of the Institute of Research on Religion, Nanjing University

Ding was born in 1915. He studied theology in the U.S.A. From the late forties to the early fifties, he worked as a clerk in the World Christian Student Alliance.

1951		Ding returns to China
1953		Identified as director of the Nanjing Union Theological Seminary
1962,	May	Identified as vice-chairman of the Council of Self-Administration of the Protestant Church
1964,	May	Identified as bishop and director of the Institute of Protestant Theology in Nanjing
	Sep	Elected deputy for Jiangsu Province to the 3rd NPC
1967		Disappears during the Cultural Revolution
1972,	Sep	First appearance after the Cultural Revolution: Present at mourning ceremonies for He Xiangning in Nanjing
1978,	Feb	Elected for Jiangsu Province to the 5th NPC
	Mar	Elected member of the Standing Committee of the 5th CPPCC
1979,	Jun	Member of the Committee to Examine Proposals at the 2nd Session of the 5th NPC
	Aug	Identified as vice-chairman of the 3rd Committee for Patriotic Movement of Christianity in China; and identified as director of the Institute of Research on Religion, Nanjing University

Ding Guoyu (Ting Kuo-yü) 丁国钰

Posts held

CCP
Member of the CCP 11th Central Committee

Military
Major-general

Others
Chairman of the CPPCC, Beijing Municipality Branch

1953,	Nov	Identified as a member of the Armistice Committee in Korea
1955,	Mar	Appointed ambassador to Afghanistan (until Jul 1958)
1956,	Apr	Identified as a PLA major-general
1958,	Dec	Appointed ambassador to Pakistan (until Jul 1966)

1966,	Nov	Identified as secretary of Beijing Municipality CP
1967,	Oct	Appointed member of the Standing Committee, Revolutionary Committee of Beijing Municipality
1970,	Oct	Member of a friendship delegation, led by Zeng Siyu, to North Korea; receives Korean Order "National Flag," 2nd class
1971,	Mar	Reelected secretary of Beijing Municipality CP (until Oct 1977)
1972,	Jul	Identified as deputy CP secretary and vice-chairman of the Revolutionary Committee of Qinghua University
1973,	Aug	Elected member of the Central Committee of the 10th CCP Congress (reelected to the 11th Central Committee in 1977)
1974,	Mar	Identified as vice-chairman of the Revolutionary Committee of Beijing Municipality (until 1977)
1977,	Oct	Identified as 3rd secretary of Beijing Municipality CP (until Oct 1978)
	Dec	Identified as chairman of the CPPCC, Beijing Municipality Branch

Ding Hao (Ting Hao)　　丁 浩

Posts held

Government
Ambassador to Kuwait

1965,	Feb	Identified as deputy director of the Western Europe Department of the Ministry of Foreign Affairs
	Nov	Identified as counselor at the embassy in Denmark
1971,	Jan	Identified as chargé d'affaires ad interim in Chile; last appearance until 1977
1977,	Sep	Appointed ambassador to Kuwait

Ding Keze (Ting K'e-tse)　　丁可则

Posts held

CCP
Member of the CCP 11th Central Committee
Member of the Standing Committee of Jiangsu Province CP

During the early phase of the Cultural Revolution Ding served in the Construction Corps of Heilongjiang Province as a youth sent to the countryside.

1973,	Aug	Elected to first term as member of the CCP Central Committee by the 10th Party Congress
	Dec	Identified as chairman of the Trade Union of Wuxi Municipality (no later reference in this post)
1977,	May	Identified as vice-chairman of the Revolutionary Committee of Jiangsu Province (until Mar 1979) and as member of the Standing Committee of Jiangsu Province CP

Ding Ling (Ting Ling) (f)　　丁 玲

Posts held

Others
Member of the 5th CPPCC

Ding was born in 1904 in Changde, Hunan Province. She attended a middle school in Changsha and subsequently studied at Shanghai University. She began to write short stories in 1927. In 1930 she joined the League of Left-Wing Writers. After the execution of Hu Yepin, with whom she had lived since 1924 and whose son she had borne, she joined the CCP in 1931. In 1933 she was temporarily imprisoned by the KMT Government. In 1936 she went to Yan'an to lecture in Chinese literature at the Red Army College. In Yan'an she married the journalist and actor Chen Ming in 1937. In 1941 she edited the literary page of Jiefang Ribao (Liberation Daily). From 1943 she was engaged in cultural work for the PLA. In 1948 she was elected a council member of the Federation of Literary and Art Circles, North China Branch. She was a member of a delegation led by Cai Chang to the 2nd Congress of the Women's International Democratic Federation in Budapest in December 1948. In March 1949 she was elected a member of the Executive Council of the Democratic Women's Federation (until September 1957). Shortly afterwards she became head of the Literary and Art Section, Propaganda Department of the CCP Central Committee. In July 1949 she was elected vice-chairman of the Literary and Art Workers Association. In September she took part in the 1st CPPCC.

1949,	Oct	Appointed member of the Cultural and Educational Commission of the Government Administrative Council; elected council member of the Sino-Soviet Friendship Association; member of a delegation to the USSR
	Dec	Identified as director of the Central Literary Institute
1951,	Feb	During a session of the Propaganda Department of the CCP Central Committee, Ding is criticized for having contravened the Party's literary and art policy
1952,	Mar	Delegate to the centenary celebrations of Gogol's death in Moscow; awarded the Stalin Prize
1953,	Sep	Elected vice-chairman of the Writers Union
1954,	May	Identified as council member of the Association for Cultural Relations with Foreign Countries
	Aug	Elected deputy for Shandong Province to the 1st NPC
1955		In connection with the campaign against Hu Feng, Ding is accused of having followed a "rightist" literary policy. She refuses to accept this criticism and resigns from the Writers Union
1957		Ding is one of the main targets of the "Anti-Rightist Campaign" following the Hundred Flowers Period, during which Zhou Yang is her major opponent. She again refuses to admit to her alleged mistakes and is eventually dismissed from all Party and non-Party posts as a rightist deviationist.

1958–1976   For much of the following two decades, she stays on a farm in Northeast China where she raises chickens and pigs. During the Cultural Revolution she is imprisoned for five years.

1979,   Jun   The most brilliant Chinese female writer reappears after 22 years; by-elected member of the 5th CPPCC at its 4th Plenum

Nov   Ding is at present working on a new novel, Bitterly Cold Days

Publications

The Diary of Miss Shafei
In the Dark
Water
Mother
The Birth of a Person
The Diary of a Person Committing Suicide
Sunshine over the Sanggan River (winner of Stalin Award)

Ding Xuesong (Ting Hsüeh-sung) (f) 丁雪松

Posts held

Government
Ambassador to the Netherlands

NPC
Deputy for Sichuan Province to the 5th NPC

1961,   Mar   Member of a women's delegation to Japan
1964,   Dec   Identified as vice-chairman of the Institute of Foreign Affairs (until Cultural Revolution)
1971,   Aug   Identified as a cadre of the Sino-African Friendship Association
1972,   Apr   Identified as secretary-general of the Association for Friendship with Foreign Countries
Nov   Identified as a cadre of the Sino-Soviet Friendship Association
1973,   Oct   Identified as vice-chairman of the Association for Friendship with Foreign Countries (until Dec 1978)
1975,   Apr   Deputy head of a troupe of artists to Trinidad/Tobago, Guiana, and Venezuela
1976,   Jan   Identified as a cadre of the State Council
1977,   Apr   Head of the Shanghai Dance and Drama Troupe visiting France and Canada
Sep   Head of a friendship delegation to Iceland, Sweden, Norway, Finland, and Denmark
1978,   Feb   Elected deputy for Sichuan Province to the 5th NPC
1979,   Jan   Appointed ambassador (first female ambassador in the history of PRC) to the Netherlands

Ding Yimin (Ting Yi-min) 丁毅民

Posts held

Provincial Administration
Vice-chairman of the People's Government, Ningxia Autonomous Region

Ding belongs to the Hui minority.

1977,   Dec   Elected vice-chairman of the Revolutionary Committee, Ningxia Autonomous Region (until Dec 1979)
1980,   Jan   Elected vice-chairman of the People's Government, Ningxia Autonomous Region

Dong Bian (Tung Pien) (f) 董边

Posts held

Mass Organization
Secretary of the Women's Federation

1952,   Sep   Identified as deputy director of the Women of New China
1953,   Apr   Elected member of the Standing Committee, Democratic Women's Federation (until 1957)
1954,   Sep   Member of a women's delegation to Romania
1957,   Sep   Identified as secretary of the Women's Federation
1958,   Nov   Elected deputy for Shandong Province to the 2nd NPC (reelected in 1964 to the 3rd NPC)
1964,   Mar   Identified as director and chief editor of Zhongguo Funü (Women in China)
1966,   May   Branded as a black gangster and purged
1978,   Sep   First appearance after the Cultural Revolution: Elected secretary of the Women's Federation

Dong Chuncai (Tung Ch'un ts'ai) 董纯才

Posts held

Government
Vice-minister of education

Others
Chairman of the Association for the Popularization of Science, Technology, and Inventions

1950,   Apr   Identified as director of the Education Department of the Northeast People's Government (until Nov 1952)
1952,   Sep   Member of a cultural and educational delegation to Eastern Europe
Nov   Identified as vice-minister of education (until Apr 1965)
1954,   Aug   Elected deputy for Shandong Province to the 1st NPC
1956,   Feb   Identified as a member of the State Committee for the Popularization of the Common Spoken Language
Mar   Identified as vice-chairman of the Association for the Elimination of Illiteracy
Aug   Elected a member of the Central Committee of the Association for Promoting Democracy
1959,   Sep   Appointed member of the Overseas Chinese Affairs Commission (until Cultural Revolution), and member of the State Commission for Cultural Relations with Foreign Countries (until Cultural Revolution)

1960, Mar Identified as vice-chairman of the Sino-Latin-American Friendship Association
1961, Aug Member of an educational delegation to the People's Republic of Mongolia
1966 Dong disappears
1978, Sep First appearance after the Cultural Revolution: Identified as advisor of the Ministry of Education
1979, Apr Identified as vice-minister of education
Aug Elected chairman of the Association for the Popularization of Science, Technology, and Inventions

Dong Qiwu (Tung Ch'i-wu) 董其武

Posts held

NPC
Member of the Standing Committee of the 5th NPC
Deputy for the PLA to the 5th NPC

Military
Colonel-general

Others
Member of the Standing Committee of the 5th CPPCC

Dong was born in 1900 in Hejin, Hebei Province. He graduated in military studies from Binye Military Academy in Taiyuan in 1924. In 1925 he commanded a reserve regiment of the Nationalist Revolutionary Army. In 1926 he served in the army led by Zhang Fakui, from 1927 in units under Fu Zuoyi. From 1930 to 1934 he was regiment commander in various divisions of the Nationalist Revolutionary Army. After additional military training he was promoted to the rank of major-general in 1936 and appointed brigade commander. In 1937 he was made commander of the 101st Division. He was promoted to the rank of lieutenant-general in 1939 and appointed commander of the Provisional 4th Army in 1940. In 1942 he commanded the 4th Cavalry Army, in 1944 the 35th Army. In 1945 he was director of the Political Department of the 12th War Zone. In 1946 he commanded the Military District of Suiyuan Province. In October of that year he was appointed governor of Suiyuan. In July 1949, following a pledge of allegiance to the Nationalist Government, he was appointed deputy commander of the Northwest China Military Headquarters. Two months later he went over to the communists. As deputy commander of Suiyuan Military District he took part in September in the founding session of the 1st CPPCC.

1949, Oct Appointed chairman of the People's Government of Suiyuan Province (until Jan 1953)
Dec Appointed vice-chairman of Suiyuan Military and Administrative Council (until Jan 1953)
1953, Jan Appointed member of the North China Administrative Council (until Sep 1954)
1954, Aug Elected deputy for the PLA to the 1st NPC (reelected in 1959 and 1964 to the 2nd and 3rd NPCs)
Sep Appointed member of the National Defense Council (until Cultural Revolution)
1955, Sep Appointed colonel-general; conferred the order "Liberation," 1st class

1959, Apr Elected member of the Standing Committee of the 3rd CPPCC (confirmed in 1965 and 1978 by the 4th and 5th CPPCCs)
1975, Jan Elected member of the Standing Committee by the 4th NPC (confirmed in Mar 1978 by the 5th NPC)
1978, Feb Elected deputy for the PLA to the 5th NPC
1979, Jun Member of the Draft Laws Committee at the 2nd Session of the 5th NPC

Dong Tianzhen (Tung T'ien-chen) 董天禎

Posts held

NPC
Member of the Standing Committee of the 5th NPC
Deputy for Qinghai Province to the 5th NPC

1975, Jan Elected member of the Standing Committee by the 4th NPC (confirmed in Mar 1978 by the 5th NPC)
1977, May Identified as a cadre in Qinghai Province
1978, Feb Elected deputy for Qinghai Province to the 5th NPC

Dong Zhiwen (Tung Chih-wen) 董志文

Posts held

CCP
Secretary of Hunan Province CP

1977, Nov Identified as secretary of Hunan Province CP

Du Chunyong (Tu Ch'un-yung) 杜春永

Posts held

Government
Vice-minister of building materials

1973, Mar Identified as director a bureau of the State Capital Construction Commission; member of a government delegation to Sri Lanka
1979, Apr Identified as vice-minister of building materials

Du Jinfang (Tu Chin-fang) (f) 杜近芳

Posts held

Mass Organization
Vice-chairman of the Youth Federation

1960, Mar Identified as an actress of the Beijing Opera
1963, Jul Identified as vice-chairman of the Youth Federation
1964, Sep Elected deputy for Hebei Province to the 3rd NPC

1966		Du disappears
1975,	Sep	First appearance after the Cultural Revolution
1979,	May	Elected vice-chairman of the Youth Federation

Du Ping (Tu P'ing) 杜 平

Posts held

CCP
Alternate member of the CCP 11th Central Committee

Military
Lieutenant-general
Political commissar of Nanjing Military Region
Secretary of the Party Committee of Nanjing Military Region

Du was born in 1905 in Puning, Guangdong Province. In 1932 he served as political commissar of an intelligence group of the 1st Front Army. As director of the Political Department of a regiment, later a division, of the 1st Front Army, he took part in the Long March of 1934-35. In 1937 he was political commissar of the 770th Regiment, 129th Division, 8th Route Army. He later served as political commissar of various units, eventually in 1949 as director of the Political Department of the 13th Army Group.

1950		Service in the Korean War as political commissar of the 15th Army Group
	Oct	Identified as deputy director of the Political Department, Chinese People's Volunteers in Korea
1954		Identified as director of the Political Department of Shenyang Military Region
1955,	Sep	Appointed lieutenant-general
1958,	Jul	Identified as deputy political commissar of Shenyang Military Region (until May 1963)
	Oct	Du temporarily served as private in a company
1963,	May	Identified as deputy political commissar of Nanjing Military Region
1964,	Dec	Identified as 3rd political commissar of Nanjing Military Region
1967,	Aug	Identified as 2nd political commissar of Nanjing Military Region (until Aug 1969)
1968,	Mar	With the establishment of the Revolutionary Committee of Jiangsu Province, Du is elected a member of the Standing Committee (no later mention in this post)
1969,	Apr	Elected to first term as member of the CCP Central Committee by the 9th Party Congress (until Aug 1977)
	Aug	Identified as political commissar of Nanjing Military Region
1970,	Dec	Elected secretary of Jiangsu Province CP (no later mention in this post)
1977,	Aug	Demoted from member to alternate member of the CCP Central Committee by the 11th Party Congress
1978,	Oct	Identified as secretary of the Party Committee of Nanjing Military Region

Du Qian (Tu Ch'ien) 杜 前

Posts held

Others
Vice-president of the Sports Federation

1964,	Feb	Identified as vice-chairman of the Shanghai Commission for Physical Culture and Sports; head of a sports delegation to Cuba
1965,	May	Head of a basketball team to Cuba
1966,	Jun	Identified as chairman of the Shanghai Sports Association; thereafter disappears
1979,	Mar	First appearance after the Cultural Revolution: Identified as vice-president of the Sports Federation
	Jul	Appointed member of the National Games Organizing Committee

Du Runsheng (Tu Jun-sheng) 杜 润生

Posts held

Government
Vice-minister of the State Agricultural Commission

Du was born in 1909 in Taigu, Shanxi Province. He graduated from Beijing Normal University. In 1941 he was secretary-general of the Education Department, Shanxi-Hebei-Shandong-Henan Border Region. In 1944 he became director of the 5th Administrative District, Taihang Administrative Office. In June 1946 he represented Liu Bocheng at the Taiyuan Center of the Military Mediation Executive Commission and was concurrently the representative of the CCP at its Dongxin Executive Subcommittee. In the following year he served as deputy director of the Taihang Administrative Office.

1949,	Dec	Identified as secretary-general of the Central-South Bureau, CCP Central Committee, and as deputy director of its Land Reform Committee (until 1953)
1953,	Jan	Identified as vice-chairman of the Farm Output Verification Committee, Central-South Administrative Council
1954,	Nov	Identified as deputy director of the 7th Staff Office of the State Council (until 1956)
	Dec	Elected council member of the Sino-Soviet Friendship Association
1956,	Mar	Identified as deputy secretary-general of the State Scientific Planning Commission (until May 1957)
1957,	Nov	Member of a scientific and technological delegation to the USSR
1958,	Mar	Identified as deputy director of the Rural Work Department, CCP Central Committee
1959,	Jun	Identified as deputy secretary-general of the Academy of Sciences
1961,	Oct	Identified as secretary-general of the Academy of Sciences
1967,	Feb	Denounced as an anti-Party element and purged

1979,   Sep First appearance after the Cultural Revolution: Identified as vice-minister of the State Agricultural Commission; member of a government delegation, led by Wang Renzhong, to Yugoslavia, Denmark, the Netherlands, and Belgium

Du Xinbo (Tu Hsin-po)   杜 新 波

Posts held

CCP
Member of the Standing Committee, Tianjin Municipality CP

Provincial Administration
Vice-chairman of the Revolutionary Committee of Tianjin Municipality

Others
Director of the Board of Directors, China International Trust and Investment Corporation

1959,   Nov Identified as director of the Department of Finance and Trade, Hebei Province CP
1964,   Oct Vice-chairman of the Hebei Branch, Sino-Soviet Friendship Association; head of a Hebei Province delegation to the USSR
1979,   Sep First appearance after the Cultural Revolution
         Oct Appointed director of the Board of Directors, China International Trust and Investment Corporation; identified as vice-chairman of the Revolutionary Committee of Tianjin Municipality, and as a member of the Standing Committee of Tianjin Municipality CP

Du Xingyuan (Tu Hsing-yüan)   杜 心 源

Posts held

CCP
Secretary of Sichuan Province CP

NPC
Deputy for Fujian Province to the 5th NPC

1950,   Oct Identified as director of the Propaganda Department of the 4th Field Army
1952,   Sep Identified as director of the Propaganda Department, Political Department of Central-South China Military Region
1957,   Jun Appointed assistant minister of the 2nd Ministry of Machine Building (until Feb 1958)
1959,   Sep Appointed vice-minister of the 1st Ministry of Machine Building (until Sep 1960)
1960,   Sep Appointed vice-chairman of the State Economic Commission (until Nov 1962)
1962,   Nov Appointed vice-minister of water conservancy and electric power (until 1977)
1970,   May Head of a government delegation to Guinea
1972,   Jun Head of a government delegation to North Korea; identified as Chinese director of

the Joint Sino-Korean Hydro-Electric Power Corporation Yalu
1974,   Nov Head of a government delegation to North Korea
1978,   Feb Elected deputy for Fujian Province to the 5th NPC
1979,   Jan Elected secretary of Sichuan Province CP

Du Xinyuan (Tu Hsin-yüan)   杜 星 垣

Posts held

CCP
Secretary of Sichuan Province CP

Government
Member of the Birth Planning Leading Group under the State Council

NPC
Deputy for Sichuan Province to the 5th NPC

Provincial Administration
Chairman of the People's Congress of Sichuan Province

Du was born in Shanxi Province. In 1947 he was identified as a member of the Provisional Peasants Federation of Shanxi-Suiyuan Border Region.

1950,   Jul Appointed member of the Cultural and Educational Committee of Southwest China Military and Administrative Council (until Sep 1954); identified as director of the Propaganda Department of West Sichuan CP
1951,   Oct Identified as council member of the West Sichuan Administrative Office
1952,   Aug Identified as director of the Cultural and Educational Office, People's Government of Sichuan Province
         Nov Identified as director of the Propaganda Department of Sichuan Province CP and as council member of Sichuan People's Government
1959,   Oct Identified as secretary of Sichuan Province CP and as chairman of the Sichuan Branch, Sino-Soviet Friendship Association
1965,   Nov Identified as vice-chairman of the Sichuan Branch, CPPCC
1966   Disappears during the Cultural Revolution
1975,   Dec First appearance after the Cultural Revolution: Named in his former post as secretary of Sichuan Province CP
1978,   Feb Elected deputy for Sichuan Province to the 5th NPC
         Jul Appointed member of the Birth Planning Leading Group under the State Council
         Oct Identified as chairman of the CPPCC, Sichuan Branch
1979,   Jun Member of the Credentials Committee at the 2nd Session of the 5th NPC
         Dec Elected chairman of the People's Congress of Sichuan Province

Du Xueran (Tu Hsüeh-jan) 杜学然

Posts held

CCP
Alternate member of the CCP 11th Central Committee

Du is a miner in Henan.

1977, Aug Elected alternate member of the CCP Central Committee by the 11th Party Congress

Du Yi (Tu Yi) 杜 易

Posts held

Government
Ambassador to Mali

1972, Feb Identified as chargé d'affaires ad interim in Burundi
1977, May Identified as counselor at the embassy in Algeria (until 1978)
1979, May Appointed ambassador to Mali

Du Yi (Tu Yi) 杜 易

Posts held

CCP
Secretary of Guangxi Autonomous Region CP

NPC
Deputy for Guangxi Autonomous Region to the 5th NPC

Mass Organization
Chairman of the Peasants Federation of Guangxi Autonomous Region

Du belongs to the Zhuang minority.

1974, Oct Identified as member of the Standing Committee of Guangxi Autonomous Region CP (until Dec 1974)
       Dec Identified as secretary of Guangxi Autonomous Region CP; elected chairman of the Peasants Federation of Guangxi Autonomous Region
1977, Dec Elected vice-chairman of the Revolutionary Committee of Guangxi (until Dec 1979)
1978, Feb Elected deputy for Guangxi Autonomous Region to the 5th NPC

Du Yide (Tu Yi-te) 杜义德

Posts held

CCP
Member of the CCP 11th Central Committee

Military
Vice-admiral
Political commissar of the PLA Navy

Du was born in Ji County, Hebei Province. In 1941 he was commander of the Weinan Detachment in Shandong. In 1946 he commanded the 2nd Military Subdistrict of South Shandong Military District. In 1947 he was political commissar of the 6th Column, Central Plains Field Army. In 1949 he served as deputy commander of the 3rd Corps in the 2nd Field Army.

1950   Identified as commander of South Sichuan Military District and as member of the Southwest China Military and Administrative Council
1951   Service in the Korean War as troop commander of the People's Volunteers
1953   Identified as political commissar of Lüda (Lüshun and Lüda) Garrison
1955   Identified as director of the Political Department of the PLA Navy; identified as vice-admiral
1961   Identified as deputy commander of the PLA Navy
1965, Dec Identified as deputy political commissar of the PLA Navy
1967   Purged as a result of criticism during the Cultural Revolution
1972, Mar First appearance after the Cultural Revolution
1975, Sep Identified in his former post as deputy political commissar of the PLA Navy (until May 1978)
1977, Aug Elected member of the CCP Central Committee by the 11th-Party Congress
1978, Jun Identified as political commissar of the PLA Navy; member of a military friendship delegation to Romania

Du Yuming (Tu Yü-ming) 杜聿明

Posts held

NPC
Deputy for Shanghai Municipality to the 5th NPC

Military
Lieutenant-general

Others
Member of the Standing Committee of the 5th CPPCC

Du was commander of the Northeast China Safety Preservation Headquarters in 1948. In 1949 he served as deputy commander of Suzhou Headquarters when he was captured by communists troops and sentenced as a war criminal.

1959, Dec Pardoned as a war criminal
1964, Dec Special delegate to the 4th CPPCC
1978, Feb Elected deputy for Shanghai Municipality to the 5th NPC
       Mar Elected member of the Standing Committee of the 5th CPPCC
1979, Jun Member of the Budget Committee at the 2nd Session of the 5th NPC

Du is the father-in-law of the American-Chinese Physics Nobel Prize winner, Yang Zhenning.

Du Yuyun (Tu Yü-yün)　杜毓芸

<u>Posts held</u>

Government
Assistant minister in the Ministry of
Foreign Trade

1950,   Jul   Appointed council member of the People's
Government of Pingyuan Province; identi-
fied as director of the Commerce Department of that government
1955,   May   Appointed trade attaché at the embassy in
India (until about 1960)
1965,   Nov   Appointed assistant minister in the Ministry of Foreign Trade
1967   Disappears during the Cultural Revolution
1972,   Nov   First appearance after the Cultural Revolution: Again named in his former post as
assistant minister in the Ministry of Foreign Trade

Du Ziduan (Tu Tzu-tuan)　杜子端

<u>Posts held</u>

Government
Vice-minister of light industry

1964,   Mar   Identified as acting director, Administration of Food Industry, Ministry of Light
Industry
1977,   Sep   Identified as vice-minister of light industry
         Oct   Head of a scientific and technical delega-
tion to Albania
1978,   May   Head of a light industry delegation to
Yugoslavia

Duan Huanjing (Tuan Huan-ching)　段焕竞

<u>Posts held</u>

Military
Major-general
Deputy commander of Nanjing Military
Region

Duan was born in 1911 in Jiangxi Province. He joined the
Red Army in 1932. After attending a course at the Red
Army School in 1934 he was appointed battalion commander. In 1935 he was chief of staff of a guerrilla unit
operating in the border area of Hunan-Jiangxi where he
was severely wounded in 1936. In July 1938 Duan commanded a battalion of the New 4th Army. in 1940 he was
made commander of the New 6th Regiment, also New
4th Army. He was again wounded in combat against the
Japanese. In 1946 he led a brigade of the East China Field
Army; two years later he became commander of the
31st Division of the same army. In 1949 he was deputy
commander of the 29th Army, 3rd Field Army.

1950,   Oct   Duan serves concurrently as commander
of Xiamen Garrison. He leads his units in
an attack on the Jinmen Islands which
ends in total defeat
1952   Service in the Korean War as commander
of the 23rd Corps

1955,   Sep   Promoted to rank of major-general; identified as deputy commander of Jiangxi
Military District
1962   Identified as commander of Jiangsu Military District (until 1966)
1970,   Jun   Identified as military leader in Nanjing
Military Region
1971,   Aug   Member of a military delegation to Albania and Romania
         Oct   Identified as deputy commander of
Nanjing Military Region

Duan Junyi (Tuan Chün-yi)　段君毅

<u>Posts held</u>

CCP
Member of the CCP 11th Central Committee
1st secretary of Henan Province CP

Military
1st political commissar of Henan Military
District

Duan was born in 1913 in Puyang, Shandong Province. He
graduated in 1937 from the Engineering College of Jinan
University. In the summer of 1937 he was one of the
leading representatives of the National Students Federation. After the Marco Polo Bridge Incident he and Jiang
Nanxiang together led students from Beijing and Tianjin to
Nanjing for military training. In 1947 he was head of the
Administration Office of Hebei-Shandong-Henan CP, one
year later secretary of Hubei-Henan District CP.

1950,   Jul   Appointed vice-chairman of the Financial
and Economic Committee and director of
the Industry Department of Southwest
China Military and Administrative Council
1952,   Aug   Appointed vice-minister of the 1st Ministry of Machine Building (until Aug 1958)
1954,   Aug   Elected deputy for Shandong Province to
the 1st NPC
1958,   Aug   Appointed vice-minister of the 2nd Ministry of Machine Building (until Sep 1960)
1960,   Sep   Appointed minister of the 1st Ministry of
Machine Building
1967   Criticized as a capitalist-roader and relieved of all posts
1971,   Aug   First appearance after the Cultural Revolution: Elected secretary of Sichuan Prov-
ince CP (until 1976)
1973,   Aug   Elected to first term as member of the
CCP Central Committee by the 10th Par-
ty Congress
1974,   Jan   Identified as vice-chairman of the Revolutionary Committee of Sichuan Province
(until 1976)
1977,   Feb   Identified as minister of railways (until
Oct 1978)
         Aug   Elected member of the CCP Central
Committee by the 11th Party Congress
1978,   Feb   Article in <u>HQ</u>: "Railway Transportation
Should March in the Van of the Rapid
Development of the National Economy"
         Aug   Head of a railways delegation to Romania
and Sweden

Sep   Identified as 1st secretary of the CP, and chairman of the Revolutionary Committee, of Henan Province (the latter post until Aug 1978) and as 1st political commissar of Henan Military District

Duan Yun (Tuan Yün)　　段　雲

Posts held

CCP
Member of the Commission for Inspecting Discipline under the CCP Central Committee

Government
Vice-minister of the State Planning Commission

Others
Director of the Board of Directors, China International Trust and Investment Corporation

During the final phase of the Revolutionary War Duan served as secretary of the CP Bureau in Shanxi-Suiyuan District.

1950,	Mar	Appointed deputy director of the Administration Office and member of the Educational and Cultural Committee of Central-South China Military and Administrative Council (until Aug 1954)
1951,	Aug	Identified as director of the Finance Department of Central-South China Military and Administrative Council
1954,	Sep	Elected member of the Federation of Supply and Marketing Cooperatives
	Nov	Appointed deputy director of the Premier's Office in the State Council (until Apr 1955)
1955,	Apr	Appointed deputy director of the 5th Staff Office of the State Council (until Sep 1959)
1959,	Sep	Appointed deputy director, Office of Finance and Commerce of the State Council (until Cultural Revolution)
1964,	Sep	Elected deputy for Shandong Province to the 3rd NPC
1967		Disappears during the Cultural Revolution
1973,	Oct	First appearance after the Cultural Revolution: Identified as vice-minister of the State Planning Commission
1978,	Mar	Advisor to an economic delegation to Japan
	Nov	Member of a government delegation led by Wang Zhen to Great Britain
	Dec	Appointed member of the Commission for Inspecting Discipline under the CCP Central Committee
1979,	Oct	Appointed director of the Board of Directors of the China International Trust and Investment Corporation

Nov   Head of an economic investigation group to Greece

Duan Zijun (Tuan Tzu-chün)　　段子俊

Posts held

Government
Vice-minister of the 3rd Ministry of Machine Building

Others
President of the Society of Astronautics and Aeronautics

1951,	Aug	Identified as director of the Bureau of Aviation Industry, Ministry of Heavy Industry
1953,	Feb	Identified as deputy director, 4th Bureau of the 2nd Ministry of Machine Building
1963,	Oct	Appointed vice-minister of the 3rd Ministry of Machine Building
1967,	Jun	Branded as a revisionist and purged
1974,	Sep	First appearance after the Cultural Revolution
1978,	Sep	Identified as president of the Society of Astronautics and Aeronautics
1979,	Jan	Identified as vice-minister of the 3rd Ministry of Machine Building
	Jun	Head of a delegation to the Le Bourget airshow in France

Dun Xingyun (Tun Hsing-yün)　　顿星云

Posts held

Military
Vice-admiral

Others
Member of the Standing Committee of the 5th CPPCC

In 1931 Dun led a company of the 2nd Red Army. In 1936 he commanded the 16th Regiment of the 2nd Red Army and in 1939 a regiment of the 120th Division, 8th Route Army. He was commander of the 4th Independent Brigade, 2nd Column, Northwest Field Army, in 1947, and in 1949 deputy commander of the 2nd Army, 1st Field Army.

1950		Dun receives naval training in the USSR
1951		Identified as commander of Lüda (Lüshun-Lüda) Naval Base
1955,	Sep	Appointed vice-admiral; conferred the order "Liberation," 1st class
1966,	Feb	Identified as commander of the North China Sea Fleet (until 1969); subsequently disappears
1975,	Jul	Reactivated after the Cultural Revolution
1978,	Mar	Elected member of the Standing Committee of the 5th CPPCC

Fan Chaoli (Fan Ch'ao-li)　范朝利

Posts held

NPC
Deputy for the PLA to the 5th NPC

Military
Lieutenant-general
Deputy commander of Jinan Military Region

In 1937 Fan served as chief of staff of the 769th Regiment in the 8th Route Army. In 1944 he commanded a subdistrict in Taihang Military District and in 1947 the 10th Column of the Central Plains Field Army. In early 1949 he was commander of the 10th Brigade in the 2nd Field Army.

1949,	Oct	After the occupation of Chongqing Fan is appointed commander of South Sichuan Military District and member of the South Sichuan Administrative Bureau
1952		Identified as deputy commander of Sichuan Military District
1955,		Identified as deputy commander of Jinan Military Region
	Sep	Identified as lieutenant-general
1967,	Mar	Elected member of the Standing Committee, Revolutionary Committee of Shandong Province (no known later mention in this post)
1975,	May	Again identified as deputy commander of Jinan Military Region
1978,	Feb	Elected deputy for the PLA to the 5th NPC

Fan Deling (Fan Te-ling)　樊德玲

Posts held

CCP
Member of the CCP 11th Central Committee

NPC
Member of the Standing Committee of the 5th NPC
Deputy for Hebei Province to the 5th NPC

1969,	Apr	Elected alternate member of the CCP Central Committee by the 9th Party Congress (until Aug 1973)
1971,	Jan	Identified as a miner in the Kailuan Coal Mine, Hebei Province; article published by NCNA on 14 January: "The Revolutionary Line of Mao Zedong"
1973,	Jul	Elected chairman of the Hebei Trade Union
	Aug	Elected member of the CCP Central Committee by the 10th Party Congress (confirmed in 1977 by the 11th Party Congress)
1974,	Aug	Head of a workers delegation to Romania (30th anniversary of liberation)
1975,	Jan	Elected member of the Standing Committee of the 4th NPC (reelected in 1978 to the 5th NPC)
1978,	Feb	Elected deputy for Hebei Province to the 5th NPC

Fan Jin (Fan Chin) (f)　范瑾

Posts held

Provincial Administration
Vice-chairman of the People's Congress of Beijing Municipality

In the mid-thirties Fan worked as a reporter of Xinhua Ribao (New China Daily) and with Zhou Deyu organized the Beihuang Drama Company performing anti-Japanese dramas. In 1937 she studied at the Central Party School in Yan'an. She married Huang Jing (died 1958) and followed him to work in the Shanxi-Chahar-Hebei Border Area. In 1949 she worked in Tianjin while Huang Jing was mayor of Tianjin.

1953,	Jan	Fan visits the Editing Department of the Pravda in Moscow as a member of a journalists' delegation headed by Deng Tuo
	Dec	Identified as director of the Propaganda Department of Beijing Municipality CP
1954,	Aug	Elected deputy for Beijing to the 1st NPC (reelected to the 2nd and 3rd NPCs in 1958 and 1964)
1957,	Sep	Elected member of the Executive Committee of the Women's Federation; identified as council member of the Sino-Syrian Friendship Association
1958,	Feb	Identified as a council member of the China-United Arab Republic Friendship Association
1960,	Mar	Elected member of the Standing Committee of the 2nd NPC; elected vice-chairman of the Journalists' Association
	Dec	Identified as a council member of the Sino-Cambodian Friendship Association
1963,	Apr	Vice-head of a journalists' delegation to the Afro-Asian Journalists' Conference in Jakarta (head: Mei Yi)
	Aug	Identified as president and editor-in-chief of RMRB
1964,	Mar	Identified as a member of the Standing Committee of Beijing Municipality CP
	Sep	Elected vice-mayor of Beijing (until Cultural Revolution)
	Nov	Member of a Party and government delegation to Tirana for the celebration of the 20th anniversary of the liberation of Albania
1966,	Jun	Accused of being an accomplice of Peng Zhen and a loyal executor of the "Three-Family Village" and purged
1974,	Sep	First appearance after the Cultural Revolution
1979,	Dec	Elected vice-chairman of the People's Congress of Beijing Municipality

Fan Muhan (Fan Mu-han)　范暮韩

Posts held

Government
Vice-minister of the 6th Ministry of Machine Building

1956,	Nov	Identified as member of the State Planning Commission

1960,	Dec	Appointed vice-chairman of the State Planning Commission
1965,	Jul	Identified as vice-minister of the 1st Ministry of Machine Building
1966,	May	Head of a government delegation to Hungary; subsequently disappears
1978,	May	First appearance after the Cultural Revolution
1979,	Jul	Identified as vice-minister of the 6th Ministry of Machine Building

Fan Rusheng (Fan Ju-sheng) 范儒生

Posts held

CCP
Member of the Commission for Inspecting Discipline of the CCP Central Committee
Secretary of Tianjin Municipality CP

1952,	Dec	Identified as deputy director of the Organization Department of Beijing Municipality CP
1955,	May	Identified as director of the Organization Department of Beijing Municipality CP
1958,	Oct	Identified as secretary of Beijing Municipality CP (until Apr 1967)
1967		Disappears during the Cultural Revolution
1978,	Dec	First appearance after the Cultural Revolution: Appointed member of the Commission for Inspecting Discipline of the CCP Central Committee
1979,	May	Identified as secretary of Tianjin Municipality CP

Fan Xixian (Fan Hsi-hsien) 范希贤

Posts held

Provincial Administration
Vice-governor of Guangdong Province

Others
Vice-chairman of the Foreign Trade Fair in Guangzhou

1960,	Dec	Identified as member of the People's Council of Guangdong Province
1973,	Jun	Identified as member of the Standing Committee, Revolutionary Committee of Guangdong Province
1977,	Oct	Identified as vice-chairman of the Revolutionary Committee of Guangdong Province (until Dec 1979) and as vice-chairman of the Foreign Trade Fair in Guangzhou
1979,	Dec	Elected vice-governor of Guangdong Province

Fan Zhongzhi (Fan Chung-chih) 范忠志

Posts held

NPC
Member of the Standing Committee of the 5th NPC
Deputy for Hubei Province to the 5th NPC

| 1978, | Feb | Elected deputy for Hubei Province to the 5th NPC |
| | Mar | Elected member of the Standing Committee of the 5th NPC |

Fan Ziyu (Fan Tzu-yü) 范子喻

Posts held

Military
Major-general
Deputy director of the Logistics Department of the PLA

Fan took part in the Long March having been appointed chief of the Supplies Unit of the 2nd Front Army in 1934. In 1937 he was deputy chief of the Supplies Department of the 120th Division, 8th Route Army. In 1949 he headed the Supplies Department of the 62nd Corps, 18th Army.

1950		Appointed chief of the Supplies Department of the 2nd Field Army and of Southwest China Military Region
1960		Fan wins swimming competitions organized by PLA generals stationed in Beijing
1964,	Aug	Identified as major-general and as head of the 2nd Department (Material Supplies) in the Logistics Department of PLA
1968		At the end of the Cultural Revolution Fan is one of the group of military officers transferred to the Ministry of Commerce
1972,	Dec	Identified as minister of commerce (until 1977)
1974,	May	Fan heads the relief group in an earthquake area in Yunnan Province
1976,	Sep	Head of a government delegation to Botswana
1978,	Jun	Identified as deputy director of the Logistics Department of the PLA

Fan Zuokai (Fan Tso-k'ai) 樊作楷

Posts held

Government
Assistant minister of foreign affairs

1959,	Nov	Identified as deputy secretary of the Rural Work Committee of Wuhan CP
1970,	Sep	Appointed ambassador to Somalia (until Jan 1975)
1975,	Sep	Appointed ambassador to Mali (until Dec 1978)
1979,	Aug	Identified as assistant minister of foreign affairs

Fang Gao (Fang Kao) 方皋

Posts held

Others
Vice-president of the People's Bank of China
Vice-chairman of the Board of Directors of the Bank of China

| 1950 | | Identified as director of the Guangdong Branch of the Chinese People's Bank |

1951		Identified as director of the South China Branch of the Chinese People's Bank
	Apr	Identified as president of the College of Finance and Economics of the China Associated University
1954,	Feb	Identified as vice-chairman of the Financial and Economic Committee of Guangdong Provincial People's Government
1955,	Mar	Identified as deputy director of the Department of Communications, South China Bureau of the CCP Central Committee
1958,	May	Identified as director of the Industry and Communications Department
1961,	Dec	Identified as vice-governor of Guangdong Province
1963,	Oct	Appointed vice-president of the People's Bank of China
1964,	Apr	Member of an economic delegation to Japan
1965,	Aug	Member of a People's Bank and Bank of China delegation to Indonesia
	Dec	Fang heads a bankers' delegation to Albania
1967		Disappears during the Cultural Revolution
1972,	Apr	First appearance after the Cultural Revolution: Identified as holding his previous post as vice-president of the People's Bank
	Nov	Identified as vice-president of the Bank of China; Fang heads a bankers' delegation to North Korea
1977,	Nov	Identified as vice-chairman of the Board of Directors of the Bank of China

Fang Qian (Fang Ch'ien)　　方　谦

Posts held

Provincial Administration
Vice-governor of Jiangxi Province

| 1979, | Dec | Elected vice-governor of Jiangxi Province |

Fang Qiang (Fang Ch'iang)　　方　强

Posts held

Military
Admiral
Deputy commander of the PLA Navy

Fang was born in 1909 in Pingjiang, Hunan Province. During the Nanchang Uprising in 1927 he led a platoon under Zhu De. In 1930 he served in the Soviet Government of Pingjiang County. In 1931 he was identified as serving in the 4th Front Army. In 1933 he commanded the Guard Battalion and was seriously wounded in Fujian Province. He took part in the Long March in the Cadres Corps. In 1935 Fang became commander of a regiment in the 4th Front Army. In the following year he was taken prisoner by the KMT in Xining. In May 1937 he escaped from Lanzhou prison and went to Yan'an where he was trained at the Anti-Japan Military and Political Academy.

In 1938 Fang became commander of a regiment in the 115th Division, commanded by Lin Biao, of the 8th Route Army. The following year he accompanied Lin Biao to the USSR and studied at the Moscow Red Army Academy. He returned to China and took over the command of a division. In winter 1945 he went to Manchuria together with Lin Biao and became deputy commander of the Hejiang Military District. In 1946 Fang was promoted to the post of commander of the Fujin Military Subdistrict. The following year he became commander of the Jiamusi Military District. In 1948 he took over the command of the 30th Division under the Northeast Division, 47th Army, under the 4th Field Army, and soon took over the command of the 44th Army, 15th Army Group, 4th Field Army.

1949,	Oct	Appointed deputy commander of the South China Military Region and concurrently deputy commander of the Guangzhou Garrison Command
1950,	Mar	Identified as council member of the Guangdong Provincial People's Government and as 2nd deputy commander of the Guangdong Military District
1951,	Jun	Identified as a member of the Central-South Military and Administrative Council (until Jan 1952)
1952,	Jun	Identified as commander of the Central-South China Naval command
1953,	Oct	Identified as deputy commander of the PLA Navy (until Jan 1960)
1955,	Sep	Identified as vice-admiral
1957,	Jun	Identified as commandant of the Nanjing Naval Academy
1958,	Jan	Member of a military delegation to India (led by Ye Jianying)
1960,	Jan	Appointed vice-minister of the 1st Ministry of Machine Building (until Sep 1963)
1963,	Sep	Appointed minister of the 6th Ministry of Machine Building, responsible for the building of naval ships (until Cultural Revolution)
1965,	Jan	Identified as a member of the National Defense Council and as full admiral
	Jun	Head of a delegation to the 34th Poznan International Fair in Poland
1967,	Nov	Denounced as an agent of He Long and purged
1972,	Dec	First appearance after the Cultural Revolution
1973,	Oct	Identified as a cadre of the State Council
1975,	Jul	Identified as a leading military cadre
1977,	May	Fang disappears again until 1979
1979,	Oct	Identified as deputy commander of the PLA Navy

Fang Weizhong (Fang Wei-chung)　房维中

Posts held

Government
Vice-minister of the State Planning Commission

| 1978, | Mar | Identified as vice-minister of the State Planning Commission; deputy head of an economic delegation to Japan |

Fang Yi (Fang Yi)   方　毅

Posts held

CCP
Member of the Politburo of the CCP
Member of the CCP 11th Central Committee
Member of the Secretariat of the Central Committee

Government
Vice-premier
Minister, State Scientific and Technical Commission
Member of the State Financial and Economic Commission

NPC
Deputy for Fujian Province to the 5th NPC

Others
President of the Academy of Sciences
Honorary president of the Weiqi Chess Association

Fang was born in 1916 in Xiamen (Amoy), Fujian Province. The fact that he "understands," according to Japanese scources, Japanese, English, German, and Russian suggests that he had received a university education. In 1930 he joined the Communist Youth League and one year later the CCP. Soon later he was an editor at the Shanghai Commercial Press. After several years of imprisonment during which he learned foreign languages he was released after the Xi'an incident. He subsequently became a member of the CP Committee of Hubei Province. In 1944 he was identified as director of the Huainan Administrative Office. Several appointments followed in 1945: vice-chairman of the Administrative Council of the Jiangsu-Anhui Border Area, secretary-general of the Department of Finance and Commerce, and director of the Finance Department in the same Administrative Council. In 1946 Fang was appointed director of the Finance Department of the Government of Shandong-Anhui Border Area. In 1948 he became a member and simultaneously secretary-general of the Financial and Economic Affairs Committee in the North China People's Government. In March 1949 he became vice-chairman of the People's Government of Shandong Province. He was appointed vice-chairman of the Fuzhou Military Control Commission in August 1949 as well as vice-chairman of the People's Government of Fujian Province and director of the Finance Department (until 1952). In September 1949 he was appointed vice-chairman of the Financial and Economic Affairs Committee in East China Military Region.

1949,	Dec	Appointed member of the East China Military and Administrative Council and vice-chairman of the Financial and Economic Affairs Committee of that Administrative Council (until Dec 1952)
1951,	Jan	Appointed deputy commander of Fujian Military Region (until Aug 1952)
	Jun	Elected council member of the Sino-Soviet Friendship Association, Fujian Section (until Aug 1952)
	Nov	Appointed chairman of the Financial and Economic Affairs Committee of Fujian Province (until Aug 1952)
1952,	Aug	Elected deputy mayor of Shanghai (until Dec 1952)
	Dec	Appointed member of the East China Administrative Council and vice-chairman of the Financial and Economic Affairs Committee in the same Administrative Council (until Aug 1954)
1953,	Sep	Appointed vice-minister of finance (until Oct 1954)
1956,	Jun	Appointed as economic representative of the Chinese Government in North Vietnam (until 1961)
1958,	May	Elected alternate member of the CCP Central Committee (until Aug 1973)
1960,	May	Member of a delegation to North Vietnam headed by Zhou Enlai
1961,	Jan	Appointed vice-chairman of the State Planning Commission (until Cultural Revolution)
	Apr	Appointed deputy director of the Foreign Affairs Office and director of the Bureau for Economic Relations with Foreign Countries
	Jun	Conferred the North Vietnamese Labor Medal, 1st class
1963,	Oct	Head of a government delegation to Algiers
	Dec	Head of an economic delegation to Mali
1964,	Jan	Head of an economic delegation to Guinea
	Jun	Appointed chairman of the Commission for Economic Relations with Foreign Countries; head of the Chinese delegation to the Afro-Asian Economic Conference in Geneva
	Aug	Head of an economic and goodwill delegation to North Korea
	Sep	Elected deputy for Fujian Province to the 3rd NPC
1965,	Jun	Member of the Chinese delegation to the planned 2nd Afro-Asian Conference in Algiers
1966-1967		Fang remains political active during the Cultural Revolution and signs several agreements on economic and technical cooperation. Though attacked by Red Guards in February 1967, he continues his activities shortly afterwards. From this it may be concluded that he enjoyed the protection of Zhou Enlai
1969,	Apr	Elected alternate member of the CCP Central Committee by the 9th Party Congress (until Aug 1973)
1970,	Apr	Head of an economic and friendship delegation to Pakistan
	Jun	Member of a Party and government delegation to North Korea to attend the 20th anniversary of liberation
	Oct	Head of a government delegation to Tanzania and Zambia to open construction work on the Tanzania-Zambia Railway
1971,	Apr	The Commission for Economic Relations with Foreign Countries is transformed into the Ministry of the same name of which Fang becomes minister (until Jan 1977)
	Sep	Member of an economic delegation to Vietnam

Nov Head of an economic delegation to Albania

1972, Oct Head of a government delegation to Congo (Brazzaville), Equatorial Guinea, Cameroon, and Nigeria

1973, Aug Elected to first term as member of the CCP Central Committee by the 10th Party Congress

1974, Oct Head of a government delegation to Zambia

1977, Jan Identified as vice-president of the Academy of Sciences (until Jul 1979)

Aug Elected member of the CCP Politburo by the 11th Party Congress

1978, Feb Identified as minister of the State Scientific and Technical Commission; elected deputy for Fujian Province to the 5th NPC

Mar Appointed vice-premier

Aug Identified as honorary president of the Chinese Weiqi Chess Association

Oct Head of a government delegation to the Federal Republic of Germany and France

1979, Jan Member of a government delegation, headed by Deng Xiaoping, to the U.S.A.

Jul Appointed member of the State Financial and Economic Commission; elected president of the Academy of Sciences

1980, Feb Elected member of the Secretariat of the 11th Central Committee by its 5th Plenum

Fang is married to Yin Sen.

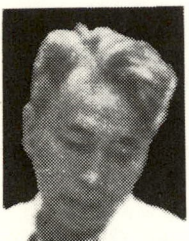

Fang Zhichun (Fang Chih-ch'un) 方志纯

Posts held

NPC
Member of the Standing Committee of the 5th NPC
Deputy for Jiangxi Province to the 5th NPC

Fang was born in 1911 in Yiyang, Jiangxi Province. When a student of Nanchang Middle School, he joined the Communist Youth League (about 1924). In 1927 he organized peasant uprisings in North Jiangxi, together with his brother Fang Zhimin (executed in 1935 by the KMT after having been taken prisoner as commander of the 10th Red Workers' and Peasants' Army). Until 1931 Fang Zhichun commanded a unit of the 10th Red Workers' and Peasants' Army. Between 1932 and 1936 he operated with a guerrilla unit in the border region of Jiangxi and Fujian Provinces. In 1937 he went to Yan'an and soon afterwards to Moscow for medical treatment. In 1940 he returned to China. Sheng Shicai, then governor of Xinjiang Province, had him imprisoned from 1942 until 1946 when he succeeded in escaping from prison. He went to Yan'an and soon afterwards was ordered to go to Manchuria where he became director of the Administrative Office of the Northwest Bureau under the CCP Central Committee. In 1948 he was identified as deputy secretary of Heilongjiang Province CP. In spring 1949 he joined the PLA forces pushing to South China.

1949, Dec Identified as vice-chairman of the People's Government of Jiangxi Province (until 1955)

1955, Feb Elected vice-governor of Jiangxi Province (until Sep 1965)

1956, Aug Identified as secretary of Jiangxi Province CP

1958, Nov Appointed president of Ruijin University (until 1960?)

1960, Sep Identiifed as president of the Scientific and Technical University of Jiangxi Province

1965, Aug Identified as acting governor of Jiangxi Province

Sep Elected governor of Jiangxi Province

1967, Sep Denounced as a follower of Liu Shaoqi and purged

1977, Oct First appearance after the Cultural Revolution

Nov Identified as vice-chairman of the Revolutionary Committee of Jiangxi Province (until Dec 1979)

1978, Feb Elected deputy for Jiangxi Province to the 5th NPC

Mar Elected member of the Standing Committee of the 5th NPC

1979, Jun Member of the Committee to Examine Proposals at the 2nd Session of the 5th NPC

Fang Zhida (Fang Chih-ta) 方知达

Posts held

CCP
Deputy director, United Front Work Department of the CCP Central Committee

1979, Apr Identified as deputy director, United Front Work Department of the CCP Central Committee

Fang Zhongru (Fang Chung-ju) 方仲如

Posts held

Others
Member of the Standing Committee of the 5th CPPCC

Fang was born in Xianyang, Shaanxi Province, and attended Weibei Middle School. In 1934-35 he took part in the Long March. He subsequently served as political commissar in various units and was political commissar and director of the Logistics Department of the 1st Field Army in early 1949.

1950, Jun Identified as mayor of Xi'an Municipality (until 1957)

1953, Oct Identified as secretary, Xi'an Municipality CP

1954, Aug Elected deputy for Xi'an Municipality to the 1st NPC

1956, Dec Elected 1st secretary, Xi'an Municipality CP (until Aug 1958)

1957, Aug Identified as secretary of Shaanxi Province CP (until 1965)

1958, Aug Elected deputy for Shaanxi Province to the 2nd NPC (confirmed in 1964 by the 3rd NPC)

1962,	May	Elected chairman of the Shaanxi Section, CPPCC (until 1965)
1963		Identified as member of the Control Committee of the CCP Central Committee
1965,	Aug	Identified as member, Northwest Bureau of the CCP Central Committee and as secretary of Gansu Province CP
1967		Disappears during the Cultural Revolution
1978,	Mar	First appearance after the Cultural Revolution: Elected member of the Standing Committee of the 5th CPPCC

Fei Xiaotong (Fei Hsiao-t'ung)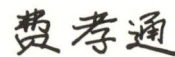

Posts held

Government
Member of the State Nationalities Affairs Commission

Others
Member of the Standing Committee of the 5th CPPCC
Vice-chairman of the China Democratic League
President of the Society of Sociology
Deputy director of the Institute of Ethnology, Academy of Social Sciences

Fei was born in 1910 in Wujiang County, Jiangsu Province. He graduated from the Social Sciences Department of Yanjing (Yenching) University in Beijing in 1933. He then continued his studies at Qinghua University and later at London University which awarded him a Ph.D. degree. In 1939 he returned to China and was appointed professor of social anthropology at the National Yunnan University. At the invitation of the U.S. State Department he went to the United States in 1943 to work at first at Harvard University, then at the University of Chicago and at the Institute of Pacific Relations in New York. After his return he lectured at Qinghua University as professor of anthropology. At the end of 1946 he went to England for a short period of time to work mainly at the London School of Economics.

1949,	Oct	Appointed member of the Culture and Education Commission of the Government Administrative Council; appointed council member of the Institute of Foreign Affairs
1950		Identified as professor in the Social Sciences Department of Qinghua University
1951,	Oct	Appointed member of the Nationalities Affairs Commission of the Government Administration Council (until 1954); identified as executive secretary of the Sino-Soviet Friendship Association (until Dec 1954) and as vice-president of the Central Institute of National Minorities
1953,	Nov	Identified as council member of the Political Science and Law Society
1954,	Aug	Elected deputy for Jiangsu Province to the 1st NPC
1956,	Feb	Elected member of the Central Committee, China Democratic League (until 1958)
	Oct	Appointed deputy director of the Bureau of Experts Administration under the State Council (until 1959?)

1957,	May	Appointed vice-chairman of the Nationalities Affairs Commission under the State Council (until Jan 1958)
1957		During the "Hundred Flowers Movement" he expresses doubts regarding CCP policy which he repeatedly defies. He is then criticized as a rightist deviationist.
1958,	Feb	Following self-criticism, Fei is cleared of the charge of "rightist deviationist"
1959,	Apr	Elected member of the 3rd CPPCC (confirmed in 1964 by the 4th CPPCC)
1967		Disappears during the Cultural Revolution
1972,	May	First appearance after the Cultural Revolution: Fei is present at a reception given for the American professor John King Fairbank
1978,	Mar	Elected member of the Standing Committee of the 5th CPPCC; and elected president of the Society of Sociology
1979,	May	Appointed member of the State Nationalities Affairs Commission
	Oct	Elected vice-chairman of the Central Committee, China Democratic League
	Dec	Identified as deputy director of the Institute of Ethnology, Academy of Social Sciences

Publications

1939	Peasant Life in China
1945	Earthbound China
1947	Systems of Child Rearing
	Rural China
1948	Rural Reconstruction
	Gentry Power and Imperial Power
1953	China's Gentry

Fei Yimin (Fei Yi-min)

Posts held

NPC
Deputy for Guangdong Province to the 5th NPC

Others
Vice-chairman of the Board of Directors, Jinan University
Member of the Standing Committee of the 5th CPPCC
President of Dagong Bao

Fei was born in Wuxian, Jiangsu Province. He studied in France. In 1949 he was appointed president of the Hong Kong edition of Dagong Bao.

1958,	Dec	Elected member of the 2nd National Committee, CPPCC
1962,	Apr	Identified as a member of the Standing Committee, Journalists' Association
1967,	May	Leads activities in front of the Hong Kong Government House
1975,	Jan	Member of the Presidium of the 4th NPC
1978,	Feb	Member of the Presidium of the 5th NPC
	Mar	Elected member of the Standing Committee of the 5th CPPCC
	Oct	Identified as vice-chairman of the Board of Directors, Jinan University
1979,	Jun	Identified as president of Dagong Bao

Feng Bohua (Feng Po-hua) 冯伯华

Posts held

Government
Vice-minister of chemical industry

1978, Jun Identified as vice-minister of chemical industry
Jul Head of a chemical delegation to Romania

Feng Depei (Feng Te-p'ei) 冯德培

Posts held

Others
Member of the Standing Committee of the 5th CPPCC
Vice-president, Shanghai Branch of the Academy of Sciences
Director of the Shanghai Institute of Physiology.

Feng was born in 1906 in Linhai, Zhejiang Province. He studied at Fudan University in Shanghai, then at Chicago University where he obtained an M.A. degree, and eventually at London University which awarded him a Ph.D. in 1933 for his work on muscular nerve physiology. Among his teachers were A.V. Hill, Adrian and Myerhoff. In 1934 he was appointed to a professorship at the Union Medical College in Beijing. In 1935 he was awarded a prize by the Chinese Cultural Fund for his scientific research work and was elected research fellow to the Academia Sinica. He was subsequently appointed director of the Preparatory Office for the Establishment of the Pharmacological Research Institute of the Academia Sinica. In 1949 he was acting director of the Medical Institute of the Academia Sinica.

1950, Mar Identified as member of the Cultural and Educational Committee, East China Military and Administrative Council
Jun Appointed director of the Institute of Physiology and Biochemistry, Academy of Sciences
1953, Feb Member of an Academy of Sciences delegation to the USSR
1954, Aug Elected deputy for Shanghai Municipality to the 1st NPC (confirmed in 1958 and 1964 by the 2nd and 3rd NPCs)
1955, May Identified as member of the Department of Biology and Earth Sciences, Academy of Sciences
1957, Dec Member of an Academy of Sciences delegation to the USSR
1958, Nov Identified as vice-president of the Shanghai Institute of Sciences
1959, Nov Identified as vice-president of the Shanghai Branch, Academy of Sciences, and as director of the Institute of Physiology of the Academy of Sciences
Dec Identified as vice-chairman of the Sino-Soviet Friendship Association, Shanghai Branch
1964, Jan Identified as vice-president of the East China Branch of the Academy of Sciences
1967 Disappears during the Cultural Revolution
1978, Feb First appearance after the Cultural Revolution

Mar Elected member of the Standing Committee of the 5th CPPCC; identified as vice-president of the Shanghai Branch, Academy of Sciences
Jul Identified as director of the Shanghai Institute of Physiology

Publications

Outline of Physiology; Change of Free Acid Content Stimulated Nerve

Feng Ding (Feng Ting) 冯定

Posts held

Others
Vice-president of Beijing University
Vice-chairman of the Society of Philosophy, Beijing Branch

Feng was born circa 1903 in Cixi County, Zhejiang Province. He graduated from the Moscow Sun Yat-sen University in 1930. From 1937 he held the following posts: chief editor of Resist the Enemy News, published by the New 4th Army; vice-president of the Central China College, Anti-Japan Military and Political Academy. In 1949 he served as director of the Propaganda Department, East China Bureau of the CCP Central Committee.

1950, Jan Identified as vice-chairman of the Cultural and Educational Committee, East China Military and Administrative Council
1952 Identified as member of the Society of Philosophy (until 1961)
1955, Jun Identified as member of the Department of Philosophy and Social Sciences, Academy of Sciences
1958, Jun Identified as professor of Beijing University
1960, Mar Identified as council member of the Sino-Latin-American Friendship Association
1961, May Identified as vice-chairman of the Society of Philosophy, Beijing Branch
1966, Jul Branded as a revisionist and purged
1979, Jan First appearance after the Cultural Revolution: Identified as vice-president of Beijing University
Jul Identified as vice-chairman of the Society of Philosophy, Beijing Branch

Publications

Communist View of Life
Simple Truth
Historical Mission of the Working Class

Feng Jixin (Feng Chi-hsin) 冯纪新

Posts held

CCP
Secretary of Gansu Province CP

NPC
Deputy for Gansu Province to the 5th NPC

Provincial Administration
Governor of Gansu Province

1953, Jan Identified as chairman of the Control Committee, People's Government of Heilongjiang Province

Jul Identified as secretary of Heilongjiang Province CP (until 1964)

1964, Sep Identified as vice-governor of Jiangsu Province (until Cultural Revolution)

1965, Mar Identified as member of the Standing Committee of Jiangsu Province CP (until Cultural Revolution)

1968 Disappears during the Cultural Revolution

1973, Mar First appearance after the Cultural Revolution

1977, Dec Elected vice-chairman of the Revolutionary Committee of Gansu Province (until Dec 1979)

1978, Feb Elected deputy for Gansu Province to the 5th NPC

May Identified as secretary of Gansu Province CP

1979, Dec Elected governor of Gansu Province

Feng Pinde (Feng P'in-te) 冯品德

Posts held

CCP
Alternate member of the CCP 11th Central Committee

1973, Aug Elected to first term as alternate member of the CCP Central Committee by the 10th Party Congress

1976, Apr Identified as a cadre in Shanghai

Feng Tianshun (Feng T'ien-shun) 冯天顺

Posts held

Government
Manager-general of the Insurance Company
Acting manager-general of the Bank of China

1973, May Identified as acting director of the London Branch, Bank of China

1975, Nov Identified as manager-general of the Insurance Company

1976, Feb Head of an insurance delegation to North Korea and Vietnam

1978, Oct Head of an insurance delegation to Japan

Dec Identified as acting manager-general of the Bank of China

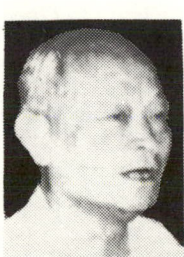

Feng Wenbin (Feng Wen-pin) 冯文彬

Posts held

CCP
Deputy director of the General Office, CCP Central Committee
Vice-president of the Party School under the CCP Central Committee
Associated dean of Academic Affairs of the Party School

Others
Member of the Standing Committee of the 5th CPPCC

Feng was born in 1911 in Pingjiang County, Hunan Province. In 1919 his family moved to Shanghai where he attended primary school for one year and then an evening school. From 1920 to 1925 he first worked as a child laborer in a match factory and then as an apprentice in a coal store. In 1925 he became a member of the Communist Youth League and in 1928 of the CCP. In 1929 he joined the 4th Red Army in Fujian Province. In 1931 he became political commissar of the Wireless Column of that army. In 1932 he became secretary of Fujian Province CP. In 1935 he was appointed secretary of the Communist Youth League. From 1936 he was mainly engaged in youth work. In 1944 he became director of the Youth Work Committee in the Politburo of the CCP. From 1947 he was head of the Youth Department of the CCP Central Committee (until 1953). He was elected member of the Executive Committee of the Federation of Labor in 1948 and in the following year secretary and member of the Central Committee, New Democratic Youth League. In September 1949 he took part in the 1st CPPCC.

1949, Oct Appointed member of the Supreme People's Court and council member of the Sino-Soviet Friendship Association

1950, Jul Identified as member of the Provisional Board of Directors of the Federation of Cooperatives

1951, Sep Member of a delegation to the World Peace Conference of Youths and Students

1952, Sep Identified as director of the Industry Department, Tianjin Municipality CP

1953, May Identified as member of the Financial and Economic Committee of Tianjin People's Government. Subsequently disappears

1977, Oct Identified as cadre of a department of the CCP Central Committee

1978, Mar Elected member of the Standing Committee of the 5th CPPCC

Aug Identified as associated dean of Academic Affairs of the Party School under the CCP Central Committee

1979, May Identified as vice-president of the Party School under the CCP Central Committee

Aug Identified as deputy director of the General Office, CCP Central Committee

Feng Xuan (Feng Hsüan) 冯铉

Posts held

CCP
Member of the CCP 11th Central Committee
Deputy director of the International Liaison Department of the CCP Central Committee

During 1946-47 Feng was head of the secretariat of the Beijing Headquarters of the CCP and KMT Military Subcommittee.

1950, Dec Appointed envoy to Switzerland (until Jul 1956)

1956, Jul Appointed ambassador to Switzerland (until Apr 1959)

1958,	Jul	Elected deputy for Sichuan Province to the 2nd NPC (until Dec 1964)
1959,	Apr	Appointed deputy secretary-general of the State Council (until Mar 1965)
1961,	May	Member of the delegation led by minister of Foreign Affairs Chen Yi to the Laos Conference in Geneva
	Jul	Elected vice-chairman of the Sino-Latin American Friendship Association
1963,	Jul	Identified as a leading cadre of a department of the CCP Central Committee
1964,	Sep	Elected deputy for Jilin Province to the 3rd NPC
1965,	Mar	Appointed deputy secretary-general of the Standing Committee of the 3rd NPC
1966,	Mar-Apr	Feng accompanies President Liu Shaoqi on state visits to Pakistan, Afghanistan, and Burma
1972,	Jul	Identified as a leading cadre in the International Liaison Department of the CCP Central Committee
1973,	Aug	Elected to first term as member of the CCP Central Committee by the 10th Party Congress
	Nov	Identified as deputy director of the International Liaison Department of the CCP Central Committee

Feng Yongshun (Feng Yung-shun) 封永順

Posts held

Military
Major-general
Deputy director of the Logistics Department of the PLA

1955,	Sep	Conferred the order "Liberation," 1st class
1957,	May	Identified as major-general and as deputy director of the PLA Logistics Department. Subsequently disappears
1969,	Oct	Identified as military leader in Beijing
1971,	Jun	Identified as deputy director of the PLA Logistics Department

Feng Yujiu (Feng Yü-chiu) 馮于九

Posts held

Government
Ambassador to Hungary

Feng was born in 1912. In 1948 he was a cadre of the Communications Department of the North China People's Government.

1950,	Feb	Identified as deputy director of the General Bureau of Highways in the Ministry of Communications
1951		Identified as deputy director of the Transportation Bureau under the Ministry of Communications
1956,	Oct	Appointed assistant minister of communications (until Jan 1959)
1960,	Dec	Appointed director of the Oceanic Transportation Bureau under the Ministry of Communications

1965,	Jan	Appointed ambassador to Norway (until 1967)
1969,	Jul	Appointed ambassador to Mauritania (until Apr 1973)
1973,	Nov	Appointed ambassador to Nigeria (until Jan 1979)
1979,	Apr	Appointed ambassador to Hungary

Feng Yunhe (Feng Yün-ho) (f) 鄧云鶴

Posts held

Others
Member of the Standing Committee of the 5th CPPCC

Feng was born in 1899(?) in a carpenter's familiy. As a child she worked as a maid servant. In 1923 she entered the Beijing Teachers' College for Women. In 1927 she went to the United States to study chemical engineering. In 1932 she became the first woman to receive a doctorate at Ohio State University. Afterwards, working in research laboratories at the University of Berlin, she developed a process for making rayon fiber from bamboo, rice and sorghum stalks. Around 1938 she returned to China and was appointed a commissioner in the National Government's Economic Committee. In Chongqing she was later a cofounder of the China National Construction Association. In September 1949 she took part in the 1st CPPCC. She has continued her research for making textile fibers from ramie, first in Shanghai, later in Guangzhou.

1954,	Aug	Elected deputy for Shandong Province to the 1st NPC (confirmed in 1958 by the 2nd NPC)
1958,	Feb	Identified as advisor at the Ministry of Textile Industry
1964,	Sep	Elected deputy for Shandong Province to the 3rd NPC
1967		Disappears during the Cultural Revolution
1978,	Feb	First appearance after the Cultural Revolution
	Mar	Elected member of the Standing Committee of the 5th CPPCC

Feng Zhanwu (Feng Chan-wu) 馮占武

Posts held

CCP
Alternate member of the CCP 11th Central Committee

1969,	Apr	Elected to first term as alternate member of the CCP Central Committee by the 9th Party Congress
1974,	Oct	Identified as vice-chairman of the Revolutionary Committee of Jilin Province (until Dec 1977)
1977,	Aug	After election as alternate member of the CCP 11th Central Committee Feng disappears; probably purged

Feng Zhi (Feng Chih)   冯 至

<u>Posts held</u>

NPC
Deputy for Beijing Municipality to the 5th NPC

Others
Director of the Institute of Foreign Literature of the Academy of Social Sciences

Feng was born in 1905 in Zhuo, Hebei Province, as the son of a salt-works director. After attending the 4th Municipal Middle School in Beijing, he studied literature at Beijing University from 1923 to 1928. He was subsequently employed as assistant by that university. From 1930 to 1935 he studied at Berlin and Heidelberg Universities in Germany and received his Ph.D. from the latter in 1935 for his study "Die Analogie von Natur und Geist als Stilprinzip in Novalis Dichtung" (The Analogy between Nature and Spirit as a Stylistic Principal in the Poetry of Novalis). After his return to China he was appointed professor at Beijing University and around 1940 professor at the Southwest Associated University.

1950,	Feb	Identified as member of the Federation of Literary and Art Circles and as member of the Writers' Association; Feng visits a number of eastern European countries
1951		Professor at the Foreign Literature Department of Beijing University (until 1964)
1952,	Dec	Member of a delegation to the World Peace Congress in Vienna
1954,	Jan	Identified as professor at Beijing University
	Aug	Elected deputy for Henan Province to the 1st NPC
1955,	Jun	Identified as member of the Philosophy and Social Sciences Department at the Academy of Sciences
1963,	Dec	Head of a writers' delegation to Cuba
1966,	Apr	Identified as council member of the Writers' Association
1967		Disappears during the Cultural Revolution
1978,	Jan	First appearance after the Cultural Revolution
	Feb	Elected deputy for Beijing Municipality to the 5th NPC
	May	Identified as director of the Institute of Foreign Literature of the Academy of Social Sciences
1979,	Jun	Head of a delegation of the Academy of Social Sciences to the Federal Republic of Germany

Fu Chongbi (Fu Ch'ung-pi)   付 崇 碧

<u>Posts held</u>

NPC
Deputy for the PLA to the 5th NPC

Military
Deputy commander of Beijing Military Region
Commander of Beijing Garrison

Fu's career begun in the 1st Front Army. At the outbreak of the Anti-Japanese War he led a company in the

regiment commanded by Yang Chengwu of the 115th Division, 8th Route Army. From 1940 to 1945 he continued to serve under Yang and rose to the post of regiment commander. In 1946 he became political commissar of a brigade in the 2nd Column in Shaanxi-Chahar-Hebei Military Region and one year later director of the Political Department of the 2nd Column.

1951		Appointed political commissar of the 63rd Corps
	Feb	Fu enters the Korea War with the 63rd Corps
1952		Made commander of the 63rd Corps
1955,	Sep	Conferred the order of "Liberation," 1st class
1964,	Dec	Elected member of the National Committee of the CPPCC
1965,	Jul	Appointed deputy commander of Beijing Military Region (until Mar 1968)
1966,	Aug-Nov	Fu is present at five Red Guard parades for Mao Zedong
1967,	Apr	With the establishment of the Revolutionary Committee for Beijing, Fu is elected vice-chairman; identified as commander of Beijing Garrison (in both posts until about Mar 1968)
1968,	Mar	Fu is criticized and disappears
1974,	Sep	Reactivated after the Cultural Revolution
1975,	Jul	Identified as deputy commander of Beijing Military Region
1978,	Feb	Elected deputy for the PLA to the 5th NPC
	Mar	Identified as commander of Beijing Garrison

Fu Hao (Fu Hao)   符 浩

<u>Posts held</u>

Government
Ambassador to Japan

Prior to the establishment of PRC, Fu had served as head of the Political Department of a PLA unit and had in addition become known as secretary of the Social Department in the CCP Central Committee.

1950,	Dec	Appointed counselor, embassy in PR Mongolia (until 1954)
1954,	May	Identified as commissar of the Asian Affairs Department in the Ministry of Foreign Affairs (until Aug 1955)
1955,	Mar	Adivisor to a Chinese trade delegation to Japan
	Sep	Appointed counselor, embassy in India; in this capacity repeatedly chargé d'affaires in India (until Jun 1962)
1970,	Nov	Identified as director of the General Office in the Ministry of Foreign Affairs (until Apr 1972); member of a Chinese government delegation attending 10th anniversary celebrations of independence in Mauritania
1971,	Sep	Member of a government delegation to France
	Nov	Appointed one of the three Chinese representatives at the 26th UN General Assembly

1972, Apr Identified as vice-minister of foreign affairs (until Sep 1974)
1974, Sep Appointed ambassador to North Vietnam (until Apr 1977)
1977, Jul Appointed ambassador to Japan

Fu is married to Jiao Ling.

Fu Maoji (Fu Mao-chi) 傅懋勣

Posts held

Government
Member of the State Nationalities Affairs Commission

Others
Deputy director, Institute of Nationalities of the Academy of Social Sciences
Vice-chairman of the Nationality Research Society

1959, Oct Identified as deputy director of the Institute of Minority Languages, Academy of Sciences (until 1966)
1978, Sep Identified as deputy director of the Institute of Nationalities, Academy of Social Sciences
1979, May Elected vice-chairman of the Nationality Research Society; appointed member of the State Nationalities Affairs Commission

Fu Qiutao (Fu Ch'iu-t'ao) 付秋涛

Posts held

NPC
Member of the Standing Committee of the 5th NPC
Deputy for the PLA to the 5th NPC

Military
Colonel-general

Fu was born in 1905. In the summer of 1934 he led an unsuccessful attack from the Jiangxi Soviet on Xishan near Nanchang which was held by KMT troops. During the Long March his task was to disrupt enemy activities with his guerrilla units in the Hunan-Hubei-Jiangxi Border Area. In July 1937 he was appointed commander of the Hunan-Hubei-Jiangxi Military Region. In 1940 he commanded a unit of the New 4th Army operating in South Anhui. In 1942 he was CP secretary of Anhui-Hubei-Jiangxi Border Area.

1949, Oct Appointed member of the East China Military and Administrative Council (until Dec 1952)
1950, Jan Appointed chairman of the Xuzhou Military Control Commission
Feb? Appointed deputy secretary of the Shandong Subbureau, East China Bureau of the CCP Central Committee
Mar Appointed vice-chairman of the People's Government of Shandong (probably until Dec 1950)

Oct Appointed deputy director of the Troop Strength Department of the Revolutionary Military Council (until 1952)
1952 Identified as deputy director of the Organization Department, General Staff of the Revolutionary Military Council (probably until Sep 1954)
1954, Sep Appointed director of the Personnel Department, General Staff of the PLA (until 1958)
1955, Sep Made colonel-general; awarded the orders of "1st August," "Independence and Freedom," and "Liberation," all 1st class
1958, Oct Elected deputy for the PLA to the 2nd NPC; appointed director of the Mobilization Department, General Staff of PLA
1959, Apr Appointed member of the National Defense Council
1969, May Organizer of the National Militia Conference in Beijing
1965, Oct Head of a military delegation to Algeria
1974, Sep Reactivated after the Cultural Revolution
1975, Jan Elected member of the Standing Committee by the 4th NPC (confirmed in 1978 by the 5th NPC)
1978, Feb Elected deputy for the PLA to the 5th NPC
1979, Jun Member of the Committee to Examine Proposals at the 2nd Session of the 5th NPC

Fu Yutian (Fu Yü-t'ien) 付雨田

Posts held

CCP
Secretary of Jiangxi Province CP

Provincial Administration
Vice-governor of Jiangxi Province

1953, May Identified as secretary of Changchun Municipality CP and as mayor of Changchun
1954, Aug Elected deputy for Changchun Municipality to the 1st NPC
1957, Jun Identified as assistant minister of urban construction (until 1958)
1960, Feb Identified as vice-chairman of Guangxi Autonomous Region (until Feb 1967)
1962, Sep Identified as secretary of Guangxi Autonomous Region CP (until Feb 1967)
1967, Feb Branded as a follower of Liu Shaoqi
1978, Dec First appearance after the Cultural Revolution
1979, Apr Identified as secretary of the CP, and as vice-chairman of the Revolutionary Committee (until Dec 1979), of Jiangxi Province
Dec Elected vice-governor of Jiangxi Province

Fu Zhong (Fu Chung)    付 鍾

Posts held

NPC
Member of the Standing Committee of the
5th NPC
Deputy for the PLA to the 5th NPC

Military
Colonel-general
Deputy director of the General Political
Department of the PLA
Deputy director of the All-Army Physical
Culture Guidance Committee

Others
Vice-chairman of the Federation of Literary and Art Circles

Fu was born in 1897 in Sichuan Province. He spent the period from 1919 to 1922 as a worker-student in France and was one of the cofounders of the France Section of the CCP. He returned to China via the USSR. In 1925 the 4th CCP Congress elected him member of the Central Committee. He was confirmed in this post in 1928 by the 6th Congress. Having been engaged in underground activities in Sichuan he became a member of the Political Department of the 4th Front Army in 1933 and one year later director of this department. He took part in the Long March serving in the 4th Front Army. In 1937 he became instructor at the Anti-Japan Military and Political Academy. Shortly afterwards he was made director of the Political Department of the 129th Division in the 8th Route Army. In 1944 he was editor-in-chief of Xinhua Ribao (New China Daily) published in Chongqing. From 1947 onward he worked in the General Political Department of the PLA. In September 1949 he participated in the CPPCC as representative for the PLA (until 1954).

1949,	Oct	Elected council member of the Sino-Soviet Friendship Association (until Dec 1954)
1950		Appointed deputy director of the General Political Department of the PLA
1954,	Sep	Elected deputy for the PLA to the 1st NPC
1955,	Sep	Made lieutenant-general
1959,	Jan	Made colonel-general
	Apr	Appointed member of the National Defense Council
1960,	Aug	Elected vice-chairman of the Federation of Literary and Art Circles
1967		Fu disappears although there were no known charges against him
1974,	Sep	First appearance after the Cultural Revolution
1975,	Dec	Identified as a high-ranking military personage in the Central Leadership
1977,	Jul	Identified as deputy director of the General Political Department of the PLA
1978,	Feb	Elected deputy for the PLA to the 5th NPC
	Jun	Identified as vice-chairman of the Federation of Literary and Art Circles; identified as deputy director of the All-Army Physical Culture Guidance Committee
1979,	Jun	Member of the Draft Laws Committee at the 2nd Session of the 5th NPC
	Jul	Appointed member of the National Games Organizing Committee

Gan Chunlei (Kan Ch'un-lei) 甘春雷

Posts held

Others
Member of the Standing Committee of the
5th CPPCC

Gan belongs to the Hui minority. During the Anti-Japanese War he was director of the Political Department, 7th Military Sub-District of Shanxi-Hebei Military District.

1951,	Oct	Identified as secretary of Cang County CP, Hebei Province
	Dec	Identified as deputy director of the Staff Office of the Nationalities Affairs Commission, Government Administative Council
1953,	May	Identified as secretary-general of the Cultural Association for Hui Minorities
1954,	Dec	Elected member of the 2nd CPPCC (confirmed in 1969 and 1964)
1956,	Feb	Identified as director of the Staff Office of the State Council's Nationalities Affairs Commission
1957,	May	Appointed vice-chairman of the Nationalities Affairs Commission (until 1959)
1960,	Jul	Identified as secretary, CP of Ningxia Autonomous Region (until Cultural Revolution)
1968		Disappears during the Cultural Revolution
1978,	Mar	First appearance after the Cultural Revolution: Elected member of the Standing Committee of the 5th CPPCC

Gan Cisen (Kan Tz'u-sen) 甘祠森

Posts held

Others
Member of the Standing Committee and deputy secretary-general of the 5th CPPCC
Vice-chairman of the Central Committee, Revolutionary Committee of the Chinese KMT

1964,	Oct	Elected deputy for Sichuan Province to the 3rd NPC
1972,	Sep	Identified as member of the Standing Committee, Central Committee of the Chinese KMT Revolutionary Committee
1978,	Mar	Elected member of the Standing Committee of the 5th CPPCC
1979,	Jun	Identified as deputy secretary-general of the 5th CPPCC
	Oct	Elected vice-chairman of the Central Committee, Revolutionary Committee of the Chinese KMT

Gan Gu (Kan Ku) 甘苦

Posts held

Provincial Administration
Vice-chairman of the People's Government of Guangxi Autonomous Region

Gan belongs to the Zhuang minority.

1979,	Dec	Elected vice-chairman of the People's Government of Guangxi Autonomous Region

Gan Weihan (Kan Wei-han) 甘渭汉

Posts held

NPC
Deputy for the PLA to the 5th NPC

Military
Lieutenant-general
Political commissar of Shenyang Military Region
3rd secretary, CP Secretariat of Shenyang Military Region

Gan was born in 1909 in Jiangxi Province. From 1931 to 1936 he served as political commissar in various units of the 4th Front Army. From 1937 he belonged to the 129th Division of the 8th Route Army. In 1944 he became deputy political commissar, and in 1947 political commissar, of the New 4th Army.

1950		Service in the Korean War
1951,	Mar	Identified as deputy director of the Political Department, Northeast Military Region
	May	Identified as deputy political commissar of Northeast Military Region
1955,	Sep	Appointed lieutenant-general
1960,	Dec	Identified as director of the Cadres Administration Department of the PLA General Political Department (until 1966)
1961,	Jan	Member of a friendship delegation led by Zhou Enlai to Burma
1963,	Jul	Article in the RMRB of 29 July: "People's Liberation Army Officers Serve as Privates"
1966,	Jul	Identified as military leader in Chengdu Military Region
1967,	Apr	Branded as an anti-Mao-Lin element and purged
1977,	Oct	First appearance after the Cultural Revolution
1978,	Feb	Elected deputy for the PLA to the 5th NPC
	Mar	Identified as political commissar of Shenyang Military Region (until Jul 1978)
	Jul	Identified as 2nd political commisar of Shenyang Military Region and as 3rd secretary of the CP Secretariat, Shenyang Military Region
1979,	Jan	Identified as political commissar of Shenyang Military Region

Gan Yetao (Kan Yeh-t'ao) 甘野陶

Posts held

Government
Ambassador to Madagascar

Before the foundation of PRC, Gan served in various posts as political commissar in the PLA, the most significant of which was director, Political Department of the 1st Field Army.

1953,	Aug	Identified as attaché at the embassy in North Korea (until Feb 1956)
1956,	Feb	Identified as counselor at the embassy in Indonesia (until Jan 1959)
1959,	Jan	Appointed ambassador to Finland (until Jun 1962)
1964,	Apr	Identified as director of the Department of Agreements and Laws in the Ministry of Foreign Affairs (until about 1966)
1973,	Feb	Appointed ambassador to Afghanistan (until Jun 1977)
1979,	Aug	Appointed ambassador to Madagascar

Gan Ziyu (Kan Tzu-yü)　　　甘子玉

Posts held

Government
Vice-minister of the State Planning Commission

1961,	Aug	Gan publishes an article on economic affairs in HQ
1978,	Nov	Identified as vice-minister of the State Planning Commission
1979,	Oct	Member of a government delegation headed by Hua Guofeng to France, the Federal Republic of Germany, Great Britain and Italy

Gan Zuchang (Kan Tsu-ch'ang)　　　甘祖昌

Posts held

NPC
Member of the Standing Committee of the 5th NPC
Deputy for Jiangxi Province to the 5th NPC

Gan was born in 1905 in Yanbei, Lianhua County, on the Jinggang Mountain range in Jiangxi Province. In 1927 he joined the Red Workers' and Peasants' Army. In 1934-35 he took part in the Long March. He was severely wounded three times during the Revolutionary War.

1957		Gan, serving as director of the Logistics Department in Xinjiang Military Region, is discharged on account of his injuries and returns to his native village
Later		Gan distinguishes himself by initiating and implementing agricultural and irrigation projects in his native village
1975,	Jan	Elected member of the Standing Committee of the 4th NPC (confirmed in 1978 by the 5th NPC)
1978,	Feb	Elected deputy for Jiangxi Province to the 5th NPC

Gao Dengbang (Kao Teng-pang)　　　高登榜

Posts held

NPC
Deputy secretary-general of the Standing Committee, NPC

Others
Deputy secretary-general of the Academy of Sciences

In 1949 Gao served as director of the Communications Department in the 1st Field Army.

1950,	Mar	Identified as deputy director of the Communications Department, Northwest Military and Administrative Council (until May 1952)
	Sep	Identified as deputy political commissar of the Railways Work Department, Northwest Military and Administrative Council
1954,	Feb	Appointed director of the Administrative Office, Ministry of Railways (until Mar 1956)
1956,	Mar	Identified as director of the State Government Organs Administrative Bureau (until Feb 1966)
1959,	Sep	Appointed deputy secretary-general of the State Council (until Feb 1966)
1960,	Sep	Identified as director of the Cooking School under the State Government Organs Administrative Bureau
1966,	Feb	Identified as deputy director of the Staff Office for Foreign Affairs under the State Council
1967,	Jun	Denounced as counterrevolutionary revisionist and purged
1975,	Sep	First appearance after the Cultural Revolution
1978,	Sep	Identified as deputy secretary-general of the Academy of Sciences
1979,	Nov	Appointed deputy secretary-general of the NPC Standing Committee

Gao Fuyou (Kao Fu-yu)　　　高富友

Posts held

Government
Deputy director, Bureau of Government Offices Administration under the State Council
Member of the State Nationalities Affairs Commission

1961,	Jan	Identified as director of the State Foreign Experts Administration (until Apr 1963)
1963,	Apr	Identified as deputy director of the Government Administration Bureau (until Cultural Revolution)
1967		Disappears during the Cultural Revolution
1976,	Jan	First appearance after the Cultural Revolution
1979,	Jan	Identified as deputy director of the Bureau of Government Offices Administration under the State Council
	May	Appointed member of the State Nationalities Affairs Commission
	Jul	Appointed deputy secretary-general of the National Games Organizing Committee

Gao Houliang (Kao Hou-liang)　高厚良

Posts held

CCP
Alternate member of the CCP 11th Central Committee

NPC
Deputy for the PLA to the 5th NPC

Military
Major-general
Political commissar of the PLA Air Force
2nd secretary, CP Secretariat of the Air Force

1964,	Nov	Identified as major-general in Nanjing Military Region
1974,	May	Identified as military leader in Beijing
1976,	May	Identified as deputy political commissar of the Air Force (until 1977)
1977,	Jun	Identified as 2nd secretary, CP Secretariat of the Air Force
	Aug	Elected alternate member of the CCP Central Committee by the 11th Party Congress
1978,	Feb	Elected deputy for the PLA to the 5th NPC
	May	Identified as political commissar of the Air Force

Gao Jianzhong (Kao Chien-chung)　高建中

Posts held

Government
Deputy director of the Protocol Department in the Ministry of Foreign Affairs

1972,	Jul	Identified as deputy director of the Protocol Department in the Ministry of Foreign Affairs
1975,	Mar	Member of a friendship delegation led by Chen Yonggui to Mexico
1978,	Jan	Member of a government delegation led by Deng Xiaoping to Burma and Nepal
	Jul	Member of a government delegation led by Geng Biao to Trinidad and Tobago, Jamaica, and Guyana
	Oct	Member of a government delegation led by Deng Xiaoping to Japan

Gao Kelin (Kao K'e-lin)　高克林

Posts held

NPC
Member of the Standing Committee of the 5th NPC
Deputy for Shaanxi Province to the 5th NPC
Vice-chairman of the Legal Commission under the NPC Standing Committee

Gao was born in 1910 in Shenmu County, Shaanxi Province. As a student at Shaanxi Normal School he joined the Communist Youth League in 1930. From 1931 to 1938 he served with Li Jingquan in guerrilla units operating in the Daqingshan Area. In 1941 he was identified as deputy director of the Institute of Minority Affairs in Yan'an. In 1948 he was secretary of Suiyuan Province CP. In June 1949 he was identified as deputy political commissar of Suiyuan Military Region (until Aug 1952). In September of that year Gao was elected member of the CPPCC.

1949,	Dec	Appointed vice-chairman of the Military and Administrative Council of Suiyuan Province
1952,	Aug	Relieved of his posts as secretary of Suiyuan Province CP and as political commissar of Suiyuan Military Region. Elected secretary of Shaanxi Province CP (until Sep 1953)
1953,	Jan	Following the reorganization of North China Military and Administrative Council into North China Administrative Council, Gao is appointed council member
	Sep	Appointed deputy chief procurator (until 1963)
1954,	Sep	Elected deputy for Guizhou Province to the 1st NPC
1956,	Sep	Elected alternate member of the CCP Central Committee and member of the Central Control Commission of the CCP Central Committee
1958,	Oct	Appointed vice-chairman of the Sino-German-Democratic-Republic Friendship Association
1959,	Sep	Head of a friendship delegation to the German Democratic Republic
1964,	Sep	Elected deputy for Shaanxi Province to the 3rd NPC
1965,	Mar	Identified as secretary of the Northwest China Bureau in the CCP Central Committee
1967		Branded as a "three-anti element" and purged
1978,	Feb	First appearance after the Cultural Revolution: Elected deputy for Shaanxi Province to the 5th NPC
	Mar	Elected member of the Standing Committee of the 5th NPC
1979,	Feb	Appointed vice-chairman of the Legal Commission under the NPC Standing Committee
	Jun	Vice-chairman of the Draft Laws Committee at the 2nd Session of the 5th NPC

Gao Qiyun (Kao Ch'i-yün)　高敬云

Posts held

CCP
Secretary of Shandong Province CP

1954,	Feb	Identified as deputy secretary of Jinan Municipality CP
1960		Identified as member of the People's Council of Shandong Province
1964,	Sep	Elected deputy for Shandong Province to the 3rd NPC
1966,	Mar	Identified as vice-governor of Shandong Province
1967		Disappears during the Cultural Revolution

1977, Aug First appearance after the Cultural Revolution: Identified as member of the Standing Committee of Shandong Province CP (until Feb 1979) and as vice-chairman of the Revolutionary Committee of Shandong Province (reelected to latter post in Dec 1977; until Dec 1979)

1979, Mar Identified as secretary of Shandong Province CP

Gao Rui (Kao Jui)　　高　锐

Posts held

Military
Deputy director of the PLA Military Science Academy

1971, Aug Identified as 2nd secretary of Ningxia Autonomous Region CP (until?)

1975, Aug Identified as military leader in Lanzhou Military Region

       Dec Identified as military leader in Beijing

1978, Aug Identified as deputy director of the PLA Military Science Academy; member of a military delegation led by Su Yu to North Korea

Gao Tie (Kao T'ieh)　　高　铁

Posts held

Others
Vice-president of Beijing University

1965, Nov Identified as vice-president of the Harbin Technical University

1978, Sep Identified as vice-president of Beijing University

Gao Wenhua (Kao Wen-hua)　　高文华

Posts held

Others
Member of the Standing Committee of the 5th CPPCC

Gao was born circa 1905 in Hunan Province. In 1927 he joined the CCP. He was a supporter of the "Li Lisan-line" before he became involved in underground work first in Wuhan and then in Shanghai around 1934. In 1937 he worked under Xu Teli in Hunan.

1949, Dec Identified as deputy secretary of Hunan Province CP

1950, Mar Identified as member of Hunan Province People's Government

1952, Nov Identified as vice-minister of light industry (until Jun 1957)

1957, Jun Appointed vice-minister of aquatic products (until Cultural Revolution)

1958, Jul Elected deputy for Hunan Province to the 2nd NPC (reelected in 1964 to the 3rd NPC)

1959, Apr Elected member of the Standing Committee of the 3rd CPPCC (confirmed in 1965 for the 4th CPPCC)

1967   Disappears during the Cultural Revolution

1978, Feb First appearance after the Cultural Revolution

       Mar Elected member of the Standing Committee of the 5th CPPCC

Gao Wenli (Kao Wen-li)　　高文礼

Posts held

Government
Vice-minister of public security

NPC
Deputy for Shandong Province to the 5th NPC

1978, Feb Elected deputy for Shandong Province to the 5th NPC

       Oct Identified as vice-minister of public security

1979, Jun Member of the Law Drafting Committee under the 2nd Session of the 5th NPC

       Jul Appointed member of the National Games Organizing Committee

Gao Xiu (Kao Hsiu)　　高　修

Posts held

Government
Vice-minister of commerce

NPC
Deputy for Shandong Province to the 5th NPC

1964, Apr Appointed vice-minister of commerce

1966   Disappears during the Cultural Revolution

1970, May First appearance after the Cultural Revolution

1972, Nov Identified in his former post as vice-minister of commerce

1978, Feb Elected deputy for Shandong Province to the 5th NPC

       Mar Deputy head of a trade delegation to Japan

Gao Yang (Kao Yang)　　高　扬

Posts held

Government
Minister of state farms and land reclamation

Gao is a native of Liaoning Province.

1950   Identified as deputy secretary of Shenyang Municipality CP and as director of the Organization Department of Shenyang Municipality CP

       Apr Appointed chairman of the People's Government of Liaodong Province (until Jun 1952)

1951, Oct Identified as member of the Northeast China People's Government (until Aug 1953)

1953,	Jan	Appointed member of the Northeast China Administrative Council (until Aug 1954)
	Sep	Appointed secretary of Liaodong Province CP (until Aug 1954)
1954,	Aug	Elected deputy for Liaoning Province to the 1st NPC (reelected in 1958 and 1964 to the 2nd and 3rd NPCs)
1956,	Sep	Appointed member of the Central Control Commission of the CCP Central Committee
1958,	Oct	Appointed deputy director of the Industrial Labor Department of the CCP Central Committee
1962,	Jul	Appointed minister of chemical industry (until Cultural Revolution)
1967		Disappears during the Cultural Revolution
1977,	Dec	First appearance after the Cultural Revolution: Elected vice-chairman of the Revolutionary Committee of Jilin Province (until May 1979)
1978,	Feb	Identified as secretary of Jilin Province CP (until May 1977)
1979,	Jun	Identified as minister of state farms and land reclamation

Gao Yangwen (Kao Yang-wen) 高扬文

Posts held

Government
Minister of coal industry

Gao was born in 1917 in Shandong Province. In April 1949 he was elected a member of the New Democratic Youth League Central Committee.

1950		Identified as director of the Organization Department of the New Democratic Youth League
1952		Identified as alternate secretary of the New Democratic Youth League (until 1953)
1955,	Feb	Identified as assistant minister of metallurgical industry (until May 1957)
1957,	Jun	Identified as vice-minister of metallurgical industry (until Mar 1965)
1964,	Sep	Elected deputy for Shandong Province to the 3rd NPC
1965,	Mar	Identified as vice-chairman of the State Economic Commission (until May 1966)
1966,	Aug	Identified as secretary of Beijing Municipality CP
1967,	Apr	Elected member of the Standing Committee, Revolutionary Committee of Beijing Municipality
1968,	Mar	Branded as a "three-anti element" and purged
1973,	Oct	First appearance after the Cultural Revolution
1978,	Sep	Identified as vice-minister of metallurgical industry (until Jan 1980)
1980,	Feb	Appointed minister of coal industry

Gao Yi (Kao Yi) 高沂

Posts held

Government
Vice-minister of education

Gao was born in 1915 in Shandong Province.

1951,	Oct	Identified as deputy director, Administration Council of the Northeast China People's Government
1958,	Jul	Identified as assistant to the president of Qinghua University
1959,	Nov	Identified as deputy secretary of Qinghua University CP
1962,	Nov	Appointed vice-president of Qinghua University
1965,	Jul	Appointed vice-minister of higher education
1967		Disappears during the Cultural Revolution
1977,	Oct	First appearance after the Cultural Revolution
	Dec	Identified as vice-minister of education
1978,	Oct	Member of a government delegation led by Fang Yi to the Federal Republic of Germany and France
1979,	Jul	Delegation to the 37th Session of the International Conference on Education in Geneva

Gao Zhanxiang (Kao Chan-hsiang) 高占祥

Posts held

Mass Organization
Secretary of the Communist Youth League
Vice-chairman of the Youth Federation

1964,	Jul	Elected member of the Communist Youth League Central Committee
1978,	Oct	Elected secretary of the Communist Youth League
1979,	Apr	Head of a youth delegation to Japan
	May	Elected vice-chairman of the Youth Federation

Gao Zhiguo (Kao Chih-kuo) 高治国

Posts held

CCP
Deputy secretary of Yunnan Province CP

1954,	May	Identified as director of the Administration of Power Industry, Southwest Administrative Council
1955,	Aug	Appointed assistant minister of power industry (until 1958)
1961,	Apr	Identified as 1st secretary, CP of Yunnan Province University
1963,	Oct	Identified as president of Yunnan Province University
1965,	Dec	Identified as secretary of Yunnan Province CP
1968		Disappears during the Cultural Revolution
1977,	Dec	First appearance after the Cultural Revolution: Elected vice-chairman of the Revolutionary Committee of Yunnan Province (until Dec 1979)
1979,	Jan	Identified as member of the Standing Committee of Yunnan Province CP (until May 1979)
	May	Identified as deputy secretary of Yunnan Province CP

Ge Buhai (Ke Pu-hai)  葛步海

Posts held

Government
Ambassador to Zambia

1950		Identified as secretary of the Democratic Youth League in Pingyuan Province
1951,	Oct	Elected council member of the Pingyuan Province People's Government
1953,	Mar	Identified as deputy secretary of the North China Work Committee, Democratic Youth League
	Jul	Elected member of the Democratic Youth League Central Committee
1954,	Mar	Identified as secretary of the North China Work Committee, Democratic Youth League
	Aug	Elected deputy for Hebei Province to the 1st NPC
1955,	Jan	Identified as counselor at the embassy in Czechoslovakia (until Jun 1960)
1960,	Aug	Identified as deputy director of the Protocol Department in the Ministry of Foreign Affairs
1964,	Sep	Identified as acting director of the Protocol Department in the Ministry of Foreign Affairs (until about 1966)
1972,	Apr	Appointed ambassador to Uganda (until Feb 1978)
1978,	Mar	Appointed ambassador to Zambia

Ge Shiying (Ke Shih-ying) 葛士英

Posts held

CCP
Member of the Standing Committee of Gansu Province CP

NPC
Deputy for Gansu Province to the 5th NPC

Provincial Administration
Vice-governor of Gansu Province

1950,	Jan	Identified as deputy secretary-general of the Gansu Province People's Government
1954,	Dec	Identified as member of the Gansu Province People's Council
1958,	Mar	Identified as vice-chairman of the Commission for the Tao River Project
	Aug	Identified as vice-governor of Gansu Province (until Cultural Revolution)
1967		Disappears during the Cultural Revolution
1977,	Dec	First appearance after the Cultural Revolution: Elected vice-chairman of the Revolutionary Committee of Gansu Province (until Dec 1979)
1978,	Feb	Elected deputy for Gansu Province to the 5th NPC
	Aug	Identified as member of the Standing Committee of Gansu Province CP
	Oct	Member of a friendship delegation to Japan
1979,	Dec	Elected vice-governor of Gansu Province

Geng Biao (Keng Piao)  耿飚

Posts held

CCP
Member of the Politburo of the CCP 11th Central Committee
Member of the CCP 11th Central Committee

Government
Vice-premier

NPC
Deputy for Hebei Province to the 5th NPC

Military
Major-general

Geng was born in 1909 in Liling County, Hunan Province. Around 1927 he joined a Communist guerrilla group. He joined the Red Workers-Peasants Army in 1930 which was based in the Jiangxi Soviet and commanded by Mao Zedong and Zhu De. In 1934-35 he took part in the Long March. Geng Biao commanded the regiment of the 1st Front Army which in January 1935 occupied the town of Zunyi where a few days later the CCP Conference took place from which Mao Zedong emerged as leader of the Party. Geng further distinguished himself during the crossing of the River Wu in Guizhou Province. From 1936 to 1937 he first attended a course, and then lectured, at the Red Army Academy. From 1938 to 1944 he commanded a brigade, later a column, of Shaanxi-Chahar-Hebei Military Region. In January 1946 he was head of the Communist Section of a joint KMT-CCP Military Committee to conduct peace negotiations with the rank of major-general. In late 1947 he served as chief of staff of Shaanxi-Chahar-Hebei Military Region. In the following year he was deputy commander of the 2nd Army, Northeast Field Army, and in early 1949 became commander of the 19th Army.

1950,	Jun	Appointed ambassador to Sweden (until Feb 1956)
	Nov	Appointed envoy to Denmark (until Mar 1955)
1951,	Mar	Appointed envoy to Finland (until Sep 1954)
1956,	Feb	Appointed ambassador to Pakistan (until Jan 1960)
1957,	Jun	Geng accompanies a Pakistani military delegation to China
1960,	Jan	Appointed vice-minister of foreign affairs (until Sep 1963)
	Aug	Member of a government delegation led by Minister of Foreign Affairs Chen Yi to Burma
1961,	Mar	Member of a government delegation led by Premier Zhou Enlai to Indonesia
1963,	Mar	Head of the Chinese section of the Sino-Pakistani Border Committee
	Sep	Appointed ambassador to Burma (until Mar 1967)
1965,	Jul	Geng accompanies Ne Win on his state visit to China
1969,	Apr	Elected member of the CCP Central Committee by the 9th Party Congress (confirmed in 1973 and 1977 by the 10th and 11th Congresses)

	Aug	Appointed ambassador to Albania (until Dec 1970)
1971,	Mar	Identified as director, International Liaison Department of the CCP Central Committee (until Mar 1979); member of a Party and government delegation to Vietnam
	Jul	Member of a Party and government delegation to North Korea
1974,	Aug	Member of a Party and government delegation to Romania
	Nov	Member of a Party and government delegation to Albania
1975,	Sep	Deputy head of a Party and government delegation to North Korea
1977,	Aug	Elected member of the CCP Politburo by the 11th Party Congress
1978,	Feb	Elected deputy for Hebei Province to the 5th NPC
	Mar	Appointed vice-premier
	May	Member of a Party and government delegation led by Hua Guofeng to North Korea
	Jun	Head of a government delegation to Pakistan to attend the inauguration of the Karakorum Road built with Chinese aid
	Jul	Head of a government delegation to Trinidad and Tobago, Jamaica, Guiana, and Malta
	Oct	Head of a government delegation to Congo (Brazzaville), Guinea, Mali, Ghana, and Nigeria (until Nov)
	Dec	Head of a government delegation to Algeria attending the funeral of Houri Boumedienne
1979,	May	Member of a government delegation to Sweden, Norway, Finland, and Iceland

Geng is married to Zhao Lanxiang.

Geng Changsuo (Keng Ch'ang-so) 耿长锁

Posts held

Provincial Administration
Vice-chairman of the People's Congress of Hebei Province

Geng was born in 1900 in Wugong, Raoyang County, Hebei Province. Since 1943 he was engaged in agricultural cooperation work.

1952,	May	Geng is commended as an agricultural labor model
1954,	Aug	Elected deputy for Hebei Province to the 1st NPC (reelected in 1958 and 1964 to the 2nd and 3rd NPCs)
1958,	Apr	Identified as chairman of Wugong People's Commune
1968,	Feb	Appointed vice-chairman of the Revolutionary Committee of Hebei Province
1971,	May	Elected member of the Standing Committee of Hebei Province CP (no later mention in this post)
1979,	Jul	First reference to Geng, after a full decade, as vice-chairman of the Revolutionary Committee of Hebei Province (until Jan 1980)
1980,	Feb	Elected vice-chairman of the People's Congress of Hebei Province

Geng Daoming (Keng Tao-ming) 耿道明

Posts held

Others
Director of the People's Insurance Company
Vice-chairman, Board of Directors of the Bank of China

1965,	Dec	Identified as director of the Political Department, People's Bank of China
1972,	Apr	Identified as vice-president of the Bank of China
1973,	Apr	Head of a bankers' delegation to Albania, Algeria, Lebanon, and Great Britain
	May	
1975,	Mar	Identified as acting manager-general of the Bank of China (until 1976)
	Apr	Head of an insurance delegation to North Korea
1976,	Mar	Identified as vice-chairman, Board of Directors of the Bank of China
1977,	Nov	Head of a banking delegation to Nepal

Geng Qichang (Keng Ch'i-ch'ang) 耿起昌

Posts held

CCP
Member of the CCP 11th Central Committee
Secretary of Henan Province CP

1957,	Oct	Identified as secretary of Xinxiang Special District CP; publication of an article in Rural Work Bulletin on intensive cultivation at the Mengzhuan People's Commune in Hui County
1968,	Jan	Elected vice-chairman of the newly established Revolutionary Committee for Henan Province (until Nov 1977)
1969,	Apr	Elected alternate member of the CCP Central Committee by the 9th Party Congress (until Aug 1973)
1971,	Mar	Elected secretary of Henan Province CP
1973,	Aug	Elected member of the CCP Central Committee by the 10th Party Congress (confirmed in 1977 by the 11th Party Congress)

Geng's last public appearance was in August 1977. According to unconfirmed reports, he has been purged.

Gong Dafei (Kung Ta-fei) 宫达非

Posts held

Government
Vice-minister of foreign affairs

1953,	Aug	Identified as 1st secretary at the embassy in Burma
1957,	Sep	Elected council member of the Sino-Syrian Friendship Association
1958,	Sep	Elected council member of the Sino-Iraq Friendship Association
	Oct	Appointed council member of the Institute of Foreign Affairs

1959, Jul Identified as deputy director of the West Asia and Africa Department in the Ministry of Foreign Affairs (until 1960)

1960, Aug Identified as counselor at the embassy in Morocco (until 1963)

1963, Oct Identified as deputy director of the West Asia and Africa Department in the Ministry of Foreign Affairs

1965, Mar Identified as deputy director of the Africa Department in the Ministry of Foreign Affairs (until 1969)

May-Jun Member of a Chinese government delegation under Ji Pengfei to Guinea, Morocco, Ghana, Mali, Congo (Brazzaville), Central African Republic

Sep-Oct Member of a Chinese government delegation under Chen Yi to Pakistan, Syria, Algeria, Mali, Guinea, and Afghanistan

1970, Feb Identified as deputy director of the West Asia and Africa Department in the Ministry of Foreign Affairs (until Nov 1970)

Dec Member of a government delegation to Iraq; appointed ambassador to Iraq (until Jan 1973)

1971, Mar Gong conducts negotiations in Kuwait for the establishment of diplomatic relations

1973, Jan Appointed ambassador to Zaire (until Jul 1978)

1976, Aug Gong conducts negotiations in the Central African Republic for the reestablishment of diplomatic relations

1978, Aug Identified as assistant minister of foreign affairs

1979, Dec Identified as vice-minister of foreign affairs

Gong Tianmin (Kung T'ien-min) 巩天民

Posts held

Others
Member of the Standing Committee of the 5th CPPCC

In September 1949 Gong took part in the 1st CPPCC as a delegate representing Industrial and Commercial Circles.

1953, Oct Identified as vice-chairman of the Federation of Industry and Commerce (until Cultural Revolution?)

1954, Aug Elected deputy for Shenyang Municipality to the 1st NPC

Dec Elected member of the 2nd CPPCC (confirmed in 1959 and 1964)

1955, Mar Identified as vice-chairman of the CPPCC Liaoning Province Section

1958, Jun Identified as vice-governor of Liaoning Province

1959, Mar Elected deputy for Liaoning Province to the 2nd NPC (reelected in 1964 to the 3rd NPC)

1965, Jan Elected member of the Standing Committee of the 4th CPPCC

1967 Disappears during the Cultural Revolution

1978, Mar First appearance after the Cultural Revolution: Elected member of the Standing Committee of the 5th CPPCC

Gong Weizhen (Kung Wei-chen) 宫維桢

Posts held

CCP
Member of the Standing Committee of Jiangsu Province CP

Provincial Administration
Vice-governor of Jiangsu Province

1954, Aug Elected deputy for Jiangsu Province to the 1st NPC (reelected to the 2nd and 3rd NPCs in 1958 and 1964)

1979, May First appearance after the Cultural Revolution

Jul Member of the National Games Organizing Committee

Sep Identified as member of the Standing Committee of Jiangsu Province CP and vice-chairman of the Revolutionary Committee of Jiangsu Province (until Dec 1979)

Dec Elected vice-governor of Jiangsu Province

Gong Zirong (Kung Tzu-jung) 龔子荣

Posts held

CCP
Secretary of Guangdong Province CP

1954, Oct Identified as deputy secretary-general of the State Council (until Mar 1965)

1956, Sep Elected alternate member of the CCP Control Commission (until 1962)

1958, Oct Identified as deputy director of the General Office of the CCP Central Committee

1963 Identified as member of the CCP Control Commission

1965, Jan Elected member of the Standing Committee of the 4th CPPCC

1967 Disappears during the Cultural Revolution

1979, May First appearance after the Cultural Revolution: Identified as secretary of Guangdong Province CP

Gu Dachun (Ku Ta-ch'un) 顾大椿

Posts held

CCP
Secretary of Hubei Province CP
Acting 1st secretary of Wuhan Municipality CP

NPC
Deputy for Hubei Province to the 5th NPC

Mass Organization
Vice-president of the Federation of Trade Unions

1953, May Identified as member of the Executive Council of the Federation of Trade Unions (until Jan 1967)

1955, Oct Identified as director of the Production Department of the Federation of Trade Unions (until Nov 1957)

1957, Aug Elected deputy secretary-general of the 8th Trade Unions' Congress

1959, Apr Elected member of the 3rd CPPCC (reelected in 1964 by the 4th CPPCC)

1961, Apr Head of a trade union delegation to Albania

1966, Oct Elected vice-chairman of the Federation of Trade Unions

1967, Jan Accused as a counterrevolutionary revisionist and disappears

1973, Oct First appearance after the Cultural Revolution

1977, May Identified as secretary of Hubei Province CP

       Nov Identified as acting 1st secretary of Wuhan Municipality CP

1978, Jan Elected vice-chairman, Revolutionary Committee of Hubei Province (until Dec 1979)

       Feb Elected deputy for Hubei Province to the 5th NPC

       Apr Identified in his previous post as vice-chairman of the Federation of Trade Unions (confirmed Nov 1979)

1979, May Identified as 1st secretary of the Hubei Province Discipline Inspection Committee

Gu Fangzhou (Ku Fang-chou) 顾方舟

Posts held

Others
Vice-president of the Academy of Medical Sciences

1978, Sep Identified as vice-president of the Academy of Medical Sciences

Gu Gengyu (Ku Keng-yü) 古耕禹

Posts held

Others
Member of the Standing Committee of the 5th CPPCC
Director of the Board of Directors, China International Trust and Investment Corporation
Vice-chairman of the Executive Committee, Federation of Industrialists and Businessmen

After graduating from St. John's University in Shanghai, Gu entered his father's business in 1925. Shortly afterwards he went to Sichuan to work for the Sichuan Animal Products Company. In 1947 he visited Great Britain.

1956   Identified as chief of the Animal Products Trade Section of Guangzhou Export Commodities Fair; identified as manager of China Animal Products Export Company (the latter post until Cultural Revolution)

1957   Six months' visit of Great Britain, France, the Federal Republic of Germany, and Switzerland

1959, Apr Delegate representing the China Democratic National Construction Association at the 3rd CPPCC; elected a member of the 3rd CPPCC (confirmed in 1964 by the 4th CPPCC)

1967   Disappears during the Cultural Revolution

1978, Mar Elected member of the Standing Committee of the 5th CPPCC

1979, Jan Identified as advisor to the China National Native Produce and Animal By-Products Import and Export Corporation

       Oct Appointed director of the Board of Directors, China International Trust and Investment Corporation; elected vice-chairman of the Executive Committee, Federation of Industrialists and Businessmen

       Dec Member of a CPPCC delegation to Romania

Gu Gongxu (Ku Kung-hsü) 顾功叙

Posts held

NPC
Deputy for Zhejiang Province to the 5th NPC

Others
Deputy director of the Institute of Geophysics, Academy of Sciences
President of the Geophysics Society
Member of the UNESCO International Advisory Committee on Earthquake Risks

Gu was born in 1907. In 1926 he was awarded an M.A. degree by the Colorado School of Mines in the United States. He then continued his studies at the California Institute of Technology.

1950, Jun Identified as deputy director of the Institute of Geophysics at the Academy of Sciences

1954, Aug Elected deputy for Zhejiang Province to the 1st NPC (reelected in 1958 and 1964 to the 2nd and 3rd NPCs)

1955, May Identified as member of the Standing Committee, Department of Earth Sciences of the Academy of Sciences

1958, Sep Elected president of the Geophysics Society

1967   Disappears during the Cultural Revolution

1971, Jul First appearance after the Cultural Revolution

1975, Nov Identified as vice-chairman of the Revolutionary Committee, Institute of Geophysics of the Academy of Sciences; head of a seismological study group visiting Japan

1976, May Head of a geophysical study group visiting Iran

1977, Aug Identified as chairman of the National Committee for Geodesy and Geophysics; head of a delegation to the General Assembly of the International Union of Geodesy and Geophysics

       Dec Identified as president of the Geophysics Society; identified as member of the UNESCO International Advisory Committee on Earthquake Risks

1978,   Feb Elected deputy for Zhejiang Province to
              the 5th NPC
         Apr Identified as deputy director of the Insti-
              tute for Geophysics, Academy of Sciences

Gu Kangle (Ku K'ang-lo)   顾康乐

Posts held

NPC
Member of the Standing Committee of the
5th NPC
Deputy for Tianjin Municipality to the
5th NPC

1964,   Sep Elected deputy for Sichuan Province to
              the 3rd NPC
1973,   Oct Identified as a scientist
1975,   Mar Identified as deputy to the 4th NPC
1978,   Feb Elected deputy for Tianjin Municipality to
              the 5th NPC
         Mar Elected member of the Standing Commit-
              tee of the 5th NPC

Gu Ming (Ku Ming)   顾 明

Posts held

Government
Vice-minister of the State Foreign Investment Commission
Vice-minister of the State Planning Commission

NPC
Deputy for Shanghai Municipality to the
5th NPC

1962,   Mar Appointed deputy director of the Beijing
              College of Light Industry (until 1965)
1965,   Feb Appointed member of the Economics
              Commission under the State Council (un-
              til 1966)
1966,   Jan Appointed vice-chairman of the Capital
              Construction   Commission   (until
              about 1967)
1972,   May First appearance after the Cultural Revo-
              lution: Identified as vice-minister of the
              State Planning Commission; deputy head
              of the Chinese delegation to the UN Con-
              ference on the Environment in Stockholm
1978,   Feb Elected deputy for Shanghai Municipality
              to the 5th NPC
         May Head of an economic delegation to Great
              Britain and France
         Nov Head of a government delegation to Yugo-
              slavia
1980,   Feb Appointed vice-minister of the State For-
              eign Investment Commission

Gu Mu (Ku Mu)   谷 牧

Posts held

CCP
Member of the CCP 11th Central Com-
mittee
Member of the Secretariat of the Central
Committee

Government
Vice premier
Minister of the State Capital Construction
Commission
Member of the State Financial and Eco-
nomic Commission

NPC
Deputy for Shandong Province to the
5th NPC

Military
Political commissar of the PLA Capital
Construction Engineering Corps

Others
Vice-chairman of the Central Patriotic
Health Campaign Committee

Gu was born in 1914 in Rongchen County, Shandong
Province. He joined the Communist Youth League in 1931
and the CCP the following year. He took part in the
activities of the League of Left-wing writers in Beijing.
During the Anti-Japanese War he served as secretary of
the Binhai Area Party Committee, political commissar of
the Binhai Military Sub-district and as Secretary of the
Central-South Shandong Party Committee.

1950,   Nov Identified as mayor of Jinan and member
              of the People's Government of Shandong
              Province (probably until Jul 1952)
1952,   Aug Identified as director of the Propaganda
              Department of Shanghai Municipality CP
              (until 1954)
1954,   Oct Appointed vice-chairman of the Construc-
              tion Commission under the State Council
              (until Nov 1956)
1956,   Nov Appointed vice-chairman of the Economic
              Commission (until Apr 1965)
1957,   Sep Appointed deputy director of the 3rd Staff
              Office under the State Council (abolished
              in Sep 1959)
1959,   Mar Elected deputy for Shandong Province to
              the NPC (confirmed in 1964 by the
              3rd NPC)
1964,   Apr Identified as director of the Political
              Work Department, CCP Central Commit-
              tee Department of Industry and Communi-
              cations
1965,   Mar Appointed chairman of the Capital Con-
              struction Commission
1967   Disappears during the Cultural Revolution
1972,   Dec Reactivated after the Cultural Revolution
1973,   Jun Identified in his previous post as minister
              of the Capital Construction Commission
              under the State Council
         Aug Elected to first term as member of the
              CCP Central Committee by the 10th Par-
              ty Congress
1975,   Jan Elected vice-premier by the 4th NPC
              (confirmed in 1978 by the 5th NPC)

1978, Feb Elected deputy for Shandong Province to the 5th NPC
Apr Appointed vice-chairman of the Central Patriotic Health Campaign Committee
May Head of a government delegation to France, Belgium, Switzerland, Denmark, Federal Republic of Germany
1979, Apr Identified as political commissar of the PLA Capital Construction Engineering Corps
Jul Appointed member of the State Financial and Economic Commission
Sep Head of a government delegation to Japan
1980, Feb Elected member of the Secretariat of the 11th Central Committee by its 5th Plenum

Gu is married to Mou Feng.

Gu Xiaobo (Ku Hsiao-po)　谷小波

Posts held

Government
Ambassador to Jordan

1952, Apr Vice-chairman of the Trade Union of Tianjin Municipality (until Aug 1955)
1953, May Elected member of the Executive Council of the Federation of Trade Unions
1955, Aug Elected chairman of the Tianjin Trade Union
1958, Jul Identified as vice-chairman of the Trade Union of Hebei Province (until 1960)
Oct Elected deputy for Hebei Province to the 2nd NPC
1959 Identified as vice-president of the Tianjin Radio Broadcast Correspondence University
1962, Apr Appointed ambassador to Sudan (until 1965)
1973, Jun Appointed ambassador to Benin (until Oct 1977)
1977, Dec Appointed ambassador to Jordan

Gu Xiulian (Ku Hsiu-lien) (f)　顾秀莲

Posts held

CCP
Alternate member of the CCP 11th Central Committee

Government
Vice-minister of the State Planning Commission

1970, Oct Identified as a cadre in the State Council
1973, Oct Identified as vice-minister of the State Planning Commission
1977, Aug Elected alternate member of the CCP Central Committee by the 11th Party Congress

Gu Yunting (Ku Yün-t'ing)　谷云亭

Posts held

CCP
Secretary of Tianjin Municipality CP

NPC
Deputy for Tianjin Municipality to the 5th NPC

1950, Mar Identified as deputy director of the Organization Department of Hebei Province CP
1955, May Identified as deputy secretary of Hebei Province CP (until 1957)
1957, Jun Identified as secretary of Hebei Province CP (until May 1958)
1958, May Identified as secretary of Tianjin Municipality CP (until Cultural Revolution)
1959, Feb Identified as member of the Standing Committee of Hebei Province CP (until Cultural Revolution)
1968 Disappears during the Cultural Revolution
1977, Dec First appearance after the Cultural Revolution: Identified as secretary of Tianjin Municipality CP
1978, Feb Elected deputy for Tianjin Municipality to the 5th NPC

Gu Zhibiao (Ku Chih-piao)　谷志标

Posts held

NPC
Deputy for Sichuan Province to the 5th NPC

Provincial Administration
Vice-chairman of the People's Congress of Sichuan Province

Others
Member of the Standing Committee of the 5th CPPCC

Around 1941 Gu served as deputy commander of Shanxi-Suiyuan Military District. In 1949 he was deputy director of the Public Security Bureau of West Sichuan Administrative Office.

1957, Jun Identified as procurator of Sichuan Province Procuracy; by-elected deputy for Sichuan Province to the 1st NPC (confirmed in 1958 and 1964 by the 2nd and 3rd NPCs)
1965, Dec Elected vice-chairman of the CPPCC in Sichuan
1966 Disappears during the Cultural Revolution
1978, Feb First appearance after the Cultural Revolution: Elected deputy for Sichuan Province to the 5th NPC
Mar Elected member of the Standing Committee of the 5th CPPCC
1979, Dec Elected vice-chairman of the People's Congress of Sichuan Province

Gu Zhuoxin (Ku Cho-hsin) 顾卓新

<u>Posts held</u>

CCP
Secretary of Anhui Province CP

Provincial Administration
Chairman of the People's Congress of Anhui Province

Gu was born in 1910 in Liaoning Province. In 1946 he was secretary of the Finance Department in the Government of Shanxi-Hebei-Shandong-Henan Border Region. In 1948 he was vice-governor of Songjiang Province, and in mid-1949 director of the Finance Department of the Northeast China People's Government (until 1952).

1950,	Aug	Appointed director of the Planning Committee for Financial and Economic Affairs, Northeast China People's Government (until Sep 1954)
1954,	Nov	Vice-chairman of the State Planning Commission (until Sep 1963)
1959,	Feb	Member of an economic delegation to Moscow
	Apr	Elected member of the National Committee, 3rd CPPCC (reelected in 1964 to the 4th CPPCC)
1961,	Apr	Member of an economic delegation to Moscow
1963,	Oct	Appointed secretary of the Northeast Bureau in the CCP Central Committee and director of the Planning Committee
1968,	May	Accused as Liu Shaoqi's agent in Liaoning and relieved of his posts
1977,	Jun	First appearance after the Cultural Revolution: Gu is posted to Anhui Province on instruction of Hua Guofeng and the CCP Central Committee
	Oct	Identified as secretary of Anhui Province CP
1978,	Jan	Elected vice-chairman of the Revolutionary Committee of Anhui Province (until Dec 1979)
	Oct	Member of a government delegation to the Federal Republic of Germany and France under Fang Yi
1979,	Dec	Elected chairman of the People's Congress of Anhui Province

Guan Jian (Kuan Chien) (f) 关 健

<u>Posts held</u>

NPC
Deputy for Shanghai Municipality to the 5th NPC

Mass Organization
Vice-president of the Women's Federation
President of the Shanghai Women's Federation

1961,	Feb	Identified as president of the Shanghai Women's Federation
1964,	Sep	Elected deputy for Shanghai Municipality to the 3rd NPC
1967		Disappears during the Cultural Revolution

1973,	Feb	Identified as member of the Revolutionary Committee of Shanghai Municipality (until Oct 1977)
1978,	Feb	Elected deputy for Shanghai Municipality to the 5th NPC
	Jul	Elected president of the Shanghai Women's Federation
	Sep	Elected vice-president of the Women's Federation
1979,	Apr	Head of a women's delegation to Sudan
	Jun	Member of the Draft Laws Committee at the 2nd Session of the 5th NPC

Guan Junting (Kuan Chün-t'ing) 官峻亭

<u>Posts held</u>

CCP
Secretary of Zhejiang Province CP

NPC
Deputy for the PLA to the 5th NPC

Military
Commander of Zhejiang Military District

1978,	Feb	Elected deputy for the PLA to the 5th NPC
1978,	Jun	Identified as commander of Zhejiang Military District
	Oct	Identified as secretary of Zhejiang Province CP

Guan Ruiwu (Kuan Jui-wu) (f) 关瑞梧

<u>Posts held</u>

Others
Member of the Standing Committee of the 5th CPPCC

1963,	Sep	Identified as member of the Executive Committee of the Women's Federation
1975,	Sep	Identified as a cadre of the Cultural and Art Circles
1978,	Mar	Elected member of the Standing Committee of the 5th CPPCC

Guan Shanfu (Kuan Shan-fu) 关山复

<u>Posts held</u>

Government
Member of the State Nationalities Affairs Commission

NPC
Deputy for Beijing Municipality to the 5th NPC

Others
Deputy chief procurator, Supreme People's Procuratorate

Guan belongs to the Manchu minority. He was born in 1906 in Jilin Province. He graduated from the Beijing Normal University. He joined the CCP when a student. After graduation he returned to Manchuria and participated in anti-Japan guerrilla activities led by Zhou Baozhong. About 1937 he studied at the Anti-Japanese Military and Political Academy in Yan'an. Later he served as deputy director of the Propaganda Department in the Jilin-Liaoning Administrative Office under the Manchuria CP. After the Japanese surrender he served inter alia as secretary-general of Jilin Province CP.

1952		Identified as deputy secretary-general of the United Front Work Department under the Northeast Bureau of the CCP Central Committee
1953,	Jan	Identified as a member of the Northeast Administrative Council (until Sep 1954)
1954,	Aug	Elected deputy for Jilin Province to the 1st NPC (reelected in 1958 and 1964 to the 2nd and 3rd NPCs)
1955,	Sep	Identified as director of the United Front Work Department, Jilin Province CP
1956,	Jul	Identified as secretary of Jilin Province CP (until Cultural Revolution)
1957,	Nov	Head of a Jilin Province delegation to the celebration ceremonies of the October Revolution in Vladivostok
1964,	Apr	Identified as director of the Propaganda Department in the Northeast China Bureau of the CCP Central Committee (until Cultural Revolution)
1965,	Apr	Member of a CCP delegation to North Korea (head: Song Renqiong)
1967,	Jun	Denounced as a counterrevolutionary and purged
1977,	Oct	First appearance after the Cultural Revolution
1978,	Feb	Elected deputy for Beijing Municipality to the 5th NPC
1979,	May	Appointed member of the State Nationalities Affairs Commission
1980,	Feb	Appointed deputy chief procurator, Supreme People's Procuratorate

Guan Xuesi (Kuan Hsüeh-szu)

Posts held

Provincial Administration
Vice-governor of Sichuan Province

1977,	Dec	Elected vice-chairman of the Revolutionary Committee of Sichuan Province (until Dec 1979)
1979,	Dec	Elected vice-governor of Sichuan Province

Guan Zehai (Kuan Tse-hai)

Posts held

CCP
Alternate member of the CCP 11th Central Committee

1977,	Aug	Elected alternate member of the CCP Central Committee by the 11th Party Congress
	Sep	Identified as a cadre in Yunnan Province

Guo Chao (Kuo Ch'ao)

Posts held

CCP
Secretary of Fujian Province CP

Provincial Administration
Vice-governor of Fujian Province

1949,	Oct	Appointed deputy director of the Personnel Department under the Ministry of Trade
1950,	Jul	Identified as deputy director of the Organization Department of Guizhou Province CP
1958,	Nov	Identified as vice-governor of Yunnan Province (until Aug 1968)
1960,	May	Identified as secretary of Yunnan Province CP (until Aug 1968)
1968,	Aug	Guo disappears
1973,	Apr	First appearance after the Cultural Revolution
	Oct	Identified as deputy secretary of Yunnan Province CP (until 1977)
1979,	Oct	Identified as secretary of Fujian Province CP and as vice-chairman of the Revolutionary Committee, Fujian Province (latter post until Dec 1979)
	Dec	Elected vice-governor of Fujian Province

Guo Cheng (Kuo Ch'eng)

Posts held

Provincial Administration
Vice-chairman of the People's Government of Guangxi Autonomous Region

Guo belongs to the Zhuang minority and was born in Guangxi Province.

1954,	Sep	Elected deputy for Guangxi Province to the 1st NPC (reelected in 1958 and 1964 to the 2nd and 3rd NPCs)
	Oct	Identified as vice-chairman of the Financial and Economic Committee, People's Government of West Guangxi Province
1955,	Feb	Identified as a member of the People's Council of Guangxi Province
	Sep	Identified as vice-chairman of the Planning Committee, People's Council of Guangxi Province
1962,	Nov	Identified as director of the Finance Department, People's Council of Guangxi Province
1966		Guo disappears
1979,	Dec	First appearance after the Cultural Revolution: Elected vice-chairman of the People's Government of Guangxi Autonomous Region

Guo Dihuo (Kuo Ti-huo)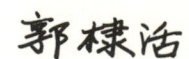

Posts held

NPC
Deputy for Guangdong Province to the 5th NPC

Provincial Administration
Vice-governor of Guangdong Province

Others
Member of the Standing Committee of the 5th CPPCC
Vice-chairman of the China Democratic National Construction Association
Director of the Board of Directors, China International Trust and Investment Corporation

Guo was born in 1898 in Australia. He studied textile industry at New Bedford Textile School in the United States. After his return to China in 1926 he was first submanager and later manager of the Shanghai Wing On Textile Company. In 1949 he was in addition chairman of the Preparatory Committee for the Shanghai Textile Industry Trade Union. In September of that year he took part in the 1st CPPCC.

1950,	Jan	Identified as member of the East China Military and Administrative Council and as member of the Shanghai People's Government
1951,	May	Identified as member of the Financial and Economic Committee of Shanghai People's Government
1953,	Oct	Elected member of the Executive Committee and of the Standing Committee of the Federation of Industry and Commerce
1954,	Aug	Elected deputy for Shanghai Municipality to the 1st NPC; identified as assistant manager-general of the Wing On Textile Company
	Nov	Identified as member of the Board of Directors, representing private shares, of the Bank of China
1955,	Apr	Elected member of the Standing Committee, China Democratic National Construction Association (until Mar 1960)
1956,	Oct	Elected vice-chairman of the Returned Overseas Chinese Association (until Cultural Revolution)
	Nov	Member of an NPC delegation to the USSR, Romania, and Czechoslovakia
1958,	Aug	Identified as vice-governor of Guangdong Province
	Sep	Elected deputy for Guangdong Province to the 2nd NPC (confirmed in 1964 by the 3rd NPC
1959,	Feb	Identified as member of the Standing Committee of Guangdong Province CP
	Apr	Elected member of the Standing Committee of the 3rd CPPCC (confirmed in 1965 by the 4th CPPCC)
1960,	Mar	Identified as vice-chairman of the China Democratic National Construction Commission
1967		Disappears during the Cultural Revolution
1972,	Feb	First appearance after the Cultural Revolution
1978,	Feb	Elected deputy for Guangdong Province to the 5th NPC
	Mar	Elected member of the Standing Committee of the 5th CPPCC
1979,	Jun	Member of the Committee to Examine Proposals at the 2nd Session of the 5th NPC

| | Oct | Appointed director of the Board of Directors, China International Trust and Investment Corporation; reelected vice-chairman of the China Democratic National Construction Association |
| | Dec | Elected vice-governor of Guangdong Province |

Guo Feng (Kuo Feng)

Posts held

CCP
Secretary of Liaoning Province CP
1st secretary of Shenyang Municipality CP

| 1979, | Dec | Identified as secretary of Liaoning Province CP |
| 1980, | Jan | Identified as 1st secretary of Shenyang Municipality CP |

Guo Fenglian (Kuo Feng-lien) (f) 郭风莲

Posts held

CCP
Alternate member of the CCP 11th Central Committee
Member of the Standing Committee of Shanxi Province CP
Secretary, CP of Dazhai Production Brigade

NPC
Member of the Standing Committee of the 5th NPC
Deputy for Shanxi Province to the 5th NPC

Others
Vice-chairman of the Revolutionary Committee of Dazhai Production Brigade

Guo was born in 1948 in a family of poor peasants in Shanxi Province.

1961		After finishing elementary school Guo starts as a farm laborer in Dazhai
1963		Following a flood catastrophe in Dazhai, Guo distinguishes herself as leader of a female shock team called "Iron Maidens Team"
1966		Member of the CCP
1973		Elected secretary, CP of Dazhai Production Brigade (successor of Chen Yonggui)
	Apr	Identified as member of the Standing Committee, Revolutionary Committee of Shanxi Province (until May 1977) and as vice-chairman, Revolutionary Committee of Dazhai Production Brigade (until May 1974)
1974,	May	Identified as chairman of the Revolutionary Committee of Dazhai Production Brigade
	Sep	Deputy head of a goodwill delegation to Japan
1975,	Sep	Member of a friendship delegation under Chen Yonggui to Mexico

Guo Hongtao

1977,   May   Identified as vice-chairman of the Revolutionary Committee of Shanxi Province (until Jun 1979?) and as member of the Standing Committee of Shanxi Province CP

        Aug   Elected alternate member of the CCP Central Committee by the 11th Party Congress

1978,   Feb   Elected deputy for Shanxi Province to the 5th NPC

        Mar   Elected member of the Standing Committee of the 5th NPC

        Jul   Advisor to an agricultural delegation to the United States

1979,   Jun   Member of the Credentials Committee at the 2nd Session of the 5th NPC

Guo Hongtao (Kuo Hung-t'ao)   郭洪涛

Posts held

Government
Vice-minister of the State Economic Commission
Member of the State Nationalities Affairs Commission

Others
Member of the Standing Committee of the 5th CPPCC

Guo was born in 1904 in Mizhi, Shaanxi Province. In 1927 he joined the Communists and was appointed secretary of Shaanxi Province CP. Shortly afterwards he was arrested by the Nationalist Government and held a prisoner until 1933. In 1935 he was made deputy secretary of the Shaanxi-Gansu-Shanxi Border District CP. In 1937 he organized guerrilla bases in Shandong Province. In 1940 he was secretary of Shandong Province CP. In 1945 he headed the Railways Department of the Northeast Democratic Joint Army.

1949,   Oct   Identified as director of the Tianjin Railway Administrative Bureau

1952,   Aug   Identified as vice-minister of railways (until 1958?)

1954,   Nov   Identified as deputy director of the 6th Administrative Office under the State Council (until Sep 1959)

1958,   Jul   Identified as deputy commander of the PLA Railway Corps (until Cultural Revolution?)

        Oct   Appointed vice-chairman of the State Economic Commission (until Cultural Revolution)

1967,   May   Branded as a traitor and "three-anti element" and purged

1976,   Jan   First appearance after the Cultural Revolution

1978,   Mar   Elected member of the Standing Committee of the 5th CPPCC

        Oct   Identified as vice-minister of the State Economic Commission

1979,   May   Appointed member of the State Nationalities Affairs Commission

Guo Huaruo (Kuo Huao-jo)   郭化若

Posts held

NPC
Member of the Standing Committee of the 5th NPC
Deputy for the PLA to the 5th NPC

Military
Lieutenant-general
Deputy commandant of the PLA Academy of Military Science

Guo was born in 1906 in Jiangsu (Fujian?) Province. In 1925 he graduated from a course at Whampoa Military Academy and in 1927 he studied at the Moscow Artillery School. Following his return to China in 1928 he served as chief of staff of the Central Red Army Headquarters and as instructor at the Red Army School. After the Long March he lectured in Yan'an at the Anti-Japan Military and Political Academy. In 1945 he became commandant of the Artillery School. In 1945 he commanded a column of the New 4th Army. In 1949 he was political commissar of the 9th Army, 3rd Field Army.

1949,   Oct   Identified as commander of Wusong-Shanghai Garrison District

        Dec   Identified as member of the East China Military and Administrative Council (until 1953)

1951,   Jun   Identified as commander of the 33rd Army

1953,   Jan   Appointed member of the East China Administrative Council (until 1954)

1955,   Sep   Appointed lieutenant-general

1957,   Aug   Identified as deputy commander of Nanjing Military Region (until Cultural Revolution)

1959,   Apr   Elected member of the Standing Committee of the 4th CPPCC (confirmed in 1965 by the 5th CPPCC)

1967   Disappears during the Cultural Revolution

1974,   Feb   First appearance after the Cultural Revolution

1975,   May   Referred to as member of the Standing Committee of the 4th CPPCC

1978,   Feb   Identified as commandant of the PLA Academy of Military Science; elected deputy for the PLA to the 5th NPC

        Mar   Elected member of the Standing Committee of the 5th NPC

Guo Jian (Kuo Chien) (f)   郭 建

Posts held

Government
Vice-minister of communications

Guo was born in 1913. In 1935 she took part in anti-Japanese activities as a student of Qinghua University.

1950   Identified as director of the Industry and Commerce Department in the North Jiangsu Administrative Office

1953,   Aug   Identified as vice-chairman of the Financial and Economic Affairs Committee of Shanghai People's Government

1955,   Feb   Identified as a member of Shanghai People's Government
1957,   Sep   Elected member of the Executive Committee of the Women's Federation (until Cultural Revolution)
1958,   Nov   Identified as chairman of the Shanghai Municipal Women's Federation (until 1961)
         Dec   Member of a women's delegation to Cambodia and Vietnam
1961,   Jan   Deputy head of a delegation to the Afro-Asian Women's Conference in Cairo
         Mar   Head of a women's delegation to Japan
         Oct   Elected secretary of the Women's Federation
         Dec   Member of a women's delegation to Indonesia
1962,   Mar   Member of a delegation to the World Conference of Women for Disarmament in Vienna
         Sep   Member of a women's delegation to Cuba
         Nov   Member of a delegation to the Executive Meeting of the International Women's Democratic Federation in the German Democratic Republic
         Dec   Identified as vice-chairman of the Sino-Cuban Friendship Association
1963,   Jun   Deputy head of a delegation to Moscow
1964,   Feb   Head of a women's delegation to Guinea
         Mar   Head of a delegation to the 6th Conference of the Afro-Asian People's Solidarity Committee in Algeria
         May   Deputy head of a trade union delegation to Romania
         Sep   Elected deputy for Hunan Province to the 3rd NPC
         Oct   Head of a women's delegation to Bulgaria
1965,   Jan   Elected member of the Standing Committee of the 3rd NPC
         Jun   Elected vice-chairman of the Afro-Asian Solidarity Committee
         Oct   Head of a delegation to the International Women's Democratic Federation Meeting in Salzburg, Austria
1966,   Feb   Head of a women's delegation to Congo and Iraq
1967   Disappears during the Cultural Revolution
1977,   Nov   First appearance after the Cultural Revolution: Identified as vice-minister of communications
1978,   Apr   Appointed member of the Patriotic Health Campaign Committee
         Oct   Head of a Society of Civil Engineering delegation to the United States

Guo Qinan (Kuo Ch'i-nan)

Posts held

Provincial Administration
Vice-governor of Shanxi Province

1979,   Dec   Elected vice-governor of Shanxi Province

Guo Rongchang (Kuo Jung-ch'ang)

Posts held

CCP
Secretary of Guangdong Province CP

1976,   May   Identified as secretary of Guangdong Province CP
1977,   Jun   Identified as vice-chairman of the Revolutionary Committee of Guangdong Province (until 1977)

Guo Ruiren (Kuo Jui-jen)

Posts held

NPC
Deputy for Fujian Province to the 5th NPC

Provincial Administration
Vice-governor of Fujian Province

1961,   Mar   Identified as vice-chairman of the Federation of Returned Overseas Chinese, Fujian Province Branch
1964,   Sep   Elected deputy for Fujian Province to the 3rd NPC
1978,   Feb   Elected deputy for Fujian Province to the 5th NPC
1979,   Dec   Elected vice-governor of Fujian Province

Guo Shushen (Kuo Shu-shen)   郭述申

Posts held

CCP
Deputy secretary of the Commission for Inspecting Discipline under the CCP Central Committee

NPC
Member of the Standing Committee of the 5th NPC
Deputy for Liaoning Province to the 5th NPC

Guo was born in Hubei Province. In 1935 he was deputy director, and around 1936 director, of the Political Department, 15th Army Group of the Red Army. In 1946 he was head of the Political Department in Western Manchuria Military District.

1951,   Oct   Identified as member of the People's Government of Lüda (Lüshun-Dairen)
1953,   Sep   Identified as deputy secretary of Lüda Municipality CP
1957,   Oct   Identified as 1st secretary of Lüda Municipality CP
1958,   Dec   Elected deputy for Liaoning Province to the 2nd NPC
1963   Identified as member of the Control Committee of the CCP Central Committee
1964   Disappears
1974,   Nov   First appearance after the Cultural Revolution

1978, Feb Elected deputy for Liaoning Province to the 5th NPC
Mar Elected member of the Standing Committee of the 5th NPC
Dec Elected deputy secretary of the Commission for Inspecting Discipline under the CCP Central Committee

Guo Tixiang (Kuo T'i-hsiang) 郭体祥

Posts held

Provincial Administration
Vice-governor of Anhui Province

1978, Jan Elected vice-chairman of the Revolutionary Committee of Anhui Province (until Dec 1979)
1979, Dec Elected vice-governor of Anhui Province

Guo Wei (Kuo Wei) 郭渭

Posts held

CCP
Secretary-general of RMRB

1962, Oct Identified as managing director of the RMRB Publishing House
1976, Jan Identified as a cadre of a CCP Central Committee department
Dec Identified as a cadre of RMRB
Apr Identified as secretary-general of RMRB; Guo visits the Federal Republic of Germany

Guo Weicheng (Kuo Wei-ch'eng) 郭维城

Posts held

Government
Minister of Railways

Military
Major-general
Deputy commander of the PLA Railway Corps

Guo was born in 1912 in Liaoning Province. He is a graduate of Fudan University. In 1945 he was head of the Qiqihar Railway Bureau.

1955, Jul Identified as major-general and 2nd deputy commander of the PLA Railway Corps
1956, Oct Identified as deputy commander of the PLA Railway Corps
1974, Sep First appearance after the Cultural Revolution
1977, Jan Identified as deputy commander of the PLA Railway Corps and as 1st secretary, CP of Zhengzhou Railway Bureau
Jul Identified as vice-minister of railways (until Nov 1978)
1978, Sep Head of a railways delegation to France and the Federal Republic of Germany
Nov Identified as vice-minister of railways

Dec Identified as secretary of the Party Group of the Ministry of Railways
1979, Mar Head of a railway delegation to Japan
Jul Appointed member of the National Games Organizing Committee
Nov Head of a railway delegation to Great Britain

Guo Xianrui (Kuo Hsien-jui) 郭献瑞

Posts held

Provincial Administration
Vice-mayor of Beijing Municipality

Guo was born in Shanxi Province. Around 1947 he was deputy director of the Supply and Marketing Department of Shaanxi-Gansu-Ningxia Border District.

1950 Identified as director of the Association of Cooperatives of Hebei Province
1952, Jul Identified as deputy director of the North China Association of Cooperatives and as member, Board of Directors of the Federation of Cooperatives (until Nov 1953)
1953, Oct Identified as member of the Executive Committee, Federation of Industry and Commerce (until 1956)
Nov Identified as member, Board of Directors of the Federation of Supply and Marketing Cooperatives (until 1957)
1957, Dec Identified as vice-chairman, Board of Directors of the Federation of Supply and Marketing Cooperatives (until Cultural Revolution)
1960, Aug Appointed vice-minister of commerce (until Jul 1961)
1963, Nov Identified as director of the Financial and Trade Administrative Office, North China Bureau of the CCP Central Committee
1967 Disappears during the Cultural Revolution
1977, Dec First appearance after the Cultural Revolution: Elected vice-chairman of the Revolutionary Committee of Beijing Municipality (until Dec 1979)
1979, Dec Elected vice-mayor of Beijing Municipality

Guo Xilan (Kuo Hsi-lan) 郭锡兰

Posts held

CCP
Secretary of Tibet Autonomous Region CP

Provincial Administration
1st vice-chairman of the People's Government of Tibet Autonomous Region

Guo was born in 1918 in Shanxi Province.

1954, Jun Identified as council member of the People's Government of Xikang Province
1957, Dec Identified as secretary general, Work Committee of Tibet CP
1958, Nov Identified as political commissar of Tibet Military Region

1965,	Aug	Elected deputy for Tibet Autonomous Region to the 3rd NPC
	Sep	With the reorganization of the Work Committee of Tibet CP into the Secretariat of Tibet Autonomous Region CP, Guo is appointed secretary; elected vice-chairman of Tibet Autonomous Region (equivalent of provincial vice-governor)
1971,	May	Identified as vice-chairman of the Revolutionary Committee of Tibet Autonomous Region (until Aug 1979)
1973,	Jun	Identified as member of the Standing Committee of Tibet Autonomous Region CP (until May 1977)
1977,	May	Identified as deputy secretary of Tibet Autonomous Region (until Nov 1977)
	Nov	Elected secretary of Tibet Autonomous Region CP
1979,	Aug	Elected 1st vice-chairman of the People's Government of Tibet Autonomous Region

Guo Yaoqing (Kuo Yao-ch'ing) 郭耀卿

Posts held

CCP
Alternate member of the CCP 11th Central Committee
Secretary of Nanning Municipality CP

Guo belongs to the Zhuang minority.

1973,	Jun	Elected vice-chairman of the Trade Unions of Guangxi Autonomous Region (no later mention in this post)
	Aug	Elected to first term as alternate member of the CCP Central Committee by the 10th Party Congress
1974,	Dec	Guo takes part in the Peasants' Congress of Guangxi Autonomous Region
1975,	Sep	Identified as deputy secretary of Nanning Municipality CP (until Jun 1977)
1977,	Jun	Identified as secretary of Nanning Municipality CP
1978,	Sep	Identified as political commissar of the Nanning Militia Division

Guo Yingfu (Kuo Ying-fu) 郭暎福

Posts held

NPC
Member of the Standing Committee of the 5th NPC
Deputy for Beijing Municipality to the 5th NPC

Others
Chairman, Trade Union of the Beijing Railway Administration

Guo became known as head of the "Mao Zedong-Locomotive" team.

| 1975, | Jan | Elected member of the Standing Committee of the 4th NPC (confirmed in 1978 by the 5th NPC) |

| | Sep | Identified as chairman, Trade Union of the Beijing Railway Administration |
| 1977, | May | Member of an NPC delegation to Romania under Seypidin |

Guo Yingqiu (Kuo Ying-ch'iu) 郭影秋

Posts held

NPC
Deputy for Beijing Municipality to the 5th NPC

Others
Member of the Standing Committee of the 5th CPPCC

Guo was born in 1908 in Shandong Province.

1950		Identified as director of the Political Department, 2nd Field Army, and as secretary-general of the South Sichuan Administrative Office
1953,	Jan	Identified as vice-chairman of the People's Government of Yunnan Province
1955,	Feb	Identified as governor of Yunnan Province (until Mar 1957)
1956,	Jan	Identified as deputy secretary of Yunnan Province CP (until Mar 1957)
1957,	Nov	Identified as president of Nanjing University (until May 1963)
1958,	Oct	Elected deputy for Jiangsu Province to the 2nd NPC
1963,	May	Identified as vice-president of Beijing People's University
1964,	Sep	Elected deputy for Beijing Municipality to the 3rd NPC
1967,	May	Branded as a counterrevolutionary revisionist and purged
1972,	Mar	First appearance after the Cultural Revolution
1978,	Feb	Elected deputy for Beijing Municipality to the 5th NPC
	Mar	Elected member of the Standing Committee of the 5th CPPCC

Guo Yufeng (Kuo Yü-feng) 郭玉峯

Posts held

CCP
Member of the CCP 11th Central Committee

1958,		Identified as deputy director, Political Department of the 64th Corps
1960		Identified as director, Political Department of Dalian Garrison
1968		Identified as director, Subdepartment of Military Administration, United Front Work Department of the CCP Central Committee
1969,	Apr	Elected alternate member of the CCP Central Committee by the 9th Party Congress (until Aug 1973)
1972,	Sep	Deputy head of a delegation of Party workers to North Korea; identified as a

cadre in the Organization Department of the CCP Central Committee

| 1973, | Aug | Elected to first term as member of the CCP Central Committee by the 10th Party Congress |
| 1975, | Sep | Identified as director of the Organization Department of the CCP Central Committee (until Oct 1977) |

Guo has presumably been purged since his last public appearance in October 1977.

Guo Zhi (Kuo Chih)   郭　志

Posts held

CCP
Secretary of Hebei Province CP

NPC
Deputy for Hebei Province to the 5th NPC

Provincial Administration
Vice-governor of Hebei Province

1974,	Jan	Identified as member of the Standing Committee of Hebei Province CP
1977,	Aug	Identified as secretary of the CP (until Nov 1978), and as vice-chairman of the Revolutionary Committee, of Hebei Province (until Jan 1980)
1978,	Feb	Elected deputy for Hebei Province to the 5th NPC
	Oct	Member of a friendship delegation to Japan
	Nov	Identified as secretary of Hebei Province CP
1980,	Feb	Elected vice-governor of Hebei Province

Guo Ziheng (Kuo Tzu-heng)   郭子恒

Posts held

Government
Vice-minister of public health

Others
Vice-president of the Medical Association

1978,	Jul	Identified as vice-president of the Medical Association
1979,	Jun	Identified as vice-minister of public health
	Nov	Attends the 2nd International Symposium on the Health Program of the WHO Member Nations in Belgrade

Hai Yuzhen (Hai Yü-chen)   海玉琛

Posts held

NPC
Member of the Standing Committee of the
5th NPC
Deputy for Jilin Province to the 5th NPC

Hai belongs to the Mongolian minority.

| 1978, | Feb | Elected deputy for Jilin Province to the 5th NPC |
| | Mar | Elected member of the Standing Committee of the 5th NPC |

Han Dongshan (Han Tung-shan)   韩东山

Posts held

Military
Major-general

Provincial Administration
Vice-chairman of the People's Congress,
Hubei Province

Others
Member of the Standing Committee of the
5th CPPCC

Han was born in Henan Province. Between 1933 and 1935 he commanded first a battalion and later a regiment of the 25th Division, 9th Corps, 4th Front Army. In 1936 he was made commander of the 25th Division. Towards the end of that year he attended a course at the Anti-Japan Military and Political Academy. In April 1937, when Zhang Guotao came under attack, Han was one of the initiators of an attempted coup against Mao Zedong. As a result he was sentenced to five years imprisonment but released shortly afterwards at the beginning of the Anti-Japanese War. In autumn 1937 Han commanded the Reserve Regiment of the 129th Division in the 8th Route Army. From 1945 to 1946 he commanded a brigade in the Central Plains Field Army.

1950		Appointed chief of staff of Hubei Military District
1952		Appointed deputy commander of Hubei Military District and council member of the People's Government of Hubei Province
1955,	Sep	Promoted to rank of major-general; appointed commander of Hubei Military District (until 1964)
1964		Appointed deputy commander of Wuhan Military Region
1966,	Jan	Identified as deputy commander of Wuhan Military Region (repeatedly referred to in this post during the Cultural Revolution and subsequently until 1971, later again from 1974 to 1975)
1978,	Mar	Elected member of the Standing Committee of the 5th CPPCC
1980,	Jan	Elected vice-chairman of the People's Congress, Hubei Province

Han Fudong (Han Fu-tung)   韩复东

Posts held

Military
Major-general
Deputy director of the Military Training
Department under the PLA General Staff
Chairman of the PLA Sports Commission
Deputy secretary-general of the All-Army
Physical Culture Guidance Committee
Chairman of the PLA Sports Commission

Others
Vice-chairman of the Sports Federation

1955,	Oct	Present at PLA Marksmanship Athletic Meeting
1957		Identified as director of the Athletic Bureau of the General Training Supervision Division of the PLA
1958,	Sep	Member of the Committee for the 1st All-China Athletic Meeting
	Oct	Head of a team attending the 1st International Summer Athletic Meeting among Friendly Forces in the Democratic Republic of Germany
1960,	May	Identified as senior colonel
1961,	Feb	Delegate at the Winter Sport Competitions in Poland
1962,	Nov	Head of a football team visiting North Korea
1963,	Jan	Head of a football team visiting Burma
	Feb	Delegate at a session of the Sports Council of the Friendly Forces of the Socialist Countries in Romania
1964,	Sep	Identified as deputy director of the Military Training Division of PLA General Staff
1967		Disappears during the Cultural Revolution
1974,	Aug	First appearance after the Cultural Revolution: Identified as holding his previous post as deputy director of the Military Training Department of the PLA General Staff
1975,	May	Identified as a cadre of the Physical Training Organization of the PLA
1977,	Feb	Han heads a PLA sports delegation to Iran
	Dec	PLA observer at a conference of the International Sports Council in Damascus; head of a sports delegation to Iran
1978,	Apr	Identified as a cadre in the Mountaineering Association
	Jun	Identified as deputy secretary-general of the All-Army Physical Culture Guidance Committee
	Jul	Identified as chairman of the PLA Sports Commission
1979,	Jan	Head of a PLA sports delegation to the 33rd Session of the International Military Sports Council in Thailand
	Jul	Appointed deputy secretary-general of the National Games Organizing Committee
	Sep	Identified as deputy director of the Military Training Department under the PLA General Staff; and as vice-chairman of the Sports Federation

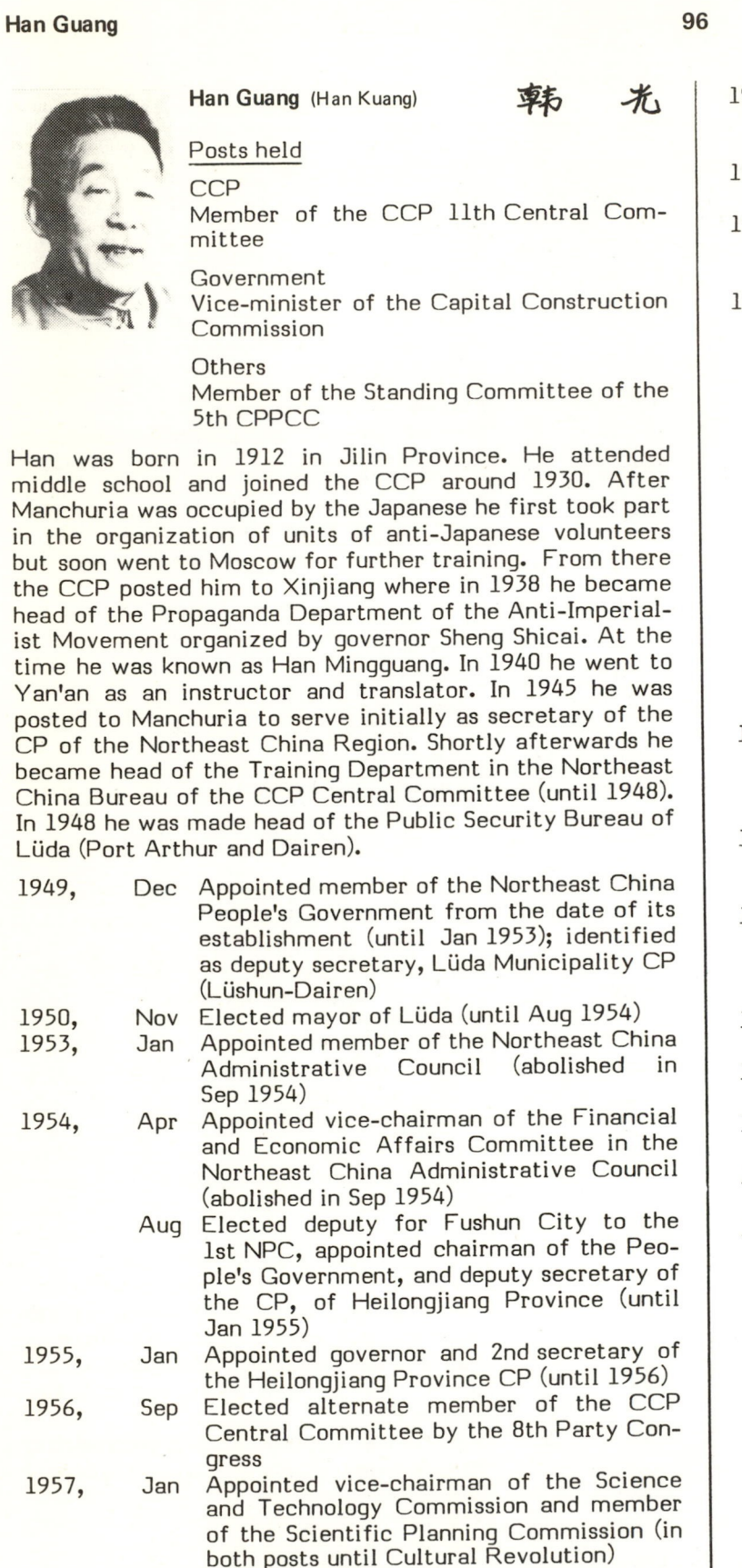

Han Guang (Han Kuang) 韩 光

Posts held

CCP
Member of the CCP 11th Central Committee

Government
Vice-minister of the Capital Construction Commission

Others
Member of the Standing Committee of the 5th CPPCC

Han was born in 1912 in Jilin Province. He attended middle school and joined the CCP around 1930. After Manchuria was occupied by the Japanese he first took part in the organization of units of anti-Japanese volunteers but soon went to Moscow for further training. From there the CCP posted him to Xinjiang where in 1938 he became head of the Propaganda Department of the Anti-Imperialist Movement organized by governor Sheng Shicai. At the time he was known as Han Mingguang. In 1940 he went to Yan'an as an instructor and translator. In 1945 he was posted to Manchuria to serve initially as secretary of the CP of the Northeast China Region. Shortly afterwards he became head of the Training Department in the Northeast China Bureau of the CCP Central Committee (until 1948). In 1948 he was made head of the Public Security Bureau of Lüda (Port Arthur and Dairen).

1949,	Dec	Appointed member of the Northeast China People's Government from the date of its establishment (until Jan 1953); identified as deputy secretary, Lüda Municipality CP (Lüshun-Dairen)
1950,	Nov	Elected mayor of Lüda (until Aug 1954)
1953,	Jan	Appointed member of the Northeast China Administrative Council (abolished in Sep 1954)
1954,	Apr	Appointed vice-chairman of the Financial and Economic Affairs Committee in the Northeast China Administrative Council (abolished in Sep 1954)
	Aug	Elected deputy for Fushun City to the 1st NPC, appointed chairman of the People's Government, and deputy secretary of the CP, of Heilongjiang Province (until Jan 1955)
1955,	Jan	Appointed governor and 2nd secretary of the Heilongjiang Province CP (until 1956)
1956,	Sep	Elected alternate member of the CCP Central Committee by the 8th Party Congress
1957,	Jan	Appointed vice-chairman of the Science and Technology Commission and member of the Scientific Planning Commission (in both posts until Cultural Revolution)
1959,	Mar	Elected chairman of the 2nd NPC for Liaoning Province
	Oct	Chairman of the Chinese section in the Sino-Soviet Commission for Technical and Scientific Cooperation
1960,	Nov	Head of a cultural delegation to Hungary
1961,	Dec	Article in HQ (1961, No. 24) on problems of industry and technology
1964,	Sep	Elected deputy for Heilongjiang Province to the 3rd NPC

1965,	Jan	Elected member of the Standing Committee of the 3rd NPC (until Cultural Revolution)
1966-1967		Attacked during the Cultural Revolution and disappears in 1967
1975,	Jan	First appearance after the Cultural Revolution at mourning ceremonies for Li Fuchun on 15 January
1978,	Mar	Elected member of the Standing Committee of the 5th CPPCC
	Apr	Identified as vice-minister of the Capital Construction Commission (probably in this post already since 1975)
	Dec	Elected member of the Central Committee by the 3rd Plenum of the CCP 11th Central Committee

Han Kehua (Han K'e-hua) 韩 克华

Posts held

Government
Former ambassador to France

1954,	May	Elected member of the Standing Committee, Wuhan Municipality CP
	Jun	Appointed deputy director of the Wuhan Planning Office
1958,	Jun	Identified as director of the Department of State-Operated Industry of Hubei Province CP
1960,	May	Identified as vice-governor of Hubei Province
	Nov	Identified as member of the Standing Committee of Hubei Province CP
1964,	Aug	Appointed ambassador to Hungary (until 1967)
1970,	Sep	Appointed ambassador to Guinea (until Jun 1974)
1974,	Sep	Appointed ambassador to Italy (until Jun 1977)
1977,	Aug	Identified as ambassador to France (until Jan 1980)
1978,	Jan	Han accompanies Prime Minister Barre on his visit to China

Han Liancheng (Han Lien-ch'eng) 韩 练成

Posts held

Military
Lieutenant-general

Others
Member of the Standing Committee of the 5th CPPCC

Han was born in 1904 in Lanzhou, Gansu Province. In 1946 he commanded the 46th Army of the Nationalist Government. In the following year he went over to the Communists in Shandong Province.

1949,	Dec	Identified as member of the Northwest China Military and Administrative Council (until Jan 1953) and as deputy commander of the Lanzhou Military Control Commission

1953,	Jan	Appointed member of the Northwest China Administrative Council
	Dec	Identified as deputy chief of staff of Northwest China Military Region and identified as deputy chief of staff of the 1st Field Army
1954,	Aug	Elected deputy for Shandong Province to the 1st NPC
	Sep	Appointed member of the National Defense Council (until 1965); awarded the order "Liberation," 1st class
1957,	Jun	Identified as chief of staff of Lanzhou Military Region and as lieutenant general
1962,	Jan	Elected vice-governor of Gansu Province
1964,	Sep	Elected deputy for Gansu Province to the 3rd NPC
1968,	Jan	Criticized as an anti-Party sectionalist and purged
1978,	Mar	First appearance after the Cultural Revolution: Elected member of the Standing Committee of the 5th CPPCC

Han Nianlong (Han Nien-lung)　韩念龙

Posts held

Government
Vice-minister of foreign affairs

Han was political commissar of a Red Army division. With the rank of colonel he was a member of the Communist Section of the Beijing Executive Headquarters of the KMT and CCP Military Subcommittee in 1946.

1949,	Oct	As political commissar of an army in the 3rd Field Army Han is appointed deputy political commissar of the Wusong-Shanghai Garrison Headquarters after the occupation of Shanghai
1951,	Sep	Appointed ambassador to Pakistan (until Feb 1956)
1956,	May	Appointed ambassador to Sweden (until Dec 1959)
1959,	Jan	Appointed assistant minister in the Ministry of Foreign Affairs (until Apr 1964)
1960,	May	Appointed concurrently head of the Staff Office in the Ministry of Foreign Affiars; member of a government delegation to PR Mongolia headed by Premier Zhou Enlai
1964,	Apr	Appointed vice-minister of foreign affairs
1965,	Mar	Member of a government delegation led by Minister of Foreign Affairs Chen Yi to Afghanistan, Pakistan, and Nepal
1966-1968		Han continues unharmed as vice-minister of foreign affairs throughout the Cultural Revolution
1971,	Mar	Member of a Party and government delegation to North Vietnam headed by Premier Zhou Enlai
1973,	Feb	Deputy head of a Chinese delegation to the Vietnam Conference in Paris
1975,	Feb	Member of a Chinese delegation to the crowning ceremonies for King Birendra of Nepal

	Apr	Member of a government delegation to Pakistan
	Aug	Member of a Party and government delegation attending the 30th anniversary celebrations of the Democratic Republic of Vietnam in Hanoi
1977,	Feb	Member of a government delegation to Burma headed by Deng Yingchao
1978,	Jan	Member of a government delegation to Kampuchea, Burma, and Nepal headed by Deng Yingchao
	Jun	Deputy head of a government delegation to Pakistan (head: Geng Biao)
	Oct	Member of a government delegation to Japan (head: Deng Xiaoping)
	Nov	Member of a Party and government delegation to Kampuchea (head: Wang Dongxing)
1979,	Apr	Head of a government delegation to North Vietnam
	May	Accompanies Deng Yingchao to North Korea
	Sep	Chairman of the Chinese delegation to the 34th Session of the UN General Assembly

Han is married to Wang Zhen, deputy director of the Information Department in the Ministry of Foreign Affairs.

Han Ningfu (Han Ning-fu)　韩宁夫

Posts held

CCP
Secretary of Hubei Province CP
2nd president of the Party School of Hubei Province

NPC
Deputy for Hubei Province to the 5th NPC

Provincial Administration
Governor of Hubei Province

1950		Identified as secretary-general of the People's Government of Hubei Province
1957,	Oct	Identified as deputy director and secretary of the CP of the Wuhan Iron and Steel Complex
1961,	Oct	Identified as director of Wuhan Iron and Steel Complex
1964,	Sep	Elected vice-governor of Hubei Province (until Cultural Revolution)
1967		Disappears during the Cultural Revolution
1973,	Jan	First appearance after the Cultural Revolution: Identified as secretary of Hubei Province CP
	Sep	Identified as vice-chairman of the Revolutionary Committee of Hubei Province (until Dec 1979)
1977,	Oct	Appointed 2nd president of the Party School of Hubei Province CP
1978,	Feb	Elected deputy for Hubei Province to the 5th NPC
1980,	Jan	Elected governor of Hubei Province

Han Peixin (Han P'ei-hsin)   韩培新

Posts held

Government
Vice-minister of light industry

Others
Vice-president of the Light Industry Society

1975,	Oct	Identified as vice-chairman of the Revolutionary Committee of Jiangsu Province (until 1977)
1976,	Apr	Identified as member of the Standing Committee of Jiangsu Province CP
1977,	May	Identified as secretary of Jiangsu Province CP (until 1977)
1978,	Jun	Identified as vice-minister of light industry
1979,	Dec	Elected vice-president of the Light Industry Society

Han Ronghua (Han Jung-hua)

Posts held

Mass Organization
Vice-chairman of the Federation of Trade Unions

| 1978, | Oct | Elected vice-chairman of the Federation of Trade Unions |
| 1979, | Jun | Head of a trade union delegation to Guinea, Guinea Bissau, and Cape Verde |

Han Xianchu (Han Hsien-ch'u)   韩先楚

Posts held

CCP
Member of the CCP 11th Central Committee
Member of the Standing Committee, Military Council under the CCP Central Committee

Military
Colonel-general
Commander of Lanzhou Military Region

Han was born in 1911 in Lishan County, Hubei Province. In 1931 he joined the 4th Front Army of the Communist forces in which he soon rose to the post of battalion commander in the 73rd Division. In 1932 he commanded a regiment in the 4th Front Army. In the winter of 1943-35 his unit was surrounded by KMT troops but managed to flee to Shaanxi. In autumn 1935 he was given the command of the 73rd Division in the 15th Red Army Corps. In early 1937 he attended a course at the Anti-Japan Military and Political Academy and in August of that year became commander of the 687th Regiment, 115th Division, 8th Route Army. In the following year he commanded the 689th Regiment operating in Shandong until 1945.

In September 1945, after the Japanese capitulation, Han led his troops to Manchuria where they were incorporated into the Northeast Democratic Joint Army. In early 1947 he served in Linjiang as commander of the 3rd Column of the Northeast Field Army. In late 1948 the 4th Field Army began moving south and Han was appointed deputy commander of the 12th Army Corps in February 1949 after the occupation of Beijing. When Hunan Province had been occupied he was appointed deputy commander of Hunan Military District in August 1949. He then took part in the occupation of Guangxi and Guangdong Provinces.

1950,	Mar	Appointed council member of the People's Government of Guangdong Province
	Apr	After the occupation of Hainan Island Han is appointed chairman of the Hainan Military and Administrative Council
	Oct	Representative in North Korea, at first as vice-chairman of the Joint Chiefs of Staff of PRC, North Korea, and the USSR
1951		Commander of the 13th Army Corps of the Chinese People's Volunteers
1952,	Jan	As deputy chief of staff of the Chinese People's Volunteers Han takes part in the cease-fire negotiations in Panmunjom
1953		Training at the Military Academy of the PLA
1954,	Sep	Appointed member of the National Defense Council (until Cultural Revolution)
1955,	Sep	Promoted to rank of colonel-general; awarded the orders of "Independence and Freedom" and "Liberation," both 1st class
1958,	May	Elected alternate member, 8th Central Committee of the CCP (until Apr 1969)
End of year		Appointed commander of PLA Fujian Front (until Jan 1974)
1965,	Nov	Identified as deputy chief of PLA General Staff (until Cultural Revolution)
1966-1967		In spite of repeated Red Guard attacks during the Cultural Revolution Han retains his position
1968,	Aug	With the establishment of the Revolutionary Committee of Fujian Province Han is elected chairman (until Jan 1974)
1969,	Apr	Elected to first term as member of the CCP Central Committee by the 9th Party Congress
1971,	Apr	Elected 1st secretary of Fujian Province CP (until Jan 1974)
1974,	Jan	Identified as commander of the Lanzhou Military Region (Han is one of eight commanders of military regions given new postings in the course of a military reshuffle)
1980,	Feb	Identified as member of the Standing Committee, Military Council under the CCP Central Committee

Han Xu (Han Hsü)   韩叙

Posts held

Government
Director of the American and Oceanian Affairs Department, Ministry of Foreign Affairs

| 1959, | Apr | Identified as an official in the Protocol Department of the Ministry of Foreign Affairs |

1964,	Jul	Appointed counselor at the embassy in the USSR (until Mar 1965)
1969,	Sep	Identified as deputy director of the Protocol Department in the Ministry of Foreign Affairs
1970,	Apr	Member of a Party and government delegation to North Korea headed by Premier Zhou Enlai
1972,	Dec	Identified as director of the Protocol Department in the Ministry of Foreign Affairs (until Mar 1973)
1973,	Feb	Member of the Chinese delegation to the Vietnam Conference in Paris
	Mar	Appointed deputy head of the PRC Liaison Office in Washington (this Office functioned as an embassy) (until Jan 1979)
1979,	Mar	Identified as director of the American and Oceanian Affairs Department, Ministry of Foreign Affairs

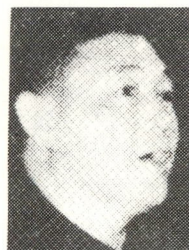

Han Ying (Han Ying) 韩 英

Posts held

CCP
Member of the CCP 11th Central Committee

Mass Organization
1st secretary of the Communist Youth League

Others
Member of the Standing Committee of the 5th CPPCC

Han was born in 1935 in Liaoning Province as the son of a poor peasant. In the 1960s he had been an engineer, later director of a mine under Datong Coal Mining Administration in Shanxi Province.

1969,	Apr	Elected alternate member of the CCP Central Committee by the 9th Party Congress (until Aug 1973)
1970,	Apr	Han reports on the 1970 economic plan for Shanxi Province in Taiyuan, the provincial capital
1971,	Jul	Identified as member of the Standing Committee of Shanxi Province CP (until Nov 1974); identified as vice-chairman of the Revolutionary Committee of Shanxi Province (until Oct 1978)
1973,	Aug	Elected to first term as member of the CCP Central Committee by the 10th Party Congress
1974,	Nov	Identified as secretary of Shanxi Province CP (until Oct 1978)
1978,	May	Member of an economic delegation to Great Britain and France (head: Gu Ming); identified as chairman of the Preparatory Committee for the 10th Congress of the Communist Youth League
	Oct	Elected 1st secretary of the Communist Youth League
1979,	Mar	Head of a delegation of the Communist Youth League to Romania and Yugoslavia

	Jun	Head of a delegation of the Communist Youth League to North Korea
	Jul	By-elected member of the Standing Committee of the 5th CPPCC

Han Yutong (Han Yü-t'ung) (f) 韩 幽 桐

Posts held

Others
Deputy director of the Institute of Law, Academy of Sciences

Han belongs to the Hui minority. She was born in 1909 in Heilongjiang Province. After attending the College of Law at Beijing University, she studied international law at the Imperial University in Tokyo. She married the journalist and professor Zhang Youyu probably during this stay in Japan. After her return she was awarded a professorship at the Northwestern Associated University. In 1945 she joined the China Democratic League. In October 1947 she took part in the 2nd Conference of the International Federation of Democratic Women in Budapest.

1949,	Oct	Appointed member of the Northeast People's Government and director of the Education Department of Songjiang Province
	Dec	Appointed deputy director of the Secondary School Education Department of the Ministry of Education
1950,	Mar	Identified as director of the Education Bureau of the People's Government of Tianjin Municipality
1952,	Apr	Identified as deputy director of the North China Branch, Supreme People's Court
1954,	Aug	Elected deputy for Heilongjiang Province to the 1st NPC (confirmed in 1958 and 1964 by the the 2nd and 3rd NPCs)
	Nov	Identified as associate presiding judge of the Supreme People's Court (until 1960)
1957,	Dec	Elected member of the Executive Committee of the Federation of Democratic Women
1958,	Jul	Elected member of the Afro-Asian Solidarity Committee; elected council member of the World Peace Council
	Sep	Identified as council member of the Sino-Iraq Friendship Association
	Dec	Identified as director of the People's High Court of Ningxia Autonomous Region (until 1964)
1961,	Mar	Member of a jurists' delegation to Japan
1962,	Oct	Member of a delegation to the Afro-Asian Legal Conference in Conakry; head of a women's delegation to Algeria
1963,	Jun	Member of a delegation to the Congress of the World Women's League in Moscow
	Sep	Member of a jurists' delegation to Tanganyika, Zaire and Guinea (until Nov 1963)
	Dec	Elected council member of the Asian-African Society
1964,	Mar	Head of a delegation to the 8th Congress of the World Federation of Democratic Jurists in Budapest
	Jul	Member of a delegation to the 10th World Conference against Atomic Bombs in Japan

Oct   Elected secretary of the Political Science and Law Society

Nov   Member of a jurists' delegation to Japan; identified as deputy director of the Research Institute of Law, Academy of Sciences

1965,   Sep   Head of a scientists' delegation to Somalia, Tanzania, Mali, and Sudan (until Oct 1965)

1967   Disappears during the Cultural Revolution

1978,   Feb   Identified as deputy director of the Law Institute of the Academy of Sciences

1979,   Dec   Head of a jurists delegation to Austria

Han Zheyi   (Han Che-yi)   韩哲一

Posts held

CCP
Secretary, Shanghai Municipality CP

NPC
Deputy for Shanghai Municipality to the 5th NPC

Provincial Administration
Vice-mayor of Shanghai Municipality
Director of the Shanghai Industry and Communications Office

Han was born in Shandong Province.

1949,   Oct   Appointed vice-chairman of the People's Government of Pingyuan Province

1950,   Aug   Identified as vice-chairman of the Financial and Ecomomic Committee in the same People's Government

1953,   Jan   Appointed member of the North China Administrative Council

1954,   Aug   Identified as member of the State Planning Commission (until Sep 1954) and as director of its Bureau of Allocation of Supplies (until 1956)

Oct   Identified as vice-chairman of the State Planning Commission (until 1960)

1956,   Dec   Identified as director of the Bureau of Allocation of Supplies under the State Council (until Mar 1958)

1958,   Mar   Appointed vice-chairman of the State Economic Commission (until 1963)

1961,   Mar   Identified as alternate secretary of the East China Bureau of the CCP Central Committee

1965,   Dec   Elected deputy for Shanghai Municipality to the 3rd NPC

1966,   Jul   Identified as secretary of the East China Bureau of the CCP Central Committee

1967   Disappears during the Cultural Revolution

1977,   Dec   First appearance after the Cultural Revolution: Elected vice-chairman of the Revolutionary Committee of Shanghai Municipality (until Dec 1979)

1978,   Jan   Identified as secretary, Shanghai Municipality CP

Feb   Elected deputy for Shanghai Municipality to the 5th NPC

May   Head of an economic delegation to Great Britain and France

Jun   Identified as director of the Shanghai Industry and Communications Office

1979,   Jun   Member of the Budget Committee, 2nd Session of the 5th NPC

Dec   Elected vice-mayor of Shanghai Municipality

Hao Deqing   (Hao Te-ch'ing)   郝德青

Posts held

Government
Director of the Institute of Foreign Affairs

NPC
Member of the Standing Committee of the 5th NPC
Deputy for Tianjin Municipality to the 5th NPC

Hao was born in October 1906 in Shanxi Province.

1950   Identified as member of the West Sichuan Administrative Office

1952,   Aug   Identified as council member of the People's Government of Sichuan Province

1954,   Jul   Identified as secretary of Chengdu Municipality CP

Sep   Appointed ambassador to Hungary (until Apr 1961)

1961,   Jul   Appointed ambassador to North Korea (until Nov 1965)

1965,   Nov   Appointed deputy director of the Office of Foreign Affairs in the State Council

1966,   Apr   Elected vice-chairman of the Association for Cultural Relations with Foreign Countries

1971,   Febr   Appointed ambassador to Norway (until Sep 1972)

1972,   Nov   Appointed ambassador to the Netherlands (until Oct 1974)

1974,   Dec   Appointed ambassador to Iran (until Jan 1977)

1977,   Mar   Identified as director of the Institute of Foreign Affairs

Jun   Head of a delegation of the Institute of Foreign Affairs to Canada and the U.S.A.

1978,   Feb   Elected deputy for Tianjin Municipality to the 5th NPC

Mar   Elected member of the Standing Committee of the 5th NPC

Sep   Head of a delegation of the Institute of Foreign Affairs to the Federal Republic of Germany and Luxemburg

Nov   Head of a delegation of the Institute of Foreign Affairs to Australia

1979,   Jun   Member of the Committee to Examine Proposals at the 2nd Session of the 5th NPC

Hao Jianxiu (Hao Chien-hsiu) (f) 郝建秀

Posts held

CCP
Member of the CCP 11th Central Committee
Member of the Standing Committee of Shandong Province CP

Government
Vice-minister of textile industry

Mass Organizations
Vice-chairman of the Women's Federation
Chairman of the Women's Federation of Shandong Province
Vice-chairman of the Trade Union of Shandong Province

Hao was born in 1935 as the daughter of a laborer in Qingdao. Before the establishment of PRC she attended school for one year.

1951		As a worker at the State Operated Cotton Factory No. 6 in Qingdao she introduces a new spinning method, propagated as the "Hao Jianxiu Work Method." She is declared a "National Model Worker in Industry"
1952,	Dec	Hao obtains a scholarship from Shandong University to attend middle school
1953		Continues her studies at the Crash-Course-Middle-School affiliated with Beijing University
	Apr	Elected member of the Executive Council of the Women's Federation
	Sep	Elected member of the Central Committee of the Democratic Youth League
1954,	Sep	Elected deputy for Shandong Province to the 1st NPC (reelected in 1958 and 1964 to the 2nd and 3rd NPCs)
1958		Continues her studies at the East China Institute of Weaving and Spinning
1962		Graduates as an engineer from the East China Institute of Weaving and Spinning and returns to Cotton Factory No. 6 in Qingdao
1964		Identified as deputy director of Cotton Factory No. 6 in Qingdao
	Jul	Elected member of the Central Committee of the Communist Youth League (until Cultural Revolution)
1967,	Jan	Elected member of the Revolutionary Committee of Qingdao Municipality
1968,	Jun	Identified as member of the Standing Committee of the Revolutionary Committee of Cotton Factory No. 6
1971,	Jul	Identified as vice-chairman of the Revolutionary Committee of Qingdao Municipality
1973,	Jul	Elected vice-chairman of the Trade Union of Shandong Province
1975,	Apr	Elected chairman of the Women's Federation of Shandong Province
1977,	Jan	Identified as member of the Standing Committee of Shandong Province CP
	Aug	Elected member of the CCP Central Committee by the 11th Party Congress
1978,	Mar	Identified as vice-minister of textile industry

	Sep	Elected vice-chairman of the Women's Federation

Hao Ting (Hao T'ing) 郝汀

Posts held

Military
Colonel

Others
Director of the Foreign Affairs Bureau of the Academy of Sciences

Hao was born in 1915 in Henan Province. In 1946 Hao was a member of the Communist delegation with the rank of colonel at the peace negotiations with the KMT.

1950,	Dec	Identified as attaché at the embassy in Sweden
1953,	Oct	Identified as attaché at the diplomatic mission in Denmark
1955,	Feb	Identified as chargé d'affaires ad interim in Denmark (until 1956)
1958,	Jul	Appointed ambassador to Afghanistan (until May 1965)
1965,	May	Elected member of the Standing Committee of the Afro-Asian Solidarity Committee (until Cultural Revolution)
1967		Disappears during the Cultural Revolution
1976,	Apr	First appearance after the Cultural Revolution: Identified as director of the Foreign Affairs Bureau of the Academy of Sciences
1979,	Jan	Member of a delegation of the Academy of Sciences to Japan

Hao Xiushan (Hao Hsiu-shan) 郝秀山

Posts held

Provincial Administration
Vice-chairman of the People's Government of Inner Mongolia

1979,	Dec	Elected vice-chairman of the People's Government of Inner Mongolia

Hao Zhongshi (Hao Chung-shih) 郝中士

Posts held

Government
Vice-minister of agriculture

Others
Vice-president of the Academy of Agriculture and Forestry

Hao was born in 1918 in Jiangsu Province. For the revolutionary period it is only known that he studied around 1937 in Yan'an at the Anti-Japanese Military and Political Academy.

1949,	Dec	Appointed deputy director of the Committee for Rural Reform in Central-South China Military and Administrative Council

1950,	Mar	Identified as secretary-general of Hubei Province CP
1954,	Feb	Identified as deputy secretary of Guangxi Province CP
	Sep	Identified as vice-chairman of the Guangxi People's Government
1955,	Feb	Elected vice-governor of Guangxi Province
1957,	Jun	Because of mismanagement in Guangxi Province Hao (together with others, among them 1st CP secretary Chen Man-yuan) is relieved of his posts as vice-governor and CP secretary
1962,	Nov	Identified as deputy director of the Staff Office of Agriculture and Forestry in the State Council (until about 1967)
1970,	Oct	Identified as a cadre in the Ministry of Agriculture and Forestry
1972,	Jul	Head of an agricultural delegation to Japan; identified as vice-president of the Academy of Agriculture and Forestry
1973,	Mar	Identified as acting chairman of the Agronomy Society (until Sep 1975)
	Nov	Identified as vice-minister of agriculture and forestry (until Feb 1979); head of the Chinese delegation to the 17th Food and Agriculture Organization (FAO) Conference in Rome
1974,	Nov	Head of the Chinese delegation to the 18th FAO Conference in Rome
	Dec	Head of a government delegation to Upper Volta and Nigeria
1975,	Sep	Identified as acting chairman of the Agronomy Society (until 1977)
1979,	Feb	Identified as vice-minister of agriculture
	Apr	Head of an agricultural delegation to Thailand

He Biao (Ho Piao) 賀 彪

Posts held

Military
Deputy director of the PLA Logistics Department
Head of the Health Section under the PLA Logistics Department

He, believed to be a relative (brother?) of He Long, was born around 1900 in Hunan Province. In 1928 he joined the Red Army led by He Long, having until then practiced medicine. He was subsequently active in the Red Army Medical Services: director of the Health Department, 2nd Front Army (1933); director of the Health Section, 120th Division (commanded by He Long), 8th Route Army; director of the Health Section of Shanxi-Suiyuan Military District (1940); director of the Health Section, 1st Field Army.

1950,	Jan	Identified as director of the Health Department of Northwest Military and Administrative Council
1951,	Apr	Identified as director of the Health Department of Northwest Military Region
1954,	Oct	Appointed vice-minister of public health (until Cultural Revolution)
1958,	Aug	Head of a health delegation to the People's Republic of Mongolia

	Oct	Identified as vice-chairman of the Sino-Albanian Friendship Association
1961,	May	Head of a health delegation to the German Democratic Republic and to Hungary (6th Conference of Socialist Countries' Ministries of Health)
1962,	May	Identified as council member of the Sino-PR-Mongolian Friendship Association
1964,	Dec	Elected member of the 4th CPPCC
1967		Disappears during the Cultural Revolution
1975,	Sep	First appearance after the Cultural Revolution
1978,	Oct	Identified as deputy director of the PLA Logistics Department and as head of the Health Section under the PLA Logistics Department; He leds an army surgeons delegation of the PLA to Pakistan

He Bingzhang (Ho Ping-chang) 賀秉章

Posts held

Government
Vice-minister of coal industry

Others
President of the Coal Mining Society

1955,	Nov	Identified as assistant minister in the Ministry of Coal Industry
1959,	Apr	Identified as chairman of the editorial board of the journal Coal Industry
1959,	Sep	Appointed vice-minister of coal industry (until 1961)
1966		Disappears during the Cultural Revolution
1975,	Jun	Reactivated after the Cultural Revolution as director of the Scientific Coal Research Institute in Beijing; head of a delegation to a conference of the International Organization Committee of the World Mining Conference in Düsseldorf, FR Germany
	Nov	Identified as president of the Coal Mining Society
1976,	May	Head of a delegation to the World Mining Conference in Düsseldorf, FR Germany
1978,	Feb	Identified as vice-minister of coal industry
	May	Head of a scientific and technological delegation to North Korea
1979,	Oct	Identified as chairman of the Chinese section, Sino-Korean Committee of Scientific and Technical Cooperation

He Cehui (Ho Ts'e-hui) (f) 何沢慧

Posts held

Others
Deputy director of the Institute of High Energy Physics of the Academy of Sciences

He was born in 1914. In 1940 she was awarded a doctorate by Berlin University. She then worked at the Curie Institute in France. Around this time she married Qian

Sanqiang with whom she jointly developed a new technique for splitting uranium atoms. Her most significant contributions to science are the demonstration of elastic collision of positive and negative electrons in a cloud chamber and the discovery of ternary fission of uranium with nuclear emulsion. Finally, she observed what she suspected to be the quarternary fission. She returned to China around 1948. After the foundation of the PRC she was initially head of the Counter Section of the Low Energy Accelerator Laboratory, Institute of Atomic Energy, Academy of Sciences.

1953		Identified as researcher at the Modern Physics Institute, Academy of Sciences
	Apr	Identified as a member of the Executive Committee of the Women's Federation
	Jun	Member of a delegation to the World Democratic Women's Conference in Copenhagen
1957,	Jan	He wins the 3rd prize of the Academy of Sciences' Science Awards for her paper "Research into the Process of Preparing Nuclear Emulsoid"
1958,	Dec	Elected deputy for Henan Province to the 2nd NPC (confirmed in 1964 for the 3rd NPC)
1967		Disappears during the Cultural Revolution
1978,	Feb	First appearance after the Cultural Revolution
	Mar	Identified as deputy director, Institute High Energy Physics, Academy of Sciences
	Oct	Member of a government delegation led by Fang Yi to the Federal Republic of Germany and France

He is married to Qian Sanqiang.

He Changgong (Ho Ch'ang-kung) 何长工

Posts held

Military
Deputy commandant of the PLA Military Academy

Others
Member of the Standing Committee of the 5th CPPCC
President of the Society on the Historical Figures of the CCP

He was born in 1900 in Huarong, Hunan Province. He attended Yueyang Middle School and a technical middle school in Hunan. In 1919 he went to France as a worker-student. In 1920 he joined the CCP. After a year of studies in Belgium he returned to China in 1924 and joined the trade union movement in Hunan. At the end of 1927 he joined the Communist units on Jinggangshan. In 1933 he was head of the Red Army College in Juichin. During the Long March he was political commissar of the 8th Red Army. In the dispute within the Communist Party he took the side of Zhang Guotao, for which he was criticized in 1936. In the following year he lectured at the Anti-Japan Military and Political Academy of which he became vice-president in 1940. He retained this post until 1947 when the university was moved to Manchuria. In 1948 he became president of the Northeast Military and Political College as well as military council member of the Northeast People's Government. In September 1949 he took part in the 1st CPPCC.

1949,	Oct	Appointed vice-minister of heavy industry (until Aug 1952) and member of the Financial and Economic Committee of the Government Administration Council
1951,	Aug	Identified as director of the Aviation Industry Bureau in the Ministry of Heavy Industry
1952,	Aug	Appointed vice-minister of geology (until Cultural Revolution)
1958,	Jul	Elected deputy for Hunan Province to the 2nd NPC
1959,	Apr	Elected member of the Standing Committee of the 3rd CPPCC (confirmed in 1965 by the 4th CPPCC)
	Nov	Elected vice-chairman of the Committee on Terrestrial Stratification
1960,	Sep	Head of a geologists' delegation to Hungary
1966,	Oct	He is publicly branded as a deviationist and relieved of his posts
1975,	May	First appearance after the Cultural Revolution
1978,	Mar	Elected member of the Standing Committee of the 5th CPPCC
	Oct	Identified as deputy commandant of the PLA Military Academy
1979,	Dec	Elected president of the Society on the Historical Figures of the CCP

He Cheng (Ho Ch'eng)   贺诚

Posts held

CCP
Member of the CCP 11th Central Committee

Military
Lieutenant-general
Deputy director of the Logistics Department of the PLA

Others
Member of the Standing Committee of the 5th CPPCC

During the Long March He served as director of the Health Department of the 1st Front Army. In 1937 he became deputy director of the Health Department of the 8th Route Army. From 1946 to 1948 he was director of the Health Department in the Rear Service Department of the CCP Military Council. In September 1949 He represented science workers at the 1st CPPCC.

1949,	Dec	Appointed vice-minister of public health (until Jan 1956) and director of the Health Department of the Revolutionary Military Council (until Jan 1953)
1952,	Aug	Appointed honorary chairman of the Medical Society
1953,	Jan	Appointed director of the Health Department in the General Logistics Department of the PLA (until Jan 1956)
1954,	Aug	Elected deputy for Sichuan Province to the 1st NPC

1955		Promoted to the rank of lieutenant-general
1956,	Jan	He is accused of having sabotaged the policy of combining Chinese with Western medicine and is relieved of his posts. He then works in a number of medical institutes
1965,	Jan	Elected member of the Standing Committee of the 4th CPPCC
	Jun	Identified as deputy director of the Logistics Department of Chengdu Military Region
1967		Disappears during the Cultural Revolution
1973,	May	First appearance after the Cultural Revolution
1977,	Jun	Identified as deputy director of the Logistics Department of the PLA
	Aug	Elected member of the CCP Central Committee by the 11th Party Congress
	Sep	He's wife, Zhou Yuehua, dies on 17 September 1977
1978,	Mar	Elected member of the Standing Committee of the 5th CPPCC

He Chenghua (Ho Ch'eng-hua)　何承华

Posts held

CCP
Member of the Standing Committee of Shaanxi Province CP

Provincial Administration
Vice-governor of Shaanxi Province

1953,	Oct	Identified as secretary-general of Gansu Province CP
1960,	Jan	Identified as secretary of Gansu Province CP (until Jan 1968)
1968,	Jan	He disappears
1979,	Oct	First appearance after the Cultural Revolution: Identified as a member of the Standing Committee of Shaanxi Province CP and vice-chairman of the Revolutionary Committee, Shaanxi Province (until Dec 1979)
	Dec	Elected vice-governor of Shaanxi Province

He Dongchang (Ho Tung-ch'ang)　何功楷

Posts held

CCP
Member of the Commission for Inspecting Discipline under the CCP Central Committee

NPC
Deputy for Beijing Municipality to the 5th NPC

Others
Vice-president of Qinghua University

1960,	Dec	Identified as deputy secretary, Qinghua University CP

1964,	Sep	Elected deputy for Anhui Province to the 3rd NPC
1967,	Mar	Branded as a counterrevolutionary revisionist and purged
1973,	May	First appearance after the Cultural Revolution: Identified as vice-chairman of the Revolutionary Committee of Qinghua University
1977,	Nov	Identified as deputy secretary, Qinghua University CP
1978,	Feb	Elected deputy for Beijing Municipality to the 5th NPC
	Dec	Appointed member of the Commission for Inspecting Discipline of the CCP Central Committee
1979,	May	Identified as vice-president of Qinghua University

He Gongkai (Ho Kung-k'ai)　何功楷

Posts held

Government
Ambassador to Tanzania

1956,	Aug	Identified as deputy director of the Western Europe and Africa Department in the Ministry of Foreign Affairs (until Mar 1957)
	Nov	Elected council member of the Sino-Egyptian Friendship Association
1957,	Mar	After reorganization of the Regional Departments in the Ministry of Foreign Affairs, identified as deputy director of the West Asian and Africa Department (until Jun 1963)
1960,	Aug	Identified as member of the Institute of Foreign Affairs
1963,	Jun	Appointed counselor, embassy in the United Arab Republic (until 1967)
1970,	Jul	Identified as deputy director of the West Asia and Africa Department in the Ministry of Foreign Affairs (until Aug 1972)
	Sep	Member of a government delegation to Mali
1971,	Oct	Member of the Chinese government delegation to the 2500th anniversary celebration in Iran
	Nov	Member of the Chinese delegation taking part in the celebrations of the 10th anniversary of independence in Tanzania
1972,	Aug	Identified as director of the Africa Department in the Ministry of Foreign Affairs (until Jan 1980)
1975,	Jun	Member of the Chinese delegation to the celebrations of independence in Mozambique
1978,	Jun	Member of a government delegation to Zaire headed by Minister of Foreign Affairs Huang Hua
	Jul/Aug	Member of a government delegation to Somalia, Gabon, and Cameroon headed by Chen Muhua
	Oct	Member of a government delegation to Congo (Brazzaville) headed by Geng Biao
1980,	Feb	Appointed ambassador to Tanzania

He Guangqian (Ho Kuang-ch'ien) 何广乾

Posts held

Others
Deputy director of the Building Research Institute
Acting chairman of the Architectural Society

1974,	Jun	Identified as acting chairman of the Architectural Society
1975,	Sep	Head of an architectural delegation to the United States
1976,	Jun	Identified as vice-chairman of the Revolutionary Committee, Institute of Building Research under the State Capital Construction Commission
1977,	Aug	Member of the presidium of the 11th CCP Congress
1978,	Oct	Identified as deputy director of the Building Research Institute; head of a delegation to the 13th Congress of the International Union of Architects in Mexico

He Guangwen (Ho Kuang-wen) 何光文

Posts held

Others
Vice-president of the Academy of Agricultural Sciences

| 1978, | Aug | Identified as vice-president of the Academy of Agricultural Sciences |

He Guangyu (Ho Kuang-yü) 何光宇

Posts held

NPC
Deputy for the PLA to the 5th NPC

Military
Major-general
Deputy commander of Lanzhou Military Region

In 1949 He had been deputy chief of staff of the 5th Corps under the 2nd Field Army.

1952		Identified as commander of the (17th?) Corps of the 5th Army
1954,	Aug	Identified as deputy commander of Guizhou Military District
1955,	Sep	Promoted to the rank of major-general
1965,	Aug	Identified as commander of Guizhou Military District (until 1975?)
1969,	Aug	Identified as vice-chairman of the Revolutionary Committee of Guizhou Province (until 1970?)
1971,	May	Elected deputy secretary of Guizhou Province CP (until 1975)
1977,	Mar	Identified as commander of Gansu Military District (until mid-1978?)
1978,	Feb	Elected deputy for the PLA to the 5th NPC
1979,	Oct	Identified as deputy commander of Lanzhou Military Region

He Haoju (Ho Hao-chü) 何郝炬

Posts held

Provincial Administration
Vice-governor of Sichuan Province

Others
Director of the Board of Directors, China International Trust and Investment Corporation

1977,	Dec	Elected vice-chairman of the Revolutionary Committee of Sichuan Province (until Dec 1979)
1978,	Oct	Member of a friendship delegation to Japan
1979,	Oct	Appointed director of the Board of Directors of the China International Trust and Investment Corporation
	Dec	Elected vice-governor of Sichuan Province

He Jifeng (Ho Chi-feng) 何基沣

Posts held

Military
Lieutenant-general

Others
Member of the Standing Committee of the 5th CPPCC

He was born in 1897 in Gaocheng, Hebei Province. He was one of the 9th graduating class of Baoding Military Academy. From 1923 he served as an officer in the Nationalist Army with the following posts: battalion commander (1925); colonel and commander of the 47th Regiment, 16th Mixed Brigade (1926); major-general and commander of the 14th Brigade, 5th Division (1928); commander of the 110th Brigade, 37th Division, 29th Army (1932); deputy commander of the Beijing Students Military Training Corps (1934); lieutenant-general and commander of the 77th Army (1938); commander of the 77th Army (1943); deputy commander of the 33rd Army Group (1943); deputy commander of the 3rd Pacification Zone (1946); deputy commander of the Xuzhou Garrison Command (1947). In November 1948 he went over to the Communists with 20,000 men. In 1949 he was appointed by the Communists commander of the 34th Army, 3rd Field Army. In September of that year he took part in the 1st CPPCC.

1953,	Feb	Appointed member of the North China Administrative Council (until 1954)
1954,	Aug	Elected deputy for Shandong Province to the 1st NPC
	Oct	Appointed vice-minister of water conservancy (until Feb 1958)
1955,	Sep	Conferred the order "Liberation," 1st class
1958,	Sep	Appointed vice-minister of agriculture (until Cultural Revolution)
1963,	Nov	Identified as vice-president of the Water Conservancy Society
1967		Disappears during the Cultural Revolution
1975,	Mar	First appearance after the Cultural Revolution: Referred to as deputy to the NPC
1976,	Jan	Identified as military leader of Guangdong Military District
1978,	Mar	Elected member of the Standing Committee of the 5th CPPCC

He Jingzhi (Ho Ching-chih)　賀敬之

Posts held

Government
Vice-minister of culture

1976,	Dec	Identified as author of the modern opera Bai-mao nü (The White Haired Girl)
1978,	Jan	Identified as vice-minister of culture
1979,	Jul	Head of a Beijing Opera troupe to North Korea

He Jinnian (Ho Chin-nien)　賀晋年

Posts held

CCP
Alternate member of the CCP 11th Central Committee

Military
Colonel-general
Deputy commander of the Armored Forces of the PLA

He was born in Shaanxi Province. He took part in the North Shaanxi Uprising and in 1934 set up the 27th Red Army of which he became commander in 1935. In 1936 he studied at the Workers and Peasants Institute of the Red Army. In 1945 he was deputy commander of Jilin-Heilongjiang Military Region. Towards the end of 1946 he served with parts of the 359th Brigade and a cavalry unit in the Manchurian Border Area. He was deputy commander of an army corps in the 4th Field Army in 1949.

1950,	Aug	Identified as deputy commander of Northeast China Military Region and as a member of the Northeast China Military and Administrative Council
1953,	Jan	Appointed acting commander of North East China Military Region following the transfer of Gao Gang to Beijing
1954,	Sep	In connection with the Gao Gang Affair He is relieved of his posts
1955,	Sep	Promoted to rank of colonel-general
1972,	Dec	Identified as deputy commander of the Armored Forces of the PLA
1977,	Aug	Elected alternate member of the CCP Central Committee by the 11th Party Congress
	Sep	Member of a military delegation to France and Romania
1978,	Jun	Member of a military delegation to Yugoslavia headed by Yang Yong

He Kang (Ho K'ang)　何　康

Posts held

Government
Vice-minister of the State Agricultural Commission
Vice-minister of agriculture

He was born in 1923 in Fujian Province.

1957,	Sep	Identified as deputy director of the Office of Experts Administration under the State Council

1963		Identified as vice-chairman of the Grain Cultivation Society and as chairman of the Preparatory Committee for the Tropical Plant Society
1964,	Sep	Elected deputy for Guangdong Province to the 3rd NPC
1967		Disappears during the Cultural Revolution
1978,	Mar	First appearance after the Cultural Revolution: Identified as vice-minister of agriculture and forestry (until Feb 1979)
	Apr	Appointed member of the Committee for the Patriotic Health Campaign
	Jul	Deputy head of an agricultural delegation to the United States
1979,	Feb	Head of an agricultural delegation to Yugoslavia
	Apr	Appointed vice-president of the Recommendation and Examination Committee in charge of classifying inventions under the State Scientific and Technical Commission
	Jun	Identified as vice-minister of the State Agricultural Commission
	Aug	Identified as vice-minister of agriculture

He Lanjie (Ho Lan-chieh)　何兰阶

Posts held

Others
Vice-president of the Supreme People's Court

1952,	Apr	Identified as vice-president of the North China Branch of the Supreme People's Court (abolished in Sep 1954) and as deputy chief-justice for criminal law in the Supreme People's Court (until Nov 1954)
1954,	Nov	Identified as chief-justice in the Supreme People's Court
1963		Identified as chief-justice for civilian law in the Supreme People's Court
1964,	Sep	Elected deputy for Hubei Province to the 3rd NPC
1966,	Mar	Appointed vice-president of the Supreme People's Court
	Oct	Ho is attacked by Red Guards and denounced as a "Person of the Type of Wang Guangmei" (wife of the main victim of the Cultural Revolution, president Liu Shaoqi)
1973,	Apr	First appearance after the Cultural Revolution: Again referred to in the position of a vice-president of the Supreme People's Court
1978,	Mar	Confirmed by the 5th NPC as vice-president of the Supreme People's Court

He Liliang (Ho Li-liang) (f)　何理良

Posts held

Government
Deputy director of the Department of International Organizations and Conferences, Agreements and Laws in the Ministry of Foreign Affairs

1973,   Mar   Deputy representative at the UN Seabed Conference

         Aug   Member of a government delegation led by Huang Zhen to Mexico

1976,   Mar   Identified as representative of the Chinese mission at the UN

         Jul   Member of the Chinese delegation to the UN Seabed Conference

1977,   Aug   Identified as deputy director of the Department of International Organizations and Conferences, Agreements and Laws of the Ministry of Foreign Affairs

         Sep   Alternate representative of the Chinese delegation to the 32nd UN General Assembly

         Oct   Member of a government delegation led by Huang Hua to Canada

1978,   Mar   Member of a government delegation led by Li Xiannian to the Philippines and Bangladesh

         Sep   He accompanies Huang Hua to Greece

         Oct   Member of a government delegation led by Deng Xiaoping to Japan

He is the wife of Huang Hua.

He Lüting (Ho Lü-t'ing) 贺绿汀

Posts held

Others
Member of the Standing Committee of the 5th CPPCC
Vice-president of the Musicians Union

He was born in Shaoyang, Hunan Province. He studied at the Shanghai Conservatory. With his composition "The Cowboy's Flute" he won a prize in 1934. He organized the Chongqing Symphony Orchestra after 1938. Later he went to Yan'an and lectured at the Lu Xun Institute of Arts. There he composed among other things "The East Is Red" and "Guerrilla Song." In September 1949 he took part in the 1st CPPCC.

1950,   Mar   Elected member of the Federation of Literary and Art Circles

         May   Identified as vice-president of the Central College of Music and as vice-chairman of the Musical Workers' Association

1952,   Dec   Member of a delegation to the World Peace Conference

1954,   May   Elected council member of the Association for Cultural Relations with Foreign Countries

         Aug   Elected deputy for Shanghai Municipality to the 1st NPC

1958,   Oct   Identified as vice-chairman of the Sino-Hungarian Friendship Association

1962,   Mar   Delegate attending the 3rd Musical Composers' Congress in Moscow

1966,   Jun   Identified as president of the Shanghai Music Conservatory

         Jul   Branded as an anti-Party and anti-socialist element and purged

1977,   Dec   First appearance after the Cultural Revolution

1978,   Mar   Elected member of the Standing Committee of the 5th CPPCC

1979,   Oct   Identified as vice-president of the Musicians Union; head of a delegation to the 18th General Assembly of the International Music Council of UNESCO in Australia

He Minxue (Ho Min-hsüeh) 贺敏学

Posts held

CCP
4th secretary, Discipline Inspection Commission of Fujian Province CP

NPC
Deputy for Fujian Province to the 5th NPC

Provincial Administration
Vice-chairman of the People's Congress of Fujian Province

Others
Member of the Standing Committee of the 5th CPPCC

In 1943 He was chief of staff of the Joint Defense Anti-Japan Volunteers of the Shandong-Jiangsu Military District.

1959,   Feb   Identified as vice-governor of Fujian Province (until 1968)

1961,   May   Identified as secretary of Fujian Province CP (until 1968)

1964,   Sep   Elected deputy for Fujian Province to the 3rd NPC

1968   He disappears

1978,   Feb   First appearance after the Cultural Revolution: Elected deputy for Fujian Province to the 5th NPC

1979,   Jul   By-elected member of the Standing Committee of the 5th CPPCC

         Dec   Elected vice-chairman of the People's Congress of Fujian Province, and as 4th secretary, Discipline Inspection Commission, Fujian Province CP

He Qifang (Ho Ch'i-fang) 何其芳

He was born in 1910 in Sichuan Province. As a child he studied classical Chinese. He subsequently attended a modern middle school in Chengdu and graduated in 1936 from Beijing University. Already in 1924 he was co-editor with Ye Shengtao, Wan Jiabo and others of the journal Literary Quarterly. In 1936 he was awarded a literary prize by the paper Dagong Bao. In the following year he lectured at the Lu Xun Academy of Art in Yan'an. In May 1949 he was elected a member of the National Committee of the Federation of Democratic Youth which he represented as a delegate at the 1st CPPCC in September.

1949,	Oct	Elected council member of the Sino-Soviet Friendship Association (until 1954)
	Dec	Elected deputy director of the Editorial Board, Federation of Literary and Art Circles
1953,	Sep	Identified as member, Standing Committee of the Union of Chinese Writers
1954,	May	Identified as council member of the Association for Cultural Relations with Foreign Countries
1955,	Jun	Identified as member of the Department of Philosophy and Social Sciences, Academy of Sciences (until Cultural Revolution)
	Dec	Identified as member of the Editorial Board of Renmin Wenxue (People's Literature)
1960,	Jul	Member of an Afro-Asian solidarity delegation to Vietnam
	Nov	Identified as secretary of the Union of Chinese Writers and as director of the Literary Institute of the Academy of Sciences
1961		Identified as chief editor of Wenxue Zazhi (Literary Review)
1964,	Oct	Elected deputy for Sichuan Province to the 3rd NPC
1967		Disappears during the Cultural Revolution
1979,	Jul	He is officially rehabilitated from the charge of "reactionary academic"

Publications

Verse	A Prophecy
	The Song of Night
	The Song of Day
Prose	The Record of the Painted Dream
	Works on Deep Impressions
	Sketches on a Homecoming Trip

He Qingji (Ho Ch'ing-chi) 贺庆积

Posts held

Military
Major-general

Others
Member of the Standing Committee of the 5th CPPCC

He was born in 1919 in Jiangxi Province. During the Anti-Japanese War he was deputy commander of a regiment in the 120th Division, 8th Route Army. In 1948 he commanded the 28th Division of the Northeast Field Army.

1957,	Oct	Identified as commander of Liaoning Military District (until 1963)
1958,	Sep	Identified as major-general
1967		Disappears during the Cultural Revolution
1978,	Mar	First appearance after the Cultural Revolution: Elected member of the Standing Committee of the 5th CPPCC

He Tingyi (Ho T'ing-yi) 何廷一

Posts held

CCP
Member of the Commission for Inspecting Discipline under the CCP Central Committee

NPC
Deputy for the PLA to the 5th NPC

Military
Major-general
Deputy commander of the Air Force of the PLA

He was born in 1912.

1955,	Sep	Awarded the order of "Liberation," 1st class
1956,	Jun	Identified as a major-general in the Air Force
1965,	Sep	Identified as deputy chief of staff of the Air Force
1967,	Nov	He is denounced as a supporter of He Long and disappears
1976,	Jan	First appearance after the Cultural Revolution
	May	Identified as deputy commander of the PLA Air Force
1978,	Feb	Elected deputy for the PLA to the 5th NPC
	Dec	Elected member of the Commission for Inspecting Discipline under the CCP Central Committee

He Xian (Ho Hsien) 何贤

Posts held

NPC
Deputy for Guangdong Province to the 5th NPC

Others
Member of the Standing Committee, 5th CPPCC
Director of the Board of Directors, China International Trust and Investment Corporation
Vice-chairman of the Board of Directors, Jinan University
Chairman, Chinese General Chamber of Commerce of Macao

1960,	Nov	Identified as president of the Chinese Chamber of Commerce of Macao
1978,	Feb	Elected deputy for Guangdong Province to the 5th NPC
	Mar	Elected member of the Standing Committee, 5th CPPCC
	Oct	Identified as vice-chairman of the Board of Directors, Jinan University
1979,	Oct	Appointed director of the Board of Directors, China International Trust and Investment Corporation; identified as chairman, Chinese General Chamber of Commerce of Macao

He Yang (Ho Yang) 何扬

Posts held

Government
Ambassador to Greece

| 1972, | Jun | Identified as chargé d'affaires in Cyprus |
| 1975, | Aug | Appointed ambassador to Greece |

He Ying (Ho Ying)　何　英

Posts held

Government
Vice-minister of foreign affairs

In 1949 He was a political commissar of a division of the PLA.

1952,	Mar	Appointed consul-general in Jakarta with the rank of envoy (until Oct 1952)
	Oct	Appointed deputy director of the Asia Department in the Ministry of Foreign Affairs (until Sep 1954)
1954,	Sep	Appointed ambassador to the People's Republic of Mongolia (until Sep 1959)
1959,	Sep	Appointed deputy director of the 1st Asia Department in the Ministry of Foreign Affairs (until Jan 1960)
1960,	Jan	Appointed director of the West Asia and Africa Department in the Ministry of Foreign Affairs (until Feb 1962)
	Apr	Elected council member of the Sino-African Friendship Association
1962,	Feb	Appointed ambassador in Tanganyika (until Jul 1964)
	Oct	He conducts negotiations in Kampala leading to the establishment of diplomatic relations between PRC and Uganda
1963,	Apr	Appointed to concurrent post as ambassador to Uganda (until Apr 1964)
	Dec	He conducts negotiations in Zanzibar and Burundi leading to the establishment of diplomatic relations
1964,	Jul	Appointed ambassador to Tanzania (until about 1967)
1965,	Feb	He accompanies President Nyerere of Tanzania on his state visit to China
1970,	Jul	Identified as deputy director of the West Asia and Africa Department in the Ministry of Foreign Affairs (until May 1972)
	Sep	Member of a delegation headed by Guo Moruo to attend the funeral of president Nasser of Egypt
1972,	May	Identified as vice-minister of foreign affairs
1974,	Jul	Head of a government delegation to Iraq
1975,	Apr	Member of a government delegation to Iran headed by Li Xiannian
1976,	Jul	Member of a government delegation to Zambia and Tanzania (inauguration of the Tan-Zam Railway) and to Zaire
1977,	Nov	He accompanies Deng Yingchao to Iran
1978,	Jun	He visits Kuwait and Jordan
	Nov	Member of a friendship delegation to Sudan and Turkey (head: Ulanhu)
1979,	Jan	Member of a government delegation to Tanzania, Mozambique, Zambia, Zaire, and Pakistan (head: Li Xiannian)
	Oct	He visits Kenya, Somalia, Oman, Lebanon, and the Yemen Arab Republic

He is married to Wang Hao.

He Yiran (Ho Yi-jan)　颀亦然

Posts held

Provincial Administration
Vice-chairman of the People's Government of Guangxi Autonomous Region

1977,	Dec	Elected vice-chairman of the Revolutionary Committee of Guangxi Autonomous Region (until Dec 1979)
1979,	Dec	Elected vice-chairman of the People's Government of Guangxi Autonomous Region

He Yixiang (Ho Yi-hsiang)　何以祥

Posts held

CCP
Member of the Standing Committee of Shanghai Municipality CP

Military
Major-general
Deputy commander of Nanjing Military Region
Commander of Shanghai Garrison

He was born in 1912. He joined a communist guerrilla unit in Sichuan Province in 1930. In 1945 he commanded a division in Shandong Military District. In the following year he became commander of the 3rd Column, East China Field Army. In 1949 he was chief of staff of the 11th Army Group, 3rd Field Army which occupied Nanjing in April.

1953,	Dec	Identified as chief of staff of Shandong Military District
1963,	Nov	Identified as major-general in Zhejiang Military District
1964,	Oct	Identified as acting director of the National Defense Athletic Association
1965,	Jun	Identified as deputy commander of Zhejiang Military District
1967		Disappears during the Cultural Revolution
1978,	Jun	Identified as commander of Shanghai Garrison
1979,	May	Identified as member of the Standing Committee of Shanghai Municipality CP
	Jun	Identified as deputy commander of Nanjing Military Region
	Oct	Identified as deputy head of Shanghai Municipal Air Defense Leading Group

He Youfa (Ho Yu-fa)　何友发

Posts held

CCP
Secretary of Jilin Province CP

NPC
Deputy for the PLA to the 5th NPC

Military
Commander of Jilin Military District

In 1946 He commanded a regiment in the Shanxi-Chahar-Hebei Field Army. In the following year he was made commander of the 12th Brigade of this Field Army which was reorganized in 1948 to form the North China Field Army. In 1949 he became deputy commander of the 192nd Division, 64th Corps, 19th Army.

1951,	Feb	He is transferred with his unit to the Korean War
1952		Appointed commander of the 192nd Division
1955		Identified as chief of staff of the 64th Army
1959		Appointed deputy commander of the 64th Corps
1967		Appointed commander of Jilin Military District
	Mar	Elected vice-chairman of the Revolutionary Committee of Jilin Province (until 1977)
1971,	Mar	Elected secretary of Jilin Province CP
1978,	Feb	Elected deputy for the PLA to the 5th NPC

He Zhengwen (Ho Cheng-wen) 何正文

Posts held

Military
Major-general
Deputy chief of PLA General Staff

During the revolutionary period He served in the 4th Front Army. In 1949 he was chief of staff of a corps in the 2nd Field Army.

1949,	Nov	Identified as chief of staff of the 3rd Army Corps stationed in Chongqing
1952		Identified as chief of staff of Sichuan Military District
1955,	Jul	Identified as deputy commander of Chengdu Military Region (active in this Military Region until 1966)
	Sep	Promoted to rank of major-general
1967,	May	After the reorganization of Chengdu Military Region He disappears
1974,	May	Reactivated after the Cultural Revolution
	Sep	Renewed mention as deputy commander of Chengdu Military Region (until Dec 1974); head of a militia delegation to Syria
	Dec	Identified as deputy chief of PLA General Staff
1975,	Oct	Head of a military delegation to Sweden
1976,	Sep	Head of a military delegation to Mexico
1977,	Feb	Head of a military delegation to Sri Lanka
1978,	Oct	Head of a military friendship delegation to Sudan and Somalia

He is married to Wan Lin.

He Zhihua (Ho Chih-hua) 贺志华

Posts held

Government
Vice-minister of light industry

1963,	Oct	Head of an expert group sent to Algeria

for the study of industrial and technological conditions (until Jan 1964)

1979,	Sep	Identified as vice-minister of light industry

He Zhuguo (Ho Chu-kuo) 何柱国

Posts held

Others
Member of the Standing Committee of the 5th CPPCC

1979,	Jul	By-elected member of the Standing Committee of the 5th CPPCC

Hong Peilin (Hung P'ei-lin) 洪沛霖

Posts held

Provincial Administration
Vice-governor of Jiangsu Province

1962,	Aug	Identified as director of the Jiangsu Provincial Department of Public Health
1979,	Jun	Identified as vice-chairman of the Revolutionary Committee of Jiangsu Province (until Dec 1979)
	Dec	Elected vice-governor of Jiangsu Province

Hong Xuezhi (Hung Hsüeh-chih) 洪学智

Posts held

CCP
Member of the CCP 11th Central Committee

NPC
Member of the Standing Committee of the 5th NPC
Deputy for the PLA to the 5th NPC

Military
Colonel-general
Director of the 2nd Office for National Defense

Hong was born in 1911 in Jiangxi Province. During the revolutionary period he served as a troop leader in the Red Army. By the end of the Anti-Japanese War he was chief of staff of the 3rd Division of the New 4th Army. In 1948 he commanded a unit of the Communist forces in Manchuria. At the beginning of the following year Hong was deputy commander of an army corps. With this unit which belonged to the 4th Field Army commanded by Lin Biao he took an important part in the battles against KMT Troops from Manchuria to South China.

1949,	Dec	Identified as commander of Guangdong Military Region and as member of the Guangzhou Military Control Commission (probably until 1950)
1950,	Apr	Appointed political commissar of the 16th Corps which shortly afterwards was dispatched to the Korean War

1952		Identified as director of the Logistics Department of the Chinese People's Volunteers in Korea
1954,	Sep	Elected deputy for the PLA to the NPC (until Mar 1959)
	Oct	Appointed member of the National Defense Council (until Mar 1959) and deputy director of the Logistics Department of the PLA (until Dec 1956)
1955,	Sep	Promoted to rank of colonel-general; conferred the orders of "1st August," "Independence and Freedom," and "Liberation," all 1st class
1956,	Sep	Elected alternate member of the CCP Central Committee by the 8th Party Congress
	Dec	Appointed director of the Logistics Department of the PLA (until Oct 1959)
1957,	Nov	Member of a military delegation to the USSR
1958,	Jul	Hong disappears
1977,	Oct	First appearance after the Cultural Revolution
1978,	Feb	Elected deputy for the PLA to the 5th NPC
	Mar	Elected member of the Standing Committee of the 5th NPC
	May	Identified as director of the General Office for National Defense Industry (until Feb 1979)
1979,	Feb	Identified as director of the 2nd Office of National Defense
	Jun	Vice-chairman of the Committee to Examine Proposals at the 2nd Session of the 5th NPC
	Sep	By-elected member of the CCP 11th Central Committee
	Oct	Co-author (with Li Zhimin and Deng Hua) of an article in Jiefangjün Bao (Liberation Army) on 25th Oct., "Heroism Shines Forever, Internationalism Inspires All People - Cherishing the Memory of Peng Dehuai"

Hong Yi (Hung Yi)   洪　毅

Posts held

Provincial Administration
Vice-governor of Hebei Province

1977,	Dec	Elected vice-chairman of the Revolutionary Committee of Hebei Province (until Jan 1980)
1980,	Feb	Elected vice-governor of Hebei Province

Hou Defeng (Hou Te-feng)   侯德封

Posts held

Others
Member of the Standing Committee of the 5th CPPCC

1950,	Sep	Identified as member of the Guidance Committee on the Chinese Geological Work Plan; identified as chief-technician

of the Nanjing Institute of Geological Investigation

1954,	Feb	Identified as council member of the Geological Society
	Jun	Identified as director of the Institute of Geology of the Academy of Sciences
1955,	May	Identified as member of the Department of Biology and Earth Sciences of the Academy of Sciences
1956,	Jan	Elected member of the 2nd CPPCC
1958,	Jul	Elected deputy for Sichuan Province to the 2nd NPC (reelected in 1964 to the 3rd NPC)
1967		Disappears during the Cultural Revolution
1974,	Feb	First appearance after the Cultural Revolution: Present at the mourning ceremonies for Zhu Kezhen
1978,	Mar	Elected member of the Standing Committee of the 5th CPPCC

Hou Deyuan (Hou Te-yüan)   侯德原

Posts held

Government
Vice-minister of posts and telecommunications

1959,	Mar	Elected deputy for Henan Province to the 2nd NPC (reelected to the 3rd NPC in 1964)
1979,	Sep	Identified as vice-minister of posts and telecommunications

Hou Jie (Hou Chieh)   侯　捷

Posts held

Provincial Administration
Vice-chairman of Tibet Autonomous Regional People's Government

1960,	Feb	Identified as deputy director of the Industry and Communications Department of Tibet CP
1962,	Dec	Identified as director of the Communications Department of Tibet Autonomous Region
1965,	Dec	Identified as member of the Standing Committee of Tibet Autonomous Region CP
1979,	Aug	Elected vice-chairman of Tibet Autonomous Regional People's Government

Hou Jie (Hou Chieh)   侯　杰

Posts held

CCP
Member of the Standing Committee of Heilongjiang Province CP

Provincial Administration
Vice-governor of Heilongjiang Province

1977,	Dec	Elected vice-chairman of the Revolutionary Committee of Heilongjiang Province (until Dec 1979)
1979,	Jan	Elected member of the Standing Committee of Heilongjiang Province CP
	Dec	Elected vice-governor of Heilongjiang Province

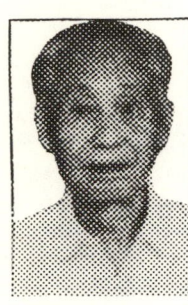

Hou Jingru (Hou Ching-ju) 侯镜如

Posts held

Military
Lieutenant-general

Provincial Administration
Vice-chairman of the People's Congress, Beijing Municipality

Others
Member of the Standing Committee of the 5th CPPCC

Hou was born in 1902 in Yuncheng, Henan Province. He was a member of the 1st graduating class of Whampoa Military Academy and then served in the Nationalist Army, successively as chief of staff of the 91st Army, commander of the 21st Division, deputy commander of the 92nd Army, commander of the 92nd Army, and commander of the 17th Army Group. He eventually reached the rank of lieutenant-general. In 1949 Hou fled to Hong Kong.

1952		Return to the PRC
1954,	Dec	Elected member of the 2nd CPPCC (reelected in 1959 and 1964)
1956,	Feb	Elected alternate member of the Central Committee of the KMT Revolutionary Committee
1958,	Dec	Elected member of the Central Committee of the KMT Revolutionary Committee
1959,	Apr	Appointed member of the National Defense Council
1967		Disappears during the Cultural Revolution
1972,	Sep	First appearance after the Cultural Revolution
1978,	Mar	Elected member of the Standing Committee of the 5th CPPCC
1979,	Dec	Elected vice-chairman of the People's Congress, Beijing Municipality

Hou Tong (Hou T'ung) 侯桐

Posts held

Others
Vice-chairman of the Association for Friendship with Foreign Countries

Hou visited France on several occasions before the foundation of the PRC.

| 1963 | | Identified as vice-chairman of the Committee for Promotion of International Trade |
| 1964, | Mar | Visit to the International Trade Fair in Lyon, France; he later visits Paris and Venice |

	Oct	Hou heads a delegation to the Chinese Economic Construction Exhibition in Ethiopia
	Dec	Hou signs an economic agreement in Vienna
1965,	Jun	Elected member of the Committee for World Peace
1966,	May	Head of a delegation to the 5th Conference of the Afro-Asian Economic Cooperation Conference in Casablanca, Morocco
1967		Disappears during the Cultural Revolution
1979,	Feb	First appearance after the Cultural Revolution: Identified as vice-chairman of the Association for Friendship with Foreign Countries
	May	Head of a friendship delegation to Columbia and Venezuela

Hou Xianglin (Hou Hsiang-lin) 侯祥麟

Posts held

Government
Vice-minister of petroleum industry

Others
Member of the Standing Committee of the 5th CPPCC
President of the Society of Petroleum

Hou received a Ph.D. degree in the United States in the 1940s. He is a former president of the Academy of Petrochemical Sciences and considered China's leading expert in the Petrochemical Industry.

1978,	Mar	Elected member of the Standing Committee of the 5th CPPCC
	Jun	Identified as vice-minister of petroleum industry
	Dec	Elected president of the Society of Petroleum
1979,	Jan	Identified as member of the Department of Technology, Academy of Sciences

Hou Yefeng (Hou Yeh-feng) 侯野烽

Posts held

Government
Ambassador to Iraq

1965,	Aug	Member of a government delegation to Congo (Brazzaville)
	Nov	Identified as deputy director of the Africa Department in the Ministry of Foreign Affairs (until about 1967)
1972,	Feb	Appointed ambassador to Tunisia (until May 1977)
1977,	Sep	Appointed ambassador to Iraq

Hu Bingyun (Hu Ping-yün)   胡炳云

Posts held

CCP
Secretary of Shaanxi Province CP

NPC
Deputy of the PLA to the 5th NPC

Military
Major-general
Deputy commander of Lanzhou Military Region
Commander of Shaanxi Military District

Hu took part in the Long March. He subsequently served as regiment commander in the New 4th Army. In 1946 he commanded a brigade, and in 1949 a corps of the 3rd Field Army.

1952,	Sep	Identified as commander of Fuzhou Garrison
1955		Identified as chief of staff of Fujian Military District
1959,	Aug	Identified as major-general
1960,	Feb	Identified as deputy commander of Lanzhou Military Region
1964,	Feb	Identified as commander of Shaanxi Military District (until Sep 1967)
1967,	Sep	Transferred to the Central Military Leadership
1970,	Oct	Hu disappears for unknown reasons
1974,	Oct	Referred to as a cadre in Sichuan, then disappears until 1977
1977,	Jul	Identified as commander of Shaanxi Military District, a post Hu had already held from 1964 to 1967
1978,	Feb	Elected deputy for the PLA to the 5th NPC
	Sep	Identified as secretary of Shaanxi Province CP and as deputy commander of Lanzhou Military Region

Hu Chengfang (Hu Ch'eng-fang) 胡成放

Posts held

Government
Ambassador to Chile

1960,	Sep	Identified as deputy director of the 1st Asia Department in the Ministry of Foreign Affairs
1962,	Dec	Identified as counselor at the embassy in Czechoslovakia (until 1965)
1973,	Feb	Appointed ambassador to Iraq (until 1974)
1978,	Mar	Appointed ambassador to Chile

Hu Dehua (Hu Te-hua) (f)   胡德华

Posts held

Mass Organization
Secretary of the Communist Youth League

Others
President of the Young Pioneers Work Society

1964,	Jul	Elected member, Central Committee of the Communist Youth League
	Sep	Elected deputy for Zhejiang Province to the 3rd NPC
1977,	Oct	Identified as cadre of a department in the CCP Central Committee
1978,	Oct	Elected secretary of the Communist Youth League
1979,	Jul	Identified as chairman of the CYL Summer Camp Committee
	Aug	Elected president of the Young Pioneers Work Society

Hu Dingyi (Hu Ting-yi)   胡定一

Posts held

Government
Consul-general in San Francisco

1966,	Mar	1st secretary of the embassy in Ghana; declared persona non grata by the Ghanaian government
1973,	Jun	Identified as embassy counselor in Great Britain (until 1975)
1979,	Oct	Appointed consul-general in San Francisco

Hu Han (Hu Han)   胡含

Posts held

Others
Director of the Institute of Genetics, Academy of Sciences

| 1979, | Dec | Identified as director of the Insitute of Genetics, Academy of Sciences |

Hu Hong (Hu Hung)   胡宏

Posts held

CCP
Secretary of Jiangsu Province CP

Government
Member of the Birth Planning Leading Group under the State Council

NPC
Deputy for Jiangsu Province to the 5th NPC

1975,	Oct	Identified as vice-chairman of the Revolutionary Committee of Jiangsu Province (until Dec 1979)
1977,	May	Identified as secretary of Jiangsu Province CP
1978,	Feb	Elected deputy for Jiangsu Province to the 5th NPC
	Jul	Identified as member of the Birth Planning Leading Group under the State Council

Hu is married to Min Huasheng.

Hu Jiabin (Hu Chia-pin)   胡嘉宾

Posts held

Government
Vice-minister of the State Nationalities Affairs Commission

1958		Identified as member of the State Nationalities Affairs Commission
1978,	Aug	First appearance after the Cultural Revolution
1979,	Apr	Identified as vice-minister of the State Nationalities Affairs Commission

Hu Jindi (Hu Chin-ti) (f)   胡金娣

Posts held

CCP
Alternate member of the CCP 11th Central Committee
Member of the Standing Committee of Shaanxi Province CP

Mass Organization
Vice-chairman, Trade Union of Shaanxi Province

1973,	Aug	Elected to first term as alternate member of the CCP Central Committee by the 10th Party Congress
1975,	Jan	Hu appears at a Daqing symposium in Xian capital city of Shaanxi Province
1976,	Dec	Identified as vice-chairman of the Trade Union of Shaanxi Province
1977,	Oct	Identified as member of the Standing Committee of Shaanxi Province CP

Hu Jingrui (Hu Ching-jui)   胡景瑞

Posts held

Government
Former ambassador to Equatorial Guinea

1970,	Nov	Identified as consul in the consulate general in Dacca (until the post is closed in Jan 1972)
1972,	May	Identified as chargé d'affaires in Mauritius (until 1973)
1974,	Aug	Appointed ambassador to Equatorial Guinea (until Aug 1979)

Hu Jiwei (Hu Chi-wei)   胡绩伟

Posts held

CCP
Chief editor of RMRB

NPC
Deputy for Sichuan Province to the 5th NPC

1950,	Mar	Identified as deputy director of the Information Bureau in the Northwest China Military and Administrative Council

1954,	May	Identified as associate editor of RMRB
1956,	Apr	Head of a delegation of journalists to the USSR
1958,	Jun	Identified as deputy editor-in-chief of RMRB
1964,	Oct	Elected deputy for Sichuan Province to the 3rd NPC
1967		Disappears during the Cultural Revolution
1976,	Jan	First appearance after the Cultural Revolution: Identified as a cadre in a department of the CCP Central Committee
	Nov	Hu is present at a reception for a press delegation from Iran
1977,	Apr	Identified as chief editor of RMRB
1978,	Feb	Elected deputy for Sichuan Province to the 5th NPC
	May	Head of a RMRB delegation to North Korea
	Jul	Head of a delegation of journalists to Yugoslavia and Romania

Hu Juewen (Hu Chüeh-wen)   胡厥文

Posts held

NPC
Vice-chairman of the Standing Committee of the 5th NPC
Deputy for Shanghai Municipality to the 5th NPC

Others
Member of the Standing Committee, 5th CPPCC
Chairman of the China Democratic National Construction Association

Hu was born in 1895 in Jiating County, Jiangsu Province. After studying at a Beijing industrial institute he worked as an engineer at the Iron Works of Hanyang in 1918. In 1919 he became head of the Engineering Department of Dongji University in Shanghai. In 1921 he established and managed a machine factory in Shanghai. In 1924 he became manager of the Hengda Textile Factory, and in 1930 established a factory for electric motors in Huangtu. In 1933 he founded the China United Machine Company. In 1937, after the outbreak of the Anti-Japanese War, he played a significant role in the evacuation of important factories into the interior. These he subsequently managed with headquarters in Chongqing. In 1945 he founded, together with Huang Yanpei and Shi Fuliang, the China Democratic National Construction Association. He was invited by the Communists to take part as the association's representative in the 1st CPPCC which elected him a member of its National Committee.

1949,	Oct	Appointed member, Committee of Financial and Economic Affairs, Government Administration Council (until Sep 1954)
	Dec	Appointed member, East China Military and Administrative Council (until Jan 1953)
1952,	Jun	Member of the Preparatory Committee, Federation of Industry and Commerce
	Jul	Elected member of the Standing Committee of the China Democratic National Construction Association

1953,	Jan	Appointed member of the East China Administrative Council (until Sep 1954)
	Nov	With the establishment of the Federation of Industry and Commerce, Hu is elected a member of its Standing Committee
1954,	Aug	Elected deputy for Shanghai Municipality to the 1st NPC (reelected in 1958 and 1964 to the 2nd and 3rd NPC
1955,	Apr	Elected vice-chairman of the China Democratic National Construction Association
1957,	Jul	Head of a China Democratic National Construction Association delegation to the Party Congress of the Socialist Unity Party of Germany in the German Democratic Republic
1959,	Apr	The 2nd NPC elects Hu a member of its Standing Committee (confirmed in this post in 1965 by the 3rd NPC)
	Jul	Elected chairman of the Shanghai Division of the Sino-Soviet Friendship Association
1962,	Jul	Elected deputy mayor of Shanghai (until Cultural Revolution)
1966-1969		Hu survives the Cultural Revolution without coming under attack
1970-1974		Hu is named on numerous occasions as a member of the Standing Committee, NPC, and occasionally also as vice-chairman of the China Democratic National Construction Association (until Oct 1979)
1975,	Jan	The 4th NPC elects Hu one the 22 vice-chairmen of its Standing Committee
1978,	Feb	Elected deputy for Shanghai Municipality to the 5th NPC
	Mar	Elected member of the Standing Committee of the 5th CPPCC
1979,	Oct	Elected chairman of the China Democratic National Construction Association

Hu is married to Shen Fangcheng.

Hu Keshi (Hu K'e-shih)   胡克实

Posts held

Others
Member of the Standing Committee of the 5th CPPCC
Vice-president of the Academy of Sciences

Hu was born in 1921 in Hubei Province. He studied at Beijing University. In 1935 he took part in the Beijing Student Movement of 9 December. He was then engaged in communist propaganda work among students and railway workers in North China. In April 1949 he was elected an alternate member of the Central Committee and director of the Organization Department, New Democratic Youth League (until 1953).

1950,	Mar	Identified as deputy secretary of the Youth Committee in the Central-South China Bureau of the CCP Central Committee
1952,	Jan	Appointed member of the Political and Legislative Committee in the Central-South Military Administration Council

1953,	Jun	Elected member of the Standing Committee and secretary of the New Democratic Youth League (until May 1957)
1954,	Jul	Member of a youth delegation to North Korea
	Aug	Elected deputy for Hubei Province to the 1st NPC
1955,	Apr	Head of a youth delegation to the USSR
1957,	Feb	Head of a youth delegation to the USSR
	May	Elected secretary and member of the Standing Committee of the Communist Youth League (until Apr 1967)
1958,	Apr	Head of a guest delegation to the 13th Congress of the Soviet Communist Youth League
1959,	May	Head of a Communist Youth League delegation to the 6th Congress of the Democratic Youth League of the German Democratic Republic
1961,	Mar	Head of Communist Youth League delegation to North Vietnam
	Jul	Head of a friendship delegation to Cuba
1965,	Jan	Elected member of the Standing Committee of the 4th CPPCC as a representative of the Communist Youth League
1967,	Apr	Hu is denounced as a supporter of Liu Shaoqi and disappears
1973,	May	First appearance after the Cultural Revolution
1975,	Jan	Confirmed as member of the Standing Committee, CPPCC
1977,	Dec	Identified as a cadre in the Academy of Sciences
1978,	Mar	Appointed vice-president of the Adademy of Sciences. Elected member of the Standing Committee of the 5th CPPCC
	Oct	Head of an Academy of Sciences delegation to Sweden and Great Britain

Hu Liangcai (Hu Liang-ts'ai)   胡良才

Posts held

CCP
Alternate member of the CCP 11th Central Committee
Member of the Standing Committee, Xinjiang Autonomous Region CP

Mass Organization
Chairman of the Trade Union of Xinjiang Autonomous Region

1968,	Nov	Identified as a worker in Xinjiang
1969,	Apr	Elected to first term as alternate member of the CCP Central Committee by the 9th Party Congress
	Aug	Identified as vice-chairman of the Revolutionary Committee of Xinjiang Province (until Aug 1979)
1973,	Sep	Elected chairman of the Xinjiang Trade Union
1978,	Jun	Identified as member of the Standing Committee, Xinjiang Autonomous Region CP

Hu Lijiao (Hu Li-chiao)   胡立教

Posts held

CCP
Member of the CCP 11th Central Committee
2nd secretary of Henan Province CP

NPC
Deputy for Henan Province to the 5th NPC

Provincial Administration
Chairman of the Standing Committee of Henan Province People's Congress

Hu was born in 1914. He took part in the Long March as a member of the "Little Devils."

1950		Identified as director of the Organization Department of the East China Bureau in the CCP Central Committee
	Mar	Appointed vice-chairman of the People's Control Committee of the East China Military and Administrative Council
1952,	Aug	Appointed vice-chairman of the Labor Employment Committee in the East China Military and Administrative Council
1954,	Oct	Appointed vice-minister of finance (until 1958)
1957		Identified as director of the Cadre School of the Ministry of Finance (until Jul 1958)
1958,	Jul	Identified as 1st secretary, Songjiang District, Heilongjiang Province CP
1961,	Dec	Identified as deputy director of the People's Bank (until Jan 1966)
1964,	Oct	Elected deputy for Guizhou Province to the 3rd NPC
1966,	Jan	Identified as acting president of the People's Bank
1967		Disappears during the Cultural Revolution
1974,	Sep	First appearance after the Cultural Revolution
1975,	Oct	Identified as deputy secretary of Henan Province CP (until Oct 1977)
1976,	Jan	Identified as vice-chairman of the Revolutionary Committee of Henan Province (until Nov 1977)
1977,	Aug	Elected member of the CCP Central Committee by the 11th Party Congress
	Oct	Identified as 2nd secretary of Henan Province CP
	Nov	Identified as 1st vice-chairman of the Revolutionary Committee of Henan Province (until Dec 1977)
	Dec	Elected vice-chairman of the Revolutionary Committee of Henan Province (until Sep 1979)
1978,	Feb	Elected deputy for Henan Province to the 5th NPC
1979,	Sep	Elected chairman of the Standing Committee of Henan Province People's Congress

Hu is married to Gu Ming.

Hu Ming (Hu Ming)   胡 明

Posts held

Government
Vice-minister of textile industry

NPC
Deputy for Liaoning Province to the 5th NPC

Hu was born in India. During the thirties he worked as a translator in Shanghai. In 1947 he was political commissar in the Jiangsu-Anhui Military Border Region. As a delegate representing peasant organizations he took part in the 1st CPPCC in September 1949.

1952,	Aug	Identified as member of the Employment Commission in the East China Military and Administrative Council
1954,	Oct	Identified as member of the State Planning Commission (until Apr 1957)
1956,	Mar	Identified as director of the Planning Bureau for Light and Textile Industry of the State Planning Commission
1957,	Jun	Appointed vice-minister of food industry (until Feb 1958)
1958,	Apr	Identified as secretary, Lüda Municipality CP (Lüshun-Dairen)
	Dec	Elected deputy for Liaoning Province to the 2nd NPC (reelected in 1964 by the 4th NPC)
1959,	Jun	Identified as mayor of Lüda
1964,	Aug	Identified as acting 1st secretary, Lüda Municipality CP
1967,	Jan	Publicly accused as a counterrevolutionary revisionist and purged
1978,	Feb	First appearance after the Cultural Revolution: Elected deputy for Liaoning Province to the 5th NPC
	May	Identified as vice-minister of textile industry

Hu Qiaomu (Hu Ch'iao-mu)   胡乔木

Posts held

CCP
Member of the CCP 11th Central Committee
Member of the Secretariat of the CCP Central Committee
Director of the Office of the Committee for the Editing and Publication of the Works of Mao Zedong

NPC
Member of the Standing Committee of the 5th NPC
Deputy for Tianjin Municipality to the 5th NPC
Vice-chairman of the Legal Commission under the NPC Standing Committee

Others
President of the Academy of Social Sciences
Advisor to the Lu Xun Studies Society

Hu was born in 1912 in Yancheng, Jiangsu Province. His familiy were wealthy landowners. His father, a well-known politician, had at one time been a member of the Beijing Parliament. After attending middle school in Yangzhou, Jiangsu Province, Hu studied physics at the Beijing Qinghua University from 1930 to 1932. In 1935 he joined the CCP. Until 1937 he was mainly active as a propaganda cadre for the CP of Shanghai. After 1937 he was primarily engaged in journalism and publishing work in the then CP Central Organization in Shaanxi Province. At this time he helped to edit the journal Chinese Youth together with Jiang Nanxiang. In 1945 he succeeded Chen Boda as Mao Zedong's secretary whom he accompanied from August to October of that year at the negotiations with Chiang Kai-shek. Little is known about Hu's activities for the following years until 1948 when he was appointed director of the Xinhua News Agency. In September the following year he was elected a member of the National Committee of the 1st CPPCC.

1949,	Oct	Identified as member of the National Committee of the Federation of Democratic Youth; member of the Standing Committee of the Association for the Reform of the Chinese Language, council member of the Sino-Soviet Friendship Association and member of the Central Committee of the New Democratic Youth League
1950		Appointed council member of the Peace Council; identified as deputy director of the Propaganda Department under the CCP Central Committee
1951		Hu publishes his book Thirty Years of the CCP which reaches 2.8 million copies by the end of 1952
1954,	Oct	Elected deputy for Jiangsu Province to the 1st NPC; elected member of the Standing Committee of the 1st NPC; identified as deputy secretary-general of the CCP Central Committee
1956,	Sep	Elected member of the CCP Central Committee by the 8th Party Congress, alternate member of the Secretariat, and deputy director of the Propaganda Department
	Oct?	Appointed vice-chairman of the Committee to Phoneticize the Chinese Language
	Nov?	Member of a CCP delegation to Moscow
1957,		Member of a CCP delegation to Moscow
1959,	Apr	Elected member of the Standing Committee of the 2nd NPC
1960,	Nov	Member of a CCP delegation to Moscow
1966		With all other cadres in the field of propaganda, Hu immediately comes under attack in the Cultural Revolution. In August he is relieved of all posts.
1967,	Jan	In a demonstration of public criticism Hu is humiliated by Red Guards and denounced as a supporter of Liu Shaoqi and as a "three-anti element." He disappears after this incident.
1974,	Sep	First appearance after the Cultural Revolution
1975,	Sep	Identified as a cadre in a department of the CCP Central Committee
1978,	Feb	Elected deputy for Tianjin Municipality to the 5th NPC
	Mar	Elected member of the Standing Committee of the 5th NPC; appointed president of the Academy of Social Sciences
	Dec	Elected member of the Central Committee by the 3rd Plenum of the 11th CCP Central Committee
1979,	Jan	Head of a friendship delegation to Japan
	Feb	Appointed vice-chairman of the Legal Commission under the Standing Committee of the 5th NPC
	Jun	Vice-chairman of the Draft Laws Committee, 2nd Session of the 5th NPC
	Sep	Identified as deputy secretary-general of the CCP Central Committee
	Nov	Head of a delegation of the Academy of Social Sciences to Romania and Yugoslavia
	Dec	Elected advisor to the Lu Xun Studies Society
		Since 1979 Hu also holds the post of director of the Office of the Committee for the Editing and Publication of the Works of Mao Zedong.
1980,	Feb	Elected member of the Secretariat of the 11th CCP Central Committee by its 5th Plenum

Hu is married to Gu Yu.

Hu Qili (Hu Ch'i-li)

胡啟立

Posts held

Mass Organization
Secretary of the Communist Youth League
Chairman of the Youth Federation

Others
Member of the Standing Committee of the 5th CPPCC
Vice-president of Qinghua University

Hu was born in Youlin County, Shaanxi Province. He is a graduate of Beijing University.

1954,	Mar	Identified as secretary of the Communist Youth League Committee of Beijing University
	Jul	Member of a youth delegation to North Korea
	Aug	Identified as vice-chairman of the Students' Federation
1958,	Apr	Elected member of the Standing Committee of the Youth Federation
1960,	Mar	Identified as council member of the Sino-Latin-American Friendship Association
	Apr	Identified as council member of the Sino-African Society
	Sep	Head of a students' delegation to Morocco
1961,	Aug	Head of a students' delegation to North Vietnam
1962,	Mar	Head of a youth delegation to Cuba
	Dec	Head of a students' delegation to Cuba
1964,	Jul	Elected alternate secretary of the Communist Youth League
	Oct	Elected deputy for Heilongjiang Province to the 3rd NPC

1965,   Jan   Elected vice-chairman of the Youth Federation

         Mar   Head of a youth delegation to Congo, Egypt, Guinea, Tanzania, and Mauritania (until Apr)

1967,   May   Branded as a follower of Liu Shaoqi and purged

1978,   Sep   Identified as vice-president of Qinghua University

         Oct   Elected secretary of the Communist Youth League

1979,   May   Elected chairman of the Youth Federation

         Jul   By-elected member of the Standing Committee of the 5th CPPCC

         Nov   Head of a youth delegation to the U.S.A.

         Dec   Head of a youth delegation to the Federal Republic of Germany and France

Hu Shangli (Hu Shang-li)　　胡 尚 礼

Posts held

CCP
Secretary of Henan Province CP

NPC
Deputy for Henan Province to the 5th NPC

Military
Political commissar of Henan Military District

1976,   Sep   Identified as political commissar of Henan Military District

1977,   Dec   Elected vice-chairman of the Revolutionary Committee of Henan Province (until Aug 1979)

1978,   Jan   Identified as secretary of Henan Province CP

         Feb   Elected deputy for Henan Province to the 5th NPC

Hu Sheng (Hu Sheng)　　胡 绳

Posts held

NPC
Member of the Standing Committee of the 5th NPC

Deputy for Shanghai Municipality to the 5th NPC

Hu was born in 1908 in Shandong Province. In August 1948 he joined the Communist-established North China People's Government. He was appointed vice-chairman of the Committee for Compilation and Examination of Publications of the People's Government's Education Department. With the foundation of the Federation of Democratic Youth in May 1949 he was elected a member of its National Committee (until June 1953). In September of that year Hu took part in the CPPCC.

1949,   Oct   Appointed a board member of the Committee for Reforming the Chinese Written Language

         Dec   Appointed director of the General Office and deputy director of the Bureau of Compilation and Translations, Publications Administration in the Government Administration Council

1951,   Mar   Identified as secretary-general, Propaganda Department of the CCP Central Committee

1954,   Aug   Elected deputy for Shandong Province to the 1st NPC

1955,   Jun   Appointed member of the Department of Philosophy and Social Sciences in the Academy of Sciences

1957,   Jun   Appointed a member of the Scientific Planning Commission under the State Council

1958,   Apr   Elected vice-chairman of the Youth Federation (until Jan 1965)

         Jul   Identified as a council member of the Peace Council (until Cultural Revolution)

         Sep   Identified as deputy director, Political Research Office of the Higher Party School

1961,   Feb   Member of a friendship delegation to the USSR; identified as deputy editor-in-chief of the journal HQ (until Cultural Revolution)

1964,   Sep   Elected deputy for Shanghai Municipality to the 3rd NPC

1966   Together with all other cadres in the field of propaganda, Hu disappears during the Cultural Revolution

1973,   Oct   First appearance after the Cultural Revolution: Mentioned as a cadre of the State Council

1975,   Jan   Elected member of the Standing Committee by the 4th NPC (confirmed in 1978 by the 5th NPC)

1978,   Feb   Elected deputy for Shanghai Municipality to the 5th NPC

Important publications by Hu Sheng:

1946   Systems of Thought and Study
1948   Imperialism and Chinese Politics
1950-1952   "Treatises on the Fundamental Knowledge of the Social Sciences," jointly written with co-authors Yu Guangyuan and Wang Huide; appeared in 29 issues of the journal Xuexi (Study) which continued after 1958 as HQ

Hu Song (Hu Sung)　　胡 松

Posts held

CCP
Alternate member of the CCP 11th Central Committee

1977,   Aug   Elected alternate member of the CCP Central Committee by the 11th Party Congress; identified as member of the (Shiwu?) Production Brigade of (Nada?) People's Commune in Dan County on Hainan Island, Guangdong Province

Hu Yaobang (Hu Yao-pang)   胡耀邦

<u>Posts held</u>

CCP
Member of the Standing Committee of the Politburo
Member of the Politburo of the CCP 11th Central Committee
Member of the CCP 11th Central Committee
Secretary-general of the Secretariat of the CCP 11th Central Committee
Vice-president of the CCP Central Committee's Party School
3rd secretary of the CCP Central Committee's Commission for Inspecting Discipline

NPC
Member of the Standing Committee of the 5th NPC
Deputy for Anhui Province to the 5th NPC

Hu was born in 1915 in Liuyang, Hunan Province. During the Autumn Harvest Uprising in 1927 he joined the so-called Children's Corps. In 1933 he was engaged in youth work for the Central Party Leadership of the Jiangxi-Soviet. During 1934-35 he took part in the Long March. At the end of 1935 he was head of the Organization Department of the Communist Youth League. From 1936 he studied at the Anti-Japan Military and Political Academy. In 1941 he headed the Organization Department of the General Political Department, 18th Army Corps. In 1947 he was identified as director of the Organization Department of the Revolutionary Military Council. In early 1949 Hu was head of the Political Department of the 3rd Regiment, PLA 2nd Field Army. In April of that year he was identified as a member of the Central Committee, New Democratic Youth League. In September the CPPCC elected him a member of its National Committee (until Dec 1964).

1949,   Dec   Identified as director of the Political Department of the 18th Army Corps; director of the North Sichuan Administrative Bureau; and political commissar of North Sichuan Military Region (until Aug 1952)

1950,   Jul   Appointed member of the Southwest China Military and Administrative Council (probably until Aug 1952)

1952,   Aug   Elected secretary of the New Democratic Youth League

1953,   May   Elected member of the Executive Council, Federation of Trade Unions (until Dec 1957)

         Jul   Head of a delegation attending a session of the World Federation of Democratic Youth in Bucharest; elected vice-chairman of the World Federation (until Aug 1959)

1954,   Aug   Elected deputy for Shandong Province to the 1st NPC (until Dec 1964)

         Sep   Elected member of the Standing Committee by the 1st NPC (confirmed in this post in 1959, 1965, and 1975 by the 2nd, 3rd, and 4th NPCs)

1956,   Mar   Appointed vice-chairman of the State Council Commission for Elimination of Illiteracy

         Sep   Elected member of the CCP Central Committee by the 8th Party Congress (until Cultural Revolution)

1957,   May   With the reorganization of the New Democratic Youth League into the Communist Youth League, Hu is elected 1st secretary (until about 1964)

         Jul   Head of a delegation to the 6th World Youth Festival in Moscow

1962,   Sep   Head of a friendship delegation to Albania

1964,   Oct   Elected deputy for Sichuan Province to the 3rd NPC

1965,   Mar   Identified as 3rd secretary of the Northwest China Bureau in the CCP Central Committee and as acting 1st secretary of Shaanxi Province CP (until Cultural Revolution)

1966,   Jan   Hu is again engaged in youth work for the Central Leadership

1967,   Jan   Hu is attacked by Red Guards as a member of Liu Shaoqi's anti-Party clique and disappears

1972,   Apr   First appearance after the Cultural Revolution

         Sep   Referred to as member of the Standing Committee of the 3rd NPC (until Jan 1975)

1975,   Nov   Referred to as a cadre in the Academy of Sciences

1976,   Jan   Referred to as a cadre of the State Council

1977,   Aug   Elected member of the CCP Central Committee by the 11th Party Congress

         Oct   Identified as vice-president of the CCP Central Committee's Party School

         Dec   Identified as director of the CCP Central Committee's Organization Department (until Dec 1978)

1978,   Feb   Elected deputy for Anhui Province to the 5th NPC

         Mar   Elected member of the Standing Committee of the 5th NPC

         Nov   Member of a Party and government delegation led by Wang Dongxing to Kampuchea

         Dec   Elected member of the Politburo by the 3rd Plenum of the 11th Central Committee and 3rd secretary of the Central Committee's newly established Commission for Inspecting Discipline

1979,   Jan   Identified as director of the CCP Central Committee's Propaganda Department (until Feb 1980) and as secretary-general (mishuzhang) of the CCP Central Committee

         Jun   Chairman of the Credentials Committee of the 2nd Session of the 5th NPC

1980,   Feb   Elected member of the Standing Committee of the Politburo by the 5th Plenum of the 11th Central Committee and officially elected as secretary-general (zongshuji) of the Secretariat of the CCP Central Committee

Hu Yimin (Hu Yi-min)   胡亦民

Posts held

CCP
Secretary of Liaoning Province CP

Provincial Administration
Vice-governor of Liaoning Province

1954,	Nov	Identified as deputy secretary, Shenyang Municipality CP
1956,	Sep	Identified as secretary, Shenyang Municipality CP
1958,	Dec	Elected secretary-general of Liaoning Province CP
1960,	Dec	Identified as member of the Standing Committee of Liaoning Province CP
1962,	Apr	Identified as alternate member of the Secretariat, Liaoning Province CP
1966,	Nov	At the height of the Cultural Revolution Hu withdraws from political life
1973,	Jun	Identified as secretary of Liaoning Province CP
1977,	Mar	Identified as vice-chairman of the Revolutionary Committee of Liaoning Province (until Dec 1979)
1980,	Jan	Elected vice-governor of Liaoning Province

Hu Yuzhi (Hu Yü-chih)   胡愈之

Posts held

NPC
Member of the Standing Committee of the 5th NPC
Deputy for Liaoning Province to the 5th NPC

Others
Vice-chairman of the Standing Committee, 5th CPPCC
Vice-chairman of the Central Committee, China Democratic League
Chairman of the Esperanto League
Honorary chairman, Publishers' Association

Hu was born in 1897 in Shangyu, Zhejiang Province. As a child he received a classical education. He continued his studies at the modern Shaoxing Middle School where Lu Xun was one of his teachers, and subsequently enrolled at the Foreign Language School in Hangzhou. Around 1920 he went to Shanghai to work as an editor for the well-known Commercial Press. In 1921 he became editor-in-chief of the Dongfang Zazhi (Eastern Journal), one of the most prestigious journals in China. Here Hu became known for his articles on domestic and foreign policy. At the same time he translated a number of European literary works into Chinese. He spent the year 1930-31 in the United States and in the USSR advocating the Esperanto movement. On his way between these two countries he probably attended lectures on international law at the University of Paris. In 1931 his widely known book Impressions of Moscow was published. In 1933 he joined the "China League for Civil Rights" organized by Song Qingling. In 1934 he was co-editor of the journal Shijie Zhishi (World Knowledge). In 1937, when Shanghai

was occupied by the Japanese at the beginning of the Anti-Japanese War, he published several anti-Japanese articles in the journal Dikang (Resistance). In 1938 he left for Wuchang and later proceeded to Hankou where he worked under Guo Moruo in the Propaganda Department of the Central Military Council. After a short period, however, he established together with Fan Changjiang the International News Agency in Ruilin. In 1940 Hu published the newspaper Nan Yang Siang in Singapore, supported by Tan Kah-kee (Chen Jiageng). At the outbreak of the Pacific War one year later, he took a leading part in organizing anti-Japanese resistance by the overseas Chinese. When Singapore fell to the Japanese Hu fled to Indonesia and remained there until the end of the Anti-Japanese War. In 1945 he returned first to Singapore, again editing various newspapers there, and in 1948 via Hong Kong to the Communist-occupied part of North China. After Beijing was occupied by Communist forces in March 1949 Hu became editor-in-chief of the newspaper GMRB. Six months later he took part in the CPPCC.

1950,	Oct	Appointed director of the Publications Office and member of the Commission of Cultural and Educational Affairs in the Government Administration Council (until Sep 1954); elected board member of the Association for Reforming the Written Chinese Language and council member of the Sino-Soviet Friendship Association (until Dec 1964)
1950,	Dec?	Appointed deputy director of the Institute of Foreign Affairs; elected member, Standing Committee of the Democratic League (until May 1953)
1952,	May	Elected council member of the Sino-Indian Friendship Association (until about 1962)
1953,	May	Elected secretary-general of the China Democratic League (until Dec 1958)
1954,	Apr	Elected deputy for Shanghai Municipality to the 1st NPC (until Mar 1959)
	Oct	Elected member of the Standing Committee of the 1st NPC
	Nov	Appointed vice-chairman, Committee for Reforming the Written Chinese Language; member of a delegation to the World Peace Council session at Stockholm
	Dec	Elected member, Standing Committee of the CPPCC
1955,	Jun	Elected vice-chairman of the Sino-Indonesian Friendship Association (until 1966)
1956,	Mar	Elected board member of the World Peace Council (until Cultural Revolution)
1958,	Dec	Elected vice-chairman of the Democratic League
	Jul	Member of a delegation to the International Disarmament Conference in Stockholm
1959,	Mar	Elected deputy for Liaoning Province to the NPC and deputy secretary-general of the NPC
	May	Member of a delegation to the World Peace Council session in Stockholm
	Sep	Appointed vice-minister of culture (until Cultural Revolution)
1960,	Mar	Elected vice-chairman of the Sino-Latin-American Friendship Association (until Cultural Revolution)
1961,	Aug	Member of an NPC delegation to Indone-

sia and Burma

1962, Apr Appointed vice-chairman of the newly established Asia-Africa Society (until Cultural Revolution)

1964, Feb Head of a friendship delegation to Nepal

       Jun Head of a cultural delegation to Romania

       Dec Identified as vice-chairman of the Sino-Soviet Friendship Association (until Cultural Revolution)

1965, Jan Elected member of the Standing Committee by the 3rd NPC

       Aug Identified as vice-chairman of the Sino-Nepalese Friendship Association (until Cultural Revolution)

1966-1969 Hu survives the Cultural Revolution without coming under attack

1970-1974 Hu appears on numerous state functions in his capacity as Standing Committee member of the NPC

1975, Jan Confirmed as member of the NPC Standing Committee by the 4th NPC (again confirmed in 1978 by the 5th NPC)

1978, Feb Elected deputy for Liaoning Province to the 5th NPC

       Mar Elected member of the Standing Committee, 5th CPPCC (until Jun 1979)

1979, Jun Member of the Draft Laws Committee at the 2nd Session of the 5th NPC

       Sep Identified as chairman of the Esperanto League

       Oct Elected vice-chairman of the Central Committee of the China Democratic League

       Dec Elected honorary chairman, Publishers' Association

Hu is married to Shen Zijin.

Hu Zhaoheng (Hu Chao-heng)　　胡昭衡

Posts held

Government
Vice-minister of public health
Member of the Birth Planning Leading Group under the State Council

Hu was born in Henan Province.

1953, Dec Identified as deputy director of the Propaganda Department, CP of Inner Mongolia

1954, Aug Identified as council member of the People's Government, Inner Mongolian Autonomous Region

1958, Mar Identified as director of the Propaganda Department, CP of Inner Mongolia (until 1960)

1960, Apr Identified as alternate secretary, CP of Inner Mongolia (until 1963)

1963, Jun Identified as secretary, CP of Tianjin Municipality

1964, Jan Identified as mayor of Tianjin

       Oct Elected deputy for Hebei Province to the 3rd NPC (until Cultural Revolution)

       Dec Identified as member of the Standing Committee of Hebei Province CP (until Cultural Revolution)

1967, Sep Identified as member of the Preparatory Group for Tianjin Revolutionary Committee

1968, Jul Branded as a renegade and purged

1978, Jun First appearance after the Cultural Revolution: Identified as vice-chairman of the Revolutionary Committee of Tianjin (until Dec 1978)

       Jul Identified as member of the Birth Planning Leading Group under the State Council

       Sep Identified as member of the Standing Committee, CP of Tianjin Municipality (until Dec 1978)

1979, Feb Identified as vice-minister of public health

Hu Ziang (Hu Tzu-ang)　　胡子昂

Posts held

NPC
Member of the Standing Committee of the 5th NPC
Deputy for Sichuan Province to the 5th NPC

Others
Vice-chairman of the 5th CPPCC
Vice-chairman of the China National Democratic Construction Association
Chairman of the Executive Committee, Federation of Industrialists and Businessmen

Hu was born in 1899 (1891?, 1900?) in Chongqing, Sichuan Province. After completing his studies at the Beijing University's College of Agriculture he became principal of a middle school in his native province. Until the beginning of the Anti-Japanese War in 1937 he successively held the following positions: director of the Border Affairs Department in the 24th Sichuan Army under Liu Wenhui; director of the Chongqing Waterworks. After 1937 he worked for the government in a number of important fields. In addition, he founded the Huagang Bank in Chongqing during this period. Before the Communist forces occupied Chongqing he left for Hong Kong. In September 1949 he took part in the 1st CPPCC.

1949, Oct Appointed member of the Financial and Economic Affairs Committee in the Government Administration Council (until Oct 1954)

       Dec Elected a member of the Standing Committee of the China National Democratic Construction Association

1950, Jan Appointed member, Southwest China Military and Administrative Council, and member of that council's Financial and Economic Affairs Committee (until Jan 1953); appointed deputy mayor of Chongqing

1953, Jan Appointed a member of the Southwest China Administrative Council (until Oct 1954)

       Dec Elected vice-chairman of the Federation of Industry and Commerce at its first session

1954,	Aug	Elected deputy for Chongqing Municipality to the 1st NPC
1955,	Apr	Elected vice-chairman of the China Democratic National Construction Association (reelected Oct 1979)
1956,	Nov	Deputy head of an NPC delegation to the USSR, Romania, and Czechoslovakia
1957,	Sep	Appointed chairman of the Sino-Syrian Friendship Association
1958,	Feb	Appointed chairman of the Sino-Egyptian Friendship Association
	Oct	Elected deputy for Sichuan Province to the 2nd NPC (reelected in 1964 by the 3rd NPC)
1965,	Jan	Elected member of the Standing Committee by the 3rd NPC (confirmed in this post by the 4th and 5th NPCs in 1965 and 1978)
	Mar	Member of an NPC delegation to Guinea, Mali, the Central African Republic, and Congo
1966-1969		Hu survives the Cultural Revolution without coming under attack
1970-1975		Hu represents the Standing Committee of NPC on occasions of domestic political importance
1978,	Feb	Elected deputy for Sichuan Province to the 5th NPC
	Mar	Elected vice-chairman of the 5th CPPCC
1979,	Jun	Vice-chairman of the Budget Committee of the 2nd Session of the 5th NPC
	Oct	Elected chairman of the Executive Committee, Federation of Industrialists and Businessmen

Hu Ziying (Hu Tzu-ying) (f) 胡子婴

Posts held

Others
Member of the Standing Committee of the 5th CPPCC
Director of the Board of Directors, China International Trust and Investment Corporation
Vice-chairman and secretary-general of the Federation of Industrialists and Businessmen

Hu was born in 1903 in Shanghai. In the early thirties she worked in several banks in Shanghai. In 1945 she founded the Women's Association for Promoting Democracy in Shanghai and joined the China Democratic National Construction Association. In early 1949 she was elected a member of the Executive Committee, Federation of Democratic Women, and member of the Federation of Democratic Youth. In September she took part in the 1st CPPCC.

1949,	Oct	Elected member of the Committee for the Defense of World Peace (until 1958)
	Nov	Appointed deputy secretary-general of the Financial and Economic Commission, Government Administration Council (until 1954)
	Oct	Identified as member of the Standing Committee, Central Committee of the China Democratic National Construction Association
1950,	Dec	Identified as member of the People's Government of Shanghai (until Feb 1955)
1951,	Jul	Identified as member of the Financial and Economic Committee of Shanghai People's Government
1953,	Apr	Elected member of the Executive Committee of the Democratic Women's Federation (until 1957)
1954,	Aug	Elected deputy for Shanghai Municipality to the 1st NPC (reelected in 1958 and 1964 to the 2nd and 3rd NPCs)
1955,	Jun	Member of a delegation to the World Peace Congress in Helsinki
	Dec	Identified as secretary-general of the Shanghai Municipal Federation of Industry and Commerce
1956,	May	Identified as vice-chairman of the Shanghai Women's Federation
1959,	Apr	Elected member of the Standing Committee of the 3rd CPPCC
	Sep	Appointed vice-minister of commerce (until Cultural Revolution)
1964,	May	Identified as acting secretary-general of the Federation of Industry and Commerce
1967		Disappears during the Cultural Revolution
1973,	Mar	First appearance after the Cultural Revolution
1978,	Mar	Elected member of the Standing Committee of the 5th CPPCC
1979,	Oct	Appointed director of the Board of Directors of the China International Trust and Investent Corporation; elected vice-chairman and secretary-general of the Federation of Industrialists and Businessmen

Hua Guofeng (Hua Kuo-feng) 华国锋

Posts held

CCP
Member of the Standing Committee of the Politburo
Member of the CCP 11th Central Committee
Chairman of the CCP 11th Central Committee
Chairman of the Military Council in the CCP Central Committee
President of the Party School in the CCP 11th Central Committee

Government
Premier

NPC
Deputy for Beijing Municipality to the 5th NPC

Hua was born in 1921 in Jiaocheng County, Shanxi Province. His family were poor peasants who had to flee to North Shaanxi following a natural catastrophe when Hua was still a child. He graduated from primary school, when he was 13 years old. When the Communist forces entered this area after the Long March in 1935 Hua immediately "joined the revolution," i.e. he served in the Red Army from the age of 15.

1949,	Aug	Secretary, Xiangyin County CP, Hunan Province. Under Hua's leadership a land

reform is carried out which proceeds "very calmly"

1951, Jun Appointed secretary, Xiangtan County CP, Hunan Province

1955 In the movement to establish rural cooperatives Xiangtan County performs best in Hunan Province (by March there were 12,000 rural cooperatives in the province of which Xiangtan County had 40%)

1956 Hua is made head of a large-scale irrigation project in Shaoshan, the birthplace of Mao Zedong, which was designed to irrigate 66,600 hectares of arable land. This project was discontinued in 1959 as a result of "intervention by Liu Shaoqi's rightist deviationist policies" and only taken up again in 1965.

Aug Identified as member of the Standing Committee of Hunan Province CP

Oct Identified as director of the Cultural and Educational Bureau in the Provincial Government of Hunan

1958, Jul Elected vice-governor of Hunan Province

Sep Identified as alternate member of the Secretariat of Hunan Province CP

1959, Oct At Mao Zedong's recommendation Hua is elected secretary of Hunan Province CP

1961? During an inspection tour of Hunan Province Mao Zedong meets Hua and "listened twice to his report on Maotien and had a high opinion of him" (In Maotien a project "for transforming nature" was carried out).

1963 Hua visits Changshou People's Commune in Pingjiang County which had been severely effected by drought

Oct Hua heads a Party delegation of Hunan Province to attend a symposium on problems of agricultural production in Guangdong

1964 Hua heads an "investigation of Lingxien County" (Shuikou Pass, occupied three times by Mao Zedong during 1927, is located in this county)

Sep Elected deputy for Hunan Province to the 3rd NPC

1966, Jun The Shaoshan irrigation project under Hua is completed

1967, Jul? At Zhou Enlai's recommendation Hua takes part in the preparatory meeting for the establishment of the Revolutionary Committee of Hunan Province

Sep Together with other members of the Preparatory Committee for the establishment of the Revolutionary Committee of Hunan Province Hua is received by Mao Zedong in Changsha

1968, Apr With the establishment of the Revolutionary Committee for Hunan Province, Hua is elected vice-chairman (until Jul 1970)

1969, Apr Elected member of the CCP Central Committee by the 9th Party Congress (confirmed in this post in 1973 by the

10th Congress); in the same month construction of the mausoleum for Yang Kaihui (first wife of Mao Zedong) is started "with the mighty support of Hua"

1970, Jul Identified as acting chairman of the Revolutionary Committee of Hunan Province (until about 1974)

Dec Hunan is the first province which elects a new Party Secretariat after the Cultural Revolution; Hua becomes 1st secretary

1971, May Hua is transferred to Beijing. According to unofficial reports he was shortly afterwards secretary general of a special group entrusted with the investigation of the fall of Lin Biao and his supporters

Jul Hua inspects Xinjian County in Jiangxi Province and the Fujian Front

1972, Nov Identified as political commissar of Guangzhou Military Region (until about 1974)

1973, Feb Identified as 1st political commissar of Hunan Military District (until about 1974)

Aug Elected member of the Politburo by the CCP 10th Congress

1975, Jan Elected vice-premier and minister of public security by the 4th NPC (the latter post until 1977)

1976, Feb Identified as acting premier

Apr Identified as premier and 1st vice-chairman of the CCP Central Committee

Oct Identified as chairman of the CCP Central Committee and as chairman of the Military Council in the CCP Central Committee

1977, Aug Hua is confirmed by the 11th Party Congress as chairman of the CCP Central Committee and as member of the Standing Committee of the Politburo

Oct Appointed president of the Party School in the CCP Central Committee

1978, Feb Elected deputy for Beijing Municipality to the 5th NPC

May Head of a Party and government delegation to North Korea

Aug Head of a Party and government delegation to Romania, Yugoslavia, and Iran

1979, Oct Head of a government delegation to France, the Federal Republic of Germany, Great Britain, and Italy (until Nov)

Hua's family

Hua has four children who attended elementary school in Zhongshan Street in Changsha during his period in Hunan. His youngest daughter, Xiaoli, graduated in 1974 from Beijing Higher School No. 166 and since then has worked as an "intellectual youth" at Xujiawa Production Brigade in Pinggu County in the outskirts of Beijing. According to the left-wing orientated paper Zheng Ming published in Hong Kong, Hua is married to Han Zhijun, also a native of Shanxi Province, who was born in 1931. In September 1978 Han was elected a member of the Standing Committee of the National Women's Federation.

Hua Luogeng (Hua Lo-keng)   华罗庚

Posts held

NPC
Member of the Standing Committee of the 5th NPC
Deputy for Beijing Municipality to the 5th NPC

Others
Vice-president of the Academy of Sciences
Director of the Institute of Mathematics, Academy of Sciences
Vice-chancellor of the Beijing University of Science and Technology
Vice-chairman of the Central Committee, China Democratic League

Hua was born in 1910 in Jindan County, Jiangsu Province. After elementary and middle school he studied at a vocational school in Shanghai. Since his parents were unable to support further studies financially he was forced to return to his hometown. He helped his father in running a small business and continued his mathematical studies at the same time. At the of age of 19 he published a treatise "On Mathematics" which caught the attention of the mathematician Xiong Qinglai, then head of the Mathematics Department of Qinghua University. Xiong personally went to Jindan to take Hua into the university as his assistant. Already during this period Hua's articles appeared in American, English, Soviet, Japanese, and Indian science journals. In 1936 he was made a professor of mathematics. In the same year he was awarded a research scholarship for a period of study at the University of Cambridge. After his return to China he received a professorship at the Southwest Associated University in Kunming in 1938. During 1945-46 he was a guest lecturer in the USSR and, from the end of 1946, at the University of Illinois. He returned to China from the U.S.A. in February 1950.

1950,	Feb	Appointed director of the Mathematics Department of Qinghua University
	Oct	Elected member of the Peace Council
1951,	Jan	Hua joins the Democratic League
	Feb	Appointed director of the Institute of Mathematics, Academy of Sciences
1953,	Feb	Identified as vice-chairman of the Mathematics Society; member of a delegation of scientists to the USSR
1954,	May	Elected board member, Association for Cultural Relations with Foreign Countries
	Jun	Delegate to a conference on disarmament in Stockholm and to a special meeting of the World Peace Council in East Berlin
	Aug	Elected deputy for Beijing Municipality to the 1st NPC (until Mar 1959)
	Dec	Elected council member of the Sino-Soviet Friendship Association
1955,	Apr	Delegate to the Conference of Asian Nations in New Delhi
	Jun	Appointed member of the Standing Committee, Department of Mathematics, Physics, and Chemistry at the Academy of Sciences
1956,	Feb	Elected member of the Standing Committee of the Democratic League

	Mar	Appointed member of the Scientific Planning Commission (until Nov 1958)
	Jun	Elected member, Standing Committee of the NPC, in a by-election
1958,	Sep	Elected board member of the Science and Technology Society
	Oct	Elected deputy for Jiangsu Province to the 2nd NPC (until Dec 1964)
1960,	Sep	Identified as director, Department of Applied Mathematics and Electronic Calculating Machines at the University of Science and Technology
	Nov	Identified as director, Institute of Electronic Calculating Techniques at the Academy of Sciences
1961,	Apr	Appointed vice-chancellor, University of Science and Technology
1963,	Jul	Identified as deputy director, Department of Mathematics, Physics, and Chemistry at the Academy of Sciences, and as director of the Institute of Mathematics at the Academy of Science and Technology
1964,	Sep	Elected deputy for Beijing Municipality to the 3rd NPC
1973,	Apr	Member of a delegation of the Sino-Japanese Friendship Association to Japan
1974,	Fall	Hua visits several provinces and lectures on "Time saving methods in the search of the best technical solution"
1975,	Jan	Reelected member of the Standing Committee by the 4th NPC (confirmed in 1978 by the 5th NPC)
1976,	Jun	Identified as director of the Institute of Mathematics of the Academy of Sciences
	Dec	Article in RMRB of 27 December: "Work Not for Yourself But for the People"
1977,	Oct	Identified as vice-chancellor, University of Science and Technology
1978,	Feb	Elected deputy for Beijing Municipality to the 5th NPC
	Mar	Appointed vice-president of the Academy of Sciences
	Oct	Head of a delegation of scientists to North Korea
1979,	Jan	Identified as member of the Department of Mathematics, Physics and Chemistry, Academy of Sciences
	Jun	Member of the Budget Committee at the 2nd Session of the 5th NPC
	Oct	Elected vice-chairman of the Central Committee, China Democratic League
	Nov	Visits to France, the Federal Republic of Germany, and Great Britain

Hua Yingdong (Hua Ying-tung)

Posts held

Others
Director of the Board of Directors, China International Trust and Investment Corporation

1979,	Oct	Appointed director of the Board of Directors, China International Trust and Investment Corporation; identified as a Hong Kong businessman

Hua Yuqing (Hua Yü-ch'ing)   华煜卿

<u>Posts held</u>

NPC
Deputy for Hubei Province to the 5th NPC

Provincial Administration
Vice-governor of Hubei Province

Others
Director of the Board of Directors, China International Trust and Investment Corporation
Vice-chairman of the Executive Committee, Federation of Industrialists and Businessmen
Chairman of the Hubei Branch, Federation of Industrialists and Businessmen

1960,	May	Identified as vice-mayor of Wuhan
1961,	Apr	Identified as chairman of the Wuhan Branch, China Democratic National Construction Association
1978,	Feb	First appearance after the Cultural Revolution: Elected deputy for Hubei Province to the 5th NPC
1979,	Jun	Member of the Committee to Examine Proposals, 2nd Session of the 5th NPC
	Oct	Appointed director of the Board of Directors, China International Trust and Investment Corporation; elected vice-chairman of the Executive Committee, Federation of Industrialists and Businessmen; identified as chairman of the Hubei Branch, Federation of Industrialists and Businessmen
1980,	Jan	Elected vice-governor of Hubei Province

Huan Xiang (Huan Hsiang)   宦乡

<u>Posts held</u>

Others
Vice-president of the Academy of Social Sciences

Huan was born in 1910 in Zunyi, Guizhou Province. He grew up in Hankou and there attended the middle school affiliated with Boone University, an American missionary college. He then studied engineering sciences at Jiaotong University in Shanghai and later political science at Waseda University in Japan. Around 1935 he returned to China to work for the Customs Department of Shanghai. During the Anti-Japanese War, from 1937 to 1945, he was editor-in-chief of the army paper <u>The Daily Front</u>. After leaving this paper he first wrote for the monthly <u>New China</u> until 1947 and then became deputy editor-in-chief of the Shanghai <u>Wenhui Bao</u> in which he sharply attacked the Nationalist Government. At this time he joined the CCP. At the end of 1947 he went to Hong Kong where he joined the Democratic League. In 1948 he moved to the "Liberated Areas." In March 1949 he was a member of the delegation led by Guo Moruo to the World Peace Conference in Prague. In June of that year he was elected a member of the Standing Committee of the Preparatory Committee for the Chinese Journalists' Association (until 1954). In September 1949 he took part as a freelance worker in the session of the 1st CPPCC which elected him deputy secretary-general.

1949,	Oct	Appointed director of the Western Europe and Africa Department in the Ministry of Foreign Affairs (until Jun 1954); elected secretary of the Sino-Soviet Friendship Association (until Dec 1954); elected member of the National Committee of the Peace Council
	Dec	Appointed member of the Institute of Foreign Affairs
1954,	Apr	Member of a delegation to the Geneva Indochina Conference headed by Zhou Enlai
	Sep	Appointed chargé d'affaires in Great Britain (until Mar 1962)
1961,	Jul	Advisor to the Chinese delegation at the Laos Conference in Geneva
1962,	Jan	Advisor to the Chinese delegation at the Laos Conference in Geneva
1964,	Apr	Appointed assistant minister at the Ministry of Foreign Affairs (until Cultural Revolution)
	Oct	Elected deputy for Guizhou Province to the 3rd NPC
	Dec	Identified as a member of the Standing Committee of the Institute of Foreign Affairs
1965,	Sep	Huan accompanies Minister of Foreign Affairs Chen Yi to Pakistan, Syria, Algeria, Guinea (disappears afterwards)
1976,	Apr	First appearance after the Cultural Revolution: Appointed ambassador to Belgium and to the European Community (until Mar 1978)
	Sep	Appointed ambassador to Luxemburg (until Mar 1978)
1978,	Sep	Appointed vice-president of the Academy of Social Sciences
	Nov	Head of an economic delegation to Yugoslavia and Romania
1979,	Apr	Head of a delegation to the Academy of Social Sciences to the U.S.A.
	Dec	Head of a scientific delegation to Japan

Huang Bingwei (Huang Ping-wei)   黄秉维

<u>Posts held</u>

NPC
Member of the Standing Committee of the 5th NPC
Deputy for Beijing Municipality to the 5th NPC

Others
Director of the Institute of Geography at the Academy of Sciences

1955,	May	Identified as a member of the Department of Biology and Earth Sciences at the Academy of Sciences
1956		Identified as vice-president of the Geographic Society
1957,	Mar	Identified as acting director of the Institute of Geography at the Academy of Sciences
1962,	Jan	Identified as director of the Institute of Geography at the Academy of Sciences

Apr Elected council member of the Sino-African Society
1964, Sep Elected deputy for Guangdong Province to the 3rd NPC
1966, Mar Identified as deputy director of the Institute of Geography at the Academy of Sciences
1967 Disappears during the Cultural Revolution
1974, Feb First appearance after the Cultural Revolution: Identified as director of the Institute of Geography at the Academy of Sciences; head of a delegation of scientists to Australia and New Zealand
1978, Feb Elected deputy for Beijing Municipality to the 5th NPC
Mar Elected a member of the Standing Committee of the 5th NPC
Sep Head of a delegation of geographers to the United States

Huang Changshui (Huang Ch'ang-shui)

黄长水

Posts held

NPC
Deputy for Guangdong Province to the 5th NPC

Others
Vice-chairman of the Executive Committee of the Federation of Industrialists and Businessmen

Huang was born in 1905 (1908?) in Huian, Fujian Province. He graduated from the Shanghai Jinan University. Around 1937 he was vice-chairman of an anti-Japanese association organized by overseas Chinese in the Philippines. In the forties Huang went to Hong Kong. Until 1949 he held the following positions there: Board chairman of the Chuan Chang Company; chairman of the Hong Kong-Philippines Import and Export Company; chairman of the Hong Kong Commercial and Industrial Club; director of the Chamber of Commerce of Fujianese in Hong Kong. In September 1949 he took part in the 1st CPPCC as a delegate of overseas Chinese.

1949, Oct Appointed member of the Overseas Chinese Affairs Commission under the Government Administrative Council
1950, Apr Identified as vice-chairman of the Hong Kong-Macao Branch Committee for Promoting the Sale of Government Bonds
1952, Jun Elected vice-chairman of the Preparatory Committee for the Federation of Industry and Commerce
Aug Elected chairman of the Guangzhou Branch of the Federation of Industry and Commerce (until Cultural Revolution)
1953, Jan Identified as vice-mayor of Guangzhou (until 1958); appointed member of the Central-South Administrative Council
Oct Identified as chairman of the Board of Directors of the Guangzhou Investment Corporation
Dec Elected vice-chairman of the Federation of Industry and Commerce (until Cultural Revolution)

1954, Aug Elected deputy for overseas Chinese to the 1st NPC (reelected in 1958 and 1964 to the 2nd and 3rd NPCs)
1955, Apr Elected member of the Standing Committee of the China Democratic National Construction Association
1956, Feb Identified as a member of the Foreign Trade Arbitration Committee
Oct Appointed vice-chairman of the State Overseas Chinese Affairs Commission; elected vice-chairman of the Association for Returned Overseas Chinese (both posts held until Cultural Revolution)
1957, May Huang criticizes the CCP bureaucracy at a forum of Democratic Parties in Guangzhou
1961, Sep Huang goes to Hong Kong to attend his mother's funeral
1967 Huang disappears
1972, Sep First appearance after the Cultural Revolution
1978, Feb Elected deputy for Guangdong Province to the 5th NPC
1979, Oct Elected vice-chairman of the Executive Committee of the Federation of Industrialists and Businessmen

Huang Dingchen (Huang Ting-ch'en)

Posts held

黄鼎臣

Others
Member of the Standing Committee of the 5th CPPCC
President of the Permanent Council of the Anti-Tuberculosis Association
Chairman of the Central Committee, China Zhi Gong Dang (Chih Kung Tang)

Huang was born in 1901 in Haifeng, Guangdong Province. He studied medicine from 1921 to 1928 at Tokyo University. After his return he worked as a physician in Shanghai, Macao, and Guangzhou. From 1929 to 1937 he was imprisoned for suspected membership in the CCP. He then resumed his work as a doctor in Guangzhou and Guilin. After the Japanese capitulation he set up a clinic in Guangzhou as a cover for the Communists Liaison Office. In 1947 he joined the China Zhi Gong Party and became a member of its Standing Committee and director of the Organization Department. In 1949 he took part in the 1st CPPCC.

1949, Oct Appointed deputy director of the Medical Administration in the Ministry of Public Health (until Cultural Revolution)
1953, Aug Identified as president of the Association for Prevention of Tuberculosis
1954, Aug Elected deputy for Guangdong Province to the 1st NPC (reelected in 1958 and 1964 to the 2nd and 3rd NPCs)
1956, Apr Elected member of the Standing Committee of the China Zhi Gong Party (until Cultural Revolution)
Jun Identified as vice-president of the Medical Society (until Cultural Revolution)
Oct Identified as member of the Standing Committee, Association of Returned Overseas Chinese

1965,   Jun   Identified as member of the Committee
                 for the Defense of World Peace
1967   Disappears during the Cultural Revolution
1972,   Sep   First appearance after the Cultural Revo-
                 lution: Present at the mourning ceremo-
                 nies for He Xiangming
1976,   Nov   Identified as deputy to the NPC
1978,   Mar   Identfied as member of the Standing
                 Committee of the 5th CPPCC
         Jun   Identified as president of the Permanent
                 Council, Anti-Tuberculosis Association
1979,   Oct   Elected chairman of the Central Commit-
                 tee of the China Zhi Gong Dang

Huang Ganying (Huang Kan-ying) (f) 黄甘英

Posts held

CCP
Member of the Commission for Inspecting
Discipline under the CCP Central Com-
mittee

Mass Organization
Vice-president and secretary of the
Women's Federation

Others
Member of the Standing Committee of the
5th CPPCC

1959,   Nov   Member of a women's delegation to Chile
1960,   Aug   Member of a women's delegation to Japan
1961,   Jan   Secretary-general of a delegation to the
                 Afro-Asian Solidarity Conference in Cairo
         Mar   Member of a women's delegation to Japan
         Aug   Identified as director of the International
                 Liaison Department of the Women's Fed-
                 eration (until 1964)
         Oct   Elected secretary of the Women's Federa-
                 tion
1962,   Jan   Member of a women's delegation to Mali
1963,   Mar   Secretary-general of a women's delegation
                 attending a session of the World Women's
                 League in Moscow
1964,   May   Deputy head of a trade union delegation
                 to Romania
         Jul   Head of a women's delegation to Indonesia
         Sep   Elected deputy for Guangdong Province to
                 the 3rd NPC
1965,   Jan   Head of a women's delegation to the
                 Preparatory Meeting of the 2nd Afro-
                 Asian Women's Conference in Cairo
         Mar   Member of a NPC delegation to Guinea,
                 Mali, Central African Republic, and
                 Congo (Brazzaville)
         May   Member of a delegation to the Afro-Asian
                 Solidarity Conference in Ghana
1967   Disappears during the Cultural Revolution
1978,   Mar   First appearance after the Cultural Revo-
                 lution: Elected member of the Standing
                 Committee of the 5th CPPCC
         Sep   Elected vice-president and secretary of
                 the Women's Federation
         Dec   Head of a women's delegation to Japan;
                 appointed member of the Commission for
                 Inspecting Discipline under the CCP Cen-
                 tral Committee

1979,   May   Head of a women's delegation to the
                 U.S.A.
         Nov   Head of a women's delegation to the
                 Preparatory Meeting of the World
                 Women's Conference in New Delhi

Huang Hou (Huang Hou)  黄 厚

Posts held

Military
Commander of Inner Mongolia Military
District

1979,   Jun   Identified as commander of Inner Mongo-
                 lia Military District

Huang Hu (Huang Hu)  黄 乎

Posts held

Others
Vice-president of the Academy of Medical
Sciences

1964,   Jul   Identified as vice-president of the Acade-
                 my of Medical Sciences; head of a medical
                 delegation to Afghanistan
1966   Disappears during the Cultural Revolution
1978,   Jun   First appearance after the Cultural Revo-
                 lution: Identified in his former post as
                 vice-president of the Academy of Medical
                 Sciences

Huang Hua (Huang Hua)   黄 华

Posts held

CCP
Member of the CCP 11th Central Committee

Government
Minister of foreign affairs

NPC
Deputy for Hebei Province to the 5th NPC

Huang was born in 1913 in Hebei Province. His original
name was Wang Rumei which he changed to Huang Hua in
the mid-thirties when he studied at the American Yanjing
University in Beijing. To avoid arrest he joined the
American journalist Edgar Snow on his way to the
Communist-controlled areas in 1936. He was Edgar Snow's
interpreter during the talks with Mao Zedong in Yan'an on
which the famous book Red Star over China is based. Also
during this period at Yan'an Huang temporarily served as
Zhu De's secretary. Subsequently engaged in youth and
organization work, he eventually functioned as an interpreter at the Beijing negotiations between the CCP and
the KMT in 1946 in the position of head of the Information
Department of the CCP Section. After the then Chinese
capital had been occupied by Communist forces in
May 1949 Huang negotiated with the remaining foreign
ambassadors on behalf of the CCP.

1950		Head of the Foreign Residence Affairs Department of Shanghai (until 1952)
1953,	Jan	Transferred to the Ministry of Foreign Affairs
	Oct	Chinese representative at the Peace Negotiations in Panmunjong
1954,	Apr	Advisor to the delegation led by Zhou Enlai to the Indochina Conference in Geneva
	Oct	Appointed director of the Western Europe and Africa Department in the Ministry of Foreign Affairs (until Dec 1956)
1955,	Apr	Advisor to a delegation led by Zhou Enlai to the Bandung Conference
	Dec	Appointed director of the Western Europe Department in the Ministry of Foreign Affairs (until Jan 1959) and head of the Research Department in the Institute of Foreign Affairs
1958		Sent to Warsaw to take part in the Sino-American ambassadorial talks at the time of confrontation in the Taiwan Strait
1960,	Aug	Appointed ambassador to Ghana (until Dec 1965)
1961,	Dec	PRC representative at the independence celebrations in Tanganyika
1964,	Feb	Negotiations with the minister of foreign affairs in Congo (Brazzaville)
	Nov	Negotiations in Dahomey
1966,	Jan	Appointed ambassador to the United Arab Republic (until Jun 1970; Huang is the only diplomat who was not recalled to Beijing for self-criticism during the Cultural Revolution)
1971,	Jul	Appointed ambassador to Canada (until Nov 1971)
	Nov	Appointed permanent representative of the PRC to the UN (until Nov 1976)
1972,	Jan	Head of the Chinese delegation to the special session of the UN in Addis Abeba
1973,	Aug	Elected to first term as member of the CCP Central Committee by the 10th Party Congress
1976,	Dec	Appointed minister of foreign affairs
1977,	Sep	Head of the Chinese delegation to the 32nd UN General Assembly
	Oct	Head of a government delegation to Canada
1978,	Feb	Elected deputy for Hebei Province to the 5th NPC
	Mar	Member of a government delegation led by Li Xiannian to the Philippines and Bangladesh
	Aug	Member of a Party and government delegation led by Hua Guofeng to Romania, Yugoslavia, and Iran
	Sep	Member of a Party and government delegation led by Deng Xiaoping to North Korea; visit to Greece, afterwards head of the Chinese delegation at the UN General Assembly
	Oct	Visits to Italy and Great Britain; Huang accompanies Deng Xiaoping to Japan, Thailand and Singapore (until November).
1979,	Jan	Huang accompanies Deng Xiaoping to the U.S.A.
	Oct	Huang accompanies Hua Guofeng to

France, the Federal Republic of Germany, Great Britain and Italy (until 6th Nov).

Nov   Huang pays a three-day official visit to Yugoslavia after accompanying Hua Guofeng on European tour; visits to Burma and Nepal

Huang is married to He Liliang.

Huang Huoqing (Huang Huo-ch'ing)

Posts held

黄火青

CCP
Member of the CCP 11th Central Committee

NPC
Deputy for Liaoning Province to the 5th NPC

Others
Chief procurator of the Supreme People's Procuracy

Huang was born in 1900 in Hubei Province. In 1919 he took part in the May 4th Movement. He joined the CCP in 1926. During the following years he was active in students and peasants movements and also in political work in the Red Army. In 1934-35 Huang took part in the Long March. In 1936 he was a cadre in the 4th Red Front Army commanded by Zhang Guotao who had opposed orders by Mao Zedong.

1949,	Oct	Elected council member of the Sino-Soviet Friendship Association (until Dec 1954)
1952,	May	Appointed chairman of the trade union of Tianjin Municipality (until Mar 1953)
	Aug	Appointed acting secretary of Tianjin Municipality CP (until Mar 1953)
1953,	Mar	Identified as secretary of Tianjin Municipality CP (until Aug 1956)
	May	Appointed member of the Executive Council, Federation of Trade Unions (until about 1956)
	Nov	Elected chairman, Tianjin Section of the Sino-Soviet Friendship Association (until 1958)
1954,	Oct	Elected deputy for Tianjin Municipality to the 1st NPC (until Mar 1959) and member of the Standing Committee of the NPC (until Mar 1959)
1955,	Jan	Elected mayor of Tianjin Municipality (until 1958)
1956,	Aug	Appointed 1st secretary of Tianjin Municipality CP (until 1958)
	Sep	Elected alternate member of the CCP Central Committee by the 8th Party Congress
1958,	Oct	Identified as 1st secretary of Liaoning Province CP
1960,	Feb	Identified as political commissar of Liaoning Military District
1963,	Jun	Identified as secretary of the Northeast Bureau in the CCP Central Committee
	Oct	Member of a delegation of the Northeast Bureau, CCP Central Committee, to North Korea

1967,	Jan	Branded as a counterrevolutionary revisionist and purged
1977,	Oct	First appearance after the Cultural Revolution
1978,	Feb	Elected deputy for Liaoning Province to the 5th NPC
	Mar	Appointed chief procurator of the Supreme People's Procuracy
	Dec	By-elected member of the CCP 11th Central Committee at its 3rd Plenum

Huang Jiasi (Huang Chia-szu) 黄家驷

<u>Posts held</u>

Government
Vice-president of the Recommendation and Examination Committee in Charge of Classifying Inventions under the Scientific and Technical Commission

Others
President of the Academy of Medical Sciences
Vice-president of the Medical Society

Huang became known as a professor of thorax-surgery at the Shanghai Medical College. In June 1949 he was appointed a member of a preparatory committee set up by the Communists for a conference of natural scientists.

1952,	Sep	Appointed deputy director of the Shanghai Medical College (until Sep 1958)
1953,	Jan	Delegate at the World Peace Council Session in Vienna
	May	Delegate at a World Medical Conference in Vienna
1954,	Aug	Elected deputy for Jiangxi Province to the 1st NPC
1955,	Jan	Delegate at a congress of Soviet surgeons
	Jun	Appointed member of the Department of Biology, Geology, and Geography of the Academy of Sciences
1957,	Jun	Appointed member of the Scientific Planning Commission under the State Council
	Nov	Member of a scientific and technical delegation visiting the USSR
1958,	Jul	Delegate at the International Disarmament Conference in Stockholm
	Sep	Elected vice-chairman of the Science and Technology Association (until Cultural Revolution)
1959,	Sep	Appointed president of the Academy of Medical Sciences; elected council member of the World Federation of Scientific Workers
1960,	Aug	Appointed director of a medical college (until Cultural Revolution)
1961,	Jun	Appointed corresponding member of the Soviet Academy of Medical Sciences (until about 1964)
1964,	Sep	Identified as vice-chairman of the Medical Society (until Cultural Revolution)
1965,	Jun	Elected vice-chairman of the Afro-Asian Solidarity Committee (until Cultural Revolution)
1968,	Sep	Huang is accused as a "capitalist-roader" and disappears

1974,	May	Reactivated after the Cultural Revolution; head of a delegation to the World Health Organization Conference in Geneva
1978,	Jun	Identified as vice-president of the Medical Society
	Sep	Article in <u>China Reconstructs</u>: "Surgery in China"
1979,	Jan	Appointed chairman of the 1st Academic Committee of the Academy of Medical Sciences
	Apr	Appointed vice-president of the Recommendation and Examination Committee in Charge of Classifying Inventions, under the State Scientific and Technical Commission
	May	Head of a medical delegation to the U.S.A.

Huang Jingbo (Huang Ching-po) 黄静波

<u>Posts held</u>

Provincial Administration
Vice-governor of Guangdong Province

1958,	Mar	Identified as vice-minister of food industry
1978,	Feb	Identified as vice-chairman of the Revolutionary Committee of Guangdong Province (until Dec 1979)
1979,	Dec	Elected vice-governor of Guangdong Province

Huang Jiqing (Huang Chi-ch'ing) 黄汲清

<u>Posts held</u>

Others
Member of the Standing Committee of the 5th CPPCC
President of the Society of Geology

Huang was born in 1904 in Sichuan Province. He graduated from Beijing University in 1928. In 1939 he obtained his doctorate in geology at Neuchatel University in Switzerland.

1950,	Jul	Identified as member of the Southwest China Military and Administrative Council
1953,	Jan	Identified as member of the Southwest Administrative Council
1954,	Jun	Identified as member of the Examination Committee of the Ministry of Geology
	Aug	Elected deputy for Sichuan Province to the 1st NPC (reelected in 1958 and 1964 to the 2nd and 3rd NPCs)
1955,	Jun	Identified as member of the Standing Committee, Department of Biology and Earth Sciences at the Academy of Sciences
1956,	Feb	Elected member, Central Committee of the Jiusan Society
	Mar	Identified as member of the State Scientific Planning Commission

	Jun	Identified as deputy director of the Department of Biology and Earth Sciences at the Academy of Sciences
1967		Disappears during the Cultural Revolution
1977,	Oct	First appearance after the Cultural Revolution
1978,	Mar	Elected member of the Standing Committee of the 5th CPPCC
1979,	Jan	Identified as member of the Department of Geology and Geography, Academy of Sciences
	Mar	Elected president of the Society of Geology (Huang is a specialist in tectonics)

Huang Juxiang (Huang Chü-hsiang) 黄菊香

Posts held

NPC
Member of the Standing Committee of the 5th NPC
Deputy for Guangdong Province to the 5th NPC

1978,	Feb	Elected deputy for Guangdong Province to the 5th NPC
	Mar	Elected member of the Standing Committee of the 5th NPC

Huang Kai (Huang K'ai) 黄 凯

Posts held

Government
Vice-minister of petroleum industry

NPC
Deputy for Sichuan Province to the 5th NPC

1959,	Jun	Relieved of post of assistant minister in the Ministry of Petroleum Industry
1964,	Oct	Identified as deputy secretary of Yan'an Municipality CP
1978,	Feb	Elected deputy for Sichuan Province to the 5th NPC
	Jul	Identified as vice-minister of petroleum industry

Huang Kecheng (Huang K'e-ch'eng)

Posts held  黄克诚

CCP
Member of the CCP 11th Central Committee
Permanent secretary of the Commission for Inspecting Discipline under the CCP Central Committee

NPC
Deputy for the PLA to the 5th NPC

Others
Member of the Standing Committee of the 5th CPPCC

Huang was born in 1899 in Yongxing County, Hunan Province. In 1924 he completed the 1st training course at Whampoa Military Academy. He joined the CCP in 1927 and during the same year helped to organize the Autumn Harvest Uprising in Hunan. In 1928 he joined the Jinggangshan Soviet which had been set up by Mao Zedong in the Jiangxi-Hunan Border Area. He took part in the Long March of 1934-35 and then acted temporarily as head of the Organization Department of the CCP Central Committee in Yan'an. In 1937 Huang was made head of the 5th Branch School of the Anti-Japan Military and Political Academy. When the New 4th Army (commander: Chen Yi, political commissar: Liu Shaoqi) was set up in 1941, Huang became commander of the 3rd Division and concurrently commander of the North Jiangsu Region. In 1945 he was elected an alternate member of the CCP Central Committee. After the end of the Anti-Japanese War Huang was one of the military officers under Lin Biao organizing troops in Manchuria. Serving in the forces commanded by Lin Biao, Huang contributed decisively to the defeat of Nationalist Government's troops as well as to the occupation of Tianjin and Beijing In January 1949 he became chairman of the Tianjin Military Control Commission but continued to take part in the campaigns of the 4th Field Army. After Hunan Province had been occupied without resistance Huang was appointed vice-chairman of the Military and Political Council of Hunan, political commissar of Hunan Military Region, and member of the Hunan Military Control Commission. In the summer of 1949 he was in addition appointed member of the Central-South China Military and Political Council and was later given the command of the 12th Army Corps, 4th Field Army. He was elected a member of the Standing Committee of the CPPCC in September 1949.

1950		The 12th Army Corps, commanded by Huang, is part of the "People's Volunteers" Forces crossing the Yalu River. Huang is elected a member of the CCP Central Committee in a by-election after the death of Ren Bishi
1952		Appointed a member of the newly established State Planning Commission
	Oct	Appointed deputy chief of staff of the Revolutionary Military Council (until Sep 1954)
1954,	Sep	Elected deputy for the PLA to the 1st NPC (probably until Mar 1959), member of the Standing Committee of the NPC (probably until Mar 1959), and director of the Logistics Department of the PLA (probably until 1956)
	Oct	Appointed vice-minister of National Defense (until Sep 1959)
1955,	Sep	Promoted to rank of army-general, conferred the orders of "1st August," "Independence and Freedom," and "Liberation," all 1st class
1956,	Sep	Reelected member of the CCP Central Committee by the 8th Party Congress and member of the Secretariat of the CCP Central Committee (until Sep 1962 at the latest)
1958,	Oct	Appointed chief of PLA General Staff (probably until summer 1959)
1959		Demoted following the purge of Peng Dehuai

1965,   Dec   Identified as vice-governor of Shanxi Province

1967,   Aug   Branded as a rightist opportunist and purged

1977,   Aug   First appearance after the Cultural Revolution

1978,   Feb   Elected deputy for the PLA to the 5th NPC

          Mar   Elected a member of the Standing Committee of the 5th CPPCC

          Dec   By-elected member of CCP 11th-Central Committee at its 3rd Plenum; appointed permanent secretary of the Commission for Inspecting Discipline under the CCP Central Committee

1979,   Jan   Article in Jiefangjun Bao (Liberation Army), 1st Jan: "A Red Heart Shines Like the Sun and Moon, Uprightness Will Be Remembered for Ages - Mourning Peng Dehuai"

Huang Kun (Huang K'un) 黄 崑

Posts held

Others
Member of the Standing Committee of the 5th CPPCC
Director of the Institute of Semi-Conductors of the Academy of Sciences

Huang was born in 1919 in Zhejiang Province.

1959,   Mar   Identified as professor of physics at Beijing University

1964,   Sep   Elected deputy for Beijing Municipality to the 3rd NPC

1972,   Jul   Present at a reception given by Zhou Enlai for the American-Chinese Nobel prize winner Yang Zhenning

1977,   Dec   Identified as director of the Institute of Semi-Conductors of the Academy of Sciences

1978,   Mar   Elected member of the Standing Committee of the 5th CPPCC

          Oct   Deputy head of an Academy of Sciences delegation to Sweden and Great Britain

Huang Mingda (Huang Ming-ta) 黄 明 达

Posts held

Government
Ambassador to Afghanistan

1965,   Apr   Identified as counselor at the embassy in Burma (until 1966)

1970,   Jun   Identified as chargé d'affaires in India (until Oct 1971)

1973,   Mar   Appointed ambassador to Sri Lanka and the Maldive Islands (until May 1977)

1977,   Sep   Appointed ambassador to Afghanistan

Huang Minwei (Huang Min-wei) 黄 民 伟

Posts held

CCP
Member of the Commission for Inspecting Discipline under the CCP Central Committee

Mass Organization
Vice-chairman of the Federation of Trade Unions

1957,   Dec   Identified as chairman of the Trade Union of Electric Industry Workers (until Sep 1960)

1960,   Oct   Identified as chairman of the Trade Union of Water Conservancy and Energy

1961,   Mar   Head of a trade union delegation to Cuba

          Apr   Identified as acting chairman of the Trade Union of Agriculture and Forestry

          Jul   Head of a trade union delegation to Ghana and Chile

1962,   Apr   Identified as member of the Executive Committee of the Federation of Trade Unions

          May   Head of a trade union delegation to Poland

1964,   Mar   Head of a trade union delegation to Ghana

1965,   Aug   Identified as secretary of the Federation of Trade Unions

1967   Disappears during the Cultural Revolution

1978,   Apr   First appearance after the Cultural Revolution: Referred to in his previous post as secretary of the Federation of Trade Unions

          Oct   Elected vice-chairman of the Federation of Trade Unions

          Dec   Appointed member of the Commission for Inspecting Discipline under the CCP Central Committee

Huang Oudong (Huang Ou-tung) 黄 欧 东

Posts held

CCP
Member of the CCP 11th Central Committee
2nd secretary of Liaoning Province CP

NPC
Deputy for Liaoning Province to the 5th NPC

Provincial Administration
Chairman of the People's Congress of Liaoning Province

Others
President, Liaoning Branch of the Sino-Korean Friendship Association
Chairman of the CPPCC, Liaoning Branch

Huang was born in 1907 in Pingxiang, Jiangxi Province. He joined the CCP as a young man and in 1934-35 he took part in the Long March. In 1937 he commanded a regiment in the 129th Division of the 8th Route Army, in 1945 he was promoted to the post of commander of a brigade in the same division. At the end of that year he was transferred to Manchuria where he became head of the Supplies Department in Nongjiang Military District. In 1948 he headed the Construction Department in Heilongjiang Province.

1949,	Oct	During the merger of Liaoning and Liaobei Provinces and their subsequent division into the provinces of Liaodong, Liaoshi, and Shenyang Municipality, Huang is appointed CP secretary and deputy mayor of Shenyang (until Jun 1952)
1952,	Jun	Appointed mayor, and 2nd secretary of the CP, of Shenyang Municipality
1954,	Aug	Elected deputy for Shenyang Municipality to the 1st NPC (until Mar 1959); with the merger of Liaodong and Liaoning Provinces to form the province of Liaoning, Huang is appointed secretary of the provincial CP (until Sep 1956)
1956,	Sep	Elected alternate member of the CCP Central Committee by the 8th Party Congress (until Cultural Revolution); appointed 1st secretary of Liaoning Province CP (until Jun 1958)
1958,	Jun	Appointed 2nd secretary of Liaoning Province CP (until Cultural Revolution)
	Dec	Elected governor of Liaoning Province (until Cultural Revolution)
1959,	Oct	Elected deputy for Liaoning Province to the 2nd NPC
1960,	Sep	Identified as chairman of the Liaoning Section, Sino-Soviet Friendship Association (until about 1964)
1962,	Aug	Identified as chairman of the People's Council of Liaoning Province (until Cultural Revolution)
1963,	Jun	Identified as secretary of the Northeast China Bureau of the CCP Central Committee (until Cultural Revolution)
1966		Huang disappears during the Cultural Revolution
1973,	Feb	Reactivated after the Cultural Revolution: Identified as vice-chairman of the Revolutionary Committee of Liaoning Province (until Jan 1980)
	Apr	Identified as secretary of Liaoning Province CP (until Nov 1977)
1977,	Aug	Elected member of the CCP Central Committee by the 11th Party Congress
	Nov	Identified as 3rd secretary of Liaoning Province CP (until Dec 1978)
1978,	Aug	Identified as president, Liaoning Branch of the Sino-Korean Friendship Association; identified as chairman of the CPPCC, Liaoning Branch
	Dec	Identified as 2nd secretary of Liaoning Province CP
1980,	Feb	Elected chairman of the People's Congress of Liaoning Province; by-elected deputy for Liaoning Province to the 5th NPC

Huang Rong (Huang Jung)  黄　荣

Posts held

CCP
Member of the Commission for Inspecting Discipline under the CCP Central Committee

Government
Member of the State Nationalities Affairs Commission

NPC
Deputy of Guangxi Autonomous Region to the 5th NPC

Provincial Administration
Chairman of the People's Congress of Guangxi Autonomous Region

Huang belongs to the Zhuang minority. He served in the Nationalist Government as a military officer and later went over to the Communists.

1954,	Aug	Elected deputy for Guangxi Province to the 1st NPC (reelected in 1958 and 1964 to the 2nd and 3rd NPCs)
1958,	Feb	Identified as member of the Minorities Committee of the NPC
1964,	Nov	Identified as vice-chairman of the CPPCC in Guangxi
1967		Disappears during the Cultural Revolution
1977,	Dec	First appearance after the Cultural Revolution: Elected vice-chairman of Guangxi Revolutionary Committee (until Dec 1979)
1978,	Feb	Elected deputy for the Guangxi Autonomous Region to the 5th NPC
	Dec	Appointed member of the Commission for Inspecting Discipline under the CCP Central Committee
1979,	May	Appointed member of the State Nationalities Affairs Commission
	Jun	Vice-chairman of the Committee to Examine Proposals at the 2nd Session of the 5th NPC
	Dec	Elected chairman of the People's Congress of Guangxi Autonomous Region

Huang Rongchang (Huang Jung-ch'ang)

Posts held   黄　荣昌

NPC
Member of the Standing Committee of the 5th NPC
Deputy for Sichuan Province to the 5th NPC

Huang was born in 1924 and has been a carpenter. He reportedly improved or designed more than 200 pieces of equipment.

1954,	Oct	Elected deputy for Sichuan Province to the 1st NPC (reelected in 1958 and 1964 to the 2nd and 3rd NPCs)
1959,	Nov	Identified as director of the Department for Bridge Construction in the Ministry of Railways and as secretary of Chengdu Railways Office CP

1966,	Feb	Identified as deputy chief-engineer of Chongqing Iron and Steel Company
1978,	Feb	Elected deputy for Sichuan Province to the 5th NPC
	Mar	Elected member of the Standing Committee of the 5th NPC; identified as worker-engineer at Chongqing Iron and Steel Company

Huang Ronghai (Huang Jung-hai)   黄荣海

Posts held

CCP
Alternate member of the CCP 11th Central Committee

Military
Lieutenant-general
Deputy commander of Guangzhou Military Region

Huang was born in Jiangxi Province. He joined the Communist Armored Forces around 1930. During the Long March he served in the Political Department of the 1st Army Corps. In 1945 he commanded a regiment of the 7th Division operating in Zhili Gulf Military District. In 1947 he was deputy commander of the 17th Division, 6th Column of the Northeast Field Army. In January 1949 he was made commander of the 128th Division, 43rd Corps, 4th Field Army.

1951-1953		Chief of staff of the 43rd Corps serving in Korea
from 1955		Deputy commander of the 43rd Corps
1956 (?)		Training at Nanjing Military Academy
1958,	Oct	Identified as major-general
1963,	Aug	Identified as lieutenant-general
1965,	Jan	Identified as commander of Guangdong Military District (until about 1970)
1968,	Feb	With the establishment of the Revolutionary Committee for Guangdong Province, Huang is elected vice-chairman (until about 1973); elected concurrently chairman of the Revolutionary Committee of Guangzhou Municipality (until about 1972)
1969,	Apr	Elected to first term as alternate member of the CCP Central Committee by the 9th Party Congress
1971,	May	Identified as deputy commander of Guangzhou Military Region; elected 1st secretary of Guangzhou Municipality CP (until 1972)

Huang Shixie (Huang Shih-hsieh)   黄世燮

Posts held

Government
Ambassador to Yemen People's Democratic Republic

1965,	Apr	Appointed counselor at the embassy in Ghana (until Nov 1966)
1972,	Jun	Appointed ambassador to Rwanda (until Aug 1977)
1977,	Nov	Appointed ambassador to Yemen People's Democratic Republic

Huang Shuze (Huang Shu-tse)   黄树则

Posts held

Government
Vice-minister of public health

Others
Member, Central Patriotic Health Campaign Committee

1961,	Jun	Identified as director of the Health Care Office in the Ministry of Public Health (until 1963)
1965,	Apr	Appointed vice-minister of public health (until Cultural Revolution)
1973,	Jan	Reactivated after the Cultural Revolution
	May	Identified as vice-minister of public health; head of a delegation to the World Health Organization Conference in Geneva
1974,	Aug	Head of a delegation to the UN Conference on World Population in Budapest
1975,	Dec	Head of a health delegation to Korea
1978,	Apr	Appointed a member of the Central Patriotic Health Campaign Committee
	Sep	Head of a health delegation to Burma

Huang Wei (Huang Wei)   黄维

Posts held

Military
General

Others
Member of the Standing Committee of the 5th CPPCC

Huang was commanding general of the KMT Forces at the Huai-Hai Battle of December 1948 when he was captured by communist troops; he was later sentenced as a war criminal.

| 1975, | Mar | Pardoned as war criminal |
| 1978, | Mar | Elected member of the Standing Committee of the 5th CPPCC |

Huang Xinbai (Huang Hsin-pai)   黄辛白

Posts held

Government
Vice-minister of education

1952,	Jul	Identified as member of the East China Branch of the Athletic Federation
1957,	Sep	Identified as deputy director of the Department of Industrial Education, Ministry of Higher Education
1964,	Sep	Elected deputy for Jiangsu Province to the 3rd NPC
1965,	Aug	Appointed vice-minister of higher education
1966,	Apr	Elected vice-chairman of the Association for Cultural Relations and Friendship with Foreign Countries
1967		Disappears during the Cultural Revolution

1972, Sep First appearance after the Cultural Revolution: Identified as vice-chairman of the Revolutionary Committee of Beijing University (until 1977)

1975, Nov Head of a higher education delegation to France

1979, Jul Identified as vice-minister of education

Nov Head of an education delegation to Thailand

Dec Head of an educational delegation to Nepal and Kuwait

Huang Xinting (Huang Hsin-t'ing) 黄新廷

Posts held

CCP
Alternate member of the CCP 11th Central Committee

Military
Lieutenant-general
Commander of the Armored Forces of the PLA

Huang became a member of the Communist Youth League in 1929. Shortly afterwards he joined a guerrilla unit in the 2nd Front Army. In 1935 he commanded the 12th Regiment, 4th Division, 2nd Army of the 2nd Front Army, in which he took part in the Long March. In August 1937 he became commander of the 761st Regiment, 358th Brigade, 120th Division of the 8th Route Army. This unit operated in Central Hebei in 1939. During the following years he served as commander of the Military District and an independent brigade. In 1945 he commanded a brigade of the 1st Column in the Northeast Field Army and two years later he was chief of staff of the 1st Column. He was made deputy commander when the 1st Column was renamed 1st Corps in February 1949.

1951 Huang is first deputy commander and later commander of the 1st Army in the 1st Field Army

1952 For service in the Korean War the 1st and 3rd Corps of the 1st Field Army are regrouped into the 1st Corps of which Huang is made commander

1953, Apr Huang leads the 1st Corps in combat at the Injim River (until Jun)

Jul Huang attends a course at the Nanjing Military Academy (until 1955)

1955, Jul Identified as lieutenant-general and deputy commander of Chengdu Military Region

1960, Jul Identified as commander of Chengdu Military Region

1964, Sep Elected deputy for Chengdu Military Region to the 3rd NPC

1965, Jan Appointed member of the National Defense Council

1967, May Criticized in connection with He Long and relieved of all posts

1974, Jul Reactivated after the Cultural Revolution

1975, Sep Identified as commander of the PLA Armored Forces

1977, Aug Elected alternate member of the CCP Central Committee by the 11th Party Congress

Huang Yan (Huang Yen) 黄岩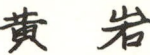

Posts held

Provincial Administration
Vice-chairman of the People's Congress of Anhui Province

Others
Member of the Standing Committee of the 4th CPPCC

Huang was born in 1917 in Liuan, Anhui Province. At the age of 14 he became a Young Pioneer leader in the Soviet Government in Liuan. In 1941 he was deputy commander of a guerrilla unit under the New 4th Army operating in Hebei Province. In 1945 he was CP secretary of the Jiangsu-Anhui Border Region, and in 1949, deputy secretary, CP of North Anhui District. In September 1949 he took part in the 1st CPPCC.

1949, Dec Identified as deputy political commissar of North Anhui Military District (until 1952)

1950, Mar Identified as member of the Land Reform Committee of the East China Military and Administrative Council

1952, Aug Identified as 2nd secretary of Anhui Province CP and as vice-governor of Anhui Province (until 1955)

1954, Aug Elected deputy for Anhui Province to the 1st NPC (reelected in 1958 and 1964 to the 2nd and 3rd NPCs)

1955, Mar Identified as governor of Anhui Province (until Cultural Revolution)

1957, May Identified as secretary of Anhui Province CP (until 1963)

1964, Jan Identified as alternate secretary of Anhui Province CP (until Cultural Revolution)

1968, Apr Branded as an agent of Liu Shaoqi and purged

1978, Feb First appearance after the Cultural Revolution

Mar Elected member of the Standing Committee of the 5th CPPCC

1979, Dec Elected vice-chairman of the People's Congress of Anhui Province

Huang Yu (Huang Yü) 黄取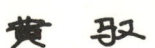

Posts held

NPC
Deputy for Anhui Province to the 5th NPC

Provincial Administration
Vice-governor of Anhui Province

1959, Dec Identified as director of the Department for Industrial Work, Anhui Province CP

1978, Feb Elected deputy for Anhui Province to the 5th NPC

1979, Dec Elected vice-governor of Anhui Province

Huang Yukun (Huang Yü-k'un)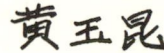

Posts held

Military
Major-general
Deputy director, General Political Department of the PLA

Huang was born in 1920 in Jiangxi Province. In 1934 he was a clerk at 3rd Army Headquarters. In 1937 he served in the 115th Division of the 8th Route Army. In 1947 he became political commissar of a division in the 1st Column of the Northeast Field Army.

1950		Huang is transferred to the Air Force and serves as a political commissar of an Air Force division, later of the Air Force Corps, in Korea
1955,	Sep	Promoted to rank of major-general of the Air Force
1957		Appointed deputy political commissar of Shenyang Military Region
1961,	Jul	Appointed political commissar of Beijing Military Region
1965,	Mar	Appointed director of the Political Department of the Air Force
1975,	Sep	Identified as deputy director, General Political Department of the PLA
1979,	Sep	Head of a delegation of vacationing PLA officers to Romania

Huang Yun (Huang Yün)

Posts held

Provincial Administration
Vice-chairman of the People's Government of Guangxi Autonomous Region

1979,	Dec	Elected vice-chairman of the People's Government of Guangxi Autonomous Region

Huang Zhaotian (Huang Chao-t'ien)

Posts held

CCP
Member of the Standing Committee of Jiangsu Province CP

NPC
Deputy for the PLA to the 5th NPC

Military
Colonel
Commander of Jiangsu Military District

Huang was born in 1916 in Xingguo County, Jiangxi Province, of a family of peasants. He joined the Red Army in 1929. In 1935 he was chief of a company in the 1st Front Army. In 1937 he attended a course at the Anti-Japan Military and Political Academy and was subsequently given the command of a company in the 115th Division, 8th Route Army. In 1947 he commanded the 1st Division, 1st Column of the East China Field Army. In 1949 he was deputy commander of the 58th Division of the 3rd Field Army.

1950,	Oct	Identified as commander of the 58th Division
1955,	Sep	Promoted to rank of colonel
1961		Identified as deputy commander of Wenzhou Garrison
1970,	Jun	Identified as commander of Jiangsu Military District
1977,	Dec	Elected member of the Standing Committee of Jiangsu Province CP
1978,	Feb	Elected deputy for the PLA to the 5th NPC

Huang Zhen (Huang Chen)

Posts held

CCP
Member of the CCP 11th Central Committee
1st deputy director, Propaganda Department in the CCP Central Committee

Government
Minister of culture

Military
Major-general

Others
Member of the Standing Committee of the 5th CPPCC

Huang was born in 1908 in Anhui Province. He graduated from the Shanghai Art Academy and joined the CCP in 1931. In early 1934 he commanded the 13th Regiment of the 3rd Front Army under Peng Dehuai. After crossing the Jinsha River during the Long March he wrote the plays "A Broken Sandal" and "March Forward with Force." Before the end of the Long March he served in the 15th Army Corps. In 1937 Huang functioned primarily as a political officer in various units in North China. With the rank of major-general he headed the 1946 negotiations between the CCP and KMT in Beijing where he was arrested by the latter and imprisoned for one year. In 1947 he served as political commissar in the Shanxi-Hebei-Shandong-Henan Field Army and was then transferred to the units commanded by Qin Jiwei.

1950,	Jun	Appointed ambassador to Hungary (until Jun 1954)
1954,	Sep	Appointed ambassador to Indonesia (until Apr 1961)
1961,	Apr	Appointed vice-minister of foreign affairs (until Apr 1964)
1962,	Nov-Dec	Visits to Burma, Ceylon, Indonesia, United Arab Republic, Ghana, and Guinea to inform the respective governments of the Chinese position in the Sino-Indian border conflict
1963,	Apr-May	Visits to Indonesia, Burma, Cambodia, and North Vietnam (there present during the negotiations between Liu Shaoqi and Ho Chi Min)
	Dec-1964, Feb	Member of a government delegation headed by Zhou Enlai to the United Arab Republic, Algeria, Morocco, Albania, Tunisia, Ghana, Mali, Guinea, Burma, Indonesia, and Ceylon

1964,   Apr   Head of a Chinese delegation to Jakarta for preliminary talks on the planned 2nd Afro-Asian Conference in Indonesia; appointed ambassador to France (until Mar 1973, suspended from early 1967 to May 1969 while answering criticism in Beijing)

       Oct   Elected deputy for Anhui Province to the 3rd NPC

1969,   Apr   Elected to first term as member of the CCP Central Committee by the 9th Party Congress

1970-1973   In his capacity as ambassador to France, Huang conducts preparatory negotiations for the establishment of diplomatic relations with Chile, San Marino, Turkey, Belgium, Australia, and Spain, as well as with the American secretary of state Henry Kissinger in preparation of the Richard Nixon visit in February 1972. In October 1972 Huang heads the Chinese delegation to the 17th UNESCO session in Paris.

1973,   Mar   Appointed head of the PRC Liaison Office in Washington (equivalent to ambassador) (until Nov 1977)

1977,   Dec   Identified as minister of culture and deputy director of the Propaganda Department in the CCP Central Committee (until Sep 1979)

1978,   Mar   Elected member of the Standing Committee, 5th CPPCC

1979,   May   Head of a cultural delegation to North Korea

       Sep   Identified as 1st deputy director of the Propaganda Department under the CCP Central Committee

       Oct   Head of a cultural delegation to Romania, Yugoslavia, Turkey, Syria, Jordan, and Tunisia (until Nov)

Huang is married to Zhu Lin who was elected a member of the Executive Council of the Womens's Federation in 1963.

Huang Zhengqing (Huang Cheng-ch'ing) 黄正清

Posts held

Provincial Administration
Vice-governor of Gansu Province

Huang belongs to the Tibetan minority (his Tibetan name is Lozong Tsewong) and was born in Xikang Province. In May 1945 he was elected member of the 6th Central Executive Committee of the KMT.

1949,   Dec   Identified as a member of the People's Government of Gansu Province

1950,   Mar   Identified as deputy director of the Department of Agriculture and Forestry of the People's Government of Gansu Province

       Jun   Identified as a member of the Northwest Military and Administrative Committee (until Jan 1953)

1952,   Aug   Identified as deputy director of the Department of Animal Husbandry under the Northwest Military and Administrative Committee

1953,   Jan   Identified as vice-chairman of the Northwest Administrative Committee

       Sep   Elected chairman of the Tibetan Autonomous Zhou Gannan in Gansu

1954,   Aug   Elected deputy for Gansu Province to the 1st NPC (reelected in 1958 to the 2nd NPC)

       Dec   Elected vice-governor of Gansu Province (until Sep 1964)

1959,   Apr   Appointed member of the National Defense Council

1960,   Jun   Identified as vice-chairman of the CPPCC, Gansu Branch

1964   Huang disappears

1979,   Dec   First appearance after the Cultural Revolution: Elected vice-governor of Gansu Province

Huang Zhigang (Huang Chih-kang) 黄志刚

Posts held

CCP
2nd secretary of Tianjin Municipality CP

NPC
Deputy for Tianjin Municipality to the 5th NPC

Provincial Administration
Vice-chairman of the Revolutionary Committee of Tianjin Municipality

1957,   Mar   Identified as director of the Propaganda Department of Shanxi Province CP

1959,   Oct   Identified as alternate secretary of Shanxi Province CP

1963,   Jul   Identified as director of the Propaganda Department, North Bureau of the CCP

1966,   Mar   Identified as alternate secretary, North Bureau of the CCP

1967,   Apr   Branded as a "three-anti element" and purged

1977,   May   First appearance after the Cultural Revolution

       Dec   Identified as 2nd secretary of Tianjin Municipality CP; elected vice-chairman of the Revolutionary Committee of Tianjin

1978,   Feb   Elected deputy for Tianjin Municipality to the 5th NPC

Huang Zhizhen (Huang Chih-chen) 黄知真

Posts held

CCP
Member of the CCP 11th Central Committee
Secretary of Hubei Province CP

Government
Member of the Birth Planning Leading Group under the State Council

Provincial Administration
Vice-governor of Hubei Province

During the Long March Huang remained in East Jiangxi as the leader of a guerrilla unit. After the outbreak of the Anti-Japanese War his unit was incorporated into the New 4th Army as the 5th Regiment of its 3rd Detachment. In 1945 he was temporarily deputy director of the Organization Department of the City of Qiqihar. In July 1949 he was identified as secretary of the CP of Shangyao County in Jiangxi Province.

1954		Identified as director of the United Front Work Department of Jiangxi Province CP
1955,	Jan	Identified as vice-chairman, CPPCC of Jiangxi Province, and as member of the People's Government Council of Jiangxi
1962,	Mar	Identified as alternate member, Secretariat of Jiangxi Province CP
1964,	Sep	Elected deputy for Jiangxi Province to the 3rd NPC
1966		Disappears during the Cultural Revolution
1972,	Apr	Reactivated after the Cultural Revolution
1973,	Mar	Identified as member of the Standing Committee of Jiangxi Province CP
	Apr	Identified as secretary of Jiangxi Province CP (until 1978)
	Aug	Elected alternate member of the CCP Central Committee by the 10th Party Congress
1977,	May	Identified as vice-chairman of the Revolutionary Committee of Jiangxi Province (until 1978)
	Aug	Elected member of the CCP Central Committee by the 11th Party Congress
1978,	Jul	Identified as member of the Birth Planning Leading Group under the State Council
1979,	May	Identified as secretary of Hubei Province CP
	Aug	Identified as vice-chairman of the Revolutionary Committee of Hubei Province (until Dec 1979)
1980,	Jan	Elected vice-governor of Hubei Province

Huang Zhong (Huang Chung)   黄　中

Posts held

Government
Vice-minister of the Physical Culture and Sports Commission

Others
Vice-president of the Athletic Federation

1952,	Jun	Appointed deputy secretary-general of the Athletic Federation (until Oct 1956)
1954,	Feb	Appointed deputy secretary-general of the Physical Culture and Sports Commission (until Oct 1956)
1956,	Oct	Appointed vice-chairman of the Physical Culture and Sports Commission and of the Athletic Federation
1960,	Feb	Appointed member of the Spare Time Education Committee
1961,	Jul	Identified as vice-chairman of the Sino-Hungarian Friendship Association
1962,	Apr-Jun	Head of a group of ping-pong players visiting Guinea, United Arab Republic, Mali, and Sudan

1963,	Nov	Head of a sports delegation to Indonesia
	Apr	Head of a sports delegation to Indonesia
	Jun	Appointed vice-chairman of the Preparatory Committee for the Games of the New Emerging Forces (GANEFO)
1964,	May	Head of a sports delegation to Cuba
	Aug	Head of a delegation attending the Executive Council Meeting of the Committee for the Games of the New Emerging Forces in Indonesia; appointed vice-chairman of the National Committee for the Games of the New Emerging Forces
1965,	Apr	Head of a sports delegation to Indonesia
	May	Head of a sports delegation to Cambodia
	Jun	Member of a group of 35 Chinese delegates to the planned 2nd Afro-Asian Conference in Algier
1966,	Jan	Head of a sports delegation to Cambodia
	Apr	Elected vice-chairman of the Association for Cultural Relations and Friendship with Foreign Countries
1967,	May	Branded as a counterrevolutionary element and purged
1975,	Sep	First appearance after the Cultural Revolution
1976,	Jan	Identified as a cadre of the Physical Culture and Sports Commission
	Oct	Head of a delegation to the 3rd Asian-African-Latin-American Table-Tennis Games in Mexico
1978,	Jul	Identified as vice-minister of the Physical Culture and Sports Commission
	Sep	Identified as vice-president of the Athletic Federation
	Dec	Deputy head of a sports delegation to the 8th Asian Games in Bangkok
1979,	Jul	Appointed member and deputy secretary-general of the National Games Organizing Committee

Huang Zuoqin (Huang Tso-ch'in) 黄作勤

Posts held

NPC
Member of the Standing Committee of the 5th NPC
Deputy for Guangxi Autonomous Region to the 5th NPC

1975,	Jan	Elected member of the Standing Committee of the 4th NPC (confirmed in 1978 by the 5th NPC)
1978,	Feb	Elected deputy for Guangxi Autonomous Region to the 5th NPC

Huang Zuozhen (Huang Tso-chen) 黄作珍

Posts held

CCP
Alternate member of the CCP 11th Central Committee
Secretary, CP of Beijing Municipality

Military
Major-general

Others
Member of the Central Patriotic Health Campaign Committee

1955,	Sep	Promoted to rank of major-general
1966,	Oct	Identified as deputy political commissar of Beijing Military Region
1967,	Apr	Elected member of the Standing Committee of the newly established Revolutionary Committee of Beijing (until Nov 1970)
	Aug	Identified as 2nd political commissar of Beijing Garrison (until about 1969)
	Nov	Huang is present at a reception given by Mao Zedong for revolutionary cadres and graduates of courses on Mao Zedong Thought
1968,	Jan	Huang is present at a reception given by Mao Zedong for revolutionary military cadres
	Feb	Identified as secretary-general of the Revolutionary Committee of Beijing (until about 1971)
	May	Present at a reception given by Mao Zedong for revolutionary activists
1969,	Apr	Elected to first term as alternate member of the CCP Central Committee by the 9th Party Congress
1970,	Nov	Identified as vice-chairman of the Revolutionary Committee of Beijing (until Feb 1979?)
1971,	Mar	Elected secretary of Beijing Municipality CP
1978,	Apr	Appointed member, Central Patriotic Health Campaign Committee

Hui Shigong (Hui Shih-kung) 惠世恭

Posts held

CCP
Member of the Standing Committee of Shaanxi Province CP

NPC
Deputy for Shaanxi Province to the 5th NPC

Provincial Administration
Vice-governor of Shaanxi Province

1954,	Dec	Identified as member of the Shaanxi People's Government
1958		Identified as director of the Industry Department in the Shaanxi People's Government
1963,	Dec	Elected vice-governor of Shaanxi Province (until May 1968)
1964,	May	Identified as member of the Standing Committee of Shaanxi Province CP (until May 1968)
1968		Disappears during the Cultural Revolution
1977,	Oct	First appearance after the Cultural Revolution: Identified as vice-chairman of the Revolutionary Committee of Shaanxi Province (until Dec 1979)
1978,	Jan	Identified as member of the Standing Committee of Shaanxi Province CP
	Feb	Elected deputy for Shaanxi Province to the 5th NPC
1979,	Dec	Elected vice-governor of Shaanxi Province

Hui Yuyu (Hui Yü-yü) 惠浴宇

Posts held

CCP
Secretary of Jiangsu Province CP

NPC
Deputy for Jiangsu Province to the 5th NPC

Provincial Administration
Governor of Jiangsu Province

Hui was born in 1906 in Shaanxi Province. During the Civil War he was director of the Political Department of the 3rd Field Army. After Jiangsu Province had been occupied by the communists and divided into North and South Jiangsu, Hui was appointed director of the North Jiangsu Administrative Office (until Nov 1952).

1950,	Oct	Appointed vice-chairman of the Committee for Harnessing the Huai River
1952,	Nov	After North and South Jiangsu are reunited to form Jiangsu Province, Hui is appointed member of its People's Council
1954		Identified as mayor and secretary of the CP of Nanjing Municipality (until Feb 1955)
	Sep	Elected deputy for Jiangsu Province to the 1st NPC (reelected in 1958 and 1964 to the 2nd and 3rd NPCs)
1955,	Feb	Elected governor of Jiangsu Province (until Cultural Revolution)
	Jul	Identified as secretary of Jiangsu Province CP (until Cultural Revolution)
1967		Disappears during the Cultural Revolution
1977,	Dec	First appearance after the Cultural Revolution: Elected vice-chairman of the Revolutionary Committee of Jiangsu Province (until Dec 1979)
1978,	Feb	Elected deputy for Jiangsu Province to the 5th NPC
	May	Identified as member of the Standing Committee of Jiangsu Province CP (until Mar 1979)
1979,	Feb	Elected chairman of the Jiangsu Province CPPCC
	Mar	Identified as secretary of Jiangsu Province CP
	Jun	Member of the Committee to Examine Proposals at the 2nd Session of the 5th NPC
	Sep	Head of a Jiangsu Provincial delegation to Japan
	Dec	Elected governor of Jiangsu Province

Hui is married to Gu Qing.

Huo Shilian (Huo Shih-lien) 霍士廉

Posts held

CCP
Member of the CCP 11th Central Committee

Government
Minister of agriculture

NPC
Deputy for Ningxia Autonomous Region to the 5th NPC

1950   Identified as director of the Civil Affairs Department in the People's Government of Zhejiang Province

1951,   Feb   Elected secretary-general of the Zhejiang People's Government

        Sep   Elected member of the People's Council of Zhejiang

1954,   Dec   Vice-chairman of Zhejiang Province (until Jan 1955)

1955,   Jan   Vice-governor of Zhejiang Province (until about Nov 1955)

1957,   Feb   Secretary of Zhejiang Province CP (until about Nov 1965)

        Apr   Chairman of the Zhejiang Section of the Sino-Soviet Friendship Association (until about Nov 1965)

        May   Appointed president of Zhejiang University (until Mar 1958)

1958,   Jan   Elected deputy for Zhejiang Province to the 2nd NPC in a by-election

1960,   May   Visit to Poland

1965,   Dec   Identified as 1st secretary of Shaanxi Province CP and as secretary of the Northwest China Bureau in the CCP Central Committee

1967   Disappears during the Cultural Revolution

1973,   Jun   Reactivated after the Cultural Revolution: Identified as secretary of Shaanxi Province CP (until Jan 1977)

        Jul   Identified as vice-chairman of the Revolutionary Committee of Shaanxi Province (until Jan 1977)

1977,   Jan   Identified as chairman of the Revolutionary Committee and as 1st secretary of the CP of Ningxia Autonomous Region (until Feb 1979)

        Aug   Elected member of the CCP Central Committee by the 11th Party Congress

1978,   Feb   Elected deputy for Ningxia Autonomous Region to the 5th NPC

1978,   Oct   Identified as 1st political commissar of Ningxia Military District (until Feb 1979)

1979,   Feb   Appointed minister of agriculture

        Jul   Head of a delegation to the World Conference on Agrarian Reform and Rural Development in Rome

        Aug   Head of an agriculture delegation to Great Britain and the Federal Republic of Germany

Ismail Amat (Szu-ma-yi Ai-mai-t'i) 司马义·艾买提

Posts held

CCP
Member of the CCP 11th Central Committee
Secretary of Xinjiang Autonomous Region CP
1st deputy secretary of the Xinjiang Party School

Military
Political commissar of Xinjiang Military Region

Provincial Administration
Chairman of Xinjiang People's Government

Ismail Amat belongs to the Uighur minority. He was born in 1934 in Xinjiang. His family were poor peasants living in Qira County, Hotan Prefecture, at the foot of the Kunlong Mountain range.

until 1960		Amat is active in the People's Commune Movement
1960		Amat is sent to the Central Party School of the CCP Central Committee for advanced studies. He is subsequently made deputy secretary of the CP of a county administration and deputy director of the Department of Political Work in Culture and Education of Xinjiang Autonomous Region
1973,	Aug	Elected member of the CCP Central Committee
1974,	Jun	Identified as secretary of Xinjiang Autonomous Region CP, and as vice-chairman of the Revolutionary Committee of Xinjiang Autonomous Region (latter post until Aug 1979)
1976,	Apr	Identified as political commissar of Xinjiang Military Region
1977,	Nov	Identified as 1st deputy director of the Xinjiang Party School
1979,	Sep	Elected chairman of the Xinjiang People's Government

Janabil (Chia-na-pu-erh) 贾那布尔

Posts held

CCP
Alternate member of the CCP 11th Central Committee
Deputy secretary of Xinjiang Autonomous Region CP
1st secretary, CP of the Autonomous Zhou of the Kazakhs, Ili

Provincial Administration
Vice-chairman of the People's Government of Xinjiang Autonomous Region
Chairman of the Revolutionary Committee, Autonomous Zhou of the Kazakhs, Ili

Janabil was born in 1933 in a family of poor shepherds. He belongs to the Kazakhs minority.

1973,	Aug	Elected to first term as alternate member of the CCP Central Committee by the 10th Party Congress
1975,	Feb	Identified as vice-chairman of the Revolutionary Committee and as member of the Standing Committee of the CP of Xinjiang Autonomous Region
	Sep	Identified as chairman of the Revolutionary Committee and as 1st secretary of the CP, Ili Autonomous Zhou of the Kazakhs
1976,	Feb	Identified as vice-chairman of the Revolutionary Committee of Xinjiang Autonomous Region (until Aug 1979)
	Nov	Head of a friendship delegation to North Korea
1977,	May	Identified as deputy secretary of Xinjiang Autonomous Region CP
1979,	Sep	Elected vice-chairman of Xinjiang Autonomous Region's People's Government

Jargal

Posts held

Provincial Administration
Vice-chairman of the People's Government of Inner Mongolia Autonomous Region

Jargal belongs to the Mongol minority.

1979,	Dec	Elected vice-chairman of the People's Government of Inner Mongolia Autonomous Region

Ji Changshan (Chi Ch'ang-shan) 吉长山

Posts held

NPC
Member of the Standing Committee of the 5th NPC
Deputy for Shanghai Municipality to the 5th NPC

1978,	Feb	Elected deputy for Shanghai Municipality to the 5th NPC
	Mar	Elected member of the Standing Committee of the 5th NPC

Ji Chunguang (Chi Ch'un-kuang) 冀春光

Posts held

CCP
Deputy secretary of Qinghai Province CP

Provincial Administration
Vice-chairman of the Standing Committee, Qinghai Province People's Congress

1950		Identified as CP secretary of Yushu County, Qinghai Province
1951,	Feb	Identified as council member of the People's Government of Qinghai

1956,   Sep   Identified as director of the United Front Work Department of Qinghai Province CP

1963,   Dec   Identified as vice-governor of Qinghai Province (until Cultural Revolution)

1966,   Feb   Identified as deputy secretary of Qinghai Province CP (until Cultural Revolution)

1967   Disappears during the Cultural Revolution

1973,   Dec   First appearance after the Cultural Revolution: Identified as member of the Standing Committee of Qinghai Province CP (until Aug 1979)

1974,   Oct   Identified as director of the Office of Agriculture and Animal Husbandry of the Qinghai Revolutionary Committee

1977,   Dec   Elected vice-chairman of the Revolutionary Committee of Qinghai (until Aug 1979)

1979,   Sep   Elected vice-chairman of the Standing Committee, Qinghai People's Congress; identified as deputy secretary of Qinghai Province CP

Ji Fang (Chi Fang)   季 方

Posts held

NPC
Member of the Standing Committee of the 5th NPC
Deputy for Jiangsu Province to the 5th NPC

Others
Vice-president of the 5th CPPCC
Chairman of the Chinese Peasants' and Workers' Democratic Party

Ji was born in 1890 in Haimen County, Jiangsu Province. After graduating from Baoting Military Academy he became an instructor at Whampoa Military Academy in 1925. In the following year he was made head of the Organization Department of the Political Department for the forces taking part in the Northern Expedition. After the KMT-Communist rift in 1927 he was engaged in the publication of various journals in Shanghai. In 1930 he joined the Provisional Action's Committee of the KMT founded by Deng Yanda which was also known under the name of "Third Party" (in 1947 renamed "Democratic Peasants and Workers Party"). Together with Cai Tingkai and Jiang Guangnai Ji was involved in the establishment of the Revolutionary People's Government of Fujian in 1933. After the collapse of that government he returned to Shanghai where he was active in the underground movement against the Nationalist Government which eventually led to his arrest and long imprisonment. During the Anti-Japanese War he was again arrested and imprisoned in Shanghai by the Japanese supported government of Wang Jingwei. After his release he joined the New 4th Army in North Jiangsu. In September 1949 he participated in the CPPCC as delegate for East China.

1949,   Oct   Appointed vice-minister of communications (until Sep 1954)

         Dec   Elected director of the General Office of the Sino-Soviet Friendship Association

1951,   Nov   Elected member of the Central Executive Bureau of the Democratic Peasants and Workers Party

1954,   Sep   Elected deputy for Jiangsu Province to the 1st NPC

         Oct   Elected member of the Standing Committee of the 1st NPC

1955,   Feb   Elected vice-governor of Jiangsu Province (until Dec 1958)

1958,   Dec   Elected chairman of the Democratic Peasants and Workers Party (until the Cultural Revolution) after the previous chairman Zhang Bojun had been reprimanded

1959,   Apr   Elected member of the Standing Committee of the CPPCC (until about 1973)

1964,   Dec   Elected member of the Standing Committee of the 3rd NPC (confirmed in this post in 1975 and 1978 by the 4th and 5th NPCs)

1978,   Feb   Elected deputy for Jiangsu Province to the 5th NPC

1979,   Jan   Identified again as chairman of the Chinese Peasants' and Workers' Democratic Party (reelected in Oct 1979)

         Jun   Member of the Draft Laws and of the Credentials Committee, 2nd Session of the 5th NPC

Ji Guixin (Chi Kuei-hsin)   冀桂昕

Posts held

CCP
Alternate member of the CCP 11th Central Committee

1977,   Aug   Elected alternate member of the CCP Central Committee by the 11th Party Congress

Ji Pengfei (Chi P'eng-fei)   姬鹏飞

Posts held

CCP
Member of the CCP 11th Central Committee
Director of the International Department of the CCP Central Committee

Government
Vice-premier
Secretary-general of the State Council

NPC
Deputy for Peking Municipality to the 5th NPC

Ji was born in 1909 as the son of a middle peasant in Yongji County in Shanxi Province. After elementary school he attended middle schools in Yongji and Xi'an. After graduating in medicine from the Military Medical College in Xi'an he served as a medical officer in a unit of the 2nd Army Group of the Nationalist Government. In 1929 he was transferred to a unit of the 26th Army commanded by the Warlord Feng Yuxiang. When in 1931 his unit was to be sent against the Communist forces in Jiangxi Province, it revolted and changed sides. During the Long March of 1934-1935 Ji was active in the Medical Department of the CCP Military Committee of which he subsequently became director.

During the Anti-Japanes War Ji served in various units mainly as director of political departments. As his latest assignment he held this post in a brigade of the New 4th Army commanded by the later minister of foreign affairs Chen Yi. His last posts during the Revolutionary War against the KMT Forces were deputy political commissar of the 7th Army Corps, 3rd Field Army, and director of the Political Department of Hangzhou Garrison.

1950,	Oct	Appointed head of the Chinese diplomatic mission to East Berlin, German Democratic Republic, with the rank of ambassador
1953,	Oct	Appointed ambassador to the German Democratic Republic (until Jan 1955)
1955,	Jan	Appointed vice-minister of foreign affairs (until Apr 1971)
	Jul	Appointed council member of the Institute of Foreign Affairs
	Aug	Member of a delegation to North Korea led by Zhu De
1960,	May	Member of a delegation to PR Mongolia led by Zhou Enlai
	Sep	Ji takes part in the mourning ceremony for Wilhelm Pieck in East Berlin
1961,	May	Member of a delegation to the Geneva Laos Conference headed by foreign minister Chen Yi
1963,	Sep	Member of a delegation to North Korea headed by president Liu Shaoqi
1964,	Oct	Elected deputy for Shanxi Province to the 3rd NPC
1965,	May	Ji visits Morocco, Guinea, Mali, Ghana, and Congo (Brazzaville)
1966,	Nov	Ji is present at several receptions given by Mao Zedong for the Red Guards
1967		Though repeatedly attacked by Red Guards, Ji remains unchallenged in his position as vice-minister of foreign affairs. In this office he is primarily responsible for relations with African and Asian countries.
1970,	Apr	Ji accompanies premier Zhou Enlai to North Korea
1971,	Apr	Identified as acting minister of foreign affairs (until Feb 1972)
1972,	Jan	Identified as minister of foreign affairs after the death of Chen Yi (until Oct 1974)
	Feb	Head of the Chinese delegation to the Vietnam Conference in Paris
1973,	Jun	Head of a government delegation to Great Britain, France, Iran, and Pakistan
	Aug	Elected to first term as member of the CCP Central Committee by the 10th Party Congress (reelected by the 11th Congress in 1977)
1975,	Jan	Elected member of the Standing Committee (until Mar 1978) and secretary-general of the Standing Committee of the 4th NPC (until Sep 1979)
1976,	Nov	Deputy head of an NPC delegation to Iran and Kuwait
	Dec	Head of a friendship delegation to Romania and Yugoslavia
1977,	Apr	Member of a delegation led by Deng Yingchao to Sri Lanka
	Sep	Deputy head of a NPC delegation to Australia and New Zealand
1978,	Feb	Elected deputy for Beijing Municipality to the 5th NPC
	Mar	Elected vice-chairman of the 5th NPC (until Sep 1979)
	Jun	Ji heads an NPC delegation to Venezuela, Mexico, and Canada
	Dec	Ji heads a friendship delegation to Iraq, Niger, Benin, Togo, Sierra Leone, and Gambia
1979,	Mar	Identified as director of the International Liaison Department, CCP Central Committee
	Sep	Appointed vice-premier
1980,	Feb	Appointed secretary-general of the State Council

Ji is married to Xu Hanbing.

Ji Xianlin (Chi Hsien-lin)　　李羡林

Posts held

Others
Vice-president of Beijing University

Ji obtained a doctorate in Indology under Professor Waldschmitt in Göttingen, Germany, around 1936.

1958,	Oct	Identified as a professor at Beijing University
1961,	Jan	Identified as a member of the Department of Philosophy and Social Sciences, Academy of Sciences
	Jul	Identified as director of the Department of Oriental Languages at Peking University
1962,	Dec	Member of a delegation to Iraq
1967		Disappears during the Cultural Revolution
1978,	Sep	First appearance after the Cultural Revolution: Identified as vice-president of Beijing University

Ji Yinglin (Chi Ying-lin)　　纪英林

Posts held

CCP
Alternate member of the CCP 11th Central Committee

1959,	Mar	Elected deputy for Jilin Province to the 2nd NPC (reelected in 1964 to the 3rd NPC)
1977,	Aug	Elected alternate member of the CCP Central Committee by the 11th Party Congress

Ji Zhongpu (Chi Chung-p'u)　　李钟朴

Posts held

Others
President of the Academy of Traditional Chinese Medicine

| 1950, | Apr | Identified as director of the Department of Medical Education, Ministry of Public Health |
| 1978, | Mar | Identified as president of the Academy of Traditional Chinese Medicine |

Ji Zongquan (Chi Tsung-ch'üan)   季宗权

Posts held

Government
Vice-minister of public health

| 1979, | Feb | Identified as vice-minister of public health |

Jia Chongzhi (Chia Ch'ung-chih)   贾冲之

Posts held

Provincial Administration
Vice-governor of Shanxi Province

1949,	Oct	Identified as deputy director of the Industrial Department, People's Government of Shanxi Province
1952,	Sep	Identified as director of the Industrial Department, People's Government of Shanxi Province
1963,	Feb	Identified as president of the Shanxi Mining College
1965,	Dec	Elected vice-governor of Shanxi Province
1967,	Mar	Jia disappears
1979,	Dec	First appearance after the Cultural Revolution: Elected vice-governor of Shanxi Province

Jia Huaiji (Chia Huai-chi)   贾怀齐

Posts held

Government
Ambassador to Guinea-Bissau and ambassador to the Republic of Cape Verde

1976,	Feb	Appointed ambassador to Guinea-Bissau
1976,	Apr	Conducts negotiations in the Republic of Cape Verde for the establishment of diplomatic relations
	Oct	Appointed ambassador to the Republic of Cape Verde

Jia is married to Ai Youmei.

Jia Huisheng (Chia Hui-sheng)   贾慧生

Posts held

Vice-minister of coal industry

1976,	Jan	Identified as a government cadre
1978,	Feb	Identified as vice-minister of coal industry; head of a coal industry study group visiting the Federal Republic of Germany
	Apr	Head of a coal industry study group to Yugoslavia

Jia Jun (Chia Chün)   贾俊

Posts held

CCP
Secretary of Shanxi Province CP

| 1977, | Dec | Elected vice-chairman of the Revolutionary Committee of Shanxi Province (until Dec 1979) |
| 1979, | Sep | Identified as secretary of Shanxi Province CP |

Jia Ruoyu (Chia Jo-yü)   贾若瑜

Posts held

Military
Major-general
Dean of the PLA Military Academy

Jia was born in Hunan Province. In 1934-35 he took part in the Long March. From 1946 to 1948 he served in Jiaodong Military District, and in 1949 he became chief of staff of the 32nd Army.

1960,	Aug	Identified as director of the Military Museum in Beijing (until Cultural Revolution)
1965,	Jul	Identified as secretary-general of the General Political Department of the PLA (until Cultural Revolution)
1967		Disappears during the Cultural Revolution
1978,	Aug	First appearance after the Cultural Revolution: Identified as dean of the PLA Military Academy

Jia Shi (Chia Shih)   贾石

Posts held

Government
Vice-minister for foreign trade

1949		Identified as director of the Finance Department of Shenyang Municipality
1950,	Jul	Identified as deputy director of the Foreign Trade Department in the Ministry of Commerce (until Oct 1952)
1952,	Oct	Identified as deputy director of the 2nd Bureau in the Ministry of Foreign Trade (until Apr 1958)
1958,	Apr	Identified as director of the 2nd Bureau in the Ministry of Foreign Trade (until Aug 1960)
1960,	Aug	Appointed assistant minister in the Ministry of Foreign Trade (until Apr 1964)
1964,	Apr	Appointed vice-minister for foreign trade
1967,	Feb	Head of a trade delegation to Romania
	Jun	Head of a trade delegation to Poland
	Oct	Identified as vice-chairman of the Council for Promoting International Trade
	Nov	Head of a trade delegation to Pakistan
1968,	Mar	Head of a trade delegation to North Korea
1969,	Sov	Jia disappears for unknown reasons
1975,	Sep	First reappearance
1977,	Apr	Renewed mention as vice-minister for foreign trade
1978,	Jul	Jia heads a trade delegation to Syria and Jordan

Jia Tingsan (Chia T'ing-san) 贾庭三

Posts held

CCP
3rd secretary of Beijing Municipality CP

NPC
Deputy for Guizhou Province to the 5th NPC

Provincial Administration
Chairman of the People's Congress of Beijing Municipality

Jia was born in 1912 in Tang County, Hebei Province.

1949,	Nov	Identified as director of the Beijing Municipal Industrial Bureau
1953,	Feb	Identified as director of the Industry Department, CP of Beijing Municipality
1955,	Feb	Elected deputy mayor of Beijing
1957,	Sep	Jia heads the delegation of the People's Council of Beijing to Yugoslavia
1958,	May	Identified as member of the Standing Committee, CP of Beijing Municipality
1964,	Sep	Elected deputy for Beijing Municipality to the 3rd NPC
1967		During the Cultural Revolution Jia is heavily attacked and dismissed from his offices
1971,	May	First appearance after the Cultural Revolution: Elected deputy secretary of Guizhou Province CP (until 1977)
1973,	Apr	Identified as vice-chairman of the Revolutionary Committee of Guizhou Province (until Oct 1978)
1977,	Sep	Identified as secretary of Guizhou Province CP (until Mar 1978)
1978,	Feb	Elected deputy for Guizhou Province to the 5th NPC
	Apr	Identified as 2nd secretary of Guizhou Province CP (until Jun 1978)
	Oct	Identified as 3rd secretary of Beijing Municipality CP
1979,	May	Elected vice-chairman of the Revolutionary Committee of Beijing Municipality (until Dec 1979)
	Dec	Elected chairman of the People's Congress of Beijing Municipality

Jia Yibin (Chia Yi-pin) 贾亦斌

Posts held

Others
Member of the Standing Committee of the 5th CPPCC
Vice-chairman of the Central Committee, Revolutionary Committee of the Chinese KMT

1961,	Feb	Identified as vice-chairman, Shanghai Section of the Kuomintang
1978,	Mar	Elected member of the Standing Committee of the 5th CPPCC
1979,	Oct	Elected vice-chairman of the Central Committee, Revolutionary Committee of the Chinese KMT

Jia Yunbiao (Chia Yün-piao) 贾云标

Posts held

Provincial Administration
Vice-governor of Shanxi Province

In 1947 Jia was commissioner of the Taihang Administrative Office.

1964,	Oct	Identified as vice-governor of Shanxi Province (until Cultural Revolution)
1967		Disappears during the Cultural Revolution
1977,	Dec	First appearance after the Cultural Revolution: Identified as vice-chairman of the Revolutionary Committee of Shanxi Province (until Dec 1979)
1979,	Dec	Elected vice-governor of Shanxi Province

Jiamuxiang Luosangjiumei Tudanquejinima (Jamyang Lozang Jigme Thubtan Chuji Nima) 嘉木样 罗藏久若土丹却 吉尼玛

Posts held

Others
Member of the Standing Committee of the 5th CPPCC

Jiamuxiang belongs to the Tibetan minority.

1978,	Mar	Elected member of the Standing Committee of the 5th CPPCC

Jian Xianren (Chien Hsien-jen) (f) 蠡先任

Posts held

CCP
Member of the Commission for Inspecting Discipline under the CCP Central Committee

Others
Member of the Standing Committee of the 5th CPPCC

1978,	Mar	Elected member of the Standing Committee of the 5th CPPCC
	Dec	Appointed member of the Commission for Inspecting Discipline under the CCP Central Committee

Jiang Baodi (Chiang Pao-ti) (f) 蒋宝娣

Posts held

CCP
Alternate member of the CCP 11th Central Committee
Member of the Standing Committee of Zhejiang Province CP

Mass Organization
Chairman of the Trade Union of Zhejiang Province

1969, Apr Elected to first term as alternate member of the CCP Central Committee by the 9th Party Congress (confirmed in 1973 and 1977)

1973, Jul Elected chairman of the Trade Union of Zhejiang Province (reelected in Aug 1978); identified as member of the Standing Committee of Zhejiang Province CP (re-elected in May 1978)

1974, Jul Identified as member of the Standing Committee, Revolutionary Committee of Zhejiang Province (until Dec 1977)

1977, Dec Elected vice-chairman of the Revolutionary Committee of Zhejiang Province (until Dec 1979)

Jiang Chunfang (Chiang Ch'un-fang)   姜椿芳

Posts held

Others
Member of the Standing Committee of the 5th CPPCC

In the early 30's Jiang was active in the underground communist movement in Manchuria. In 1937 he worked for the Translation News edited by Xia Yan in Shanghai. In the following year he co-edited together with Mei Yi the Daily Translation News. In 1941 he was chief editor of Time Weekly and in the following year chief editor of Soviet Literature and Art Weekly.

1954, Feb Identified as deputy director of the Bureau for Compilation and Translation of Works of Marx, Engels, Lenin, and Stalin in the CCP Central Committee; until 1959, subsequently disappeared until Mar 1978

1978, Mar Elected member of the Standing Committee of the 5th CPPCC

1979, Nov Identified as leading member of the China Encyclopedia Publishing House

Jiang Feng (Chiang Feng)   江丰

Posts held

Others
Chairman of the Artists' Association

Jiang was born in 1910. In 1937 he went to Yan'an where he became dean of the Art Department of the Lu Xun Art Institute.

1949 Appointed vice-president of the Central Academy of Fine Arts; elected vice-chairman of the Artists' Association (both posts held until early 1958)

1954, Aug Elected deputy for Shanghai Municipality to the 1st NPC (he lost this mandate in Jan 1958)

1957 Jiang is criticized as a rightist and disappears

1978, Jan First appearance after his purge in 1957

1979, Nov Elected chairman of the Artists' Association

Jiang Hua (Chiang Hua)   江华

Posts held

CCP
Member of the CCP 11th Central Committee

NPC
Deputy for Tianjin Municipality to the 5th NPC

Others
President of the Supreme People's Court

Jiang was born in 1905 in Shandong Province. In 1941 he was engaged as political commissar of Shandong Military Region in Communist guerrilla activities in his native province. After the occupation of Hangzhou he was appointed mayor of that city in April 1949 (until 1952).

1952 Appointed deputy secretary of Zhejiang Province CP

1955, Jan Elected member of the People's Council of Zhejiang Province

Feb Appointed chairman of Zhejiang Section, CPPCC

1956, Sep Elected alternate member of the CCP Central Committee by the 8th Party Congress; identified as 1st secretary of Zhejiang Province CP (until Cultural Revolution)

1957, Mar Identified as political commissar of Zhejiang Military Region (until Cultural Revolution)

1963, Jun Member of the Funeral Committee for Shen Junru

1965, Dec Identified as secretary of the East China Bureau in the CCP Central Committee (until Cultural Revolution)

1967 Disappears during the Cultural Revolution

1973, Aug First appearance after the Cultural Revolution: Mentioned during the 10th CCP Congress which elected him alternate member of its Central Committee, a post he had already held from 1956 until the Cultural Revolution

1975, Jan Appointed president of the Supreme People's Court

1977, Aug Elected member of the CCP Central Committee by the 11th Party Congress

1978, Feb Elected deputy for Tianjin Municipality to the 5th NPC

May Article in HQ, May 1978: "Act in Strict Accordance with the New Constitution"

Jiang is married to Wu Zhonglian.

Jiang Liyin (Chiang Li-yin)   江礼银

Posts held

CCP
Member of the CCP 11th Central Committee
Secretary of Fujian Province CC

NPC
Member of the Standing Committee of the 5th NPC
Deputy for Fujian Province to the 5th NPC

Mass Organization
Chairman, Trade Union of Fujian Province

Jiang is a worker in the Locomotive Department of the Fuzhou Railway Bureau and first became known there.

1969, Apr Elected to first term as member of the CCP Central Committee by the 9th Party Congress (confirmed in 1973 and 1977)

1973, Jul Elected chairman of the Trade Union of Fujian Province; identified as member of the Standing Committee of Fujian Province CP (until Jun 1975)

1975, Jun Identified as secretary of Fujian Province CP

1978, Feb Elected deputy for Fujian Province to the 5th NPC

Apr Last appearance; probably purged

Jiang Ming (Chiang Ming)   江　明

Posts held

Government
Vice-minister of the Scientific and Technical Commission

In the early 1940s Jiang served in the Central China Bureau of the CCP. In 1942 he followed Liu Shaoqi to Yan'an. In 1949 he was head of the Trade Administrative Bureau in the North China People's Government.

1950, Jun Identified as chief of the Trade Planning Office, Planning Department, Financial and Economic Committee of the Government Administrative Council (until 1952)

1952, Apr Identified as deputy director of the Foreign Trade Department in the Ministry of Trade (until 1954)

1953, Nov Deputy head of a trade delegation to Moscow

1954, Dec Identified as director of the 1st Bureau in the Ministry of Foreign Trade (until 1955)

1955, Jun Identified as vice-minister of foreign trade (until Cultural Revolution)

Sep Head of a delegation to the Damascus International Fair

Dec Head of a trade delegation to Syria, Lebanon, and Saudi Arabia (until Jan 1956)

1956, Oct Head of a trade delegation to Egypt

1957, Sep Identified as council member of the Sino-Syrian Friendship Association

1958, Feb Identified as a council member of the Sino-Egyptian Friendship Association

1959, Jan Head of a trade delegation to the People's Republic of Mongolia

1960, Feb Head of a trade delegation to North Korea

1964, Oct Identified as director of the Bureau of Customs Administration in the Ministry of Foreign Trade (until Cultural Revolution)

Nov Head of a trade delegation to Romania

1965, Feb Head of a trade delegation to Poland, Hungary, Czechoslovakia (until Apr 1965)

1967 Disappears during the Cultural Revolution

1978, Jun First appearance after the Cultural Revolution: Identified as vice-minister of the Scientific and Technical Commission

1979, Aug Head of a delegation to the UN Conference on Science and Technology for Development in Vienna

Jiang Nanxiang (Chiang Nan-hsiang)   蔣南翔

Posts held

CCP
Member of the CCP 11th Central Committee

Government
Minister of education
Vice-minister of the Scientific and Technical Commission

NPC
Member of the Standing Committee of the 5th NPC
Deputy for Tianjin Municipality to the 5th NPC

Jiang was born in 1910 in Shaoxing, Zhejiang Province. He graduated from Qinghua University in Beijing. About 1932 he joined the CCP and was one of the leading Party cadres at Qinghua University. At the beginning of the Sino-Japanese War he went to Yan'an. After training in the USSR he was together with Hu Qiaomu co-editor of the journal Zhongguo Qingnian (Chinese Youth). In 1949 he was elected deputy secretary of the Central Committee of the New Democratic Youth League. At this time he was head of a sub-division of the Youth Work Committee of the CCP Central Committee and the Central League School of the Youth League (until 1950). He was elected member of the National Committee of the CPPCC in September 1949 representing the Youth League (until December 1954).

1949, Oct Appointed member of the Committee of Cultural and Educational Affairs in the Government Administration Council (until Oct 1954)

1950, Oct Appointed member of the Peace Council (until Jul 1958)

1951, Oct Appointed council member and secretary of the Sino-Soviet Friendship Association (until Dec 1954)

1952, Sep Appointed secretary of the Youth League CC (until 1953)

Nov Appointed dean of Qinghua University

1953, Feb Elected member of the Standing Committee of the CPPCC in a by-election (until Dec 1954)

1954, Aug Elected deputy for Beijing Municipality to the 1st NPC

1956, Sep Elected alternate member of the CCP Central Committee by the 8th Party Congress

1957, May Elected member of the Communist Youth League (probably until Jul 1964)

Sep Appointed 1st secretary of Qinghua University CP

1958, Oct Appointed chairman of the Sino-Albanian Friendship Association

1960, Jan Appointed vice-minister for education (until Oct 1964)

1961, Feb Member of a CCP delegation to Albania

1964, Oct Appointed vice-minister for higher education (until Jan 1965)

1965, Jan Appointed minister for higher education

1966 Jiang is attacked as a supporter of Peng Zhen and branded as "black gangster of the Three-Family Village"

1974,	Sep	First appearance after the Cultural Revolution
1977,	Jul	Identified as vice-chairman of the Revolutionary Committee of Tianjin Municipality (until fall 1977)
	Dec	Identified as vice-minister of the State Scientific and Technical Commission
1978,	Feb	Elected deputy for Tianjin Municipality to the 5th NPC
	Mar	Elected member of the Standing Committee of the 5th NPC
1979,	Feb	Identified as minister of education
	Jun	Member of the Credentials Committee, 2nd Session of the 5th NPC
	Sep	Head of a government delegation to Italy, the Netherlands, and Great Britain; by-elected member of the CCP 11th Central Committee by its 4th Plenum

Jiang Ping (Chiang P'ing)　　江　平

Posts held

Government
Vice-minister of the State Nationalities Commission

| 1978, | Dec | Identified as a cadre of the State Nationalities Commission |
| 1979, | May | Identified as vice-minister of the State Nationalities Commission |

Jiang Weiqing (Chiang Wei-ch'ing)　江渭清

Posts held

CCP
Member of the CCP 11th Central Committee
1st secretary of Jiangxi Province CP

NPC
Deputy for Jiangxi Province to the 5th NPC

Military
Political commissar of Fuzhou Military Region
1st political commissar of Jiangxi Military District
Member of the Standing Committee, CP Secretariat of Fuzhou Military Region

Jiang is a native of Jiangsu Province. During the final phase of the Anti-Japanese War he served as political commissar in the 6th Division of the New 4th Army. In 1946 he worked as a cadre in the Central China Bureau of the CCP Central Committee in Anhui Province. During the following years he was again political commissar in various military units. After the occupation of Nanjing in April 1949 he became a member of the Nanjing Military Control Commission headed by Liu Bocheng as well as deputy secretary of the Nanjing CP. In September of the same year he represented the 3rd Field Army as a delegate to the 1st CPPCC.

| 1950, | Mar | Appointed member of the Control Commission, East China Military and Adminis- |

trative Council (until Jan 1953); deputy secretary of the CP of Nanjing Municipality (until Nov 1953); member of the Nanjing People's Government (until Nov 1953) and chairman of the Trade Union in Nanjing (until Nov 1953)

1953,	Jan	Appointed member of the East China Administrative Council (probably until 1954)
	Nov	Appointed 2nd secretary of Jiangsu Province CP (until Jan 1955)
1955,	Jan	Appointed secretary of Jiangsu Province CP (until Jul 1956)
1956,	Jul	Appointed 1st secretary of Jiangsu Province CP (until Cultural Revolution)
	Sep	Elected alternate member of the CCP Central Committee by the 8th Party Congress (until Cultural Revolution)
	Dec	Identified as chairman of the Jiangsu Section, CPPCC (until Cultural Revolution)
1960,	Feb	Identified as political commissar of Jiangsu Military Region (until Cultural Revolution)
1965,	Dec	Identified as chairman of the Nanjing Section, CPPCC (until Cultural Revolution)
1966,	Mar	Identified as member of the Secretariat, East China Bureau of the CCP Central Committee
1973,	Aug	Reelected alternate member of the CCP Central Committee by the 10th Party Congress (this occasion also marks Jiang's first appearance after the Cultural Revolution after his disappearance at the end of 1966)
1975,	Jan	Identified as 1st secretary of Jiangxi Province CP
	May	Identified as chairman of the Revolutionary Committee of Jiangxi (until Dec 1977). The ideological party journal HQ of May 1975 publishes an article by Jiang: "Continue to Strengthen the Dictatorship of the Proletariat in Rural Areas"
1976,	Sep	Identified as 1st political commissar of Jiangxi Military District
1977,	Jun	Identified as member of the Standing Committee, CP Secretariat of Fuzhou Military Region
	Aug	Elected member of the CCP Central Committee by the 11th Party Congress
1978,	Feb	Elected deputy for Jiangxi Province to the 5th NPC
	Jun	Identified as political commissar of Fuzhou Region

Jiang Wen (Chiang Wen)　　江　文

Posts held

NPC
Deputy for the PLA to the 5th NPC

Military
Director of the Department of Communications, PLA General Staff

Around 1933 Jiang attended the School of Telephone Communications in Ruijin. In 1937 he was in charge of the

Field Communications Company, 115th Division of the 8th Route Army. Two years later he commanded a field communications battalion in Shanxi Military District. In 1947 he was head of the Field Communications Department in the Headquarters of Northeast China Field Army. In 1949 he was chief of the Field Communications Department of the 4th Field Army.

1950		Jiang heads the Field Communications Unit of the Chinese People's Volunteers in North Korea
1958		Identified as commandant of the Field Communications School of the PLA
1959		Concurrently, identified as head of the Field Communications Department in the General Staff of the PLA
1964,	Sep	Elected deputy for the PLA to the 3rd NPC
1971,	May	Identified as a military officer in Wuhan Military Region
1974,	Jan	Identified as deputy commander of Wuhan Military Region (until 1975)
1977,	Sep	Identified as head, Signals Department of the Headquarters of the General Staff; member of a military delegation to France and Romania
1978,	Feb	Elected deputy of the PLA to the 5th NPC
	Jun	Member of a military goodwill delegation, led by Zhang Aiping, to Sweden and Italy
1979,	May	Identified as director of the Communications Department, PLA General Staff

Jiang Xieyuan (Chiang Hsieh-yüan) 江燮元

Posts held

CCP
Alternate member of the CCP 11th Central Committee

Military
Deputy commander of Guangzhou Military Region

Jiang was born in 1912 in Longshi, Jiangxi Province. He probably took part in the Long March in the 1st Front Army which was commanded by Lin Biao. In 1938 he was commander of a battalion in 115th Division (commanded by Lin Biao) of the 8th Route Army. In 1945 he was assigned as regiment commander to East Shandong Military District. In the following year he commanded the 34th Regiment, 12th Corps, Northeast China Joint Democratic Army. In 1948 he was commander of the 12th Division, Northeast China Field Army. One year later he commanded the 133rd Division of the 4th Field Army.

1950		Identified as chief of staff of the 41st Corps
about 1955		Training at a military academy
1961		Identified as deputy commander of the 41st Corps
1966		Identified as commander of the 41st Corps and as commander of Shantou Garrison
1967		Identified as deputy chief of staff of Guangzhou Military Region
1968,	Jan	Identified as deputy commander of Guangzhou Military Region
1969,	Apr	Elected to first term as member of the CCP Central Committee by the 9th Party Congress (confirmed 1973 by the

10th Congress)

| 1977, | Aug | Jiang is demoted from member to alternate member of the CCP Central Committee by the 11th Party Congress |

Jiang Xueshan (Chiang Hsüeh-shan) 江雪山

Posts held

Military
Commander of Hainan Island Military District

Jiang was born in 1917 in Jiangxi Province. He joined the Red Army at the age of about seventeen. From 1942 (?) until 1945 he served initially as company, later battalion, commander in Shandong Military District. He was appointed deputy commander of the 34th Regiment, 12th Division, Northeast Field Army, in 1947. In 1949 he became commander of the 367th Regiment, 123rd Division, 41st Army, 4th Field Army.

1954,	Aug	Elected deputy for the PLA to the 1st NPC (reelected in 1958 and 1964 to the 2nd and 3rd NPCs)
1956,	Sep	Identified as deputy commander of the 123rd Division
1961,	Mar	Identified as commander of the 123rd Division
1965,	Jun	Identified as deputy commander of the 41st Army
1976,	Jan	Identified as commander of Hainan Island Military District

Jiang Yi (Chiang Yi) 姜一

Posts held

CCP
Secretary of Shaanxi Province CP

Provincial Administration
Vice-governor of Shaanxi Province

Jiang was born in 1919 in Shanxi Province.

1957,	Nov	Identified as 1st secretary of Huanggang District CP, Hubei Province (until Cultural Revolution)
1965,	Nov	Identified as alternate member of the Secretariat of Hubei Province (until Cultural Revolution)
1967		During the Cultural Revolution Jiang is criticized as a capitalist-roader
1968,	Feb	With the establishment of the Revolutionary Committee of Hubei Province, Jiang is elected member of its Standing Committee
1971,	Mar	With reestablishment of the Party Secretariat in Hubei Province, Jiang is elected CP secretary (until Aug 1977)
1977,	Sep	Identified as secretary of Shaanxi Province CP
	Dec	Elected vice-chairman of Shaanxi Province Revolutionary Committee (until Dec 1979)
1978,	Jul	Deputy head of an agricultural delegation to the U.S.A.
1979,	Dec	Elected vice-governor of Shaanxi Province

Jiang Ying (Chiang Ying) 蔣　英

Posts held

Others
Member of the Standing Committee of the
5th CPPCC

1978,   Mar   Elected member of the Standing Committee of the 5th CPPCC

Jiang Yizhen (Chiang Yi-chen) 江一真

Posts held

CCP
2nd secretary of Hebei Province CP

Government
Vice-chairman, Committee for Patriotic
Health Campaign
Vice-chairman, Birth Planning Leading
Group under the State Council

Others
Member of the Standing Committee of the
5th CPPCC

Provincial Administration
Chairman of the People's Congress of
Hebei Province

1951   Identified as vice-chairman of the Fujian
Peasants' Federation and as vice-chairman
of the Land Reform Committee, People's
Government of Fujian Province
1952,   Aug   Appointed director of the Agriculture and
Forestry Department in the Fujian Peo-
ple's Government
1955,   Jan   Elected vice-governor of Fujian Province
Feb   Identified as president of the Fujian College of Agriculture (until 1957)
Aug   Identified as deputy secretary of Fujian
Province CP
1956,   Jun   Elected secretary of Fujian Province CP
Sep   Appointed member of the Ballot Committee of the CCP 8th National Congress
1959,   Feb   Elected governor of Fujian Province (until
Dec 1962); elected deputy for Fujian
Province to the 2nd NPC (reelected to the
3rd NPC in 1964)
1962,   Oct   Appointed vice-minister of state farms
and land reclamation (until Sep 1964)
1964,   Oct   Appointed vice-minister of agriculture
(until Cultural Revolution)
1967,   Jan   Branded as "three-anti" element and paraded through the streets of Beijing as a
deviationist
1974,   Sep   First appearance after the Cultural Revolution
1977,   Nov   Identified as minister of public health
(until Apr 1979)
1978,   Mar   Elected member of the Standing Committee, 5th CPPCC
Apr   Appointed vice-chairman of the Committee for Patriotic Health Campaign
Jul   Appointed vice-chairman of the Birth
Planning Leading Group under the State
Council

Dec   Jiang heads a public health delegation to
North Korea
1979,   May   Identified as 2nd secretary of Hebei CP
and vice-chairman of the Revolutionary
Committee of Hebei Province
Nov   Article in RMRB, 11 November, "Life Is
Like a Burning Fire," commemorating the
40th anniversary of the death of the Canadian surgeon Norman Bethune
1980,   Feb   Elected chairman of the People's Congress
of Hebei Province

Jiang Yonghui (Chiang Yung-hui) 江拥辉

Posts held

CCP
Member of the CCP 11th Central Committee

Military
Major-general
Deputy commander of Shenyang Military
Region

Jiang distinguished himself as a guerrilla fighter during
the revolutionary period. In 1945 he was commander of
the 2nd Regiment, 1st Division, Northeast Field Army. In
January 1946 he was wounded during the fighting in
Liaoning Province. In 1948 he was given the command of
the 1st Division; after the reorganization of the Northeast
Combat Units he became commander of the 112th Division of the 4th Field Army.

1952   Receives training at the Beijing Military
School and is made commander of the
64th Army
1958,   Dec   Identified as major-general in Shenyang
Military Region
1965   Identified as deputy chief of staff in
Shenyang Military Region
1968,   Sep   Identified as deputy commander of
Shenyang Military Region
1969,   Apr   Elected to first term as member of the
CCP Central Committee by the 9th Party
Congress

Jiang Zehan (Chiang Tse-han)   江泽涵

Posts held

Others
Vice-president of the Society of Mathe-
matics
President of the Beijing Society of Mathe-
matics
Member of the Department for Mathe-
matics, Physics, and Chemistry of the
Academy of Sciences

1962,   Sep   Identified as vice-president of the Society
of Mathematics
1977,   Feb   First appearance after the Cultural Revolution
1978,   Apr   Identified in his former position as vice-
president of the Society of Mathematics

1979, Jan Identified as member of the Department for Mathematics, Physics, and Chemistry of the Academy of Sciences

Nov Identified as a professor of Beijing University and as president of the Beijing Society of Mathematics

Jiang Zemin (Chiang Tse-min) 江泽民

Posts held

Others
Vice-chairman of the Society of Mechanical Engineering

1950 Identified as director of the Military Engineering Department of Northeast Military Region

Dec Identified as commercial counselor of the Chinese embassy in the USSR

1956, Oct Identified as assistant minister of the 1st Ministry of Machine Building (until Sep 1959)

1960 Identified as vice-chairman of the Society of Mechanical Engineering

1963, Aug Identified as vice-chairman of the Scientific and Technical Association, Beijing Branch

1976, Jan First appearance after the Cultural Revolution

1978, Sep Identified in his former post as vice-chairman of the Society of Mechanical Engineering

Oct Identified as adviser to the 1st Ministry of Machine Building

Jiao Linyi (Chiao Lin-yi) 焦林义

Posts held

CCP
Member of the CCP 11th Central Committee
Standing secretary of Guangdong Province CP

NPC
Deputy for Guangdong Province to the 5th NPC

Others
Chairman of the Revolutionary Committee of Guangzhou Municipality

1952 Identified as 2nd secretary of Dongjiang Region CP, Guangdong Province

1955, Nov Identified as deputy mayor of Guangzhou (until Cultural Revolution)

1958, Oct Elected deputy for Guangdong Province to the 2nd NPC (until 1974)

Nov Identified as secretary of Guangzhou CP (until Mar 1965)

1965, Mar Elected 2nd secretary of Guangzhou CP (until Mar 1973)

1966, Jul Identified as acting 1st secretary of Guangzhou CP

1969, Apr The 9th Party Congress elects Jiao alternate member of the CCP Central Committee (until Aug 1973)

Aug Identified as vice-chairman of the Revolutionary Committee of Guangzhou (until Mar 1973)

1972, Mar Identified as member of the Standing Committee of Guangdong Province CP (until Jul 1975)

1973, Mar Identified as 1st secretary of Guangzhou CP (until Mar 1979); identified as chairman of the Revolutionary Committee of Guangzhou

May Identified as vice-chairman of the Revolutionary Committee of Guangdong (until Dec 1979)

Aug Elected to first term as member of the CCP Central Committee by the 10th Party Congress

1975, Jul Identified as secretary of Guangdong Province CP

1978, Feb Elected deputy for Guangdong Province to the 5th NPC

Apr Elected standing secretary of Guangdong Province CP

Jiao Liren (Chiao Li-jen) 焦力人

Posts held

Government
Vice-minister of petroleum industry

1958, Jun Identified as CP secretary and chairman of the oil production area of Yumen and as director of the Yumen School of Engineering

1972, Sep Deputy head of a petroleum study group to Canada

1975, Dec Identified as vice-minister of petroleum and chemical industry

1978, Jul Identified as vice-minister of petroleum industry

Jiao Ruoyu (Chiao Jo-yü) 焦若愚

Posts held

Government
Minister of the 8th Ministry of Machine Building

1949 Identified as deputy mayor of Shenyang (until Aug 1954)

1953, Sep Identified as vice-chairman of the Sino-Soviet Friendship Association of Shenyang Municipality

1954, Aug Elected deputy for Shenyang Municipality to the 1st NPC (until Mar 1959)

Nov Identified as secretary of Shenyang Municipality CP

1956, Sep Identified as 1st secretary of Shenyang Municipality CP

1960, May Identified as member of the Standing Committee, Liaoning Province CP

1965,	Nov	Appointed ambassador to North Korea (until about 1967)
1971,	Dec	Appointed ambassador to Peru (until Jan 1976)
1977,	May	Appointed ambassador to Iran (until Aug 1979)
1979,	Sep	Appointed minister of the 8th Ministry of Machine Building

Jiao Shanmin (Chiao Shan-min)　焦善民

Posts held

Government
Vice-minister for textile industry

1950,	Jun	Identified as director of the Planning Office for Light Industry in the Central Bureau for Financial and Economic Planning of the Government Administration Council
1955,	Jan	Appointed assistant minister in the Ministry for Construction
1957,	Jun	Appointed vice-minister for building materials
1958,	Feb	Identified as secretary of Gansu Province CP
1966,	Oct	Appointed vice-minister for textile industry
1967		Attacked during the Cultural Revolution and removed from his offices
1970,	Nov	Reactivated after the Cultural Revolution
1972,	Apr	Identified as vice-minister for light industry (until 1977)
1977,	Oct	Head of an industrial delegation to North Vietnam
1978,	May	Identified as vice-minister of textile industry
	Nov	Head of a textile study group to Japan

Jin Baosheng (Chin Pao-sheng)　金宝生

Posts held

Government
Member of the State Nationalities Affairs Commission

NPC
Deputy for Guangxi Autonomous Region to the 5th NPC

Provincial Administration
Vice-chairman of the People's Government of Guangxi Autonomous Region

Jin belongs to the Yao minority.

1954,	Aug	Elected deputy for Guangxi Province to the 1st NPC (reelected in 1958 and 1964 to the 2nd and 3rd NPCs)
1962,	Nov	Identified as secretary of Dayao Shan County CP
1978,	Feb	First appearance after the Cultural Revolution: Elected deputy for Guangxi Autonomous Region to the 5th NPC

1979,	May	Appointed member of the State Nationalities Affairs Commission
	Dec	Elected vice-chairman of the People's Government of Guangxi Autonomous Region

Jin Cheng (Chin Ch'eng)　金　城

Posts held

Others
Member of the Standing Committee of the 5th CPPCC

Jin was born in Hebei Province. In 1939 he was director of the Public Relations Department of the Shaanxi-Gansu-Ningxia Border District Government.

1949,	Nov	Identified as vice-chairman of the Sino-Soviet Friendship Association, Hebei Branch
1950,	Apr	Identified as director of the Propaganda Department of Hebei Province CP
1952,	Jan	Identified as director of the 2nd Office of the United Front Work Department in the CCP Central Committee
1956,	Feb	Identified as assistant minister in the Ministry of Aquatic Products (until Jul 1959)
1959,	Sep	Appointed vice-minister of aquatic products (until Jun 1964)
1963,	Nov	Identified as deputy director of the United Front Work Department in the CCP Central Committee (until Cultural Revolution)
1967		Disappears during the Cultural Revolution
1975,	Sep	First appearance after the Cultural Revolution
1978,	Mar	Elected member of the Standing Committee of the 5th CPPCC

Jin Guixiang (Chin Kuei-hsiang) (f)　

Posts held

NPC
Member of the Standing Committee of the 4th NPC
Deputy for Hebei Province to the 4th NPC

Government
Member of the Birth Planning Leading Group under the State Council
Member of the Education Ministry Party Group

1964,	Sep	Member of a women's delegation to Albania
1975,	Jan	Elected member of the Standing Committee of the 4th NPC (confirmed in 1978 by the 5th NPC)
1978,	Feb	Elected deputy for Hebei Province to the 5th NPC
	Jul	Appointed member of the Birth Planning Leading Group under the State Council
	Oct	Identified as member of the Education Ministry Party Group

Jin Jianzhong (Chin Chien-chung) 金建中

Posts held

NPC
Deputy for Gansu Province to the 5th NPC

Others
Director of the Lanzhou Institute of Physics, Academy of Sciences
President of the Vacuum Society

1978,	Feb	Elected deputy for Gansu Province to the 5th NPC
1979,	Dec	Elected president of the Vacuum Society; identified as director of the Lanzhou Institute of Physics, Academy of Sciences

Jin Ming (Chin Ming) 金 明

Posts held

CCP
1st secretary of Hebei Province CP

Jin was born in 1908 in Shandong Province. He served as Mao Zedong's orderly during Jinggangshan times. In 1934-35 he took part in the Long March. In 1942 he served in Huaihai District, North Jiangsu. He became deputy political commissar of Hunan Military District in August 1949.

1950,	Mar	Identified as member of the People's Government of Hunan Province
	Jul	Identified as chairman, Land Reform Committee of Hunan People's Government
1952,	Feb	Identified as vice-chairman of Hunan Province (until Feb 1955)
	Oct	Identified as deputy secretary of Hunan Province CP
1953,	Feb	Identified as secretary of Hunan Province CP (until Feb 1955)
	Sep	Appointed vice-minister of finance (until Dec 1961)
1958,	Nov	Elected deputy for Shandong Province to the 2nd NPC (reelected in 1964 to the 3rd NPC)
1961,	Oct	Identified as alternate secretary, Central-South Bureau of the CCP Central Committee
1963,	Mar	Identified as council member of the Sino-Laotian Friendship Association
1965,	Apr	Identified as secretary, Central-South Bureau of the CCP Central Committee
1968,	Jan	Branded as a capitalist-roader and purged
1978,	Dec	First appearance after the Cultural Revolution
1979,	Apr	Identified as secretary-general of the State Council (until Jan 1980)
	Jul	Appointed member of the State Financial and Economic Commission (until Jan 1980)
1980,	Jan	Identified as 1st secretary of Hebei Province CP

Jin Minghan (Chin Ming-han) 金明汉

Posts held

CCP
Alternate member of the CCP 11th Central Committee
Member of the Standing Committee, Jilin Province CP

NPC
Deputy for Jilin Province to the 5th NPC

1964		Identified as deputy secretary, CP of Yanbian Autonomous Zhou of the Koreans
1977,	Aug	Elected alternate member of the CCP Central Committee by the 11th Party Congress
1978,	Jan	Identified as member of the Standing Committee of Jilin Province CP
	Feb	Elected deputy for Jilin Province to the 5th NPC
1979,	Jun	Member of the Committee to Examine Proposals at the 2nd Session of the 5th NPC

Jin Shanbao (Chin Shan-pao) 金善宝

Posts held

NPC
Deputy for Zhejiang Province to the 5th NPC

Others
President of the Academy of Agricultural Sciences
Vice-chairman of the Agronomy Society
Director of the Science and Technology Committee under the Ministry of Agriculture
Vice-chairman of the Jiusan (Chiu-san) Society

Jin, a wheat expert, was born in 1910 in Zhuji, Zhejiang Province. In 1949 he lectured at the College of Agriculture of Nanjing University.

1950,	Mar	Appointed deputy director of the Agriculture and Forestry Department in the Central-South China Military and Administrative Council (reorganized in December 1952)
	May	Elected deputy mayor of Nanjing
1952,	Mar	Elected vice-chairman of the Agricultural Sciences Society (until Sep 1959)
	Sep	Elected member of the Jiusan Society Central Committee (probably until 1959)
	Dec	Appointed deputy director of the Agriculture and Forestry Department in the Central-South China Administrative Council (until Sep 1954)
1954,	Aug	Elected deputy for Jiangsu Province to the 1st NPC; appointed director of the Nanjing College of Agriculture

1955,   Feb   Elected member of the People's Council, Jiangsu Province
         Jun   Appointed member of the Biology, Geology, and Geography Department in the Academy of Sciences
1956,   Mar   Jin becomes a CCP member
1957,   Mar   Appointed vice-president of the Academy of Agricultural Sciences (until Oct 1965)
         May   Appointed member of the Scientific Planning Commission, State Council
1958,   Dec   Elected member of the Standing Committee, Jiusan Society Central Committee
1963,   Sep   Identified as vice-chairman of the Agricultural Society; identified as chairman of the Society for the Study of Crops
1965,   Oct   Appointed president of the Academy of Agricultural Sciences
1977,   Jun   Identified as president of the Academy of Agriculture and Forestry Sciences (until 1978)
1978,   Feb   Elected deputy for Zhejiang Province to the 5th NPC
1979,   May   Identified as director of the Science and Technology Committee under the Ministry of Agriculture
         Sep   Identified as president of the Academy of Agricultural Science
         Oct   Elected vice-chairman of the Central Committee, Jiusan (Chiu-san) Society

Jin Tairan (Chin T'ai-jan) (f)　　金太然

Posts held

CCP
Member of the Standing Committee of Jilin Province CP

Provincial Administration
Vice-chairman of the Revolutionary Committee of Jilin Province

Jin belongs to the Korean minority.

1977,   Jan   Identified as vice-chairman of the Revolutionary Committee of Jilin Province
         Dec   Identified as member of the Standing Committee of Jilin Province CP

Jin Xiying (Chin Hsi-ying)　　金熙英

Posts held

Government
Vice-minister of the State Planning Commission

1978,   Jan   Identified as vice-minister of the State Planning Commission
         Mar   Advisor to a coal industry study group visiting the Federal Republic of Germany and Yugoslavia (until Apr 1978)

Jin Xun (Chin Hsün)　　金逊

Posts held

CCP
Member of the Standing Committee of Jiangsu Province CP

NPC
Deputy for Jiangsu Province to the 5th NPC

Provincial Administration
Vice-governor of Jiangsu Province
Director of the Finance Office, People's Government of Jiangsu Province

1978,   Feb   Elected deputy for Jiangsu Province to the 5th NPC
         Jul   Identified as a member of the Standing Committee, Jiangsu Province CP
         Aug   Identified as director of the Finance Office, People's Government of Jiangsu Province
1979,   Dec   Elected vice-governor of Jiangsu Province

Jin Zhao (Chin Chao)　　金照

Posts held

Government
Deputy director of the Central Broadcasting Administration

1955,   Mar   Identified as deputy director of the Central Broadcasting Administrative Bureau (until 1966)
1960,   Aug   Identified as a council member of the Sino-Vietnamese Friendship Association
1962,   Dec   Identified as council member of the Sino-Cuban Friendship Association
1966   Jin disappears
1972,   Nov   First appearance after the Cultural Revolution
1973,   Mar   Identified as deputy director of the Central Broadcasting Administration
1977,   Apr   Head of a broadcasting delegation to Iran
1979   Jun   Head of a broadcasting delegation to Yugoslavia

Jin Zhaodian (Chin Chao-tien)　　金昭典

Posts held

CCP
Secretary of Fujian Province CP

Provincial Administration
Vice-governor of Fujian Province

1964,   Sep   Elected deputy for Hubei Province to the 3rd NPC
1977,   Jan   Identified as secretary of Fujian Province CP
         Oct   Identified as vice-chairman of the Revolutionary Committee of Fujian Province (until Dec 1979)
1979,   Dec   Elected vice-governor of Fujian Province

Jin Zhifu (Chin Chih-fu) 金血夫

Posts held

Others
Vice-president of the Federation of Trade Unions

In 1949 Jin was chairman of the Preparatory Committee of the Coal Miners' Trade Union.

1953,	May	Delegate of the Fushun Municipality Trade Union to the 7th Congress of the Federation of Trade Unions
	Oct	Identified as a council member of the World Federation of Trade Unions
1954,	Oct	Elected deputy for Fushun Municipality to the 1st NPC
1955,	Apr	Head of a coal miners' delegation to Scotland
1956,	Dec	Identified as chairman of the Coal Miners' Trade Union
1957,	Apr	Elected alternate council member of the 4th World Federation of Trade Unions
1959,	Mar	Elected deputy for Hebei Province to the 2nd NPC
	Jun	Identified as chairman of the Liaoning Province Trade Union (until Cultural Revolution)
1960,	Jun	Elected council member of the Sino-African Friendship Association
1962,	Apr	Head of a trade union delegation to North Vietnam
1963,	Apr	Head of a trade union delegation to Cuba
1964,	Apr	Head of a trade union delegation to Czechoslovakia
	Sep	Elected deputy for Liaoning Province to the 3rd NPC
1965,	Jun	Identified as a member of the Committee for World Peace
1966		Jin disappears
1979,	Nov	First appearance after the Cultural Revolution: By-elected vice-president of the Federation of Trade Unions

Jing Shuping (Ching Shu-p'ing) 经叔平

Posts held

Others
Director of the Board of Directors, China International Trust and Investment Corporation
Deputy secretary-general of the Federation of Industrialists and Businessmen

Jing was born in Zhejiang Province in 1918.

1963		Identified as deputy secretary-general of the Federation of Industry and Commerce
1976,	Nov	First appearance after the Cultural Revolution
1979,	Apr	Member of a trade delegation headed by Rong Yiren to the Federal Republic of Germany, Switzerland, and France
	Oct	Appointed director of the Board of Directors, China International Trust and Investment Corporation; identified as deputy secretary-general of the Federation of Industrialists and Businessmen

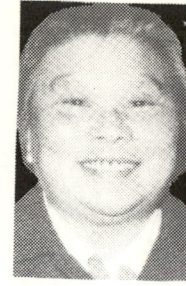

Kang Keqing (K'ang K'e-ch'ing) (f) 康克清

Posts held

CCP
Member of the CCP 11th Central Committee

NPC
Member of the Standing Committee of the 5th NPC
Deputy for Jiangxi Province to the 5th NPC

Mass Organizations
Vice-chairman of the Women's Federation

Others
Vice-chairman of the 5th CPPCC
Vice-chairman of the Patriotic Health Campaign Committee
Member of the Executive Council of the Welfare Institute

Kang was born in 1910 in Wan'an, Jiangsu Province, as the daughter of a fisherman. When she was one month old her parents gave her away to a peasant family. In 1927 she joined the Communist Youth League. In 1928 she ran away from her foster parents and the prospect of a marriage which they had arranged for her. She then began to organize armed Communist guerrilla units for the Red Army. In 1929, at the age of 20, she married the then 43-year-old commander of the Communist forces Zhu De at the Communist Base on Jinggangshan. In 1930 she became involved with women's work. In 1931 she managed a youth school. In 1932 she was head of a group of female volunteers. After six months training at the Red Army College, the college gave her a lectureship in 1933; she was concurrently commander of the Women's Department in the Red Army. Shortly afterwards she was in charge of supervising field medical services. In 1934-35 she took part in the Long March during which she was engaged in organizational and propaganda work. From 1936 to 1937 she studied at first at the Party School and later at the Anti-Japan Military and Political Academy. She was subsequently made director of the Political Department of the 8th Route Army. In August 1940 she accompanied her husband Zhu De to negotiations with generals of the Nationalist Army in Luoyang and Xi'an. In December 1948 Kang was a member of the Preparatory Committee for the foundation of the Democratic Women's Federation. With its establishment in 1949, Kang was elected a member of the Standing Committee (until Sep 1957). In September 1949 she took part as delegate at the 1st CPPCC which elected her a member of its National Committee (until Jan 1975).

1949,	Oct	Elected council member of the Sino-Soviet Friendship Association (until Dec 1954)
1950,	Oct	Member of the Chinese Delegation to the session of the World Peace Council in Warsaw
1952,	Jun	Elected member of the Standing Committee of the Athletic Federation (until Oct 1956)
1953,	Oct	Kang is deputy head of a delegation to the Chinese People's Volunteers in Korea
1954,	Aug	Elected deputy for Henan Province to the 1st NPC (reelected in 1958 to the 2nd NPC)
1955,	Sep	Elected secretary of the Democratic Women's Federation (until Sep 1957)
1957,	Sep	Elected vice-chairman of the Women's Federation (successor of the former "Democratic Federation")
1958,	Jul	Elected member of the Standing Committee, Chinese section of the World Peace Council (until about 1964)
1964,	Oct	Elected deputy for Jiangxi Province to the 3rd NPC
1975,	Jan	Elected member of the Standing Committee of the 4th NPC (confirmed in 1978 by the 5th NPC)
1977,	Aug	Elected member of the CCP Central Committee by the 11th Party Congress
1978,	Feb	Elected deputy for Jiangxi Province to the 5th NPC
	Mar	Elected vice-chairman of the 5th CPPCC
	Apr	Appointed vice-chairman of the Patriotic Health Campaign Committee; identified as vice-chairman of the Women's Federation
	Jun	Identified as member of the Executive Council of the Welfare Institute
1979,	Jun	Vice-chairman of the Credentials Committee at the 2nd Session of the 5th NPC
	Oct	Head of a CCP friendship delegation to North Korea

Kang Lin (K'ang Lin) 康林

Posts held

CCP
Alternate member of the CCP 11th Central Committee

Military
Deputy commander of Beijing Military Region

Kang was born in 1917 in Jiangxi Province. In 1934 he served in the bodyguard of Chen Yi who at the time of the Long March remained with his guerrilla units in the area of the former Jiangxi Soviet. In 1938 these units became the nucleus of the New 4th Army. In 1945 Kang commanded an independent regiment in the Central China Military Region. In 1949 he was made commander of the 72nd Division, 24th Corps, 3rd Field Army.

1951-1953		Deputy commander of the 24th Corps in the Korean War
1968,	Aug	Elected member of the Standing Committee, Revolutionary Committee of Fujian Province (no later mention in this post)
	Sep	Identified as commander of the 28th Corps
1969,	Apr	Elected to first term as alternate member of the CCP Central Committee by the 9th Party Congress
1972,	May	Identified as deputy commander of Beijing Military Region
	Jun	Deputy head of a military delegation to Algeria
1977,	Oct	Member of a military delegation led by Wang Shangrong to Tunisia

Kang Maozhao (K'ang Mao-chao) 康矛召

Posts held

Government
Ambassador to Belgium, Luxembourg, and
the European Community

Before the foundation of PRC Kang served as political
commissar in the PLA.

1950,	Dec	Appointed cultural attaché in India
1955,	Jul	Member of the Chinese delegation to Katmandu to negotiate the establishment of diplomatic relations
	Aug	Appointed attaché at the embassy in Nepal
1956,	Jul	Appointed attaché at the embassy in Afghanistan
1957,	Jul	Identified as counselor at the embassy in Afghanistan (until May 1959)
1959,	Jun	Identified as deputy director of the Information Department in the Ministry of Foreign Affairs (until Jun 1964)
1960,	Apr	Kang accompanies Premier Zhou Enlai to Burma and India
1964,	Oct	Identified as chargé d'affaires ad interim in Yugoslavia (until 1966)
1969,	Jun	Appointed ambassador to Cambodia (until Aug 1974)
1975,	Jan	Appointed ambassador to Mauritania (until Feb 1978)
1978,	May	Appointed ambassador to Belgium
	Jun	Appointed ambassador to Luxembourg and the European Community

Kang is married to Yang Lin.

Kang Shien (K'ang Shih-en) 康世恩

Posts held

CCP
Member of the CCP 11th Central Committee

Government
Vice-premier
Minister of the Economy Commission
Member of the State Financial and Economic Commission

Others
Vice-chairman, Central Patriotic Health
Campaign Committee

Kang was born in Chahar into a landlord family in 1913.
As a student Kang joined the 8th Route Army in 1937 into
which the Communist forces had been reorganized following the United Front with the KMT.

1950,	Mar	Identified as member of the Financial and Economic Affairs Committee, Northwest China Military and Administrative Council
1952,	Jan	Identified as director of the Petroleum Administration Bureau, Northwest China Military and Administrative Council
	Aug	In the course of the "three-anti-campaign," Kang is criticized as a bourgeois individualist

1953,	Jul	Appointed director of the Petroleum Administration Bureau in the Ministry of Fuel Industy (until Jul 1955)
1955,	Aug	Appointed assistant minister in the Ministry of Petroleum Industry (until Oct 1956)
	Oct	Head of a petroleum delegation to the USSR
1956,	Oct	Appointed vice-minister of petroleum industry (until May 1967)
1964,	Sep	Elected deputy for Heilongjiang Province to the 3rd NPC
1966,	Nov	In the course of the Cultural Revolution Kang is attacked as a collaborator of Liu Shaoqi and Deng Xiaoping
1967,	May	Accused of being a henchman of Yu Qiuli and purged
1971,	May	First appearance after the Cultural Revolution
1973,	Sep	Identified as a cadre in the Ministry of Fuel and Chemical Industry (until Jan 1975)
1975,	Jan	Appointed minister of petroleum and chemical industry (until Feb 1978)
1977,	Aug	Elected member of the CCP Central Committee by the 11th Party Congress
1978,	Mar	Appointed minister of the Economy Commission and vice-premier
	Apr	Appointed vice-chairman of the Central Patriotic Health Campaign Committee
1979,	May	Head of a government delegation to Brazil and the U.S.A.
	Jul	Appointed member of the State Financial and Economic Commission

Kang Yonghe (K'ang Yung-ho) 康永和

Posts held

Government
Director of the State Bureau of Labor
1st deputy head of the Leading Group for
Educated Youth Settled in the Countryside

NPC
Deputy for Shanxi Province to the
5th NPC

Mass Organization
Vice-chairman of the Federation of Trade
Unions

Kang was born in 1915. In 1937 he was elected chairman
of the Communist Workers' Federation in Shanxi Province.
In the same year he organized workers of Taiyuan City to
form guerrilla units against the Japanese. In 1948 Kang
was elected a member of the General Council, World
Federation of Trade Unions, and member of the Executive
Council of the Chinese Federation of Trade Unions. In
September 1949 he represented the Federation of Trade
Unions at the CPPCC which elected him a member (until
Apr 1959).

1949,	Nov	Elected chairman of the Shanxi Trade Union (probably until Feb 1952)
1950,	Aug	Appointed council member of the Shanxi People's Government
1952,	Apr	Appointed chairman of the North China

Labor Committee of the Federation of Trade Unions

1953, May Elected board member and member of the Executive Council by the 7th Congress of the Federation of Trade Unions

Sep Delegate at the 3rd Congress of the World Federation of Trade Unions in Vienna

Nov Head of a trade union delegation to the USSR

1954, Aug Elected deputy for Shanxi Province to the 1st NPC

1957, May Guest at the May Day celebrations in Jakarta

Sep Delegate at the 4th Congress of the World Federation of Trade Unions in Leipzig

Dec In addition to his other posts, Kang is elected a member of the Secretariat by the 8th Congress of the Federation of Trade Unions

1958, Jan Identified as alternate member of the Executive Council, World Federation of Trade Unions

Sep Elected member of the Sino-Iraq Friendship Association

1960, Jun Elected member of the Standing Committee of the World Federation of Trade Unions; elected council member of the Sino-African Friendship Association

Oct Head of a trade union delegation to Cuba

1961, Jan Member of a delegation to the 22nd session of the Executive Council, World Federation of Trade Unions, in East Berlin

Sep Head of a delegation to the Joint Conference of the World Federation of Trade Unions and the Confederation of Free German Trade Unions (FDGB) in East Berlin

Nov Head of a friendship delegation to Moscow to attend the 44th anniversary of the October Revolution

1962, Apr Head of a trade union delegation to Outer Mongolia

May Head of a trade union delegation to the World Federation of Trade Unions Congress in Budapest

Jul Delegate at a session of the World Peace Council in Moscow; deputy head of a delegation to the Conference against Atomic Bombs in Tokyo

Aug Head of a trade union delegation to Japan

Nov Member of a CCP delegation to the 8th Congress of CP Bulgaria in Sofia

Dec Head of a delegation to the 5th Congress of the Polish Federation of Trade Unions in Warsaw

1964, Apr Delegate at a session of the World Federation of Trade Unions in Sofia

Nov Member of a solidarity delegation to North Vietnam

1965, Jan Delegate at the 47th session of the Executive Council, World Federation of Trade Unions

May Head of a trade union delegation to North Vietnam

Jun Elected vice-chairman of the Afro-Asian Solidarity Committee

Jul Head of a trade union delegation to the 26th session of the Executive Council, World Federation of Trade Unions in Prague

Sep Head of a trade union delegation to North Korea

Oct Head of a delegation to the 6th World Federation of Trade Unions' Congress in Warsaw

1966, May Head of a delegation to the 32nd Executive Council Session of the World Federation of Trade Unions in Cyprus

Nov Head of a trade union delegation to Japan

1967 Disappears during the Cultural Revolution

1974, Jul First appearance after the Cultural Revolution: Identified as director of the Labor Bureau under the State Planning Commission

1977, Nov Identified as director of the State Bureau of Labor

1978, Feb Elected deputy for Shanxi Province to the 5th NPC

Apr Identified as vice-chairman of the Federation of Trade Unions

1979, Jan Identified as 1st deputy head of the Leading Group for Educated Youth Settled in the Countryside

Jun Member of the Credentials Committee and the Draft Laws Committee at the 2nd Session of the 5th NPC

Nov Article in RMRB of 28 November, "Practice Distribution According to Labor and Oppose Egalitarianism"

Kang Zhijie (K'ang Chih-chieh)   康至杰

Posts held

Provincial Administration
Vice-chairman of the People's Government, Ningxia Autonomous Region

1980, Jan Elected vice-chairman of the People's Government, Ningxia Autonomous Region

Ke Bonian (K'e Po-nien)   柯柏年

Posts held

Government
Deputy director of the Institute of Foreign Affairs

Ke was born in 1907 in Guangdong Province. He graduated in law from the Sun Yat-sen University and subsequently continued his studies in the United States. He then moved to Australia and Singapore. In Singapore he worked for the CP Malaya. After his return to China he joined the CCP in 1932. He became known with his edition of a dictionary of economics and a handbook on the United States which appeared in 1933. In 1946 he headed the Compilation and Translation Department of the Military Mediation Commission. Around 1948 he became head of the Research Office, International Liaison Department of the CCP.

1949, Dec Appointed director of the America and Australia Department in the Ministry of Foreign Affairs (until Nov 1954)

1951,	Sep	Elected council member of the International Federation of Democratic Jurists
1952,	Apr	Delegate at the Conference of the International Federation of Democratic Jurists in Vienna
1953,	Apr	Elected vice-chairman of the Society of Political Science and Law
1954,	Jan	Head of a delegation to the Vienna Conference of the International Federation of Democratic Jurists
	Apr	Advisor to a delegation led by Zhou Enlai to the Indochina Conference in Geneva
	Nov	Appointed ambassador to Romania (until Apr 1959)
1960,	Apr	Elected council member of the Sino-African Friendship Association
	Jul	Elected member of the Society of Political Science and Law
	Oct	Deputy head of a delegation to the 7th Congress of the International Federation of Democratic Jurists in Sofia
1961,	Mar	Deputy head of a jurists' delegation to Japan
1963,	Oct	Appointed ambassador to Denmark (until about 1967)
1971,	Oct	First appearance after the Cultural Revolution
1972,	Jun	Identified as a cadre at the Institute of Foreign Affairs
1973,	Jun	Identified as deputy director of the Institute of Foreign Affairs

Ke Hua (K'e Hua)　　　柯 华

Posts held

Government
Ambassador to Great Britain and Northern Ireland

Ke was born in 1915 in Guangdong Province.

1955,	Mar	Identified as director of the Protocol Department in the Ministry of Foreign Affairs (until Oct 1957)
1957,	Oct	Appointed director of the West Asia and Africa Department in the Ministry of Foreign Affairs (until Jan 1960)
1958,	Oct	Deputy head of a trade delegation to Morocco
1960,	Mar	Appointed ambassador to Guinea (until May 1964)
	Oct	Ke conducts negotiations in Mali for the establishment of diplomatic relations
1964,	Sep	Appointed director of the Africa Department in the Ministry of Foreign Affairs (until Cultural Revolution)
1965,	Apr	Identified as council member of the Institute of Foreign Affairs
	Jun	Member of a government delegation to Pakistan, United Arab Republic, and Tanzania
1972,	Sep	Appointed ambassador to Ghana (until Aug 1974)
1975,	Apr	Identified as director of the Asia Department in the Ministry of Foreign Affairs (until Jul 1975)

	Dec	Appointed ambassador to the Philippines (until Apr 1978)
1978,	Sep	Appointed ambassador to Great Britain and Northern Ireland

Ke-li-gen (Kergen)

Posts held

Others
Member of the Standing Committee of the 5th CPPCC

1978,	Mar	Elected member of the Standing Committee of the 5th CPPCC

Ke Ligeng (K'e Li-keng)　　克力更

Posts held

CCP
Director of the United Front Work Department, Inner Mongolia Autonomous Region CP

Provincial Administration
Vice-chairman of the People's Congress, Inner Mongolia Autonomous Region
Chairman of the Nationalities Affairs Commission of the People's Government, Inner Mongolia Autonomous Region

Ke belongs to the Mongol minority.

1949		Identified as chairman of the Supervision Committee, Inner Mongolia Autonomous Region; as secretary of the Working Committee of the Inner Mongolia Branch of the Communist Youth League; and as vice-chairman of the Inner Mongolian Peace Council
1954		Identified as a member of the Inner Mongolian People's Council
1978,	May	First appearance after 1956
	Sep	Identified as director of the United Front Work Department, Inner Mongolia Autonomous Region CP
1979,	Aug	Identified as chairman of the Nationalities Affairs Commission, People's Government of Inner Mongolia Autonomous Region
	Dec	Elected vice-chairman of the People's Congress of Inner Mongolia Autonomous Region

Ke-you-mu-mai-ti Ni-ya-zi (Keyum Matniyaz)　　克允木·买提尼牙孜

Posts held

NPC
Member of the Standing Committee of the 5th NPC
Deputy for Xinjiang Autonomous Region to the 5th NPC

Keyum belongs to the Uighur minority. Before the foundation of PRC he was a farm laborer.

1952		Identified as oil driller at the Karamai Oil Field in Xinjiang
1964		Received by Mao Zedong
1973		Keyum attends a cadre training course at the Central Institute for Nationality Minorities
1975,	Jan	Elected member of the Standing Committee by the 4th NPC (confirmed in 1978 by the 5th NPC)
1978,	Feb	Elected deputy for Xinjiang Autonomous Region to the 5th NPC

Ke Zhao (K'e Chao)　　柯　召

Posts held

NPC
Deputy for Sichuan Province to the 5th NPC

Others
Vice-chairman of the Central Committee of the Jiusan Society
Vice-president of Sichuan University

1958,	Sep	Elected deputy for Sichuan Province to the 2nd NPC (reelected in 1964 to the 3rd NPC)
1963,	Mar	Identified as vice-president of Sichuan University
1978,	Feb	First appearance after the Cultural Revolution: Elected deputy for Sichuan Province to the 5th NPC
	Jul	Identified as a council member of the Mathematical Society and in his former position as vice-president of Sichuan University
1979,	Oct	Elected vice-chairman of the Central Committee of the Jiusan Society

Kong Anmin (K'ung An-min)　　孔安民

Posts held

NPC
Deputy for Hunan Province to the 5th NPC

Provincial Administration
Vice-chairman of the People's Congress of Hunan Province

1960,	Jun	Identified as deputy secretary of Changsha Municipality CP
1965,	May	Identified as political commissar of Changsha Subdistrict in Hunan Military District
1977,	Dec	Identified as vice-chairman of the Revolutionary Committee of Hunan Province (until Dec 1979)
1978,	Feb	Elected deputy for Hunan Province to the 5th NPC
1979,	Dec	Elected vice-chairman of the People's Congress of Hunan Province

Kong Congzhou (K'ung Ts'ung-chou)　　孔从周

Posts held

Military
Lieutenant-general
Deputy commander of the PLA Artillery

Others
Member of the Standing Committee of the 5th CPPCC

In 1937 Kong commanded the 7th Division of the 38th Nationalist Army and in the following year the 55th Division of the same army. In 1941 he became deputy commander of the 38th Army. In 1946 he went over to the Communists with his former 55th Division which was then incorporated into the Shanxi-Hebei-Shandong-Henan Field Army as the 38th Army. In 1949 Kong was commander of the 9th Army, 1st Field Army.

1950		Service in the Korean War (until 1953)
1955,	Sep	Appointed lieutenant-general; conferred the orders of "Independence and Freedom" and "Liberation," both 1st class
1957		Identified as commandant of the PLA Artillery School (until 1971)
1959,	Apr	Appointed member of the National Defense Council (until 1974)
1978,	Mar	Elected member of the Standing Committee of the 5th CPPCC
	May	Identified as deputy commander of the PLA Artillery

Kong Fei (K'ung Fei)　　孔　飞

Posts held

CCP
Secretary of Inner Mongolia Autonomous Region CP

Provincial Administration
Chairman of the People's Government, Inner Mongolia Autonomous Region

Kong was born in 1911 as the son of a peasant familiy in the Horqin Left Wing Middle Banner of the Jirem League, Inner Mongolia. He joined the CCP in 1936 after graduating from the Department of Border Politics in the Northeast China University, and engaged in research work at a nationalities institute in Yan'an. Subsequently he became a column commander and division commander in a Communist army operating in Inner Mongolia.

1955,	Aug	Identified as deputy commander of Inner Mongolia Military Region (until Cultural Revolution)
1957,	May	Identified as major-general
1967		Disappears during the Cultural Revolution
1978,	May	First appearance after the Cultural Revolution
	Nov	Identified as secretary of the CP, and chairman of the Revolutionary Committee, Inner Mongolia Autonomous Region (latter post until Dec 1979)
1979,	Dec	Elected chairman of the People's Government, Inner Mongolia Autonomous Region

Kong Qingde (K'ung Ch'ing-te) 孔庆德

Posts held

NPC
Deputy for the PLA to the 5th NPC

Military
Lieutenant-general
Deputy commander of Wuhan Military Region
Member of the Standing Committee, CP Secretariat of Wuhan Military Region

Kong joined the Communist forces in 1930. In 1937 he commanded the Reserve Regiment of the 385th Brigade, 129th Division of the 8th Route Army. In 1946 he was commander of South Hebei Military District. In the following year he commanded the 2nd Column of the Central Plains Field Army.

1950,	Jul	Identified as deputy commander of Henan Military District
1958,	Dec	Identified as lieutenant-general
1959,	Mar	Identified as deputy commander of Wuhan Military Region
1971,	Mar	Elected secretary of the newly established CP Secretariat of Hubei Province (until 1976?)
1977,	Jun	Identified as member of the Standing Committee, CP Secretariat of Wuhan Military Region
1978,	Feb	Elected deputy for the PLA to the 5th NPC

Kong Shiquan (K'ung Shih-ch'üan) 孔石泉

Posts held

CCP
Member of the CCP 11th Central Committee

Military
Lieutenant-general
2nd political commissar of Chengdu Military Region

Kong served in 1948 as deputy political commissar of the 8th Column, Northeast Field Army, and in the following year as deputy commander of the 15th Corps of the 4th Field Army.

1949,	Dec	Identified as deputy director of the Political Department of Guangdong Military District
1950,	Sep	Appointed director of the Political Department of Guangdong Military District and of the 15th Corps
	Nov	Identified as member of the Rural Reform Committee, People's Government of Guangdong Province
1952		Appointed deputy political commissar of Jiangxi Military District after the 15th Corps is abolished
1955,	Sep	Promoted to rank of lieutenant-general; conferred the order "Liberation," 1st class
1958,	Dec	Kong holds a post at the Political Academy of the PLA

1966,	Oct	Identified as political commissar of Guangxi Military District
1967,	Aug	At the height of the Cultural Revolution, Kong is involved in armed fights between rival "rebel groups" in Guangzhou, for which he is sharply attacked
	Sep	Kong is present at a speech held by Premier Zhou Enlai on the situation in Canton
	Nov	Identified as 3rd political commissar of Guangzhou Military Region
	Dec	Identified as member of the preparatory group for the establishment of the Revolutionary Committee of Guangdong Province
1968,	Feb	With the establishment of the Revolutionary Committee of Guangdong Province, Kong is elected 1st vice-chairman (until Oct 1977)
	Mar	Identified as political commissar of Guangzhou Military Region (until May 1977)
1969,	Apr	Elected to first term as member of the CCP Central Committee by the 9th Party Congress
1970,	Dec	With the reestablishment of the Secretariat of Guangdoung Province CP after the Cultural Revolution, Kong is elected secretary (until Oct 1977)
1977,	Oct	Identified as 2nd political commissar of Chengdu Military Region

Kong Xiangzhen (K'ung Hsiang-chen) 孔祥桢

Posts held

Others
Member of the Standing Committee of the 5th CPPCC

Kong was born in 1908 in Shanxi Province. During the 1930s he was active in the Communist underground in North China.

1950,	Jan	Identified as director of the Organization Department in the Central-South China Bureau of the CCP Central Committee
1950,	Mar	Identified as director of the Labor Employment Committee of the Central-South Military and Administrative Council (until 1953)
1953,	Oct	Identified as chairman of the Central-South Work Committee of the Trade Unions
1954,	Jun	Identified as director of the Urban Work Department, Central-South Bureau of the CCP Central Committee
	Sep	Elected deputy for Henan Province to the 1st NPC
	Oct	Appointed vice-chairman of the State Construction Commission (until Feb 1958)
1957,	Apr	Appointed vice-minister of communications (until Apr 1960)
1959,	Apr	Elected member of the 3rd CPPCC (reelected in 1964 by the 4th CPPCC)
1960,	Apr	Appointed vice-minister of light industry (until Apr 1965)

1965,	Jan	Elected member of the Standing Committee of the 4th CPPCC
	Apr	Appointed vice-minister of the 1st Ministry of Light Industry
1967,	Jun	Branded as a traitor and purged
1978,	Feb	First appearance after the Cultural Revolution
	Mar	Elected member of the Standing Committee of the 5th CPPCC

Kong Xiao (K'ung Hsiao)　　孔　筱

Posts held

Government
Deputy director of the General Administrative Bureau for Travel and Tourism in China
Deputy manager-general of the China International Travel Service

1973,	Feb	Identified as deputy director of the General Administrative Bureau for Travel and Tourism in China
1977,	Sep	Deputy head of a friendship delegation to North Korea
1978,	Apr	Identified as deputy manager-general of the China International Travel Service; deputy head of a tourism delegation to Mexico, Argentina, Venezuela, and Panama
	Oct	Head of a tourism delegation to Burma

Kong Yuan (K'ung Yüan)　　孔　原

Posts held

CCP
Member of the CCP 11th Central Committee

NPC
Deputy secretary-general of the Standing Committee of the 5th NPC

Others
Member of the Standing Committee of the 5th CPPCC

Kong Yuan was born under the name of Chen Tiesheng in Pingxiang County, Jiangxi Province. As a student at Pingxiang Middle School he joined the Red Army. There is as yet no record of his career until his appointment as secretary of Fushun Municipality CP following the Japanese capitulation in 1945.

1949,	Oct	Appointed member of the Financial and Economic Affairs Committee of the Government Administration Council (until Oct 1954); director of the Customs Administration (until Oct 1954)
1953,	Jan	Appointed vice-minister of foreign trade (until Oct 1957)
1954,	Apr-Sep	Head of a trade delegation to Indonesia to sign a trade agreement
	Oct	Head of a trade delegation to India to sign a trade agreement
1955,	Nov	Head of a trade delegation to Yugoslavia
1956,	Jan	Head of a trade delegation to Hungary

	Feb	Head of a trade delegation to Yugoslavia to sign a trade agreement
	Jul	Head of a trade delegation to Czechoslovakia
1957,	Apr	Head of a trade delegation to Czechoslovakia and Hungary
1958,	Mar	Appointed deputy director of the Staff Office for Foreign Affairs
	May	Elected alternate member of the CCP Central Committee
	Oct	Elected deputy for Jiangsu Province to the 2nd NPC (until Mar 1959)
1959,	Apr	Appointed member of the Standing Committee of the 3rd CPPCC (until Dec 1964)
1960,	Aug	Member of a government delegation led by Minister of Foreign Affairs Chen Yi to Afghanistan
1963,	Jul	Identified as a cadre in a department of the CCP Central Committee
	Dec	Member of a delegation led by Zhou Enlai to ten African countries and to Albania
1964,	Feb	Member of a delegation led by Zhou Enlai to Burma, Indonesia, and Pakistan
	Oct	Elected deputy for Guizhou Province to the 3rd NPC
1965,	Jan	Elected member of the Standing Committee of the 3rd NPC
1966,		Attacked as a "three-anti element" during the Cultural Revolution and relieved of all posts
1974,	Sep	First appearance after the Cultural Revolution
1977,	Aug	Elected member of the CCP Central Committee by the 11th Party Congress
1978,	Mar	Elected member of the Standing Committee of the 5th CPPCC
1979,	Feb	Appointed deputy secretary-general of the Standing Committee of the 5th NPC

Kong Zhaonian (K'ung Chao-nien)　孔照年

Posts held

CCP
Member of the CCP 11th Central Committee

Military
Deputy commander of the PLA Navy

1973,	Aug	Elected to first term as member of the CCP Central Committee by the 10th Party Congress
1974,	Feb	Identified as military leader
1975,	Feb	Identified as deputy commander of the PLA Navy
1978,	Jun	Member of a military delegation to Yugoslavia under Yang Yong

Kou Qingyan (K'ou Ch'ing-yen)　　冠庆延

Posts held

CCP
Member of the Standing Committee of Guangdong Province CP

NPC
Deputy for Guangdong Province to the
5th NPC

Kou was born in 1906(?) in Jiangxi Province.

1950,   Sep   Identified as deputy director of the Public
                Security Department, People's Govern-
                ment of Hunan Province (until Sep 1951)
1951,   Sep   Identified as deputy director of the Public
                Security Department, People's Govern-
                ment of Guangdong Province
1953,   Oct   Identified as director of the Public Securi-
                ty Department, People's Government of
                Guangdong Province (until about 1954)
1954,   Aug   Appointed chief procurator of Guangdong
                Province; elected deputy for Guangdong
                Province to the 1st NPC (until Mar 1959)
1960,   May   Identified as director of the Political and
                Judicial Office of Guangdong Province CP
                (until 1963)
1964,   Feb   Identified as member of the Standing
                Committee of Guangdong Province CP
                (until Cultural Revolution)
         Sep   Elected deputy for Guangdong Province to
                the 3rd NPC
1965,   Dec   Elected vice-governor of Guangdong Prov-
                ince (until Cultural Revolution)
1971,   Nov   Reactivated after the Cultural Revolu-
                tion: Identified as member of the Standing
                Committee, Revolutionary Committee of
                Guangdong Province
1975,   Sep   Identified as vice-chairman of the Revolu-
                tionary Committee of Guangdong Prov-
                ince (until Dec 1979)
1978,   Feb   Elected deputy for Guangdong Province to
                the 5th NPC
         Jun   Identified as member of the Standing
                Committee of Guangdong Province CP

Kuang Yaming (K'uang Ya-ming) 匡 业 明

Posts held

Provincial Administration
Vice-chairman of the People's Congress of
Jiangsu Province

Others
President of Nanjing University

1952,   Aug   Identified as director of the Propaganda
                Department, East China Bureau of the
                CCP Central Committee (until 1954)
1955,   Jun   Identified as president of the Northeast
                People's University (until Oct 1958)
1957,   Nov   Member of a delegation of scientists to
                the USSR
1958,   Oct   Identified as president of Jilin University
                (until May 1963)
1961,   Aug   Article in HQ: "On the Relationship Be-
                tween Teachers and Students"
1963,   May   Identified as president of Nanjing Univer-
                sity (until Cultural Revolution)
1964,   Oct   Elected deputy for Jiangsu Province to
                the 3rd NPC

1966,   Jun   Branded as a counterrevolutionary ele-
                ment and purged
1978,   May   First appearance after the Cultural Revo-
                lution: Identified as president and 1st par-
                ty secretary of Nanjing University
         Dec   Head of a delegation of college presidents
                to Japan
1979,   Dec   Elected vice-chairman of the People's
                Congress of Jiangsu Province

Kui Bi (K'uei Pi)

Posts held

NPC
Member of the Standing Committee of the
5th NPC
Deputy for the Inner Mongolian Autonomous Region to the 5th NPC

Others
Chairman of the CPPCC, Inner Mongolian
Section

Kui, who belongs to the Mongolian minority, was born in
1903 in the Banner of Tümet of the Bayin Tala League. As
a child he received no school education. In 1923 he went
together with Ulanhu and Ji Yatai to Beijing to attend the
School for Mongolians and Tibetans. In Beijing he joined
the Socialist Youth League in 1924. At the end of that
year he was given the task by the CCP to organize the
Association for Promoting the National Assembly in
Suiyuan Special District. In March of the following year
he was a representative at the National Assembly convened by Sun Yat-sen. At this time he also joined the
CCP. In 1925 (or 1926) he was one of the Communist
students at the Beijing School for Mongolians and Tibetans
who were sent to study in Outer Mongolia. There Kui
completed his studies at the Higher Party School in 1929.
His next known appearance was at the end of 1945 as
political commissar and director of the Organization
Department, Executive Council of the Federation of the
Movement for an Autonomous Inner Mongolia (until
April 1946). In September 1949 he took part in the CPPCC
in Beijing which elected him a member of its National
Committee (until December 1954).

1949,   Oct   Appointed member of the Minorities Af-
                fairs Commission of the Government Ad-
                ministration Council (until Oct 1954)
         Dec   Appointed council member (until
                Jun 1954) and director of the Civil Affairs
                Department (until Jan 1953) of the Peo-
                ple's Government of Inner Mongolian
                Autonomous Region; vice-chairman of the
                People's Government of Suiyuan (until
                Jun 1954); member of the Inner Mongolia
                Subbureau, North China Bureau of the
                CCP Central Committee
1950,   Feb   Appointed chairman of the Council for
                Minorities Affairs of Suiyuan Province
                (until Jun 1954)
         Mar   Appointed member of the Military and
                Administrative Council of Suiyuan Prov-
                ince (until Jun 1954)
1954,   Jun   Appointed member of the Standing Com-
                mittee and director of the Organization
                Department, Inner Mongolia Subbureau,

North China Bureau of the CCP Central Committee (until Jan 1956); elected vice-chairman of the Inner Mongolian Autonomous Region

Sep   Elected deputy for the Inner Mongolian Autonomous Region to the 1st NPC (reelected in 1958 and 1964 to the 2nd and 3rd NPCs)

1956, Jun   Appointed vice-chairman of the Nationalities Affairs Commission of the NPC

Jul   Identified as secretary, Inner Mongolian Autonomous Region CP

Sep   Elected alternate member of the CCP Central Committee by the 8th Party Con-gress

1959, Sep   Member of an NPC delegation to the People's Republic of Mongolia

1967   Purged together with Ulanhu

1978, Feb   First appearance after the Cultural Revolution: Elected deputy for Inner Mongolian Autonomous Region to the 5th NPC

Mar   Elected member of the Standing Committee of the 5th NPC

Dec   Identified as vice-chairman of the CPPCC, Inner Mongolia Section

1979, Jun   Member of the Credentials Committee at the 2nd Session of the 5th NPC

Lai Jifa (Lai Chi-fa) 赖际发

Posts held

Others
Member of the Standing Committee of the
5th CPPCC

Lai was born in 1906 in Sichuan (Fujian?) Province. In 1938 he commanded an independent detachment of the 149th Division. In 1940 he was political commissar in the 2nd Subdistrict of Taihang Military District. In 1948 he commanded the 18th Detachment in Northwest Shanxi Military District. From October of that year until October 1949 he was deputy director, Department of State-Operated Industry of the North China People's Government.

1950,	Mar	Appointed director, General Office of the Ministry of Heavy Industry (until Aug 1952)
1952,	Aug	Appointed vice-minister of heavy industry (ministry abolished in May 1956)
1954,	Sep	Elected deputy for Sichuan Province to the 1st NPC (until Dec 1964)
1955,	May	Member of a Party and government delegation to the German Democratic Republic
1956,	May	Appointed vice-minister of the newly established Ministry of Construction Materials (until Feb 1958)
1959,	Sep	Appointed vice-minister of the Ministry of Construction (reorganized in Mar 1965)
1965,	Jan	Elected member of the Standing Committee of the 4th CPPCC
	Mar	Appointed minister of construction materials (until about 1972)
1969,	Apr	Elected member of the CCP Central Committee by the 9th Party Congress (until Aug 1973)
1970,	Oct	Head of a government delegation to Romania
	Nov	Head of a government delegation to Mauritania
1973,	May	Identified as vice-chairman of the Capital Construction Commission (until 1975?)
	Nov	Head of a government delegation to Guinea
1978,	Mar	Reelected member of the Standing Committee by the 5th CPPCC

Lai Yali (Lai Ya-li) 赖业力

Posts held

Government
Permanent representative of the PRC to the UN

Lai was born in 1910 in Sichuan Province. In May 1949 he was elected a member of the National Committee of the Federation of Democratic Youth. In September of that year he took part in the 1st CPPCC as a delegate representing the KMT Revolutionary Committee.

1949,	Oct	Appointed deputy director, Administrative Office of the Ministry of Foreign Affairs (until Feb 1956)
	Dec	Identified as council member of the Institute of Foreign Affairs
1955,	Aug	Member of the delegation under Wang Bingnan at the Sino-American Talks in Geneva
1956,	Feb	Identified as counselor at the embassy in Moscow
	Oct	Identified as counselor at the embassy in Switzerland
1961,	Jan	Appointed ambassador to Mali (until May 1965)
1965,	Jun	Identified as director of the Protocol Department of the Ministry of Foreign Affairs
1966,	Mar	Member of a delegation under Liu Shaoqi to Pakistan and Afghanistan
1967		Disappears during the Cultural Revolution
1975,	Sep	First appearance after the Cultural Revolution: Member of the Chinese delegation to the 30th UN General Assembly
1976,	Mar	Head of a delegation to the UN Conference on the Law of the Sea in New York
1977,	May	Identified as acting permanent representative of the PRC to the UN
1978,	Feb	Identified as permanent representative of the PRC to the UN

Lai is married to Zhu Hong.

Lai Yi (Lai Yi) 赖毅

Posts held

Military
Lieutenant-general

Others
Member of the Standing Committee of the
5th CPPCC

Lai was born in Hunan Province. In 1927 he joined the Communist Youth League and the Red Army. From about 1938 he served in the Political Department, 4th Division of the New 4th Army.

1950,	Dec	Identified as member of the North Jiangsu Administrative Office and as political commissar of North Jiangsu Military District
1959,	Apr	Identified as lieutenant-general and as deputy political commissar of Nanjing Military Region (until 1962?)
1962		Identified as alternate member of the Control Committee of the CCP Central Committee
1978,	Mar	Elected member of the Standing Committee of the 5th CPPCC

Lan Ganting (Lan Kan-t'ing) 蓝干亭

Posts held

CCP
Deputy secretary of Jilin Province CP

1957,	May	Identified as director of the Propaganda Department of Jilin Province CP
1959,	Nov	Identified as secretary general of Jilin Province CP
1965,	Nov	Identified as secretary of Jilin Province CP (until Cultural Revolution)

1970,   Jun   Identified as vice-chairman of the Revolutionary Committee of Jilin Province (until 1977)

   Oct   Head of a friendship delegation representing Jilin Province to North Korea at the 20th anniversary of the entry of Chinese People's Volunteers into the Korean War

1971,   Mar   Elected member of the Standing Committee of Jilin Province CP (until Oct 1977)

1977,   Oct   Identified as deputy secretary of Jilin Province CP

Lan Kaimin (Lan K'ai-min)   兰凯民

Posts held

Provincial Administration
Vice-governor of Hebei Province

1977,   Dec   Elected vice-chairman of the Revolutionary Committee of Hebei Province (until Feb 1980)

1980,   Feb   Elected vice-governor of Hebei Province

Lan Rongyu (Lan Jung-yü)   蓝荣玉

Posts held

CCP
Member of the Standing Committee of Fujian Province CP

Provincial Administration
Vice-chairman of the Standing Committee of the People's Congress, Fujian Province

Lan was born in 1914.

1949,   Oct   Appointed director of the Civil Affairs Department, Fujian Province

1952,   Nov   Identified as a member of the People's Government, Fujian Province

1955,   Feb   Appointed president of the People's Higher Court, Fujian Province (until 1957)

1957,   May   Identified as vice-governor of Fujian Province (until Cultural Revolution)

   Aug   Identified as a member of the Standing Committee, Fujian Province CP (until Cultural Revolution)

1968,   Sep   Elected vice-chairman of the Revolutionary Committee, Fujian Province, on its foundation

1969,   Apr   Elected alternate member of the Central Committee by the 9th CCP Party Congress (until Aug 1973)

1972,   Oct   Lan disappears for two and a half years

1975,   Feb   Identified as a member of the Standing Committee of Fujian Province CP

1978,   Jan   Reelected vice-chairman of the Revolutionary Committee of Fujian Province (until Dec 1979)

1979,   Dec   Elected vice-chairman of the Standing Committee, People's Congress of Fujian Province

Lan Tinghui (Lan T'ing-hui)   蓝庭辉

Posts held

NPC
Deputy for the PLA to the 5th NPC

Military
Deputy commander of the PLA Railway Corps

1971,   May   Identified as military leader in Beijing

1975,   Aug   Member of a delegation of PLA veterans to Algeria; identified as deputy commander of the PLA Railway Corps

1978,   Feb   Elected deputy for the PLA to the 5th NPC

Langdun Gonggawangqiu (Namdon Kunga Wongchug)   朗顿滚噶旺秋

Posts held

Provincial Administration
Vice-chairman of the Standing Committee, Tibet Autonomous Regional People's Congress

Others
Vice-chairman of the Tibet Branch, 5th CPPCC

Langdun belongs to the Tibetan minority.

1959,   Apr   Identified as member of the Standing Committee, Preparatory Committee for the Establishment of Tibet Autonomous Region

1961,   Sep   Identified as vice-chairman of the Preparatory Committee for the Establishment of Tibet Autonomous Region

   Dec   Identified as vice-chairman, Tibet Branch of the CPPCC

1965,   Sep   Elected vice-chairman of Tibet Autonomous Regional People's Congress

1966   Disappears during the Cultural Revolution

1977,   Jan   First appearance after the Cultural Revolution

1978,   Nov   Identified as vice-chairman of the Tibet Branch, 5th CPPCC

1979,   Aug   Elected vice-chairman of the Standing Committee, Tibet Autonomous Regional People's Congress

Lei Jieqiong (Lei Chieh-ch'iung) (f)   雷洁琼

Posts held

Mass Organization
Vice-president of the Women's Federation

Provincial Administration
Vice-mayor of Beijing Municipality

Others
Member of the Standing Committee of the 5th CPPCC
Vice-chairman of the Central Committee, China Association for Promoting Democracy
Professor of Law at Beijing University

Lei was born in 1905 in Guangdong Province. She studied law in the United States. At the founding session of the Democratic Women's Federation in April 1949 she was elected a member of its Standing Committee. In September of that year she took part in the 1st CPPCC.

1949,	Oct	Appointed member of the Commission of Culture and Education of the Government Administrative Council (until 1954)
1951,	Feb	Identified as council member of the Beijing Municipal Government and as professor at Yanjing University
	Nov	Elected member of the Committee for the Protection of Children
1953,	Jan	Appointed member of the Committee for the Implementation Campaign of the Marriage Laws
	Jun	Member of a delegation under Cai Chang to the World Congress of Women in Denmark; identified as council member of the newly established Political Science and Law Association
1954,	Jan	Member of a delegation to an international conference of law workers in Austria
	Aug	Elected deputy for Guangdong Province to the 1st NPC (reelected in 1959 and 1964 to the 2nd and 3rd NPCs)
1956,	Oct	Identified as deputy director of the Bureau of Foreign Experts Administration under the State Council
1958,	Jun	Identified as member of the Beijing Standing Committee of the CPPCC
1967		Disappears during the Cultural Revolution
1975,	Jul	First appearance after the Cultural Revolution: Identified as member of the Standing Committee of the China Association for Promoting Democracy (until Oct 1979)
1978,	Mar	Elected member of the Standing Committee of the 5th CPPCC
	Apr	Identified as professor of law at Beijing University
	Sep	Elected vice-president of the Women's Federation
1979,	Jan	Head of a women's delegation to Iraq
	Oct	Elected vice-chairman of the Central Committee, China Association for Promoting Democracy
	Dec	Elected vice-mayor of Beijing Municipality

Lei Renmin (Lei Jen-min)   雷任民

Posts held

Others
Vice-chairman of the Board of Directors, China International Trust and Investment Corporation

Lei was born in 1910 in Shanxi Province. In 1928 when a student of Taiyuan Normal School he joined the CCP. During the Anti-Japanese War he was engaged in guerrilla activities in North Shanxi. In August 1948 he was appointed deputy director of the Civil Affairs Department under the North China People's Government.

1949,	Oct	Appointed director of the General Office, Ministry of Internal Affairs

1951,	Oct	Identified as vice-minister of trade (until Aug 1952)
1952,	Apr	Member of a delegation to the International Economic Conference in Moscow
	Aug	Appointed vice-minister of foreign trade (until May 1967)
1953,	Oct	Elected member of the Executive Committee of the Federation of Industry and Commerce
1954,	Apr	Advisor of the PRC delegation to the Indochina Conference in Geneva (head: Zhou Enlai)
1955,	Apr	Head of a trade delegation to Japan
	Jul	Appointed council member of the Institute of Foreign Affairs (until May 1967)
	Aug	Elected vice-chairman of the Committee for the Promotion of International Trade
1957,	Apr	Appointed member of the State Commission of Overseas Chinese Affairs (until May 1967)
1958,	Sep	Head of a trade delegation to Tunisia and Morocco
1959,	Jun	Head of a trade delegation to Ceylon (now Sri Lanka)
1960,	Dec	Member of a friendship delegation to Burma
1964,	Dec	Deputy head of a PRC delegation to hold talks with the Presidium of the Italian Committee for World Peace in Rome (head: Liao Chengzhi)
1965,	Jan	Head of a trade delegation to Burma
	Jun	Head of a trade delegation to Sweden, Denmark, Norway, Finland
1966,	Apr	Head of a trade delegation to Egypt, Zambia, and Tanzania
1967,	May	Denounced as a counterrevolutionary revisionist and purged
1979,	Oct	First appearance after the Cultural Revolution: Appointed vice-chairman of the Board of Directors, China International Trust and Investment Corporation

Lei Yang (Lei Yang)   雷 杨

Posts held

Government
Former ambassador to Gambia

1954		Appointed director of the Propaganda Department, Northwest Bureau of the CCP Central Committee
1960		Appointed counselor at the embassy in Burma (until Jul 1961)
1964,	Oct	Identified as director of the Training Department of the Ministry of Foreign Affairs (until about 1966)
1969,	Aug	Identified as chargé d'affaires ad interim in Poland (until about 1972)
1970,	Jan	Appointed chief representative at the Sino-American Ambassadorial Talks in Warsaw
1975,	May	Appointed ambassador to Gambia (until Nov 1979)

Li Baoguang (Li Pao-kuang) (f) 李宝光

Posts held

CCP
Deputy secretary of Henan Province CP

Mass Organization
Vice-president and secretary of the Women's Federation
Member of the Standing Committee of the 5th CPPCC

Li was elected alternate member of the Executive Committee of the Federation of Democratic Women in March 1949.

1950,	Jul	Identified as council member of the Henan Provincial People's Government and as chairman of the Henan Federation of Democratic Women
1952,	Sep	Identified as deputy director of the Rural Work Department of the Federation of Democratic Women
1953,	Apr	Elected member of the Executive Committee of the Federation of Democratic Women
1956,	Mar	Elected member of the 2nd CPPCC
1957,	May	Elected member of the Communist Youth League Central Committee
	Sep	Identified as secretary of the Federation of Democratic Women
1960,	Oct	Head of a women's delegation to Hungary
1964,	Oct	Elected deputy for Hebei Province to the 3rd NPC
1967		Disappears during the Cultural Revolution
1974,	Sep	First appearance after the Cultural Revolution: Identified as a cadre of a department in the CCP Central Committee
1978,	Mar	Elected member of the Standing Committee of the 5th CPPCC
	Sep	Elected vice-president and secretary of the National Women's Federation
1979,	Jun	Head of a women's work organizers delegation to North Korea
	Dec	Identified as deputy secretary of Henan Province CP

Li Baohua (Li Pao-hua) 李葆华

Posts held

CCP
Member of the CCP 11th Central Committee

Others
President of the People's Bank

Li was born in 1908 in Leting County, Hebei Province. He is the eldest son of Li Dazhao, cofounder of the CCP. He joined the CCP in 1928. In 1937 he was given the task together with two other cadres to establish the Shanxi-Chahar-Hebei Party District which was subordinated under the North China Bureau of the CCP Central Committee. In 1945 he was elected alternate member of the CCP Central Committee by the 7th Party Congress (until September 1956). In spring 1949 he was identified as deputy secretary of Beijing Municipality CP. In September of that year he took part in the 1st CPPCC.

1949,	Oct	Elected council member of the Sino-Soviet Friendship Association (until 1954); appointed vice-minister of water conservancy (until Feb 1958)
1956,	Sep	Elected member of the CCP Central Committee by the 8th Party Congress
1958,	Feb	Following reorganization of the ministry, Li is appointed vice-minister of water conservancy and electric power (until Apr 1963)
1960,	May	Member of a government delegation to Poland
1961,	Mar	Identified as secretary of the East China Bureau of the CCP Central Committee (until Cultural Revolution)
1962,	Sep	Identified as 1st secretary of Anhui Province CP (until Feb 1967)
1964,	Oct	Elected deputy for Anhui Province to the 3rd NPC (until Feb 1967)
1965,	Apr	Identified as 3rd secretary, East China Bureau of the CCP Central Committee (until Feb 1967)
	Jun	Identified as 1st political commissar of Anhui Military Region (until Jan 1967)
1966,	Mar	Identified as chairman of the CPPCC, Anhui Section (until Feb 1967)
	Sep	At the beginning of the Cultural Revolution Li is accused of having "followed the reactionary capitalist line"
	Nov	Li receives injuries in demonstrations against him
1967,	Feb	Condemned as an "agent of the Chinese Khrushchev in Anhui," relieved of all posts and disappears
1973,	Aug	First appearence after the Cultural Revolution: Elected to first term as member of the CCP Central Committee by the 10th Party Congress
	Nov	Identified as a cadre in Guizhou Province
1974,	Feb	Identified as 2nd secretary of Guizhou Province CP and as vice-chairman of the Revolutioanry Committee of Guizhou Province (until 1977)
1978,	Mar	Appointed president of the People's Bank
1979,	Jun	Head of a People's Bank delegation to Yugoslavia and Sweden
	Nov	Article in HQ: "Bringing the Role of the Bank as Economic Lever into Full Play"

Li Benshan (Li Pen-shan) 李本善

Posts held

Provincial Administration
Vice-chairman of the Tibet Autonomous Regional People's Government

1960,	Sep	Identified as deputy director of the Department of Agriculture and Animal Husbandry of Tibet CP
1966,	Mar	Identified as secretary of Xigaze District CP
1973,	Nov	Identified as member of the Standing Committee of Tibet CP (until Nov 1977) and as 1st secretary of Lhasa CP (until 1975?)
1979,	Aug	Elected vice-chairman of the Tibet Autonomous Regional People's Government

Li Binsan (Li Pin-san)   李彬三

Posts held

Provincial Administration
Vice-chairman of the People's Government, Inner Mongolia Autonomous Region

1960,	Jan	Identified as deputy director of the Department for Industrial Work, Inner Mongolia Autonomous Region CP
1979,	Dec	Elected vice-chairman of the People's Government, Inner Mongolia Autonomous Region

Li Boning (Li Po-ning)   李伯宁

Posts held

Government
Vice-minister of water conservancy

1958,	Apr	Identified as deputy director of the Capital Construction Department, Ministry of Water Conservancy and Electric Power
1978,	Feb	Identified as vice-minister of water conservancy and electric power (until Feb 1979)
1979,	May	Identified as vice-minister of water conservancy

Li Buxin (Li Pu-hsin)   李步新

Posts held

CCP
Deputy director of the Organization Department of the CCP Central Committee

Others
Member of the Standing Committee of the 5th CPPCC

1950,	Jan	Identified as 1st secretary of South Anhui District CP and as secretary of Wuhu Municipal Committee CP
	Mar	Identified as deputy director of the Civil Affairs Department, East China Military Administrative Council (until Oct 1952)
1952,	Oct	Identified as deputy director of the Organization Department, East China Bureau of the CCP Central Committee
1954,	Aug	Elected deputy for Anhui Province to the 1st NPC (reelected in 1958 to the 2nd NPC)
1963,	Nov	Identified as deputy director of the Organization Department of the CCP Central Committee
1973,	Oct	Identified as a cadre of a department in the CCP Central Committee
1978,	Mar	Elected member of the Standing Committee of the 5th CPPCC
	Nov	Identified as deputy director of the Organization Department in the CCP Central Committee
1979,	Nov	Member of a CCP delegation, led by Ulanhu, to Romania to attend the 12th Congress of the Romanian CP

Li Chang (Li Ch'ang)   李　昌

Posts held

CCP
Member of the CCP 11th Central Committee

NPC
Member of the Standing Committee of the 5th NPC
Deputy for Shanghai to the 5th NPC

Others
Vice-president of the Academy of Sciences
1st vice-president of the University of Science and Technology

Li was born in 1916 in Fujian Province. In 1935, when a student of Beijing's Qinghua University, he was active in student demonstrations against Japan, later known as the "December 9 Movement." In 1936 he joined the Communist Youth League and became secretary of its Qinghua University Branch. In 1937 he acted as general chief of the "Pioneers for National Liberation." Soon afterwards he went to Yan'an. After the outbreak of the Sino-Japanese War he went to Taiyuan with the headquarters of the "Pioneers for National Liberation" and when Japanese troops occupied Taiyuan some months later, they proceeded to Linfen, Shanxi Province. In 1938 the Nationalist Government dissolved that organization. In spring 1949 he became a member of the Youth Department under the CCP Central Committee. In May that year he was elected member of the Federation of Democratic Youth (until August 1953).

1950,	Jan	Appointed member of the East China Military and Administrative Council
	Mar	Identified as secretary of the Work Committee of the East China Youth League
1951,	Mar	Deputy leader of a youth delegation to the USSR
1952,	Sep	Identified as secretary of the New Democratic Youth League
1954,	Jun	Identified as president of the Harbin Polytechnical University (until 1965)
	Aug	Elected deputy for Harbin to the 1st NPC
1956,	Sep	Elected alternate member of the CCP 8th Central Committee
1960,	Nov	Identified as 1st secretary of Harbin Polytechnical University CP
1964,	Jul	Head of a goodwill delegation to Cuba
	Nov	Appointed vice-chairman of the Commission for Cultural Relations with Foreign Countries (until Cultural Revolution)
1965,	May	Member of a delegation to the USSR to attend the celebrations for the 20th anniversary of the Defeat of Fascists; subsequently the delegation visited Romania
	Jun	Elected vice-chairman of the Chinese Committee for World Peace
1966,	Mar	Head of a cultural delegation to Iraq, Syria, Egypt, and the Yemen Arab Republic
1967,	May	Denounced as a follower of Liu Shaoqi and purged
1974,	Sep	First appearance after the Cultural Revolution
1975,	Jan	Elected member of the Standing Committee of the 4th CPPCC

1977,	Mar	Identified as a cadre of the Academy of Sciences
1978,	Feb	Elected deputy for Shanghai to the 5th NPC
	Mar	Elected member of the Standing Committee of the 5th NPC; appointed vice-president of the Academy of Sciences
	Jun	Head of a delegation of the Academy of Sciences to The Netherlands and the Federal Republic of Germany
	Sep	Identified as 1st vice-president of the University of Science and Technology
1979,	Sep	Head of a scientific delegation to Japan; by-elected member of the CCP 11th Central Committee

Li Chang'an (Li Ch'ang-an) 李昌安

Posts held

CCP
Alternate member of the CCP 11th Central Committee

1977,	Aug	Elected alternate member of the CCP Central Committee by the 11th Party Congress
	Oct	Li attends the National Day celebrations in Beijing

Li Changlin (Li Ch'ang-lin) 李长林

Posts held

Military
Deputy commander of Xinjiang Military Region

1964,	Oct	Elected deputy for the PLA to the 4th NPC
1974,	Jan	Identified as deputy commander of Xinjiang Military Region; member of a military delegation to Pakistan
1978,	Jun	Member of a government delegation under Geng Biao to Pakistan to attend the opening ceremonies for the Karakorum Road

Li Chao (Li Ch'ao) 李超

Posts held

Government
Ambassador to Surinam

1961,	Feb	Identified as secretary-general of the Sino-Albanian Friendship Association
1964,	Sep	Identified as deputy director of the Protocol Department of the Ministry of Foreign Affairs
1965,	Aug	Identified as counselor at the embassy in Iraq (until about 1967)
1973,	Jul	Appointed ambassador to Jamaica (until Nov 1976)
1977,	Jul	Appointed ambassador to Surinam

Li Chaobo (Li Ch'ao-po) 李超伯

Posts held

Government
Vice-minister of the Capital Construction Commission
Director, Office of the Environmental Protection Leading Group under the State Council

Others
President of the Environmental Society

1949,	Dec	Identified as member of the Financial and Economic Affairs Committee in the South Sichuan Administrative Office (until Aug 1952)
1953,	Jan	Identified as deputy secretary-general of the Financial and Economic Affairs Committee in the South Sichuan Administrative Office
1954,	Nov	Appointed deputy director of the State Bureau of Statistics (until Apr 1957)
1957,	Apr	Appointed assistant minister of chemical industry (until Jan 1959)
1960,	May	Appointed vice-minister of chemical industry (until Dec 1962)
1963,	Sep	Appointed member of the State Economic Commission (until Dec 1964) and deputy director of the Administrative Bureau of Supplies under the State Council (until Nov 1964)
1967		Disappears during the Cultural Revolution
1977,	Sep	First appearance after the Cultural Revolution: Identified as secretary of the CP, and as vice-chairman of the Revolutionary Committee, of Gansu Province (until May 1978)
1978,	Jul	Identified as director, Office of the Environmental Protection Leading Group under the State Council
	Aug	Identified as vice-minister of the Capital Construction Commission
	Oct	Head of an environmental delegation to Japan
1979,	Mar	Elected president of the Environmental Society
	Aug	Head of a delegation to a symposium on the inter-relationship between resources, environment, population and development under the auspices of the UN in Stockholm

Li Chengfang (Li Ch'eng-fang) 李成芳

Posts held

CCP
Alternate member of the CCP 11th Central Committee

Military
Lieutenant-general
1st political commissar of Wuhan Military Region

Li was born in 1911 in Macheng, Hubei Province. At the age of 16 he joined the Red Workers and Peasants Army.

In 1934-35 he took part in the Long March. He then attended a course at the Anti-Japan Military and Political Academy. From 1937 he served in the 129th Division of the 8th Route Army. In 1945 he commanded a brigade, and two years later a division. During the Battle of Huaihai his units contributed decisively to the breakthrough to the south. In January 1949 he was appointed commander of the 11th Corps, 2nd Field Army. Three months later his troops occupied the Chang Jiang crossing and reached Guangdong, through Zhejiang and Fujian Provinces.

1950,	Aug	Elected council member of the People's Government of Yunnan Province
1953		Identified as deputy commander of Yunnan Military District
1955,	Sep	Promoted to rank of major-general
1958		Appointed deputy commander of Wuhan Military Region
1959,	Oct	Identified as lieutenant-general
1961		Training at the PLA Political Academy
1963,	Feb	Identified as deputy commander of Kunming Military Region
1965,	Jan	Appointed member of the National Defense Council (until Cultural Revolution)
1967,	May	Accused as a traitor
	Jul	Li disappears following self-criticism
1973,	May	First appearance after the Cultural Revolution
	Oct	Identified as a cadre of the State Council
1975,	Jan	Appointed minister of the 5th Ministry of Machine Building by the 4th NPC (until 1977)
1977,	Aug	Elected alternate member of the CCP Central Committee by the 11th Party Congress
1978,	Jan	Identified as 1st political commissar of Wuhan Military Region

Li Chuan (Li Ch'uan)   李　川

Posts held

Others
Vice-chairman of the Council for Promotion of International Trade

1965,	Nov	Head of the Chinese Economic Fair in the Central African Republic
1966,	Feb	Identified as director of the Liaison Office of the Committee for Promotion of International Trade
1972,	Apr	Head of a delegation to the Paris Fair; identified as vice-chairman of the Council for Promotion of International Trade
	May	Head of a trade delegation to Mexico
	Jun	Head of an exhibition delegation to the Poznan Fair in Poland
1974,	Oct	Head of an exhibition delegation to Australia
1975,	Mar	Head of a trade delegation to Japan
	Sep	Head of a trade delegation to the United States
1976,	Sep	Head of an exhibition delegation to the Philippines
1977,	Apr	Head of an exhibition delegation to Nagoya, Japan
1979,	Feb	Head of an exhibition delegation to Thailand

Li Chuli (Li Ch'u-li)   李初梨

Posts held

Military
Major-general

Others
Member of the Standing Committee of the 5th CPPCC

Li was born in 1900 in Sichuan Province. He is a graduate of the Imperial University in Tokyo. After his return to China in 1924 he cofounded with Guo Moruo the Creation Society and engaged in left-wing writing. In 1931 he was arrested by the Nationalist Government for subversive activities. Released in 1937, he went to Yan'an and became active in the Shanxi-Chahar-Hebei Border Region. In 1945 he was political commissar in East Hebei Military District. In July 1946 he was appointed head of the Executive Group of the Military Mediation Executive Committee for talks with KMT authorities. In 1949 he was made deputy director of the Propaganda Department in the Northeast China Bureau of the CCP Central Committee.

1949,	Oct	Appointed director of the Liaison Department of the Overseas Chinese Affairs Commission (until 1951)
1954,	Aug	Elected deputy for Sichuan Province to the 1st NPC (reelected in 1958 to the 2nd NPC)
1955,	May	Identified as deputy director of the Overseas Chinese Affairs Department of the CCP Central Committee
	Jul	Identified as council member of the Institute of Foreign Affairs
1962,	Sep	Identified as director of the Organization Department in the CCP Central Committee
1965,	Jan	Elected member of the Standing Committee of the 4th CPPCC
1967,	Jun	Branded as a renegade and purged
1978,	Feb	First appearance after the Cultural Revolution
	Mar	Elected member of the Standing Committee of the 5th CPPCC

Li Chunqing (Li Ch'un-ch'ing)   李纯青

Posts held

Others
Member of the Standing Committee of the 5th CPPCC
Vice-chairman of the General Office, Taiwan Democratic Self-government League

Li was born in 1915 in Fujian Province and studied in Japan. As chief-editor of  Dagong Bao he was elected a member of the Preparatory Committee for the Journalists' Association in July 1949.

| 1951, | May | Identified as deputy chief-editor of the Shanghai Dagong Bao |
| 1954, | Aug | Elected deputy for Tianjin Municipality to the 1st NPC; identified as vice-chairman of the Taiwan Democratic Self-Government League |

	Dec	Elected member of the Standing Committee of the 2nd CPPCC
1955,	Jul	Identified as council member of the Institute of Foreign Affairs
1956,	Nov	Member of a NPC delegation to the USSR and Eastern Europe (until Jan 1957)
1964,	Dec	Elected member of the 4th CPPCC
1967		Disappears during the Cultural Revolution
1974,	May	First appearance after the Cultural Revolution
1978,	Mar	Elected member of the Standing Committee of the 5th CPPCC
1979,	Oct	Reelected vice-chairman of the General Office of the Taiwan Democratic Self-government League

Li Da (Li Ta)

Posts held

CCP
Member of the CCP 11th Central Committee

Military
Colonel-general
Deputy chief of PLA General Staff
Director of the All-Army Physical Culture Guidance Committee

Li was born in 1905 in Shaanxi Province. At the end of 1927 he joined the Communist forces under Mao Zedong in Jinggangshan. In the late twenties or early thirties he studied at the Red Army Academy in Moscow. In 1934-35 he took part in the Long March, serving in its final phase in the 2nd Front Army commanded by He Long. After the outbreak of the Anti-Japanese War and the reorganization of the Communist forces into the 8th Route Army, Li was appointed chief of staff of the 129th Division in 1937. In 1940 he took part in the famous Battle of the 100 Regiments in Southwest Shanxi. In 1946 he was chief of staff of Shanxi-Hebei-Shandong-Henan Military District under the command of Liu Bocheng. As chief of staff of Liu Bocheng's Central Plains Field Army, renamed 2nd Field Army in 1948, Li contributed decisively to the victories of this unit which pushed forward to Sichuan in late 1949.

1950,	Jan	Li continues as chief of staff of the 2nd Army; appointed member of the Southwest China Military and Administrative Council; identified as deputy commander of Southwest China Military Region
1953,	Jun	Posted to Korea as chief of staff of the Chinese People's Volunteers
1954,	Sep	Appointed vice-minister of national defense (until Sep 1959)
1955,	Sep	Promoted to rank of colonel-general; awarded the orders of "1st August," "Independence and Freedom," and "Liberation," all 1st class
1957,	Sep	Li accompanies Minister of Defense Stoph of the German Democratic Republic on his tour of China
1959,	Mar	Elected deputy for the PLA to the 2nd NPC
	Apr	Appointed member of the National Defense Council (until Cultural Revolution)

	Jun	Identified as chairman of the National Defense Athletic Association
	Sep	Appointed vice-chairman of the Physical Culture and Sports Commission under the State Council (until Cultural Revolution)
1961,	Jul	Head of a defense athletic delegation to the USSR
	Sep	Li accompanies British Field-Marshal Montgomery on a tour of China
1963,	Nov	Head of a defense athletic delegation to Albania
1964,	Sep	Elected deputy for Shaanxi Province to the 3rd NPC
	Oct	Head of a sports delegation to North Vietnam
1965,	Jan	Elected member of the Standing Committee of the 3rd NPC (until Jan 1975)
1967		Li disappears during the Cultural Revolution
1972,	Nov	First appearance after the Cultural Revolution: Referred to as deputy chief of PLA General Staff
1973,	Aug	Elected to first term as member of the CCP Central Committee by the 10th Party Congress
1974,	May	Head of a PLA friendship delegation to North Korea
	Jul	Head of a military delegation to Tanzania
1975,	Jan	Member of the presidium of the 4th NPC
1978,	Jun	Identified as director of the All-Army Physical Culture Guidance Committee
1979,	Jun	Head of an army officers' vacation group to Romania
	Jun	Appointed member of the National Games Organizing Committee

Li Daigeng (Li Tai-keng)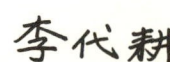

Posts held

Government
Vice-minister of power industry

Others
Acting president of the Civil Engineering Society

1954,	Jun	Identified as director of the Shanghai Electric Industry Administration
1955,	Nov	Identified as assistant minister of electric power industry
1958,	Dec	Deputy head of an economic delegation to Hungary
1961,	Jul	Identified as vice-minister of water conservancy and electric power (until Cultural Revolution)
1967		Disappears during the Cultural Revolution
1977,	Dec	First appearance after the Cultural Revolution: Identified as vice-minister of water conservancy and electric power (until Feb 1979)
1978,	Jul	Identified as acting president of the Civil Engineering Society; head of an electric engineering delegation to the United States and Japan
1979,	Jun	Identified as vice-minister of power industry

Li Dehua (Li Te-hua) 李德华

Posts held

Government
Deputy secretary-general of the Institute of Foreign Affairs

1962,	Nov	Identified as counselor at the embassy in Sweden (until 1976)
1972,	Jan	Identified as chargé d'affaires ad interim in Lebanon (until 1976)
1978,	Aug	Identified as deputy secretary-general of the Institute of Foreign Affairs

Li Dengying (Li Teng-ying) 李登瀛

Posts held

CCP
Secretary of Gansu Province CP

Provincial Administration
Vice-chairman of the People's Congress of Gansu Province

1950,	May	Identified as member of the Standing Committee of North Sichuan District CP
	Jun	Identified as director of the Control Commission of North Sichuan Administration Office
1952,	Apr	Identified as deputy director of the Rural Work Department in the Northwest China Bureau of the CCP
1954,	Nov	Appointed deputy director of the General Office in the State Council
1956,	Mar	Appointed deputy secretary-general of the Scientific Planning Commission (until Jun 1957)
	Sep	Appointed deputy director of the Staff Office of Agriculture and Forestry under the State Council (until Dec 1960)
1961,	Feb	Identified as member of the Standing Committee of the Rural Work Department, Northeast China Bureau of the CCP Central Committee
1964,	Oct	Identified as chairman of the Committee for Water and Soil Conservation in the Middle Reaches of the Yellow River under the State Council
1966	Jan	Identified as director of the Rural Work Department, Northwest China Bureau of the CCP Central Committee
1967		Disappears during the Cultural Revolution
1977,	Oct	First appearance after the Cultural Revolution: Identified as vice-chairman of the Revolutionary Committee of Shaanxi Province (until Feb 1978)
	Dec	Elected vice-chairman of the Revolutionary Committee of Gansu Province (until Dec 1979)
1978,	May	Identified as secretary of Gansu Province CP
1979,	Apr	Head of a friendship delegation to Romania
	Dec	Elected vice-chairman of the People's Congress of Gansu Province

Li Desheng (Li Te-sheng) 李德生

Posts held

CCP
Member of the Politburo of the CCP 11th Central Committee
Member of the CCP 11th Central Committee

NPC
Deputy for the PLA to the 5th NPC

Military
Major-general
Commander of Shenyang Military Region
1st secretary, CP Secretariat of Shenyang Military Region

Li was born in 1916 in Hong'an (Huang'an), Hubei Province. Around 1932 he joined the 4th Front Army. In 1934-35 he took part in the Long March. He rose to the post of detachment and battalion commander in 1936. In 1937 the Communist forces were reorganized into the 8th Route Army, and Li became detachment leader in a regiment of the 129th Division. In 1940 he served as battalion commander in the South Hebei Independent Brigade. In 1943 he commanded a regiment. His 49th Regiment was noted for distinguished service in July 1947 at the Battle of Xiangyang and was titled the "Heroes Regiment of Xiangyang." In 1948 Li's regiment was integrated into the Central Plains Field Army and took part in the Huaihai Battle. When the Central Plains Field Army was reorganized in February 1949 to form the 2nd Field Army, Li was made commander of the 35th Division. In November 1949 his forces played a decisive role in the occupation of Chongqing.

1951,	Mar	Li is detached with his 35th Division to join the Chinese People's Volunteers in Korea
1952		Appointed chief of staff of the 12th Army, Chinese People's Volunteers
1953,	Feb	In charge of coastal defense in the Wonsan and Singosan area
1954		Training at the PLA Military Academy in Nanjing
1955,	Sep	Promoted to rank of major-general
1958		Identified as commander of the 12th Army
1960		Lin Biao calls upon military commanders to return to basic service. Accordingly, Li serves in the 2nd Detachment under Guo Xingfu, 1st Battalion, 100th Regiment, 34th Division, as a private. This was the origin of the "Teaching Method of Guo Xingfu" which was to gain significance.
1967,	Jan	At the height of the Cultural Revolution, Li with his 12th Army intervened, apparently at the instruction of the central Party leadership, in the conflict between the Red Guards and the old Party leadership of Jiangsu Province which had already led to a large number of casualties. Thanks to his intervention 2,000 arrested Red Guards were released. This incident represented the first active intervention of a PLA unit in the Cultural Revolution.
	May	As before in Nanjing, Li intervenes with his units at the instruction of the CCP Central Committee in Anhui Province. He

succeeds in restoring discipline among the conflicting groups after power struggles had led to a chaotic situation.

Jul Following the "Wuhan Incident" Li's 12th Army itself becomes a target of Red Guard attacks with the declared aim to drive away the 12th Army. After Red Guards had occupied the Staff Headquarters of the 34th Division and physically attacked officers and troops and confiscated weapons, Li ordered his soldiers to withdraw without resistance and requested further instructions from the central Party leadership. This moderate course of action won Li special praise from Jiang Qing, the wife of Mao Zedong, who was then 1st vice-chairman of the Cultural Revolutionary Group of the CCP Central Committee, because Li had contributed to the avoidance of bloodshed.

Oct Appointed commander of Anhui Military District (until Jan 1974)

1968, **Apr** Elected chairman of the newly established Revolutionary Committee of Anhui Province (until Jan 1974)

1969, **Apr** Elected to first term as member of the CCP Central Committee by the 9th Party Congress and alternate member of the Politburo (latter post until Aug 1973)

1970, **Sep** Identified as director of the Political Department of the PLA (until about 1974)

1971, **Jan** Elected 1st secretary of the new CP Secretariat of Anhui Province (until Jan 1974)

Jul Deputy head of a government and Party delegation to North Korea to attend the 10th anniversary of the signing of the Friendship Treaty

Aug Head of a military delegation to Albania and Romania

1973, **Aug** Confirmed by the 10th CCP Congress in his former Party post and, in addition, elected member of the Standing Committee of the Politburo (latter post until Aug 1977)

Sep Head of a friendship delegation to North Korea

1974, **Jan** Identified as commander of Shenyang Military Region

1977, **Jun** Identified as 1st secretary, CP Secretariat of Shenyang Military Region

1978, **Feb** Elected deputy for the PLA to the 5th NPC

Sep 13 Article in RMRB: "Participate in the Struggle and Maintain Contact with the People"

Li Dongye (Li Tung-yeh)　　李东冶

Posts held

Government
Vice-minister of metallurgical industry

Others
Secretary, Anshan Iron and Steel Company CP

Li was born in Shanxi Province.

1949, **Nov** Identified as director of the Social Work Department of Rehe Province CP

1950, **Jan** Identified as director of the Public Security Department of Rehe People's Government

Apr Identified as deputy chief procurator, Northeast China Branch of the Supreme People's Procuracy

1958, **Oct** Identified as director of the Political and Judicial Department of Liaoning Province

1960, **Jun** Identified as secretary of Liaoning Province CP (until 1968)

1968 Li disappears

1979, **Jul** First appearance after the Cultural Revolution: Identified as vice-minister of metallurgical Industry and as secretary of the CP of Anshan Iron and Steel Company

Li Eding (Li O-ting)　　李鹗鼎

Posts held

Government
Vice-minister of power industry

1979, **May** Identified as vice-minister of power industry

Li Enqiu (Li En-ch'iu)　　李恩求

Posts held

Government
Former ambassador to Czechoslovakia

1952, **Apr** Appointed counselor at the embassy in Poland

1954, **Aug** Identified as chargé d'affaires ad interim in Romania

1955, **Sep** Appointed vice-chairman of the Institute of Foreign Affairs under the Ministry of Foreign Affairs

1958, **Sep** Elected council member of the Sino-Polish Friendship Association

1961, **Jun** Identified as deputy director of the Agreements and Laws Department in the Ministry of Foreign Affairs

1962, **Oct** Identified as secretary of the Political Science and Law Society

1963, **Jul** Appointed chargé d'affaires in the Netherlands

1966, **Jul** Li is declared persona non grata and expelled by the Dutch Government because of his involvement in the alleged murder of the Chinese engineer Xu Zicai

1971, **Jan** Identified as a cadre of the Association for Friendship with Foreign Countries

1973, **Mar** Identified as council member of the Association for Friendship with Foreign Countries

Sep Identfied as vice-chairman of the Association for Friendship with Foreign Countries

1974, **Aug** Head of a friendship delegation to Romania; identified as vice-chairman of the Sino-Romanian Friendship Association

1975, **Jun** Appointed ambassador to Czechoslovakia (until Sep 1978)

Li Erzhong (Li Erh-chung) 李尔重

Posts held

CCP
Secretary of Hebei Province CP

1949,	Nov	Identified as director of the Propaganda Department of Wuhan Municipality CP
1952		Identified as chairman of the Culture and Education Committee in the Central-South China Military and Administrative Council
1954,	Oct	Identified as 3rd secretary of Wuhan Municipality CP (until Oct 1955)
1955,	Oct	Identified as 2nd secretary of Wuhan Municipality CP (until May 1957)
1957,	May	Identified as deputy secretary of Wuhan Municipality CP (until Oct 1957)
	Oct	Identified as secretary of Wuhan Municipality CP; identified as member of the Standing Committee of Hubei Province CP
1961,	May	Identified as director of the Propaganda Department in the Central-South Bureau of the CCP Central Committee (until Mar 1963)
1965,	Feb	Identified as member of the Standing Committee in the Central-South China Bureau of the CCP Central Committee (until Cultural Revolution)
1966,	Mar	Identified as director of the Agriculture Committee in the Central-South China Bureau of the CCP Central Committee (until Cultural Revolution)
1975,	Jul	First appearance after the Cultural Revolution: Identified as vice-chairman of the Revolutionary Committee of Guangdong Province (until 1977)
	Nov	Identified as member of the Standing Committee of Guangdong Province CP
1977,	Sep	Identified as secretary of Shaanxi Province CP (until Mar 1979)
1978,	Jun	Identified as vice-principal of the Party School of Shaanxi Province CP
1979,	Mar	Identified as standing secretary of Shaanxi Province CP
	Sep	Member of a government delegation led by Wang Renzhong to Yugoslavia, Denmark, The Netherlands, and Belgium; identified as vice-chairman of the Revolutionary Committee of Shaanxi Province (until Dec 1979)
1980,	Jan	Identified as secretary of Hebei Province CP

Li Feiping (Li Fei-p'ing) 李非平

Posts held

Government
Vice-minister of metallurgical industry

1978,	Aug	Identified as vice-minister of metallurgical industry

Li Fenglan (Li Feng-lan) (f) 李风兰

Posts held

NPC
Member of the Standing Committee of the 5th NPC
Deputy for Shaanxi Province to the 5th NPC

1958,	Nov	Elected deputy for Hebei Province to the 2nd NPC
1973,	Apr	Identified as a peasant in Hu County, Shaanxi Province; amateur painter
1975,	Jan	Elected member of the Standing Committee of the 4th NPC (confirmed in 1978 by the 5th NPC)
1978,	Feb	Elected deputy for Shaanxi Province to the 5th NPC

Li Fenglou (Li Feng-lou) 李风楼

Posts held

NPC
Deputy for Beijing Municipality to the 5th NPC

Others
President of the Football Association

1962,	Oct	Identified as deputy director of the Department for Ball Games under the State Commission for Physical Culture and Sports
1964,	Sep	Identified as vice-president of the Football Association
1966,	Jul	Identified as a council member of the Sports Federation; after this Li disappears
1978,	Feb	First appearance after the Cultural Revolution; elected deputy for Beijing Municipality to the 5th NPC
1979,	Jul	Identified as president of the Football Association

Li Fengping (Li Feng-p'ing) 李丰平

Posts held

CCP
Secretary of Zhejiang Province CP

Provincial Administration
Governor of Zhejiang Province

1949,	Dec	Identified as director of the Public Security Department of Zhejiang People's Government
1951,	Sep	Identified as council member of Zhejiang People's Government
1955,	Jan	Identified as vice-governor of Zhejiang (until 1963)
1957,	May	Identified as secretary of Zhejiang Province CP (until 1963)
1963,	Feb	Identified as secretary of Anhui Province CP (until 1966)
1966,	May	Identified as secretary of Zhejiang Province CP (until Cultural Revolution)

1968,	Jul	Branded as a capitalist-roader and purged
1978,	May	First appearance after the Cultural Revolution: Elected secretary of Zhejiang Province CP
1979,	Jul	Identified as vice-chairman of the Revolutionary Committee of Zhejiang Province (until Dec 1979)
	Dec	Elected governor of Zhejiang Province

Li Fuke (Li Fu-k'e)   李夫克

Posts held

Military
Deputy commandant of the PLA Military and Political Academy

1970,	Oct	Identified as a military cadre
1976,	Feb	Identified as deputy commandant of the PLA Military and Political Academy; deputy head of a military delegation to Pakistan

Li Fuquan (Li Fu-ch'üan)   李夫全

Posts held

CCP
Member of the Standing Committee of Hubei Province CP

Provincial Administration
Vice-governor of Hubei Province

1973,	May	Identified as member of the Standing Committee of Hubei Province CP
1974,	Mar	Identified as vice-chairman of the Revolutionary Committee of Hubei Province (until Dec 1979)
1980,	Jan	Elected vice-governor of Hubei Province

Li Fuzhong (Li Fu-chung)   李福忠

Posts held

NPC
Member of the Standing Committee of the 5th NPC
Deputy for Sichuan Province to the 5th NPC

1978,	Feb	Elected deputy for Sichuan Province to the 5th NPC
	Mar	Elected member of the Standing Committee of the 5th NPC

Li Guang (Li Kuang)   黎光

Posts held

Government
Vice-minister of railways

1963,	Sep	Identified as deputy director of the Political Department, Ministry of Railways
1978,	Jun	Identified as vice-minister of railways

Li Guangjun (Li Kuang-chün)   李光军

Posts held

Military
Deputy commander of Wuhan Military Region

1971,	Aug	Identified as a cadre of Wuhan Military Region
1972,	Jan	Identified as deputy commander of Wuhan Military Region
	Mar	Li disappears for unknown reasons
1976,	Jan	First reappearance
1979,	Dec	Again identified as deputy commander of Wuhan Military Region

Li Gui (Li Kuei)   李贵

Posts held

CCP
Deputy director of the United Front Work Department of the CCP Central Committee

NPC
Vice-chairman of the Nationalities Committee of the 5th NPC
Deputy for Inner Mongolia Autonomous Region to the 5th NPC

1965,	Dec	Identified as 1st secretary of Hohhot Municipality
1966,	Aug	Branded as a black gangster
1977,	Nov	First appearance after the Cultural Revolution: Identified as deputy director of the United Front Work Department of the CCP Central Committee
1978,	Feb	Elected deputy for Inner Mongolia Autonomous Region to the 5th NPC
1979,	Jun	Member of the Credentials Committee at the 2nd Session of the 5th NPC
	Jul	Identified as vice-chairman of the Nationalities Committee of the 5th NPC

Li Guocai (Li Kuo-ts'ai)   李国才

Posts held

Government
Vice-minister of chemical industry

1975		Li becomes known as a national worker; identified as member of the Standing Committee of Jilin Municipality CP, as vice-chairman of the Revolutionary Committee of Jilin Municipality and as chairman of the Jilin Municipality Trade Union
1976,	Jan	Identified as vice-minister of petroleum and chemical industry
1979,	Jan	Identified as vice-minister of chemical industry

Li Guohao (Li Kuo-hao)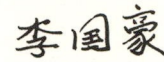

Posts held

NPC
Deputy for Shanghai Municipality to the 5th NPC

Others
President of the Shanghai Dongji University

1978, Feb Elected deputy for Shanghai Municipality to the 5th NPC
1979, Apr Identified as president of the Shanghai Dongji University
May Li gives lectures on bridge-building and mechanics in the Federal Republic of Germany

Li Haifeng (Li Hai-feng) (f)

Posts held

Mass Organization
Secretary of the Communist Youth League
Vice-chairman of the Youth Federation

Li was born in 1949. She became known as head of an oil-extraction team in Daqing.

1975, Jun Identified as member of the Standing Committee of Heilongjiang Province CP (no later mention in this post) and as secretary of the Communist Youth League of Daqing Oil Field
1978, Oct Elected secretary of the Communist Youth League
1979, May Elected vice-chairman of the Youth Federation
Jul Appointed member of the National Games Organizing Committee

Li Helin (Li Ho-lin)

Posts held

NPC
Deputy for Beijing Municipality to the 5th NPC

Others
Director of the Lu Xun Museum in Beijing

1964, Aug Identified as director of the Chinese Literature Department at Nankai University
1978, Feb Elected deputy for Beijing Municipality to the 5th NPC
Oct Identified as director of the Lu Xun Museum in Beijing

Li Hua (Li Hua)

Posts held

Government
Vice-minister of metallurgical industry

Others
Vice-president of the Metallurgical Society

1979, Jan Identified as vice-minister of metallurgical industry and as vice-president of the Metallurgical Society

Li Huamin (Li Hua-min)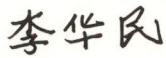

Posts held

CCP
Alternate member of the CCP 11th Central Committee

Military
Major-general
Deputy commander of Shenyang Military Region

In 1948 Li commanded the 21st Division of the 7th Column, Northeast Field Army. In January 1949 he was appointed deputy commander of the 44th Corps, 4th Field Army.

1953 Li serves in the Korean War as commander of the 54th Corps
1955, Sep Promoted to rank of major-general
1963 Identified as chief of staff of Guangzhou Military Region
1968 Identified as deputy commander of Wuhan Military Region (until 1977)
1969, Apr Elected to first term as alternate member of the CCP Central Committee by the 9th Party Congress
1978, May Identified as deputy commander of Shenyang Military Region

Li Huang (Li Huang)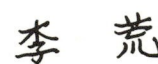

Posts held

CCP
Secretary of Liaoning Province CP
1st secretary of Lüda Municipality CP

In September 1949 Li was a participant at the 1st CPPCC.

1950, Apr Identified as director of the Northeast Daily News and as member of the Cultural and Educational Committee of the Northeast Military and Administrative Council (until 1954)
1953, Jul Identified as deputy secretary of Liaoxi Province CP
1954, Nov Identified as deputy secretary of Liaoning Province CP
1956, Sep Identified as secretary of Liaoning Province CP (until Cultural Revolution)
1959, Dec Identified as vice-president, Liaoning Branch of the Sino-Soviet Friendship Association
1960, Aug Head of a delegation to North Korea representing Liaoning Province; identified as chairman of the Sino-Korean Friendship Association, Liaoning Branch
1964, Aug Elected deputy for Liaoning Province to the 3rd NPC

1966		Disappears during the Cultural Revolution
1978,	Aug	First appearance after the Cultural Revolution: Identified as 1st secretary of Lüda Municipality CP and as secretary of Liaoning Province CP
1979,	Jul	Appointed member of the National Games Organizing Committee

Li Jiacheng (Li Chia-ch'eng)　　李嘉诚

Posts held

Others
Director of the Board of Directors, China International Trust and Investment Corporation

1979,　Oct　Appointed director of the Board of Directors, China International Trust and Investment Corporation; identified as a Hong Kong businessman

Li Jian'an (Li Chien-an)　　李建安

Posts held

Provincial Administration
Vice-governor of Guangdong Province

1963,　Mar　Identified as deputy director of the Economic Committee of Guangdong People's Council

1977,　Aug　Identified as vice-chairman of the Revolutionary Committee of Guangdong Province (until Dec 1979)

1979,　Dec　Elected vice-governor of Guangdong Province

Li Jianbai (Li Chien-pai)　　李剑白

Posts held

CCP
Secretary of Heilongjiang Province CP
1st secretary of Harbin Municipality CP

Others
Chairman of the Revolutionary Committee of Harbin Municipality

1952,　Aug　Identified as director of the Propaganda Department of Heilongjiang Province CP

1953,　Jan　Identified as deputy secretary of Heilongjiang Province CP

1961,　Feb　Identified as secretary of Heilongjiang Province CP

1967,　Jan　Branded as a capitalist-roader

1976,　Sep　First appearance after the Cultural Revolution: Identified as secretary of Harbin Municipality CP

　　　　Oct　Identified as chairman of the Revolutionary Committee of Harbin Municipality

1978,　Feb　Identified as secretary of Heilongjiang Province CP

　　　　Sep　Identified as 1st secretary of Harbin Municipality CP

1979,　Jul　Appointed member of the National Games Organizing Committee

Li Jianping (Li Chien-p'ing)　　李建平

Posts held

Government
Vice-minister of light industry

NPC
Deputy for Beijing Municipality to the 5th NPC

1953,　Jul　Identified as director of the Coal Production Bureau under the Northeast China Administrative Council

1955,　Nov　Appointed assistant minister of coal industry (until Oct 1957)

1959　　　　Identified as director of the Administrative Bureau of Coal Mines under the People's Government of Liaoning Province

1960,　Jan　Appointed vice-minister of coal industry (until Cultural Revolution)

1973,　Oct　First appearance after the Cultural Revolution

1974,　Sep　Identified as vice-minister of fuel and chemical industry (until 1977?)

1978,　Feb　Elected deputy for Beijing Municipality to the 5th NPC

1979,　Apr　Identified as vice-minister of light industry

Li Jianzhen (Li Chien-chen) (f)　　李坚真

Posts held

CCP
Alternate member of the CCP 11th Central Committee
Secretary of Guangdong Province CP
Secretary of the Discipline Inspection Committee, Guangdong Province CP

Provincial Administration
Chairman of the People's Congress of Guangdong Province

Li was born in 1904 in Fengshun County, Guangdong Province. Forced by poverty her parents betrothed and sold her as a child to another family. In 1927 she joined the CCP and shortly afterwards took part in an uprising in the East River Area, after the failure of which she joined the 11th Red Army commanded by Gu Dacun as a propaganda worker. From 1930 to 1933 she served in the Fujian Soviet. In 1934 she went to the Jiangxi Soviet from where she joined the Long March in that year. During the march she was at first head of a women's group of the 1st Cadre Company and later worked in a field medical unit. In 1937 she was identified as director of the Women's Department in the Government of Shaanxi-Gansu-Ningxia Border Region. In 1945 she was secretary of the CP in Changting County, Fujian Province. In April 1949 she was elected a member of the Executive Council of the Democratic Women's Federation (until March 1953). In September of the same year she took part in the CPPCC.

1949, Dec Appointed member of the Central-South China Military and Administrative Council; identified as secretary of the Women's Work Committee, Central-South China Subbureau of the CCP Central Committee (until Nov 1954)

1954, Aug Elected deputy for Guangdong Province to the 1st NPC

1955, Feb Elected member of the People's Council of Guangdong Province

Apr Appointed 1st secretary of Central Guangdong District CP

1956, Sep Elected alternate member of the CCP Central Committee by the 8th Party Congress (until Cultural Revolution)

1958, Feb Appointed secretary of the Control Commission of Guangdong Province CP (until Cultural Revolution)

1960, Oct Identified as secretary of Guangdong Province CP (until Cultural Revolution)

1966 Disappears during the Cultural Revolution

1973, Jul First appearance after the Cultural Revolution: Identified as vice-chairman of the Revolutionary Committee of Guangdong Province (until Dec 1979)

1974, Dec Elected chairman of the newly established Peasants' Federation of Guangdong Province (no later mention in this post)

1975, Aug Head of a friendship delegation to North Korea

1977, Aug Elected alternate member of the CCP Central Committee by the 11th Party Congress

Dec Identified as secretary of Guangdong Province CP

1979, Jun Identified as secretary of the Discipline Inspection Committee, Guangdong Province CP

Dec Elected chairman of the People's Congress of Guangdong Province

---

Li Jiliang (Li Chi-liang)

Posts held

CCP

1977, Aug Elected alternate member of the CCP 11th Central Committee by the 11th Party Congress

Sep Identified as a laborer in the oil drilling area of Maoming, Guangdong Province

---

Li Jinde (Li Chin-te) 李金德

Posts held

Others
Member of the Standing Committee of the 5th CPPCC

Before the foundation of PRC Li was temporarily deputy director of the Office of Confidential Material, General Office of the CCP Central Committee.

1949, Dec Identified as director of the Office of Confidential Material in the Government Administration Council

---

1955, Mar Appointed deputy director of the State Council Secretariat (until Apr 1959)

1965, Mar Appointed deputy secretary-general of the 4th CPPCC and head of the Secretariat Office (until Cultural Revolution)

Aug Identified as a cadre of the United Front Work Department in the CCP Central Committee (until Cultural Revolution)

1972, Mar First appearance after the Cultural Revolution

1973, Sep Identified as a cadre of the United Front Work Department in the CCP Central Committee (until 1977)

1975, Mar Appointed deputy secretary-general, Standing Committee of the 4th NPC (until 1977)

1978, Mar Elected member of the Standing Committee of the 5th CPPCC

Li Jing (Li Ching)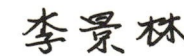

Posts held

Government
Vice-minister of petroleum industry

Others
Director of the Xinjiang Petroleum Administrative Bureau

1960, Aug Recalled from his post as deputy director of the Changchun Institute of Geology

1966, Mar Identified as deputy CP secretary of Jilin Institute of Technology

Sep Denounced as an "anti-Party element" and purged

1979, Oct First appearance after the Cultural Revolution: Identified as vice-minister of petroleum industry and as director of the Xinjiang Petroleum Administrative Bureau

---

Li Jinglin (Li Ching-lin) 李景林

Posts held

Others
Member of the Standing Committee of the 5th CPPCC

Li belongs to the Hui minority. In 1939 he was active in the Shaanxi-Gansu-Ningxia Border Region.

1949, Dec Identified as vice-chairman of Ningxia Province (until Sep 1954)

1950, Jan Identified as member of the Financial and Economic Affairs Committee of the Northwest Military and Administrative Council

1955, Jan Identified as 3rd secretary of Gansu Province CP

1956, Oct Identified as secretary of Gansu Province CP

1958, Mar Identified as chairman of the Tao River Project Committee

Oct Elected deputy for Ningxia Autonomous Region to the 2nd NPC (confirmed in 1964 by the 3rd NPC)

1962,	Nov	Identified as secretary of Ningxia Autonomous Region CP
1967		Disappears during the Cultural Revolution
1978,	Feb	First appearance after the Cultural Revolution
	Mar	Elected member of the Standing Committee of the 5th CPPCC

Li Jingquan (Li Ching-ch'üan)　李井泉

Posts held

CCP
Member of the CCP 11th Central Committee

NPC
Vice-chairman of the Standing Committee of the 5th NPC
Deputy for Shanxi Province to the 5th NPC

Li was born in 1908 as the son of a landlord in Huichang, Jiangxi Province. In the mid-1920s he studied at the KMT Peasants' Institute in Guangzhou, of which Mao Zedong was head. In 1931 he was political commissar of the Guard Regiment of the 1st Front Army and in 1934 director of the Political Department of its 4th Division. In that year he went from Jiangxi to Xikang to lead a guerrilla unit. After the outbreak of the Anti-Japanese War in 1937 he became political commissar of the CCP Military Region of Suiyuan-Inner Mongolia. In 1941 he commanded a guerrilla unit of the 120th Division, 8th Route Army. In 1947 he was political commissar of Shanxi-Suiyuan Military Region and secretary-general of the Joint Defense Army Headquarters for Shaanxi-Gansu-Ningxia-Suiyuan-Shanxi. After Chengdu had been occupied by the forces under He Long in December 1949, Li was appointed chairman of the Chengdu Military Commission.

1950,	Jan	Appointed deputy political commissar of Southwest China Military Region
	Mar	Appointed chairman of the West Sichuan Administrative Office
	May	Appointed member of the Southwest China Military and Administrative Council (until Jan 1953)
1952,	Aug	Appointed chairman of the People's Government of Sichuan (until 1955); secretary of Sichuan Province CP and political commissar of Sichuan Military Region (until Sep 1954)
1953,	Jan	Appointed member of the Southwest China Administrative Council (until Sep 1954)
1954,	Sep	Appointed political commissar of Chengdu Military Region (until Mar 1964)
1955,	Jan	Elected member of the People's Council of Sichuan Province and chairman of the Sichuan Section, CPPCC
1956,	Jul	Appointed 1st secretary of Sichuan Province CP (probably until May 1965)
	Sep	Elected member of the CCP Central Committee by the 8th Party Congress (until Cultural Revolution)
1958,	May	Elected member of the Politburo by the 5th Session of the 8th Central Committee (until Cultural Revolution)
1960,	Nov	Member of a CCP delegation under Liu

		Shaoqi to attend the anniversary of the October Revolution in Moscow
1961,	Oct	Identified as 1st secretary of the Southwest China Bureau of the CCP Central Committee (until Cultural Revolution)
1964,	Mar	Identified as 1st political commissar of Chengdu Military Region (until Cultural Revolution)
	Oct	Elected deputy for Sichuan Province to the 3rd NPC
1965,	Jan	Elected vice-chairman of the Standing Committee of the 3rd NPC (until Cultural Revolution)
1966-1967		Li is severely attacked during the Cultural Revolution. Having been initially accused of collaboration with He Long, he is publicly branded in June 1967 by 80,000 demonstrators as an anti-Party-element, antisocialist, opponent of Mao Zedong thought, governor of his own kingdom, and as a tyrant. As a result of this public stage trial he is relieved of all posts
1973,	Aug	Renewed election as member of the CCP Central Committee by the 10th Party Congress. This is also Li's first appearance after the Cultural Revolution with the withdrawal of all previous accusations and his complete rehabilitation
1975,	Jan	Elected vice-chairman, Standing Committee of the 4th NPC (confirmed in this post in 1978 by the 5th NPC)

Li is married to Xiao Li.

Li Jingzhao (Li Ching-chao)　李景昭

Posts held

Government
Vice-minister of the State Capital Construction Commission

1966,	Sep	Appointed vice-minister of building construction
1967		Disappears during the Cultural Revolution
1973,	Oct	First appearance after the Cultural Revolution
1978,	Apr	Identified as vice-minister of the State Capital Construction Commission
1979,	May	Head of a government friendship delegation to Zaire to attend the opening of the Palais du Peuple constructed with Chinese aid.

Li Jukui (Li Chü-k'uei)　李聚奎

Posts held

NPC
Member of the Standing Committee of the 5th NPC
Deputy for the PLA to the 5th NPC

Military
Colonel-general

Li was born in 1906 in Hunan Province. He is believed to have studied in Moscow around 1927. In July 1928 he took part in the Pingjiang Uprising organized by Peng Dehuai. Peng's forces joined the base set up by Mao Zedong in Jinggangshan in November 1928. During the Long March Li commanded the 1st Division of the 1st Front Army. In 1937 he served in the 129th Division of the 8th Route Army. He was operating with combat units in Shandong Province when in 1939 his troops were integrated into the 115th Division of the 8th Route Army. In 1949 Li was chief of staff of the 4th Field Army.

1951,	Feb	Identified as director of the Logistics Department of Northeast China Military Region
1955,	Jul	Appointed minister of petroleum industry (until Feb 1958)
	Sep	Promoted to rank of major-general
1958,	Mar	Identified as political commissar of the Logistics Department of the PLA (until Cultural Revolution)
1959,	Apr	Appointed member of the National Defense Council (until Cultural Revolution)
1964,	Oct	Elected deputy for the PLA to the 3rd NPC
1967,	Mar	Criticized as a follower of He Long and subsequently disappears
1974,	Jul	First appearance after the Cultural Revolution
1975,	Jan	Elected member of the Standing Committee by the 4th NPC (confirmed by the 5th NPC in 1978)
1978,	Feb	Elected deputy for the PLA to the 5th NPC

Li Kaixin (Li K'ai-hsin)

Posts held

Government
Director of the State Bureau of Supplies

NPC
Deputy for Tianjin Municipality to the 5th NPC

1956,	Nov	Identified as member of the State Economic Commission
1965,	Nov	Identified as vice-chairman of the State Economic Commission
1967,	Mar	Branded as a renegade and purged
1974,	Sep	First appearance after the Cultural Revolution: Identified as a cadre in the State Council
1976,	Oct	Identified as director of the State Bureau of Supplies
1978,	Feb	Elected deputy for Tianjin Municipality to the 5th NPC

Li Ke (Li K'e)

Posts held

Government
Vice-minister of economic relations with foreign countries

Li was born in 1920 in Anhui Province.

1960,	Jan	Appointed director of the Department for Economic Cooperation with Foreign Countries in the Main Office for Economic Relations with Foreign Countries
1964,	Jun	Appointed director of the Department for Economic Relations with Foreign Countries in the Commission for Economic Relations with Foreign Countries
1965,	Sep	Identified as director of the 3rd Department of the Commission for Economic Relations with Foreign Countries
1973,	May	Identified as vice-minister of economic relations with foreign countries
1977,	Dec	Head of an economic delegation to Kuwait
1978,	Jul	Head of an economic delegation to Zambia and Tanzania

Li Kechang (Li K'e-ch'ang)

Posts held

Provincial Administration
Vice-governor of Zhejiang Province

| 1979, | Dec | Elected vice-governor of Zhejiang Province |

Li Kuisheng (Li K'uei-sheng)

Posts held

Government
Vice-minister of coal industry
Member of the Patriotic Health Campaign Committee

1964,	Sep	Elected deputy for Heilongjiang Province to the 3rd NPC
1978,	Apr	Appointed member of the Patriotic Health Campaign Committee
	Jul	Identified as vice-minister of coal industry

Li Li (Li Li) 李 立

Posts held

Others
Member of the Standing Committee of the 5th CPPCC

Li was born in about 1916 in Ji'an, Jiangxi Province. In 1934-1935 he took part in the Long March. In 1936 he studied at the Anti-Japan Military and Political Academy. In 1947 he was deputy secretary of the Jilin Municipality CP. In 1949 he served as political commissar of the 142nd Division of the 48th Army.

1949,	Nov	Identified as a political commissar in a sub-district of Jiangxi Military District
1950,	Jan	Identified as secretary of Ji'an District CP, Jiangxi Province
1954,	Sep	Identified as secretary of Luoyang Municipality CP

1956,   Feb   Identified as 1st secretary of Luoyang Municipality CP

1958,   Nov   Identified as secretary of Henan Province CP (until 1964)

1963,   Sep   Identified as director of the Organization Department of the Central-South Bureau under the CCP Central Committee (until Cultural Revolution)

1965,   Feb   Identified as secretary of Guizhou Province CP (until Cultural Revolution)

         Jul   Elected governor of Guizhou Province (until Cultural Revolution)

1966,   Dec   Li is accused of being a follower of the Liu Shaoqi clique and forced to self-criticism

1967,   Dec   Li emerges after self-criticism

         Feb   Elected vice-chairman of the Revolutionary Committee of Guizhou Province (until 1977)

1969,   Apr   Elected alternate member of the CCP Central Committee by the 9th Party Congress (until 1973)

1971,   May   Elected deputy secretary of Guizhou Province CP (until 1977)

1977,   May   Li disappears for unknown reasons, probably because there are evidences for his close relations to the "Gang of Four"

1979,   Jul   By-elected member of the Standing Committee of the 5th CPPCC

Li Li (Li Li)   李 力

<u>Posts held</u>

Provincial Administration
Vice-chairman of the People's Government, Ningxia Autonomous Region

1974,   Sep   Identified as chairman of the Revolutionary Committee, National Institute of Minorities

1980,   Jan   Elected vice-chairman of the People's Government, Ningxia Autonomous Region

Li Li'an (Li Li-an)   李力安

<u>Posts held</u>

CCP
Secretary of Heilongjiang Province CP

NPC
Deputy for Heilongjiang Province to the 5th NPC

1959,   Nov   Identified as director of a section in the Finance and Commerce Department of the CCP Central Committee

1964,   Sep   Identified as deputy director of the Organization Department of the CCP Central Committee

1966,   Feb   Identified as secretary of Heilongjiang Province CP

         Jun   Li is attacked by Red Guards

1974,   Aug   First appearance after the Cultural Revolution: Identified as secretary of Heilongjiang Province CP

1978,   Feb   Elected deputy for Heilongjiang Province to the 5th NPC

Li Lianbi (Li Lien-pi)   李连壁

<u>Posts held</u>

Government
Ambassador to Congo (Brazzaville)

1953,   Jun   Elected member of the Federation of Democratic Youth

1962,   May   Identified as deputy director of the 2nd Asia Department in the Ministry of Foreign Affairs

         Oct   Identified as attaché at the embassy in Poland

1964,   Jul   Identified as counselor at the embassy in Poland (until about 1966)

1972,   May   Appointed ambassador to Belgium (until Feb 1976)

1973,   Dec   Appointed concurrently ambassador to Luxemburg (until Feb 1976)

1975,   Sep   Appointed concurrently ambassador to the European Community (until Feb 1976)

1976,   Aug   Appointed ambassador to Congo (Brazzaville)

Li Lianqing (Li Lien-ch'ing)   李连庆

<u>Posts held</u>

Government
Deputy director of the Central Broadcasting Administration

Others
Director of the China Central Television Station

1960,   Feb   Identified as 1st secretary, embassy in the German Democratic Republic

1967,   Feb   Identified as deputy director of the USSR and Eastern Europe Department in the Ministry of Foreign Affairs (until about 1971)

1973,   Apr   Identified as counselor at the embassy in Tokyo (until 1975)

1977,   Mar   Identified as deputy director of the Central Broadcasting Administration

1978,   Aug   Head of a radio and television broadcasting delegation to Sweden, the Federal Republic of Germany, and France

1979,   Aug   Identified as director of the China Central Television Station

Li Ligong (Li Li-kung)　　李立功

Posts held

CCP
Member of the Commission for Inspecting Discipline under the CCP Central Committee
Secretary of Beijing Municipality CP

Government
Member of the Birth Planning Leading Group under the State Council

1954,	Nov	Identified as member of the Communist Youth League Central Committee (until Cultural Revolution)
1966,	Jun	Identified as 1st secretary of Beijing Communist Youth League (until Cultural Revolution)
1967		Disappears during the Cultural Revolution
1977,	Dec	First appearance after the Cultural Revolution: Elected vice-chairman of the Revolutionary Committee of Beijing (until Dec 1979)
1978,	Jul	Appointed member of the Birth Planning Leading Group under the State Council
	Sep	Identified as secretary of Beijing Municipality CP
	Dec	Appointed member of the Commission for Inspecting Discipline under the CCP Central Committee

Li Lin (Li Lin) (f)　　里　林

Posts held

Provincial Administration
Vice-chairman of the People's Government, Guangxi Autonomous Region

1979,	Dec	Elected vice-chairman of the People's Government, Guangxi Autonomous Region

Li Linchuan (Li Lin-ch'uan)

Posts held

Government
Vice-minister of posts and telecommunications

1973,	Aug	Identified as director of the Department for Telecommunications under the Ministry of Posts and Telecommunications
1977,	Jun	Identified as director of the Directorate-General of Telecommunications under the Ministry of Posts and Telecommunications
1979,	Sep	Identified as vice-minister of posts and telecommunications

Li Linzhi (Li Lin-chih)　　李林枝

Posts held

NPC
Deputy for Sichuan Province to the 5th NPC

Provincial Administration
Vice-chairman of the People's Congress of Sichuan Province

1950,	Jul	Identified as member of the North Sichuan District Committee CP and as secretary of Suining District CP
1952,	Jan	Identified as council member of the Sichuan People's Government
1964,	Jul	Identified as 1st secretary of Suining District CP
1966,	Jan	Identified as vice-governor of Sichuan Province
1967		Disappears during the Cultural Revolution
1973,	Nov	First appearance after the Cultural Revolution: Identified as a cadre in Sichuan
1977,	Dec	Elected vice-chairman of the Revolutionary Committee of Sichuan (until Dec 1979)
1978,	Feb	Elected deputy for Sichuan Province to the 5th NPC
1979,	Dec	Elected vice-chairman of the People's Congress of Sichuan Province

Li Liyin (Li Li-yin)　　李力殷

Posts held

Government
Deputy director of the General Office of the State Council

Others
Member of the Standing Committee of the 5th CPPCC

1960,	Sep	Identified as counselor at the embassy in Burma
1963,	Oct	Identified as deputy director of the General Office of the Ministry of Foreign Affairs
1967		Disappears during the Cultural Revolution
1973,	Oct	First appearance after the Cultural Revolution: Identified as a cadre of the State Council
1978,	Mar	Elected member of the Standing Committee of the 5th CPPCC
	Oct	Identified as deputy director of the General Office of the State Council; member of a government delegation led by Deng Xiaoping to Japan
	Nov	Member of a delegation led by Deng Xiaoping to Thailand and Singapore

Li Maozhi (Li Mao-chih)　　李懋之

Posts held

Military
Deputy commander of the PLA Artillery

1977,	Sep	Identified as deputy commander of the PLA Artillery; member of a military delegation led by Yang Chengwu to France and Romania

Li Mengfu (Li Meng-fu)　李梦夫

Posts held

Government
Deputy director of the General Office of the State Council

NPC
Deputy for Beijing Municipality to the 5th NPC

1955,	Mar	Identified as deputy director of the State Bureau of Foreign Experts Administration
1956,	Nov	Identified as deputy director of the State Bureau of Foreign Experts Administration (until Jan 1961)
1961,	Jan	Identified as deputy director of the Government Offices Administration Bureau (until Apr 1963)
1963,	Apr	Identified as deputy director of the State Council Secretariat
1967,	Mar	Branded as a counterrevolutionary revisionist and purged
1972,	Mar	First appearance after the Cultural Revolution: Identified as a cadre of the State Council
1978,	Feb	Elected deputy for Beijing Municipality to the 5th NPC
	Jul	Identified as deputy director of the General Office of the State Council

Li Menghua (Li Meng-hua)　李梦华

Posts held

Government
Vice-minister of the Physical Culture and Sports Commission

NPC
Deputy for Tianjin Municipality to the 5th NPC

Others
Vice-president of the Sports Federation
President of the Weiqi Chess Association

1953,	Apr	Identified as director of the Southwest Office of the Youth Federation
	May	Identified as member of the New Democratic Youth League Central Committee
	Jun	Identified as member of the National Committee of the Youth Federation (until May 1957)
1955,	Jul	Head of a youth delegation to the 5th International Youth Festival in Warsaw
1956,	May	Identified as council member of the Sino-Pakistani Friendship Association
1957,	Jul	Deputy head of a youth delegation to the 6th International Youth Festival in Moscow
1958,	Mar	Appointed vice-chairman of the Youth Federation
1960,	Dec	Identified as vice-chairman of the Physical Culture and Sports Commission and as vice-chairman of the Athletic Association
1963,	Apr	Deputy head of a table tennis delegation to the 27th International Championship of Table Tennis in Prague
	Oct	Deputy head of a delegation to the 1st Games of New Emerging Forces (GANEFO) in Jakarta
1966,	Nov	Deputy head of a delegation to the 1st Asian GANEFO in Phnom Penh
1967,	Nov	Branded as a follower of He Long and purged
1973,	May	First appearance after the Cultural Revolution: Identified as a cadre of the State Council
	Oct	Head of a sports delegation to Japan
1977,	Jun	Head of a sports delegation to Romania
1978,	Feb	Elected deputy for Tianjin Municipality to the 5th NPC
	Jul	Identified as vice-minister of the Physical Culture and Sports Commission
	Oct	Identified as vice-president of the Sports Federation and as president of the Athletic Association (the latter post until Oct 1979)
	Nov	Identified as president of the Weiqi Chess Association
1979,	Jul	Appointed member of the National Games Organizing Committee
	Nov	Head of a sports delegation to Brazil and Venezuela

Li Ming (Li Ming)　黎　明

Posts held

NPC
Deputy for the PLA to the 5th NPC

Government
Deputy director-general of the General Administration of Civil Aviation

Li was born in Guangxi Province; he belongs to the Zhuang minority.

1949,	Dec	Identified as member of the Hainan Military and Administrative Council
1950,	Jul	Identified as council member of the Guangzhou Municipal People's Government
1952,	Jun	Identified as deputy commander of Liuzhou South District of Guangxi Military District
1954,	Aug	Elected deputy for Guangxi Province to the 1st NPC (reelected in 1958 and 1964 to the 2nd and 3rd NPCs)
1964,	Apr	Identified as deputy director-general of the General Administration of Civil Aviation
	May	Member of a goodwill delegation to Cambodia to inaugurate the direct aviation link between China and Cambodia
	Aug	Identified as vice-chairman of the Aviation Association
1967		Disappears during the Cultural Revolution
1978,	Feb	First appearance after the Cultural Revolution: Elected deputy for the PLA to the 5th NPC
	Apr	Identified as deputy director-general of the General Administration of Civil Aviation
	May	Deputy head of a goodwill delegation to Yugoslavia to inaugurate the direct aviation link between China and Yugoslavia

Li Peifu (Li P'ei-fu)   李培福

Posts held

Provincial Administration
Vice-chairman of the People's Congress of
Gansu Province

Li was born in 1912 in Sichuan Province. Around 1941 he
served as commander of the East Gansu Military District
of Shaanxi-Gansu-Ningxia Border Region.

1952		Identified as member of the Gansu Provincial People's Government
1953,	Nov	Identified as director of the Civil Affairs Department of Gansu People's Government
1954,	Dec	Identified as vice-governor of Gansu Province
1957,	Oct	Identified as alternate secretary of Gansu Province CP
1958,	Jun	Identified as deputy director of the Rural Work Department of Gansu Province CP
1967		Disappears during the Cultural Revolution
1977,	Dec	First appearance after the Cultural Revolution: Elected vice-chairman of the Revolutionary Committee of Gansu Province (until Dec 1979)
1979,	Dec	Elected vice-chairman of the People's Congress of Gansu Province

Li Pu (Li P'u)   李　普

Posts held

Government
Deputy director of XNA

1978,	Jun	Identified as deputy director of XNA
	Jul	Deputy head of a delegation of journalists visiting Yugoslavia and Romania

Li Qi (Li Ch'i)   李　琦

Posts held

Government
Vice-minister of education
Member of the Central Patriotic Health
Campaign Committee
Chairman of the National Commission of
the PRC for UNESCO

Others
Member of the Standing Committee of the
5th CPPCC
Vice-president of the Society of Education

Li was born in 1918 in Hebei Province.

1949,	Dec	Appointed advisor to the Government Administration Council
1955,	Apr	Appointed deputy director of the Premier's Office (until Apr 1958)
1957,	May	Identified as 1st secretary of Taiyuan Municipality CP (until 1961)
1963,	Dec	Appointed vice-minister of culture (until Cultural Revolution)

1965,	Jul	Head of a friendship delegation to Cuba
	Oct	Head of a cultural delegation to North Korea
1966,	Apr	Head of a cultural delegation to Congo (Brazzaville) and Guinea
	May	Elected vice-chairman of the Association for Cultural Relations and Friendship with Foreign Countries (until Cultural Revolution)
1967		With all other cadres in the field of culture Li is relieved of all posts and disappears
1973,	Apr	First appearance after the Cultural Revolution: Member of a Sino-Japanese Friendship Association delegation to Japan; referred to as a writer
	Jul	Identified as a cadre in the Science and Education Group under the State Council (until Jan 1975)
1975,	Mar	Identified as a cadre in the Ministry of Culture
1977,	Oct	Identified as vice-minister of education
1978,	Mar	Elected member of the Standing Committee of the 5th CPPCC
	Apr	Appointed member of the Central Patriotic Health Campaign Committee
	Jul	Head of a delegation of educationalists to the 4th UNESCO Regional Conference on Asia and Oceania in Sri Lanka
	Oct	Identified as vice-president of the Education Society; advisor to an educational delegation to the United States under Zhou Peiyuan; head of the Chinese delegation to the 20th Session of the UNESCO General Conference in Paris
1979,	Feb	Elected chairman of the National Commission of the PRC for the UNESCO
	Jul	Appointed member of the National Games Organizing Committee

Li Qiang (Li Ch'iang)   李　强

Posts held

CCP
Member of the CCP 11th Central Committee

Government
Minister of foreign trade

NPC
Deputy for Shanghai Municipality to the
5th NPC

Li was born in 1905 in Jiangsu Province. As a member of
the CCP, he was selected by the Party to study
broadcasting technology in 1929 after he had recently
graduated from university in a technical subject. His
further training took place in the French Concession of
Shanghai. There Li installed the first secret transmitter
for the CCP in 1930 using a specially equipped shop as a
cover. This transmitter established the first radio contact
between the Party center and its bases in North, South,
and Central China. During the same year the first training
course for radio operators was held in Shanghai, probably
under Li's supervision.

Following this nothing is known about Li for nearly two decades. He reappeared in 1948 when he was elected a member of the Executive Council of the Workers' Federation (predecessor of the trade unions). On this occasion it also became known that he had received training as a radio specialist at the Moscow Council for Posts and Telecommunications.

With the establishment of the PRC in October 1949 Li was immediately installed in a responsible technical position, being one of the few outstanding technical experts available.

1949,	Oct	Appointed director of the Telecommunications Bureau in the Ministry of Posts and Telecommunications and as director of the Broadcasting Bureau of the News Administration (latter being controlled by Beijing Radio)
1950,	Feb	Li as a member of the Party and government delegation under Mao Zedong and Zhou Enlai signs agreements on the establishment of postal and telecommunications links in Moscow; these are the first official agreements entered into by the government of PRC and the USSR
	Sep	Designated as PRC delegate to the Session of the International Telecommunications Union and the International Conference on High Frequency Radio Technology in Florence (for political reasons Li is prevented from participating)
	Jul	Identified as director of the Broadcasting Bureau in the Ministry of Posts and Telecommunications (until Aug 1952)
1952,	Aug	End of Li's career as a radio specialist; appointed vice-minister of foreign trade (until Oct 1973). In this capacity Li is posted to the Chinese embassy in Moscow as trade counselor (until 1955)
1955,	Jun	Appointed member of the Department of Technical Sciences, Academy of Sciences
	Dec	Head of a technical and scientific delegation to Moscow
1956,	Jun	Acting chairman of the Chinese section, Sino-Soviet Committee for Scientific and Technical Cooperation (active until 1959)
1959,	Jun	Appointed deputy secretary-general of the Scientific Planning Commission under the State Council (until Nov 1958)
	Aug	Identified as vice-chairman of the Electronics Society (until 1961); head of a trade delegation to Poland and Czechoslovakia
1960,	May	Head of a trade delegation to North Korea
	Jun	Head of a trade delegation to PR Mongolia
1961,	Mar	Deputy head of an economic delegation to the USSR
	Apr	Appointed deputy director of the Central Office for Economic Relations with Foreign Countries (raised to the status of a state council commission in Jun 1964)
1962,	Aug	Head of a trade delegation to the USSR
	Dec	Head of a trade delegation to Poland
1963,	Apr	Head of a trade delegation to the USSR
	Oct	Head of a trade delegation to North Korea and North Vietnam

1964,	Aug	Member of a Party and government delegation to Romania under Li Xiannian to attend the 15th Anniversary of Liberation
	Oct	Member of a Party and government delegation to the German Democratic Republic under Ulanhu to attend its 15th Anniversary; elected deputy for Anhui Province to the 3rd NPC
1965,	Mar	Appointed vice-chairman of the Commission for Economic Relations with Foreign Countries (the commission is made a ministry in Apr 1971)
	Apr	Head of a trade delegation to the USSR
	Dec	Head of a trade delegation to North Korea
1967,	Nov	Member of a Party and government delegation to Albania to attend the 25th Anniversary of Liberation
1969,	Apr	Elected to first term as member of the CCP Central Committee by the 9th Party Congress
1971,	Sep	Member of an economic delegation under Li Xiannian to North Vietnam
	Dec	Head of a trade delegation to North Korea
1973,	Jan	Identified as acting minister of foreign trade
	Oct	Identified as minister of foreign trade
1974,	Jan	Head of a trade delegation to Albania
	Nov	Head of a trade delegation to Iran
	Dec	Head of a trade delegation to Romania
1975,	Jan	Member of the Presidium of the 4th NPC; head of a trade delegation to Sri Lanka
	Feb	Head of a trade delegation to Pakistan
	Dec	Head of a trade delegation to Burma
1976,	Feb	Head of a trade delegation to Albania
	Mar	Head of a trade delegation to Kampuchea
1977,	Jan	Head of a trade delegation to Yugoslavia and Romania
	Nov	Head of a trade delegation to Great Britain and France
1978,	Feb	Elected deputy for Shanghai Municipality to the 15th NPC
	Mar	Head of a trade delegation to Egypt, Belgium, Luxembourg
	Apr	Head of a trade delegation to the European Community and the Federal Republic of Germany
	Oct	Head of a trade delegation to New Zealand and Australia
	Nov	Head of a trade delegation to Bangladesh
	Dec	Conferred the 1978 International Gold Mercury Prize for Individuals in acknowledgement of his contribution to the development of productivity and international cooperation; head of a trade delegation to the Philippines, Macao, and Hong Kong
1979,	Mar	Head of a trade delegation to Thailand, Malaysia, and Singapore
	Apr	Head of a trade delegation to The Netherlands, Denmark, and Ireland
	Jun	Vice-chairman of the Credentials Committee at the 2nd Session of the 5th NPC
	Oct	Head of a trade delegation to Canada and the U.S.A.
1980,	Jan	Friendship visit to Japan

Li is married to Wei Huandu.

Li Qiaoyun (Li Ch'iao-yün) (f) 李巧云

Posts held

CCP
Alternate member of the CCP 11th Central Committee

NPC
Deputy for Beijing Municipality to the 5th NPC

1977,	Aug	Elected alternate member of the CCP Central Committee by the 11th Party Congress
	Dec	Elected vice-chairman of the Revolutionary Committee of Beijing Municipality (until Nov 1979?)
1978,	Feb	Elected deputy for Beijing Municipality to the 5th NPC

Li Qiming (Li Ch'i-ming) 李敬明

Posts held

CCP
Member of the CCP 11th Central Committee
Standing secretary of Yunnan Province CP

Government
Member of the Birth Planning Leading Group under the State Council

Li was born in 1908 in Shanxi Province. In 1944 he was deputy director of the Public Security Department of Shaanxi-Gansu-Ningxia Border Government. In 1947 he was deputy director of the Social Work Department in the Northwest China Bureau of the CCP Central Committee.

1950,	Mar	Appointed deputy director of the Public Security Department, Northwest Military and Administrative Council (until Jan 1953)
1953,	Jan	Appointed director of the Public Security Department, Northwest Administrative Council
1956		Identified as member of the Standing Committee of Shaanxi Province CP (until Feb 1961)
1957,	Mar	Elected vice-governor of Shaanxi Province (until Dec 1963)
1961,	Feb	Elected secretary of Shaanxi Province CP (until May 1968)
1963,	Apr	Identified as acting governor of Shaanxi Province
	Dec	Elected governor of Shaanxi Province
1964,	Sep	Elected deputy for Shaanxi Province to the 3rd NPC
1968,	May	Attacked as a renegade, secret agent and capitalist-roader
1977,	Aug	First appearance after the Cultural Revolution: Elected member of the CCP Central Committee by the 11th Party Congress
	Sep	Identified as secretary of the CP, and vice-chairman of the Revolutionary Committee, of Yunnan Province (latter post until Dec 1977)
1978,	Sep	Identified as a member of the Birth

Planning Leading Group under the State Council

1979,	Sep	Elected standing secretary of Yunnan Province CP

Li Qin (Li Ch'in) (f) 李琴

Posts held

Government
Deputy editor-in-chief of XNA
Member of the Birth Planning Leading Group under the State Council

NPC
Deputy for Beijing Municipality to the 5th NPC

Mass Organization
Secretary of the Women's Federation

1974,	Sep	Identified as a cadre in a department of the CCP Central Committee
1977,	Mar	Identified as a cadre of XNA
1978,	Feb	Member of a Party delegation under Hua Guofeng to North Korea; elected deputy for Beijing Municipality to the 5th NPC
	Jul	Appointed member of the Birth Planning Leading Group under the State Council
	Sep	Elected secretary of the Women's Federation
1979,	Oct	Identified as deputy editor-in-chief of XNA

Li Qing (Li Ch'ing) 黎靖

Posts held

Government
Vice-minister of communications

1956,	Dec	Identified as director of the State Navigation Bureau
1973,	May	Identified as director of the Chinese Shipping Register
	Nov	Head of a delegation to the Inter-Governmental Maritime Consultative Conference in London
1975,	Jun	Identified as director of the State Bureau for Harbor Superintendency (until 1976)
1976,	Apr	Li disappears until November 1979
1979,	Nov	Identified as vice-minister of communications; head of a delegation to the 11th Assembly of the Inter-Governmental Maritime Consultative Organization

Li Qingchuan (Li Ch'ing-ch'uan) 李青川

Posts held

Government
Vice-minister of the Physical Culture and Sports Commission

1970,	Jun	Identified as a cadre of the Physical Culture and Sports Commission
1972,	Jun	Head of a sports delegation to Romania

1974,   Sep   Head of a sports delegation to Albania
1977,   Aug   Identified as vice-minister of the Physical Culture and Sports Commission
1979,   Jul   Appointed member of the National Games Organizing Committee
        Nov   Head of a sports delegation to Syria and Iraq

Li Qingkui (Li Ch'ing-k'uei)　李庆逵

Posts held

NPC
Deputy for Jiangsu Province to the 5th NPC

Others
President of the Society of Pedology

1959,   Mar   Elected deputy for Jiangsu Province to the 2nd NPC (reelected in 1964 to the 3rd NPC)
1962   Identified as chairman of the Society of Pedology
1965,   Mar   Deputy director of the Nanjing Institute of Pedology
        Oct   Member of a delegation of scientists to Cuba
1967   Disappears during the Cultural Revolution
1978,   Feb   First appearance after the Cultural Revolution: Elected deputy for Guangdong Province to the 5th NPC
        Jun   Identified as president of the Society of Pedology and as professor at Nanjing Institute of Pedology, Academy of Sciences; head of a delegation to the International Conference on Soil Science in Canada

Li Qingwei (Li Ch'ing-wei)　李庆伟

Posts held

CCP
Secretary of Henan Province CP

Provincial Administration
Vice-governor of Henan Province

1950,   Jul   Identified as member of Henan People's Government
1953,   Nov   Identified as member of the Federation of Supply and Marketing Cooperatives
1956,   Nov   Identified as vice-governor of Henan Province (until Cultural Revolution)
1965,   May   Identified as member of the Standing Committee of Henan Province CP
1967   Disappears during the Cultural Revolution
1975,   Oct   First appearance after the Cultural Revolution: Identified as member of the Standing Committee of Henan Province CP
1977,   Jan   Identified as director of the Agricultural Bureau, Revolutionary Committee of Henan Province
        Dec   Elected vice-chairman of the Revolutionary Committee of Henan Province (until Sep 1979)

1978,   Dec   Identified as deputy secretary of Henan Province CP (until Mar 1979)
1979,   Apr   Identified as secretary of Henan Province CP
        Sep   Elected vice-governor of Henan Province

Li Qitao (Li Ch'i-t'ao)　李琦涛

Posts held

Government
Vice-minister of education

1950,   Sep   Identified as member of the Executive Council of the Welfare Association
1952,   Jan   Identified as deputy secretary, Shanghai Section of the New Democratic Youth League, and as director of the Organization Department, Youth Work Department of Shanghai Municipality CP
1953,   Jul   Elected member of the Central Committee, New Democratic Youth League (until May 1957)
1955,   Feb   Elected council member of Shanghai People's Government
        May   Elected 1st secretary of the New Democratic Youth League, Shanghai Section
1956,   Aug   Elected chairman of the Federation of Democratic Youth, Shanghai Section (until Jul 1960)
1957,   May   Elected member of the Communist Youth League's Central Committee (successor of the New Democratic Youth League)
1959,   Nov   Head of a delegation of the Shanghai Communist Youth League to Leningrad
1960,   Mar   Elected secretary and member of the Standing Committee of the Communist Youth League
        Nov   Head of a Communist Youth League delegation to North Korea
1961,   Mar   Member of a guest delegation to the 3rd Congress of the Vietnamese Youth League
1962,   Aug   Head of a delegation to the 7th Conference of the International Student Union in Leningrad
1963,   Apr   Head of a youth delegation to Cuba
        Nov   Head of a youth delegation to Albania
1964,   Sep   Elected deputy for Anhui Province to the 3rd NPC
        Oct   Elected vice-chairman of the Commission for Cultural Relations with Foreign Countries
        Dec   Identified as acting secretary-general of the Sino-Soviet Friendship Association
1965,   May   Member of a delegation to Moscow to attend the 20th anniversary of victory over German Fascism
1966,   May   Head of a cultural delegation to Vietnam
1967   Attacked as an anti-Mao element during the Cultural Revolution
1977,   Jul   First appearance after the Cultural Revolution: Identified as a cadre in the Ministry of Education
        Oct   Identified as vice-minister of education

Li Qiyang (Li Ch'i-yang) (f)　　李屺阳

Posts held

Provincial Administration
Vice-governor of Gansu Province

1960,	Apr	Identified as secretary of Lanzhou Municipality CP
1964,	Sep	Elected deputy for Gansu Province to the 3rd NPC
1979,	Dec	Elected vice-governor of Gansu Province

Li Quanzhong (Li Ch'üan-chung)　李权中

Posts held

Government
Deputy manager-general of the China International Travel Service

1964,	Aug	Identified as deputy manager-general of the China International Travel Service
1965,	Dec	Appointed deputy director of the China Travel Administration
1971		Li disappears for unknown reasons
1977,	Feb	First reappearance
1978,	Jun	Identified as deputy manager-general of the China International Travel Service

Li Renjun (Li Jen-chün)　　李人俊

Posts held

Government
Vice-minister of the State Planning Commission

1949		Identified as member of the People's Government Council of Shandong Province and as director of its Department of Industry and Mines
1950,	Feb	Member of the Financial and Economic Affairs Committee in the East China Military and Administrative Council (until Jun 1954)
1952,	Aug	Appointed vice-minister of fuel industry (until Aug 1955)
1953,	Sep	Head of a delegation to Romania to discuss scientific and technical cooperation
1955,	Aug	Appointed vice-minister of petroleum industry (until Oct 1964)
1965,	Nov	Appointed minister of building construction (until Mar 1956)
1973,	Mar	First appearance after the Cultural Revolution
1974,	Nov	Identified as vice-minister of the Planning Commission
1978,	Jan	Advisor to a petroleum industry delegation to the United States and Japan

Li Renlin (Li Jen-lin)　　李人林

Posts held

Government
Vice-minister of the State Capital Construction Commission

NPC
Deputy for the PLA to the 5th NPC
Military
Director of the Capital Construction Engineering Corps

Li was born in 1918 as the son of a fisherman in Tianmen County, Anhui Province. At the age of 14 he joined the guerrilla force under He Long. In 1934-35 he took part in the Long March. From 1938 he served in the 5th Division of the New 4th Army, commanded by Li Xiannian.

1950,	Jan	Identified as secretary of Enshi District Committee CP
	Mar	Identified as council member of the People's Government of Hubei Province
1955,	Sep	Conferred the order of "Liberation," 1st class
1964,	Sep	Elected deputy for Hubei Province to the 3rd NPC
1966,	Apr	Identified as deputy director of the Industrial and Communication Political Department of the CCP Central Committee
1967,	Apr	Branded as a renegade and purged
1974,	May	First appearance after the Cultural Revolution
1977,	Jul	Identified as director of the Capital Construction Engineering Corps
1978,	Feb	Elected deputy for the PLA to the 5th NPC
	Jun	Identified as vice-minister of the State Capital Construction Commission

Li Renzhi (Li Jen-chih)　　李任之

Posts held

CCP
Member of the CCP 11th Central Committee
Secretary of Hubei Province CP
1st secretary of Wuhan Municipality CP

Others
Mayor of Wuhan Minicipality

In 1943 Li served as political commissar of a regiment of the New 4th Army which was operating in Anhui Province. In 1946 he was a Party cadre in Huaibei District under the Central China Bureau of the CCP.

1952,	Aug	Identified as secretary of Huainan Municipality CP and as head of the Huainan Mining Administration Bureau; identified as council member, People's Government of Anhui Province
1956,	Oct	Identified as secretary of Anhui Province CP, temporarily responsible for industry (until Cultural Revolution)

1964,	Sep	Elected vice-governor of Anhui Province (until Cultural Revolution)
1968,	Apr	Elected vice-chairman of the newly established Revolutionary Committee of Anhui Province (until Jan 1979)
1971,	Jan	With the establishment of the CP Secretariat of Anhui Province, Li is elected deputy secretary (until Jul 1973)
1973,	Jul	Identified as secretary of Anhui Province CP (until Jan 1979)
	Aug	Elected to first term as member of the CCP Central Committee by the 10th Party Congress
1977,	Sep	Head of a friendship delegation to North Korea
1978,	Feb	Deputy head of a coal industry study group visiting the Federal Republic of Germany
	Mar	Identified as secretary of Hubei Province CP and as 1st secretary of Wuhan Municipality CP
	Apr	Deputy head of a coal industry study group visiting Yugoslavia
1979,	Dec	Elected mayor of Wuhan Municipality

Li Rinai (Li Jih-nai)　　厉　日耐

Posts held

CCP
Alternate member of the CCP 11th Central Committee
Secretary of Shandong Province CP

Government
Member of the Birth Planning Leading Group under the State Council

1973,	Aug	Elected to first term as alternate member of the CCP Central Committee by the 10th Party Congress
1975,	Mar	Identified as secretary, CP of Lijiazhai Production Brigade of Dashan People's Commune in Junan County, Shandong Province (Mao Zedong quotation: "The village of Lijiazhai is a good example for the transformation of China in the spirit of Yugong who moved mountains")
	May	Elected vice-chairman of the Peasants' Federation of Shandong Province (no later mention in this post)
1977,	Jan	Identified as secretary of Shandong Province CP and as vice-chairman of the Revolutionary Committee of Shandong Province (until Dec 1979)
1978,	Jul	Identified as member of the Birth Planning Leading Group under the State Council

Li Rui (Li Jui)　　李　瑞

Posts held

Provincial Administration
Vice-governor of Heilongjiang Province

| 1960, | May | Identified as a member of the Standing Committee, Heilongjiang Province CP, |

and concurrently director of its Organization Department

1966,	Jan	Identified as alternate secretary of Heilongjiang Province CP
1967,	Jan	Li disappears
1979,	Dec	First appearance after the Cultural Revolution: Elected vice-governor of Heilongjiang Province

Li Rui (Li Jui)　　李　锐

Posts held

Government
Vice-minister of power industry

1950,	May	Identified as director of the News and Publications Bureau of the People's Government of Hunan Province
	Jul	Identified as member of the Land Reform Committee of Hunan People's Government
1955,	Nov	Identified as assistant minister of electric power (until Feb 1958) and as director of the General Bureau for Hydroelectric Construction of that ministry
1956,	Mar	Identified as member of the Yellow River Planning Commission under the State Planning Commission
	Jun	Identified as vice-president of the Hydro-engineering Society
1958,	Feb	Appointed assistant minister of water conservancy and electric power
	Aug	Appointed vice-minister of water conservancy and electric power (until Sep 1959)
1967,	May	Branded as anti-Party element and purged
1979,	Feb	First appearance after the Cultural Revolution: Identified as vice-minister of the 4th Ministry of Machine Building (until May 1979)
	May	Identified as vice-minister of power industry; member of a government delegation, led by Kang Shien, to the U.S.A.

Publications

1953-1954	The Early Revolutionary Activities of Comrade Mao Zedong
1956	The Harnessing and Development of the Yellow River
1956	Some Fundamental Problems Concerning the Total Utilization Plan for the Yellow River

Li Ruihuan (Li Jui-huan)　　李瑞环

Posts held

NPC
Member of the Standing Committee of the 5th NPC
Deputy for Beijing Municipality to the 5th NPC

Li was born in 1935.

| 1973, | Apr | Identified as vice-chairman of the Beijing Trade Union |

1977,	Apr	Identified as director-general of the Work Site for the Mao Zedong Memorial Hall in Beijing
1978,	Feb	Elected deputy for Beijing Municipality to the 5th NPC
	Mar	Elected member of the Standing Committee of the 5th NPC
	Jun	Member of an NPC delegation led by Ji Pengfei to Venezuela, Mexico, and Canada
1979,	Apr	Li is named a national model worker

 **Li Ruishan** (Li Jui-shan)   李瑞山

Posts held

CCP
Member of the CCP 11th Central Committee

Government
Vice-minister of the State Agricultural Commission

NPC
Deputy for Shaanxi Province to the 5th NPC

1954,	Jun	Appointed deputy director of the Financial and Economic Affairs Committee of Hunan People's Government as well as director of the Rural Work Department of Hunan Province CP
1955,	Sep	Identified as deputy secretary of Hunan Province CP
1956,	Sep	Elected secretary of Hunan Province CP
1958,	Jan	Identified as deputy secretary of Hunan Province CP
	May	Identified as secretary of Hunan Province CP (until Cultural Revolution)
1959,	Aug	Identified as 1st secretary of Changsha Municipality CP (until Cultural Revolution)
1968,	May	Elected chairman of the newly established Revolutionary Committee of Shaanxi Province (until Dec 1978)
1969,	Apr	Elected to first term as member of the CCP Central Committee by the 9th Party Congress
	Oct	Identified as 1st political commissar of Shaanxi Military District (until Dec 1978)
1970,	Jun	Identified as political commissar of Lanzhou Military Region (until Dec 1978)
1971,	Mar	Elected 1st secretary of Shaanxi Province CP (until Dec 1978)
1978,	Jun	Identified as principal of the Shaanxi Party School (until Dec 1978)
1979,	Apr	Identified as vice-minister of the State Agricultural Commission
	May	Advisor of an agricultural delegation, headed by Wang Feng, to the U.S.A.
	Jun	Member of the Budget Committee at the 2nd Session of the 5th NPC

Li Shanyi (Li Shan-yi)   李善一

Posts held

Government
Former ambassador to Cuba

1969,	Aug	Identified as chargé d'affaires ad interim in Cuba (until 1971)
1972,	May	Identified as chargé d'affaires ad interim in Mexico
1973,	Jun	Identified as counselor at the embassy in Mexico (until 1974)
1975,	Jun	Identified as ambassador to Cuba (until Apr 1979)

Li Shaoyu (Li Shao-yü)   李绍禹

Posts held

Government
Vice-president of the People's Bank

1951,	Jan	Identified as member of the Economic Committee, People's Government of Henan Province, and as director of Henan People's Bank
1952,	Aug	Identified as manager-general, Central-South Branch of the Bank of China
1955,	Aug	Identified as director, Commercial Credit Bureau of the Bank of China
1956,	Jul	Identified as manager-general of the Agricultural Bank of China
1957,	Aug	Identified as assistant to the director of the People's Bank
1961,	Mar	Identified as deputy manager-general of Bank of China
	Apr	Appointed vice-president of the People's Bank
1963,	Feb	Head of a delegation to the Conference of the Ministers of Finance of the Socialist Countries in Prague
1966		Li disappears
1979,	Jun	First appearance after the Cultural Revolution: Identified as vice-president of the People's Bank; deputy head of a People's Bank delegation to Yugoslavia and Sweden

Li Shi (Li Shih)   李石

Posts held

Government
Ambassador to the Central African Republic

1953,	Dec	Identified as 1st secretary at the embassy in North Korea (until 1954)
1959,	Jun	Appointed counselor at the embassy in Sudan (until about 1963)
1973,	Aug	Identified as chargé d'affaires ad interim in Kenya
1976,	Nov	Appointed ambassador to the Central African Republic

Li Shiji (Li Shih-chi) (f)   李世济

Posts held

Others
Member of the Standing Committee of the 5th CPPCC

1978,	Feb	Delegate to the 5th CPPCC representing the Literary and Art Circles
	Mar	Elected member of the Standing Committee of the 5th CPPCC

Li Shijun (Li Shih-chün)   李世俊

Posts held

CCP
Member of the CCP 11th Central Committee

1950		Li holds a post in a district committee under the South China Bureau of the CCP Central Committee
1951		Identified as director of the Plant Pest Control Department in the Ministry of Agriculture
1952,	Dec	Member of a delegation led by Qian Sanqiang to the Academy of Sciences in the USSR
1953,	Sep	Identified as director of the General Administration Bureau of Agriculture in the Ministry of Agriculture
1955,	Mar	Member of a delegation to the Asian Conference in India
1957		Identified as president of the Southwest Agricultural College; subsequently disappears
1977,	Aug	Elected member of the CCP Central Committee by the 11th Party Congress

Li Shinong (Li Shih-nung)   李世农

Posts held

CCP
Secretary of Anhui Province CP

NPC
Deputy for Anhui Province to the 5th NPC

Provincial Administration
Vice-chairman of the People's Congress, Anhui Province

Li was born about 1916 as the son of a rich peasant's family. After criticisms for "escapism" in 1944 and 1947 he disappeared from the communist scene.

1950,	Jan	Identified as deputy secretary of North Anhui Province District CP
	Mar	Identified as a member of the People's Control Committee under the East China Military and Administrative Council (until Jun 1954)
1953		Identified as director of the Organization Department of Anhui Province CP
1955,	Mar	Identified as vice-governor of Anhui Province
1956,	Jan	Identified as deputy secretary of Anhui Province CP
1957,	May	Identified as secretary of Anhui Province CP
1958,	Jan	Expelled from all positions after having been referred to as an anti-Party rightist
1963,	Mar	Identified in his former position as secretary of Anhui Province CP

1967,	Jan	Again expelled from his Party position
1978,	Feb	First appearance after the Cultural Revolution: Elected deputy for Anhui Province to the 5th NPC
1979,	Feb	Identified as 1st secretary of the Committee for Inspecting Discipline under the Anhui Province CP
	Apr	Identified as secretary of Anhui Province CP
	Dec	Elected vice-chairman of the People's Congress, Anhui Province

Li Shiying (Li Shi-ying)   李士英

Posts held

Others
Deputy chief procurator of the Supreme People's Procuratorate

Li was born in Henan Province. In June 1949 he was director of the Public Security Bureau, People's Government of Shanghai Municipality.

1949,	Oct	Appointed member of the Supreme People's Procuratorate
1950,	Feb	Identified as director of the Public Security Department under the East China Military and Administrative Council
1953,	Dec	Identified as vice-governor of Shandong Province (until Feb 1955)
1955,	Aug	Identified as deputy chief of the Supreme People's Procuratorate (until Sep 1962)
1958,	Aug	Identified as secretary of the Political Science and Law Society
1961		Identified as a member of the Standing Committee of the Control Committee under the CCP Central Committee (until 1963)
1962,	Jan	Identified as vice-governor of Jiangsu Province (until Cultural Revolution)
	Apr	Identified as secretary of Jiangsu Province CP (until Cultural Revolution)
1964,	Sep	Elected deputy for Jiangsu Province to the 3rd NPC
1966,	Oct	Li disappears
1978,	Dec	First appearance after the Cultural Revolution: Appointed deputy chief procurator of the Supreme People's Procuratorate

Li Shizhang (Li Shih-chang)   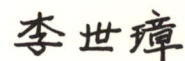

Posts held

NPC
Deputy for Jiangxi Province to the 5th NPC

Provincial Administration
Vice-governor of Jiangsu Province

Others
Member of the Standing Committee of the 5th CPPCC

Vice-chairman of the Central Committee, Revolutionary Committee of the Chinese KMT

Li was born in Henan Province. In September 1949 he took part in the 1st CPPCC as a delegate representing the Three People's Principles Comrades Association.

1949,	Dec	Identified as secretary-general of the People's Control Commission of the Government Administration Council
1950,	Mar	Identified as member of the Central Committee, KMT Revolutionary Committee
1954,	Aug	Elected deputy for Henan Province to the 1st NPC (confirmed in 1964 by the 2nd NPC)
	Oct	Appointed vice-minister of supervision (until 1959)
1956,	Feb	Elected member of the Standing Committee of the KMT Revolutionary Committee
1959,	Sep	Identified as vice-governor of Jiangxi Province (until Cultural Revolution)
1964,	Oct	Elected deputy for Jiangxi Province to the 3rd NPC
1967		Disappears during the Cultural Revolution
1978,	Feb	First appearance after the Cultural Revolution: Elected deputy for Jiangxi Province to the 5th NPC
	Mar	Elected member of the Standing Committee of the 5th CPPCC
1979,	Oct	Elected vice-chairman of the Central Committee, Revolutionary Committee of the Chinese KMT
	Dec	Elected vice-governor of Jiangsu Province

Li Shoubao (Li Shou-pao) 李超伯

Posts held

Others
Vice-chairman of the Youth Federation

1962,	Jul	Member of a Peace Council delegation to Moscow
1963,	Sep	Member of a Red Cross delegation to Poland
1964,	Jul	Member of a delegation to the 10th World Conference against Atomic Bombs in Japan
1979,	May	Elected vice-chairman of the Youth Federation

Li Shoulin (Li Shou-lin) 李守林

Posts held

CCP
Alternate member of the CCP 11th Central Committee

1964,	Sep	Elected deputy for Shaanxi Province to the 3rd NPC
1969,	Apr	Elected to first term as alternate member of the CCP Central Committee by the 9th Party Congress (confirmed in 1973 and 1977 by the 10th and 11th Congresses)

Li Shu (Li Shu) 黎澍

Posts held

Others
Chief editor of Lishi Yanjiu (Historical Studies)
Deputy director of the Institute of Modern History, Academy of Social Sciences
Editor of the bi-monthly Zhongguo Shehui Kexue (Social Science in China)

Li was born in 1918.

1961,	Jan	Identified as managing editor of Lishi Yanjiu (Historical Studies)
	Dec	Identified as deputy director of the Institute of Modern History, Academy of Sciences
1966,	Oct	Accused as a follower of Zhou Yang and purged
1978,	May	Identified as chief editor of Lishi Yanjiu (Historical Studies)
1979,	Apr	Identified as deputy director of the Institute of Modern History under the Academy of Social Sciences
	Dec	Identified as editor of the bi-monthly Zhongguo Shehui Kexue (Social Science in China)

Li Shubin (Li Shu-pin) 栗树彬

Posts held

CCP
Secretary-general, Propaganda Department of the CCP Central Committee

Mass Organization
Secretary of the Federation of Trade Unions

1960,	Jun	Identified as chairman of the Mountaineering Association
1962,	Apr	Identified as member of the Executive Council of the Federation of Trade Unions and as director of the Sports Department, Executive Council of the Federation of Trade Unions; head of a trade union delegation to Hungary
1965,	Sep	Identified as vice-chairman of the Trade Union of Light Industry; head of a trade union delegation to Czechoslovakia and Poland
	Dec	By-elected deputy for Shandong Province to the 3rd NPC
1966,	May	Head of a trade union delegation to Romania
	Aug	Identified as secretary of the Federation of Trade Unions; subsequently disappears
1978,	Apr	First appearance after the Cultural Revolution: Identified as secretary of the Federation of Trade Unions
	Aug	Identified as secretary-general, Propaganda Department of the CCP Central Committee

Li Shude (Li Shu-te) 李树德

Posts held

Government
Chargé d'affaires ad interim in Belgium, Luxembourg, and the European Community

1954,	Jun	Member of a trade delegation to Great Britain
1959,	Sep	Identified as director of the Agricultural Customs Administration under the Ministry of Finance
1960,	Nov	Identified as vice-minister of finance (until Oct 1962)
1961,	Feb	Deputy head of a trade delegation to Finland
1977,	Jul	First appearance after the Cultural Revolution: Identified as commercial counselor to the Chinese embassy at the European Community
1978,	Mar	Identified as chargé d'affaires ad interim at the embassy in Belgium
	Apr	Identified as chargé d'affaires ad interim at the embassy in Luxembourg
	May	Identified as chargé d'affaires ad interim at the European Community

Li Shuiqing (Li Shui-ch'ing) 李水清

Posts held

CCP
Member of the CCP 11th Central Committee

Government
Vice-minister of communications

Military
Major-general

Li was born in 1905. In 1942 he served as political commissar of a military subdistrict near Beijing. In 1948 he commanded the 199th Division of the 20th Army Group. In March 1949 this unit belonged to the forces which occupied Taiyuan, the provincial capital of Shanxi.

1951		Li is posted to Korea with his unit to serve with the Chinese People's Volunteers
1952		Appointed chief of staff of the 67th Corps
1954		Appointed deputy commander of the 67th Corps
1957		Appointed commander of the 67th Corps and commander of Qingdao Garrison; identified as major-general
1958		Li serves as a private in a detachment
1961,	Mar	Identified as commander of the 67th Army
1968,	Feb	Identified as deputy commander of Jinan Military Region
1969,	Apr	Elected to first term as member of the CCP Central Committee by the 9th Party Congress
1970,	Jan	Identified as a leading cadre in the Revolutionary Committee of Shandong Province and as military leader in Jinan Military Region (until Mar 1971)

1971,	Mar	Identified as minister of the 1st Ministry of Machine Building (until 1976)
	Jun	Head of a government delegation to Romania
	Dec	Head of a government delegation to Pakistan
1972,	Jun	Head of a government and military delegation to Algeria
	Aug	Head of a government delegation to Sweden, Norway, and Finland
1974,	Oct	Head of a government delegation to Algeria
1976,	Jul	Identified as deputy commander of Nanjing Military Region (until 1977?)
1979,	Oct	Identified as vice-minister of communications; head of a government delegation to the 11th Conference of the Inter-governmental Maritime Consultative Organization (I.M.C.O.)

Li Shuying (Li Shu-ying) (f) 李淑英

Posts held

NPC
Deputy for Hebei Province to the 5th NPC

Others
Member of the Standing Committee of the 5th CPPCC

1953,	Apr	Identified as member of the Executive Council of the Democratic Women's Federation (until Cultural Revolution)
	May	Identified as member of the Executive Council of the Federation of Trade Unions (until Dec 1957)
1957,	Dec	Elected alternate member of the Executive Council, Federation of Trade Unions (until Cultural Revolution)
1959,	Aug	Identified as vice-chairman of the Trade Union of Light Industry Workers (until Cultural Revolution)
1962,	Dec	Identified as council member of the Sino-Cuban Friendship Association
1965,	Jan	Elected member of the Standing Committee of the 4th CPPCC (confirmed in 1978 by the 5th CPPCC)
	Jul	Head of a trade union delegation to Japan
1973,	Oct	Reactivated after the Cultural Revolution
1978,	Feb	Elected deputy for Hebei Province to the 5th NPC

Li Shuzheng (Li Shu-cheng) (f) 李淑铮

Posts held

Mass Organization
Secretary of the Women's Federation

1961,	May	Member of a youth delegation to Ecuador
1962,	Aug	Member of a youth delegation attending the World Youth Festival in Helsinki
	Oct	Identified as deputy director of the Foreign Relations Department of the Communist Youth League

1964,   Jul   Elected alternate secretary of the Communist Youth League
        Nov   Head of a student delegation to Bulgaria
1967   Disappears during the Cultural Revolution
1978,   Sep   First appearance after the Cultural Revolution: Elected secretary of the Women's Federation

Li Su (Li Su)   李 苏

Posts held

Others
Deputy secretary-general of the Academy of Sciences

1959,   Jan   Appointed director of the College of Chemistry in Beijing
1960,   Jul   Appointed vice-minister of chemical industry
1962,   Jul   Head of a scientific and technical delegation to Hungary
1967,   Nov   Head of a scientific and technical delegation to North Korea
1978,   Jun   Identified as deputy secretary-general of the Academy of Sciences
        Oct   Member of a government delegation to the Federal Republic of Germany and France under Fang Yi

Li Tao (Li T'ao)   李 涛

Posts held

Government
Vice-minister of textile industry

1950,   May   Identified as deputy secretary of Shenyang Municipality CP
        Oct   Identified as director of the Department of Agriculture and Forestry of Liaodong Province
1952,   Jun   Identified as chairman of Liaodong Province
1954,   Aug   Elected deputy for Liaodong Province to the 1st NPC; identified as vice-chairman of Liaoning Province
1955,   Feb   Identified as secretary of Liaoning Province CP (until Oct 1958)
1958,   Jun   Li is accused as a supporter of the anti-Party clique around Wang Zheng and relieved of his posts
1977,   Nov   First appearance after the Cultural Revolution
1979,   Apr   Identified as vice-minister of textile industry

Note

It cannot be ruled out that the dates up to 1958 and those after, respectively, belong to two different persons.

Li Tianxiang (Li T'ien-hsiang)   李 天 相

Posts held

Government
Vice-minister of petroleum industry

Others
Deputy general manager of the China National Petroleum Corporation

Li is a college graduate who received his training after 1949. He is noted for his successes in developing China's petroleum mining industry and improving petroleum technology and equipment, particularly drilling chisels.

1978,   Sep   Identified as vice-minister of petroleum industry
        Nov   Identified as deputy general manager of the China National Petroleum Corporation

Li Tiezheng (Li T'ieh-cheng)   李 铁 铮

Posts held

Others
Member of the Standing Committee of the 5th CPPCC

1979,   Jul   By-elected member of the Standing Committee of the 5th CPPCC

Li Tinggui (Li T'ing-kuei)   李 庭 桂

Posts held

CCP
Deputy secretary of Guizhou Province CP

NPC
Deputy for Guizhou Province to the 5th NPC

Provincial Administration
Vice-governor of Guizhou Province

1958,   Aug   Identified as director of the Finance and Commerce Department of Guizhou Province CP
1966,   Aug   Identified as member of the Standing Committee of Guizhou Province CP
1967,   Jan   Li is relieved of his posts
1973,   Dec   First appearance after the Cultural Revolution: Identified as a cadre in Guizhou
1975,   Apr   Identified as member of the Standing Committee of Guizhou Province CP (until Mar 1978)
1977,   Jan   Identified as vice-chairman of the Revolutionary Committee of Guizhou Province (until Jan 1980)
1978,   Feb   Elected deputy for Guizhou Province to the 5th NPC
        Apr   Elected deputy secretary of Guizhou Province CP
1979,   Jun   Member of the Budget Committee at the 2nd Session of the 5th NPC
1980,   Jan   Elected vice-governor of Guizhou Province

Li Tingquan (Li T'ing-ch'üan)

Posts held

Government
Ambassador to Czechoslovakia

1967,	Nov	Identified as chargé d'affaires ad interim in Albania
1969,	May	Identified as counselor at the embassy in Albania (until Dec 1970)
1971,	Nov	Identified as deputy director of the USSR and Eastern Europe Department in the Ministry of Foreign Affairs
1972,	Nov	Identified as acting director of the USSR and Eastern Europe Department in the Ministry of Foreign Affairs
1973,	Aug	Appointed ambassador to Romania (until Nov 1978)
1978,	May	Li accompanies Party head Ceausescu on his tour of China
1979,	Jun	Appointed ambassador to Czechoslovakia

Li is married to Wang Yixian.

Li Tingzan (Li T'ing-tsan)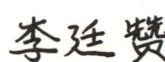

Posts held

Government
Deputy director of the State Bureau of Surveying and Cartography

Others
President of the Surveying and Cartographic Society

1959,	Sep	Identified as deputy director of the State Bureau of Surveying and Cartography (until Aug 1960)
1960,	Aug	Appointed director of the State Bureau of Surveying and Cartography (until Oct 1962)
1962,	Oct	Appointed deputy director of the State Bureau of Surveying and Cartography
1963		Identified as president of the Society of Surveying and Cartography; subsequently disappears
1979,	Jul	First appearance after the Cultural Revolution; identified as deputy director of the State Bureau of Surveying and Cartography and as president of the Society of Surveying and Cartography

Li Weihan (Li Wei-han)

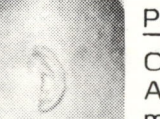

Posts held

CCP
Advisor to the United Front Work Department under the CCP Central Committee

Others
Vice-chairman of the Standing Committee of the 5th CPPCC

Li was born in 1896 near Liling, Hunan Province. At the age of 20 he joined the "Study Society" established by Mao Zedong and Cai Hesen in Changsha. In 1920 he went to France as a worker-student and there he was one of the cofounders of the French Section of the CCP in 1922. Following his return to China shortly afterwards he became a close supporter of Mao Zedong. He joined the CCP in 1923. In May 1927 a serious quarrel arose between the two men when Li in his capacity as secretary of Hunan Province CP withdrew the Communist troops, under orders to attack Changsha, at the approach of the KMT forces. Although he was criticized by the 8th CCP Congress in 1928, it nevertheless elected him an alternate member of the CCP Central Committee. During the years 1928-1930 he was engaged in underground work in Shanghai and later moved to the Jiangxi-Soviet where he probably established close contact to the Moscow Group within the CCP. In 1934-35 Li took part in the Long March as a commander and political commissar of a column of the Red Army. He was head of the Party School in Yan'an from 1937 to 1939. From 1944 until about March 1965 he was in charge of the United Front Work Department of the CCP Central Committee. In January 1946 he was a member of the Communist delegation led by Zhou Enlai to the Political Consultative Conference in Chongqing. In September 1949 he was one of the chief organizers of the CPPCC.

1949,	Oct	Appointed secretary-general of the Government Administration Council, member of the Political and Legal Affairs Committee, chairman of the Minorities Affairs Committee, and one of the leading cadres of the Sino-Soviet Friendship Association
1951,	May	Li signs the Tibet Agreement
1954,	Oct	Appointed director of the 8th Staff Office under the State Council (until Sep 1959), elected deputy for Hunan Province to the 1st NPC Congress (until Oct 1964), and vice-chairman of the Standing Committee of the NPC (until Dec 1964)
1956,	Sep	Elected member of the CCP Central Committee by the 8th Party Congress
1964,	Oct	Elected deputy for Xinjiang Autonomous Region to the 3rd NPC
1967,	Jun	Branded as a counterrevolutionary revisionist and purged
1978,	Feb	First appearance after the Cultural Revolution
	Mar	Elected member of the Standing Committee of the 5th CPPCC (until Jul 1979)
1979,	Mar	Identified as advisor to the United Front Work Department under the CCP Central Committee
	Jul	By-elected vice-chairman of the 5th CPPCC

Li Wenjie (Li Wen-chieh)

Posts held

Others
Director of the Board of Directors, China International Trust and Investment Corporation
Member of the Central Committee, China Democratic National Construction Association

1961,	Nov	Identified as vice-mayor of Tianjin Municipality

1979,	Oct	First appearance after the Cultural Revolution: Appointed director of the Board of Directors, China International Trust and Investment Corporation; appointed member of the Central Committee, China Democratic National Construction Association

Li Wenqing (Li Wen-ch'ing) 李文清

Posts held

Military
Major-general
Deputy commander, Chengdu Military Region

Li is a native of Songzi, Hubei Province. In 1930 he served in the 11th Regiment of the 2nd Front Army. Two years later he commanded the 15th Regiment of the 5th Division under the same army. In 1937 he was chief of staff of a regiment in the 120th Division of the 8th Route Army. In 1945 he commanded the 3rd Brigade of the 120th Division. In spring 1949 he became chief of staff of the 3rd Army.

1950		Identified as deputy commander of the North Sichuan Military Subdistrict
1958,	Jan	Identified as deputy commander of Chengdu Military Region and as major-general
1965,	Dec	Identified as commander of Sichuan Military District
1967,	Apr	Li is seriously wounded during the fights with Red Guards in Chengdu and disappears
1976,	Oct	First appearance after the Cultural Revolution
1978,	Sep	Identified as a military cadre in Chengdu
1980,	Feb	Identified as deputy commander, Chengdu Military Region

Li Wenyao (Li Wen-yao) 李文耀

Posts held

Others
President of the Athletics Association

1957,	May	Elected member of the Central Committee of the Communist Youth League (CYL)
1962,	Oct	Identified as a member of the Standing Committee of the Athletics Association and as vice-chairman of the Table Tennis Association
1964,	Jul	Elected member of the Standing Committee, Central Committee of the CYL
	Aug	Member of a CYL delegation to Indonesia
1965,	Jan	Elected vice-chairman of the Youth Federation
	Jun	Head of a youth delegation to Mali
	Nov	Head of a table tennis team to Sweden

1966,	Apr	Head of a table tennis team to Czechoslovakia and Syria
	Jun	Head of a youth delegation to Bulgaria
	Nov	Li disappears
1978,	May	First appearance after the Cultural Revolution
	Sep	Head of a weight-lifting group sent to the U.S.A.
	Dec	Deputy head of a sports delegation to the 8th Asian Games in Bangkok
1979,	Oct	Identified as president of the Athletics Association

Li Wenyi (Li Wen-yi) (f) 李文宜

Posts held

Others
Member and deputy secretary-general of the Standing Committee of the 5th CPPCC
Vice-chairman of the Central Committee, China Democratic League

Li was born in 1902 in Xiakou, Hubei Province. Since about 1940 she served as secretary of Procuracy at the Yunnan Provincial High Court and during this period also established the Yunnan Provincial Women's Federation. In 1945 she was elected a member of the Executive Committee of the China Democratic League. In 1947 she joined the Communists. In March 1949 she was elected a member of the Standing Committee of the Federation of Democratic Women. She represented this federation as a delegate at the 1st CPPCC in September 1949.

1949,	Oct	Elected member of the Standing Committee of the Sino-Soviet Friendship Association
	Dec	Member of a delegation to the Conference of the International Federation of Democratic Women in Hungary; identified as deputy director of the Administrative Office of the Ministry of Labor
1954,	Aug	Elected deputy for Hubei Province to the 1st NPC (reelected in 1958 and 1964 to the 2nd and 3rd NPCs)
1956,	Feb	Elected member of the Standing Committee of the China Democratic League
1959,	Apr	Elected member of the 3rd CPPCC
1961,	Jun	Identified as acting secretary-general of the Democratic League
1967		Disappears during the Cultural Revolution
1973,	Mar	First appearance after the Cultural Revolution
1978,	Mar	Elected member of the Standing Committee of the 5th CPPCC
	Aug	Identified as deputy secretary-general of the 5th CPPCC
1979,	Oct	Elected vice-chairman of the Central Committee of the China Democratic League

Li Xiannian (Li Hsien-nien)　　李先念

<u>Posts held</u>

CCP
Vice-chairman of the 11th CCP Central Committee
Member of the Standing Committee, Politburo of the 11th CCP Central Committee
Member of the Politburo of the 11th CCP Central Committee
Member of the CCP Central Committee

Government
Vice-premier
Vice-chairman of the State Financial and Economic Commission

NPC
Deputy for Hubei Province to the 5th NPC

Military
Army general

Others
Chairman of the Central Patriotic Health Campaign Committee

Li was born in 1905 (1906?) as the son of poor peasants in Hong'an (Huang'an) County, Hubei Province. As a young man he was trained as a carpenter. In 1926 he joined the KMT forces on their Northern Expedition when they reached his native province. After the rift between the KMT and the CCP in 1927 he joined the CCP. He first distinguished himself as a Communist Party worker during the following years when he established a Soviet in Hubei of which he became chairman. During the Long March he served as army captain and political commissar in a number of smaller units of the Communist Army. In 1936 the units under his command were defeated in Gansu Province. He again appeared in 1939 in his native province of Hubei as commander of a strong guerrilla force. In 1941 he commanded 60,000 men, and in that year his troops were integrated into the New 4th Army to form the 5th Division. Around 1944 Li was made commander of Central China Military Region. In 1945 the 7th CCP Congress elected Li to his first term as a member of the Central Committee. With the exception of a short period of service as a troop commander in North China, Li operated in Central China after the Japanese capitulation, eventually as deputy commander of the 4th Field Army. After his troops had occupied Wuhan in 1949 Li was made chairman of the Provincial Government of Hubei.

1949, Oct Appointed member of the Revolutionary Military Council (until Sep 1954) and of the Central-South China Military and Administrative Council (until Dec 1952)

1952   Appointed mayor of Wuhan (until 1954)

      Dec Appointed member of the Central-South China Administrative Council (until Sep 1954)

1954, Sep Appointed vice-premier and member of the National Defense Council; elected deputy for Hubei Province to the 1st NPC; appointed army-general

      Nov Head of a delegation to Albania to attend the 10th Anniversary of Liberation. In Tirana he signs a credit and trade agreement with Albania

1956, Jul Head of a delegation to Ulan Bator to attend the 35th Anniversary of the Mongolian Revolution

      Sep Elected member of the Politburo by the 8th CCP Congress

1957, Jun Appointed minister of finance (until Jan 1975?)

      Oct Member of a delegation under Mao Zedong to conduct negotiations in Moscow

      Nov Head of the Chinese delegation to the funeral ceremonies for the Czech cadre Zapotozki

1958, May Elected member of the CCP Central Committee Secretariat at the 2nd Session of the 8th CCP Central Committee (until Cultural Revolution)

1959, Sep Appointed director of the Financial and Economic Affairs Bureau in the State Council (until Cultural Revolution)

1961, Feb Head of a CCP delegation to Albania

1962, Nov Appointed vice-chairman of the State Planning Commission (until 1972)

1964, Aug Head of a Party and government delegation to Romania

      Nov Head of a Party and government delegation to Albania

1966, Apr Head of a government delegation to Cambodia

1969, Apr Li is confirmed by the 9th CCP Congress in his post as member of the Central Committee and as member of the CCP Politburo (again confirmed by the 10th Congress in 1973)

1974, Aug Head of a Party and government delegation to the 30th Anniversary Celebrations of Liberation in Romania

1975, Apr Head of a government delegation to Iran and Pakistan

1977, Aug Elected vice-chairman of the CCP Central Committee by the 11th Party Congress

1978, Jan Elected deputy for Hubei Province to the 5th NPC

      Mar Head of a government delegation to the Philippines

      Apr Appointed chairman of the Central Patriotic Health Campaign Committee

1979, Jan Head of a government delegation to Tanzania, Mozambique, Zambia, and Zaire

      Jul Appointed vice-chairman of the State Financial and Economic Commission

Li is married to Lin Jiamei.

Li Xiebo (Li Hsieh-po)　　李颉伯

<u>Posts held</u>

Government
Vice-minister of railways

1978, Aug Identified as vice-minister of railways

Li Ximing (Li Hsi-ming)   李锡铭

Posts held

Government
Vice-minister of power industry

1975,	Oct	Identified as a government cadre
1976,	Mar	Identified as vice-minister of water conservancy and electric power (until Feb 1979) and as acting chairman of the Society of Electro-Engineering (until Jul 1978)
	Dec	Head of a delegation to North Korea for negotiations on the Yalu Power Station
1977,	Jun	Identified as acting chairman of the Society of Electro-Engineering
1979,	Jan	Head of a delegation to North Korea to the Yalu River Hydroelectric Power Company Board Meeting
	Jun	Identified as vice-minister of power industry

Li Xuan (Li Hsüan)   李 轩

Posts held

Government
Deputy director of the National General Geological Bureau

NPC
Deputy for Sichuan Province to the 5th NPC

1953,	Oct	Identified as deputy director of the Ore-Prospecting Engineering Department of the Ministry of Geology
1961,	Jan	Appointed vice-minister of geology (until Cultural Revolution)
1973,	Apr	Identified as director of the Office of Economic Aid under the Ministry of Communications (until 1977)
1978,	Feb	Elected deputy for Sichuan Province to the 5th NPC
	May	Identified as deputy director of the National General Geological Bureau

Li Xuezhi (Li Hsüeh-chih)   李学智

Posts held

CCP
Alternate member of the CCP 11th Central Committee
1st secretary of Ningxia Autonomous Region CP

1964,	Mar	Identified as secretary of Jinhua Government District CP, Zhejiang Province
1977,	Aug	Elected alternate member of the CCP Central Committee by the 11th Party Congress
1978,	Apr	Elected secretary of Ningxia Autonomous Region CP (until May 1979)

1979,	May	Identified as 1st secretary of the CP and as chairman of the Revolutionary Committee of Ningxia Autonomous Region (until Jan 1980)
	Aug	Deputy head of an agricultural delegation to Great Britain and the Federal Republic of Germany

Li Yanlu (Li Yen-lu)   李延祿

Posts held

NPC
Member of the Standing Committee of the 5th NPC
Deputy for Heilongjiang Province to the 5th NPC

Li was born in Yanji County, Jilin Province. After the Shenyang Incident he founded the "Anti-Japanese National Salvation Army" together with Li Du and Ma Zhanshan of the Northeast Army, becoming chief of staff of this force in 1931. After Li Du had been forced to withdraw into the USSR with parts of this army, Li organized the remainder to form the new Joint Anti-Japanese Army in Heilongjiang Province in 1933. In 1935 he applied to Chiang Kai-shek for support from the Nationalist Government for this army, but eventually discarded this plan after two years of unsuccessful negotiations. In 1938 he joined the Communist forces and started training the cadres for Manchuria. He later organized guerrilla activities in the Rehe area. In February 1946 he was appointed chairman of the People's Government of Hejiang Province (until October 1949) which later became part of Heilongjiang Province.

1949,	Oct	Appointed vice-chairman of the People's Government of Songjiang Province (until Jun 1954)
1953		Identified as member of the Northeast China Administrative Council (until Sep 1954)
1954,	Jun	Identified as vice-chairman of the People's Government of Heilongjiang Province (until Feb 1955)
	Aug	Elected deputy for Heilongjiang Province to the 1st NPC (confirmed in 1958 and 1964 for the 2nd and 3rd NPCs)
1955,	Feb	Appointed vice-governor of Heilongjiang Province (until Cultural Revolution)
1957,	Nov	Identified as member of Heilongjiang Province CP (until Cultural Revolution)
1958,	Nov	Head of a friendship delegation of Heilongjiang Province to Chabarowsk in the USSR
1965,	Jan	Elected member of the Standing Committee of the 3rd NPC
1967		Disappears during the Cultural Revolution
1973,	May	First appearance after the Cultural Revolution: Named in his former post as member of the Standing Committee of the NPC
1975,	Jan	Confirmed by the 4th NPC as member of the Standing Committee (again confirmed in 1978 by the 5th NPC)
1978,	Feb	Elected deputy for Heilongjiang Province to the 5th NPC

Li Yanshou (Li Yen-shou)　李衍援

Posts held

Government
Deputy director of the Central Broadcasting Administration

1973,　Apr　Identified as member of the Standing Committee of Hubei Province CP (until 1977)

1978,　Jul　Identified as deputy director of the Central Broadcasting Administration

　　　Dec　Head of a broadcasting delegation to the Philippines

Li Yaowen (Li Yao-wen)　李耀文

Posts held

CCP
Alternate member of the CCP 11th Central Committee

Military
Major-general

Others
Political commissar of the National Defense Scientific and Technological Commission

Li served as political commissar of a division in the 8th Column, East China Field Army, in 1948. In 1949 he held the post of political commissar, 26th Corps, 3rd Field Army.

1950,　Nov　Service in the Korean War
1955　　　Appointed deputy director of the Political Department of Jinan Military Region
　　　Sep　Promoted to rank of major-general
1958　　　Identified as director of the Political Department of Jinan Military Region
1964　　　Identified as deputy political commissar of Jinan Military Region
1967,　Feb　Elected member of the Standing Committee, Revolutionary Committee of Shandong Province
1969,　Feb　Referred to as military leader in Jinan Military Region
1970,　Jul　Recalled to Beijing
1971,　Jul　Member of a Party and government delegation to North Korea
1972,　Apr　Appointed ambassador to Tanzania (until Jan 1976)
1973,　Jan　Appointed concurrently ambassador to Madagascar (until Jun 1974)
1977,　Aug　Elected alternate member of the CCP Central Committee by the 11th Party Congress
　　　Oct　Identified as political commissar of the National Defense Scientific and Technological Commission

Li Yilin (Li Yi-lin)　李艺林

Posts held

Government
Vice-minister of chemical industry

1964,　Oct　Appointed vice-minister of chemical industry; elected deputy for Jilin Province to the 3rd NPC

1966,　Mar　Head of a trade delegation to the Leipzig Fair

1967　　　Disappears during the Cultural Revolution

1974,　Sep　First appearance after the Cultural Revolution

　　　Nov　Identified as vice-minister of fuel and chemical industry (until Jan 1975)

1975,　Nov　Identified as vice-minister of petroleum and chemical industry (until Feb 1978)

1978,　Sep　Identified as vice-minister of chemical industry

Li Yimeng (Li Yi-meng)　李一氓

Posts held

CCP
Deputy director of the International Liaison Department of the CCP Central Committee
Deputy secretary of the Commission for Inspecting Discipline under the CCP Central Committee

Li was born in 1902 in Chengdu, the provincial capital of Sichuan. After graduating in economics (?) in Shanghai he joined the "Creation Society" founded by Guo Moruo and others and started a literary career. Particularly his short novels found recognition at the time. During the Northern Expedition in 1926 Li served in the Political Department of the Nationalist Revolutionary Army's Headquarters. After the rift between the KMT and the Communists in the following year he continued to work for the latter. In 1933 he joined the Jiangxi-Soviet established by Mao Zedong where he was given charge of the Bureau of Political Security in the Secret Service Department. During the Long March he was director of the Propaganda Section in the Political Department of the 1st Front Army. After a short period as secretary of Shaanxi Province CP he went to Shanghai in 1938 to work underground. Around 1940 he joined the New 4th Army. In 1943 he was successively director of the Huaihai Administrative Office and chairman of the Jiangsu-Anhui Border Government. In 1946 he was criticized for failing to oppose the KMT forces moving into Jiangsu. He eventually reappeared in April 1949 as 1st vice-chairman of the Administrative Office of Lüda (Lüshun-Dalian).

1951,　Apr　Member of the Chinese delegation to the 1st Session of the World Peace Council in East Berlin

1952,　Jul　Appointed council member of the World Peace Council

1953,　Dec　Member of a delegation to the World Peace Council Session in Vienna

1954,　May　Member of a delegation to the World Peace Council Session in East Berlin

　　　Aug　Elected deputy for Sichuan Province to the 1st NPC

　　　Jul　Elected secretary of the World Peace council (until 1957)

1955,　Jan　Delegate at the World Peace Council Session in Vienna

　　　Mar　Elected council member of the Association for Cultural Relations with Foreign Countries

Jun   Member of a delegation to the World Peace Council Congress in Helsinki

1956,   Mar   Present at the Council Session of World Peace Council in Stockholm

1958,   Mar   Appointed ambassador to Burma (until Sep 1963)

1964,   Apr   Appointed deputy director of the Staff Office for Foreign Affairs under the State Council (until 1966)

        Dec   Appointed deputy director of the Institute of Foreign Affairs (until 1967)

1965,   Jun   Elected vice-chairman of the Chinese Section of the World Peace Council (until 1967)

1967   Disappears during the Cultural Revolution

1974,   Sep   First appearance after the Cultural Revolution

1975,   Oct   Identified as deputy director of the International Liaison Department of the CCP Central Committee

1978,   Mar   Head of a delegation of CCP workers to Yugoslavia and Romania

        Dec   Appointed deputy secretary of the Commission for Inspecting Discipline under the CCP Central Committee

Li Yiqing (Li Yi-ch'ing)   李一清

Posts held

Government
Vice-minister of posts and tecelommunications

Li was born in 1907 in Xiyang, Shanxi Province. Circa 1941 he was head of the Public Security Bureau of Shanxi-Hebei-Shandong-Henan Border Region Government. In early 1949 he was director of the West Hunan Administrative Office.

1949,   Dec   Identified as member of the Central-South China Military and Administrative Council

1950,   Jul   Identified as vice-chairman of the Financial and Economic Commission of Central-South China Administrative Council (until 1954)

1957,   Oct   Identified as general manager of the Wuhan Iron and Steel Company (until 1961)

1961,   Oct   Identified as alternate secretary of the CCP Central-South Bureau (until 1965)

1963,   Feb   Identified as chairman of the Scientific and Technological Commission of the CCP Central-South Bureau

1965,   Mar   Identified as secretary of the CCP Central-South Bureau

1967   Disappears during the Cultural Revolution

1978,   Oct   First appearance after the Cultural Revolution: Identified as vice-minister of posts and telecommunications

Li Yizhang (Li Yi-chang)   李毅章

Posts held

CCP
Member of the Standing Committee of Jiangxi Province CP

NPC
Deputy for Jiangxi Province to the 5th NPC

Provincial Administration
Vice-chairman of the People's Congress of Jiangxi Province

1977,   Oct   Identified as member of the Standing Committee of Jiangxi Province CP

1978,   Feb   Elected deputy for Jiangxi Province to the 5th NPC and vice-chairman of the Revolutionary Committee of Jiangxi Province (latter post until Dec 1979)

1979,   Dec   Elected vice-chairman of the People's Congress of Jiangxi Province

Li Youjiu (Li Yu-chiu)   李友九

Posts held

Government
Vice-minister of agriculture

NPC
Deputy for Gansu Province to the 5th NPC

Li was born in 1917 in Fujian Province.

1960,   Mar   Identified as secretary of Guangxi Autonomous Region CP

1967,   May   Branded as a capitalist-roader and purged

1977,   Dec   First appearance after the Cultural Revolution: Elected vice-chairman of the Revolutionary Committee of Gansu Province (until May 1978)

1978,   Feb   Elected deputy for Gansu Province to the 5th NPC

        May   Identified as vice-minister of agriculture and forestry (until Feb 1979)

        Aug   Deputy head of an agricultural delegation to Romania, Federal Republic of Germany, and France

1979,   Jul   Identified as vice-minister of agriculture; head of an agriculture delegation to North Korea

Li Youwen (Li Yu-wen)   栗又文

Posts held

NPC
Deputy for Jilin Province to the 5th NPC

Others
Member of the Standing Committee of the 5th CPPCC

Li was born in 1909 in Liaobei Province. He is a graduate of the Sun Yat-sen University in Moscow. From 1946 to 1947 he was vice-chairman of the People's Government of Liaobei Province.

1949,   Dec   Appointed member and secretary-general of the Northeast People's Government (until 1952)

1952,   Aug   Identified as chairman of the People's Government of Jilin Province (until Feb 1955)

1954, Aug Elected deputy for Jilin Province to the 1st NPC (reelected in 1958 and 1964 to the 2nd and 3rd NPCs)

1955, Feb Identified as governor of Jilin (until Cultural Revolution)

1957, Oct Identified as secretary of Jilin Province CP (until Cultural Revolution)

1967 Disappears during the Cultural Revolution

1978, Feb First appearance after the Cultural Revolution: Elected deputy for Jilin Province to the 5th NPC

Mar Elected member of the Standing Committee of the 5th CPPCC

Li Yuan (Li Yüan)   黎　原

Posts held

CCP
Alternate member of the CCP 11th Central Committee

Military
Major-general
Deputy director of the PLA General Logistics Department
Deputy director of the PLA Capital Construction Engineering Corps

Li was born in 1911 in Hunan Province. He is a graduate of Whampoa Military Academy. He joined the CCP in 1930. In 1948 he was commander of a regiment of the 29th Division, Northeast Field Army.

1950, Identified as deputy chief of staff of the 140th Division, 47th Army

1951, Apr Identified as deputy commander of the 140th Division

1952, Jun Identified as commander of the 140th Division

1964, Oct Identified as major-general

Nov Identified as deputy chief of staff of Guangzhou Military Region

1966 Identified as commander of the 47th Army based in Changsha, Hunan Province

1967, Sep Li is received by Mao Zedong in Changsha; identified as head of the Preparatory Group for the Revolutionary Committee of Hunan Province

1968, Apr With the establishment of the Hunan Revolutionary Committee, Li is elected chairman (nominally until 1977)

1969, Apr Elected alternate member of the CCP Central Committee by the 9th Party Congress (confirmed in this post in 1973 and 1977 by the 10th and 11th Congresses)

1970, Apr Li disappears for unknown reasons, possibly ill health

1976, Sep Present at mourning ceremonies for Mao Zedong in Lanzhou

1977, Jul Identified as deputy commander of Lanzhou Military Region

Oct Identified as responsible person of the Science and Technology Leadership Group of Lanzhou Military Region

1978, Dec Identified as deputy director of the PLA General Logistics Department

1979, Apr Identified as deputy director of the PLA Capital Construction Engineering Corps

Li Yuanru (Li Yüan-ju)   李元如

Posts held

Government
Vice-minister of the 4th Ministry of Machine Building
Director-general of the General Broadcasting and Television Industry Bureau under the 4th Ministry of Machine Building

1978, Aug Identified as vice-minister of the 4th Ministry of Machine Building and as director general of the General Broadcasting and Television Industry Bureau under the 4th Ministry of Machine Building; deputy head of a broadcasting and television delegation to Sweden, Federal Republic of Germany, France

Li Yuchi (Li Yü-ch'ih)   李玉池

Posts held

Government
Ambassador to Somalia

1959, Jan Appointed embassy counselor to the embassy in Afghanistan (until Nov 1962)

1979, Oct Appointed ambassador to Somalia

Li Yukui (Li Yü-k'uei)   李玉奎

Posts held

Government
Vice-minister of posts and telecommunications

1956, May Appointed assistant minister in the Ministry of Posts and Telecommunications (until Jan 1959)

Sep Identified as director, Investment Administration in the Ministry of Posts and Telecommunications

1964, Feb Appointed vice-minister of posts and telecommunications (until Cultural Revolution)

1966 Disappears during the Cultural Revolution

1971, Nov First appearance after the Cultural Revolution

1973, Jan Identified as deputy director of the Bureau of Posts and Telecommunications

Oct Identified as vice-minister of posts and telecommunications

1979, Apr Head of a telecommunications delegation to Canada

Sep Head of a posts and telecommunications delegation to France, Belgium, and the Netherlands

Li Yunchang (Li Yün-ch'ang)   李运昌

Posts held

Others
Member of the Standing Committee of the 5th CPPCC

Li was born in 1908 in Leting, Hebei Province. He is a nephew of Li Dazhao, one of the cofounders of the CCP. After training at the Northwest Military Academy he went to Guangdong to join the Communists. In 1937 he commanded the Anti-Japan United Forces in Fengrun, Hebei Province. In the following year he was made commander of the 4th Column of the Shanxi-Chahar-Hebei Military District. In 1940 he commanded the Shanxi-Rehe-Chahar Military District and in 1945 the Hebei-Rehe-Liaoning Military District. He took part in the 1st CPPCC in September 1949 as a delegate representing the Northeastern Region.

1949,	Dec	Identified as vice-minister of communications (until Jul 1958)
1959,	Apr	Elected member of the Standing Committee of the 3rd CPPCC (confirmed by the 4th CPPCC in 1965)
1963		Identified as member of the Central Control Commission of the CCP Central Committee
1966		Disappears during the Cultural Revolution
1979,	Jun	First appearance after the Cultural Revolution
	Jul	By-elected a member of the Standing Committee of the 5th CPPCC

Li Yunchuan (Li Yün-ch'uan) 李云川

Posts held

Government
Ambassador to Switzerland

Li was born in 1919 in Shandong Province.

1956,	Jan	Identified as secretary-general of the Machine Building Trade Union
1957,	Nov	Identified as vice-chairman of the Machine Building Trade Union; in this capacity head of a delegation to Japan
1960,	Jul	Identified as chairman of the Machine Building Trade Union
1962,	Aug	Deputy head of a delegation of the Machine Building Trade Union to Japan
	Oct	Head of a delegation of the Machine Building Trade Union to the USSR
1963,	Apr	Identified as director of the International Liaison Department of the Chinese Federation of Trade Unions
	Oct	Identified as member of the Standing Council of the Sino-Japanese Friendship Association
1964,	Sep	Elected deputy for Heilongjiang Province to the 3rd NPC
	Oct	Identified as council member of the Institute of Foreign Affairs
1965,	Feb	Appointed ambassador to Dahomey
1966,	Jan	Following the severing of diplomatic relations between Dahomey and the PRC, Li returns to Beijing
1970,	Mar	Appointed ambassador to North Korea (until 1976)
1976,	Aug	Appointed ambassador to Switzerland

Li Yunhe (Li Yün-ho) 李惲和

Posts held

Provincial Administration
Vice-chairman of the People's Government, Ningxia Autonomous Region

1960,	May	Identified as deputy director of the Department for Industry and Communications, Xinjiang Autonomous Region CP
1974,	Oct	Identified as a member of the Standing Committee of Xinjiang CP and as director of the Office for Industry and Communications, Xinjiang Revolutionary Committee
1977,	May	Identified as deputy secretary of Xinjiang CP (until Jan 1979?)
1980,	Jan	Elected vice-chairman of the People's Government, Ningxia Autonomous Region

Li Yutang (Li Yü-t'ang) 李玉堂

Posts held

Government
Vice-minister of the 5th Ministry of Machine Building

NPC
Deputy for Tianjin Municipality to the 5th NPC

1952,	Aug	Identified as council member of the People's Government of Shanxi Province
1966,	Jan	Appointed vice-minister of the 5th Ministry of Machine Building
1967		Disappears during the Cultural Revolution
1973,	Oct	First appearance after the Cultural Revolution: Referred to as a cadre of the State Council
1978,	Feb	Elected deputy for Tianjin Municipality to the 5th NPC
	Oct	Identified as vice-minister of the 5th Ministry of Machine Building
1979,	May	Head of a machine building delegation to Pakistan to attend the foundation stone laying for a Chinese-aided factory at Wah

Li Zewang (Li Tse-wang) 李则望

Posts held

Government
Ambassador to Poland

1959,	Feb	Identified as counselor at the embassy in Moscow (until Apr 1960)
1964,	Apr	Identified as deputy director of the America and Australia Department in the Ministry of Foreign Affairs (until 1965)
1971,	Nov	Identified as chargé d'affaires ad interim in Tanzania (until 1972)
1973,	Mar	Appointed ambassador to Hungary (until Dec 1976)
1977,	Apr	Appointed ambassador to Poland

Li Zhaoji (Li Chao-chi)　李兆吉

Posts held

Government
Vice-minister of the 4th Ministry of Machine Building

Others
Director of the Communications Engineering Research Institute
Council member of the Electronics Society

1971,	Aug	Deputy head of a telecommunications delegation to Chile, Great Britain, Switzerland, and France (until Sep)
1976,	Nov	Identified as council member of the Electronics Society; deputy head of an electronics delegation to Japan
1978,	Apr	Identified as director of the Communications Engineering Research Institute
	May	Identified as vice-minister of the 4th Ministry of Machine Building

Li Zhen (Li Chen) (f)　李貞

Posts held

NPC
Member of the Standing Committee of the 5th NPC
Deputy for the PLA to the 5th NPC

Military
Major-general

Li was born in Liuyang, Hunan Province, in 1910. She was given away by her parents at the age of six. In 1926 she escaped from her husband's family and joined the CCP the following year. She took part in the Long March, 1934-1935. In 1938 she served as director of the Cadres Section under the Political Department of the 120th Division, 8th Route Army. Later on she headed the Cadres Section of the Shanxi-Suiyuan-Shaanxi-Gansu-Ningxia Joint Forces Command. In 1945 she took over the Cadres Section under the Political Department of the Northwest Field Army. In March 1949 she was elected member of the Executive Committee of the Federation of Democratic Women. In September that year she was delegated by the 1st Field Army to the 1st CPPCC.

1951,	Nov	Identified as secretary-general of the Political Department of the Chinese People's Volunteers (CPV) to the Korean War
1953,	Jan	Identified as director of the Political Department of the CPV
	Apr	Elected member of the Executive Committee of the Federation of Democratic Women
	Oct	Deputy head of a women's delegation to attend the celebration of the 36th anniversary of the October Revolution in Moscow
1954,	Aug	Elected deputy for Hunan Province to the 1st NPC (reelected in 1958 and 1964 to the 2nd and 3rd NPCs)
1955,	Sep	Identified as deputy director of the Politi-

		cal Department of the PLA Navy; appointed major-general (the only female major-general of the PLA); awarded the order of "Liberation," 1st class
1956,	Nov	Identified as director of the Cadres Section under the PLA General Political Department
1958,	Dec	Identified as deputy chief procurator of the PLA Military Procuratorate
1964,	Sep	Head of a women's delegation to Albania
1967-1976		Li survives the Cultural Revolution unharmed and is mentioned as a military cadre on several occasions in connection with matters of inner-Chinese importance
1978,	Feb	Elected deputy for the PLA to the 5th NPC
	Mar	Elected member of the Standing Committee of the 5th NPC

Li Zhen (Li Chen)　李振

Posts held

Military
Major-general
Deputy political commissar, Logistics Department of the PLA

Li was born in 1905 as the son of a wealthy farmer in Henan Province. He is a university graduate. In 1934-35 he took part in the Long March. He then served as battalion commander and later as regiment commander in the 129th Division of the 8th Route Army. In 1946 he was head of the Public Security Bureau in Beihai District. In 1947 he was political commissar of the 18th Brigade, 6th Column of the Central Plains Field Army. In February 1949 he was appointed political commissar of the 36th Division, 12th Corps of the 2nd Field Army.

1950,	May	Appointed member of the People's Supervisory Committee in the Southwest China Military and Administrative Council (until Sep 1954)
	Sep	Appointed political commissar of the 12th Corps
1955,	Sep	Promoted to rank of major-general
1957		Identified as deputy director of the Political Department of Liaoning Military District (until Jul 1958)
1958,	Jul	Identified as deputy director of the Political Department of Shenyang Military Region (until 1963)
1963,	Sep	Identified as director of the Political Department in the Ministry of Railways
1967,	Jan	Appointed vice-minister of public security (until Oct 1972); in this capacity entrusted with the investigation of offenses committed by Chief of General Staff Luo Ruiqing
1969,	Apr	Elected member of the CCP Central Committee by the 9th Party Congress (until Aug 1977)
1972,	Oct	Identified as minister of public security (until Jan 1975)
1975,	Dec	Identified as deputy political commissar of the PLA Logistics Department
1978,	Sep	Last appearance; probably purged

Li Zhen (Li Chen)　　李　震

Posts held

CCP
Secretary of Shandong Province CP

1977, Sep　Identified as vice-chairman of the Revolutionary Committee, and as secretary of the CP, of Shandong Province (first post until Dec 1979)

1978, May　Head of a friendship delegation to North Korea

Li Zhengguang (Li Cheng-kuang)　　李正光

Posts held

Government
Vice-minister of textile industry

1958, Aug　Deputy director of the Technical Department of the Ministry of Textile Industry

1963, May　Identified as vice-chairman of the Society of Textile Technology

1978, Jul　Identified as vice-minister of textile industry

Li Zhengting (Li Cheng-t'ing)　　李正亭

Posts held

Government
Director of the Bureau of Weights and Measures under the State Council

1957, Sep　Identified as deputy director, Rural Work Department of Henan Province CP

1964, Apr　Appointed vice-minister of labor

1968, Feb　Branded as a follower of Liu Shaoqi and purged

1977, Oct　First appearance after the Cultural Revolution

1979, Apr　Identified as director of the Bureau of Weights and Measures under the State Council

Li Zhimin (Li Chih-min)　　李志民

Posts held

CCP
Member of the CCP 11th Central Committee

Military
Colonel-general
Political commissar of Fuzhou Military Region
Member of the Standing Committee, CP Secretariat of Fuzhou Military Region

Li was born in 1909 in Hunan Province. He joined the CCP in 1927. In 1931 he was political commissar of a regiment of the 2nd Division, 3rd Front Army. In 1948 he was head of the Political Department of the 2nd Corps, Northeast Field Army. In the following year he was appointed political commissar of the 19th Corps.

1949, Nov?　Appointed council member of the People's Government of Shaanxi Province

1950, Jun　Appointed member of the Northwest Military and Administrative Council (until Jan 1953)

1953, Feb　Appointed director of the Political Department, Chinese People's Volunteers in Korea

1954, Aug　Elected deputy for the PLA to the 1st NPC (until Mar 1959)

1956, Sep　Elected alternate member of the CCP Central Committee by the 8th Party Congress

1958, Feb　Identified as colonel-general

1963, Oct　Head of a military delegation to Algeria; identified as political commissar of the PLA Military Academy

1967　At the height of the Cultural Revolution Li is branded as a "three-anti element" and relieved of all posts

1973, Aug　First appearance after the Cultural Revolution: Elected member of the CCP Central Committee by the 10th Party Congress

Oct　Identified as political commissar of Fuzhou Military Region

1975, Oct　Head of a friendship delegation to North Korea

1977, Jun　Identified as member of the Standing Committee, CP Secretariat of Fuzhou Military Region

1979, Oct　Co-author (with Hong Xuezhi and Deng Hua) of an article in Jiefangjun Bao (Liberation Army) on 25th Oct, "Heroism Shines Forever, Internationalism Inspires All People - Cherishing the Memory of Comrade Peng Dehuai"

Li Zhizhong (Li Chih-chung)　　李执中

Posts held

Provincial Administration
Vice-governor of Jiangsu Province

1977, Dec　Elected vice-chairman of the Revolutionary Committee of Jiangsu Province (until Dec 1979)

1979, Dec　Elected vice-governor of Jiangsu Province

Li Zhongxuan (Li Chung-hsüan)　　李钟玄

Posts held

Military
Deputy commander of Beijing Military Region
Deputy commander of Beijing Garrison

1965, Aug　Identified as military attaché at the embassy in Indonesia

1977, Oct　Identified as deputy commander of Beijing Garrison

1978, Apr　Identified as deputy commander of Beijing Military Region

Li Zhongyuan (Li Chung-yüan)   李中垣

Posts held

Provincial Administration
Vice-chairman of the Revolutionary Committee of Tianjin Municipality

Military
Deputy commander of Qingdao Garrison

1977,	Dec	Elected vice-chairman of the Revolutionary Committee of Tianjin Municipality
1979,	Aug	Identified as deputy commander of Qingdao Garrison

Li Zhuang (Li Chuang)   李 庄

Posts held

CCP
Deputy chief-editor of RMRB

1963,	Apr	Identified as director of the Home Department and member of the Editorial Department of RMRB
1964,	Oct	Elected deputy for Hebei Province to the 3rd NPC
1966		Disappears during the Cultural Revolution
1977,	Mar	First appearance after the Cultural Revolution
	Apr	Identified as deputy chief-editor of RMRB
1979,	May	Head of a RMRB delegation to North Korea

Li Zhuoran (Li Cho-jan)   李卓然

Posts held

Others
Member of the Standing Committee of the 5th CPPCC

Li was born in 1903 in Hunan Province. He studied in France and later in the USSR at the Moscow Workers' University and at the Leningrad Military and Political University. In 1930 he returned to China and worked in the Jiangxi Soviet Area. In 1933 he was appointed deputy director of the General Political Department of the Red Army. During the Long March he was head of the Political Department of the 5th Army. In 1936 he lectured at the Anti-Japan Military and Political Academy. In 1940 he was director of the Propaganda Department in the Northwest China Bureau of the CCP Central Committee; In 1946 deputy director of the Propaganda Department in the Northeast China Bureau of the CCP Central Committee, and from 1948 director of the department. In August 1949 he was made a member of the Northeast China People's Government and director of its Cultural and Educational Committee.

1953,	Jan	Appointed vice-chairman of the Northeast China Administrative Council
1954,	Sep	Identified as deputy director of the Propaganda Department of the CCP Central Committee (until Cultural Revolution)
	Dec	Elected member of the 2nd CPPCC (re-elected in 1959 and 1964 to the 3rd and 4th CPPCCs)

1955,	Mar	Li criticizes Gao Gang during a session of the CCP Central Committee
1958,	Sep	Identified as council member of the Sino-Korean Friendship Association
1967		Disappears during the Cultural Revolution
1975,	Oct	First appearance after the Cultural Revolution
1978,	Mar	Elected member of the Standing Committee of the 5th CPPCC

Li Zichao (Li Tzu-ch'ao)   李子超

Posts held

CCP
Secretary of Shandong Province CP

NPC
Deputy for Shandong Province to the 5th NPC

1977,	Apr	Identified as vice-chairman of the Revolutionary Committee of Shandong Province (until Dec 1979)
	Sep	Identified as member of the Standing Committee of Shandong Province CP (until Jan 1980)
1978,	Feb	Elected deputy for Shandong Province to the 5th NPC
1980,	Feb	Identified as secretary of Shandong Province CP

Li Ziyuan (Li Tzu-yüan)   李子元

Posts held

CCP
Member of the CCP 11th Central Committee
Secretary of Sichuan Province CP

1952,	Jan	Identified as member of the Rural Reform Committee of Guangdong Province People's Government
1956,	Feb	Identified as deputy director of the Rural Work Department of Guangdong Province CP (until Jan 1958)
1958,	Feb	Identified as director of the Rural Work Department of Guangdong Province CP (until Jan 1960)
1963,	Feb	Identified as member of the Standing Committee of Guangdong Province CP (until Feb 1965)
	May	Elected secretary-general of Guangdong Province CP (until Jan 1965)
1965,	Mar	Identified as alternate member of the Secretariat of Guangdong Province CP
1967,	Oct	Li is accused as a follower of Zhao Ziyang and disappears
1975,	Dec	First appearance after the Cultural Revolution: Identified as a cadre in Sichuan
1977,	Jan	Identified as secretary of Sichuan Province CP (reelected in Jan 1979)
	Aug	Elected member of the CCP Central Committee by the 11th Party Congress
	Dec	Elected vice-chairman of the Revolutionary Committee of Sichuan Province (until Feb 1979?)

Li Zugen (Li Tsu-ken)   李祖根

Posts held

CCP
Alternate member of the CCP 11th Central Committee

Mass Organization
Vice-chairman of the Trade Union of Jiangxi Province

1973,   Aug   Elected vice-chairman of the Trade Union of Jiangxi Province; elected to first term as alternate member of the CCP Central Committee by the 10th Party Congress

Lian Guan (Lien Kuan)   连贯

Posts held

Government
Deputy director of the Office of Overseas Chinese Affairs under the State Council

Others
Vice-chairman of the Federation of Returned Overseas Chinese

Lien was born in Dapu, Guangdong Province. He took part in the 1st CPPCC in September 1949 as a delegate representing the Liberated Areas of South China.

1949,   Oct   Appointed member of the Overseas Chinese Affairs Commission in the Government Administration Council (until 1964); appointed director of the 3rd Office, United Front Work Department of the CCP Central Committee (until?)

1957,   Oct   Identified as deputy secretary-general, Standing Committee of the NPC (until Cultural Revolution)

1958,   Nov   Elected deputy for the Overseas Chinese to the 2nd NPC (reelected in 1964 to the 3rd NPC)

1961,   Aug   Member of an NPC delegation led by Guo Moruo to Indonesia and Burma

1963,   Mar   Identified as chairman of the China-Laos Friendship Association

1964,   Dec   Appointed council member of the Institute of Foreign Affairs

1965,   Mar   Member of an NPC delegation to Africa
1967   Disappears during the Cultural Revolution

1972,   Sep   First appearance after the Cultural Revolution

1973,   Oct   Identified in his former post as chairman of the China-Laos Friendship Association (no later mention in this post)

1974,   Sep   Identified in his former post as deputy secretary-general of then NPC (until Jan 1975)

1978,   Jun   Identified as deputy director of the Office of Overseas Chinese Affairs under the State Council

1979,   Jan   Identified as vice-chairman of the Federation of Returned Overseas Chinese and as vice-chairman of the Board of Directors, Guanzhou Overseas Chinese University

Liang Biye (Liang Pi-yeh)   梁必业

Posts held

CCP
Member of the CCP 11th Central Committee

NPC
Member of the Standing Committee of the 5th NPC
Deputy for the PLA to the 5th NPC

Military
Lieutenant-general
Deputy director of the General Political Department of the PLA

Liang was born in 1900 in Jiangxi (Hunan?) Province. In 1945 he was identified as political commissar of the 1st Division, 1st Column of the Joint Democratic Northeast Army. In 1949 he was deputy political commissar of the 13th Army Corps.

1950,   Oct   Identified as deputy director of the Organization Department, Political Department of Central-South China Military Region

         Dec   Appointed member of the Supervisory Committee of Central-South China Military and Administrative Council

1955,   Jun   Identified as deputy director of the Political Department of Central-South China Military Region

         Sep   Conferred the order "Liberation," 1st class; promoted to rank of lieutenant-general

1957,   Oct   Identified as deputy political commissar and director of the Political Department of the Chinese People's Volunteers in Korea (until their withdrawal in Oct 1958)

1958,   Oct   Conferred the North Korean order "National Flag," 2nd class

1960,   Jun   Identified as military leader in Jinan Military Region (until 1962)

1961,   Mar   Member of a military delegation to Outer Mongolia

1962,   Apr   Identified as deputy director of the General Political Department of the PLA (until Cultural Revolution)

1964,   Sep   Elected deputy for the PLA to the 3rd NPC (until Cultural Revolution)

1965,   Sep   Deputy head of a government delegation to the 10th Anniversary celebrations of Xinjiang Autonomous Region

1966,   Apr   Liang is attacked by Red Guards as "a sworn supporter of Luo Ruiqing"

         Dec   Liang is branded as a "three-anti element" and relieved of all posts

1973,   May   First appearance after the Cultural Revolution

1975,   Jan   Elected member of the Standing Committee by the 4th NPC (confirmed by the 5th NPC in 1978); identified as deputy director of the General Political Department of the PLA

1977,   Aug   Elected member of the CCP Central Committee by the 11th Party Congress

1978,   Feb   Elected deputy for the PLA to the 5th NPC

Jun   Member of a military friendship delegation to Romania

1979,   Jun   Member of the Credentials Committee at
the 2nd Session of the 5th NPC

Liang Buting (Liang Pu-t'ing)   梁步庭

Posts held

CCP
1st secretary of Qinghai Province CP

1953,   Jun   Identified as a member of the Central
Committee of the New Democratic Youth
League (until May 1957)
1954,   Apr   Member of a delegation to the May Day
celebration in Moscow
1957,   May   Elected secretary and member of the
Standing Committee of the Communist
Youth League
Dec   Elected member of the 8th Executive
Committee of the Federation of Trade
Unions
1958,   Dec   Head of a youth delegation to Bulgaria
and Czechoslovakia
1961,   Nov   Head of a youth delegation to Albania
1964,   Oct   Appointed deputy director of the State
Office for Agriculture and Forestry
1966   Liang disappears
1978,   Aug   First appearance after the Cultural Revolution: Identified as secretary of Qinghai
Province CP (until Jan 1979)
1979,   Jan   Identified as 2nd secretary of Qinghai
Province CP (until Jan 1979)
1980,   Jan   Identified as 1st secretary of Qinghai
Province CP

Liang Changwu (Liang Ch'ang-wu)   梁昌武

Posts held

Government
Vice-minister of forestry
Deputy director of the State General
Forestry Bureau

1954,   Jul   Appointed council member of the Federation of Supply and Marketing Cooperatives
1961,   Jul   Appointed vice-minister of forestry (until
Cultural Revolution)
1970,   Jun   First appearance after the Cultural Revolution
1971,   Nov   Identified as vice-minister of agriculture
and forestry (until Feb 1979)
1975,   Jan   Head of an agricultural delegation to
Albania
1977,   Apr   Head of a forestry delegation to North
Korea
Nov   Head of an agricultural delegation to
Cameroon
1978,   Oct   Identified as deputy director of the State
General Forestry Bureau
1979,   Sep   Identified as vice-minister of forestry

Liang Chengye (Liang Ch'eng-yeh)   梁成业

Posts held

NPC
Deputy for Guangxi Autonomous Region
to the 5th NPC

Provincial Administration
Vice-chairman of the People's Government, Guangxi Autonomous Region

Others
Chairman of the Revolutionary Committee, Guilin Municipality

Liang belongs to the Zhuang minority.

1978,   Feb   Elected deputy for Guangxi Autonomous
Region to the 5th NPC
1979,   Jun   Member of the Budget Committee at the
2nd Session of the 5th NPC
Jul   Identified as chairman of the Revolution-
ary Committee, Guilin Municipality
Dec   Elected vice-chairman of the People's
Government, Guangxi Autonomous Region

Liang Huaxin (Liang Hua-hsin)   梁华新

Posts held

CCP
Secretary-general of Guangxi Autonomous
Region CP
Member of the Standing Committee of
Guangxi CP

Provincial Administration
Vice-chairman of the People's Congress of
Guangxi Autonomous Region

Others
Member of the Standing Committee of the
5th CPPCC

Liang belongs to the Zhuang minority.

1954,   Aug   Elected deputy for Guangxi Province to
the 1st NPC (confirmed by the 2nd and
3rd NPCs)
1965,   Nov   Identified as director of the Nationalities
Affairs Committee of Guangxi Autono-
mous Region
1973,   Dec   Identified as director of the United Front
Work Department of Guangxi CP (un-
til 1974?)
1977,   Jul   Identified as secretary-general of
Guangxi CP
Sep   Identified as member of the Standing
Committee of Guangxi CP
1978,   May   Elected member of the Standing Committee of the 5th CPPCC
1979,   Dec   Elected vice-chairman of the People's
Congress of Guangxi Autonomous Region

Liang Jiquan (Liang Chi-ch'üan)   梁吉泉

Posts held

CCP
Member of the Standing Committee of
Guangxi Autonomous Region CP

NPC
Member of the Standing Committee of the 5th NPC
Deputy for Guangxi Autonomous Region to the 5th NPC

Mass Organization
Secretary of the Communist Youth League of Guangxi Autonomous Region

Liang belongs to the Zhuang minority.

1973,	Jun	Elected secretary of the Communist Youth League in Guangxi Autonomous Region
1974,	Jun	Identified as member of the Standing Committee of Guangxi Province CP
1975,	Jan	Elected member of the Standing Committee of the 4th NPC (confirmed in 1978 by the 5th NPC)
1978,	Feb	Elected deputy for Guangxi Autonomous Region to the 5th NPC
1979,	Jun	Member of the Credentials Committee at the 2nd Session of the 5th NPC

Liang Kaixuan (Liang K'ai-hsüan) 梁凯轩

Posts held

Provincial Administration
Vice-governor of Jiangxi Province

| 1979, | Dec | Elected vice-governor of Jiangxi Province |

Liang Lingguang (Liang Ling-kuang) 梁灵光

Posts held

Government
Minister of light industry

Liang served in the Northward Advance Column of the New 4th Army in 1939. In 1945 he was commander of the 9th Regiment, 3rd Brigade, 1st Division of the New 4th Army. In 1948 he commanded the 9th Military Subdistrict of Central Jiangsu Military District. In early 1949 he was made chief of staff of the 29th Army (until April 1952), and in September of that year mayor of Xiamen.

1950,	Oct	Identified as council member of the People's Government of Fujian Province
1956,	Jun	Identified as member of the Standing Committee of Fujian Province CP and as director of its Industrial Work Department
	Aug	Elected vice-governor of Fujian Province (until Aug 1968)
1959,	Feb	Elected deputy for Fujian Province to the 2nd NPC
1960,	May	Elected alternate member of the Secretariat of Fujian Province CP (until Aug 1968)
1968		Disappears during the Cultural Revolution
1976,	Apr	First appearance after the Cultural Revolution: Identified as member of the Standing Committee of the CP, and as vice-

chairman of the Revolutionary Committee, of Fujian Province (until Feb 1978)

| 1978, | Mar | Appointed minister of light industry |

Liang Shangli (Liang Shang-li)

Posts held

Others
Vice-chairman of the Executive Committee, Federation of Industrialists and Businessmen

| 1979, | Oct | Elected vice-chairman of the Executive Committee, Federation of Industrialists and Businessmen |

Liang Weilin (Liang Wei-lin) 梁威林

Posts held

Provincial Administration
Vice-governor of Guangdong Province

Liang was born in Guangdong Province.

1955,	May	Identified as director of the Hong Kong Branch of NCNA (acting as PRC representative) in Hong Kong (until Dec 1971)
1964,	Sep	Elected deputy for Guangdong Province to the 3rd NPC
1977,	Dec	Elected vice-chairman of the Revolutionary Committee of Guangdong Province (until Dec 1979)
1979,	Dec	Elected vice-governor of Guangdong Province

Liang Wenqi (Liang Wen-ch'i)

Posts held

Others
President of the Tropical Crops Society

| 1979, | Jan | Identified as president of the Tropical Crops Society |

Liang Wenying (Liang Wen-ying) 梁文英

Posts held

CCP
Member of the Standing Committee of Yunnan Province CP
Director of the Propaganda Department of Yunnan Province CP

1975,	Feb	Identified as member of the Standing Committee of Yunnan Province CP and as deputy director of the Propaganda Department of Yunnan Province CP
1978,	Apr	Identified as director of the Propaganda Department of Yunnan Province CP
1979,	Mar	Identified as vice-chairman of the Revolutionary Committee of Yunnan (until Dec 1979)

Liang Xiang (Liang Hsiang)   梁 湘

Posts held

CCP
Member of the Standing Committee of Guangdong Province CP
2nd secretary of Guangzhou Municipality CP

Others
Vice-chairman of the Revolutionary Committee of Guangzhou Municipality

1960, Sep   Identified as CP secretary and deputy mayor in Guangzhou (until Cultural Revolution)
1976, Jan   Identified as vice-chairman of the Revolutionary Committee of Guangzhou
1977, May   Identified as member of the Standing Committee of Guangdong Province CP
      Oct   Identified as 2nd secretary of Guangzhou Municipality CP
      Dec   Elected vice chairman of the Revolutionary Committee of Guangdong Province (until Dec 1979)

Liao Chengmei (Liao Ch'eng-mei)   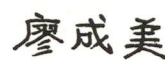廖成美

Posts held

Military
Major-general
Commander of the 2nd Artillery of the PLA

In 1947 Liao served as regiment commander in the East China Field Army. In 1949 he was made commander of the 88th Division, 30th Army, 3rd Field Army.

1950   Identified as a cadre of the East China Security Forces
1964, Aug   Identified as major-general of the PLA in Nanjing Military Region
1968, Mar   Identified as military leader of the PLA Unit 6408 based in Anhui Province
      Apr   Elected vice-chairman of the Anhui Provincial Revolutionary Committee (until 1969?)
      Sep   Liao is recalled to the Central Leadership; identified as political commissar of the Higher Artillery Technical School
1977, Sep   Identified as commander of the PLA 2nd Artillery (probably in this post since 1974)

Liao Chengzhi (Liao Ch'eng-chih)   廖承志

Posts held

CCP
Member of the CCP Central Committee

Government
Head of the Overseas Chinese Affairs Office under the State Council

NPC
Vice-chairman of the 5th NPC
Deputy for Guangdong Province to the 5th NPC

Others
Chairman of the Sino-Japanese Friendship Association
Honorary chairman of the Federation of Returned Overseas Chinese

Liao was born in 1908 in Tokyo. His father, Liao Zhigao, who was the closest confidant of Sun Yat-sen, was murdered in Guangzhou in 1925. His mother, He Xiangning, had been chairman of the Standing Committee of the NPC from 1954 until her death at the age of 95 in 1972. Liao received his first school education at a Catholic school in Japan. In 1919 he returned to China to continue his studies at a school attached to Lingnan University in Guangzhou. After the murder of his father he went back to Japan to study at Waseda University but was expelled from university in 1928 because of revolutionary activities. He then traveled to Europe as a seaman and, after being arrested in Hamburg for distributing Communist propaganda, was deported from Germany. He returned to China via the USSR. In 1932 the Nationalist Government ordered Liao's arrest in Shanghai, but he was released on his mother's personal petition to Chiang Kai-shek. He then joined the Red Army in Sichuan. Commanded by Zhang Guotao, these forces merged in 1935 during the Long March with Mao Zedong's and Zhu De's army from the Jiangxi-Soviet. After the Long March Liao was appointed director of the Publications Office of the CCP Central Committee in 1936. Until 1938 he was concurrently editor of the Liberation Press and head of NCNA. During the Anti-Japanese War Liao was secretary in the South China Bureau of the CCP Central Committee which concentrated its activities on Guangdong Province and Hong Kong. From 1942 to the beginning of 1946 Liao was imprisoned by the Nationalist Government. While under detention he was elected alternate member of the CCP Central Committee (until 1956) by the 7th Party Congress in 1945. In 1947 Liao was made head of the Peasants Department of the CCP Central Committee and in 1949, member of the Central Committee. In April of that year he was elected deputy secretary of the New Democratic Youth League and in July headed the Chinese delegation to the International Youth Festival in Budapest. In May 1949 he was elected chairman of the Federation of Democratic Youth which he represented as delegate at the CPPCC in September.

1949, Oct   Appointed member of the Political and Legal Affairs Committee and vice-chairman of the Overseas Chinese Affairs Committee
1951, Feb   Appointed deputy director, United Front Work Department of the CCP Central Committee
1952, Dec   Member of the Chinese delegation to the World Peace Council Session in Vienna
1953, Mar   Member of the Chinese delegation at Stalin's funeral in Moscow
      Jul   Elected secretary, Central Committee of the New Democratic Youth League
      Nov   Delegate at the Executive Council Session of the World Peace Council in Vienna
1954, May   Delegate at a special session of the Executive Council of the World Peace Council in East Berlin

Jun Delegate at an international conference on problems of détente in Stockholm

Oct Elected deputy for the Overseas Chinese to the 1st NPC (reelected in 1959 and 1964 to the 2nd and 3rd NPCs) and member of the Standing Committee of the NPC

1955, Apr Member of the Chinese delegation to the Afro-Asian Conference in Bandung

Jun Deputy head of the Chinese delegation to the Peace Council Session in Helsinki

Jul Appointed member of the Institute of Foreign Affairs (until Cultural Revolution)

1956, Feb Elected-vice chairman of the Afro-Asian Solidarity Committee (until Jul 1958)

Sep Elected member of the CCP Central Committee by the 8th Party Congress (until Apr 1969)

1957, May Member of the Chinese delegation to the Peace Conference in Colombo

Dec Deputy head of a Red Cross delegation to Japan

1958, Mar Appointed deputy director of the Foreign Affairs Office (until about 1962)

Jul Elected chairman of the Afro-Asian Solidarity Committee (until 1965)

1959, Apr Appointed chairman of the Overseas Chinese Affairs Commission (until 1964)

May Elected vice-chairman of the Sino-Soviet Friendship Association (until 1962)

1960, Feb Appointed chairman of the Commission for Receiving and Resettling Returned Overseas Chinese (until 1965)

Apr Head of the Chinese delegation to the 2nd Afro-Asian Solidarity Conference in Guinea; elected council member of the Sino-African Friendship Association

May Member of a government delegation led by Zhou Enlai to Cambodia

Jul Delegate to board meeting of the World Peace Council in Stockholm

Nov Member of a CCP delegation to Moscow

1961, Jan Appointed chancellor of the Overseas Chinese University (until 1965)

Mar Head of the Chinese delegation to the World Peace Council Session in New Delhi

Dec Head of the Chinese delegation to the World Peace Council Session in Stockholm

1963, Apr Appointed chairman of the Commission for Receiving and Resettling Overseas Chinese returned from Indonesia (until 1965)

Oct Appointed chairman of the Sino-Japanese Friendship Association

Nov Head of the Chinese delegation to the World Peace Council Session in Warsaw

1964, Nov Head of a Peace Council delegation to Italy

1965, May Head of the Chinese delegation to the 4th Afro-Asian Solidarity Conference in Winneba (Ghana)

1967 Liao is attacked by Red Guards during the Cultural Revolution and disappears

1971, Aug First appearance after the Cultural Revolution

1972, Jan Reactivated as chairman of the Sino-Japanese Friendship Association

1973, Apr Head of a delegation of the Sino-Jananese Friendship Association to Japan

Aug Reelected member of the CCP Central Committee by the 10th Party Congress (confirmed in 1977 by the 11th Congress)

1975, Jan Elected member of the Standing Committee by the 4th NPC

1977, May Deputy head of an NPC delegation led by Seypidin to Romania

1978, Feb Elected deputy for Guangdong Province to the 5th NPC

Mar Elected vice-chairman of the 5th NPC

Sep Identified as head of the Overseas Chinese Affairs Office under the State Council

Oct Member of a government delegation led by Deng Xiaoping to Japan

Dec Identified as honorary chairman of the Federation of Overseas Chinese

1979, Jan Identified as president of the Overseas Chinese University in Quanzhou, Fujian Province

May Head of a friendship delegation to Japan

Liao is married to Jing Puchun.

Liao Hansheng (Liao Han-sheng) 廖汉生

Posts held

CCP
Member of the CCP 11th Central Committee

NPC
Deputy for the PLA to the 5th NPC

Military
Political commissar of Nanjing Military Region
Lieutenant-general
1st political commissar of Shenyang Military Region

Liao was born in 1910 in Liling County, Hunan Province. In 1929 he joined the Communist guerrilla forces operating under He Long in the Henan-Hubei Border Area. In 1934-35 he took part in the Long March. During the Anti-Japanese War he served as political commissar of the 6th Division, 2nd Front Army, and subsequently as political commissar of the 715th Regiment, 358th Brigade, 120th Division (commander: He Long) of the 8th Route Army. In the following year he was appointed deputy political commissar of the 358th Brigade. He was promoted to the post of political commissar of this brigade in 1945. In the following year he was made deputy political commissar of the 1st Column in the Shaanxi-Gansu-Ningxia Border Area and in 1947 political commissar of the 1st Column, Northeast Liberation Army. In 1949 he was appointed political commissar of the 1st Corps, 1st Field Army.

1949, Oct Appointed member of the Northwest China Military and Administrative Council (until Jan 1953) and chairman of Qinghai Military and Administrative Council

1950, Mar Identified as vice-chairman of the People's Government of Qinghai Province and as deputy commander of Qinghai Military Region (until 1954)

<table><tr><td>1953,</td><td>Jan</td><td>Appointed member of the Northwest China Administrative Council (until 1955)</td></tr></table>

1953, Jan Appointed member of the Northwest China Administrative Council (until 1955)

1954, Apr Appointed deputy political commissar of Northwest China Military Region (until 1956)

Oct Elected deputy for the PLA to the 1st NPC (until Mar 1959); appointed vice-minister of National Defense and member of the National Defense Council (until 1966)

1955, Sep Appointed lieutenant-general; awarded the orders of "1st August," "Independence and Freedom," and "Liberation," all 1st class

1956, Sep Elected alternate member of the CCP Central Committee by the 8th Party Congress (until Cultural Revolution)

1957, Nov Appointed head of the PLA Military Academy (no later mention in this post)

1962, Sep Identified as military leader in the Beijing Area

1964, Sep Elected deputy for the PLA to the 3rd NPC (until Cultural Revolution)

1965, Feb Identified as secretary of the North China Bureau of the CCP Central Committee (until Cultural Revolution)

1973, May First appearance after the Cultural Revolution

1975, Apr Identified as political commissar of Nanjing Military Region

1977, Aug Identified as 1st secretary, CP Secretariat of Nanjing Military Region; elected member of the CCP Central Committee by the 11th Party Congress (first post until Jan 1980)

Dec Identified as 1st political commissar of Nanjing Military Region (until Jan 1980)

1978, Feb Elected deputy for the PLA to the 5th NPC

Jun Deputy head of a military delegation led by Yang Yong to Yugoslavia

1979, Mar Head of a military friendship delegation to Gabon, Cameroon, and Equatorial Guinea

1980, Feb Identified as 1st political commissar of Shenyang Military Region

Liao Jingdan (Liao Ching-tan) 廖井丹

Posts held

CCP
Deputy director, Propaganda Department of the CCP Central Committee

Liao was born in 1916 in Sichuan Province. He attended the Party School of the Red Army in Yan'an.

1950, Jan Identified as deputy director of the Propaganda Department, Southwest Bureau of the CCP Central Committee

Jul Identified as director, Information and Publication Bureau of the Southwest Military and Administrative Council and as secretary-general of the Cultural and Educational Committee

1954, Aug Elected deputy for Sichuan Province to the 1st NPC (confirmed in 1958 and 1961 by the 2nd and 3rd NPCs)

1955, Mar Identified as secretary of Chengdu Municipality CP

1957, May Identified as 1st secretary of Chengdu Municipality CP

1959, Oct Identified as member of the Standing Committee of Sichuan Province CP (until 1965)

1964, Jan Identified as vice-chairman of the Weiqi Chess Association; head of a chess delegation to Japan

1966, Jan Identified as secretary of Sichuan Province CP

1968, Oct Elected member of the Revolutionary Committee of Chengdu Municipality; subsequently disappears

1977, Dec First appearance after the Cultural Revolution: Identified as deputy director, Propaganda Department of the CCP Central Committee

Liao Mosha (Liao Mo-sha) 廖沫沙

Posts held

Others
Advisor to the Beijing Journalism Society

Liao was born in 1907. In the 1930s he worked as a journalist in Shanghai. He was elected a member of the Preparatory Committee for the Journalists' Association in July 1949.

1957, Feb Identified as director of the Education Department of Beijing Municipality CP

1958, Nov Member of a workers' delegation to Moscow

1959, Dec Identified as vice-chairman of the Beijing Branch, Sino-Soviet Friendship Association

1961, Feb Member of a friendship delegation to Moscow

Sep Identified as director of the United Front Work Department of Beijing Municipality CP (until Cultural Revolution)

1961-1964 Liao publishes together with Wu Han and Deng Tuo several essays entitled "Notes of the Three-Family Village" in Qianxian (Frontline), an organ of Beijing Municipality CP

1962, Dec Elected vice-chairman of the Beijing Branch, CPPCC

1964, Apr Head of a Peace Council delegation to Japan

1966, May Branded as a revisionist in connection with his activities in the "Three-Family Village" and purged

1979, Feb First appearance after the Cultural Revolution

1980, Feb Elected advisor to the Beijing Journalism Society

Publications

1943 A Tour of Hsienyang
1944 O Phoenix! O Phoenix!
1947 Departure from Yin

Liao Rongbiao (Liao Jung-piao) 廖容标

Posts held

Military
Lieutenant-general
Deputy commander of Nanjing Military Region (?)

In 1938 Liao commanded the 3rd Detachment of the Shandong Column. In 1941 he was commander of an independently operating brigade of the Shandong Column. In 1945 he commanded the 4th Division of Shandong Military District. He was identified as commander of the 32nd (?) Corps, 3rd Field Army, in early 1949.

1950		Identified as commander of Shandong Military District and concurrently of Jinan Garrison
1951		Identified as deputy commander of the East China Security Commando based in Shanghai (until early 1955)
1955,	Jul	Identified as deputy commander of Shanghai Garrison
	Sep	Appointed lieutenant-general and commander of Shanghai Garrison (until 1959)
1959,	Oct	Identified as commander of Anhui Military District
1967		Identified as deputy commander of Nanjing Military Region
1978,	Dec	Named as advisor of Nanjing Military Region

Liao Shengdong (Liao Sheng-tung) 廖生东

Posts held

CCP
Member of the Standing Committee of Guangxi Autonomous Region CP

Provincial Administration
Vice-chairman of the People's Government of Guangxi Autonomous Region

1961,	Jan	Identified as director of the Department of Finance and Commerce, People's Council of Guangxi Autonomous Region
1965,	Aug	Member of a banking delegation to Indonesia
1975,	Dec	Identified as member of the Standing Committee of Guangxi CP
1977,	Dec	Elected vice-chairman of the Revolutionary Committee of Guangxi Autonomous Region (until Dec 1979)
1979,	Dec	Elected vice-chairman of the People's Government of Guangxi Autonomous Region

Liao Shiquan (Liao Shih-ch'üan) 廖诗权

Posts held

Government
Vice-minister of railways

NPC
Deputy for Sichuan Province to the 5th NPC

1960,	Jan	Identified as director of the Chengdu Railway Bureau
1978,	Feb	Elected deputy for Sichuan Province to the 5th NPC
	Aug	Identified as vice-minister of railways and as 2nd secretary, CP of Zhengzhou Railway Bureau

Liao Zhigao (Liao Chih-kao) 廖志高

Posts held

CCP
Member of the CCP 11th Central Committee
1st secretary of Fujian Province CP

NPC
Deputy for Fujian Province to the 5th NPC

Military
Political commissar of Fuzhou Military Region
1st political commissar of Fujian Military District
Member of the Standing Committee, CP Secretariat of Fuzhou Military Region

Provincial Administration
Chairman of the People's Congress of Fujian Province

Liao was born in 1908 in Qianning County, Xikang Province. After graduating from Qinghua University in Beijing he returned to Xikang to become a teacher in Yaan. In nearby Maogong the main Communist forces under Mao Zedong were joined by the 4th Front Army under Zhang Guotao during the Long March in the winter of 1934-35. Here Liao joined the Red Army. He served during the latter part of the Long March in a vanguard unit under Liu Bocheng. Subsequently, he studied at the Central Party School in Yan'an. From about 1937 he was engaged in guerrilla tasks in his native province of Xikang and Sichuan.

1949,	Nov	Appointed director of the Yaan Military Control Committee in Xikang Province
1950,	Feb	Appointed political commissar of Xikang Military Region (until Jul 1955)
	Mar	Appointed secretary of the CP, and governor, of Xikang Province (until Jul 1955)
	Jul	Appointed member of the Southwest China Military and Administrative Council (until Feb 1953)
	Oct	Appointed chairman of the Financial and Economic Affairs Committee of Xikang Province
1953,	Feb	Appointed member of the Southwest China Administrative Council (until Nov 1954)
1954,	Aug	Elected deputy for Xikang Province (abolished in 1955) to the 1st NPC
	Sep	Appointed member of the Nationalities Affairs Committee of the NPC (until Dec 1964)
1956,	Nov	Appointed secretary of Sichuan Province CP

1958,	May	Elected alternate member of the CCP Central Committee (until Cultural Revolution)
	Jul	Elected deputy for Sichuan Province to the 2nd NPC (until Cultural Revolution)
1965,	May	Identified as 1st secretary of Sichuan Province CP and as secretary of the Southwest China Bureau of the CCP Central Committee (until Cultural Revolution)
	Dec	Elected chairman of the Sichuan Section, CPPCC (until Cultural Revolution)
1967,	Jan	In the Cultural Revolution Liao is accused of being a sworn follower of Li Jingquan and disappears
1973,	Aug	First appearance after the Cultural Revolution: Elected alternate member of the CCP Central Committee by the 10th Party Congress (until Aug 1977)
1975,	Jan	Identified as 1st secretary of the CP, and as chairman of the Revolutionary Committee, of Fujian Province (latter post until Dec 1979)
	Feb	Identified as political commissar of Fuzhou Military Region and as 1st political commissar of Fujian Military District
1977,	Jun	Identified as member of the Standing Committee, CP Secretariat of Fuzhou Military Region
	Aug	Elected member of the CCP Central Committee by the 11th Party Congress
1978,	Feb	Elected deputy for Fujian Province to the 5th NPC; article in HQ: "Give Free Rein to the Masses to Smash the Assaults of Urban and Rural Capitalist Forces"
1979,	Aug	Head of a Party workers delegation to Romania
	Dec	Elected chairman of the People's Congress of Fujian Province

Lin Bin (Lin Pin)　　　林　彬

Posts held

Military
Major-general
Deputy commander, Armored Forces of the PLA

In 1948 Lin commanded the 43rd Brigade, 15th Column, 1st Army Corps. In the following year he was made commander of the 184th Division, 62nd Corps, 18th Army (until 1953).

1953		Training at the Military Academy of the PLA
1959		Identified as deputy commander, Armored Forces of the PLA; identified as major-general
1965,	Oct	Again referred to as deputy commander of the PLA Armored Forces; last mention in this post in Mar 1977
1975,	Jun	Identified as military leader in Lanzhou Military Region
1977,	Mar	Member of a military delegation to Pakistan

Lin Chao (Lin Ch'ao)　　　林　超

Posts held

Provincial Administration
Vice-governor of Yunnan Province

1961,	Oct	Identified as professor of the Geology and Geography Department, Beijing University
1979,	Dec	Elected vice-governor of Yunnan Province

Lin Haiyun (Lin Hai-yün)　　　林海云

Posts held

Others
Member of the Standing Committee of the 5th CPPCC

Before the establishment of PRC Lin held a post of director, Foreign Business Office, Department of Trade of North China People's Government.

1949,	Oct?	Appointed director, General Office of the Ministry of Commerce (until Jun 1950)
1950,	Mar	Appointed director, Foreign Trade Department of the Ministry of Commerce (until Oct 1952)
1954,	Dec	Appointed director, Customs Administration of the Ministry of Foreign Trade (probably until 1961)
1955,	Jun	Appointed assistant minister in the Ministry of Foreign Trade (until Oct 1956)
1956,	May	Head of a trade delegation to Finland
	Oct	Appointed vice-minister of foreign trade
1958,	Apr	Head of a trade delegation to the German Democratic Republic
1962,	Dec	Head of a trade delegation to Burma
1963,	Jan	Head of a trade delegation to Pakistan
	Dec	Head of a trade delegation to Cuba
1964,	Sep	Elected deputy for Fujian Province to the 3rd NPC
1965,	Feb	Identified as acting minister of foreign trade (until Feb 1971)
	Nov	Head of a trade delegation to Albania
1966,	Apr	Report to the Standing Committee of the NPC on the work of the Ministry of Foreign Affairs
1970,	Jan	Head of a trade delegation to Albania and Guinea
1971,	Feb	Lin disappears until May 1973
1973,	May	Named as a cadre of the State Council
1975,	May	Mentioned among the vice-ministers of foreign trade, presumably holding same post (probably until 1977)
1978,	Mar	Elected member of the Standing Committee of the 5th CPPCC

Lin Hao (Lin Hao)　　　林　浩

Posts held

Military
Commandant of the PLA Political Academy

1974,	Sep	Identified as a military cadre
1979,	Jul	Identified as commandant of the PLA Political Academy

Lin Hujia (Lin Hu-chia) 林乎加

Posts held

CCP
Member of the 11th CCP Central Committee
1st secretary of Beijing Municipality CP

NPC
Deputy for Beijing Municipality to the 5th NPC

Military
1st political commissar of Beijing Military Region
1st political commissar of Beijing Garrison

Provincial Administration
Mayor of Beijing Municipality

Lin was born in 1916 in Shanghai where he received a university education.

1951,	Jan	Appointed council member of Zhejiang People's Government; director of the Rural Work Department of Zhejiang CP
	Mar	Identified as director of the Propaganda Department of Zhejiang CP
1955,	Oct	Identified as deputy secretary of Zhejiang Province CP
1957,	May	Identified as secretary of Zhejiang Province CP (until Apr 1967)
1967,	Apr	Branded as a rightist deviationist opportunist and relieved of his posts
1974,	Sep	First appearance after the Cultural Revolution
1977,	Jan	Identified as secretary of the CP, and vice-chairman of the Revolutionary Committee, of Shanghai Municipality (until Jun 1978)
	Aug	Elected member of the CCP Central Committee by the 11th Party Congress
1978,	Jun	Identified as 1st secretary of the CP, and chairman of the Revolutionary Committee, of Tianjin Municipality (until Oct 1978)
	Oct	Identified as 1st secretary of the CP, and chairman of the Revolutionary Committee, of Beijing Municipality (latter post until Dec 1979)
1979,	May	By-elected deputy for Beijing Municipality to the 5th NPC
	Nov	Head of a Beijing friendship delegation to Japan
1979,	Dec	Elected mayor of Beijing Municipality
1980,	Feb	Identified as 1st political commissar of Beijing Military Region, and as 1st political commissar of Beijing Garrison

Lin Jixin (Lin Chi-hsin) 林基鑫

Posts held

Government
Deputy manager-general of the Bank of China

1964,	Jun	Member of a delegation to an international economics forum in Pyongyang, North Korea
1971,	Jul	Head of a banking delegation to Vietnam
	Dec	Identified as deputy manager-general of the Bank of China
1972,	Apr	Member of a delegation to the UN Conference on Trade and Development (UNCTAD) in Santiago
1975,	Aug	Chinese representative to the 7th Special Meeting of the UN General Assembly

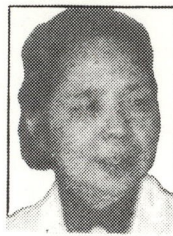

Lin Lanying (Lin Lan-ying) (f) 林兰英

Posts held

NPC
Deputy for Beijing Municipality to the 5th NPC

Others
Deputy director of the Institute of Semiconductors, Academy of Sciences

Lin was born in 1918 in Putian, Fujian Province. She lectured in physics at Xiehe University before leaving for the United States in 1948. She obtained a Ph.D. degree at the University of Pennsylvania in 1955.

1957,	Jan	Lin returns to China
1959,	Jul	Identified as research fellow of the Semiconductors Institute of the Academy of Sciences
1962,	Apr	Elected vice-chairman of the Youth Federation
1964,	Oct	Elected deputy for Guizchou Province to the 3rd NPC (confirmed in 1974 by the 4th NPC)
1965,	Jan	Elected member of the Standing Committee of the 3rd NPC
1977,	Dec	Identified as deputy director of the Institute of Semiconductors of the Academy of Sciences
1978,	Feb	Elected deputy for Beijing Municipality to the 5th NPC
	Mar	Lin is engaged in revising the Horizontal Bridgeman Method and seeking new materials for semiconductors
1979,	Jun	Member of the Committee to Examine Proposals at the 2nd Session of the 5th NPC

Lin Lin (Lin Lin) 林林

Posts held

Others
Vice-chairman of the Association for Friendship with Foreign Countries
President of the Society for the Study of Japanese Literature

Lin was born in Fujian Province. He is a graduate of Beijing University and later continued his studies in Japan from 1933 to 1936.

1953, Mar Identified as director of the Literature and Art Section in the Propaganda Department, South China Bureau of the CCP Central Committee

Dec Appointed deputy director of the Cultural Bureau, People's Government of Guangdong Province

1955, Mar Elected member of the Standing Committee, Guangzhou Section of the Union of Chinese Writers

Jun Identified as secretary-general of the Sino-Indonesian Friendship Association (until 1966)

Oct Identified as cultural attaché at the embassy in India

1959, Apr Identified as deputy secretary-general of the Association for Cultural Relations with Foreign Counties

Aug Identified as deputy secretary-general, Liaison Committee with the Permanent Bureau of Afro-Asian Writers

1960, Jan Deputy head of a cultural delegation to Burma

Apr Elected member of the Standing Committee of the Sino-African Friendship Association (until Cultural Revolution)

1961, Mar Member of a delegation to the Conference of Afro-Asian Writers in Japan

1963, Sep Head of a delegation of artists to Japan

Oct Identified as deputy secretary-general of the Sino-Japanese Friendship Association (until Cultural Revolution)

1965, Jun Elected member of the Afro-Asian Solidarity Committee (until Cultural Revolution)

1966, Apr Elected secretary of the newly established Association for Cultural Relations and Friendship with Foreign Countries (until Cultural Revolution)

1967   Disappears during the Cultural Revolution

1973, Jun First appearance after the Cultural Revolution: Referred to as vice-chairman of the Association for Friendship with Foreign Countries

1979, Nov Elected president of the Society for the Study of Japanese Literature

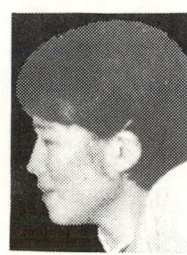

Lin Liyun (Lin Li-yün) (f)   林丽韫

Posts held

CCP
Member of the CCP 11th Central Committee

NPC
Member of the Standing Committee of the 5th NPC
Deputy for Taiwan to the 5th NPC

Mass Organization
Vice-president of the Women's Federation

Others
Council member of the Sino-Japanese Friendship Association

Lin was born in 1933 on Taiwan.

1971, Feb Present at receptions given by Premier Zhou Enlai for delegations from Japan

1973, Apr Identified as council member of the Sino-Japanese Friendship Association; member of a delegation of this association to Japan

Aug Elected to first term as member of the CCP Central Committee by the 10th Party Congress

1974, Oct Head of a group of the Central Philharmonic Society to Japan

1975, Jan Elected member of the Standing Committee of the 4th NPC (reelected 1978 to the 5th NPC)

1976, Sep Article in RMRM of 30 September: "We Are Determined to Liberate Taiwan"

1978, Feb Elected deputy for Taiwan to the 5th NPC

Sep Elected vice-president of the Women's Federation

1979, Apr Deputy head of an NPC delegation, led by Deng Yingchao, to Japan

Jun Member of the Credentials Committee at the 2nd Session of the 5th NPC

Jul Appointed member of the National Games Organizing Committee

Sep Head of a delegation of the Women's Federation to the 25th Conference of the International Alliance of Women in Monrovia

Oct Head of a women's delegation to Sierra Leone and Niger

Lin Mohan (Lin Mo-han)   林默涵

Posts held

Government
Vice-minister of culture

Others
Vice-chairman of the Federation of Literary and Art Circles

Lin was invited to attend the 1st National Congress of Writers and Artists organized by the Communists in June 1949 in Beijing. In the event, he did not take part, however, because he was unable to obtain transport to Beijing from Hong Kong where he was working at the time.

1950   In Beijing appointed member of the Culture and Education Committee, Planning Committee of the Government Administration Council (until Sep 1954)

1953, Oct Appointed member of the Union of Chinese Writers

1957, Sep Identified as deputy secretary of the Association of Literary and Art Circles

1958, Sep Appointed director of the Literature Division, Propaganda Department of the CCP Central Committee

1959, Sep Appointed vice-minister of culture (until Cultural Revolution)

1961, Aug Identified as deputy director, Propaganda Department of the CCP Central Committee

1962, Aug Lin addresses the Conference of Stage Authors in Guangzhou

Dec Member of a cultural delegation to Cuba;
appointed vice-chairman of the Sino-Cuban Friendship Association

1964, Sep Elected deputy for Fujian Province to the 3rd NPC

1967, Dec Branded as a counterrevolutionary and purged

1978, Jan First appearance after the Cultural Revolution: Identified as vice-minister of culture

1979, Nov Elected vice-chairman of the Federation of Literary and Art Circles

Lin Ping (Lin P'ing)  林 平

Posts held

Government
Ambassador to Australia

Lin was born in 1920 in Zhejiang Province.

1955, Aug Identified as assistant at the Sino-American Ambassadorial Talks in Warsaw

1959, Oct Identified as deputy director of the America and Australia Department in the Ministry of Foreign Affairs

1960, Mar Identified as council member of the Sino-Latin-American Friendship Association

1962, Dec Identified as council member of the Sino-Cuban Friendship Association

1965, Jun Appointed head of the Chinese Trade Mission in Chile (until 1970)

1971, Jun Appointed ambassador to Chile (until Feb 1973)

1973, Jul Identified as director of the America and Oceania Department in the Ministry of Foreign Affairs (until Oct 1978)

1978, Nov Appointed ambassador to Australia

Li is married to Zhi Ni.

Lin Qiaozhi (Lin Ch'iao-ch ih) (f) 林巧稚

Posts held

NPC
Member of the Standing Committee of the 5th NPC
Deputy for Beijing Municipality to the 5th NPC

Mass Organization
Vice-president of the Women's Federation

Others
Vice-president of the Academy of Medical Sciences
Director, Department of Obstetrics and Gynaecology at the Anti-Imperialist Hospital in Beijing
Vice-president of the Medical Association

Lin was born circa 1920 in Fujian Province. She studied medicine in the United States.

1950, Aug Identified as council member of the Medical Society

1951, Nov Elected member of the National Committee for the Protection of Children

1953, Apr Elected member of the Executive Council of the Women's Federation; identified as principal professor, Department of Obstetrics and Gynaecology at Beijing Medical College

1954, Mar Identified as vice-chairman of the Beijing Women's Federation

       Aug Elected deputy for Beijing Municipality to the 1st NPC (reelected in 1958 and 1964 to the 2nd and 3rd NPCs)

1955, May Identified as member of the Department of Biology and Earth Sciences, Academy of Sciences

1957, Mar Identified as chairman of the Birth Control Committee in the Medical Society

       May Identified as vice-chairman of the Medical Society

1959, Apr Elected member of the Standing Committee of the 3rd CPPCC (until Dec 1964)

1960, Oct Identified as council member of the Sino-Albanian Friendship Association (until Cultural Revolution)

1964, Mar Identified as vice-president of the Academy of Medical Sciences

1965, Jan Elected member of the Standing Committee of the 3rd NPC (confirmed in this post by the 4th and 5th NPCs in 1975 and 1978)

1971, Nov Identified as director, Department of Obstetrics and Gynecology at the Anti-Imperialist Hospital in Beijing

1972, Oct Member of a medical delegation to the United States, Canada, and France

1974, Nov Head of a goodwill delegation to Iran for the inauguration of the direct airlink between Beijing and Teheran

1978, Feb Elected deputy for Beijing Municipality to the 5th NPC

       Jun Identified as vice-president of the Medical Association

       Sep Elected vice-president of the Women's Federation; identified as advisor of the Popular Science Writers' Society

       Nov Member of a friendship delegation to Great Britain, Belgium, and France

1979, Jun Member of the Committee to Examine Proposals at the 2nd Session of the 5th NPC

Lin Shaonan (Lin Shao-nan) (f)  林少南

Posts held

Provincial Administration
Vice-governor of Hubei Province

Lin is the widow of Zhang Tixue, former member of the CCP Central Committee and 1st secretary of Hubei Province CP, who died on 3 September 1973.

1978, Jan Elected vice-chairman of the Revolutionary Committee of Hubei Province (until Dec 1979)

1980, Jan Elected vice-governor of Hubei Province

Lin Song (Lin Sung)

Posts held

Government
Ambassador to Equatorial Guinea

1972,	Jul	Identified as embassy counselor in Zambia
1976,	Jan	Identified as embassy counselor in Burundi (until 1979)
1980,	Jan	Appointed ambassador to Equatorial Guinea

Lin Tie (Lin T'ieh)

Posts held

NPC
Member of the Standing Committee of the 5th NPC
Deputy for Hebei Province to the 5th NPC

Lin was born in 1904 in Sichuan Province. He studied at the Guangdong Agricultural Institute. In 1946 he was identified as political commissar of a district in Shaanxi-Hebei-Chahar Military Region. In the following year he was CP secretary of Central Hebei. In September 1949 he took part in the CPPCC as a delegate representing North China.

1949,	Nov?	Appointed member of the People's Government of Hebei Province
1950		Elected secretary of Hebei Province CP (until Aug 1956)
1952,	Nov	Elected chairman of Hebei Province (until Feb 1955); identified as political commissar of Hebei Military Region (probably until 1957)
1954,	Aug	Elected deputy for Hebei Province to the 1st NPC
1955,	Feb	Appointed governor of Hebei Province after reorganization of the Provincial Government (until Nov 1958)
1956,	Aug	Appointed 1st secretary of Hebei Province CP
	Sep	Elected member of the CCP Central Committee by the 8th Party Congress
1960,	Apr	Guest delegate for the CCP at the CP Belgium Congress in Brussels
1965,	Apr	Identified as 3rd Secretary, North China Bureau of the CCP Central Committee
1967,	Apr	Branded as a member of the "Liu-Deng Clique"
1974,	Sep	First appearance after the Cultural Revolution
1978,	Feb	Elected deputy for Hebei Province to the 5th NPC
	Mar	Elected member of the Standing Committee of the 5th NPC

Lin Weixian (Lin Wei-hsien)

Posts held

NPC
Deputy for the PLA to the 5th NPC

Military
Lieutenant-general
Deputy commander of Wuhan Military Region

Lin was born in 1911 as the son of poor peasants in Jincai, Lihong County, Anhui Province. In 1928 he served in the 4th Front Army under Xu Xiangqian. In 1932 he became a member of the CCP. During the Long March he was ordered to stay behind with his regiment in Heshan with a guerrilla unit of 1,700 men. This unit was reorganized in 1935 to form the 28th Red Army. In 1941 he commanded a regiment of the New 4th Army and was concurrently secretary of Anhui Province CP. In 1945 he was appointed commander of the 21st Brigade, New 4th Army. In 1946 Lin commanded the 7th Division, 3rd Column of the Northeast China Liberation Army. In 1949 he was commander of the 22nd Corps of the 3rd Field Army.

1950		Appointed deputy commander of Shanghai Garrison
1951		Identified as commander of the Security Forces in East China Military Region
1955,	Jul	Appointed lieutenant-general; identified as commander of Zhejiang Military District (until 1964)
1959,	Apr	Appointed member of the National Defense Council (until Cultural Revolution)
1964,	Nov	Identified as deputy commander of Nanjing Military Region (until 1969)
1970,	May	Identified as deputy commander of Wuhan Military Region
1978,	Feb	Elected deputy for the PLA to the 5th NPC

Lin Xiude (Lin Hsiu-te)

Posts held

Government
Deputy director of the Office of Overseas Chinese Affairs under the State Council

Others
Member of the Standing Committee of the 5th CPPCC

Lin is a native of Fujian Province.

1954		Identified as director of the United Front Work Department of Fujian Province CP
1955,	Feb	Identified as council member of Fujian Province People's Government
1956,	Feb	Identified as vice-chairman of the Fujian Section, CPPCC
1958,	Mar	Professorship for socialist education at the Teachers' College in Fujian; identified as member of the Standing Committee of Fujian Province CP (until Aug 1960)
1960,	Jun	Member of the Presidium, National Conference of Literary and Art Workers
	Aug	Identified as alternate member of the Secretariat of Fujian Province CP (until 1964)
1963,	Jan	Identified as 1st secretary of Fuzhou Municipality CP
1964,	Apr	Identified as vice-chairman of the Overseas Chinese Affairs Commission under the State Council (until Cultural Revolution)

	Dec	Delegate at the 4th CPPCC representing the Overseas Chinese (confirmed in 1978 by the 5th CPPCC)
1965,	Jan	Elected member of the Standing Committee of the 4th CPPCC
1966		Disappears during the Cultural Revolution
1973,	May	First appearance after the Cultural Revolution: Referred to in his former post as member of the Standing Committee, CPPCC (confirmed in this post in Jan 1975 by the 5th CPPCC)
1975,	Sep	Named as a cadre of the State Council
1978,	Apr	Identified as deputy director of the Office of Overseas Chinese Affairs under the State Council

Lin Yi (Lin Yi)　　　　林　毅

Posts held

Government
Vice-minister of the 6th Ministry of Machine Building

1979,	Oct	Identified as vice-minister of the 6th Ministry of Machine Building

Lin Yinru (Lin Yin-ju)　　　林菌如

Posts held

Provincial Administration
Vice-chairman of the People's Congress of Shaanxi Province

1959,	Apr	Identified as deputy director of the Financial and Trade Department of Shaanxi Province CP
1964,	Sep	Identified as vice-governor of Shaanxi Province (until Cultural Revolution)
1967		Disappears during the Cultural Revolution
1979,	Jan	First appearance after the Cultural Revolution: Identified as vice-chairman of the Revolutionary Committee of Shaanxi Province (until Dec 1979)
	Dec	Elected vice-chairman of the People's Congress of Shaanxi Province

Lin Yiping (Lin Yi-p'ing)　　　林依平

Posts held

NPC
Member of the Standing Committee of the 5th NPC
Deputy for the PLA to the 5th NPC

1978,	Feb	Elected deputy for the PLA to the 5th NPC
	Mar	Elected member of the Standing Committee of the 5th NPC

Lin Yishan (Lin Yi-shan)　　　林一山

Posts held

NPC
Member of the Standing Committee of the 5th NPC
Deputy for Hubei Province to the 5th NPC

Others
Chairman of the Chang Jiang Valley Long-range Planning Commission

Lin served in the 4th Field Army in 1949.

1949,	Dec	Identified as director of the Chang Jiang River Conservancy Commission
1950,	Nov	Identified as member of the Huai River Control Commission
1951,	Mar	Identified as member of the Financial and Economic Committee of the Central-South Military and Administrative Council
1952,	Apr	Identified as deputy director of the Jing River Stream-dividing Engineering Commission
1954,	Jul	Identified as director of the Chang Jiang River Conservancy Commission
1958,	Jan	Identified as director of the Chang Jiang River Planning Office under the Ministry of Water Conservancy and Power
1967		Disappears during the Cultural Revolution
1976,	Jan	First appearance after the Cultural Revolution attending the mourning ceremonies for Zhou Enlai
1978,	Feb	Elected deputy for Hubei Province to the 5th NPC
	Mar	Elected member of the Standing Committee of the 5th NPC
1979,	Oct	Identified as chairman of the Chang Jiang Valley Long-range Planning Commission

Lin Yixin (Lin Yi-hsin)　　　林一心

Posts held

CCP
Secretary of Fujian Province CP

Others
Member of the Standing Committee of the 5th CPPCC
Vice-chairman of the Board of Directors of Quanzhou Overseas Chinese University

1950,	Jan	Identified as secretary of Xiamen Municipality CP
1952,	Jul	Identified as member of Fujian Province CP
	Sep	Identified as deputy director of Fujian Province CP
1954,	Aug	Elected deputy for Fujian Province to the 1st NPC (reelected in 1959 and 1964 to the 2nd and 3rd NPCs)
1955		Identified as deputy secretary of Fujian Province CP (until Feb 1957)
1957		Identified as secretary of Fujian Province CP

1960,	Feb	Appointed chairman of the Committee of Fujian Province for Receiving and Resettling Returned Overseas Chinese (until Cultural Revolution)
1965,	Aug	Appointed vice-chairman of the Overseas Chinese Affairs Commission under the State Council (until Cultural Revolution)
1972,	Sep	Reactivated after the Cultural Revolution
1975,	Jul	Identified as secretary of Fujian Province CP
1978,	Mar	Elected member of the Standing Committee of the 5th CPPCC
	Jun	Identified as vice-chairman of the Revolutionary Committee of Fujian Province (until Dec 1979)

Lin Zesheng (Lin Tse-sheng)　林泽生

Posts held

Government
Vice-minister of metallurgical industry

1955,	Jan	Appointed assistant minister of heavy industry (until May 1956)
1957,	Sep	Appointed vice-minister of metallurgical industry (until Sep 1959)
1959,	Sep	Appointed vice-minister of metallurgical industry
1972,	Sep	Lin disappears followed by public appearance only in 1974 and Jan 1975
1977,	Jul	Renewed mention as vice-minister of metallurgical industry

Lin Zhaonan (Lin Chao-nan)　林兆南

Posts held

Government
Chargé d'affaires ad interim, Chinese embassy in Iran

1956,	Jul	Identified as attaché at the embassy in Egypt (until 1964)
1964,	Apr	Identified as deputy director of the West Asia and Africa Department in the Ministry of Foreign Affairs (until Sep 1964); member of a delegation led by Minister of Foreign Affairs Chen Yi to the Preparatory Session of the 2nd Afro-Asian Conference in Jakarta
	Sep	After reorganization identified as deputy director of the West Asia and North Africa Department in the Ministry of Foreign Affairs
1975,	Nov	First appearance after the Cultural Revolution: Identified in his former post as deputy director of the West Asia and North Africa Department in the Ministry of Foreign Affairs (until 1977)
1976,	May	Member of a government delegation to Sudan
1977,	Jun	Identified as acting director of the West Asia and Africa Department in the Minis-

try of Foreign Affairs (until 1978)

| | Sep | Alternate representative, Chinese delegation to the 32nd UN General Assembly |
| 1978, | Sep | Identified as chargé d'affaires ad interim, Chinese embassy in Iran |

Lin Zhenfeng (Lin Chen-feng)　林震峰

Posts held

Government
Deputy manager-general of the Insurance Company

1965,	Aug	Identified as deputy manager-general of the Insurance Company
1966		Lin disappears
1973,	Nov	First appearance after the Cultural Revolution: Identified as holding his former post as deputy manager-general of the Insurance Company
1974,	Jun	Head of a delegation to the 3rd African Insurance Conference in Zaire and to Tanzania
1975,	Jul	Head of an insurance delegation to Nigeria
1977,	Oct	Head of a delegation to the 3rd World Insurance Congress in the Philippines
1978,	Aug	Head of an insurance delegation to Mozambique
1979,	Jun	Head of an insurance delegation to Kenya

Lin Zhong (Lin Chung)　林　中

Posts held

CCP
Director of the Political Department of the Foreign Ministry

Government
Assistant minister of foreign affairs

1958,	Jun	Identified as deputy director of the Personnel Department of the Ministry of Foreign Affairs
1962,	Nov	Identified as counselor, embassy in Hungary (until 1964)
1965,	May	Identified as counselor, embassy in Bulgaria (until about 1966)
1969,	Jul	Identified as counselor, embassy in Albania (until 1970)
1971,	Aug	Appointed ambassador to Algeria (until Mar 1975)
1975,	Jun	Appointed ambassador to Mozambique (until Jan 1977)
1978,	May	Identified as assistant minister of foreign affairs
	Oct	Member of a government delegation led by Geng Biao to Congo, Guinea, Mali, Ghana, and Nigeria
1979,	Aug	Identified as director of the Political Department of the Foreign Ministry

Lin Zongtang (Lin Tsung-t'ang) 林宗棠

Posts held

Government
Deputy director of a department under the State Scientific and Technological Commission

NPC
Deputy for Shanghai Municipality to the 5th NPC

1978, Feb Elected deputy for Shanghai Municipality to the 5th NPC; identified as assistant chief engineer of the Shanghai Heavy Machinery Plant who designed China's first 10,000 ton hydraulic press

1979, Jun Identified as deputy director of a department under the State Scientific and Technological Commission; identified as chief engineer of the High-Energy Physics Experimental Center; identified as deputy chief engineer for the construction of the laboratory of the high-energy accelerator

Ling Qing (Ling Ch'ing) 凌青

Posts held

Government
Director of the Department for International Organizations and Conferences, Agreements and Laws, Ministry of Foreign Affairs

1965, Jan 1st secretary at the embassy in Indonesia
Jun Deputy director of the Department of International Relations in the Ministry of Foreign Affairs (until about 1966)

1971, Apr Deputy director of the Western Europe, America and Australia Department in the Ministry of Foreign Affairs (until Aug 1972)

1972, Aug Deputy director of the Department of International Organizations and Conferences, Agreements and Laws in the Ministry of Foreign Affairs (until Sep 1975)

1973, Feb Member of the Chinese delegation to the Vietnam Conference in Paris
Sep Member of the Chinese delegation to the UN General Assembly

1974, Jun Deputy head of the Chinese delegation to the UN Law of the Sea Conference

1975, Oct Appointed ambassador to Venezuela (until Jan 1978)

1976, Jul Head of the Chinese delegation to the UN Law of the Sea Conference

1977, Sep Representative of the Chinese delegation to the 23rd UN General Assembly

1978, May Deputy head of a delegation to the UN General Assembly on Disarmament in New York
Aug Identified as director of the Department for International Organizations and Conferences, Agreements and Laws in the Ministry of Foreign Affairs

1979, Jul Deputy head of the Chinese delegation to the Indochina Refugee Conference in Geneva

Ling Yun (Ling Yün) 凌云

Posts held

Government
Vice-minister of public security

NPC
Deputy for Shanghai Municipality to the 5th NPC

Ling was born in 1917.

1964, Feb Identified as vice-minister of public security (until 1966)
Sep Elected deputy for Shandong Province to the 3rd NPC

1966 Disappears during the Cultural Revolution
1975, Sep First appearance after the Cultural Revolution
Dec Identified as vice-minister of public security

1978, Feb Elected deputy for Shanghai Municipality to the 5th NPC

1979, Jun Member of the Committee to Examine Proposals at the 2nd Session of the 5th NPC
Oct Member of the delegation, led by Hua Guofeng, to France, the Federal Republic of Germany, Great Britain, and Italy

Liu Ang (Liu Ang) (f) 刘昂

Posts held

Government
Vice-minister of agricultural machinery

1959, Mar Elected deputy for Sichuan Province to the 2nd NPC (reelected in 1964 to the 3rd NPC)

1960, May Identified as deputy director of the Premier's Secretariat (until 1966)

1973, Mar First appearance after the Cultural Revolution
Dec Identified as vice-minister of the 1st Ministry of Machine Building (until 1978)

1979, Sep Identified as vice-minister of agricultural machinery

Liu Baitao (Liu Pai-t'ao) 刘白涛

Posts held

Government
Vice-minister of railways

Others
Secretary, CP of the Shanghai Railway Bureau

1978, Sep Identified as secretary, CP of the Shanghai Railway Bureau and as vice-minister of railways

Liu Baiyu (Liu Pai-yü)　　刘白羽

Posts held

NPC
Deputy for the PLA to the 5th NPC

Military
Director of the Cultural Section, PLA
General Political Department

Others
Vice-chairman of the Writers' Union
Council member of the Sino-Soviet
Friendsip Association

Liu was born in 1915 in Hebei Province. He went to Yan'an in 1938. In 1946 he worked for New China Daily. He took part in the Battle of Sipingjie in 1947. In 1949 he was a reporter for NCNA. In July 1949 he was elected a member of the Federation of Literary and Art Circles (until Cultural Revolution). In September of that year he took part in the 1st CPPCC as a delegate representing the 4th Field Army.

1950,	Nov	Member of a delegation to the USSR; identified as deputy director, Cultural Section of the PLA Political Department
1951,	Jul	Awarded the Stalin prize for the scenario entitled "The Victory of the Chinese People"
	Oct	Member of a cultural delegation to India and Burma
1952,	Oct	Identified as council member of the Sino-Indian Friendship Association
1953,	Nov	Identified as council member of the Union of Chinese Writers
1954,	May	Identified as council member of the Association for Cultural Relations with Foreign Countries
	Aug	Elected deputy for Hebei Province to the 1st NPC (reelected in 1958 to the 2nd NPC)
1956,	Dec	Elected secretary of the Union of Chinese Writers
1958,	Feb	Identified as vice-chairman of the Sino-Albanian Friendship Association
1960,	Apr	Elected member of the Standing Committee of the Sino-African Friendship Association (until Cultural Revolution)
	Aug	Elected vice-chairman of the Union of Chinese Writers
	Dec	Head of a literary delegation to Ceylon
1961,	Mar	Head of a literary delegation to Japan
1962,	Apr	Head of a literary delegation to North Korea
1964,	Sep	Elected deputy for Beijing Municipality to the 3rd NPC
1965,	Mar	Deputy head of a literary delegation to Japan
	Apr	Identified as vice-minister of culture (until Cultural Revolution)
	Jun	Elected vice-chairman of the Afro-Asian Solidarity Committee (until Cultural Revolution)
1967,	Feb	Branded as a counterrevolutionary revisionist
1976,	Jan	First appearance after the Cultural Revolution attending the mourning ceremonies for Zhou Enlai

1977,	Nov	Identified as council member of the Sino-Soviet Friendship Association and director of the Cultural Section, PLA General Political Department
1978,	Feb	Elected deputy for the PLA to the 5th NPC
	Jun	Identified as vice-chairman of the Chinese Writers' Union

Liu Bing (Liu Ping)　　刘冰

Posts held

Provincial Administration
Vice-governor of Gansu Province

1979,	Dec	Elected vice-governor of Gansu Province

Liu Bocheng (Liu Po-ch'eng)　　刘伯承

Posts held

CCP
Member of the Politburo of the CCP
11th Central Committee
Member of the CCP 11th Central Committee

NPC
Vice-chairman of the Standing Committee of the 5th NPC
Deputy for the PLA to the 5th NPC

Military
Marshal

Liu Bocheng was born in 1892 in Kai County, Sichuan Province, as the son of a traveling musician. Thanks to his father's wish to secure a better future for his son, Liu received an expensive school education. However, as the son of a musician, placed at the bottom of the social hierarchy in traditional China, Liu was not admitted to the Xiucai examination although he qualified in all other respects. Eventually, he enrolled at the Military Academy in Chengdu, provincial capital of Sichuan, from which he graduated shortly before the Revolution of 1911. He began his career as a young officer in the forces under General Xiong Kewu who fought the Manchu Garrisons after the Revolution. During the following years Liu repeatedly distinguished himself for bravery and was wounded several times. Following the loss of one eye during this period, he became known as the "one-eyed dragon" (du-yan long). Under the influence of Sichuan scholar and revolutionary Wu Yuzhang, Liu began to support the Communist cause in the early 1920s. He joined the CCP in May 1926 and temporarily served as leader of guerrilla units in Sichuan. Shortly afterwards he joined the Northern Expedition in the summer of 1926 as commander of the 15th Army and concurrently functioned as liaison officer with the forces under Yang Sen in Sichuan. In August 1927 Liu played a significant roll in the Nanchang Uprising. After its failure he left for the USSR to study initially at the Moscow Infantry School and from 1928 to 1930 at the Red Army University (Frunze Military Academy). According to unconfirmed reports, Liu is thought to have served under the Soviet General Galen who fought Zhang Xueliang in Manchuria in 1929. In the summer of 1930 Liu Bocheng returned to China under orders to take Nanchang. After the failure of this operation he withdrew with his troops to East Hunan. In 1931 the joined the main Communist forces in Jiangxi Soviet. There he served as head of the Red Army Academy during the following three years. In 1932 he was appointed concurrently chief of staff, Headquarters of the Communist Armored Forces. During the Long March Liu Bocheng commanded vanguard units, successfully leading his troops through the most difficult terrain in Xikang. The hostile mountain tribes of the Miao living in that area allowed the Communist forces unhindered passage after Liu, who spoke their language, had pledged friendship with the tribal chief. In the inner-Party struggles during the Long March, Liu took the side of Mao Zedong. After the outbreak of the Anti-Japanese War in 1937 he was made commander of the 129th Division, one of the three divisions of the reorganized 8th Route Army. These forces were originally based in Shanxi and Hebei and later extended their operations to Henan and Shandong. In spring 1944 the headquarters for Shanxi-Hebei-Shandong-Henan-Anhui were set up under Liu's command. During this period his troops dug an extensive tunnel system along the northern embankment of the Huang He which served both as protection against artillery fragments and as an easily defended communications network. This tactic was later also employed by the Chinese in the Korean War. In August 1945 Liu was elected for the first time member of the CCP Central Committee by the 7th Party Congress. After the Japanese capitulation he continued as commander of the forces in the Shanxi-Hebei-Shandong-Henan Region. In June 1946 his troops crossed the Huang He and the Longhai Railway and pushed forward via Kaifeng to Dongshan before they were forced to retreat to the northern bank of the Huang He. From 1947 to 1948 Liu's troops operated along the railway between Beijing and Hankou. In 1948 they were reorganized to form the 2nd Field Army which subsequently played a significant role in the war against the KMT forces in South China. In April 1949 Liu occupied Nanjing and eventually reached Yunnan having pushed through Guizhou and Sichuan. In September 1949 he was elected a member of the CPPCC.

1949,	Oct	Appointed 1st deputy secretary of the CCP Central Committee, council member of the newly established Sino-Soviet Friendship Association, member of the Central Government Administration Council, and member of the Revolutionary Military Council (until Sep 1954)
1951		Appointed director of the PLA Military Academy (until 1958)
1954,	Jun	Appointed vice-chairman of the Revolutionary Military Council (until Sep 1954)
	Sep	Elected deputy for the PLA to the NPC; appointed vice-chairman of the National Defense Council as well as director of the Training Department of the PLA (until 1957); elected vice-chairman of the Standing Committee of the NPC
1955,	Sep	Appointed marshal
1956,	Sep	Elected member of the CCP Politburo by the 8th Party Congress (confirmed in this post by the 9th to 11th Congresses)
1975,	Jan	Elected vice-chairman of the 4th NPC (confirmed in this post in 1978 by the 5th NPC)
1978,	Feb	Elected deputy for the PLA to the 5th NPC

Note

Due to the near total loss of his eye-sight, Liu has not taken part in public occasions since his reelection as member of the Politburo in August 1977.

Liu Changyi (Liu Ch'ang-yi)  刘昌毅

Posts held

Military
Vice-admiral
Deputy commander of Guangzhou Military Region

In the early 1940s Liu commanded a brigade (of the New 4th Army?). In 1949 he was deputy commander of a corps of the 3rd Field Army.

1950		Transferred to the Navy
1955		Identified as deputy commander of the North China Sea Fleet and as rear-admiral
1958,	Feb	Identified as vice-admiral, based in Lüda (Lüshun-Dalian)
1959,	Apr	Elected council member of the 3rd CPPCC (confirmed in this post in 1964)
1967		Disappears during the Cultural Revolution
1975,	Mar	First appearance after the Cultural Revolution: Identified as deputy commander of Nanjing Military Region (until 1978)
1979,	Apr	Identified as deputy commander of Guangzhou Military Region

Liu Chonggui (Liu Ch'ung-kuei) 刘重桂

Posts held

CCP
Alternate member of the CCP 11th Central Committee
2nd secretary of Guangxi Autonomous Region CP

Military
Senior colonel
Political commissar of Guangxi Military District

1961,	Aug	Identified as military attaché in North Vietnam with the rank of senior colonel (until 1964)
1964,	Sep	Identified as deputy commander of Guangxi Military District
1970,	May	Identified as vice-chairman of the Revolutionary Committee of Guangxi Autonomous Region (until Dec 1979); identified as 2nd political commissar of Guangxi Military District (until Dec 1970)
1971,	Jan	Identified as political commissar of Guangxi Military District
	Feb	With the reestablishment of the CP Secretariat of Guangxi Autonomous Region, Liu is elected deputy secretary (until Aug 1974)
1974,	Aug	Identified as secretary of Guangxi Autonomous Region CP (until Apr 1977)

1977,   Apr Identified as 2nd secretary of Guangxi Autonomous Region CP
          Aug Elected alternate member of the CCP Central Committee by the 11th Party Congress

Liu Chun (Liu Ch'un)   刘 春

Posts held

Government
Former ambassador to Tanzania and the Seychelles

Liu is a former student of Beijing University. During the Anti-Japanese War he served in the 8th Route Army and as a political cadre in Shanxi-Hebei-Chahar Military Region.

1955   Promoted to rank of major-general
1960   Identified as director of the Political Department, Armored Forces of the PLA
1961,   Nov Identified as deputy head of the Economic and Cultural Mission in Khang Khay, Laos
1962,   Jul Identified as chargé d'affaires ad interim in Laos
          Sep Appointed ambassador to Laos (until about 1970)
1963,   Mar Liu accompanies the king of Laos on his visit to China
1964,   Apr Liu accompanies the prime minister of Laos on his visit to China
          Oct Liu accompanies Prince Souphannouvong on his visit to China
1970,   Oct Member of a friendship delegation to North Korea; conferred the Korean order "National Flag," 2nd class
1971,   Aug Identified as director of the Asia Department in the Ministry of Foreign Affairs
1972,   May Appointed ambassador to Turkey (until Mar 1976)
1974,   Jul Liu accompanies the foreign minister of Turkey on his visit to China
1976,   May Appointed ambassador to Tanzania (until Oct 1979)
1978,   Apr Appointed concurrently ambassador to the Seychelles (until Sep 1979)

Liu Chunqiao (Liu Ch'un-ch'iao)   刘春樵

Posts held

CCP
Member of the CCP 11th Central Committee
Member of the Standing Committee of Hunan Province CP

Provincial Administration
Vice-chairman of the People's Congress of Hunan Province

Liu was born circa 1920 in Changde, Hunan Province. As a child he was forced to support himself by begging. Later he worked for eighteen years as a farm laborer. He became known as Representative of Progressive Producers in Hunan Province.

1969,   Jan Identified as chairman of the Revolutionary Committee of Caijiagang People's Commune in Changde County, Hunan Province
          Apr Elected alternate member of the CCP Central Committee by the 9th Party Congress (until Aug 1977)
1970,   Apr Identified as secretary of Caijiagang People's Commune CP
1971,   Aug Identified as member of the Standing Committee of Hunan Province CP
1973,   Dec Elected vice-chairman of the Peasants' Federation of Hunan Province (no later mention in this post)
1977,   Aug Elected member of the CCP Central Committee by the 11th Party Congress
1979,   Dec Elected vice-chairman of the People's Congress of Hunan Province

Liu Dagang (Liu Ta-kang)   柳大纲

Posts held

NPC
Deputy for Beijing Municipality to the 5th NPC

Others
Director of the Institute of Chemistry, Academy of Sciences

1959,   Mar Identified as deputy director of the Institute of Chemistry, Academy of Sciences
1960,   Nov Identified as director of the Institute of Chemistry, Academy of Sciences
1964,   Sep Elected deputy for Jiangsu Province to the 3rd NPC
          Oct Identified as deputy director of the Institute of Applied Chemistry, Academy of Sciences
1967   Disappears during the Cultural Revolution
1974,   Sep First appearance after the Cultural Revolution
1977,   Dec Identified as director of the Institute of Chemistry, Academy of Sciences
1978,   Feb Elected deputy for Beijing Municipality to the 5th NPC

Liu Danian (Liu Ta-nien)   刘大年

Posts held

NPC
Member of the Standing Committee of the 5th NPC
Deputy for Shanghai Municipality to the 5th NPC

1953,   May Member of a delegation of the Chinese Academy of Sciences to the USSR
1954,   Apr Identified as secretary of the Academy of Sciences
1955,   Feb Identified as deputy chief-editor of the monthly Lishi Yanjiu (Historical Research)
          May Identified as member of the Department of Philosophy and Social Sciences of the Academy of Sciences

1960,	Oct	Identified as deputy director of the Institute of Modern History of the Academy of Sciences (until Jan 1967)
1962,	Jan	Liu attends a conference of Pakistani historians in Dacca
1963,	Dec	Delegate at a conference of historians in Japan
1964,	Sep	Elected deputy for Hunan Province to the 3rd NPC
1965,	Oct	Appointed member of the Peparatory Committee for the celebrations of the 100th birthday of Sun Yat-sen
1966,	Oct	On 25 October Liu is branded by the official news agency Xinhua as a member of a group of anti-Party elements, as an anti-socialist historian, and sworn supporter of Li Shu, Deng Tuo, Wu Han, Jian Bozan, and Hou Wailu
1967,	Jan	An article in RMRB of 8 January refers to Liu as an "accomplice of Zhou Yang" (a leading propaganda cadre). In addition, he is accused of having disregarded instructions by Mao Zedong; subsequently disappears
1972,	Jul	First appearance after the Cultural Revolution
1975,	Jan	Elected member of the Standing Committee by the 4th NPC (confirmed in 1978 by the 5th NPC)
1978,	Feb	Elected deputy for Shanghai Municipality to the 5th NPC

Publications since 1955

The Reactionary Nature of Liu Shangming's Thought on Problems of the Chinese Feudal and Land System
On Emperor Kang Xi, the Revolution of 1911, and the Opposition against Manchu Rule
Historical Science in New China
Problems of Modern History in China
The Evaluation of a History of Asia

Liu Daosheng (Liu Tao-sheng)   刘道生

Posts held

CCP
Alternate member of the CCP 11th Central Committee

Military
Vice-admiral
1st deputy commander of the PLA Navy

Liu was born circa 1916 in Jiangxi Province. He joined the Communist forces in Hunan-Jiangxi Border Area as a youth in the early 1930s. In 1933 he attended a course at the Red Army Academy in Ruijin where Deng Xiaoping and Liu Bocheng were among his teachers. In 1934 he was transferred to the Political Department of the 22nd Division in Guangdong-Jiangxi Military Region which during the Long March suffered heavy casualties in battles with KMT troops. After the Long March he served as deputy director of the Political Department of a regiment. In 1938 he held the post of political commissar, 4th Military Subdistrict of Shaanxi-Hebei-Chahar Military Region. In 1942 he was commander of the 10th Military Subdistrict of the same military region. He was appointed political

commissar of Shanxi-Chahar Military District of Shanxi-Chahar-Hebei Military Region in 1945. In the following year he served as political commissar of a column of the Shanxi-Chahar-Hebei Field Army. In 1947 he was appointed deputy director of the Political Department of the same field army.

1950		Identified as political commissar and director of the Political Department of the Navy Headquarters
1954,	Aug	Identified as deputy political commissar of Central-South China Naval Headquarters
1955,	Sep	Conferred the orders "1st August," "Independence and Freedom," and "Liberation," all 1st class; promoted to rank of vice-admiral
1958,	Aug	Identified as deputy commander of the Navy
	Sep	Elected deputy for Jiangsu Province to the 2nd NPC
1964,	Sep	Elected deputy for the PLA to the 3rd NPC
1966		During the Cultural Revolution Liu is attacked together with the political commissar of the Navy, Su Zhenhua, and disappears
1972,	Jul	First appearance after the Cultural Revolution
1973,	Mar	Identified as holding his previous post of deputy commander of the Navy
	Jul	Member of a military delegation to Albania
1977,	Aug	Elected alternate member of the CCP Central Committee by the 11th Party Congress
	Sep	Member of a military delegation to France and Romania
1978,	Jul	Identified as 1st deputy commander of the Navy

Liu Ding (Liu Ting)   刘鼎

Posts held

Others
Member of the Standing Committee of the 5th CPPCC
Vice-president of the Society of Mechanical Engineering

Liu joined the CCP in 1924. In 1925 he was arrested in Germany. Subsequently he is believed to have studied in the USSR. In 1931 he was twice arrested by the Nationalist Government in China and temporarily imprisoned. He then worked for the "Association for Students in the USSR," an organ of the KMT "Blue Shirt Society." From 1948 he was deputy director of the Enterprise Department of North China People's Government. In June 1949 he was elected member of the Standing Committee, Preparatory Committee for the Conference of Natural Science Workers which he represented as delegate at the 1st CPPCC.

| 1949, | Oct | Appointed vice-minister of heavy industry (until 1952) |

	Aug	Identified as member of the Standing Committee, Federation of Scientific Societies
1952,	Aug	Identified as vice-minister of the 2nd Ministry of Machine Building (until 1955)
1955,	Feb	Identified as assistant minister of the 2nd Ministry of Machine Building (until 1957)
	Aug	Identified as council member of the Society of Mechanical Engineering
1957,	May	Identified as vice-minister of the 2nd Ministry of Machine Building (until 1959)
1959,	Sep	Appointed vice-minister of the 1st Ministry of Machine Building (until 1960)
1960,	Sep	Appointed vice-minister of the 3rd Ministry of Machine Building (until Cultural Revolution)
1961,	Apr	Identified as deputy director of the General Office of Economic Relations with Foreign Countries under the State Council
1962		Identified as vice-president of the Society of Mechanical Engineering
1967		Disappears during the Cultural Revolution
1978,	Mar	First appearance after the Cultural Revolution: Elected member of the Standing Committee of the 5th CPPCC
	Sep	Identified as vice-president of the Society of Mechanical Engineering

Liu Fang (Liu Fang)　　刘　放

Posts held

Government
Vice-minister of the 6th Ministry of Machine Building

1950,	Jun	Identified as director of the Mining Bureau of Fushun Municipality
1953,	Aug	Identified as deputy director, General Control Bureau of Petroleum of the Ministry of Industry
	Sep	Member of a delegation to the 1st Sino-Romanian Scientific and Technical Conference
1954,	Oct	Identified as trade counselor at the embassy in the USSR
1955,	Aug	Appointed assistant minister of the Ministry of Petroleum Industry (until Sep 1959)
1957,	Nov	Member of a scientific and technical delegation to the USSR
1959,	Sep	Appointed vice-minister of petroleum industry (until Dec 1963)
1962,	Jul	Head of a government delegation to Iraq
1964,	Feb	Appointed ambassador to Romania (until Dec 1965)
1966		Disappears during the Cultural Revolution
1974,	Sep	First appearance after the Cultural Revolution
	Oct	The Vietnamese press refers to Liu as the "vice-minister of national defense industry"
1977,	Oct	Identified as acting president of the Society of Shipbuilding Engineers; head of a shipping delegation to Japan
1979,	Jun	Identified as vice-minister of the 6th Ministry of Machine Building

Liu Faxiu (Liu Fa-hsiu)　　刘发秀

Posts held

Military
Deputy commander of Xinjiang Military Region

| 1977, | Mar | Identified as military leader in Xinjiang |
| 1978, | Jun | Identified as deputy commander of Xinjiang Military Region |

Liu Fei (Liu Fei)　　刘　斐

Posts held

NPC
Member of the Standing Committee of the 5th NPC
Deputy for Hunan Province to the 5th NPC

Military
Lieutenant-general

Others
Vice-chairman of the Central Committee, Revolutionary Committee of the Chinese KMT

Liu was born in 1898 in Liling, Hunan Province. In 1923 he was chief of a company, and one year later lieutenant-colonel in the Guangzhou Headquarters of the Nationalist Revolutionary Army. In 1925 he posted to the Front Headquarters of the Joint Expedition Forces of Yunnan-Guangxi with the rank of colonel. He attended an infantry school and a military academy in Japan from 1927 to 1934. In 1935, with the rank of major-general, he was head of the Training Department of the School for Military Cadres in Guangxi. After the outbreak of the Anti-Japanese War in 1937 he was appointed a member of the National Defense Council of the KMT Central Committee and, in addition, made head of the Operational Department, 1st Ministry of the Military Council. In 1938 he was made director of the 1st Department in the Ministry of Military Order, eventually to rise to the post of vice-minister in 1940. In 1945 he became a member of the National People's Congress of the KMT Government. In the same year he was elected alternate member of the KMT Executive Council. His appointment as deputy chief of general staff, responsible for counterintelligence and war planning, followed in 1946. In April 1949 he was one of the KMT negotiators at a last attempt to secure a ceasefire agreement with the Communists in Beijing. After the failure of the negotiations he changed over to the Communists. Carrying out secret instructions by the Communists, he unsuccessfully attempted from Hong Kong to persuade the provincial commanders of Hunan, Guangxi, and Guangdong to capitulate in June 1949. In September 1949 he took part in the 1st CPPCC organized by the Communists.

| 1949, | Oct | Appointed deputy head of the Research Group for National Defense of the Revolutionary Military Council |
| | Dec | Appointed member of the Central-South China Military and Administrative Council; elected member of the Standing Committee, Central Committee of the KMT Revolutionary Committee |

1950-1953		Liu is entrusted with various administrative posts in the Central-South China Administrative Council, primarily in the field of irrigation
1954,	Aug	Elected deputy for Hunan Province to the 1st NPC (reelected in 1958, 1964, and 1975 to the 2nd, 3rd, and 4th NPCs)
	Sep	Appointed member of the National Defense Council (until 1974); appointed member of the Legislative Council of the 1st NPC
1959,	Apr	Elected member of the Standing Committee of the 3rd CPPCC (confirmed in 1965 by the 4th CPPCC; until Dec 1974)
1975,	Jan	Elected member of the Standing Committee by the 4th NPC (confirmed in 1978 by the 5th NPC)
1978,	Feb	Elected deputy for Hunan Province to the 5th NPC
1979,	Jun	Member of the Draft Laws Committee at the 2nd Session of the 5th NPC
	Oct	Elected vice-chairman of the Central Committee, Revolutionary Committee of the Chinese KMT

Publications

The Philosophy of War
The Philosophy of Tactics
Modern Military Technology
Modern Knowledge on National Defense

Liu Fu (Liu Fu)   刘　溥

Posts held

Government
Ambassador to Mexico

1969,	Aug	Identified as chargé d'affaires ad interim, embassy in the German Democratic Republic
1972,	Jun	Appointed ambassador to Malta (until May 1977)
1977,	Aug	Appointed ambassador to Mexico
1979,	Apr	Visit to Ecuador and received by that country's foreign minister

Liu Fusheng (Liu Fu-sheng)   刘夫生

Posts held

CCP
Secretary of Hunan Province CP
Secretary-general of Hunan CP

Provincial Administration
Vice-governor of the Revolutionary Committee of Hunan Province

1976,	May	Identified as member of the Standing Committee of Hunan Province CP (until Jun 1977)
	Nov	Identified as secretary-general of Hunan CP
1977,	Jun	Identified as secretary of Hunan CP
	Dec	Elected vice-chairman of the Revolutionary Committee of Hunan Province (until Dec 1979)
1979,	Dec	Elected vice-governor of the Revolutionary Committee of Hunan Province

Liu Fuzhi (Liu Fu-chih)   刘　復之

Posts held

Government
Vice-minister of culture

NPC
1st deputy secretary-general of the NPC Standing Committee's Legal Commission

In 1948 Liu was deputy head of the Security Department, Political Department of the Shanxi-Chahar-Hebei Field Army. In 1949 he was deputy head of the 3rd Office, North China Bureau of the CCP.

1949,	Dec	Appointed deputy director of the General Office, Ministry of Public Security
1964,	Feb	Appointed vice-minister of public security
1967		Disappears during the Cultural Revolution
1971,	Jun	First appearance after the Cultural Revolution
1972,	May	Identified in his former post as vice-minister of public security
1973,	Feb	Liu disappears for unknown reasons until 1978
1978,	Jan	Identified as vice-minister of culture (until Jul 1978)
	Jul	Appointed member of the Birth Planning Leading Group under the State Council (until May 1979)
	Aug	Identified as vice-minister of public security (until Nov 1978)
	Nov	Identified as vice-minister of culture
1979,	Nov	Appointed 1st deputy secretary-general of the NPC Standing Committee's Legal Commission

Liu Gang (Liu Kang)   刘　刚

Posts held

CCP
Secretary of Tianjin Municipality CP

Provincial Administration
Vice-chairman of the Revolutionary Committee of Tianjin Municipality

1954,	Apr	Identified as 3rd secretary of Henan Province CP
1958,	Aug	Identified as director of Tractor Factory No. 1 in Luoyang
1960,	Aug	Appointed vice-president of the Northwest Technical University in Xi'an
1963,	Oct	Identified as alternate member of the Secretariat, Northwest Bureau of the CCP Central Committee
1965,	Jul	Identified as director of the Propaganda Department, Northwest Bureau of the CCP Central Committee
1968,	Jun	Branded as a counterrevolutionary
1978,	May	First appearance after the Cultural Revolution
1979,	May	Identified as vice-chairman of the Revolutionary Committee of Tianjin Municipality
	Jul	Identified as secretary of Tianjin Municipality CP

Liu Geng (Liu Keng) 刘 庚

Posts held

Provincial Administration
Vice-governor of Shaanxi Province

1957,	Mar	Identified as mayor of Xi'an Municipality
1959,	Oct	Identified as secretary of the Xi'an Municipality CP
1964,	Jan	Identified as chairman of the Shaanxi Branch, Chinese Peace Council
1965		Liu disappears
1979,	Dec	First appearance after the Cultural Revolution: Elected vice-governor of Shaanxi Province

Liu Guangtao (Liu Kuang-t'ao) 刘光涛

Posts held

CCP
Member of the CCP 11th Central Committee

In 1947 Liu served as political commissar of the 8th Division, 3rd Column, Northeast China Field Army. In 1949 he was head of the Political Department, 40th Corps, 4th Field Army.

1964,	Nov	Identified as political commissar, 40th Corps of the PLA
1969,	Oct	Identified as leading cadre in the Revolutionary Committee of Heilongjiang Province and in Heilongjiang Military District
1970,	May	Identified as deputy political commissar of Shenyang Military Region and as 2nd political commissar of Heilongjiang Military District (no later mention in this post); identified as vice-chairman of the Revolutionary Committee of Heilongjiang Province (until Aug 1971)
1971,	Aug	Elected 2nd secretary of the CP Secretariat of Heilongjiang Province newly established after the Cultural Revolution (until Mar 1977); identified as 1st vice-chairman of the Revolutionary Committee of Heilongjiang Province (until Mar 1977)
1973,	Aug	Elected alternate member of the CCP Central Committee by the 10th Party Congress (until Aug 1977)
1976,	Sep	Identified as political commissar of Heilongjiang Military District (until Mar 1977)
1977,	Mar	Identified as 1st secretary of the CP, and chairman of the Revolutionary Committee, of Heilongjiang Province as well as 1st political commissar of Heilongjiang Military District (until Dec 1977)
	Aug	Elected member of the CCP Central Committee by the 11th Party Congress
	Dec	Liu disappears; probably purged

Liu is married to Wei Shenghua.

Liu Haiqing (Liu Hai-ch'ing) 刘海清

Posts held

Military
Major-general
Deputy commander of Beijing Military Region

Liu was born in 1914 in Pingjiang, Hunan Province. He joined the Red Army in 1928 and took part in the Pingjiang Uprising. After the failure of this uprising he moved with the units of Peng Dehuai to the Communist base on Jinggangshan. He is believed to have taken part in the Long March serving in the 3rd Front Army. In 1937 he was commander of a company of the 115th Division, 8th Route Army. Sent to Manchuria after the Japanese capitulation in 1945, he commanded a regiment of the Northeast Field Army, after 1949 in the 4th Field Army.

1950		Service in the Korean War, initially as chief of staff, later as deputy commander of the 112th Division, 38th Army
1955		Appointed commander of the 113th Division of the 38th Army
1956?		After return from Korea training at the Military Academy of the PLA
1963		Identified as major-general
1966,	Oct	Identified as deputy commander of the 38th Army
1971,	May	With the reestablishment of the CP Secretariat of Hebei Province, Liu is elected secretary (no later mention in this post)
1972		Identified as deputy commander of Beijing Military Region

Liu Haiquan (Liu Hai-ch'üan) 刘海泉

Posts held

Provincial Administration
Vice-governor of Sichuan Province

1977,	Dec	Elected vice-chairman of Sichuan Province (until Dec 1979)
1979,	Jul	Appointed member of the National Games Organizing Committee
	Dec	Elected vice-governor of Sichuan Province

Liu Hegeng (Liu Ho-keng) 刘和赓

Posts held

Provincial Administration
Vice-governor of Hubei Province

1980,	Jan	Elected vice-governor of Hubei Province

Liu Hekong (Liu Ho-k'ung) 刘鹤孔

Posts held

Government
Vice-minister of the 1st Ministry of Machine Building

1979,	Sep	Identified as vice-minister of the 1st Ministry of Machine Building

Liu Houming (Liu Hou-ming)

Posts held

Mass Organization
Vice-chairman of the Youth Federation

1979,   Mar   Identified as vice-chairman of the Youth Federation
         Jun   Head of a youth delegation to Zaire, Somalia, Tanzania, and Zambia

Liu Huaqing (Liu Hua-ch'ing)   刘华清

Posts held

Government
Vice-minister of the State Scientific and Technological Commission

Military
Rear-admiral
Assistant to the chief of PLA General Staff

In 1946 Liu served as political commissar of the 8th Division, 3rd Column of the Central Plains Field Army, and two years later as political commissar of the 3rd Column. In 1949 he was head of the political Department, 11th Corps of the 2nd Field Army.

1950   Transferred to the Navy
1955,   Sep   Conferred the order of "Liberation," 1st class (an award for distinguished service against the KMT Armored Forces after 1945)
1958,   Oct   Identified as rear-admiral of the PLA in the region of Lüda (Lüshun-Dairen)
1967,   Jan   Appointed vice-chairman of the Scientific and Technological Commission for National Defense; identified as member of the Cultural Revolutionary Group of the PLA
1968,   Mar   Identified as 1st vice-chairman of the Scientific and Technical Commission for National Defense
         Jun   Liu is asked to offer self-criticism
         Aug   Attacked together with Nie Rongzhen under the charge of having established an "independent kingdom" in the Scientific and Technological Commission for National Defense (Nie survives these accusations while Liu dissappears)
1975,   Sep   Reactivated after the Cultural Revolution
1978,   Nov   Identified as vice-minister of the State Scientific and Technological Commission; member of a delegation led by Wang Zhen to Great Britain
1979,   Dec   Identified as assistant to the chief of PLA General Staff; head of a military delegation to Yugoslavia

Liu Jianfu (Liu Chien-fu)   刘坚夫

Posts held

CCP
Member of the Standing Committee of Beijing Municipality CP

Provincial Administration
Vice-mayor of Beijing

1977,   Dec   Elected vice-chairman of Beijing Municipality (until Dec 1979)
1979,   Mar   Identified as member of the Standing Committee of Beijing Municipality CP
         Dec   Elected vice-mayor of Beijing Municipality

Liu Jianxun (Liu Chien-hsün)   刘建勋

Posts held

CCP
Member of the CCP 11th Central Committee

NPC
Deputy for Henan Province to the 5th NPC

Liu was born in 1908 in Yangcheng County, Shanxi Province. He joined the CCP in 1935. In 1938 he was political commissar of the 3rd Detachment of a "Dare-To-Die Corps." In 1945 he was identified as political commissar of the 13th Military Subregion, Taihang Military Region. During the peace negotiations between the KMT and the Communists chaired by General George Marshall in 1946 he temporarily served with the rank of lieutenant-colonel as section chief of the Military Subcommittee comprising three members.

1950,   Mar   Identified as 2nd deputy secretary of Hubei Province CP (until 1952)
1951,   Oct   Appointed member of the Central-South China Military and Administrative Council (abolished in 1953) and chairman of the People's Government of Hubei Province
1952   Identified as political commissar of Hubei Military Region and as 2nd secretary of Hubei Province CP (until Jan 1956)
1953,   Jan   Appointed member of the Central-South China Administrative Council (until 1955)
1954,   Aug   Elected deputy for Hubei Province to the 1st NPC
1955   Identified as deputy secretary of Hubei Province CP (until Jan 1956)
1956,   Jan   Appointed deputy director, Rural Work Department of the CCP Central Committee, and 1st secretary of Guangxi Province CP (after Mar 1958 Autonomous Region), probably until Oct 1961
1958,   May   Elected alternate member of the CCP Central Committee
1960,   Feb   Appointed vice-chairman of the Commission for Receiving and Resettling Returned Overseas Chinese
1962,   Jul   Identified as 1st secretary of Henan Province CP (until May 1978)
1964,   Sep   Elected member of the People's Council of Henan; identified as chairman of the Henan Section, CPPCC
1965,   Jul   Identified as secretary, Central-South China Bureau of the CCP Central Committee (until Cultural Revolution)
1966   Liu is one of the few 1st provincial CP secretaries who survived the Cultural Revolution without loss of influence

1968,   Jan   With the establishment of the Revolution-
                ary Committee of Henan Province, Liu is
                elected chairman
         Dec   Identified as 1st political commissar of
                Henan Military District
1969,   Apr   Elected to first term as member of the
                CCP Central Committee by the 9th Party
                Congress
1971,   Mar   With the reestablishment of the Party
                Secretariat of Henan Province after the
                Cultural Revolution, Liu is elected
                1st secretary (until May 1978)
1977,   Dec   Identified as director of the Party School
                of Henan
1978,   Feb   Elected deputy for Henan Province to the
                5th NPC
         Apr   Disappears and probably purged

Liu Jianzhang (Liu Chien-chang)   刘建章

Posts held

Government
Vice-minister of railways
Member of the Patriotic Health Campaign
Committee

NPC
Deputy for Tianjin Municipality to the
5th NPC

Others
Vice-president of the Sports Federation
Chairman of the Board of Directors,
Society of Railways

In 1936 Liu was an employee in the administration of a
cooperative in Yan'an. Later he was appointed council
member of the People's Government of Shanxi-Hebei-
Shandong-Henan Border Area. In 1948 he was vice-
minister of communications of North China People's
Government and head of its Communications Department.

1951   Identified as director of the Railway
                Administration Bureau of Zhengzhou (un-
                til 1952)
1954,   Jul   Identified as member of the National
                Committee of Supply and Marketing Co-
                operatives
         Oct   Appointed vice-minister of railways (until
                Cultural Revolution)
         Dec   Member of a communications delegation
                to North Vietnam
1955,   Feb   Head of a railway delegation to North
                Korea
1963,   Jun   Deputy head of a delegation of architects
                to Cuba and Mexico
1966   Disappears during the Cultural Revolution
1975,   Apr   First appearance after the Cultural Revo-
                lution: Named in his former post as vice-
                minister of railways
         Sep   Head of a railway delegation to North
                Korea
1978,   Feb   Elected deputy for Tianjin Municipality to
                the 5th NPC
         Apr   Appointed member of the Patriotic Health
                Campaign Committee

1979,   Jul   Appointed member of the National Games
                Organizing Committee
         Sep   Identified as vice-president of the Sports
                Federation
         Nov   Elected chairman of the Board of Direc-
                tors, Society of Railways

Liu Jie (Liu Chieh)   刘杰

Posts held

CCP
Standing secretary of Henan Province CP

Provincial Administration
Governor of Henan Province

In 1945 Liu served as member of Chahar Province CP.

1949,   Dec   Identified as member of the People's
                Government of Henan Province (until
                Jun 1954)
1950,   Jul   Identified as deputy secretary of Henan
                Province CP
         Nov   Identified as director of the Industry
                Department and as vice-chairman of the
                Financial and Economic Committee of
                Central-South China Military and Admin-
                istrative Council (until Aug 1952)
1952,   Aug   Identified as vice-minister of geology (un-
                til Apr 1957)
1955,   May   Identified as deputy director of the
                3rd General Office under the State Coun-
                cil (until Apr 1957)
1956,   Mar   Delegate to the International Conference
                in Moscow on the Establishment of a Joint
                Institute of Nuclear Research
1959,   Sep   Appointed vice-minister of the 2nd Minis-
                try of Machine Building
1960,   Sep   Appointed minister of the 2nd Ministry of
                Machine Building
1964,   Sep   Elected member of the 4th CPPCC
1966   Liu disappears
1978,   Dec   First appearance after the Cultural Revo-
                lution: Identified as vice-chairman of the
                Revolutionary Committee and as member
                of the Standing Committee of Henan
                Province CP (until Sep 1979)
1979,   Sep   Elected governor of Henan Province; iden-
                tified as standing secretary of Henan
                Province CP

Liu Jinfeng (Liu Chin-feng)

Posts held

Provincial Administration
Vice-chairman of the Revolutionary Committee, Tianjin Municipality

1979,   Dec   Identified as vice chairman of the Revolu-
                tionary Committee, Tianjin Municipality

Liu Jingfan (Liu Ching-fan) 刘景苑

Posts held

Government
Vice-minister of civil affairs

Others
Member of the Standing Committee of the 5th CPPCC

Liu was born in Shaanxi Province. In 1935 he joined a Communist guerrilla unit in his native province. In 1941 he was deputy secretary-general of Shaanxi-Gansu-Ningxia Border Region, and in 1949 acting chairman of that regional government.

1949,	Dec	Identified as vice-chairman of the People's Control Committee of the Government Administration Council
1951,	Dec	Identified as secretary-general of the Austerity Examination Committee of the Government Administration Council
1954,	Aug	Elected deputy for Henan Province to the 1st NPC
	Oct	Appointed vice-minister of supervision (until Apr 1955)
1955,	May	Appointed vice-minister of geology (until Apr 1965)
1967		Disappears during the Cultural Revolution
1975,	Sep	First appearance after the Cultural Revolution
1978,	Mar	Elected member of the Standing Committee of the 5th CPPCC
	Oct	Identified as vice-minister of civil affairs

Liu Jingji (Liu Ching-chi) 刘靖基

Posts held

Others
Member of the Standing Committee of the 5th CPPCC
Member of the Central Committee, China Democratic National Construction Association
Director of the Board of Directors, China International Trust and Investment Corporation
Vice-chairman of the Executive Committee, Federation of Industrialists and Businessmen

In 1949 Liu had been general manager of the Anda Textile Mill in Shanghai.

1954,	Aug	Elected deputy for Shanghai Municipality to the 1st NPC (confirmed in 1958 and 1964 by the 2nd and 3rd NPCs)
1961,	Feb	Identified as vice-chairman of the Shanghai Section, CPPCC
1963,	Dec	Identified as chairman of the Shanghai Branch, Federation for Promotion of Industry and Commerce
1967		Disappears during the Cultural Revolution
1977,	Apr	First appearance after the Cultural Revolution: Named in his former post as vice-chairman of the Shanghai Section, CPPCC
1978,	Nov	Elected member of the Standing Committee of the 5th CPPCC

1979,	Jan	Identified as member of the Central Committee, China Democratic National Construction Association; as vice-chairman of the Shanghai Branch, CPPCC; and as chairman of the Shanghai Branch, Federation of Industry and Commerce
	Oct	Appointed director of the Board of Directors, China International Trust and Investment Corporation; elected vice-chairman of the Executive Committee, Federation of Industrialists and Businessmen

Liu Jingping (Liu Ching-p'ing) 刘景平

Posts held

CCP
Secretary of Inner Mongolia Autonomous Region CP

NPC
Deputy for Inner Mongolia Autonomous Region to the 5th NPC

1951,	May	Identified as minister of commerce, Inner Mongolia Autonomous Region
1954,	Aug	Elected council member of the People's Government of Inner Mongolia
1970,	Aug	Elected vice-chairman of the Revolutionary Committee of Inner Mongolia (reelected in Dec 1977)
1975,	Feb	Identified as secretary of Inner Mongolia Autonomous Region CP (until Dec 1979)
1978,	Feb	Elected deputy for Inner Mongolia Autonomous Region to the 5th NPC

Liu Jingzhi (Liu Ching-chih) 刘敬之

Posts held

CCP
Member of the Commission for Inspecting Discipline under the CCP Central Committee

Government
Deputy director of NCNA

1953,	Jun	Identified as deputy director of the Press Office, Northeast Bureau of the CCP Central Committee
1960,	Jul	Identified as chief-editor of Jilin Ribao (Jilin Daily)
1965,	Jun	Identified as deputy director of the Propaganda Department, Northeast Bureau of the CCP Central Committee
1967,	Mar	Branded as a counterrevolutionary revisionist and purged
1978,	Aug	Identified as deputy director of NCNA
	Dec	Appointed member of the Commission for Inspecting Discipline under the CCP Central Committee
1979,	Jul	Appointed member of the National Games Organizing Committee
	Sep	Head of a NCNA delegation to North Korea

Liu Jiping (Liu Chi-p'ing)　刘季平

Posts held

Others
President of the Society of Libraries
Chief librarian of Beijing Library

In 1946 Liu served as director of the Education Department of Jiangsu-Anhui Border Regional Government.

1950, Mar Identified as director of the Department of Culture and Education of South Jiangsu Administrative Office (until 1952)

1952, Oct Identified as council member of the Sino-Soviet Friendship Association, Shanghai Branch

1953, May Identified as deputy mayor of Shanghai Municipality (until 1960)

1957, Jan Identified as director, Department of Health and Education of Shanghai Municipality CP

1959, Oct Identified as secretary of Shandong Province CP

1963, Sep Identified as vice-minister of education (until Jan 1967)

1964, Sep Elected deputy for Anhui Province to the 3rd NPC

1965, Jan Head of a friendship delegation to North Vietnam

1967, Jan Branded as a counterrevolutionary revisionist and purged

1973, Mar First appearance after the Cultural Revolution

1974, Oct Identified as curator of Beijing Library

1978, Oct Identified as chief librarian of Beijing Library

1979, Aug Elected president of the Society of Libraries

Liu Junxiu (Liu Chün-hsiu)　刘俊秀

Posts held

CCP
Member of the Standing Committee of Jiangxi Province CP

NPC
Deputy for Jiangxi Province to the 5th NPC

Provincial Administration
Vice-chairman of the People's Congress of Jiangxi Province

Liu was born in 1904 in Suichuan, Jiangxi Province. He joined the CCP in 1926 and served as Party secretary in his native town during the early 1930s. In 1936 he attended a training course at the Party School in Yan'an and was subsequently appointed director of the Organization Department of Shanxi-Suiyuan Regional CP. After the Japanese capitulation in 1945 he was posted to Manchuria as director of the Mass Movement Department. In 1947 he became a member of the Standing Committee of Jilin Province CP and director of its Organization Department. He was identified as director of the Organization Department of Jiangxi Province CP in June 1948.

1950   Identified as member of the Jiangxi People's Government and as vice-chairman of its Financial and Economic Committee, as well as chairman of the Peasants' Federation of Jiangxi (until?)

1953, Jan Identified as deputy secretary of Jiangxi Province CP

1954, Aug Elected deputy for Jiangxi Province to the 1st NPC (reelected in 1959 and 1964 to the 2nd and 3rd NPCs)

1957, Jan Identified as secretary of Jiangxi Province CP

1959   Identified as president of the Cadre School of Jiangxi CP

1965, Mar Elected vice-chairman of the Peasants' Federation of Jiangxi

1967   Disappears during the Cultural Revolution

1972, Dec First appearance after the Cultural Revolution

1973, Apr Identified as member of the Standing Committee of Jiangxi Province CP

1976, Sep Identified as member of the Standing Committee, Revolutionary Committee of Jiangxi Province (until Oct 1977)

1977, Oct Identified as vice-chairman of the Revolutionary Committee of Jiangxi (until Dec 1979)

1978, Feb Elected deputy for Jiangxi Province to the 5th NPC

1979, Dec Elected vice-chairman of the People's Congress of Jiangxi Province

Liu Kun (Liu K'un)　刘琨

Posts held

Government
Vice-minister of forestry

1958, Mar Identified as deputy director, Afforestation Bureau of the Ministry of Forestry

1964, Feb Deputy director of the General Office of State Forests, Ministry of Forestry

Sep Elected deputy for Hunan Province to the 3rd NPC

1966   Liu disappears

1978, Aug First appearance after the Cultural Revolution: Identified as deputy director of the Forestry Administration Bureau of the Ministry of Agriculture and Forestry

1979, May Identified as vice-minister of forestry

Liu Lanbo (Liu Lan-po)　刘澜波

Posts held

CCP
Member of the CCP 11th Central Committee

Government
Minister of power industry

Liu was born in 1908 in Anlong, Liaoning Province. He moved to Yan'an around 1940. In 1946 he was identified as member of the Northeast China Administrative Council.

In 1949 he joined the Northeast China People's Government and concurrently held the posts of chairman of the People's Government of Liaodong Province and deputy secretary of Liaodong Province CP.

1950,	May	Appointed vice-minister of fuel industry (divided into three separate ministries in Jun 1955)
1954,	Oct	Elected deputy for Benxi Municipality to the 1st NPC (until Mar 1959)
1955,	Jun	Appointed minister of electric power (until Feb 1958)
	Nov	Head of a scientific and technical delegation to Czechoslovakia
1956,	Sep	Elected alternate member of the CCP Central Committee by the 8th Party Congress
1958,	Jun	Appointed vice-minister of water conservancy and electric power
1959,	Mar	Elected deputy for Liaoning Province to the 2nd NPC
1962,	Apr	Member of an NPC delegation to North Korea
1963		Identified as board member of the Electrotechnical Society
1965,	Jan	Elected member of the Standing Committee of the 3rd NPC
1967,	Mar	Branded as a bourgeois counterrevolutionary and disappears
1979,	Feb	First appearance after the Cultural Revolution: Appointed minister of power industry
	Sep	By-elected member of the CCP 11th Central Committee

Liu Lantao (Liu Lan-t'ao) 刘澜涛

Posts held

CCP
Member of the CCP 11th Central Committee
1st deputy director of the United Front Work Department under the CCP Central Committee

Others
Vice-chairman of the 5th CPPCC

Liu was born in 1910 in Mizhi, Shaanxi Province. He attended middle school in his native town and subsequently studied law at Beijing University. He joined the CCP as a student in 1928. In 1930 he was appointed secretary in the CCP Special Committee. In 1938 he was secretary of the CP Regional Committee in Shaanxi-Chahar-Hebei Border Area, and in 1940 deputy secretary of the regional CP and deputy political commissar of Shensi-Chahar-Hopei Military Region. In 1945 the 7th CCP Congress elected him an alternate member of its Central Committee (until Sep 1956). In January 1949 he was appointed director of North China Revolutionary College. Concurrently, he served as 3rd secretary, North China Bureau of the CCP Central Committee. In September of that year he took part in the CPPCC.

1950,	Sep	Appointed director of the North China Department, General Office of the Central Government Council (until May 1952)
1952		Appointed member of the State Planning Commission (abolished in 1957)
1954,	Oct	Elected deputy for Hebei Province to the 1st NPC (until Sep 1964) and member of the Standing Committee of the NPC
1956,	Sep	Elected member of the Central Committee, alternate member of the Central Committee's Secretariat, and deputy secretary of the Central Control Commission of the CCP Central Committee
1963,	Oct	Identified as 1st secretary, Northwest China Bureau of the CCP Central Committee
1964,	Sep	Elected deputy for Shaanxi Province to the 3rd NPC
1965,	Jan	Elected vice-chairman of the CPPCC
	Oct	Identified as political commissar of Lanzhou Military Region
1967,	Jan	Branded as a reactionary anti-Party element and purged
1978,	Dec	First appearance after the Cultural Revolution
1979,	Jan	Identified as secretary-general of the 5th CPPCC (until Sep 1979)
	Mar	Identified as 1st deputy director of the United Front Work Department under the CCP Central Committee
	Jul	By-elected vice-chairman of the 5th CPPCC
	Sep	By-elected member of the CCP 11th Central Committee

Liu Liangmo (Liu Liang-mo) 刘良模

Posts held

Others
Member of the Standing Committee of the 5th CPPCC
Vice-chairman of the Shanghai Section, Returned Overseas Chinese Federation

In May 1949 Liu was elected an alternate member of the Federation of Democratic Youth; at the time he was Program director of the Chinese YMCA Association.

1949,	Oct	Elected member of the Peace Committee
	Nov	Elected alternate member of the Central Committee, China Democratic League
1953,	Jun	Identified as member of the Standing Committee, Federation of Democratic Youth
1954,	Jul	Elected member of the Standing Committee, Committee of Protestant Churches for Three-self Patriotic Movement
1955,	May	Identified as vice-chairman, Shanghai Committee for Promoting Patriotism among Protestants
1958,	Apr	Elected vice-chairman of the Youth Federation (successor of the Democratic Youth Federation)
1959,	Apr	Elected member of the 3rd CPPCC
1962,	Apr	Elected member of the Standing Committee of the Youth Federation
1964,	Dec	Delegate representing religious circles at the 4th CPPCC
1965,	Jan	Elected member of the Standing Committee of the 4th CPPCC

1967		Disappears during the Cultural Revolution
1978,	Feb	First appearance after the Cultural Revolution
	Mar	Elected member of the Standing Committee of the 5th CPPCC
	May	Identified as vice-chairman of the Shanghai Section, Returned Overseas Chinese Federation

Liu Lin (Liu Lin) 刘 林

Posts held

CCP
Member of the Standing Committee of Jiangsu Province CP

Military
Deputy commander of Jiangsu Military District

Provincial Administration
Vice-governor of Jiangsu Province

1958,	Apr	Identified as secretary of Nanjing Municipality CP
1970,	Jun	Identified as a cadre of the Jiangsu Military District
1977,	May	Identified as deputy commander of Jiangsu Military District
	Dec	Identified as a member of the Standing Committee of Jiangsu Province CP
1979,	Dec	Identified as vice-governor of Jiangsu Province

Liu Mingbang (Liu Ming-pang) 刘名榜

Posts held

Provincial Administration
Vice-chairman of the Standing Committee, Henan Provincial People's Congress

1954,	Oct	Elected deputy for Henan Province to the 1st NPC (reelected in 1958 and 1964 to the 2nd and 3rd NPCs)
1959,	Feb	Identified as secretary of the Legal Committee, Henan Province CP
1965,	Jan	Identified as a member of the Standing Committee, Henan Province CP
1966	Aug	Liu disappears
1979,	Sep	First appearance after the Cultural Revolution: Elected vice-chairman of the Standing Committee, Henan Provincial People's Congress

Liu Minghui (Liu Ming-hui) 刘明辉

Posts held

CCP
Alternate member of the CCP 11th Central Committee
2nd secretary of Yunnan Province CP

Provincial Administration
Governor of Yunnan Province

Liu is a native of Jiangxi Province.

1950		Elected council member of the People's Government of Chongqing Municipality
1951,	Apr	Identified as director of the Public Security Bureau, People's Government of Chongqing Municipality
1952,	Jul	Elected mayor of Chongqing Municipality
1955,	Feb	Appointed vice-governor of Yunnan Province
1957,	Apr	Member of a delegation to Burma
1958,	Mar	Identified as secretary of Yunnan Province CP; member of a delegation of Yunnan CP to North Vietnam
1959,	Jul	Elected chairman, Yunnan Province Section of the 2nd CPPCC
1960,	Dec	Head of a delegation of Yunnan CP to Burma
1964,	Jan	Identified as acting governor of Yunnan Province (until Feb 1965)
	Sep	Elected deputy for Yunnan Province to the 3rd NPC
1967		At the height of the Cultural Revolution Liu is criticized together with the 1st secretary of Yunnan Province CP, Yan Hongyan, as a counterrevolutionary revisionist, but suffers no loss of influence
1968,	Aug	With the establishment of the Revolutionary Committee for Yunnan Province, Liu is elected vice-chairman (until Dec 1979)
1972,	Nov	Identified as member of the Standing Committee of Yunnan Province CP (until Oct 1973)
1973,	Oct	Identified as deputy secretary of Yunnan Province CP (until Sep 1975)
1975,	Sep	Identified as secretary of Yunnan Province CP (until May 1979)
1977,	Aug	Elected alternate member of the CCP Central Committee by the 11th Party Congress
1979,	May	Identified as 2nd secretary of Yunnan Province CP
	Jun	Head of a friendship delegation to North Korea
	Dec	Elected governor of Yunnan Province

Liu Nianzhi (Liu Nien-chih) 刘念智

Posts held

NPC
Deputy for Shanghai Municipality to the 5th NPC

Others
Vice-chairman of the Executive Committee of the Federation of Industrialists and Businessmen

1978,	Feb	Elected deputy for Shanghai Municipality to the 5th NPC
1979,	Jun	Member of the Budget Committee of the 2nd Session of the 5th NPC
	Oct	Elected vice-chairman of the Executive Committee of the Federation of Industrialists and Businessmen

Liu Ningyi (Liu Ning-yi)   刘宁一

Posts held

Others
Member of the Standing Committee and deputy secretary-general of the 5th CPPCC

Liu was born in 1905 in Mancheng County, Hebei Province. As a laborer at the coal mine in Kailuan he took part in the May 30 Movement in 1925, which first brought him into contact with the Communist movement. From 1927 he worked in a Communist underground organization in his native province, but was soon arrested and sentenced to ten years imprisonment. After his release he first went to Shanghai and, in 1943, to Yan'an. As chairman of the Preparatory Committee for the foundation of the Workers Federation he took part in the Council Session of the World Federation of Trade Unions in Moscow in June 1946, which elected him a council member. In August 1948 he was elected vice-chairman and director of the International Liaison Department by the 6th Workers Congress in Harbin. He took part in the 1st Congress of the World Peace Council in Paris in April 1949 as deputy head of the Chinese delegation. In September 1949 he was elected a member of the Standing Committee of the CPPCC (until December 1954).

1950,	May	Head of a delegation to the May Day celebrations in Prague
	Oct	Secretary of the Chinese delegation to the 2nd World Peace Council Conference
1952,	May	Appointed member of the Council for Promotion of International Trade
	Dec	Delegate at the World Peace Council Session
1953,	Feb	Elected secretary-general, Liaison Committee for the Asia and Pacific Zone, World Peace Council
	May	Elected member of the new Board and of the Secretariat of the Federation of Trade Unions (until Dec 1957)
	Jun	Delegate at the session of the Executive Council of the World Peace Council in Budapest
	Sep	Head of the Chinese delegation to the 3rd Congress of the World Federation of Trade Unions
	Oct	Vice-chairman of the Executive Bureau of the World Federation of Trade Unions (until Oct 1957)
	Nov	Elected council member of the World Peace Council
1954,	Mar	Delegate to the 25th Session of the Executive Council, World Federation of Trade Unions, in Vienna
	May	Appointed council member of the Association for Cultural Relations with Foreign Countries
	Jun	Delegate to the International Conference on Problems of Détente in Stockholm
	Jul	Appointed council member of the Institute of Foreign Affairs
	Sep	Elected deputy for Shandong Province to the 1st NPC (until Oct 1964) and member of the Standing Committee of the NPC
	Nov	Head of the Chinese delegation to the Council Session of the World Peace Council in Stockholm
	Dec	Elected vice-chairman of the Sino-Soviet Friendship Association
1955,	Mar	Delegate to a conference of Asian countries in India
	Jun	Secretary-general of the Chinese delegation to the session of the World Peace Council in Helsinki
	Aug	Head of a delegation to the World Conference against Atomic Bombs in Hiroshima
	Sep	Head of a friendship delegation to Yugoslavia
	Dec	Delegate to the Council Session of the World Peace Council in Helsinki
1956,	Feb	Elected vice-chairman of the Sino-Soviet Friendship Association; head of a trade union delegation to the 4th Congress of the Italian Trade Unions in Rome
	Mar	Deputy head of the Chinese delegation to a special session of the World Peace Council in Stockholm
	May	Delegate to the 8th Annual Meeting of the Indian Federation of Trade Unions in Surat; secretary-general of the Chinese delegation to the session of the World Peace Council in Helsinki
	Sep	Elected member of the CCP Central Committee by the 8th Party Congress
1957,	Apr	Member of a CCP delegation to the 12th Congress of the CP Belgium
	May	Delegate to the Peace Conference in Colombo
	Nov	Member of the Chinese delegation to the anniversary of the October Revolution in Moscow
	Dec	Member of the Chinese delegation to the Afro-Asian Solidarity Conference in Cairo
1958,	Mar	Appointed deputy director of the Staff Office of Foreign Affairs (until Sep 1959)
	Jul	Elected vice-chairman of the Peace Council
	Aug	Elected chairman of the Federation of Trade Unions following the death of Lai Ruoyu
	Sep	Appointed chairman of the Sino-Iraq Friendship Association
1959,	Jan	Member of the CCP guest delegation attending the 21st CPSU Congress
1960,	Jul	Delegate to the World Conference against Atomic Bombs in Tokyo
	Nov	Member of the CCP delegation to the 43rd anniversary of the October Revolution in Moscow
1961,	Mar	Head of the delegation to the session of the World Peace Council in New Delhi
	Apr	Head of a delegation to the session of the Afro-Asian Solidarity Organization in Bandung
	Dec	Head of the delegation to the session of the World Peace Council in Stockholm
1962,	Dec	Appointed chairman of the Sino-Cuban Friendship Association
1963,	Jan	Head of a delegation to the 3rd Afro-Asian Solidarity Conference in Moshi, Tanganyika
	Apr	Delegate to the Congress of the CP New Zealand in Auckland
	Jul	Member of the CCP delegation led by

Deng Xiaoping to ideological talks in Moscow

Oct   Head of the CCP delegation to the National Day celebrations in Algeria

Nov   Deputy head of a delegation to the session of the World Peace Council in Warsaw

1964,   Jul   Head of a delegation to the 10th World Conference against Atomic Bombs in Japan

Oct   Elected deputy for Hebei Province to the 3rd NPC; identified as member of the Institute of Foreign Affairs

Nov   Head of a solidarity delegation to North Vietnam

1965,   Jan   Elected vice-chairman and secretary-general of the Standing Committee of the NPC

Mar   Head of an NPC delegation to Guinea, Mali, Central Africa, and Congo (Brazzaville)

May   Member of a Party and parliamentary delegation to Indonesia

Jun   Elected vice-chairman of the Afro-Asian Solidarity Committee

Jul   Head of a delegation to the 11th World Conference against Atomic Bombs in Tokyo

1966,   Apr   Head of a Party delegation to the 21st Congress of the CP New Zealand

1968,   Apr   Branded as a counterrevolutionary revisionist and purged

1979,   Jun   First appearance after the Cultural Revolution

Jul   By-elected a member of the Standing Committee of the 5th CPPCC

Sep   Elected deputy secretary-general of the 5th CPPCC

Liu Peirong (Liu P'ei-jung)   刘佩荣

Posts held

Government
Vice-minister of the 4th Ministry of Machine Building

1978,   Dec   Identified as vice-minister of the 4th Ministry of Machine Building

Liu Peng (Liu P'eng)   刘 鹏

Posts held

Provincial Administration
Vice-governor of Shandong Province

1960,   Mar   Identified as director of the Construction Bureau for the Miyun Dam

1978,   Jan   Identified as vice-chairman of the Revolutionary Committee of Shandong Province (until Dec 1979)

1979,   Dec   Elected vice-governor of Shandong Province

Liu Qinghai (Liu Ch'ing-hai)   刘清海

Posts held

Military
Deputy commander of Lanzhou Military Region

1977,   Jul   Identified as deputy commander of Lanzhou Military Region

Liu Ruilong (Liu Jui-lung)   刘瑞龙

Posts held

Others
Member of the Standing Committee of the 5th CPPCC

Liu was born in Nantong County, Jiangsu Province. He studied in the USSR. In 1928 he was elected a member of the CCP Central Committee by the 6th Party Congress. He then served as head of the Southeast Cadres Training Class. In 1933 he was director of the Propaganda Department of Sichuan Province CP. In 1941 he was a member of the CCP Committee of Hubei-Jiangsu-Anhui Border Region and concurrently director of the Border Region Administrative Office. In 1945 he served in the United Front Work Department, Central China Bureau of the CCP Central Committee.

1950,   Mar   Identified as vice-chairman of the Land Reform Committee, East China Military and Administrative Council (until Jun 1952) and as secretary of the Rural Work Department, East China Bureau of the CCP Central Committee

1952,   Aug   Appointed vice-minister of agriculture (until Jan 1961)

1955,   Feb   Head of an agricultural delegation to Burma

1957,   Apr   Appointed member of the Overseas Chinese Affairs Commission under the State Council

May   Identified as vice-chairman of the Water and Soil Conservation Commission under the State Council

1958,   Oct   Identified as chairman of the Sino-Bulgarian Friendship Association (until Cultural Revolution)

1960,   Oct   Head of a scientific and technical delegation to Bulgaria and Albania

1964,   Apr   Identified as head of the Agricultural Administration Office, East China Bureau of the CCP Central Committee

1967,   Mar   Branded as a renegade and purged

1978,   Mar   First appearance after the Cultural Revolution: Elected member of the Standing Committee of the 5th CPPCC

Liu Ruiqing (Liu Jui-ch'ing)   刘瑞庆

Posts held

CCP
Alternate member of the CCP 11th Congress

1977,   Aug Elected alternate member of the CCP Central Committee by the 11th Party Congress

1978,   Feb Identified as a miner of Maan Coal Mine in Guangdong Province

Liu Shaowen (Liu Shao-wen)　刘绍文

Posts held

NPC
Deputy for Beijing Municipality to the 5th NPC

Military
Lieutenant-general

Others
Member of the Standing Committee of the 5th CPPCC

Liu served in the 1st Front Army during the Long March. In 1938 he was political instructor of a company of the so called Independent Regiment, 115th Division, 8th Route Army. In 1941 he was political instructor of the 3rd Regiment, 5th Military Subregion of Shanxi-Chahar-Hebei Military Region. He served as political commissar of a division in the same military region in 1948. One year later he was appointed political commissar of a division of the reorganized North China Field Army.

1950-1953   Service in the 65th Corps in the Korean War
1954   Identified as director of the Political Department, 65th Corps
1955   Identified as political commissar of the 65th Corps
         Sep   Promoted to rank of major-general
1958,   Mar   Identified as lieutenant-general
1959,   Nov   Identified as deputy political commissar of Shanxi Military District
1962   Identified as deputy political commissar of Beijing Garrison
1965,   Dec   Identified as 2nd political commissar of Beijing Garrison
1967,   Mar   With the establishment of the Revolutionary Committee of Beijing, Liu is elected a member of the Standing Committee (last mention in this post in Jul 1972); identified as 3rd political commissar of Beijing Garrison (no later mention in this post)
1971,   Mar   Elected secretary of the newly established CP Secretariat of Beijing (until 1975)
1978,   Feb   Elected deputy for Beijing Municipality to the 5th NPC
         Mar   Elected member of the Standing Committee of the 5th CPPCC

Liu Shihong (Liu Shih-hung)　刘世洪

Posts held

CCP
Secretary of Hunan Province CP

Military
Senior-colonel
Political commissar of Hunan Military District

Provincial Administration
Vice-chairman of the People's Congress of Hunan Province

1957,   Jun Identified as director of the Cadre Department in Shanxi Military District
1959,   Mar Identified as deputy director of the Political Department in Shanxi Military District
1965,   Mar Identified as deputy political commissar of Shanxi Military District
1972,   Nov Identified as secretary of the CP, and chairman of the Revolutionary Committee of Taiyuan Municipality
         Dec Identified as member of the Standing Committee of Shanxi Province CP
1976,   Jan Identified as a cadre in Hunan
         Apr Identified as secretary of Hunan Province CP and as political commissar of Hunan Military District
1979,   Dec Elected vice-chairman of the People's Congress of Hunan Province

Liu Shunyuan (Liu Shun-yüan)　刘顺元

Posts held

CCP
Deputy secretary of the Commission for Inspecting Discipline under the CCP Central Committee

Others
Member of the Standing Committee of the 5th CPPCC

In 1938 Liu served in the Fujian-Guangdong-Jiangxi Border Region, in 1948 he was political commissar of Jinan Garrison, and in the following year secretary of Jinan Municipality CP.

1952   Identified as deputy chief of the Planning Bureau, Financial and Economic Committee of the East China Military and Administrative Council
         Dec   Identified as deputy secretary-general of the East China Military and Administrative Council (until 1954)
1955,   Feb   Identified as vice-governor of Jiangsu Province (until 1958)
         Jul   Identified as alternate member of Jiangsu Province CP
1956,   Jul   Identified as member of Jiangsu Province CP (until Cultural Revolution)
1965,   Dec   Identified as vice-chairman, Nanjing Branch of the CPPCC
1967   Disappears during the Cultural Revolution
1978,   Feb   First appearance after the Cultural Revolution
         Mar   Elected member of the Standing Committee of the 5th CPPCC
         Dec   Appointed deputy secretary of the Commission for Inspecting Discipline under the CCP Central Committee

Liu Shuqing (Liu Shu-ch'ing)   刘述卿

Posts held

Government
Ambassador to Norway

1960,	Jan	Identified as 2nd secretary at the embassy in the USSR
1972,	Apr	Appointed ambassador to Poland (until Jan 1977)
1977,	May	Identified as ambassador to Norway

Liu Shuzhou (Liu Shu-chou)   刘述周

Posts held

Others
Vice-chairman of the Science and Technology Association

1950,	Dec	Identified as secretary-general of the People's Government of Nanjing Municipality
1954,	Nov	Identified as deputy director of the United Front Work Department of Shanghai Municipality CP
1955,	May	Identified as vice-chairman of the Shanghai Section, CPPCC (until 1964)
	Dec	Identified as director of the United Front Work Department of Shanghai Municipality CP
1956,	Jun	By-elected deputy for Shanghai Municipality to the 1st NPC (reelected in 1958 and 1964 to the 2nd and 3rd NPCs)
	Sep	Identified as deputy mayor of Shanghai Municipality (until 1964)
1958,	Nov	Identified as alternate member of Shanghai Municipality CP (until 1962) and as president of the Shanghai Branch of the Academy of Sciences
1959,	Nov	Deputy head of a friendship delegation to the USSR
1962,	Nov	Identified as secretary of Shanghai Municipality CP
1963,	Sep	Identified as president of Jiaotong University
1965,	Jul	Identified as deputy director, United Front Work Department of the CCP Central Committee
1967,	Apr	Branded as a counterrevolutionary revisionist and purged
1975,	Sep	First appearance after the Cultural Revolution
1978,	Jun	Identified as vice-chairman of the Science and Technology Association

Liu Tianfu (Liu T'ien-fu)   刘田夫

Posts held

CCP
Secretary of Guangdong Province CP

NPC
Deputy for Guangdong Province to the 5th NPC

Provincial Administration
Vice-governor of Guangdong Province

Others
Chairman of the Guangzhou Export Commodities Fair

1952,	Nov	Elected 2nd secretary, CP District Committee of West Guangdong
1953,	Dec	Identified as deputy director of the General Office of Central-South China Military Region
1957,	Sep	Identified as director of the Industry Department of Guangdong Province CP
1958,	Apr	Appointed vice-chairman of the Scientific Work Committee of Guangdong People's Government
	Sep	Elected vice-governor of Guangdong Province (until Cultural Revolution)
1960,	May	Identified as alternate member of the Secretariat of Guangdong Province CP (until Apr 1962)
1962,	Apr	Identified as secretary of Guangdong Province CP
1965,	Jul	Identified as alternate member of the Secretariat, Central-South China Bureau of the CCP Central Committee (until Cultural Revolution)
1967		Disappears during the Cultural Revolution
1973,	Jan	First appearance after the Cultural Revolution: Identified as vice-chairman of the Revolutionary Committee of Guangdong Province (until Dec 1979)
	Dec	Identified as member of the Standing Committee of Guangdong Province CP (until Nov 1977)
1974,	Apr	Vice-chairman of the Guangzhou Export Commodities Fair
1975,	Mar	Head of the a friendship delegation to Laos to inaugurate the direct airlink between China and Laos
1977,	Oct	Identified as vice-chairman of the Guangzhou Export Commodities Fair
	Nov	Identified as secretary of Guangdong Province CP
1978,	Feb	Elected deputy for Guangdong Province to the 5th NPC
1979,	Apr	Identified as chairman of the Guangzhou Export Commodities Fair
	Dec	Elected vice-governor of Guangdong Province

Liu Tiesheng (Liu T'ieh-sheng)   刘铁生

Posts held

Government
Former ambassador to Hungary

1960,	Jan	Identified as counselor at the embassy in Poland (until 1972)
1977,	Mar	Appointed ambassador to Hungary (until 1978)

Liu Wei (Liu Wei)   刘 伟

Posts held

CCP
Member of the CCP 11th Central Committee

Government
Minister of the 2nd Ministry of Machine Building

During the final phase of the revolutionary period Liu served as director of the political department of an army.

1949,	Dec	Appointed director of the 8th Bureau, Ministry of Public Security
1955,	May	Appointed vice-minister of geology (until Apr 1957)
1956,	Aug	Identified as deputy director of the Locomotive and Railway Carriage Factory in Lüda
1961,	Mar	Appointed vice-minister of the 2nd Ministry of Machine Building (until Cultural Revolution)
1969,	Apr	Elected member of the CCP Central Committee by the 9th Party Congress (confirmed in this post in 1973 and 1977 by the 10th and 11th Congresses)
1978,	Mar	Appointed minister of the 2nd Ministry of Machine Building

Liu Weiming (Liu Wei-ming)   刘维明

Posts held

CCP
Alternate member of the CCP 11th Central Committee

Mass Organization
Secretary of the Communist Youth League
Vice-chairman of the Youth Federation

1977,	Mar	Identified as vice-chairman of the Revolutionary Committee of Guangdong Province (until Oct 1978)
	Aug	Elected alternate member of the CCP Central Committee by the 11th Party Congress
1978,	Oct	Elected secretary of the Communist Youth League
1979,	May	Elected vice-chairman of the Youth Federation

Liu Xiangsan (Liu Hsiang-san)   刘向三

Posts held

Government
Vice-minister of water conservancy

1949		Identified as director, Administration Bureau of the Northeast Coal Mine
1951,	Jan	Identified as director, Administration Bureau Coal Mine in the Ministry of Fuel Industry

1955,	Feb	Identified as assistant minister in the Ministry of Fuel Industry (until Aug 1955)
	Aug	Appointed assistant minister in the Ministry of Coal Industry (until Apr 1957)
1957,	Apr	Appointed vice-minister of coal industry (until Jun 1964)
1967		Disappears during the Cultural Revolution
1975,	Apr	First appearance after the Cultural Revolution
1977,	Feb	Identified as vice-minister of water conservancy and electric power (until Feb 1979)
	May	Identified as vice-minister of water conservancy

Liu Xiao (Liu Hsiao)   刘晓

Posts held

Others
Member of the Standing Committee of the 5th CPPCC

Liu was born in 1907 in Xingtan, Hunan Province. He joined the CCP already in 1927 and began his Party career as a trade union cadre in Shanghai under Liu Shaoqi. In 1934 he was a member of the Central Executive Committee of the Soviet Government under Mao Zedong, which was based in Ruijin, Jiangxi Province. During the Long March he was a cadre in the Political Department, 1st Army Corps of the Red Army. In 1942 he was appointed secretary of Jiangsu Province CP. In 1945 the 7th CCP Congress elected Liu an alternate member of its Central Committee. In September 1949 he was elected member of the CPPCC.

1950,	Feb	Appointed member of the East China Military and Political Council and chairman of its Control Committee; identified as deputy secretary of Shanghai CP (probably until Jan 1955)
1955,	Jan	Appointed ambassador to the USSR (until Oct 1962)
1956,	Feb	Member of the CCP guest delegation to the 20th Congress of the CPSU
	Sep	Elected member of the CCP Central Committee
1957,	Apr	Liu accompanies Woroschilow on his tour of China
1961,	May	Member of the Chinese delegation to the Laos Conference in Geneva
1963,	May	Appointed vice-minister of foreign affairs (until Mar 1967)
1964,	Nov	Member of the CCP delegation to Moscow attending the 47th anniversary of the October Revolution
1965,	Jan	Elected member of the Standing Committee of the CPPCC
1967,	Apr	Appointed ambassador to Albania
1968,	May	Branded as a counterrevolutionary revisionist and purged
1978,	Feb	First appearance after the Cultural Revolution
	Mar	Elected member of the Standing Committee of the 5th CPPCC

Liu Xichang (Liu Hsi-ch'ang) 刘锡昌

Posts held

CCP
Member of the CCP 11th Central Committee
Member of the Standing Committee of the Beijing Municipality CP

Mass Organization
Vice-chairman of the Trade Union of Beijing

1967   As a worker at Guanghua Sawmill in Beijing, Liu is one of the "Red Rebels" there

Apr   With the establishment of the Revolutionary Committee of Beijing, Liu is elected a member of the Standing Committee (until Jun 1976)

May   Identified as member of the presidium, Conference of Revolutionary Workers and Employees in Beijing

Jun   Member of a Red Guard delegation to the 5th Congress of the Albania Youth Federation in Tirana

Nov   Liu addresses a mass demonstration in Beijing on the 23rd Anniversary of the Liberation of Albania

1969,   Apr   Elected to first term as member of the Standing Committee by the 9th Party Congress

Sep   Identified as chairman of the Revolutionary Committee of Guanghua Sawmill

1971,   Apr   Elected member of the Standing Committee after reestablishment of the CP Secretariat of Beijing

1973,   Apr   Elected vice-chairman of the Trade Union of Beijing

1976,   Jun   Identified as vice-chairman of the Revolutionary Committee of Beijing Municipality (until Nov 1977)

Liu Xigeng (Liu Hsi-keng) 刘锡更

Posts held

Government
Vice-minister of agriculture

1977,   Dec   Elected vice-chairman of the Revolutionary Committee of Jiangsu Province (until May 1978)

1978,   May   Deputy head of an agricultural delegation to Japan

Jun   Identified as vice-minister of agriculture and forestry (until Feb 1979)

1979,   May   Identified as vice-minister of agriculture

Liu Xing (Liu Hsing) 刘型

Posts held

Others
Member of the Standing Committee of the 5th CPPCC

Liu was born in Shaoyang, Hunan Province. In 1927 he took part in the Autumn Harvest Uprising in his native province. He subsequently followed Mao Zedong to the Jinggangshan.

1950,   Jan   Identified as member of the People's Government of Hunan Province (until 1953)

Mar   Identified as secretary-general of Hunan Province CP

1951,   Dec   Identified as chief procurator of Hunan People's Procuracy (until 1953)

1953,   Jan   Appointed director of the Beijing Institute of Geology (until Jul 1958)

1958,   Nov   Appointed vice-minister of state farms and land reclamation (until Cultural Revolution)

1959,   Apr   Elected member of the 3rd CPPCC (confirmed in 1964 by the 4th CPPCC)

Sep   Identified as member of the Overseas Chinese Affairs Commission under the State Council (until Cultural Revolution)

1967   Disappears during the Cultural Revolution

1974,   Sep   First appearance after the Cultural Revolution

1978,   Mar   Elected member of the Standing Committee of the 5th CPPCC

Liu Xingyuan (Liu Hsing-yüan) 刘兴元

Posts held

CCP
Member of the CCP 11th Central Committee

Military
Lieutenant-general

Liu was born in 1914 in Shandong (Hunan?) Province. In 1940 he was head of the Political Department of a unit of the New 4th Army, and in 1943 of Pinghai Military District in Shandong. In 1945 he was made chief of staff of the 3rd Division, New 4th Army. In 1947 he became political commissar of the 1st Column, Northeast Field Army. In January 1949 he was appointed head of the Cadre Department, Political Department of the 4th Field Army; he concurrently held the same post in the Central-South China Military Council (until about 1953).

1955,   Jun   Identified as deputy political commissar of Guangzhou Military Region

Sep   Appointed lieutenant-general; identified as political commissar of South China Air Force Headquarters

1963,   Dec   Identified as 2nd political commissar of Guangzhou Military Region

1964,   Sep   Elected deputy for the PLA to the 3rd NPC

1965,   Jan   Identified as member of the National Defense Council (until Cultural Revolution)

1969,   Apr   Elected to first term as member of the CCP Central Committee by the 9th Party Congress

May   Identified as chairman of the Revolutionary Committee of Guangdong Province (until Apr 1972), and as 1st political com-

missar of Guangzhou Military Region
(until Apr 1972)

1970,	Dec	Elected 1st secretary of the newly established CP Secretariat of Guangdong Province (until Jul 1972)
1973,	Feb	Identified as 1st secretary of the CP, and as chairman of the Revolutionary Committee, of Sichuan Province (until Jan 1976), as well as 1st political commissar of Chengdu Military Region (until Jan 1976)
1976,	Jan	Identified as commander of Chengdu Military Region (until Oct 1977)
1976,	Apr	Identified as vice-chairman of the Revolutionary Committee of Sichuan Province (until Nov 1977)
1977,	Aug	Reelected member of the CCP Central Committee; subsequently disappears and probably purged

Liu Xinquan (Liu Hsin-ch'üan) 刘新权

Posts held

CCP
Deputy director of the International Liaison Department under the CCP Central Committee

In 1948 Liu was head of the Political Department of the 14th Division, 5th Column, Northeast Field Army. In the following year he served as deputy political commissar of a division of the 42nd Corps, 4th Field Army.

1950,	Sep	Identified as member of the Presidium, Congress of the Battle Heroes
1951		Identified as political commissar of a division
1953		Identified as political commissar of the 42nd Corps
1959,	Nov	Identified as major-general of a PLA unit in Guangdong Province
1960,	May	Appointed assistant minister in the Ministry of Foreign Affairs (until Apr 1964)
1964,	Apr	Appointed vice-minister of foreign affairs (until Jun 1966)
1966,	Jun	Branded as a counterrevolutionary revisionist on the charge of having suppressed Red Guards' activities at the Beijing Institute of Foreign Languages
1970,	Nov	Appointed ambassador to the USSR (until Mar 1976)
1976,	Sep	Appointed ambassador to Albania (last mention on this post: Nov 1977)
1979,	Jun	Identified as deputy director of the International Liaison Department under the CCP Central Committee

Liu Xiwen (Liu Hsi-wen) 刘希文

Posts held

Government
Vice-minister of foreign trade

Others
Director of the Board of Directors of the China International Trust and Investment Corporation

1955,	Feb	Identified as deputy director of the 3rd Bureau, Ministry of Foreign Trade
1960,	May	Identified as director of the 4th Bureau, Ministry of Foreign Trade
1963, Dec-		Member of a delegation under Zhou Enlai
1964, Feb		visiting ten African nations
	Apr	Appointed assistant minister in the Ministry of Foreign Trade (until May 1977)
1970,	Mar	Identified as Chinese representative at the Sino-Japanese Memorandum Trade Office
	Nov	Identified as a cadre in the Council for Promotion of International Trade (until 1972)
1973,	Sep	Head of an economic and trade delegation to Japan
1975,	Oct	Head of the Chinese pavilion at the That Luang Fair in Laos
1977,	May	Identified as vice-minister of foreign trade
	Sep	Head of an exhibition group to Japan
1978,	Aug	Head of a delegation to the Conference of Trade Ministers of the UN Economic and Social Committee for Asia and the Pacific in India
1979,	Mar	Identified as president of the Chinese section of the Sino-Japanese Joint Committee for the Long-term China-Japan Trade Agreement; head of a trade delegation to Japan
	May	Head of the Chinese delegation to the 5th UN Conference on Trade and Development (UNCTAD) Session in Manila
	Oct	Appointed director of the Board of Directors of the China International Trust and Investment Corporation

Liu Xiyao (Liu Hsi-yao) 刘西尧

Posts held

CCP
Alternate member of the CCP 11th Central Committee

Provincial Administration
Vice-governor of Sichuan Province

1949		Identified as secretary, CP of Hongshan District, Hubei Province
1950		Identified as member of the Financial and Economic Committee and as vice-chairman of the Land Reform Committee of the People's Government of Hubei Province
1953,	Dec	Identified as 1st deputy secretary of Hubei Province CP (until Mar 1954)
1957,	Feb	Appointed vice-chairman of the State Technology Commission (reorganized in Nov 1958)
	Nov	Member of a scientific and technical delegation to the USSR
1959,	Sep	Appointed vice-chairman of the Science and Technology Commission (until Sep 1963)
1963,	Oct	Disappears until 1969

1969,	Apr	Elected to first term as alternate member of the CCP Central Committee by the 9th Party Congress
1972,	Jul	Identified as head of the Science and Education Group in the State Council (until 1973)
1975,	Jan	Appointed minister of the 2nd Ministry of Machine Building (until 1976)
1977,	Jan	Identified as minister of education (until Jan 1979)
1979,	Dec	Elected vice-governor of Sichuan Province

Liu Xuechu (Liu Hsüeh-ch'u) 刘雪初

Posts held

Government
Vice-minister of education

| 1978, | Dec | Identified as vice-minister of education |
| 1979, | Jul | Appointed member of the National Games Organizing Committee |

Liu Xuexin (Liu Hsüeh-hsin) 刘学新

Posts held

Government
Vice-minister of metallurgical industry

Others
Vice-president of the Metals Society

1977,	Dec	Identified as vice-minister of metallurgical industry
1978,	Aug	Identified as vice-president of the Metals Society
1979,	Jun	Member of a government delegation, led by Ma Yi, to Sweden.

Liu Ya'nan (Liu Ya-nan) 刘亚南

Posts held

NPC
Deputy for Hunan Province to the 5th NPC

Provincial Administration
Vice-governor of Hunan Province

1977,	Nov	Elected vice-chairman of the Revolutionary Committee of Hunan Province (until Dec 1979)
1978,	Feb	Elected deputy for Hunan Province to the 5th NPC
1979,	Jul	Appointed member of the National Games Organizing Committee
	Dec	Elected vice-governor of Hunan Province

Liu Yangqiao (Liu Yang-ch'iao) 刘仰崎

Posts held

Government
Vice-minister of education

Others
Secretary-general of the Academy of Social Sciences
Secretary of the Bureau of Foreign Affairs, Academy of Social Sciences

In 1946 Liu served as political commissar of the 6th Subdistrict of Shaanxi-Suiyuan Military District.

1951,	Jan	Identified as deputy secretary-general, Southwest Bureau of the CCP Central Committee
	Sep	Identified as member of the Cultural and Educational Committee of the Southwest Military and Administrative Council
1956,	Mar	Identified as director of the Administrative Office, Industrial Work Department of the CCP Central Committee
1958,	Mar	Identified as vice-president and 1st Party secretary of Wuhan University
1959,	Jun	Identified as vice-president of the Wuhan Branch, Academy of Sciences
1960,	Apr	Identified as secretary of Hubei Province CP
1964,	Dec	Appointed vice-minister of higher education (until Cultural Revolution)
1967,	Jan	Branded as a capitalist-roader and purged
1973,	Mar	First appearance after the Cultural Revolution at the mourning ceremonies for He Wei (former minister of education)
	May	Identified as a cadre of the State Administrative Bureau for Museums and Archaeological Data
1974,	Dec	Head of a delegation to the United States for an exhibition of archaeological discoveries
1975,	Oct	Identified as a cadre of the Department of Philosophy and Social Sciences, Academy of Sciences
1978,	Apr	Identified as secretary of the Bureau of Foreign Affairs of the Academy of Social Sciences
	May	Identified as secretary-general of the Academy of Social Sciences
1979,	Mar	Head of a delegation of the Academy of Social Sciences to Australia
	May	Identified as vice-minister of education

Liu Yaxiong (Liu Ya-hsiung) (f) 刘亚雄

Posts held

Others
Member of the Standing Committee, 5th CPPCC

Liu joined the CCP in 1921. From 1923 until 1924, when she studied at the Beijing Girls Normal College, she was also active in the Chinese Students Federation. In 1945 Liu worked in the Shanyin (Daiyue) Administrative Office. In 1949 she held the post of secretary of Changchun Municipality CP. In the same year she was elected a member of the Executive Council of the Women's Federation (until 1967). As a delegate of that Federation Liu joined the 1st CPPCC in September of that year.

| 1952, | Nov | Identified as vice-minister of labor (until Jun 1964) |

1954,   Aug   Elected deputy for Changchun Municipality to the 1st NPC

1958,   Jul   Elected deputy for Jilin Province to the 2nd NPC (reelected in 1964 to the 3rd NPC)

1963   Identified as a member of the Central Control Commission, CCP Central Committee

1965,   Jan   Elected a member of the Standing Committee of the 3rd NPC

1967,   Mar   Denounced as a follower of Liu Shaoqi and purged

1979,   Jul   First appearance after the Cultural Revolution: By-elected member of the Standing Committee, 5th CPPCC

Liu Yi (Liu Yi)   刘 毅

Posts held

Government
Director of the Counselor's Office under the State Council
Deputy director of the General Office of the State Council

NPC
Deputy for Beijing Municipality to the 5th NPC

1974,   Sep   Identified as a State Council cadre

1978,   Feb   Elected deputy for Beijing Municipality to the 5th NPC

        Sep   Identified as deputy director of the General Office of the State Council; head of a friendship delegation to North Korea

1979,   Jan   Identified as director of the Counselor's Office under the State Council

        Jun   Member of the Committee to Examine Proposals at the 2nd Session of the 5th NPC

Liu Yifu (Liu Yi-fu)   刘亦夫

Posts held

Provincial Administration
Vice-governor of Zhejiang Province

1962,   Jul   Identified as member of the People's Government of Zhejiang Province

1977,   Dec   Elected vice-chairman of the Revolutionary Committee of Zhejiang Province (until Dec 1979)

1979,   Dec   Elected vice-governor of Zhejiang Province

Liu Yin (Liu Yin)   刘 寅

Posts held

Government
Vice-minister of the 4th Ministry of Machine Building

NPC
Deputy for Jiangxi Province to the 5th NPC

Others
President of the Electronics Society

In September 1949 Liu was chairman of a preparatory committee for the establishment of the Trade Union for Telecommunications Workers.

1950,   Mar   Elected chairman of the Trade Union for Postal and Telecommunications Workers (until Aug 1953)

1954,   Nov   Appointed vice-minister of the 2nd Ministry of Machine Building (until Feb 1958 when this ministry was incorporated into the 1st Ministry of Machine Building)

1958,   Jun   Identified as vice-minister of the 1st Ministry of Machine Building (until 1960)

1960,   Sep   Appointed vice-minister of the 3rd Ministry of Machine Building (until Sep 1963)

1961,   Oct   Head of a scientific and technical delegation to North Korea

        Nov   Identified as vice-chairman of the Electronics Society

1963,   Jun   Appointed vice-minister of the 4th Ministry of Machine Building (until Cultural Revolution)

1964,   Oct   Elected deputy for Jiangxi Province to the 3rd NPC

1966   Disappears during the Cultural Revolution

1973,   Oct   First appearance after the Cultural Revolution: Identified as a cadre of the State Council

1975,   Apr   Identified as vice-minister of the 4th Ministry of Machine Building; identified as vice-president of the Electronics Society

1976,   Nov   Head of an electronics delegation to Japan

1978,   Feb   Elected deputy for Jiangxi Province to the 5th NPC

1979,   May   Head of an electronics delegation to the Federal Republic of Germany

        Sep   Identified as president of the Electronics Society

Liu Ying (Liu Ying)   刘 英

Posts held

CCP
Member of the Commission for Inspecting Discipline under the CCP Central Committee
Member of the Standing Committee of Hebei Province CP

1977,   Dec   Elected vice-chairman of the Revolutionary Committee of Hebei Province (until Jan 1980)

1978,   Jan   Identified as member of the Standing Committee of Hebei Province CP

        Dec   Appointed member of the Commission for Inspecting Discipline under the CCP Central Committee

Liu Yingxian (Liu Ying-hsien)   刘英仙

Posts held

Government
Ambassador to Sao Tomé and Principe

1964,   Aug   Identified as 1st secretary at the embassy in Congo (Brazzaville)

1972,   Mar   Identified as chargé d'affaires ad interim in Congo (Brazzaville)

1974,   Aug   Appointed ambassador to Gabon (until Nov 1979)

         Oct   Liu accompanies President Bongo of Gabon on his tour of China

1975,   Jul   PRC representative at the celebrations of independence in Sao Tomé

1976,   May   Appointed ambassador to Sao Tomé and Principe

Liu is married to Li Xiyou.

Liu Yongsheng (Liu Yung-sheng) 刘永生

Posts held

NPC
Deputy for Fujian Province to the 5th NPC

Provincial Administration
Vice-chairman of the People's Congress of Fujian Province

Liu was born in 1893 in Fujian Province. One of his teachers at primary school was Zhang Dingcheng, under whose influence he joined the CCP in 1928. During the years until 1934 he rose from company to regiment commander serving in the units commanded by Zhang. In March 1938 Liu was ordered to remain in Southwest Fujian with 150 soldiers while Zhang Dingcheng led his forces north. Starting with only twelve men at the end of that year, Liu had soon established a guerrilla base comprising 20,000 soldiers. After the end of the Anti-Japanese War Liu continued as commander of guerrilla units in Fujian. He was appointed commander of Fujian-Guangdong-Jiangxi Border Region in 1949 and subsequently incorporated his troops into the 4th Field Army.

1949,   Oct   Identified as commander of Fujian Military District

1950,   Apr   Elected member of the Fujian Province CP Committee

         Oct   Elected council member of Fujian Province

         Dec   Identified as deputy commander of Fujian Military District

1954,   Aug   Elected deputy for Fujian Province to the 1st NPC (reelected in 1958 and 1964 to the 2nd and 3rd NPCs)

1957   Identified as major-general

         Dec   Identified as deputy commander of Fuzhou Garrison

1959,   Feb   Elected governor of Fujian (until Cultural Revolution)

         Aug   Identified as commander of Fujian Military District (until 1963)

1968,   Aug   Elected member of the Standing Committee of the newly established Revolutionary Committee of Fujian Province; subsequently disappears

1975,   Aug   First appearance after the Cultural Revolution: Identified as vice-chairman of the Revolutionary Committee of Fujian Province (until Dec 1979)

1978,   Feb   Elected deputy for Fujian Province to the 5th NPC

1979,   Dec   Elected vice-chairman of the People's Congress of Fujian Province

Liu is married to Huang Yueying.

Liu Yongyuan (Liu Yung-yüan) 刘永源

Posts held

Military
Major-general
Deputy commander of Shenyang Military Region

1964,   Sep   Identified as deputy commander of Shenyang Military Region (since 1976 only referred to as military leader)

Liu Yu'e (Liu Yü-o) (f) 刘玉娥

Posts held

CCP
Member of the Standing Committee of Hunan Province CP

Mass Organization
Vice-chairman of the Federation of Trade Unions
Chairman of the Hunan Provincial Trade Unions
Secretary of the Communist Youth League of Hunan Province

1973,   May   Elected secretary of the Communist Youth League of Hunan Province

         Aug   Identified as member of the Standing Committee of Hunan Province CP

1978,   Oct   Elected vice-chairman of the Federation of Trade Unions

         Dec   Elected chairman of the Hunan Provincial Trade Unions

Liu Zhen (Liu Chen) 刘震

Posts held

CCP
Member of the CCP 11th Central Committee

Military
Colonel-general

Liu Zhen was born in 1909 in Hubei Province. In 1935 he was identified as troop leader and political commissar of various units of the Red Army. In the summer of that year he was wounded near Yuanzhaitou. In 1936 he studied at the Anti-Japan Military and Political Academy in North Shaanxi. In 1941 he was commander of the 10th Brigade, 4th Division, New 4th Army. After the Japanese capitulation in 1945 he went to Manchuria with Lin Biao, where he was appointed commander of Jilin-Heilongjiang Military Region. In January 1949 his troops were involved as part of the Northeast Field Army in the battle at Tianjin.

1950,	Oct	Identified as deputy commander of an army corps
1951,	Oct	Appointed council member of the Northeast China People's Government (until Jan 1953)
1957,	Nov	Identified as colonel-general of the Air Force; member of a military delegation to the USSR
1958,	May	Elected alternate member of the CCP Central Committee
1959		Identified as deputy commander of the Air Force
1965,	Sep	Identified as head of the Air Force Academy
1967,	Jan	Liu is accused of having conspired with Cheng Jun to stage a coup d'état with the support of He Long
	Sep	Liu faces a "struggle session" in front of 40,000 people
1977,	Aug	First appearance after the Cultural Revolution: Elected member of the CCP Central Committee by the 11th Party Congress
	Sep	Identified as commander of Xinjiang Military Region (until Feb? 1979) and as 3rd secretary of Xinjiang Autonomous Region CP (until Feb 1978)
1978,	Mar	Identified as 2nd secretary of Xinjiang Autonomous Region CP (until Feb? 1979)
1979,	Feb	Identified as 2nd secretary of the Party Committee of Xinjiang Military Region (until Feb? 1979)

Liu is married to Li Ling.

Liu Zhenhua (Liu Chen-hua)   刘振华

Posts held

CCP
Alternate member of the CCP 11th Central Committee

Military
Deputy political commissar, Shenyang Military District

Before the foundation of PRC, Liu served in the 4th Field Army.

1950		Identified as director of the Political Department of a division of the PLA
1969,	Apr	Elected to first term as alternate member of the CCP Central Committee by the 9th Party Congress
	May	Identified as political commissar of a corps of the PLA
1971,	Feb	Appointed ambassador to Albania (until May 1976)
1976,	Jul	Identified as vice-minister of foreign affairs (until Feb 1979)
1980,	Jan	Identified as deputy political commissar, Shenyang Military Region

Liu is married to Liu Junxiao.

Liu Zhijian (Liu Chih-chien)   刘志坚

Posts held

CCP
Alternate member of the CCP 11th Central Committee

Military
Lieutenant-general
1st Political commissar, Kunming Military Region

Liu was born in 1905 in Hunan Province. In 1930 he joined a Communist federation of trade unions. Shortly afterwards he was elected chairman of the trade union of his native town of Changshoukai. Also in 1930, he joined the Communist Youth League and became a member of the Political Work Department in the companies of the 3rd Army Group of the Red Army. In 1937 he was head of the Propaganda Subdepartment of the Political Department, 129th Division, 8th Route Army. He is believed to have spent the period from 1939 to 1944 in the USSR. In 1947 he was head of the Political Department of an Army Corps in Shanxi-Hebei-Shandong-Henan Military Region. In early 1949 he was appointed deputy political commissar and director of the Political Department of the 4th Army, 2nd Field Army.

1950		Appointed director of the Propaganda Department, General Political Department of the Revolutionary Military Council
1955,	Sep	Appointed major-general, conferred the orders "1st August," "Independence and Freedom," and "Liberation," all 1st class
1957,	Jun	Member of a military delegation to the USSR
1958,	Jan	Appointed deputy director, General Political Department of the PLA
	Apr	Identified as lieutenant-general; deputy head of a Defense Sports delegation to a meeting in Leipzig
1962,	Dec	Appointed vice-chairman of the Sino-Cuban Friendship Association
1963,	Sep	Head of a friendship delegation to the USSR
1964,	Oct	Elected deputy for the PLA to the 3rd NPC
1965,	Jan	Appointed member of the National Defense Council
1967,	Feb	Liu is denounced as an anti-Mao element and disappears
1974,	Sep	First appearance after the Cultural Revolution
1975,	Dec	Identified as political commissar of Kunming Military Region (until Feb 1979)
1977,	Aug	Elected alternate member of the CCP Central Committee by the 11th Party Congress
1978,	Oct	Identified as secretary of the CP Committee of Kunming Military Region (until May 1979)
1979,	Feb	Identified as 1st political commissar, and as 2nd secretary of the CP Committee, of Kunming Military Region
	Oct	Head of a military delegation to Algeria

Liu Zhiping (Liu Chih-p'ing)　刘志平

Posts held

Government
Deputy director of the State Oceanography Bureau

1964, Oct Appointed deputy director of the State Oceanography Bureau; thereafter Liu disapppears

1974, Nov First appearance after the Cultural Revolution: Identified as acting chairman of the Oceanography Society (until 1975)

1978, Sep Identified as deputy director of the State Oceanography Bureau

Liu Zhiqiang (Liu Chih-ch'iang)　柳志强

Posts held

CCP
Alternate member of the CCP 11th Central Committee

1977, Aug Elected alternate member of the CCP Central Committee by the 11th Party Congress

Sep Identified as a cadre in Hunan Province; believed to be a model worker of the Hunan Rubber Plant

Liu Zhonghou (Liu Chung-hou)　刘仲侯

Posts held

Government
Vice-minister of education
Member of the State Nationalities Affairs Commission

1977, Jul Identified as a cadre in the Ministry of Education

Nov Identified as vice-minister of education

1979, May Appointed member of the State Nationalities Affairs Commission

Liu Zhongqian (Liu Chung-ch'ien)　刘众前

Posts held

Provincial Administration
Vice-governor of Shandong Province

1979, Dec Elected vice-governor of Shandong Province

Liu Zhongrong (Liu Chung-jung)　刘仲容

Posts held

Others
Member of the Standing Committee of the 5th CPPCC

Vice-chairman of the Central Committee, Revolutionary Committee of the Chinese KMT

Liu was born in 1906 in Yiyang, Hunan Province. He returned to China in 1927 after having studied at the Sun Yat-sen University in Moscow. According to reports from Taiwan, he was a Communist agent inside the KMT from about 1936.

1954, Dec Elected member of the 2nd CPPCC (re-elected in 1958 to the 3rd CPPCC)

1955, Jan Identified as director of the Beijing Institute of Foreign Languages (from 1959 deputy director)

1956, Mar Identified as member of the Central Committee of the Chinese KMT Revolutionary Committee

1964, Sep Elected deputy for Hunan Province to the 3rd NPC

1967 Disappears during the Cultural Revolution

1972, Sep First appearance after the Cultural Revolution

1978, Mar Elected member of the Standing Committee of the 5th CPPCC

1979, Oct Elected vice-chairman of the Central Committee, Revolutionary Committee of the Chinese KMT

Liu Zhuofu (Liu Cho-fu)　刘卓甫

Posts held

Government
Director of the State Bureau for Commodity Prices

Liu took part in the 11th Olympic Games in Berlin as a player of the Chinese basketball team in August 1936. In 1938 he worked in the Central Hebei Administrative Office. Two years later he was transferred to the 120th Division of the 8th Route Army. Between 1942 and 1945 he was with the Independent 4th Brigade in Northwest Shanxi. In 1949 he was deputy manager of the Northwest Trading Corporation.

1950, Jul Identified as deputy director of the Trade Department of the Southwest Military and Administrative Council (until 1954)

1954, Nov Identified as vice-minister of commerce (until Sep 1955)

1955, Sep Appointed vice-minister for the procurement of farm products (until Dec 1956)

1957, Apr Identified as vice-minister of urban services (until Mar 1958)

1958, Mar Identified as vice-governor of Yunnan Province (until Sep 1963)

1959, Oct Identified as secretary of Yunnan Province CP (until Sep 1963)

1960, Jun Head of a Yunnan Province delegation to North Vietnam

1963, Sep Appointed vice-chairman of the State Commission for Price Control (until Feb 1967)

1967, Feb Denounced as a bourgeois element and purged

1978, Feb First appearance after the Cultural Revolution: Elected deputy for Hebei Province to the 5th NPC

1979, Oct Identified as director of the State Bureau for Commodity Prices

Liu Zihou (Liu Tzu-hou)　刘子厚

Posts held

CCP
Member of the CCP 11th Central Committee

Military
Political commissar of Beijing Military Region

Liu was born in 1911 in Hebei Province. After the Japanese attack on Mukden (today Shenyang) in 1931 he was dismissed as a student in Beijing because of anti-Japanese activities. He subsequently went to Manchuria to join guerrilla units fighting the Japanese. There he established his first contacts with the Communist resistance. He joined the CCP around 1936. After the outbreak of the Anti-Japanese War he went to Henan Province where he became the secretary of the Magistrate of Xinyang. When Xinyang was occupied by the Japanese in October 1928, he again joined the anti-Japanese guerrilla forces. In 1929 he joined the Communist forces attached to Eyuwan (Hubei-Henan-Anhui) Soviet. Little is known about Liu's activities during the following two decades. From his subsequent career, however, it may be concluded that he served with guerrilla units in Central China during this period. In 1948 he was identified as director of the Administration Office of a border area and as director of the Organization Department of Hubei Province CP.

1949,	Nov	Appointed member of the Control Commission of Central-South China Military and Administrative Council (until Jan 1953)
1950,	Mar	Appointed member of the People's Government of Hubei Province
1952,	May	Appointed vice-governor of Hubei Province and member of the Central-South China Military and Administrative Council
1953,	Mar	Appointed 2nd secretary of Hubei Province CP (until Jul 1955)
1954,	Oct	Appointed chairman of the Provincial Government of Hubei Province (until Feb 1955)
1955,	Feb	Elected governor of Hubei Province (until Apr 1958)
1957,	Apr	Appointed director of the Sanmen Gorge Construction Bureau
	Nov	Appointed 1st secretary of Sanmen CP
1958,	Apr	Elected governor of Hebei Province
	May	Elected alternate member of the CCP Central Committee
	Aug	Identified as secretary of Hebei Province CP
	Nov	Elected deputy for Hebei Province to the 2nd NPC
1964,	Mar	Identified as 2nd secretary of Hebei Province CP
1965,	Jul	Identified as secretary, North China Bureau of the CCP Central Committee
1966-1967		Liu is one of the few provincial cadres who survives the Cultural Revolution, though severely attacked by the Red Guards, without loss of influence
1968,	Feb	Elected 1st vice-chairman of the newly established Revolutionary Committee of Hebei Province (until Nov 1979)
1969,	Apr	Elected to first term as member of the CCP Central Committee by the 9th Party Congress
1971,	May	Elected 1st secretary of the new CP Secretariat of Hebei Province after the Cultural Revolution (until Jan 1980)
1974,	Aug	Head of a friendship delegation to North Korea
1975,	Mar	Identified as political commissar of Beijing Military Region
1979,	Mar	Liu is forced to make a self-criticism for Hebei CP's slowness in carrying out Party policies and clearing up problems left over from the Cultural Revolution

Liu is married to Liu Dong.

Liu Zimo (Liu Tzu-mo)　刘子漠

Posts held

Provincial Administration
Vice-chairman of the People's Government of Xinjiang Autonomous Region

1963,	Apr	Identified as director of the Finance Department of Xinjiang Autonomous Region
1979,	Jun	Identified as vice-chairman of the Revolutionary Committee of Xinjiang Autonomous Region (until Sep 1979)
	Sep	Elected vice-chairman of the People's Government of Xinjiang Autonomous Region

Liu Zongzhuo (Liu Tsung-cho)　刘宗卓

Posts held

CCP
Deputy chief editor of HQ

NPC
Deputy for Beijing Municipality to the 5th NPC

1977,	May	Identified as deputy chief editor of HQ
1978,	Feb	Elected deputy for Beijing Municipality to the 5th NPC

Long Feihu (Lung Fei-hu)　龙飞虎

Posts held

NPC
Deputy for the PLA to the 5th NPC

Military
Deputy commander of Fuzhou Military Region
Member of the Standing Committee, CP Secretariat of Fuzhou Military Region

1970,	Apr	Identified as director of the Logistics Department of Fuzhou Military Region

1977,   Jan   Identified as deputy commander of Fuzhou Military Region

        Jun   Identified as member of the Standing Committee, CP Secretariat of Fuzhou Military Region

1978,   Feb   Elected deputy for the PLA to the 5th NPC

Lu Beijian (Lu Pei-chien)

Posts held

Government
Vice-minister of finance

1978,   Sep   Identified as vice-minister of finance

Lu Da (Lu Ta)   路达

Posts held

Government
Vice-minister of metallurgical industry

NPC
Deputy for Tianjin Municipality to the 5th NPC

Others
Vice-president of the Metals Society

Lu was born in 1914 in Zhejiang Province. From 1933 to 1937 he studied metallurgy at Berlin Technical University.

1957,   Apr   Identified as deputy secretary-general of the China Council for the Promotion of International Trade; member of a delegation of this council to the Federal Republic of Germany

1963,   Jan   Head of a metallurgical industry delegation to Switzerland, Austria, Federal Republic of Germany, and France (until May 1963)

1978,   Feb   Elected deputy for Tianjin Municipality to the 5th NPC

        Apr   Identified as vice-minister of metallurgical industry and as vice-president of the Metals Society

Lu Dadong (Lu Ta-tung)    鲁大东

Posts held

CCP
Member of the CCP 11th Central Committee
Standing secretary of Sichuan Province CP
1st secretary of Chongqing Municipality CP

Provincial Administration
Governor of Sichuan Province

Others
Chairman of the Revolutionary Committee of Chongqing Municipality

1950   Identified as secretary of Leshan District CP, Sichuan Province

1954,   May   Identified as director of the Industrial Department of Chongqing CP

1955,   Oct   Identified as deputy secretary of Chongqing Municipality CP (until May 1957)

1957,   May   Identified as secretary of Chongqing Municipality CP (until Jun 1972)

1968,   Jun   Elected vice-chairman of the Revolutionary Committee of Chongqing Municipality (until Apr 1974)

1969,   Apr   Elected to first term as alternate member of the CCP Central Committee by the 9th Party Congress

1972,   Jun   Identified as member of the Standing Committee, Revolutionary Committee of Sichuan Province (until Nov 1977), and as 2nd secretary of Chongqing Municipality CP (until 1976)

1974,   Apr   Identified as chairman of the Revolutionary Committee of Chongqing Municipality

1976,   May   Identified as 1st secretary of Chongqing Municipality CP

1977,   Apr   Identified as secretary of Sichuan Province CP

        Aug   Elected member of the CCP Central Committee by the 11th Party Congress

        Dec   Elected vice-chairman of the Revolutionary Committee of Sichuan Province (until Dec 1979)

1979,   Jan   Elected standing secretary of Sichuan Province CP

        Dec   Elected governor of Sichuan Province

Lu Dingyi (Lu Ting-yi)   陆定一

Posts held

CCP
Member of the CCP 11th Central Committee

Others
Vice-chairman of the 5th CPPCC

Lu Dingyi was born in 1906 in Wushi, Jiangsu Province. He joined the CCP in 1925. Following his graduation in a technical subject from Jiaotong University in Shanghai he continued his studies for a short period in the United States and then in the USSR. As a student Lu joined the CCP. After his return from abroad he joined the Ruijin Soviet to take the post of secretary-general of the Communist Youth League. In 1928 he took part in the 6th CCP Congress in Moscow and in a Comintern congress as a delegate representing the Chinese Communist Youth League. After his return to China he became head of the Propaganda Department of the Communist Youth League in 1930. In the following year he went to Ruijin. In 1933 he was active as a cadre in the Propaganda Department of the Red Army General Political Department. He continued to be engaged in this work during the Long March. In 1937 he became head of the Propaganda Department of the 1st Front Army and shortly afterwards, of the 8th Route Army. From roughly this period Lu was head of the Propaganda Department of the CCP Central Committee, a post in which he was only briefly replaced by Xi Zhongxun from late 1952 to 1953. In 1942 he became deputy director of the Propaganda Department of the 18th Army. He was elected a member of the Central Committee by the 7th CCP Congress in 1945. In 1946 he was one of the Communist delegates at the negotiations with the Nationalist Government in Chongqing and later in Nanjing. In September 1949 he was a member of the CPPCC which later elected him a member of its National Committee.

1949,	Oct	Appointed vice-chairman of the Culture and Education Committee of the Central People's Government, and vice-chairman of the Preparatory Committee for the Research Institute of New Political Science, member of the Association for the Reform of the Chinese Language, and council member of the Sino-Soviet Friendship Association
1950		Identified as member of the Peace Council
1954,	Oct	Elected deputy for Jiangsu Province to the 1st NPC and member of its Standing Committee (until Mar 1959)
1956,	May	On 26 May Lu delivers a later famous speech on the subject of "Let a hundred flowers blossom"
	Sep	Elected alternate member of the Politburo by the 8th CCP Congress (until Cultural Revolution)
1957,	Oct	Member of the Chinese delegation to the anniversary celebrations of the October Revolution in Moscow
1959,	Apr	Appointed vice-premier
1960,	Nov	Member of the CCP delegation to the Conference of the 81 Communist Parties in Moscow
1962,	Sep	Elected member of the CCP Central Committee Secretariat by the 10th Session of the 8th CCP Central Committee
1965,	Jan	Appointed minister of culture
	May	Head of a Party and government delegation to the German Democratic Republic
1966,	Dec	Branded as a counterrevolutionary revisionist and purged
1979,	Jan	First appearance after the Cultural Revolution
	Jul	By-elected vice-chairman of the 5th CPPCC
	Sep	By-elected member of the CCP 11th Central Committee

Lu Guang (Lu Kuang)   鲁 光

Posts held

CCP
Member of the Standing Committee of Heilongjiang Province CP

Provincial Administration
Vice-governor of Heilongjiang Province

1960,	Apr	Identified as deputy director of the Industrial Work Department of Heilongjiang Province CP
1977,	Dec	Elected vice-chairman of the Revolutionary Committee of Heilongjiang Province (until Dec 1979)

1978,	May	Identified as member of the Standing Committee of Heilongjiang Province CP
1979,	Dec	Elected vice-governor of Heilongjiang Province

Lu Jiaxi (Lu Chia-hsi)    卢嘉锡

Posts held

NPC
Deputy for Fujian Province to the 5th NPC

Others
Director of the Chemistry Department of the Beijing University of Science and Technology
Director of the Fujian Institute on the Structure of Matter, Academy of Sciences

1961,	Apr	Identified as vice-president of Fuzhou University and as chairman of the Scientific and Technical Association, Fujian Branch
1964,	Sep	Elected deputy for Fujian Province to the 3rd NPC
1967		Disappears during the Cultural Revolution
1978,	Feb	First appearance after the Cultural Revolution: Elected deputy for Fujian to the 5th NPC
	Mar	Identified as director of the Fujian Institute on the Structure of Matter, Academy of Sciences
	Jun	Head of a delegation to the 3rd International Symposium on Nitrogen Fixation
	Ovt	Identified as director of the Chemistry Department of the Beijing University of Science and Technology

Lu Jindong (Lu Chin-tung)    路金栋

Posts held

Government
Vice-minister of the Physical Culture and Sports Commission

Others
Vice-president of the Sports Federation

1953,	Jul	Elected member of the Communist Youth League Central Committee; identified as deputy director, Organization Department of the Communist Youth League
1960,	Mar	Identified as member of the Standing Committee, Central Committee of the Youth League
1964,	Jul	Elected secretary of the Youth League (until Cultural Revolution)
	Oct	Elected deputy for Hebei Province to the 3rd NPC
1965,	Apr	Member of a youth delegation to Albania
1967		Disappears during the Cultural Revolution
1973,	Oct	First appearance after the Cultural Revolution
1975,	Oct	Identified as a cadre of the Physical Culture and Sports Commission

1976,   May Head of a sports delegation to Thailand
1978,   May Head of a sports delegation to Singapore
        Jun Identified as vice-minister of the Physical
             Culture and Sports Commission
1979,   Mar Identified as vice-president of the Sports
             Federation
        Jul Appointed member of the National Games
             Organizing Committee

Lu Jinlong (Lu Chin-lung)

Posts held

CCP
Alternate member of the CCP 11th Central Committee
Deputy secretary, CP of Xuzhou Mining Bureau in Jiangsu Province

Lu is a model industrial worker.

1973,   Aug Elected to first term as alternate member
             of the CCP Central Committee
1977,   May Identified as deputy secretary, CP of
             Xuzhou Mining Bureau in Jiangsu Province

Lu Ping (Lu P'ing)

Posts held

Government
Vice-minister of the 7th Ministry of Machine Building

Others
Honorary president of the Vacuum Society

As a student of Beijing University Lu was engaged in the
"December 9 Student Movement" in 1935. About 1938 he
went to Yan'an to work in youth affairs. In 1946 he was
secretary of Kowloon (Hong Kong) CP. In 1948 he was
elected director of the Youth Work Committee of the
Federation of Trade Unions (until December 1952). In
April 1949 he was elected member of the Standing
Committee of the New Democratic Youth League (until
December 1952). In September that year Lu attended the
1st CPPCC.

1949,   Oct Appointed council member of the Sino-
             Soviet Friendship Association (until
             Dec 1954)
1950,   Jul Identified as director of the Political
             Department of the Ministry of Railways
1952,   Dec Identified as director of the Harbin Rail-
             way Administration Bureau (until
             Nov 1954)
1954,   Oct Identified as vice-minister of railways
             (until Oct 1957)
1957,   Oct Identified as vice-president of Beijing
             University (until Jun 1960)
1958,   Sep Elected deputy for Heilongjiang Province
             to the 2nd NPC
        Oct Identified as vice-president of the Sino-
             Romanian Friendship Association (until
             Jul 1961)
1960,   Mar Elected council member of the Sino-Latin
             American Friendship Association
        Jun Identified as president of Beijing Universi-

ty (until Cultural Revolution)
1961,   Aug Identified as president of the Sino-Roma-
             nian Friendship Association
1964,   Sep Elected deputy for Beijing Municipality to
             the 3rd NPC
1966,   May Attacked by the first big character poster
             (Dazi Bao) posted by Nie Yuanzi
        Jun Denounced as a revisionist and purged
1979,   Dec First appearance after the Cultural Rev-
             olution: Elected honorary president of the
             Vacuum Society; identified as vice-minis-
             ter of the 7th Ministry of Machine Build-
             ing

Lu Sheng (Lu Sheng)

Posts held

Military
Lieutenant-general
Member of the Standing Committee,
CP Secretariat of Fuzhou Military Region

Others
Member of the Standing Committee of the
5th CPPCC

In 1934 Lu commanded an independent battalion of the
Red 3rd Regiment in Fujian Province, and in 1937 a
regiment of the New 4th Army. In 1941 he was
commander of the 3rd Brigade, 1st Division, New 4th Army. He was appointed director of the Political Department of the 4th Column, East China Field Army, in 1946
and in 1949 political commissar of the 23rd Army,
3rd Field Army.

1953   Identified as political commissar of Fujian
             Military District
1955,   Sep Appointed lieutenant-general
1959,   Jul Identified as director of the Political
             Department of Fuzhou Military Region
1964,   Aug Identified as deputy political commissar
             of Fuzhou Military Region (until a-
             bout 1976)
1977,   Jun Identified as member of the Standing
             Committee, CP Secretariat of Fuzhou
             Military Region
1978,   Mar Elected member of the Standing Commit-
             tee of the 5th CPPCC
        Jun Identified as advisor in Fuzhou Military
             Region

Lu Shenghe (Lu Sheng-ho)

Posts held

NPC
Member of the Standing Committee of the
5th NPC
Deputy for Liaoning Province to the
5th NPC

1978,   Feb Elected deputy for Liaoning Province to
             the 5th NPC
        Mar Elected member of the Standing Commit-
             tee of the 5th NPC

Lu Tianji (Lu T'ien-chi)　　　鹿田计

Posts held

CCP
Member of the CCP 11th Central Committee
Member of the Standing Committee of Shandong Province CP

Mass Organization
Chairman of the Trade Unions of Shandong Province

Lu originally became known as a miner of Zhaozhuang Coal Mine in Shandong Province.

1969,	Apr	Elected to first term as member of the CCP Central Committee by the 9th Party Congress
1973,	Jul	Elected chairman of the Trade Unions of Shandong Province
1977,	Jan	Identified as member of the Standing Committee of Shandong Province CP

Lu Weizhao (Lu Wei-chao)　　　陆维钊

Posts held

Government
Ambassador to Syria

1963,	Jul	Identified as counselor at the embassy in North Vietnam (until about 1967)
1970,	Sep	Identified as deputy director of the Asia Department in the Ministry of Foreign Affairs
1972,	Dec	Identified as director of the Asia Department in the Ministry of Foreign Affairs (until Feb 1974)
1974,	Sep	Appointed ambassador to Pakistan (until Apr 1979)
1979,	Sep	Appointed ambassador to Syria

Lu Xuzhang (Lu Hsü-chang)　　　卢绪章

Posts held

Government
Director of the General Administration of Travel and Tourism

Lu was born in 1911 in Zhejiang Province. Before 1949 he was manager of Guang Da Hua Hong, a Hong Kong overseas trade company.

1950,	Feb	Appointed deputy director of the Commerce Department of the East China Military and Administrative Council
	Mar	Appointed manager of the China Import and Export Corporation
1952,	Apr	Member of a delegation to the 1st International Economic Conference in Moscow
1953,	Sep	Identified as director of the 3rd Bureau, Ministry of Foreign Trade
1955,	Apr	Elected member of the Central Committee of the National Construction Associa-

		tion; deputy head of a trade delegation to Japan
	Jun	Appointed assistant minister of foreign trade (until Oct 1956)
1956,	Mar	Head of an economic delegation to PR Mongolia
	Oct	Appointed vice-minister of foreign trade
	Dec	Appointed member of the Standing Committee, Federation of Industry and Commerce
1958,	Jan	Head of a trade delegation to Yugoslavia
	Mar	Head of a trade delegation to Albania
	Dec	Head of a trade delegation to Egypt
1959,	May	Head of a trade delegation to Finland
1960,	Jul	Head of a trade delegation to Cuba
1961,	Jan	Head of a trade delegation to Egypt
	Feb	Head of a trade delegation to Mali
	Apr	Chinese representative at independence celebrations in Sierra Leone
1963,	Mar	Head of a trade delegation to Great Britain, Switzerland, The Netherlands, Burma, and Hong Kong (until May 1963)
1964,	Jul	Head of a trade delegation to Mali
	Aug	Representative of the Chinese Government attending the 1st Anniversary of the Congolese Revolution in Brazzaville
	Sep	Head of a trade delegation to Niger, Dahomey, and the Central African Republic
	Oct	Head of a trade delegation to Ceylon
	Dec	Representative of the Chinese Government attending the independence celebrations in Kenya
1967		Disappears during the Cultural Revolution
1976,	Jan	First appearance after the Cultural Revolution at mourning ceremonies for Zhou Enlai
1978,	May	Identified as director of the International Travel Service
1979,	Jan	Identified as director of the General Administration for Travel and Tourism

Lu Yu (Lu Yü)　　　陆禹

Posts held

Provincial Administration
Deputy mayor of Beijing Municipality

1957,	Jun	Identified as deputy director of the Department for Industrial Work, Beijing Municipality CP
1979,	Dec	Elected deputy mayor of Beijing Municipality

Lu Zhenfan (Lu Chen-fan)　　　陆锁藩

Posts held

Others
Member of the Standing Committee of the 5th CPPCC

1954,	Jul	Identified as deputy commissioner of Duyun Special District in Guizhou Province
	Aug	Elected deputy for Guizhou Province to the 1st NPC

1959, Jan Identified as deputy director of the Agricultural Department of Guizhou Province

Apr Elected member of the 3rd CPPCC (confirmed in 1964 by the 4th CPPCC)

1978, Mar Elected member of the Standing Committee of the 5th CPPCC

Lu Zhian (Lu Chih-an)

Posts held

CCP
Secretary of Qinghai Province CP

1970, Oct Identified as political commissar of Qinghai Military District (until 1976)

1971, Mar Elected deputy secretary of Qinghai Province CP (until 1978)

1979, Apr Identified as secretary of Qinghai Province CP

Lu Zhongyang (Lu Chung-yang) 卢忠阳

Posts held

CCP
Alternate member of the CCP 11th Central Committee
Member of the Standing Committee of Henan Province CP
1st CP secretary of a people's commune

Others
Chairman of the Revolutionary Committee of a people's commune in Jia County, Henan Province

1958 Lu returns to his native village having attended a state school

1970-1972 Studies at Qinghua University

1973, Aug Elected to first term as alternate member of the CCP Central Committee by the 10th Party Congress

1974, Jul Identified as 1st CP secretary of a people's commune

1975, Apr Identified as chairman of the Revolutionary Committee of a people's commune in Jia County, Henan Province

1977, Oct Identified as member of the Standing Committee of Henan Province CP

Lü Cunjie (Lü Ts'un-chieh) (f)

Posts held

CCP
Alternate member of the CCP 11th Central Committee
Secretary, CP of Fenggengkou Production Brigade of Tongguo People's Commune, Huzhu Autonomous County of the Tu in Qinghai Province

Mass Organization
Vice-chairman of the Women's Federation of Qinghai Province

Lü belongs to the Tu minority. She became known as an agricultural worker of "Red Star" Production Brigade in Songtuo People's Commune, Qinghai Province.

1969, Apr Elected alternate member of the CCP Central Committee by the 9th Party Congress (confirmed in 1973 and 1977 by the 10th and 11th congresses)

1973, Sep Elected vice-chairman of the Women's Federation of Qinghai Province

1974, Nov Identified as member of Qinghai Province CP

1975, Mar Identified as secretary of the CP of Fenggengkou Production Brigade, Tongguo People's Commune in Huzhu Autonomus County of the Tu

Lü Dong (Lü Tung)

Posts held

Government
Minister of the 3rd Ministry of Machine Building

Others
Member of the Standing Committee of the 5th CPPCC

Lü was first identified as a cadre in 1945. At the time he was head of the 1st Bureau of Central Shanxi Administrative Office.

1950, Apr Appointed deputy director of the Industry Department of Northeast China People's Government (until Aug 1952)

1952, Aug Appointed vice-minister of heavy industry (abolished in May 1956)

1957, Jun Appointed vice-minister of metallurgical industry (until Jul 1964)

1964, Jul Appointed minister of metallurgical industry

1967, Jan Branded as an anti-Party element and disappears

1973, May First appearance after the Cultural Revolution

1978, Mar Appointed minister of the 3rd Ministry of Machine Building; elected member of the Standing Committee of the 5th CPPCC

Nov Head of an aviation experts delegation to the Federal Republic of Germany, France, and Great Britain

Lü He (Lü Ho)

Posts held

CCP
Alternate member of the CCP 11th Central Committee

Others
Secretary of the CP, and chairman of the Revolutionary Committee, of Taiping Production Brigade in Zhongxing People's Commune, Gannan County, Heilongjiang Province

Lü was first known as a model agricultural worker.

1964,	Oct	Elected deputy for Heilongjiang Province to the 3rd NPC
1969,	Feb	Identified as member of the Revolutionary Committee of Heilongjiang Province, as vice-chairman of the Revolutionary Committee of Nenjiang District, as well as chairman of the Revolutionary Committee of Taiping Production Brigade in Gannan County
	Apr	Elected alternate member of the CCP Central Committee by the 9th Party Congress (confirmed in 1973 and 1977 by the 10th and 11th congresses)
1970,	May	Identified as secretary, CP of Taiping Production Brigade

 **Lü Ji** (Lü Chi)

Posts held

NPC
Member of the Standing Committee of the 5th NPC
Deputy for Shanghai Municipality to the 5th NPC

Others
President of the Union of Musicians

Lü was born in 1906. In 1935 Lü took part in the "December 9 Student Movement" in Beijing. He was one of the signatories of a letter of protest against acts of brutality committed by Italian sailors in Shanghai in 1937. Having moved to Yan'an, he became widely known as the composer of many revolutionary songs. In May 1949 he was elected a member of the National Committee of the Federation of Democratic Youth, and in July of that year member of the National Committee of the Federation of Literary and Art Circles (until Cultural Revolution), as well as president of the Union of Musicians. In September he took part in the 1st CPPCC.

1949,	Nov	Identified as director of the Central Institute of Music under the Ministry of Culture
1954,	Apr	Member of a friendship delegation to the USSR
	May	Identified as council member of the Association for Cultural Relations with Foreign Countries
	Jun	Member of a cultural delegation to Poland
	Aug	Elected deputy for Hunan Province to the 1st NPC (reelected in 1958 and 1964 to the 2nd and 3rd NPCs)
1958,	Mar	Head of a cultural delegation to Japan; identified as council member of the the Sino-United Arab Republic Friendship Association
1959,	Nov	Identified as council member of the Sino-Albanian Friendship Association
1961,	Jul	Head of a delegation of artists visiting PR Mongolia
1962,	Apr	Member of a cultural delegation to North Korea
1963,	Oct	Identified as council member of the Sino-Japanese Friendship Association
1967,	Jan	Branded as a revisionist and purged

1975,	Sep	First appearance after the Cultural Revolution
1977,	Aug	Head of a Central Philharmonic Society delegation to North Korea
1978,	Feb	Elected deputy for Shanghai Municipality to the 5th NPC
	Mar	Elected member of the Standing Committee of the 5th NPC
	Jun	Identified in his former post as president of the Union of Musicians (reelected Nov 1979)

Lü Jianguang (Lü Chien-kuang) 吕剑光

Posts held

Government
Vice-minister of public security
Member of the Patriotic Health Campaign Committee
Member of the Birth Planning Leading Group under the State Council

1978,	Apr	Identified as member of the Patriotic Health Campaign Committee
	Jul	Identified as member of the Birth Planning Leading Group under the State Council
1979,	Feb	Identified as vice-minister of public security
	Nov	Head of a delegation of the Ministry of Public Security to Thailand

Lü Jianren (Lü Chien-jen) 吕剑人

Posts held

CCP
Secretary of Shaanxi Province CP

1953,	Jun	Identified as director of the United Front Work Department of Xinjiang Province CP
1954,	Aug	Elected deputy for Xinjiang Province to the 1st NPC (reelected to the 2nd and 3rd NPCs in 1959 and 1964)
1956,	Nov	Identified as secretary of Xinjiang Autonomous Region CP (until Sep 1968)
1959,	Apr	Appointed member of the Nationalities Affairs Committee of the 2nd NPC (reappointed in 1964 to the 3rd NPC)
1968,	Sep	Denounced as a follower of Liu Shaoqi
1978,	Dec	First appearance after the Cultural Revolution
1979,	Sep	Identified as secretrary of Shaanxi Province CP and vice-chairman of the Revolutionary Committee, Shaanxi Province (until Dec 1979)

Lü Kebai (Lü K'e-pai)

Posts held

Government
Vice-minister of the State Capital Construction Commission

In the mid 1940s Lü was secretary-general of the Finance Department of Shaanxi-Gansu-Ningxia Border Regional Government.

1950,	Jun	Identified as deputy director of the Financial and Currency Planning Office of the Central Financial and Economic Planning Bureau under the Government Administration Council
1956,	Nov	Identified as member of the State Economic Commission (until Sep 1959)
1959,	Sep	Appointed member of the State Capital Construction Commission (until Jan 1961)
1961,	Jan	Appointed member of the State Planning Commission
1965,	Apr	Appointed vice-chairman of the State Capital Construction Commission
1967		Disappears during the Cultural Revolution
1978,	Apr	First appearance after the Cultural Revolution
	May	Identified as vice-minister of the State Capital Construction Commission

Lü Qing (Lü Ch'ing)　　　吕　涛

Posts held

Government
Vice-minister of state farms and land reclamation

1954,	Oct	Identified as deputy political commissar of Heilongjiang Military District
1955,	Jan	Identified as a member of Heilongjiang Province CP
1964,	Sep	Elected deputy for Heilongjiang Province to the 3rd NPC
1979,	Oct	First appearance after the Cultural Revolution: Identified as vice-minister of state farms and land reclamation

Lü Shuxiang (Lü Shu-hsiang)　　吕叔湘

Posts held

NPC
Member of the Standing Committee of the 5th NPC
Deputy for Shanghai Municipality to the 5th NPC

Others
Director of the Institute of Linguistics, Academy of Social Sciences
Chief editor of Zhongguo Yuwen (The Chinese Language)

Lü at one time served as editor of Kai Ming Bookstore and as professor at Kunming Associated University and at the National Central University.

1950		Identified as deputy director of the Institute of Philology of the Academy of Sciences
1953,	May	Member of a delegation of the Academy of Sciences to the USSR

1954,	Dec	Elected member of the National Committee of the 2nd CPPCC (confirmed in 1959 by the 3rd CPPCC)
1955,	May	Identified as member of the Department of Philosophy and Social Sciences of the Academy of Sciences
1958,	Mar	Identified as director of the Institute of Linguistics at the Academy of Sciences
1962,	Apr	Identified as deputy secretary-general of the Sino-Soviet Friendship Association
1964,	Sep	Elected deputy for Jiangsu Province to the 3rd NPC
1967		Disappears during the Cultural Revolution
1973,	Oct	First appearance after the Cultural Revolution
1975,	Mar	Identified as deputy to the 4th NPC
1978,	Feb	Elected deputy for Shanghai Municipality to the 5th NPC
	Mar	Elected member of the Standing Committee of the 5th NPC
	May	Identified as director of the Institute of Linguistics, Academy of Social Sciences, and as chief editor of Zhongguo Yuwen

Publications

1951	Talks on Rhetoric
1953	Learning Chinese Grammar
1954	The Work and the Accomplishment of Soviet Linguists
1955	Exercises in Grammar and Rhetorics
1956	Digest Essentials of Chinese Grammar
1957	The Auxiliary Words in Chinese Classical Language
1961	The Use of New Phonetical Spelling Method for Chinese
1964	Chinese Studying English
1978	Problems in the Grammatical Analysis of Contemporary Chinese

Lü Wei (Lü Wei)　　　律　巍

Posts held

Government
Deputy director of the State Oceanography Bureau

1978,	Apr	Identified as deputy director of the State Oceanography Bureau
	Sep	Head of an oceanograhpic delegation to Japan

Lü Xuguo (Lü Hsü-kuo)　　吕需国

Posts held

CCP
Alternate member of the CCP 11th Central Committee

1977,	Aug	Elected alternate member of the CCP Central Committee by the 11th Party Congress

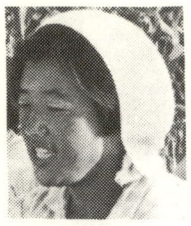

Lü Yulan (Lü Yü-lan) (f)   呂玉兰

Posts held

CCP
Member of the CCP 11th Central Committee
Secretary of Hebei Province CP
1st secretary of Linxi County CP, Hebei Province

Government
Member of the Birth Planning Leading Group under the State Council

NPC
Member of the Standing Committee of the 5th NPC
Deputy for Hebei Province to the 5th NPC

Lü was born circa 1940 in Linxi County, Hebei Province.

1966,	Jun	Identified as vice-chairman of the Federation of Poor and Lower-Middle Peasants in Hebei Province
	Jul	Identified as secretary, CP of Tongliushanku Production Brigade, Changsanzhai People's Commune (later renamed Xiapaosi People's Commune) in Linxi County, Hebei Province
	Sep	Named as a model student of the works of Mao Zedong
1968,	Feb	Appointed member of the newly established Revolutionary Committee of Hebei Province
	May	Identified as vice-chairman of the Revolutionary Committee of Linxi County
1969,	Apr	Elected to first term as member of the CCP Central Committee by the 9th Party Congress
1970,	Jun	Member of a Party and government delegation to North Korea to attend the 20th anniversary of the War of Liberation; identified as vice-chairman of the Revolutionary Committee of Hebei Province (until 1979?)
1971,	May	Identified as deputy secretary of Hebei Province CP (until Sep 1976)
1972,	Oct	Head of a youth delegation to Albania
1975,	Jan	Elected member of the Standing Committee of the 4th NPC (confirmed in Mar 1978 by the 5th NPC)
	Feb	Identified as 1st secretary of Linxi County CP
1977,	Jun	Identified as secretary of Hebei Province CP
1978,	Feb	Elected deputy for Hebei Province to the 5th NPC
	Jul	Appointed member of the Birth Planning Leading Group under the State Council

Lü Zhengcao (Lü Cheng-ts'ao)   呂正操

Posts held

CCP
Member of the CCP 11th Central Committee

Military
Colonel-general
1st political commissar, Railway Engineering Corps of the PLA

Lü was born in 1901 in Haicheng, Liaoning Province. In 1921 he served as a bodyguard in the Headquarters of the General Inspector of Manchuria. From 1922 to 1924 he studied at the Northeast Military Academy which he left with the rank of lieutenant. In the following year he joined the Nationalist Northeast Army, rising to the rank of colonel by 1933. In March of that year he took part with his military unit in battles with the Japanese near Lamadong and Jielingkou. After further military training at the officers' school in Lushan he went over to the Communists in spring 1937. He was noted for distinguished service during the Anti-Japanese War. In February 1938 he was appointed commander of Central Hebei Military District. During this period he also attended a course at the Anti-Japan Military and Political Academy in Yan'an.

From 1940 to 1943 Lü was successively commander of Central Hebei Military Region and of Shanxi-Suiyuan Military Region. He was elected alternate member of the CCP Central Committee by the 7th Party Congress in June 1945. Two months later, after the Japanese capitulation, he was transferred to Manchuria. In June 1946 he was identified as deputy commander of the Northeast China Joint Democratic Army (renamed Northeast China People's Liberation Army in January 1948). One month later he was appointed deputy director of the Political Department of the Northeast China Railway Security Corps. His appointment as deputy director of the Railway Department of the Revolutionary Military Council followed in January 1948. In September 1949 Lü took part in the CPPCC as a delegate representing the PLA Headquarters.

1949,	Oct	Appointed vice-minister of railways (until Jan 1965)
1950		Appointed director of the General Bureau of Technology in the Ministry of Railways; identified as deputy commander of the PLA Railway Corps
1954,	Aug	Elected deputy for Benxi Municipality to the 1st NPC (until Mar 1959)
	Oct	Appointed member of the National Defense Council
	Dec	Elected member of the Standing Committee of the CPPCC (until Dec 1964); head of a communications delegation to North Vietnam
1955,	Sep	Awarded the orders "Independence and Freedom" and "Liberation," both 1st class
1956,	Sep	Elected member of the CCP Central Committee by the 8th Party Congress
1958,	Dec	Elected deputy for Liaoning Province to the 2nd NPC
1961,	Jun	Head of a railway delegation to Budapest
1963,	Jun	Head of a railway delegation to the 8th Conference of the Socialist Countries' Ministers of Railways in Warsaw
1964,	Jan	Head of a railway delegation to North Korea
	Mar	Identified as colonel-general
	Jun	Head of a railway delegation to the USSR
1965,	Jan	Appointed minister of railways (until Cultural Revolution)
	Mar	Head of a railway delegation to the

10th Conference of the Socialist Countries' Ministers of Railways in Hanoi

1967, Jan At the height of the Cultural Revolution Lü is paraded through the streets of Beijing as a deviationist

1974, Jul First appearance after the Cultural Revolution

1975, Jan Elected member of the Standing Committee by the 4th NPC (not confirmed by the 5th NPC)

1976, Aug Identified as political commissar of the PLA Engineering Corps (until Feb 1979)

1977, Aug Elected member of the CCP Central Committee by the 11th Party Congress

1979, Feb Identified as 1st political commissar of the PLA Railway Engineering Coprs

Lü Zhixian (Lü Chih-hsien)　呂志先

Posts held

Government
Ambassador to North Korea

1954, Nov Identified as director of the Propaganda Department of Zhejiang Province CP

1958, Apr Identified as 1st secretary of Jinhua Special District CP, Zhejiang Province

Aug Identified as secretary-general of Zhejiang Province CP

1964, Jan Identified as chancellor of Hangzhou University

1965, Sep Appointed ambassador to Mauretania (until 1967)

1970, Sep Appointed ambassador to Hungary (until Jan 1973)

1973, Mar Appointed ambassador to Congo (Brazzaville) (until May 1976)

1976, Sep Appointed ambassador to North Korea

Luo Fanqun (Lo Fan-ch'ün)　罗范群

Posts held

CCP
Secretary of Guangzhou Municipality CP

Others
Deputy director of the Guangzhou Export Commidities Fair

Luo was born in 1912 in Xinning, Guangdong Province. After the Long March he attended a course at the Communist Anti-Japan Military and Political Academy. In September 1949 he took part in the 1st CPPCC.

1951, Dec Elected mayor of Shantou, Guangdong Province

1952 Identified as secretary of Chaoan-Shantou District CP

1953 Identified as 2nd CP secretary and mayor of Shantou

1954, Jun Elected member of the People's Government of Guangdong Province

1956, Jun Appointed director of the 8th Office of Guangdong People's Government and deputy director of the United Front Work Department of Guangdong Province CP

1958, Sep Elected deputy for Guangdong Province to the 2nd NPC (reelected in 1964 to the 3rd NPC)

1961, May Elected vice-governor of Guangdong Province (until Cultural Revolution) and director of the United Front Work Department of Guangdong Province CP (until 1962)

1966 Disappears during the Cultural Revolution

1973, Feb First appearance after the Cultural Revolution

Aug Identified as vice-chairman of the Revolutionary Committee of Guangzhou Municipality

Oct Deputy director of the Guangzhou Export Commodities Fair (subsequently of the respective spring and autumn fairs until autumn 1978)

Nov Identified as secretary of Guangzhou Municipality CP

1975, Aug Head of a friendship delegation to North Korea

Luo Guibo (Lo Kuei-po)　罗贵波

Posts held

CCP
2nd secretary of Shanxi Province CP

Provincial Administration
Governor of Shanxi Province

Luo was born in 1911 in Guangdong Province. He was educated in France where he joined the Communist International. He became a member of the CCP in 1927. In 1934-35 he took part in the Long March. He was head of the Propaganda Department of the 120th Division and of Shanxi-Suiyuan Subbureau of the Central Committee in 1938. In 1939 he was identified as political commissar of the 358th Brigade, 8th Route Army. At the end of that year Luo became political commissar of the Provisional Headquarters of the New Shanxi Army following the "Shanxi New Army Incident." This army was commanded by Xu Fanting who had successfully revolted against Yan Xishan, KMT commander of the 2nd War Region. After the occupation of Taiyuan by Communist troops in April 1949 Luo was appointed a member of the Military Control Commission of Taiyuan.

1950? Appointed director of the General Office of the Revolutionary Military Council (probably until Aug 1954)

1954, Aug Appointed ambassador to North Vietnam (until Oct 1957)

1955, Jul Luo accompanies Ho Chi-minh on a state visit to China

1956, Sep Elected alternate member of the CCP Central Committee by the 8th Party Congress (until Apr 1969)

1957, Jul Luo accompanies Ho Chi-minh on a visit to Beijing

Oct Appointed vice-minister of foreign affairs

1959, Jul Head of a delegation to Iraq

1970, Oct Still active as vice-minister of foreign affairs, Luo disappears for unknown reasons

1978, Dec First appearance thereafter

1979, Mar Identified as 2nd secretary of Shanxi Province CP

Dec Elected governor of Shanxi Province

Luo Libin (Lo Li-pin) 罗立斌

Posts held

CCP
Member of the Standing Committee, Guangxi Autonomous Region CP

Provincial Administration
Vice-chairman of the People's Government, Guangxi Autonomous Region

1962,	Dec	Identified as deputy director of the Propaganda Department, Guangxi Autonomous Region CP
1978,	Jun	Identified as a member of the Standing Committee, People's Government of Guangxi Autonomous Region
1979,	Dec	Elected vice-chairman of the People's Government, Guangxi Autonomous Region

Luo Qingchang (Lo Ch'ing-ch'ang) 罗青长

Posts held

CCP
Member of the CCP 11th Central Committee

NPC
Member of the Standing Committee of the 5th NPC
Deputy secretary-general, Standing Committee of the 5th NPC
Deputy for Sichuan Province to the 5th NPC

Luo was born in 1918 in Hubei Province. During the Anti-Japanese War he was private secretary to Lin Zuhan, then director of the Xi'an Office of the 8th Route Army. In 1947 he was head of the 1st Section, Department of Social Affairs of the CCP Central Committee.

1954,	Mar	Identified as deputy director of the Premier's Office in the State Council (until Mar 1965)
1960,	May	Luo accompanies Premier Zhou Enlai on state visits to Burma, Nepal, India, and the People's Republic of Mongolia
1963,	Apr	Luo accompanies President Liu Shaoqi on state visits to Indonesia, Burma, Cambodia, and North Vietnam
1964,	Oct	Elected deputy for Sichuan Province to the 3rd NPC; member of a delegation led by minister of Foreign Affairs Chen Yi to Algeria
	Nov	Member of a delegation to the independence celebrations in Cambodia
1965,	Mar	Appointed deputy secretary-general of the State Council (until Jan 1975); member of a government delegation under Premier Zhou Enlai to Romania, Albania, Algeria, United Arab Republic, Pakistan, and Burma (until Apr 1965)
	Apr	Member of a delegation to the 10th anniversary celebrations of the Bandung Conference to Indonesia; member of a government delegation under Zhou Enlai to Burma

	Jun	Member of a government delegation under Zhou Enlai to Pakistan and Tanzania
1966-1968		Owing to his close association with Zhou Enlai Luo survives the Cultural Revolution uncriticized and without loss of influence
1969,	Apr	Identified as a cadre in the United Front Work Department of the CCP Central Committee
1973,	Aug	Elected to first term as member of the CCP Central Committee by the 10th Party Congress
1975,	Mar	Appointed deputy secretary-general, Standing Committee of the 4th NPC (confirmed in 1978 by the 5th NPC)
1978,	Feb	Elected deputy for Sichuan Province to the 5th NPC
	Mar	Elected member of the Standing Committee of the 5th NPC
	Nov	Member of a Party and government delegation under Wang Dongxing to Campuchea
1979,	Jan	Article in RMRB of 9 January: "The Indelible Impression - Recalling Premier Zhou's Sincere Reminder to Me during the Great Cultural Revolution"
	Apr	Deputy head of an NPC delegation, led by Deng Yingchao, to Japan
	Jun	Vice-chairman of the Committee to Examine Proposals at the 2nd Session of the 5th NPC

Luo Qiong (Lo Ch'iung) (f) 罗琼

Posts held

Mass Organization
1st secretary of the Women's Federation
Vice-president of the Women's Federation

Others
Member of the Standing Committee of the 5th CPPCC

Luo was born in Jiangsu Province. In April 1949 she was elected a member of the Executive Council and director of the Propaganda Department of the Democratic Women's Federation (until April 1953).

1949,	Sep	Participant at the founding session of the 1st CPPCC
1951,	Nov	Elected member of the Committee for the Protection of Children
1953,	Jan	Member of the Chinese delegation to the World Peace Council Session
	Feb	Elected deputy secretary-general and member of the Standing Committee of the Democratic Women's Federation
	Apr	Elected secretary of the Democratic Women's Federation (until Sep 1957)
1954,	Aug	Elected deputy for Jiangsu Province to the 1st NPC (reelected in 1958 and 1964 to the 2nd and 3rd NPCs)
1955,	Jun	Deputy head of the Chinese delegation to the World Conference of Mothers in Switzerland
1957,	Sep	Following reorganization of the Democratic Women's Federation into the Wom-

en's Federation, Luo is confirmed as secretary and member of the Standing Committee

1958,   Apr   Elected 1st secretary of the Women's Federation

1964,   Dec   Elected member of the Standing Committee of the 3rd NPC

1966   Disappears during the Cultural Revolution

1974,   Sep   First appearance after the Cultural Revolution: Named in a former post as member of the Standing Committee of the 3rd NPC subsequently disappears until 1978

1978,   Mar   Elected member of the Standing Committee of the 5th CPPCC

       Sep   Elected vice-president and 1st secretary of the Women's Federation

1979,   Apr   Head of a women's delegation to Yugoslavia and Romania

Luo Qiuyue (Lo Ch'iu-yüeh) (f)   罗秋月

Posts held

CCP
Member of the Standing Committee of Hunan Province CP

NPC
Deputy for Hunan Province to the 5th NPC

Provincial Administration
Vice-chairman of the People's Congress of Hunan Province

Mass Organization
Chairman of the Women's Federation of Hunan Province

1970,   Dec   Elected member of the Standing Committee of the newly established Party Secretariat of Hunan Province

1971,   Mar   Identified as member of the Standing Committee, Revolutionary Committee of Hunan Province (until Nov 1977)

1973,   May   Deputy head of a women's delegation to North Korea

       Sep   Elected chairman of the Women's Federation of Hunan Province

1977,   Dec   Elected vice-chairman of the Revolutionary Committee of Hunan (until Dec 1979)

1978,   Feb   Elected deputy for Hunan Province to the 5th NPC

       Oct   Member of a friendship delegation to Japan

1979,   Dec   Elected vice-chairman of the People's Congress of Hunan Province

Luo Shigao (Lo Shih-kao)   罗士高

Posts held

Others
Vice-chairman of the Association for Friendship with Foreign Countries

Luo is a native of Guangdong Province.

1950   Identified as secretary-general of the People's Government of Chongqing Municipality

1951,   Oct   Identified as deputy mayor of Chongqing

1957,   May   Appointed ambassador to Albania (until Jul 1964); subsequently disappears until 1978

1978,   Aug   Identified as vice-chairman of the Association for Friendship with Foreign Countries

       Oct   Head of a friendship delegation to Niger, Upper Volta, Benin, Mali, Gambia, Guinea Bissau, Mauritania, and Tunisia

1979,   May   Head of a friendship delegation to Sudan, Kuwait, and Oman

Luo Shuzhang (Lo Shu-chang) (f)   罗叔章

Posts held

NPC
Member of the Standing Committee of the 5th NPC
Deputy for Tianjin Municipality to the 5th NPC

Others
Vice-chairman of the Executive Committee, Federation of Industrialists and Businessmen

Luo was born in 1907 (1906?) in Hunan Province. As a young woman she went to Shanghai to take a position as a teacher. There she joined the National Salvation Society. In the early 1930s she worked as a teacher in various countries of Southeast Asia. Having returned to China in 1937 she became active in a number of women's organizations. Around 1939 she founded a cooperative for manufacturers of pharmaceuticals in Chongqing. Later she organized an association of small and medium-sized factories. Her first contacts with the Communists during this period soon led to her active participation in the labor movement. She returned to Shanghai after the Japanese capitulation in 1945 where she was in charge of setting up a branch factory for a pharmaceutical company. In Shanghai she joined the Democratic League in which she soon rose to a leading position. Around 1947 she went to Manchuria to join the Communists. She was elected secretary-general of the Preparatory Committee for the foundation of the Democratic Women's Federation in March 1949, and eventually member of its Standing Committee. In September of that year she attended the 1st CPPCC as a delegate. In the same month she was elected secretary-general of the National Democratic Construction Association.

1949,   Oct   Appointed deputy director, General Office of the People's Government Council; member of the Peace Council; deputy secretary-general of the Sino-Soviet Friendship Association

       Nov   Appointed member of the Financial and Economic Council in the Government Administration Council

1950   Identified as member of the Executive Council and director of the Construction Department of the Democratic Women's Federation

1952,   Jun   Reelected member of the Preparatory Committee for the Federation of Industry and Commerce

1953   Identified as member of the Committee for the Implementation of the New Marriage Law

1954,   Oct   Elected deputy for Hunan Province to the 1st NPC (reelected in 1958 and 1964 to the 2nd and 3rd NPCs); appointed vice-minister of labor (until Apr 1957)

        Dec   Elected deputy secretary-general of the 2nd CPPCC

1955,   Apr   Elected member of the Standing Committee, Central Committee of the Democratic Women's Federation

1957,   Jun   Appointed vice-minister of food industry (until this ministry was abolished in Feb 1958)

1958,   Jul   Appointed vice-minister of light industry (until Feb 1965)

1959,   Feb   Elected vice-chairman of the Federation of Industry and Commerce (until Cultural Revolution)

        Nov   Head of a women's delegation to Chile to attend a congress of women representatives of Latin-American countries

1960,   Mar   Head of a women's delegation to Moscow for the 50th anniversary of Women's Day

        Oct   Head of a scientific and technical delegation to Hungary

1961,   Dec   Identified as chairman of the Chinese Section of the Sino-Albanian Committee for Scientific and Technical Cooperation

1962,   Nov   Head of a scientific and technical delegation to Albania

1964,   Nov   Head of a scientific and technical delegation to Albania

1965,   Jan   Elected deputy secretary-general and member of the Standing Committee of the 3rd NPC (reelected to the latter post in Jan 1975 and Mar 1978 for the 4th and 5th NPCs)

        Feb   Appointed vice-minister of the 1st Ministry of Light Industry (until Mar 1965)

1978,   Feb   Elected deputy for Tianjin Municipality to the 5th NPC

1979,   Oct   Elected vice-chairman of the Executive Committee, Federation of Industrialists and Businessmen

Luo Shuzhen (Lo Shu-chen) (f)   罗淑珍

Posts held

Government
Vice-minister of posts and telecommunications

1959,   Feb   Elected deputy for Beijing Municipality to the 2nd NPC (confirmed in 1964 by the 3rd NPC)

1964,   Aug   Identified as postal worker

1973,   Apr   Elected vice-chairman of the Trade Union of Beijing

        Oct   Identified as a cadre of the State Council

1976,   Jan   Identified as vice-minister of posts and telecommunications

Luo Tian (Lo T'ien)   罗 天

Posts held

CCP
Member of the Standing Committee of Guangdong Province CP
Secretary of Hainan Island CP

Provincial Administration
Vice-chairman of the People's Congress of Guangdong Province

Mass Organization
Vice-chairman of the Peasants' Federation of Guangdong Province

1953,   Aug   Identified as director of the Organization Department, Regional Committee of East Guangdong

1956,   Oct   Identified as 1st secretary of Shantou District CP

1960,   Feb   Appointed vice-chairman of the Committee for Receiving and Resettling Returned Overseas Chinese under the Guangdong Provincial Administration

1961,   Nov   Elected vice-governor of Guangdong Province (until Cultural Revolution)

1968,   Mar   Elected member of the Standing Committee, Revolutionary Committee of Guangdong Province (until Aug 1975)

1974,   Dec   Elected vice-chairman of the Peasants' Federation of Guangdong Province

1975,   Aug   Identified as vice-chairman of the Revolutionary Committee of Guangdong Province (until Dec 1979)

1976,   Dec   Identified as secretary of Hainan Island CP

1978,   Nov   Identified as member of the Standing Committee of Guangdong Province CP

1979,   Dec   Elected vice-chairman of the People's Congress of Guangdong Province

Luo Yuchuan (Lo Yü-ch'uan)   罗玉川

Posts held

Government
Minister of forestry
Director of the State Forestry Administration Bureau

NPC
Deputy for Beijing Municipality to the 5th NPC

In 1946 Luo was secretary of Central Hebei District CP and director of its Administration Office.

1949,   Oct   Appointed vice-minister of agriculture (until Jul 1950)

1950,   Jul   Appointed vice-governor of Pingyuan Province (until Nov 1952)

1952,   Aug   Appointed vice-minister of forestry (until Dec 1956) and deputy director of the Yellow River Flood Prevention General Headquarters

1956,   Oct   Appointed vice-minister of timber industry (until Feb 1958)

1958,	Feb	Appointed vice-minister of forestry (until Apr 1967)
	Oct	Elected deputy for Hebei Province to the 2nd NPC (reelected in 1964 to the 3rd NPC)
1967,	Apr	Branded as a capitalist-roader and disappears
1974,	Sep	First appearance after the Cultural Revolution
1976,	Aug	Identified as a cadre in the Ministry of Agriculture and Forestry
1977,	May	Identified as vice-minister in the Ministry of Agriculture and Forestry (until Feb 1979)
1978,	Feb	Elected deputy for Beijing Municipality to the 5th NPC
	Aug	Identified as director of the State Forestry Administration Bureau; head of a forestry delegation to Austria and Romania
1979,	Feb	Identified as minister of the newly established Ministry of Forestry

Luo Yuru (Lo Yü-ju)   罗钰如

Posts held

Government
Deputy director of the State Oceanography Bureau

Others
President of the Society of Oceanography

1975,	Aug	Identified as acting president of the Society of Oceanography; head of a delegation of that Society to Japan
1976,	Mar	Member of a delegation to the UN Conference on the Law of the Sea
	Jul	Member of a delegation to the UN Conference on the Law of the Sea

1977,	May	Member of a delegation to the UN Conference on the Law of the Sea
	Oct	Identified as deputy director of the State Oceanography Bureau; deputy head of a delegation to the 10th Session of the UN Educational, Scientific and Cultural Organization (UNESCO) Intergovernmental Oceanographic Commission in Paris
1978,	Apr	Head of an oceanographic delegation to the U.S.A.
	Aug	Identified as president of the Society of Oceanography

Luosangcucheng (Lo-sang-tz'u-ch'eng)   洛桑慈诚

Posts held

Provincial Administration
Vice-chairman of the People's Government of Tibet Autonomous Region

Luosang belongs to the Tibetan minority. He was born in 1928.

1964,	Dec	Elected deputy for Tibet Autonomous Region to the 3rd NPC
1965,	Sep	Elected chairman of Tibet People's Court
1966		Disappears during the Cultural Revolution
1975,	Dec	First appearance after the Cultural Revolution: Referred to as vice-chairman of the Revolutionary Committee of Tibet Autonomous Region (until Aug 1979)
1977,	Jan	Identified as member of the Standing Committee of Tibet Autonomous Region CP (until Nov 1977)
	Mar	Identified as director of the Department for Farm Production and Livestock under the Tibet Revolutionary Committee
	Aug	Elected vice-chairman of the People's Government of Tibet Autonomous Region

Ma Bin (Ma Pin) 马 宾

Posts held

Government
Vice-minister of the State Commission for
Foreign Investment
Vice-minister of metallurgical industry

NPC
Deputy for Liaoning Province to the
5th NPC

Others
Vice-president of the Metals Society

Ma was born in 1913.

1978,	Feb	Elected deputy for Liaoning Province to the 5th NPC
	Nov	Identified as vice-minister of metallurgical industry and as secretary, CP of Anshan Iron and Steel Company
1979,	Jan	Identified as vice-president of the Metals Society
	Feb	Identified as deputy director-general of the Paoshan Iron and Steel Company to be built by Nippon Steel Corporation
	Sep	Identified as vice-minister of the State Commission for Foreign Investment

Ma Changyan (Ma Ch'ang-yen) 马长奂

Posts held

NPC
Deputy for Anhui Province to the 5th NPC

Provincial Administration
Vice-chairman of the People's Congress of
Anhui Province

In 1942 Ma commanded a regiment of the New 4th Army. In 1947 he was commander of the 5th South District of Jianghuai Military District. In the following year he was appointed deputy commander of the 36th Division, East China Field Army, and in 1949 commander of the 90th Division, 30th Army, 3rd Field Army.

1952,	Aug	Identified as member of the People's Government of Anhui Province
1956,	May	Identified as vice-governor of Anhui Province (until Cultural Revolution)
	Jun	Identified as secretary-general of the Huai River Regulation Project
1967		Disappears during the Cultural Revolution
1973,	Mar	First appearance after the Cultural Revolution: Identified as member of the Standing Committee, Revolutionary Committee of Anhui Province (until 1977)
1978,	Jan	Elected vice-chairman of the Revolutionary Committee of Anhui Province (until Dec 1979)
	Feb	Elected deputy for Anhui Province to the 5th NPC
1979,	Dec	Elected vice-chairman of the People's Congress of Anhui Province

Ma Dayou (Ma Ta-yu) 马大猷

Posts held

Others
Deputy director of the Electronics Society
Deputy director of the Institute of Acoustics, Academy of Sciences

Ma was born in 1914. He was awarded a doctorate by Harvard University in 1940.

1950,	Aug	Elected member of the Standing Committee and director of the Secretariat of the Natural Sciences Association (until Sep 1958)
1951		Identified as director of the School of Engineering of Beijing University
1955		Identified as leading member of the Preparatory Committee for the Changchun Branch of the Academy of Sciences
1956,	Jun	Identified as vice-chairman of the Preparatory Committee for the Electronics Society (until 1961)
1959,	Jan	Identified as deputy director of the Electronics Research Institute; identified as research fellow at the Institute of Applied Physics of the Academy of Sciences
	Jul	Vice-chairman of the Preparatory Committee for the Electronics Research Institute of the Academy of Sciences
1961		Identified as member of the Editorial Board of the Journal Zhongguo Kexue (Scienta Sinica)
1962,	Mar	Identified as director of the Electronics Research Institute of the Academy of Sciences (until Cultural Revolution)
1963		Identified as vice-chairman of the Electronics Society
1964,	Sep	Elected deputy for Guangdong Province to the 3rd NPC
1966		Disappears during the Cultural Revolution
1973,	Oct	Reactivated after the Cultural Revolution as vice-chairman of the Electronics Society
1978,	Mar	Identified as research fellow at the Institute of Physics, Academy of Sciences
1979,	Mar	Identified as deputy director of the Institute of Acoustics, Academy of Sciences

Ma Guishu (Ma Kuei-shu)

Posts held

Provincial Administration
Vice-governor of Shanxi Province

1954,	Apr	Identified as deputy secretary of Taiyuan Municipality CP
1957,	Feb	Identified as 2nd secretary of Taiyuan Municipality CP
1961,	May	Identified as 1st secretary of Taiyuan Municipality CP
1962,	Nov	Identified as a member of the Standing Committee of Shaanxi Province CP

1965,	May	Identified as deputy secretary of Tibet Autonomous Region CP
	Sep	Identified as secretary of Tibet Autonomous Region CP
1968		Denounced as a counterrevolutionary revisionist and purged
1979,	Dec	First appearance after the Cultural Revolution: Elected vice-governor of Shanxi Province

Ma Haoqian (Ma Hao-ch'ien) 马浩讦

Posts held

NPC
Member of the Standing Committee of the 5th NPC
Deputy for Anhui Province to the 5th NPC

1978,	Feb	Elected deputy for Anhui Province to the 5th NPC
	Mar	Elected member of the Standing Committee of the 5th NPC

Ma Hengchang (Ma Heng-ch'ang) 马恒昌

Posts held

NPC
Member of the Standing Committee of the 5th NPC
Deputy for Heilongjiang Province to the 5th NPC

Ma was born circa 1918. He orginally distinguished himself as an industrial worker.

1954,	Oct	Elected deputy for Shenyang Municipality to the 1st NPC
1959,	Mar	Elected deputy for Heilongjiang Province to the 2nd NPC (confirmed in Oct 1964 by the 3rd NPC)
1966		Disappears during the Cultural Revolution
1975,	Jan	First appearance after the Cultural Revolution: Elected member of the Standing Committee by the 4th NPC (confirmed in Mar 1978 by the 5th NPC)
1977,	Mar	Identified as chief mechanical engineer of Qiqihar No. 2 Machine Tool Works
1978,	Feb	Elected deputy for Heilongjiang Province to the 5th NPC
1979,	Jun	Member of the Committee to Examine Proposals at the 2nd Session of the 5th NPC

Ma Hong (Ma Hung) 马洪

Posts held

Others
Vice-president of the Academy of Social Sciences

1979,	Jul	Identified as vice-president of the Academy of Social Sciences

Ma Hui (Ma Hui) 马辉

Posts held

CCP
Member of the CCP 11th Central Committee
Secretary of Hebei Province CP

Military
Major-general
Commander of Hebei Military District

Provincial Administration
Vice-chairman of the People's Congress of Hebei Province

Ma was born in 1910. In 1947 he commanded the 4th Brigade of Shanxi-Chahar-Hebei Field Army. In February 1949 he was appointed commander of the 201 Division of the 20th Army Corps.

1951		Service in the Korean War as troop commander
1954,	Sep	Return from Korea
1955,	Sep	Promoted to rank of major-general
1962		Identified as deputy commander of Hebei Military District
1965,	Jun	Identified as commander of Hebei Military District
1966,	Oct	Identified as member of the Standing Committee of Hebei Province CP
1968,	Feb	Elected vice-chairman of the newly established Revolutionary Committee of Hebei Province (until Jan 1980)
1971,	May	Elected secretary of the newly established CP Secretariat of Hebei Province
1977,	Aug	Elected member of the CCP Central Committee by the 11th Party Congress
1980,	Feb	Elected vice-chairman of the People's Congress of Hebei Province

Ma Huizhi (Ma Hui-chih) 马辉之

Posts held

NPC
Member of the Standing Committee of the 5th NPC

Others
Member of the Standing Committee of the 5th CPPCC

Ma was born in 1911 in Hunan Province. During the Anti-Japanese War he served as secretary of Shanxi-Chahar-Rehe Border District CP. In 1946 he was made concurrently member of the Standing Committee of the Trade Union of that border district. In 1948 he was elected a member of the Executive Committee of the Federation of Trade Unions.

1950,	Sep	Identified as deputy procurator of the Northeast Procuracy (until 1951)
1951,	Sep	Identified as vice-chairman of the Northeast People's Government Control Committee (until 1954)
1953,	Jan	Appointed member of the Northeast China Administrative Council (until Sep 1954)
1955,	May	Appointed vice-minister of communications (until 1967)

1965,   Sep   Head of a delegation to the National Day
                celebrations in Yemen Arab Republic
1967,   Apr   Branded as a revisionist and purged
1979,   Jun   First appearance after the Cultural Revo-
                lution: By-elected a member of the
                5th CPPCC
         Jul   By-elected a member of the Standing
                Committee of the 5th NPC

Ma Jikong (Ma Chi-k'ung)   马继孔

Posts held

CCP
Secretary of Jiangsi Province CP

Ma was born in Hunan Province. In 1946 he served in
Shanxi-Hebei-Shandong-Henan Border District and in 1949
as director of the Administrative Office of the Nanjing
Military Control Commission.

1950,   Aug   Identified as council member and secre-
                tary-general of the People's Government
                of Yunnan Province
1953,   Jan   Identified as secretary of Kunming Munic-
                ipality CP
1955,   Apr   Identified as deputy secretary of Yunnan
                Province CP
1956,   Jan   Identified as secretary of Yunnan Prov-
                ince CP
1958,   Aug   Identified as president of the Yunnan
                Branch of the Aceademy of Sciences
         Nov   Elected deputy for Yunnan Province to
                the 2nd NPC
1965,   Oct   Identified as secretary of Gansu Prov-
                ince CP
1967,   Apr   Branded as a counterrevolutionary revi-
                sionist and purged
1977,   Dec   First appearance after the Cultural Revo-
                lution: Elected vice-chairman of the Rev-
                olutionary Committee of Gansu Province
                (until 1978)
1978,   Aug   Identified as secretary of Gansu Prov-
                ince CP (until Dec 1978)
1979,   Jan   Identified as secretary of Jiangxi Prov-
                ince CP and as vice-chairman of the
                Revolutionary Committee of that prov-
                ince (latter post until Dec 1979)
         Jul   Appointed member of the National Games
                Organizing Committee

Ma Jinhua (Ma Chin-hua) (f)   马金花

Posts held

CCP
Alternate member of the CCP 11th Central Committee

Mass Organization
Vice-chairman of the Women's Federation
of Ningxia Autonomous Region

Ma belongs to the Hui (Moslem) minority. She was born in
1938 as the daughter of a farm worker in Guyuan County,
Ningxia Province. Until the foundation of PRC she had no
opportunity to receive a school education. Later she
became known as the first woman from a rural provincial
area who not only learned to read and write but also
became the first female cadre and militia commander.

1961   Ma joins the CCP
1964   Identified as secretary, CP of Malian
                Production Brigade of Qiying People's
                Commune in her native county of Guyuan
1973,   Aug   Elected vice-chairman of the Women's
                Federation of Ningxia; elected alternate
                member of the CCP Central Committee
                by the 10th Party Congress (confirmed in
                1977 by the 11th Congress)

Ma Ming (Ma Ming)   马 明

Posts held

CCP
Alternate member of the CCP 11th Central Committee

Ma was born circa 1935 as the son of a poor peasant. At
the age of eight he had to beg together with his mother.

1954   Member of the Ma Wanshui Production
                Group at Longyan Iron-ore Mine which
                distinguished itself by high performance
1966   Head of the Ma Wanshui Production Group
1973,   Aug   Elected alternate member of the CCP
                Central Committee by the 10th Party
                Congress (confirmed in 1977 by the
                11th Congress)
1974,   May   Identified as head of the Tunneling Team
                at Longyan Iron-ore Mine in Hebei Prov-
                ince

Ma Muming (Ma Mu-ming)   马牧鸣

Posts held

Government
Ambassador to Spain

1959,   Aug   Identified as 1st secretary at the embassy
                in India
1964,   Jul   Identified as deputy director of the Infor-
                mation Department in the Ministry of
                Foreign Affairs
1973,   Oct   Identified as chargé d'affaires ad interim
                in India (until 1975)
1974,   Jun   Head of the Chinese delegation to the
                crowning ceremonies of the King of Bhu-
                tan
1976,   Sep   Appointed ambassador to Spain
1978,   Jun   Ma accompanies the King of Spain on his
                visit to China

Ma is married to Zhang Xiuhua.

Ma Qingnian (Ma Ch'ing-nien) 马青年

Posts held

Others
Member of the Standing Committee of the
5th CPPCC

Provincial Administration
Chairman of the People's Congress, Ningxia Autonomous Region

Ma belongs to the Hui minority.

1950,	Mar	Identified as chairman of the Nationalities Affairs Committee of the People's Government of Gansu Province
1952,	Jun	Identified as member of the Nationalities Affairs Committee of the Northwest Military and Administrative Council
1957,	Jul	Identified as vice-governor of Gansu Province (until 1964)
1958,	Mar	Identified as member of the Commission for the Tao River Project
	Oct	Elected deputy for Gansu Province to the 2nd NPC (confirmed in 1964 by the 3rd NPC)
1959,	Apr	Appointed member of the NPC's Nationalities Committee
1965,	Mar	Member of an NPC delegation led by Liu Ningyi to Guinea, Mali, Central African Republic, and Congo
1967		Disappears during the Cultural Revolution
1978,	Feb	First appearance after the Cultural Revolution
	Mar	Elected member of the Standing Committee of the 5th CPPCC
1980,	Jan	Elected chairman of the People's Congress, Ningxia Autonomous Region

Ma Sizhong (Ma Szu-chung) 马思忠

Posts held

CCP
Alternate member of the CCP 11th Central Committee
Member of the Standing Committee of Ningxia Autonomous Region CP

Provincial Administration
Vice-chairman of the People's Government, Ningxia Autonomous Region

Ma belongs to the Hui minority.

1964,	Oct	Elected deputy for Ningxia Autonomous Region to the 3rd NPC
1977,	Aug	Elected alternate member of the CCP Central Committee by the 11th Party Congress
	Dec	Elected vice-chairman of the Revolutionary Committee of Ningxia Autonomous Region (until Dec 1979)
1979,	Sep	Identified as member of the Standing Committee of Ningxia Autonomous Region CP
1980,	Jan	Elected vice-chairman of the People's Government, Ningxia Autonomous Region

Ma Teng'ai (Ma T'eng-ai) 马腾霭

Posts held

Provincial Administration
Vice-chairman of the People's Government, Ningxia Autonomous Region

Ma belongs to the Hui minority and was born in 1919 in Chuanji, Ningxia. In 1947 he was vice-chairman of the KMT Ningxia Provincial Political Consultative Conference. In August 1949 he went over to the Communists.

1950,	Jan	Identified as Islam Imam of Ningxia Province and as vice-governor of Ningxia (latter post until Sep 1953)
1953,	May	Identified as vice-president of the Association for Promoting Hui Nationality Culture
	Jun	Elected member of the Standing Committee of the Youth Federation
1954,	Aug	Elected deputy for Gansu Province to the 1st NPC
1955,	Mar	Identified as magistrate of Wuzhong Hui Autonomous District in Ningxia
1956,	May	Identified as council member of the Sino-Pakistan Friendship Association
	Nov	Member of an NPC delegation visiting the USSR, Romania, and Czechoslovakia
1958,	Feb	Identified as council member of the Sino-United Arab Republic Friendship Association
	Oct	Elected vice-chairman of Ningxia Autonomous Region; elected deputy for Ningxia to the 2nd NPC (reelected in 1958 to the 3rd NPC)
1963,	Oct	Identified as vice-chairman of the Islamic Association
1966		Ma disappears
1980,	Jan	First appearance after the Cultural Revolution: Elected vice-chairman of the People's Government, Ningxia Autonomous Region

Ma Wanli (Ma Wan-li) 马万里

Posts held

CCP
Deputy director of the Propaganda Department of Qinghai Province CP

Provincial Administration
Vice-governor of Qinghai Province

1977,	Sep	Identified as deputy director of the Propaganda Department of Qinghai Province CP
	Dec	Elected vice-chairman of the Revolutionary Committee of Qinghai Province (until Aug 1979)
1979,	Jul	Appointed member of the National Games Organizing Committee
	Sep	Elected vice-governor of Qinghai Province

Ma Wanqi (Ma Wan-ch'i)

Posts held

Others
Director of the Board of Directors, China International Trust and Investment Corporation
Vice-chairman of the General Chamber of Commerce of Macao

1979, Oct   Appointed director of the Board of Directors, China International Trust and Investment Corporation; identified as vice-chairman of the General Chamber of Commerce of Macao

Ma Weihua (Ma Wei-hua) 马伟华

Posts held

NPC
Deputy for the PLA to the 5th NPC

Military
Major-general
Deputy commander of Beijing Military Region

In 1938 Ma served in the units under Yang Chengwu in Shanxi-Chahar-Hebei Border Region. In 1940 he was chief of staff of the 42nd Regiment in Shanxi-Chahar-Hebei Military Region. In 1946 he commanded a regiment of Shanxi-Chahar-Hebei Field Army. He was made chief of staff of the 1st Division, 3rd North China Army Corps, in 1948. In February 1949 he was appointed deputy commander of the 196th Division of the 66th Army.

1950		Service with his unit in the Korean War
1951,	Jan	The 66th Army under Ma's command successfully penetrates South Korean positions
	Feb	Ma's troops capture an American artillery battalion near Hoeng Song
1952,	Sep	Appointed chief of staff of the 66th Army
1955		Identified as deputy commander of the 66th Army
	Sep	Identified as major-general
1957,	Feb	Identified as chief of staff of Beijing Military Region
1968,	Mar	Ma is relieved of all posts because of his connection with the Yang Chengwu Incident
1970,	Oct	Identified as military leader in Beijing Military Region
1972,	Dec	Identified as deputy commander of Beijing Military Region
1978,	Feb	Elected deputy for the PLA to the 5th NPC
	Jun	Member of a military delegation led by Yang Yong to Yugoslavia

Ma Wendong (Ma Wen-tung) 马文东

Posts held

Provincial Administration
Vice-governor of Yunnan Province

1979,	Jun	Identified as vice-chairman of the Revolutionary Committee of Yunnan Province (until Dec 1979); deputy head of a friendship delegation to North Korea
	Dec	Elected vice-governor of Yunnan Province

Ma Wenrui (Ma Wen-jui) 马文瑞

Posts held

CCP
Member of the CCP 11th Central Committee
1st secretary of Shaanxi Province CP

NPC
Deputy for Anhui Province to the 5th NPC

Provincial Administration
Chairman of the People's Congress of Shaanxi Province

Ma was born in 1909 in Shaanxi Province. He joined the CCP already as a young man. He served in Northwest China throughout the Revolutionary Period. There he held among others the offices of secretary of East Shaanxi CP in Shaanxi-Gansu-Ningxia Border Area, and director of the Organization Department, Northwest Bureau of the CCP Central Committee.

1949,	Dec?	Appointed member of the Northwest China Military and Political Council (until 1953)
1953		Appointed member of the Northwest China Administrative Council and chairman of the Control Committee of this council (until Sep 1954); identified as 3rd secretary, Northwest China Bureau of the CCP Central Committee
1954,	Sep	Appointed minister of labor
1956,	Sep	Elected alternate member of the CCP Central Committee by the 8th Party Congress
1959,	Jun	Received in Moscow by Khrushchev; head of a delegation to the Poznan Fair in Poland
1961,	Feb	Article in HQ: "Human Labor Resources in Socialist Construction"
1967,	Jan	Ma is branded as a counterrevolutionary revisionist and relieved of his posts
1974,	Sep	First appearance after the Cultural Revolution
1977,	Jul	Identified as vice-minister of the State Planning Commission (until Dec 1978)
	Aug	Elected member of the CCP Central Committee by the 11th Party Congress
1978,	Feb	Elected deputy for Anhui Province to the 5th NPC
	Aug	Appointed vice-president of the Party School of the CCP Central Committee (until Dec 1978)

1979,   Jan   Identified as 1st secretary of Shaanxi
               Province CP
         Dec   Elected chairman of the People's Congress
               of Shaanxi Province

Ma Xin (Ma Hsin)   马 信

Posts held

CCP
Member of the Commission for Inspecting
Discipline under the CCP Central Com-
mittee

NPC
Deputy for Ningxia Autonomous Region to
the 5th NPC

Provincial Administration
Chairman of the People's Government of
Ningxia Autonomous Region

Ma belongs to the the Hui minority.

1951   Identified as council member and as depu-
               ty director of the Agriculture and Forest-
               ry Department, People's Government of
               Rehe Province
1958,   Oct   Identified as chairman of the Planning
               Commission of Ningxia Autonomous Re-
               gion
1964,   Sep   Elected vice-chairman of Ningxia Autono-
               mous Region (until Cultural Revolution)
1968   Disappears during the Cultural Revolution
1977,   Dec   First appearance after the Cultural Revo-
               lution: Elected vice-chairman of the Rev-
               olutionary Committee of Ningxia Autono-
               mous Region (until Dec 1979)
1978,   Dec   Appointed member of the Commission for
               Inspecting Discipline under the CCP Cen-
               tral Committee
1980,   Jan   Elected chairman of the People's Govern-
               ment, Ningxia Autonomous Region; by-
               elected deputy for Ningxia Autonomous
               Region to the 5th NPC

Ma Xingyuan (Ma Hsing-yüan)   马兴元

Posts held

CCP
Member of the CCP 11th Central Com-
mittee
Secretary of Fujian Province CP

Provincial Administration
Governor of Fujian Province

1959   Identified as deputy director of the Rural
               Work Department of Fujian Province CP
1975,   Jul   Identified as secretary of Fujian Prov-
               ince CP
1977,   Aug   Elected member of the CCP Central
               Committee by the 11th Party Congress
1978,   Jan   Elected vice-chairman of the Revolution-
               ary Committee of Fujian Province (until
               Dec 1979)
         May   Advisor to an agricultural delegation to
               Japan

1979,   Dec   Elected governor of Fujian Province

Ma Xiuzhong (Ma Hsiu-chung)   马秀中

Posts held

Provincial Administration
Vice-chairman of the Revolutionary Committee of Tianjin Municipality

1977,   Dec   Elected vice-chairman of the Revolution-
               ary Committee of Tianjin Municipality

Ma Yi (Ma Yi)   马仪

Posts held

Government
Vice-minister of the State Economic
Commission

1972,   May   Identified as a cadre of the 1st Ministry of
               Machine Building
1973,   Apr   Identified as vice-minister of the 1st Min-
               istry of Machine Building (until 1977)
         May   Head of a scientific and technical delega-
               tion to Hungary
1974,   Oct   Identified as chairman of the Chinese
               section, Sino-Hungarian Commission on
               Scientific and Technical Cooperation
1975,   Oct   Head of a scientific and technical delega-
               tion to Hungary
1977,   Nov   Head of a scientific and technical delega-
               tion to Hungary
1978,   Feb   Identified as vice-minister of the State
               Planning Commission (until Jul 1978)
         Aug   Identified as vice-minister of the State
               Economic Commission
1979,   Jun   Head of a government delegation to Swe-
               den
         Sep   Head of an economic delegation to Japan
         Dec   Head of an economic delegation to Hunga-
               ry

Ma Yinchu (Ma Yin-ch'u)   马寅初

Posts held

NPC
Deputy for Beijing Municipality to the
5th NPC

Others
Member of the Standing Committee of the
CPPCC
Honorary president of Beijing University

Ma Yinchu (alias Ma Yuanshan) was born in 1882 (1881?) in
Cheng County, Zhejiang Province. After attending middle
school in Shanghai he studied mineralogy at Beiyang
University in Tianjin. In 1907 he went to the United Stated
to study economics at Yale and Columbia Universities.
After receiving a doctorate in 1910 he returned to China
where he lectured at Beijing National University, as well
as at Jiatong, Zhejiang, and Chongqing Universities, until
the Communist takeover. In 1918 he was one of the
cofounders of the Society for the Study of Marxism. When
this society developed into the nucleus of the later

Communist Party, Ma canceled his membership before the CCP was founded. From 1928 to 1947 Ma, who had quickly established himself as the leading Chinese economist, was a member of the Legislative Yuan. He nevertheless criticized the Nationalist Government's economic policy during the Anti-Japanese War with the result that he was imprisoned for one year because of his Communist leaning. After the end of the war he continued his criticism of various government policies and in addition supported a numer of antigovernment student movements in Shanghai and Hangzhou. In September 1949 he took part in the CPPCC which elected him a member of its National Committee.

1949,	Oct	Appointed member of the Government Administration Council and vice-chairman of its Financial and Economic Committee
1950,	Jan	Appointed chancellor of Zhejiang University (until Aug 1951)
	Jun	Identified as council member of the Sino-Soviet Friendship Association
1951,	Aug	Appointed chancellor of Beijing University (until Apr 1960)
1954,	Aug	Elected deputy for Zhejiang Province to the 1st NPC (probably until Dec 1964)
	Nov	Appointed board member of the People's Bank (probably until 1959)
	Dec	Elected vice-chairman of the Sino-Soviet Friendship Association (probably until 1959)
1955,	Jun	Appointed member of the Institute of Philosophy and Social Sciences of the Academy of Sciences
1957,	Aug	Publication of New Principles on Chinese Population, which contained criticism of official government policy. This criticism shortly afterwards led to his purge
1961,	Jan	Identified as member of the Department of Philosophy and Social Sciences of the Academy of Sciences
1965,	Jan	Elected member of the Standing Committee of the CPPCC
1966		Disappears during the Cultural Revolution
1974,	May	First appearance after the Cultural Revolution: Identified as holding his former post of vice-chairman, CPPCC (until Feb 1978)
1978,	Mar	Elected member of the Standing Committee of the 5th CPPCC
1979,	Jul	GMRB of 7 July publishes an article by Gong Ming, "Nothing Can Be Accomplished Without Democracy - the Reputation of Ma Yinchu Should Be Restored"
	Sep	Appointed honorary president of Beijing University
	Dec	By-elected deputy for Beijing Municipality to the 5th NPC

Publications

1925	China's Foreign Trade
1929	On Chinese Banks
1932	Ma Yinchu's Essays on Problems of the Economy
1935	China's Economic Reform
1945	Ma Yinchu's Essays during the War Period
1957	New Principles on Chinese Population
1958	My Economic Theories, Philosophical Thoughts, and Political Convictions

Ma is married to Wang Zhongzhen.

Ma-yi-nu-er (Ma·yi·nu·erh) (f)   玛依努尔

Posts held

Provincial Administration
Vice-chairman of the Standing Committee of the People's Congress, Xinjiang Autonomous Region

Mass Organizations
Vice-president of the Women's Federation
President of the Xinjiang Women's Federation

Ma belongs to the Uighur minority.

1978,	Sep	Elected vice-president of the Women's Federation; identified as president of the Women's Federation of Xinjiang Autonomous Region
1979,	Sep	Elected vice-chairman of the Standing Committee, People's Congress of Xinjiang Autonomous Region
	Nov	Head of a women's delegation to France

Ma Yuhuai (Ma Yü-huai)   马玉槐

Posts held

CCP
Secretary of Ningxia Autonomous Region CP

Ma who belongs to the Hui minority was born in 1917 in Renqiu County, Hebei Province. After attending Tongren Middle School in Baoding he held the following posts successively from 1938 to 1949: chairman of the Central Hebei Region; member of the Islamic Anti-Japan National Salvation Association; deputy political commissar of the 9th Military Subdistrict of Central Hebei Military District; chairman of the Beijing Municipal Islam Work Committee. In September 1949 he was appointed president of the Islam College.

1949,	Oct	Appointed member of the Nationalities Affairs Commission of the Government Administration Council (until Sep 1954)
1952,	Jul	Secretary-general of the Preparatory Committee for the Islamic Association
1953,	May	Elected vice-chairman of the Islamic Association (until Cultural Revolution)
1954,	May	Identified as member of the Standing Committee, Association for Cultural Relations with Foreign Countries
	Aug	Elected deputy for Beijing Municipality to the 1st NPC
	Sep	Appointed member of the Nationalities Committee of the NPC (until Cultural Revolution)
1955,	Apr	Identified as president of the Islamic Theology College
	Jun	Identified as vice-chairman of the Sino-Indonesian Friendship Association (until 1960)
	Jul	Head of an Islamic delegation to Mecca
1956,	Feb	Deputy head of a cultural delegation to Egypt

1958,   Feb   Head of an Islamic delegation to the Afro-Asian Islamic Conference in Bandung
        Oct   Elected vice-chairman of Ningxia Autonomous Region; elected deputy for Ningxia to the 2nd NPC (confirmed in 1964 by the 3rd NPC); elected secretary of Ningxia CP (until Cultural Revolution)
1960,   Apr   Elected council member of the Sino-African Society
1962,   Jan   Head of an Islamic delegation to Indonesia
1965,   Feb   Head of an Islamic delegation to the Afro-Asian Islamic Conference in Indonesia
1968,   Apr   Branded as a revisionist and purged
1977,   Dec   First appearance after the Cultural Revolution: Elected vice-chairman of the Revolutionary Committee of Ningxia Autonomous Region (until Dec 1979)
1978,   Apr   Elected secretary of Ningxia Autonomous Region CP

Ma Yunhan (Ma Yün-han)   马云汉

Posts held

Others
Vice-chairman of the Council for the Promotion of International Trade

1977,   Aug   Identified as vice-chairman of the Council for the Promotion of International Trade
        Dec   Head of an exhibition delegation to the United Arab Emirates
1978,   Sep   Head of a trade delegation to the Democratic Republic of Germany and to Ireland
1979,   Jul   Head of a trade delegation to Jordan

Mahsut Teibov (Mai·ho·su·te T'ieh·yi·po·fu)   买合蘇德铁衣波夫

Posts held

Others
Member of the Standing Committee of the 5th CPPCC

1978,   Mar   Elected member of the Standing Committee of the 5th CPPCC

Mao Diqiu (Mao Ti-ch'iu)   毛迪秋

Posts held

NPC
Member of the Standing Committee of the 5th NPC
Deputy for Hunan Province to the 5th NPC

Mao was born in Hunan Province. His father, Mao Fuxuan, who was secretary of the 1st Party Group founded by Mao Zedong in Shaoshan, was executed by the Nationalist Government.

1968,   Nov   Identified as vice-chairman of the Revolutionary Committee of Shaoshan
1969,   Oct   Identified as chairman of the Shaoshan Production Brigade
1975,   Jan   Elected member of the Standing Committee of the 4th NPC (confirmed in Mar 1968 by the 5th NPC)
        Feb   Identified as CP secretary of the Shaoshan Brigade, Shaoshan People's Commune
1976,   Nov   Member of an NPC delegation to Iran and Kuwait
1978,   Feb   Elected deputy for Hunan Province to the 5th NPC

Mao Dun

see **Shen Yanbing**

Mao Lianjue (Mao Lien-chüeh)   毛联珏

Posts held

CCP
Secretary of Beijing Municipality CP

NPC
Deputy for Beijing Municipality to the 5th NPC

1975,   Nov   Identified as deputy secretary-general of Beijing Revolutionary Committee
1977,   Aug   Identified as member of the Standing Committee of Beijing Municipality CP (until May 1978)
        Dec   Elected vice-chairman of the Revolutionary Committee of Beijing Municipality (until Dec 1979)
1978,   Feb   Elected deputy for Beijing Municipality to the 5th NPC
        Jun   Identified as secretary of Beijing Municipality CP

Mao Lin (Mao Lin)   茅林

Posts held

Government
Vice-minister of metallurgical industry

1975,   Feb   Identified as secretary of the CP, and as vice-chairman of the Revolutionary Committee, of Gansu Province (until 1978)
1979,   May   Identified as vice-minister of metallurgical industry

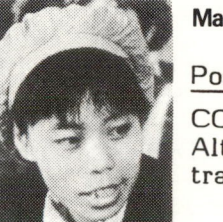

Mao Xinxian (Mao Hsin-hsien) (f)   毛信贤

Posts held

CCP
Alternate member of the CCP 11th Central Committee

Mao is a model worker at the Shanghai No. 27 Weaving Mill. She was commended for a weaving record of 400,000 meters of good quality cloth without a flaw.

1977,   Aug   Elected alternate member of the CCP Central Committee by the 11th Party Congress

Mao Yisheng (Mao Yi-sheng)　茅以昇

Posts held

NPC
Member of the Standing Committee of the
5th NPC
Deputy for Beijing Municipality to the
5th NPC

Others
Chairman of the Civil Engineering Society
President of the Institute of Railway
Research of the Ministry of Railways
Vice-president of the Scientific and Tech-
nical Association
Deputy director of the Committee for the
Promotion of International Measurement
Director of the Board of Directors, China
International Trust and Investment Corpo-
ration
Vice-chairman of the Jiusan (Chiu-san)
Society
Honorary president of the Association for
Popularization of Science and Technology
and Inventions

Mao was born in 1895 in Dantu, Jiangsu Province. He
graduated from Jiaotong University in Tangshan in 1916.
One year later he continued his studies at Cornell
University in the United States and was awarded a
doctorate at the Carnegie Institute of Technology in 1920.
From 1921 he held a professorship at the Engineering
College in Tangshan. In 1924 he became head of the
Engineering Department of the East Asia University, and
in 1925 head of the Engineering College of Haihe. He
served as a technical advisor to the Nationalist Government's Ministry of Communications in 1927. In 1928 he
was appointed professor at the National Beiyang University. In 1934 he was technical advisor to the Ministry of
Industry and Commerce. In 1930 he became head of the
National Beiyang University. He was head of the Engi-
neering Bureau responsible for the construction of the
bridge across the Qiantang Jiang in 1934, and in 1936
director of the Nationalist Government's Water Conservancy Bureau. In 1941 he became head of the Chinese
Engineering Society as well as head of the Bridge
Construction Bureau of the Ministry of Communications.
He was appointed chancellor of Jiaotong University in
Shanghai in 1945 and concurrently council member of the
Economic Affairs Committee of Academia Sinica. In
September 1949 Mao took part in the founding session of
the CPPCC as a delegate representing natural science
workers.

1950, Aug Identified as chancellor of Jiaotong University (until Nov 1952)
1951, Feb Identified as director of the Railways
Research Institute at the Ministry of
Railways
1953, Sep Elected chairman of the Civil Engineering
Society
1954, Aug Elected deputy for Jiangsu Province to
the 1st NPC (reelected in 1958 and 1964
to the 2nd and 3rd NPCs)
       Dec Elected council member of the Sino-
Soviet Friendship Association
1955, Feb Identified as chairman of the Technical
Advisory Committee for the construction
of the Chang Jiang bridge in Wuhan

       Apr Identified as deputy director of the Sci-
ence and Technology Department of the
Academy of Sciences
       Dec Member of a delegation of scientists to
Japan
1956, Mar Appointed member of the Scientific Planning Commission under the State Council
       Apr Member of a cultural delegation to Iraq
       Jun By-elected member of the Standing Com-
mittee of the 1st NPC (confirmed in this
post in 1959, 1965, 1975, and 1978 by the
2nd through 5th NPCs)
1957, Aug Participant at a technical congress in
England
1958, Sep Elected vice-chairman of the Science and
Technology Association
       Dec Elected vice-chairman of the Jiusan Soci-
ety
1962, Feb Article in the Peking RMRB entitled
"Talks on Bridges"
1963, Jul Elected vice-chairman of the Science and
Technology Association (reactivated in
this post in 1978)
1973, May Head of an engineering delegation to
Japan
1976, Sep Head of an engineering delegation to
Japan; identified as president of the Institute of Railway Research of the Ministry
of Railways
1978, Feb Elected deputy for Beijing Municipality to
the 5th NPC
       Dec Identified as chairman of the Beijing
Branch of the Scientific and Technical
Association
1979, Mar Identified as deputy director of the Committee for the Promotion of International
Measurement
       Jun Head of a delegation of the Scientific and
Technical Association to the U.S.A.;
member of the Credentials Committee
and Draft Laws Committee at the
2nd Session of the 5th NPC
       Aug Elected honorary president of the Associ-
ation for Popularization of Science and
Technology and Inventions
       Oct Elected director of the Board of Direc-
tors, China International Trust and Investment Corporation; reelected vice-chairman of the Jiusan Society

Mao Zhiyong (Mao Chih-yung)　毛致用
Posts held

CCP
Member of the CCP 11th Central Committee
1st secretary of Hunan Province CP

NPC
Deputy for Hunan Province to the
5th NPC

Military
1st political commissar of Hunan Military
District

Mass Organization
Vice-chairman of the Peasants' Federation
of Hunan Province

1973, Aug Identified as secretary of Hunan Province CP (until May 1977)
       Dec Identified as vice-chairman of the Peasants' Federation of Hunan Province
1977, Jun Appointed 1st secretary of the CP, and chairman of the Revolutionary Committee, of Hunan Province (latter post until Dec 1979), as well as 1st political commissar of Hunan Military District
       Aug Elected member of the CCP Central Committee by the 11th Party Congress
1978, Feb Elected deputy for Hunan Province to the 5th NPC; article in HQ: "The Fundamental Way to Do a Good Job of Building Political Power Is to Link with the Masses"
1979, Aug Head of a Party workers delegation to Romania

Mei Jiasheng (Mei Chia-sheng) 梅嘉生

Posts held

Military
Rear-admiral
Deputy commander of the PLA

Mei was born in Danyang, Jiangsu Province. He is a university graduate. In 1945 he served as deputy commander of the 1st Military Subdistrict of Central-Jiangsu Military District. He was appointed commander of the River Defense Command of the 7th Division, New 4th Army, circa 1946.

1955, Sep Awarded the order "Liberation," 1st class
1964, Apr Identified as rear-admiral
1965, Nov Identified as deputy commander of the East China Sea Fleet
1967   Disappears during the Cultural Revolution
1974, Sep First appearance after the Cultural Revolution
1976, Dec Identified as deputy commander of the PLA Navy

Mei Songlin (Mei Sung-lin) 梅松林

Posts held

CCP
Alternate member of the CCP 11th Central Committee

Mei is a member of the "Hard Bones 6th Company."

1977, Aug Elected alternate member of the CCP Central Committee by the 11th Party Congress

Mei Yi (Mei Yi) 梅 益

Posts held

Others
Deputy secretary-general of the Academy of Social Sciences
Director of the Planning Bureau of the Academy of Social Sciences

Mei was born in 1915 in Shantou, Guangdong Province. He became well known by his numerous translations from Russian. In 1937 he worked for Translation News and Solidarity Weekly in Shanghai, and in 1938 for Daily Translation News and The Leader. In 1946 he was spokesman of the CCP Liaison Office in Nanjing. He was elected a member of the Executive Council of the Federation of Democratic Youth in May 1949 and in September represented this federation as a delegate at the 1st CPPCC.

1949, Dec Appointed deputy director of the Broadcasting Administration Bureau under the News Administration of the Government Administration Council (until 1952)
1950, Jun Identified as associate editor of XNA
1952, Sep Identified as director of the State Broadcasting Administration Bureau (until Cultural Revolution)
1954, May Elected council member of the Association for Cultural Relations with Foreign Countries (until Cultural Revolution)
       Aug Elected deputy for Yunnan Province to the 1st NPC
       Sep Elected vice-president of the Journalists' Association (until Cultural Revolution)
1957, Nov Member of a cultural delegation to the USSR
1958, Mar Appointed member of the Commission for Cultural Relations with Foreign Counties (until Cultural Revolution)
       Sep Elected deputy for Guangdong Province to the 2nd NPC (confirmed in 1958 by the 3rd NPC)
       Dec Identified as vice-chairman of the Sino-Romanian Friendship Association
1960, Mar Elected vice-chairman of the Journalists' Association (until Cultural Revolution)
1961, Dec Head of a delegation of journalists to Cuba
1962, Feb Head of a delegation of journalists to Ecuador, Chile, Brazil, and Great Britain (until Apr)
       Dec Identified as council member of the Sino-Cuban Friendship Association
1963, Apr Head of a delegation of journalists to the Conference of Afro-Asian Journalists in Jakarta
1964, May Head of a broadcasting delegation to North Korea
       Aug Head of a broadcasting delegation to North Vietnam
1965, Jun Elected vice-chairman of the Afro-Asian Solidarity Committee
1967, May Branded as a counterrevolutionary revisionist
1978, Dec First appearance after the Cultural Revolution
1979, Feb Identified as director of the Planning Bureau of the Academy of Social Sciences
       Apr Identified as deputy secretary-general of the Academy of Social Sciences
       Jun Head of a delegation of the Academy of Social Sciences to the U.S.A.

Meng Dongbo (Meng Tung-po) 孟东波

Posts held

NPC
Deputy for Sichuan Province to the 5th NPC

Provincial Administration
Vice-governor of Sichuan Province

1949,	Nov	Identified as a council member and secretary-general of the People's Government, Shandong Province (until 1952)
1952,	Oct	Identified as secretary-general of the People's Government, Fujian Province
	Nov	Identified as a council member of the People's Government, Fujian Province (until 1954)
1959,	Jan	Identified as director of the Sichuan Metallurgical Industrial Plant
1964,	Sep	Identified as a member of the People's Council, Sichuan Province, and as director of its Metallurgical Department
1965,	Dec	Identified as vice-governor of Sichuan Province
1966		Meng disappears
1978,	Feb	First appearance after the Cultural Revolution: Elected deputy for Sichuan Province to the 5th NPC
1979,	Nov	Identified as vice-chairman of the Revolutionary Committee of Sichuan Province (until Dec 1979)
	Dec	Elected vice-governor of Sichuan Province

Meng Fulin (Meng Fu-lin) 孟富林

Posts held

NPC
Deputy for Anhui Province to the 5th NPC

Provincial Administration
Vice-governor of Anhui Province

1978,	Feb	Elected deputy for Anhui Province to the 5th NPC
1979,	Dec	Elected vice-governor of Anhui Province

Meng Jiaqin (Meng Chia-ch'in) 孟家芹

Posts held

Provincial Administration
Vice-governor of Anhui Province

1978,	Jan	Elected vice-chairman of the Revolutionary Committee of Anhui Province (until Dec 1979)
1979,	Dec	Elected vice-governor of Anhui Province

Meng Jimao (Meng Chi-mao) 孟继懋

Posts held

NPC
Member of the Standing Committee of the 5th NPC
Deputy for Beijing Municipality to the 5th NPC

1955,	Feb	Identified as member of the Medical Research Commission under the Ministry of Public Health
1956,	Aug	Identified as member of the Standing Committee of the Medical Association
1960		Identified as head of the Beijing Chishuitan Hospital
1963,	Sep	Identified as director of the Surgical Section of the Medical Association
1964,	Sep	Elected deputy for Beijing Municipality to the 3rd NPC
1965,	Jan	Elected member of the Standing Committee of the 3rd NPC
1975,	Sep	Having survived the Cultural Revolution, Meng disappears until 1978
1978,	Feb	Elected deputy for Beijing Municipality to the 5th NPC
	Mar	Elected member of the Standing Committee of the 5th NPC

Meng Qi (Meng Ch'i) 孟琦

Posts held

Provincial Administration
Vice-governor of Yunnan Province

1961,	Sep	Identified as deputy mayor of Baotou Municipality
1977,	Dec	Elected vice-chairman of the Revolutionary Committee of Inner Mongolia Autonomous Region (until mid-1979)
1979,	Dec	Elected vice-governor of Yunnan Province

Meng Xiande (Meng Hsien-te) 孟宪德

Posts held

CCP
Member of the Standing Committee of Guangdong Province CP

Provincial Administration
Vice-governor of Guangdong Province

1960,	May	Identified as 1st secretary of Zhanjiang District CP, Guangdong Province
1977,	Dec	Elected vice-chairman of the Revolutionary Committee of Guangdong Province (until Dec 1979)
1978,	Oct	Identified as member of the Standing Committee of Guangdong Province CP
1979,	Dec	Elected vice-governor of Guangdong Province

Meng Ying (Meng Ying) 孟英

Posts held

Government
Ambassador to PR Mongolia

During the final phase of the Revolutionary War, Meng served as political commissar of the 3rd Subdistrict, Central Shandong Military District.

1950,	Dec	Identified as counselor at the embassy in Burma

1956,	Jan	Identified as counselor at the embassy in PR Mongolia (until Jan 1961)
1961,	Mar	Identified as deputy director of the West Asia and African Department of the Ministry of Foreign Affairs (until 1963)
1962,	Dec	Member of a delegation led by Huang Zhen to the United Arab Republic, Ghana, and Guinea
1963,	Mar	Appointed ambassador to Zanzibar (until Jul 1964)
1964,	Sep	Identified as deputy director of the Asia Department in the Ministry of Foreign Affairs
	Dec	Appointed ambassador to the Central African Republic (until Jan 1966); subsequently disappears until 1978
1978,	Aug	Appointed ambassador to the PR Mongolia

Meng is married to Wang Hongyu.

Meng Yue (Meng Yüeh)

Posts held

Government
Ambassador to Bulgaria

| 1970, | Apr | Appointed ambassador to Mali (until 1973?) |
| 1975, | Sep | Appointed ambassador to Bulgaria |

Mi Guojun (Mi Kuo-chün) 米国钧

Posts held

Government
Ambassador to Fiji

Mi was born in 1917.

1964,	Aug	Identified as technical advisor to the Association for the Promotion of International Trade
1966,	Feb	Identified as representative of the Association for the Promotion of International Trade in Austria
1973,	Feb	Identified as chargé d'affaires ad interim in Japan
1974,	Aug	Identified as counselor at the embassy in Japan
1977,	Apr	Appointed ambassador to Fiji
1978,	Jun	Mi accompanies the prime minister of Fiji on his visit to China
1979,	Mar	Mi visits Nauru
	Jul	Mi takes part in independence celebrations of Kiribati

Mi Yong (Mi Yung) 廩鐥

Posts held

Government
Ambassador to Morocco

| 1961, | Apr | Identified as director of the Bureau for International Transports, Ministry of Railways |

1964,	Sep	Identified as deputy director, State Office of Foreign Experts Affairs
1966,	Feb	Mi disappears
1972,	Nov	First appearance after the Cultural Revolution
	Dec	Mi disappears again until July 1978
1979,	Sep	Identified as ambassador to Morocco

Miao Jiurui (Miao Chiu-jui) 苗九锐

Posts held

Government
Ambassador to Chad

1971,	Oct	Identified as consul in Karachi
1972,	Oct	Identified as consul-general in Karachi
1977,	Sep	Appointed ambassador to Chad

Miao Piyi (Miao P'i-yi) 苗丕一

Posts held

Provincial Administration
Vice-chairman of the Standing Committee, Tibet Autonomous Regional People's Congress

Circa 1939 Miao served as commander of the 31st Regiment, Independent Brigade of the Jiangsu-Anhui-Henan Border District.

1956,	Mar	Identified as commander of the 53rd Division, 18th Army, which occupied Tibet
1957		Identified as vice-chairman of the Qamdo District People's Liberation Council
1965,	Aug	Elected secretary of the Tibet Autonomous Regional CP Committee and member of the Tibet Autonomous Regional People's Congress; elected deputy for Tibet to the 3rd NPC
1968,	Sep	Elected vice-chairman of the Tibet Revolutionary Committee
1971,	May	Miao disappears for unknown reasons
1979,	Aug	First reappearance: Elected vice-chairman of the Standing Committee, Tibet Autonomous Regional People's Congress

Miao Yuntai (Miao Yün-t'ai) 繆雲台

Posts held

Others
Member of the Standing Committee of the 5th CPPCC
Director of the Board of Directors, China International Trust and Investment Corporation

Miao was born in 1894. From 1945 until 1947 he was a minister without portfolio in the Executive Yuan of the Chinese National Government. In 1949 he emigrated to the U.S.A.

| 1973 | | First visit to the PRC |
| 1976 | | Second visit to the PRC |

1979,   Jun Miao returns to China to stay
         Jul By-elected member of the Standing Committee of the 5th CPPCC
         Oct Appointed director of the Board of Directors, China International Trust and Investment Corporation

Min Xuesheng (Min Hsüeh-sheng) 闵学胜

Posts held

Military
Major-general
Deputy commander of Wuhan Military Region
Member of the Standing Committee, CP Secretariat of Wuhan Military Region

During the Revolutionary Period Min served around 1938 as regiment commander in the 129th Division, 8th Route Army.

1954   Identified as deputy commander of the PLA Railway Corps serving in Korea
1958,   Jan Identified as deputy chief of staff of Wuhan Military Region
1960,   Oct Identified as major-general
1965,   Dec Identified as chief of staff of Wuhan Military Region
1970,   Sep Identified as deputy commander of Wuhan Military Region
1977,   Jun Identified as member of the Standing Committee, CP Secretariat of Wuhan Military Region

Min Yu (Min Yü) 闵予

Posts held

Government
Vice-minister of petroleum industry

Others
Chief engineer for geology at Daqing Oil Field
Deputy director-general of the Petroleum Society

Min is a college graduate trained after 1949. He has contributed to the development of Daqing Oil Field and to the maintenance of its stable and high yield.

1978,   Jun Identified as chief engineer for geology at Daqing Oil Field
         Jul Identified as vice-minister of petroleum industry
1979,   Feb Head of a scientific and technical delegation to Mexico
         Sep Head of a delegation to the 10th World Petroleum Congress in Bucharest; identified as deputy director-general of the Petroleum Society

Mo Naiqun (Mo Nai-ch'ün) 莫乃群

Posts held

NPC
Deputy for Guangxi Autonomous Region to the 5th NPC

Provincial Administration
Vice-chairman of the People's Government of Guangxi Autonomous Region

Ma was born in Guangxi Province. He studied in Japan. In the mid-forties he was chief editor of the Hong Kong Wenhui Bao. In 1947 he was editor of the China Economic Yearbook published by the Pacific Economic Research Institute, Hong Kong. In 1949 he decided to work for the Communists.

1949,   Dec Identified as council member of the People's Government, Guangxi Province
1950,   Mar Elected member of the South China Branch of the China Democratic League
1951,   May Identified as a member of the Financial and Economic Committee, People's Government of Guangxi Province
1952,   Feb Identified as vice-chairman of the Guangxi People's Government (until Feb 1955)
1953,   Nov Elected member of the presidium of the Federation of Industry and Commerce
1954,   Aug Elected deputy for Guangxi to the 1st NPC (reelected in 1958 and 1964 to the 2nd and 3rd NPCs)
1955,   Feb Elected vice-governor of Guangxi Province (until Jul 1960)
1956,   Feb Elected member of the Central Committee, China Democratic League
1960,   Jul Elected vice-chairman of Guangxi Autonomous Region
1961,   Dec Identified as vice-chairman of the Sino-North Vietnamese Friendship Association, Guangxi Branch
1968   Mo disappears
1978,   Feb First appearance after the Cultural Revolution: Elected deputy for Guangxi Autonomous Region to the 5th NPC
1979,   Jun Member of the Committee to Examine Proposals at the 2nd Session of the 5th NPC
         Dec Elected vice-chairman of the People's Government, Guangxi Autonomous Region

Mo Wenxiang (Mo Wen-hsiang) 莫文祥

Posts held

Government
Vice-minister, 3rd Ministry of Machine Building

1979,   Sep Identified as vice-minister of the 3rd Ministry of Machine Building

Mo Yanzhong (Mo Yen-chung) 莫燕忠

Posts held

Government
Ambassador to Burma

1957,   Apr Identified as counselor at the embassy in Vietnam (until 1962?)
1963,   May Identified as counselor at the embassy in Indonesia (until 1965)
1977,   Nov Appointed ambassador to Burma

Mou Haixiu (Mou Hai-hsiu)　　牟海秀

Posts held

Provincial Administration
Vice-governor of Sichuan Province

1979,　Dec　Elected vice-governor of Sichuan Province

Mu Lin (Mu Lin)　　穆林

Posts held

CCP
Member of the Standing Committee of Jilin Province CP

Provincial Administration
Vice-chairman of the Revolutionary Committee of Jilin Province

1951,　Jan　Identified as vice-chairman of the Land Reform Committee of the People's Government of Shandong Province

1953,　Dec　Identified as deputy secretary of the Rural Work Department of Shandong Province CP

1959,　Mar　Identified as member of the Standing Committee of Shandong Province CP (until Mar 1966) and as 1st secretary of Linyi CP (until 1963)

1963,　Dec　Elected vice-governor of Shandong Province

1966,　Mar　Identified as secretary of Shandong Province CP

　　　　Sep　Head of a friendship delegation to Albania

1967,　Feb　Elected member of the Standing Committee of the newly established Revolutionary Committee of Shandong Province (until Nov 1969)

1969,　Nov　Identified as vice-chairman of the Revolutionary Committee of Shandong Province (until 1977)

1972,　Mar　Identified as member of the Standing Committee of Shandong Province CP (until 1977)

1977,　Dec　Identified as member of the Standing Committee of Jilin Province CP; elected vice-chairman of the Revolutionary Committee of Jilin Province

Mu Qing (Mu Ch'ing)　　穆青

Posts held

CCP
Cadre of a department of the CCP Central Committee

NPC
Deputy for Tianjin Municipality to the 5th NPC

Government
Deputy director of XNA

1959,　Apr　Identified as deputy director of XNA
1966　　　　Disappears during the Cultural Revolution
1972,　Oct　First appearance after the Cultural Revolution: Referred to in his former post as deputy director of XNA
1973,　Nov　Visit to Yugoslavia
1976,　Jan　Identified as a cadre of a department of the CCP Central Committee
　　　　Dec　Head of a delegation of journalists to Kampuchea
1978,　Feb　Elected deputy for Tianjin Municipality to the 5th NPC
　　　　Apr　Head of a delegation of journalists to Guyana, Venezuela, Peru, and Mexico
1979,　Oct　Head of a journalists delegation to Italy and Spain

Mu·sha·yeh·fu (Mushayef)　　木沙也夫

Posts held

Provincial Administration
Vice-chairman of the Standing Committee of the People's Congress of Xinjiang Autonomous Region

Others
Member of the Standing Committee of the 5th CPPCC

Mu-sha-ye-fu belongs to the Uighur minority.

1964,　Apr　Identified as director of the Bureau of Civil Affairs of Xinjiang Autonomous Region

1978,　Mar　Elected member of the Standing Committee of the 5th CPPCC

1979,　Sep　Elected vice-chairman of the Standing Committee of the People's Congress of Xinjiang Autonomous Region

Na·mu·la (Na-mu-la)　　　　那木拉

<u>Posts held</u>

NPC
Member of the Standing Committee of the 5th NPC
Deputy for Inner Mongolia Autonomous Region to the 5th NPC

| 1978, | Feb | Elected deputy for Inner Mongolia Autonomous Region to the 5th NPC |
| | Mar | Elected member of the Standing Committee of the 5th NPC |

Ngapoi Ngawang Jigmi (Ah·p'ei Ah·wang Chin·mei)

阿沛阿旺晋美

<u>Posts held</u>

NPC
Vice-chairman of the 5th NPC
Deputy for Tibet Autonomous Region to the 5th NPC

Military
Lieutenant-general

Provincial Administration
Chairman of the Standing Committee of the People's Congress of Tibet Autonomous Region

Ngapoi Ngawang Jigmi, who belongs to the Tibetan minority, was born in 1909 in present-day Qinghai Province as the son of an aristocrat. His father was governor of Qamdo, the eastern part of Tibet, and commander of the Tibetan armored forces. After studying in Great Britain, he returned to Tibet in 1932 and subsequently joined the Tibetan Army. As a cabinet member under the Dalai Lama, he later advocated reformist policies. After the Communist forces occupied this region in 1950 after 36 years of Tibetan independence, Ngapoi served as governor of Qamdo.

1950,	Oct	Captured by Communist troops entering Qamdo, a Tibetan Military Region under his control as a kaloon of the Tibetan local government
	Dec?	Released and returned to Lhasa
1951,	Apr	Head of a Tibetan delegation to the peace negotiations with the Chinese in Beijing
	May	Tibetan signatory of the "Agreement on the Peaceful Liberation of Tibet"; returned to Tibet via India accompanied by Zhang Jingwu
	Sep	Appointed member of the Minorities Commission under the State Council (until Aug 1954)
	Nov	By-elected member of the CPPCC (until Dec 1954)
1952		Identified as deputy commander of Tibet Military Region (until 1977)
1954,	Aug	Elected deputy for Tibet to the 1st NPC (reelected to the 2nd through 5th NPCs)
	Sep	Appointed member of the National Defense Council (until Cultural Revolution)
1955,	Sep	Appointed lieutenant-general; conferred the order "Liberation," 1st class
1956,	Apr	Appointed member of the Preparatory Committee for the establishment of Tibet

Autonomous Region (PCTAR)

	May	Appointed secretary general of PCTAR
1959,	Apr	Elected vice-chairman of the CPPCC (until Dec 1964)
	Dec	Appointed vice-chairman of PCTAR
1961,	Aug	Identified as head of a cadre school in Lhasa
	Sep	Ngapoi accompanies the Banqen Lama to Beijing
1962,	Jan	Report on Tibet to the CPPCC in Beijing
	Aug	Ngapoi accompanies the Banqen Lama on his return to Tibet; appointed vice-chairman of the Election Committee for Tibet Autonomous Region
1965,	Jan	Elected member of the Standing Committee of the NPC
	Mar	Identified as acting chairman of PCTAR
	Sep	Appointed executive chairman of the presidium, 1st session of the 1st People's Congress of Tibet; elected chairman of Tibet Autonomous Region
1968,	Sep	Elected vice-chairman of the newly established Revolutionary Committee of Tibet Autonomous Region (until Aug 1979)
1969-1974		Numerous public appearances, primarily in his capacity as vice-chairman of the Standing Committee of the NPC, usually in Beijing occasionally in Lhasa
1975,	Jan	Confirmed as vice-chairman of the Standing Committee by the 4th NPC (again in Mar 1978 by the 5th NPC)
1979,	Aug	Elected chairman of the Standing Committee of the People's Congress of Tibet Autonomous Region

Ni Guyin (Ni Ku-yin) (f)　　　仉谷音

<u>Posts held</u>

NPC
Member of the Standing Committee of the 5th NPC
Deputy for Shanghai Municipality to the 5th NPC

1964,	Jul	Elected alternate member of the Communist Youth League
1978,	Feb	Elected deputy for Shanghai Municipality to the 5th NPC
	Mar	Elected member of the Standing Committee of the 5th NPC; identified as outstanding Shanghai primary school teacher with 26 years of experience

Ni Zhifu (Ni Chih-fu)　　　仉志福

<u>Posts held</u>

CCP
Member of the Politburo of the CCP 11th Central Committee
Member of the CCP 11th Central Committee

NPC
Deputy for Beijing Municipality to the 5th NPC

Mass Organizations
Chairman of the Federation of Trade Unions
President of the Trade Union Cadre School

Ni was born in 1932 in Shanghai as the 3rd child of a peasant. His father died before Ni was one year old. In 1944, under Japanese occupation, he worked as an errand-boy for a Japanese oil company. After the War he attended elementary school for three years from 1945. In 1948 he started as an apprentice at a Shanghai printing machine factory. After the Communist victory in 1949 he remained with this privately owned factory. He joined the trade union in 1950.

1952		Ni attends an eight months' course as worker technician
1953		As a mechanic of Yongding Machine Tool Factory, Ni is sent to Beijing having developed a new drilling device in the course of a campaign for technical innovations which has become known as "Ni Zhifu Drilling Head"
1958		Ni joins the CCP
1962		Promoted engineer
1966-1968		Active participation in the criticism movement during the Cultural Revolution
1969,	Apr	Elected member of the CCP Central Committee by the 9th Party Congress (confirmed in this post in 1973 by the 10th Congress)
1970,	Oct	Head of a workers delegation to Chile
1971,	Mar	Elected member of the Standing Committee following the reestablishment of the CP Secretariat of Beijing after the Cultural Revolution (until Sep 1973)
1972,	Oct	Identified as deputy secretary, CP of Yongding Machine Tool Factory
	Dec	Identified as vice-chairman of the Revolutionary Committee of Yongding Machine Tool Factory
1973,	Apr	Elected chairman of the Trade Union of Beijing
	Aug	Elected alternate member of the Politburo by the 10th CCP Congress (until Aug 1977)
	Sep	Deputy head of a friendship delegation to North Korea; identified as commander of Beijing Workers Militia; identified as secretary of Beijing Municipality CP (until Nov 1976)
1976,	Apr	Identified as vice-chairman of the Revolutionary Committee of Beijing Municipality (until Oct 1978)
	Nov	Following the purge of the Gang of Four, Ni is posted as 2nd CP secretary to the former Regional Center of Shanghai (until Oct 1978)
	Dec	Identified as 1st vice-chairman of the Revolutionary Committee of Shanghai (until Oct 1978)
1977,	Jul	Identified as 2nd secretary of Beijing Municipality CP
	Aug	Elected member of the Politburo by the 11th CCP Congress
	Nov	Identified as chairman of the Trade Union of Beijing
1978,	Feb	Elected deputy for Beijing Municipality to the 5th NPC
	Oct	Elected chairman of the Federation of Trade Unions
	Nov	Identified as president of the Trade Union Cadre School
1979,	Sep	Head of a trade unions delegation to North Korea

Nie Fengzhi (Nieh Feng-chih) 聂凤智

Posts held

CCP
Member of the CCP 11th Central Committee

Military
Lieutenant-general
Commander of Nanjing Military Region
Secretary of the CP Committee of Nanjing Military Region

Nie was born in 1917 in Shanxi Province. In 1934-35 he took part in the Long March. He was commander of the 3rd Military Subregion of East Shandong Military District in 1945 and concurrently commander of the 5th Division. At the end of that year he became commander of the 6th Division of the Shandong Field Army. In early 1947 he commanded the 25th Division of the East China Field Army, and at the end of that year the 9th Column of this Field Army. In March 1949 he was commander of an army belonging to the 3rd Field Army. In the summer of that year he was appointed chief of staff at the East China Military and Administrative Academy.

1950,	Dec	Appointed commander of the 4th Army of the Air Force which was engaged in training Air Force units for service in Korea
1952-1953		Nie is entrusted with the strategic command of the Chinese People's Volunteers Air Force units operating in Korea. There he puts forth his views on "flexible operation" of aircraft into action. This was based on the principle "fight only under favourable conditions" in contradiction to the strategy "fight under all circumstances," advocated by Peng Dehuai and the Soviet advisors
1954		Identified as commander of the Air Force in East China Military Region
1955,	Jan	Identified as commander of the Air Force in Nanjing Military Region
1957,	Aug	Identified as deputy commander of Nanjing Military Region in addition to his post as commander of the Air Force in Nanjing Military Region; identified as lieutenant-general
1960		Disappears for unknown reasons
1975,	Jun	Identified as deputy commander of Nanjing Military Region
1977,	May	Identified as commander of Nanjing Military Region
	Aug	Elected member of the CCP Central Committee by the 11th Party Congress
1978,	Oct	Identified as secretary of the CP Committee of Nanjing Military Region

Nie is married to He Ming.

Nie Rongzhen (Nieh Jung-chen) 聶榮臻

Posts held

CCP
Member of the Politburo of the CCP
11th Central Committee
Member of the CCP 11th Central Committee
Vice-chairman of the Military Council of
the CCP Central Committee

NPC
Vice-chairman of the Standing Committee
of the 5th NPC
Deputy for the PLA to the 5th NPC

Military
Marshal

Nie was born in 1899 in Jiangjin, Sichuan Province, as the son of a landlord. He attended middle school in Chongqing where he joined the "May 4th Movement" in 1919. At the end of that year he went to France as a worker-student studying in Grenoble and Paris. He then studied natural sciences for another two years at the Université du Travail in Charleroi, Belgium. During this period he was employed, probably during term vacations, in the weapons factory of Schneider-Creusot, in Renault automobile factories, and in the Thomson Electrical Equipment Factory. Nie joined the Communist Youth League in 1922 and the CCP one year later. He was in Berlin temporarily together with Lu Fuchun in 1923. In 1924 he went to Moscow to study military sciences at the Far East University of the University of the Red Army.

He returned to China in late 1925. Under Zhou Enlai he served initially as political instructor of the 5th and 6th training course at Whampoa Military Academy. In mid-1926 he took part in the Northern Expedition. After the rift between the KMT and the Communists in 1927 he became political commissar of the army commanded by Ye Ting which took part in the Nanchang Uprising. After the failure of this uprising Nie left together with Ye for Hong Kong via the Hailufeng Soviet. In December 1927 he took part in the equally unsuccessful Guangzhou Uprising. Nie spent the following three years in Hong Kong.

In 1930 he traveled to North China where he was entrusted by the Party with organizational tasks in Beijing, Tianjin, and in the coal mining district of Tangshan. In 1931 Nie served at first on the Shanghai Military Advisory Committee of the Party Center, and then moved to the Jiangxi Soviet set up by Mao Zedong and Zhu De. After a brief period as deputy director of the Red Army Political Department Nie became political commissar in the 1st Army Corps commanded by Lin Biao. He retained this post until approximately summer 1934. In February 1934 he was elected a member of the Central Executive Council of the Chinese Soviet Republic (Jiangxi Soviet). Having been temporarily posted to the military forces under Chen Yi as political commissar, Nie again served under Lin Biao during the Long March. After the outbreak of the Anti-Japanese War and the reorganization of the Communist armored forces into the 8th Route Army, of which the 1st Front Army was now commanded by Lin Biao as the 115th Division, Nie was appointed deputy commander in addition to his former post as political commissar. After victory against the Japanese at the battle of Pingxing Pass, Lin Biao let the main force of

the 115th Division southward while Nie was ordered to establish the first Communist guerrilla base in the Japanese occupied area in the Wutai Mountain range with the remaining 2,000 men. Thanks to his extraordinary negotiating skills, Nie succeeded in winning local administrations over to his side and in setting up effective operational bases against the Japanese. In the years until 1943 Nie recruited some 150,000 soldiers in this area of which the majority, however, was detached to units of other guerrilla bases after basic training, leaving some 64,000 men under his command. From mid-1943 Nie served in the Communist Central Base in Yan'an where he was elected a member of the Central Committee by the 7th CCP Congress in June 1945. Immediately afterwards he returned to his base in the Wutain Maintain range as commander. After the Japanese capitulation in August 1945, Nie's forces occupied the stragically important city of Zhangjiakou (Kalgan) through which Lin Biao could move his troops into Manchuria. In 1948 Nie was appointed commander of North China Military Region (until 1954) after his units had occupied the strategic city of Shijiazhuang in late 1947, an important railway junction south of Beijing. He held the concurrent post of 2nd secretary, North China Bureau of the CCP (until 1954), the area correspoding under the Party administration to that under his military control. In August 1948 Shijiazhuang became the capital of North China People's Government under Dong Biwu and thus the direct predecessor of the PRC. In the winter of 1948-49 the forces under Nie and Lin Biao proceeded to move against the Beijing-Tianjin region, controlled by 500,000 soldiers under the KMT General Fu Zuoyi. Following short battles near Tianjin, Nie was chief responsible negotiator of the Communists with the KMT, leading to the surrender of Beijing in January 1949 (with the foundation of the PRC in October 1949, Fu Zuoyi was appointed minister of water conservancy and electric power, a post he held until three months before his death in April 1975). After the occupation of Beijing, Nie was appointed commander of Beijing and Tianjin Garrisons (until 1955). During the following months he was a member of two further delegations negotiating an agreement with the KMT to end the war. These negotiations failed, however, because the Communists at this point were unwilling to settle for less than unconditional capitulation. From July to August 1949 Nie served once more in the military when the troops under Peng Dehuai had met unexpectedly strong resistance by the units of KMT General Hu Zongnan in Shaanxi Province. This resistance was broken when Nie arrived with two armies in support of Peng. On 8 September 1949 Nie succeeded Ye Jianying as mayor of Beijing (until Feb 1951) and as chairman of the Military Commission of Beijing. In the same month he took part in the 1st CPPCC.

1949,	Oct	Appointed member of the Central Government Council; member of the Revolutionary Military Council; deputy chief of PLA General Staff
1950,	Sep	Identified as acting chief of PLA General Staff. In this capacity he informs the U.S.A. through the Indian ambassador in Beijing, Panikkar, that China would not watch American troops aproaching the Yalu "with their hands in their laps." One month later the "Chinese People's Volunteers" intervened in the Korean War.
1951		Identified as member of North China Administrative Council (until 1954)

1952, Feb Head of a Party and government delegation to the mourning ceremonies for Tschoibalsan in the People's Republic of Mongolia

Dec Appointed member of the Government Administration Council (until Sep 1954)

1954, Sep Elected deputy for the PLA to the 1st NPC (until Mar 1959) and member of the Standing Committee of the NPC (until Jul 1957); appointed vice-chairman of the National Defense Council (until Cultural Revolution)

1955, Sep Appointed one of the marshals of the PLA; awarded the order "1st August," "Independence and Freedom," and "Liberation," all 1st class

Dec Member of a Party delegation led by Zhu De to the 2nd Conference of the Romanian Workers Party

1956, Jan Member of a delegation to celebrations of the 80th birthday of President Wilhelm Pieck of the German Democratic Republic; the delegation subsequently visits Hungary, Czechoslovakia, and Poland. In Prague, Nie takes part in a session of the Political Consultative Council of the Warsaw Pact Powers as official Chinese observer

Feb Present with Zhu De at the opening session of the famous 20th CPSU Party Congress. On his return one day later, while Zhu remained in Moscow, Nie visits the PR Mongolia

Apr Head of a Party delegation to the 3rd Congress of the Korean Workers Party

Sep The 8th Party Congress confirms Nie in his post as member of the CCP Central Committee

Oct Appointed vice-premier (until 1974)

1957, Mar Head of a government delegation to the independence celebrations in Ghana. Nie returns to China traveling via London, Bern, and Prague

May Appointed chairman of the Scientific Planning Commission (until Nov 1958 when it was joined with the Technical Commission to form the Science and Technology Commission)

1958, Jul Elected deputy for Sichuan Province to the 2nd NPC (confirmed in Dec 1964 by the 3rd NPC)

Nov Appointed chairman of the Science and Technology Commission under the State Council (until 1966)

1959, Oct Head of a Party and government delegation to the 10th anniversary celebrations of the German Democratic Republic

1961, Mar Identified as vice-chairman, Military Council of the CCP Central Committee

1967, Jan Identified as member of the Politburo of the CCP Central Committee (until Mar 1969). Around this time the Staff Office of National Defense Industry is established, shortly afterwards renamed Scientific and Technological Commission for National Defense under the State Council. According to non-Chinese sources Nie was chairman of this commission.

His leadership in the Scientific Planning Commission (1957-1958), the Science and Technology Commission (1958-1966), the Staff Office of National Defense Industry, as well as the Scientific and Technological Commission for National Defense, points to the organizational development of the nuclear and missile capability, the coordination of which was the primary responsibility of each of these agencies.

May Having come under attack with other leading cadres during the Cultural Revolution, Nie warns in a speech of 24 May of the damage for China resulting from an interruption of the nuclear and missile program. He survived the Cultural Revolution without loss of influence.

1969, Apr Confirmed as member of the CCP Central Committee by the 9th Party Congress, but not as member of the Politburo

1973, Aug Reelected member of the CCP Central Committee by the 10th Party Congress

1975, Jan Elected vice-chairman of the Standing Committee by the 4th NPC (confirmed in 1978 by the 5th NPC)

1977, Aug Elected member of the CCP Politburo by the 11th Party Congress

Sep Article in HQ: "Restore and Carry Forward the Party's Fine Style of Work"

1978, Feb Elected deputy for the PLA to the 5th NPC

Nie has been married to Zhang Ruihua since about 1930. By 1938 they had two children.

Nie Zhen (Nieh Chen)

Posts held

Others
Member of the Standing Committee of the 5th CPPCC
Deputy secretary-general of the 5th CPPCC

1959, Feb Identified as vice-chairman of the Sino-Bulgarian Friendship Association

1961, Jan Identified as deputy director of the Beijing Institute of Socialism

Feb Identified as vice-president of the Beijing People's University

1966 Nie disappears

1978, Feb First appearance after the Cultural Revolution

Apr Identified as deputy secretary-general of the 5th CPPCC

1979, Jul By-elected member of the Standing Committee of the 5th CPPCC

Niu Peizong (Niu P'ei-tsung)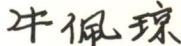

Posts held

Others
Member of the Standing Committee of the 5th CPPCC

Niu was born in 1908 in Dingxiang, Shanxi Province. He joined the CCP in 1928. In 1938 he belonged to the Sacrifice and National Salvation League in Shanxi Province founded by Bo Yibo. In 1940 Niu commanded the 21st Brigade of the Dare-to-die Column of that League. Two years later he headed the Taiyuan Administrative Office. In 1949 he became chairman of the People's Government of Henan Province (until 1952).

1950,	Mar	Identified as vice-chairman of the Financial and Economic Committee of the Central-South Military and Administrative Council (until 1954)
1954,	Oct	Identified as deputy director of the 5th General Office of the State Council (until Sep 1959)
1956,	Jun	Identified as deputy director of the General Office of the NPC
1957,	Jul	Appointed member of the Central Relief Commission of the State Council
1959,	Sep	Appointed deputy director of the State Office of Finance and Trade (until 1967)
1967		Niu disappears
1979,	Jun	First appearance after the Cultural Revolution
	Jul	By-elected member of the Standing Committee of the 5th CPPCC

Niu Ruizhou (Niu Jui-chou) 牛瑞调

Posts held

CCP
Member of the Standing Committee of Tibet Autonomous Region CP

Provincial Administration
Vice-chairman of the People's Government of Tibet Autonomous Region

1977,	Nov	Elected member of the Standing Committee of Tibet CP
	Dec	Elected vice-chairman of the Revolutionary Committee of Tibet (until Aug 1979)
1979,	Aug	Elected vice-chairman of the People's Government of Tibet Autonomous Region

Niu Yinguan (Niu Yin-kuan) 牛荫冠

Posts held

Government
Director of the Federation of Supply and Marketing Cooperatives

Niu was born in 1911 in Shanxi Province. In 1936 he worked under Bo Yibo in his native province organizing the Sacrifice and National Salvation League. In 1948 he was head of the Central Shanxi Administration Office.

1950		Identified as director of the Finance Department of the Jiangxi Province People's Government
1952		Identified as vice-chairman of the Jiangxi Province People's Government
1962,	Oct	Appointed vice-minister of commerce (until Cultural Revolution)
1963,	Dec	Identified as director of the Beijing College of Commerce
1966		Disappears during the Cultural Revolution
1975,	Sep	First appearance after the Cultural Revolution
1979,	Jun	Appointed director of the Federation of Supply and Marketing Cooperatives

Nyapoi Cedan Zhoigar
(Ah·p'ei Ts'ai·t'an Cho·ke) (f)

Posts held 阿沛才担卓嘎

NPC
Deputy for Tibet Autonomous Region to the 5th NPC

Mass Organization
Vice-chairman of the Women's Federation
Vice-president of Tibet Women's Federation

Nyapoi is the wife of Ngapoi Ngawang Jigmi and belongs to the Tibetan minority.

1959,	Apr	Elected member of the 3rd CPPCC
	Jun	Identified as member of the Standing Committee of the Preparatory Committee for Tibet Autonomous Region
1964,	Oct	Elected deputy for Tibet Autonomous Region to the 3rd NPC
1965,	Feb	Identified as president of Tibet Women's Federation
1973,	Jul	Identified as vice-president of Tibet Women's Federation
1975,	Mar	Identified as deputy to the 4th NPC (re-elected Feb 1978 to the 5th NPC)
1978,	Sep	Elected vice-chairman of the Women's Federation

Ou Mengjue (Ou Meng-chüeh) (f)   欧梦觉

Posts held

Provincial Administration
Vice-chairman of the People's Congress of
Guangdong Province

Ou was born in 1903 in Guangdong Province. From 1923
until 1925 she studied at the Guangzhou Kunwei Middle
School and joined the CCP. About 1926 she married a
teacher of that school, Tan Tiandu. In March 1927 she
attended the 5th Congress of the CCP in Wuhan. In 1931
she was arrested, for a short time, by the KMT. About
1938 she studied at the Central Party School in Yan'an.
The following years she worked in the Women's Department of the CCP Central Committee. In January 1949
she was elected member of the Preparatory Committee of
the Democratic Women's Federation. In September that
year she took part in the 1st CPPCC.

1949,   Dec   Appointed council member of the People's
              Government of Guangdong Province; iden-
              tified as director of the South China
              Branch of NCNA and as a council member
              of the Sino-Soviet Friendship Association
              (until Dec 1954)

1952,   Feb   Identified as deputy director of the Or-
              ganization Department, South China
              Branch under the CCP Central Committee
              (until Oct 1954)

1953,   Apr   Elected member of the Executive Com-
              mittee of the Democratic Women's Feder-
              ation (until Sep 1957)

1954,   Aug   Elected deputy for Guangdong Province to
              the 1st NPC

        Oct   Identified as secretary of the Women's
              Work Committee of the South China
              Bureau under the CCP Central Commit-
              tee; identified as director of the Organi-
              zation Department, South China Bureau
              under the CCP Central Committee

1955,   Sep   Elected director of the Organization De-
              partment, Guangdong Province CP

        Dec   Identified as a member of the Standing
              Committee, Guangdong Province CP (until
              Dec 1956)

1956,   Sep   Elected alternate member of the CCP
              8th Central Committee

1957,   Jan   Identified as secretary of Guangdong
              Province CP

        Feb   Identified as vice-chairman of the Sino-
              Soviet Friendship Association, Guangdong
              Branch

1960,   Nov   Identified as secretary of Guangzhou Mu-
              nicipality CP

        Dec   Elected chairman of the CPPCC, Guang-
              dong Branch

1964,   Sep   Elected deputy for Guangdong Province to
              the 3rd NPC

1967,   Jan   Denounced as a counterrevolutionary
              "three-anti element" and an accomplice of
              Tao Zhu

1979,   Dec   First appearance after the Cultural Revo-
              lution: Elected vice-chairman of the Peo-
              ple's Congress, Guangdong Province

Ou Tangliang (Ou T'ang-liang) (f)   区棠亮

Posts held

CCP
Deputy director, International Liaison Department of the CCP Central Committee

NPC
Member of the Standing Committee of the
5th NPC
Deputy for Tianjin Municipality to the
5th NPC

Ou is a native of Guangxi Province. She graduated from
Yanjing University. As a representative of the "Federation
of Students in the Liberated Areas" she took part in a
council session of the Communist International Students
Federation in September 1948 in Paris. In April 1949 she
was elected alternate member of the Executive Council,
New Democratic Youth League, and one month later
member of the Administrative Council of the Federation
of Democratic Youth.

1950   Identified as head of the International
              Liaison Department of the Federation of
              Democratic Youth

        Oct   Elected member of the National Commit-
              tee of the Chinese Peace Council

1952   Identified as alternate member, Secretari-
              at of the Federation of Democratic Youth

        Dec   Member of a delegation to the World
              Peace Council Session in Vienna

1953,   Apr   Elected member of the Standing Commit-
              tee by the 2nd Congress of the Democrat-
              ic Women's Federation

        Jun   Elected vice-chairman of the Federation
              of Democratic Youth and secretary of the
              New Democratic Youth League (then the
              only woman in the leadership of both
              organizations)

        Aug   Head of a delegation to the 4th Congress
              of the World Federation of Democratic
              Youth in Bukarest

1954,   May   Elected member of the Standing Commit-
              tee, Association for Cultural Relations
              with Foreign Countries; elected deputy
              for Guangxi Province to the 1st NPC
              (reelected in 1958 and 1964 to the 2nd and
              3rd NPCs)

        Jun   Identified as council member of the World
              Federation of Democratic Youth (until
              about 1962)

        Dec   Elected council member of the Sino-
              Soviet Friendship Association

1955,   Aug   Head of a delegation to the 5th Congress
              of the World Federation of Democratic
              Youth in Warsaw

1957,   Jan   Member of an NPC delegation led by Peng
              Zhen to the USSR, Romania, Czechoslova-
              kia, Bulgaria, Albania, and Yugoslavia

        May   Elected member of the Standing Commit-
              tee of the Communist Youth League

1958,   Apr   Elected vice-chairman of the Federation
              of Democratic Youth and member of the
              Democratic Women's Federation

        Jul   Elected secretary-general of the Peace
              Council; member of a Chinese delegation
              to the World Peace Council Session in
              Stockholm

Sep Elected council member of the Sino-Iraq Friendship Association (until Cultural Revolution)

1959, May Member of a delegation to the World Peace Council Session in Stockholm

Jul Elected member of the Afro-Asian Solidarity Committee

1960, Apr Elected member of the Sino-African Friendship Association (until Cultural Revolution)

Dec Member of a delegation to Cuba

1961, Mar Member of the Chinese delegation to the World Peace Council Session in New Delhi

1962, Mar Member of a delegation to the World Women's Conference on Disarmament in Vienna

Jul Member of a delegation to the World Conference on Total Disarmament and International Peace in Moscow

Dec Elected council member of the Sino-Cuban Friendship Association (until Cultural Revolution)

1963, Jun Deputy head of a delegation to the World Women's Conference in Moscow

1965, Jan Elected member of the Standing Committee by the 3rd NPC

Jun Elected vice-chairman of the Peace Council and of the Afro-Asian Solidarity Committee

1967 Disappears during the Cultural Revolution

1972, Apr First appearance after the Cultural Revolution

Aug Identified as a cadre of the International Liaison Department of the CCP Central Committee

Sep Identified in her former post as member of the Standing Committee of the NPC

1975, Jan Reelected member of the Standing Committee by the 4th NPC (confirmed in Mar 1978 by the 5th NPC)

1978, Feb Elected deputy for Tianjin Municipality to the 5th NPC

Mar Identified as deputy director, International Liaison Department of the CCP Central Committee

1979, Jun Member of the Committee to Examine Proposals at the 2nd Session of the 5th NPC

Ou Zhifu (Ou Chih-fu)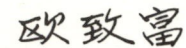

Posts held

Military
Major-general
Deputy commander of Guangzhou Military Region

Ou belongs to the Zhuang minority. He was born circa 1910 in Guangxi Province. During the Revolutionary Period he served in the Red Army, reaching the rank of regiment commander in the 8th Route Army in 1941. In 1946 he was brigade commander and in 1948 division commander. In 1949 he commanded the 142nd Division of the 4th Field Army.

1950 Identified as deputy commander of the 48th Army

1952 Identified as commander of the 48th Army

1953 After the 48th Army was dissolved, Ou probably attended the PLA Military Academy

1958 Identified as commander of Guangxi Military District (until Jun 1971) and as major-general

1964, Oct Elected deputy for Guangxi Autonomous Region to the 3rd NPC

1968, Aug Elected vice-chairman of the newly established Revolutionary Committee of Guangxi Autonomous Region (until circa 1972)

1969, Dec Identified as deputy commander of Guangzhou Military Region

Pagbalha Geleg Namgyai (Pebala Gelieh Namje)

Posts held 帕巴拉·卓列朗杰

NPC
Deputy for Tibet Autonomous Region to the 5th NPC
Provincial Administration
Vice-chairman of the People's Government of Tibet Autonomous Region

Others
Vice-chairman of the 5th CPPCC

Pagbalha who belongs to the Tibetan minority, is a living Buddha from the monastery of Qamdo. He was born in 1940.

1950		Elected deputy director of the Liberation Committee of Qamdo
1953,	Jun	Elected council member of the Buddhist League
1956,	Apr	With the establishment of the Preparatory Committee for the foundation of Tibet Autonomous Region (PCTAR), Pagbalha is elected a member
1958,	Feb	Identified as member of the Standing Committee of PCTAR
1959,	Mar	Elected deputy for Tibet to the 2nd NPC
	Apr	Elected vice-chairman of the CPPCC
	Nov	He accompanies the Banqen Erdeni on a tour in China (until Feb 1960)
1960,	Feb	Identified as vice-chairman of PCTAR (until Sep 1965)
1961,	Sep	Pagbalha accompanies the Banqen Lama to Beijing
1962,	May	Pagbalha accompanies the Banqen Lama to the May Day celebrations in Beijing
1963,	Oct	Identified as director of the Religious Affairs Committee of PCTAR (until Sep 1965)
1965,	Sep	Elected member of the Tibetan People's Congress and vice-chairman of Tibet Autonomous Region (until Cultural Revolution)
1972,	Jan	First appearance after the Cultural Revolution: Named in his former post as vice-chairman of the 4th CPPCC (confirmed in 1978 by the 5th CPPCC)
1973,	Oct	Pagbalha gives an interview in Lhasa on the development of Tibet
1975,	Jan	Member of the Presidium of the 4th NPC
1978,	Feb	Elected deputy for Tibet Autonomous Region to the 5th NPC
1979,	Jan	Identified as vice-chairman of the Reception Committee for Returned Tibetan Compatriots
	Aug	Elected vice-chairman of the People's Government of Tibet Autonomous Region

Pan Fei (P'an Fei)   潘 非

Posts held

CCP
Deputy chief editor of RMRB (People's Daily)
Cadre of a department of the CCP Central Committee

1959		Correspondent for NCNA and RMRB in London
1960,	Apr	Identified as deputy director for International Affairs, Board of Editors of RMRB (until 1964)
1963,	Feb	Identified as member of the Editorial Department of RMRB
1973,	May	Head of a delegation of journalists to the Federal Republic of Germany
1974,	Sep	Identified as a cadre of a department of the CCP Central Committee
	Nov-Dec	Head of a delegation of journalists to Zambia, Tanzania, North Yemen, and South Yemen
1977,	Apr	Identified as deputy chief editor of RMRB

Pan Meiying (P'an Mei-ying) (f)   盤美英

Posts held

CCP
Alternate member of the CCP 11th Central Committee
Deputy secretary of He County CP, Guangxi Autonomous Region

Others
Vice-chairman of the Revolutionary Committee of He County, Guangxi Autonomous Region

Pan belongs to the Yao minority. She was born in 1930 as the daughter of very poor peasants in He Xian, Guangxi Province. At the age of 10 she entered service for a landlord. She received her first schooling after the Communist take-over.

1969,	Apr	Elected alternate member of the CCP Central Commitee by the 9th Party Congress (confirmed in 1973 and 1977 by the 10th and 11th Congresses)
	Jun	Identified as vice-chairman of Huangshi Production Brigade, Butou People's Commune, He County
1972,	Mar	Identified as secretary, CP of Huangshi Production Brigade
1975,	May	Identified as member of the Standing Committee, Revolutionary Committee of Guangxi Autonomous Region
1976,	Dec	Member of a delegation of Party organizers to North Korea
1977,	Aug	Last appearance; probably purged

Pan Qi (P'an Ch'i)   潘 琪

Posts held

Government
Vice-minister of communications

1947		Identified as director of the Education Department of Andong Province People's Government
1948		Identified as director of the Civil Affairs Department of Andong Province People's Government

1950,	Mar	Identified as deputy director of the Civil Affairs Department of Central-South China Military Administrative Council (until Sep 1951)
1951,	Aug	Identified as deputy director of the Personnel Department of Central-South China Military and Administrative Council (until Aug 1952)
1953,	Feb	Appointed director of the Road Bureau in the Ministry of Communications (until Jun 1954)
1954,	Jun	Appointed vice-minister of communications (until Jun 1964)
1964,	Jun	Appointed vice-minister of the 6th Ministry of Machine Building
1966		Disappears during the Cultural Revolution
1975,	Oct	First appearance after the Cultural Revolution
1976,	Apr	Identified as holding his former post as vice-minister of communications
1978,	Apr	Head of a government delegation to Laos
	Jun	Deputy head of a government delegation under Geng Biao to inaugurate the Karakorum Highway to Pakistan
	Jul	Deputy head of a government delegation under Chen Muhua to Somalia, Gabon, and Cameroon

Pan Ruizheng (P'an Jui-cheng)　潘瑞征

Posts held

Provincial Administration
Vice-governor of Shanxi Province

| 1979, | Dec | Elected vice-governor of Shanxi Province |

Pan Shixing (P'an Shih-hsing)　潘时兴

Posts held

CCP
Alternate member of the CCP 11th Central Committee

| 1977, | Aug | Elected alternate member of the CCP Central Committee by the 11th Party Congress |

Pan Shu (P'an Shu)　潘菽

Posts held

Others
Member of the Standing Committee of the 5th CPPCC
President of the Psychology Society
Vice-chairman of the Central Committee, Jiusan (Chiu-san) Society

Pan was born in 1898 in Yixing, Jiangsu Province. He graduated from Nanjing University in 1920 and received his Ph.D. at Chicago University in 1924. After his return to China in 1921 he held a professorship at the National Central University for many years. In 1944 he founded together with Xu Deheng and others the Democratic Science Society which was renamed Jiusan Society one year later. In 1949 he joined the Communists and in June of that year was elected a member of the Preparatory Committee for the 1st Natural Science Workers Conference (until 1960).

1950,	Jan	Identified as member of the East China Military and Administrative Council
	Mar	Identified as chairman of the Nanjing University Administrative Committee as well as member of the Cultural and Educational Committee of the East China Military and Administrative Committee (until Jan 1953)
	Dec	Identified as member of Nanjing People's Government and as member of the Jiusan Society Central Committee
1952,	Sep	Elected member of the Standing Committee of the Jiusan Society (until 1956)
	Nov	Identified as president of Nanjing University and as council member of the People's Government of Jiangsu Province
1953,	Jan	Identified as member of the Cultural and Educational Committee of the East China Administrative Council (until 1956)
1954,	Aug	Elected deputy for Jiangsu Province to the 1st NPC (confirmed in 1958 and 1964 to the 2nd and 3rd NPCs)
1955,	Jun	Identified as member of the Department of Biology, Geology, and Geography of the Academy of Sciences; elected president of the Psychological Association
1956,	Mar	Pan joins the CCP
	Dec	Identified as director of the Psychological Institute of the Academy of Sciences
1958,	Dec	Elected vice-chairman of the Jiusan Society; identified as member of the Scientific and Technological Association
1967		Disappears during the Cultural Revolution
1977,	Feb	First appearance after the Cultural Revolution
1978,	Mar	Elected member of the Standing Committee of the 5th CPPCC
	Jul	Identified as president of the Psychology Society
1979,	Oct	Elected vice-chairman of the Central Committee of the Jiusan Society

Pan Yan (P'an Yen)　泮焱

Posts held

Military
Deputy commander of Beijing Military Region
Commander of Beijing Garrison

Provincial Administration
Vice-chairman of the People's Congress of Beijing Municipality

1968,	Dec	Identified as chief of staff of the PLA Navy (until 1976)
1971,	Aug	Member of a military delegation to Albania and Romania
1979,	Dec	Elected vice-chairman of the People's Congress of Beijing Municipality

1980,   Feb   Identified as deputy commander of the Beijing Military Region and as commander of Beijing Garrison

Pan Zhenwu (P'an Chen-wu)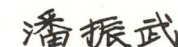

Posts held

CCP
Secretary of Hubei Province CP

Military
Major-general
Deputy political commissar of Wuhan Military Region
Member of the Standing Committee, CP Secretariat of Wuhan Military Region

Pan was born in Jiangxi Province. In 1931 he served in the Political Department of the 1st Front Army in which took part in the Long March. He was head of the Subdepartment of Enemy Work in the Political Department of the 115th Division, 8th Route Army, in 1938. In 1946 he was political commissar of a regiment of the 2nd Division, Northeast China Joint Democratic Field Army. In the following year he served as political commissar of the Logistics Department of a corps of the Northeast Field Army. In 1945 he was appointed deputy political commissar of the Logistics Department, 4th Field Army.

1950   Identified as deputy political commissar of the Logistics Department, 4th Field Army
1954,   Oct   Identified as political commissar of the Central-South China Military Region
1959,   Aug   Identified as military attaché with the rank of major-general at the embassy in Moscow (until summer 1963)
1963,   Sep   Identified as deputy director of the General Office in the Ministry of National Defense
1965,   Jun   Identified as member of the Standing Committee of the Afro-Asian Solidarity Committee (until Cultural Revolution)
1969,   Dec   Identified as deputy political commissar of Wuhan Military Region
1970,   Jun   Identified as vice-chairman of the Revolutionary Committee of Hubei Province
1971,   Mar   Elected secretary of the new CP Secretariat of Hubei Province after the Cultural Revolution (last mention in this post in 1976)
1977,   Jun   Identified as member of the Standing Committee, CP Secretariat of Wuhan Military Region
1978,   Nov   Identified as advisor in Wuhan Military Region

Pei Changhui (P'ei Ch'ang-hui) 裴昌会

Posts held

NPC
Member of the Standing Committee of the 5th NPC
Deputy for Sichuan Province to the 5th NPC

Provincial Administration
Vice-chairman of the People's Congress of Sichuan Province

Others
Vice-chairman of the Central Committee, Revolutionary Committee of the Chinese KMT

Pei was born in 1899 in Shandong Province. He went over to the Communists in 1949 as commander of the 7th Army Group and concurrently deputy commander of the Sichuan-Shaanxi-Gansu Border Regional Pacification Command under the Nationalist Government.

1950,   Mar   Identified as vice-chairman of North Sichuan Administrative Office
         Jul   Identified as member of the Southwest Military and Administrative Council
1953,   Jan   Identified as member of the Southwest Administrative Council
1954,   Aug   Elected deputy for Sichuan Province to the 1st NPC (reelected in 1958 and 1964 to the 2nd and 3rd NPCs)
         Sep   Appointed member of the National Defense Council
1955,   Sep   Awarded the order "Liberation," 1st class
1956,   Mar   Elected member of the Central Committee, Revolutionary Committee of the Chinese KMT
1958,   Sep   Identified as deputy mayor of Chongqing
1967   Disappears during the Cultural Revolution
1978,   Feb   First appearance after the Cultural Revolution: Elected deputy for Sichuan Province to the 5th NPC
         Mar   Elected member of the Standing Committee of the 5th NPC
1979,   Jun   Member of the Budget Committee at the 2nd Session of the 5th NPC
         Oct   Elected vice-chairman of the Central Committee, Revolutionary Committee of the Chinese KMT
         Dec   Elected vice-chairman of the People's Congress of Sichuan Province

Pei Jianzhang (P'ei Chien-chang)

Posts held

Government
Ambassador to Libya

Pei was born in 1927 in Shandong Province.

1971,   May   Identified as acting chargé d'affaires in Great Britain
1973,   May   Appointed ambassador to New Zealand (until Apr 1979)
1976,   May   Pei accompanies the prime minister of New Zealand on his visit to China
1977,   Oct   Appointed ambassador to Papua New Guinea (until Apr 1979)
1979,   Sep   Appointed ambassador to Libya

Pei is married to Pan Jin.

Pei Lisheng (P'ei Li-sheng) 裴丽生

Posts held

Others
Vice-chairman of the Science and Technology Association

Pei was born in 1907 in Yuanzu, Shanxi Province. He graduated from Qinghua University and later studied at Moscow University. He joined the CCP at a young age. As a middle school teacher in Shanxi, he became active in 1936 in the Sacrifice for National Salvation League established by Yan Xishan. Around 1939 he went to Yan'an, initially as a cadre in the Social Affairs Department of the CCP Central Committee. In 1946 he was appointed director of the Shanyin (Daiyue) Administrative Office and in early 1949 mayor of Taiyuan.

1949,	Dec	Identified as vice-chairman of Shanxi
1950,	Aug	Identified as director of the Industry Department of Shanxi People's Government
1952,	Mar	Identified as governor of Shanxi Province (until 1957)
1953,	Dec	Identified as 2nd secretary of Shanxi Province CP (until 1957)
1956,	Mar	Identified as member of the State Scientific Planning Commission
1958,	Apr	Identified as secretary-general of the Academy of Sciences
	Dec	Elected member of the Standing Committee of the Jiusan Society (until Cultural Revolution)
1959,	Apr	Identified as vice-president of the Stratigraphy Society
1960,	Feb	Head of a delegation of the Academy of Sciences to the USSR
	Aug	Appointed vice-president of the Academy of Sciences (until Cultural Revolution)
1964,	Oct	Elected deputy for Shanxi Province to the 3rd NPC
1966,	Apr	Head of a delegation of scientists to Albania
1967,	Feb	Branded as a "three-anti element" and purged
1978,	Apr	First appearance after the Cultural Revolution: Identified as vice-chairman of the Science and Technology Association
1979,	May	Head of a science and technology delegation to the U.S.A.

Pei Wenzhong (P'ei Wen-chung) 裴文中

Posts held

Others
Deputy director-general of the Society of Archaeology

Pei was born in 1904 in Gu'an County, Hebei Province. He graduated from Beijing University and subsequently continued his studies at the Paris Research Institute of Ancient Creatures and at London University. Having returned to China, he conducted archaeological excavations in Northern China where he discovered the skull of the Peking Man near Zhoukoudian, Beijing Municipality. In 1934 he was appointed a research fellow of the Geological Research Institute of the Academia Sinica. He concurrently served as head of the excavation site of Zhoukoudian. In 1935 he returned to London University for further research. In 1949 he took part in the World Peace Congress meeting in Paris.

1949,	Oct	Appointed council member of the Sino-Soviet Friendship Association
1950,	Apr	Identified as council member of the People's Government of Hebei Province
	Aug	Identified as council member of the Federation for Dissemination of Science and Technology
1952,	Jun	Identified as member of the Committee for Higher Education of the North China Administrative Council
1953,	Mar	Elected council member of the Jiusan Society
1955,	May	Identified as member of the Department of Biology, Geology and Geography of the Academy of Sciences
	Jun	Identified as council member of the Sino-Indonesian Friendship Association
1956,	Feb	Identified as director of the Institute for Vertebrate Paleontology and Paleo-Anthropology of the Academy of Sciences
1958,	Jan	Appointed honorary member of the Royal British Anthropological Institute
1966		Pei disappears
1973,	Mar	First appearance after the Cultural Revolution
1979,	Apr	Elected deputy director-general of the Society of Archaeology

Pei Xianbai (P'ei Hsien-pai) 裴先白

Posts held

NPC
Deputy for Shanghai Municipality to the 5th NPC

Provincial Administration
Vice-mayor of Shanghai Municipality

Others
Director of the Board of Directors, China International Trust and Investment Corporation

1978,	Feb	Elected deputy for Shanghai Municipality to the 5th NPC
	May	Identified as vice-chairman of the Revolutionary Committee of Shanghai Municipality (until Dec 1979)
1979,	Oct	Appointed director of the Board of Directors, China International Trust and Investment Corporation
	Dec	Elected vice-mayor of Shanghai Municipality

Peng Chong (P'eng Ch'ung) 彭 冲

Posts held

CCP
Member of the Politburo of the CCP
11th Central Committee
Member of the CCP 11th Central Committee
Member of the Secretariat, CCP
11th Central Committee

NPC
Deputy for Shanghai to the 5th NPC

Provincial Administration
Mayor of Shanghai Municipality

Others
Vice-president of the 5th CPPCC

Peng was born in 1915 in Zhangzhou, Fujian Province. He joined the Communist Youth League in 1933 and CCP the following year. At the beginning of the 1930s he engaged in underground Party work. During the Anti-Japanese War, he took part in building some base areas in Southern Jiangsu. In 1938 he was appointed political commissar of a regiment in the New 4th Army and later as deputy political commissar of a division.

1950		Identified as director of the United Front Work Department of Fujian Province CP
	Nov	Elected vice-chairman of the People's Government of Fujian Province
1951,	Sep	Council member of the People's Government of Fujian Province (until Aug 1954)
1955,	Jun	Identified as mayor of Nanjing Municipality (until Dec 1959)
	Aug	Identified as 1st secretary of Nanjing Municipality CP (until 1960)
1958,	Nov	Elected deputy for Jiangsu Province to the 2nd NPC (confirmed in 1964 to the 3rd NPC)
1959,	Jan	Identified as member of the Standing Committee of Jiangsu Province CP (until May 1960)
1960,	May	Identified as alternate member of the Secretariat of Jiangsu Province CP (until Aug 1965)
	Oct	Identified as vice-chairman of the Jiangsu Section of the CPPCC
1961,	Jul	Identified as vice-chairman of the Jiangsu Branch of the Sino-Soviet Friendship Association (until Cultural Revolution)
1962,	Jul	Again identified as 1st secretary of Nanjing Municipality CP
	Sep	Head of a friendship delegation of Jiangsu Province to the USSR
1965,	Aug	Identified as secretary of Jiangsu Province CP (until about 1967)
1968,	Mar	With the establishment of the Revolutionary Committee of Jiangsu Province, Peng is elected vice-chairman (until Dec 1974)
1969,	Apr	Elected alternate member of the CCP Central Committee by the 9th Party Congress
1970,	Dec	Elected deputy secretary of the new CP Secretariat of Jiangsu Province after the Cultural Revolution (until Feb 1975)
1974,	Dec	Identified as chairman of the Revolutionary Committee of Jiangsu Province (until Nov 1976)
1975,	Feb	Identified as 1st secretary of Jiangsu Province CP (until Nov 1976)
1976,	Dec	Appointed 3rd secretary of the CP, and 2nd vice-chairman of the Revolutionary Committee, of Shanghai Municipality (until Dec 1978)
1977,	Jun	Identified as 2nd political commissar of Nanjing Military Region (until Feb 1980)
	Aug	Elected member of the CCP Central Committee and member of its Politburo by the 11th Party Congress
	Dec	Article in HQ: "Make Full Use of and Actively Develop Shanghai's Industry so as to Make Still Greater Contributions to the Realization of the Four Modernizations"
1978,	Feb	Elected deputy for Shanghai to the 5th NPC
	Mar	Elected vice-president of the 5th CPPCC
	Sep	Deputy head of a Party and government delegation to North Korea under Deng Xiaoping
	Oct	Identified as head of the CCP Central Committee's Anti-schistosomiasis Leading Group
1979,	Jan	Identified as 1st secretary of the CP (until Feb 1980), and chairman of the Revolutionary Committee, of Shanghai Municipality (latter post until Dec 1979)
	Feb	Identified as 1st secretary of the Shanghai Garrison Command CP Committee (until Feb 1980)
	Jun	Head of a Shanghai delegation to the Federal Republic of Germany, Spain and Italy
	Dec	Elected mayor of Shanghai Municipality (until Feb 1980)
1980,	Feb	Elected member of the newly set up Secretariat under the CCP 11th Central Committee

Peng is married to Luo Ping.

Peng Deqing (P'eng Te-ch'ing) 彭德清

Posts held

Government
Vice-minister of communications

Military
Rear-admiral

Peng was born in 1915 in Jiangxi Province. He joined the CCP at a young age. In 1942 he was political commissar of a regiment of the New 4th Army which was conducting guerrilla war in Jiangsu Province. He was appointed director of the Political Department of the 10th Brigade, 6th Division, New 4th Army, in late 1945. In 1947 he commanded the 12th Division of the East China Field Army.

| 1951, | Jan | Appointed deputy commander of the 22nd Army, 3rd Field Army |
| 1954 | | Identified as commander of the 27th Army, 3rd Field Army |

1956, Jun Identified as rear-admiral and as deputy commander of the East China Sea Fleet (until 1965)

1959 Identified as commander of Xiamen Naval Base in Fujian Province

1960 Identified as commander of the Navy Unit 1072

1965, Apr Identified as vice-minister of communications

1966, Apr Head of a shipping delegation to Albania to the 5th Session of the Administrative Council, Joint Sino-Albanian Shipping Corporation

1967 Disappears during the Cultural Revolution

1975, Sep First appearance after the Cultural Revolution

Oct Identified as holding his former post as vice-minister of communications

1976, Apr Head of a shipping delegation to Albania to the 11th Session of the Administrative Council, Joint Stock Sino-Albanian Shipping Company

1979, Apr Head of a shipping delegation to the U.S.A.

Peng Dixian (P'eng Ti-hsien) 彭迪先

Posts held

NPC
Deputy for Sichuan Province to the 5th NPC

Provincial Administration
Vice-governor of Sichuan Province

Others
Member of the Standing Committee of the 5th CPPCC
Vice-chairman of the Central Committee of the China Democratic League

Peng was born in 1909 in Meishan, Sichuan Province. After graduating from Kyushu Imperial University in Japan he worked as an assistant in the Economics Department of that university. There he translated Kanae Hatano's On Modern Economics into Chinese. In 1945 he joined the China Democratic League and became chairman of its West Sichuan Committee.

1950, Jan Identified as member of the Cultural and Educational Committee of Southwest Military and Administrative Council

1952, Aug Identified as member of the Sichuan People's Government Committee

1953, Jan Identified as president of Sichuan University (until 1961)

1954, Oct Elected deputy of Sichuan Province to the 1st NPC (reelected in 1958 and 1964 to the 2nd and 3rd NPCs)

1956, Feb Elected member of the Central Committee of the China Democratic League

1959, Sep Identified as chairman of the Sichuan Branch, China Democratic League

1965, Sep Identified as vice-chairman of the Sichuan Branch of the CPPCC

1967 Disappears during the Cultural Revolution

1978, Feb First appearance after the Cultural Revolution: Elected deputy for Sichuan Province to the 5th NPC

Mar Elected member of the Standing Committee of the 5th CPPCC

1979, Jun Member of the Committee to Examine Proposals at the 2nd Session of the 5th NPC

Oct Elected vice-chairman of the Central Committee of the China Democratic League

Dec Elected vice-governor of Sichuan Province

Peng Guangwei (P'eng Kuang-wei) 彭光伟

Posts held

Government
Ambassador to Nepal

1962, Sep Identified as chairman of the Trade Unions of Sichuan Province

1963, Apr Head of a trade union delegation to Hungary

1964, Oct Elected deputy for Sichuan Province to the 3rd NPC

1972, Jun Appointed ambassador to the German Democratic Republic (until Nov 1977)

1978, Oct Appointed ambassador to Nepal

Peng is married to Cai Guilan.

Peng Hua (P'eng Hua) 彭华

Posts held

Government
Ambassador to Guinea

1960, Jan Identified as deputy director of the Cultural Office of Yunnan Province; deputy head of a cultural delegation to Burma

1961, May Advisor to the Chinese delegation at the Laos Conference in Geneva

Jun Press official in Geneva

1964, Sep Identified as acting director of the Cultural Office of Yunnan Province

1971, Jun Identified as deputy director of the Information Department of the Ministry of Foreign Affairs (until Oct 1972)

1972, Oct Identified as director of the Information Department of the Ministry of Foreign Affairs (until Aug 1974)

1973, Feb Member of the Chinese delegation to the Vietnam Conference in Paris

1977, Jan Appointed ambassador to Guinea

Peng Mengyu (P'eng Meng-yü) 彭梦庚

Posts held

NPC
Deputy for Jiangxi Province to the 5th NPC

Provincial Administration
Vice-chairman of the People's Government, Inner Mongolia Autonomous Region

1955,	Feb	Identified as member of the People's Council of Jiangxi Province
1957,	Oct	Identified as secretary-general of the People's Council of Jiangxi Province
1958,	Jun	Elected vice-governor of Jiangxi Province (until Jan 1968)
1968		Disappears during the Cultural Revolution
1977,	May	First appearance after the Cultural Revolution: Identified as deputy secretary-general of Jiangxi Province CP; head of a friendship delegation to Romania
	Sep	Identified as member of the Standing Committee of the CP, and as vice-chairman of the Revolutionary Committee, of Jiangxi Province
1978,	Feb	Elected deputy for Jiangxi Province to the 5th NPC
	Oct	Last appearance in Jiangxi Province
1979,	Dec	Elected vice-chairman of the People's Government, Inner Mongolia Autonomous Region

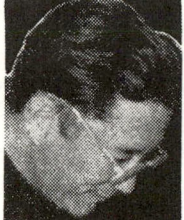

Peng Min (P'eng Min)   彭 敏

Posts held

Government
Vice-minister of the Capital Construction Commission

Peng joined the CCP at a young age. In 1948 he repaired a bridge across the Sunghua Jiang (Sungari) with the help of Soviet advisers as commander of a railway corps unit of the PLA. Shortly afterwards he supervised the repair of the important railway links between Siping and Changchun and between Tianjin and Bukou.

1950		Appointed commander of the PLA Railway Corps. For two years commander of the PLA units of the Railway Corps serving in the Korean War
1951		Severely wounded in action in Korea
until 1953		Hospitalized
1954,	Jun	Appointed director of the Construction Bureau for the Chang Jiang Bridge near Wuhan
1958,	Oct	Appointed vice-chairman of the Committee for Construction of the Chang Jiang Bridge near Nanjing
1960,	Apr	Identified as head of the Engineering Bureau for the Construction of the Huang He Bridge
1963,	May	Appointed vice-chairman of the Science and Technology Commission under the State Council (until Cultural Revolution)
1966		Disappears during the Cultural Revolution
1972,	Apr	First appearance after the Cultural Revolution: Identified as vice-minister of communications (until Dec 1975)
1975,	Dec	Identified as vice-minister of the Capital Construction Commission
1978,	May	Member of a government delegation led by Gu Mu to France, Switzerland, Belgium, Denmark, Federal Republic of Germany

Peng Mingzhi (P'eng Ming-chih)   彭明治

Posts held

NPC
Member of the Standing Committee of the 5th NPC
Deputy for the PLA to the 5th NPC

In 1940 Peng was commander of the Jiangsu-Shandong-Henan Detachment. In 1945 he served as brigade commander in the 3rd Division of the New 4th Army.

1950,	Jan	Identified as commander of Nanning Garrison
	Mar	Identified as council member of the People's Government of Guangxi Province
	Jul	Appointed ambassador to Poland (until Sep 1952)
1955		Identified as commander of Wuhan Garrison
1959,	Apr	Elected member of the 3rd CPPCC (confirmed in 1964 by the 4th CPPCC)
1969,	Oct	Identified as military leader in Beijing
1974,	Aug	Identified as head of the Intelligence Subdepartment of the PLA General Staff
1978,	Feb	Elected deputy for the PLA to the 5th NPC
	Mar	Elected member of the Standing Committee of the 5th NPC

Peng Zhen (P'eng Chen)   彭 真

Posts held

CCP
Member of the Politburo, 11th Central Committee
Member of the CCP 11th Central Committee

NPC
Vice-chairman of the Standing Committee, 5th NPC
Acting secretary-general of the Standing Committee, 5th NPC
Chairman of the Legal Commission, 5th NPC
Deputy for Beijing Municipality to the 5th NPC

Peng was born in 1902 in Shanxi Province as the son of a poor peasant. After great hardship during his youth he first had an opportunity to attend middle school at the age of 21. At this time he also joined the Communist Youth League. Shortly afterwards he served as a cadre of labor organizations in his native province and temporarily as secretary of the Trade Union. In 1923 he was arrested. He joined the CCP in 1923. In 1936 he was a member of the North China Bureau of the CCP Central Committee. After further imprisonment he served as political commissar of the 115th Division, 8th Route Army, in 1937. Peng was subsequently entrusted with organizational tasks, first in Shanxi-Chahar-Hebei Border Region and later in Hebei-Rehe-Liaoning Border Region. At this time he served concurrently as secretary of the North China Bureau of the CCP Central Committee. In 1945 Peng was elected a member of the CCP Central Committee by the 7th Party Congress in Yan'an. At the end of the Anti-

Japanese War he was posted to Manchuria to serve under Lin Biao as political commissar. At this time he was appointed concurrently director of the Northeast Bureau of the CCP Central Committee. In September 1949 Peng was elected a member of the National Committee of the CPPCC.

1949, Oct Appointed member of the Central Government Administration Council and vice-chairman of the Political and Legislative Council of the Government Administration Council. Identified as secretary of Beijing Municipality CP

1950, Jul Elected vice-chairman of the Peace Council (until Jul 1958)

1951, Oct Elected mayor of Beijing; by-elected member of the Politburo of the CCP Central Committee

1954, Sep Elected vice-chairman and secretary-general (until Jan 1965) of the Standing Committee of the NPC; elected deputy for Beijing Municipality to the 1st NPC

Dec Elected vice-chairman of the CPPCC

1955 Identified as 1st secretary of Beijing Municipality CP (until Jun 1966)

1956, Sep Elected member, Secretariat of the CCP Central Committee

Nov Head of a delegation to the USSR and several Eastern European countries

1960, Jun Head of a Party delegation to Romania
Nov Head of a Party delegation to Moscow

1961, Oct Member of a Party delegation to the 22nd Congress of the CPSU

1962, Apr Head of an NPC delegation to North Korea

Sep Head of an NPC delegation to North Vietnam

1963, Jul Deputy head of a CCP delegation for ideological discussions in Moscow

1964, Nov Head of a planned CCP delegation to Japan (entry permit refused by the Japanese authorities)

1965, May Head of a CCP and NPC delegation to Indonesia for the 45th anniversary of the CPI

1966, Jun Peng is replaced by Li Xuefeng as 1st secretary of Beijing Municipality CP

Dec Peng disappears after several criticism sessions

1979, Jan First appearance after the Cultural Revolution

Feb Appointed chairman of the Legal Commission under the NPC Standing Committee

May By-elected deputy for Beijing Municipality to the 5th NPC

Jul By-elected vice-chairman of the Standing Committee, 5th NPC

Sep By-elected member of the CCP 11th Central Committee and its Politburo

Nov Appointed acting secretary-general, Standing Committee of the 5th NPC; article in HQ: "Some Questions on the Socialist Legal System"

Ping Jiesan (P'ing Chieh-san)   平杰三

Posts held

CCP
Deputy director, United Front Work Department of the CCP Central Committee
Member of the Commission for Inspecting Discipline of the CCP Central Committee

Government
Member of the State Nationalities Affairs Commission

Others
Member of the Standing Committee of the 5th CPPCC

Ping was born in 1903 in Hebei Province. He is a graduate of Beijing University and later studied at the Sun Yat-sen University in Moscow.

1951, Apr Identified as director of the United Front Work Department, North China Bureau of the CCP Central Committee

1954, Aug Elected deputy for Hebei Province to the 1st NPC

1956, Apr Identified as deputy director, United Front Work Department of the CCP Central Committee (until Cultural Revolution)

1959, Apr Elected member of the Standing Committee of the 3rd CPPCC (confirmed in 1965 by the 4th CPPCC)

1965, Jan Elected secretary-general of the 4th CPPCC

1967, Jan Branded as a counterrevolutionary revisionist and purged

1978, Dec First appearance after the Cultural Revolution: Elected member of the Commission for Inspecting Discipline of the CCP Central Committee

1979, Jan Identified as deputy director, United Front Work Department of the CCP Central Committee and as member of the State Nationalities Affairs Commission

Jul By-elected member of the Standing Committee of the 5th CPPCC

Qi Shouliang (Ch'i Shou-liang) 齐寿良

Posts held

CCP
1st CP secretary of Changsha Municipality

NPC
Deputy for Hunan Province to the 5th NPC

Provincial Administration
Vice-chairman of the People's Congress of Hunan Province

Others
Vice-chairman of the Revolutionary Committee of Changsha Municipality

1959, Mar Identified as 1st CP secretary of the Autonomous Zhou West Hunan

1977, Mar Identified as 1st CP secretary and chairman of the Revolutionary Committee of Changsha Municipality

Dec Identified as vice-chairman of the Revolutionary Committee of Hunan Province (until Dec 1979)

1978, Feb Elected deputy for Hunan Province to the 5th NPC

May Deputy head of an agricultural delegation to Japan

1979, Dec Elected vice-chairman of the People's Congress of Hunan Province

Qi Tao (Ch'i T'ao) 齐涛

Posts held

Others
Vice-president of the Academy of Medical Sciences

1978, Nov Identified as vice-president of the Academy of Medical Sciences

Qi Tian (Ch'i T'ien) 祁田

Posts held

Government
Vice-minister of the 1st Ministry of Machine Building

1978, Apr Identified as vice-minister of the 1st Ministry of Machine Building; head of an engineering delegation to Yugoslavia

Qi Zisheng (Ch'i Tzu-sheng) 齐子升

Posts held

NPC
Member of the Standing Committee of the 5th NPC
Deputy for Tianjin Municipality to the 5th NPC

1978, Feb Elected deputy for Tianjin Municipality to the 5th NPC

Mar Elected member of the Standing Committee of the 5th NPC

Apr Identified as a steel worker at Steel Plant No. 1 in Tianjin

Qi Zonghua (Ch'i Tsung-hua) 齐崇华

Posts held

Government
Deputy director of the Western Europe Department in the Ministry of Foreign Affairs

1964, Dec Member of a peace council delegation to Italy

1973, Sep Member of the Chinese delegation to the 28th UN General Assembly

1974, Sep Member of the Chinese delegation to the 29th UN General Assembly

1975, Apr Identified as deputy director of the Western Europe Department in the Ministry of Foreign Affairs

May Member of a government delegation under Deng Xiaoping to France

1978, Sep Qi accompanies the minister of foreign affairs Huang Hua to Greece

Qian Changzhao (Ch'ien Ch'ang-chao) 钱昌照

Posts held

Others
Member of the Standing Committee of the 5th CPPCC
Vice-chairman of the Central Committee, Revolutionary Committee of the Kuomintang
Director of the Board of Directors, China International Trust and Investment Corporation

Qian was born in 1900 in Zhangsu County, Jiangsu Province. He studied at London University and Oxford University. After his return to China he became an official in the Nationalist Government in 1928. From 1931 to 1932 he was vice-minister of education, from 1932 to 1934 deputy secretary-general of the Planning Committee of the National Defense Council, then until 1938 deputy secretary-general of the National Resources Commission in the same council. At the end of 1938 he was appointed vice-chairman of the National Resources Commission in the Ministry of Economics. In 1945 he was elected alternate member of the Executive Committee of the 6th KMT Central Committee. One year later he became chairman of the National Resources Commission. In September 1949 he accepted an invitation by the Communists to attend the 1st CPPCC as a specially invited delegate. The conference elected him a member of its National Committee.

1949, Oct Appointed member of the Financial and Economic Committee in the Government Administration Council

Dec Identified as deputy director of the Planning Bureau in the Financial and Economic Committee

1954, Sep Elected deputy for Shandong Province to the 1st NPC (reelected to the 2nd and 3rd NPCs)

1956, Feb Elected member of the Central Committee, Revolutionary Committee of the KMT

1958, Dec Elected member of the Standing Committee, Central Committee of the KMT Revolutionary Committee

1967 Disappears

1971, May First appearance attending the mourning ceremony for Li Siguang

1972, Sep Renewed mention as member of the Standing Committee of the KMT Revolutionary Committee

1978, Mar Elected member of the Standing Committee of the 5th CPPCC

1979, Oct Elected vice-chairman of the Central Committee, Revolutionary Committee of the Chinese KMT; appointed director of the Board of Directors, China International Trust and Investment Corporation

Qian is married to Shen Xingyuan.

Qian Chuanjun (Ch'ien Ch'uan-chün)

 钱傅钧

Posts held

Government
Vice-minister of metallugical industry

1976, Jan Identified as a government cadre
1978, Jul Identified as vice-minister of metallugical industry

Qian Junrui (Ch'ien Chün-jui)   钱俊瑞

Posts held

Others
Director of the Institute of World Economics, Academy of Social Sciences
Advisor of the Society for the Study of the Future

Qian was born in 1903 in Wuxi, Jiangsu Province. He studied at the College of Education in Jiangsu and, after graduation, in Japan. He joined the CCP in 1926. In 1934 he became a member of the Institute of Chinese Agricultural Research where he was chief editor of two scientific journals. During the Anti-Japanese War he at first worked as a writer in Shanghai and later as a culture and propaganda worker in the New 4th Army. During the final phase of the war he was head of the Control Committee for Cultural Affairs in the Central China Bureau of the CCP Central Committee. From 1946 to 1947 he was head of the Beijing News Agency Xinhua (NCNA) and concurrently served in the communist section of the headquarters of representatives of the CCP, KMT and the Americans trying to negotiate a settlement. After Beijing had been occupied by the Communists in spring 1949, Qian became head of the Culture and Education Bureau of the Beijing Military Control Commission. He was concurrently dean of the North China University and vice-chairman of the Higher Education Commission in the North China People's Government. In May 1949 he was elected vice-chairman of the Democratic Youth League. In June of that year he took part as China representative in the 2nd Congress of the World Federation of Trade Unions in Warsaw.

1949, Oct Appointed vice-minister of education and member of the Committee of Cultural and Educational Affairs in the Government Administration Council

Dec? Appointed secretary-general of the Sino-Soviet Friendship Association (until 1960?)

1953, Mar Member of the government delegation attending the funeral ceremonies for Stalin in Moscow

1954, Apr Head of a friendship delegation to the USSR

Sep Elected deputy for Jiangsu Province to the 1st NPC (until Dec 1964)

Oct Confirmed as vice-minister of culture (until Sep 1963); appointed deputy director of the 2nd Office, State Council (until Sep 1959)

1955, Jun Appointed member of the Department of Philosophy and Social Sciences, Academy of Sciences

1956, Jul Head of a cultural delegation to Moscow; Qian signs an agreement on cultural cooperation

Sep Elected alternate member of the CCP Central Committee by the 8th Party Congress

1957, Oct Deputy head of a Party delegation attending the 40th anniversary celebrations of the October Revolution in Moscow

1959, Sep Appointed deputy director of the Office of Culture and Education (until Jul 1959)

Nov Member of a Party delegation attending the October Revolution celebrations in Moscow

1960, Feb Appointed member of the Spare-time Education Committee

1964, Dec Special delegate at the CPPCC

1967, Jun Branded as a capitalist-roader and purged

1979, Jan First appearance after the Cultural Revolution: Identified as director of the Institute of World Economics of the Academy of Social Sciences

Feb Qian attends the 9th Annual Symposium of the European Management Forum in Davos, Switzerland

Mar Appointed advisor of the Society for the Study of the Future

Qian Liren (Ch'ien Li-jen)    钱李仁

Posts held

Government
Permanent delegate to UNESCO

1953, Jun Identified as deputy secretary-general of the Federation of Democratic Youth and as member of the Central Committee of the New Democratic Youth League

	Jul	Member of a delegation to the 4th World Festival of Youth and Students in Bucharest
1956,	May	Identified as secretary-general of the Students' Federation
	Jun	Head of a students' delegation to the Afro-Asian Students' Conference in Indonesia
1957,	Jul	Member of a delegation to the 6th World Youth Festival in Moscow
1958,	Apr	Elected member of the Standing Committee of the Federation of Youth (successor of the Federation of Democratic Youth)
	Sep	Identified as member of the Sino-Iraq Friendship Association
1959,	May	Identified as director of the International Liaison Department of the Communist Youth League
1960,	Apr	Head of a youth delegation to Cuba
1961,	Feb	Head of a youth delegation to Finland and Sweden
	Jul	Deputy head of a youth delegation to Moscow
	Nov	Head of a students' delegation to Czechoslovakia
1962,	Aug	Deputy head of a delegation to the 8th World Festival of Youth and Students in Helsinki
1963,	Oct	Head of a students' delegation to Algeria
1964,	Jan	Head of a youth delegation to Mali, Ghana, Senegal, Tanganyika, Kenya, and Somalia (until Feb)
1965,	May	Member of a delegation to the 4th Afro-Asian Solidarity Conference in Winneba, Ghana
	Jul	Member of a delegation to the 2nd World Conference against Atomic Bombs in Japan
1966,	Jan	Member of a delegation to the Afro-Asian-Latin American People's Solidarity Conference in Cuba
1967		Disappears during the Cultural Revolution
1974,	Aug	First appearance after the Cultural Revolution: Member of a friendship delegation to Romania
1975,	Apr	Identified as member of the Standing Committee of the Association for Friendship with Foreign Countries
1978,	Feb	Identified as permanent delegate to UNESCO
	Jul	Member of the Chinese delegation to the 4th UNESCO Regional Conference on Asia and Oceania in Sri Lanka

Qian Min (Ch'ien Min)　　　钱　敏

Posts held

Government
Minister of the 4th Ministry of Machine Building

1977,	Dec	Elected vice-chairman of the Revolutionary Committee of Sichuan Province (until Jul 1978)
1978,	Apr	Elected 1st secretary, CP of Chongqing Municipality (until Jul 1978)

	Aug	Appointed minister of the 4th Ministry of Machine Building
	Nov	Head of a delegation of the 4th Ministry of Machine Building to France

Qian Qichen (Ch'ien Ch'i-ch'en)　钱其琛

Posts held

Government
Director of the Information Department of the Ministry of Foreign Affairs

1960,	Feb	2nd secretary, embassy in the USSR (until 1962)
1974,	Aug	Ambassador to Guinea (until Nov 1976)
	Sep	Appointed concurrently ambassador to Guinea Bissau (until Oct 1975)
1977,	Jan	Identified as director of the Information Department in the Ministry of Foreign Affairs
1978,	Aug	Deputy head of a journalists delegation to U.S.A.
1979,	Aug	Head of a journalists delegation to the Netherlands, Denmark and Greece

Qian Renyuan (Ch'ien Jen-yüan)　钱人元

Posts held

Others
Deputy director of the Institute of Chemistry, Academy of Sciences

1959,	Nov	Identified as professor of chemistry, Academy of Sciences
1964,	Oct	Elected deputy for Jiangxi Province to the 3rd NPC
1972,	Oct	Member of a delegation of scientists to Great Britain
1975,	Sep	Member of a study group on molecular crystals visiting Japan
1978,	Feb	Qian is commended for outstanding scientific achievements
1979,	Mar	Identified as deputy director of the Institute of Chemistry, Academy of Sciences

Qian Sanqiang (Ch'ien San-ch'iang)　钱三强

Posts held

NPC
Deputy for Tianjin Municipality to the 5th NPC

Others
Vice-president of the Academy of Sciences
Vice-president of the Physics Society
President of Zhejiang University

Qian was born in 1912 in Shaoxing (or Wuxing), Zhejiang Province. His father, Qian Xuontong, was an historian and one of the leaders of the "May Fourth Movement" of 1919. He was also a well-known contributor to the journal Xin Qingnian (New Youth).

Qian studied physics at Qinghua University in Beijing, graduating in 1936. During the following year he did research in the Physics Department in the Academia Sinica. Having won a Chinese government scholarship, he went to France at the end of 1937 together with his wife, Dr. He Cehui, who had obtained her doctorate at the University of Shanghai. From 1937 to 1944 he studied nuclear physics at the prestigeous Curie Institute in Paris. In 1943 he received a doctorate in physics from the University of Paris. From 1946 to 1947 he continued his studies at the French Academy of Sciences under Professor Joliot-Curie. He was awarded the 1946 Physics Prize of the French Academy of Sciences for a new technique for fission of uranium atoms he had discovered together with his wife. During the same year he served as advisor to the Chinese Nationalist Government Delegation to the Paris UNESCO Conference and was appointed to the board of directors of the (communist) World Federation of Scientific Workers. In 1948 Qian returned to China to assume a professorship in nuclear physics at Qinghua University.

He remained in Beijing when the capital was occupied by Communist forces in 1949. In April of that year he was a member of the Communist delegation to the World Peace Congress in Prague. In May he was elected a member of the Standing Committee of the Federation of Democratic Youth (shortly afterwards he was elected a member of the Communist World Federation of Democratic Youth; until 1958).

In June 1949 he became a member of the Preparatory Committee for a Conference of Chinese National Scientists. In September 1949 Qian took part in the 1st CPPCC.

1949,	Oct	Appointed member of the Executive Council of the Sino-Soviet Friendship Association; appointed member of the Cultural and Educational Committee in the Government Administration Council
1950,	Jun	Identified as director of the Physics Department of Qinghua University; appointed deputy director, Planning Bureau of the Academy of Sciences, and deputy director of the Institute of Modern Physics
	Nov	Member of the Chinese delegation to the 2nd World Peace Conference in Warsaw and to the World Youth Conference in Vienna (According to Le Figaro, 12 May 1966, Qian and his wife conducted extensive field research in 1950 for the exploration of uranium deposits and other radioactive minerals in China, mainly in Xinjiang and Manchuria)
1951,	Mar	Identified as director of the Institute of Modern Physics, Academy of Sciences (in 1958 this institute was renamed Institute of Atomic Energy)
1953,	Jan	Elected vice-chairman of the Physics Society
	Mar	Member of the Chinese delegation to the funeral ceremonies for Stalin; member of the Chinese delegation to the Oslo session of the World Peace Council; visit to Sweden
	May	Member of the Chinese delegation to the session of the (Communist) World Federation of Scientific Workers

	Dec	Member of the Chinese delegation to the Vienna session of the World Peace Council
1953,	Feb-May	Head of a delegation of 26 Academy of Sciences representatives to Moscow to promote scientific cooperation between China and the USSR (Qian's stay in Moscow coincides with the death of Stalin; Qian is a member of the delegation headed by Zhou Enlai to attend the funeral)
	Jun	Elected member of the World Peace Council
1954,	Apr	Appointed secretary-general of the Academy of Sciences (until May 1961)
	Aug	Elected deputy for Shandong Province to the 1st NPC
1955,	Oct	Appointed member of the Mathematics, Physics and Chemistry Department of the Academy of Sciences
1956,	Mar	Appointed member of the State Council Commission for Scientific Planning; delegate in Moscow at a Communist Block Conference for the establishment of the nuclear research centre in Dubna (near Moscow)
1957,	May	Reports to the Academy of Sciences on China's contribution to the nuclear research center in Dubna (this implies Qian's own substantial participation in the project)
	Jun	In the course of a rectification campaign, Qian attacks several scientists, among them nuclear physicist Qian Weichang, who is subsequently denounced as a rightist deviationist
	Nov	Member of a workers delegation to Moscow to celebrate the 40th anniversary of the October Revolution
1958,	Aug	Appointed director of the Institute of Atomic Energy, Academy of Sciences
	Sep	Appointed member of the Scientific and Technical Association
1960,	Dec	Represents the PRC at a conference of the eleven Communist countries participating in the nuclear research center in Dubna
1961,	May	Appointed deputy secretary-general of the Academy of Sciences (until May 1964)
1964,	Sep	Elected deputy for Heilongjiang Province to the 3rd NPC
1968		In the course of the Cultural Revolution Qian is criticized as a "capitalist-roader" and as a "secret agent"
1973,	Apr	First appearance after the Cultural Revolution
1975,	Oct	Identified as secretary-general of the Academy of Sciences
	Nov	Identified as again holding the post of director, Institute of Atomic Energy, Academy of Sciences (until Sep 1978)
1977,	Jun	Head of an Academy of Sciences delegation to Australia
	Dec	Head of an Academy of Sciences delegation to Romania and Yugoslavia
1978,	Feb	Elected deputy for Tianjin Municipality to the 5th NPC
	Mar	Appointed vice-president of the Academy of Sciences

Jun Head of a delegation of the Academy of Sciences to Belgium and France

Aug Identified as vice-president of the Physics Society

1979, Jan Identified as member of the Department for Mathematics, Physics and Chemistry, Academy of Sciences

Feb Appointed president of Zhejiang University

Mar Appointed deputy director of the Committee for the Promotion of International Measurement

Jun Member of the Committee to Examine Proposals at the 2nd Session, 5th NPC

Qian is married to He Cehui.

Qian Weichang (Ch'ien Wei-ch'ang) 钱伟长

Posts held

Others
Professor at Qinghua University

Qian is a nuclear physicist who worked among others at the California Institute of Technology. He is believed to have been an assistant to Qian Xuesen, probably already at California Institute of Technology. He returned to China in 1946. Before the establishment of the PRC he already belonged to several organizations founded by the Communists. In May 1949 he was elected member of the Standing Committee of the Democratic Youth League (until 1958) and one month later member of the Preparatory Committee for the 1st National Conference of Scientific Workers.

1950, Aug Elected member of the Standing Committee of the Federation of Scientific Societies (until Sep 1958)

Dec Identified as dean of studies at Qinghua University in Beijing (until Mar 1955)

1951, Oct Member of a cultural delegation to India and Burma

1952, May Elected vice-chairman of the Sino-Burmese Friendship Association (until Nov 1959)

Sep Identified as deputy director of the Organizations Department, Federation of Scientific Societies (until Sep 1958)

1954, May Elected board member of the Federation for Cultural Relations with Foreign Countries (until 1958)

Aug Elected deputy for Jiangsu Province to the 1st NPC (until Mar 1959)

1955, Jun Identified as member of the Mathematics, Physics and Chemistry Department of the Academy of Sciences

1956, Jun Conferred the title of "Academician" by the Polish Academy of Sciences

Dec Identified as vice-president of Qinghua University (until 1958)

1957, Jan Awarded a 2nd prize of the Academy of Sciences for his paper "Concerning the Question of Major Bending for Elastic Circular and Thin Plate"

Feb Identified as council member of the Mechanics Society

Mar Identified as member of the State Council Commission for Scientific Planning (until Mar 1958)

Jun Qian is one of five professors who signed the article "Some Views on the Question Concerning Our Country's Regulations Governing Science" in GMRB. This was one of the statements encouraged by the just started "One Hundred Flowers Movement" which invited frank criticism. Having gone too far, however, it was stamped as a "Reactionary Science Program", especially because it took the view that laymen should not be permitted to set guidelines for experts

1958 Because of his heretical views Qian is denounced as as rightest deviationist and relieved of all posts

1960, Nov Qian is officially rehabilitated from the charge of rightist deviationism

1972, Jul First appearance after the Cultural Revolution at a reception given by Premier Zhou Enlai for Yang Zhenning (U.S.-Chinese Nobel Prize winner for physics)

Oct Member of a scientific delegation to Great Britain

Qian Xinzhong (Ch'ien Hsin-chung) 钱信忠

Posts held

CCP
Deputy head, Anti-schistosomiasis Leading Group of the CCP Central Committee

Government
Minister of public health

NPC
Member of the Standing Committee of the 5th NPC
Deputy for Shanghai Municipality to the 5th NPC

Others
President of the Chinese Red Cross Society
President of the Medical Association

Qian was born in 1911 in Shanghai. In his youth he studied German. He took part in the 1st CPPCC in Sep 1949 representing the 2nd Field Army.

1950, Jul Identified as director of the Health Department in Southwest China Military Region and as member of the Southwest China Military and Administration Council as well as director of its Health Department (until 1953)

Aug Identified as member of the Standing Committee of the Federation of Scientific Societies (until 1958)

1953, Feb Identified as member of the Southwest China Administrative Council and as director of its Health Department (until Nov 1954)

1955,	Feb	Identified as member of the Medical Research Committee in the Ministry of Public Health
1957,	May	Identified as member of the Scientific Planning Commission of the State Council (until Nov 1958)
	Sep	Appointed vice-minister for public health
	Nov	Member of a scientific-technical delegation to the USSR
1958,	Sep	Identified as member of the Scientific and Technical Association
1959,	Sep	Member of the Chinese section in the Sino-Soviet Committee for Scientific and Technical Cooperation
1961,	Oct	Identified as member of the Executive Council of the Chinese Red Cross Society
1962,	Apr	Deputy head of a health delegation to Cuba
	May	Deputy head of a health delegation to CSSR
	Jul	Head of a delegation to the International Cancer Congress in Moscow
	Sep	Identified as vice-chairman of the China-Ceylon Friendship Association
1963,	Nov	Head of a health delegation to North Korea
1964,	Sep	Elected deputy for Jiangsu Province to the 3rd NPC
	Oct	Head of a medical delegation to Egypt to the 1st Afro-Asian Medical Conference
1965,	Apr	Elected chairman of the Chinese Red Cross Society
1966		Attacked by the Red Guards during the Cultural Revolution
1972,	Dec	Reactivated after the Cultural Revolution
1973,	Dec	Confirmed in the post of vice-minister for public health (until Apr 1979)
1974,	Jan	Head of a medical delegation to Romania
	Oct	Head of a medical delegation to North Vietnam
1975,	Apr	Identified as a cadre in the Chinese Red Cross Society
1978,	Feb	Elected deputy for Shanghai Municipality to the 5th NPC
	Mar	Elected member of the Standing Committee of the 5th NPC; head of a government delegation to Gabon
	Apr	Appointed member of the Committee for Patriotic Health Campaign; identified as president of the Chinese Medical Association
	May	Chief delegate to the 31st World Health Organization (WHO) Conference in Geneva
	Jun	Head of a public health delegation to the Federal Republic of Germany and Great Britain
	Aug	Identified as president of the Red Cross Society
	Oct	Identified as deputy head of the Anti-schistosomiasis Leading Group under the CCP Central Committee
1979,	Jan	Head of a public health delegation to Japan
	Apr	Appointed minister of public health; head of a public health delegation to Denmark
	Sep	Head of a public health delegation to Australia and New Zealand
	Oct	Special envoy of the PRC to the celebrations of the 25th anniversary of the Algerian Revolution
	Dec	Identified as deputy leader of the CCP Central Committee's group in charge of snail fever prevention in thirteen South China provinces

Qian Xuesen (Ch'ien Hsüeh-sen) 钱学森

Posts held

CCP
Alternate member of the CCP 11th Central Committee

Government
Vice-chairman of the Science and Technology Commission for National Defense

NPC
Deputy for the PLA to the 5th NPC

Others
President of the Society of Mechanics and Automation
Advisor of the Society for the Study of the Future
Deputy director of the Committee for the Promotion of International Measurement

Qian was born in 1912 in Shanghai as the son of a businessman. He graduated in 1934 having studied engineering at the Jiaotong University in Shanghai. In September 1935 he went to the U.S.A., having won a scholarship. During his first year in the U.S.A. he studied aeronautics and aerodynamics at the Massachusetts Institute of Technology and completed his studies with a Master's degree. He then went to the California Institute of Technology where he became a favorite student of Professor Theodor von Karman, a leading scientist in the field of aerodynamics, who interested him in jet propulsion for supersonic aircraft. In the course of his work under professor von Karman Qian was introduced to rocket research to which he contributed the "Qian Formula" for jet propulsion named after him. In 1938 he was awarded a doctorate under von Karman and became an assistant. Very shortly afterward he was given an assistant professorship in charge of the Laboratory for Supersonic Research.

During World War II Qian worked as director of the Rocket Section in the U.S. National Defense Scientific Advisory Board. At the recommendation of Professor von Karman he was made a colonel of the U.S. National Defense Scientific Advisory Board (headed by General Henry "Hap" Arnold) and director of its Rocket Section in 1945. After Germany's capitulation he headed the American group of scientists sent to dismantle the German rocket center in Peenemünde and ship it to the U.S.A.

In 1946 Qian was made a professor at the Massachusetts Institute of Technology - at the age only 34 the youngest professor in the history of this institute.

In the summer of 1947 he returned to Shanghai and married Jiang Ying, the daughter of General Jiang Baili.

In Shanghai he was offered the presidency of Jiaotong University, a position he could not take up because the then minister for education of the Chinese Nationalist

Government objected that he was too young. He then returned to the U.S.A. in September 1947 as a professor at the California Institute of Technology and from 1949 until 1955 as director of the Guggenheim Jet Propulsion Laboratory. He specialized in propulsion systems for rockets and in atomic physics. He was appointed Goddard professor of jet propulsion by the California Institute of Technology. In 1950 Qian decided to return to the PRC, which had been established on 1 October 1949. However, with the outbreak of the Korean War he was accused of having been a Communist in the 1930s and prevented from leaving the country by the FBI. In addition, in Honolulu eight crates Qian had already sent off to China were found to contain scientific documents and research notes. As a result he was arrested. After 15 days he was released on $15,000 bail, and he continued his research at California Institute of Technology.

In 1955 Sino-American ambassadorial talks in Warsaw secured the release of nine Americans detained by China and Qian was permitted to return. Together with his wife, his son Qian Yonggang and daughter Qian Yongzhen, as well as 800 kg of scientific documents and notes he eventually returned to China via Hong Kong in October 1955.

1955,	Nov	Qian is appointed head of the Preparatory Committee for the foundation of the Institute of Mechanics in the Academy of Sciences
1956,	Jan	Elected member of the 2nd CPPCC
	Feb	With the establishment of the Institute of Mechanics in the Academy of Sciences, Qian is appointed director
	Mar	Appointed member of the State Council Commission for Scientific Planning (until Nov 1958)
	May	Appointed member of the editorial staff of the bi-monthly Kexue Tongbao (Science Bulletin); Qian participates in a congress for aerodynamics in Poland
1957,	Jan	Qian wins the first prize of the Academy of Sciences Science Award for 1956; the award is for his dissertation written in the U.S.A., "Engineering Cybernetics," discussing theories of automatic control and regulation of various technical systems (the prize consisted of a medal, a certificate and 10,000 yuan).
	Feb	Elected chairman of the Dynamics Society
	May	Appointed member of the Department of Mathematics, Physics and Chemistry at the Academy of Sciences
	Sep	Appointed member of the Executive Council of the International Federation of Automatic Control
1958,	Apr	Appointed head of the Preparatory Committee for the Automation Society
	Sep	Elected deputy for Guangdong Province to the 2nd NPC (reelected to the 3rd NPC in September 1964); with the foundation of the Scientific and Technical Association, Qian is elected a member
	Dec	Appointed chairman of the Compilation, Translation, and Publication Committee of the Academy of Sciences; Qian joins the CCP
1959,	May	Appointed director of the Department of Mechanics, University of Science and Technology
1961,	Jan	Appointed member of the editorial board of the monthly Zhongguo Kexue (Scientic Sinica)
	Nov	Elected chairman of the Automation Society
1964,	Dec	Member of the Presidium of the 3rd NPC
1966-1968		Qian survives the Cultural Revolution without coming under attack and is repeatedly seen participating in official occasions
1969,	Apr	Elected to first term as alternate member of the CCP Central Committee by the 9th Party Congress
1975,	Jul	Qian's name tops the list of representatives of the Scientific and Technical Commission for National Defense named on the occasion of the PLA's anniversary
1978,	Feb	Elected deputy for the PLA to the 5th NPC
	Jul	Identified as vice-chairman of the Science and Technology Commission for National Defense
	Nov	Identified as president of the Society of Mechanics and Automation
1979,	Jan	Identified as member of the Department for Mathematics, Physics, and Chemistry, Academy of Sciences
	Mar	Appointed advisor of the Society for the Study of the Future; appointed deputy director of the Committee for the Promotion of International Measurement

Qian is married to Jiang Ying, who is a teacher in vocal-music at the Central Conservatory of Music. She studied music in Germany.

Publications by Qian after his return to the PR China:

1956	"Allow Science and Technology to Progress Rapidly" (Gongren Ribao, 12 May 1956)
	"An Old and Yet Young Branch of Science" (RMRB, 11 June 1956)
	"On aircraft and Guided Missiles and the Computers That Control Them" (GMRB, 8 October 1956)
	"The Realization of Interplanetary Traffic" (GMRB, 19 November 1956)
1957	"The Scientific and Technical Significance of the USSR's Artificial World Satelite" (GMRB, 3 November 1957)
	"The Beginning of the Space Age" (Dagong Bao, 29 December 1957)
1958	"The Utilization of Collective Wisdom Is the Only Truly Good Method" (RMRB, 29 April 1958)
	"Break Out of the Solar System and Create a Greater Universe" (RMRB, 4 October 958)
1959	"On Space Rockets and Interplanetary Flight" (RMRB, 8 January 1959)
	"The Space Rocket" (HQ, February 1959)
	"The Essential Tasks of the Chinese University of Science and Technology" (RMRB, 26 May 1959)
1960	"The New Position of the USSR in Conquering Space" (RMRB, 19 January 1960)
1961	"General Education in Science and Tech-

nology" (GMRB, 10 June 1961)

"The Subject and Aim of Modern Dynamics" (RMRB, 10 November 1961)

1962 "Lectures on Physics" (Scientific Press, February 1962)

1963 "Survey of Developments in Interplanetary Flight" (Scientific Press, February 1963)

"A Bright Future for Scientific and Technical Support to Agriculture" (HQ, 1963, No.19)

"Labor Organization and Management in Science and Technology" (HQ, 1963, No.22)

1964 "The Tremendous Significance of Scientific Experimentation" (Popular Science, 1964, No.8)

1977 "Science and Technology Must Catch Up with and Surpass Advanced World Levels Before the End of the Century" (HQ, 1977, No.7)

1978 Theory of Engineering Control

Qian Zhengying (Ch'ien Cheng-ying) (f)

钱正英

Posts held

CCP
Member of the CCP 11th Central Committee

Government
Minister of water conservancy

Others
Chairman of the Association of Hydraulic Engineering

Qian was born in 1922. She studied engineering sciences at Datong University in Shanghai. In 1942 she joined the Communist New 4th Army. In spring 1949 she was elected a member of the Executive Council of the Democratic Women's Federation. In June of that year she was appointed a member of the Huang He Water Conservancy Commission.

1950, Feb Appointed deputy director of the Water Conservancy Department in the East China Military and Administrative Council

Oct Appointed member of the Huai River Harnessing Commission as well as deputy director and chief-engineer of its technical division

1952, Nov Appointed vice-minister of water conservancy

1954, Aug Elected deputy for Guangxi Province to the 1st NPC (until 1964)

1957, May Elected vice-chairman of the newly established Commission for Harnessing the Huai River and its Tributaries

1958, Feb Vice-minister of the new joint Ministry of Water Conservancy and Electric Power (until Dec 1974)

May Appointed vice-chairman of the Grand Canal Commission

1959, Nov Head of a women's delegation to the USSR attending the 42nd anniversary of the Socialist Revolution

1964, Sep Elected deputy for Zhejiang Province to the 3rd NPC

1970, Nov Head of a Ministry of Water Conservancy and Electric Power delegation to Albania

1972, Nov Head of an irrigation delegation to Sri Lanka

1973, Aug Elected to first term as member of the CCP Central Committee by the 10th Party Congress

Dec Identified as chairman of the Association of Hydraulic Engineering

1975, Jan Appointed minister of water conservancy and electric power (until Feb 1979)

1978, May Member of a government delegation led by Gu Mu to France, Belgium, Switzerland, Denmark, and the Federal Republic of Germany

1979, Feb Appointed minister of water conservancy; identified as responsible person of the Office in Charge of Farmland Capital Construction

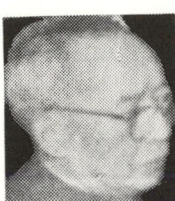

Qian Zhiguang (Ch'ien Chih-kuang)

钱之光

Posts held

CCP
Member of the CCP 11th Central Committee

Government
Minister for textile industry

Qian was born in 1905 in Shanghai. After training in business administration he joined the Jiangxi Soviet in 1932 in which he was made head of the Commerce Department. After the Long March he became head of the CCP Commerce Department in 1935. In 1939 he was deputy director of the CCP Liaison Department in Xi'an. From 1940 to 1943 he headed the Liaison Department of the 18th Army Group in Chongqing.

1949, Oct Appointed vice-minister for textile industry (until 1970); appointed member of the Financial and Economic Affairs Committee in the Government Administration Council (until Sep 1954)

1952, Jun Member of the Preparatory Committee of the Federation of Industry and Commerce

1959, Apr Elected deputy for Shandong Province to the 2nd NPC (until Dec 1974)

1969, Apr Elected to first term as member of the CCP Central Committee by the 9th Party Congress

1970, Jul Identified as minister for light industry (until Feb 1978); head of a government delegation to Iraq

1971, Apr Head of a delegation to the Zagreb Trade Fair in Yugoslavia

1978, Mar Appointed minister for textile industry

Qiao Jiaxin (Ch'iao Chia-hsin)

乔加欣

Posts held

Provincial Administration
Vice-chairman of the People's Government, Tibet Autonomous Region

1977,	Dec	Elected vice-chairman of the Revolutionary Committee of Tibet Autonomous Region (until Aug 1979)
1979,	Jul	Appointed member of the National Games Organizing Committee
	Aug	Elected vice-chairman of the People's Government, Tibet Autonomous Region

Qiao Mingbu (Ch'iao Ming-pu)   乔明甫

Posts held

CCP
Secretary of Henan Province CP

Provincial Administration
Vice-chairman of the Standing Committee, Henan Provincial People's Congress

In 1936 Qiao worked for the Communists in Shanxi Province.

1963,	Jul	Identified as deputy director of the Organization Department of the CCP Central Committee
1967,	Apr	Purged in connection with Bo Yibo
1978,	Dec	First appearance after the Cultural Revolution
1979,	Mar	Identified as secretary of Henan Province CP
	Sep	Elected vice-chairman of the Standing Committee, Henan Provincial People's Congress

Qiao Peixin (Ch'iao P'ei-hsin)   乔培新

Posts held

Others
Honorary chairman of the Bank of China

1950		Identified as director of the Northwest China Branch of the People's Bank of China (until 1953)
1951,	Feb	Identified as deputy director of the Agricultural Bank of China (a People's Bank subsidiary) (until Mar 1955)
1953,	Dec	Identified as director of the Northwest China Branch of the People's Bank of China (until 1955)
1955,	Mar	Identified as director of the Agricultural Bank of China; identified as deputy director-general of the People's Bank of China; Identified as member of the State Council Commission for Overseas Chinese Affairs (until Sep 1959)
	May	Identified as director-general of the Bank of China (until Cultural Revolution)
1958,	May	Head of a government delegation to the German Democratic Republic
1959,	Dec	Head of a government delegation to the PR Mongolia
1971,	Jun	Identified as vice-president of the People's Bank of China
	Dec	Identified as acting president of the People's Bank of China (also identified in this office in 1972, 1973, 1975)

1972,	Oct	Head of a banking delegation to Albania and Romania
	Dec	Head of a banking delegation to Tanzania
1974,	Jul	Identified as acting director of the Bank of China
1975,	Apr	Head of a banking delegation to Japan
	Nov	Head of a banking delegation to North Korea
1976,	Mar	Identified as chairman of the board of directors of the Bank of China
1978,	Jun	Identified as vice-president of the Bank of China (until Jul 1979)
1979,	May	Head of a banking delegation to France and Italy
	Jul	Identified as honorary chairman of the Bank of China

Qiao Shi (Ch'iao Shih)   乔石

Posts held

CCP
Deputy director of the International Liaison Department in the CCP Central Committee

1964,	Nov	Member of a solidarity delegation to North Vietnam
1965,	Jun	Elected secretary of the Afro-Asian Solidarity Committee (until Cultural Revolution)
1978,	Mar	Identified as deputy director of the International Liaison Department in the CCP Central Committee; deputy head of a delegation of CCP workers to Yugoslavia and Romania
	Aug	Member of a Party and government delegation under Hua Guofeng to Romania, Yugoslavia, and Iran

Qiao Xiaoguang (Ch'iao Hsiao-kuang)

Posts held   乔晓光

CCP
Member of the CCP 11th Central Committee
1st secretary, CP of Guangxi Autonomous Region

NPC
Deputy for Guangxi Autonomous Region to the 5th NPC

Military
1st political commissar of Guangxi Military District

1950		Identified as secretary of Changde District CP, Hunan Province
1952		Identified as secretary-general of Guangxi Province CP and as director of the Organizations Department of Guangxi CP (until 1954)
1956,	Feb	Appointed ambassador to North Korea (until Jul 1961)

Dec Appointed secretary of Guangxi Autonomous Region CP

1965, Jul Identified as 2nd secretary of Guangxi Autonomous Region CP (until Cultural Revolution)

1966, Oct Identified as acting 1st secretary of Guangxi Autonomous Region CP

1972, Aug Identified as member of the Standing Committee, Revolutionary Committee of Guangxi Autonomous Region
Identified as member of the Standing Committee of Guangxi Autonomous Region CP (until Aug 1974)

1973, Oct Identified as vice-chairman of the Revolutionary Committee in Guangxi (until Feb 1977)

1974, Aug Identified as secretary of Guangxi CP (until May 1976)

1975, Jan Identified as head of the Birth Planning Group in Guangxi Autonomous Region; member of the presidium of the 4th NPC

Nov Head of a friendship delegation to Pakistan and Sri Lanka

1976, May Identified as 2nd secretary of Guangxi CP (until Feb 1977)

1977, Feb Identified as 1st CP secretary, and as chairman of the Revolutionary Committee, in Guangxi (latter post until Dec 1979)

Mar Identified as 1st political commissar of Guangxi Military District

Aug Elected member of the CCP Central Committee by the 11th Party Congress

1978, Feb Elected deputy for Guangxi Autonomous Region to the 5th NPC

Qiao Zhimin (Ch'iao Chih-min) 乔志敏

Posts held

Provincial Administration
Vice-governor of Sichuan Province

1977, Dec Elected vice-chairman of the Revolutionary Committee of Sichuan Province (until Dec 1979)

1979, Dec Elected vice-governor of Sichuan Province

Qin Chuan (Ch'in Ch'uan) 秦 川

Posts held

CCP
Deputy editor-in-chief of the Peking RMRB

Government
Member of the Birth Planning Leading Group under the State Council

1978, Apr Identified as deputy editor-in-chief of the Beijing RMRB

Jul Identified as member of the Birth Planning Leading Group under the State Council

Qin Hezhen (Ch'in Ho-chen) 秦和珍

Posts held

CCP
Secretary of Shandong Province CP

NPC
Deputy to the 5th NPC for Shandong Province

Provincial Administration
Vice-governor of Shandong Province

1973, Jun Identified as member of the Standing Committee, Shandong Province CP

1977, Jan Identified as CP secretary and vice-chairman of the Revolutionary Committee of Shandong Province (latter post until Dec 1979)

1978, Feb Elected deputy for Shandong Province to the 5th NPC

1979, Dec Elected vice-governor of Shandong Province

Qin Jialin (Ch'in Chia-lin) 秦加林

Posts held

Government
Ambassador to Denmark

From 1945 to 1947 Qin was editor of the Yanfu News at the Communist guerrilla base in Yanfu, Jiangxi Province.

1957, Jun Appointed counselor at the Chinese mission in Great Britain (until Oct 1962)

1962, Oct Appointed deputy director of the Information Department in the Ministry of Foreign Affairs (until Mar 1965)

1965, Mar Appointed director of the Information Department in the Ministry of Foreign Affairs (until about 1967)

1969, Jun Appointed ambassador to Syria (until May 1974)

1974, Aug Identified as director of the Information Department in the Ministry of Foreign Affairs (until Dec 1976)

1977, Aug Identified as ambassador to Denmark

Qin Jiwei (Ch'in Chi-wei) 秦基伟

Posts held

CCP
Member of the CCP 11th Central Committee
2nd secretary of the Party Committee, Beijing Military Region

NPC
Deputy for the PLA to the 5th NPC

Military
Lieutenant-general
Commander of Beijing Military Region

Qin was born about 1910 in Qiliping, Huanggang County, Hubei Province. In 1927 he took part in the Huanggang Uprising before joining a guerrilla unit which was integrated in 1929 into the Red Workers and Peasants Army led by Xu Xiangqian. After this force was reorganized to form the 4th Front Army in autumn 1931, Qin was given the command of the 2nd Company, Pistol Battalion, Headquarter Forces. In the Left Route Column under Zhang Guotao he took part in the Long March and with a small Security Force successfully broke the encirclement of the Ma-Jia Army near Yongchang in December 1936. In March 1936 he was captured by KMT troops, but escaped two months later and fled to Yan'an. From September 1937 to March 1938 he attended a course at the Anti-Japan Military and Political Academy. In 1940 he commanded an independent brigade in the Taihang Area. In 1944 he was chief of staff of Taihang Military District. In 1947 he was made commander of the 9th Column, Central Plains Military Region. In early 1949 he commanded the 15th Corps, 4th Army, 2nd Field Army.

1950		As corps commander Qin is concurrently commander of South Yunnan Military District
1951,	Mar	In the Korea War Qin leads a division which already after two months suffers heavy casualties
1952,	Oct	Distinguished service in repelling an attack by one U.S. and two South Korean divisions
1954,	Mar	Appointed commander of Yunnan Military District (until Oct 1958)
1955,	Mar	Appointed deputy commander of Kunming Military Region (until Oct 1958)
	Sep	Promoted to rank of lieutenant-general
1958,	Jul	Elected deputy for the PLA to the 2nd NPC (reelected in Sep 1964 to the 3rd NPC)
	Oct	Identified as commander of Kunming Military Region (until Cultural Revolution)
1960,	Dec	Head of the military delegation as part of the 400-member friendship delegation led by Zhou Enlai to Burma
1961,	Mar	Member of the Chinese delegation to the New Delhi World Peace Council Session
1965,	Jan	Appointed member of the National Defense Council (until Cultural Revolution)
1967		Disappears during the Cultural Revolution
1973,	May	First appearance after the Cultural Revolution
1974,	Jan	Identified as commander of Chengdu Military Region (until Dec 1975)
	Oct	Head of a military delegation to Algeria
1973,	Aug	Elected to first term as member of the CCP Central Committee by the 10th Party Congress
1976,	Apr	Identified as 2nd political commissar of Beijing Military Region (until Oct 1978)
1977,	May	Head of the Group for Solution of the Baoding Problem
1978,	Feb	Elected deputy for the PLA to the 5th NPC
	Nov	Identified as 1st political commissar of Beijing Military Region (until Dec 1979)
1979,	Oct	Identified as 2nd secretary of the Party Committee, Beijing Military Region
1980,	Jan	Identified as commander of Beijing Military Region

Qin Lisheng (Ch'in Li-sheng)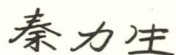

Posts held

NPC
Deputy for Beijing Municipality to the 5th NPC

Government
Vice-chairman of the National Commission of the PRC for UNESCO

1950,	Oct	Identified as deputy secretary of Xikang Province CP and as council member of the People's Government of Xikang Province
1951,	Mar	Identified as member of the Rural Reform Committee in the Southwest China Military and Administrative Council (until Jan 1953)
1960,	Sep	Identified as deputy secretary-general of the Academy of Sciences (until Cultural Revolution)
1962,	Jul	Head of a delegation of the Academy of Sciences to Moscow
1967,	Feb	Branded as an anti-Party element and disappears
1971,	May	First appearance after the Cultural Revolution: Renewed mention in his previous post as deputy secretary-general of the Academy of Sciences (until Feb 1979)
1972,	Feb	Head of an Academy of Sciences delegation to Cuba for the 10th anniversary of the Sciences Academy
1976,	Mar	Head of a delegation of scientists to Zaire
1978,	Feb	Elected deputy for Beijing Municipality to the 5th NPC
	Sep	Deputy head of an Academy of Sciences delegation under Zhou Peiyuan to Japan
1979,	Feb	Appointed vice-chairman of the National Commission of the PRC for U.N.E.S.C.O.
	Dec	Head of a scientific delegation to Egypt

Qin Lizhen (Ch'in Li-chen)

Posts held

Government
Ambassador to New Zealand

1950		Identified as director of the Visa Department in the Ministry of Foreign Affairs
1955,	Oct	Identified as deputy director of the Consular Department in the Ministry of Foreign Affairs (until Jun 1958)
1958,	Jun	Identified as director of the Consular Department in the Ministry of Foreign Affairs (until Feb 1962)
1959,	Sep	Appointed member of the State Council Commission for Overseas Chinese Affairs
1962,	Apr	Appointed Ambassador to Norway (until Jan 1965)
1965,	Feb	Appointed ambassador to Zambia (until 1972)
1974,	Jan	Identified as director of the Consular Department in the Ministry of Foreign Affairs (until Jul 1974)
	Jul	Appointed ambassador to Sweden (until May 1979)
1979,	Dec	Appointed ambassador to New Zealand

Qin Tianzhen (Ch'in T'ien-chen)   秦天真

Posts held

Provincial Administration
Vice-governor of Guizhou Province

1980,   Jan   Elected vice-governor of Guizhou Province

Qin Wencai (Ch'in Wen-ts'ai)   秦文彩

Posts held

Government
Vice-minister of petroleum industry

1979,   Mar   Identified as vice-minister of petroleum industry

Qin Yingji (Ch'in Ying-chi)   覃应机

Posts held

CCP
Member of the CCP 11th Central Committee
Secretary of Guangxi Autonomous Region CP

Provincial Administration
Chairman of the People's Government of Guangxi Autonomous Region

Qin belongs to the Zhuang minority; he was born in 1915 in Donglan County, Guangxi Province. He joined the Worker-Peasant Red Army in 1929. In Yan'an he attended the Nationalities College and the Anti-Japan Military and Political Academy. During the Anti-Japanese War he served as regiment and deputy division commander in the New 4th Army.

1949   Identified as director of the Public Security Department of the People's Government of Hebei Province (until Mar 1950)
1950,   Mar   Identified as council member of the People's Government of Guangxi Province
         Jul   Identified as director of the Public Security Department of Guangxi Provincial Government as well as commander of the 6th Division, Public Security Forces (until 1951)
1952   Identified as chairman of the Guixi Autonomous Zhou of the Zhuang (until 1956)
1953,   Jan   Appointed member of the Central-South China Administrative Council (until Sep 1954)
1954,   Aug   Elected deputy for Guangxi Province to the 1st NPC (reelected in 1959 and 1964 to the 2nd and 3rd NPCs)
         Sep   Identified as vice-chairman of the People's Government of Guangxi Province (until 1955)
1955,   Feb   Identified as vice-governor of Guangxi Province (until Cultural Revolution)
1957,   May   Identified as secretary of Guangxi Province CP (until Cultural Revolution)

1958   Qin retains his post after Guangxi obtains the status of Autonomous Region
1960,   Aug   Identified as chairman of the Guangxi Section, Sino-Vietnamese Friendship Association
1966   Disappears during the Cultural Revolution
1972,   Oct   First appearance after the Cultural Revolution
         Dec   Identified as member of the Standing Committee, Revolutionary Committee of Guangxi Autonomous Region (until Aug 1974)
1974,   Aug   Identified as vice-chairman, Revolutionary Committee of Guangxi Autonomous Region (until Dec 1979), and as secretary of Guangxi Autonomous Region CP
1975,   Apr   Head of a friendship delegation to North Korea
1977,   Aug   Elected member of the CCP Central Committee by the 11th Party Congress
1979,   Mar   Identified as chairman of the Guangxi Branch, CPPCC
         Dec   Elected chairman of the People's Government of Guangxi Autonomous Region

Qin Zhongda (Ch'in Chung-ta)   秦仲达

Posts held

Government
Vice-minister of chemical industry

1978,   Jan   Identified as director of a department in the Ministry of Petroleum and Chemical Industry (until Mar 1978)
         Jul   Identified as vice-minister of chemical industry

Qiu Chunfu (Ch'iu Ch'un-fu)   邱纯甫

Posts held

Government
Vice-minister of the State Economic Commission

Others
Director of the Board of Directors, China International Trust and Investment Corporation

1978,   Dec   Identified as vice-minister of the State Economic Commission
1979,   Oct   Appointed director of the Board of Directors, China International Trust and Investment Corporation

Qiu Guoguang (Ch'iu Kuo-kuang)   邱国光

Posts held

Military
Deputy commander of Guangzhou Military Region

During the revolutionary period Qiu served in the 1st Front Army and in the 4th Field Army.

1963,	Aug	Identified as major-general in Guangzhou Military Region
1964,	Jan	Identified as director of the Logistics Department in Guangzhou Military Region
1968,	Jan	Identified as member of the Preparatory Group for the foundation of the Guangdong Province Revolutionary Committee
	Feb	Elected vice-chairman of the Revolutionary Committee of Guangdong Province (until about 1971)
1969,	Apr	Elected member of the CCP Central Committee by the 9th Party Congress (until Aug 1973)
1971,	Nov	Identified as member of the Standing Committee of Guangdong Province CP (until about 1972); identified as deputy commander of Guangzhou Military Region

Note

Qiu belonged to the Lin Biao faction which explains his rise to the CCP Central Committee in 1969. After the fall of Lin Biao, Qiu was relieved of all posts, but probably still holds that of a deputy commander of Guangzhou Military Region.

Qu Geping (Ch'ü Ke-p'ing)　　曲格平

Posts held

Government
First permanent representative of the PRC to the UN Environment Program
Deputy head of the Office of the Environmental Protection Leading Group under the State Council
Council member of the Society of Environment

1974,	Sep	Identified as an environment cadre
1975,	Jul	Head of an environmental delegation to Japan
1976,	Mar	Identified as first permanent representative of the PRC to the UN Environment Program
1978,	May	Deputy head of a delegation to the 5th Conference of the UN Environment Program in Nairobi
1979,	Apr	Identified as deputy head of the Office of the Environmental Protection Leading Group under the State Council; head of a delegation to the 7th Session of the Governing Council, UN Environment Program in Nairobi
	Aug	Advisor to the Chinese delegation to the Symposium on the Interrelationship between Resouces, Environment, Population and Development under the joint auspices of the UN and the Swedish government in Stockholm
	Sep	Identified as council member of the Society of Environment

Qu Wu (Ch'ü Wu)　　屈武

Posts held

NPC
Deputy for Shaanxi Province to the 5th NPC

Others
Member of the Standing Committee of the 5th CPPCC
Vice-chairman of the Revolutionary Committee of the Chinese KMT

Qu was born in Shaanxi Province in 1898. As president of the Shaanxi Student Union he participated in the "May 4th Movement" in 1919. From 1926 to 1929 he studied at Moscow University. After his return he served in the Nationalist Government until 1949 holding the following offices: member of the KMT Legislative Yuan; director of the Civil Affairs Department of Xinjiang Provincial Government, and mayor of Dihua (Ürümqi). He went over to the Communists in September 1949.

1949,	Dec	Appointed member of the Northwest China Military and Administrative Council (until Jan 1953) and mayor of Ürümqi (until 1950)
1950,	Sep	Appointed deputy secretary-general of the Government Administration Council (until 1954)
1952,	Nov	Identified as member of the Solidarity Committee of the KMT Revolutionary Committee
1953,	Jan	Appointed member of the Northwest Administrative Council
1954,	Aug	Elected deputy for Henan Province to the 1st NPC (confirmed in 1958 by the 2nd NPC)
	Sep	Appointed deputy secretary-general of the Standing Committee of the 1st NPC
	Dec	Identified as deputy secretary-general of the Central Committee, KMT Revolutionary Committee
1956,	Feb	Elected member of the Standing Committee of the KMT Revolutionary Committee
1957,	Jul	Identified as deputy director of the Office of Counselors under the State Council (until Jan 1959)
1958,	Mar	Member of an NPC delegation to Finland
	May	Appointed vice-chairman of the Commission for Cultural Relations with Foreign Countries (until Nov 1965)
	Sep	Head of a troupe of performers visiting Switzerland
1959,	Apr	Elected member of the Standing Committee of the 3rd CPPCC (confirmed in 1965 by the 4th CPPCC)
	Jun	Head of a cultural delegation to Afghanistan
	Aug	Identified as chairman of the Sino-Hungarian Friendship Association
1960,	Feb	Head of a troupe of performers visiting Sudan
	Apr	Elected vice-chairman of the Sino-African Friendship Association
	Jun	Head of a troupe of performers visiting Morocco
1961,	Apr	Head of a friendship delegation to Hungary

1967		Disappears during the Cultural Revolution
1974,	Sep	First appeareance after the Cultural Revolution: Identified as holding his previous post as member of the Standing Committee of the 4th CPPCC
1978,	Feb	Elected deputy for Shaanxi Province to the 5th NPC
	Mar	Elected member of the Standing Committee of the 5th CPPCC
1979,	May	Member of an NPC delegation, led by Deng Yingchao, to Japan
	Oct	Elected vice-chairman of the Central Committee, Revolutionary Committee of the Chinese KMT

Raidi (Je-ti) 热 地

Posts held

CCP
Alternate member of the CCP 11th Central Committee
Secretary of Tibet Autonomous Region CP
Secretary of the Commission for Inspecting Discipline of Tibet CP

Mass Organization
Chairman of the Peasants' Federation of Tibet

Provincial Administration
Vice-chairman of the Standing Committee, People's Congress of Tibet Autonomous Region

Raidi belongs to the Tibetan minority.

1975,	Sep	Identified as secretary of Tibet CP
	Dec	Identified as chairman of the Peasants' Federation of Tibet
1977,	Aug	Elected alternate member of the CCP Central Committee by the 11th Party Congress
	Dec	Elected vice-chairman of the Revolutionary Committee of Tibet Autonomous Region (until Aug 1979)
1979,	Feb	Elected secretary of the Commission for Inspecting Discipline of Tibet CP
	Aug	Elected vice-chairman of the Standing Committee, People's Congress of Tibet Autonomous Region

Ran Guiying (Jan Kuei-ying) (f) 冉桂英

Posts held

CCP
Alternate member of the CCP 11th Central Committee

1977,	Aug	Elected alternate member of the CCP Central Committee by the 11th Party Congress

Ran Yannong (Jan Yen-nung) 冉砚农

Posts held

Provincial Administration
Vice-governor of Guizhou Province

1959,	Nov	Identified as deputy director of the Rural Work Department of Wuhan CP
1977,	Dec	Elected vice-chairman of the Revolutionary Committee of Guizhou Province (until Dec 1979)
1980,	Jan	Elected vice-governor of Guizhou Province

Rao Bin (Jao Pin) 饶 斌

Posts held

Government
Vice-minister of the 1st Ministry of Machine Building

NPC
Deputy for Hubei Province to the 5th NPC

Rao was born in 1913 in Jilin Province. He studied at Shanghai University. In 1937 he served in the 120th Division of the 8th Route Army. In 1949 he was mayor of Harbin.

1949,	Dec	Identified as member of the Northeast People's Government
1950,	Jan	Identified as deputy 1st secretary of Harbin Municipality CP
	Jun	Identified as secretary of Songjiang Province (until Jun 1954)
1951,	Oct	Identified as vice-chairman of Songjiang (until Jun 1954)
1954,	Feb	Identified as manager of Changchun No. 1 Automobile Manufacturing Plant
1960,	Jan	Appointed vice-minister of the 1st Ministry of Machine Building (until Jun 1961)
1961,	Jul	Appointed vice-chairman of the State Economic Commission (until Oct 1963)
1967		Disappears during the Cultural Revolution
1978,	Feb	First appearance after the Cultural Revolution: Elected deputy for Hubei Province to the 5th NPC
	Jun	Identified as vice-minister of the 1st Ministry of Machine Building

Rao Shoukun (Jao Shou-k'un) 饶守坤

Posts held

Military
Vice-admiral
Commander of JInan Military Region

Before 1945 Rao was a leader of a Red Army regiment, which carried out three-year guerrilla war in the Central Soviet Zone. In 1946 he commanded a brigade of the Central China Field Army.

1955,	Sep	Awarded the order "Liberation," 1st class
1958,	Dec	Identified as vice-admiral and deputy commander of the East China Sea Fleet
1967,	Aug	Disappears during the Cultural Revolution
1979,	Jan	First appearance after the Cultural Revolution: Identified as commander of the North China Sea Fleet (until Jan 1980)
1980,	Feb	Identified as commander of Jinan Military Region

Rao Xing (Jao Hsing) 饶 兴

Posts held

Government
Director of the Central Meteorological Bureau

1950,	Jun	Identified as a member of the Financial and Economic Committee, North Sichuan Administrative Office
	Jul	Identified as secretary-general of the CCP North Sichuan District Committee
1956,	Oct	Identified as assistant minister of water conservancy (until Oct 1957)
1957,	Nov	Identified as deputy director of the Central Meteorological Bureau (until Oct 1964)
1964,	Mar	Head of a meterorological delegation to North Vietnam
	Sep	Elected deputy for Hunan to the 3rd NPC
	Oct	Identified as director of the Central Meteorological Bureau
1968,	Apr	Denounced as a bourgeois counterrevolutionary and purged
1974,	May	First appearance after the Cultural Revolution
1975,	Sep	Identified as a cadre of the Central Meteorological Bureau
1978,	Dec	Rao heads a meteorological delegation to Japan
1979,	Sep	Identified as director of the Central Meteorological Bureau

Rao Xingli (Jao Hsing-li)   饶兴礼

Posts held

CCP
Member of the CCP 11th Central Committee
Member of the Standing Committee of Hubei Province CP

Provincial Administration
Vice-chairman of the People's Congress, Hubei Province

Mass Organization
Chairman of the Peasants' Federation of Hubei Province

Rao has distinguished himself as a model agricultural worker.

1954,	Aug	Elected deputy for Hubei Province to the 1st NPC (reelected in 1959 and 1964 to the 2nd and 3rd NPC)
1956,	Mar	Marked out as model agricultural worker, special class; identified as chairman of the Production Cooperative "October" in Xishui County, Hubei Province
1958,	Dec	Member, Presidium of the National Congress of Progressive Production Cooperatives
1966,	May	Identified as vice-chairman of the Federation of Poor and Lower-Middle Peasants of Hubei Province
1968,	Feb	Elected vice-chairman of the newly established Revolutionary Committee of Hubei Province (until 1977)
1969,	Apr	Elected to first term as member of the CCP Central Committee by the 9th Party Congress
1972,	Jan	Identified as member of the Standing Committee of Hubei Province

| 1973, | Dec | Elected chairman of the Peasants' Federation of Hubei Province |
| 1980, | Jan | Elected vice-chairman of the People's Congress, Hubei Province |

Rao Zhengxi (Jao Cheng-hsi)   饶正锡

Posts held

CCP
Member of the Commission for Inspecting Discipline under the CCP Central Committee

Military
Lieutenant-general
Deputy director of the PLA General Logistics Department

Rao was born in Hubei Province. In 1949 he was deputy political commissar of the 1st Field Army.

1949,	Dec	Identified as member of the Xinjiang Subbureau of the CCP Central Committee and as member of the Xinjiang People's Government
1952,	Aug	Identified as mayor, and as secretary of the CP, of Ürümqi (until 1953)
1953,	Nov	Identified as director of the Public Health Division, General Logistics Department of the People's Revolutionary Military Council
1955,	Sep	Appointed lieutenant-general; awarded the order "Liberation," 1st class
1957,	Dec	Identfied as director of the Public Health Division of the PLA General Logistics Department
1958,	Jan	Member of a military delegation to India
	Jul	Identified as deputy director of the PLA General Logistics Department
1967,	Sep	Branded as a "three-anti element" and purged
1974,	Jul	First appearance after the Cultural Revolution
1978,	Apr	Identified as deputy director of the PLA General Logistics Department
	Dec	Appointed member of the Commission for Inspecting Discipline under the CCP Central Committee

Redi (Je-ti)

see **Raidi**

Ren Baige (Jen Pai-ke)   任白戈

Posts held

Others
Member of the Standing Committee of the 5th CPPCC

Ren was born in Sichuan Province. At one time he was a book-dealer in Shanghai. In early 1949 he served as director of the Culture Section in the Political Department of the 2nd Field Army. In July of that year he was elected member of the Association of Literary and Art Circles which he represented as delegate at the 1st CPPCC in September 1949.

1949,   Oct   Elected council member of the Sino-Soviet Friendship Association (until 1954)

         Dec   Identified as member of the Cultural and Educational Committee of the Southwest Military and Administrative Council (until 1954) and as director of the Propaganda Department of Chongqing Municipality CP

1950,   Jun   Identified as deputy director of the Cultural and Educational Department of the Southwest Military and Administrative Council

1954,   May   Identified as council member of the Association for Cultural Relations with Foreign Countries

         Aug   Elected deputy for Chongqing Municipality to the 1st NPC

1955,   Jan   Elected vice-governor of Sichuan Province (until Jul 1958); identified as mayor of Chongqing (until Cultural Revolution)

         Oct   Identified as deputy secretary of Chongqing Municipality CP (until 1956)

1956,   Aug   Identified as secretary of Chongqing Municipality CP (until 1959)

1958,   Jul   Elected deputy for Sichuan Province to the 2nd NPC

1959,   Nov   Identified as 1st secretary of Chongqing Municipality CP (until Cultural Revolution)

1968,   Jun   Branded as a collaborator of Li Jingquan and purged

1975,   Sep   First appearance after the Cultural Revolution

1978,   Mar   Elected member of the Standing Committee of the 5th CPPCC

Ren Gengqing (Jen Keng-ch'ing)　　任耕卿

Posts held

Provincial Administration
Vice-chairman of the People's Government, Guangxi Autonomous Region

1979,   Dec   Elected vice-chairman of the People's Government, Guangxi Autonomous Region

Ren Jiyu (Jen Chi-yü)　　任继愈

Posts held

NPC
Deputy for Shanghai Municipality to the 5th NPC

Others

Director of the Institute of Research on World Religion, Academy of Social Sciences
President of the Society for the Study of Tibetan Buddhism

1974,   Sep   Identified as a cadre in the field of science

1978,   Feb   Elected deputy for Shanghai Municipality to the 5th NPC

         Apr   Identified as a cadre of the Institute of Research on World Religion

1979,   Feb   Identified as director of the Institute of Research on World Religion, Academy of Social Sciences

         Apr   Identified as president of the Society for the Study of Tibetan Buddhism

Ren Mingdao (Jen Ming-tao)　　任明道

Posts held

CCP
Member of the Standing Committee of Sichuan Province CP

1956   Identified as secretary, CP of Aba Autonomous Zhou of the Tibetans in Sichuan

1962,   Jan   Elected 1st secretary, CP of Aba Autonomous Zhou of the Tibetans in Sichuan

1965,   Sep   Elected secretary of Tibet Autonomous Region CP

1967   Disappears during the Cultural Revolution

1965,   Nov   First appearance after the Cultural Revolution: Identified as vice-chairman of the Revolutionary Committee of Sichuan Province (until Mar 1979?)

1976,   Jun   Identified as member of the Standing Committee of Sichuan Province CP; head of a friendship delegation to Romania

1978,   Feb   Elected deputy to Sichuan Province to the 5th NPC

Ren Puzhai (Jen P'u-chai)　　任朴斋

Posts held

Government
Vice-minister of the State Capital Construction Commission

1960,   Dec   Identified as director of the Construction Bureau under the Ministry of Building Construction

1971,   Aug   Identified as vice-minister for building construction (until Jan 1975); head of a government delegation to Algeria

1973,   Apr   Identified as acting chairman of the Society of Building Construction

1978,   May   Identified as vice-minister of the State Capital Construction Commission; member of an economic delegation to England and France

Ren Quansheng (Jen Ch'üan-sheng)　　任泉生

Posts held

Government
Vice-minister of commerce

Ren was born in Shandong Province.

1950, May Identified as council member of the People's Government of Liaodong Province (until Jun 1954)

Nov Appointed director of the Commerce Department in the People's Government of Liaodong (until Jun 1954)

1953, Feb Identified as head of the Northeast Storage Department under the Ministry of Commerce

1957, Apr Identified as chairman of the Association of Paper and Writing Utensils

1958, Jun Identified as director of the Bureau of Textile Trade in the Ministry of Commerce

1964, Apr Appointed vice-minister of commerce (until Cultural Revolution)

1973, Nov Reactivated after the Cultural Revolution: Identified in his previous post as vice-minister of commerce

1979, Jul Appointed member of the National Games Organizing Committee

Ren Rong (Jen Jung) 任 荣

Posts held

CCP
Member of the CCP 11th Central Committee
1st secretary of Tibet Autonomous Region CP

NPC
Deputy for the Tibet Autonomous Region to the 5th NPC

Military
Major-general
1st political commissar of Tibet Military District

Ren's career started in the 1st Front Army. In 1938 he was head of the Propaganda Department of Central Military District in the Military Region of Shaanxi-Gansu-Ningxia Border Area. In 1947 he was political commissar of a division in the 9th Column of the Northeast Liberation Army. In the following year he became head of the Political Department of this 9th Column which was renamed 46th Corps in February 1949.

1951 Appointed deputy political commissar of the 46th Corps in the 4th Field Army and sent to the Korean War with this unit

1952 Appointed political commissar of the 46th Corps

1954 Appointed director of the Organization Department in the Political Department of the Chinese People's Volunteers in Korea

1955, Sep Promoted to rank of major-general

1956 Appointed deputy director of the Political Department of the Chinese People's Volunteers in Korea

1957, Feb Identified as director of the Political Department of the Chinese People's Volunteers in Korea

1960, Nov Identified as major-general; identified as a member of the Chinese section of the Cease-fire Commission in Panmunjong

1965, Sep Identified as deputy political commissar of Tibet Military Region

1967, Aug At the height of the Cultural Revolution Ren is publicly denounced as an "ally of the bandits" without, however, suffering any political setbacks

Oct Ren delivers a speech at a demonstration on the occasion of the Chinese National Day in Lhasa

1968 Ren is present at several important occasions in Beijing

Sep Elected vice-chairman of the newly established Revolutionary Committee of Tibet Autonomous Region (until Aug 1979)

1970, Jun Identified as political commissar of Tibet Military Region (this Military Region is reduced to the status of Military District in 1971)

1971, Aug Elected 1st secretary of the newly established CP Secretariat of Tibet Autonomous Region

1973, Aug Elected alternate member of the CCP Central Committee by the 10th Party Congress (until Aug 1977)

1975, Sep Identified as 1st political commissar of Tibet Military District

1976, Dec Head of a friendship delegation of Party organizers to North Korea

Aug Elected member of the CCP Central Committee by the 11th Party Congress

1978, Feb Elected deputy for the Tibet Autonomous Region to the 5th NPC

1979, Aug Identified as chairman of the Tibet CPPCC

Ren Sizhong (Jen Szu-chung) 任思忠

Posts held

CCP
Member of the CCP 11th Central Committee

Military
Major-general
Deputy political commissar of Jinan Military Region

Ren was born in 1914. In 1947 he was political commissar of a regiment in the Northeast Field Army and in 1949 headed the Political Department of the 135th Division of the 4th Field Army.

1951-1953 Ren serves in the Korean War as deputy political commissar of the 135th Division

1955, Sep Promoted to rank of major-general

1960 Identified as political commissar of the 42nd Army based in Guangzhou Military Region

1967 Identified as director of the Political Department of Guangzhou Military Region

1969, Apr Elected to first term of the CCP Central Committee by the 9th Party Congress

1971, May Identified as political commissar of Guangzhou Military Region (until about 1974)

1975, May Transferred to Shandong Province

1977, Mar Identified as deputy political commissar of Jinan Military Region

Ren Xinmin (Jen Hsin-min) 任新民

Posts held

NPC
Member of the Standing Committee of the
5th NPC
Deputy for Shanghai Municipality to the
5th NPC

Others
Director of the Research Institute of
Space Technology
President of the Space Flight Society

1964,	Sep	Elected deputy for Beijing Municipality to the 3rd NPC
1973,	Oct	First appearance after the Cultural Revolution: Referred to as a scientist
1978,	Feb	Elected deputy for Shanghai Municipality to the 5th NPC
	Mar	Elected member of the Standing Committee of the 5th NPC
	Jul	Identified as director of the Research Institute of Space Technology
	Aug	Identified as president of the Space Flight Society; head of a Space Flight Society delegation to Japan
	Nov	Head of a space technology delegation to the U.S.A.
1979,	Jun	Member of the Committee to Examine Proposals at the 2nd Session of the 5th NPC

Ren Zhibin (Jen Chih-pin) 任质斌

Posts held

CCP
Alternate member of the CCP 11th Central Committee
Member of the Standing Committee of
Anhui Province CP
Secretary-general of Anhui Province CP

Ren served in the New 4th Army in 1945.

1951,	Feb	Appointed council member of Shandong People's Government
	Sep	Identified as secretary-general of the Shandong Subbureau in the CCP Central Committee
1962,	Jul	Identified as secretary of Anhui Province CP (until 1967)
1967,	Jan	Disappears following criticism
1974,	Feb	First appearance after the Cultural Revolution (in Anhui Province)
1977,	Aug	Elected alternate member of the CCP Central Committee by the 11th Party Congress
	Oct	Identified as member of the Standing Committee of Anhui Province CP
1978,	May	Identified as secretary-general of Anhui Province CP

Ren Zhiheng (Jen Chih-heng) 任之恒

Posts held

Vice-minister of coal industry

1978,	May	Identified as vice-minister of coal industry

Ren Zhongyi (Jen Chung-yi) 任仲夷

Posts held

CCP
Member of the CCP 11th Central Committee
1st secretary of Liaoning Province CP

NPC
Deputy for Liaoning Province to the
5th NPC

Military
1st political commissar of Liaoning Military District

Ren was born in Hebei Province.

1951,	Oct	Identified as secretary of the Democratic Youth League of Lüshun-Dalian Municipality
1954,	Aug	Elected deputy for Harbin Municipality to the 1st NPC
	Nov	Identified as 2nd secretary of Harbin CP
1956,	Sep	Ren reports to the 8th CCP Congress on the development of production in Harbin; identified as 1st secretary of Harbin CP (until Cultural Revolution)
1958,	Sep	Elected deputy for Heilongjiang Province to the 2nd NPC (until Aug 1964)
1961,	Feb	Identified as secretary of Heilongjiang Province CP (until Cultural Revolution)
1973,	May	Reactivated after the Cultural Revolution: Identified as secretary of Heilongjiang Province CP (until Mar 1977)
	Aug	Identified as vice-chairman of the Revolutionary Committee of Heilongjiang Province (until Mar 1977)
1977,	Mar	Identified as 1st vice-chairman of the Revolutionary Committee and as 2nd secretary of the CP of Liaoning Province (until Sep 1978)
	Aug	Elected member of the CCP Central Committee by the 11th Party Congress
1978,	Feb	Elected deputy for Liaoning Province to the 5th NPC
	Sep	Identified as 1st secretary of the CP, and as chairman of the Revolutionary Committee, of Liaoning Province (until Jan 1980), as well as 1st political commissar of Liaoning Military District
1979,	Jun	Member of the Credentials Committee at the 2nd Session of the 5th NPC
	Jul	Head of a Liaoning Provincial delegation to North Korea
	Sep	Head of a delegation of workers of the CCP to Romania and Yugoslavia

Renzeng Wangjie　　仁增旺杰
(Jen-tseng Wang-chieh, Rigdzin Wanggyual)

<u>Posts held</u>

CCP
Alternate member of the CCP 11th Central Committee
Member of the Standing Committee of Tibet CP
Secretary of Lhünze County CP
Secretary, CP of Nyama People's Commune

Renzeng, who was born in 1936, initially worked as a slave. He became known as an agricultural model worker having made land arable at an elevation of 4,200 m in Nyama People's Commune. Nyama People's Commune has since been known as "a Dazhai on the Tibetan plateau."

1974,	Mar	Identified as member of the Standing Committee of Tibet CP
	Nov	Identified as secretary, CP of Nyama People's Commune
1976,	Jul	Identified as secretary of Lhünze County CP and as secretary, CP of Nyama People's Commune
1977,	Aug	Elected alternate member of the CCP Central Committee by the 11th Party Congress

Rong Gaotang (Jung Kao-t'ang)　　荣高棠

<u>Posts held</u>

Government
Vice-minister of the State Physical Culture and Sports Commission

Others
Vice-president of the Sports Federation

Rong was born in 1912. From 1946 to 1947 he was director of the Communist Administration Department in the Executive Department, Military Mediation Committee. In April 1949 he was elected a member of the Standing Committee of the Central Committee, secretary general and director of the General Office of the New Democratic Youth League. One month later he was elected a member of the Central Committee of the Federation of Democratic Youth. In September of that year he took part in the 1st CPPCC.

1950,	Oct	Appointed secretary-general of the Preparatory Committee for the Athletic Federation; elected member of the Peace Council
1952,	Jun	With the establishment of the Athletic Federation, Rong is elected vice-chairman and secretary-general(until Oct 1956)
	Oct	Identified as member of the Secretariat of the New Democratic Youth League (until May 1957)
1953,	May	Identified as director of the Military and Sports Department of the New Democratic Youth League (until May 1957)
	Jun	Identified as secretary-general of the Physical Culture and Sports Commission in the Government Administration Council

1954,	Jul	Head of the Chinese team at the Olympic Games in Helsinki
	May	Elected council member of the Association for Cultural Relations with Foreign Countries
	Jul	Head of the Chinese team to the Soviet National Sports Competitions
	Aug	Elected deputy for Hubei Province to the 1st NPC
	Oct	Appointed vice-chairman of the Physical Culture and Sports Commission
1955,	Jun	Delegate at a session of the Olympic Committee in Paris
1956,	Mar	Head of the Chinese team at the Table-Tennis World Championship in Japan
1958,	Oct	Appointed vice-chairman of the China-German Democratic Republic Friendship Association
1962,	Nov	Head of a group of table-tennis players visiting Japan
1963,	Jun	Appointed vice-chairman of the Preparatory Committee for the Games of the New Emerging Forces
	Oct	Head of the Chinese sports team at the Games of the New Emerging Forces in Jakarta
1964,	Feb	Head of a sports group visiting Cuba
	Mar	Head of a sports group visiting Albania
	Aug	Elected chairman of the National Committee, Games of the New Emerging Forces
	Sep	Head of a sports group visiting North Korea
1965,	Apr	Head of the Chinese table-tennis team at the World Championship in Yugoslavia
1967,	Jan	Branded as a counterrevolutionary revisionist
1979,	Feb	First appearance after the Cultural Revolution
	Mar	Elected vice-president of the Sports Federation
	Jul	Appointed vice-chairman and secretary-general of the National Games Organizing Committee
	Aug	Identified as vice-minister of the State Physical Culture and Sports Commission

Rong is married to Guan Ping.

Rong Yiren (Jung Yi-jen)　　荣毅仁

<u>Posts held</u>

NPC
Member of the Standing Committee of the 5th NPC
Deputy for Shanghai Municipality to the 5th NPC

Others
Vice-president of the 5th CPPCC
Chairman of the Board of Directors, China International Trust and Investment Corporation
Vice-chairman of the Executive Committee of the Federation of Industrialists and Businessmen
Managing director of the Bank of China

Rong was born in 1916 in Jiangsu Province. When Shanghai was occupied by the Communists in spring 1949 he was deputy director of Sangsong Cotton Mills and Fuxin Flour Company which were both owned by his family.

1950,	Mar	Appointed member of the Financial and Economic Committee in the East China Military and Administrative Council (until Dec 1952)
	Dec	Elected council member of the Shanghai People's Government (until Feb 1955)
1952,	Oct	Appointed director of the Administrative Council of Sangsong Cotton Mills
	Dec	Appointed member of the Financial and Economic Committee in the East China Administrative Council (until 1954)
1953,	Oct	Appointed vice-chairman of the newly established Federation of Industry and Commerce
1954,	Aug	Elected deputy for Shanghai Municipality to the 1st NPC and vice-chairman, Shanghai Section of the Federation of Industry and Commerce
1955,	Feb	Elected member of the People's Council of Shanghai
1956,	Mar	Delegate at the special session of the World Peace Council in Stockholm
1957,	Apr	Elected deputy mayor of Shanghai Municipality (until Cultural Revolution)
1959,	Apr	Elected member of the Standing Committee, CPPCC (until Cultural Revolution)
	Sep	Appointed vice-minister of textile industry (until Cultural Revolution)
1961,	Jan	Member of a friendship delegation led by Zhou Enlai to Burma
1966		Rong disappears during the Cultural Revolution
1972,	Jan	Reactivated after the Cultural Revolution
	Mar	Identified as member of the Standing Committee of the CPPCC
1973,	Apr	Member of a delegation of the Sino-Japanese Friendship Association to Japan
1975,	Jan	Elected member of the Standing Committee by the 4th NPC (confirmed in 1978 by the 5th NPC)
1978,	Feb	Elected deputy for Shanghai Municipality to the 5th NPC
	Mar	Elected vice-president of the 5th CPPCC
1979,	Jan	Identified as vice-chairman of the Federation of Industry and Commerce (until Oct 1979)
	Apr	Head of a delegation to the Hanover Fair (Federal Republic of Germany) and to Switzerland and France; identified as managing director of the Bank of China
	Jun	Member of the Draft Law Committee at the 2nd Session of the 5th NPC
	Oct	Head of an investment delegation to the U.S.A.; appointed chairman of the Board of Directors and president of the China International Trust and Investment Corporation; elected vice-chairman of the Executive Committee of the Federation of Industrialists and Businessmen

Rong is married to Yang Jianqing (born 1917).

Rong Zihe (Jung Tzu-ho)   戊子和

Posts held

Others
Member of the Standing Committee of the 5th CPPCC

Rong was born circa 1905 in Lingqiu, Shanxi Province. He is a graduate of Shanxi University. In 1935 he was a member of the Shanxi National Salvation Sacrifice League. In 1938 he led the Shanxi 3rd Dare-to-Die Column operating in Shanxi-Henan Border Region. He joined the guerrilla forces under Bo Yibo in 1940. In 1941 he served as vice-chairman of the Shanxi-Hebei-Shandong-Henan Border Government. In 1948 he was a member and minister of finance of the North China People's Government.

1949,	Oct	Appointed vice-minister of finance (until Jul 1961)
1954,	Dec	Identified as managing director of the Bank of Communications
1964,	Jul	Member of a friendship delegation to Cuba
1965,	Jun	Identified as director of the Finance and Trade Office, Northeast Bureau of the CCP Central Committee
1967		Disappears during the Cultural Revolution
1978,	Dec	First appearance after the Cultural Revolution
1979,	Jul	By-elected a member of the Standing Committee of the 5th CPPCC

Rouzi Tuerdi (Jou·tz'u T'u·erh·t'i, Ruzi Turdi)

肉孜·土
尔迪

Posts held

CCP
Alternate member of the CCP 11th Central Committee
Secretary of Turpan County CP in Xinjiang Autonomous Region

Others
Chairman of the Revolutionary Committee of Turpan County in Xinjiang Autonomous Region

Rouzi belongs to the Uighur minority. He was born in 1921 in Turpan County, Xinjiang, as the son of poor peasants. At the age of eight he worked together with his father as a farm laborer in the service of a landlord. He is said to have owned his first pair of trousers at the age of twelve.

1952	Rouzi is one of the first Uighurs to join the CCP
1955	Rouzi organizes the first cooperative in Turpan County
1958	He establishes the first people's commune in Turpan County
1962	Rouzi initiates the utilization of melted snow from the Tianshan which eventually leads to the construction of a canal involving 1,000 members of his people's commune
1964	Responsible for the afforestation of protective belts of forests

1966		Identified as vice-chairman of Turpan County
1969,	Apr	Elected alternate member of the CCP Central Committee by the 9th Party Congress (confirmed in 1973 and 1977 by the 10th and 11th Congresses)
1971,	Jan	Identified as chairman of the Revolutionary Committee, and as secretary of the CP, of Turpan County
1973,	Nov	Article in HQ: "The Implementation of a Correct Political Line Requires a Correct Attitude towards the Masses"
1977,	Aug	Last appearance; probably purged

Ru Fuyi (Ju Fu-yi)　　茹夫一

Posts held

NPC
Deputy for Sichuan Province to the 5th NPC

Military
Deputy commander of Chengdu Military Region

Provincial Administration
Vice-chairman of the Revolutionary Committee of Sichuan Province

1960,	Jan	Identified as chief of staff of Chengdu Military Region
1977,	Feb	Identified as a cadre in Sichuan
	Dec	Elected vice-chairman of the Revolutionary Committee of Sichuan Province
1978,	Feb	Elected deputy for Sichuan Province to the 5th NPC
1980,	Feb	Identified as deputy commander of Chengdu Military Region

Rui Ban (Jui Pan)　　瑞板

Posts held

NPC
Member of the Standing Committee of the 5th NPC
Deputy for Yunnan Province to the 5th NPC

1975,	Jan	Member of the presidium of the 4th NPC
1978,	Feb	Elected deputy for Yunnan Province to the 5th NPC
	Mar	Elected member of the Standing Committee of the 5th NPC

Rui Mu (Jui Mu)　　芮沐

Posts held

Others
Director of the Board of Directors, China International Trust and Investment Corporation

Rui studied in Germany and France.

1962,	Jan	Identified as professor of law, Beijing University
	Feb	Identified as a council member of the Association of Political Science and Law
1979,	Oct	Appointed director of the Board of Directors, China International Trust and Investment Corporation; identified as a professor in the Department of Law, Beijing University

Sa Kongliao (Sa K'ung-liao)   萨空了

Posts held

Government
Member of the State Nationalities Affairs
Commission

Others
Member of the Standing Committee of the
5th CPPCC
Deputy secretary-general of the 5th
CPPCC
Vice-chairman of the Central Committee
of the China Democratic League

Sa was born in 1905 in Beijing of a Mongolian family from Sichuan. He is a graduate of Beijing University. He joined the CCP as a student. In 1933 he was concurrently editor of a special supplement to the Beijing Evening News, the World, and lecturer in journalism at the Minguo University in Beijing. In 1935 he was a cofounder of the National Salvation Society. In 1936 he became chief editior of the Shanghai newspaper Li Bao. After the outbreak of the Anti-Japanese War in 1937, he left occupied Shanghai together with Mao Dun (Shen Yanbing) and other left-wing writers via Hong Kong to Dihua (now Ürümqi), to work as chief editor of the Xinjiang Ribao (Xinjiang Daily) and as lecturer at Xinjiang University. Prosecuted by the then governor of Xinjiang, Sheng Shicai, he fled to Hong Kong in 1938. There he edited the daily Guangming in 1939. When Hong Kong was occupied by the Japanese in 1941 he moved to Guilin in Guangxi Province where he was arrested in 1943 because of anti-government activities. In prison he wrote Remarks on Vocational Training for Youths, General Thoughts on Scientific Journalism, From Hong Kong to Sinkiang, and the novelette The Coward. In addition, he translated several European works during this period. In June 1944 he was moved to a reeducation camp in Chongqing, and released in June 1945. After the Japanese capitulation Sa went to Hong Kong as editor of Huashang Newspaper. In May 1949 he was elected a member of the Standing Committee of the Federation of Democratic Youth. Two months later he was a member of the Preparatory Committee for the foundation of the Chinese Journalists' Association (until 1954). In September 1949 he took part as a delegate representing the National Salvation Society in the 1st CPPCC which elected him a member of its National Committee (until Dec 1954).

1950,	Oct	Appointed council member of the Sino-Soviet Friendship Association (until Dec 1954); member of the Association for the Reform of the Chinese Written Language; deputy director of the News Administration in the Government Administration Council (until Aug 1952)
	Dec	Appointed director of the Bureau of Press Photos in the News Administration (until Aug 1952); elected a member of the 1st Central Committee of the Democratic League (until Jan 1956); appointed secretary-general of the daily GMRB
1951,	Oct	Appointed member of the Minorities Affairs Commission (until Sep 1954)
1952,	Aug	Appointed deputy director of the Press Administration (until Sep 1954)
1953,	Jan	Identified as chairman of the Nationalities Press
	May	Identified as vice-chairman of the Propaganda Council, Democratic League (until Feb 1956)
1954,	May	Appointed member of the Standing Committee, Association for Cultural Relations with Foreign Countries (until Cultural Revolution)
	Aug	Elected deputy for Sichuan Province to the 1st NPC (reelected in 1958 and 1964 to the 2nd and 3rd NPCs)
	Oct	Appointed vice-chairman of the Minorities Affairs Commission (until Sep 1959)
	Nov	Member of a cultural delegation to Albania
1958,	Sep	Elected a member of the Sino-Iraq Friendship Association (until Cultural Revolution)
	Dec	Elected director of the Propaganda Department of the Democratic League (until Cultural Revolution)
1959,	Apr	Elected member of the Standing Committee of the 3rd CPPCC
1960,	Apr	Elected council member of the Sino-African Friendship Association (until Cultural Revolution)
	Aug	Elected member of the Literary Society (until Cultural Revolution)
	Nov	Elected council member of the Sino-Albanian Friendship Association (until Cultural Revolution)
1961,	Mar	Member of a government delegation to Indonesia
	Jul	Appointed vice-chairman of the Sino-Indonesian Friendship Association (until 1966)
1963,	Apr	Head of an opera troupe to Hong Kong and Macao (until Jun)
1964,	Dec	Reelected member of the Standing Committee of the CPPCC
1965,	Jan	Deputy head of a friendship delegation to Indonesia
1966		Disappears during the Cultural Revolution
1973,	Mar	First appearance after the Cultural Revolution: Identified in his former post as member of the Standing Committee of the 4th CPPCC (confirmed in Mar 1978 by the 5th CPPCC)
1978,	Aug	Identified as deputy secretary-general of the 5th CPPCC
1979,	May	Appointed member of the State Nationalities Affairs Commission
	Oct	Elected vice-chairman of the Central Committee of the China Democratic League

Se·yin·ba·ya·er (Se·yin·pa·ya·erh)   色音巴
雅尔

Posts held

Government
Member of the State Nationalities Affairs
Commission

Provincial Administration
Vice-chairman of the Revolutionary Committee of Jilin Province

Se-yin-ba-ya-er belongs to the Mongolian minority.

1977,	Dec	Elected vice-chairman of the Revolutionary Committee of Jilin Province
1978,	Oct	Head of an animal husbandry delegation to Australia
1979,	May	Appointed member of the State Nationalities Affairs Commission

Sengqen Losang Gyancan
(Seng-ch'en Lo·sang Gyants'an)

生钦·洛桑·坚赞

Posts held

NPC
Deputy for Tibet to the 5th NPC

Provincial Administration
Vice-chairman of the People's Congress, Tibet Autonomous Region

Sengqen belongs to the Tibetan minority. His Tibetan name is Zanchhen Lozong Geltseng.

1964,	Dec	Elected deputy for Tibet to the 3rd NPC
1978,	Feb	Elected deputy for Tibet to the 5th NPC
1979,	Aug	Elected vice-chairman of the People's Congress, Tibet Autonomous Region
1980,	Feb	Member of an NPC delegation to Thailand (head: Deng Yingchao)

Seypidin Äzizi (Saifudin)

赛福鼎

Posts held

CCP
Alternate member of the CCP Politburo
Member of the CCP 11th Central Committee

NPC
Vice-chairman of the Standing Committee of the 5th NPC
Deputy for Xinjiang Autonomous Region to the 5th NPC

Seypidin was born in 1916 in Xinjiang. He belongs to the Uighur nationality, the largest minority group in Xinjiang. From circa 1938 to 1942 he studied political science at the Central Asian University in Moscow. He joined the CPSU during this period. In 1944 Seypidin organized uprisings against the Chinese in the areas of Ili, Tacheng, and Ashan. He then played an important role in the foundation of the "People's Republic of East Turkestan," of which he became minister of education in January 1945.

In 1946 Seypidin joined the Beijing inspired "Coalition Government of Xinjiang under the Chinese General Zhang Zhizhong (1891-1969). In this government he held the post of education commissar. In 1947 he resigned from this coalition government to return to Ili from where he organized the resistance against the Chinese Nationalist Government. Under Seypidin's initiative the "People's Republic of East Turkestan" was renamed "League for the Protection of Democracy and Self-Government in Xinjiang" in 1948. At the same time, the independence movement organized by Seypidin joined the CCP.

1949,	Sep	Elected member of the CPPCC (until Dec 1954)

	Oct	Appointed member of the Government People's Council and vice-chairman of the Nationalities Affairs Commission (until Sep 1954)
	Dec	Appointed vice-chairman of the Provincial Government of Xinjiang and member of the Military and Political Council. At approximately this time appointed member of the Peace Council (until Jul 1958)
1950,	Feb	Visit to Moscow, presumably to apply for permission to cancel his CPSU membership and to join the CCP (at the same time Mao Zedong was conducting negotiations in Moscow)
later:		In the course of 1950 Seypidin joins the CCP and is appointed 4th secretary of Xinjiang CP
1953,	Jan	After the Northwest China Military and Administrative Council is abolished, Seypidin is appointed vice-chairman of the newly established Northwest China Administrative Council
later:		Appointed member of the Committee for Drafting a New Chinese Constitution
1954,	Sep	Elected deputy for Xinjiang to the 1st NPC. Subsequently elected vice-chairman of the Standing Committee of the NPC. Following the reorganization of the Central Government in autumn 1954, Seypidin is relieved of all administrative posts. At the same time he becomes a member of the newly established National Defense Council as well as vice-governor of Xinjiang.
	Dec	Elected vice-chairman of the Sino-Soviet Friendship Association (until about 1963)
1955,	Oct	The status of Xinjiang Province is changed to Xinjiang Autonomous Region of which Seypidin is installed as chairman (equivalent to governor) and secretary of the CP; appointed deputy commander of Xinjiang Military Region (until 1972)
1956,	Sep	Elected alternate member of the CCP Central Committee by 8th Party Congress
1957,	Jul-Aug	Head of a NPC delegation to Moscow and Helsinki
1959,	Mar	Elected deputy for Xinjiang Autonomous Region to the 2nd NPC
	Apr	Seypidin condemns the Tibetan Uprising in an article in RMRB
	May	Elected vice-chairman of the Sino-Soviet Friendship Association
	Aug	Seypidin receives Ho Chi-minh arriving in Ürümqi from the USSR
1960,	Aug	Elected vice-chairman of the Federation of Literary and Art Circles (until Cultural Revolution)
1961,	Oct	Present at the October celebrations in Beijing
1962,	Sep	Deputy head of a NPC delegation to PR Vietnam
1964,	Jun	Appointed chancellor of Xinjiang University in Ürümqi (until Cultural Revolution)
1966,	Aug	Identified as chairman of the Sino-Pakistani Friendship Association (no later mention in this post)
1968,	Sep	Elected vice-chairman of the newly established Revolutionary Committee of

Xinjiang Autonomous Region (until Aug 1973)

1969, Apr Elected member of the CCP Central Committee by the 9th Party Congress (confirmed in 1973 and 1977 by the 10th and 11th Congresses)

Aug Identified as deputy commander of Xinjiang Military Region (until Oct 1973)

1971, May Identified as 2nd secretary of Xinjiang Autonomous Region CP (until Jul 1973)

1973, Jul Identified as 1st secretary of Xinjiang Autonomous Region CP (until Jan 1978)

Aug Identified as chairman of the Revolutionary Committee of Xinjiang Autonomous Region (until Jan 1978); elected to first term as alternate member of the CCP Politburo by the 10th Party Congress

Oct Identified as 1st political commissar of Xinjiang Military Region (until Jan 1978)

1975, Jan Elected vice-chairman of the Standing Committee by the 4th NPC

Oct Article in HQ 10/1975 on the 20th anniversary of Xinjiang Autonomous Region

1977, May Head of a NPC delegation to Romania

Oct Article in RMRB: "The People of Various Nationalities in Xinjiang Cherish the Memory of Chairman Mao"

Nov Appointed director of the Party School of Xinjiang CP (until Jan 1978)

1978, Feb Elected deputy for Xinjiang Autonomous Region to the 5th NPC

Mar Confirmed by the 5th NPC as vice-chairman

Seypidin is married to Ahyimu.

Sha Qianli (Sha Ch'ien-li)　沙千里

Posts held

NPC
Deputy secretary-general of the 5th NPC
Member of the Standing Committee of the 5th NPC
Deputy for Shanghai Municipality to the 5th NPC
Vice-chairman of the Legal Commission under the 5th NPC Standing Committee

Others
Vice-chairman of the Executive Committee, Federation of Industrialists and Businessmen

Sha was born in 1901 in Suzhou, Jiangsu Province. He graduated from the Shanghai School of Law in 1929 and subsequently practiced in Shanghai. In 1935 he was one of the cofounders of the National Salvation Society which supported a united front between the KMT and the CCP against the Japanese. Sha was one of the seven leading cadres arrested following the rejection of this united front. When he was released in 1937 he joined the Communist oriented National United Front against the Japanese. As a delegate representing the National Salvation Society, which was abolished shortly afterwards, Sha took part in the CPPCC in 1949.

1949, Oct Appointed vice-minister of commerce (ministry abolished in Aug 1952)

Dec Identified as council member of the Sino-Soviet Friendship Association (until Nov 1951)

1952, Apr Head of a trade delegation to Moscow

Aug Appointed vice-minister of the newly established Ministry of Economics (until Sep 1954)

1953, Oct Appointed secretary-general of the Federation of Industry and Commerce at its founding session

1954, Sep Elected deputy for Jiangsu Province to the 1st NPC appointed minister of local industries (abolished in May 1956)

1955, May Member of a government delegation to the German Democratic Republic

1956, May Appointed minister of light industry (until Feb 1958)

1958, Feb Appointed minister of food (until Cultural Revolution)

Nov Identified as member of the Central Committee of the National Construction Association

1975, Jan Elected member of the Standing Committee by the 4th NPC (confirmed in Mar 1978 by the 5th NPC)

Mar Appointed deputy secretary-general of the 4th NPC (confirmed in Mar 1978 by the 5th NPC)

1978, Feb Elected deputy for Shanghai Municipality to the 5th NPC

1979, Feb Elected vice-chairman of the Legal Commission under the NPC Standing Committee

Jun Vice-chairman of the Draft Laws Committee at the 2nd Session of the 5th NPC

Oct Elected vice-chairman of the Executive Committee of the Federation of Industrialists and Businessmen

Shan Huaixiang (Shan Huai-hsiang) 单怀香

Posts held

NPC
Deputy for Shaanxi Province to the 5th NPC
Member of the Standing Committee of the 5th NPC

1978, Feb Elected deputy for Shaanxi Province to the 5th NPC

Mar Elected member of the Standing Committee of the 5th NPC

Shang Kan (Shang K'an)　尚侃

Posts held

Military
Commander of Henan Military District

1978, Mar Identified as deputy commander of Henan Military District

Aug Identified as commander of Henan Military District

Shang Zhitian (Shang Chih-t'ien) 尚志田

Posts held

Provincial Administration
Vice-governor of Qinghai Province

1979,	Sep	Elected vice-governor of Qinghai Province

Shang Zijin (Shang Tzu-chin) 尚子锦

Posts held

Provincial Administration
Vice-governor of Hunan Province

1955,	Jun	Identified as director of the Commerce Department, People's Government of Hunan Province
1957,	May	Identified as deputy director of the Office of Finance, Food, and Commerce of Hunan People's Government
1958,	Jul	Elected vice-governor of Hunan Province (until Cultural Revolution)
	Sep	Identified as alternate member of Hunan Province CP
1965,	Jul	Article in Dagong Bao (L'Impartial): "Commerce Must Concentrate Primarily on Rural Areas"
1967		Disappears during the Cultural Revolution
1971,	Jul	First appearance after the Cultural Revolution: Identified as vice-chairman of the Revolutionary Committee of Hunan Province (reelected in Nov 1977) (until Dec 1979)
1976,	Jul	Head of a friendship delegation to Albania
1979,	Dec	Elected vice-governor of Hunan Province

Shao Feng (Shao Feng) 邵 风

Posts held

Provincial Administration
Vice-governor of Yunnan Province

1979,	Dec	Elected vice-governor of Yunnan Province

Shao Gongwen (Shao Kung-wen) 邵公文

Posts held

Government
Manager-general of the China Publication Center

1959,	Oct	Identified as director of Zhongguo Guoji Shudian (China Publication Center)
1964,	Apr	Shao visits Vietnam
1977,	Dec	First appearance after the Cultural Revolution
1978,	Aug	Identified as manager-general of the China Publication Center

Shao Jingwa (Shao Ching-wa) (f) 邵井蛙

Posts held

CCP
Secretary of Ningxia Autonomous Region CP

1950,	Jul	Elected vice-chairman of the Trade Union of Textile Workers (reelected in Aug 1953)
1956,	Apr	Member of the Presidium of the National Congress of Progressive Workers
1957,	Dec	Elected member of the Executive Council of the Federation of Trade Unions (until Cultural Revolution)
1965,	Apr	Elected chairman of the Trade Union of Textile Workers (until Cultural Revolution)
1971,	Aug	Elected deputy secretary of the new CP Secretariat of Ningxia Autonomous Region after the Cultural Revolution (until Apr 1978)
	Oct	Identified as vice-chairman of the Revolutionary Committee of Ningxia Autonomous Region (reelected in Dec 1977)
1977?		Elected vice-chairman of the Revolutionary Committee of Ningxia Autonomous Region (until Dec 1979)
1978,	Apr	Elected secretary of Ningxia Autonomous Region CP

Shao Rongbin (Shao Jung-pin) 邵荣宾

Posts held

NPC
Member of the Standing Committee of the 5th NPC
Deputy for Shanghai Municipality to the 5th NPC

1978,	Feb	Elected deputy for Shanghai Municipality to the 5th NPC
	Mar	Elected member of the Standing Committee of the 5th NPC

Shen Chuyun (Shen Ch'u-yün) (f) 沈初云

Posts held

CCP
Alternate member of the CCP 11th Central Committee

Shen became known as a Hangzhou textile worker.

1977,	Aug	Elected alternate member of the CCP Central Committee by the 11th Party Congress

Shen Guang (Shen Kuang) 申 光

Posts held

Government
Vice-minister of posts and telecommunications

Shen was born in Shandong Province. Before 1949 he was director of the Supplies Department in the Central Bureau of Telecommunications in Beijing.

1949,　Oct　Appointed director of the General Office in the Ministry of Posts and Telecommunications (until Jan 1955)

1955,　Jan　Appointed assistant minister in the Ministry of Posts and Telecommunications (until Apr 1956)

1956,　Apr　Appointed vice-minister of posts and telecommunications (until Cultural Revolution)

1961,　Oct　Head of a postal delegation to Cuba

1972,　Oct　Identified as deputy director of the Bureau of Telecommunications under the State Council (until 1973)

1973,　Oct　Identified as vice-minister of posts and telecommunications

Shen Hong (Shen Hung)　　沈　鴻

Posts held

Government
Vice-minister of the 1st Ministry of Machine Building

NPC
Member of the Standing Committee of the 5th NPC
Deputy for Shanghai Municipality to the 5th NPC

Others
Vice-president of the Society of Mechanical Engineering

Shen was born in Shanghai. Without previous schooling he entered the firm of a cotton trader as an apprentice. Gifted with an extraordinary talent for mechanics, he set up a machine tool factory in Shanghai as a youth. After the outbreak of the Anti-Japanese War in 1937 he moved his factory to Hankou (today: Wuhan) where he first came into contact with the CCP of which he became a member. After the Japanese occupation of Hankou he went to the Communist base in Shaanxi as chief engineer of the Anzhai Arsenal which produced light firearms as well as agricultural and textile equipment. As the "father of industry in the border region" he laid the foundation for light industry in the Communist controlled areas. In 1944 he was praised as a "labor hero." In 1948 he worked as an engineer in the Industrial Bureau of Shanxi-Chahar-Hebei Border Region. He was appointed engineer of the Industrial Department of North China People's Government (predecessor of PRC) in August 1948. In September 1949 he took part in the 1st CPPCC as a delegate representing the trade unions.

1950,　Jan　Member of a delegation led by Zhou Enlai to Moscow where it is joined by Mao Zedong to sign several agreements

　　　　Jun　Appointed director of the Department of Heavy Industry, Planning Bureau of the Financial and Economic Commission of the Government Administration Council

1954,　Aug　Elected director of the Organization Department of Engineering Society

1955,　Apr　Appointed vice-minister of the 3rd Ministry of Machine Building (until May 1956)

1957,　Jun　Appointed vice-minister of electrical equipment (until Nov 1957)

　　　　Nov　Identified as vice-minister of coal industry (until Sep 1959); head of a delegation to Yugoslavia

1959,　Sep　Identified as vice-minister of the Ministry of Agricultural Machinery (until Dec 1961)

1960,　May　Elected vice-chairman of the Society of Mechanical Engineering

1961,　Dec　Identified as vice-minister of the 1st Ministry of Machine Building

1963,　Nov　Head of a scientific and technological delegation to Hungary

1964,　Sep　Elected deputy for Heilongjiang Province to the 3rd NPC

1966,　Jul　Head of a scientific and technical delegation to Hungary

1970,　Sep　First reference after the Cultural Revolution to Shen in his former post as vice-minister of the 1st Ministry of Machine Building

1978,　Feb　Elected deputy for Shanghai Municipality to the 5th NPC

　　　　Mar　Elected member of the Standing Committee of the 5th NPC

　　　　Sep　Identified as vice-president of the Society of Mechanical Engineering

1979,　Jun　Member of the Draft Laws Committee at the 2nd Session of the 5th NPC

Shen Jian (Shen Chien)　　申　健

Posts held

CCP
Deputy director of the International Liaison Department of the CCP Central Committee

Others
Member of the Standing Committee of the 5th CPPCC

Shen was born circa 1923. He graduated in English from the Beijing Teachers College.

1949,　Oct　Identified as director of the Secretariat of the General Office, Military Council of the Central People's Government (until Sep 1950)

1950,　Sep　Identified as counselor at the embassy in India (until Jul 1958)

1958,　Jul　Identified as deputy director of the America and Australia Department in the Ministry of Foreign Affairs (until Feb 1959)

1959,　Feb　Identified as director of the America and Australia Department in the Ministry of Foreign Affairs (until Nov 1960)

1960,　Mar　Identified as council member of the Sino-Latin-American Friendship Association

　　　　Nov　Appointed ambassador to Cuba (until Jan 1964)

1964,　Dec　Identified as vice-chairman of the Institute of Foreign Affairs

1966-1969　Shen survives the Cultural Revolution without coming under attack

1971,	Mar	Identified as a cadre of the International Liaison Department of the CCP Central Committee
1973,	Aug	Identified as deputy director of the International Liaison Department of the CCP Central Committee
1974,	Feb	Head of a Wuhan acrobatic troupe visiting South America
	Aug	Deputy head of a friendship delegation to North Korea
1975,	Feb	Head of a Wuhan acrobatic troupe visiting Senegal
	Aug	Member of a Party and government delegation to Hanoi to attend the 30th anniversary celebrations of the Democratic Republic of Vietnam
1977,	Apr	Head of a friendship delegation to North Korea
	Dec	Member of a Party and government delegation to Kampuchea under Chen Yonggui
1978,	Mar	Elected member of the Standing Committee of the 5th CPPCC
	May	Member of a Party and government delegation to North Korea under Hua Guofeng
	Nov	Member of a Party and government delegation to Kampuchea under Wang Dongxing
1979,	Feb	Head of a Party delegation to Mexico to the 50th anniversary of the foundation of the Revolutionary Institutional Party

Shen Ling (Shen Ling)   沈　頷

Posts held

Provincial Administration
Vice-governor of Qinghai Province

1960,	Nov	Identified as 1st secretary, CP of Yushu Autonomous Zhou in Qinghai Province
1977,	Dec	Elected vice-chairman of the Revolutionary Committee of Qinghai Province (until Aug 1979)
1979,	Sep	Elected vice-governor of Qinghai Province

Shen Maogong (Shen Mao-kung)   申茂功

Posts held

CCP
Alternate member of the CCP 11th Central Committee

Shen became known as a worker at Cotton Mill No. 6 in Zhengzhou, the capital city of Henan Province.

1966		At the beginning of the Cultural Revolution Shen is head of the "Worker-Rebels Headquarters" in Henan Province
1967,	Oct	Elected chairman of the Workers Congress of Zhengzhou
1968,	Jan	With the establishment of the Revolutionary Committee of Henan Province Shen is elected a member of its Standing Committee (until about 1973)
1969,	Apr	Elected member of the CCP Central Committee by the 9th Party Congress (until Aug 1973)

1971,	Mar	Elected member of the Standing Committee of Henan Province CP
	Apr	Member of a workers delegation to Albania
1972,	Jul	Head of a workers delegation to Romania
1973,	Aug	Demoted to alternate member of the CCP Central Committee by the 10th Party Congress (confirmed in 1977 by the 11th Congress)
	Sep	Elected chairman of the Trade Unions of Henan Province (no later mention in this post)
1979,	Sep	Named a "counterrevolutionary, to be dealt with seriously" by XNA on 26 September

Shen Ping (Shen P'ing)   沈　平

Posts held
Government
Director of the Asia Department in the Ministry of Foreign Affairs

1952,	Oct	Identified as deputy director of the Public Relations Office in the Ministry of Foreign Affairs
1955,	Jul	Appointed consul-general in Geneva (until Apr 1959)
1959,	Apr	Appointed deputy director of the 1st Asia Department in the Ministry of Foreign Affairs (until Dec 1962)
1961,	Mar	Member of a government delegation to Indonesia
1962,	Dec	Appointed counselor at the Chinese Mission in Great Britain
1967,	Sep	Identified as chargé d'affaires ad interim in Great Britain (until Apr 1969)
1970		Head of a bureau in the Ministry of Foreign Affairs
1971,	Apr	Appointed ambassador to Italy (until Jun 1974)
1975,	Aug	Identified as director of the Asia Department in the Ministry of Foreign Affairs; member of a Party and government delegation to Hanoi to attend the 30th anniversary celebrations of the Democratic Republic of Vietnam
1978,	Jan	Member of a government delegation to Kampuchea under Deng Yingchao
	Jun	Member of a government delegation led by Geng Biao to Pakistan
	Oct	Member of a government delegation led by Deng Xiaoping to Japan

Shen Qizhen (Shen Ch'i-chen)   沈其震

Posts held

Others
Vice-president of the Academy of Medical Sciences
Vice-president of the Red Cross Society
Vice-chairman of the Central Committee, China Peasants and Workers Democratic Party

In 1946 Shen was head of the Medical Department of the New 4th Army.

1951,	Oct	Identified as director of the Lüda Medical College
1952,	Dec	Identified as director of the Sanitation Research Institute under the Ministry of Public Health
1953,	Feb	Member of an Academy of Sciences delegation to the USSR
1954,	Aug	Elected deputy for Hunan Province to the 1st NPC (reelected in 1958 and 1964 to the 2nd and 3rd NPCs)
1955,	Jun	Identified as member of the Department of Biology and Geology, Academy of Sciences
1960,	May	Identified as council member of the Sino-German Democratic Republic Friendship Association
	Oct	Identified as vice-president of the Academy of Medical Sciences
1962,	Jun	Member of an Academy of Sciences delegation to Hungary
1967,	Feb	Identified as director of the Sanitation Research Institute under the Ministry of Public Health; subsequently disappears
1974,	Sep	First appearance after the Cultural Revolution
1978,	Oct	Identified as vice-president of the Academy of Medical Sciences
1979,	Feb	Elected vice-president of the Red Cross Society
	Oct	Elected vice-chairman of the Central Committee of the China Peasants and Workers Democratic Party
	Dec	Member of a CPPCC delegation to Romania

Shen Tu (Shen T'u)　　沈　图

Posts held

Government
Director-general of the General Administration of Civil Aviation

1954,	Oct	Appointed manager of the Sino-Soviet Civil Aviation Corporation
1955,	Jan	Member of a delegation led by Wu Faxian to civil aviation negotiations in Moscow
1959,	Apr	Identified as deputy director of the Bureau of Civil Aviation in the Ministry of Communications (until Mar 1962)
	Jun	Head of an aviation delegation to Ceylon
1962,	Mar	The Bureau of Civil Aviation in the Ministry of Communications is reorganized into the Civil Aviation Administration under the State Council, of which Shen becomes vice-chairman
	Oct	Head of a delegation visiting an aircraft factory in France
1963,	Aug	Head of an aviation delegation to Pakistan
	Nov	Head of an aviation delegation to Cambodia
1965,	Jul	Head of an aviation delegation to Burma
1966,	Feb	Head of an aviation delegation to the USSR for revision of the Sino-Soviet Agreement on Civil Aviation
1967		Disappears during the Cultural Revolution
1973,	Oct	First appearance after the Cultural Revolution: Identified in his former post as deputy director-general of the Civil Aviation Administration; head of an aviation delegation to Switzerland
1974,	Sep	Head of a delegation to a session of the International Civil Aviation Organization (ICAO) in Montreal
1975,	Sep	Head of an aviation delegation to the Federal Republic of Germany
1976,	Apr	Head of an aviation delegation to North Korea
1977,	Sep	Head of an aviation delegation to Canada to attend the 22nd meeting of the International Civil Aviation Organization
1978,	Jan	Identified as director-general of the Civil Aviation Administration
	Nov	Head of a delegation to the 14th Meeting of the Civil Aviation Directors of the Asian Pacific Region in Kathmandu, Nepal
1979,	Jan	Head of a civil aviation delegation to Thailand and Burma

Shen Xinfa (Shen Hsin-fa)　　沈新发

Posts held

CCP
Member of the Standing Committee of Inner Mongolia Autonomous Region CP

Provincial Administration
Vice-chairman of the People's Congress of Inner Mongolia Autonomous Region CP

1950,	Apr	Identified as deputy secretary of the Control Committee of Inner Mongolia Autonomous Region CP
1964,	Sep	Elected vice-chairman of Inner Mongolia Autonomous Region
1967		Relieved of all posts during the Cultural Revolution
1972,	Mar	Identified as vice-chairman of the Revolutionary Committee of Inner Mongolia Autonomous Region (until Dec 1979)
	Sep	Identified as member of the Standing Committee of Inner Mongolia Autonomous Region CP
1979,	Dec	Elected vice-chairman of the People's Congress of Inner Mongolia Autonomous Region CP

Shen Yanbing (Shen Yen-ping)　　沈雁冰

Posts held

NPC
Deputy for Shandong Province to the 5th NPC

Others
Vice-chairman of the 5th CPPCC
Honorary chairman of the Federation of Literary and Art Circles
President of the Union of Chinese Writers
President of the Lu Xun Studies Society

Shen, who became internationally known under his pen-name Mao Dun, was born in 1896 in Tongxiang, Zhejiang Province. After completing elementary school he studied at Hehai Technical College in Nanjing and subsequently continued his studies at Beijing University. He earned first literary recognition as editor of the Commercial Press and as publisher of a journal for short stories. During the Northern Expedition in 1926 he was in charge of publications in the Department of Political Training. Later in Shanghai he wrote the famous trilogy Shi (Darkness) comprising Disillusion, Agitation, and Pursuit. During the Anti-Japanese War he spent a period of time at the Communist base in Yan'an. The drama Before and After the Qingming Festival was written in Chongqing. After the Japanese capitulation Shen became head of the Literature Department at Xinjiang Academy. He visited the USSR in 1946. In 1948 he published a monthly in Hong Kong for short stories. In September 1949 the 1st CPPCC elected him a member of its Standing Committee.

1949,	Oct	Appointed member of the Central People's Government Council (until Oct 1954) and minister of culture (until Jan 1965)
	Dec	Elected vice-chairman of the Sino-Soviet Friendship Association
1950		Identified as chairman of the Union of Chinese Writers (reelected Nov 1979) and as vice-chairman of the Federation of Literary and Art Circles
	Nov	Elected vice-chairman of the World Peace Council (until about 1963)
1953,	Jan	Head of a cultural delegation to Poland
1954,	Aug	Elected deputy for Shandong Province to the 1st NPC (reelected in 1958 and 1964 to the 2nd and 3rd NPCs)
1956		Identified as vice-chairman of the Afro-Asian Solidarity Committee (until Cultural Revolution)
1958,	Oct	Identified as chairman of the Sino-Polish Friendship Association (until Cultural Revolution)
1960,	Aug	Head of a cultural delegation to Poland
1965,	Jan	Elected vice-chairman of the 4th CPPCC
1967-1969		Shen survives the Cultural Revolution without coming under personal attack
1978,	Feb	Elected deputy for Shandong Province to the 5th NPC
	Mar	Reelected vice-chairman by the 5th CPPCC
1979,	Nov	Elected honorary chairman of the Federation of Literary and Art Circles
	Dec	Elected president of the Lu Xun Studies Society

Publications

1927-1928	Huanmie, Dongyao, Zhiqiu (Disillusion, Agitation, and Pursuit)
1930	Hong (uncompleted) (The Rainbow)
later:	Lu (The Road)
1931	Sanren Xing (Three Travel Companions)
1931-1932	Ziye (Midnight)
1932	Lin Jia Puzi (The Shop of Family Lin)
	Fushi (Corruption)
1945	Qingming Qianhou (Before and After the Qingming Festival)
	Wild Rose
	Bandits
	Spring Silkworms

Collected Short Stories
Essays
The Study of Chinese Mythology
Talks on Western Literature

Shen Yuan (Shen Yüan)   沈　元

Posts held

Others
President of the Society of Aeronautics and Astronautics
Deputy director of the Beijing Aeronautical Engineering Institute

1963,	Sep	Identified as deputy director of the Beijing Aeronautical College
1964,	Mar	Identified as president of the Aeronautics Society
1967		Disappears during the Cultural Revolution
1978,	Apr	First appearance after the Cultural Revolution: Identified as president of the Aeronautics Society (until Feb 1979)
	May	Identified as member of the Beijing Aeronautical Engineering Institute
1979,	Mar	Identified as deputy director of the Beijing Aeronautical Engineering Institute
	Jun	Identified as president of the Society of Aeronautics and Astronautics; member of a scientific and technical delegation, led by Pei Lisheng, to the U.S.A.

Shen Yue (Shen Yüeh)   沈　越

Posts held

CCP
Secretary of Liaoning Province CP

1979,	Aug	Identified as secretary of Liaoning Province CP

Shen Yunpu (Shen Yün-p'u)   申云浦

Posts held

Provincial Administration
Vice-governor of Guizhou Province

1980,	Jan	Elected vice-governor of Guizhou Province

Shen Zhendong (Shen Chen-tung)   沈振东

Posts held

Government
Director of the State Oceanography Bureau

1973,	Oct	Identified as a government cadre
1977,	Oct	Identified as director of the State Oceanography Bureau; head of a delegation to the 10th Conference of the UN Educational, Scientific and Cultural Organization (UNESCO) Intergovernmental Oceanographic Commission in Paris

Shen Zhiwei (Shen Chih-wei)　　申志伟

Posts held

Government
Deputy director of the America and Oceania Department in the Ministry of Foreign Affairs

Shen was born in 1925 in Henan Province.

1971,	May	Identified as counselor at the embassy in Bulgaria (until Jun 1972)
1972,	Nov	Identified as chargé d'affaires ad interim in Greece (until 1974)
1975,	Jul	Identified as deputy director of the America and Oceania Department in the Ministry of Foreign Affairs
1978,	Aug	Member of a government delegation led by Geng Biao to Trinidad and Tobago, Jamaica, and Guyana

Shen Zhongyi (Shen Chung-yi)　　沈仲义

Posts held

Government
Vice-minister of the 4th Ministry of Machine Building

1964,	Sep	Elected deputy for Gansu Province to the 3rd NPC
1974,	Sep	First appearance after the Cultural Revolution
1977,	Sep	Member of a military delegation to France and Romania
1978,	Dec	Identified as vice-minister of the 4th Ministry of Machine Building

Sheng Wan (Sheng Wan) (f)　　盛婉

Posts held

NPC
Member of the Standing Committee of the 5th NPC
Deputy for Henan Province to the 5th NPC

Mass Organization
Vice-chairman of the Trade Unions of Henan Province

1973,	Sep	Elected vice-chairman of the Trade Unions of Henan Province
1978,	Feb	Elected deputy for Henan Province to the 5th NPC
	Mar	Elected member of the Standing Committee of the 5th NPC

Shi Bangzhi (Shih Pang-chih)　　石邦智

Posts held

Provincial Administration
Vice-chairman of the People's Congress of Hunan Province

Shi, who belongs to the Miao minority, was born in 1916 in Hunan Province. During the revolutionary period he was leader of a guerrilla unit in West Hunan.

1953,	Jan	Appointed chairman of the People's Government of the West Hunan Autonomous Zhou of the Miao
1954,	Aug	Elected deputy for Hunan Province to the 1st NPC (reelected in 1958 and 1964 to the 2nd and 3rd NPCs)
1956,	Mar	Member of a government delegation to Tibet
1957,	Sep	Elected chairman of the newly established West Hunan Autonomous Zhou of the Miao and Tujia
1958,	Jul	Elected member of the People's Committee for Defense of World Peace
1967		Disappears during the Cultural Revolution
1977,	Dec	Elected vice-chairman of the Revolutionary Committee of Hunan (until Dec 1979)
1979,	Dec	Elected vice-chairman of the People's Congress of Hunan Province

Shi Chuan (Shih Ch'uan)　　石川

Posts held

CCP
Member of the Standing Committee, Hubei Province CP

Provincial Administration
Vice-governor of Hubei Province

1979,	May	Identified as a member of the Standing Committee, Hubei Province CP
1980,	Jan	Elected vice-governor of Hubei Province

Shi Guanghua (Shih Kuang-hua)　　石光华

Posts held

Provincial Administration
Vice-chairman of the People's Government, Inner Mongolia Autonomous Region

1960,	Jun	Identified as 1st secretary of the Jirem League CP, Inner Mongolia
1979,	Dec	Elected vice-chairman of the People's Government, Inner Mongolia Autonomous Region

Shi Huaibi (Shih Huai-pi)　　史怀璧

Posts held

Government
Member of the State Nationalities Affairs Commission

NPC
Deputy for Shanxi Province to the 5th NPC

Shi was born in 1907 in Wuxing, Shanxi Province. He is a graduate of Taiyuan Police Training School. From 1938 to

1948 he served in the administration of Tunliu County and Taiyuan Municipality.

1949,	Dec	Appointed director of the Administration Office of the Ministry of Labor
1958		Identified as director of the Research Office of the NPC's Standing Committee
	Apr	Member of a delegation of jurists to Japan
1964,	Jan	Identified as vice-governor of Yunnan Province (until Jan 1966)
1966,	Feb	Appointed vice-chairman of the Commission for Cultural Relations with Foreign Countries
	May	Head of a cultural delegation to Afghanistan and Pakistan
1967		Disappears during the Cultural Revolution
1973,	Oct	First appearance after the Cultural Revolution: Identified as deputy secretary-general of the Revolutionary Committee of Shanxi Province
1977,	May	Identified as vice-chairman of the Revolutionary Committee of Shanxi Province (reelected in Dec 1977; until Dec 1979)
1978,	Feb	Elected deputy for Shanxi Province to the 5th NPC
1979,	May	Appointed member of the State Nationalities Affairs Commission
	Jun	Member of the Committee to Examine Proposals at the 2nd Session of the 5th NPC

Shi Laihe (Shih Lai-ho)　　史来贺

Posts held

NPC
Member of the Standing Committee of the 5th NPC
Deputy for Henan Province to the 5th NPC

1964,	Sep	Elected deputy for Henan Province to the 3rd NPC
1974,	Feb	Identified as CP secretary of the Liuzhuang Production Brigade, Chiliying People's Commune, Henan Province
1978,	Feb	Elected deputy for Henan Province to the 5th NPC
	Mar	Elected member of the Standing Committee of the 5th NPC

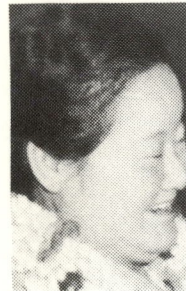

Shi Liang (Shih Liang) (f)　　史良

Posts held

NPC
Vice-chairman of the Standing Committee of the 5th NPC
Vice-chairman of the NPC Legal Commission
Deputy for Shanghai to the 5th NPC

Mass Organization
Vice-chairman of the Women's Federation

Others
Vice-president of the 5th CPPCC
Chairman of the Central Committee, China Democratic League

Shi was born in 1900 in Wuxi, Kiangsu Province. After attending one of the first modern girls schools in China she graduated from the Shanghai College of Political Science and Law. She was a veteran of the "May 4th Movement" and the Northern Expedition and subsequently worked for the Nanjing Court of Criminal Law. After various administrative posts she was one of the cofounders of the National Salvation Society in 1931 which was close to the Communists. In 1935 she was arrested by the Nationalist Government together with six other leading cadres of this society. Having escaped from prison she surrendered to the authorities, a nationally reported incident which eventually led to her release in 1937. During the Anti-Japanese War she worked together with Deng Yingchao, the wife of Zhou Enlai, primarily in the women's movement. In 1945 she played an important role in the foundation of the Democratic League. After the Japanese capitulation in 1945 she settled in Shanghai as a lawyer. In September 1949 she was a delegate at the 1st CPPCC which elected her a member.

1949,	Dec	Elected member of the Central Committee of the Democratic League (until May 1953); appointed member of the Legislative Council in the Government Administration Council
1951,	Oct	Elected council member of the Sino-Soviet Friendship Association (until about 1963)
1953		Identified as vice-chairman of the Committee for the Implementation of the Marriage Laws
	Apr	Elected vice-chairman of the Democratic Women's Federation (until Cultural Revolution)
	May	Elected vice-chairman of the Democratic League (until Dec 1958)
1954,	Aug	Elected deputy for Jiangsu Province to the 1st NPC (reelected in 1958 and 1964 to the 2nd and 3rd NPCs)
	Oct	Appointed minister of justice (until Apr 1959)
1955,	Jul	Head of a delegation of jurists to the USSR
1958,	Jul	Appointed council member fo the Peace Council (until about 1964)
1959,	Apr	Elected member of the Standing Committee of the 2nd NPC (confirmed in 1965 and 1975 by the 3rd and 4th NPCs); elected member of the Standing Committee of the 3rd CPPCC (reelected in 1965 by the 4th CPPCC)
1967-1969		Shi survives the Cultural Revolution without coming under attack
1975,	Jan	Reelected member of the Standing Committee of the 4th NPC (confirmed in Mar 1968 by the 5th NPC)
1978,	Feb	Elected deputy for Shanghai Municipality to the 5th NPC
	Mar	Elected vice-president of the 5th CPPCC
	Sep	Reelected vice-chairman of the Women's Federation
1979,	Feb	Elected vice-chairman of the NPC Legal Commission
	Jun	Vice-chairman of the Draft Laws Committee at the 2nd Session of the 5th NPC
	Jul	By-elected vice-chairman of the Standing Committee of the 5th NPC

Oct   Elected chairman of the Central Committee of the China Democratic League

Shi Lide (Shih Li-te)   史立德

Posts held

Others
Deputy director of the Supply and Marketing Cooperatives

1963,   Oct   Identified as deputy director of the Supply and Marketing Cooperatives; head of a Supply and Marketing Cooperatives delegation to Japan; identified as council member of the Sino-Japanese Friendship Association

1966,   Feb   Shi disappears

1979,   Jun   Identified as deputy director of the Supply and Marketing Cooperatives

Shi Lin (Shih Lin)   石 林

Posts held

Government
Vice-minister of economic relations with foreign countries

NPC
Deputy for Shanghai Municipality to the 5th NPC

1965,   Jun   Designated advisor to the 2nd Afro-Asian Solidarity Conference in Algiers which was canceled

1973,   May   Identified as vice-minister of economic relations with foreign countries

1977,   Jan   Head of a government delegation to Pakistan

1978,   Feb   Elected deputy for Shanghai Municipality to the 5th NPC

Oct   Head of a government delegation to the Philippines

Nov   Head of a scientific and technical delegation to Romania

1979,   Mar   Head of a scientific cooperation delegation to Bangladesh

Jun   Member of the Draft Laws Committee at the 2nd Session of the 5th NPC

Shi Qingsheng (Shih Ch'ing-sheng)   史清盛

Posts held

Provincial Administration
Vice-chairman of the People's Government, Guangxi Autonomous Region

1979,   Dec   Elected vice-chairman of the People's Government, Guangxi Autonomous Region

Shi Ruwei (Shih Ju-wei)   施汝为

Posts held

Others
Director of the Institute of Physics at the Academy of Sciences
Vice-president of the Physics Society

1954   Shi takes part in the 13th Session of the (Communist) World Federation of Scientific Workers in Vienna; identified as council member of the Beijing Section of the Physics Society

1955,   May   Identified as member of the Department of Mathematics, Physics, and Chemistry of the Academy of Sciences

1956,   Nov   Identified as acting director of the Research Institute of Applied Physics of the Academy of Sciences

1960,   Sep   Identified as director of the Research Institute of Applied Physics of the Academy of Sciences

1964,   Oct   Elected deputy for Guangxi Autonomous Region to the 3rd NPC

1972,   Jun   Identified as director of the Institute of Physics at the Academy of Sciences; head of a delegation of physicists to the Congress of Canadian Physicists

1978,   Aug   Identified as vice-president of the Physics Society

Shi Xiangsheng (Shih Hsiang-sheng)   史向生

Posts held

Others
Vice-president of the Academy of Agronomy

1955,   Feb   Identified as vice-governor of Henan Province (until Dec 1958)

1957,   Sep   Identified as secretary of Henan Province CP (until 1959)

1966,   Mar   Identified as vice-president of the Beijing Agricultural University

1967,   Apr   Branded as a "three-anti element"

1978,   Aug   First appearance after the Cultural Revolution: Identified as vice-president of the Academy of Agronomy

Shi Yi (Shih Yi) (f)   史 毅

Posts held

Provincial Administration
Vice-governor of Henan Province

1977,   Dec   Elected vice-chairman of the Revolutionary Committee of Gansu Province (until 1978?)

1979,   Sep   Elected vice-governor of Henan Province

Shi Yizhi (Shih Yi-chih)　时逸之

Posts held

Provincial Administration
Vice-chairman of the People's Congress,
Shaanxi Province

Shi was born in 1910 in Yangcheng, Shanxi Province. In 1932 he joined the CCP. In the late thirties he studied at the Taiyuan Branch of the Anti-Japan Military and Political Academy. In 1940 he served in the Shanxi-Henan Office of the CCP. The following year he was made director of the 4th Administrative District under the Shanyin (Daiyue) Administrative Office. In 1946 he headed the Civil Affairs Section of the Taiyuan Administrative Office. Circa 1948 he became director of the Political Department of the 4th Army.

1949,	Dec	Identified as deputy director of the South Shaanxi Administrative Office and as secretary-general of the Shaanxi Provincial People's Government
1950,	Mar	Identified as a member of the Financial and Economic Committee, Shaanxi Provincial People's Government
1955,	Nov	Identified as vice-governor of Shaanxi Province
1961,	Mar	Identified as secretary of Xi'an Municipality CP
1962		Shi disappears
1979,	Sep	First appearance after the Cultural Revolution: Identified as vice-chairman of the Revolutionary Committee, Shaanxi Province
	Dec	Elected vice-chairman of the People's Congress, Shaanxi Province

Shi Yulin (Shih Yü-lin)　史五林

Posts held

Provincial Administration
Vice-chairman of the People's Congress of
Ningxia Autonomous Region

1977,	Dec	Elected vice-chairman of the Revolutionary Committee of Ningxia Autonomous Region (until Dec 1979)
1980,	Jan	Elected vice-chairman of the People's Congress of Ningxia Autonomous Region

Shi Zhongqin (Shih Chung-ch'in) (f)　石钟琴

Posts held

NPC
Member of the Standing Committee of the
5th NPC
Deputy for Shanghai Municipality to the
5th NPC

Shi was born in 1948. She became known as a ballerina.

1978,	Feb	Elected deputy for Shanghai Municipality to the 5th NPC
	Mar	Elected member of the Standing Committee of the 5th NPC

Shi Ziming (Shih Tzu-ming)　史梓铭

Posts held

Government
Ambassador to Burundi

1958,	Dec	Identified as director of the Heavy Tool Machine Factory in Wuhan
1970,	Apr	Appointed ambassador to Finland (until Jul 1975)
1978,	Mar	Appointed ambassador to Burundi
1979,	Mar	Accompanies President Bagazi of Burundi to China

Shu Tong (Shu T'ung)　舒同

Posts held

Others
Member of the Standing Committee of the
5th CPPCC

Shu was born in 1906 in Dongxiang, Jiangxi Province. In 1921 he graduated from the 1st Normal School in Jiangxi. He joined the CCP in 1927. In 1931 he was head of the Subdepartment of Propaganda in the Political Department of the 2nd Division, 1st Army Corps of the Red Army. In 1934-35 he took part in the Long March. During the Anti-Japanese War he was head of the Political Department in Shanxi-Chahar-Hebei Border Region, and in 1946 head of the Political Department of the New 4th Army. In the following year he was appointed director of the Political Department of Shandong Military Region. He was identified as director of the Political Department of the 3rd Army as well as director of the Propaganda Department, East China Bureau of the CCP Central Committee, in 1949.

1949,	Dec	Appointed director of the Political Department of East China Military Region and of the 3rd Field Army; identified as director of the Propaganda Department, East China Bureau of the CCP Central Committee
1950,	Feb?	Appointed member of the East China Military and Administrative Council and director of the Cultural and Educational Committee of the Military and Administrative Council
1952,	Aug	Appointed chairman of the Supervisory Committee of Institutions of Higher Education in East China
	Sep	Appointed chairman of the Study Committee on Party Cadres, East China Bureau of the CCP Central Committee
	Nov	Elected vice-chairman of the East China Section of the Peace Council
1953,	Jan	Elected secretary of Jiangsu Province CP (until Jan 1955)
	Mar	Elected vice-chairman of the East China Section of the Sino-Soviet Friendship Association
1954,	Aug	Elected deputy for Shandong Province to the 1st NPC (reelected in 1958 to the 2nd NPC)
1955,	Jan	Elected 1st secretary of Shandong Province CP (probably until 1959)

	Mar	Elected member of Shandong People's Government
1956,	Sep	Elected member of the CCP Central Committee by the 8th Party Congress
1958,	Sep	Identified as political commissar of Jinan Military Region (until about 1959)
1964,	Sep	Elected deputy for Shaanxi Province to the 3rd NPC
1965,	Jul	Identified as secretary of Shaanxi Province CP
1967,	Mar	Branded as an anti-Mao element and purged
1977,	Dec	First appearance after the Cultural Revolution: Elected vice-chairman of the Revolution Committee of Shaanxi Province (until mid-1978?)
1979,	Jul	By-elected member of the Standing Committee of the 5th CPPCC

Shuai Mengqi (Shuai Meng-ch'i) (f) 帅孟奇

Posts held

Others
Member of the Standing Committee of the 5th CPPCC

Shuai was born in 1897 in Hunan Province. She studied in the USSR at a young age. After her return to China in 1930 involvement in organizing workers in Shanghai led to several terms of imprisonment. In 1949 she was elected a member of the Executive Council of the Federation of Democratic Women, and in September of the same year she was a delegate representing that federation at the CPPCC (member until December 1957).

1949,	Oct	Appointed member of the People's Control Commission in the Government Administration Council
1954,	Aug	Elected deputy for Hunan Province to the 1st NPC
1956,	May	Head of a women's delegation to North Vietnam
	Sep	Elected alternate member of the CCP Central Committee by the 8th Party Congress as well as member of the Central Control Commission
1957,	Oct	Identified as deputy director of the Organization Department of the CCP Central Committee
	Sep	Elected member of the Executive Council of the Women's League
1961		Identified as member of the Standing Committee, Central Control Commission of the CCP Central Committee
1965,	Jan	Elected member of the Standing Committee of the 3rd NPC
1967		Disappears during the Cultural Revolution
1978,	Dec	First appearance after the Cultural Revolution
1979,	Jul	By-elected member of the Standing Committee of the 5th CPPCC

Si-ma-yi Ya-sheng-nuo-fu (Szu-ma-yi Ya-sheng-no-fu) 司马益亚生诺夫

Posts held

Provincial Administration
Vice-chairman of Xinjiang Autonomous Regional People's Government

Si-ma-yi belongs to the Uighur minority.

1959,	Mar	Elected deputy for Xinjiang Province to the 2nd NPC (reelected 1964 to the 3rd NPC
1960,	Jul	Identified as director of the Rural Work Department of Xinjiang Autonomous Region CP
1979,	Sep	Elected vice-chairman of Xinjiang Autonomous Regional People's Government

Situ Huimin (Szu-t'u Hui-min) 司徒慧敏

Posts held

Government
Vice-minister of culture
Member of the State Nationalities Affairs Commission

1959,	Jul	Identified as deputy director of the Film Industry Administration, Ministry of Culture
1960,	Feb	Identified as deputy director of the Cinema Bureau, Ministry of Culture
1962,	Mar	Identified as council member of the Sino-Czechoslovakian Friendship Association
1967		Disappears during the Cultural Revolution
1975,	Sep	First appearance after the Cultural Revolution
1978,	Jul	Identified as a cadre of the Cinema Bureau of the Ministry of Culture
	Aug	Identified as vice-minister of culture
1979,	May	Appointed member of the State Nationalities Affairs Commission

Song Chengzhi (Sung Ch'eng-chih) 宋承志

Posts held

Military
Major-general
Commander of the PLA Artillery

In 1948 Song was deputy division commander of the Artillery Column of Northeast Field Army.

1950		Service with the 4th Field Army in the Korean War
1951		Identified as deputy commander of the Artillery Command of Northeast Military Region
1957		Identified as commander, Artillery Command in Shenyang Military Region
1963,	Sep	Identified as major-general
1965,	Feb	Identified as deputy commander of the PLA Artillery

Song has since been present every year on military occasions involving the Central Leadership.

1977,	Mar	Member of a military delegation to Pakistan
1978,	Jun	Member of a military delegation to Yugoslavia; identified as commander of the PLA Artillery

Song Hanyi (Sung Han-yi) 宋寒毅

Posts held

Government
Ambassador to Sudan

1974,	Jul	Appointed ambassador to Morocco (until Jan 1979)
1979,	May	Appointed ambassador to Sudan

Song Jiehan (Sung Chieh-han) 宋洁涵

Posts held

CCP
Secretary of Jilin Province CP

Provincial Administration
Vice-chairman of the Revolutionary Committee of Jilin Province

1959,	Mar	Elected deputy for Jilin Province to the 2nd NPC
1960,	Jun	Identified as 1st secretary of Changchun Municipality CP (until 1966)
1962,	May	Identified as chairman of the Changchun Section of the CPPCC
1965,	Oct	Identified as alternate secretary of Jilin Province CP
1967		Disappears during the Cultural Revolution
1977,	Dec	First appearance after the Cultural Revolution: Elected vice-chairman of the Revolutionary Committee of Jilin Province
1978,	Jan	Identified as deputy secretary of Jilin Province CP (until Aug 1979)
1979,	Aug	Identified as secretary of Jilin Province CP

Song Jiwen (Sung Chi-wen) 宋季文

Posts held

Government
Vice-minister of light industry

Song was born in 1920 in Dingyuan, Anhui Province.

1949,	Oct	Identified as director of the Financial Bureau of the Nanjing People's Government and as member of the Financial and Economic Committee of the East China Military and Administrative Council (until 1954 after that council had been reorganized into the East China Administrative Council in 1953)
1953,	Jan	Identified as director of the Tax Bureau, Shanghai People's Government

1955,	Oct	Identified as director of the Office of Finance, Food, and Trade of Shanghai People's Government
1957,	Jan	Identified as deputy mayor of Shanghai Municipality (until Cultural Revolution)
1962,	Mar	Identified as member of the Standing Committee of Shanghai Municipality CP (until Cultural Revolution)
1964,	Sep	Elected deputy for Shanghai Municipality to the 3rd NPC
1967,	Jan	Branded as a revisionist and paraded through Shanghai
1977,	Dec	First appearance after the Cultural Revolution: Elected president of Shanghai Higher People's Court
1978,	Jan	Identified as vice-minister of light industry

Song Kanfu (Sung K'an-fu) 宋侃夫

Posts held

Mass Organization
Vice-chairman of the Federation of Trade Unions

Song was born in Jiangxi Province.

1949,	Dec	Identified as secretary of Sha Municipality CP in Hubei Province
1950,	Mar	Identified as council member of the People's Government of Hubei Province
	Oct	Identified as chairman of the Trade Unions of Hubei Province
1952,	Nov	Identified as vice-mayor of Wuhan Municipality (until Jan 1955)
1955,	Jan	Elected mayor of Wuhan Municipality
	Mar	Elected 2nd secretary of Wuhan Municipality CP (until Jan 1956)
1956,	Jan	Elected 1st secretary of Wuhan Municipality CP (until Cultural Revolution)
1962,	Jun	Identified as secretary of Hubei Province CP (until Cultural Revolution)
1968,	Jun	Denounced as an anti-Party element and purged
1974,	Jan	First appearance after the Cultural Revolution
1975,	Aug	Identified as secretary of Hubei Province (until 1977)
1978,	Oct	Elected vice-chairman of the Federation of Trade Unions

Song Lin (Sung Lin) 宋 林

Posts held

CCP
Member of the Standing Committee of Qinghai Province CP

Provincial Administration
Vice-governor of Qinghai Province

1977,	Dec	Elected vice-chairman of the Revolutionary Committee of Qinghai Province (until Aug 1979)
1978,	May	Identified as member of the Standing Committee of Qinghai Province CP
1979,	Sep	Elected vice-governor of Qinghai Province

Song Ping (Sung P'ing)   宋 平

Posts held

CCP
Member of the CCP 11th Central Committee
1st secretary of Gansu Province CP

NPC
Deputy for Gansu Province to the 5th NPC

Military
2nd political commissar of Lanzhou Military Region
1st political commissar of Gansu Military District

1960		Identified as secretary-general of Taiyuan Municipality CP
1973,	Jul	Identified as secretary of Gansu Province CP
	Aug	Identified as vice-chairman of the Revolutionary Committee of Gansu Province
1975,	Feb	Head of a government delegation to the Chinese Trade and Economic Exhibition in Jamaica
1976,	Sep	Eulogy in Gansu for Mao Zedong
1977,	Jun	Appointed 1st secretary of the CP, and chairman of the Revolutionary Committee, of Gansu Province (latter post until Dec 1979) as well as 1st political commissar of Gansu Military District
	Jul	Identified as 2nd political commissar of Lanzhou Military Region
	Aug	Elected member of the CCP Central Committee by the 11th Party Congress
1978,	Feb	Elected deputy for Gansu Province to the 5th NPC

Song Qingling (Soong Ching Ling) (f) 宋庆龄

Posts held

NPC
Vice-chairman of the Standing Committee of the 5th NPC
Deputy for Shanghai Municipality to the 5th NPC

Mass Organization
Honorary president of the National Women's Federation
Honorary president of the Lu Xun Studies Society

Song Qingling, the widow of Dr. Sun Yat-sen and eldest sister of the wife of Chiang Kai-shek, was born in 1890 in Shanghai. At the age of 14 she began to study in the U.S.A. She received a doctorate from Wesleyan College in Middletown, Connecticut. When Sun Yat-sen was proclaimed provisional president of China, Sung served as a secretary in the Presidential Office. After Yuan Shikai banned the KMT led by Sun Yat-sen, she followed Sun to Japan where they were married in 1914. Until his death in 1925 she remained his closest assistant. In 1926 she was elected a member of the KMT Central Executive Committee and a year later a member of the Nationalist Government Council. She strongly condemned the rift between the KMT and CCP in the spring of 1927. Immediately afterwards she traveled to Europe and the USSR accompanied by Comintern agent Borodin and by Chen Youren, the former minister of foreign affairs of the Nationalist Government at Wuhan. She returned to China in 1929, and two years later founded the League for the Protection of Human Rights. In 1938, after the outbreak of the Anti-Japanese War, she established the China Defense League in Hong Kong. Its chief objective was to raise funds, which were mostly made available to the Communists, for the struggle against the Japanese. In 1941 she visited the Communist occupied parts of North China were she devoted herself to setting up military hospitals. After the Japanese capitulation she took part in the Political Consultative Conference convened by the KMT in Chongqing, and subsequently settled in Shanghai. There she reorganized the China Defense League which was to become the China Welfare Fund with the main aim of providing financial assistance to the Communists. In September 1949 she attended the 1st CPPCC which elected her a member of its National Committee.

1949,	Oct	Elected vice-chairman of the Central People's Government Council, and vice-chairman of the Sino-Soviet Friendship Association (until Dec 1954)
1950,	Apr	Elected chairman of the Relief Association; identified as honorary chairman of the Women's Federation
1951,	Nov	Elected chairman of the Committee for the Protection of Children; awarded the Stalin Prize
1954,	Sep	Elected deputy for Shanghai Municipality to the 1st NPC and member of the Standing Committee of the NPC (until Mar 1959)
	Dec	Elected vice-chairman of the CPPCC (until Apr 1959) and chairman of the Sino-Soviet Friendship Association
1957,	Nov	Member of the delegation to the Moscow celebrations of the 40th anniversary of the October Revolution
1959,	Apr	Elected vice-president of the PRC (until Jan 1975)
1964,	Feb	Visit to Ceylon at the invitation of Prime Minister Bandaranaike
1975,	Jan	Elected vice-chairman by the 4th NPC (confirmed in Mar 1978 by the 5th NPC)
1978,	Feb	Elected deputy for Shanghai Municipality to the 5th NPC
	Sep	Elected honorary president of the National Women's Federation
1979,	Dec	Elected honorary president of the Lu Xun Studies Society

Song Qingyou (Sung Ch'ing-yu)   宋庆友

Posts held

CCP
Alternate member of the CCP 11th Central Committee
Member of the Standing Committee of Shandong Province CP

Mass Organization
Vice-chairman of the Trade Union of Shandong Province

1973,   Jul   Elected vice-chairman of the Trade Union of Shandong Province

         Aug   Elected to first term as alternate member of the CCP Central Committee by the 10th Party Congress

1977,   May   Identified as member of the Standing Committee of Shandong Province CP

Song Renqiong (Sung Jen-ch'iung) 宋任穷

<u>Posts held</u>

CCP
Member of the CCP 11th Central Committee
Member of Secretariat of the 11th Central Committee
Director of the Organization Department of the CCP Central Committee

NPC
Deputy for Sichuan Province to the 5th NPC

Military
Army general

Others
Vice-chairman of the 5th CPPCC

Song was born in 1909 in Liuyang County, Hunan Province. He graduated from the Liuyang High School and joined the CCP in 1926. Later he graduated from Whampoa Military Academy. In 1927 he came to Jinggangshan and served in the 4th Red Army. In 1932 he worked in the Political Department of the 5th Red Regiment (reorganization of the 26th Route Army of the Nationalist Army which had defected to the Communists). Political commissar of this regiment was then Xiao Jingguang, and director of its Political Department was Liu Bocheng. In 1934-35 Song took part in the Long March, serving as political commissar of the Red Army Cadre Corps. In 1936 he served in the 28th Army Group of the Red Army. At the beginning of the Anti-Japanese War Song was political commissar of the 129th Division. In 1938 he operated with a cavalry regiment in Hebei Province. In 1942 he organized the "Death Corps" in Shanxi Province. From 1943 he lectured at the Central Academy of the CCP. In 1945 he was elected alternate member of the CCP Central Committee by the 7th Party Congress (until September 1956). During the Civil War he was successively commander of South Hebei and of Central Hebei Military Regions and commissar of the 4th Army Corps. When Nanjing was occupied in April 1949 by the 2nd Field Army commanded by Liu Bocheng, Song was appointed chairman of the Nanjing Military Control Commission.

1950,   Mar   Identified as deputy political commissar of Southwest China Military Region; appointed chairman of Yunnan Military Control Commission and member of Southwest China Military and Political Council

1952,   Aug   Appointed vice-chairman of Southwest China Military and Political Council (until Feb 1953)

1953,   Feb   Appointed vice-chairman of Southwest China Administrative Council; identified as 1st secretary of the Southwest China Bureau of the CCP Central Committee; identified as member of Yunnan People's Government (all posts until Jun 1954)

1954,   Jul?   Song is recalled to Beijing

         Oct   Appointed member of the National Defense Council

1955,   Sep   Promoted to rank of army general; conferred the orders "1st August," "Independence and Freedom," and "Liberation," all 1st class

1956,   Sep   Elected member of the CCP Central Committee by the 8th Party Congress; identified as deputy secretary-general of the CCP Central Committee

         Nov   Appointed minister of the 3rd Ministry of Machine Building (until Feb 1958)

1958,   Feb   Appointed minister of the 2nd Ministry of Machine Building into which the 3rd Ministry has been incorporated

         Nov   Elected deputy for Yunnan Province to the 2nd NPC (until Sep 1964)

1961,   Oct   Identified as 1st secretary, Northeast China Bureau of the CCP Central Committee

1963,   Oct   Member of a delegation of the Northeast China Bureau of the CCP Central Committee to North Korea

1964,   Apr   Identified as political commissar of Shenyang Military Region

1965,   Jan   Elected vice-chairman of the CPPCC

         Dec   Identified as 1st political commissar of Shenyang Military Region

1966,   Aug   Elected alternate member of the Politburo of the 8th Central Committee by its 11th Plenum

1966-1967   Song is repeatedly attacked by Red Guards

1968,   May   Branded as a renegade, traitor, and "the biggest capitalist-roader of the Party in the Northeast Area"

         Jul   Publicly humiliated in Beijing; subsequently disappears

1974,   Sep   First appearance after the Cultural Revolution

1978,   Feb   Elected deputy for Sichuan Province to the 5th NPC

         Mar   Reelected vice-chairman of the 5th CPPCC; appointed minister of the 7th Ministry of Machine Building (until Dec 1978)

         Dec   Elected member of the CCP Central Committee by the 3rd Plenum of the 11th Central Committee

1979,   Jan   Identified as director of the Organization Department of the CCP Central Committee

         Jun   Vice-chairman of the Credentials Committee at the 2nd Session of the 5th NPC

         Jul   Head of a Party workers delegation to Yugoslavia and Romania

1980,   Feb   Elected member of the Secretariat of the CCP 11th Central Committee by its 5th Plenum

Song Shilun (Sung Shih-lun) 宋时轮

Posts held

CCP
Member of the CCP 11th Central Committee

NPC
Deputy for the PLA to the 5th NPC

Military
Colonel-general
Director of the PLA Academy of Military Science

Song was born in 1907 in Hunan Province. He attended a middle school in his native province. After taking a course at Whampoa Military Academy he served as an officer of the Nationalist Army in Fujian Province. In the late 1920s he joined the Communists and led a guerrilla unit in Jiangxi Province. In 1930 he was chief of staff of the 20th Red Army. In 1933 he graduated from a course at the Red Army Military Academy in Ruijin. In 1934-35 he took part in the Long March. In 1937 he was commander of a regiment in the 115th Division (commander: Lin Biao), 8th Route Army. In 1938 he commanded parts of the 8th Route Army in Eastern Hebei Province where he became widely known by organizing uprisings in 17 counties and strikes in the coal mines of Kailuan. At the end of that year he took a course at the Party School in Yan'an and was subsequently appointed commander of the 7th Division of the New 4th Army. His appointments as commander of the 10th Column and concurrently commander of Bohai Military District followed the organization of the East China Field Army. In 1948 he commanded the Army Group of the 3rd Field Army and in 1949 he was made concurrently commander of Shanghai-Wusong Garrison (until February 1950).

1949,	Dec	Appointed member of the East China Military and Administrative Council (until Jan 1953)
1950,	Oct	Commander of the Eastern Front, Chinese People's Volunteers in Korea
1954,	Sep	Appointed member of the National Defense Council (until Cultural Revolution)
1955		Identified as head of the Infantry School in Nanjing
	Sep	Promoted to rank of colonel-general and awarded the orders "1st August," "Independence and Freedom," "Liberation," all 1st class
1956,	Sep	Elected alternate member of the CCP Central Committee by the 8th Party Congress (until Cultural Revolution)
1958		Identified as deputy head of the Academy of Military Science (until Cultural Revolution)
1962,	Jul	Head of a military delegation to Iraq
1967		During the Cultural Revolution criticized as follower of He Long and disappears
1972,	Sep	First appearance after the Cultural Revolution
1973,	Aug	Elected alternate member of the CCP Central Committee by the 10th Party Congress (until Aug 1977)
	Sep	Identified as head of the PLA Academy of Military Science; head of a friendship delegation of the PLA to North Korea;

awarded the Korean order "National Flag," 1st class

| 1977, | Aug | Elected member of the CCP Central Committee by the 11th Party Congress |
| 1978, | Feb | Elected deputy for the PLA to the 5th NPC |

Song Xiaopeng (Sung Hsiao-p'eng) 宋筱蓬

Posts held

Provincial Administration
Vice-governor of Guizhou Province

| 1977, | Dec | Elected vice-chairman of the Revolutionary Committee of Guizhou Province (until Dec 1979) |
| 1980, | Jan | Elected vice-governor of Guizhou Province |

Song Xilian (Sung Hsi-lien) 宋希濂

Posts held

Military
Lieutenant-general

Others
Member of the Standing Committee of the 5th CPPCC

In 1949 Song commanded the Sichuan-Hunan-Hubei Border Region of the Pacification Headquarters under the Nationalist Government. After his capture by the Communists he was convicted as a war criminal.

1959,	Dec	Song is pardoned
1964,	Dec	Special delegate to the 4th CPPCC
1978,	Mar	Elected member of the Standing Committee of the 5th CPPCC

Song Yangchu (Sung Yang-ch'u) 宋养初

Posts held

Government
Vice-minister of the State Capital Construction Commission
Minister of building materials

NPC
Deputy for Shanghai Municipality to the 5th NPC

1950		Identified as deputy director of Education, School of the New Democratic Youth League
1953,	Mar	Identified as deputy director of that school
1954,	Oct	Appointed member of the State Planning Commission
1955,	Dec	Identified as director of the Planning Bureau for Heavy Industry under the Planning Commission
1959,	Sep	Appointed vice-chairman of the Planning Commission (until Jun 1964)

1964,	Apr	Appointed vice-chairman of the Economy Commission (until Jan 1966)
1965,	Apr	Appointed vice-chairman of the Capital Construction Commission
1978,	Feb	Elected deputy for Shanghai Municipality to the 5th NPC
	May	Head of a Capital Construction delegation to Japan
1979,	Apr	Appointed minister of building materials

Song Yimin (Sung Yi-min) 宋一民

Posts held

Provincial Administration
Vice-governor of Shandong Province

1977,	Dec	Elected vice chairman of the Revolutionary Committee of Shandong Province (until Dec 1979)
1979,	Dec	Elected vice-governor of Shandong Province

Song Yiping (Sung Yi-p'ing) 宋一平

Posts held

NPC
Deputy for Beijing Municipality to the 5th NPC

Others
Vice-president and secretary-general of the Academy of Social Sciences

Song was born in Shanxi Province. In 1937 he worked in the Northwest Youth National Salvation Association. The following year he was engaged in youth work in the CCP Chang Jiang Bureau. In 1941 he was trained at the Young Cadres School in Yan'an. In September 1945 he accompanied Jiang Nanxiang to lead a youth work team from Yan'an to Northeast China. The following year he founded the Northeast Democratic Youth League. In May 1949 he was elected member of the Executive Committee of the New Democratic Youth League. In September that year he attended the 1st CPPCC.

1952,	Sep	Identified as secretary of the New Democratic Youth League
1954,	Sep	Identified as 3rd secretary of Wuhan Municipality CP
1956,	Oct	Identified as secretary of Wuhan Municipality CP (until Apr 1965)
1958,	Dec	Elected deputy for Hubei Province to the 2nd NPC (reelected to the 3rd NPC in 1964)
1961,	Jun	Head of a Hubei Province delegation to the Ukraine
1965,	Apr	Appointed vice-chairman of the State Commission for Cultural Relations with Foreign Countries (until Cultural Revolution)
	Sep	Head of a government cultural delegation to France
1966,	Feb	Head of a cultural delegation to North Korea
	Apr	Elected vice-chairman of the Association

		for Cultural and Friendly Relations with Foreign Countries
1968,	Feb	Denounced as an anti-Mao element and purged
1974,	Apr	First appearance after the Cultural Revolution
1978,	Feb	Elected deputy for Beijing Municipality to the 5th NPC
1979,	Jun	Identified as secretary-general of the Academy of Social Sciences
	Nov	Identified as vice-president of the Academy of Social Sciences

Song Youtian (Sung Yu-t'ien) 宋友田

Posts held

CCP
Member of the Standing Committee of Shaanxi Province CP

Provincial Administration
Vice-governor of Shaanxi Province

1977,	Jul	Identified as a member of the Standing Committee of Shaanxi Province CP
1979,	Dec	Elected vice-governor of Shaanxi Province

Song Zhenming (Sung Chen-ming) 宋振明

Posts held

Government
Minister of petroleum industry

1976,	Jan	Identified as a cadre of the State Council
	May	Identified as secretary of the CP, and chairman of the Revolutionary Committee, of Daqing Oil Field
	Nov	Identified as vice-minister of petroleum and chemical industry (until Feb 1978)
1977,	Apr	Speech at the Daqing Conference
1978,	Mar	Appointed minister of petroleum industry
	Jul	Head of a government delegation to Iraq
	Aug	Head of a government delegation to Iran
1979,	May	Member of a government delegation, headed by Kang Shien, to Brazil and the U.S.A.

Song Zhenting (Sung Chen-t'ing) 宋振庭

Posts held

CCP
Dean of education of the Party School under the CCP Central Committee

Song was born in 1920. In 1937 he studied at the Anti-Japan Military and Political Academy in Yan'an.

1955,	Mar	Identified as deputy director of the Propaganda Department of Jilin Province CP (until 1960)

1956,	Oct	Identified as director of the Cultural and Educational Department of Jilin Province CP (until Cultural Revolution)
1958,	Jul	Identified as professor at Northeast People's University
1960,	May	Identified as director of the Propaganda Department of Jilin Province CP
1962,	Feb	Identified as member of the Standing Committee of Jilin Province CP
1967,	Aug	Branded as a counterrevolutionary revisionist and purged
1977,	Dec	Identified as member of the Standing Committee of Jilin Province CP; elected vice-chairman of the Revolutionary Committee of Jilin Province (until Mar 1979)
1978,	Apr	Identified as director of the Propaganda Department of Jilin Province CP (until Mar 1979)
	Jul	Article in RMRB of 8 July: "The Story of Lenin Reminds Me of a Test Question"
1979,	Jul	Identified as dean of education of the Party School under the CCP Central Committee

Song Zhiguang (Sung Chih-kuang)　宋之光

Posts held

Government
Assistant minister of foreign affairs

Song was born in 1916 in Guangdong Province.

1958,	Mar	Identified as director of the Western Europe Department in the Ministry of Foreign Affairs
1964,	Feb	Identified as counselor at the embassy in France (until Jul 1970)
1970,	Sep	Appointed ambassador to the German Democratic Republic (until Apr 1972)
1972,	Jul	Appointed ambassador to Great Britain (until Dec 1977)
1978,	Jan	Identified as assistant minister of foreign affairs
	Sep	Song accompanies minister of foreign affairs Huang Hua to Greece, Italy, and Great Britain
	Nov	Member of a friendship delegation led by Ji Pengfei to Iraq, Niger, Benin, Togo, Sierra Leone, Gambia

Song is married to Zhang Ru.

Song Zhihe (Sung Chih-ho)　宋致和

Posts held

CCP
Secretary of Xinjiang Autonomous Region CP

Provincial Administration
Vice-chairman of the People's Government of Xinjiang Autonomous Region

Song was born in 1915 in Dongshan, Hebei Province. He studied at the China College in Beijing. Around 1937 he joined the CCP. In 1940 he held an administrative office in Shanxi-Chahar-Hebei Border Region. In 1943 he was secretary-general of the Administrative Office of Chahar-Hebei. He was appointed a member of the People's Council of Henan Province in 1949.

1950,	Aug	Appointed mayor of Zhengzhou
1955,	Feb	Identified as member of the People's Government of Henan Province
1959,	Jul	Identified as secretary of Henan Province CP (until 1965)
1965,	Aug	Appointed vice-minister of material allocation (until Cultural Revolution)
1970,	Mar	Identified as vice-chairman of the Revolutionary Committee of Xinjiang Autonomous Region (reelected in Feb 1978)
1971,	May	Elected secretary of the new CP Secretariat of Xinjiang Autonomous Region
1979,	Sep	Elected vice-chairman of the People's Government of Xinjiang Autonomous Region

Song Zhong (Sung Chung)　宋　中

Posts held

Others
Secretary-general of the Chinese Olympic Committee

1971,	Mar	Identified as acting chairman of the Table-Tennis Association (until 1978); deputy secretary-general of a table-tennis team visiting Japan
1972,	Jun	Identified as council member of the International Table-Tennis Association; delegate at its meeting in Yugoslavia
1973,	Jan	Head of a sports delegation to Nigeria
	Feb	Identified as secretary-general of the Athletic Federation
	Mar	Deputy head of the Chinese team to the 32nd Table-Tennis World Championship
	Dec	Deputy head of a sports delegation to Iran
1974,	Mar	Identified as honorary secretary-general of the Asian Table-Tennis Championships in Japan; head of the Chinese team competing in this championship
1975,	Jun	Head of the Chinese team to the 2nd Afro-Asian-Latin-American Table-Tennis Competitions in Lagos
	Dec	Head of the Chinese team to the Southeast Asian Games in Bangkok
1976,	Mar	Head of the Chinese delegation to the meeting of the Asian Badminton Association in Bangkok
	Apr	Head of the Chinese delegation to the 3rd Congress of the Asian Table-Tennis Association in Pyongyang
1977,	Jul	Head of a delegation to the 5th Arab Table-Tennis Competitions in Rabat
1978,	May	Head of a sports delegation to Mexico, Venezuela, Ecuador, Peru, Argentina, and Chile
1979,	Mar	Identified as secretary-general of the Chinese Olympic Committee; delegate to the Executive Board Session of the I.O.C. in Lausanne
	Jun	Head of a sports delegation to Italy and Puerto Rico

Jul   Appointed member of the National Games Organizing Committee

Oct   Delegate to the Executive Board Conference of the I.O.C. in Nagoya

Soong Ching Ling (f) 宋庆龄

see **Song Qingling (f)**

Su Buqing (Su Pu-ch'ing) 苏步青

Posts held

NPC
Member of the Standing Committee of the 5th NPC
Deputy for Shanghai Municipality to the 5th NPC

Provincial Administration
Vice-chairman of the People's Congress of Shanghai Municipality

Others
President of Fudan University
Vice-president of the Mathematics Society
Vice-chairman of the Central Committee, China Democratic League

Su was born in 1902 in Zhejiang Province. Though having attended only three years of elementary school and four years of middle school, his school selected him to study in Japan. In 1919 he was enrolled at Tokyo Industrial School. In 1924 he began to study mathematics. After graduation he continued his mathematical studies, supporting himself as a library clerk. Having returned to China in 1931 he was given a lecturership at Zhejiang University. In 1946 he was appointed by this university director of the Department of Mathematics.

1950,   Aug   Elected member of the Federation of Natural Science Workers

1954,   May   Appointed dean of the Shanghai Fudan University (until 1957)

1955,   Jun   Identified as member of the Department of Physics, Mathematics, and Chemistry of the Academy of Sciences

        Dec   Member of a delegation of scientists to Japan

1956,   Feb   Elected member of the Afro-Asian Solidarity Committee; elected member of the China Democratic League;
in 1956 Su is awarded the 2nd Class Prize by the Academy of Sciences

1957,   Jun   Identified as vice-president of Fudan University

1958,   May   Delegate to a mathematical conference in Romania

        Jun   Visit to Hungary

        Nov   Elected deputy for Shanghai Municipality to the 2nd NPC (reelected in 1964 to the 3rd NPC)

1959,   May   Su joins the CCP; identified as director of the Mathematics Institute, Shanghai Branch of the Academy of Sciences

1960   Identified as vice-president of the Mathematics Society

1967   Disappears during the Cultural Revolution

1978,   Feb   First appearance after the Cultural Revolution: Elected deputy for Shanghai Municipality to the 5th NPC

        Mar   Elected member of the Standing Committee of the 5th NPC

        Apr   Identified as vice-president of the Mathematics Society

        Jun   Identified as president of Fudan University

        Dec   Identified as chairman of the Shanghai Scientific and Technological Association

1979,   May   Head of a scientific delegation to Japan

        Oct   Elected vice-chairman of the Central Committee of the China Democratic League

        Dec   Elected vice-chairman of the People's Congress of Shanghai Municipality

Su Gang (Su Kang) 苏钢

Posts held

CCP
Secretary of Guizhou Province CP

Provincial Administration
Governor of Guizhou Province

1960,   Jun   Identified as member of the Standing Committee of Hunan Province CP (until Jul 1965)

1965,   Jul   Identified as alternate member of the CP Secretariat of Hunan Province CP (until Cultural Revolution)

1967   Disappears during the Cultural Revolution

1977,   Jan   First appearance after the Cultural Revolution: Identified as a cadre in Hunan Province

        Jul   Identified as deputy secretary of Guizhou Province CP and as vice-chairman of the Revolutionary Committee of Guizhou Province (until Dec 1979)

1978,   Apr   Elected secretary of Guizhou Province CP

1980,   Jan   Elected governor of Guizhou Province

Su Jing (Su Ching) 苏静

Posts held

CCP
Member of the 11th CCP Central Committee

Government
Vice-minister of the State Planning Commission
Vice-chairman of the Birth Planning Leading Group under the State Council

Military
Lieutenant-general

Others
Member of the Standing Committee of the 5th CPPCC

Su was born in 1914 in Fujian Province. In 1932 he first led a company and later a battalion of the 1st Front Army. In 1935 he received military training in the USSR. In 1938 he served as deputy commander of the 359th Brigade, 120th Division, 8th Route Army. He was head of the 1st Office of the 4th Field Army Headquarters in early 1949. In September of that year he took part in the 1st CPPCC as a delegate representing the 4th Field Army.

1950		Identified as member of the Central-South China Military and Administrative Council (until Nov 1952)
	Aug	Identified as deputy chief of staff of the Central-South China Military Region
1951-1953		Service in the General Staff of the Chinese People's Volunteers in the Korean War
1954		Identified as deputy director of the Operational Department, General Staff of the Chinese People's Volunteers in Korea
1955,	Sep	Appointed lieutenant-general; conferred the order "Liberation," 1st class
1956		Identified as deputy commander of Guangdong Military Region (until 1957)
1957		Identified as deputy director of the Department for Inspection of Combat Strength, General Staff of the PLA
1969,	Apr	Elected to first term as member of the CCP Central Committee by the 9th Party Congress
1975,	Sep	Identified as vice-minister of the Planning Commission
1978,	Mar	Elected member of the Standing Committee of the 5th CPPCC
	Jul	Appointed vice-chairman of the Birth Planning Leading Group under the State Council

Su Yiran (Su Yi-jan)   苏毅然

Posts held

CCP
Member of the CCP 11th Central Committee
Secretary of Shandong Province CP

Military
1st political commissar of Shandong Military District

Provincial Administration
Vice-governor of Shandong Province

1950,	Dec	Identified as council member of South Anhui Administrative Region
1952,	Aug	Identified as director of the Public Security Bureau of South Anhui Administrative Region
1955,	Mar	Identified as member of the People's Council of Anhui Province
1957		Identified as vice-governor, and as member of the Standing Committee of the CP, of Anhui Province (until 1963)
1959,	Feb	Identified as alternate member of the Secretariat of Anhui Province CP (until 1963)
1963		Transferred to Shandong

1964,	Aug	Identified as secretary of Shandong Province CP
1967		Disappears during the Cultural Revolution
1971,	Feb	First appearance after the Cultural Revolution: Identified as vice-chairman of the Revolutionary Committee of Shandong Province
	Apr	With the reestablishment of the CP Secretariat of Anhui Province, Su is elected deputy secretary (until Jan 1977)
1977,	Jan	Identified as secretary of Shandong Province CP
	Aug	Elected member of the CCP Central Committee by the 11th Party Congress
1978,	Sep	Identified as 1st political commissar of Shandong Military District
1979,	Dec	Elected vice-governor of Shandong Province

Su Yu (Su Yü)   苏羽

Posts held

CCP
Secretary of Anhui Province CP

1950,	Jul	Identified as vice-chairman of the People's Court of Shandong Province (until about 1956)
1959,	Nov	Identified as deputy director of the Industrial Production Committee and as director of the Bureau of Metallurgical Industry of Liaoning Province (until 1963)
1963,	Jul	Identified as vice-governor of Liaoning Province (until Cultural Revolution)
1967		Disappears during the Cultural Revolution
1973,	Mar	Identified as vice-chairman of the Revolutionary Committee of Liaoning Province (until 1978)
1976,	Aug	Identified as secretary of Liaoning Province CP (until 1978); head of a friendship delegation to Romania
1978,	Sep	Identified as secretary of Dandong Municipality CP; head of a friendship delegation to North Korea
1979,	Mar	Identified as secretary of Anhui Province CP
	Apr	Identified as vice-chairman of the Revolutionary Committee of Anhui Province (until Dec 1979)

Su Yu (Su Yü)   粟裕

Posts held

CCP
Member of the CCP 11th Central Committee
Member of the Standing Committee, Military Council of the CCP Central Committee

Government
Vice-minister of national defense

Military
Army general

NPC
Member of the Standing Committee of the 5th NPC
Deputy for the PLA to the 5th NPC

Though born in Fujian Province in 1909 (1908? 1910?), Su spent his childhood in Hunan, where he joined the Communist Youth League as a student at the 2nd Provincial Teachers College. In 1927 he was dismissed from school because of communist agitation and subsequently joined the Student Battalion of the 4th Army commanded by Ye Ting in Wuchang. At the same time he joined the CCP. He took part in the Nanchang Uprising of 1 August 1927 after the failure of which he joined Mao Zedong's Soviet on Jinggangshan.

During the Long March it was his task to organize guerrilla units in Jiangxi Province. At the beginning of the Anti-Japanese War Su Yu's units formed the nucleus of the New 4th Army which was organized by Ye Ting to comprise those Communist units operating south of the Chang Jiang. In 1940 he became commander of one of the seven divisions of that army. After the Anti-Japanese War Su succeeded in significantly strengthening his division by incorporating a large number of units of the army under the command of Wang Jingwei. From then on Su's forces became known as the Central China Field Army which, however, continued to operate under the 4th Field Army. Su was elected an alternate member of the CCP Central Committee by the 7th Party Congress in 1945 (until September 1956). At the beginning of the war against the KMT forces Su operated in the area of North Jiangxi and South Shandong. He was appointed deputy commander of the East China Field Army set up in late 1946; this army was reorganized in 1948 to form the 3rd Field Army commanded by Chen Yi. After the occupation of Shanghai in June 1949 Su was appointed vice-chairman of the Shanghai Military Control Commission. In September of that year he was elected a member of the CPPCC.

1949,	Oct	Appointed member of the Revolutionary Military Council; vice-chairman of the East China Military and Political Council as well as deputy commander of East China Military Region
	Nov	Su succeeds Liu Bocheng as chairman of Nanjing Military Control Commission
1950,	Feb	Elected council member of the Sino-Soviet Friendship Association
1952,	Apr	Appointed deputy chief of General Staff (probably until Oct 1954)
	Aug	Member of a delegation led by Zhou Enlai to Moscow
1954,	Sep	Elected deputy for the PLA to the 1st NPC. Appointed chief of General Staff (until Oct 1958) and member of the National Defense Council
1955,	Sep	Promoted to rank of army general. Conferred the orders "1st August," "Independence and Freedom," and "Liberation," all 1st class
1956,	Sep	Elected member of the CCP Central Committee by the 8th Party Congress
1957,	Nov	Member of a military delegation led by Peng Dehuai to the USSR
1958,	Feb	Member of a delegation to North Korea
1959,	Sep	Appointed vice-minister of national defense
1965,	Jan	Elected member of the Standing Commit-

tee of the 3rd NPC

1969,	Apr	Reelected member of the CCP Central Committee by the 9th Party Congress
1975,	Jan	Confirmed by the 4th NPC as member of the Standing Committee (reelected in Mar 1978 by the 5th NPC)
	Jun	Identified as member of the Military Council of the CCP Central Committee
1977,	Jul	Identified as member of the Standing Committee, Military Council of the CCP Central Committee; article in RMRB of 29 July: "In Memory of Chen Yi"
1978,	Feb	Elected deputy for the PLA to the 5th NPC
	Aug	Head of a military delegation to North Korea; conferred the Korean order "National Flag," 1st class
1979,	May	Member of a friendship delegation to Japan

Su is married to Zhu Jing.

Su Zhan (Su Chan)  苏　展

Posts held

Provincial Administration
Vice-mayor of Beijing Municipality

| 1975, | Nov | Identified as a cadre of the National Earthquake Bureau |
| 1979 | | Elected vice-mayor of Beijing Municipality |

 **Su Ziheng** (Su Tzu-heng) 苏、子衡

Posts held

Others
Member of the Standing Committee of the 5th CPPCC
Vice-chairman of the General Office, Taiwan Democratic Self-government League

Su was born in Taiwan; he is a graduate in chemistry.

1959,	Apr	Delegate of the League for Self-Government of Taiwan at the 3rd CPPCC
1965,	Jan	Elected member of the Standing Committee by the 4th CPPCC
1967		Disappears during the Cultural Revolution
1973,	Feb	First appearance after the Cultural Revolution
1978,	Mar	Reelected member of the Standing Committee by the 5th CPPCC
	Dec	Identified as professor of chemistry
1979,	Jun	Identified as research fellow at the Institute of Photo-sensitivity, Academy of Sciences
	Oct	Elected vice-chairman of the General Office, Taiwan Democratic Self-government League

Sun Chengpei (Sun Ch'eng-p'ei) 孙承佩

Posts held

Others
Member of the Standing Committee of the 5th CPPCC
Vice-chairman of the Central Committee, Jiusan (Chiu-san) Society

1954,	Dec	Elected member of the 2nd CPPCC
1956,	Feb	Elected member of the Jiusan Society
1958,	Dec	Elected member of the Standing Committee and secretary-general of the Jiusan Society
1965,	Mar	Elected deputy secretary-general of the 4th CPPCC
1967		Disappears during the Cultural Revolution
1973,	Mar	First appearance after the Cultural Revolution
1978,	Mar	Elected member of the Standing Committee of the 5th CPPCC
1979,	Oct	Elected vice-chairman of the Central Committee of the Jiusan Society
	Dec	Deputy head of a CPPCC delegation to Romania

Sun Daguang (Sun Ta-kuang) 孙大光

Posts held

Government
Minister of geology
Director of the National General Geological Bureau

NPC
Deputy for Shanghai Municipality to the 5th NPC

Sun was born in 1917.

1949,	Oct	Identified as director of the Northeast China Shipping Bureau (probably until 1953)
1953,	Sep	Appointed director, Planning Department of the Ministry of Communications (probably until Jan 1955)
	Oct	Identified as director of Northeast China Naval Academy (until Jun 1954)
1955,	Jan	Assistant minister of the Ministry of Communications (until Jul 1958)
	Jun	Head of a delegation to the International Coastal Shipping Conference in Scheveningen
1958,	Jul	Appointed vice-minister of communications (until Jul 1964)
1959,	Jan	Appointed chairman of the Law of the Sea Arbitrage Commission of the Council for Promotion of International Trade
1962,	May	Identified as Chinese chairman of the Sino-Albanian Shipping Corporation; head of a delegation to its first session in Albania; visit to the United Arab Republic
1964,	Jul	Appointed minister of communications
	Oct	Elected deputy for Anhui Province to the 3rd NPC
1965,	Jan	Elected member of the National Defense Council

1966,	Mar	Head of a communications delegation to North Vietnam
	Apr	Sun disappears
1974,	Sep	First appearance after the Cultural Revolution
1975,	Dec	Identified as director of the National General Geological Bureau
1978,	Feb	Elected deputy for Shanghai Municipality to the 5th NPC
	May	Head of a geological delegation to the Federal Republic of Germany and France
1979,	Apr	Head of a geological delegation to the U.S.A. and Canada
	Sep	Appointed minister of geology

Sun Fuling (Sun Fu-ling) 孙孚凌

Posts held

Others
Director of the Board of Directors, China International Trust and Investment Corporation

Sun inherited the Beijing Fuxing Mill in 1948.

1960,	Jun	Identified as a member of the Standing Committee of the Association for Industry and Commerce
1963		Identified as deputy secretary-general of the Association for Industry and Commerce
1973,	Nov	First appearance after the Cultural Revolution
1979,	May	Identified as a member of the Revolutionary Committee of Beijing Municipality
	Oct	Appointed director of the Board of Directors, China International Trust and Investment Corporation; identified as deputy director of the Bureau of Foreign Trade, Beijing Municipality

Sun Guozhi (Sun Kuo-chih) 孙国冶

Posts held

CCP
Secretary of Hunan Province CP

NPC
Deputy for Hunan Province to the 5th NPC

Provincial Administration
Governor of Hunan Province

1958,	Sep	Identified as deputy director of the Transport Department of Hunan Province CP
1959,	Jan	Identified as director of the Communications and Transport Department of Hunan Province CP
1964,	Apr	Identified as director of the Bureau of Irrigation, Agriculture, and Forestry of Hunan People's Council
1966,	Aug	Identified as secretary of Hunan Province CP
1968		Disappears during the Cultural Revolution

1973,   Aug   First appearance after the Cultural Revolution: Identified as member of the Standing Committee of Hunan Province CP (until May 1977)

1977,   Jan   Identified as chairman of the Planning Committee, Revolutionary Committee of Hunan Province

         May   Identified as secretary of Hunan Province CP

         Nov   Elected vice-chairman of the Revolutionary Committee of Hunan Province (until Dec 1979)

1978,   Feb   Elected deputy for Hunan Province to the 5th NPC

         May   Member of an economic delegation to Great Britain and France

1979,   Jun   Member of the Credentials Committee at the 2nd Session of the 5th NPC

         Dec   Elected governor of Hunan Province

Sun Hao (Sun Hao)   孙　浩

Posts held

Government
Ambassador to Kampuchea

1972,   Aug   Identified as counselor at the Cambodian Exile Government in Beijing

1974,   Aug   Appointed ambassador to the Cambodian Exile Government in Beijing

1975,   Sep   Ambassador in Phnom Penh

Sun Hongzhen (Sun Hung-chen)   孙洪珍

Posts held

Military
Deputy director of the Logistics Department of the PLA

1973,   Sep   Identified as deputy director of the PLA Logistics Department

1974,   May   Deputy head of a PLA Friendship delegation to North Korea

Sun Jingwen (Sun Ching-wen)   孙敬文

Posts held

Government
Minister of chemical industry

NPC
Deputy for Tianjin Municipality to the 5th NPC

Sun was born in Hebei Province. In 1949 he was head of the Propaganda Department of Chahar Province.

1949,   Oct   Identified as director of the Propaganda Department of Chahar Province CP

1950,   Jun   Identified as mayor of Zhangjiakou

         Jul   Elected member of the People's Government of Chahar Province

1951   Identified as vice-governor of Chahar Province (until 1954)

1952,   Jan   Identified as 2nd secretary of Chahar Province CP (until 1954)

1954,   Aug   Identified as director of the Urban Construction Bureau of the Ministry of Building (until Apr 1955)

         Oct   Appointed member of the State Construction Commission (until Jan 1958)

1957,   Jun   Appointed vice-minister of urban construction (until Feb 1958)

1958,   Apr   Appointed vice-minister of building (until Sep 1959)

1959,   Sep   Appointed vice-minister of petroleum industry (until Cultural Revolution)

1965,   Apr   Appointed vice-chairman of the State Capital Construction Commission (until Cultural Revolution)

1967   Disappears during the Cultural Revolution

1975,   Jun   First appearance after the Cultural Revolution: Identified as vice-chairman of the Revolutionary Committee of Tianjin Municipality (until Dec 1975)

         Sep   Identified as member of the Standing Committee of Tianjin Municipality CP (until Dec 1975)

1976,   Apr   Identified as vice-minister of petroleum and chemical industry (until Feb 1978)

1978,   Jan   Head of a petroleum delegation to the U.S.A. and Japan

         Feb   Elected deputy for Tianjin Municipality to the 5th NPC

         Mar   Appointed minister of chemical industry

Sun Jixian (Sun Chi-hsien)   孙继先

Posts held

Military
Lieutenant-general
Deputy commander of Jinan Military Region

Sun was born in 1907 (1912?) in Shandong Province. In 1935 he commanded a battalion of the 1st Front Army. During the Long March his unit had a significant part in the battles preceding the crossing of the River Dadu. In 1937 he was battalion commander in the 129th Division of the 8th Route Army. At the end of that year he established a military base in Southern Hebei with parts of the 129th Division. He was appointed commander of the 2nd Subdistrict of Shandong Military District in 1939, and in 1944 commander of the 3rd Subdistrict of Shandong Military District. In 1946 his units were incorporated into the East China Field Army followed by Sun's appointment as commander of the 22nd Division. In July 1947 he led the 8th Column of East China Field Army. In February 1949 he was made commander of the 22nd Army of the 3rd Field Army.

1955,   Mar   Identified as a graduate of Nanjing Military Academy

         Sep   Promoted to rank of lieutenant-general

1963   Identified as deputy commandant of Nanjing Military Academy

1966,   Mar   Identified as deputy commandant of Beijing Military Academy (until about 1967)

1972,   Jun   First appearance after the Cultural Revolution: Identified as deputy commander of Jinan Military Region

Sun Junren (Sun Chün-jen)　孫俊人

Posts held

Government
Vice-minister of the 4th Ministry of Machine Building

Others
Vice-president of the Electronics Society
Deputy director of the Institute of Electronics, Academy of Sciences

1963		Identified as vice-president of the Electronics Society
1965,	May	Identified as head of the Chinese Section, Sino-Cuban Commission for Scientific and Technical Cooperation
1966		Sun disappears
1978,	May	First appearance after the Cultural Revolution: Identified as vice-president of the Electronics Society; head of an electronics delegation to the U.S.A.
	Jul	Identified as secretary-general of the Electronics Society
	Dec	Identified as vice-minister of the 4th Ministry of Machine Building
1979,	Jul	Identified as deputy director of the Institute of Electronics, Academy of Sciences

Sun Lanfeng (Sun Lan-feng)　孫兰峰

Posts held

NPC
Deputy for Inner Mongolia Autonomous Region to the 5th NPC

Provincial Administration
Vice-chairman of the People's Congress of Inner Mongolia Autonomous Region

Others
Member of the Standing Committee of the 5th CPPCC

Sun was born in Teng County, Shandong Province. From 1939 to 1943 he was commander of the 3rd Army of the 8th KMT War Zone. In 1948 he commanded the 11th KMT Army and served concurrently as acting governor of Chahar Province. In 1949 he went over to the Communists together with Fu Zuoyi. In September of that year he took part in the 1st CPPCC which elected him a member (confirmed in 1954, 1958, and 1964).

1949,	Oct	Identified as vice-chairman of Suiyuan People's Government and as vice-chairman of Suiyuan Military and Administrative Council (until 1954)
1954,	Mar	Identified as vice-chairman of the Inner Mongolia Branch of the CPPCC
	Apr	Identified as member of the Commission for Construction of the New Mausoleum for Genghis Khan
	Jun	Identified as vice-chairman of Inner Mongolia Autonomous Region (until Cultural Revolution)
1957,	Feb	Identified as vice-chairman of the Inner Mongolia Branch of the Sino-Soviet Friendship Association

1967		Disappears during the Cultural Revolution
1978,	Feb	First appearance after the Cultural Revolution: Elected deputy for Inner Mongolia to the 5th NPC
	Mar	Elected member of the Standing Committee of the 5th CPPCC
1979,	Jan	Identified as vice-chairman of the Inner Mongolia Branch of the CPPCC
	Dec	Elected vice-chairman of the People's Congress of Inner Mongolia Autonomous Region

Sun Ping (Sun P'ing)

Posts held

CCP
Deputy director, International Liaison Department, CCP Central Committee

1979,	Sep	Identified as deputy director, International Liaison Department, CCP Central Committee; head of a CCP delegation to Tunisia

Sun Pinghua (Sun P'ing-hua)　孫平化

Posts held

Others
Secretary-general and vice-chairman of the Sino-Japanese Friendship Association

Sun was born in 1917 in Liaoning Province; he studied at the Technical University in Tokyo.

1955,	Mar	Member of a commerce delegation to Japan; identified as deputy director of the Liaison Office, Association of Cultural Relations with Foreign Countries
1960,	Aug	Identified as council member of the Institute of Foreign Affairs
1963,	Oct	Elected secretary-general of the Sino-Japanese Friendship Association
1964,	Jun	Identified as deputy secretary-general of the Association for Cultural Relations with Foreign Countries (until Cultural Revolution)
	Aug	Appointed head of the Tokyo Liaison Office of the Liao Chengzhi Office (until early 1968)
1968		Disappears during the Cultural Revolution
1972,	Jul	First appearance after the Cultural Revolution: Head of a dance and drama troupe visiting Japan
1973,	Apr	Identified in his former post as secretary-general of the Sino-Japanese Friendship Association; deputy head of a delegation of this association to Japan
1974,	Sep	Deputy head of a goodwill delegation to Japan on the occasion of resumption of civil aviation between China and Japan
1975,	Sep	Deputy head of a friendship delegation to Japan
1979,	Jan	Identified as vice-chairman of the Sino-Japanese Friendship Association

Sun Qimeng (Sun Ch'i-meng)   孙起孟

Posts held

NPC
Deputy for Anhui Province to the 5th NPC

Others
Member of the Standing Committee and deputy secretary general of the 5th CPPCC
Vice-chairman of the Central Committee, China Democratic National Construction Association
Vice-chairman of the Executive Committee, Federation of Industrialists and Businessmen

Sun was born in 1908 as the son of a merchant in Xiuning, Anhui Province. He graduated in law from Suzhou University. In 1932 he was editor of the Shanghai newspaper Shenbao. In the following year he became secretary to General Gu Chudong, then commander of the Sichuan Headquarters for Fighting the Communists. Shortly afterwards he became secretary to the governor of Guizhou, Wu Zhongxin. In 1934 he was principal of a middle school in Guizhou. At the end of that year he moved to Shanghai to became chief-secretary of the Association for Vocational Training headed by Huang Yanpei. During the Anti-Japanese War he was head of a branch of this association in Yunnan Province and concurrently of a sparetime middle school. In 1945 he was one of the cofounders of the China Democratic National Construction Association together with Huang Yanpei, Hu Quewen and others. In 1948 he was chief-editor of the Hong Kong newspaper Wenhui Bao. In early 1949 he was a member of the Preparatory Committee for the 1st CPPCC in Shijiazhuang. In September of that year he took part in the 1st CPPCC as a delegate representing the National Construction Association.

1949,	Oct	Appointed deputy secretary-general of the Government Administration Council (until Sep 1954); director of the Personnel Bureau of the Government Administration Council (until Oct 1950); member of the Peace Council (until Jul 1958)
1950,	Oct	Appointed vice-minister of personnel (until Sep 1954)
1952,	Oct	Elected member of the Standing Committee of the Federation of Industry and Commerce (until Dec 1956)
1954,	Apr	Elected deputy for Anhui Province to the 1st NPC (reelected in 1958 and 1964 to the 2nd and 3rd NPCs); elected member of the Standing Committee (until Dec 1964) and deputy secretary-general of the 1st NPC (until Apr 1959)
	Dec	Elected member of the Standing Committee of the 2nd CPPCC (reelected in 1975 to the 5th CPPCC)
1967		Disappears during the Cultural Revolution
1974,	Sep	First appearance after the Cultural Revolution: Identified in his former post as member of the Standing Committee of the CPPCC (confirmed Mar 1978)
1978,	Feb	Elected deputy for Anhui Province to the 5th NPC
1979,	Jun	Identified as deputy secretary general of the 5th CPPCC; member of the Credentials Committee at the 2nd Session of the 5th NPC
	Oct	Elected vice-chairman of the Central Committee of the China Democratic National Construction Association

Sun Shengwei (Sun Sheng-wei)   孙盛渭

Posts held

Government
Ambassador to Sri Lanka

1960,	Apr	Identified as counselor at the embassy in Burma (until about 1962)
1970,	Oct	Identified as chargé d'affaires ad interim in Burma
1971,	Aug	Appointed ambassador to Kuwait (until May 1977)
1977,	Sep	Appointed ambassador to Sri Lanka

Sun Suochang (Sun So-ch'ang)   孙锁昌

Posts held

Government
Director of a department in the Ministry of Foreign Trade

1971,	Nov	Identified as director of the 3rd Department in the Ministry of Foreign Trade
1973,	Oct	Head of a government delegation to Argentina
	Nov	Head of an exhibition delegation to The Netherlands
1974,	Apr	Identified as deputy director of a bureau in the Ministry of Foreign Trade
	May	Head of a trade delegation to Sweden and the Federal Republic of Germany
	Dec	Head of a trade delegation to Finland
1975,	Feb	Deputy head of a government delegation to Jamaica
	Mar	Head of a delegation to Australia and New Zealand
	Aug	Head of a trade delegation to Papua New Guinea
1976,	Jun	Head of a trade delegation to Mexico; identified as deputy director of a department in the Ministry of Foreign Trade
1977,	Mar	Head of a trade delegation to Canada
	Jun	Head of a trade delegation to Norway and Denmark
1978,	Jan	Head of a trade delegation to the European Community in Brussels
	Jun	Head of a trade delegation to Switzerland and Sweden
	Nov	Identified as director of a department in the Ministry of Foreign Trade
1979,	May	Head of a trade delegation to Australia

Sun Xiaocun (Sun Hsiao-ts'un)   孙晓村

Posts held

Others
Member of the Standing Committee of the 5th CPPCC
Managing director of the Bank of China
Director of the Board of Directors, China International Trust and Investment Corporation
Vice-chairman of the Central Committee, China Democratic National Construction Association

During the 1930s Sun was vice-chairman of the National Resources Commission of the Nationalist Government. In 1936 he was a member of the China Agricultural Economy Study Association. In early 1949 he was elected a member of the Preparatory Committee of the China New Economic Society. In September of that year he took part in the 1st CPPCC as a delegate representing the National Salvation Association.

1949,	Oct	Appointed member of the Financial and Economic Commission of the Government Administration Council (until 1954)
	Dec	Identified as manager of China Vegetable Oil Company
1950,	Mar	Identified as member of the Standing Committee of China Democratic National Construction Association
1951,	Oct	Identified as director of the Beijing Agricultural College (until Feb 1960)
1953,	Feb	Identified as vice-chairman of the Beijing Branch of the Sino-Soviet Friendship Association
1954,	May	Identified as member of the Standing Committee of the Association for Cultural Relations with Foreign Countries (until Cultural Revolution)
	Aug	Elected deputy for Shandong Province to the 1st NPC (reelected in 1958 and 1964 to the 2nd and 3rd NPCs)
1955,	Apr	Elected member of the Standing Committee of China Democratic National Construction Association
1956,	Feb	Elected member of the Asian Solidarity Committee (until 1958)
1957		Identified as member of the Editorial Board of Jingji Yanjiu (Economic Research)
1958,	Jul	Identified as secretary-general of the Administrative Office, Chang Jiang River Basin Planning Committee
	Oct	Identified as vice-chairman of the Sino-Vietnamese Friendship Association (until Cultural Revolution)
1959,	Apr	Elected member of the Standing Committee of the 3rd CPPCC (confirmed in 1965 to the 4th CPPCC)
1960,	Aug	Head of a friendship delegation to North Vietnam
1965,	Apr	Identified as council member of the Sino-Romanian Friendship Association
1967,	Jun	Branded as a henchman of Liu Shaoqi and purged
1972,	Oct	First appearance after the Cultural Revolution: Referred to as member of the

1978,	Mar	Standing Committee of the 4th CPPCC Elected member of the Standing Committee of the 5th CPPCC
1979,	Oct	Identified as managing director of the Bank of China; appointed director of the Board of Directors of the China International Trust and Investment Corporation; elected vice-chairman of the Central Committee of the China Democratic National Construction Association

Sun Xiaofeng (Sun Hsiao-feng)   孙晓风

Posts held

Government
Vice-minister of petroleum industry
Member of the Patriotic Health Campaign Committee under the State Council

1965,	Feb	Appointed vice-minister of petroleum industry (until Dec 1970)
1967,	Oct	Acting chairman of the Chinese Section, Sino-Romanian Committee for Scientific and Technical Cooperation
1968,	Feb	Chairman of the Chinese Section, Sino-Albanian Committee for Scientific and Technical Cooperation
1969,	Dec	Head of a scientific and technical delegation to Albania
1970,	Sep	Head of a scientific and technical delegation to Romania
1971,	Jan	Identified as vice-minister of fuel and chemical industry (until Jan 1975)
	Dec	Head of a scientific and technical delegation to North Korea
1973,	May	Head of a scientific and technical delegation to Romania
	Oct	Head of a scientific and technical delegation to North Korea
1975,	Jan	Identified as vice-minister of petroleum and chemical industry (until Feb 1978)
	Nov	Head of a scientific and technical delegation to North Korea
1976,	Apr	Head of a scientific and technical delegation to Romania
1978,	Apr	Appointed member of the Patriotic Health Campaign Committee under the State Council
	Jun	Identified as vice-minister of petroleum industry

Sun Xuemei (Sun Hsüeh-mei) (f)   孙雪梅

Posts held

CCP
Alternate member of the CCP 11th Central Committee

1977,	Aug	Elected alternate member of the CCP Central Committee by the 11th Party Congress

Sun Yefang (Sun Yeh-fang)　　孙冶方

Posts held

Others
Advisor to the Institute of Economics of the Academy of Social Sciences

The economist Sun Yefang was born circa 1905. He joined the CCP in 1924 and started studying in the USSR in the following year. In 1938 he was entrusted with cultural work in Shanghai. In 1941 Sun served with the Central China Party School. In 1949 he was deputy director of the Industry Department of East China Military and Administrative Council and member of its Financial and Economic Committee (until June 1954).

1950,	Dec	Identified as president of the College of Finance and Economics in Shanghai (until 1953)
1954,	Nov	Appointed deputy director of the State Statistical Bureau (until Aug 1961)
1956,	Jul	Member of a delegation of the Statistical Bureau to the USSR
1958,	Apr	Identified as director of the Institute of Economics of the Academy of Sciences
1959,	May	Visit to the USSR
1960,	Apr	Participant at the forum "The Role of the National Economy under Socialism" in Prague
1961,	Sep	Visit to the USSR; subsequently branded as as rightist deviationist
1964		Sun is accused of having joined the opposition to the Party line
1966,	Jun	Branded as a reactionary bourgeois revisionist and subsequently imprisoned for more than seven years
1977,	Dec	First appearance after the Cultural Revolution
1978,	Apr	Identified as advisor of the Institute of Economics of the Academy of Social Sciences
	Nov	Deputy head of an economic delegation to Yugoslavia and Romania

Publications

1937	Co-editor of <u>National Salvation Handbook</u>
1940	Translation of <u>Concise Dictionary of Philosophy</u> by M. Rozentale and P. Udena
1979	<u>Several Theoretical Questions Concerning Socialist Economy</u>

Sun Yi (Sun Yi)　　孙　毅

Posts held

Military
Lieutenant-general

Others
Member of the Standing Committee of the 5th CPPCC
Vice-president of the PLA Armymen's Association

Sun was born in 1902 in Hebei Province. He attended Baoding Military Academy, and in 1937 joined the CCP.

He then served successively as commander of a regiment, brigade, and division of the Shanxi-Chahar-Hebei Border Region. In 1946 he was deputy commander of Central Hebei Military District, and two years later commanded the 7th Column of the Hebei Military District. In 1949 he was commander of the 68th Army.

1950,	Mar	Identified as council member of Hebei Province People's Government
1951,	Feb	Identified as commander of Hubei Province; later service in the Korean War where he commanded an army
1952,	Mar	Identified as commander of the 16th Army Group of the 4th Field Army
1953		Returned from Korea; identified as deputy commander of North China Military Region
1955,	Sep	Awarded the orders "1st August," "Independence and Freedom," and "Liberation," all 1st class; appointed lieutenant-general
1959,	Feb	Identified as deputy director of the Department of Military Schools, General Staff of the PLA
1978,	Mar	Elected member of the Standing Committee of the 5th CPPCC
1979,	Nov	Identified as vice-president of the PLA Armymen's Association

Sun Youyu (Sun Yu-yü)　　孙友余

Posts held

Government
Vice-minister of the 1st Ministry of Machine Building

1963		Identified as vice-chairman of the Preparatory Committee of the Society of Measuring Techniques and Instruments
1965,	Nov	Appointed vice-minister of the 1st Ministry of Machine Building (until Cultural Revolution)
1967		Disappears during the Cultural Revolution
1973,	Mar	First appearance after the Cultural Revolution: Identified in his former post as vice-minister of the 1st Ministry of Machine Building
1974,	Sep	Head of a scientific and technical delegation to Czechoslovakia
1976,	Nov	Head of a scientific and technical delegation to Czechoslovakia
1978,	May	Deputy head of an economic delegation to Great Britain and France
	Aug	Member of a delegation led by Hua Guofeng to Yugoslavia

Sun Yuting (Sun Yü-t'ing)　　孙雨亭

Posts held

CCP
Deputy secretary of Yunnan Province CP

Government
Member of the State Nationalities Affairs Commission

Provincial Administration
Vice-chairman of the People's Congress,
Yunnan Province

In 1948 Sun was deputy secretary of the 9th District Committee of the Shaanxi-Shanxi District CP. The following year he became director of the Political Department of the 5th Army Group under the 2nd Field Army.

1950,	Jun	Identified as deputy director of the Civil Affairs Department, Southwest China Military and Administrative Council
1951,	Feb	Identified as a member of the Land Reform Committee, Southwest China Military and Administrative Council
1952,	Aug	Identified as vice-chairman of the Nationalities Affairs Committee, Southwest China Military and Administrative Council
1956,	Oct	Identified as secretary of the Border Work Committee, Yunnan Province CP
1958		Identified as director of the United Front Work Department, Yunnan Province CP
	Mar	Elected vice-chairman of the 2nd CPPCC, Yunnan Branch
1959,	Oct	Identified as secretary of Yunnan Province CP (until Cultural Revolution)

1967,	Aug	Denounced as a counterrevolutionary revisionist and purged
1979,	Apr	First appearance after the Cultural Revolution: Identified as deputy secretary of Yunnan Province CP
	May	Appointed member of the State Nationalities Affairs Commission
	Dec	Elected vice-chairman of the People's Congress, Yunnan Province

Sun Ziyuan (Sun Tzu-yüan)　　孙子元

Posts held

Provincial Administration
Vice-chairman of the People's Congress of Heilongjiang Province

1978,	Jan	Elected vice-chairman of the Revolutionary Committee of Heilongjiang Province
1979,	Dec	Elected vice-chairman of the People's Congress of Heilongjiang Province

Tan Guansan (T'an Kuan-san)　譚冠三

<u>Posts held</u>

Others
Member of the Standing Committee of the
5th CPPCC

Tan was born in 1908. From 1937 to 1940 he served in the
115th Division of the 8th Route Army. In 1947 he was
deputy political commissar of the 11th Column, Central
Plains Field Army. In early 1949 he was identified as
political commissar of the 18th Corps, 2nd Field Army.

1950,	Apr	Identified as political commissar of the PLA units occupying Tibet
1951,	Apr	Member of the Chinese delegation conducting negotiations with the Tibetans in Beijing
	Nov?	Appointed deputy secretary of the Work Committee of Tibet CP (until Sep 1965)
1952,	Feb	Appointed political commissar of the newly established Tibet Military Region
1956,	Apr	Identified as member of the Preparatory Committee for the Establishment of Tibet Autonomous Region (until Sep 1965)
1959,	Mar	Acting representative of the Chinese Central Government in Tibet during the uprising
	Dec	Elected chairman of the Tibet Section, CPPCC (until Sep 1965)
1962,	Jun	Identified as lieutenant-general
1965,	Jan	Elected member of the Standing Committee of the CPPCC
	Sep	Identified as secretary of Tibet CP (until Cultural Revolution)
1967,	Jul	Identified as vice-chairman of the Supreme People's Court (last mention in this post in May 1970); subsequently disappears
1975,	Dec	Renewed mention as member of the Standing Committee of the CPPCC (confirmed in Mar 1978 by the 5th CPPCC)

Tan Jiazhen (T'an Chia-chen)　談家楨

<u>Posts held</u>

NPC
Deputy for Shanghai Municipality to the
5th NPC

Others
Member of the Standing Committee of the
5th CPPCC
Vice-president of Fudan University

1961,	Dec	Identified as vice-president of Fudan University and as professor of genetics
1964,	Sep	Elected deputy for Shanghai Municipality to the 3rd NPC
1966		Disappears during the Cultural Revolution
1978,	Feb	First appearance after the Cultural Revolution: Elected deputy for Shanghai Municipality to the 5th NPC
	Mar	Elected member of the Standing Committee of the 5th CPPCC
	Jun	Identified as vice-president of Fudan University

Tan Liren (T'an Li-jen)　談立人

<u>Posts held</u>

Provincial Administration
Vice-governor of Liaoning Province

1979,	May	Identified as vice-chairman of the Revolutionary Committee of Liaoning Province (until Jan 1980)
	Jun	Identified as director of the Liaoning Provincial Economic Commission
1980,	Jan	Elected vice-governor of Liaoning Province

Tan Qilong (T'an Ch'i-lung)　譚启龙

<u>Posts held</u>

CCP
Member of the CCP 11th Central Committee
2nd secretary of Sichuan Province CP

Tan was born in 1912 as the son of a peasant in Jiangxi
Province (or, according to different sources, in 1911 in
Liling, Hunan Province). As political cadre of a guerrilla
unit he was severely wounded in July 1937 fighting KMT
troops in the area of Hunan-Hubei-Jiangxi Border Region.
His life was saved by the United Front between KMT and
the CCP against the Japanese agreed upon immediately
afterwards. In 1943 he was identified as political
commissar of a guerrilla unit in Zhejiang Province. In 1944
he held the same post in the East Zhejiang Corps, a unit of
the New 4th Army. In autumn 1945 these troops were
transferred to Shandong Province. Circa 1948 Tan held the
post of political commissar in the 7th Army Corps
operating in Zhejiang. In May 1949 he was appointed
deputy secretary of Zhejiang Province CP as well as
deputy political commissar of Zhejiang Military Region and
as secretary of the Youth Work Department of the
CCP Central Committee.

1950,	Mar	Elected member of the East China Military and Administrative Council
1951,	Sep	Appointed vice-chairman of the Provincial Government of Zhejiang (until Nov 1952)
1952,	Aug	Appointed secretary of Zhejiang Province CP and political commissar of Zhejiang Military Region (until Dec 1954)
	Nov	Appointed chairman of the Provincial Government of Zhejiang (until Dec 1954)
1954,	Dec	Appointed acting chairman of Shandong Province (until Mar 1955)
1955,	Jan	Appointed 2nd secretary of Shandong Province CP (until Sep 1956) and chairman of the Shandong Section, CPPCC
1956,	Sep	Elected alternate member of the CCP Central Committee by the 8th Party Congress; appointed secretary of Shandong Province CP (probably until Oct 1961)
1958,	Nov	Appointed governor of Shandong Province (probably until Feb 1964); elected deputy for Shandong Province to the 2nd NPC
1961,	Oct	Identified as 1st secretary of Shandong Province CP (until 1966)
1964,	Oct	Identified as 1st political commissar of Jinan Military Region (until about 1967)

1966,	Jan	Identified as secretary, East China Bureau of the CCP Central Committee (until Cultural Revolution)
1969,	Apr	Confirmed alternate member of the CCP Central Committee by the 9th Party Congress (until Aug 1973)
1970,	Oct	Identified as a cadre of Fujian Province
1971,	Apr	Elected secretary of Fujian Province CP (until Oct 1972)
1972,	Jan	Identified as vice-chairman of the Revolutionary Committee of Fujian Province (until Oct 1972)
	Oct	Identified as a cadre of Zhejiang Province
1973,	Feb	Identified as secretary of Zhejiang Province CP (until Jun 1973)
	Jun	Identified as 1st secretary of Zhejiang Province CP (until Mar 1977)
	Jul	Identified as chairman of the Revolutionary Committee of Zhejiang Province and as 1st political commissar of Zhejiang Military District (until Mar 1977)
	Aug	Elected to first term as member of the CCP Central Committee by the 10th Party Congress
1977,	Mar	Identified as chairman of the Revolutionary Committee (until Aug 1979), and as 1st secretary of the CP, of Qinghai Province (until Dec 1979), as well as 1st political commissar of Qinghai Military District
1978,	Feb	Elected deputy for Qinghai Province to the 5th NPC
1979,	Mar	Head of a Party workers' delegation to Romania
	Apr	Head of an agricultural and animal husbandry delegation to Australia and New Zealand
	Aug	Elected chairman of the Standing Committee of the People's Congress of Qinghai Province
1980,	Jan	Identified as 2nd secretary of Sichuan Province CP

Tan is married to Yan Yongjie.

Tan Shanhe (T'an Shan-ho) 譚善和

Posts held

CCP
Alternate member of the CCP 11th Central Committee

Military
Major-general
Commander of the PLA Engineering Corps

NPC
Deputy for the PLA to the 5th NPC

1951		Service in Korea as commander of the Engineering Corps, Chinese People's Volunteers
1955		Promoted to rank of major-general
1956?		Tan attends a course of the PLA Military Academy
1965,	May	Referred to as military leader in Beijing
1974,	Feb	First appearance after the Cultural Revolution

1975,	Sep	Identified as military leader in Beijing
1977,	Jun	Identified as commander of the PLA Engineering Corps
	Aug	Elected alternate member of the CCP Central Committee by the 11th Party Congress
1978,	Feb	Elected deputy for the PLA to the 5th NPC
	Aug	Member of a military delegation led by Su Yu to North Korea

Tan Weixu (T'an Wei-hsü) 淡維煦

Posts held

Provincial Administration
Vice-governor of Shaanxi Province

| 1979, | Dec | Elected vice-governor of Shaanxi Province |

Tan Wenzhen (T'an Wen-chen) (f) 譚文英

Posts held

CCP
Alternate member of the CCP 11th Central Committee

| 1977, | Aug | Elected alternate member of the CCP Central Committee by the 11th Party Congress |
| | Oct | Present at National Day celebrations in Beijing |

Tan Yubao (T'an Yü-pao) 譚余保

Posts held

NPC
Member of the Standing Committee of the 5th NPC
Deputy for Hunan Province to the 5th NPC

Provincial Administration
Vice-chairman of the People's Congress of Hunan Province

Tan was born in 1897 in Hunan Province. In 1933 he was chairman of the Hunan-Jiangxi Soviet Government. During the Long March he stayed behind in Hunan-Jiangxi Border Region with a small guerrilla unit which was later incorporated into the New 4th Army. In 1935 he was secretary, CP of the Hunan-Jiangxi Regional Committee. Two years later he served in Yan'an. In September 1949 he was elected a member of the 1st CPPCC.

1950,	Mar	Identified as vice-chairman of the People's Government of Hunan Province (until 1955)
1951,	Feb	Identified as member of the Control Committee, Central-South Military and Administrative Council
1954,	Aug	Elected deputy for Hunan Province to the 1st NPC (confirmed by the 2nd and 3rd NPCs)

1955,	Feb	Elected vice-governor of Hunan Province (until Sep 1964)
	Dec	Identified as deputy secretary of Hunan Province CP
1956,	Nov	Identified as secretary of Hunan Province CP
1957,	Sep	Identified as principal of Hunan Party School
1962,	Sep	Identified as member of the Control Committee, CCP Central Committee
1964,	Jul	Identified as member of the Central-South Bureau of the CCP Central Committee
1965,	Jun	Identified as member of the Standing Committee, Central-South Bureau of the CCP Central Committee
1967		Disappears during the Cultural Revolution
1975,	Jan	First appearance after the Cultural Revolution: Member of the Presidium of the 4th NPC
1978,	Feb	Elected deputy for Hunan Province to the 5th NPC
	Mar	Elected member of the Standing Committee of the 5th NPC
1979,	Dec	Elected vice-chairman of the People's Congress of Hunan Province

Tan Yunhe (T'an Yün-ho) 譚云鶴

Posts held

Government
Vice-minister of public health

1958,	Sep	Identified as deputy secretary-general of Heilongjiang Province CP
1960,	Jan	Identified as member of the Standing Committee of Heilongjiang Province CP
1978,	Mar	Identified as vice-minister of public health
1979,	May	Delegate to the 32nd UN World Health Assembly in Geneva

Tan Zheng (T'an Cheng) 譚政

Posts held

NPC
Member of the Standing Committee of the 5th NPC
Vice-chairman of the NPC Legal Commission
Deputy for the PLA to the 5th NPC

Military
Army general

Tan was born in 1903 in Hunan Province. He joined the CCP in 1927 and during the same year took part in the Nanchang Uprising. In 1928 he joined the Soviet founded by Mao Zedong on Jinggangshan where he served temporarily as Mao's personal secretary. During the years until 1934 he took part in numerous battles against KMT troops, and eventually in the Long March. During the entire period of the Anti-Japanese War he served as political commissar of the Reserve Corps commanded by Xiao Jingguang in Shaanxi-Gansu-Ningxia Border Region. In 1945 Tan was elected an alternate member of the CCP

Central Committee by the 7th Party Congress (until September 1956). After the Japanese capitulation he was in charge of recruiting troops in Manchuria under Lin Biao. In early 1948 he was appointed political commissar of the Northeast PLA organized there, a post he retained after these forces, renamed 4th Field Army, began their campaign throughout China in 1949 from Manchuria. Until the occupation of Central and South China Tan served in this army and at the same time served temporarily as vice-chairman of Tianjin Military Control Commission, later as chairman of the same commission in Wuhan.

1949,	Oct	Appointed member of the Central-South China Military and Political Council, chairman of the Control Commission of that council; confirmed as political commissar of the 4th Field Army; appointed deputy political commissar of Central-South China Military Region and 3rd secretary, South China Subbureau, Central-South China Bureau of the CCP Central Committee
1954,	Sep	Elected deputy for the PLA to the 1st NPC (until Dec 1964) and member of its Standing Committee (until Mar 1959)
	Oct	Appointed member of the National Defense Council (until Dec 1959), vice-minister of national defense (until Mar 1965), and deputy director of the Political Department of the PLA (until Dec 1956)
1955,	Sep	Appointed army general; conferred the order of "1st August," "Independence and Freedom," and "Liberation," all 1st class
1956,	Sep	Elected member of the Central Committee and of the Secretariat of the CCP Central Committee (until Sep 1962)
	Dec	Identified as director of the General Political Department of the PLA (until Sep 1964)
1957,	Nov	Member of a military delegation to the USSR
1966,	Mar	Identified as vice-governor of Fujian Province
1967,	Sep	Branded as an anti-Party element and disappears
1975,	Jan	First appearance after the Cultural Revolution
	Sep	Named as cadre of the Central Military Leadership
1978,	Feb	Elected deputy for the PLA to the 5th NPC
	Mar	Elected member of the Standing Committee of the 5th NPC
1979,	Feb	Elected vice-chairman of the NPC Legal Commission
	Jun	Vice-chairman of the Draft Laws Committee at the 2nd Session of the 5th NPC

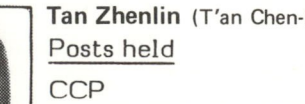

Tan Zhenlin (T'an Chen-lin) 譚震林

Posts held

CCP
Member of the CCP 11th Central Committee

NPC
Vice-chairman of the 5th NPC
Deputy for Hunan Province to the 5th NPC

Tan Zhenlin was born in 1902 as the son of a mining company employee in You County, Hunan Province. His school education was limited to three years. He joined the CCP in 1926, and in 1927 took part in the Autumn Harvest Uprising which had been organized by Mao Zedong. He later followed Mao Zedong into the Jinggangshan region and became political commissar of the 12th Red Army. He served temporarily also as commander and political commissar of Fujian-Guangdong-Jiangxi Military District. Tan did not take part in the Long March. Instead, he had been assigned special duties which required him to stay behind with Chen Yi, Zhang Dingcheng, and Deng Zihui. Under the pseudonym of Lin Zhun he organized the "South China Volunteers Resistance against Japan" during the Anti-Japanese War and commanded the 3rd Division of the New 4th Army. In 1941 he was made commander of the 6th Division, New 4th Army, in which he served concurrently as political commissar. In 1942 Tan was made secretary of the Jiangxi-Anhui Border Region CP. At about the same time he was posted to the New 4th Army's 2nd Divison (commander: Luo Binghui) as political commissar. The 7th CCP Congress elected Tan an alternate member of the Central Committee in 1945. He later became secretary of Zhejiang Province CP and in 1948, commander of a 3rd Field Army division. After the occupation of Hangzhou he was appointed chairman of the Hangzhou Military Control Council in May 1949.

1949,	Oct	Appointed member of the East China Military and Administrative Council; chairman of the Land Reform Committee, East China Military and Administrative Council; chairman of the Zhejiang Provincial Government (until Nov 1952); secretary of Zhejiang Province CP; deputy political commissar of the 3rd Field Army; and commander of Zhejiang Military District
1952,	Aug	Appointed vice-chairman of the East China Military and Administrative Council (until Dec 1952)
	Nov	Appointed chairman of Jiangsu Provincial Government (until Feb 1955)
	Dec	Appointed vice-chairman of the East China Administrative Council (until Feb 1954)
1954,	Dec	Elected member of the Standing Committee of the CPPCC (probably until 1959)
1955,	Feb	Appointed deputy secretary general of the CCP Central Committee (probably until Sep 1956)
1956,	Feb	Member of the CCP guest delegation led by Zhu De to the 20th CPSU Congress
	Sep	Elected member of the CCP Central Committee by the 8th Party Congress and member of the Politburo (until Cultural Revolution)
1958,	Nov	Elected deputy for Shanghai Municipality to the 2nd NPC
1959,	Apr	Appointed vice-premier (until Cultural Revolution)
	Nov	Head of a Party delegation to Hungary
1962,	Nov	Appointed vice-chairman of the Planning Commission and director of the Staff Office of Agriculture and Forestry under the State Council (until Cultural Revolution)
1967,	Feb	At the height of the Cultural Revolution, Tan participates in the "February Adverse

Current" opposing the decisions passed by the 10th Plenum of the CCP Central Committee in an attempt to outlaw the Red Guards

	May	Tan disappears
1973,	Aug	First appearance after the Cultural Revolution: Tan is elected to first term as member of the CCP Central Committee by the 10th Party Congress
1975,	Jan	Elected vice-chairman by the 4th NPC (confirmed in Mar 1978 by the 5th NPC)
1977,	Jul	Article in RMRB of 29 July: "In Memory of Chen Yi"
1978,	Feb	Elected deputy for Hunan Province to the 5th NPC

Tang Aoqing (T'ang Ao-ch'ing)   唐敖庆

<u>Posts held</u>

Others
President of Jilin University

1950?		Tang returns to China
1958,	Aug	Elected deputy for Jilin Province to the 2nd NPC (reelected in 1964 to the 3rd NPC)
1960,	Jun	Identified as vice-president of Jilin University (until Cultural Revolution); identified as deputy director of Jilin Branch, Academy of Sciences
1966		Tang disappears
1977,	Jun	First apprearance after the Cultural Revolution
	Oct	Identified as professor of the Chemistry Department, Jilin University
1978,	Mar	Identified as a specialist in the field of quantum chemistry
1979,	Aug	Identified as president of Jilin University; honored with the title "special-class model worker"

Tang Hongguang (T'ang Hung-kuang)

唐宏光

<u>Posts held</u>

Provincial Administration
Vice-chairman of the People's Congress of Liaoning Province

1958,	May	Identified as secretary-general of the Liaoning Branch of the Peace Council
1964,	Dec	Identified as vice-chairman, Liaoning Branch of the Sino-Soviet Friendship Association; head of a friendship delegation to the USSR
1978,	Feb	Identified as vice-chairman of the Revolutionary Committee of Liaoning Province (until Jan 1980)
1980,	Feb	Elected vice-chairman of the People's Congress of Liaoning Province

Tang Ke (T'ang K'e)   唐 克

<u>Posts held</u>

CCP
Member of the CCP 11th Central Committee

Government
Minister of metallurgical industry

Tang was born in 1918.

1952		Identified as deputy director of the Petroleum Administration Bureau of the Ministry of Fuel Industry
1964,	Apr	Identified as chairman of the Petroleum and Natural Gas Exploration and Exploitation Corporation
1965,	Feb	Appointed vice-minister of petroleum industry
	Sep	Member of a government delegation to the opening of a Chinese exhibition on economic construction in Bucharest
1966,	May	Head of a petroleum industry delegation to Albania
1967		During the Cultural Revolution, Tang is branded as a "corrupt element"
1971,	Feb	First appearance after the Cultural Revolution: Identified as a cadre of the Ministry of Fuel and Chemical Industry
	Dec	Identified as vice-minister of fuel and chemical industry (until Mar 1976)
1972,	May	Head of a delegation to the UN Conference on Environmental Pollution in Stockholm
	Sep	Head of a petroleum study group visiting Canada
1974,	Dec	Head of a delegation to Venezuela, Mexico, and Trinidad/Tobago
1976,	Mar	Identified as vice-minister of metallurgical industry (until Jul 1977)
1977,	Jul	Identified as minister of metallurgical industry
	Aug	Elected member of the CCP Central Committee by the 11th Party Congress
1978,	Apr	Head of an iron and steel delegation to Austria, Great Britain, Federal Republic of Germany, France, and the Netherlands
1979,	Feb	Head of a metallurgical delegation to the U.S.A.
	Apr	Head of a metallurgical delegation to Japan

Tang Kebi (T'ang K'e-pi) (f)   唐 克 碧

<u>Posts held</u>

CCP
Alternate member of the CCP 11th Central Committee
Member of the Standing Committee of Sichuan Province CP

NPC
Deputy for Sichuan Province to the 5th NPC

1973,	Aug	Elected alternate member of the CCP Central Committee by the 10th Party Congress (confirmed in 1977 by the 11th Congress)
1975,	Jan	Elected member of the Standing Committee by the 4th NPC (until Feb 1978)
1976,	Dec	Identified as secretary of Sichuan Province CP (until Dec 1978); deputy head of a friendship delegation of Party organizers to North Korea
1978,	Feb	Elected deputy for Sichuan Province to the 5th NPC
1979,	Jan	Demoted by the secretary to rank of Standing Committee member of Sichuan Province CP

Tang Liang (T'ang Liang)   唐 亮

<u>Posts held</u>

CCP
Alternate member of the CCP 11th Central Committee

Military
Colonel-general
Leading cadre in the Central Military Leadership

Tang was born in 1908 in Linyang County, Hunan Province, as the son of a laborer. He received no school education. His military career began in 1930 as political instructor of the 1st Company, 2nd Division, 8th Corps, 3rd Red Army. In 1941 he was identified as director of the Political Department of Hebei-Shandong-Henan Military Region, and in 1947 as political commissar of an army corps operating in Shandong Province. In June 1948 he was appointed director of the Political Department of East China Field Army which was shortly afterwards renamed 3rd Field Army.

1949,	Oct	Appointed deputy secretary of Nanjing Municipality CP
	Nov	Appointed vice-chairman of Nanjing Military Control Committee; elected member of the Presidium of the People's Congress of Nanjing
	Dec	Elected deputy mayor of Nanjing (until Dec 1950); appointed member of the East China Military and Administrative Council (until Dec 1952)
1952,	Dec	Appointed member of the East China Administrative Council (until Aug 1954)
1953,	Jan	Appointed director of the Political Department of East China Military Region (until Aug 1954)
1954,	Mar	Appointed deputy political commissar of East China Military Region (until Aug 1954)
	Aug	Elected deputy for Shandong Province to the 1st NPC (until Mar 1959)
	Sep	Appointed member of the National Defense Council (until Cultural Revolution)
	Nov?	Appointed political commissar of Nanjing Military Region (until 1965)
1955,	Sep	Promoted to rank of colonel-general; conferred the orders of "Independence and Freedom" and "Liberation," both 1st class

1958,	May	Elected alternate member of the CCP Central Committee
1965,	Jul	Appointed 2nd political commissar of Nanjing Military Region
1969,	Apr	Reelected alternate member of the CCP Central Committee by the 9th Party Congress (confirmed in this post in 1973 and 1977 by the 10th and 11th Party Congresses)
1974		Identified as a leading cadre in an unknown position of the Central Military Leadership

Tang Peisong (T'ang P'ei-sung) 汤佩松

Posts held

Others
Research fellow at the Laboratory of Plant Physiology and Biochemistry at the Beijing Institute of Botany, Academy of Sciences
Chairman of the Botany Society

Tang was born in 1903.

1959,	Apr	Identified as director of the Institute of Plant Physiology, Academy of Sciences
1963,	Nov	Identified as vice-president of the Society of Plant Physiology, and as deputy director of the Institute of Botany, Academy of Sciences
1964,	Sep	Elected deputy for Hubei Province to the 3rd NPC
1967		Disappears during the Cultural Revolution
1977,	Feb	First appearance after the Cultural Revolution
	Jul	Identified as a research fellow at the Laboratory of Plant Physiology and Biochemistry at the Beijing Institute of Botany, Academy of Sciences
1978,	Feb	Member of the Presidium of the 5th CPPCC
	Nov	Identified as president of the Botany Society

Tang Tianji (T'ang T'ien-chi) 唐天际

Posts held

NPC
Member of the Standing Committee of the 5th NPC
Deputy for the PLA to the 5th NPC

Military
Lieutenant-general

Tang was born in 1905 in Hunan Province. After graduating from the 1st Training Course of Whampoa Military Academy, he took part in the Northern Expedition in 1926 serving in the 36th Army. In 1927 he joined the Communists who initially appointed him company leader under He Long. In 1928 he served in the battalion commanded by Lin Biao in Ruijin. Tang took part in the Long March as director of the Political Department of a division of the 3rd Front Army. In late 1935 he served in a unit of the 15th Army Corps. In 1937 he was political commissar of the 344th Brigade, 115th Division, 8th Route Army. In 1938 he led a guerrilla unit in the border area of Shanxi-Henan. He later commanded the 6th Brigade of the Shanyin (Daiyue) Column. In 1946 he was commander of the Shanxi-Hebei-Honan-Shandong Border Region Column. Circa 1947 he was transferred to Manchuria as deputy commander of Yanji Military District. He was appointed deputy political commissar of Jilin Military District in 1948. In May 1949 he was identified as deputy political commissar and director of the Political Department of Wuhan Garrison, and three months later as deputy political commissar of Hunan Military District.

1949,	Dec	Identified as political commissar of the 21st Army Group
1950,	Mar	Identified as member of the People's Government of Hunan Province
1951		Identified as political commissar of the 12th Army Group and as commander of Hunan Military District
1952,	Jun	Appointed vice-chairman of a committee on problems of flood control of the River Jin
	Oct	Appointed vice-chairman of the Financial and Economic Committee of Central-South China Military Administrative Council (until Jan 1953)
1953,	Jan	Appointed vice-chairman of the Financial and Economic Committee of Central-South China Administrative Council
	Oct	Identified as political commissar of the Air Defense Forces (until 1958)
1954,	Sep	Identified as deputy director of the PLA Logistics Services (until about 1963); promoted to rank of lieutenant-general; conferred the orders of "1st August" and "Liberation," both 1st class
1959,	Apr	Elected member of the Standing Committee of the 3rd CPPCC (reelected in Jan 1965 by the 4th CPPCC)
1969,	Oct	Last appearance in spite of having survived the Cultural Revolution without apparent loss of influence
1974,	May	First appearance after five years of absence: Renewed mention as member of the Standing Committee of the CPPCC (until Feb 1978)
1978,	Feb	Elected deputy for the PLA to the 5th NPC
	Mar	Elected member of the Standing Committee of the 5th NPC

Tang Wensheng (T'ang Wen-sheng) (f) 唐闻生

Posts held

CCP
Alternate member of the CCP 11th Central Committee

Government
Deputy director of the America and Oceania Department of the Ministry of Foreign Affairs

Tang is the daughter of Tang Mingzhao, since 1972 under-secretary-general for Political Affairs and Decolonization of the UN.

1972,   Feb   Present as interpreter at the visit of President Richard Nixon
1973,   Jun   Member of a delegation led by Ji Pengfei to Great Britain, France, and Iran
         Aug   Elected alternate member of the CCP Central Committee by the 10th Party Congress (confirmed in 1977 by the 11th Congress)
         Sep   Interpreter at the reception given by Mao Zedong for Pompidou; interpreter at the reception given by Zhou Enlai for the prime minister of New Zealand
         Nov   Interpreter at the reception given by Mao for the prime minister of Australia
1974,   Feb   Interpreter at the reception given by Mao for the president of Zambia
         Mar   Interpreter at the reception given by Mao for the president of Tanzania
         Nov   Identified as deputy director of the America and Oceania Department of the Ministry of Foreign Affairs

Tang Yuanbing (T'ang Yüan-ping) 汤元炳

Posts held

Provincial Administration
Vice-governor of Zhejiang Province

Others
Director of the Board of Directors, China International Trust and Investment Corporation
Vice-chairman of the Central Committee, China Democratic National Construction Commission

1961,   Mar   Identified as vice-chairman of the Zhejiang Section, 3rd CPPCC
1979,   Oct   Appointed director of the Board of Directors, China International Trust and Investment Corporation; elected vice-chairman of the Central Committee, China Democratic National Construction Commission; identified as chairman of the Federation of Industrialists and Businessmen, Zhejiang Province
         Dec   Elected vice-governor of Zhejiang Province

Tang Zian (T'ang Tzu-an) 唐子安

Posts held

Military
Major-general
Deputy commander of Shenyang Military Region

Tang was born in 1909 in Hunan Province. In 1937 he commanded a battalion of an independent regiment in the 115th Division, 8th Route Army. He was in charge of guerrilla activities in 1938 in a unit commanded by Yang Dezhi. In 1939 he was appointed regiment commander in the column commanded by Yang Cheng in Shanxi-Chahar-Hebei Military Region. In 1946 he was brigade commander in Hebei-Shandong-Henan Military Region. In 1949 he served as deputy commander of the 64th Army, North China Field Army.

1951   Service as troop commander in the Korean War (until 1955)
1953   Appointed commander of the 64th Army
1955,   May   Appointed deputy chief of staff of Shenyang Military Region; promoted to rank of major-general
1960,   Jul   Identified as chief of staff of Shenyang Military Region
1966,   Oct   Identified as deputy commander of Shenyang Military Region
1967   Position unknown during the Cultural Revolution
1973,   Jul   First appearance after the Cultural Revolution holding his former post as deputy commander of Shenyang Military Region

Tao Hanzhang (T'ao Han-chang) 陶汉章

Posts held

Military
Major-general
Deputy commandant of the PLA Military Academy

Tao was born in 1917 in Jiangxi Province. During the final phase of the Revolutionary War he served in the Northeast Field Army.

1955,   Sep   Promoted to rank of major-general
1960   Identified as deputy chief of staff of Guangzhou Military Region
1964,   Feb   Identified as deputy commander of Guangxi Military District
1965   Identified as chief of staff of Guangzhou Military Region
1967   Disappears during the Cultural Revolution
1974,   May   First appearance after the Cultural Revolution: Identified as deputy commander of the PLA Military and Political Academy (until the academy is divided in Jan 1978 to form the Military Academy and the Political Academy)
         Jun   Deputy head of a military friendship delegation to Tanzania
1978,   Oct   Head of a delegation of the Academy of Military Science to Great Britain
1979,   Sep   Identified as deputy commandant of the PLA Military Academy

Tao Qi (T'ao Ch'i) 陶琦

Posts held

Government
Vice-minister of communications

1959,   Jan   Appointed member of the Law of the Sea Commission
1965,   Mar   Head of the Chinese Section, Administrative Council of the Sino-Albanian Shipping Corporation
         Apr   Appointed vice-minister of communications

1970,	Apr	Head of the Chinese Section, Administrative Council of the Sino-Albanian Shipping Corporation
1975,	Jan	Head of an economic delegation to Nepal
1979,	May	Deputy head of a government and military delegation, led by Zhang Zhen to Sudan

Tao Tao (T'ao T'ao) (f)　　陶　涛

Posts held

Government
Vice-minister of chemical industry
Member of the Birth Planning Leading Group under the State Council

Others
Chairman of the Board of Directors, Chemical Industry Society

1975,	Nov	Identified as vice-minister of petroleum and chemical industry (until 1977)
1977,	Aug	Tao is referred to as a member of the family of Zhu Yi during the mourning ceremonies for Zhu, former deputy departmental director in the Overseas Chinese Commission and deputy director of the Counselor's Office in the State Council
1978,	Jun	Identified as vice-minister of chemical industry
	Jul	Appointed member of the Birth Planning Leading Group under the State Council
	Dec	Identified as chairman of the Board of Directors, Chemical Industry Society

Tao Xijin (T'ao Hsi-chin)　　

Posts held

NPC
Vice-chairman of the Legal Commission under the NPC Standing Committee
Deputy for Beijing Municipality to the 5th NPC

Military
Major-general

In the mid 1930s Tao worked for the National Salvation Sacrifice League founded by Bo Yibo. He was criticized as being self-willed. In 1946 he served as chief of the Communist Section of a military mediation subcommittee with the rank of major-general. In 1948 he was appointed secretary-general of the North China People's Government.

1949,	Dec	Identified as secretary-general of the Political and Legal Commission of the Government Administration Council
1950,	Dec	Appointed vice-minister of North China affairs (until 1951)
1953		Identified as council member of the Political Science and Law Society
	Dec	Identified as vice-chairman of the Legislative Affairs Commission under the Government Administration Council

1954,	Nov	Identified as director of the Bureau of Legal Affairs, and as director of the Counselor's Office under the State Council (until Jun 1959), as well as deputy secretary-general of the State Council (until Sep 1959)
1957,	Nov	Member of a delegation to the Afro-Asian Legal Work Conference in Damascus
1978,	Oct	First appearance after the Cultural Revolution
1979,	Feb	Appointed vice-chairman of the Legal Commission under the NPC Standing Committee
	May	By-elected deputy for Beijing Municipality to the 5th NPC

Tao Zhiyue (T'ao Chih-yüeh)　　陶峙岳

Posts held

NPC
Member of the Standing Committee of the 5th NPC
Deputy for the PLA to the 5th NPC

Military
Colonel-general

Provincial Administration
Vice-chairman of the People's Congress of Hunan Province

Others
Member of the Standing Committee of the 5th CPPCC

Tao was born in 1892 in Ningxiang, Hunan Province. He graduated from Baoding Military Academy in 1916. From 1917 to 1925 he served first as battalion, later as regiment commander, of the Hunan Army. In 1928 he was appointed commander of the 3rd Division, 40th Army, which took part in the Northern Expedition. As commander of the 8th Division he operated from 1932 onwards in the area of Jiangsu and Gansu Provinces against Communist units. In 1937 he commanded the 76th, and one year later the 1st, Army. He was appointed deputy commander of the 34th Army Group in 1940. In 1943 he became commander of the 37th Army Group. In 1944 he commanded the Henan Garrison Headquarters. During the following year he was appointed deputy commander of the 8th War Zone. In 1946 he was commander of Xinjiang. As military commander of Xinjiang, he went over to the Communists in September 1949.

1949,	Oct	Appointed commander of the 22nd Army Group of the PLA
1950,	Jan	Appointed member of the Northwest China Military and Administrative Council (until Jan 1953)
1951,	Nov	Elected member of the 1st CPPCC
1953,	Jan	Appointed member of the Northwest China Administrative Council
1954,	Aug	Elected deputy for the PLA to the 1st NPC (reelected in 1959 and 1964 to the 2nd and 3rd NPCs)
	Sep	Appointed member of the National Defense Council (until Cultural Revolution); appointed commander of the Production and Construction Corps of Xinjiang (until Cultural Revolution)

1955,	Sep	Appointed colonel-general; conferred the order "Liberation," 1st class
1957,	Nov	Identified as deputy commander of Xinjiang Military Region (until Cultural Revolution)
1959,	Apr	Elected member of the Standing Committee by the 3rd CPPCC (confirmed in this post in Jan 1965 by the 4th CPPCC)
1966		Disappears during the Cultural Revolution
1974,	Mar	First appearance after the Cultural Revolution
1975,	Jan	Elected member of the Standing Committee by the 4th NPC (confirmed in Mar 1978 by the 5th NPC)
1978,	Feb	Elected deputy for the PLA to the 5th NPC
	Mar	Elected member of the Standing Committee of the 5th CPPCC
1979,	Jun	Member of the Committee to Examine Proposals at the 2nd Session of the 5th NPC
	Dec	Elected vice-chairman of the People's Congress of Hunan Province

Tian Bao (T'ien Pao)
Tibetan name: Sanggyai Yexe

天　宝
（桑吉悦希）

Posts held

CCP
Member of the CCP 11th Central Committee
Secretary of Tibet Autonomous Region CP

NPC
Deputy for Tibet Autonomous Region to the 5th NPC

Military
2nd political commissar of Tibet Military District

Provincial Administration
Chairman of the People's Government of Tibet Autonomous Region

Tian belongs to the Tibetan minority; he was born in 1917 in Tangba, Xikang Province (today: Sichuan Province). He and both of his brothers are Lamas. With the establishment of the Poba Government following the occupation of Tangba by Red Army troops in 1935, Tian was appointed director of the Youth Department and head of the Young Pioneers Group as well as political commissar of the newly established Poba Division which joined the Red Army on its march to Shaanxi. In 1944 Tian graduated from a course at the Nationalities Institute in Yan'an. In September 1949 he represented the minorities as a delegate at the CPPCC which elected him a member of its National Committee (until 1954).

1949,	Oct	Appointed member of the Minorities Commission of the Government Administration Council (until Oct 1954)
1950,	Jul	Appointed member of the Southwest China Military and Administrative Council (until Feb 1953)
	Oct	Appointed council member of the People's Government of Xikang Province (until Jan 1955)

	Dec	Appointed chairman of the Autonomous Region of the Tibetans in Xikang Province (until Jul 1955)
1952,	Oct	Elected council member of the People's Government of Sichuan Province (until Jan 1955)
1953,	Feb	Appointed member of the Southwest China Aministrative Council (until Nov 1954); by-elected member of the Standing Committee of the CPPCC (until Dec 1954)
1954,	Sep	Elected deputy for Sichuan Province to the 1st NPC
1955,	Jan	Elected vice-governor of Xikang Province (abolished in Jul 1955)
	Jul	Elected vice-governor of Sichuan Province
1956,	Jun	Appointed vice-chairman of the Minorities Committee of the NPC (until Dec 1964)
	Sep	Elected alternate member of the CCP Central Committee by the 8th Party Congress
1957,	Dec	Identified as 1st secretary, CP of Ganzi Autonomous Zhou of the Tibetans
1958,	Aug	Identified as member of the Standing Committee of Sichuan Province CP (until Cultural Revolution)
1968,	May	Elected vice-chairman of the Revolutionary Committee of Sichuan Province (until 1969)
1969,	Apr	Elected to first term as member of the CCP Central Committee by the 9th Party Congress
	Aug	Identified as vice-chairman of the Revolutionary Committee of Tibet Autonomous Region (until Aug 1979)
1970,	Sep	Identified as political commissar of Tibet Military District (until Oct 1976)
1971,	Aug	Elected secretary of Tibet Autonomous Region CP
1976,	Oct	Identified as 2nd political commissar of Tibet Military District
1978,	Feb	Elected deputy for Tibet Autonomous Region to the 5th NPC
	Sep	Head of a Tibetan friendship delegation to Nepal
1979,	Jan	Identified as chairman of the Reception Committee for Returned Tibetan Compatriots
	Jun	Member of the Credentials Committee at the 2nd Session of the 5th NPC
	Aug	Elected chairman of the People's Government of Tibet Autonomous Region

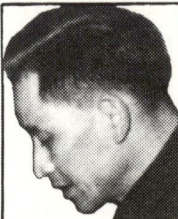

Tian Fuda (T'ien Fu-ta)

田富达

Posts held

Government
Member of the State Nationalities Affairs Commission

NPC
Deputy for Taiwan to the 5th NPC

Others
Vice-chairman of the Council of the General Office, Taiwan Democratic Self-Government League

Tian, who belongs to the Gaoshan minority, was born in Xinzhu, Taiwan. In 1946 he served as a soldier in the 70th Army of the National Government Forces. In 1949 he was taken prisoner by the Communist forces. In September 1949 he attended the session of the 1st CPPCC.

1949,	Oct	Appointed member of the State Nationalities Affairs Commission (until Cultural Revolution)
1954,	Jul	Elected deputy for Fujian Province to the 1st NPC (reelected to the 2nd and 3rd NPCs in 1958 and 1964)
1961,	Jun	Tian graduates from the Central Nationalities Institute
1962,	Feb	Elected member of the Central Committee of the Taiwan Democratic Self-Government League
1967		Tian disappears
1972,	Sep	First appearance after the Cultural Revolution
1978,	Feb	Elected deputy for Taiwan to the 5th NPC
1979,	May	Appointed member of the State Nationalities Affairs Commission
	Oct	Elected vice-chairman of the Council of the General Office, Taiwan Democratic Self-Government League

Tian Ping (T'ien P'ing)　田　平

Posts held

Government
Ambassador to Sierra Leone

1958,	Jun	Identified as deputy director of the Personnel Department of the Ministry of Foreign Affairs
1961,	Jul	Appointed counselor at the embassy in the German Democratic Republic (until Cultural Revolution)
1967		Disappears during the Cultural Revolution
1975		Identified as deputy director of the Consular Department of the Ministry of Foreign Affairs
1976,	Feb	Appointed consul-general in Osaka (until May 1978)
1978,	Oct	Appointed ambassador to Sierra Leone

Tian Xiuquan (T'ien Hsiu-ch'üan) (f)　田秀涓

Posts held

Government
Member of the Birth Planning Leading Group under the State Council

Mass Organization
Secretary of the Women's Federation

Tian was born in Hebei Province. In 1948 she served as director of the North China Women's Work Committee. In 1949 she was deputy director of the Women's Work Department, North China Bureau of the CCP Central Committee, and deputy director of the Organization Department of the Democratic Women's Federation.

| 1950, | Jul | Identified as chairman of the Hebei Provincial Federation of Democratic Women |

1953,	Apr	Elected member of the Standing Committee, Federation of Democratic Women (until Sep 1957)
1954,	Oct	Elected deputy for Hebei Province to the 1st NPC (reelected in 1958 and 1964 to the 2nd and 3rd NPCs)
1955,	Jan	Identified as director of the Department of Children's Welfare, Federation of Democratic Women
1957,	Aug	Member of an NPC delegation to Finland
	Sep	Elected secretary of the Federation of Democratic Women
	Dec	Identified as member of the Federation of Handicrafts Industry Cooperatives
1964,	Apr	Identified as council member of the Sino-Vietnamese Friendship Association
1967		Disappears during the Cultural Revolution
1978,	Jul	First appearance after the Cultural Revolution: Appointed member of the Birth Planning Leading Group under the State Council
	Sep	Elected secretary of the Women's Federation

Tian Ying (T'ien Ying)　田　英

Posts held

Provincial Administration
Vice-governor of Hubei Province

| 1978, | Jan | Elected vice-chairman of the Revolutionary Committee of Hubei Province (until Jan 1979) |
| 1980, | Jan | Elected vice-governor of Hubei Province |

Tian Zhidong (T'ien Chih-tung)　田志东

Posts held

Government
Former ambassador to Madagascar

1961,	Jan	Identified as 1st secretary at the embassy in Mali
1963,	Dec	Identified as councelor at the embassy in Mali (until about 1966)
1971,	May	Identified as councelor at the embassy in France (until Sep 1973)
1974,	Jun	Appointed ambassador to Madagascar (until Mar 1979)

Tian Zhong (T'ien Chung)　田　仲

Posts held

Provincial Administration
Vice-chairman of Xinjiang Autonomous Regional People's Government

| 1954, | Sep | Identified as deputy director, South Xinjiang Administrative Office of Xinjiang People's Government |
| 1957, | May | Identified as secretary-general of the People's Government of Xinjiang |

1961,	Feb	Identified as vice-chairman of the Sino-Soviet Friendship Association, Xinjiang Branch
1964,	Apr	Elected vice-chairman of Xinjiang Autonomous Region
	Nov	Elected deputy for Xinjiang to the 3rd NPC
1967,	Mar	Identified as deputy director of the Xinjiang Production Office; subsequently disappears
1978,	Mar	First appearance after the Cultural Revolution: Identified as secretary-general of the Revolutionary Committee of Xinjiang
	Aug	Identified as vice-chairman of the Revolutionary Committee of Xinjiang (until Aug 1979)
1979,	Sep	Elected vice-chairman of Xinjiang Autonomous Regional People's Government

Tie Ying (T'ieh Ying)   铁 瑛

Posts held

CCP
Member of the CCP 11th Central Committee
1st secretary of Zhejiang Province CP

NPC
Deputy for Zhejiang Province to the 5th NPC

Military
1st political commissar of Zhejiang Military District
1st secretary, CP Secretariat of Zhejiang Military District

Provincial Administration
Chairman of the People's Congress of Zhejiang Province

1965		Identified as political commissar of Zhoushan County, Zhejiang Province
1972,	Jun	Identified as secretary of Zhejiang Province CP
	Sep	Identified as vice-chairman of the Revolutionary Committee of Zhejiang Province
1973,	Aug	Elected alternate member of the CCP Central Committee by the 10th Party Congress (until Aug 1977)
1977,	Mar	Identified as chairman of the Revolutionary Committee (until Dec 1979), and as 1st secretary of the CP, of Zhejiang Province as well as 1st political commissar of Zhejiang Military District
	Aug	Elected member of the CCP Central Committee by the 11th Party Congress
	Nov	Identified as 1st secretary, CP Secretariat of Zhejiang Military District
1978,	Feb	Elected deputy for Zhejiang Province to the 5th NPC
	Oct	Head of a Party workers delegation to Romania and Yugoslavia
1979,	Dec	Elected chairman of the People's Congress of Zhejiang Province

Tie is married to Su Peilan.

Ting Mao (T'ing Mao)   廷 懋

Posts held

CCP
2nd secretary of Inner Mongolia Autonomous Region CP

Military
Major-general
2nd political commissar of Inner Mongolia Military District

Provincial Administration
Chairman of the People's Congress of Inner Mongolia Autonomous Region

Ting belongs to the Mongolian minority. He was born in 1913 in Liaoning Province. He joined the CCP in 1936 and subsequently served as battalion political instructor and regimental political commissar. Around 1938 he studied at the Anti-Japan Military and Political Academy in Yan'an. In 1943 he was battalion instructor of the Daqingshan Detachment, Shanxi-Suiyuan Military District. In 1947 he was made deputy director of the Political Department of Inner Mongolia Military District.

1952,	Oct	Identified as director of the Political Department of Inner Mongolia Military Region
1955,	Aug	Identified as deputy political commissar of Inner Mongolia Military Region
1956,	Sep	Identified as major-general
1957,	Aug	Conferred the order "Liberation and Freedom"
1961,	Aor	Identified as deputy political commissar of Inner Mongolia Military Region (until Cultural Revolution)
1967		Disappears during the Cultural Revolution
1979,	Jun	First appearance after the Cultural Revolution: Identified as 2nd political commissar of Inner Mongolia Military District
	Jul	Identified as 2nd secretary of Inner Mongolia Autonomous Region CP
	Dec	Elected chairman of the People's Congress of Inner Mongolia Autonomous Region

Tomur Dawamat (T'ieh·mu·erh Ta·wa·mai·t'i)

Posts held

CCP
Secretary of Xinjiang Autonomous Region CP

Government
Vice-minister of the State Nationalities Affairs Commission

NPC
Member of the Standing Committee of the 5th NPC
Deputy for Xinjiang Autonomous Region to the NPC

Provincial Administration
Chairman of the Standing Committee of Xinjiang Autonomous Region People's Congress

Tomur belongs to the Uighur minority. He was born in 1925 and worked as a hired farmhand before 1949.

1950		Tomur becomes a village chief
1952		Tomur joins the CCP
1955		Student at Beijing Central Nationalities College (until 1956)
1956		Identified as secretary of Toksun County CP in the Turpan Basin (until 1960) (the first county Party secretary of minority nationality in Sinkiang)
1960,	May	Identified as 1st secretary of Toksun County CP
1964,	Jul	Identified as vice-chairman of Xinjiang Autonomous Region
	Nov	Elected deputy for Xinjiang to the 3rd NPC
1968,	Sep	With the establishment of a Revolutionary Committee for Xinjiang Autonomous Region, Tomur is elected a member of the Standing Committee; subsequently disappears until 1976
1976,	Sep	Present at the mourning ceremonies for Mao Zedong in Ürümqi
1978,	Feb	Elected deputy for Xinjiang to the 5th NPC; elected vice-chairman of the Revolutionary Committee of Xinjiang
	Mar	Elected member of the Standing Committee of the 5th NPC
	Apr	Identified as secretary of Xinjiang Autonomous Region CP
1979,	May	Appointed vice-minister of the State Nationalities Affairs Commission
	Jun	Member of the Credentials Committee at the 2nd Session of the 5th NPC
	Sep	Elected chairman of the Standing Committee of Xinjiang Autonomous Region People's Congress

Tong Dalin (T'ung Ta-lin)　童大林

Posts held

Government
Vice-minister of the State Science and Technology Commission

1965,	Jun	Identified as a cadre of a department of the CCP Central Committee; member of a Party and government delegation to the German Democratic Republic
1978,	Mar	Identified as vice-minister of the State Science and Technology Commission
1979,	May	Deputy head of a scientific and technical delegation to the U.S.A.

Tong Guogui (T'ung Kuo-kuei)　童国贵

Posts held

CCP
Member of the Standing Committee of Hunan Province CP
Military
Major-general
Commander of Hunan Military District

Tong was born in Hubei Province. In 1937 he commanded a battalion of the 129th Division, 8th Route Army. He later served with guerrilla units in the Taihang Mountains. In 1948 he became commander of the 9th Brigade, 3rd Column in Hebei-Shandong-Henan Military Region. In 1949 he commanded the 33rd Division, 2nd Field Army.

1950		The 33rd Division commanded by Tong is reorganized into the Independent Division and assigned coastal defense duty in Shandong Province as a precaution against American attacks
1951		Tong commands a unit in the Korean War
1953		After return from Korea appointed chief of staff of the 26th Corps
1955,	Sep	Promoted to rank of major-general
1958		Identified as deputy commander of the 26th Corps
1961		Identified as commander of the 26th Corps
1964		Identified as commander of Shandong Military District (until 1974)
1967,	Feb	With the establishment of the Revolutionary Committee of Shandong Province, elected a member of the Standing Committee (no later mention in this post)
1975,	Dec	Identified as commander of Hunan Military District
1976,	Nov	Identified as secretary of Hunan Province CP (until May 1977)
1977,	May	Identified as member of the Standing Committee of Hunan Province CP
	Nov	Elected vice-chairman of the Revolutionary Committee of Hunan Province (until Dec 1979)

Tong Shaosheng (T'ung Shao-sheng)　童少生

Posts held

NPC
Deputy for Sichuan Province to the 5th NPC

Provincial Administration
Vice-chairman of the People's Congress of Sichuan Province

Others
Member of the Standing Committee of the 5th CPPCC
Vice-chairman of the Standing Committee, China Democratic National Construction Association
Director of the Board of Directors, China International Trust and Investment Corporation

Tong was born in 1904 in Chongqing, Sichuan Province. After leaving school he was employed in a shipping business. In 1949 he was manager of the Min Sheng Industrial Company in Chongqing.

1951,	Oct	Identified as council member of the People's Government of Chongqing (until 1954)
1953,	Nov	Elected member of the Executive Committee, Federation of Industry and Commerce

1954,	Aug	Elected deputy for Sichuan Province to the 1st NPC (reelected in 1958 and 1964 to the 2nd and 3rd NPCs)
1958,	Oct	Identified as vice-governor of Sichuan (until 1968)
1968		Disappears during the Cultural Revolution
1978,	Mar	First appearance after the Cultural Revolution: Elected member of the Standing Committee of the 5th CPPCC
1979,	Jan	Identified as member of the Standing Committee, China Democratic Construction Association (until Oct 1979)
	Jun	Member of the Committee to Examine Proposals at the 2nd Session of the 5th NPC
	Oct	Appointed director of the Board of Directors of the China International Trust and Investment Corporation; elected vice-chairman of the Standing Committee, China Democratic National Construction Association
	Dec	Elected vice-chairman of the People's Congress of Sichuan Province

Tong Xiaopeng (T'ung Hsiao-p'eng) 童小鵬

Posts held

CCP
Deputy director, United Front Work Department of the CCP Central Committee

Others
Member of the Standing Committee of the 5th CPPCC

In 1936 Tong attended a course for regiment commanders at the Worker-Peasant Red Army College in Yan'an.

1956		Identified as secretary-general, United Front Work Department of the CCP Central Committee
	Sep	Supervisor of ballots at the 8th CCP Congress
1958,	Apr	Identified as director of the Premier's Secretariat
	Jul	Elected deputy for Sichuan Province to the 2nd NPC (reelected in 1964 to the 3rd NPC)
1959,	Sep	Appointed deputy secretary-general of the State Council
1960,	Dec	Member of a government delegation to Burma to attend the 13th anniversary celebrations of Independence
1963,	Dec–	Member of a government delegation led
1964,	Feb	by Zhou Enlai to Egypt, Algeria, Morocco, Albania, Tunisia, Ghana, Mali, Guinea, Sudan, Ethiopia, Somalia
	Feb	Member of a government delegation led by Zhou Enlai to Burma, Pakistan, Ceylon
1972,	Sep	First appearance after the Cultural Revolution
1973,	Sep	Identified as a cadre of the United Front Work Department, CCP Central Committee
1977,	Nov	Identified as deputy director, United Front Work Department of the CCP Central Committee
1978,	Mar	Elected member of the Standing Committee of the 5th CPPCC

Tuo-hu-ti Sha-bi-er (T'o-hu-t'i Sha-pi-erh) 托手提沙比尔

Posts held

Provincial Administration
Vice-chairman of Xinjiang Autonomous Regional People's Government

Tuo-hu-ti belongs to the Uighur minority.

1979,	Sep	Elected vice-chairman of Xinjiang Autonomous Regional People's Government

Ulanhu (Ulanfu)   乌蓝夫

Posts held

CCP
Member of the Politburo of the CCP
11th Central Committee
Member of the CCP 11th Central Committee
Director, United Front Work Department
of the CCP Central Committee

NPC
Vice-chairman of the Standing Committee
of the 5th NPC
Deputy for Inner Mongolia Autonomous
Region to the 5th NPC

Military
Colonel-general

Others
Vice-president of the 5th CPPCC

Ulanhu was born in 1904 in the Banner of Tumd, Suiyuan Province. His family were feudal aristocrats of Mongolian origin. Ulanhu received a Chinese education, and from 1922 to 1924 he studied together with his brother Yun Ren at the Mongolian-Tibetan School in Beijing. There he also joined the Communist Youth League. In 1925 he took part in the 1st Congress of the People's Revolutionary Council of Inner Mongolia in Zhangjiakou. In the winter of 1925 he started to study Marxism-Leninism and technical subjects at the Far East University in Moscow. He returned to China in 1930 to teach elementary school in his native town. Besides his work he developed strong political interests which were initially aimed at Mongolian independence. In 1935 Ulanhu served in the forces of Fu Zuoyi which reconquered Darhan Muminggan Lianheqi (Bailingmiao). In the spring of 1937 he joined the Suiyuan Security Forces and became instructor in its Political Department headed by Bai Haifeng. From 1937 to about 1939 Ulanhu commanded a brigade of the Mongolian Independence Banner stationed in Yimeng. In 1939 he went to Yan'an to become head of the Nationalities Institute of the Anti-Japan Military and Political Academy. At the same time he held a post in the Commission for Minority Affairs in the Shaanxi-Gansu-Ningxia Border Region Government. His main task during this period was, however, the recruiting and training of Mongolian cadres. In 1944 he set up the Democratic Anti-Japanese Government in the Ju-League in Suiyuan. He was elected an alternate member of the Central Committee by the 7th CCP Congress in 1945. After the Japanese capitulation and the occupation of Zhangjiakou, Chahar Province, by Communist forces, he was sent into that area to persuade the Eastern Mongolia Autonomous Government to join the Communists. This led in February 1946 to the establishment of a joint Committee for Autonomy of which Ulanhu was elected chairman. By 1947 he had succeeded in establishing control over the Eastern Mogolian Autonomous Government and felt thus encouraged to proclaim the Inner Mongolia Autonomous Region. Ulanhu was then elected chairman of the new Autonomous Region which was, however, not recognized by the Nationalist Government. In 1949 he took part in the 1st CPPCC in Beijing and was elected a member of the Standing Committee of its 1st National Committee.

1949,	Oct	Appointed member of the Central Government Administration Council; vice-chairman of the Minority Affairs Commission, Central Government Administration Council; member of the Political and Legal Affairs Committee; director of the General Office, Sino-Soviet Friendship Association; chairman of the Inner Mongolia Autonomous Region; commander and political commissar, Inner Mongolia Military Region (since 1949 Ulanhu probably also served as secretary of the Inner Mongolia Autonomous Region CP)
1950		Identified as vice-chairman of the newly established Suiyuan Military and Administrative Council (abolished in 1952)
1952,	Feb	Identified as member of the newly established North China Administrative Council and as chairman of the reorganized Suiyuan Provincial Government; identified as secretary, Suiyuan Office of the CCP Central Committee
1954,	Sep	Appointed vice-premier; chairman of the Minority Affairs Commission; member of the National Defense Council; vice-chairman of the Sino-Soviet Friendship Association; member of the Peace Council; elected deputy for the Inner Mongolia Autonomous Region to the 1st NPC
1955		Identified as 1st secretary of Inner Mongolia Autonomous Region CP
	Sep	Appointed colonel-general; awarded the order "Liberation," 1st class
1956,	Apr	Head of a delegation attending the crowning ceremonies for King Mahendra of Nepal
	Sep	Elected alternate member of the Politburo by the 8th CCP Congress
1957,	Jun	Identified as president of the University of Hohhot
	Oct	Member of a delegation to the October Revolution celebrations in the USSR
1959,	Aug	Head of a delegation to Mongolia
1961,	May	Head of a CCP guest delegation to the 16th CP France Congress in Paris; identified as chairman, Inner Mongolia Division of the CPPCC
	Jun	Head of a delegation to Mongolia for the 40th anniversary celebrations of the Revolution
1964,	Oct	Head of a Party and government delegation to the 15th founding anniversary of the German Democratic Republic in East Berlin
1965,	Jul	Identified as 2nd secretary, North China Office of the CCP Central Committee
1967		At the height of the Cultural Revolution Ulanhu is branded as a "ruler in an independent kingdom" and is dismissed from all offices
1973,	Aug	First appearance after the Cultural Revolution: Elected a member of the CCP Central Committee by the 10th Party Congress
1975,	Jan	Elected vice-chairman of the Standing Committee by the 4th NPC
	Aug	Deputy head of a delegation to Hanoi for the 30th founding anniversary of the Democratic Republic of Vietnam

1976,	Nov	Head of an NPC delegation to Iran and Kuwait
1977,	Jul	Identified as director, United Front Work Department of the CCP Central Committee
	Aug	Elected member of the Politburo, CCP Central Committee, by the 11th Party Congress
	Sep	Head of an NPC delegation visiting Australia and New Zealand
1978,	Feb	Elected deputy for Inner Mongolia Auton-

omous Region to the 5th NPC

	Mar	Elected vice-president of the 5th CPPCC
	Nov	Head of a friendship delegation to Sudan and Turkey
1979,	Jun	Secretary-general of the 2nd Session of the 5th NPC
	Nov	Head of a Party delegation to Romania to attend the 12th Congress of the Romanian CP

Ulanhu is married to Yun Liwen.

Wa-zha-mu-ji (Wachamuchi)   瓦渣木基

<u>Posts held</u>

Others
Member of the Standing Committee of the 5th CPPCC

Wa-zha-mu-ji, who belongs to the Yi minority, was born in Xikang Province.

1950,	Jul	Identified as member of the Nationalities Affairs Committee, Southwest Military and Administrative Council
1951,	Sep	Identified as member of the People's Government of Xikang Province
1952,	Oct	Identified as chairman of Liangshan Autonomous District of the Yi
1954,	Aug	Elected deputy for Xikang Province to the 1st NPC
1958,	Jul	Elected deputy for Sichuan Province to the 2nd NPC (confirmed in 1964 by the 3rd NPC)
1959,	Nov	Identified as secretary of Liangshan Autonomous Zhou of the Yi
1962,	Oct	Identified as chairman of Liangshan Autonomous Zhou of the Yi
1964,	Oct	Identified as member of the Sichuan Provincial People's Council
1978,	Mar	First appearance after the Cultural Revolution: Elected Member of the Standing Committee of the 5th CPPCC

Wan Da (Wan Ta)   万达

<u>Posts held</u>

CCP
Member of the CCP 11th Central Committee
2nd secretary of Hunan Province CP

Provincial Administration
Chairman of the People's Congress of Hunan Province

1952,	Mar	Identified as deputy secretary of Yiyang District CP in Hunan Province
1957,	May	Identified as director, Rural Work Department of Hunan Province CP
1965,	Dec	Identified as secretary of Hunan Province CP
1970,	Jan	Identified as member, Standing Committee of the Revolutionary Committee of Hunan (until May 1970)
	May	Identified as vice-chairman of the Revolutionary Committee of Hunan Province (until Dec 1979)
	Dec	Elected member of the Standing Committee of Hunan Province CP (until Aug 1973)
1973,	Aug	Identified as secretary of Hunan Province CP (until Mar 1979)
	Dec	Elected vice-chairman of the Peasants Federation of Hunan Province (no later mention in this post)
1977,	Aug	Elected member of the CCP Central Committee by the 11th Party Congress

1979,	Apr	Identified as 2nd secretary of Hunan Province CP
	Dec	Elected chairman of the People's Congress of Hunan Province

Wan Fu (Wan Fu)   万复

<u>Posts held</u>

Government
Deputy director of the China Travel and Tourism Administrative Bureau

1965,	Feb	Appointed deputy director of the China Travel and Tourism Administration; thereafter disappears
1977,	Sep	First appearance after the Cultural Revolution: Identified as deputy director of the China Travel and Tourism Administrative Bureau
1978,	Oct	Head of a friendship delegation to Romania

Wan Li (Wan Li)   万里

<u>Posts held</u>

CCP
Member of the CCP 11th Central Committee
Member of the Secretariat of the 11th Central Committee

NPC
Deputy for Anhui Province to the 5th NPC

Wan was born in 1916 in Dongping, Shandong Province. He studied in France. In 1936 he joined the CCP. During the Anti-Japanese War he served as secretary-general of Hebei-Shandong-Henan Border Region CP and in organizing guerrilla activities behind the Japanese lines. In the summer of 1949 he was head of the Construction Bureau of Nanjing Municipality.

1950,	Jul	Appointed member of the Southwest China Military and Administrative Council and deputy director of its Industry Department
1952,	Nov	Appointed vice-minister of construction
1955,	Apr	Appointed director of the Urban Planning Bureau under the State Council (until May 1956)
1956,	May	Appointed minister of urban planning (until Feb 1958)
1958,	Feb	Appointed secretary of Beijing Municipality CP
	Aug	Elected deputy mayor of Beijing
1962,	Dec	Elected vice-chairman of the Beijing Section, CPPCC
1963,	Jun	Member of a delegation led by Liu Shaoqi to North Korea
1964,	Sep	Elected deputy for Beijing Municipality to the 3rd NPC
1966,	Dec	Publicly branded as a "bourgeois reactionary" and follower of Liu Shaoqi

1971,   Mar   First appearance after the Cultural Revolution: Elected member of the Standing Committee of Beijing Municipality CP (until Nov 1974)

1974,   Nov   Identified as secretary of Beijing Municipality CP (until Jan 1975)

1975,   Jan   Appointed minister of railways (until about May 1977)

         Sep   Head of a railway delegation to North Korea

1976,   Apr   Wan is dismissed following the Tian'anmen Incident

1977,   May   First appearance after the purge of the Gang of Four: present at May Day celebration in Beijing

         Jun   Appointed 1st secretary of the CP, and chairman of the Revolutionary Committee (until Dec 1979), of Anhui Province as well as 1st political commissar of Anhui Military District (until Feb 1980)

         Aug   Elected member of the CCP Central Committee by the 11th Party Congress

1978,   Feb   Elected deputy for Anhui Province to the 5th NPC; article in HQ: "Conscientiously Implement the Party's Economic Policy in the Rural Areas"

         Oct   Head of a friendship delegation to Japan

1979,   Oct   Head of a Anhui Provincial delegation to Maryland, U.S.A.

         Dec   Identified as 1st secretary of Anhui Military District Party Committee (until Feb 1980)

1980,   Feb   Elected member of the Secretariat of the CCP 11th Central Committee by its 5th Plenum

Wan Yi (Wan Yi)   万　毅

<u>Posts held</u>

Military
Lieutenant-general

Others
Member of the Standing Committee of the 5th CPPCC

Wan was born in 1904 in Haicheng County, Liaoning Province. After attending Jiangwutang Military Academy in Manchuria he joined the Nationalist Army. Among other units he commanded the 3rd Regiment of the Northeast Army under Commander Zhang Xueliang. He joined the CCP circa 1933. At the beginning of the Anti-Japanese War he was commander of a brigade in the 111th Division of the Nationalist Army operating in Shandong-Jiangxi Border Area. In 1939 he was able to force his division commander to join the Communists. In early 1945 he was director of the Communist Administration Office for the provinces of Jiangxi and Anhui. In April of that year he was elected alternate member of the CCP Central Committee by the 7th Party Congress. In August 1945 he was posted to Manchuria where he served during the following year as deputy commander of the Joint Democratic Northeast Army. In 1948 he was appointed a member of the Northeast China Administrative Council. When in the same year the Joint Democratic Northeast Army was renamed Northeast Field Army, Wan was made

commander of its 1st Army Corps. In early 1949 the Northeast Army was again renamed, now 4th Field Army, and Wan was appointed commander of one of its Special Corps.

1950,   Mar   Appointed member of the Central-South China Military and Administrative Council (until Jul 1950)

         Jul   Appointed deputy commander of the Artillery Forces in Central-South China Military Region (until Aug 1962)

1952,   Aug   Appointed vice-minister of the 2nd Ministry of Machine Building (until Nov 1954)

1954,   Oct   Elected deputy for Shenyang Municipality to the 1st NPC (until Mar 1959); appointed member of the National Defense Council (until Mar 1959)

1955,   May   Advisor to the Chinese delegation attending the Congress on the Defense of Peace and Security of European Nations in Warsaw as observer

1955,   Sep   Promoted to rank of lieutenant-general; conferred the order of "Independence and Freedom" and "Liberation," both 1st class

1956,   Sep   Reelected alternate member of the CCP Central Committee by the 8th Party Congress

1957,   Jun   Appointed member of the Scientific Planning Commission (until Nov 1958)

1958,   Sep   Appointed vice-chairman of the Science and Technology Association

1967,   Nov   Branded as a trusted follower of Peng Dehuai and purged

1977,   Oct   First appearance after the Cultural Revolution

1978,   Mar   Elected member of the Standing Committee of the 5th CPPCC

Wang Bicheng (Wang Pi-ch'eng)   王必成

<u>Posts held</u>

CCP
Member of the CCP 11th Central Committee

NPC
Deputy for the PLA to the 5th NPC

Military
Lieutenant-general

Wang was born in 1912 in Jiangsu (Hunan?) Province as the son of poor peasants. In 1938 he served as battalion commander in the New 4th Army. In that army he rose to regiment commander in 1940 and brigade commander in 1941. In 1945 he was made commander of the 6th Division, New 4th Army. In 1947 he commanded the 6th Column of East China Field Army. In 1949 he served as commander of the 24th Corps, 7th Army Corps, 3rd Field Army, later as deputy commander of Zhejiang Military District.

1951   Identified as member of the People's Government of Zhejiang Province and as commander of Zhejiang Military District

1952,   Aug   Appointed deputy commander of the 9th Army Group, Chinese People's Volunteers in Korea

1953,	Feb	Identified as commander of the 9th Army Group (until 1955)
1954,	Aug	Elected deputy for the PLA to the 1st NPC
1955,	Sep	Appointed lieutenant-general
	Dec	Appointed commander of Shanghai Garrison (until 1961)
1961,	Sep	Identified as deputy commander of Nanjing Military Region (until about 1967)
1964,	Oct	Elected deputy for the PLA to the 3rd NPC
1970,	May	Identified as 1st deputy commander of Kunming Military Region (until Nov 1972)
1971,	Jun	Elected 2nd secretary of Yunnan Province CP (until 1975)
1972,	Nov	Identified as 1st vice-chairman of the Revolutionary Committee of Yunnan (until 1975); identified as commander of Kunming Military Region (until Dec 1978)
1973,	Aug	Elected member of the CCP Central Committee by the 10th Party Congress (confirmed by the 11th Congress in 1977)
1976,	Jan	Identified as secretary of the CP, and as vice-chairman of the Revolutionary Committee, of Yunnan Province (until Dec 1978)
1978,	Feb	Elected deputy for the PLA to the 5th NPC
1979,	Jan	Identified as commander of Wuhan Military Region (until Jan 1980)

Wang Bin (Wang Pin)

Posts held

Government
Vice-minister of forestry

1976,	Aug	Identified as deputy director of the Forestry Bureau under the Ministry of Agriculture and Forestry
	Oct	Head of a forestry study group visiting Finland, Denmark, Sweden, and Norway
1979,	Nov	Identified as vice-minister of forestry

Wang Bingnan (Wang Ping-nan)   王炳南

Posts held

Others
Chairman of the Association for Friendship with Foreign Countries
Member of the Standing Committee of the 5th CPPCC

Wang was born in 1908 in Sanyuan, Shaanxi Province, as the son of a wealthy landlord. As a young man he served as secretary to Yang Hucheng, an influential warlord in Shaanxi and a friend of his father's. He was sent to Germany to study by Yang. In Berlin Wang joined the 3rd Communist International and the CCP. There he married Anna von Kleist who lectured at Humboldt University until at least 1962. In 1936 Wang returned to China to work initially for Yang Hucheng. He was involved in the "Xi'an Incident," in which Chiang Kai-shek was arrested by the Communists, and subsequently served in the Communist Headquarters in Yan'an. At the time of the CCP-KMT alliance, Wang was liaison officer for the Communists in Chongqing and at the same time personal secretary to Zhou Enlai. During the negotiations between the CCP and the KMT chaired by General Marshall in Nanjing in 1945, Wang acted as chief secretary on the Communist side.

1949,	Oct	Appointed director of the General Office in the Ministry of Foreign Affairs (until Sep 1954). Identified as board member of the Institute of Foreign Affairs and of the Sino-Soviet Friendship Association (until Dec 1954)
	Nov	Appointed director of the USSR and East Europe Department in the Ministry of Foreign Affairs
1954,	Apr	Secretary-general of the Chinese delegation at the Indochina Conference in Geneva
	Oct	Appointed assistant minister in the Ministry of Foreign Affairs (until Mar 1955)
1955,	Jan	Appointed ambassador to Poland (until Apr 1964). From August 1955 to April 1964 he conducts 120 ambassadorial talks in this capacity with the U.S. ambassador in Warsaw, at the time the only official channel of communication between Beijing and Washington
1957,	Jan	Wang accompanies a Polish government delegation led by Cyrankiewicz to China
1958,	Dec	Elected deputy for Liaoning Province to the 2nd NPC
1961,	May-Jul	Member of the Chinese delegation to the Geneva Laos Conference
1964,	Apr	Appointed vice-minister of foreign affairs (until Cultural Revolution)
	Sep	Elected deputy for Shaanxi Province to the 3rd NPC
1967,	Jan	Accused of "collaboration with foreign countries" and relieved of all posts; subsequently disappears
1975,	Aug	First appearance after the Cultural Revolution: Identified as chairman of the Association for Friendship with Foreign Countries
1976,	Mar	Head of a friendship delegation to Japan
1977,	Sep	Head of a friendship delegation to Iran, Somalia, Iraq
	Oct	Head of a friendship delegation to North Korea
1978,	Feb	Head of a friendship delegation to Pakistan, Bangladesh, and India
	Mar	Elected member of the Standing Committee of the 5th CPPCC
	Apr	Head of a friendship delegation to Romania
1979,	Mar	Head of a friendship delegation to Thailand and the Philippines
	May	Head of a friendship delegation to the Federal Republic of Germany, Austria, and Italy (until July)
	Aug	Head of a friendship delegation to the U.S.A. and Canada

Wang Bingqian (Wang Ping-ch'ien) 王丙乾

Posts held

Government
Vice-minister of finance

1963,	Jul	Identified as director of the Budget Department of the Ministry of Finance
1973,	Jun	Identified as vice-minister of finance
1979,	Jun	Member of the Committee to Examine Proposals at the 2nd Session of the 5th NPC

Wang Bingshi (Wang Ping-shih) 汪冰石

Posts held

CCP
Member of the Standing Committee of Jiangsu Province CP

Provincial Administration
Vice-governor of Jiangsu Province

1977,	Dec	Elected vice-chairman of the Revolutionary Committee (until Dec 1979) and member of the Standing Committee of Jiangsu Province CP
1979,	Dec	Elected vice-governor of Jiangsu Province

Wang Bingxiang (Wang Ping-hsiang) 王秉祥

Posts held

Provincial Administration
Vice-governor of Gansu Province

1952,	Aug	Identified as director of the Personnel Department, People's Government of Gansu Province
1959,	Dec	Identified as vice-governor of Gansu Province
1960,	Jan	Identified as secretary of Gansu CP
	Mar	By-elected deputy for Gansu Province to the 2nd NPC
1964,	Apr	Wang disappears
1979,	Dec	Elected vice-governor of Gansu Province

Wang Bingyun (Wang Ping-yün) 王秉鋆

Posts held

Government
Member of the State Nationalities Affairs Commission

Provincial Administration
Vice-governor of Guizhou Province

Wang belongs to the Buyi minority.

1979,	May	Appointed member of the State Nationalities Affairs Commission
1980,	Jan	Elected vice-governor of Guizhou Province

Wang Boping (Wang Po-p'ing) 王博平

Posts held

Provincial Administration
Vice-governor of Zhejiang Province

1977,	Dec	Elected vice-chairman of the Revolutionary Committee of Zhejiang Province (until Dec 1979)
1979,	Dec	Elected vice-governor of Zhejiang Province

Wang Caoli (Wang Ts'ao-li) 王操犁

Posts held

Provincial Administration
Vice-governor of Heilongjiang Province

1960,	Aug	Identified as director of the Rural Work Department, Heilongjiang Province CP
1979,	Dec	Elected vice-governor of Heilongjiang Province

Wang Chaozhu (Wang Ch'ao-chu) 王超柱

Posts held

CCP
Member of the 11th CCP Central Committee

Wang was born in 1918 in Changqing County, Shandong Province, as the son of poor peasants. At the age of eight he became an orphan and two years later earned his own living as a child laborer. At the age of fourteen he was called up by the Japanese occupation forces for forced labor. After the Communist take-over he received training as a bridge construction worker.

1959		Wang joins the CCP
1960		Promoted worker-engineer
later		Wang contributes to the construction of the Chang Jiang Bridge in Nanjing (completed in 1968) as one of the responsible engineers
1969,	Apr	Elected member of the CCP Central Committee by the 9th Party Congress (confirmed in 1973 and 1977 by the 10th and 11th Congresses)
1970,	Aug	Identified as vice-chairman of the Revolutionary Committee of Jiangsu Province (until about May 1973)
1973,	Jun	Elected chairman of the Trade Union of Hubei Province (until 1978?)
1974,	Jun	Head of a workers delegation to Tanzania

Wang Chenghan (Wang Ch'eng-han) 王诚汉

Posts held

NPC
Deputy for the PLA to the 5th NPC

Military
Major-general
Deputy commander of Chengdu Military Region

Wang was born in Hubei Province. In 1936 he was battalion commander in the 25th Army; in 1937 he held the same rank in the 386th Brigade, 129th Division, 8th Route Army. In 1945 he commanded a regiment in Shanyin (Daiyue) Military District. He was commander of the 39th Brigade of North China Field Army in 1948 and from 1949 commander of the 181st Division, 2nd Field Army.

1951		Service in the Chinese People's Volunteers in the Korean War as commander of the 181st Division
1952		Identified as chief of staff of the 60th Army, Chinese People's Volunteers
1955,	Sep	Promoted to rank of major-general
1958		Identified as commander of the 60th Army
1964,	Mar	Identified as deputy commander of Tibet Military Region
1967		Disappears during the Cultural Revolution
1973,	Mar	Identified as deputy commander of Chengdu Military Region
1978,	Feb	Elected deputy for the PLA to the 5th NPC

Wang Chongli (Wang Ch'ung-li) 王崇理

Posts held

Government
Ambassador to Jamaica

1955,	Feb	Identified as a cadre of the Ministry of Foreign Affairs
1960,	Mar	Appointed consul-general in Damascus
1961,	Nov	Identified as counselor at the embassy in Syria
1964,	Oct	Identified as deputy director of a department in the Ministry of Foreign Affairs
1970,	Jun	Identified as a cadre of the Asia Department in the Ministry of Foreign Affairs
1972,	Jul	Identified as consul-general in Geneva (until 1975?)
	Aug	Appointed deputy permanent representative at the UN Offices in Geneva (until 1975?)
1977,	Mar	Appointed ambassador to Jamaica
1979,	Feb	Chinese government representative at the celebrations of St. Lucia's independence

Wang Chonglun (Wang Ch'ung-lun) 王崇伦

Posts held

NPC
Deputy for Liaoning Province to the 5th NPC

Mass Organization
Vice-chairman of the Federation of Trade Unions
Director of the Production Department, Federation of Trade Unions

Others
Vice-chairman of the Revolutionary Committee of Anshan Iron and Steel Company

Wang was born in 1927. He is a national model worker; in the 1950s he was responsible for eight innovations in the manufacture of cutting tools.

1959,	Aug	Elected deputy for Liaoning Province to the 2nd NPC (reelected in 1964 to the 3rd NPC)
1973,	Apr	Identified as worker-engineer; member of a friendship delegation to Japan
1978,	Jan	Identified as vice-chairman of the Revolutionary Committee of Anshan Iron and Steel Company
	Feb	Elected deputy for Liaoning Province to the 5th NPC
	Jun	Member of an NPC delegation led by Ji Pengfei to Venezuela, Mexico, Canada
	Jul	Promoted to chief mechanical engineer of the Anshan Iron and Steel Company
	Oct	Elected vice-chairman of the Federation of Trade Unions
1979,	Apr	Identified as director of the Production Department of the Federation of Trade Unions
	Jun	Member of the Budget Committee at the 2nd Session of the 5th NPC
	Jul	Appointed member of National Games Organizing Committee

Wang Chongzhi (Wang Ch'ung-chih)

Posts held

Provincial Administration
Vice-governor of Shanxi Province

1979,	Dec	Elected vice-governor of Shanxi Province

Wang Chuan (Wang Ch'uan) 王川

Posts held

Government
Vice-minister of the 5th Ministry of Machine Building

1976,	Jan	Identified as a cadre of the State Council
1978,	Apr	Identified as vice-minister of the 5th Ministry of Machine Building

Wang Chuanbin (Wang Ch'uan-pin) 王傳斌

Posts held

Government
Ambassador to Niger

1957,	Mar	Identified as member of the Central Committee of the Communist Youth League
1960,	Apr	Member of a delegation to the Afro-Asian Solidarity Conference in Conakry

	Oct	Identified as deputy secretary-general of the Youth Federation and the Communist Youth League
1961,	Apr	Head of a youth delegation to Ceylon
1962,	Apr	Elected secretary-general of the Youth Federation (until May 1964)
1963,	Jun	Head of a youth delegation to Japan
1965,	Mar	Identified as deputy secretary-general of the Afro-Asian Solidarity Committee (until Jun 1966)
	May	Head of a delegation to the Afro-Asian Solidarity Conference in Ghana
	Jun	Elected secretary of the Peace Council and elected secretary and vice-chairman of the Afro-Asian Solidarity Committee
1966,	Apr	Wang disappears
1972,	Jul	Identified as council member of the Sino-African Friendship Association
1973,	Oct	Identified as consul-general in San Marino
1974,	Oct	Identified as embassy counselor of the Chinese embassy in Italy (until Mar 1979)
1979,	Sep	Identified as ambassador to Niger

Wang Chun (Wang Ch'un)　　王　纯

Posts held

CCP
Secretary of Beijing Municipality CP

Provincial Administration
Deputy mayor of Beijing Municipality

1950,	Mar	Identified as chairman of the Beijing Branch, Federation of Supply and Marketing Cooperatives
	Dec	Identified as member of the Financial and Economic Committee of Beijing People's Government
1952,	Aug	Identified as council member of the Federation of Supply and Marketing Cooperatives (until Nov 1953)
1957,	Jul	Identified as chairman of the Planning Committee of Beijing People's Government
1960,	Jul	Identified as deputy mayor of Beijing (until Cultural Revolution)
1963,	Nov	Head of an urban construction delegation to North Korea
1967		Disappears during the Cultural Revolution
1977,	Dec	First appearance after the Cultural Revolution: Elected vice-chairman of the Revolutionary Committee of Beijing (until Dec 1979)
1979,	Mar	Identified as secretary of Beijing Municipality CP
	Dec	Elected deputy mayor of Beijing Municipality

Wang Congwu (Wang Ts'ung-wu)　王从吾

Posts held

CCP
Deputy secretary of the Commission for Inspecting Discipline under the CCP Central Committee

Others
Member of the Standing Committee of the 5th CPPCC

Wang was born in 1905 in Henan Province. As a child he went begging with his mother and brothers and sisters. He joined the CCP around 1927 and was engaged in underground work in his native province. Circa 1930 he was sent to Moscow to study at the Sun Yat-sen University. After his return to China, Wang was successively political commissar of a division, an army corps, and an army. In addition, he temporarily served as director of the Organization Department, Central Plains Bureau of the CCP Central Committee, and as CP secretary of Hebei-Shandong-Henan Border Area. In April 1945 Wang was elected an alternate member of the CCP Central Committee by the 5th Party Congress (until September 1956).

1951		Identified as director of the Rural Work Department and of the Organization Department, as well as chairman of the Committee for Inspecting Discipline, North China Bureau of the CCP Central Committee (until 1954)
1952,	Jan	Appointed member of the North China Administrative Council (until Sep 1954)
1953,	Jul	Appointed 1st deputy secretary, North China Bureau of the CCP Central Committee (until 1954)
1954,	Dec	Elected member of the Standing Committee of the CPPCC (until Dec 1964)
1956,	Apr	Member of a CCP delegation to the 2nd Congress of the Korean Workers Party in Pyongyang
	Sep	Elected member of the CCP Central Committee by the 8th Party Congress as well as member and deputy secretary of the Central Control Commission of the CCP Central Committee
1959,	Nov	Member of a CCP delegation to the Congress of the Socialist Workers Party of Hungary in Budapest
1961,	Dec	Identified as director of the Central Party School (until May? 1963); identified as deputy director of the Organization Department of the CCP Central Committee
1963		Identified as member of the Standing Committee, Central Control Commission of the CCP Central Committee
1965,	Jan	Elected member of the Standing Committee of the CPPCC
1967,	May	Branded as a "three-anti element" and purged
1978,	Feb	First appearance after the Cultural Revolution
	Mar	Elected member of the Standing Committee of the 5th CPPCC
	Dec	Appointed deputy secretary of the Commission for Inspecting Discipline under the CCP Central Committee

Wang Daheng (Wang Ta-heng) 王大珩

Posts held

NPC
Deputy for Jilin Province to the 5th NPC

Others
Director of the Changchun Institute of Optical and Precision Machinery of the Academy of Sciences
President of the Optical Society

Wang was born in 1915.

1963		Identified as vice-chairman of the Preparatory Committee for the Society of Measurement Technology and Instruments
1964,	Oct	Elected deputy for Jilin Province to the 3rd NPC
1978,	Feb	Elected deputy for Jilin Province to the 5th NPC
	Jun	Identified as deputy director of the Changchun Institute of Optical and Precision Machinery
	Nov	Identified as director of the Changchun Institute of Optical and Precision Machinery
1979,	Jan	Identified as vice-chairman of the Jilin Branch, CPPCC
	Dec	Elected president of the Optical Society

Wang Daohan (Wang Tao-han) 汪道涵

Posts held

Government
Vice-minister of the State Foreign Investment Control Commission
Vice-minister for economic relations with foreign countries

Others
President of the Society of Mechanical Engineering

Wang was born in Liling, Hunan Province. During the final phase of the Revolutionary War he served as deputy director of the South of Huai River Administrative Office of Jiangsu-Anhui Border Area.

1949,	Nov	Identified as director of the Finance Department of Zhejiang Province People's Government
1950,	Feb	Identified as member of the East China Military and Administrative Council and as director of its Industry Department (until 1952)
1952,	Aug	Identified as vice-minister of the 1st Ministry of Machine Building; advisor of a delegation to Moscow under Zhou Enlai
1953,	Sep	Head of a scientific and technical delegation to the German Democratic Republic
	Oct	Elected Executive Committee member of the Federation of Industry and Commerce
1954,	Aug	Identified as vice-president of the Mechanical Engineering Society
1957,	May	Identified as member of the State Scientific Planning Commission

	Nov	Member of a scientific and technical delegation to the USSR
1958,	Sep	Elected member of the Science and Technology Association
1961,	Nov	Identified as president of the Mechanical Engineering Society (until Cultural Revolution)
1963,	Jul	Head of a scientific and technical delegation to Czechoslovakia
1964,	Nov	Appointed vice-chairman of the Commission for Economic Relations with Foreign Countries (until Cultural Revolution)
1965,	Sep	Member of a delegation led by Chen Yi to Pakistan, Syria, Algeria, Guinea, and Mali
1966,	Mar	Member of a delegation led by Liu Shaoqi to Pakistan and Afghanistan
	Apr	Member of a delegation led by Chen Yi to Cambodia; head of an economic delegation to Mali
1967		Disappears during the Cultural Revolution
1978,	Sep	First appearance after the Cultural Revolution: Identified as vice-minister for economic relations with foreign countries; identified as president of the Society of Mechanical Engineering
1979,	Sep	Identified as vice-minister of the State Foreign Investment Control Commission

Wang Daren (Wang Ta-jen) 王大任

Posts held

CCP
Secretary of Jilin Province CP

NPC
Deputy for Shanxi Province to the 5th NPC

Wang was born in 1910 in Hunan Province. From 1943 to 1945 he served as political commissar of a regiment in the 129th Division, 8th Route Army. In 1946 he was director of the Political Department of a brigade, also in the 129th Division. At the end of that year he held the same post in the 16th Brigade of the same division.

1950		Identified as director of the Propaganda Department of Taiyuan Municipality CP (provincial capital of Shanxi) and as council member of Taiyuan People's Government
1951,	Feb	Identified as member of the Standing Committee of Taiyuan CP
1953,	Oct	Identified as secretary of Taiyuan CP (until 1957)
1956,	Dec	Identified as director of the Department of Culture and Education of Shanxi Province CP
1958,	Nov	Elected alternate member of the Secretariat of Shanxi Province CP (until Sep 1964)
1964,	Oct	Elected secretary of Shanxi Province CP (until Cultural Revolution)
1967,	Oct	Accused as a "three-anti element" and "capitalist-roader" by Red Guards; subsequently disappears
1974,	Nov	First appearance after the Cultural Revolution

1975,	Jan	Member of the Presidium of the 4th NPC
	Dec	Identified as deputy secretary of Shanxi Province CP (until Mar 1977)
1977,	Apr	Identified as secretary of Shanxi Province CP (reelected in Mar 1978) (until Oct 1979)
	Dec	Elected vice-chairman of the Revolutionary Committee of Shanxi Province (until Oct 1979)
1978,	Feb	Elected deputy for Shanxi Province to the 5th NPC
1979,	Dec	Identified as secretary of Jilin Province CP

Wang De (Wang Te)　　王　德

Posts held

CCP
Secretary of Guangdong Province CP

Wang was born in 1911 in Hunan Province. In 1930 he was one of the leading cadres of Fujian Province CP who in May of that year freed a number of arrested Communists by force.

1952,	Oct	Identified as secretary of West Guangdong District CP (probably until 1953)
1954,	Oct	Identified as 2nd secretary of Guangzhou Municipality CP
1955,	May	Identified as 1st secretary of Guangzhou Municipality CP (until Mar 1965)
	Jun	Elected chairman of the Guangzhou Section, CPPCC
1959,	Feb	Elected vice-chairman of the Guangdong Section of the CPPCC
	May	Identified as alternate member of the Secretariat of Guangdong Province CP (until Nov 1962)
1962,	Nov	Identified as secretary of Guangdong Province CP
	Dec	Elected member of the People's Council of Guangzhou Municipality
1965,	Jul	Identified as alternate member of the Secretariat, Central-South China Bureau of the CCP Central Committee
1967,	Oct	Branded as a renegade and follower of Tao Zhu and purged
1979,	May	First appearance after the Cultural Revolution: Identified as secretary of Guangdong Province CP

Wang Derun (Wang Te-jun)　　王德润

Posts held

Military
Deputy commander of the PLA Artillery

| 1975, | Feb | Identified as deputy commander of Lanzhou Military Region |
| 1978, | Jun | Identified as deputy commander of the PLA Artillery; member of a military goodwill delegation to Congo and Zaire headed by Chi Haotian |

Wang Dezhao (Wang Te-chao)　　汪　德昭

Posts held

Others
Director of the Institute of Acoustics, Academy of Sciences
President of the Society of Acoustics
President of the Society of Instruments and Meters
Council member of the Society of Oceanography

Wang was born in 1902. Following a post as assistant at Beijing Normal University he studied in France where he received a doctorate in 1941. He then remained in France as a student of nuclear physics.

1956		Returns to China
1958,	Nov	Elected deputy for Anhui Province to the 2nd NPC (reelected in 1964 to the 3rd NPC)
1961,	Feb	Identified as director of the Electronics Institute of the Academy of Sciences
1964,	Sep	Identified as director of the Institute of Acoustics of the Academy of Sciences
1965		Member of a delegation of scientists to France
1966		Wang disappears
1973,	Jun	First appearance after the Cultural Revolution: Representative of PRC to the UN Seabed Committee Session in Geneva
1975,	Mar	Identified as council member of the Society of Oceanography; head of an oceanographical delegation to Japan
1979,	Apr	Elected president of the Society of Instruments and Meters; identified as director of the Institute of Acoustics of the Academy of Sciences
	Jun	Identified as president of the Society of Acoustics

Wang Dong (Wang Tung)　　王　东

Posts held

Government
Ambassador to Canada

1954,	Dec	Identified as 1st secretary of the embassy in Albania (until May 1956)
1960,	Aug	Identified as deputy director, Bureau of Film Administration, Ministry of Culture
1964,	Feb	Identified as counselor at the embassy in Romania (until Dec 1966)
1969,	Jun	Appointed ambassador to Sweden (until Dec 1971)
1972,	Apr	Identified as deputy director of the Western Europe, America, and Australia Department in the Ministry of Foreign Affairs
	Oct	Following reorganization of this department, Wang is identified as director of the Western Europe Department in the Ministry of Foreign Affairs (until Apr 1974)
1974,	Apr	Wang disappears for unknown reasons until 1977
1977,	Jul	Appointed ambassador to Canada

Wang Dongbao (Wang Tung-pao) 王东保

Posts held

Military
Major-general
Deputy commander of Chengdu Military Region

Wang was born in 1917. In 1932 he joined the 1st Front Army. He was political instructor of a company of the 1st Front Army in 1935, and in 1937 political instructor of a battalion of the 115th Division, 8th Route Army. In 1941 he served as political commissar of the 20th Regiment, New 4th Army. He was commander of a regiment in the Northeast Democratic Joint Army in 1945. In 1947 he was promoted to deputy commander of the 26th Division. In 1949 he commanded the 127th Division, 43rd Army, 4th Field Army.

1950		Identified as deputy commander of the 43rd Army and as commander of Shantou Garrison
1960		Identified as commander of the 38th Army
1965		Identified as deputy chief of staff of Shenyang Military Region
1977,	Jun	Identified as deputy commander of Chengdu Military Region
	Dec	Elected vice-chairman of the Revolutionary Committee of Sichuan Province (until Dec 1979)

Wang Douguang (Wang Tou-kuang) 王斗光

Posts held

Government
Deputy director of the Customs Administration

1960,	Mar	Identified as trade counselor in Ceylon (until Jun 1964)
1978,	Jul	Identified as deputy director of the Customs Administration; head of a customs delegation to Switzerland

Wang Duo (Wang To) 王铎

Posts held

CCP
Permanent secretary of Inner Mongolia Autonomous Region CP

NPC
Deputy for Inner Mongolia Autonomous Region to the 5th NPC

1949,	Oct	Identified as council member of the People's Government of Inner Mongolia Autonomous Region
1954,	Aug	Elected deputy for Inner Mongolia Autonomous Region to the 1st NPC
1955		Identified as deputy director, Economic Construction Committee of Inner Mongolia People's Council
	Apr	Appointed director of the Organization Department, Inner Mongolia Bureau of the CCP Central Committee

1956,	Jul	Identified as secretary of Inner Mongolia Autonomous Region CP
1967		During the Cultural Revolution Wang is accused of being an agent of Ulanhu and disappears
1975,	May	First appearance after the Cultural Revolution: Identified as vice-chairman of the Revolutionary Committee of Inner Mongolia Autonomous Region (until Dec 1979)
1977,	Jan	Identified as member of the Standing Committee of Inner Mongolia Autonomous Region CP (until Jul 1978)
	May	Head of a friendship delegation to North Korea
1978,	Feb	Elected deputy for Inner Mongolia to the 5th NPC
	Aug	Identified as secretary of Inner Mongolia Autonomous Region CP (until Aug 1979)
1979,	Jul	Elected chairman of the Inner Mongolia Federation of Philosophy and Social Sciences; appointed member of the National Games Organizing Committee
	Aug	Identified as permanent secretary (zhangwu shuji) of Inner Mongolia Autonomous Region CP

Wang Enhui (Wang En-hui) 王恩惠

Posts held

CCP
Member of the Standing Committee of Tianjin Municipality CP

NPC
Deputy for Tianjin Municipality to the 5th NPC

Provincial Administration
Vice-chairman of the Revolutionary Committee of Tianjin

1977,	Dec	Elected vice-chairman of the Revolutionary Committee of Tianjin Municipality
1978,	Feb	Elected deputy for Tianjin Municipality to the 5th NPC
	Sep	Member of a Tianjin friendship delegation to Japan
1979,	Apr	Identified as member of the Standing Committee of Tianjin Municipality CP

Wang Enmao (Wang En-mao) 王恩茂

Posts held

CCP
Member of the CCP 11th Central Committee
1st secretary of Jilin Province CP
Director of the Jilin Party School

NPC
Deputy for Jilin Province to the 5th NPC

Military
Lieutenant-general
Deputy political commissar of Shenyang Military Region
1st political commissar of Jilin Military District

Provincial Administration
Chairman of the Revolutionary Committee of Jilin Province

Wang was born in 1912 in Yongxin County, Jiangxi Province. Together with his father and two brothers he joined the first Communist fighting units in 1927. In 1934 he was political commissar of a Red Army unit. In 1936 he attended a course at the Anti-Japan Military and Political Academy in Yan'an. In 1938 he commanded a regiment of the 120th Division, 8th Route Army. In 1942 he was director of the Political Department, 359th Brigade, 8th Route Army, and two years later deputy political commissar of the 359th Brigade. In late 1944 he was transferred to Hunan where he was a cofounder of the Anti-Japan and National Salvation Army commanded by Wang Zhen (political commissar: Wang Shoudao). He served with this army in Henan Province until the Japanese capitulation. In 1946 he again joined the 359th Brigade as political commissar. In 1948 he was political commissar of a corps of the 1st Field Army.

1949,	Oct	Identified as member of the Xinjiang Bureau of the CCP Central Committee (abolished in Oct 1955); appointed political commissar of the 1st Field Army and member of the People's Government of Xinjiang (until Oct 1955)
1950,	Jul	Appointed member of the Northwest China Military and Administrative Council (abolished in Jan 1953)
1952,	Oct?	Appointed secretary of Xinjiang Province CP (until Oct 1955) and political commissar of Xinjiang Military Region
1954,	Feb?	Appointed 1st secretary of Xinjiang Province CP (until Oct 1955)
	Aug	Elected deputy for Xinjiang Province to the 1st NPC (until Mar 1959)
1955,	Sep	Appointed member of the People's Council of the newly established Xinjiang Autonomous Region; conferred the orders "1st August," "Independence and Freedom," and "Liberation," all 1st class; promoted to rank of major-general
	Oct	Appointed 1st secretary of Xinjiang Autonomous Region CP
1956,	Apr	Head of a animal husbandry delegation to the USSR
	Sep	Elected alternate member of the CCP Central Committee by the 8th Party Congress (until May 1958)
	Oct	Identified as commander of Xinjiang Military Region
1958,	May	Elected member of the CCP Central Committee
1963,	Mar	Identified as lieutenant-general
1965,	Jan	Appointed member of the National Defense Council
	Aug	Identified as secretary, Northwest China Bureau of the CCP Central Committee
1966,	Mar	Identified as 1st secretary, CP of the PLA Xinjiang Construction Corps
1968		Wang is exposed to severe criticism during the final phase of the Cultural Revolution
1969,	Apr	Demoted from member to alternate member of the CCP Central Committee by the 9th Party Congress (until Aug 1973); subsequently disappears until 1973

1973,	Sep	Present at militia demonstration in Hefei, Anhui Province
1975,	Dec	Identified as deputy political commissar of Nanjing Military Region (until late 1976)
1977,	Mar	Identified as 1st secretary of the CP, and chairman of the Revolutionary Committee, of Jilin Province as well as 1st political commissar of Jilin Military District
	Aug	Identified as deputy commander of Shenyang Military Region (until 1977); elected member of the CCP Central Committee by the 11th Party Congress
1978,	Feb	Elected deputy for Jilin Province to the 5th NPC; identified as deputy political commissar of Shenyang Military Region
	Apr	Identified as director of the Jilin Party School
	Sep	Head of a friendship delegation of Jilin Province to North Korea; article in RMRB of 2 September: "Unforgettable History, Profound Education - Restudying Chairman Mao's Talk at the Enlarged Working Conference Convened by the CCP Central Committee"
1979,	Aug	Head of a friendship delegation to Romania
	Nov	Identified as 1st secretary of Jilin Military District Party Committee

Wang Fang (Wang Fang)　　王　芳

Posts held

CCP
Deputy secretary of Zhejiang Province CP

Provincial Administration
Vice-chairman of the People's Congress of Zhejiang Province

Wang served as political commissar of the 94th Division, 32nd Army, 3rd Field Army, in 1949.

1950,	Apr	Identified as deputy commander of the Hangzhou Air Defense Command
1951,	Feb	Identified as deputy director of the Public Security Department, People's Government of Zhejiang Province
1954,	May	Identified as political commissar of the Public Security Forces of Zhejiang Province
1955,	Jan	Identified as member of the People's Government of Zhejiang Province
	Jul	Identified as director of the Public Security Department of the People's Government of Zhejiang
1964,	Sep	Elected vice-governor of Zhejiang Province (until Cultural Revolution)
1967,	Jan	Branded as a counterrevolutionary revisionist and purged
1977,	Dec	First appearance after the Cultural Revolution: Elected vice-chairman of the Revolutionary Committee of Zhejiang (until Dec 1979)
1978,	Jan	Identified as member of the Standing Committee of Zhejiang Province CP

May Elected deputy secretary of Zhejiang Province CP

1979, Dec Elected vice-chairman of the People's Congress of Zhejiang Province

Wang is married to Liu Xin.

Wang Feng (Wang Feng)   汪 锋

Posts held

CCP
Member of the CCP 11th Central Committee
1st secretary of Xinjiang Autonomous Region CP
Principal of the Xinjiang Party School

NPC
Deputy for Xinjiang Autonomous Region to the 5th NPC

Military
1st political commissar of Xinjiang Military Region
1st secretary, CP Committee of Xinjiang Military Region

Wang was born in 1906 in Lantian, Shaanxi Province. He joined the Communist Youth League as a student at Beijing University. From circa 1937 he served in Shaanxi-Gansu-Ningxia Border Region, temporarily as commander of Guanchong Garrison. In 1946 he was commander of Lushan Military District and political commissar of the 38th Red Army. In 1947 he became director of the United Front Work Department, Northwest Bureau of the CCP Central Committee (until 1952).

1950, Mar Appointed chairman of the Minorities Affairs Commission, Northwest China Military and Administrative Council (until Jan 1953)

1951 Identified as member of the Land Reform Committee of Northwest China Military and Administrative Council (until Jan 1953)

1952, Aug Appointed member of the Political and Legal Affairs Committee of Northwest China Military and Administrative Council (until Jan 1953) and director of the Northwest China Nationalities Institute

Nov Appointed vice-chairman of the Minorities Commission of the Government Administration Council

1953, Jan Appointed chairman of the Minorities Affairs Commission of Northwest China Administrative Council (abolished in Aug 1954)

1954, Sep Elected deputy for Qinghai Province to the 1st NPC (until Mar 1959)

1955, Nov Appointed deputy director, United Front Work Department of the CCP Central Committee

1956, Mar Deputy head of a delegation led by Chen Yi to Lhasa (establishment of the Preparatory Committee for Tibet Autonomous Region)

1958, May Elected alternate member of the CCP Central Committee

Jun Appointed 1st secretary of Ningxia Province CP (until Feb? 1961)

1959, Mar Elected deputy for Xinjiang Autonomous Region to the 2nd NPC (until Dec 1964)

1961, Apr Identified as 1st secretary of Gansu Province CP

1964, Apr Identified as secretary, Northwest China Bureau of the CCP Central Committee

Sep Elected deputy for Gansu Province to the 3rd NPC

1966, Sep Accused by Red Guards as "three-anti element"; subsequently disappears

1977, Aug First appearance after the Cultural Revolution: Elected member of the CCP Central Committee by the 11th Party Congress

Sep Identified as 1st vice-chairman and 2nd CP secretary of Xinjiang Autonomous Region, as well as 2nd political commissar of Xinjiang Military Region (until Jan 1978)

1978, Jan Identified as 1st secretary of the CP, and chairman of the Revolutionary Committee (latter post until Sep 1979) of Xinjiang Autonomous Region and as 1st political commissar of Xinjiang Military Region

Feb Elected deputy for Xinjiang Autonomous Region to the 5th NPC

May Identified as principal of the Xinjiang Party School

1979, May Head of an agricultural delegation to the U.S.A.

Wang Fu (Wang Fu)   王 甫

Posts held

Others
Member of the Standing Committee of the 5th CPPCC
Deputy chief procurator of the Supreme People's Procuracy

1949, Oct Identified as board member of the Beijing Branch, Sino-Soviet Friendship Association

1956, Sep Supervisor of Ballots at the 8th CCP Congress

1958, Oct Identified as deputy director, Organization Department of the CCP Central Committee (until 1964)

1964, May Identified as alternate secretary, Northwest Bureau of the CCP Central Committee

1965, Aug Identified as secretary, Northwest Bureau of the CCP Central Committee

1967 Disappears during the Cultural Revolution

1978, Feb First appearance after the Cultural Revolution

Mar Elected member of the Standing Committee of the 5th CPPCC

Dec Appointed deputy chief procurator of the Supreme People's Procuracy

Wang Fuzhi (Wang Fu-chih) 王扶之

Posts held

CCP
Alternate member of the CCP 11th Central Committee
Secretary of Shanxi Province CP

Military
Commander of Shanxi Military District

1971,	May	Identified as military leader in Beijing
1976,	Apr	Identified as commander of Shanxi Military District
1977,	Aug	Elected alternate member of the CCP Central Committee by the 11th Party Congress
	Sep	Identified as secretary of Shanxi Province CP

Wang Ganchang (Wang Kan-ch'ang) 王淦昌

Posts held

Government
Vice-minister of the 2nd Ministry of Machine Building

NPC
Member of the Standing Committee of the 5th NPC
Deputy for Sichuan to the 5th NPC

Others
Director of the Atomic Energy Institute, Academy of Sciences

Wang was born circa 1909. He studied at Berlin University which awarded him a Ph.D. degree in 1943. (Until) 1948 he was engaged in research at the University of California before returning to China.

1953,	Nov	Identified as deputy director of the Physics Institute of the Academy of Sciences (until Jul 1958)
1955,	Feb	Member of an organizational committee for general lectures on nuclear physics
	Jun	Identified as member of the Department of Mathematics, Physics, and Chemistry of the Academy of Sciences
	Aug	Member of a Chinese delegation to a conference on peaceful use of atomic energy in Geneva; subsequently to a similar conference in the USSR
1956,	Feb	Elected member, Central Committee of the Jiusan Society
1957,	Nov	Chairman of an international conference of physicists in Moscow
1958,	Jul	Appointed deputy director of the Nuclear Physics Institute, Academy of Sciences
1959,	Jan	Appointed deputy director of the Joint Atomic Research Center of Socialist States in Dubna (until Sep 1961)
1960		According to Soviet press reports of 1960, Wang was head of a group of Chinese and Soviet scientists who first succeeded in

obtaining heavy fundamental particles of XI-minus-hyperons by using a powerful proton synchroton

1964,	Sep	Elected deputy for Jiangsu Province to the 3rd NPC
1965,	Jan	Elected member of the Standing Committee of the 3rd NPC (confirmed in Jan 1975 and Jan 1978 by the 4th and 5th NPCs)
1978,	Feb	Elected deputy for Sichuan Province to the 5th NPC
	Oct	Identified as director of the Institute of Atomic Energy, Academy of Sciences
1979,	Apr	Head of a nuclear energy technology delegation to Canada
	Jun	Identified as vice-minister of the 2nd Ministry of Machine Building

Wang Guangmei (Wang Kuang-mei) (f) 王光美

Posts held

Others
Director of the Foreign Affairs Bureau, Academy of Social Sciences
Member of the 5th CPPCC

Wang was born circa 1922 in the U.S.A. She returned to China as a child to attend primary school in Beijing and later middle school in Tianjin. From 1939 to 1943 she studied physics at Furen University. She then went to Yanjing University as a postgraduate. In 1946 she served as an interpreter for the Communists on the Military Mediation Executive Commission of the CCP and KMT. At the end of that year she went to Yan'an to work for the Foreign Affairs Department of the CCP Central Committee. In summer 1948 she married Liu Shaoqi.

1957,	Sep	Elected member of the Executive Committee of the Women's Federation
1963,	Apr	Accompanies Liu to Indonesia, Burma, Cambodia, and Vietnam (until May)
	Dec	Wang conducts investigations in a test of the "Four Clean-ups Campaign" in the Taoyuan Production Brigade, Luwangzhuang People's Commune, Funing County, Hebei Province (later this test became the basis of "Taoyuan Experience", an alleged crime of Liu Shaoqi)
1964,	Oct	Elected deputy for Hebei Province to the 3rd NPC
1966,	Mar	Accompanies Liu to Pakistan, Afghanistan, and Burma (until May)
	Jun	Sent to Qinghua University to direct the Cultural Revolution movement and to make "typical examples" (later her work at the university was criticized for suppressing the students' spirit of rebellion)
1967,	Jan	Subjected to public trial three times by Red Guards
1979,	Jan	First appearance after the Cultural Revolution
	Jun	By-elected a member of the 5th CPPCC
	Aug	Identified as director of the Foreign Affairs Bureau, Academy of Social Sciences

Wang Guangying (Wang Kuang-ying) 王光英

Posts held

Others
Director of the Board of Directors, China International Trust and Investment Corporation
Vice-chairman of the Central Committee, China Democratic National Construction Association

Wang was born in Great Britain. He studied at Beijing Experimental Primary School.

1952,   Jan   Identified as a member of the Investment and Production Guidance Committee, Association of Industry and Commerce of Tianjin Municipality, and as managing director of a Tianjin chemical factory

      Jun   Elected member of the Preparatory Committee of the Federation of Industry and Commerce

1953,   Jun   Identified as a member of the Standing Committee of the Federation of Democratic Youth (until May 1959); identified as vice-chairman of the Committee for Production Increase and Austerity for Private Enterprises, Tianjin Municipality

1954,   Aug   Elected deputy for Tianjin Municipality to the 1st NPC

1955,   Feb   Identified as vice-chairman of the Federation of Democratic Youth, Tianjin Branch

      Jul   Member of a delegation to Egypt

      Oct   Identified as a member of the Executive Committee of the Federation of Industry and Commerce

1958,   Apr   Identified as vice-chairman of the Federation of Democratic Youth; elected deputy for Hebei Province to the 2nd NPC (reelected in 1964 to the 3rd NPC)

1959,   Jan   Elected chairman of the Association of Industry and Commerce, Tianjin Branch

      Max   Elected vice-chairman of the Youth Federation (successor of the Federation of Democratic Youth) (until Feb 1967)

      Jul   Deputy head of a delegation to the 7th World Youth Festival in Vienna

1967,   Feb   Denounced as a reactionary and purged

1979,   Jun   First appearance after the Cultural Revolution: By-elected member of the 5th CPPCC

      Oct   Appointed director of the Board of Directors, China International Trust and Investment Corporation; elected vice-chairman of the Central Committee, China Democratic National Construction Association

Note
Wang is an elder brother of Wang Guangmei, the widow of Liu Shaoqi.

Wang Guangyu (Wang Kuang-yü) 王光宇

Posts held

CCP
Member of the CCP 11th Central Committee
Secretary of Anhui Province CP

Wang is a native of Jiangsu Province.

1951,   Mar   Identified as member of the Land Reform Committee of North Anhui Administration Office

1954,   Jul   Identified as director of the Rural Work Department of Anhui Province CP

1955,   Mar   Identified as member of the People's Council of Anhui Province

1956,   Oct   Appointed director of the Agricultural College in Anhui

1957   Identified as vice-governor of Anhui Province (until Cultural Revolution)

1959,   Oct   Identified as secretary of Anhui Province CP (until Cultural Revolution)

1967   Disappears during the Cultural Revolution

1974,   Feb   First appearance after the Cultural Revolution: Identified as secretary of Anhui Province CP

1975,   Aug   Identified as vice-chairman of the Revolutionary Committee of Anhui Province (until Dec 1979)

1977,   Aug   Elected member of the CCP Central Committee by the 11th Party Congress

1978,   May   Advisor to an agricultural delegation to Japan

1979,   Feb   Identified as head of the Anhui Provincial Agricultural Science and Technology Leadership Group

Wang Guangzhong (Wang Kuang-chung) 王光中

Posts held

CCP
Member of the Standing Committee of Liaoning Province CP

Provincial Administration
Vice-governor of Liaoning Province

1977,   Dec   Elected vice-chairman of the Revolutionary Committee of Liaoning Province (until Jan 1980)

1978,   May   Identified as member of the Standing Committee of Liaoning Province CP

1980,   Jan   Elected vice-governor of Liaoning Province

Wang Guofan (Wang Kuo-fan) 王国藩

Posts held

CCP
Member of the CCP 11th Central Committee
Secretary of Zunhua County CP, Hebei Province

Others
Chairman of the Revolutionary Committee of Zunhua County, Hebei Province

Wang who was born in 1920 in Zunhua County, Hebei Province, joined the Communists at the age of seventeen. He became known as a member of Xipu Agricultural Cooperative in Zunhua County. This particularly poor cooperative, founded in 1952, had been cited as a "symbol of a whole nation" by Mao Zedong. Wang became an agricultural model worker known throughout China.

1958,	Jun	Elected member of the Presidium, National Congress of Model Worker Groups
	Sep	Appointed CP secretary of Xipu Production Brigade of the newly established Jianming People's Commune in Zunhua
1959,	Mar	Elected deputy for Hebei Province to the 2nd NPC (reelected in 1964 to the 3rd NPC)
1966,	Dec	Member of a trade union delegation to Iraq
1968,	Feb	Elected member of the Standing Committee of the newly established Revolutionary Committee of Hebei Province (no later mention in this post)
	Apr	Identified as chairman of the Revolutionary Committee of Xipu Production Brigade
1969,	Apr	Elected to first term as member of the CCP Central Committee by the 9th Party Congress
1971,	Jul	Identified as secretary of the CP, and chairman of the Revolutionary Committee, of Zunhua County
1975,	May	Article in HQ: "Maintain and Continue the Revolutionary Spirit by Studying the Instructions of Chairman Mao on Agricultural Cooperation"
1978,	Aug	Wang disappears; probably purged

Wang Guoquan (Wang Kuo-ch'üan)

Posts held   王国权

Government

Vice-minister of civil affairs

Wang was born circa 1916 in Henan Province. He took part in the 1st CPPCC in September 1949 as a delegate representing the Peasants Federation.

1950,	Jan	Identified as secretary of Rehe Province CP
1954,	Aug	Elected deputy for Rehe Province to the 1st NPC
1955,	Feb	Elected governor of Rehe Province
	Jul	Rehe Province is abolished as an administrative unit and devided into Hebei and Liaoning Provinces
1957,	Jun	Appointed ambassador to the German Democratic Republic (until Jan 1964)
1958,	Oct	Elected deputy for Hebei Province to the 2nd NPC
1964,	Apr	Appointed ambassador to Poland. In this capacity Wang succeeds Wang Bingnan at the Sino-American Ambassadorial Talks in Warsaw (until about 1967)
	Aug	Elected deputy for Henan Province to the 3rd NPC
1970,	Oct	Wang is reactivated after the Cultural Revolution

1971,	Aug	Identified as vice-chairman of the Sino-Japanese Friendship Association; head of a delegation to Japan to attend mourning ceremonies for the politician Matsumura
1973,	May	Appointed ambassador to Australia (until Jul 1976)
1977,	Sep	Appointed ambassador to Italy (until Sep 1978)
1980,	Apr	Identified as vice-minister of civil affairs

Wang Hairong (Wang Hai-jung) (f)

Posts held   王海容

Government

Vice-minister of foreign affairs

Wang was born in 1938 in Hunan Province. She is the daughter of Mao Zemin, a brother of Mao Zedong who was killed during the revolution in Xinjiang Province in 1943.

1966		Wang graduates in English from the Beijing Foreign Language Institute
1967		Named as a cadre of the Ministry of Foreign Affairs. During the Cultural Revolution she is an active participant in the Red Guard Movement
1970		Present at receptions given by Mao Zedong for heads of state and government of the following countries: Tanzania, Zambia (July), France (July), Sudan (August), South Yemen (August)
1971		Present at receptions given by Mao Zedong for heads of state and government of the following countries: Romania (June), Burma (August), Ethiopia (October)
	Sep	Identified as deputy director of the Protocol Department in the Ministry of Foreign Affairs (until May 1972)
	Nov	Member of the Chinese delegation to the 26th UN General Assembly in New York
1972		Present at receptions given by Mao Zedong for the heads of state and government of the following countries: Pakistan (February), U.S.A. (February), Sri Lanka (June), France (July)
	May	Identified as assistant minister in the Ministry of Foreign Affairs (until Sep 1974)
1974,	Sep	Identified as vice-minister of foreign affairs
1978,	Jul	Member of a government delegation led by Geng Biao to Trinidad/Tobago, Jamaica, Guyana

Wang Haisu (Wang Hai-su)   汪海粟

Posts held

Provincial Administration

Vice-governor of Jiangsu Province

| 1977, | Dec | Elected vice-chairman of the Revolutionary Committee of Jiangsu Province (until Dec 1979) |
| 1979, | Dec | Elected vice-governor of Jiangsu Province |

Wang Hanzhang (Wang Han-chang) 王汉章

Posts held

Provincial Administration
Vice-governor of Hubei Province

1978,	Jan	Elected vice-chairman of the Revolutionary Committee of Hubei Province (until Dec 1979)
1980,	Jan	Elected vice-governor of Hubei Province

Wang Heshou (Wang Ho-shou) 王鹤寿

Posts held

CCP
Member of the CCP 11th Central Committee
Deputy secretary of the Commission for Inspecting Discipline under the CCP Central Committee

Wang was born in 1908 in Hebei Province. He studied at Sun Yat-sen University in Moscow. In 1930 he was head of the Propaganda Department of Manchuria CP. In 1940 he worked in the Organization Department of the CCP Central Committee. In 1946 he was political commissar of Heilongjiang Military Region. In summer 1949 he was appointed a member, and minister of industry, of the newly established People's Government of Northeast China.

1952,	Aug	Appointed minister of heavy industry (ministry abolished in May 1956); member of a government delegation led by Zhou Enlai to the USSR
1954,	Dec	Elected member of the 2nd CPPCC (until Apr 1959)
1956,	May	Appointed minister of metallurgical industry (until Dec 1964 and chairman of the Construction Commission (until Feb 1958)
	Sep	Elected alternate member of the CCP Central Committee by the 8th Party Congress
1959,	Mar	Elected deputy for Hebei Province to the 2nd NPC (until 1964)
1962,	Jul	Head of the Funeral Committee for Qiu Yuzhi
1963,	Dec	Head of a government delegation to the inauguration of the blast furnace of Trai-cau Mine in North Vietnam
1964,	Sep	Elected deputy for Liaoning Province to the 3rd NPC
1965,	Jul	Identified as 1st secretary of Anshan Municipality CP
1967,	Apr	Branded as a capitalist-roader and purged
1978,	Dec	First appearance after the Cultural Revolution: Elected deputy secretary of the Commission for Inspecting Discipline under the CCP Central Committee
1979,	Sep	By-elected member of the CCP 11th Central Committee by its 4th Plenum

Wang Heting (Wang Ho-t'ing) 王和亭

Posts held

Provincial Administration
Vice-chairman of the Tibet Autonomous Regional People's Government

1979,	Aug	Elected vice-chairman of the Tibet Autonomous Regional People's Government

Wang Hui (Wang Hui) 王 辉

Posts held

CCP
Secretary of Henan Province CP
3rd secretary, CP of Zhengzhou Railway Bureau

Military
Commander of the Pioneer Corps in Wuhan Military Region

1967,	Oct	Identified as deputy commander of Henan Military District
1968,	Mar	Elected member of the Standing Committee, Revolutionary Committee of Henan, and chairman of the Revolutionary Committee of Zhengzhou, the provincial capital of Henan
1969,	Jan	Identified as military figure in the PLA Unit 154 in Wuzhi, Henan Province
1972,	Jul	Elected member of the Standing Committee of Henan Province CP and 1st secretary of Zhengzhou Municipality CP
1974,	Feb	Wang disappears for unknown reasons
1977,	Jan	First appearance after three years of absence: Identified as commander of the Pioneer Corps of Wuhan Military Region and as 3rd secretary, CP of Zhengzhou Railway Bureau
	Oct	Identified as secretary of the CP, and as vice-chairman of the Revolutionary Committee, of Henan Province (latter post until 1978)
1978,	Apr	Deputy head of an agricultural machinery study group visiting Italy, France, Great Britain, Denmark

Wang Huide (Wang Hui-te) 汪惠德

Posts held

CCP
Director of the Bureau of Translation of the Works of Marx, Engels, Lenin, and Stalin

NPC
Deputy for Beijing Municipality to the 5th NPC

1964,	Apr	Identified as member of the Editorial Department of RMRB

1966,	Jun	Participant at a scientific forum in Beijing; subsequently disappears
1974,	Apr	First appearance after the Cultural Revolution
	May	Identified as a cadre of a department of the CCP Central Committee
1978,	Feb	Elected deputy for Beijing Municipality to the 5th NPC
	Oct	Identified as director of the Bureau of Translation of the Works of Marx, Engels, Lenin, and Stalin
1979,	Apr	Head of a delegation of the Bureau of Translation of the Works of Marx, Engels, Lenin, and Stalin to Romania

Wang Jian (Wang Chien) 王 鑒

Posts held

CCP
Member of the Standing Committee of Shanghai Municipality CP

Provincial Administration
Vice-mayor of Shanghai

1977,	Dec	Elected vice-chairman of the Revolutionary Committee of Shanghai (until Dec 1979)
1978,	Jun	Identified as member of the Standing Committee of Shanghai Municipality CP
	Nov	Identified as director of the Shanghai Municipal Political and Judicial Office
1979,	Dec	Elected vice-mayor of Shanghai

Wang Jian'an (Wang Chien-an) 王建安

Posts held

NPC
Member of the Standing Committee of the 5th NPC
Deputy for the PLA to the 5th NPC

Military
Colonel-general

Wang was born in 1902 in Hong'an (Huang'an), Hubei Province. In 1933 he served as political commissar of the 4th Red Army. He studied at the Anti-Japan Military and Political Academy in Yan'an in 1936. In 1941 he was deputy commander of Shandong Military District, in 1946 he commanded the Central Shandong Military District. In the following year he was made commander of the 8th Column, East China Field Army. In early 1949 he commanded the 7th Corps of the 3rd Field Army. In May 1949 he was appointed commander of Zhejiang Military District (until 1952). In September 1949 he took part in the 1st CPPCC.

1950,	Feb	Identified as member of the East China Military and Administrative Council
1951,	Oct	Identified as commander of the East China Recruit Training Command which was responsible for training soldiers for the Korean War
1952		Service in the Korean War as commander of the 21st, 23rd, and 24th Armies

	Aug	Identified as commander of the 9th Army Group in Korea
1955		Returned from Korea; made deputy commander of Shenyang Military Region and concurrently commandant of the Harbin Military Engineering College
	Sep	Appointed colonel-general and conferred the order "Liberation," 1st class
1958,	Jul	Elected deputy for the PLA in to the 5th NPC
1959,	Apr	Appointed member of the National Defense Council
1963,	Dec	Identified as military leader of the PLA Jinan Units
1964,	Feb	Identified as 2nd political commissar of Jinan Military Region
1970,	Apr	Identified as military leader of Fuzhou Military Region (until 1975)
1978,	Feb	Elected deputy for a PLA to the 5th NPC
	Mar	Elected member of the Standing Committee of the 5th NPC
	Apr	In connection with a military demonstration in Nanchang, Wang is referred to as "advisor from the Military Commission"

Wang Jianshi (Wang Chien-shih) 王兼士

Posts held

Others
Executive director of the Board of Directors, China International Trust and Investment Corporation
Member of the Standing Committee, Shanghai Federation of Industrialists and Businessmen

Wang was born in Jiangsu Province in 1905. He received his doctorate in economics from Munich University in 1937. Before 1949 he was manager of the Zhabei Power Plant in Shanghai.

1979,	Oct	Appointed executive director of the Board of Directors, China International Trust and Investment Corporation; identified as a member of the Standing Committee, Shanghai Federation of Industrialists and Businessmen

Wang Jinchuan (Wang Chin-ch'uan) 王錦川

Posts held

Government
Ambassador to Ethiopia

1960,	Mar	Identified as director of the Foreign Affairs Bureau, People's Council of Guangdong Province
1961,	Jun	Identified as council member of the Institute of Foreign Affairs (until 1964)
1966,	Jan	Identified as counselor at the embassy in Albania (until 1967)
1971,	Dec	Identified as chargé d'affaires ad interim in North Vietnam

1972,   Jun   Identified as ambassador to Senegal (until Aug 1977)

1974,   May   Wang accompanies President Senghor of Senegal to China

1977,   Nov   Appointed ambassador to Ethiopia

Wang Jingrong (Wang Ching-jung)   王景融

Posts held

Government
Consul-general in Karachi, Pakistan

1960,   Sep   Identified as 2nd secretary at the embassy in the Arab Republic of Yemen

1971,   Sep   Identified as counselor at the embassy in Iran

1977,   Sep   Identified as consul-general in Karachi

Wang Jingzhi (Wang Ching-chih)   王静之

Posts held

Provincial Administration
Vice-chairman of the Standing Committee, Tibet Autonomous Regional People's Congress

1979,   Aug   Elected vice-chairman of the Standing Committee, Tibet Autonomous Regional People's Congress

Wang Jinling (Wang Chin-ling) (f)   王金玲

Posts held

CCP
Alternate member of the CCP 11th Central Committee

1977,   Aug   Elected alternate member of the CCP Central Committee by the 11th Party Congress

Wang Jinling (Wang Chin-ling)   王金玲

Posts held

NPC
Deputy for Heilongjiang Province to the 5th NPC

Provincial Administration
Vice-governor of Heilongjiang Province

1964,   Oct   Elected deputy for Heilongjiang Province to the 3rd NPC

1978,   Feb   Elected deputy for Heilongjiang Province to the 5th NPC

1979,   Dec   Elected vice-governor of Heilongjiang Province

Wang Jinshan (Wang Chin-shan)   王金山

Posts held

CCP
Alternate member of the CCP 11th Central Committee
Secretary of Hebei Province CP

1954,   Jul   Identified as chairman of the Federation of Supply and Marketing Cooperatives of Hebei Province

1955,   Feb   Appointed member of the People's Council of Hebei Province

1958,   Oct   Elected vice-governor of Hebei Province

1971,   Jul   Identified as vice-chairman of the Revolutionary Committee of Hebei Province (reelected in Dec 1977; until Jan 1980) and as member of the Standing Committee of Hebei Province CP (until Oct 1977)

1977,   Aug   Elected alternate member of the CCP Central Committee by the 11th Party Congress

        Oct   Identified as secretary of Hebei Province CP

Wang Jinxiang (Wang Chin-hsiang)   汪金祥

Posts held

Others
Member of the Standing Committee of the 5th CPPCC

Wang is a native of Jiangxi Province. In 1948 he was director of the Public Security Department of Northeast China Administrative Council. In September 1949 he took part in the session of the 1st CPPCC as a delegate.

1949,   Oct   Appointed member of the Supreme People's Procuracy

        Dec   Appointed member of the Northeast China People's Government

1950,   Apr   Appointed chief procurator for Northeast China (until Sep 1954)

1953,   Sep   Appointed vice-chairman of the Northeast China Administrative Council (until Sep 1954)

1954,   Feb   Identified as member of the Northeast China Bureau of the CCP Central Committee

        Oct   Appointed vice-minister of public security (until Cultural Revolution)

1965,   Jan   Elected member of the Standing Committee of the CPPCC

1967   Because of his close association with Luo Ruiqing, Wang is relieved of all posts

1975,   May   First appearance after the Cultural Revolution: Named in his former post as member of the Standing Committee of the CPPCC (confirmed in Mar 1978 by the 5th CPPCC)

Wang Jinyou (Wang Chin-yu) 王金友

Posts held

CCP
Alternate member of the CCP 11th Central Committee
Member of the Standing Committee of Zhejiang Province CP

1977,   Aug   Elected alternate member of the CCP Central Committee by the 11th Party Congress
          Oct   Identified as secretary, CP of Shangwang Production Brigade of Hongshan People's Commune, Shaoxing County, Zhejiang Province
1978,   May   Elected member of the Standing Committee of Zhejiang Province CP

Wang Jinzi (Wang Chin-tzu) 王金籽

Posts held

CCP
Secretary of Heilongjiang Province CP

NPC
Deputy for Heilongjiang Province to the 5th NPC

1975   Identified as deputy secretary of Xiyang County CP, a Dazhai-type county
1977,   Mar   Identified as secretary of Shanxi Province CP (until Oct 1979)
          Sep   Identified as vice-chairman of the Revolutionary Committee of Shanxi Province (until Oct 1978)
1978,   Feb   Elected deputy for Heilongjiang Province to the 5th NPC; elected secretary of Heilongjiang Province CP
          Sep   Identified as vice-chairman of the Revolutionary Committee of Heilongjiang CP
1979,   Sep   Identified as vice-chairman of the Revolutionary Committee of Heilongjiang Province (until Dec 1979)

Wang Jiyuan (Wang Chi-yüan) 王纪元

Posts held

Provincial Administration
Vice-governor of Liaoning Province

Others
Director of the Board of Directors, China International Trust and Investment Corporation

Wang was born in Indonesia. There he was president, and one of the cofounders, of Life News.

1952,   Nov   Identified as board member of NCNA
1953   Expelled after return to Indonesia
          Sep   Identified as deputy director of the Department of Culture, Education and Propaganda of the Overseas Chinese Affairs Commission

1954,   Dec   Elected member of the 2nd CPPCC (confirmed in 1959 for the 3rd CPPCC)
1956,   Oct   Identified as member of the Standing Committee, and as deputy secretary-general, of the Association of Returned Overseas Chinese
1960,   Sep   Identified as deputy director of NCNA
1977,   Dec   Elected vice-chairman of the Revolutionary Committee of Liaoning Province (until Jan 1980)
1979,   Oct   Elected director of the Board of Directors of the China International Trust and Investment Corporation
1980,   Jan   Elected vice-governor of Liaoning Province

Wang Jun (Wang Chün) (f) 王军

Posts held

Provincial Administration
Vice-governor of Heilongjiang Province

1963,   Apr   Identified as chairman of the Trade Unions of Harbin Municipality; head of a Heilongjiang Province trade union delegation to the May Festival in Bulgaria
1964,   May   Member of a delegation to the Congress on International Problems of Women's Work in Bucharest
1965,   Jul   Identified as wife of Lü Qian (then 1st secretary of Harbin Municipality CP)
1966,   Apr   Head of a Harbin trade union delegation to the May Festival in the German Democratic Republic; thereafter Wang disappears
1979,   Dec   First appearance after the Cultural Revolution: Elected vice-governor of Heilongjiang Province

Wang Junshao (Wang Chün-shao) 王君绍

Posts held

CCP
Alternate member of the CCP 11th Central Committee
Secretary, CP of the Gongchang Ling Mine

Wang was born in 1938 as the son of poor peasants. His father, a hired hand in the service of a landlord, died when he was a boy. Wang was then reduced to begging with his mother.

1977,   Feb   Identified as deputy secretary, CP of Anshan Iron and Steel Company
          Aug   Elected alternate member of the 11th CCP Central Committee
          Dec   The Wang Junshao Brigade, consisting of 99 men in 1977, produced 3.5 million tons of ore, double the state quota
1978,   Jan   Identified as secretary, CP of Gongchang Ling Mine
          May   Cited as a model worker

Wang Kedong (Wang K'e-tung) 王克东

Posts held

Government
Member of the State Nationalities Affairs
Commission

Provincial Administration
Vice-governor of Hebei Province

1979,   May   Appointed member of the State Nationalities Affairs Commission
1980,   Feb   Elected vice-governor of Hebei Province

Wang Kejun (Wang K'e-chün) 王克俊

Posts held

Others
Member of the Standing Committee of the
5th CPPCC

1965,   Mar   Elected deputy secretary-general of the
4th CPPCC; thereafter disappears
1973,   Mar   First appearance after the Cultural Revolution
1979,   Jul   By-elected member of the Standing Committee of the 5th CPPCC

Wang Kewen (Wang K'e-wen) 王克文

Posts held

CCP
Secretary of Shanxi Province CP

1950   Identified as member of the Financial and
Economic Council and as director of the
Finance Department, People's Government of Hubei Province
1954   Identified as secretary-general of the
People's Council of Wuhan Municipality
1955,   Jan   Elected deputy mayor of Wuhan
Jul   Appointed director of the Department of
Finance and Commerce of Wuhan CP
1957,   Oct   Identified as acting mayor of Wuhan
1959,   Feb   Identified as secretary of Wuhan Municipality CP
1966   Disappears during the Cultural Revolution
1971,   May   Elected secretary of Wuhan Municipality CP (until Feb 1973)
1973,   Feb   Elected 1st secretary of Wuhan Municipality CP and secretary of Hubei Prov-
ince CP (until Feb 1978)
1978,   Apr   Elected secretary of Shanxi Province CP

Wang Kuancheng (Wang K'uan-ch'eng) 王兜诚

Posts held

NPC
Deputy for Guangdong Province to the
5th NPC

Others
Director of the Board of Directors, China
International Trust and Investment Corpo-
ration

Vice-chairman of the Board of Directors,
Jinan University
Vice-chairman, General Chamber of Com-
merce of Hong Kong

1978,   Feb   Elected deputy for Guangdong Province to
the 5th NPC
Oct   Identified as vice-chairman of the Board
of Directors, Jinan University
1979,   Jun   Member of the Budget Committee,
2nd Session of the 5th NPC
Oct   Appointed director of the Board of Directors, China International Trust and Investment Corporation; identified as vice-
chairman of the General Chamber of
Commerce of Hong Kong

Wang Kuang (Wang K'uang) 王匡

Posts held

Others
Member of the Standing Committee of the
5th CPPCC
Director of the Hong Kong Branch of
XNA

Wang was born in 1917 in Guangdong Province. In 1942 he
was in Yan'an and was a correspondent of XNA thereafter.

1950   Identified as director of the Southern
Daily
Oct   Identified as director of the Guangdong
Branch of XNA and as a council member
of the Guangzhou Branch of the Journalists' Association
1952,   Sep   Identified as deputy director of the Propaganda Department of the South China
Subbureau, CCP Central Committee (until 1953)
1956,   Apr   Identified as director of the Propaganda
Department, Guangdong Province CP
(until 1962)
1958,   Jun   Identified as managing director of the
Shangyu magazine published in Guangdong
1960,   Aug   Member of a cultural delegation to Poland, headed by Shen Yanbing
1962,   Jan   Identified as alternate secretary of
Guangdong Province CP
Nov   Identified as director of the Propaganda
Department of the Central-South Bureau,
CCP Central Committee (until 1966)
1963   Identified as a council member of the
Association for Cultural Relations with
Foreign Countries
1967,   Sep   Denounced as a "three-anti element" and
purged
1977,   Jul   First appearance after the Cultural Revolution
1978,   Mar   Identified as director of the State Publication Administrative Bureau (until
Jul 1978)
Jul   Identified as director of the Hong Kong
Branch of XNA
1979,   Jul   By-elected member of the Standing Committee of the 5th CPPCC

Wang Kunlun (Wang K'un-lun) 王昆仑

<u>Posts held</u>

NPC
Member of the Standing Committee of the 5th NPC
Deputy for Beijing Municipality to the 5th NPC

Others
Vice-chairman of the Standing Committee of the 5th CPPCC
Vice-chairman of the Central Committee, Revolutionary Committee of the Chinese KMT

Wang was born in 1902 in Jiangsu Province. He is a graduate of Beijing University. As a student, he joined the Association of Comrades of Democracy. In 1933 he was a legislator of the Nationalist Government Legislative Yuan. In 1935 he was elected alternate member of the 5th Central Executive Committee of the KMT. In 1936 he became a member of the Propaganda Department of the KMT Central Committee. A few years later he was chairman of the left wing Sino-Soviet Cultural Association. In 1945 he left the KMT to join the Association of Comrades of Three People's Principles and went to the U.S.A. He joined the Communists in spring 1949. In May of that year he was elected a member of the Administrative Committee of the Federation of Democratic Youth and in September took part in the 1st CPPCC.

1949,	Oct	Appointed member of the Government Administration Council (until 1954)
	Nov	Elected member of the Standing Committee, Revolutionary Committee of the KMT
1950,	Oct	Elected member of the Committee for World Peace (until 1958)
1951,	Oct	Elected executive secretary of the Sino-Soviet Friendship Association (until 1954)
1954,	Aug	Elected deputy for Jiangsu Province to the 1st NPC
	Sep	Elected member of the Standing Committee of the 1st NPC (confirmed in 1959 and 1965 to the 2nd and 3rd NPCs)
1955,	Feb	Appointed deputy mayor of Beijing (until Cultural Revolution)
	May	Head of a delegation to the May Day celebrations in Moscow
1958,	Aug	Elected deputy for Beijing to the 2nd NPC (reelected in 1964 to the 3rd NPC)
1960,	Nov	Head of an opera troupe to Cambodia
	Dec	Identified as vice-chairman of the Sino-Cambodian Friendship Association
1966,	Jun	Identified as vice-chairman of the Association for Cultural Relations and Friendship with Foreign Countries. Wang disappears thereafter
1975,	Nov	First appearance after the Cultural Revolution
1976,	Mar	Identified as member of the Standing Committee of the KMT Revolutionary Committee
1978,	Feb	Elected deputy for Beijing Municipality to the 5th NPC
	Mar	Elected member of the Standing Committee, 5th NPC, and member of the Standing Committee, 5th CPPCC

1979,	Jul	By-elected vice-chairman of the 5th CPPCC
	Oct	Elected vice-chairman of the Central Committee, Revolutionary Committee of the Chinese KMT

Wang Lanxi (Wang Lan-hsi) 王兰西

<u>Posts held</u>

Government
Vice-minister of culture

Wang was born in Sichuan Province. After a career as an actor of modern drama he engaged in united front activities. In 1942 he was editor of <u>Jianghuai Ribao</u> (Jianghuai Daily). In the following year he became deputy director of the Propaganda Department of North Jiangsu District CP. In summer 1949 he was a member of a film delegation visiting the USSR. In 1949 he served as director of the Propaganda Department of Central-South Military Region.

1950,	Mar	Identified as member of the Culture and Education Committee of the Central-South Military and Administrative Council
1951,	Oct	Identified as director of the Political Department of Hunan Military District
1952,	Jun	Identified as deputy director of the Film Bureau, Ministry of Culture
1953,	jun	Identified as acting director of the Film Bureau, Ministry of Culture
	Oct	Identified as member of the Federation of Literary and Art Circles (until Cultural Revolution) and as council member of the Union of Chinese Writers
1954,	Jun	Head of a film delegation to the USSR
1956,	May	Identified as director of the Film Industry Administration under the Ministry of Culture and as assistant minister of culture (until Jan 1959)
1957,	Jun	Identified as director of the Beijing Central Film Institute (until Jan 1959)
	Nov	Member of a cultural delegation to the USSR
1960,	Aug	Identified as council member of the Union of Chinese Film Workers
1962,	Nov	Appointed director of the Culture and Education Department of Guangdong Province CP
1963,	Mar	Identified as deputy director of the Propaganda Department, Central-South Bureau of the CCP
1964,	Oct	Identified as deputy director, Political Department of Guangzhou Military Region
1965,	Dec	Identified as member of the Standing Committee of Guangdong Province CP
1966,	Jan	Identified as vice-governor of Guangdong Province (until Cultural Revolution)
1967,	Feb	Branded as a capitalist-roader and "three-anti element"
1978,	Jan	First appearance after the Cultural Revolution: Identified as vice-minister of Culture
1979,	Oct	Head of a film delegation to North Korea

Wang Lei (Wang Lei)   王　磊

Posts held

Government
Minister of commerce

Wang was born in 1914 in Shandong Province. In March 1949 he held the post of deputy manager, Northwest China Branch of the People's Bank; in September of that year he became head of the Xi'an Branch.

1950,	May	Appointed board member of the Bank of Communications
	Jul	Appointed member of the Financial and Economic Council of the Southwest China Military and Administrative Council and director of its Commerce Department
1952,	Jun	Elected member of the Preparatory Committee for the Federation of Industry and Commerce
1953,	Jan	Appointed vice-minister of commerce (until Feb 1958)
1958,	Feb	Following reorganization of the Ministry of Commerce, Wang is appointed vice-minister of the 1st Ministry of Commerce (until Sep 1958)
	Sep	Wang remains vice-minister (until Cultural Revolution) after both Commerce Ministries are rejoined
1964,	Sep	Elected deputy for Shandong Province to the 3rd NPC
1965,	May	Head of a trade delegation to North Korea
1966,	Feb	Identified as director of the Political Department, Ministry of Commerce
1970,	Jul	Identified as deputy secretary-general of the Revolutionary Committee of Beijing (until 1973)
1971,	Mar	Elected member of the Standing Committee of Beijing Municipality CP
1973,	May	Identified as vice-chairman of the Revolutionary Committee of Beijing
1974,	Sep	Deputy head of a goodwill delegation to Japan for the opening of civil aviation between the two countries
1978,	Mar	Appointed minister of commerce (until Jul 1978)
	Nov	Identified as secretary of the CP, and vice-chairman of the Revolutionary Committee, of Beijing Municipality (until Feb 1979)
1979,	Feb	Appointed minister of commerce

Wang Li (Wang Li)   王　立

Posts held

Government
Vice-minister of the 5th Ministry of Machine Building

Wang was born in 1917 in Shanxi Province.

1966,	Feb	Appointed vice-minister of the 5th Ministry of Machine Building; subsequently disappears
1974,	Sep	First appearance after the Cultural Revolution: Identified as a cadre of the State Council

1977,	Apr	Identified as vice-minister of the 5th Ministry of Machine Building
1978,	Apr	Member of a government delegation led by Chen Muhua to Romania

Wang Lin (Wang Lin)   王　林

Posts held

CCP
Secretary of Shaanxi Province CP
1st secretary of Xi'an Municipality CP (provincial capital of Shaanxi)

NPC
Deputy for Shaanxi Province to the 5th NPC

During the Long March Wang served as political instructor of a Red Army unit. In 1938 he served in Shaanxi-Gansu-Ningxia Border Region. In 1949 he became a member of the CP of Tangshan in Hebei Province.

1950,	Aug	Appointed director of the General Office, Ministry of Fuel Industry (until Oct 1954)
1954,	Aug	Elected deputy for Tianjin Municipality to the 1st NPC (until Apr 1959)
	Oct	Appointed vice-minister of fuel industry (until Jul 1950)
1955,	May	Member of a Party and government delegation to Czechoslovakia to attend the 10th anniversary of independence
	Aug	Appointed vice-minister of electric power (until Feb 1958)
	Sep	Member of a scientific and technical delegation to Czechoslovakia
1957,	Sep	Appointed member of the Huang He Project Committee (until 1958)
1958,	Jan	Appointed member of the Songhua River Basin Project Committee (until Feb 1959)
1959,	Feb	Identified as secretary of Shaanxi Province CP (until Cultural Revolution)
1963,	Oct	Identified as alternate member of the Secretariat, Northwest Bureau of the CCP Central Committee
1965,	Aug	Identified as secretary, Northwest Bureau of the CCP Central Committee
1966		Disappears during the Cultural Revolution
1976,	Sep	First appearance after the Cultural Revolution
1977,	Oct	Identified as secretary of Shaanxi Province CP and as 1st secretary of Xi'an Municipality CP
1978,	Feb	Elected deputy for Shaanxi Province to the 5th NPC
	Apr	Head of a friendship delegation of Xi'an Municipality to Japan

Wang Linhe (Wang Lin-ho)   王林鹤

Posts held

CCP
Member of the CCP 11th Central Committee

Wang became known as a model industrial worker.

1962,	Nov	Identified as vice-chairman of the Youth Federation of Shanghai
1967		Disappears during the Cultural Revolution
1977,	Aug	Elected member of the CCP Central Committee by the 11th Party Congress
	Sep	Identified as a cadre in Shanghai
1978,	Apr	Head of a workers delegation to North Korea

Wang Liusheng (Wang Liu-sheng) 王六生

Posts held

CCP
Alternate member of the CCP 11th Central Committee

Military
Major-general

In late 1946 Wang served as political commissar of the 22nd Regiment, 8th Brigade, 3rd Division, New 4th Army. In 1949 he was political commissar of the 22nd Corps, 3rd Field Army.

1951		Identified as director of the Political Department of the 22nd Corps
1953		Appointed deputy political commissar of the 22nd Corps
1955		Appointed political commissar of the 22nd Corps
1959,	Aug	Appointed deputy political commissar of Nanjing Garrision; identified as major-general
1964		Appointed 2nd political commissar of Shanghai Garrison
1966		Identified as director of the Political Department of Nanjing Military Region
1969,	Apr	Elected to first term as alternate member of the CCP Central Committee by the 9th Party Congress
	Aug	Identified as deputy political commissar of Nanjing Military Region (until 1971)
1972,	Feb	Identified as 1st political commissar of Wuhan Military Region (until Sep 1977)
	Aug	Identified as 2nd secretary of Hubei Province CP (until May 1977)
1977,	Jun	Identified as leading cadre in the Central Military Leadership

Wang Lizhi (Wang Li-chih) 王黎之

Posts held

CCP
Secretary of Sichuan Province CP

NPC
Deputy for Sichuan Province to the 5th NPC

| 1975, | Oct | Identified as secretary of Sichuan Province CP |
| 1978, | Feb | Elected deputy for Sichuan Province to the 5th NPC |

Wang Luming (Wang Lu-ming) 王路明

Posts held

Provincial Administration
Vice-governor of Heilongjiang Province

1959,	May	Identified as director of the Organization Department of Hebei Province CP
1961,	Nov	Identified as alternate secretary of Hebei Province CP
1975,	Apr	Identified as vice-chairman of the Revolutionary Committee of Hebei Province (until 1976?)
1979,	Dec	Elected vice-governor of Heilongjiang Province

Wang Maolin (Wang Mao-lin) 王茂林

Posts held

Provincial Administration
Vice-governor of Shanxi Province

| 1977, | Dec | Elected vice-chairman of the Revolutionary Committee of Shanxi Province (until Dec 1979) |
| 1979, | Dec | Elected vice-governor of Shanxi Province |

Wang Maoquan (Wang Mao-ch'üan) 王茂全

Posts held

CCP
Member of the CCP 11th Central Committee

1975,	Jan	Elected member of the Standing Committee by the 4th NPC (until Feb 1978)
1977,	Aug	Elected member of the CCP Central Committee by the 11th Party Congress
1978,	Feb	Present at Spring Festival in Shijiazhuang

Wang Meng (Wang Meng) 王猛

Posts held

CCP
Member of the CCP 11th Central Committee

Government
Minister of the Physical Culture and Sports Commission
Member of the Patriotic Health Campaign Committee

1963?		Identified as political commissar of the 38th Army
1968,	Aug	Identified as military leader of the PLA Unit 4800 in Hebei (until Oct 1969)
1971,	May	Identified as a cadre in Beijing

Oct Identified as minister of the Physical Culture and Sports Commission (until Sep 1974 when he is replaced by table-tennis world champion Zhuang Zedong at the initiative of Jiang Qing)

1973, Dec Head of a sports delegation to Iran
1974, Sep Wang disappears
1976, Apr Identified as military leader in Wuhan Military Region (until Dec 1976)
1977, Mar After the purge of Zhuang Zedong, Wang is returned as minister of the Physical Culture and Sports Commission
        Aug Elected member of the CCP Central Committee by the 11th Party Congress
        Dec Head of a sports delegation to Turkey
1978, Apr Identified as member of the Patriotic Health Campaign Committee
        May Head of a sports delegation to Tunisia
        Oct Head of a sports delegation to Yugoslavia and Romania
1979, Jun Head of a sports delegation to the Federal Republic of Germany, Great Britain and France
        Jul Appointed vice-chairman of the National Games Organizing Committee
        Nov Head of a sports delegation to Mexico

Wang Mingzhang (Wang Ming-chang)

Posts held

CCP
Member of the CCP 11th Central Committee
Member of the Standing Committee of Shanghai Municipality CP

Mass Organization
Secretary of the Shanghai Communist Youth League

1977, Aug Elected member of the CCP Central Committee by the 11th Party Congress
1978, May Identified as member of the Standing Committee of Shanghai Municipality CP
        Jun Identified as secretary of the Shanghai Communist Youth League

Wang Minsheng (Wang Min-sheng)

Posts held

Mass Organization
Secretary of the Communist Youth League

1975, Oct Identified as vice-chairman of the Revolutionary Committee of Jiangsu Province (until Feb 1979)
1976, Dec Identified as secretary of Jiangsu Province CP (until Sep 1978)
1977, Nov Head of a youth delegation to Japan
1978, Oct Elected secretary of the Communist Youth League

Wang Ning (Wang Ning)

Posts held

CCP
Member of the Standing Committee of Guangdong Province CP

Provincial Administration
Vice-governor of Guangdong Province

1964, Dec Identified as director of the Public Security Office of Guangdong Provincial Government
1977, Dec Elected vice-chairman of the Revolutionary Committee of Guangdong Province (until Dec 1979); identified as member of the Standing Committee of Guangdong Province CP
1979, Dec Elected vice-governor of Guangdong Province

Wang Ping (Wang P'ing)

Posts held

CCP
Member of the CCP 11th Central Committee
Member of the Standing Committee, Military Council under the CCP Central Committee

NPC
Member of the Standing Committee of the 5th NPC
Deputy for the PLA to the 5th NPC

Military
Colonel-general
Political commissar of the PLA General Logistics Department
Deputy director of the All-Army Physical Culture Guidance Committee

Wang was born in 1911 in Ruijin County, Jiangxi Province. He received his military training as a participant in the first training course at the Red Army Academy in Ruijin. During the Long March he served as director of the Political Department, 3rd Army Corps of the Red Army. In 1946 he served, with the rank of lieutenant-colonel, on the Subcommittee for Supervising Disarmament in the region of Hailong (Jilin Province) under the Joint Beijing Headquarters of the KMT and CCP. During the Civil War he commanded between 1947 and 1949 various regiments and divisions in the forces under Lin Biao.

1950, Jan Appointed chairman of the Datong Military Control Commission in Shanxi Province and vice-chairman of the People's Government of Chahar Province
        Jun Identified as commander of Chahar Military Region
1953, Mar Appointed director of the Cadres Department of North China Military Command
2nd half Transferred to Chinese People's Volunteers in Korea
1955, Sep Promoted to rank of colonel-general; conferred the orders "Independence and freedom" and "Liberation," both 1st class

1957,	Oct	Appointed political commissar of the Chinese People's Volunteers in Korea
1958,	Jul	Elected deputy for the PLA to the 2nd NPC
	Oct	Conferred the Korean order "National Flag," 1st class; returns to China
	Dec	Appointed political commissar of Nanjing Military Region
1959,	Apr	Appointed member of the National Defense Council
1960,	Oct	Member of a military goodwill delegation led by He Long to North Korea
1962,	Apr	Member of an NPC delegation to North Korea
1965,	Mar-Apr	Deputy head of an NPC delegation led by Liu Ningyi to Guinea, Mali, Central Africa, and Congo (Brazzaville)
1968,	Jan	Wang is accused as Mao opponent and relieved of all posts
1975,	Nov	First appearance after the Cultural Revolution
	Oct	Identified as political commissar of Wuhan Military Region (until Oct 1977)
1976,	Jun	Identified as 2nd secretary, CP Secretariat of Wuhan Military Region (until 1977)
1977,	Aug	Elected member of the CCP Central Committee by the 11th Party Congress
	Oct	Identified as 1st political commissar of Wuhan Military Region (until Dec 1977)
1978,	Feb	Elected deputy for the PLA to the 5th NPC
	Mar	Elected member of the Standing Committee of the 5th NPC
	Apr	Identified as political commissar of the PLA Logistics Department
	Jun	Identified as deputy director of the All-Army Physical Culture Guidance Committee
1979,	Jul	Appointed member of the National Games Organizing Committee
1980,	Feb	Identified as member of the Standing Committee, Military Council under the CCP Central Committee

Wang Qian (Wang Ch'ien)   王　谦

Posts held

CCP
Member of the CCP 11th Central Committee
1st secretary of Shanxi Province CP

NPC
Deputy for Shanxi Province to the 5th NPC

Military
1st political commissar of Shanxi Military District

Prior to the Communist occupation of Taiyuan Wang served, although a long-standing member of the CCP, as a Nationalist Government official, among others as secretary-general and director of the Civil Affairs Department of Shanxi Provincial Government.

1951		Identified as secretary of Changzhi District CP in Shanxi Province

1953,	Apr	Identified as deputy director of the Rural Work Department, North China Bureau of the CCP Central Committee
1955,	Feb	Identified as secretary of Shanxi Province CP (until Jul 1966)
1960,	Sep	Identified as director of the Rural Work Department of Shanxi Province CP
1965,	Dec	Elected governor of Shanxi Province (until Cultural Revolution); by-elected deputy for Shanxi Province to the 3rd NPC
1966,	Jul	Identified as 2nd secretary of Shanxi Province CP (until Cultural Revolution)
1967,	Jan	Wang is accused of having turned Shanxi Province into a center for resurrecting the capitalist system and disappears
1973,	Aug	First appearance after the Cultural Revolution: Elected alternate member of the CCP Central Committee by the 10th Party Congress (until Aug 1977)
1974,	Jan	Identified as secretary of Shanxi Province CP (until Sep 1975); identified as vice-chairman of the Revolutionary Committee of Shanxi Province (until Sep 1975)
1975,	Sep	Identified as 1st secretary of Shanxi Province CP; identified as chairman of the Revolutionary Committee of Shanxi Province (until Dec 1979)
1977,	Aug	Elected member of the CCP Central Committee by the 11th Party Congress
1978,	Feb	Elected deputy for Shanxi Province to the 5th NPC
1979,	Feb	Identified as 1st political commissar of Shanxi Military District

Wang Quanguo (Wang Ch'üan-kuo)   王全国

Posts held

CCP
Secretary of Guangdong Province CP

Provincial Administration
Vice-governor of Guangdong Province

Wang was born in 1913 in Yunxin County, Jiangxi Province. At the time of the Jiangxi Soviet he served as a soldier in the Red Army.

1952,	Oct	Identified as mayor of Guilin Municipality in Guangxi Province
1953		Appointed director of the Political Department of Henan Military District
1960		Identified as deputy political commissar of Henan Military District
1964,	Dec	Identified as 3rd political commissar of Henan Military District
1975,	Jun	Identified as vice-chairman of the Revolutionary Committee of Guangdong Province (until Dec 1979)
1977,	Feb	Identified as member of the Standing Committee of Guangdong Province CP (until Apr 1978)
1978,	Apr	Elected secretary of Guangdong Province CP
	May	Member of a government delegation led by Gu Mu to France, Switzerland, Belgium, Denmark, Federal Republic of Germany
1979,	Dec	Elected vice-governor of Guangdong Province

Wang Rensan (Wang Jen-san) 王人三

Posts held

Government
Ambassador to Liberia

1958,	Nov	Identified as deputy director of the Propaganda Department of Jiangsu Province CP
1961,	Dec	Elected 1st secretary of Suzhou Municipality CP
1965,	Mar	Identified as council member of the Institute of Foreign Affairs
	Aug	Identified as deputy director of the West Asia and North Africa Department in Ministry of Foreign Affairs (until 1966)
1973,	Apr	Appointed ambassador to Chad (until May 1977)
1977,	Jul	Appointed ambassador to Liberia

Wang Renzhong (Wang Jen-chung)

王任重

Posts held

CCP
Member of the CCP 11th Central Committee
Member of the Secretariat of the CCP Central Committee
Director of the Propaganda Department, CCP Central Committee

Government
Vice premier
Minister of the State Agricultural Commission
Chairman of the National Committee on Natural Agricultural Resources Surveying and Agricultural Zoning
Head of the State Council's Leading Group on Educated Youth Settled in the Countryside

Wang was born in 1907 in Jiangxian County, Hebei Province. He joined the CCP in 1933 and moved to the Jiangxi Soviet. In 1934-35 he took part in the Long March and subsequently studied at the North Shaanxi University in Yan'an. In 1936 he was made head of the South Hebei Administrative Office of Shanxi-Hebei-Shandong-Henan Border Government. In 1937 he was political commissar of the division commanded by Li Xiannian. In June 1949 he was appointed vice-chairman of the People's Government of Hubei Province (until February 1952).

1950,	Mar	Appointed member of the Financial and Economic Committee of Central-South China Military and Administrative Council
1952,	Feb	Appointed deputy mayor of Wuhan (until Jan 1955) and deputy secretary of Wuhan Municipality CP (until Apr 1954)
	Nov	Elected chairman of the Sino-Soviet Friendship Association, Wuhan Section (until Jan 1955)
1953,	Jan	Appointed member of the Central-South China Administrative Council
1954,	Apr	Appointed 1st secretary of Wuhan Municipality CP (until Sep 1954)
	Sep	Elected deputy for Wuhan Municipality to

		the 1st NPC (until Mar 1959); appointed 1st secretary of Hubei Province CP
1955,	Feb	Elected member of the People's Council of Hubei Province
1958,	May	Elected alternate member of the CCP Central Committee
	Jun	Lecturer at Wuhan University
1961,	Dec	Identified as 2nd secretary, Central-South China Bureau of the CCP Central Committee
1963,	Mar	Identified as political commissar of Wuhan Military Region
1967,	Jan	Branded as a bourgeois reactionary and purged
1978,	Sep	First appearance after the Cultural Revolution: Identified as 2nd secretary of the CP, and 1st vice-chairman of the Revolutionary Committee, of Shaanxi Province (until Dec 1978)
	Dec	Elected member of the CCP Central Committee by the 3rd Plenum of the 11th Central Committee; appointed vice premier
1979,	Feb	Appointed minister of the State Agricultural Commission
	Apr	Appointed chairman of the National Committee on Natural Agricultural Resources Surveying and Agricultural Zoning
	Aug	Identified as head of the State Council's Leading Group on Educated Youth Settled in the Countryside
	Sep	Head of a government delegation to Yugoslavia, Denmark, the Netherlands, Belgium and Switzerland (until Oct)
1980,	Feb	Elected member of the Secretariat of the CCP 11th Central Committee by its 5th Plenum
	Mar	Identified as director of the Propaganda Department under the CCP Central Committee

Wang Ruiting (Wang Jui-t'ing) 王瑞庭

Posts held

Government
Vice-minister of textile industry

1962,	Jun	Head of a textile expert group to Indonesia
1979,	Jul	Identified as vice-minister of textile industry

Wang Runsheng (Wang Jun-sheng)

王润生

Posts held

Government
Vice-minister of foreign trade

NPC
Deputy for Beijing Municipality to the 5th NPC

1950,	Dec	Identified as commercial attaché at the embassy in Poland

1955,	Sep	Identified as commercial attaché at the embassy in East Germany
1962,	Mar	Identified as trade counselor at the embassy in Cambodia (until May 1964)
1964,	Nov	Identified as deputy director of the 5th Department in the Ministry of Foreign Trade
1969,	Jul	Identified as director of a department in the Ministry of Foreign Trade
1971,	May	Member of a trade delegation to Chile and Peru
1972,	May	Speech at the UN Economic and Social Council
	Sep	Member of the Chinese delegation to the 27th UN General Assembly
1973,	Mar	Identified as permanent PRC representative at the UN
	Jun	Head of the Chinese delegation to the session of the UN Economic and Social Council in Geneva
	Sep	Member of the Chinese delegation to the 28th UN General Assembly
	Nov	Wang disappears for unknown reasons until 1977
1977,	Apr	Identified as vice-minister of foreign trade
	Sep	Head of a delegation to the International Fair in Bagdad
1978,	Jan	Head of a trade delegation to Bulgaria and the German Democratic Republic
	Feb	Elected deputy for Beijing Municipality to the 5th NPC
	Mar	Head of a trade delegation to Cuba
	Apr	Head of a trade delegation to Romania and Yugoslavia
	Dec	Head of a trade delegation to Sri Lanka

Wang Ruojie (Wang Jo-chieh) 王若杰

Posts held

Government
Ambassador to Mauritius

Military
Major-general

Wang was born in 1917 in Changshan, Shandong Province. He joined the CCP as a student at Jinan Normal College. From 1937 he served first in guerrilla units, later in the 3rd Field Army, becoming director of a political department of an army in 1949.

1955		Identified as director of the Political Department of Zhejiang Military District
1960		Identified as major-general
1964,	Feb	Appointed ambassador to Yemen (until Feb 1973)
1973,	Jun	Appointed ambassador to the Provisional Revolutionary Government of the Republic of South Vietnam (until 1975)
1974,	May	Wang accompanies the president of the Provisional Revolutionary Government of South Vietnam to Ürümqi, Xinjiang (enroute to Algiers)
1977,	Sep	Appointed ambassador to Mauritius

Wang is married to Zhang Lanxin.

Wang Ruoshui (Wang Jo-shui) 王若水

Posts held

CCP
Member of the Commission for Inspecting Discipline, CCP Central Committee
Deputy editor in chief of RMRB

NPC
Deputy for Beijing Municipality to the 5th NPC

1978,	Feb	Elected deputy for Beijing Municipality to the 5th NPC
	Jul	Identified as deputy editor in chief of RMRB
	Dec	Appointed member of the Commission for Inspecting Discipline under the CCP Central Committee

Wang Shangrong (Wang Shang-jung) 王尚荣

Posts held

CCP
Alternate member of the CCP 11th Central Committee

Military
Lieutenant-general
Deputy chief of the PLA General Staff

Wang was born in 1908 (1912?) in Shanxi (Jiangxi?) Province. In 1927 he took part in the Nanchang Uprising and subsequently served under Xiao Ke as commander of a regiment, later a brigade, of the Red Army. During the Long March he commanded a unit under the 2nd Front Army. In autumn 1937 he was appointed deputy commander of the 359th Brigade, 120th Division, 8th Route Army. In 1939 he commanded the 2nd Independent Brigade of the 120th Division and was concurrently commander of the 4th Subregion of Northwest Shanxi Military Region. From late 1939 to 1942 he studied at the Frunze Military Academy in the USSR. In 1946 he commanded the 1st Independent Brigade of the units under Zhang Zongxun. In early 1949 he was made commander of an army corps of the 1st Field Army, followed in September by his appointment as commander of Qinghai Military Region.

1949,	Dec	Appointed member of the People's Council of Qinghai Province
1952,	Aug	Appointed deputy director of the Department of War Operations of the General Staffs (until 1954)
1954		Appointed director of the Department of War Operations of the General Staff
1955,	Aug	Promoted to rank of lieutenant-general; conferred the orders "1st August" and "Liberation," both 1st class
1958,	May	Elected alternate member of the CCP Central Committee by the 8th Party Congress (until Cultural Revolution)
1967		During the Cultural Revolution Wang is accused of having planned the "February Coup" under Marshal He Long and relieved of all posts
1974,	Dec	First appearance after the Cultural Revolution: Identified as deputy chief of general staff

1977,   Aug Elected alternate member of the CCP Central Committee by the 11th Party Congress

        Oct Head of a military delegation to Tunisia

1979,   Sep Head of a military delegation to Belgium, Luxembourg, the Netherlands, Switzerland, and Yugoslavia

        Nov Head of a goodwill military delegation to Thailand

Wang is married to Huang Ke.

Wang Shaoyan (Wang Shao-yen) 王少岩

Posts held

NPC
Deputy for Yunnan Province to the 5th NPC

Provincial Administration
Vice-chairman of the People's Congress, Yunnan Province

Others
Director of the Executive Board, China International Trust and Investment Corporation
Chairman of the Kunming Branch of the China Democratic National Construction Association

Wang was born in Yunnan Province.

1950,   Aug Identified as a council member of the People's Government of Yunnan Province

1953,   Nov Elected member of the Executive Committee of the Federation of Industry and Commerce

1954,   Aug Elected deputy for Yunnan Province to the 1st NPC (reelected in 1958 and 1964 to the 2nd and 3rd NPCs)

1955,   Apr Elected member of the Central Committee, China Democratic National Construction Association

        Nov Elected chairman of the Federation of Industry and Commerce, Yunnan Branch

1964,   Jan Identified as vice-governor of Yunnan Province (until Aug 1968)

1968,   Aug Wang disappears

1978,   Feb First appearance after the Cultural Revolution: Elected deputy for Yunnan Province to the 5th NPC

1979,   Oct Appointed director of the Executive Board, China International Trust and Investment Corporation; identified as chairman of the China Democratic National Construction Association, Kunming Branch

        Dec Elected vice-chairman of the People's Congress of Yunnan Province

Wang Shiguang (Wang Shih-kuang) 王士光

Posts held

Government
Vice-minister of the 4th Ministry of Machine Building

1956,   Jun Identified as vice-chairman of the Preparatory Committee of the Electronics Society

1962,   Apr Identified as vice-chairman of the Electronics Society

1963,   Jun Appointed vice-minister of the 4th Ministry of Machine Building

1967   Disappears during the Cultural Revolution

1975,   Sep First appearance after the Cultural Revolution

1978,   Feb Identified as vice-minister of the 4th Ministry of Machine Building

        May Member of an economic delegation led by Gu Ming to Great Britain and France

Wang Shitai (Wang Shih-t'ai) 王世泰

Posts held

CCP
Member of the 11th CCP Central Committee

NPC
Deputy for Gansu Province to the 5th NPC

Provincial Administration
Chairman of the People's Congress of Gansu Province

Wang was born in 1909 in Luochuan County, Shaanxi Province. After attending middle school in Yan'an he engaged in guerrilla activities in his native province. In 1932 he founded a Soviet in Shaanxi-Gansu Border Region and later led a regiment in the 26th Red Army. In 1934 he was deputy commander of Shaanxi-Gansu-Ningxia Border Region. In 1941 he temporarily served under He Long as acting commander of the Joint Defense Headquarters of Shanxi-Suiyuan-Shaanxi-Gansu-Ningxia. In 1946 he was appointed commander of Shaanxi-Gansu-Ningxia Border Region Headquarters. In 1947 he commanded the 4th Corps of the 1st Field Army, and in 1949 served as political commissar of the 2nd Army Corps, 1st Field Army. In this capacity he took part in the 1st CPPCC in September.

1949,   Dec Appointed member of the Northwest China Military and Administrative Council and vice-chairman of the People's Government of Gansu Province (until Nov 1952)

1950,   Mar Appointed chairman of the Financial and Economic Committee of Northwest China Military and Administrative Council (until Aug 1952)

1951   Appointed director and political commissar of the Northwest Bureau of Railway Technology; appointed member of the Northwest Bureau of the CCP Central Committee

1952,   Aug Appointed vice-minister of railways (until Oct 1954)

1954,   Aug Elected deputy for Jiangsu Province to the 1st NPC (until Mar 1959)

        Sep Appointed member of the National Defense Council (until Cultural Revolution)

        Nov Appointed vice-chairman of the Construction Commission (until Feb 1958); head of a group of technicians visiting the USSR

Dec Head of a communications delegation to North Vietnam to sign a communications agreement

1956, Sep Elected alternate member of the CCP Central Committee by the 8th Party Congress (until Cultural Revolution)

1961, Aug Identified as secretary of Gansu Province CP (until Cultural Revolution)

1964, Sep Elected deputy for Gansu Province to the 3rd NPC

1965, Jan Elected member of the Standing Committee of the NPC (until Cultural Revolution)

Nov Identified as member of the Standing Committee, Northwest China Bureau of the CCP Central Committee (until Cultural Revolution)

1967 At the height of the Cultural Revolution Wang is accused as a capitalist-roader, as an advocate of armed struggle, and as oppressor of the masses. He is subsequently relieved of all posts and disappears

1975, Jan First appearance after the Cultural Revolution: Elected member of the Standing Committee by the 4th NPC (until Feb 1978)

1977, Aug Elected member of the CCP Central Committee by the 11th Party Congress

Dec Elected vice-chairman of the Revolutionary Committee of Gansu Province (until Dec 1979)

1978, Feb Elected deputy for Gansu Province to the 5th NPC

May Head of a goodwill delegation to Yugoslavia

1979, Jun Member of the Budget Committee at the 2nd Session of the 5th NPC

Dec Elected chairman of the People's Congress of Gansu Province

Wang Shixian (Wang Shih-hsien) 王实先

Posts held

NPC
Deputy for Jiangxi Province to the 5th NPC

Provincial Administration
Vice-governor of Jiangxi Province

1960, Jan Identified as director of the Industrial Work Department, Jiangxi Province CP

1978, Feb Elected deputy for Jiangxi Province to the 5th NPC

1979, Dec Elected vice-governor of Jiangxi Province

Wang Shoudao (Wang Shou-tao) 王首道

Posts held

CCP
Member of the CCP 11th Central Committee

Government
Vice-chairman of the Birth Planning Leading Group under the State Council

NPC
Vice-chairman of the Legal Commission under the NPC
Deputy for Guangdong Province to the 5th NPC

Others
Vice-chairman of the 5th CPPCC

Wang was born in 1904 (1903?) in Liuyang County, Hunan Province, as the son of poor peasants. He attended middle school in Changsha and later an agricultural school in Hunan Province. He joined the Communist Youth League in 1922 and in that year enrolled at the Guangdong Peasants School founded by Mao Zedong and Peng Pai. In 1925 he joined the CCP and was, after the KMT-CCP rift, entrusted with the organization of peasant uprisings and of guerrilla units in his native province. Until the Long March in which he took part as member of the Political Department, Military Commission of the Red Worker-Peasant Army, he was successively chairman of the Hunan Soviet and secretary of the CP of Jiangxi-Hubei Border Region. In 1936 he held the post of political commissar in the 15th Regiment. In addition to serving in the Secretariat of the CCP Central Committee in Yan'an, Wang was instructor at the Institute of Marxism-Leninism, the Central Research Institute, and the Central Party School. In 1943 he was made political commissar of the Expeditionary Corps of 4,000 men which operated during the following two years behind the Japanese fronts from North China to Guangdong Province. After the Anti-Japanese War this Expeditionary Corps joined the forces of Li Xiannian and Wang Shusheng in Central China. When these forces were encircled by KMT troops shortly afterwards, Wang fled to Yan'an. In 1945 he was elected an alternate member of the CCP Central Committee by the 7th Party Congress. Still in that year he was appointed director of the Political Department of Central Plains Military Region. His appointment as political commissar of the Joint Democratic Northeast Army followed in 1946. In early 1949 he was made deputy director of the Financial and Economic Committee of Northeast China Military and Administrative Council.

1949, Oct Appointed member of the Central-South China Military and Administrative Council

1950 Appointed governor of Hunan (until Mar 1952), 1st secretary of Hunan Province CP and member of the Military and Administrative Council of Hunan. Raised to member of the CCP Central Committee following the death of Ren Bishi

1952, Apr Appointed vice-minister of communications (until Feb 1958)

1954, Oct Appointed director of the 6th Staff Office of the State Council (Transport and Communications; until Sep 1959)

1956, Mar Appointed member of the newly established Scientific Planning Commission under the State Council (until Jun 1957)

Sep Confirmed as member of the CCP Central Committee by the 8th Party Congress

1957, May Delegate to the 11th Congress of CP Finland

Jun By-elected deputy for Shaanxi Province to the 1st NPC (until Mar 1959)

1958, Feb Appointed minister of communications (until Jul 1964)

1959, Mar Elected deputy for Shandong Province to

the 2nd NPC (until Dec 1964)

Jul   Head of a communications delegation to the USSR

1963, Mar   Report on the communications situation to the Standing Committee of the NPC

1964, Aug   Identified as secretary, Central-South China Bureau of the CCP Central Committee (until Cultural Revolution)

Sep   Elected deputy for Guangdong Province to the 3rd NPC

1967   Though forced to make a self-criticism during the Cultural Revolution, Wang survives without loss of influence

1968, Feb   With the establishment of the Revolutionary Committee of Guangdong Province, Wang is elected vice-chairman (until 1978)

1969, Apr   Confirmed as member of the CCP Central Committee by the 9th Party Congress (again in 1973 and 1977 by the 10th and 11th Party Congresses)

1970, Dec   Elected secretary of Guangdong Province CP (until 1978)

1972, Sep   Head of a delegation of Party workers visiting North Korea

1977, Oct   Identified as chairman of the Guangzhou Foreign Trade Fair

1978, Feb   Elected deputy for Guangdong Province to the 5th NPC

Mar   Elected vice-president of the 5th CPPCC

Jul   Appointed vice-chairman of the Birth Planning Leading Group under the State Council

Dec   Head of a friendship delegation to Laos

1979, Feb   Appointed vice-chairman of the Legal Commission under the NPC Standing Committee

Jun   Vice-chairman of the Draft Laws Committee at the 2nd Session of the 5th NPC

Wang Shouguan (Wang Shou-kuan) 王绶琯

Posts held

NPC
Deputy for Beijing Municipality to the 5th NPC

Others
Vice-president of the Society of Astronomy

Deputy director of the Beijing Astronomical Obervatory

Director of the Astrophysics Research Center of the University of Science and Technology

1978, Feb   Elected deputy for Beijing Municipality to the 5th NPC, commended for outstanding achievements in the field of astronomy

Sep   Identified as vice-president of the Society of Astronomy

Oct   Identified as deputy director of the Beijing Astronomical Observatory and as director of the Astrophysics Research Center of the University of Science and Technology

Nov   Head of a delegation of astronomers to the Federal Republic of Germany

Wang Shu (Wang Shu) 王殊

Posts held

Government
Vice-minister of foreign affairs

1959   Correspondent of NCNA in Ghana

1961   Correspondent of NCNA in Congo where he interviews the widow of Lumumba in Stanleyville (RMRB of 29 June)

1962   Correspondant of NCNA in Cuba

1972, Nov   Identified as chargé d'affaires ad interim in the Federal Republic of Germany

1974, Sep   Appointed ambassador to the Federal Republic of Germany (until Nov 1976)

1975, Oct   Wang accompanies West German chancellor Helmut Schmidt on his visit to China

1977, Apr   Identified as chief editor of HQ (until May 1978)

1978, Jun   Identified as vice-minister of foreign affairs

Wang Shucheng (Wang Shu-ch'eng) 王树成

Posts held

CCP
Deputy secretary of Henan Province CP

Provincial Administration
Vice-governor of Henan Province

1955, Dec   Identified as secretary-general of Hubei Province CP

1957, Dec   Identified as secretary of Hubei Province CP (until 1968)

1968, Feb   Elected member of the Standing Committee, Revolutionary Committee of Hubei Province (until 1974); subsequently disappears

1979, Apr   Identified as a cadre in Henan

Aug   Identified as deputy secretary of Henan Province CP and as vice-chairman of the Revolutionary Committee of Henan Province (latter post until Sep 1979)

Sep   Elected vice-governor of Henan Province

Wang Tao (Wang T'ao) 汪滔

Posts held

Government
Ambassador to Barbados

Wang was born in 1916 in Liaoning Province.

1960, Apr   Identified as counselor at the embassy in North Vietnam (until 1966)

1976, Oct   Identified as counselor at the embassy in Western Samoa (until 1978)

1979, May   Appointed ambassador to Barbados

Oct   Representative of the PRC to St. Vincent and Grenadines Independence celebrations

Wang Tingdong (Wang T'ing-tung)

王庭栋

Posts held

CCP
Secretary of Shanxi Province CP

1971, Jan Identified as vice-chairman of the Revolutionary Committee of Shanxi Province (reelected in Dec 1977) (until Dec 1979)

1973, Feb Identified as member of the Standing Committee of Shanxi Province CP (until Nov 1975)

1974, Oct Deputy head of a goodwill delegation to Pakistan for the inaugural flight of the Chinese Airline to Karachi

1975, Nov Identified as secretary of Shanxi Province CP (reelected in Mar 1978)

1978, Jul Deputy head of an agricultural delegation to the U.S.A.

Wang Wanlin (Wang Wan-lin) 王万林

Posts held

NPC
Deputy for the PLA to the 5th NPC

Military
Deputy commander, Navy of the PLA

1967, May Identified as member of the Revolutionary Committee of Beijing

1974, Jan Identified as deputy commander of the PLA Navy; member of a military delegation to Pakistan

1978, Feb Elected deputy for the PLA to the 5th NPC

Jun Member of a military goodwill delegation to Sweden and Italy under Zhang Aiping

Wang Wei (Wang Wei) 王伟

Posts held

Government
Vice-minister of public health

Wang was born in 1915 in Henan Province.

1952 Identified as chairman, Youth Work Committee of the CCP Central Committee

1953 Identified as deputy secretary, Central-South Work Committee of the New Democratic Youth League

Jul Elected member of the Standing Committee of the New Democratic Youth League (until 1957)

1954, Aug Elected deputy for Henan Province to the 1st NPC

1955, Jan Head of a youth delegation to Czechoslovakia

1957, May Elected secretary, member of the Standing Committee, of the Communist Youth League (successor to the New Democratic Youth League)

1958, Apr Elected a member of the Youth Federation

Oct Head of a youth delegation to Poland and Hungary; elected deputy for Hebei Province to the 2nd NPC (reelected in 1964 to the 3rd NPC)

1960, Feb Member of a friendship delegation to the USSR

Aug Head of a student delegation to the Executive Meeting of the International Students in Prague

1963, Jan Head of a youth delegation to Japan

Nov Head of a delegation of the Communist Youth League to North Korea

1965, Jan Identified as chairman of the Youth Federation

1967, Jan Attacked by Red Guards and purged

1978, Mar First appearance after the Cultural Revolution: Identified as vice-minister of public health (until Dec 1978)

1979, Jan Identified as president of the Youth Federation (until Apr 1979)

Apr Again identified as vice-minister of public health

(The youth cadre Wang Wei is possibly not identical with the vice-minister of public health, Wang Wei.)

Wang Weicai (Wang Wei-ts'ai) 王伟才

Posts held

Government
Vice-president of the Bank of China
Manager of the London Branch Office of the Bank of China

1973, Sep Deputy representative of the Chinese delegation to the 28th UN General Assembly in New York

1979, Sep Identified as vice-president of the Bank of China; head of a delegation to the opening of the Luxembourg Branch, Bank of China

Nov Identified as manager of the Branch Office of the Bank of China in London

Wang Weigang (Wang Wei-kang) 王维纲

Posts held

Others
Member of the Standing Committee of the 5th CPPCC
Vice-president of the Supreme People's Court
Member of the Judical Committee under the Supreme People's Court

Wang was born in 1911 in Ci County, Hebei Province. He studied at the No. 7 Teachers College in his native province. In 1930 he became head of a school of commerce in Ci County. Hitherto a member of the KMT, he joined the Communists in 1932. As a member of a guerrilla unit he was soon captured by nationalist troops and imprisoned. He was released as a result of the KMT-CCP United Front in 1937. In 1949 he served as political commissar of an army in the 2nd Field Army.

1950, Aug Identified as member of the Southwest

China Military and Administrative Council (until Jan 1953) and as deputy director of the its Justice Department (until Sep 1954)

1951,	Oct	Identified as 3rd secretary of Chongqing Municipality CP (until Jun 1954)
1953,	May	Elected member of the Executive Council, Federation of Trade Unions (until Dec 1957)
1954,	Aug	Elected deputy for Wuhan Municipality to the 1st NPC
1956,	Sep	Elected member of the Control Committee of the CCP Central Committee (until Sep 1962)
1958,	Apr	Appointed vice-minister of justice (until Apr 1959 when the ministry was abolished)
1959,	Sep	Appointed vice-president of the Supreme People's Court (until Cultural Revolution)
1962,	Sep	Elected alternate member of the Standing Committee, Control Committee of the CCP Central Committee (until Cultural Revolution)
1965,	Jan	Elected member of the Standing Committee of the 4th CPPCC
1967		Disappears during the Cultural Revolution
1975,	Oct	First appearance after the Cultural Revolution
	Dec	Identified in his former post as member of the Standing Committee of the CPPCC (confirmed in Feb 1978 by the 5th CPPCC)
1978,	Mar	Appointed vice-president of the Supreme People's Court
1979,	Nov	Appointed member of the Judical Committee under the Supreme People's Court

Wang Wenlin (Wang Wen-lin) 王文林

Posts held

Others
Vice-chairman of the Council for Promotion of International Trade
Chairman of the Maritime Arbitrage Commission under the Council for Promotion of International Trade

1964,	Apr	Head of an exhibition delegation to the fair in Casablanca
1966,	Mar	Head of the Chinese pavilion at the Leipzig Fair
1972,	Mar	Identified as vice-chairman of the Council for Promotion of International Trade
	Jun	Member of a delegation to Austria, the Netherlands, and Belgium
1974,	Nov	Head of a delegation of the Council for Promotion of International Trade to Japan
1975,	Jun	Head of an exhibition delegation to Zaire
1976,	Jun	Identified as vice-chairman of the Maritime Arbitrage Commission
	Oct	Head of an exhibition delegation to Papua New Guinea
1977,	Sep	Head of an exhibition delegation to Japan
1978,	Dec	Identified as chairman of the Maritime Arbitrage Commission under the Council for Promotion of International Trade; head of an economic and trade exhibition group to Bangladesh

Wang Xi (Wang Hsi) 王西

Posts held

Provincial Administration
Vice-chairman of the People's Government, Inner Mongolia Autonomous Region

| 1979, | Dec | Elected vice-chairman of the People's Government, Inner Mongolia Autonomous Region |

Wang Xian (Wang Hsien) 王宪

Posts held

CCP
Secretary of Beijing Municipality CP

Provincial Administration
Vice-chairman of the People's Congress of Beijing Municipality

1958,	May	Identified as deputy director of the Rural Work Department of Beijing Municipality CP
1960,	Mar	Identified as head of the Construction Bureau for the Miyun Dam
1977,	Sep	Identified as vice-chairman of the Revolutionary Committee of Beijing (until Dec 1979)
1979,	Apr	Identified as secretary of Beijing Municipality CP
	Dec	Elected vice-chairman of the People's Congress of Beijing Municipality

Wang Xiaobin (Wang Hsiao-pin) 王效斌

Posts held

Government
Vice-minister of railways

| 1978, | Jun | Identified as vice-minister of railways |

Wang Xiaoci (Wang Hsiao-tz'u) 王孝慈

Posts held

Others
Member of the Standing Committee of the 5th CPPCC

Wang was born in 1909 (?) in Hunan Province. He studied at the Whampoa Military Academy and belonged to the 5th Graduating Class. Due to his membership in the CCP he was imprisoned between 1933 and 1937. In 1939 he was political commissar of the 4th Subdistrict of the Taihang Military District. In 1943 Wang was identified as political commissar of the West Shandong Military District.

1951		Identified as vice-chairman of the Railway Labor Union
1952,	Apr	Member of a delegation to the May Festival in the USSR
1955,	May	Identified as president of the Beijing Railway College (until Apr 1959)

1961,   Dec   Elected vice-governor of Gansu Province (until Cultural Revolution)
1968,   Jan   Denounced as a follower of Liu Shaoqi and purged
1979,   Jan   First appearance after the Cultural Revolution
         Jul   By-elected member of the Standing Committee of the 5th CPPCC

Wang Xiaoyi (Wang Hsiao-yi) 王笑一

Posts held

CCP
Member of the Standing Committee of Beijing Municipality CP

Provincial Administration
Vice-mayor of Beijing Municipality

1961,   Oct   Identified as member of the Standing Committee of Hebei Province CP
1967,   Jul   Identified as a cadre of the Revolutionary Committee of Beijing
1973,   Oct   Identified as deputy secretary-general of the Revolutionary Committee of Beijing
1977,   Dec   Elected vice-chairman of the Revolutionary Committee of Beijing (until Dec 1979)
1978,   Sep   Head of a Beijing friendship delegation to Sweden, Finland, Denmark, Norway, Great Britain
1979,   Mar   Identified as member of the Standing Committee of Beijing Municipality CP
         Dec   Elected vice-mayor of Beijing Municipality

Wang Xiaoyun (Wang Hsiao-yün) 王晓云

Posts held

Government
Minister of the embassy in Tokyo

Wang was born in 1920 in Shandong Province.

1957,   Dec   Member of a Red Cross delegation to Japan
1961,   Jun   Identified as deputy secretary of the Institute of Foreign Affairs
1962,   Jul   Identified as council member of the Institute of Foreign Affairs; member of a delegation to the Conference on Total Disarmament in Moscow
1963,   Apr   Appointed deputy secretary-general of the Sino-Japanese Friendship Association
1965,   Aug   Elected member of the Afro-Asian Solidarity Committee (until Cultural Revolution)
1967,   Feb   Identified as member of the Association for Cultural Relations and Friendship with Foreign Countries (renamed Association for Friendship with Foreign Countries in 1969)
1968-1970   Numerous activities, primarily in connection with the reception of Japanese delegations to Beijing

1971,   Mar   Deputy head of the Chinese table-tennis team at the 31st World Championship in Nagoya (beginning of "ping-pong diplomacy")
1972,   Dec   Identified as deputy director of the Asia Department in the Ministry of Foreign Affairs (until Apr 1979)
1978,   Jan   Member of a government delegation led by Deng Xiaoping to Burma and Nepal
         Mar   Member of a government delegation led by Li Xiannian to the Philippines and Bangladesh
         Oct   Member of a government delegation led by Deng Xiaoping to Japan
         Nov   Member of a government delegation led by Deng Xiaoping to Singapore
1979,   May   Identified as minister of the Chinese embassy in Japan

Wang Xinsan (Wang Hsin-san) 王新三

Posts held

Government
Vice-minister of coal industry

1950,   Jun   Identified as a member of the People's Government of Fushun Municipality and as secretary of Fushun CP
1954,   Oct   Identified as a member of the State Planning Commission (until Nov 1956)
1956,   Feb   Identified as director of the Fuel Industry Planning Bureau under the State Planning Commission
         Nov   Appointed vice-chairman of the State Economic Commission (until Jun 1963)
1964,   Jun   Wang disappears
1979,   Apr   Identified as vice-minister of coal industry

Wang Xiping (Wang Hsi-p'ing) 王西萍

Posts held

Government
Vice-minister of communications

1953,   Feb   Identified as director of the 4th Bureau, 2nd Ministry of Machine Building
1957,   Jun   Appointed assistant minister of the 2nd Ministry of Machine Building (until 1959)
1978,   Dec   First appearance after the Cultural Revolution
1979,   Mar   Identified as vice-minister of communications

Wang Xiuxiu (Wang Hsiu-hsiu) (f) 王秀秀

Posts held

CCP
Member of the CCP 11th Central Committee

1977,   Aug   Elected member of the CCP Central Committee by the 11th Party Congress

Wang Xuewen (Wang Hsüeh-wen) 王学文

Posts held

Others
Member of the Standing Committee of the
5th CPPCC

Wang is a graduate of Kyoto University in Japan. He became known for his translation of Das Kapital by Marx into Chinese. In mid-1949 he was invited to join the Preparatory Committee for the establishment of the New Economic Order Research Society.

1951,	Oct	Identified as board member of the Sino-Soviet Friendship Association
1954,	Aug	Elected deputy for Jiangsu Province to the 1st NPC
1955,	May	Appointed member of the Department of Philosophy and Social Sciences, Academy of Sciences
1956,	Feb	Identified as member of the Asian Solidarity Committee
1965,	Jan	Elected member of the Standing Committee of the CPPCC
1967		Disappears during the Cultural Revolution
1973,	May	First appearance after the Cultural Revolution: Named in his former post as member of the Standing Committee of the CPPCC (confirmed in Mar 1978 by the 5th CPPCC)

Wang Xueying (Wang Hsüeh-ying) (f) 王雪莹

Posts held

Others
Member of the Standing Committee of the
5th CPPCC

1954,	Dec	Delegate representing the Democratic Women's Federation at the 2nd CPPCC (again in 1959 and 1964 at the 3rd and 4th CPPCC)
1965,	Jan	Elected member of the Standing Committee of the CPPCC
1967		Disappears during the Cultural Revolution
1973,	May	First appearance after the Cultural Revolution: Again named as member of the Standing Committee of the CPPCC (confirmed in Mar 1978 by the 5th CPPCC)

Wang Yan (Wang Yen) 王炎

Posts held

Provincial Administration
Vice-governor of Fujian Province

1978,	Jan	Elected vice-chairman of the Revolutionary Committee of Fujian Province (until Dec 1979)
	Aug	Identified as director of the Economic Committee, Revolutionary Committee of Fujian
1979,	Dec	Elected vice-governor of Fujian Province

Wang Yanchang (Wang Yen-ch'ang) 王淦昌

Posts held

Government
Ambassador to Guyana and to Trinidad and Tobago

NPC
Deputy for Beijing Municipality to the
5th NPC

1960,	Jan	Identified as consul at the Consulate-General in Bombay (until 1962?)
1969,	Aug	Identified as chargé d'affaires in Denmark (until Feb 1971)
1971,	Sep	Identified as head of the Peru Trade Office of the Council for the Promotion of International Trade
1972,	Aug	Identified as counselor at the embassy in Peru (until 1975?)
1977,	Mar	Identified as chief editor of GMRB
	May	Identified as a cadre of a department of the CCP Central Committee
1978,	Feb	Elected deputy for Beijing Municipality to the 5th NPC
	Aug	Appointed ambassador to Guyana
1979,	Nov	Appointed ambassador to Trinidad and Tobago

Wang Yang (Wang Yang) 汪洋

Posts held

Military
Deputy commander of Beijing Military Region

Wang took part in the Long March of 1934-35. In 1939 he served as regiment commander in Shandong. From 1947 to 1948 he was deputy commander of the 5th Division and chief of staff of the 2nd Column of the Northeast Field Army commanded by Lin Biao. In the following year he commanded the 116th Division, 39th Army, 4th Field Army.

1950		Service in the Korean War as commander of the 116th Division; subsequently disappears
1967,	Aug	Identified as military leader in Jilin Military District (until Dec 1971)
1972,	Mar	Identified as military leader in Beijing
1973,	May	Identified as a cadre of the State Council
1975,	Jan	Appointed minister of the 7th Ministry of Machine Building (until Feb 1978)
1978,	Sep	Identified as deputy commander of Beijing Military Region

Wang Yaohua (Wang Yao-hua) (f) 王耀花

Posts held

NPC
Member of the Standing Committee of the
5th NPC
Deputy for Ningxia Autonomous Region to the 5th NPC

1950,	Oct	Identified as deputy director of the Finance Department, People's Government of Gansu Province
1954,	Dec	Elected member of the People's Council of Gansu Province
1956,	Jun	Elected alternate member of the Secretariat of Gansu Province CP
1965		Identified as secretary of Lanzhou Municipality CP
1975,	Jan	Elected member of the Standing Committee of the 4th NPC (confirmed in Mar 1978 by the 5th NPC)
1978,	Feb	Elected deputy for Ningxia Autonomous Region to the 5th NPC

Wang Yaoting (Wang Yao-t'ing) 王耀庭

Posts held

Others
Chairman of the China Council for Promotion of International Trade

Wang became widely known when he was arrested in Rio de Janeiro by the Brazilian authorities together with eight other Chinese in April 1964. At the time Wang, in his capacity as deputy director of the Textile Import and Export Corporation, was head of the Rio de Janeiro branch of the Council for Promotion of International Trade. For alleged subversive activities Wang and the other eight Chinese were sentenced to ten years imprisonment each by the 2nd Military Court of the 1st Brazilian Region on 22 December 1964. As a result of massive protest by the Chinese authorities and a number of international organizations they were, however, released in April 1965 and celebrated as heroes on their return to China.

1972,	Sep	Head of an economic and trade exhibition in Rome
1973,	Jun	Identified as chairman of the Council for Promotion of International Trade
	Sep-Oct	Head of a trade delegation to Great Britain, France, and Switzerland
	Nov	Head of a trade delegation to the Philippines
1974,	Jul	Head of a friendship delegation to Japan
	Sep	Head of a friendship and trade delegation to Japan
1975,	May	Named as government cadre (this may be taken as evidence that the China Council for Promotion of International Trade is a government organ)
	Sep	Head of a trade delegation to Sweden and Switzerland
	Dec	Head of a trade delegation to Thailand
1976,	Apr	Head of a trade delegation to Belgium
1977,	May	Head of a trade delegation to Australia
	Jul	Head of an exhibition delegation to Sapporo, Japan
	Sep	Head of a trade delegation to the U.S.A.
1978,	Jan	Head of a trade delegation to the United Arab Emirates
	May	Head of a trade delegation to the ASEAN Trade Fair in Manila

| 1979, | Sep | Member of a government delegation, led by Gu Mu, to Japan |
| | Nov | Head of a trade delegation to India |

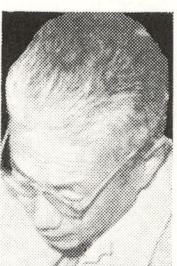

Wang Yeqiu (Wang Yeh-ch'iu) 王冶秋

Posts held

NPC
Member of the Standing Committee of the 5th NPC
Deputy for Beijing Municipality to the 5th NPC

Others
Director of the Administration Bureau for Museums and Archaeological Data

1961,	Feb	Identified as director of the Office of Cultural Objects in the Ministry of Culture
1964,	Oct	Elected deputy for Hebei Province to the 3rd NPC
1970,	Oct	Named as a "patriotic person"
1973,	Apr	Identified as director of the Administration of State Cultural Objects
	May	Head of a preparatory delegation for an exhibition of recent excavations in France
	Jun	Head of an exhibition delegation to Japan
1974,	May	Identified as director of the Administrative Bureau for Museums and Archaeological Data
	Oct	Head of an exhibition delegation to Japan
1975,	Jan	Elected member of the Standing Committee by the 4th NPC (confirmed in Mar 1978 by the 5th NPC)
1977,	Jan	Head of a delegation to a Chinese archaeology exhibition in Australia
1978,	Feb	Elected deputy for Beijing Municipality to the 5th NPC
	Apr	Present at opening of Archaeological Finds Exhibition in Hong Kong
	Sep	Visit to Sweden to attend a Lu Xun exhibition

Wang Yi (Wang Yi)   王一

Posts held

CCP
Secretary of Tianjin Municipality CP

NPC
Deputy for the PLA to the 5th NPC

Military
Commander of Tianjin Garrison

Provincial Administration
Vice-chairman of the Revolutionary Committee of Tianjin Municipality

1970,	May	Identified as commander of Tianjin Garrison and as vice-chairman of the Revolutionary Committee of Tianjin
1971,	May	Elected secretary of Tianjin Municipality CP
1978,	Feb	Elected deputy for the PLA to the 5th NPC

Wang Yilun (Wang Yi-lun)   王一伦

Posts held

CCP
Secretary of Inner Mongolia Autonomous
Region CP
1st secretary of the Discipline Inspection
Commission, Inner Mongolia Autonomous
Region CP

Provincial Administration
Vice-chairman of the People's Congress of
Inner Mongolia Autonomous Region

1956   Identified as deputy secretary of
            Heilongjiang Province CP
1965   Identified as vice-governor, and secretary
            of the CP, Heilongjiang Province
1973, Feb   Identified as vice-chairman of the Revolu-
            tionary Committee of Heilongjiang Prov-
            ince (until Nov 1977)
      May   Identified as secretary of Heilongjiang
            Province CP (until May 1979)
1979, Mar   Identified as secretary of Heilong-
            jiang CP's Commission for Inspecting Dis-
            cipline (until May 1979)
      Sep   Identified as secretary of Inner Mongolia
            Autonomous Region CP and as 1st secre-
            tary of the Discipline Inspection Commit-
            tee of that CP
      Dec   Elected vice-chairman of the People's
            Congress of Inner Mongolia Autonomous
            Region

Wang Yinglai (Wang Ying-lai)   王应睐

Posts held

NPC
Deputy for Shanghai Municipality to the
5th NPC

Others
President of the Shanghai Branch, Acad-
emy of Sciences
Director of the Institute of Biochemistry,
Academy of Sciences in Shanghai
President of the Society of Biochemistry

Wang was born in 1910. He was awarded a Ph.D. degree in
chemistry by Cambridge University in 1941.

1950, Jan   Identified as researcher of the Preparato-
            ry Office, Medical Institute of the Acad-
            emy of Sciences
      Jun   Identified as deputy director of the Insti-
            tute of Physiology and Biochemistry of
            the Academy of Sciences
1955, May   Identified as member of the Department
            of Biology and Earth Sciences of the
            Academy of Sciences
1956, Feb   Elected member of the Central Commit-
            tee of the Jiusan Society
1958, Mar   Identified as director of the Institute of
            Biochemistry, Academy of Sciences
1961, Aug   Head of a delegation to the 5th Interna-
            tional Conference of Biochemists in
            Moscow

1964, Sep   Elected deputy for Shanghai Municipality
            to the 3rd NPC
1967   Disappears during the Cultural Revolution
1974, May   First appearance after the Cultural Revo-
            lution
1977, Jun   Member of a delegation of the Academy
            of Sciences to Australia
1978, Jan   Identified as director of the Shanghai
            Institute of Biochemistry of the Academy
            of Sciences; head of a delegation of
            scientists to Japan
      Feb   Elected deputy for Shanghai Municipality
            to the 5th NPC
      Jun   Identified as president of the Shanghai
            Branch, Academy of Sciences
1979, May   Identified as president of the Society of
            Biochemistry

Wang Yingzhong (Wang Ying-chung)   王应中

Posts held

Military
Deputy commander of Liaoning Military
District

1965, May   Identified as chief of staff of Liaoning
            Military District (until 1968)
1977, Dec   Elected vice-chairman of the Revolution-
            ary Committee of Liaoning Province (until
            Jan 1980)
1979, Dec   Identified as deputy commander of
            Liaoning Military District

Wang Yiping (Wang Yiping)   王一平

Posts held

CCP
Member of the CCP 11th Central Com-
mittee
Secretary of Shanghai Municipality CP

Government
Member of the Birth Planning Leading
Group under the State Council

Provincial Administration
Vice-mayor of Shanghai Municipality

1949, Dec   Appointed director, Tax Bureau of the
            People's Government of Shanxi Province
1952, Oct   Elected council member of the Sino-
            Soviet Friendship Association, Shanghai
            Section
1954, Mar   Elected deputy vice-mayor, and secretary
            of the CP, of Fuzhou Municipality
1956   Identified as director of the Organization
            Department of Shanghai Municipality CP
1957, Sep   Identified as deputy director, Bureau of
            Food Grains of the People's Government
            of Beijing
1958, Sep   Identified as director, Bureau of Food
            Grains of the People's Government of
            Beijing
1964, Feb   Identified as alternate member, Secretari-
            at of Shanghai Municipality CP

1965,   Apr   Identified as secretary of Shanghai Munic-
              ipality CP
1966   Disappears during the Cultural Revolution
1972,   Nov   First appearance after the Cultural Revo-
              lution: Identified as vice-chairman of the
              Revolutionary Committee of Shanghai
              (until Dec 1979)
1977,   Jan   Identified as secretary of Shanghai Munic-
              ipality CP
        Aug   Elected member of the CCP Central
              Committee by the 11th Party Congress
1978,   Mar   Head of a friendship delegation to Japan
        Jun   Appointed member of the Executive Com-
              mittee of the Welfare Institute
        Jul   Appointed member of the Birth Planning
              Leading Group under the State Council
1979,   Dec   Elected vice-mayor of Shanghai Munici-
              pality

Wang Yongxing (Wang Yung-hsing) 王永幸

Posts held

NPC
Member of the Standing Committee of the
5th NPC
Deputy for Shandong Province to the
5th NPC

1965,   Dec   By-elected deputy for Shandong Province
              to the 3rd NPC; identified as secretary,
              CP of Xiatingjia Production Brigade,
              Dalüjia People's Commune, Huang County,
              Shandong Province
1978,   Feb   Elected deputy for Shandong Province to
              the 5th NPC
        Mar   Elected member of the Standing Commit-
              tee of the 5th NPC
        Jun   Member of an NPC delegation led by Ji
              Pengfei to Venezuela, Mexico, and Canada

Wang Youping (Wang Yu-p'ing) 王幼平

Posts held

Government
Vice-minister of foreign affairs
Ambassador to the USSR

NPC
Deputy for Shandong Province to the
5th NPC

Wang was born in 1910 and joined the CCP in 1931. In
1947 he served as director of the Political Department of
Henan-Anhui-Jiangsu Border Area.

1950,   Jul   Appointed ambassador to Romania (until
              Nov 1954)
1954,   Dec   Appointed ambassador to Norway (until
              Aug 1958)
1958,   Sep   Appointed ambassador to Cambodia (until
              Feb 1962)
1963,   May   Identified as advisor at the Ministry of
              Foreign Affairs; Wang accompanies the
              Chinese head of state Liu Shaoqi to
              Cambodia
1964,   Jan   Appointed ambassador to Cuba (until

              about 1967)
        Sep   Elected deputy for Shandong Province to
              the 3rd NPC
1969,   Jun   Appointed ambassador to North Vietnam
              (until Aug 1974)
1971,   Nov   Wang accompanies the Vietnamese prime
              minister Pham Van Dong on his visit to
              China
1973,   Jun   Wang accompanies the Vietnamese prime
              minister Pham Van Dong on his visit to
              China
1975,   Jan   Appointed ambassador to Malaysia (until
              Apr 1974)
1977,   Aug   Appointed ambassador to the USSR
1978,   Feb   Elected deputy for Shandong Province to
              the 5th NPC
1979,   Sep   Identified as vice-minister of foreign
              affairs; head of the Chinese delegation to
              talks on normalization in Moscow

Wang Yuexia (Wang Yüeh-hsia) (f) 王月霞

Posts held

NPC
Member of the Standing Committee of the
5th NPC
Deputy for Zhejiang Province to the
5th NPC

1978,   Feb   Elected deputy for Zhejiang Province to
              the 5th NPC
        Mar   Elected member of the Standing Commit-
              tee of the 5th NPC
1979,   Jun   Identified as Party secretary of Dongtou
              County in Zhejiang Province

Wang Yueyi (Wang Yüeh-yi) 王越毅

Posts held

Government
Ambassador to Turkey

1952   Identified as deputy director of the Mar-
              keting Bureau, Federation of Supply and
              Marketing Cooperatives
1954,   Jul   Elected member of the Federation of
              Supply and Marketing Cooperatives
1963,   Jun   Identified as vice-chairman of the Federa-
              tion of Supply and Marketing Cooperatives
1971,   Sep   Appointed ambassador to Austria (until
              Aug 1974)
1974,   Sep   Appointed ambassador to Kenya (until
              Jan 1979)
1975,   Apr   Head of the Chinese delegation to the
              3rd Session of the UN Environmental Pro-
              tection Program in Nairobi
1976,   Nov   Head of the Chinese delegation to the
              19th Session of UN Educational Scientific
              and Cultural Organization in Nairobi
1978,   May   Identified as permanent representative to
              the UN Environment Program
1979,   Mar   Appointed ambassador to Turkey

Wang Yunsheng (Wang Yün-sheng)

王芸生

Posts held

NPC
Deputy for Hebei Province to the 5th NPC

Others
Member of the Standing Committee of the 5th CPPCC
Vice-chairman of the Sino-Japanese Friendship Associations

Wang was born in 1899 in Tianjin. In the mid-1920s he became one of the best-known journalists in China, working mainly for Dagong Bao (temporarily as chief editor). In September 1949 he was invited to take part in the 1st CPPCC which elected him a member.

1949,	Dec	Appointed member of the East China Military and Administrative Council (until Jan 1953); chief editor of the Dagong Bao (until Jan 1953)
1950,	Mar	Appointed member of the Cultural and Educational Committee of the East China Military and Administrative Council (until Jan 1953)
	Dec	Appointed member of the People's Government of Shanghai (until Jun 1954)
1952,	Oct	Elected chairman of the Shanghai Section, Sino-Soviet Friendship Association
1953,	Jan	Appointed head of Dagong Bao; appointed member of the East China Administrative Council (until Jun 1954)
	Nov	Elected member of the Executive Council, Federation of Industry and Commerce (until Dec 1956)
1954,	Aug	Elected deputy for Hebei Province to the 1st NPC (reelected in 1958 and 1964 to the 2nd and 3rd NPCs)
1955,	Jun	Member of a delegation to the session of the World Peace Council in Helsinki
1956,	Feb	Appointed member of the Asian Solidarity Committee (retaining membership after the committee is renamed Afro-Asian Solidarity Committee in Jul 1958)
	Aug	Member of a delegation to the Conference against Atomic Bombs in Nagasaki
	Nov	Member of a delegation of the NPC to the USSR, Romania, and Czechoslovakia
1959,	Apr	Elected member of the Standing Committee of the 3rd CPPCC (reelected in Jan 1965 to the 4th CPPCC)
	Jun	Elected vice-chairman of the Association of Newspapers Workers (until Cultural Revolution)
1962,	Apr	Elected council member of the Afro-Asian Solidarity Committee (until Cultural Revolution)
1963,	Oct	Identified as council member of the Sino-Japanese Friendship Association
1966		Disappears during the Culutral Revolution
1973,	Feb	First appearance after the Cultural Revolution: Named in his former post as member of the Standing Committee of the CPPCC (confirmed in Mar 1978 by the 5th CPPCC)
	Aug	Identified as vice-chairman of the Sino-Japanese Friendship Association

1975,	Jan	Member of the Presidium of the 4th NPC
1976,	Nov	Head of a delegation of workers to Japan
1978,	Feb	Elected deputy for Hebei Province to the 5th NPC
1979,	Jun	Member of the Credentials Committee and of the Draft Laws Committee at the 2nd Session of the 5th NPC

Wang Yuqing (Wang Yü-ch'ing) 王玉清

Posts held

Government
Vice-minister of metallurgical industry

Others
Vice-president of the Metals Society

1953,	Jan	Identified as deputy general manager of the Anshan Iron and Steel Company
1957,	Jan	Identified as director of the Iron and Steel Industry Administrative Bureau of the Ministry of Metallurgical Industry
1964,	Jun	Appointed vice-minister of metallurgical industry
1967		Disappears during the Cultural Revolution
1978,	Nov	First appearance after the Cultural Revolution: Identified as vice-minister of metallurgical industry and as vice-president of the Metals Society

Wang Zaitian (Wang Tsai-t'ien) 王再天

Posts held

Others
Member of the Standing Committee of the 5th CPPCC

Wang was born under the name of Namjilsereng in the Left Middle Banner of the Jirem League in Inner Mongolia. He belongs to the Mongolian minority. In 1947 he held the following posts: member of the Central Committee of Inner Mongolia CP, deputy commander of Inner Mongolia Military Region, and chief procurator of Inner Mongolia. He represented Inner Mongolia as a delegate at the 1st CPPCC in September 1949.

1949,	Nov	Identified as member of the Nationalities Affairs Commission of the Government Administration Council (until Sep 1954); identified as director of the Public Security Department of Inner Mongolia Autonomous Region
	Dec	Identified as deputy commander of Inner Mongolia Military Region
1951,	Jul	Head of a delegation to Ulan Bator to attend the 30th anniversary of the Mongolian Revolution
	Nov	Appointed chief procurator of Inner Mongolia People's Procuracy
1954,	Jun	Elected vice-chairman of Inner Mongolia Autonomous Region (until Nov 1967)
	Aug	Elected deputy for Inner Mongolia to the 1st NPC (reelected in 1958 and 1964 to the 2nd and 3rd NPCs)

1955,   Dec   Member of a government delegation to the People's Republic of Mongolia

1957,   Aug   Conferred the order "Independence and Freedom," 1st class

          Nov   Member of a delegation from Inner Mongolia to the USSR

1960,   Mar   Elected council member of the Sino-Latin-American Friendship Association

          May   Elected secretary of Inner Mongolia Autonomous Region CP (until 1967)

1961,   Jul   Head of a joint delegation of Inner Mongolia and Xinjiang to Ulan Bator

1967,   Nov   Identified as member of the Standing Committee, Revolutionary Committee of Inner Mongolia Autonomous Region; subsequently disappears

1979,   Jul   First appearance after the Cultural Revolution: By-elected member of the Standing Committee of the 5th CPPCC

Wang Ze (Wang Tse)   王　　泽

Posts held

Government
Ambassador to Peru

Wang was born in 1923. He is a graduate of the Joint Southwest University.

1955,   Jun   Identified as consul-general in Mandalay (Lashio) in Burma (until Jul 1961)

1965,   Nov   Identified as consul-general in Dacca, Pakistan (until 1967)

1969,   Jul   Appointed ambassador to Nepal (until Aug 1972)

1972,   Sep   Appointed ambassador to Mauritius (until Jan 1977)

1977,   May   Appointed ambassador to Peru

Wang Zejiu (Wang Tse-chiu)

Posts held

Others
Vice-president of the Academy of Geological Sciences

1979,   Aug   Identified as vice-president of the Academy of Geological Sciences

Wang Zhanyuan (Wang Chan-yüan)   王占元

Posts held

Government
Ambassador to Cuba

Wang was born in 1925 in Hebei Province.

1959,   May   Identified as 2nd secretary at the embassy in Bulgaria (until about 1962)

1970,   Jun   Identified as counselor at the embassy in Romania (until Oct 1972)

1973,   Mar   Appointed ambassador to Guyana (until May 1979)

1975,   Sep   Appointed concurrently ambassador to Trinidad and Tobago (until May 1979)

          Nov   PRC representative at the independence celebrations in Surinam

1979,   Aug   Appointed ambassador to Cuba

Wang Zhaohua (Wang Chao-hua) 王照华

Posts held

CCP
Secretary-general, Organization Department of the CCP Central Committee

1953,   Jul   Elected member of the Central Committee, New Democratic Youth League

          Aug   Member of a delegation to the World Youth Festival in Bucharest

1954   Identified as 2nd secretary, Beijing Branch of the New Democratic Youth League

1957,   May   Elected member of the Standing Committee, Communist Youth League (successor organization to the New Democratic Youth League); identified as 1st secretary of the Communist Youth League, Beijing Branch (until Apr 1963)

1958,   Apr   Elected member of the Standing Committee, Federation of Democratic Youth

1960,   Mar   Elected secretary of the Communist Youth League (until Cultural Revolution); head of a youth delegation to the Conference of the World Federation of Democratic Youth in Guinea

          Sep   Head of a delegation to the Preparatory Conference for the World Youth Festival in Moscow

1961,   Apr   Head of a delegation to a session of the World Federation of Democratic Youth in Chile; subsequent visit to Cuba

          Jul   Head of a youth delegation to the World Youth Forum in Moscow

          Sep   Head of a youth delegation to Indonesia

1962,   Apr   Elected vice-chairman of the Federation of Democratic Youth

          May   Head of a youth delegation to Japan

          Jul   Head of a youth delegation to the World Festival in Helsinki

          Dec   Elected vice-chairman of the Sino-Cuban Friendship Association

1963,   Feb   Head of a youth delegation to the Session of the World Federation of Democratic Youth in Budapest

1964,   Jan   Head of a youth delegation to Jakarta

          Sep   Head of a youth delegation to Moscow

          Oct   Appointed council member of the Institute of Foreign Affairs (until Cultural Revolution)

          Nov   Head of a youth delegation to Algeria

1965,   Jan   Elected member of the Standing Committee of the CPPCC

          Feb   Head of a youth delegation to Indonesia

          Jun   Elected vice-chairman of the Peace Council (until Cultural Revolution)

1966,   Apr   Elected vice-chairman of the Association for Cultural Relations and Friendship with Foreign Countries (until Cultural Revolution)

1967		Disappears during the Cultural Revolution
1973,	Oct	First appearance after the Cultural Revolution: Identified as member of the Standing Committee of the CPPCC (until Feb 1978)
1978,	May	Vice-chairman of the Preparatory Committee of the 10th Congress of the Communist Youth League
1979,	May	Identified as secretary-general, Organization Department of the CCP Central Committee
	Oct	Head of a youth delegation to Japan; identified as advisor of the Youth Federation

Wang Zhaorong (Wang Chao-jung) 王昭荣

Posts held

CCP
Member of the Standing Commitee of the Jiangxi Province CP

Provincial Administration
Vice-governor of Jiangxi Province

1978,	Feb	Elected vice-chairman of the Revolutionary Committee of Jiangxi Province (until Feb 1979); identified as member of the Standing Committee of Jiangxi Province CP
1979,	Dec	Elected vice-governor of Jiangxi Province

Wang Zhaowen (Wang Chao-wen) 王朝文

Posts held

CCP
Member of the Commission for Inspecting Discipline under the CCP Central Committee
Member of the Standing Committee of Guizhou Province CP

Provincial Administration
Vice-governor of Guizhou Province

Mass Organization
Secretary of the Communist Youth League in Guizhou Province
Chairman of the Youth Federation of Guizhou Province

Wang belongs to the Miao minority.

1973,	May	Elected secretary of the Communist Youth League in Guizhou
1977,	Nov	Identified as member of the Standing Committee of Guizhou Province CP; elected vice-chairman of the Revolutionary Committee of Guizhou (until Dec 1979)
1978,	Dec	Appointed member of the Commission for Inspecting Discipline under the CCP Central Committee
1979,	Mar	Identified as chairman of the Youth Federation of Guizhou Province
1980,	Jan	Elected vice-governor of Guizhou Province

Wang Zhen (Wang Chen) (f) 王珍

Posts held

Government
Deputy director of the Information Department in the Ministry of Foreign Affairs

Wang is the wife of Han Nienlong.

1971,	Apr	Identified as deputy director of the Protocol Department in the Ministry of Foreign Affairs (until Apr 1973)
1973,	Apr	Identified as deputy director of the Information Department in the Ministry of Foreign Affairs
	May	Deputy head of a delegation of journalists visiting the U.S.A.
1977,	Oct	Deputy head of a delegation of journalists visiting Japan
1978,	Oct	Member of a government delegation led by Deng Xiaoping to Japan

Wang Zhen (Wang Chen) 王震

Posts held

CCP
Member of the Politburo of the CCP 11th Central Committee
Member of the CCP 11th Central Committee
Leading cadre of the Military Council under the CCP Central Committee

Government
Vice-premier
Member of the State Financial and Economic Commission

NPC
Deputy for Heilongjiang Province to the 5th NPC

Military
Colonel-general

Others
Chairman of the Administrative Affairs Committee, Shanghai Jiaotong University

Wang was born in 1908 as the son of poor peasants in Liuyang County, Hunan Province. After attending elementary school for three years he was forced to earn a living and worked at a train station on the Guangzhou-Hankou (today: Wuhan) railway. In 1924 he became a member of the Railway Workers Association and in 1927 he joined the CCP. Two weeks after their marriage his wife was executed following the rift between CCP and KMT. Up to 1934 Wang was successively a minor Party secretary, a participant in various peasant revolts and eventually troop leader in the army commanded by He Long. After taking part in the Long March in 1934-35 he was made commander of the 259th Brigade, 120th Division which conducted guerrilla missions in Shanxi and Hebei. During the Anti-Japanese War he led his unit from Shanxi Province to Guangdong and en route distinguished himself in numerous skirmishes. After the end of the war he returned to Northwest China. During the Civil War the units under his command contributed decisively to the victories over Hu Zongnan near Baoji and over Ma Bufang in Qinghai. In 1945 the 7th CCP Congress elected him an alternate member of the Central Committee (until Sep 1956). In autumn 1949 he was stationed in Xinjiang.

1950		Appointed member of the Northwest China Military and Political Council; member of the People's Government of Xinjiang Province; political commissar of Xinjiang Military Region and secretary of the Xinjiang Subbureau in the Northwest China Bureau of the CCP Central Committee (probably until 1945)
1952,	Aug	Appointed member of the Preparatory Committee for Xinjiang Autonomous Region; identified as acting commander of Xinjiang Military Region (probably until 1954)
	Sep	Appointed deputy commander of Northwest China Military Region (probably until 1954)
1954,	Feb	Appointed commander and political commissar of the PLA Railway Corps (probably until May 1956)
	Aug	Elected deputy for the PLA to the 1st NPC (until Mar 1959)
	Oct	Appointed member of the National Defense Council (until Cultural Revolution)
1955,	Sep	Promoted to rank of colonel-general; awarded the orders of "1st August," "Independence and Freedom," and "Liberation," all 1st class
1956,	May	Appointed minister of state farms and reclamation (until Cultural Revolution)
	Sep	Elected member of the CCP Central Committee by the 8th Party Congress
1959,	Mar	Elected deputy for Heilongjiang Province to the 2nd NPC (reelected in 1964 to the 3rd NPC)
1962,	Sep	Member of an NPC delegation to North Vietnam
1966		Although criticized during the Cultural Revolution as a supporter of He Long, Wang retains his posts
1969,	Apr	Reelected member of the CCP Central Committee by the 9th Party Congress (confirmed in 1973 by the 10th Congress)
1974,	Sep	Head of a goodwill delegation to Japan for the establishment of a direct air link between China and Japan
1975,	Jan	Appointed vice premier (reelected in Mar 1978)
1978,	Feb	Elected deputy for Heilongjiang Province to the 5th NPC
	Nov	Head of a government delegation to Great Britain and Switzerland
	Dec	Elected member of the Politburo of the CCP Central Committee by the 3rd Plenum of the 11th Central Committee
1979,	May	Identified as leading member of the Military Council under the CCP Central Committee
	Jul	Appointed member of the State Financial and Economic Commission
	Aug	Identified as chairman of the Administrative Affairs Committee of the Shanghai

		Jiaotong University
	Sep	Article in <u>RMRB</u>, 27th September: "Fight Heroically and Build Up a Pioneering Enterprise Through Arduous Labor - Some Recollections of the Liberation and Building of Xinjiang"

Wang Zhenjiang (Wang Chen-chiang)　王振江

<u>Posts held</u>

Provincial Administration
Vice-governor of Guizhou Province

1977,	Dec	Elected vice chairman of the Revolutionary Committee of Guizhou Province (until Dec 1979)
1980,	Jan	Elected vice-governor of Guizhou Province

Wang Zhenwen (Wang Chen-wen)　王振文

<u>Posts held</u>

NPC
Deputy for Xinjiang Autonomous Region to the 5th NPC

Provincial Administration
Vice-chairman of the Standing Committee of Xinjiang Autonomous Region People's Congress

1978,	Feb	Elected vice-chairman of the Revolutionary Committee of Xinjiang Autonomous Region and deputy for Xinjiang to the 5th NPC
1979,	Sep	Elected vice-chairman and secretary-general of the Standing Committee of Xinjiang Autonomous Region People's Congress

Wang Zhibang (Wang Chih-pang)　王治邦

<u>Posts held</u>

Provincial Administration
Vice-governor of Gansu Province

1979,	Dec	Elected vice-governor of Gansu Province

Wang Zhiguo (Wang Chih-kuo)　王治国

<u>Posts held</u>

CCP
Member of the Schistosomiasis Prevention Leading Group under the CCP Central Committee
Secretary of Hunan Province CP

Provincial Administration
Vice-governor of Hunan Province

Mass Organization
Vice-chairman of the Peasants Federation of Hunan Province

1973,   Aug   Identified as member of the Standing Committee of Hunan Province CP (until 1977)
        Dec   Elected vice-chairman of the Peasants Federation of Hunan Province
1977,   Oct   Elected secretary of Hunan Province CP
1978,   Oct   Identified as member of the Schistosomiasis Prevention Leading Group under the CCP Central Committee
1979,   Apr   Identified as vice-chairman of the Revolutionary Committee of Hunan Province (until Dec 1979)
        Dec   Elected vice-governor of Hunan Province

Wang Zhong (Wang Chung)   王　中

Posts held

Others
Member of the Standing Committee of the 5th CPPCC

1950   Identified as secretary of the Land Reform Committee of Hubei Province People's Government
1957,   Feb   Appointed assistant minister in the Ministry of Food Industry (until Feb 1958)
1958,   Feb   Appointed assistant minister in the Ministry of Light Industry (until Jan 1959)
1959,   Jan   Identified as vice-governor of Anhui Province (until Cultural Revolution)
1966,   Oct   Identified as member of the Standing Committee of Anhui Province CP (until 1975)
1971,   Apr   Identified as vice-chairman of the Revolutionary Committee of Anhui Province (until 1975)
1978,   Mar   Elected member of the Standing Committee of the 5th CPPCC

Wang Zhongyin (Wang Chung-yin) 王众音

Posts held

CCP
Member of the Standing Committee, Shandong Province CP

Provincial Administration
Vice-governor of Shandong Province

1953,   Jun   Identified as deputy director of the Propaganda Department, Shandong Province CP
1957,   Oct   Identified as director of the Department of Education and Culture, Shandong Province CP
1960,   Jul   Identified as director of the Propaganda Department, Shandong Province CP
1963,   Aug   Identified as vice-chairman of the Shandong Branch, Sino-Soviet Friendship Association; head of an artists' group visiting the USSR
1965,   Aug   Identified as a member of the Standing Committee, Shandong Province CP
        Dec   Elected vice-governor of Shandong Province

1967,   Feb   Wang disappears
1979,   May   First appearance after the Cultural Revolution: Identified as a member of the Standing Committee, Shandong Province CP
        Aug   Identified as vice-chairman of the Revolutionary Committee, Shandong Province (until Dec 1979)
        Dec   Elected vice-governor of Shandong Province

Wang Zhuxi (Wang Chu-hsi)   王竹溪

Posts held

Others
Vice-president of Beijing University
Vice-chairman of the Central Committee of the Jiusan (Chiu-san) Society

1962,   Apr   Identified as vice-president of Beijing University
        Sep   Identified as a physicist
1967   Disappears during the Cultural Revolution
1972,   Jul   First appearance after the Cultural Revolution: Present at the reception given by Zhou Enlai for the U.S.-Chinese Nobel Prize winner Yang Zhenning
1978,   Aug   Identified as vice-president of Beijing University; head of a university delegation to Yugoslavia and Romania
1979,   Oct   Elected vice-chairman of the Central Committee of the Jiusan (Chiu-san) Society

Wang Zigang (Wang Tzu-kang)   王子纲

Posts held

Government
Minister of posts and telecommunications

Others
Member of the Standing Committee of the CPPCC

1949,   Oct   Appointed director of the 3rd Bureau, Revolutionary Military Council of the Central People's Government; appointed director of the Bureau of Telecommunications, Ministry of Posts and Telecommunications (until 1951)
1950,   Mar   Elected member of the National Committee of the Postal Union
1952,   Sep   Appointed vice-minister of posts and telecommunications (until Cultural Revolution)
1954,   Dec   Deputy head of a telecommunications delegation to North Vietnam
1956,   Feb   Head of a telecommunications delegation to Yugoslavia and the People's Republic of Mongolia
1964,   Apr   Elected chairman of the Electronics Society (until Cultural Revolution)
1965,   Jan   Elected member of the Standing Committee of the 4th CPPCC

1966		At the beginning of the Cultural Revolution Wang is branded as a capitalist-roader and disappears
1973,	May	First appearance after the Cultural Revolution: Identified in his former post as member of the Standing Committee of the CPPCC
1976,	Nov	Identified as chairman of the Electronics Society (until Jul 1979)
1977,	May	Identified as a government cadre
	Nov	Identified as vice-minister of the 4th Ministry of Machine Building (until Oct 1978)
1978,	Nov	Identified as minister of posts and telecommunications
1979,	Sep	Head of a posts delegation to France, Belgium, and the Netherlands

Wang Ziye (Wang Tzu-yeh) 王子野

Posts held

Government
Deputy director of the State Publications Bureau

NPC
Deputy for Shanghai Municipality to the 5th NPC

1954,	Dec	Delegate representing publishing circles at the 2nd CPPCC
1960,	Apr	Identified as director of "People's Press"
1964,	Aug	Identified as council member of the Sino-Romanian Friendship Association
1967		Disappears during the Cultural Revolution
1978,	Feb	First appearance after the Cultural Revolution: Elected deputy for Shanghai Municipality to the 5th NPC
1979,	Jun	Identified as deputy director of the State Publications Bureau

Wang Ziyi (Wang Tzu-yi) 王子义

Posts held

Government
Vice-minister of the 1st Ministry of Machine Building

1978,	Apr	Identified as vice-minister of the 1st Ministry of Machine Building

Wang Zongjin (Wang Tsung-chin) 王宗金

Posts held

Government
Vice-minister of the 4th Ministry of Machine Building

1973,	Oct	Identified as deputy manager of the China Radio Appliances Corporation
1978,	Jul	Identified as vice-minister of the 4th Ministry of Machine Building

Wei Baoshan (Wei Baoshan) 韦宝善

Posts held

Government
Ambassador to Cameroon

1964,	Jun	Identified as counselor at the embassy in PR Mongolia (until 1966)
1971,	Aug	Identified as chargé d'affaires ad interim in Algeria
1972,	Aug	Identified as chargé d'affaires ad interim in Kenya
1973,	Mar	Appointed ambassador to Togo (until Jun 1974)
1974,	Sep	Appointed ambassador to Cameroon
1977,	Oct	Wei accompanies the president of Cameroon, Ahidjo, on his visit to China

Wei Chuantong (Wei Ch'uan-t'ung) 韦传统

Posts held

Military
Major-general
President of the PLA Art College

Wei was born in 1907.

1949,	Oct	Identified as deputy director of the Liaison Department, General Political Department, People's Revolutionary Military Council (until 1954)
1955,	Jun	Identified as secretary-general of the PLA General Political Department (until 1958)
	Sep	Appointed major-general; order of "Liberation," 1st class, conferred upon Wei
1958,	Mar	Identified as a member of the State Commission for Cultural Relations with Foreign Countries (until 1966)
	Jun	Identified as deputy director of the Propaganda Department, PLA General Political Department
	Sep	Secretary-general of a friendship delegation to North Korea
	Oct	Identified as vice-president of the Sino-Korean Friendship Association (until 1966)
1966		Wei disappears
1975,	Sep	First appearance after the Cultural Revolution
1978,	Feb	Identified as a member of the 5th CPPCC (literary and art circles); referred to as a poet
1979,	Sep	Identified as president of the PLA Art College

Wei Fengqi (Wei Feng-ch'i) 卫逢祺

Posts held

Provincial Administration
Vice-governor of Shanxi Province

1950,	Aug	Identified as secretary-general of the People's Government of Shanxi Province and as a member of its Financial and Economic Committee

1955,	Feb	Identified as secretary-general of the People's Council of Shanxi Province (until Oct 1964)
1964,	Oct	Elected vice-governor of Shanxi Province (until Cultural Revolution)
1967		Wei disappears
1979,	Dec	First appearance after the Cultural Revolution: Elected vice-governor of Shanxi Province

Wei Fengying (Wei Feng-ying) (f)

尉风英

Posts held

CCP
Alternate member of the CCP 11th Central Committee
Member of the Standing Committee of Liaoning Province CP

Wei was born in 1935 in Liaoning (?) Province as the daughter of a laborer. Her father died when she was three years old.

1951		Head of a street committee for women
1954		Apprentice at the Machine Building Factory of Shenyang Municipality; she soon distinguishes herself as a model apprentice working at a stamping machine; joins the CCP
1956,	Apr	Delegate to the Conference of Model Workers in Shenyang Municipality
1958		Wei organizes a spare-time group for technical innovations which succeeds in introducing 173 innovations. For this she is named a model worker of Liaoning Province
1959,	Mar	Elected deputy for Liaoning Province to the 2nd NPC (reelected in 1964 to the 3rd NPC)
1966,	Oct	In Beijing an exhibition is held under the title: "The Achievements of Comrade Wei Fengying, a Good Worker of Chairman Mao"; on that occasion named as a worker-engineer of Northeast Machine Factory
1967		Active participation in the Cultural Revolution in her native province in Liaoning; she is particularly noted for uniting three rival rebel groups
1968,	May	Elected vice-chairman of the newly established Revolutionary Committee of Liaoning Province (until Nov 1977)
1969,	Apr	Elected a member of the CCP Central Committee by the 9th Party Congress (until Aug 1973)
1970,	Oct	Member of a women's delegation to North Korea; there awarded the Korean order "National Flag," 1st class
1971,	Jun	Identified as member of the Standing Committee, Secretariat of Liaoning Province CP
1972,	Dec	Article in the weekly Peking Review: "Always Belong to the Working Class"
1973,	Aug	Elected chairman of the Women's Federation of Liaoning (until 1977?)
1974,	Mar	Head of a women's delegation to Congo, Brazzaville

| 1977, | Aug | Demoted from member to alternate member of the CCP Central Committee by the 11th Party Congress |
| 1978, | Jul | Last appearance, probably purged |

Wei Guoqing (Wei Kuo-ch'ing)   韦国清

Posts held

CCP
Member of the Politburo, CCP 11th Central Committee
Member of the CCP 11th Central Committee

Military
Major-general
Director of the General Political Department of the PLA

NPC
Vice-chairman of the 5th NPC
Deputy for the PLA to the 5th NPC

Wei belongs to the Zhuang minority. He was born in 1906 (1907?) in Donglan, Guangxi Province. After attending elementary and middle school, he participated in the Northern Expedition of 1926, serving in the 15th Division of the 7th Nationalist Revolutionary Army. He changed to the Communist side circa 1929. After taking part in the Baisi Uprising in Guangxi he became commander of a regiment in the 7th Workers-Peasants Army. In 1931 he reached the Jiangxi Soviet with his unit which was incorporated into the 3rd Front Army commanded by Peng Dehuai. Wei took part in the Long March of 1934-35. In 1938 he was made commander of a New 4th Army brigade and in 1941 of the 8th Brigade, 3rd Division, of the same army. In 1944 he commanded the 4th Division; he was identified as a major-general in 1946. At the beginning of 1949 Wei was deputy political commissar of the 10th Army Corps, 3rd Field Army, and in August of that year he served as political commissar of the same unit as well as mayor of Fuzhou.

1949,	Dec	Appointed vice-chairman, Fuzhou Military Control Commission
1950		Deputy political commissar of the newly established Fuzhou Military Region; concurrently deputy political commissar of the 10th Army Corps
1954,	Sep	Elected deputy for Guangxi Province to the 1st NPC (reelected in 1958 and 1964 to the 2nd and 3rd NPCs); elected member of the Standing Committee of the NPC (until 1956); appointed member of the National Defense Council (until Cultural Revolution)
	Oct	Appointed vice-chairman of the Commission for Minority Affairs (until May 1957)
	Dec?	Elected council member of the Sino-Soviet Friendship Association
1955,	Feb	Appointed governor, and secretary of the CP, of Guangxi Province
	Sep	Awarded orders of "1st August," "Independence and Freedom," and "Liberation," all 1st class
1956,	Sep	Elected alternate member of the CCP Central Committee by the 8th Party Congress (until Apr 1969)

1957, Sep Appointed chairman of the Preparatory Committee for the establishment of Guangxi Autonomous Region

1958, Mar Elected chairman of Guangxi Autonomous Region (until Cultural Revolution)

1961, Oct Identified as 1st secretary of Guangxi Autonomous Region CP (until Cultural Revolution)

1964, Feb Identified as 1st political commissar of Guangxi Military Region (until Cultural Revolution)

1965, Jan Elected vice-chairman of the 4th CPPCC (confirmed in Mar 1978 by the 5th CPPCC)

1966, Jun Identified as member, Central-South China Bureau of the CCP Central Committee (until about 1967)

1967, Mar Identified as political commissar of Guangzhou Military Region (until Jan 1974)

later Wei is accused by Red Guards of having "suppressed the Cultural Revolution." The CCP Central Committee subsequently announces in a statement on the situation in Guangxi that although Wei had committed errors, he had corrected them

1968, Aug Elected chairman of the newly established Revolutionary Committee of Guangxi Autonomous Region (until Oct 1975)

1969, Apr Elected member of the CCP Central Committee by the 9th Party Congress

Sep Member of a delegation led by Zhou Enlai to attend the mourning ceremonies for Ho Chi-minh

1971, Feb Elected 1st secretary of Guangxi Autonomous Region CP (until Oct 1975)

1973, Aug Confirmed as member of the CCP Central Committee by the 10th Party Congress; elected to first term as member of the CCP Politburo

1974, Jan Identified as 1st political commissar of Guangzhou Military Region (until 1978)

1974, Jan Elected vice-chairman of the Standing Committee by the 4th NPC (confirmed in Mar 1978 by the 5th NPC)

Oct Identified as 1st secretary of the CP, and chairman of the Revolutionary Committee, of Guangdong Province (until Dec 1978)

1977, Sep Identified as director of the General Political Department of the PLA

1978, Feb Elected deputy for the PLA to the 5th NPC

Dec Head of a Central Committee delegation to the Guangxi celebrations

Wei Jie (Wei Chieh) 韦 杰

<u>Posts held</u>

CCP
Member of the Standing Committee of Sichuan Province CP

NPC
Deputy for the PLA to the 5th NPC

Military
Lieutenant-general
Deputy commander of Chengdu Military Region

Wei was born in 1911 in Shandong Province. In 1932 he belonged to a guerrilla unit operating in Henan-Hubei-Anhui Border Area. During the Long March he commanded a battalion. He subsequently attended a course at the Anti-Japan Military and Political Academy. In 1937 he commanded a regiment of the 129th Division, 8th Route Army. In 1940 he was commander of the 4th Subdistrict of Hebei-Shandong-Henan Military District. In 1949 he commanded the 61st Army, 2nd Field Army.

1950, Feb Appointed commander of North Sichuan Military District

1951, Mar Service in the Korean War as commander of the 60th Army

May The 60th Army is encircled and destroyed by enemy forces. 5,000 men are captured, many of whom later went to Taiwan

1955, Sep Promoted to rank of lieutenant-general

1958, Oct Identified as deputy commander of Sichuan Military Region

1967, May Accused by Red Guards of having "suppressed the revolutionary rebels"; recalled to Beijing for self-criticism

1970, May Present at a demonstration in Chengdu.

1974, Oct After more than four years of absence Wei is again named in the post of deputy commander of Chengdu Military Region

1978, Feb Elected deputy for the PLA to the 5th NPC

1979, Jan Elected member of the Standing Committee of Sichuan Province CP

Wei Wenbo (Wei Wen-po)

<u>Posts held</u>

CCP
Deputy secretary, Commission for Inspecting Discipline, CCP Central Committee

Government
Minister of justice

Wei was born in 1905. In 1925 he studied at the Wuchang Political Science and Law School. In the same year he joined the Communist Youth League. In 1929 he was imprisoned in Beijing for a certain time. In 1939 he headed the United Front Work Section of the North Chang Jiang Command, New 4th Army. In the following year Wei became magistrate of Dingyuan County, Anhui Province. In 1941 he was deputy director of the Office of Joint Defense on Western Longhai Railroad. Two years later he went to Yan'an for political studies.

1950, Feb Identified as deputy director of the Political Committee, East China Military and Administrative Council (until 1952)

Apr Identified as chief procurator of the Supreme People's Procuratorate, East China Branch (until 1952)

1952, Nov Appointed vice-minister of justice (until Feb 1956)

1955,   Sep   Identified as deputy secretary, Shanghai Municipality CP

1956,   Oct   Identified as secretary, Shanghai Municipality CP (until Feb 1967)

1958,   May   Appointed deputy secretary of the Group for the Prevention of Schistosomiasis under the CCP Central Committee

          Nov   Identified as director of the Shanghai Institute of Socialism

1959,   Jun   Identified as director of the Rural Work Department, Shanghai Municipality CP (until Feb 1967)

1963,   Jun   Identified as alternate secretary of the East China Bureau, CCP Central Committee

1964,   Sep   Elected deputy for Jiangsu Province to the 3rd NPC

1966,   Mar   Identified as secretary of the East China Bureau, CCP Central Committee (until Feb 1967)

1967,   Feb   Denounced as a follower of Liao Shaoqi and purged

1978,   Dec   First appearance after the Cultural Revolution: Appointed deputy secretary, Commission for Inspecting Discipline, CCP Central Committee

1979,   Sep   Appointed minister of justice

Wei Xingzheng (Wei Hsing-cheng) 韦兴政

Posts held

CCP
Alternate member of the CCP 11th Central Committee

1977,   Aug   Elected alternate member of the CCP Central Committee by the 11th Party Congress

          Oct   Identified as a model quarryman of the Xiaoling Branch of Harbin Cement Plant, Heilongjiang Province

Wei Xinyi (Wei Hsin-yi) 魏心一

Posts held

NPC
Deputy for Anhui Province to the 5th NPC

Provincial Administration
Vice-governor of Anhui Province

1978,   Feb   Elected deputy for Anhui Province to the 5th NPC

1979,   Dec   Elected vice-governor of Anhui Province

Wei Yongqing (Wei Yung-ch'ing) 韦永清

Posts held

Government
Director of the Protocol Department of the Ministry of Foreign Affairs

1962,   Jun   Identified as assistant director of the Protocol Department of the Ministry of Foreign Affairs (until Mar 1965)

1965,   Sep   Identified as chargé d'affaires ad interim in Mauretania (until Nov 1967)

1971,   Sep   Identified as council member of the Institute of Foreign Affairs

1972,   Jun   Identified as chargé d'affaires ad interim in Ghana

1976,   May   Appointed ambassador to Turkey (until Sep 1978)

1978,   Oct   Identified as director of the Protocol Department of the Ministry of Foreign Affairs

1979,   Jan   Member of a government delegation, headed by Deng Xiaoping, to the U.S.A.

Wei Yuming (Wei Yü-ming) 韦玉明

Posts held

Government
Vice-minister of economic relations with foreign countries

Wei was born in 1924.

1965,   Nov   Appointed economic counselor at the embassy in Ghana (until late 1966)

1970,   Sep   Identified as a cadre of the State Council

1971,   Nov   Member of an economic delegation to Albania; subsequently disappears until 1974

1974,   Oct   Identified as director of a department of the Ministry of Economic Relations with Foreign Countries (until 1977)

          Dec   Head of an economic delegation to North Vietnam; subsequently again disappears until 1977

1977,   Feb   Identified as vice-minister of economic relations with foreign countries

1978,   Apr   Member of a government delegation led by Chen Muhua to Romania

          Aug   Head of a delegation to the UN Technical Cooperation Conference of Developing Countries in Buenos Aires

          Nov   Head of a scientific and technical delegation to Thailand

1979,   Dec   Visit to UN Industrial Development Organization headquarters in Vienna

Wei Zhenwu (Wei Chen-wu) 韦震五

Posts held

Vice-chairman of the Revolutionary Committee of Jilin Province

Wei was born in 1913. In 1949 he was head of the Department of Agriculture and Forestry of Northeast People's Government.

1954,   Oct   Identified as director of the Bureau of Northeast State Farms Administration of the Ministry of Agriculture (until 1956)

1955,   Apr   Identified as assistant minister, Ministry of Agriculture (until 1959)

1957,	Oct	Member of an agricultural delegation to Japan
1958,	Jun	Identified as director of the Institute of Agricultural Economics of the Academy of Agricultural Sciences
1960,	Apr	Appointed vice-minister of agriculture
1961,	Mar	Head of a delegation to the World Agricultural Exhibition in Cairo
1962		Identified as vice-chairman of the Preparatory Committee of the Agricultural Machinery Society
1963,	Nov	Head of a scientific and technical delegation to Bulgaria
1967		Disappears during the Cultural Revolution
1977,	Dec	First appearance after the Cultural Revolution: Elected vice-chairman of the Revolutionary Committee of Jilin Province
1978,	Sep	Advisor to an agricultural delegation to Japan

Wei Zhimin (Wei Chih-min)　卫之尼

Posts held

Provincial Administration
Vice-governor of Heilongjiang Province

| 1979, | Dec | Elected vice-governor of Heilongjiang Province |

Wen Chengyi (Wen Ch'eng-yi)　文成一

Posts held

CCP
Member of the Commission for Inspecting Discipline, CCP Central Committee

Government
Member of the State Nationalities Affairs Commission

Others
Member of the Standing Committee of the 5th CPPCC

Wen belongs to the Korean minority.

1978,	Dec	Appointed member of the Commission for Inspecting Discipline under the CCP Central Committee
1979,	May	Appointed member of the State Nationalities Affairs Commission
	Jul	By-elected member of the Standing Committee of the 5th CPPCC

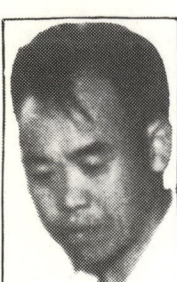

Wen Fushan (Wen Fu-shan)　温附山

Posts held

Provincial Administration
Vice-governor of Fujian Province

| 1959, | Jan | Identified as director of the Department |

of Finance and Commerce of Fujian Province CP

| 1978, | Oct | Identified as vice-chairman of the Revolutionary Committee of Fujian Province (until Dec 1979) |
| 1979, | Dec | Elected vice-governor of Fujian Province |

Wen Jiasi (Wen Chia-szu)　闻家驷

Posts held

Provincial Administration
Vice-chairman of the People's Congress of Beijing Municipality

Others
Member of the Standing Committee of the 5th CPPCC
Member of the Standing Committee, Central Committee of the Democratic League
Professor of Beijing University

Wen was born in 1900 in Hubei Province. He studied in the U.S.A. From about 1934 to 1937 he was head of the French Department of Beijing University. In 1943 he was a prominent cofounder of the Democratic League which elected him a member of its Central Committee in 1949.

1958,	Dec	Elected member of the Standing Committee, and secretary-general of the Central Committee of the Democratic League
1965,	Jan	Elected member of the Standing Committee of the 4th CPPCC
1967		Disappears during the Cultural Revolution
1972,	Oct	First appearance after the Cultural Revolution: Identified as holding his previous post as member of the Standing Committee of the CPPCC (confirmed in Mar 1978 by the 5th CPPCC)
1978,	Feb	Identified as a professor of Beijing University
1979,	Dec	Elected vice-chairman of the People's Congress of Beijing Municipality

Wen Minsheng (Wen Min-sheng)　文敏生

Posts held

CCP
Secretary of Heilongjiang Province CP
1st secretary of Harbin Municipality CP

Wen was born in 1910 in Henan Province. He is a graduate of Beijing University. During the Guangzhou Uprising in 1927 he was a platoon leader under Ye Jianying. During the Anti-Japanese War he served as political commissar of the 2nd Subdistrict in Henan-Hubei Military Region

| 1950, | Mar | Identified as secretary of Jianglin (Jingzhou) County CP, Hubei Province, and as deputy secretary-general of the Central-South China Military and Administrative Council (until Sep 1952) |
| 1952, | Jan | Identified as member of the Political and Legal Affairs Committee of Central-South China Military and Administrative Council (probably until 1954) |

Feb   Identified as deputy director of the Public Security Department of Central-South China Military and Administrative Council (until Jan 1953)

1954,   Feb   Identified as director of the Political Department of the Public Security Forces in Central-South China Military Region (until Jun 1954)

Oct   Identified as vice-chairman of the People's Government of Guangdong Province (until Feb 1955)

1955,   Jan   Appointed director of the Social Affairs Department of South China Subbureau, Central-South China Bureau of the CCP Central Committee (until Oct 1955)

Feb   Elected vice-governor of Guangdong Province (until 1956)

Oct   Identified as secretary of Guangdong Province CP (probably until May 1962)

1958,   Aug   Elected deputy for Guangdong Province to the 2nd NPC (until Dec 1964)

1962,   May   Identified as secretary of Henan Province CP (until Sep 1965)

1963,   Oct   Identified as governor of Henan Province

1964,   Sep   Elected deputy for Henan Province to the 3rd NPC

1965,   Sep   Identified as 2nd secretary of Henan Province CP

1967,   Oct   Branded as a counterrevolutionary revisionist and purged

1979,   Mar   First appearance after the Cultural Revolution: Identified as 1st secretary of Heilongjiang Province CP and as 1st secretary of Harbin Municipality CP

Dec   Head of a Harbin friendship delegation to Niigata, Japan

Wen Ning (Wen Ning)   溫 宁

Posts held

Government
Ambassador to Albania

1949   Identified as deputy director, Political Department of a PLA army corps

1950,   Dec   Identified as counselor at the embassy in Czechoslovakia (until Sep 1952)

1952,   Oct   Identified as deputy director of the USSR and Eastern Europe Department of the Ministry of Foreign Affairs (until 1954)

1954,   Jun   Identified as counselor at the embassy in Moscow (until 1959)

1979,   Apr   Appointed ambassador to Albania

Wen Xianglan (Wen Hsiang-lan) (f) 文 香 兰

Posts held

CCP
Alternate member of the CCP 11th Central Committee
Member of the Standing Committee of Henan Province CP

Mass Organization
Chairman of the Women's Federation of Henan Province

Wen was born in 1933 (1934?) in Lushan, Henan Province, as the daughter of poor peasants. In 1952 she became known as the head of an agricultural production cooperative in Lushan County.

1954   Wen joins the CCP

1955   Delegate at the National Congress of the Activists of Socialist Construction

1958,   Oct   Identified as chairman of Hezhuang People's Commune in Lushan County

Dec   Member of the Presidium, National Congress of Progressive Agricultural Work Groups

1968,   Jan   Elected member of the Standing Committee, Revolutionary Committee of Henan Province (until 1977?)

1969,   Apr   Elected to first term as alternate member of the CCP Central Committee by the 9th Party Congress; identified as chairman of the Revolutionary Committee of Hezhuang People's Commune

1973,   Apr   Identified as member of the Standing Committee of Henan Province CP

Sep   Elected chairman of the Women's Federation of Henan Province

Wen Yezhan (Wen Yeh-chan)   溫 北 湛

Posts held

Government
Deputy director of the Western Asia and Africa Department of the Ministry of Foreign Affairs

1959,   May   Identified as attaché at the embassy in Sudan (until 1961)

1973,   Jan   Identified as deputy director of the Africa Department of the Ministry of Foreign Affairs

1976,   Nov   Identified as deputy director of the Western Asia and Africa Department of the Ministry of Foreign Affairs

Weng Dujian (Weng Tu-chien)   翁 独 健

Posts held

Others
Vice-chairman of the Nationality Research Society
President of the Society of Mongolian History

1958   Identified as member of the State Nationalities Affairs Commission

1962,   Feb   Identified as professor at the 2nd Institute of History, Academy of Sciences

1979,   May   Elected vice-chairman of the Nationality Research Society

Aug   Elected president of the Society of Mongolian History

Publications

The History of the Yuan Dynasty

Wu Bo (Wu Po)

Posts held

CCP
Member of the Commission for Inspecting Discipline under the CCP Central Committee

Government
Minister of finance

Others
Member of the Standing Committee of the 5th CPPCC

In 1948 Wu served as deputy director of the Finance Department of North China People's Government.

1949,	Oct	Appointed director, General Office of the Ministry of Finance (until Sep 1954)
1952,	May	Appointed vice-minister of finance (until 1960)
1957,	May	Identified as supervisor of Public Affairs of the Bank of China
1960,	Dec	Identified as vice-president of the People's Bank
1961,	Dec	Identified as vice-minister of finance (until 1963)
1964,	Sep	Elected deputy for Anhui Province to the 3rd NPC
1967,	May	Branded as a counterrevolutionary revisionist
1975,	Sep	First appearance after the Cultural Revolution
1978,	Mar	Elected member of the Standing Committee of the 5th CPPCC
	Aug	Identified as cadre of the Ministry of Finance
	Dec	Appointed member of the Commission for Inspecting Discipline under the CCP Central Committee
1979,	Sep	Appointed minister of finance

Wu Chengqing (Wu Ch'eng-ch'ing)

Posts held

NPC
Member of the Standing Committee of the 5th NPC
Deputy for Guizhou Province to the 5th NPC

1975,	Jan	Elected member of the Standing Committee by the 4th NPC (confirmed in 1978 by the 5th NPC)
1978,	Feb	Elected deputy for Guizhou Province to the 5th NPC
	May	Identified as deputy director of the 2nd Engineering Bureau of the Ministry of Railways

Wu Dai (Wu Tai)

Posts held

Military
Major-general
Deputy political commissar of Beijing Military Region

Wu was born in Funing, Jiangsu Province. In 1933 he served in a Red Army unit as member of the Communist Youth League. In 1934 he was identified as political instructor of a company of the 2nd Front Army. In the following year he served in the Guard Company of the 1st Front Army. In 1940 he was head of the Political Department of the a regiment of the 115th Division, 8th Route Army. Later he served as political commissar of a regiment. In 1946 he was deputy director of the Political Department of the 1st Division, Democratic Joint Northeast Army. In 1948 he was appointed political commissar of the 1st Division, 1st Column, Northeast Field Army.

1950		Identified as director of the Political Department of the 38th Army
1951		Identified as deputy political commissar of the 38th Army
1953		Identified as political commissar of the 38th Army
1961,	Feb	Identified as major-general in the Lüda Area
1964,	Sep	Elected deputy for the PLA to the 3rd NPC
1965,	Dec	Appointed director of the Political Department of Beijing Military Region
1969,	Nov	Identified as deputy political commissar of Beijing Military Region
1971,	May	Elected 2nd secretary of Tianjin Municipality CP (until Aug 1977)
1974,	Apr	Identified as 1st vice-chairman of the Revolutionary Committee of Tianjin Municipality (until Nov 1977)
1975,	Oct	Deputy head of a friendship delegation to North Korea

Wu Daifeng (Wu Tai-feng)

Posts held

Others
Member of the Standing Committee of the 5th CPPCC

Wu was born in 1919. He obtained a doctorate in 1952 from Strasbourg University in France.

1974,	Jun	Identified as an historian; member of a delegation to Romania
1978,	Mar	Elected member of the Standing Committee of the 5th CPPCC

Wu Fushan (Wu Fu-shan)

Posts held

NPC
Deputy for the PLA to the 5th NPC

Military
Lieutenant-general
Deputy commander of the PLA Air Force

In 1936 Wu attended a course of the Red Army Worker-Peasants University. In the following year he served as political commissar of a regiment of the 129th Division, 8th Route Army. In 1947 he was political commissar of West Liaoning Military District, and in 1948 political

403 Wu Heng

commissar of the 7th Column, Northeast Field Army. In early 1949 he was identified as political commissar of the 44th Army, 4th Field Army.

1949,	Oct	Identified as deputy political commissar of Guangzhou Garrison
1950,	Mar	Appointed member of the People's Government of Guangzhou
1951,	Feb	Identified as deputy political commissar, Air Force Command of Central-South China Military Region
1954,	Jun	Appointed political commissar of the Air Force in Central-South China Military Region
	Sep	Appointed political commissar of the Air Force in Guangzhou Military Region
1955,	Sep	Promoted to rank of lieutenant-general
1958,	Feb	Identified as commander of the Air Force in Guangzhou Military Region
1967		Disappears during the Cultural Revolution
1973,	Oct	First appearance after the Cultural Revolution
1974,	Mar	Identified as deputy commander of Guangzhou Military Region (until 1975)
1977,	Apr	Identified as deputy commander of the PLA Air Force
	May	Deputy head of a military delegation to North Korea
	Jun	Conferred the Korean order "National Flag," 2nd class
1978,	Feb	Elected deputy for the PLA to the 5th NPC
1979,	Jun	Head of a delegation to the Aeronautics and Space Show at Le Bourget, France

Wu Guangtang (Wu Kuang-t'ang) 武光汤

Posts held

Provincial Administration
Vice-governor of Shanxi Province

Wu was born in 1915 in Shanxi Province. He graduated from Shanxi University. In 1937 he was magistrate of Yulin County in Shanxi Province. In 1940 he was magistrate of Wuxiang County in Shanxi Province and concurrently battalion commander of a Communist army unit. In 1943 Wu was appointed commissioner of the 3rd Taihang Administrative District. In June 1949 he was identified as director of the Agricultural Department of the People's Government of Shanxi Province.

1950,	Aug	Identified as director of the Agriculture and Forestry Department, People's Government of Shanxi Province (until 1952)
1955,	Feb	Elected vice-governor of Shanxi Province (until Cultural Revolution)
1966,	Jan	Identified as secretary of Shanxi Province CP (until Cultural Revolution)
1967,	Jan	Denounced as a capitalist reactionary and purged
1979,	Nov	First appearance after the Cultural Revolution
	Dec	Elected vice-governor of Shanxi Province

Wu Guixian (Wu Kuei-hsien) (f) 吴桂贤

Posts held

CCP
Member of the CCP 11th Central Committee

Wu was born circa 1937 as the daughter of poor peasants in Shaanxi Province. At the age of fourteen she was an apprentice at a cotton mill.

1963,	Jun	Identified as head of the CP cell of a work group at the state operated Northwest Cotton Mill No 1 in Xianyang, Shaanxi Province.
1964		Commended as an "activist in the study and application of Mao Zedong Thought" and named a model worker by the Ministry of Textile Industry
1966-1967		Active participation in the Cultural Revolution; elected a member of the Revolutionary Committee of a cotton mill in Xianyang
1968,	May	Article in RMRB: "Follow the Instructions of Mao Zedong and Set an Example of the Revolutionary Spirit of Promoting Production"
1969,	Apr	Elected member of the CCP Central Committee by the 9th Party Congress (confirmed in this post by the 10th Congress in 1973)
1970,	Jan	Article in the ideological journal HQ: "Fight to Defend the Revolutionary Line of Chairman Mao"
1971,	Mar	Elected deputy secretary of the new CP Secretariat of Shaanxi Province after the Cultural Revolution (until Jun 1973)
1972,	Apr	Member of a workers delegation to Albania
1973,	Jun	Identified as secretary of Shaanxi Province CP (until Jan 1975)
	Aug	Elected alternate member of the Politburo, CCP Central Committee by the 10th Party Congress (until Aug 1977)
1974,	Nov	Deputy head of a Party and government delegation to Albania
1975,	Jan	Elected one of twelve vice-premiers (only female) by the 4th NPC (until Feb 1978)
1977,	Sep	Wu disappears; probably purged

Wu Heng (Wu Heng) 武 衡

Posts held

Government
Vice-minister of the State Scientific and Technical Commission
Member of the Birth Planning Leading Group under the State Council

Others
Member of the Department of Geology and Geography, Academy of Sciences
Vice-president of the Stratigraphic Society

Wu joined the CCP as a student of geology at Qinghua University.

1953,	Feb	Member of a delegation of scientists to the USSR
1954,	Apr	Identified as deputy secretary-general of the Academy of Sciences (until Cultural Revolution)
1955,	May	Identified as member of the Department of Biology and Earth Sciences of the Academy of Sciences
1956,	Mar	Identified as deputy secretary-general of the State Scientific and Planning Commission (until 1957)
1958,	Nov	Identified as vice-chairman of the State Scientific and Technological Commission (until Cultural Revolution)
1959,	Nov	Identified as vice-chairman of the Committee on Terrestrial Stratification
1960,	Feb	Head of a scientific and technical delegation to the USSR
1961,	Apr	Deputy head of a scientific and technical delegation to the USSR
1962,	Jun	Head of a scientific and technical delegation to the USSR
1963,	Jul	Head of a scientific and technical delegation to North Vietnam
	Aug	Identified as vice-president of the Stratigraphy Society
1964,	Jun	Head of a government delegation to the 33rd Poznan International Fair in Poland
	Jul	Head of a scientific and technical delegation to the German Democratic Republic
	Dec	Head of a scientific and technical delegation to the United Arab Republic and to Algeria
1965,	Mar	Head of a scientific and technical delegation to Indonesia and Cambodia
	Jun	Head of a scientific and technical delegation to Moscow
	Dec	Head of a scientific and technical delegation to North Vietnam
1966,	Apr	Elected vice-chairman of the Association for Cultural Relations and Friendship with Foreign Countries
1967,	Feb	Branded as a counterrevolutionary revisionist and purged
1972,	Mar	First appearance after the Cultural Revolution: Named as a cadre of the State Council
1973,	May	Identified as a cadre of the Academy of Sciences
1978,	Mar	Identified as vice-minister of the State Scientific and Technical Commission
	Jul	Appointed member of the Birth Planning Leading Group under the State Council
	Dec	Head of a scientific and technical delegation to Japan
1979,	Jan	Identified as member of the Department of Geology and Geography of the Academy of Sciences
	Apr	Appointed president of the Recommendation and Examination Committee in charge of classifying inventions under the State Scientific and Technical Commission
	May	Wu visits the Federal Republic of Germany and Yugoslavia for talks on cooperation in patents
	Nov	Identified as vice-president of the Stratigraphic Society

Wu Hongbin (Wu Hung-ping, Ali) 吴鸿宾

Posts held

Provincial Administration
Vice-chairman of the People's Congress of Gansu Province

Others
Member of the Standing Committee of the 5th CPPCC

Wu belongs to the Hui minority; he was born in 1899 in Tianshui, Gansu Province. He graduated from Beijing University in 1930. When Shanghai was attacked by the Japanese in 1932 he joined the resistance movement. In 1935 he organized the Hui People Association against Japan and for National Salvation. He then became politicly active in Gansu Province. In 1945 he founded the Gansu Branch of the China Democratic League. In 1948 he became vice-chairman of the Lanzhou Military Control Commission and in the following year mayor of Lanzhou (until 1958). In September 1949 he took part in the 1st CPPCC as a delegate representing minorities; the Conference elected him a member of its Standing Committee (confirmed by the 2nd - 4th CPPCC).

1949,	Oct	Appointed member of the Nationalities Affairs Commission; member of the Chinese People's Committee for World Peace (until 1958) and council member of the Sino-Soviet Friendship Association
	Dec	Identified as member of the Northwest Military and Administrative Council
1953,	Jan	Appointed member of the Northwest Administrative Council
	May	Identified as vice-chairman of the Cultural Association of Chinese Hui People
1954,	Aug	Elected deputy for Gansu Province to the 1st NPC
	Dec	Identified as member of the People's Government of Gansu Province
1956,	Feb	Elected member of the Central Committee, China Democratic League (until 1958)
1958,	Sep	Identified as chairman of the Democratic League, Gansu Branch
	Oct	Identified as vice-chairman, Gansu Branch of the CPPCC
	Nov	Elected member of the Standing Committee of the China Democratic League
1964,	Oct	Elected deputy for Gansu Province to the 3rd NPC
1966		Disappears during the Cultural Revolution
1978,	Feb	First appearance after the Cultural Revolution
	Mar	Elected member of the Standing Committee of the 5th CPPCC
	Apr	Identified as a cadre of Gansu Province
1979,	Dec	Elected vice-chairman of the People's Congress of Gansu Province

Wu Hongxiang (Wu Hung-hsiang) 伍洪祥

Posts held

CCP
Secretary of Fujian Province CP

Provincial Administration
Vice-governor of Fujian Province

In 1934 Wu served in the 8th Independent Regiment of the Red Army in West Fujian.

1950, Oct Identified as council member of the People's Government of Fujian and as secretary of the New Democratic Youth League of Fujian Province
1954, Nov Identified as director of the Organization Department of Fujian Province CP
1955, Feb Elected member of the People's Council of Fujian Province
1956, Aug Identified as secretary of Fujian Province CP (until Cultural Revolution)
1968, Aug Elected vice-chairman of the newly established Revolutionary Committee of Fujian Province (until Dec 1979)
1976, Nov Identified as member of the Standing Committee of Fujian Province CP
1978, Oct Identified as secretary of Fujian Province CP
1979, Dec Elected vice-governor of Fujian Province

Wu Huanxing (Wu Huan-hsing) 吴桓兴

Posts held

NPC
Deputy for Beijing Municipality to the 5th NPC

Others
Member of the Standing Committee of the 5th CPPCC
Director of the Cancer Institute of the Academy of Sciences
Director of the Tumor Hospital of the Academy of Medical Sciences
Member of the Executive Committee of the International Union against Cancer

Wu is a returned overseas Chinese from Mauritius. He is a wellknown specialist for oncology and radiology and has contributed to knowledge on the prevention and treatment of cancer.

1953, Jul Identified as director of the Shanghai Radium-Therapy Sanatorium; Wu attends the International Medical Conference in Vienna
1954, Aug Elected deputy for the overseas Chinese to the 1st NPC (reelected in 1958 and 1964 to the 2nd and 3rd NPCs)
1957, Sep Identified as director of the Cancer Hospital of the Academy of Medical Sciences
      Oct Member of a delegation to the International Medical Conference in France
1967   Wu disappears
1972, Jun First appearance after the Cultural Revolution

1973, Apr Member of a delegation of the Sino-Japanese Friendship Association to Japan
1978, Feb Elected deputy for Beijing Municipality to the 5th NPC
      Mar Elected member of the Standing Committee of the 5th CPPCC
      Apr Head of a cancer study group to the U.S.A.
      May Identified as director of the Cancer Institute of the Academy of Sciences; identified as director of the Tumor Hospital of the Academy of Medical Sciences
      Jun Wu visits Great Britain and France; awarded honorary fellowship by the Royal College of Radiologists of Great Britain
      Oct Head of a delegation to the 12th International Congress on Cancer in Buenos Aires; elected member of the Executive Committee of the International Union against Cancer

Wu Huojin (Wu Huo-chin)  吴火金

Posts held

CCP
Alternate member of the CCP 11th Central Committee
Secretary, CP of Longjiao Brigade, Wu County, Jiangsu Province

1977, Aug Elected alternate member of the CCP Central Committee by the 11th Party Congress
1979, Jan Identified as secretary, CP of Longjiao Brigade, Wu County, Jiangsu Province

Wu Jieping (Wu Chieh-p'ing) 吴阶平

Posts held

Others
Vice-president of the Academy of Medical Sciences
Vice-president of the Medical Society

1960, Jun Identified as professor of Beijing University
1962   Wu treats the Indonesian Head of State Sukarno in Jakarta for a kidney disease
1966, Mar Appointed director of the 2nd Medical College in Beijing
1976, Jan Listed among those present at the mourning ceremonies for Zhou Enlai in the first place under "medical personnel"
      Apr Head of a delegation to the 29th World Health Organization Conference in Geneva
1978, Jun Identified as vice-president of the Medical Society
      Jul Identified as vice-president of the Academy of Medical Sciences
1979, Apr Wu performs a kidney transplantation at Beijing Friendship Hospital
      May Secretary-general of a medical delegation, led by Huang Jiasi, to the U.S.A.

Wu Jinghua (Wu Ching-hua) 伍精华

Posts held

Government
Vice-minister of the State Nationalities
Affairs Commission

Provincial Administration
Vice-chairman of the People's Congress of
Sichuan Province

Wu belongs to the Yi minority.

1975,	Mar	Identified as deputy to the 4th NPC
1979,	May	Identified as vice-minister of the State Nationalities Affairs Commission
	Dec	Elected vice-chairman of the People's Congress of Sichuan Province

Wu Jinquan (Wu Chin-ch'üan) 吴金全

Posts held

CCP
Alternate member of the CCP 11th Central Committee

Mass Organization
Vice-chairman of the Trade Union of
Sichuan Province

Wu became known as a 1st class model worker in agriculture of the Independent 3rd Team in Huaiyang County, Henan Province.

1952,	Jan	Participant at the 1st Henan Conference of Model Workers in Agriculture
1968		Identified as "activist in the study of Mao Zedong Thought"
1969,	Apr	Elected alternate member of the CCP Central Committee by the 9th Party Congress (confirmed in 1973 and 1977 by the 10th and 11th Congresses)
1974,	Jun	Identified as vice-chairman of the Trade Union of Sichuan Province

Wu Juenong (Wu Chüeh-nung) 吴觉农

Posts held

Others
Member of the Standing Committee of the
5th CPPCC

In September 1949 Wu took part in the session of the 1st CPPCC.

1949,	Oct	Appointed vice-minister of agriculture (until Sep 1954)
1950,	Mar	Identified as member of the Federation of National Science Workers (until 1958)
1951,	Jun	Identified as member of the Standing Committee, China Democratic National Construction Association (until Cultural Revolution)
	Oct	Identified as council member of the Sino-Soviet Friendship Association; member of a delegation to the Conference for Promoting East-West Trade in Copenhagen

1954,	Dec	As delegate representing the China Democratic National Construction Association, elected a member of the 2nd CPPCC (reelected in 1959 and 1964 to the 3rd and 4th CPPCCs)
1955,	Jun	Identified as vice-chairman of the Organization Committee of China Democratic National Construction Commission (until Cultural Revolution)
1957		Identified as vice-president of the Agricultural Society
1967,	Jun	Branded as a black element and purged
1976,	Nov	First appearance after the Cultural Revolution
1978,	Mar	Elected member of the Standing Committee of the 5th CPPCC

Wu Kaizhang (Wu K'ai-chang) 武开章

Posts held

CCP
Secretary of Shandong Province CP

1959,	Jul	Identified as secretary of Xinjiang Province CP
1977,	Dec	Elected vice-chairman of the Revolutionary Committee of Shandong Province (until Dec 1979)
1978,	Apr	Identified as secretary of Shandong Province CP

Wu Kehua (Wu K'e-hua) 吴克华

Posts held

CCP
Alternate member of the CCP 11th Central Committee

NPC
Deputy for the PLA to the 5th NPC

Military
Lieutenant-general
Commander of Guangzhou Military Region

Wu was born circa 1910. After an apprenticeship as a carpenter he enrolled at Xinjiang Military and Political School in 1929. In 1934-35 he took part in the Long March. He was sent to the USSR for further military training in 1935. In 1938 he served as staff officer in the 115th Division of the 8th Route Army. In 1940 he commanded a regiment of the Shandong Column. In 1945 he was commander of the 5th Brigade, Shandong Column. He was appointed commander of the 5th Division of the Shandong Field Army in 1943. In 1946 he commanded the 4th Column of Liaodong Military District. In 1949 he became commander of the 41st Army, 4th Field Army.

| 1950, | Mar | Appointed council member of the People's Government of Guangdong and commander of the South Bank of East River Pacification Command in Guangdong |
| 1951 | | Identified as commander of the 15th Corps, 4th Field Army, and as chief of staff of South China Military Region |

1953		Service in Korea as deputy commander of the 13th Corps, Chinese People's Volunteers
1954		Identified as chief of staff of the Air Force in Central-South China Military Region
1955,	Sep	Promoted to rank of lieutenant-general
1958,	Jun	Identified as deputy commander of Jinan Military Region (until May 1965)
1964,	Sep	Elected deputy for the PLA to the 3rd NPC
1965,	Jan	Appointed member of the National Defense Council (until Cultural Revolution)
	Jun	Identified as commander of the PLA Artillery Corps (until Cultural Revolution)
1967,	Aug	Criticized as a "three-anti element" and disappears
1974,	Jul	First appearance after the Cultural Revolution
1977,	Aug	Elected alternate member of the CCP Central Committee by the 11th Party Congress
	Oct	Identified as commander of Chengdu Military Region (until Feb 1979)
1978,	Feb	Elected deputy for the PLA to the 5th NPC
1979,	Jun	Identified as commander of Xinjiang Military Region (until Jan 1980)
1980,	Feb	Identified as commander of Guangzhou Military Region

Wu Lanting (Wu Lan-t'ing)　乌兰亭

Posts held

Military
Deputy commander of Wuhan Military Region

1970,	Feb	Identified as deputy commander of Anhui Military District
1979,	Aug	Identified as deputy commander of Wuhan Military Region

Wu Lengxi (Wu Leng-hsi)　吴冷西

Posts held

CCP
Alternate member of the CCP 11th Central Committee

NPC
Member of the Standing Committee of the 5th NPC
Deputy for Shanghai Municipality to the 5th NPC

Wu was born in 1909 in Jiangxi Province. He studied at Wuhan University and at the Lu Xun Academy of Arts. In 1937 he worked in the Marxist-Leninist Library in Yan'an as well as in the publishing sector. Shortly afterwards he was transferred to the Chang Jiang CP Bureau of the Central Plains Military District where he was temporarily deputy chief editor of the Paper of 7 July. In 1948 he served as deputy director of the Propaganda Department of Central Plains Military District. In summer 1949 he was one of the founding members of the Journalist Association.

1949,	Oct	Appointed chief editor of NCNA (until Dec 1950)
1950,	Apr	Appointed deputy director of NCNA (until Dec 1952)
1952,	Dec	Appointed director of NCNA (until Cultural Revolution)
1954,	Apr	Member of the Chinese delegation to the Geneva Indochina Conference
	May	Elected council member of the newly established Association for Cultural Relations with Foreign Countries; identified as member of the Commission for Cultural Relations with Foreign Countries
	Sep	Elected deputy for Tianjin Municipality to the 1st NPC (until Mar 1959); elected vice-chairman and secretary-general of the Journalist Association (until Mar 1960)
1958,	Dec	Identified as chief editor of RMRB (until Cultural Revolution)
1959,	Mar	Elected deputy for Guangdong Province to the 2nd NPC (reelected in 1964 to the 3rd NPC)
1960,	Mar	Elected vice-chairman of the newly established Sino-Latin-American Friendship Association; elected chairman of the Journalist Association (until Cultural Revolution)
1961,	May	Member of the Chinese delegation to the Laos Conference in Geneva
1963,	Oct	Head of a RMRB delegation to North Korea
1964,	Feb	Head of a RMRB delegation to North Vietnam
	Sep	Identified as deputy director, Propaganda Department of the CCP Central Committee (until Cultural Revolution)
1965,	Jan	Elected member of the Standing Committee of the NPC (until Cultural Revolution)
1966		With all other cadres in the culture and propaganda field, Wu is an early victim of the Cultural Revolution
1972,	Sep	First appearance after the Cultural Revolution: Named in his former post as member of the Standing Committee of the NPC
1977,	Aug	Elected alternate member of the CCP Central Committee by the 11th Party Congress
1978,	Feb	Elected deputy for Shanghai Municipality to the 5th NPC
	Mar	Elected member of the Standing Committee of the 5th NPC
1979,	Jun	Member of the Draft Laws Committee at the 2nd Session of the 5th NPC

Wu Liangping (Wu Liang-p'ing)　吴亮平

Posts held

Others
Member of the Standing Committee of the 5th CPPCC

Wu was born in 1906 in Fenghua County, Zhejiang Province, as the son of a merchant. He attended Qinji Elementary School in Fenghua (Chiang Kai-shek's former school), Nanyang Middle School in Shanghai, and eventually Amoy University and Daxia University in Shanghai. In 1925 he became a member of the Communist Youth League and was involved in anti-Japanese activities after the May 30 Incident. In late 1925 he went to Moscow to study at the Sun Yat-sen University. Before he returned to China in 1929 he traveled through Germany, France, Belgium, and England. He then worked underground in Shanghai and translated three Marxist works: History of Socialism, Anti-Dühring, and The Materialistic Interpretation of History and Dialecticism. In 1931 he was temporarily imprisoned by the Nationalist Government. He then went to the Jiangxi Soviet to lecture at the Red Army College in Ruijin. During the Long March he served in the Political Department of the 1st Front Army. In 1936 he became director of the Propaganda Department of the CCP Central Committee. He was concurrently lecturer at the Anti-Japan Military and Political Academy and interpreter for Mao Zedong.

1952		Identified as alternate secretary of Shanghai Municipality CP and as a cadre of the East China Bureau of the CCP Central Committee
1958,	Mar	Identified as vice-minister of chemical industry (until Dec 1963)
1963,	Nov	Identified as member of the State Economic Commission (until Cultural Revolution)
1967,	May	Branded as a counterrevolutionary revisionist and purged
1973,	Oct	First appearance after the Cultural Revolution
1978,	Mar	Elected member of the Standing Committee of the 5th CPPCC

Wu Maosun (Wu Mao-sun)

吴茂荪

Posts held

Government
Advisor to the Institute of Foreign Affairs

Others
Member of the Standing Committee of the 5th CPPCC
Vice-chairman of the Central Committee, Revolutionary Committee of the Chinese KMT

Wu was born in 1911 in Anhui Province. After graduating from the National Central University he worked for the Nationalist Government. From 1937 to 1945 he served as council member of the Chongqing Municipal Government. From 1946 to 1948 he studied law at Columbia University in New York. He subsequently went to Hong Kong where he joined the KMT Revolutionary Committee, from 1949 as a Central Committee member. He took part in the 1st CPPCC in September 1949 as a delegate representing the Society of Comrades of the Three People's Principles.

1949,	Dec	Identified as secretary-general of the Chinese People's Diplomacy Society
1950,	Apr	Identified as deputy director, Organization Department of the KMT Revolutionary Committee
	Oct	Identified as deputy secretary-general of the Committee for Defense of World Peace (until 1958)
1952,	Jun	Identified as council member of the Sino-Soviet Friendship Association
1953,	Jun	Elected member of the Standing Committee of the Youth Federation
1954,	May	Identified as council member of the Association for Cultural Relations with Foreign Countries
	Dec	Elected member of the 2nd CPPCC
1956,	Feb	Elected member of the Standing Committee, KMT Revolutionary Committee
1958,	Jul	Identified as member of the Standing Committee, Committee for World Peace; member of a delegation to the Conference on Disarmament and International Cooperation in Stockholm
	Oct	Elected deputy for Anhui Province to the 2nd NPC (reelected in 1964 to the 3rd NPC)
1960,	Apr	Elected council member of the Sino-African Friendship Association
1961,	Oct	Identified as member of the Executive Committee, China Red Cross Society
1963,	Aug	Identified as council member of the Sino-Afghanistan Friendship Association
1964,	Dec	Identified as vice-president of the Institute of Foreign Affairs
1965,	Mar	Member of a NPC delegation led by Liu Ningyi to Africa
1967		Disappears during the Cultural Revolution
1972,	Sep	First appearance after the Cultural Revolution: Named as a member of the Standing Committee, Revolutionary Committee of the KMT
1978,	Mar	Elected member of the Standing Committee of the 5th CPPCC
	Jul	Identified as advisor to the Institute of Foreign Affairs
1979,	Oct	Elected vice-chairman of the Central Committee, Revolutionary Committee of the Chinese KMT

Wu Nansheng (Wu Nan-sheng)

吴南生

Posts held

CCP
Secretary of Guangdong Province CP

1949,	Oct	Identified as vice-chairman of the Shantou Military Control Commission
1953,	Mar	Identified as director, Propaganda Department of the CCP Hainan District Committee
1955,	Jan	Identified as deputy secretary of the CCP Hainan District Committee
1957		Identified as deputy director, Propaganda Department of Guangdong Province CP
1961,	Apr	Identified as deputy secretary-general, Central-South Bureau of the CCP Central Committee
1967,	Jan	Branded as a capitalist-roader and purged
1977,	Oct	First appearance after the Cultural Revolution: Identified as deputy secretary of Guangdong Province CP
1978,	Apr	Identified as secretary of Guangdong Province CP

Wu Qingtong (Wu Ch'ing-t'ung) 伍庆彤

Posts held

Government
Director of the General Office of the State Council
Deputy secretary-general of the State Council

Wu was born in 1924 in Hebei Province.

1970,	Oct	Identified as a cadre of the State Council
1977,	Jul	Identified as director of the General Office of the State Council
1978,	Aug	Member of a government delegation led by Geng Biao to Trinidad and Tobago, Jamaica, and Guyana
1979,	Apr	Identified as deputy secretary-general of the State Council

Wu Quanheng (Wu Ch'üan-heng) (f) 吴全衡

Posts held

Mass Organization
Secretary of the Women's Federation

1961,	Jan	Identified as secretary of the Women's League (until Cultural Revolution)
	May	Member of a women's delegation to Tunisia
1962,	Jan	Member of a women's delegation to Mali
	Jul	Member of a delegation to the session of the World Peace Council in Moscow
	Nov	Head of a women's delegation to the session of the International Women's Federation in East Berlin
1963,	Jan	Head of a women's delegation to the Pan-American Women's Congress in Cuba
	Jun	Deputy head of a delegation to the Congress of the International Women's Federation in Moscow
	Oct	Head of a women's delegation to Algeria
1964,	Oct	Elected deputy for Sichuan Province to the 3rd NPC
1965,	Mar	Head of a women's delegation to Austria
1966,	Apr	Elected vice-chairman of the Association for Cultural Relations and Friendship with Foreign Countries
1967		Disappears during the Cultural Revolution
1978,	May	First appearance after the Cultural Revolution: Named as a cadre of the Women's Federation
	Sep	Elected secretary of the Women's Federation
1979,	Apr	Deputy head of a women's delegation to Yugoslavia

Wu Quanqing (Wu Ch'üan-ch'ing) 吴全清

Posts held

CCP
Member of the 11th CCP Central Committee

Wu became known as head of the "iron drill team" of Daqing Oil Field.

1977,	Aug	Elected member of the CCP Central Committee by the 11th Party Congress
1978,	Feb	Identified as chairman of the Revolutionary Committee of Daqing Oil Field

Wu Ruishan (Wu Jui-shan) 吴瑞山

Posts held

Military
Major-general
Deputy commander of Wuhan Military Region

Wu was born in 1910 in Anhui Province. In 1945 he commanded a regiment of the Northeast Field Army. In 1949 he was appointed deputy commander of the 135th Division, 45th Corps, 4th Field Army.

1949,	Dec	Appointed commander of the 135th Division of the 45th Corps
1951,	Mar	The 45th Corps is renamed 54th Corps; Wu serves as chief of staff of this unit with the Chinese People's Volunteers in Korea
1954?		Appointed deputy commander of the 54th Corps
1955,	Sep	Promoted to rank of major-general
1958,	Mar	Conferred the North Korean order of "Liberation"
1960		Identified as commander of the 54th Corps
1964		Identified as commander of Jiangxi Military District (until Aug 1967)
1967		Accused during the Cultural Revolution of supporting the anti-Mao faction; relieved of his posts
1970,	May	Identified as deputy commander of Fuzhou Military Region (until about 1972)
1974,	Jan	Identified as deputy commander of Wuhan Military Region

Wu Shaowen (Wu Shao-wen) 吴绍文

Posts held

Government
Vice-minister of the Ministry of Agricultural Machinery

NPC
Deputy for Sichuan Province to the 5th NPC

Others
Manager of the Agricultural Mechanization Service

1978,	Feb	Elected deputy for Sichuan Province to the 5th NPC
1979,	Oct	Identified as vice-minister of the Ministry of Agricultural Machinery and as manager of the Agricultural Mechanization Service

Wu Shaozu (Wu Shao-tsu) 伍紹祖

Posts held

Others
Chairman of the Students Federation

1965, Jan Elected chairman of the Students Federation

Dec By-elected deputy for Guangdong Province to the 3rd NPC

1967 Disappears during the Cultural Revolution

1979, Jan First appearance after the Cultural Revolution: Identified in his former post as chairman of the Students Federation

Oct Head of a youth delegation to Colombia

Wu Shengmin (Wu Sheng-min) 吳生紋

Posts held

Provincial Administration
Vice-governor of Yunnan Province

1979, Dec Elected vice-governor of Yunnan Province

Wu Shengrong (Wu Sheng-jung) 伍生榮

Posts held

CCP
Secretary of Qinghai Province CP

NPC
Deputy for the PLA to the 5th NPC

Military
Major-general
Deputy commander of, Lanzhou Military Region
Commander of Qinghai Military District

Provincial Administration
Vice-chairman of the Qinghai Province People's Congress

In 1938 Wu was commander of a battalion, later a regiment, of the 1st Training Brigade, 115th Division, 8th Route Army. In 1949 he served as deputy commander of the 16th Division, 6th Corps, 1st Field Army.

1949, Oct Appointed commander of the 16th Division

1952? Training at the Military Academy of the PLA

1955, Sep Promoted to rank of major-general; identified as deputy chief of staff of Lanzhou Military Region

1960 Identified as chief of staff of Lanzhou Military Region

1975, Feb Identified as deputy commander of Lanzhou Military Region

1977, Jul Identified as commander of Qinghai Military District

1978, Feb Elected deputy for the PLA to the 5th NPC

May Identified as secretary of Qinghai Province CP

1979, Sep Elected vice-chairman of the Standing Committee, Qinghai Province People's Congress

Wu Shihong (Wu Shih-hung) 吳仕宏

Posts held

Military
Major-general
Deputy commander of Nanjing Military Region

During the Anti-Japanese War Wu served successively as battalion commander in the 396th Brigade of the 8th Route Army and commander of the Guards Regiment of the Taiyue Column and commander of the 12th Brigade. In 1947 he became chief of staff and deputy commander of the 23rd Brigade, 8th Column, under the Shaanxi-Hebei-Shandong Field Army. In April 1949 he took over the 179th Division, 60th Army, under the 2nd Field Army.

1950, Mar Identified as commander of the Mao County Military Subdistrict of the West Sichuan Military District

1951-1953 Wu takes part in the Korean War

1955, Sep Appointed major-general and deputy commander of the 60th Army

1956 Wu returns to Nanjing from North Korea

1966, Feb Identified as commander of the 6th Army stationed in Nanjing

1969-1978 Wu was referred to as a leading military cadre of Nanjing Military Region on numerous occasions

1979, Apr Identified as deputy commander of Nanjing Military Region

Wu Su (Wu Su) 吳肅

Posts held

Provincial Administration
Vice-chairman of the People's Congress of Guizhou Province

1958, Oct Identified as secretary of Guizhou Province CP (until Cultural Revolution)

1965, Feb Identified as vice-chairman of the Preparatory Committee for the Association of Poor and Lower-Middle Peasants

1967 Disappears during the Cultural Revolution

1977, Dec First appearance after the Cultural Revolution: Elected vice-chairman of the Revolutionary Committee of Guizhou (until Dec 1979)

1980, Jan Elected vice-chairman of the People's Congress of Guizhou Province

Wu Wenjun (Wu Wen-chün) 吳文俊

Posts held

Others
Member of the Standing Committee of the 5th CPPCC
Research fellow of the Institute of Mathematics, Academy of Sciences

1950		Wu returns from the U.S.A.
1964		Identified as deputy director of the Institute of Mathematics, Academy of Sciences
1978,	Mar	Elected member of the Standing Committee of the 5th CPPCC
	Jul	Identified as research fellow of the Institute of Mathematics, Academy of Sciences
1979,	Jan	Three months study tour to the U.S.A. at the invitation of the Princeton Institute for Advanced Studies

Wu Xianen (Wu Hsien-en)　　吴先恩

Posts held

Military
Lieutenant-general
Deputy commander of Beijing Military Region

Wu is born in Hong'an (Huang'an) County, Hubei Province. In the late twenties he was leader of a small guerrilla unit operating near Hong'an in the Soviet area of Hubei-Henan-Anhui. He took part in the Long March of 1934-35 as a member of the 4th Front Army. In 1947 he served as deputy director of the Logistics Department in Shanxi-Chahar-Hebei Military District.

1950,	Sep	Appointed director of the Logistics Department of Hubei Military District; council member of the People's Government of Hubei Province and director of its Finance Department
1951		Identified as deputy director of the Logistics Department, Chinese People's Volunteers in Korea
1955,	Sep	Promoted to rank of lieutenant-general; conferred the orders "1st August" and "Liberation," both 1st class
1957		Identified as director of the Logistics Department of Beijing Military Region
1966,	Oct	Identified as deputy commander of Beijing Military Region

Wu Xianfeng (Wu Hsien-feng)　　吴先锋

Posts held

NPC
Member of the Standing Committee of the 5th NPC
Deputy for Guangdong Province to the 5th NPC

1975,	Jan	Elected member of the Standing Committee of the 4th NPC (confirmed in 1978 by the 5th NPC)
1978,	Feb	Elected deputy for Guangdong Province to the 5th NPC

Wu Xiangbi (Wu Hsiang-pi)　　吴向必

Posts held

CCP
Alternate member of the CCP 11th Central Committee
Secretary of Guizhou Province CP

Wu belongs to the Miao minority. Before the foundation of PRC he was a herdsman.

1973,	Aug	Elected to first term as alternate member of the CCP Central Committee by the 10th Party Congress
1974,	Feb	Identified as secretary of Guizhou Province CP

Wu Xianwen (Wu Hsien-wen)　　吴献文

Posts held

Others
Member of the Standing Committee of the 5th CPPCC

Before 1949 Wu worked as a researcher at the Institute of Zoology, Academia Sinica.

1950,	Jun	Identified as deputy director of the Institute of Hydrobiology of the Academy of Sciences
1955,	May	Identified as member of the Department of Biology and Earth Sciences of the Academy of Sciences
1956,	Feb	Identified as member of the Central Committee of the Jiusan Society
1959,	Apr	Elected member of the 3rd CPPCC (confirmed in 1964 by the 4th CPPCC)
1963,	Dec	Identified as vice-president of the Society of Aquatic Products
1965,	Jan	Elected member of the Standing Committee of the 4th CPPCC
	May	Identified as director of the Institute of Limnology, Academy of Sciences
1967		Disappears during the Cultural Revolution
1978,	Feb	First appearance after the Cultural Revolution
	Mar	Elected member of the Standing Committee of the 5th CPPCC

Wu Xiaoda (Wu Hsiao-ta)　　吴晓达

Posts held

Government
Consul general at Houston, U.S.A.

1959,	Jul	Identified as deputy secretary-general of the Institute of Foreign Affairs
1964,	Feb	Identified as counselor at the embassy in Kenya
1969,	Dec	Identified as a cadre of the Association for Cultural Relations and Friendship with Foreign Countries
1974,	Aug	Identified as chargé d'affaires ad interim in Guinea (until 1976)

1977,	May	Representative of PRC at the UN Seabed Conference in New York
	Sep	Alternate representative of PRC at the 32nd UN General Assembly
1978,	Sep	Alternate representative of PRC at the 33rd UN General Assembly
1979,	Apr	Representative at the Preparatory Committee for a New International Development Strategy
	Oct	Appointed consul general at Houston, U.S.A.

Wu Xihai (Wu Hsi-hai) 吴希海

Posts held

Provincial Administration
Vice-governor of Sichuan Province

1977,	Dec	Elected vice-chairman of the Revolutionary Committee of Sichuan Province (until Dec 1979)
1978,	May	Member of an economic delegation led by Gu Ming to Great Britain and France
1979,	Dec	Elected vice-governor of Sichuan Province

Wu Xinyu (Wu Hsin-yü) 武新宇

Posts held

NPC
Member of the Standing Committee and deputy secretary-general of the 5th NPC
Vice-chairman and secretary-general of the NPC Legal Commission
Deputy for Shanxi Province to the 5th NPC

Wu was born in 1902 (1905?) in Shi County, Shanxi Province. After graduating from Beijing Teachers College he continued his studies in Japan. Having returned to China he became head of a middle school in Taiyuan and later taught at a Beijing school. After the outbreak of the Anti-Japanese War he returned to Shanxi to serve as director of the Political Department of the 8th Training Regiment of the New Shanxi Army. In 1939 he joined the Communists who initially appointed him deputy director of the North Shanxi Administrative Office. Until the Communists came to power he held various similar administrative posts in North China. In September 1949 he took part in the 1st CPPCC.

1949,	Oct	Appointed vice-minister of civil affairs (until Dec 1953) and director of the Department of Social Affairs in that ministry
1954,	Aug	Elected deputy for Shanxi Province to the 1st NPC (reelected in 1958 and 1964 to the 2nd and 3rd NPCs)
	Sep	Appointed member of the Legislative Council of the NPC (until Apr 1959)
1956,	Nov	Member of an NPC delegation led by Peng Zhen to the USSR, Czechoslovakia, and Romania (until Jan 1957)

1959,	Apr	Elected member of the Standing Committee of the 2nd NPC (reelected in Jan 1965 and Jan 1975 by the 3rd and 4th NPCs)
1961,	Dec	Head of a friendship delegation to Cuba
1962,	Sep	Appointed deputy secretary-general of the 2nd NPC (confirmed in this post in Jan 1965 and Mar 1975 by the 3rd and 4th NPCs)
1964,	Oct	Elected vice-chairman of the Committee of Political and Legal Affairs (until Cultural Revolution)
1967		Disappears during the Cultural Revolution
1972,	Sep	First appearance after the Cultural Revolution
1975,	Jan	Elected member of the Standing Committee of the 4th NPC (confirmed in Mar 1978 by the 5th NPC)
	Mar	Appointed deputy secretary-general of the NPC (confirmed in Mar 1978 by the 5th NPC)
1978,	Feb	Elected deputy for Shanxi Province to the 5th NPC
1979,	Feb	Appointed vice-chairman of the Legal Commission under the NPC
	Jun	Vice-chairman of the Draft Laws Committee and member of the Credentials Committee at the 2nd Session of the 5th NPC
	Nov	Appointed secretary-general of the NPC Standing Committee's Legal Commission

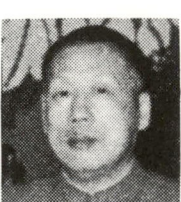

Wu Xiuquan (Wu Hsiu-ch'üan) 伍修权

Posts held

CCP
Member of the CCP 11th Central Committee

Military
Deputy chief of PLA General Staff

Others
President of the Armymen's Association

Wu was born in 1908 in Wuchang, Hubei Province. He became an active leader of the student movement already as a student at middle school in his native town. Circa 1926 he went for five years to the USSR to study political and military science at Sun Yat-sen University. After his return to China he lectured in political science at the Fudan University in Shanghai. In 1932 he was a staff member of the Red Army Headquarters and also lectured at the Red Army University. In 1934 he was deputy chief of staff of the 3rd Army Corps in which he served during the Long March. In 1936 he became head of the Foreign Affairs Department of the CCP Central Committee. In 1945 he was one of the cadres who were transferred to Manchuria with Lin Biao. After the occupation of Shenyang by Communist forces in November 1948 Wu was appointed chairman of the Shenyang Military Control Commission. In August 1949 he was appointed a member of the newly established People's Government of Northeast China.

1949,	Oct	Appointed director of the USSR and Eastern Europe Department of the Ministry of Foreign Affairs (until Aug 1952)
1950,	Jan	Member of a delegation led by Zhou Enlai to Moscow
	Nov	At the UN Security Council Wu accuses the U.S.A. of armed aggression in Taiwan and armed intervention in Korea
1951		Appointed vice-minister of foreign affairs (until Mar 1955)
1953,	Mar	Member of the Chinese delegation attending the funeral of Stalin in Moscow
1954,	Sep	Elected deputy for Sichuan Province to the 1st NPC (until Mar 1959)
1955,	Mar	Appointed ambassador to Yugoslavia (until Sep 1958)
1956,	Sep	Elected member of the CCP Central Committee by the 8th Party Congress (until Cultural Revolution)
1959,	Mar	Identified as director of the International Liaison Department of the CCP Central Committee; member of a Party delegation to Poland and Great Britain
1960,	Jun	Member of a CCP delegation to Romania
	Sep	Member of a CCP delegation to Cuba
1961,	May	Member of a CCP delegation to France
	Sep	Member of a CCP delegation to North Korea
1962,	Nov	Head of a CCP delegation to the 8th Congress of CP Bulgaria in Sofia and to the 8th Congress of CP Hungary in Budapest
	Dec	Head of a CCP delegation to Czechoslovakia
1963,	Jan	Head of a CCP delegation to the 6th Congress of the Socialist Unity Party in East Berlin
	Jul	Member of a CCP delegation led by Deng Xiaoping for ideological talks in Moscow
	Sep	Member of a delegation led by Liu Shaoqi on a state visit to North Korea
1964,	Nov	Member of a CCP delegation led by Zhou Enlai to participate in the Moscow celebrations of the 47th anniversary of the October Revolution; member of a Party and government delegation to Albania
1965,	Jan	Elected member of the Standing Committee of the CPPCC (until Cultural Revolution)
	Jul	Member of a CCP delegation to Romania
1967		Branded during the Cultural Revolution as a counterrevolutionary; subsequently disappears
1974,	Sep	First appearance after the Cultural Revolution
1975,	Jan	Elected member of the Standing Committee by the 4th NPC (until Feb 1978)
	May	Identified as deputy chief of PLA General Staff
1977,	Jun	Head of a delegation of PLA veterans to Yugoslavia
	Aug	Elected member of the CCP Central Committee by the 11th Party Congress
1978,	Nov	Head of a military goodwill delegation to the Philippines and Burma
1979,	Jun	Identified as president of the Armymen's Association

Wu is married to Xu He.

Wu Xueqian (Wu Hsüeh-ch'ien) (f) 吴学谦

Posts held

CCP
Deputy director of the International Liaison Department of the CCP Central Committee

In 1949 Wu was deputy director of the International Liaison Department of the New Democratic Youth League.

1952,	Nov	Head of a youth delegation to Indonesia
1953,	Jun	Identified as director of the International Liaison Department of the Federation of Democratic Youth
	Jul	Elected member of the Central Committee of the New Democratic Youth League; secretary-general of the Chinese delegation to the 3rd Conference, World Federation of Democratic Youth in Bucharest
1954,	May	Identified as council member of the Association for Cultural Relations with Foreign Countries (until Cultural Revolution)
	Dec	Head of a youth delegation to Vienna
1955,	Jul	Head of a youth delegation to Poland
	Nov	Head of a youth delegation to Belgium and France (until Jan 1956)
1957,	May	Elected member of the Standing Committee of the Communist Youth League (successor of the New Democratic Youth League) (until Jul 1964)
	Jul	Secretary-general of a delegation to the 6th Festival of the World Federation of Democratic Youth in Moscow
	Sep	Identified as member of the Executive Committee of the Democratic Women's Federation
1958,	Feb	Head of a youth delegation to Cairo
	Apr	Elected vice-chairman of the Federation of Democratic Youth (until 1964)
1960,	Apr	Appointed council member of the Sino-African Friendship Association; member of a delegation to the 2nd Afro-Asian People's Conference in Conakry, Guinea
1961,	Jan	Identified as member of the Sino-Afro-Asian Solidarity Committee
	Mar	Observer of the 3rd All-African People's Conference in Cairo
1962,	Jul	Member of a delegation to the Conference on Disarmament and World Peace in Moscow
1963,	Jan	Member of a delegation to the Afro-Asian Conference in Zanzibar
1964,	Jul	Member of a delegation to the 10th World Conference against Atomic Bombs in Japan
	Sep	Elected deputy for Anhui Province to the 3rd NPC
	Dec	Appointed council member of the People's Institute of Foreign Affairs
1965,	May	Member of a delegation to the Afro-Asian Conference in Accra, Ghana
	Jul	Elected vice-chairman of the Sino-Afro-Asian Solidarity Committee (until Cultural Revolution)
1967		Disappears during the Cultural Revolution

1978,   Feb   First appearance after the Cultural Revolution: Appointed member of the 5th CPPCC

         May   Identified as deputy director of the International Liaison Department of the CCP Central Committee

1979,   Dec   Head of a CP Party functionaries' delegation to Somalia, Tanzania, Zambia, Burundi, Togo, Benin, Sierra Leone, Guinea, and Senegal (until Feb 1980)

Wu Xueyi (Wu Hsüeh-yi)   吴学艺

Posts held

Government
Deputy director of the Central Meteorological Bureau

1976,   Nov   Identified as a cadre of the Central Meteorological Bureau

1979,   Apr   Identified as deputy director of the Central Meteorological Bureau and as permanent representative of PRC to the World Meteorological Organization (WMO) in Geneva

Wu Xuezhi (Wu Hsüeh-chih)   吴雪之

Posts held

Others
Member of the Standing Committee of the 5th CPPCC
Vice-chairman of the Executive Committee, Federation of Industrialists and Businessmen

1950,   Mar   Identified as director of the Trade Department, East China Military and Administrative Council

1951,   Feb   Elected vice-chairman of the Shanghai Federation of Industry and Commerce

1952,   Jun   Identified as member of the Preparatory Committee of the Federation of Industry and Commerce

1953,   Jan   Identified as vice-minister of commerce (until Feb 1958)

         Oct   Elected member of the Standing Committee, Federation of Industry and Commerce (until 1955)

1955,   Mar   Head of a delegation to the International Fair in Czechoslovakia

         Apr   Identified as vice-chairman of the Federation of Industry and Commerce (until Cultural Revolution)

1956,   Sep   Head of a delegation to the International Fair in Yugoslavia

1958,   Feb   Appointed vice-minister of the 1st Ministry of Commerce (until Sep 1958)

         Sep   Appointed vice-minister of the Ministry of Commerce (until Cultural Revolution)

1959,   Apr   Elected member of the 3rd CPPCC (confirmed in 1964 by the 4th CPPCC)

1967,   Apr   Criticized as an anti-Party element and purged

1978,   Feb   First appearance after the Cultural Revolution

         Mar   Elected member of the Standing Committee of the 5th CPPCC

         Oct   Elected vice-chairman of the Executive Committee of the Federation of Industrialists and Businessmen

Wu Yeshan (Wu Yeh-shan)   吴冶山

Posts held

Government
Vice-minister of railways

1978,   May   Identified as vice-minister of railways; member of an economic delegation led by Gu Ming to Great Britain and France

Wu Yifang (Wu Yi-fang) (f)   吴贻芳

Posts held

NPC
Deputy for Jiangsu Province to the 5th NPC

Provincial Administration
Vice-governor of Jiangsu Province

Mass Organization
Vice-president of the Women's Federation

Others
Member of the Standing Committee of the 5th CPPCC
Vice-chairman of the Central Committee, China Association for Promoting Democracy

Wu was born in 1893 as the daughter of a poor family in Sichuan Province. She attended Qinghai Middle School in Suzhou and Jinling Girls College in Nanjing. She then continued her studies in the United States and was awarded a Ph.D. by the University of Michigan. From 1925 to 1926 she was vice-president of the Chinese Students Association in the U.S.A. In 1927 she returned to China and became professor of the National Beijing Higher Girls Normal College and subsequently president of Jinling Girls College. In 1933 she took part in the International Women's Congress in Chicago as a delegate representing China. She became chairman of the Executive Committee, Association for Promoting Christianity, in 1935. In 1939 she was elected a member of the Standing Committee of the Society for Protection of Children in Wartime, and in the following year member of the Presidium, People's Political Council of the Nationalist Government. In March 1945 she was a member of the Chinese delegation to the founding session of the United Nations in San Francisco. She was subsequently appointed dean of the College of Arts and Sciences of Nanjing University. In 1946 she was appointed a member of the National Assembly for Drafting the Constitution of the Republic of China and in the following year a member of the National Assembly. Still in 1947, she was made president of the China Branch of the International Democratic Women's Federation. In September 1949 she took part in the 1st CPPCC which elected her a member of its National Committee.

1949,	Oct	Identified as professor of Yanjing University (until 1952) and as member of the Chinese People's Committee for World Peace
1951,	Nov	Identified as member of the Chinese People's Committee for Protection of Children
1952,	Nov	Identified as member of the People's Government of Kiangsu
1954,	Jul	Identified as vice-chairman of the Standing Committee, Christian Three-Self Patriotic Movement
	Aug	Elected deputy for Jiangsu Province to the 1st NPC (reelected in 1958 and 1964 to the 2nd and 3rd NPCs)
1955,	Jun	Member of a delegation to the World Peace Congress in Helsinki
	Sep	Identified as director of the Education Department of Jiangsu People's Government (until 1958)
1956,	Feb	Identified as member of the Standing Committee of the China Association for Promoting Democracy
1957,	Sep	Elected member of the Executive Committee, Democratic Women's Federation
1961,	Jan	Identified as vice-chairman of the Association for Promoting Christianity
1962,	Jan	Identified as chairman of the China Association for Promoting Democracy, Jiangsu Branch
1972,	Sep	After the mourning ceremonies for He Xiangning Wu disappears until Feb 1978
1978,	Feb	Elected deputy for Jiangsu Province to the 5th NPC
	Mar	Elected member of the Standing Committee of the 5th CPPCC
	Sep	Elected vice-president of the Women's Federation
1979,	Jun	Member of the Budget Committee at the 2nd Session of the 5th NPC
	Oct	Elected vice-chairman of the Central Committee of the China Association for Promoting Democracy
	Dec	Elected vice-governor of Jiangsu Province

Wu Yingkai (Wu Ying-k'ai)　　吴英恺

Posts held

Others
Honorary director of the Qinghai Provincial Research Institute on Cardiovascular Diseases on the Plateau
Director of the Beijing Fuwai Hospital

1954,	Sep	Elected deputy for Liaoning to the 1st NPC (reelected in 1958 and 1964 to the 2nd and 3rd NPCs)
1960,	Apr	Identified as director of the Beijing Fuwai Hospital
1961,	Oct	Identified as a member of the Executive Committee of the Chinese Red Cross Society
1977,	Oct	First appearance after the Cultural Revolution
1978,	Apr	Identified on his former post as director of the Beijing Fuwai Hospital

1979,	Jun	By-elected member of the 5th CPPCC
	Aug	Identified as honorary director of the Qinghai Provincial Research Institute on Cardiovascular Diseases on the Plateau

Wu Yubu (Wu Yü-pu)　　武玉璞

Posts held

NPC
Deputy for Tianjin Municipality to the 5th NPC
Member of the Standing Committee of the 5th NPC

1978,	Feb	Elected deputy for Tianjin Municipality to the 5th NPC
	Mar	Elected member of the Standing Committee of the 5th NPC

Wu Zhichao (Wu Chih-ch'ao)　　吴志超

Posts held

Others
Executive director of the Board of Directors, China International Trust and Investment Corporation
Vice-chairman of the Central Committee, China Democratic National Construction Commission
Chairman of the Shanghai Federation of Industrialists and Businessmen

1965,	Jul	Identified as deputy director of the Administrative Bureau for Agricultural People's Communes
1979,	Oct	Appointed executive director of the Board of Directors, China International Trust and Investment Corporation; elected vice-chairman of the Central Committee, China Democratic National Construction Commission; identified as chairman of the Shanghai Federation of Industrialists and Businessmen

Wu Zhizhong (Wu Chih-chung)　　吴执中

Posts held

Others
President of the Occupational Disease Prevention Society

1954,	Oct	Elected deputy for Shenyang Municipality to the 1st NPC
1959,	Mar	Elected deputy for Liaoning Province to the 2nd NPC (relected in 1964 to the 3rd NPC)
1964,	May	Delegate to an Afro-Asian Conference in Jakarta
1977,	Oct	First appearance after the Cultural Revolution
1979,	Oct	Elected president of the Occupational Disease Prevention Society

of Yun-

Revolu-

delegation to

ian Province to

er the Cultural Revo-

airman of the People's
inan Province

 (Wu Tso-jen) 吴作人

neld

Deputy for Shanghai Municipality to the
5th NPC

Others
President of the Central Academy of Fine
Arts
Vice-president of the Artists Association
Vice-chairman of the Federation of Liter-
ary and Art Circles

951,	Oct	Member of a cultural delegation to Burma
1952,	Jun	Identified as council member of the Sino-Indian Friendship Asociation
1953,	Oct	Identified as member of the Federation of Literary and Art Circles (until Cultural Revolution)
1954,	May	Identified as vice-president of the Fine Arts Association
	Oct	Elected deputy for Henan Province to the 1st NPC (reelected in 1958 and 1964 to the 2nd and 3rd NPCs)
1955,	Jun	Identified as vice-president of the Central Institute of Fine Arts (until Jun 1958)
1958,	Jun	Identified as president of the Central Institute of Fine Arts (until Cultural Revolution)
	Jul	Member of a delegation to the Conference on Disarmament and International Cooperation in Stockholm, Sweden
1960,	Mar	Identified as member of the Sino-Latin-American Friendship Association
1967,	May	Branded as a reactionary authority
1973,	Mar	First appearance after the Cultural Revolution
1975,	Feb	Elected deputy for Shanghai Municipality to the 4th NPC (confirmed in 1978 by the 5th NPC)
1979,	Jul	Identified as president of the Central Academy of Fine Arts and as vice-president of the Artists Association
	Nov	Elected vice-chairman of the Federation of Literary and Art Circles

ri-

gzhou

under of

吴作民

istration
of the People's Congress of
nce

andong Province. In 1949 he was
al Logistics Department of the
Corps, under the 2nd Field Army.

tified as a member of the People's
vernment of Yunnuan Province (until 1955)
Elected vice-governor of Yunnan Province
(until Cultural Revolution)
Oct Identified as a member of the Standing
Committee of Yunnan Province CP

Xi Guoguang (Hsi Kuo-kuang)   席国光

Posts held

Government
Vice-minister of public security

1978,   Jun   Identified as vice-minister of public security

Xi Jinwu (Hsi Chin-wu)   郗晋武

Posts held

CCP
Secretary, Tibetan Autonomous Region CP

Military
Commander of Tibet Military District

1975,   Feb   Identified as deputy commander of Tibet Military District
1976,   May   Identified as commander of Tibet Military District
1977,   Nov   Elected secretary, Tibetan Autonomous Region CP

Xi Yesheng (Hsi Yeh-sheng)   奚业胜

Posts held

Government
Director of a department in the Ministry of Foreign Trade

1964,   Jun   Identified as trade counselor at the embassy in Ceylon (until about 1970)
1971,   Apr   Identified as deputy director of a department in the Ministry of Foreign Affairs; member of a trade delegation to Morocco and Algeria
          Sep   Member of a trade delegation to France
1973,   Aug   Identified as director of a department in the Ministry of Foreign Trade; head of a trade delegation to Japan
1974,   Sep   Head of a trade delegation to Iran
1976,   Mar   Head of a trade delegation to the Philippines
          Nov   Head of a trade delegation to Bangladesh
1977,   Mar   Head of a trade delegation to Japan
          Sep   Head of a trade delegation to Singapore
          Oct   Head of a trade delegation to Iran
1978,   Feb   Head of a trade delegation to the Philippines
          Sep   Head of a trade delegation to Turkey
          Oct   Head of a trade delegation to Thailand

Xi Yi (Hsi Yi)   席一

Posts held

Government
Deputy director of the Foreign Affairs Bureau in the Ministry of National Defense

Others
Vice-president of the PLA Army Men's Association

1964,   Jul   Identified as senior colonel and military attaché in the German Democratic Republic
1978,   Aug   Identified as deputy director of the Foreign Affairs Bureau in the Ministry of National Defense
1979,   May   Identified as vice-president of the PLA Army Men's Association

Xi Zhanyuan (Hsi Chan-yüan)   郗占元

Posts held

Others
Deputy chief procurator, Supreme People's Procuratorate

1957,   Dec   Identified as secretary of the Federation of Trade Unions and director of their Department for Social Insurance
1959,   Mar   Elected deputy for Hebei to the 2nd NPC
1965,   Aug   Identified as vice-minister of labor. Xi disappears thereafter.
1979,   Sep   First appearance after the Cultural Revolution: Appointed deputy chief procurator, Supreme People's Procuratorate

Xi Zhongxun (Hsi Chung-hsün)   习仲勋

Posts held

CCP
Member of the CCP 11th Central Committee
1st secretary of Guangdong Province CP

Provincial Administration
Governor of Guangdong Province

Others
Member of the Standing Committee of the 5th CPPCC

Xi was born in 1908 (?) in Fuping, Shaanxi Province. He graduated from middle school and joined the Communist Youth League in 1926. After the rift between the KMT and the CCP he was imprisoned but soon escaped. He went to North Shaanxi and engaged in guerrilla activities. Later he joined the 26th Red Army and became political commissar of a battalion. In 1935 he studied at the Central Party School at Wayaobao. In 1937 he served as dean of discipline at the Central Party School. The following year he was made political commissar of the 2nd Independent Brigade under the 120th Division of the 8th Route Army. Later he was director of the Rear Services Department of the 8th Route Army. In 1945 he was elected alternate member of the 7th Central Committee of the CCP (until September 1956) and director of its Organization Department. In the fall of that year he served as deputy secretary of the Northwest Bureau under the CCP Central Committee. In 1946 he was made political commissar of the Shanxi-Suiyuan-Gansu-Shaanxi-

Ningxia Defense Army. The following year he was appointed political commissar of the North Shaanxi Field Army (commander: Peng Dehuai) which was then responsible for the protection of the Yan'an base. In 1948 he became political commissar of the Northwest Field Army and secretary of the Northwest Bureau of the CCP Central Committee. In 1949 the Northwest Field Army was renamed 1st Field Army; Xi remained political commissar. In September 1949 he took part in the 1st CPPCC meeting.

1949,	Oct	Appointed member of the Central People's Government and member of the People's Revolutionary Military Council (until 1954)
	Nov	Appointed vice-chairman of the Northwest Military and Administrative Council (chairman: Peng Dehuai) and concurrently director of its Land Reform Committee
	Dec	Elected council member of the Sino-Soviet Friendship Association; identified as political commissar of the Northwest Military Region (until Oct 1954)
1952,	Aug	Appointed vice-chairman of the Cultural and Educational Committee, Government Administrative Council (until Oct 1954)
	Nov	Identified as a member of the State Planning Commission (until Oct 1954)
1953,	Jan	Appointed vice-chairman of the Northwest Administrative Council
	Jul	Identified as director of the Propaganda Department of the CCP Central Committee (until Oct 1954)
	Sep	Identified as secretary-general of the Government Administrative Council (until Oct 1954)
1954,	Aug	Elected deputy for Xi'an Municipality to the 1st NPC
	Sep	Appointed secretary-general of the State Council
1956,	Sep	Elected member of the Central Committee by the 8th CCP Congress
1957,	Jul	Identified as vice-chairman of the Central Relief Commission
1958,	Aug	Elected deputy for Shaanxi Province to the 2nd NPC
1959,	Feb	Head of a CP delegation to the Spring Fair at Leipzig, German Democratic Republic
	Apr	Appointed vice-premier
	Sep	Head of an economic delegation to the USSR
1960,	Sep	Head of a CP delegation to the German Democratic Republic participating in the funeral ceremony for President Pieck
1962		Xi disappears
1966		During the Cultural Revolution Xi is the target of accusations because of his close relations to Peng Dehuai
1978,	Feb	First appearance after the Cultural Revolution
	Mar	Elected member of the Standing Committee of the 5th CPPCC
	Apr	Identified as 2nd secretary of Guangdong Province CP (until Dec 1978) and as vice-chairman of the Revolutionary Committee of Guangdong Province (until Apr 1979)
	Sep	Identified as 2nd political commissar of Guangzhou Military Region
	Dec	By-elected member of the CCP 11th Central Committee by its 3rd Plenum; identified as 1st secretary of Guangdong Province CP
1979,	May	Identified as chairman of the Provincial Revolutionary Committee of Guangdong Province (until Dec 1979)
	Nov	Head of a provincial delegation from Guangdong to Australia
	Dec	Elected governor of Guangdong Province

Xia Juhua (Hsia Chü-hua) (f)   夏菊花

Posts held

NPC
Member of the Standing Committee of the 5th NPC
Deputy for Hubei Province to the 5th NPC

Mass Organization
Vice-chairman of the Women's Federation of Hubei Province

Xia was born in 1937. As a young child she helped her mother and grandmother by begging for a living. At the age of five she was sold to a circus director.

1957		Xia joins the CCP
1964,	Sep	Elected deputy for Hubei Province to the 3rd NPC
1966,	Sep	Identified as member of the Wuhan Acrobatic Troupe
1973,	Jul	Elected vice-chairman of the Women's Federation of Hubei Province
1974,	Nov	Deputy head of a goodwill delegation to France for the opening of the Beijing-Paris air-link
1975,	Jan	Elected member of the Standing Committee of the 4th NPC (confirmed in this post in 1978 by the 5th NPC)
1978,	Feb	Elected deputy for Hubei Province to the 5th NPC
	Nov	Head of an acrobatic troupe to Brazil
1979,	May	Head of a Wuhan acrobatic troupe to the Philippines and Japan

Xia Nai (Hsia Nai)   夏

Posts held

NPC
Deputy for Beijing Municipality to the 5th NPC

Others
Director of the Institute of Archaeology of the Academy of Sciences
Director-general of the Archaeological Society

Xia was born in Yongjia, Zhejiang Province. He graduated from Qinghua University in Beijing and then continued his studies at London University. During and after this course of studies he took part in archaeological excavations in England, Egypt, and Palaestina. After his return to China he started excavations in the Anyang area in 1934.

1950		Identified as professor of archaeology at Zhejiang University
1952		Identified as council member of the Historical Society and as deputy director of the Institute of Archaeology of the Academy of Sciences
1955,	Jun	Identified as member of the Philosophy and Social Sciences Department
1957		Identified as professor of archaeology at Beijing University
	May	Appointed member of the Scientific Planning Commission (until Nov 1958)
1958,	Feb	Elected council member of the Sino-United Arab Republic Friendship Association
	Nov	Elected deputy for Shandong Province to the 2nd NPC
1959,	Jun	Xia joins the CCP
1962,	Sep	Identified as director of the Institute of Archaeology, Academy of Sciences
1963,	May	Delegate at the 15th Pakistan Historians Congress in Karachi
1972,	Feb	First appearance after the Cultural Revolution: Present at a reception by Premier Zhou Enlai for U.S. President Richard Nixon
	Sep	Head of an archaeological group to Albania
1973,	Apr	Head of an archaeological group to Peru and Mexico
1977,	Oct	Head of a delegation of archaeologists to Iran
1978,	Feb	Elected deputy for Beijing Municipality to the 5th NPC
1979,	Apr	Identified as director-general of the Archeological Society
	Jun	Deputy head of a delegation of the Academy of Social Sciences headed by Zhou Yang to Japan

Publications

1954	"The Present Situation of Archaeology in China" in Xinhua Yuekan (New China Monthly), 8/1954
1955	"A Critique of the Capitalist Thinking in the Hu Shi School of Archaeology" in Xinhua Yuekan, 6/1955
1956	"The Gradual Development of Archaeological Work in China" in RMRB, 28 February
1957	"The Silver Coins of the Persian Saxon Dynasty Recently Discovered in China" in Kaogu (Archaeology), 2/1957

Xia Qi (Hsia Ch'i)   夏　琦

Posts held

CCP
Secretary of Zhejiang Province CP

Provincial Administration
Vice-chairman of Zhejiang Province People's Congress

| 1971, | Nov | Identified as deputy political commissar of Zhejiang Military District (until 1976) |
| 1973, | Apr | Identified as member of the Standing Committee of Zhejiang Province CP (un- |

til 1977)

| 1978, | Aug | Identified as secretary of Zhejiang Province CP |
| 1979, | Dec | Elected vice-chairman of Zhejiang Province People's Congress |

Xia Shihou (Hsia Shih-hou)   夏世厚

Posts held

CCP
Member of the Standing Committee of Hubei Province CP

Military
Deputy commander of Hubei Military District

Provincial Administration
Vice-chairman of the Standing Committee, People's Congress of Hubei Province

1955,	Feb	Appointed member of the People's Council of Hubei Province
1962,	Oct	Identified as vice-governor of Hubei Province (until Cultural Revolution)
1966,	Jun	Identified as deputy head of the Headquarters for Fighting Drought of Hubei Province
1973,	Jun	Identified as vice-chairman of the Revolutionary Committee of Hubei Province (until Jan 1980)
1978,	Jan	Identified as member of the Standing Committee of Hubei Province CP
1979,	Aug	Identified as deputy commander of Hubei Military District
1980,	Jan	Elected vice-chairman of the Standing Committee, People's Congress of Hubei Province

Xia Siping (Hsia Szu-p'ing)   夏似萍

Posts held

Provincial Administration
Vice-chairman of the People's Government, Ningxia Autonomous Region

| 1980, | Jan | Elected vice-chairman of the People's Government, Ningxia Autonomous Region |

Xia Yan (Hsia Yen)   夏　衍

Posts held

Government
Advisor to the Ministry of Culture

Others
Member of the Standing Committee of the 5th CPPCC
Vice-chairman of the Sino-Japanese Friendship Association
Vice-chairman of the Association for Friendship with Foreign Countries
Vice-chairman of the Association of Literary and Art Circles
Chairman of the Film Artists' Association

Xia Yan (pen name) was born under the name of Shen Duanxian in 1900 in Hangzhou, Zhejiang Province. He graduated in 1919 from Hangzhou Technical College and then went to Japan to continue his studies at the Kyushu Technical Institute. After his return to China he took part in the Northern Expedition of 1926-27. In 1929 he founded a drama club which published the journal Art. From 1937 to 1948 he edited a number of newspapers and journals in Shanghai and Hong Kong. In May 1949 he was appointed deputy director of the Propaganda Department in the East China Bureau of the CCP Central Committee. Shortly afterwards he was appointed vice-chairman of the Shanghai Culture Administration and permanent member of the Association of Literary and Art Circles. In September of that year he took part in the CPPCC.

1949,	Oct	Appointed council member of the Peace Council and of the Sino-Soviet Friendship Association
	Dec	Appointed member of the East China Military and Administrative Council (until Dec 1952); appointed director of the Asia Department in the Ministry of Foreign Affairs (until Aug 1952)
1950,	Jan	Appointed director of the Shanghai Culture Bureau (until Dec 1953)
	Oct	Appointed chairman of the Shanghai Section of the Association of Literary and Art Circles
	Dec	Elected member of the Shanghai People's Government (probably until 1959)
1952,	Aug	Appointed member of the East China Administrative Council (until Feb 1954)
1953,	Sep	Elected board member of the Association of Literary and Art Circles
	Oct	Elected board member of the Union of Chinese Writers
1954,	May	Appointed council member of the Association for Cultural Relations with Foreign Countries
	Oct	Appointed vice-minister of culture (until Apr 1965); appointed director of the Shanghai People's Theater
1955,	Sep	Appointed member of the Institute of Foreign Affairs
1956,	Aug	Elected member of the Executive Council of the Welfare Institute
1958,	Mar	Elected chairman of the Sino-Czechoslovakian Friendship Association
	Nov	Elected deputy for Shandong Province to the 2nd NPC
1959,	Jul	Head of a delegation to the International Book Fair in Leipzig
1960,	Dec	Member of a cultural delegation to Cuba
1961,	Jan	Member of a cultural delegation to Burma
1962,	Feb	Deputy head of a delegation to the Conference of Afro-Asian Writers in Cairo
	Sep	Xia wins a prize as best film script-writer of 1962
1963,	Sep	Identified as vice-chairman of the Association for Cultural Relations with Foreign Countries
1965,	Jun	Criticized as a "bourgeois" author for his film script "Lin's Shop" which was based on a short novel by Mao Dun
1967,	Aug	Xia is accused of having been an agent of Liu Shaoqi in the literary and art circles and subsequently disappears
1977,	Oct	First appearance after the Cultural Revolution
1978,	Feb	Identified as vice-chairman of the Sino-Japanese Friendship Association
	Mar	Elected a member of the Standing Committee of the 5th CPPCC
	Apr	Identified as vice-chairman of the Association for Friendship with Foreign Countries
	Jun	Identified as vice-chairman of the Association of Literary and Art Circles
1979,	Jan	Identified as advisor to the Ministry of Culture
	Nov	Elected chairman of the Film Artists' Association

Xia Zhengnong (Hsia Cheng-nung) 夏征农

Posts held

CCP
Secretary of Shanghai Municipality CP
1st secretary, Fudan University CP

1951,	Oct	Identified as council member of the Sino-Soviet Friendship Association (until Dec 1954)
1953,	Dec	Identified as director of the Propaganda Department, Shandong Subbureau of the CCP Central Committee
1954,	Oct	Elected deputy for Shandong Province to the 1st NPC
1956,	Nov	Identified as secretary of Shandong Province CP
1960,	Mar	Identified as secretary of Jinan Municipality CP
1964,	Jan	Identified as director of the Propaganda Department, East China Bureau of the CCP Central Committee
1967		Disappears during the Cultural Revolution
1979,	May	First appearance after the Cultural Revolution: Identified as secretary of Shanghai CP as well as 1st secretary, Fudan University CP

Xia Zhixu (Hsia Chih-hsü) (f) 夏之栩

Posts held

Government
Vice-minister of light industry

Others
Member of the Standing Committee of the 5th CPPCC

Xia was born in 1907 in Haining County, Zhejiang Province. Her father, who died in 1911, was a minor official in Sichuan Province. In 1918 she attended the first modern girl school in Hubei Province, in Wuchang. In 1922 she joined the Socialist Youth League and shortly afterwards became a member of the CCP. At the end of 1922 she was dismissed from school because, with five other pupils, she had supported a Communist teacher who had been discharged. Subsequently, she and her mother converted their house to a base for the Communists in Wuchang. In 1924 Xia worked for the Socialist Youth

League in Beijing. In 1925 she married Zhao Shiyan who had just returned to Beijing from studies at the University of the Toilers of the Far East in Moscow and now worked in the CCP Propaganda Department. In 1926 they were both posted by the Party to Shanghai. Following the KMT-CCP rift Zhao Shiyan was arrested in July 1927 and executed because of his CCP membership. In 1929 Xia went to Moscow with her two little sons and enrolled at the same university from which her husband had received his training. Returning from the USSR at the end of 1931, she was arrested in Manzhouli and detained for six months before she was able to return to Shanghai. There she was again arrested in 1933 and only released in 1937 after the outbreak of the Anti-Japanese War under amnesty granted as a result of the KMT-CCP United Front. From 1937 to 1949 she was entrusted mainly with organizational duties both on the regional and central levels.

1950,	Mar	Appointed member of the Central-South China Military and Administrative Council (until Nov 1952)
1954,	Jul	Appointed director of the Staff Office, Ministry of Light Industry (until Feb 1955)
	Aug	Elected deputy for Guangdong Province to the 1st NPC
1955,	Feb	Appointed assistant minister in the Ministry of Light Industry (until Jun 1957)
1957,	Jun	Appointed assistant minister in the Ministry of Food Industry (abolished in Feb 1958)
1960,	May	Appointed vice-minister of light industry
1964,	Sep	Elected deputy for Zhejiang Province to the 3rd NPC
1965,	Feb	After separation of the Ministry of Light Industry into 1st and 2nd Ministries, she continues as vice-minister of the 1st Ministry
1967,	Oct	Head of a women's delegation to Albania
1971		The 1st and 2nd Ministries of Light Industry rejoin to form the Ministry of Light Industry. Xia continues as vice-minister
1978,	Mar	Elected member of the Standing Committee of the 5th CPPCC
	Apr	Appointed member of the Committee for the Patriotic Health Campaign

Xiang Kefang (Hsiang K'e-fang) 项克方

Posts held

Government
Managing director of the Bank of China
Vice-president of the Bank of China

1979,	May	Identified as managing director of the Bank of China
	Nov	Identified as vice-president of the Bank of China

Xiang Layu (Hsiang La-yü) (f) 向腊玉

Posts held

NPC
Member of the Standing Committee of the 5th NPC
Deputy for Jiangxi Province to the 5th NPC

1978,	Feb	Elected deputy for Jiangxi Province to the 5th NPC
	Mar	Elected member of the Standing Committee of the 5th NPC

Xiang Nan (Hsiang Nan) 项 南

Posts held

Government
Vice-minister of the Ministry of Agricultural Machinery

Others
Vice-president of the Society for Agricultural Machinery

1977,	Jul	Identified as vice-minister of the 1st Ministry of Machine Building (until 1978)
1978,	Apr	Identified as vice-president of the Society for Agricultural Machinery; head of a study group on agricultural machinery to Italy, France, Great Britain, and Denmark
1979,	Jun	Identified as vice-minister of the Ministry of Agricultural Machinery; head of an agricultural and livestock machinery delegation to the Philippines and Australia

Note: Xiang is possibly identical with the person of the same name who was a prominent youth cadre from 1952 until the Cultural Revolution

Xiang Shouzhi (Hsiang Shou-zhi) 向守志

Posts held

Military
Deputy commander of Nanjing Military Region

1974,	Sep	Identified as military leader in Beijing
1977,	Oct	Identified as deputy commander of Nanjing Military Region
1979,	Sep	Deputy head of a PLA touring group to North Korea

Xiang Zhaozong (Hsiang Chao-tsung) 项朝宗

Posts held

Others
Member of the Standing Committee of the 5th CPPCC

1978,	Mar	Elected member of the Standing Committee of the 5th CPPCC

Xiang Zhonghua (Hsiang Chung-hua) 向仲华

Posts held

CCP
Alternate member of the CCP 11th Central Committee

NPC
Deputy for the PLA to the 5th NPC

Military
Lieutenant-general
Political commissar of Guangzhou Military Region
CP secretary of Guangzhou Military Region

Xiang took part in the Peasants Uprisings of 1928. During the following years he served primarily as political instructor in the front army led by Peng Dehuai. In 1937 he was temporarily editor of the journal Red China as well as of a Red Army journal. In 1945 he became deputy director of the Propaganda Department, Political Department of Shaanxi-Gansu-Ningxia Military Region. After the Japanese capitulation in 1945 the journal Red China was renamed New China of which Xiang became editor-in-chief.

1953,	Dec	Identified as deputy political commissar of the Armored Forces of the PLA
1955,	Sep	Promoted to the rank of lieutenant-general; awarded the order of "Liberation," 1st class
1958,	Dec	Identified as political commissar of the PLA Armored Forces (until 1971)
1959,	Mar	Elected deputy for the PLA to the 2nd NPC (reelected in 1964 to the 3rd NPC)
1966-1969		During the Cultural Revolution Xiang is consistently referred to as a "responsible military" cadre
1972,	Jun	Identified as deputy chief of PLA General Staff (until Oct 1977)
1973,	Aug	Elected to first term as alternate member of the CCP Central Committee by the 10th Party Congress
1974,	Mar	Head of a military delegation to Peru
	Sep	Head of a military delegation to Romania
1975,	May	Head of a military delegation to Yugoslavia
1977,	Oct	Identified as political commissar of Guangzhou Military Region
1978,	Feb	Elected deputy for the PLA to the 5th NPC
	Oct	Identified as CP secretary of Guangzhou Military Region

Xiao Fangzhou (Hsiao Fang-chou) 肖 方 洲

Posts held

Others
Vice-chairman of the Committee for Promotion of International Trade

1952,	Nov	Identified as a cadre in the Administrative Office of Linan City, Zhejiang Province
1955,	Mar	Identified as deputy secretary-general of the Committee for Promotion of International Trade (until Oct 1960)
1956,	Sep	Head of the Chinese pavilion at the trade fair in Brno, Czechoslovakia
1959,	Jan	Identified as vice-chairman of the Arbitration Committee
1960,	Apr	Elected member of the Standing Committee of the Sino-African Friendship Association

	Oct	Identified as secretary-general of the Committee for Promotion of International Trade (until May 1964)
1963,	Sep	Head of the Chinese economic exhibition in Algiers
	Oct	Identified as council member of the Sino-Japanese Friendship Association
1964,	Mar	Identified as vice-chairman of the Committee for Promotion of International Trade
	May	Deputy head of the Chinese economic exhibition in Osaka
1966,	Dec	Head of a trade delegation to Turkey
1973,	Apr	Reactivated after the Cultural Revolution. Again referred to as vice-chairman of the Committee for Promotion of International Trade
	Aug	Head of an exhibition group in Turkey
1974,	Sep	Head of an exhibition delegation to Japan
1975,	Apr	Head of a trade delegation to Bahrein and the United Arab Emirates
	Jun	Head of the Chinese industrial exhibition in Cologne, Federal Republic of Germany
1976,	Nov	Head of an exhibition delegation to Bahrein
1977,	Apr	Head of an exhibition delegation to Basel, Switzerland
	Jul	Head of an exhibition delegation to Sapporo, Japan
1978,	Mar	Head of an economic delegation to the Philippines

Xiao Han (Hsiao Han) (A)   肖 寒

Posts held

CCP
Alternate member of the CCP 11th Central Committee

Government
Vice-minister of the State Economic Commission

1975,	Oct	Identified as vice-minister of coal industry
1977,	Jul	Identified as minister of coal industry (until Feb 1980)
	Aug	Elected alternate member of the CCP Central Committee by the 11th Party Congress
1980,	Mar	Identified as vice-minister of the State Economic Commission

Xiao Han (Hsiao Han) (B)   肖   寒

Posts held

CCP
Secretary of Guangxi Autonomous Region CP
Secretary of Nanning Municipality CP (provincial capital of Guangxi)

NPC
Deputy for Guangxi Autonomous Region to the 5th NPC

Provincial Administration
Vice-chairman of the People's Government, Guangxi Autonomous Region

1960,	Apr	Identified as 1st secretary of Liuzhou Municipality CP
1970,	Dec	Identified as member of the Standing Committee of the Revolutionary Committee of Guangxi Autonomous Region (last mention in this post in June 1971)
1974,	Feb	Identified as member of the Standing Committee of Guangxi Autonomous Region CP (until 1977) and as secretary of Nanning Municipality CP (until 1976)
1977,	Jun	Identified as secretary of Guangxi Autonomous Region CP
	Jul	Identified as 1st secretary of Nanning Municipality CP
1978,	Feb	Elected deputy for Guangxi Autonomous Region to the 5th NPC
1979,	Dec	Elected vice-chairman of the People's Government, Guangxi Autonomous Region

Xiao Hua (Hsiao Hua)

Posts held

CCP
Member of the CCP 11th Central Committee
Member of the Military Commission under the CCP Central Committee
Secretary of Gansu Province CP

NPC
Deputy for the PLA to the 5th NPC

Military
Colonel-general
1st political commissar of Lanzhou Military Region

Xiao was born in 1914 (1915?) in Xingguo, Jiangxi Province, as the son of a mason. He worked for the CCP already at the age of 11 to 13 and eventually gained membership in December 1928. From that date he was active as a CCP youth cadre in his home county. When Mao Zedong visited Xingguo in March 1929 a seminar was set up there at which Xiao received his first political education. He joined the Red Army in the same year. In the years up to the Long March Xiao was successively director of the Youth Department of the 1st Red Army Group, head of the Youth Department in the Red Army General Political Department, and political commissar of the Communist Youth Division which was part of the 5th Red Army Group. During the Long March he served as head of the Youth Department, Political Department of the 1st Route Army which formed the vanguard of the Communist forces during the Long March. In April 1936 he was appointed commander and political commissar in the 2nd Division of the 1st Route Army based in Gansu. Shortly afterward he was severely wounded. In March 1938 he was appointed political commissar of the 343rd Brigade, 115th Division, 8th Route Army. Four months later he became commander of the Shandong-Hebei Border Area and in March 1939 political commissar of the 115th Division which shortly afterward occupied Western Shandong. Xiao was then appointed chairman of the

Western Shandong Administrative Office and commander and political commissar of Shandong Military Region. After the end of the Anti-Japanese War Xiao became political commissar of Liaodong Military Region in 1946 and in October 1948 political commissar of the 12th Army Group, commanded by Xiao Jingguang. In April 1949 he was elected member of the Central Committee of the Youth League and one month later member of the Central Committee of the Federation of Democratic Youth. In July of the same year he led a delegation of the Federation of Democratic Youth to the 2nd Congress of the World Federation of Democratic Youth in Budapest which elected him a council member.

1949,	Nov	Head of a youth delegation to Moscow
	Dec	Appointed deputy director of the General Political Department of the Revolutionary Military Council (until Sep 1964)
1953,	Dec	Identified as director of the General Cadres Department of the Military Council
1954,	Sep	Elected deputy for the PLA to the 1st NPC (until Mar 1959)
1955,	Feb	Head of the Chinese farewell delegation to the Soviet troops leaving Lüda (Lüshun-Dalian)
	Sep	Awarded the orders of "1st August," "Independence and Freedom," and "Liberation," all 1st class; promoted to the rank of colonel-general
1956,	Sep	The 8th Party Congress elects Xiao a member of the CCP Central Committee and deputy secretary of the Central Control Commission (until Cultural Revolution)
1959,	Apr-Jun	Member of the military delegation under Peng Dehuai visiting Eastern Europe and Outer Mongolia; in Albania conferred the "Guerrilla Order," 1st class
1961		Identified as deputy secretary general of the Military Council in the CCP Central Committee (until Cultural Revolution)
	Dec	Member of a military delegation to North Vietnam
1962		After reorganization of the Central Control Commission Xiao is appointed a member as well as member of the Standing Committee and deputy secretary (until about 1964)
1964,	Sep	Appointed director of the General Political Department of the PLA (until Cultural Revolution)
1965,	Jan	Appointed member of the National Defense Council (until Cultural Revolution)
1967,	Jan	Identified as vice-chairman of the Cultural Revolutionary Group of the PLA (set up in August 1966 under Liu Zhijian who was purged in 1966). Beside Xiao the Cultural Revolutionary Group, now headed by Xu Xiangqian, comprises Yang Chengwu, Wang Xinting, Xu Liqing, Guan Feng, Xie Tangzhong, and Li Mancun as vice-chairmen. Jiang Qing, wife of Mao Zedong, acts as "advisor" to the Cultural Revolutionary Group and, in fact, sets its course. Jiang Qing is responsible for the removal of Xiao Hua by accusing him in front of a group of rebels on 19 January 1967 of

having evaded self-criticism in connection with the fall of Liu Zhijian

Aug Xiao is accused of being a supporter of Liu Shaoqi; of having followed the line of Liu Shaoqi and Deng Xiaoping of strengthening the Party inside the military; of having prevented criticism of Liu Shaoqi inside the military; of having defended Peng Dehuai (minister of National Defense until 1959); and of having called Luo Ruiqing the best chief of General Staff

1974, Sep First appearance after the Cultural Revolution

1977, May Identified as political commissar of Lanzhou Military Region

Jun Identified as 1st political commissar of Lanzhou Military Region

Aug Elected member of the CCP Central Committee by the 11th Party Congress

Sep Article in HQ: "Chairman Mao's Revolutionary Line Is a Beacon Guiding the Long March to Victory"

1978, Feb Elected deputy for the PLA to the 5th NPC

1979, Sep Identified as member of the Military Commission under the CCP Central Committee; head of a PLA touring group to North Korea

Xiao Jianguang (Hsiao Chien-kuang)

肖剑光

Posts held

Provincial Administration
Vice-governor of Gansu Province

1974, Sep Identified as a cadre of the State Council (probably vice-minister of the 5th Ministry of Machine Building)

1979, Dec Elected vice-governor of Gansu Province

Xiao Jingguang (Hsiao Ching-kuang) 肖劲光

Posts held

CCP
Member of the CCP 11th Central Committee

Government
Vice-minister of National Defense

NPC
Vice-chairman of the Standing Committee of the 5th NPC
Deputy for the PLA to the 5th NPC

Military
Admiral

Xiao was born in Changsha, the provincial capital of Hunan, in the family of a minor landlord. After attending elementary school he studied at the Hunan Teachers College in Changsha where Mao Zedong had also studied a few years previously. He completed his studies in 1920. His first contacts with Mao Zedong, who was then promoting study in the USSR, date from this period. The

year he left college Xiao went with Ren Bishi to Shanghai to attend the Russian language course organized by Comintern agent Woitinsky. At this time he joined the Socialist Youth League and around 1922 the CCP. From 1922 to 1924 he studied at the University of the Toilers of the Far East East which had been set up in 1921 and was offering three-year courses to 800 Asian students at a time. Xiao returned to China in 1924 and took part in the first training course at Whampoa Military Academy which was headed by Chiang Kai-shek. In 1926-27 he took part in the Northern Expedition. After the KMT-CCP rift he was sent to the University of the Red Army in the USSR to continue his studies. In 1934 he returned to China and was given the command of the 7th Army Corps in the Jiangxi Soviet which he also commanded during the Long March. In 1936 he organized guerrilla units in Shaanxi Province and there set up the 29th Army. (Xinhua of 1st July 1979 notices that Xiao worked as commandant of the Central Red Army Academy and as commander of the Fujian-Jiangxi Military Area Command from 1927 to 1937.) During the Anti-Japanese War he operated in the Shaanxi-Gansu-Ningxia Border Area. In 1945 the 7th CCP Congress elected him an alternate member of its Central Committee. Shortly afterward he was sent together with Lin Biao to Manchuria. During the Civil War he commanded the 12th Army Corps and was concurrently deputy commander of the 4th Field Army. After Xiao had obtained without resistance the surrender of Hunan Province from Cheng Qian in mid-1949, he was appointed chairman of the Changsha Military Control Commission. His appointment as commander of Hunan Military Region followed shortly afterward.

1949, Dec Identified as member of the Central-South China Military and Administrative Council

1950 Identified as head of the Navy Headquarters of the Revolutionary Military Council (later commander of the PLA Navy, a post he held until Feb 1980)

1954, Sep Elected deputy for the PLA to the 1st NPC

Oct Appointed member of the National Defense Council (until Cultural Revolution) and vice-minister of national defense

Dec Elected council member of the Sino-Soviet Friendship Association (until 1958)

1955, May Head of the Chinese section of the Sino-Soviet Military Commission for the takeover of Lüda (Lüshun-Dalian)

Sep Made an admiral; awarded the orders of "1st August," "Independence and Freedom," and "Liberation," all 1st class

1956, Sep Elected member of the CCP Central Committee by the 8th Party Congress (confirmed in this post in 1969, 1973, and 1977 by the 9th, 10th and 11th Congress)

1965, Jan Elected member of the Standing Committee of the 3rd NPC (confirmed in this post in 1975 and 1978 by the 4th and 5th NPC)

1969-1978 Xiao suffers no setback during the Cultural Revolution. He is one of the few cadres still holding all their previous posts today

1978, Feb Elected deputy for the PLA to the 5th NPC

Jul Identified as 2nd secretary of the PLA Navy Party Committee (until Feb 1980)

1979,   Jul   By-elected vice-chairman of the Standing Committee of the 5th NPC

Xiao Ke (Hsiao K'e)   肖 克

Posts held

CCP
Member of the CCP 11th Central Committee

Government
Vice-minister of national defense

Military
Colonel-general
Commandant, PLA Military Academy
1st political commissar, PLA Military Academy

Xiao was born in 1909 (1907?) in Jiahe County, Hunan Province, as the son of an impoverished member of the gentry. For five years he attended a traditional elementary school followed by three years of middle school and two years at a teachers training college which he left at the age of 17. He joined a gendarme regiment as an officer in 1926 and there began his career as a political officer in a company of the 24th Division commanded by Ye Ting which served as vanguard during the Northern Expedition. In 1927 he joined the CCP and shortly afterwards took part in the historic Nanchang Uprising. After its failure Xiao organized a guerrilla unit and soon put himself under the command of Zhu De's Red Army on Jingganshan. In 1929 he was made commander of a regiment of the 4th Red Army, two years later of the 17th Division, and already in 1932 of the 9th Red Army. In 1933 his unit was engaged in fighting Warlords in Hunan. Xiao subsequently became political commissar of the 6th Red Army which at the beginning of the Long March in the following year first served as vanguard and then joined the units under He Long's command to form the 2nd Regional Army in Guizhou in which Xiao again held the post of political commissar. These units reached the new Communist base in Shaanxi at the end of 1936. With the reorganization of the Red Army into the 8th Route Army after the beginning of the Anti-Japanese War, Xiao became deputy commander under He Long of the 120th Division which operated during the War in Shaanxi, Hebei, and Chahar Provinces and after the War was based in Rehe Province. In spring 1949 Xiao was appointed chief of staff of the 4th Field Army commanded by Lin Biao which contributed decisively to the defeat of the KMT armed forces during the following months.

1949,   Dec   Appointed member of the Central-South Military and Administrative Council and chief of staff of the Central-South China Military Region (until 1953)

1953   Identified as director of the Training Department in the Revolutionary Military Council (until Oct 1954)

1954,   Sep   Elected deputy for the PLA to the 1st NPC (until Mar 1959)

         Oct   Appointed member of the National Defense Council (until Cultural Revolution); vice-minister of National Defense (until Sep 1959), and deputy director of the Training Department of the PLA (until Nov 1957)

1955,   Sep   Made colonel-general; awarded the orders of "1st August," "Independence and Freedom," and "Liberation," all 1st class

1956,   Sep   Elected member of the CCP Central Committee by the 8th Party Congress (until Cultural Revolution)

1957,   Nov   Appointed director of the Training Department of the PLA (probably until Sep 1959)

1959,   Sep   Appointed vice-minister of state farms and land reclamation (until Cultural Revolution)

1962,   Aug   Xiao reports to the Standing Committee of the NPC on state farms in China

1966   Following criticism by Red Guards as a supporter of He Long, Xiao disappears

1972,   Mar   First appearance after the Cultural Revolution attending funeral of Xie Fuzhi

1973,   Aug   Identified as director of the Military and Political Academy of the PLA; elected alternate member of the CCP Central Committee by the 10th Party Congress (until Aug 1977)

1977,   Aug   Elected member of the CCP Central Committee by the 11th Party Congress

1978,   Jan   Identified as commandant, PLA Military Academy

         Oct   Head of a military delegation to Turkey

1979,   Sep   Identified as 1st political commissar of the PLA Military Academy

1980,   Mar   Identified as vice-minister of national defense

Note   Xiao is believed to be related to He Long.

Xiao Peng (Hsiao P'eng)   肖 鹏

Posts held

Government
Vice-minister of agriculture (?)
Director, State Aquatic Products Bureau

Others
Member of the Standing Committee of the 5th CPPCC
Chairman of the Fishery Association

1958,   Mar   Identified as deputy director of the Communications Department in the Provincial Government of Guangdong

1963,   Oct   Identified as vice-chairman of the Fishery Association; head of a fishery delegation to Japan

         Dec   Appointed vice-minister of marine products (until Cultural Revolution)

1972,   Apr   First appearance after the Cultural Revolution

         Jun   Identified as vice-minister of agriculture and forestry

1973,   Feb   Identified as acting chairman of the Fishery Association

1974,   Jan   Head of a government delegation to Tanzania

1975,   Apr   Member of a friendship delegation headed by Chen Yonggui to Mexico

1976,   Nov   Head of a government delegation to Mexico to attend the inauguration of president Lopez Portillo

1977, May Identified as chairman of the Fishery Association

Jul Head of a fishery delegation to Japan

Nov Head of the Chinese delegation to the 19th Food and Agriculture Organization (FAO) session in Rome

1978, Mar Elected member of the Standing Committee of the 5th CPPCC

Aug Identified as director of the State Aquatic Products Bureau

Oct Head of a fishery delegation to Japan

1979, Feb The Ministry of Agriculture and Forestry is dissolved to form the two new ministries of agriculture and forestry. Since this time Xiao probably holds the post of a vice-minister of agriculture

Dec Attends the International Symposium on Fishing Techniques in Mexico

Xiao Quanfu (Hsiao Ch'üan-fu) 肖全福

Posts held

Military
Major-general
Commander of Xinjiang Military Region

Xiao was born in 1914. Around 1939 he commanded the 14th Regiment in Hebei-Rehe-Liaoning Military District. In 1947 he was commander of the 26th Division, 9th Column, North-East China Field Army. In 1949 he was made commander of the 137th Division, 46th Corps (formerly 9th Column), 4th Field Army.

1950 Identified as deputy commander of the 46th Corps

1952 Xiao is sent with the 46th Corps to the Korean War

1953 Appointed commander of the 46th Corps

1955 Promoted to rank of major-general

1958 Xiao voluntarily serves for a period as group leader of a company

1963 Identified as deputy chief of staff of Shenyang Military Region

1965, Dec Identified as deputy commander of Shenyang Military Region (until Jan 1980)

1980, Feb Identified as commander of Xinjiang Military Region

Xiao is married to Liu Haibo.

Xiao Siming (Hsiao Szu-ming) 肖思明

Posts held

Military
Major-general

Others
Member of the Standing Committee of the 5th CPPCC

Xiao was born around 1910 in Jiangxi Province. In 1937 he was battalion commander in the 115th Division, 8th Route Army.

1952, Aug Identified as acting commander of Shanxi Military District and as member of the People's Government of Shanxi Province

1956, Oct Identified as major-general

1960, Nov Identified as commander of Hebei Military District

1965, Jun Identified as 2nd political commissar of Hebei Military District

1967, Dec Elected vice-chairman of the Revolutionary Committee of Tianjin Municipality (until 1968)

1970, Oct Identified as military leader in Beijing

1972, Jan Identified as 3rd political commissar of Wuhan Military Region

1974, Oct Identified as political commissar of Wuhan Military Region (until Jul 1975); subsequently disappears until 1978

1978, Mar Elected member of the Standing Committee of the 5th CPPCC

Xiao Tong (Hsiao T'ung) 肖桐

Posts held

Government
Director of the National Administration of Building Materials Industry

Others
Director of the Board of Directors, China International Trust and Investment Corporation
Vice-president of the Society of Architecture

1963, Aug Identified as deputy director of the Bureau of Urban Construction, Building Ministry

1978, Jan First appearance after the Cultural Revolution: Head of an architectural delegation to the Federal Republic of Germany and Austria; identified as vice-president of the Society of Architecture

Oct Appointed director of the Board of Directors, China International Trust and Investment Corporation; identified as director of the National Administration of Building Materials Industry

Xiao Wangdong (Hsiao Wang-tung) 肖望东

Posts held

CCP
Alternate member of the CCP 11th Central Committee

Military
Lieutenant-general
1st political commissar of Jinan Military Region

Xiao was born in 1909 in Jiangxi Province. In 1938 he commanded a unit of the New 4th Army. In 1945 he was director of the Political Department of the 2nd Division in the New 4th Army.

1949 Identified as political commissar of the 29th Army

Dec Appointed member of the East China Military and Administrative Council (until Jan 1953) and secretary, CP of North

Jiangsu District (until Apr 1950)

1953,	Jan	Appointed member of the East China Administrative Council
1954,	Feb	Identified as deputy director of the Political Department of East China Military Region
1955,	Sep	Promoted to rank of lieutenant-general
1956,	Feb	Appointed deputy political commissar of Nanjing Military Region (until Apr 1965)
1957,	Mar	Identified as director of the Political Department of Nanjing Military Region
1958,	Jul	Elected deputy for the PLA in Nanjing to the 2nd NPC (reelected in 1964 to the 3rd NPC)
1961,	Sep	Identified as political commissar of Nanjing Military Region (until 1964)
1965,	Jan	Appointed member of the National Defense Council (until Jul 1967)
	Apr	Appointed vice-minister of culture (until Jul 1967)
1966,	Feb	After the purge of Lu Dingyi, Xiao functions as acting minister of culture
1967,	Jul	Denounced as a capitalist-roader and counterrevolutionary revisionist (a now famous caricature depicts Xiao as a deviationist)
1976,	Apr	First appearance after the Cultural Revolution: Identified as political commissar of Jinan Military Region (until Jan 1980)
1977,	Aug	Elected alternate member of the CCP Central Committee by the 11th Party Congress
1980,	Feb	Identified as 1st political commissar of Jinan Military Region

Xiao is married to Xin Ping.

Xiao Xianfa (Hsiao Hsien-fa) 肖贤法

Posts held

Government
Director of the State Bureau of Religious Affairs

1961,	Jul	Appointed director of the State Bureau of Religious Affairs
1966,	Apr	Elected vice-chairman of the Association for Friendship with Foreign Countries; subsequently disappears
1975,	Jun	First appearance after the Cultural Revolution: Identified as a cadre of the Bureau of Religious Affairs
1979,	Jun	Identified as director of the Bureau of Religious Affairs

Xiao Xuanjin (Hsiao Hsüan-chin) 肖选进

Posts held

Military
Major-general
Deputy commander of Beijing Military Region

Xiao served as regiment commander in the 20th Division, 4th Column of the East China Field Army, from 1947 to

1948. In early 1949 he was appointed deputy commander of the 74th Division, 25th Corps, 3rd Field Army.

1951		Appointed commander of the 74th Division (previously part of the 24th Corps)
1952		Sent to Korean War with the 74th Division
1953,	Jun	The 74th Division is noted for distinguished service in a counterattack against the 9th South Korean Division
1955,	Sep	Promoted to rank of colonel; subsequently attends a course at the Military Academy of the PLA
1960		Appointed deputy commander of the 24th Corps
1964		Identified as major-general
1974		Identified as deputy commander of Beijing Military Region

Xiao Yan (Hsiao Yen) 肖岩

Posts held

Government
Vice-minister of education

1965,	Sep	Identified as deputy director of the Political Department in the Ministry of Education
1978,	Jun	Identified as vice-minister of education

Xie Bangding (Hsieh Pang-ting) 谢邦定

Posts held

Others
Vice-chairman of the Association for Friendship with Foreign Countries

Xie was born in 1921 in Jiangsu Province.

1959,	Aug	Elected secretary of the World Youth Federation
1963,	Aug	Identified as secretary-general of the Students Federation; head of a students delegation to Morocco
1964,	Jul	Identified as council member of the Youth Federation; head of a youth delegation to Mali, Congo (Brazzaville), and Dahomey (now Benin)
1965,	Feb	Identified as deputy secretary-general of the Youth Federation
1967		Disappears during the Cultural Revolution
1978,	Sep	First appearance after the Cultural Revolution: Identified as vice-chairman of the Association for Friendship with Foreign Countries
1979,	Jan	Head of a friendship delegation to Yemen Arab Republic

Xie Bangzhi (Hsieh Pang-chih) 谢邦治

Posts held

Government
Former ambassador to Finland

Xie is a native of Songjiang Province. In 1943 he headed the Rural Work Department in the CP Committee of Jiangsu-Anhui Border Area.

1950		Identified as deputy secretary of Wuhan CP
1955,	Feb	Identified as assistant minister in the Ministry of Communications (until Nov 1955)
	Nov	Identified as assistant minister in the Ministry of Supervision (until Jul 1958)
1958,	Jul	Identified as vice-minister of supervision (until Sep 1958)
	Sep	Identified as vice-minister of justice (until Apr 1959)
1961,	Apr	Identified as secretary-general, CP of Shanghai Municipality (until Apr 1962)
1962,	Jul	Appointed ambassador to Bulgaria (until about 1967)
1969,	Jul	Appointed ambassador to Afghanistan (until Jan 1973)
1973,	Oct	Appointed ambassador to Upper Volta (until Dec 1978)
1979,	Apr	Appointed ambassador to Finland (until Mar 1980)

Xie Beiyi (Hsieh Pei-yi)   謝北一

Posts held

Government
Vice-minister of the State Capital Construction Commission

Xie was born in March 1920 in Henan Province.

1956,	Nov	Appointed member of the State Economic Commission (until Dec 1964)
1963,	Sep	Appointed deputy director of the State Bureau of Allocation of Materials (until Nov 1964)
1964,	Nov	Appointed vice-minister of material allocation (until Cultural Revolution)
1965,	Apr	Appointed vice-chairman of the Capital Construction Commission
1978,	Apr	Advisor of an iron and steel industry delegation to Austria, Great Britain, Federal Republic of Germany and the Netherlands
1979,	Sep	Member of a government delegation headed by Gu Mu to Japan
	Nov	Head of an economic delegation to Japan

Xie Bingxin (Hsieh Ping-hsin) (f)   謝冰心

Posts held

NPC
Deputy for Fujian Province to the 5th NPC

Others
Member of the Standing Committee of the 5th CPPCC

Vice-chairman of the Central Committee of the China Association for Promoting Democracy
Vice-chairman of the Federation of Literary and Art Workers

Xie was born in 1902 in Minhou, Fujian Province, as the daughter of a high ranking naval officer. She received a classical Chinese education and showed literary talents and interests already at an early age. After attending the Beijing Bridgeman Girls' School she continued her studies at Yanjing University from which she graduated with a B.A. degree in 1923. Her articles reached the public for the first time in connection with the May 4th Movement in 1919. She published her first poems and short stories in 1920. From 1924 to 1926 she studied at Wellesley College, Massachusetts, from which she graduated with an M.A. degree. She continued her literary activities at college. In 1926 she returned to China as a lecturer in literature at Yanjing University. In 1929 she married Wu Wencao with whom she again visited the U.S.A. in 1936. She returned via Europe and the USSR in 1937 to become a lecturer at the Southwest Associated University in Kunming. In 1945 she was appointed a member of the People's Political Council of the Nationalist Government. In 1946 she went to Japan and lectured on modern Chinese literature at Tokyo University.

1951,	Dec	Xie returns to China
1953,	Oct	Identified as member of the Federation of Literary and Art Circles
1954,	Feb	Member of a friendship delegation to India
	May	Elected council member of the Association for Cultural Relations with Foreign Countries
	Aug	Elected deputy for Fujian Province to the 1st NPC (confirmed in 1958 and 1964 by the 2nd and 3rd NPCs)
1955,	Jun	Member of a women's delegation to the World Mothers' Conference in Switzerland
	Jul	Member of a delegation to the Anti-Atomic Bombs Conference in Hiroshima
	Aug	Identified as council member of the Sino-Indian Friendship Association
	Nov	Identified as member of the Children and Juvenile Literature Section of the Creative Committee, Chinese Writers' Union
1956,	Feb	Elected member of the Asian Solidarity Committee
	Aug	Elected member of the Central Committee, China Association for Promoting Democracy
1957,	Sep	Elected member of the Executive Committee of the Women's Federation
1958,	Apr	Member of a cultural delegation to England
	Oct	Member of a delegation to the Afro-Asian Writers' Congress in Tashkent, USSR
	Nov	Member of a workers' delegation to the USSR attenting celebrations of the October Revolution anniversary
	Dec	Elected member of the Standing Committee, Central Committee of the China Association for Promoting Democracy (until Oct 1979)
1960,	Aug	Identified as deputy director of the Children's Literature Section of the Writers' Union

1961,	Mar	Member of a writers' delegation to the Afro-Asian Conference in Tokyo
1962,	Feb	Member of a delegation to the 2nd Afro-Asian Writers' Conference in Cairo
1963,	Aug	Identified as council member of the Sino-Japanese Friendship Association and as secretary of the Writers' Union
1967		Disappears during the Cultural Revolution
1972,	Jun	First appearance after the Cultural Revolution: Present at a reception given for Han Suyin
1973,	Apr	Member of a friendship delegation to Japan
1978,	Feb	Elected deputy for Fujian Province to the 5th NPC
	Mar	Elected member of the Standing Committee of the 5th CPPCC
	Sep	Identified as advisor to the Popular Science Writers' Society
1979,	Jun	Member of the Committee to Examine Proposals of the 2nd Session of the 5th NPC
	Oct	Elected vice-chairman of the Central Commission, China Association for Promoting Democracy
	Nov	Elected vice-chairman of the Federation of Literary and Art Circles

Publications

1920	Two volumes of poetry: Spring Creek and Myriad Stars
1923	Short stories: Superman
1926	Letters to Young Readers
1931	Returning South
1936	More Letters to Young Readers
	About Women

Translation

| 1936 | The Prophet by Kahlil Gibran |

Xie Gaozhong (Hsieh Kao-chung) 謝高忠

Posts held

Provincial Administration
Vice-chairman of the People's Government of Xinjiang Autonomous Region

| 1978, | Feb | Elected vice-chairman of the Revolutionary Committee of Xinjiang Autonomous Region (until Aug 1979) |
| 1979, | Sep | Elected vice-chairman of the People's Government of Xinjiang Autonomous Region |

Xie Hechou (Hsieh Ho-ch'ou) 謝鶴籌

Posts held

Government
Vice-minister of the State Nationalities Affairs Commission

Xie belongs to the Zhuang minority; he was born in Guangxi Province.

1950,	Mar	Identified as member of the Guangxi People's Government
1954,	Jun	Identified as director of the 1st Section, Nationalities Affairs Commission
	Aug	Elected deputy for Guangxi to the 1st NPC (reelected in 1958 and 1964 to the 2nd and 3rd NPCs)
1956,	Jan	Identified as director, Political and Legal Section of the Nationalities Affairs Commission
1957,	May	Appointed vice-chairman of the Nationalities Affairs Commission (until Cultural Revolution)
1966		Disappears during the Cultural Revolution
1979,	May	Identified as vice-minister of the State Nationalities Affairs Commission

Xie Hongsheng (Hsieh Hung-sheng) 谢红胜

Posts held

Government
Vice-minister of textile industry

| 1977, | Jun | Identified as a government cadre |
| 1979, | Feb | Identified as vice-minister of textile industry; head of a textile delegation to France |

Xie Huaide (Hsieh Huai-te) 谢怀德

Posts held

CCP
Member of the Standing Committee of Shaanxi Province CP

Provincial Administration
Vice-governor of Shaanxi Province

Xie was born circa 1907 in Ganquan, Shaanxi Province. Around 1940 he served as mayor of Yan'an.

1950,	Feb	Identified as director of the Agriculture and Forestry Department of Shaanxi People's Government
1953,	Jan	Identified as council member of Shaanxi People's Government
1956,	Nov	Identified as vice-governor of Shaanxi Province (until 1964)
1961,	Jun	Identified as secretary of Shaanxi Province CP (until 1964)
1964,	Dec	Appointed vice-chairman of the State Commission for Economic Relations with Foreign Countries (until 1970)
1970,	Jun	Xie disappears for unknown reasons
1979,	Mar	First reappearance: Identified as member of the Standing Committee of Shaanxi Province CP and as vice-chairman of the Revolutionary Committee of Shaanxi Province (latter post until Dec 1979)
	Dec	Elected vice-governor of Shaanxi Province

Xie Huangtian (Hsieh Huang-t'ien) 谢荒田

Posts held

Provincial Administration
Vice-governor of Liaoning Province

1978,	May	Elected vice-chairman of the Revolutionary Committee of Liaoning Province (until Jan 1980); identified as secretary of Liaoning Province CP (until Aug 1979)
1980,	Feb	Elected vice-governor of Liaoning Province

Xie Kexi (Hsieh K'e-hsi) 谢克西

Posts held

Government
Former ambassador to Niger

1949		Appointed secretary of Yancheng CP in Jiangsu Province and member of the North Jiangsu Administrative Council
1952,	Nov	Identified as member of the People's Government of Jiangsu Province
1953,	May	Elected alternate member of the Executive Council of the Federation of Trade Unions (until Dec 1957)
1956,	Feb	Identified as chairman of the Trade Unions of Jiangsu Province
1957,	Dec	Elected member of the Executive Council of the Federation of Trade Unions
1958,	Apr	Identified as deputy director of the Department of Industry and Communications, Jiangsu CP
1962,	Aug	Appointed ambassador to Ceylon (until Dec 1965)
1975,	Mar	Appointed ambassador to Niger (until Apr 1979)

Xie is married to Zhang Ren.

Xie Li (Hsieh Li) 谢黎

Posts held

Government
Secretary-general of the Institute of Foreign Affairs

1960		Identified as chargé d'affairs in the Netherlands
1963,	Nov	Identified as director of the Western Europe Department in the Ministry of Foreign Affairs
1967		Xie disappears during the Cultural Revolution
1973,	Sep	First appearance after the Cultural Revolution: Identified as a cadre of the Institute of Foreign Affairs
1978,	Nov	Identified as secretary-general of the Institute of Foreign Affairs

Xie Ming (Hsieh Ming) 谢明

Posts held

Government
Vice-minister of finance

1979,	Jun	Identified as vice-minister of finance

Xie Tieguang (Hsieh T'ieh-kuang)

Posts held

Others
President of the Law History Society
Deputy director of the Law Institute, Academy of Social Sciences

1978,	Jun	Identified as deputy director of the Law Institute under the Academy of Social Sciences
1979,	Sep	Elected president of the Law Society

Xie Tieli (Hsieh T'ieh-li) 谢铁俪

Posts held

NPC
Member of the Standing Committee of the 5th NPC
Deputy for Shanghai Municipality to the 5th NPC

Xie was born in 1925. He is a film producer who was persecuted by Jiang Qing.

1978,	Feb	Elected deputy for Shanghai Municipality to the 5th NPC
	Mar	Elected member of the Standing Committee of the 5th NPC
1979,	Apr	Member of an NPC delegation headed by Deng Yingchao to Japan

Xie Xide (Hsieh Hsi-te) (f) 谢希德

Posts held

Others
Vice-president of Fudan University
Vice-president of the Physics Society

Xie is a specialist in surface physics. She returned to China in 1952 from the United States where she had studied theoretical physics and obtained a doctorate.

1978,	Oct	Elected vice-president of the Physics Society; identified as vice-president of Fudan University; head of a delegation to the World Conference of the International Nuclear Target Development Society in the Federal Republic of Germany

Xie is married to Zao Dianjian.

Xie Xuegong (Hsieh Hsüeh-kung) 解学恭

<u>Posts held</u>

CCP
Member of the CCP 11th Central Committee

NPC
Deputy for Tianjin Municipality to the 5th NPC

In 1949 Xie was a cadre in the Taiyuan Military Control Commission.

1950,   Aug   Identified as vice-chairman of the People's Government of Shanxi Province (until Jun 1952)

    Dec   Identified as deputy secretary of Shanxi Province CP (until Jun 1952)

1952,   Nov   Identified as vice-minister of foreign trade (until Jun 1958)

1954,   Dec   Identified as director of the College of Foreign Trade (until Jun 1958)

1956,   Feb   Head of a trade delegation to North Vietnam

1958,   Aug   Identified as secretary of Hebei Province CP (until Cultural Revolution)

1963,   May   Identified as secretary of the North China Bureau in the CCP Central Committee (until Cultural Revolution)

1964,   Sep   Elected deputy for the Inner Mongolian Autonomous Region to the 3rd NPC

1969,   Apr   Elected to first term as member of the CCP Central Committee by the 9th Party Congress

    Sep   Identified as chairman of the Revolutionary Committee of Tianjin Municipality (until Jun 1978)

1971,   May   With reestablishment of the CP Secretariat after the Cultural Revolution Xie is elected 1st CP secretary (until Jun 1978)

1975,   Jun   Head of a friendship delegation of Tianjin Municipality to Japan

1978,   Feb   Elected deputy for Tianjin Municipality to the 5th NPC

    Jun   Xie is replaced by Lin Hujia in Tianjin and has probably been purged

Xie Yunqing (Hsieh Yün-ch'ing) 解云清

<u>Posts held</u>

Provincial Administration
Vice-governor of Heilongjiang Province

1960,   Feb   Identified as deputy director of the Department for Finance and Commerce, Heilongjiang Province CP

1979,   Dec   Elected vice-governor of Heilongjiang Province

Xie Zhenghao (Hsieh Cheng-hao) 谢正浩

<u>Posts held</u>

Military
Rear-admiral
Deputy commander of the East China Sea Fleet

1964,   Apr   Identified as chief of staff of the East China Sea Fleet; identified as rear-admiral

1967,   Aug   Appointed commander of Chousan Naval Base of the East China Sea Fleet

1968,   Mar   Elected member of the Standing Committee, Revolutionary Committee of Zhejiang Province (until 1969)

1969,   Sep   Identified as vice-chairman of the Revolutionary Committee of Zhejiang Province (until 1973)

1971,   Jan   Elected deputy secretary following the establishment of a CP Secretariat in Zhejiang Province after the Cultural Revolution (until 1973)

1975,   Dec   Identified as deputy commander of the East China Sea Fleet; subsequently disappears until

1978,   Apr   Renewed mention as deputy commander of the East China Sea Fleet

Xie Zhenhua (Hsieh Chen-hua) 谢振华

<u>Posts held</u>

Military
Major-general
Deputy commander of Shenyang Military Region

In 1945 Xie commanded an independent regiment of the New 4th Army.

1952   Identified as chief of staff of the 3rd Army, Chinese People's Volunteers in Korea

1955,   Sep   Promoted to rank of major-general

1957   Appointed deputy commander of the 3rd Army

1958   Graduation from a course at the PLA Military Academy

    Aug   Identified as commander of Jilin City Garrison (until Cultural Revolution)

1967   Xie commands the 69th Corps in Shanxi Province in support of the Revolutionary Committee established there

    Oct   Identified as military leader in Shanxi Province

1970,   May   Identified as commander of Shanxi Military District (until Apr 1971)

1971,   Apr   Elected 1st secretary following the reestablishment of the CP Secretariat in Shanxi Province after the Cultural Revolution (until 1973)

1972,   Nov   Identified as chairman of the Revolutionary Committee of Shanxi Province (until 1973)

1973,   Aug   Elected alternate member of the CCP Central Committee by the 10th Party Congress (not reelected by the CCP 11th Congress in 1977)

1975   Only two appearances recorded in this year until

1978,   Aug   Identified as deputy commander of Shenyang Military Region

Xi-hou-ba (Hsi·hou·pa)   希侯巴

Posts held

CCP
Member of the CCP 11th Central Committee
Deputy secretary, Haixi Autonomous Zhou CP, Qinghai Province

Provincial Administration
Vice-govervor of Qinghai Province

Xi-hou-ba belongs to the Tibetan minority.

1976   Identified as deputy secretary, Haixi Autonomous Zhou CP
1977,   Aug   Elected member of the CCP Central Committee by the 11th Party Congress
        Dec   Elected vice-chairman of the Revolutionary Committee of Qinghai Province (until Aug 1978)
1979,   Sep   Elected vice-governor of Qinghai Province

Xin Junjie (Hsin Chün-chieh)   信俊杰

Posts held

CCP
Member of the Standing Committee of Jiangxi Province CP

Military
Commander of Jiangxi Military District

1970,   Jun   Identified as vice-chairman of the Revolutionary Committee of Hubei Province (until 1975) and as commander of Hubei Military District (until 1975)
1973,   May   Identified as member of the Standing Committee of Hubei Province CP (until 1975)
1975,   Nov   Identified as commander of Jiangxi Military District
1977,   May   Identified as member of the Standing Committee of Jiangxi Province CP
1978,   Feb   Elected vice-chairman of the Revolutionary Committee of Jiangxi Province (until Dec 1979)
1979,   Mar   Identified as head of the Political and Legal Leadership Group of Jiangxi CP

Xin Yuanxi (Hsin Yüan-hsi)   忻元锡

Posts held

Government
Vice-minister of finance

1978,   Sep   Identified as vice-minister of finance; deputy head of an economic study group to Yugoslavia and Romania

Xing Chongzhi (Hsing Ch'ung-chih)   邢崇智

Posts held

Government
Vice-minister of agriculture

1964,   Jul   Elected member of the Central Committee, Communist Youth League. Thereafter Xing disappears
1978,   May   First appearance after the Cultural Revolution: Identified as vice-chairman of the Preparatory Committee for the 10th Congress of the Communist Youth League
1979,   Sep   Identified as vice-minister of agriculture; head of an agricultural delegation to Burma
        Nov   Head of a delegation to the 20th Session of the Food and Agriculture Organization (FAO) Conference in Rome

Xing Fangqun (Hsing Fang-ch'ün)   邢方群

Posts held

Mass Organization
Alternate member, Secretariat of the Federation of Trade Unions

Others
Editor-in-chief of Gongren Ribao (Workers Daily)

1964,   Oct   Elected deputy for Yunnan Province to the 3rd NPC
1965,   Nov   Identified as editor-in-chief of Gongren Ribao
1967   Disappears during the Cultural Revolution
1979,   Jul   First appearance after the Cultural Revolution: Identified as alternate member, Secretariat of the Federation of Trade Unions, in addition to his former post as editor-in-chief of Gongren Ribao

Xing Yanzi (Hsing Yen-tzu) (f)   邢燕子

Posts held

CCP
Member of the CCP 11th Central Committee
Secretary, Tianjin Municipality CP

Provincial Administration
Vice-chairman, Revolutionary Committee of Tianjin Municipality

Mass Organization
Vice-chairman, Communist Youth League of Tianjin Municipality

Xing was born in 1940 in Tianjin. Her father was a deputy director of a factory.

1958		After graduating from middle school Xing goes to the countryside as an agricultural worker (she thus anticipated a development on her own initiative which a decade later made rural work compulsory for educated youth). She distinguishes herself by her work in Sijiazhuang Brigade of Dazhongzhuang People's Commune.
1960		Xing joins the CCP
1962,	Dec	Elected member of the 9th National Congress of the Communist Youth League
1964,	Oct	Elected deputy for Hebei Province to the 3rd NPC as well as member of the presidium
1968,	Feb	Identified as member of the Revolutionary Committee of Hebei Province
1971,	May	Elected member of Hebei Province CP and member of the CP of Baodi County
1973,	Apr	Identified as vice-chairman of the Revolutionary Committee of Dazhongzhuang People's Commune in Baodi County, Hebei Province; member of a delegation of the Sino-Japanese Friendship Association to Japan
	May	Elected vice-chairman of the Communist Youth League of Hebei Province
	Aug	Elected to first term as member of the CCP Central Committee by the 10th Party Congress
1975,	May	Identified as secretary, Tianjin Municipality CP
	Dec	Identified as deputy chairman of the Revolutionary Committee of Tianjin Municipality; head of a friendship delegation to Romania

Xing Yimin (Hsing Yi-min)　邢亦民

Posts held

NPC
Deputy secretary-general of the 5th NPC

1954,	Nov	Identified as member of the Supreme People's Court
1956,	Mar	Identified as member of the Foreign Arbitration Committee, Association for Promoting International Trade
1962,	Sep	Identified as deputy director, 2nd Court of Criminal Cases of the Supreme People's Court
1966,	Mar	Appointed vice-president of the Supreme People's Court (until 1967)
1967		Xing disappears
1978,	May	First appearance after the Cultural Revolution: Appointed deputy secretary-general of the 5th NPC

Xing Yuanlin (Hsing Yüan-lin)　幸元林

Posts held

NPC
Deputy for the PLA to the 5th NPC

Military
Deputy commander of Xinjiang Military Region

| 1978, | Feb | Elected deputy for the PLA to the 5th NPC |
| 1979, | Apr | Identified as deputy commander of Xinjiang Military Region |

Xiong Fu (Hsiung Fu)　熊復

Posts held

CCP
Editor-in-chief of HQ

NPC
Deputy for Sichuan Province to the 5th NPC

Others
Member of the Standing Committee of the 5th CPPCC

Xiong was born in 1916 in Sichuan Province. In 1946 he worked on the Chongqing Staff of the NCNA. In 1947 he went to Yan'an. In July 1949 he was elected a member of the Preparatory Committee of the Journalists' Association.

1949,	Oct	Appointed deputy director of the Propaganda Department, Central-South Bureau of the CCP Central Committee
1950,	Mar	Identified as director of the Information and Publications Bureau of the Central-South Military and Administrative Council (until 1953); identified as director of Changjiang Ribao (Yangtse River Daily)
1954,	May	Identified as council member of the Association for Cultural Relations with Foreign Countries
1955,	Sep	Member of a scientific delegation to Japan
	Dec	Identified as a researcher of No. 3 Historical Research Institute of the Academy of Sciences
1956,	Feb	Identified as a member of the Asian Solidarity Committee (until 1958)
	Apr	Appointed secretary-general of the Propaganda Department, CCP Central Committee
	Nov	Member of a delegation led by Zhou Enlai to North Vietnam, Cambodia, India, Burma, Pakistan, the USSR, Poland, Hungary, Afghanistan, Nepal, and Ceylon (until Feb 1957)
1961,	May	Advisor to the Chinese delegation at the Geneva Conference
1962,	Nov	Member of a Party delegation to Bulgaria, Hungary, Czechoslovakia, and the German Democratic Republic (until Jan 1963)
1964,	Dec	Elected a member of the 4th CPPCC
1965,	Jun	Elected a member of the Afro-Asian Solidarity Committee
1967,	Mar	Branded as a counterrevolutionary revisionist and purged

1973,	Oct	First appearance after the Cultural Revolution
1978,	Feb	Elected deputy for Sichuan Province to the 5th NPC
	Mar	Elected a member of the Standing Committee of the 5th CPPCC
	Oct	Identified as editor-in-chief of HQ
1979,	Sep	Head of an HQ delegation to Romania

Xiong Tianjing (Hsiung T'ien-ching) (f)

熊 天 荆

Posts held

Others
Member of the Standing Committee of the 5th CPPCC

Xiong was vice-chairman of the Democratic Women's Federation in the Shaanxi-Gansu-Ningxia Border Region around 1947.

1949,	Oct	Appointed director of the Relief and Pension Department in the Ministry of Civil Affairs
1954,	Mar	Identified as director of the General Office in the Ministry of Civil Affairs
1957,	Sep	Identified as director of the Rural Relief Department in the Ministry of Civil Affairs
1964,	Jul	Elected chairman of the Association of the Blind, Deaf and Dumb
	Oct	Elected deputy for Heilongjiang Province to the 3rd NPC
1967		Disappears during the Cultural Revolution
1972,	Apr	First appearance after the Cultural Revolution: Present at the mourning ceremonies for Li Dequan
1978,	Mar	Elected member of the Standing Committee of the 5th CPPCC

Xiong Xianghui (Hsiung Hsiang-hui)

熊 向 辉

Posts held

CCP
Deputy director of the Department for United Front Work, CCP Central Committee

Government
Deputy director of the Institute of Foreign Affairs

Others
Member of the Standing Committee of the 5th CPPCC

1954,	May	Identified as a council member of the Association for Cultural Relations with Foreign Countries (until 1960)
1960,	Aug	Identified as director of a department in the Ministry for Foreign Affairs
1961,	May	Advisor to the Chinese delegation at the Laos Conference in Geneva
1962,	Mar	Identified as chargé d'affaires at the Chinese Diplomatic Mission in London (until Cultural Revolution)

1972,	Apr	Appointed ambassador to Mexico (until Aug 1973)
1973,	Mar	Deputy head of the Chinese delegation to the UN Security Council Meeting in Panama
	Oct	Identified as a cadre in a department of the CCP Central Committee (until 1977)
1978,	Mar	Elected a member of the Standing Committee, 5th CPPCC
	Nov	Identified as deputy director of the Institute of Foreign Affairs; advisor to a delegation under vice premier Wang Zhen to Great Britain
1979,	Jan	Identified as deputy director of the Department for United Front Work under the CCP Central Committee

Xiong Yi (Hsiung Yi)

熊 毅

Posts held

Others
Director of the Nanjing Institute of Pedology, Academy of Sciences

1951		Xiong receives a doctor's degree at the University of Wisconsin, U.S.A.
1960,	Dec	Identified as director of the Institute of Water and Soil Conservation, Academy of Sciences
1961,	Jan	Member of a scientific delegation to the 13th Pakistan Scientific Conference in Dacca
1963,	Mar	Identified as deputy director of the Institute of Pedology, Academy of Sciences (until Cultural Revolution); member of a scientific delegation to the 15th Pakistan Scientific Conference in Lahore
1979,	Dec	First appearance after the Cultural Revolution; identified as director of the Nanjing Institute of Pedology, Academy of Sciences

Publications

1962	"Problems on the Improvement of Alkaline Soil in Hebei Province" (article in GMRB, July 1962)
1963	"On Alkaline Soil" "Prevent the Soils of North China Plain from Being Alkaline" (articles distributed to the National Working Conference on Agricultural Science and Technology)

Xiong Zuofang (Hsiung Tso-fang)

熊 作 芳

Posts held

Military
Deputy commander of Jinan Military Region

1973,	Apr	Identified as leading military in Jinan Military Region
1978,	May	Identified as deputy commander of Jinan Military Region

Xu Biaojun (Hsü Piao-chün) 许彪俊

Posts held

CCP
Alternate member of the CCP 11th Central Committee

1977, Aug Elected alternate member of the CCP Central Committee by the 11th Party Congress

Xu Binru (Hsü Pin-ju) 徐彬如

Posts held

Others
Member of the Standing Committee of the 5th CPPCC
Vice-chairman of the Central Committee, China Peasants and Workers Democratic Party

1957, May Identified as member of China Peasants and Workers Democratic Party
1961, Jul Identified as director of Beijing Revolutionary Museum
1965, Jan Identified as deputy director of Beijing Revolutionary Museum
1978, Mar Elected member of the Standing Committee of the 5th CPPCC
Aug Identified as member of the Central Presidium, China Peasants and Workers Democratic Party (until Oct 1979)
1979, Oct Elected vice-chairman of the Central Committee of China Peasants and Workers Democratic Party

Xu Binzhou (Hsü Pin-chou) 徐斌洲

Posts held

Government
Vice-minister, 1st Ministry of Machine Building

Military
Lieutenant-general

Others
Member of the Standing Committee of the 5th CPPCC

Xu commanded an independent brigade in the Shanxi-Chahar-Hebei Military Region in 1944. In 1947 he was made deputy commander of the 6th Column, North China Field Army. In early 1949 he became commander of the 68th Corps, 20th Army, under the direct command of the PLA Headquarters.

1950, Jul Xu takes part in the Korean War
1953 Visit to the Institute of Military Affairs
1958, Jun Identified as lieutenant-general and deputy political commissar at the Institute of Military Affairs
1960, Apr Appointed vice-minister of agricultural machinery
1965, Jan The Ministry of Agricultural Machinery is renamed 8th Ministry of Machine Building; Xu continues as vice-minister

1970, Jul First appearance after the Cultural Revolution after four years absence; identified as a cadre in the 1st Ministry of Machine Building
1972, Feb Identified as vice-minister, 1st Ministry of Machine Building
1977, Feb Head of a delegation to Pakistan to inaugurate a foundry and forge in Taxila
1979, Jul By-elected member of the Standing Committee of the 5th CPPCC

Xu Boxin (Hsü Po-hsin) 徐伯昕

Posts held

Others
Member of the Standing Committee of the 5th CPPCC
Deputy secretary-general of the 5th CPPCC
Vice-chairman of the China Association for Promoting Democracy

Before the foundation of PRC, Xu was a well-known publisher. He took part in the 1st CPPCC in September 1949 as a delegate representing the China Association for Promoting Democracy.

1949, Dec Identified as member of the Central Committee, China Democratic League; appointed deputy director of the General Office, Publications Administration of the Government Administrative Council (until 1952)
1950, Apr Identified as deputy secretary-general, China Association for Promoting Democracy (until Dec 1958)
1954, Aug Elected deputy for Sichuan Province to the 1st NPC (reelected in 1958 and 1964 by the 2nd and 3rd NPCs)
Dec Elected deputy secretary-general of the CPPCC
1958, Dec Elected secretary-general of the China Association for Promoting Democracy
1965, Jan Elected member of the Standing Committee of the 4th CPPCC
1967 Disappears during the Cultural Revolution
1972, Sep First appearance after the Cultural Revolution: Identified as holding his previous post as member of the Standing Committee of the 4th CPPCC
1978, Mar Elected member of the Standing Committee of the 5th CPPCC
Aug Identified as deputy secretary-general of the 5th CPPCC; identified as vice-chairman of the China Association for Promoting Democracy (reelected Oct 1979)

Xu Changyu (Hsü Ch'ang-yü) 徐昌裕

Posts held

Government
Vice-minister of the 3rd Ministry of Machine Building

Military
Major-general

| 1958, | Oct | Identified as major-general |
| 1979, | Mar | Identified as vice-minister of the 3rd Ministry of Machine Building |

Xu Chi (Hsü Ch'ih) 徐 驰

Posts held

CCP
Alternate member of the CCP 11th Central Committee

Government
Vice-minister of metallurgical industry

Others
Vice-president of the Metallurgy Society

1950,	Mar	Identified as director of the Planning Department in the Ministry of Heavy Industry
1955,	Feb	Identified as assistant minister of the Ministry of Heavy Industry (until May 1956)
1957,	Jun	Identified as assistant minister of the Ministry of Metallurgical Industry (until Sep 1959)
1959,	Sep	Appointed vice-minister of the Ministry of Metallurgical Industry (until 1966)
1968,	May	Elected vice-chairman of the Revolutionary Committee of Sichuan Province (until Feb 1978)
1969,	Apr	Elected to first term as alternate member of the CCP Central Committee by the 9th Party Congress
1971,	Aug	Elected secretary of Sichuan Province CP (until Feb 1978)
1978,	Apr	Identified as vice-minister of metallurgical industry
	Aug	Identified as vice-president of the Metallurgy Society; head of a metallurgical delegation to Canada, the U.S.A., and Mexico

Xu Chubo (Hsü Ch'u-po) 徐楚波

Posts held

Others
Member of the Standing Committee of the 5th CPPCC
Member of the Standing Committee, China Association for Promoting Democracy

Xu was born in 1899 in Wei County, Hebei Province. He graduated from the History and Geography Department of Zhili High Normal College. He then lectured at the following schools: Sino-Japanese Middle School in Tianjin, Girls Middle School attached to Beijing Normal University, Beijing Chengda Middle School, Beijing No. 1 Middle School, Datong Middle School. In September 1949 he took part in the 1st CPPCC.

| 1949, | Dec | Identified as principal of Peking No. 1 Middle School |
| 1956, | Aug | Elected member of the Standing Committee, China Association for Promoting Democracy |

1959,	Apr	Elected member of the 3rd CPPCC
1965,	Jan	Elected member of the Standing Committee, 4th CPPCC
1967		Disappears during the Cultural Revolution
1973,	May	First appearance after the Cultural Revolution
1978,	Mar	Elected member of the Standing Committee of the 5th CPPCC
	Aug	Identified as member of the Standing Committee, China Association for Promoting Democracy

Xu Daoqi (Hsü Tao-ch'i) 许道珩

Posts held

CCP
Secretary of the Hubei Province CP

1953,	Jul	Identified as director of the Propaganda Department of Hubei Province CP (until 1957)
1956,	Feb	Identified as secretary of Hubei Province CP (until Cultural Revolution)
1958,	Jan	Identified as vice-chairman of the Preparatory Committee for the Wuhan Branch of the Academy of Sciences
1960,	May	Member of a CCP delegation led by Bo Yibo to Poland
1964,	Sep	Elected deputy for Hubei Province to the 3rd NPC
1966,	Sep	Identified as head of the Cultural Revolutionary Group of Hubei Province CP
1968,	Feb	Branded as a supporter of Liu Shaoqi
1978,	Jan	First appearance after the Cultural Revolution: Elected vice-chairman of the Revolutionary Committee of Hubei Province (until Dec 1979)
1979,	Apr	Identified as secretary of Hubei Province CP
	Jul	Appointed member of the National Games Organizing Committee

Xu Deheng (Hsü Te-heng) 许德珩

Posts held

NPC
Vice-chairman of the Standing Committee of the 5th NPC
Deputy for Tianjin Municipality to the 5th NPC

Others
Vice-chairman of the 5th CPPCC
Chairman of the Jiusan Society

Xu was born in 1890 in Jiujiang County, Jiangxi Province. He studied at Beijing University and as a student leader took a major part in the May 4th Movement in 1919. After graduating in Beijing Xu went to Europe to study sociology and economics at the universities of Paris and London. After his return to China around 1924 he lectured at various universities and soon gained the reputation of a leftist professor. Together with other members of the KMT left wing he edited the journals _Revolutionary_

Review and Mass Vanguard in early 1927 which were banned, however, shortly after the rift between the CCP and the KMT. As a professor at Beijing University he was one of the strongest advocates of resistance against the Japanese following the "Incident of 18 September 1931." After the outbreak of the Anti-Japanese War in 1937 he founded a school in his home province for the training of military and political cadres. Together with two other academics Xu founded the Democracy and Science Society which was renamed Jiusan Society after the end of the Anti-Japanese War. During this period Xu returned to Beijing University. Xu organized a celebration at the Tianan Men and gave a welcoming speech for the Communist forces entering Beijing. Three months later he was sent with Guo Moruo as a delegate to the World Peace Council in Paris. After his return he was elected a member of the Standing Committee of the reorganized Beijing University. In September of that year he took part as a delegate of the Jiusan Society in the CPPCC which elected him a member of its National Committee.

1949,	Oct	Appointed member of the Committee of Political and Legal Affairs and vice-chairman of the Legislative Council (probably until 1954)
	Dec	Elected chairman of the Jiusan Society
1954,	Sep	Elected deputy for Jiangxi Province to the 1st NPC (reelected in 1959 and 1964 to the 2nd and 3rd NPCs)
1956,	Apr?	Elected chairman of the Western Pacific Fishery Study Commission
	May	Elected minister of aquatic products (until Cultural Revolution)
1965,	Jan	Elected vice-chairman, CPPCC (confirmed in 1968)
1975,	Jan	Elected one of the 22 vice-chairmen of the Standing Committee by the 4th NPC (confirmed in this post in 1978 by the 5th NPC)
1978,	Feb	Elected deputy for Tianjin Municipality to the 5th NPC
1979,	Apr	Xu becomes a member of the CCP
	Oct	Reelected chairman of the Jiusan Society

Xu Dixin (Hsü Ti-hsin)　　　許涤新

Posts held

NPC
Member of the Standing Committee of the 5th NPC
Deputy for Guangdong Province to the 5th NPC

Others
Vice-president of the Academy of Social Sciences
Director of the Institute of Economics of the Academy of Social Sciences
Honorary president of the Society of Foreign Economic Theories
Honorary president of the Insurance Society

Xu was born in 1902 in Jieyang County, Guangdong Province. As a student at the Sun Yat-sen University in Guangzhou he joined the Communist Youth League in 1925. He was dismissed from university because of Communist activities in 1927 and found employment as an elementary school teacher in Shantou. Several attempts to complete his studies at the universities of Xiamen and Fudan failed because of financial difficulties. He eventually graduated from the Shanghai Institute of Economics in 1933. Then Xu became active in Communist underground work in the Shanghai area. In 1935 he was arrested and only released in 1937 after the outbreak of the Anti-Japanese War. After initially working for the newspaper Xinhua Ribao (New China) published in Hankou (today: Wuhan), he was engaged for the remaining war period in United Front Work mainly in Hankou, Chongqing, Nanjing, and Shanghai. During this period he wrote two books on economics. In July 1949 he was elected a member of the Preparatory Committee of the Association of New Science. Two months later he was appointed vice-chairman of the Committee of Financial and Economic Affairs of East China Military Region.

1950,	Jan	Identified as vice-chairman of the Committee of Financial and Economic Affairs in the East China Military and Administrative Council, as member of the Shanghai People's Government Council and of the Shanghai Bureau of Financial and Economic Affairs (until Jun 1954)
1952,	May	Elected a member of the newly established Council for the Promotion of International Trade
	Jun	Elected a member of the Preparatory Committee for the Federation of Industry and Commerce (until Oct 1953)
	Jul	Elected a member of the Standing Committee of the National Construction Association
1953,	Oct	Elected vice-chairman of the Federation of Industry and Commerce
1954,	Jun	Elected deputy for Shandong Province to the 1st NPC (until Mar 1959)
	Aug	Appointed deputy director of the 8th Office, State Council (until Sep 1959)
	Nov	Appointed director of the Central Administration of Industry and Commerce (probably until Sep 1959)
1956,	Sep	Elected a member of the CCP Central Committee and deputy director of the United Front Work Department in the CCP Central Committee
1964,	Sep	Elected deputy for Guangdong Province to the 3rd NPC
1967		Disappears during the Cultural Revolution
1975,	Sep	First appearance after the Cultural Revolution
1977,	Nov	Article in RMRB of 22 November: "On Profits under Socialism"
1978,	Feb	Elected deputy for Guangdong Province to the 5th NPC
	Mar	Elected a member of the Standing Committee of the 5th NPC
	May	Identified as director of the Institute of Economics of the Academy of Social Sciences
	Aug	Head of a delegation of academics to the 26th Conference of the European Association of Chinese Studies in Rome
	Nov	Identified as vice-president of the Academy of Social Sciences

1979,   Jun   Vice-chairman of the Budget Committee, 2nd Session of the 5th NPC
        Oct   Elected honorary president of the Society of Foreign Economic Theories
        Dec   Elected honorary president of the Insurance Society

              Publications

1947   On the Economy
              On the Collapse of the Chinese Economy
              The Birth of New China
1948   The Road for the Chinese Economy
              The Road out for Commercialists and Industrialists
1949   New Democracy and China's Economy
1950   Brief History of Economism
              The Enlargement of Political Economy
1951   On Bureaucratic Capital
1957   An Analysis of China's Economy during the Transition Period

Xu Feiqing (Hsü Fei-ch'ing)   许飞青

Posts held

Provincial Administration
Vice-governor of Gansu Province

1979,   Dec   Elected vice-governor of Gansu Province

Xu Guanren (Hsü Kuan-jen)

Posts held

Others President of the Society for the Application of Atomic Energy in Agronomy

Xu, a renowned radiation seed breeding expert, returned from the U.S.A. in 1956.

1978,   Jun   Identified as professor of the Research Institute for Application of Atomic Energy to Agriculture, Academy of Agricultural Science
1979,   Apr   Elected president of the Society for the Application of Atomic Energy in Agronomy

Xu Guoxian (Hsü Kuo-hsien)   徐国贤

Posts held

Military
Major-general
Deputy commander, PLA Engineer Corps

Xu commanded the 718th Regiment of the 120th Division, 8th Route Army, in 1938. In 1945 he led a column of the 359th Brigade. In 1948 he commanded the 5th Brigade, 2nd Column, Northwest Field Army. He took part in the occupation of Xinjiang in 1949 as commander of the 5th Division of the 6th Army.

1950   Identified as deputy commander of the 2nd Army

1956   Identified as deputy commander of South Xinjiang Military District and as major-general
1960,   Apr   Identified as deputy commander of Xinjiang Military Region
1973,   Jul   Identified as 1st deputy commander of Xinjiang Military Region (until about 1975)
1978,   Jul   Identified as deputy commander, PLA Engineer Corps

Xu Huang (Hsü Huang)   徐晃

Posts held

Government
Ambassador to Laos

1955   Identified as deputy director of the Information Department in the Ministry of Foreign Affairs
1960,   Apr   Identified as counselor, embassy in the German Democratic Republic (until 1963?)
1964,   Oct   Identified as director of a department in the Ministry of Foreign Affairs (until?)
1977,   Dec   Appointed ambassador to Laos

Xu Jianchun (Hsü Chien-ch'un) (f)   徐建春

Posts held

CCP
Member of the Standing Committee, Shandong Province CP

Provincial Administration
Vice-chairman of the People's Congress, Shandong Province

Mass Organization
Secretary of the Communist Youth League, Shandong Province

1951   Xu, an intellectual youth, goes to the countryside
1956,   Sep   Elected member of the Central Committee, Communist Youth League (confirmed in 1964)
1958,   Jul   Identified as head of the Xiyu People's Commune in Yi County, Shandong Province
1959,   Mar   Elected deputy for Shandong Province to the 2nd NPC (relected in 1964 to the 3rd NPC)
1965,   Jan   Elected vice-chairman of the Youth Federation
1966   Xu disappears
1973,   Jun   First appearance after the Cultural Revolution; identified as secretary of the Communist Youth League, Shandong Province, and as a member of the Standing Committee of Shandong Province CP
1979,   Dec   Elected vice-chairman of the People's Congress, Shandong Province

Xu Jiansheng (Hsü Chien-sheng) 徐健生

Posts held

CCP
Deputy secretary, Guizhou Province CP
1st secretary, Guiyang Municipality CP

Provincial Administration
Chairman of the People's Congress, Guizhou Province

Before 1949 Xu once served as secretary-general of NCNA.

1950,	Jun	Identified as secretary-general of the People's Government of Guizhou Province
1954,	Jun	Identified as director of the Department of United Front Work, Guizhou Province CP
	Aug	Elected deputy for Guizhou Province to the 1st NPC (reelected in 1958 and 1964 to the 2nd and 3rd NPCs)
1955,	Feb	Identified as vice-governor of Guizhou Province (until Cultural Revolution)
1956,	Nov	Identified as a member of the Standing Committee, Guizhou Province CP
1962,	Nov	Identified as alternate secretary of Guizhou Province CP
1966,	Sep	Identified as secretary of Guizhou Province CP
1967,	Jan	Xu disappears
1972,	Jul	First appearance after the Cultural Revolution
1973,	Oct	Identified as a cadre of the CCP Central Committee (until 1976)
1977,	Dec	Identified as deputy secretary of Guizhou Province CP and as 1st secretary of Guiyang Municipality CP
1980,	Jan	Elected chairman of the People's Congress, Guizhou Province

Xu Jiatun (Hsü Chia-t'un) 许家屯

Posts held

CCP
Member of the CCP 11th Central Committee
1st secretary of Jiangsu Province CP
Director of the Party School of Jiangsu CP

NPC
Deputy for Jiangsu Province to the 5th NPC

Military
1st political commissar of Jiangsu Military District

Provincial Administration
Chairman of the People's Congress of Jiangsu Province

1950		Identified as secretary, CP of Fuzhou, Fujian Province
1954		Identified as secretary, CP of Nanjing, Jiangsu Province
1955,	Jul	Identified as deputy secretary of Jiangsu Province CP

1956,	Oct	Identified as secretary of Jiangsu Province CP (until Cultural Revolution)
1958,	Jun	Lecturer at Nanjing Technical College
	Jul	Appointed chairman of the Jiangsu Branch of the Academy of Sciences; identified as chairman of the Committee for Scientific Work of Jiangsu Province
	Oct	Elected vice-governor of Jiangsu Province (until Cultural Revolution)
1968,	Mar	Xu is relieved of all posts
1970,	Dec	Identified as vice-chairman of the Revolutionary Committee of Jiangsu Province (until Mar 1977)
1975,	Sep	Identified as secretary of Jiangsu Province CP (until Mar 1977)
1977,	Mar	Identified as 1st secretary, Jiangsu Province CP, and chairman of the Revolutionary Committee of Jiangsu Province (latter post until Dec 1979); 1st political commissar of Jiangsu Military District
	Jul	Article in HQ: "A Party Committee Should Be a Promotion Committee"
	Aug	Elected member of the Central Committee by the CCP 11th Congress
	Oct	Head of a Party workers delegation to Romania; appointed director of the Jiangsu Party School
1978,	Feb	Elected deputy for Jiangsu Province to the 5th NPC
1979,	Sep	Member of a government delegation, headed by Gu Mu, to Japan
	Nov	Head of a Jiangsu Province friendship delegation to Australia
	Dec	Elected chairman of the People's Congress of Jiangsu Province

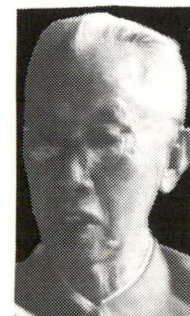

Xu Jie (Hsü Chieh) 许傑

Posts held

Government
Deputy director of the State Geological Bureau

NPC
Member of the Standing Committee of the 5th NPC
Deputy for Anhui Province to the 5th NPC

Others
Vice-president of the Geology Society

Xu was born in 1900 in Tiantai County, Zhejiang Province. He graduated from the Imperial University in Japan. He then held the following offices: chief editor of South Seas Masses News in Malaya, professor at the New China Arts College in Shanghai, and professor at the Zhongshan University in Canton.

1949,	Dec	Identified as member of the Cultural and Educational Committee, East China Military and Administrative Council (until Jun 1954)
1951		Identified as president of Anhui University
1952,	Aug	Vice-chairman of the People's Government of Anhui Province (until Feb 1955)
1954,	Jun	Appointed vice-minister of geology (until Cultural Revolution)

Aug   Elected deputy for Anhui Province to the 1st NPC (confirmed in 1958 and 1964 by the 2nd and 3rd NPCs)

1955,   May   Deputy director of the Department of Biology and Earth Sciences, Academy of Sciences

1956,   Feb   Elected member of the Standing Committee, China Democratic League

Mar   Identified as member of the Scientific Planning Commission (until 1957)

1957,   Nov   Member of a scientific and technical delegation to the USSR

1958,   Sep   Appointed honorary member of the USSR Paleontology Society

1959,   Aug   Appointed president of the Geological Research Institute

1966,   Feb   Head of a government delegation to Tanzania

1967   Disappears during the Cultural Revolution

1973,   May   First appearance after the Cultural Revolution: Identified as a cadre in the State Bureau of Geology

1977,   Jul   Head of a geologists' delegation to Romania; identified as acting president of the Geology Society (until Oct 1979)

1978,   Feb   Elected deputy for Anhui Province to the 5th NPC

Mar   Elected member of the Standing Committee of the 5th NPC

1979,   Apr   Identified as deputy director of the State Geological Bureau

Oct   Identified as vice-president of the Geological Society

Xu Leijian (Hsü Lei-chien)   住雷健

Posts held

CCP
Member of the Standing Committee, Shandong Province CP

Provincial Administration
Vice-governor of Shandong Province

1963   Identified as a member of the Executive Council, Federation of Trade Unions

1977,   May   Identified as a member of the Standing Committee, Shandong Province CP

1979,   Jul   Appointed member of the National Games Organizing Committee

Dec   Elected vice-governor of Shandong Province

Xu Liangtu (Hsü Liang-t'u)   徐良图

Posts held

Government
Vice-minister of the State Economic Commission

1977,   Nov   Identified as vice-minister of the State Planning Commission (until Sep 1978)

1978,   Oct   Identified as vice-minister of the State Economic Commission; deputy head of a delegation of that commission to Japan

Xu Liqing (Hsü Li-ch'ing)   徐立清

Posts held

CCP
Alternate member of the CCP 11th Central Committee

Military
Lieutenant-general
Deputy director, General Political Department of the PLA

Xu was born in 1907 (1908?) in Henan Province. He studied at Nankai University in Tianjin. In 1933 he joined the Jiangxi Soviet and later probably took part in the Long March. In 1936 he served as political commissar in the 1st Front Army. After studying at the Party School in Yan'an he was engaged in political work in the 115th Division of the 8th Route Army. In 1942 he became political commissar of the New 4th Army. In 1949 he commanded a division in the 1st Field Army.

1949,   Oct   Appointed director of the Political Department of Xinjiang Military Region

Dec   Appointed deputy secretary, Xinjiang Sub-bureau of the CCP Central Committee

1952,   Aug   Identified as deputy director of the Cadre Department in the Revolutionary Military Council (until Sep 1954)

1954,   Aug   Elected deputy for the PLA to the 1st NPC (reelected in 1959 and 1964 to the 2nd and 3rd NPCs)

Sep   Appointed deputy director of the Cadre Department of the PLA

1955,   Sep   Promoted to rank of lieutenant-general

1959,   Apr   Elected member of the Standing Committee of the 3rd CPPCC

1963,   Aug   Identified as deputy director of the General Political Department of the PLA (until Cultural Revolution)

1967,   Jan   Appointed deputy head of the PLA Cultural Revolution Group

Aug   Suspended from office for self-examination and then purged

1973,   Jul   First appearance after the Cultural Revolution

Oct   Identified as member of the Standing Committee of the 3rd NPC, a post to which he had never been elected

1974,   Jan   Identified as political commissar of Jinan Military Region (until 1975)

1976,   Apr   Identified as deputy director of the General Political Department of the PLA

1977,   Aug   Elected alternate member of the CCP Central Committee by the 11th Party Congress

Xu Liqun (Hsü Li-ch'ün)   许立群

Posts held

Others
Member of the Standing Committee of the 5th CPPCC

Xu was born in Jiangsu Province. In April 1949 he was elected member of the New Democratic Youth League (NDYL).

1949,	Oct	Identified as secretary of the Beijing Municipal Work Committee, NDYL
	Dec	Identified as member of the People's Control Commission of the Government Administrative Council (until 1954)
1950,	May	Member of a delegation to the celebrations of May Day in Czechoslovakia
	Aug	Member of a youth delegation to the German Democratic Republic
1951,	Jul	Identified as alternate member of the Central Committee, NDYL (until 1954)
1954,	Aug	Elected deputy for Jiangsu Province to the 1st NPC
1956,	Sep	Identified as director of the Theoretical Propaganda Section, Propaganda Department of the CCP Central Committee
1961,	Sep	Identified as deputy director of the Propaganda Department in the CCP Central Committee
1964,	Sep	Identified as deputy editor-in-chief of HQ
1966,	Dec	Accused of being a "three-anti element" and purged
1975,	Sep	First appearance after the Cultural Revolution
1978,	Mar	Elected member of the Standing Committee of the 5th CPPCC

Xu Liyi (Hsü Li-yi)　　　许力以

Posts held

Government
Deputy director of the State Publication Administration Bureau

1978,	Jul	Identified as deputy director of the State Publication Administration Bureau
	Sep	Head of a publishing delegation to Japan

Xu Maijin (Hsü Mai-chin)　　　徐迈进

Posts held

Government
Advisor of the Ministry of Culture

Others
Member of the Standing Committee of the 5th CPPCC

From about 1938 Xu served as head of the General Office of Xinhua Ribao (New China Daily News) in Chongqing and took charge of organization work for the China Association of Young Reporters led by Fan Changjiang. In May 1949 he was a member of the Cultural Affairs Committee of the Beijing Military Control Commission. He represented the journalists as a delegate at the 1st CPPCC in September.

1949,	Dec	Identified as director of the General Office, Press Administration, and director of the Broadcasting Administration Bureau, Government Administration Council (until Aug 1952)
1951,	Oct	Identified as director of the General Office, Culture and Education Committee of the Government Administration Council (until Oct 1954)

1954,	Sep	Elected deputy secretary-general of the Journalists Association
	Oct	Appointed deputy director of the Broadcasting Administration Bureau under the State Council (until Sep 1959)
1957,	Jun	Identified as deputy director of the 2nd General Office of the State Council (until Sep 1959)
1959,	Jun	Identified as deputy director of the Office of Culture and Education under the State Council (until Aug 1964)
1960,	Mar	Identified as member of the Spare-time Education Committee
	Nov	Identified as deputy director of the Cultural and Educational Section of the 3rd CPPCC
1964,	Aug	Identified as director of the Office of Culture and Education under the State Council (until Cultural Revolution)
1967		Disappears during the Cultural Revolution
1979,	Jun	First appearance after the Cultural Revolution
	Jul	By-elected member of the Standing Committee of the 5th CPPCC
	Oct	Identified as advisor of the Ministry of Culture; head of a Beijing opera troupe to Canada

Xu Mengxia (Hsü Meng-hsia)　　　许梦侠

Posts held

CCP
Secretary of Sichuan Province CP
1st secretary of Chengdu Municipality CP
1st secretary of the Discipline Inspecting Committee, Sichuan Province CP

Others
Chairman of the Revolutionary Committee of Chengdu Municipality

1958,	May	Identified as secretary of Sichuan Province CP (until Cultural Revolution)
1973,	Feb	First appearance after the Cultural Revolution: Identified as member of the Standing Committee of Sichuan Province CP and as vice-chairman of the Revolutionary Committee of Sichuan Province
1976,	Jan	Identified as secretary of Sichuan Province CP, 1st secretary of the CP, and chairman of the Revolutionary Committee, of Chengdu Municipality
1979,	Feb	Identified as 1st secretary of the Discipline Inspecting Committee, Sichuan Province CP

Xu Ming (Hsü Ming)　　　徐明

Posts held

Government
Ambassador to Algeria

Before 1960 Xu was counselor at the embassy in the German Democratic Republic.

1960,	Sep	Deputy director of the USSR and Eastern Europe Department in the Ministry of Foreign Affairs (until 1964)
1965,	Oct	Head of the Council Office, Council for the Promotion of International Trade in Rome (until about 1967)
1971,	Mar	Cadre in the Sino-Japanese Memorandum Trade Bureau
1972,	Mar	Appointed ambassador to Lebanon (until Sep 1978)
1978,	Dec	Appointed ambassador to Algeria

Xu Qihai (Hsü Ch'i-hai) 徐英海

Posts held

CCP
Member of the Standing Committee, Guangxi Autonomous Region CP

Military
Major-general

Provincial Administration
Vice-chairman of the People's Government of Guangxi Autonomous Region

Xu took part in the Long March in 1934-35.

1962,	Mar	Identified as commandant of Guangzhou PLA Military and Athletic College; identified as major-general
1968,	Jul	Identified as military leader in Guangxi
1970,	Oct	Identified as member of the Standing Committee of Guangxi Revolutionary Committee (until Nov 1977)
1971,	Jan	Identified as deputy commander of Guangxi Military District (until 1975?)
1974,	Oct	Identified as member of the Standing Committee, Guangxi Autonomous Region CP
1977,	Dec	Elected vice-chairman of Guangxi Revolutionary Committee (until Dec 1979)
1979,	Jul	Appointed member of the National Games Organizing Committee
	Dec	Elected vice-chairman of the People's Government of Guangxi Province

Xu Qin (Hsü Ch'in) 许勤

Posts held

NPC
Deputy for Jiangxi Province to the 5th NPC

Provincial Administration
Vice-governor of Jiangxi Province

| 1978, | Feb | Elected deputy for Jiangxi Province to the 5th NPC |
| 1979, | Dec | Elected vice-governor of Jiangxi Province |

Xu Qixiao (Hsü Ch'i-hsiao) 徐英孝

Posts held

NPC
Deputy for the PLA to the 5th NPC

Military
Major-general
Deputy commander of Kunming Military Region

Xu was born in 1912 in Macheng County, Hubei Province. In 1929 he joined the Red Army. In 1930 he served as platoon leader of a company in the 1st Front Army and in 1935 he led a company in the 25th Army. In 1937 he commanded a battalion in the 129th Division of the 8th Route Army. He was appointed deputy commander of the 11th Brigade in the Shanxi-Hebei-Shandong-Henan Field Army in 1947 and in 1948 concurrently commander of West Henan Military District. At the end of 1948 he took part in the battle at Lake Huai. In February 1949 he was made commander of the 43rd Division of the 2nd Field Army which occupied Yunnan in 1950.

1951		Xu undergoes military training
1955,	Sep	Promoted to rank of major-general
1964,	Aug	Identified as deputy chief of staff of Kunming Military Region
1966,	Nov	Identified as deputy commander of Kunming Military Region (until Cultural Revolution)
1973,	Aug	First appearance after the Cultural Revolution: Renewed mention as deputy commander of Kunming Military Region
1978,	Feb	Elected deputy for the PLA to the 5th NPC

Xu Ren (Hsü Jen) 徐仁

Posts held

Others
President of the Palynological Society

| 1979, | Mar | Identified as president of the Palynological Society and as head of the Paleobotany Research Laboratory of the Institute of Botany, Academy of Sciences |

Xu Shaofu (Hsü Shao-fu) 徐少甫

Posts held

CCP
Member of the Commission for Inspecting Discipline of the CCP Central Committee
Secretary of Liaoning Province CP

1956,	Sep	Identified as secretary of Shenyang Municipality CP
1962,	Oct	Identified as alternate secretary of Liaoning Province CP (until 1968)
1968		Disappears during the Cultural Revolution
1978,	Dec	First appearance after the Cultural Revolution: Appointed member of the Commission for Inspecting Discipline of the CCP Central Committee
1979,	May	Identified as secretary of Liaoning Province CP

Xu Shiyou (Hsü Shih-yu)   許世友

<u>Posts held</u>

CCP
Member of the Politburo in the CCP 11th Central Committee
Member of the CCP 11th Central Committee

NPC
Deputy for the PLA
Military
Colonel-general

Xu was born in 1906 as the son of a peasant in Henan Province. He began his military career as a company leader in the forces of warlord Wu Peifu. About 1928 he joined the Communist guerrilla units under Xu Xiangqian operating in the border area of Henan, Hubei, and Anhui Provinces. In 1931 he commanded the 34th Regiment of the 4th Front Army under Xu Xiangqian. These Communist forces had to retreat to Sichuan under the pressure of KMT troops in 1932. When the 4th Front Army joined the main Communist forces under Mao Zedong and Zhu De near Maogong in June 1935 during the Long March, Xu was commander of a cavalry regiment. His units were again separated from the main forces, and Xu eventually reached the Communist base in Shaanxi in 1936 where he took part in a course at the Anti-Japan Military and Political Academy. In April 1937 Mao Zedong initiated a campaign within the Party against Zhang Guotao who had commanded those units during the Long March in which Xu had served. Together with forty other graduates of the Military and Political Academy Xu remained loyal to Zhang and took part in a rebellion which led to his arrest. This incident did not, however, affect his further career, and after his release in 1937 he was appointed deputy commander of the 385th Brigade, 129th Division of the 8th Route Army. In 1938 he was posted to Xu Xiangqian's units operating in Shandong Province where he first commanded a brigade and in 1942 Qinghe Military District. In 1944 he was commander of Bohai Military District, and in 1945 commander of Jiaodong Military District as well as the coastal defense installations of Yantai (Chefoo) and Weihaiwei. In 1947 his units were made part of the East China Field Army, renamed 3rd Field Army in 1949. In this Army Xu remained commander of the 11th Army Corps and commander of Shandong Military District. In September of that year he was a delegate at the 1st CPPCC.

1950,	Jan	Appointed member of the East China Military and Administrative Council (abolished in 1953)
1953		Appointed member of the East China Administrative Council (abolished in 1954)
1954,	Aug	Elected deputy for the PLA to the 1st NPC (until Mar 1959)
	Sep	Appointed member of the National Defense Council
	Nov	Identified as commander of Nanjing Military Region (until Jan 1974)
1955,	Sep	Promoted to rank of colonel-general
1956,	Sep	Elected alternate member of the CCP Central Committee by the 8th Party Congress (until Apr 1969)
1959,	Sep	Appointed vice-minister of national defense (until about 1973)

1961,	Dec	Author of the book <u>The Battle of Yashan</u>
1964,	Nov	Member of a Party and government delegation to Albania
1966,	Mar	Identified as a member of the Secretariat, East China Bureau in the CCP Central Committee (until Cultural Revolution)
1967		Self-criticism during the Cultural Revolution. Under the protection of Kang Sheng Xu survives the Cultural Revolution without loss of influence
1968,	Mar	With the establishment of a Revolutionary Committee for Jiangsu Province, Xu is appointed chairman (until Dec 1973)
1969,	Apr	Elected to first term as member of the CCP Central Committee and of the Politburo by the 9th Party Congress
1970,	Dec	Elected 1st secretary of Jiangsu Province CP (until Dec 1973)
1974,	Jan	Identified as commander of Guangzhou Military Region (until Feb 1980)
1978,	Feb	Elected deputy for the PLA to the 5th NPC
	Sep	Article in <u>HQ</u>: "Chairman Mao Will Live Forever in Our Hearts - Commemorating the Second Anniversary of the Passing Away of the Great Leader and Teacher Mao"
	Oct	Identified as 1st CP secretary of Guangzhou Military Region (until Feb 1980)

Xu Wenyi (Hsü Wen-yi)   許文益

<u>Posts held</u>

Ambassador to Lebanon

1970,	Jul	Identified as chargé d'affaires ad interim in Congo (Brazzaville)
1971,	Aug	Appointed ambassador to the People's Republic of Mongolia (until Feb 1974)
1979,	Apr	Appointed ambassador to Lebanon

Xu Xiangqian (Hsü Hsiang-ch'ien)   徐向前

<u>Posts held</u>

CCP
Member of the Politburo of the CCP 11th Central Committee
Member of the CCP 11th Central Committee
Vice-chairman of the Military Council in the CCP Central Committee

Government
Vice-premier
Minister of national defense

NPC
Deputy for the PLA to the 5th NPC

Military
Marshal

Xu was born in 1902 in Wutai County, Shanxi Province, as the son of a landowner who had passed the state examination for <u>xiucai</u> (first degree) in Imperial China.

After leaving elementary school, Xu worked for a short period in a book shop, but soon returned to his studies (completed around 1923) at Taiyuan Teachers College. In 1924 he entered Whampoa Military Academy without his parents' consent to participate in its first training course and in 1925 took part in the Northern Expedition. From the following year until the summer of 1927 he held a teaching position at the Wuchang Military and Political Academy. In spring 1927 he joined the CCP. After the rift between the KMT and CCP, Xu went to Guangzhou to become active in Communist underground work. In December of the same year he was one of the organizers of the Guangzhou Uprising, after the failure of which he retreated to Hailufeng Soviet which had been founded by Peng Pai in Guangdong Province. From June 1929 he established together with Zhang Guotao a Communist base in the border region of Hubei-Henan-Anhui. Here the 31st Red Workers' and Peasants' Division was created from modest beginnings which was integrated into the 4th Army and grew within three years to a unit of 30,000 men. In 1932 Xu and his division were driven by KMT troops into Sichuan Province. From there he pushed through to join the Communist forces on the Long March during the summer of 1935. After the purge of Zhang Guotao, with whom Xu had been closely associated, he was forced to undergo self-criticism at Yan'an, and when the Red Army was reorganized in 1937 he merely received the post of deputy commander of the 129th Division. In 1938 Xu led parts of the 115th and 129th Divisions into Hebei Province under orders to operate behind the lines of the Japanese aggressors. In 1939 he set up guerrilla units in Shandong Province, in the leadership of which he played a significant role until 1941. From 1942 to 1946 he served under He Long as deputy commander at the Joint Defense Command which was in charge of the forces in the border regions of Shanxi-Suiyuan and Shaanxi-Gansu-Ningxia. In 1945 the 7th CCP Congress elected Xu a member of the Central Committee (total membership 44). In 1947 he commanded the troops in the border region of Shanxi-Hebei-Shandong-Henan and together with Peng Dehuai inflicted heavy losses on KMT forces. In 1948 his units were integrated into the North China Military Region under Nie Rongzhen, Xu taking the post of deputy commander. In April Xu occupied Taiyuan, capital of his native province Shanxi. In September 1949 he was a delegate at the 1st CPPCC in Beijing.

1949,	Oct	Elected member and chief of staff, Revolutionary Military Council (until 1954 the equivalent to the later post of a chief of PLA General Staff). These appointments Xu held only nominally because ailing health forced him to retire for several years
1954,	Sep	Elected deputy to the 1st NPC for the PLA and member of the Standing Committee of the NPC
	Oct	Appointed vice-chairman, National Defense Council
1955,	Sep	Promoted to the rank of marshal
1956,	Sep	Reelected member of the CCP Central Committee by the 8th Party Congress
1965,	Jan	Elected vice-chairman of the Standing Committee of the NPC
1967,	Jan	Identified as member of the Politburo of the CCP (until Apr 1969); identified as director, Cultural Revolutionary Group in the Military Council of the CCP Central

		Committee (until about mid-1967)
	May	Xu is criticized for sabotaging the Cultural Revolution and opposing Lin Biao
1969,	Apr	Reelected member of the CCP Central Committee by the 9th Party Congress
1972,	May	Xu accompanies the Cambodian head of State, Prince Sihanouk, on a trip to Manchuria
	Aug	Xu accompanies Prince Sihanouk on a trip to Shandong Province
1973,	Feb	Xu accompanies Prince Sihanouk through several Chinese provinces
	May	Head of a delegation to Sri Lanka to inaugurate a conference building built with Chinese aid
	Jul	Head of a military delegation to Albania
1975,	Jan	Confirmed by 4th NPC as vice-chairman of the Standing Committee
1977,	Aug	Reelected member of the Politburo by the CCP 11th Congress
	Sep	Article in RMRB Sep 19: "Always Uphold the Principle That the Party Commands the Guns"
1978,	Feb	Elected deputy for PLA Army to the 5th NPC
	Mar	Appointed minister of national defense; article in RMRB Mar 5: "Life of Service, Pillar of Strength" (in memory of Zhou Enlai)
	Aug	Article in HQ: Heighten Vigilance, Be Prepared Against War"
1979,	Oct	Article in HQ: "Strive to Achieve Modernization in National Defense" - in celebration of the 30th anniversary of the founding of the PRC

Xu's first wife died in the 1920s. He is now married to Huang Jie.

Xu Xiaobing (Hsü Hsiao-ping)   徐肖冰

Posts held

Others
Chairman of the Photographic Society
Council member of the Sino-Soviet Friendship Association

1954,	Aug	Elected deputy for Jiangsu Province to the 1st NPC (reelected in 1958 and 1964 to the 2nd and 3rd NPCs)
1964,	Jun	Identified as director of the Central Film Studio for Newsreel and Documentary Films
1965,	Feb	Identified as a council member of the Sino-Korean Friendship Association
1966		Xu disappears
1975,	Nov	First appearance after the Cultural Revolution: Identified as a council member of the Sino-Soviet Friendship Association
1978,	Feb	Elected member of the 5th CPPCC as a delegate of Literary and Art Circles
	Aug	Identified as head of the Preparatory Group of the Photographic Society
1979,	Nov	Elected chairman of the Photographic Society

Xu Ya (Hsü Ya)　　　　許　亞

Posts held
CCP
Secretary of Fujian Province CP

Provincial Administration
Vice-governor of Fujian Province

1950,　Jan　Identified as mayor of Fuzhou (until Jan 1957)
1956,　Jan　Identified as secretary, Fuzhou CP
　　　　Aug　Identified as vice-governor of Fujian Province (until Aug 1968)
1959,　Jan　Identified as member of the Standing Committee of Fujian Province CP
1962,　Jan　Identified as alternate member of the Secretariat of Fujian Province CP (until Aug 1968)
1968　　　　Disappears during the Cultural Revolution
1976,　Nov　First appearance after the Cultural Revolution: Identified as member of the Standing Committee of Fujian Province CP (until Aug 1979)
1977,　May　Identified as vice-chairman of the Revolutionary Committee of Fujian Province (until Dec 1979)
1979,　Aug　Identified as secretary of Fujian Province CP
　　　　Dec　Elected vice-governor of Fujian Province

Xu Yinsheng (Hsü Yin-sheng)　　徐寅生

Posts held

Government
1st vice-minister, Physical Culture and Sports Commission

Mass Organizations
Vice-chairman of the Youth Federation

Others
President of the Table-Tennis Association

1960,　Nov　Member of a table tennis team visiting Sweden
1965,　Jan　Elected vice-chairman of the Youth Federation
1966,　Nov　Member of a table-tennis team visiting Sweden
1971,　Mar　Member of a table-tennis team visiting Japan
1972,　May　Head of a table-tennis team visiting Japan
1973,　Mar　Identified as vice-president of the Table-Tennis Association
1975,　Jan　Deputy head of the Chinese team to the 33rd Table-Tennis World Championship in Calcutta
　　　　Feb　Elected vice-president for Asia of the International Table-Tennis Association
1976,　Jan　Head of a table-tennis team visiting Mexico
　　　　Jun　Head of a delegation to a session of the International Table-Tennis Association in Dubrovnik, Yugoslavia
1977,　Mar　Identified as 1st vice-minister of the Physical Culture and Sports Commission

1978,　Jun　Head of a table-tennis delegation to Japan
　　　　Dec　Head of a sports delegation to the 8th Asian Games in Bangkok
1979,　Apr　Identified as president of the Table Tennis Association; head of the Chinese delegation to the 35th World Table Tennis Championship in North Korea
　　　　May　Elected vice chairman of the Youth Federation
　　　　Jul　Appointed member of the National Games Organizing Committee

Xu Yiqiao (Hsü Yi-ch'iao)　　徐逸樵

Posts held

Others
Member of the Standing Committee of the 5th CPPCC

1979,　Jul　By-elected member of the Standing Committee of the 5th CPPCC

Xu Yixin (Hsü Yi-hsin)　　徐以新

Posts held

Government
Ambassador to Pakistan

Xu was born in 1906 in Jiangsu Province. From 1927 to 1930 he studied at the Sun Yat-sen University in Moscow. At the end of the Revolutionary War he served as director of Garrison Work, Political Department of the PLA Northeast Military Region.

1950,　Jun　Identified as deputy director of the USSR and Eastern Europe Department of the Ministry of Foreign Affairs
1952,　Aug　Identified as director of the USSR and Eastern Europe Department of the Ministry of Foreign Affairs; member of a government delegation led by Zhou Enlai to Moscow
1954,　Jun　Appointed ambassador to Albania (until May 1957)
1958,　Apr　Appointed ambassador to Norway (until Mar 1962)
1962,　Mar　Appointed ambassador to Syria (until Dec 1965)
1966,　Jan　Appointed vice-minister of foreign affairs
1969,　Nov　Xu disappears for unknown reasons
1979,　Aug　Appointed ambassador to Pakistan

Xu Zailian (Hsü Tsai-lien)　　許在廉

Posts held

Government
Vice-minister of coal industry

Director of the China National Mining Committee

1975,　Nov　Identified as vice-minister of coal industry

1977,	Oct	Identified as director of the China National Minining Committee
1979,	Sep	Head of a coal industry delegation to Romania

Xu Zhongfu (Hsü Chung-fu) 徐中夫

Posts held

Government
Ambassador to Argentina

1956,	Oct	Identified as counselor, embassy in Sweden (until Apr 1961)
1963,	Mar	Identified as director, General Office in the Commission for Cultural Relations with Foreign Countries
1964,	Jun	Identified as cultural officer in the United Arab Republic (until about 1967)
1971,	Jan	Identified as counselor, embassy in Canada (until 1973)
1973,	Mar	Appointed ambassador to Chile (until Oct 1977)
1978,	Jan	Appointed ambassador to Argentina

Xue Gongzhuo (Hsüeh Kung-cho) 薛公绰

Posts held

Others
Director of the Foreign Affairs Bureau of the Ministry of Public Health

Xue is a physiologist and once worked as dean of Education at the Medical College in Shenyang.

1949,	Dec	Identified as director of the Administrative Office, Ministry of Public Health
1952,	Sep	Identified as member, Central Committee of the Jiusan Society
1953,	Feb	Member of an Academy of Sciences delegation to the USSR
	Dec	Member of a medical delegation to India
1955,	Nov	Identified as vice-president of Beijing Medical College (until 1958)
1958,	Jun	Identified as secretary-general of the Medical Society
	Dec	Identified as member of the Standing Committee, Central Committee of the Jiusan Society
1960,	Nov	Identified as vice president of the Academy of Medical Sciences; head of a medical delegation to England and Denmark (until Dec 1960)
1961,	Jan	Head of a medical delegation to Norway and Finland
1964,	Dec	Delegate representing the Jiusan Society at the 4th CPPCC
1967		Disappears during the Cultural Revolution
1973,	Jun	First appearance after the Cultural Revolution
	Nov	Identified as director of the Foreign Affairs Bureau, Ministry of Public Health
1977,	Sep	Delegate at the 28th Session of World Health Organization (WHO), Western Pacific Section

Xue Guangjun (Hsüeh Kuang-chün) 薛光军

Posts held

CCP
Member of the Standing Committee of Guangdong Province CP

Provincial Administration
Vice-chairman of the People's Congress of Guangdong Province

1966,	Aug	Identified as secretary-general of the Central-South China Bureau in in the CCP Central Committee
1967,	Jan	Xue is denounced by Red Guards in Lanzhou as a renegade and disappears
1976,	Oct	First appearance after the Cultural Revolution: Identified as member of the Standing Committee, Revolutionary Committee of Guangdong
1977,	May	Identified as vice-chairman of the Revolutionary Committee of Guangdong Province (until Dec 1979)
1979,	Sep	Identified as member of the Standing Committee of Guangdong Province CP
	Dec	Elected vice-chairman of the People's Congress of Guandong Province

Xue Hongfu (Hsüeh Hung-fu) 薛宏福

Posts held

CCP
Deputy secretary of Ningxia Autonomous Region CP

Provincial Administration
Vice-chairman of the People's Government, Ningxia Autonomous Region

During the last phase of the revolutionary period Xue served in the Logistics Department of the 1st Field Army.

1949,	Dec	Elected council member, People's Government of Qinghai Province
1953,	Jan	Identified as director of the Commerce Department of Qinghai People's Government
1954,	Dec	Identified as deputy director of the Finance and Commerce Committee of Qinghai People's Government
1957,	Jan	Identified as director of the Finance and Commerce Department of Qinghai Province CP
1958,	Jun	Identified as 1st secretary, CP of the Work Committee of Qaidam (an important oil producing area)
1968,	Aug	With the establishment of the Revolutionary Committee for Qinghai Province, Xue is elected vice chairman (until Dec 1979)
1971,	Mar	Elected secretary of Qinghai Province CP (until 1976)
1978,	Apr	Elected deputy secretary of Ningxia Autonomous Region CP
1980,	Jan	Elected vice-chairman of the People's Government, Ningxia Autonomous Region

Xue Jinda (Hsüeh Chin-ta) 薛金达

Posts held

CCP
Member of the CCP 11th Central Committee

1977, Aug Elected member of the CCP Central Committee by the 11th Party Congress

Xue Jinlian (Hsüeh Chin-lien) (f) 薛金莲

Posts held

CCP
Alternate member of the CCP 11th Central Committee

Mass Organization
Secretary of the Communist Youth League of the Inner Mongolian Autonomous Region

1973 Jun Elected secretary of the Communist Youth League of the Inner Mongolian Autonomous Region
       Aug Elected to first term as alternate member of the CCP Central Committee by the 10th Party Congress

Xue Muqiao (Hsüeh Mu-ch'iao) 薛暮桥

Posts held

Government
Director of the Economics Institute under the State Planning Commission
Director of the State Statistical Bureau

Others
President of the Statistical Society

Xue is an economist who had lectured at the Anti-Japan Military and Political Academy before the foundation of the PRC and since 1943 at the University of Shandong. Since the early 1940s he has specialized on problems of Chinese agriculture. In July 1949 he was elected vice-chairman of the newly established Study Society for the New Economy (until 1953).

1949, Oct Appointed member of the Financial and Economic Committee and director of the Central Control Bureau for Private Enterprises in the Government Administration Council
       Dec Appointed secretary-general of the Financial and Economic Committee (until Aug 1952); identified as director of the Financial and Economic Committee of the CCP Central Committee (probably until 1958)
1952, May Appointed member of the Council for Promotion of International Trade
       Aug Appointed director of the Statistical Office under the State Council (until Sep 1959)
       Nov Appointed member of the Planning Commission

1954, Sep Elected deputy for Jiangsu Province to the 1st NPC (reelected in 1958 and 1964 to the 2nd and 3rd NPCs)
       Oct Appointed vice-chairman of the Planning Commission (until Sep 1959)
       Dec Member of a scientific and technical delegation to the USSR
1955, Jun Appointed member of the Department of Philosophy and Social Sciences, Academy of Sciences
1956, Mar Identified as deputy secretary-general of the State Scientific Planning Commission (until Jun 1957)
1957, Jan Identified as chairman of the Editorial Board of Jihua Jingji (Economic Planning)
1958, May Identified as professor of political economy at the Department of Economics, Beijing People's University
       Oct Identified as vice-chairman of the State Economic Commission (until Dec 1960)
1963, Sep Identified as chairman of the State Commission for Price Control (until Cultural Revolution)
1967, Feb Branded as a counterrevolutionary revisionist and purged
1975, Sep First appearance after the Cultural Revolution
1979, Mar Identified as advisor to the State Planning Commission; identified as director of the Economics Institute under the State Planning Commission
       Dec Elected president of the Statistical Society; identified as director of the State Statistical Bureau

Publications

General Knowledge of Chinese Agricultural Economics
Methods of Thinking and Methods of Study
Fundamental Problems of the Chinese Revolution and Political Economy
Questions on the Theory of Socialist Economy

Xue Renzong (Hsüeh Jen-tsung) 薛仁宗

Posts held

Government
Vice-minister of the State Economic Commission

1978, Jul Identified as vice minister of the State Economic Commission

Xue Zizheng (Hsüeh Tzu-cheng) 薛子正

Posts held

CCP
Deputy director of the United Front Work Department under the CCP Central Committee

Others
Member of the Standing Committee of the 5th CPPCC

Xue was born in 1907 in Liangshan County, Sichuan Province. He studied at Shanghai University and later in the USSR. During the revolutionary period he served successively as commander of a regiment and as political commissar of a division. From 1946 to January 1947 he served with the rank of major-general on the Subcommittee of three delegates of the joint KMT-CCP Political Consultative Conference.

1949,   Nov   Elected secretary general and council member of the Beijing People's Government

1950,   Apr   Appointed member of the Urban Planning Committee of Beijing

1955,   Feb   Elected deputy mayor of Beijing (until Aug 1957)

1956,   Dec   Appointed vice-chairman of the National Economic Commission (until Apr 1958)

1959,   Apr   Elected member of the 3rd CPPCC (until Dec 1964)

           Oct   Identified as deputy director, United Front Work Department of the CCP Central Committee (until Cultural Revolution)

1963   Identified as alternate member, Central Control Commission of the CCP Central Committee

1964,   Dec   Elected member of the 4th CPPCC

1966   Disappears during the Cultural Revolution

1979,   Feb   First appearance after the Cultural Revolution

           May   Appointed 1st deputy secretary-general of the 5th CPPCC

           Jul   By-elected member of the Standing Committee of the 5th CPPCC

           Oct   Identified as deputy director of the United Front Work Department under the CCP Central Committee

Ya-bu-long (Ya·pu·lung)   尔布龙

Posts held

CCP
Member of the Standing Committee of Qinghai Province CP

Provincial Administration
Vice-governor of Qinghai Province

Ya-bu-long belongs to the Mongolian minority.

1954		Identified as deputy secretary of a county CP in Qinghai Province
1970		Identified as director of the Animal Husbandry Bureau, Qinghai Province
1977,	Aug	Identified as a member of the Standing Committee of Qinghai Province CP
1979,	Apr	Identified as vice-chairman of the Revolutionary Committee of Qinghai Province
	Sep	Elected vice-governor of Qinghai Province

Yan Dakai (Yen Ta-k'ai)   阎达开

Posts held

CCP
Secretary of Tianjin Municipality CP

Provincial Administration
Vice-chairman of the Revolutionary Committee of Tianjin

Yan was born circa 1915 in Hebei Province. During 1936-37 he participated in the student movements in Beijing and Tianjin. He also joined the CCP at this time. In 1936 he studied at the Party School in Yan'an which appointed him head of its 3rd Department in 1938.

1954,	Jun	Identified as vice-governor of Hebei Province (until Dec 1962)
1955,	Jun	Identified as deputy secretary of Hebei Province CP
1956,	Nov	Identified as secretary of Hebei Province CP (until Dec 1967)
1967,	Oct	Identified as acting 2nd secretary of Tianjin Municipality CP; subsequently disappears until 1977
1977,	Dec	First appearance after the Cultural Revolution: Elected vice-chairman of the Revolutionary Committee of Tianjin; identified as secretary of Tianjin Municipality CP

Yan Deming (Yen Te-ming)   严德明

Posts held

Military
Major-general
Deputy commander of Guangzhou Military Region

Yan was born in 1907 in Guangdong Province. He served in the 120th Division of the 8th Route Army in 1939. In 1942 he commanded a battalion, and in 1945 a regiment, in Jilin-Heilongjiang Military District. In 1946 he was made chief of staff of a division of the Northeast Field Army. In 1949 he commanded the 139th Division, 4th Field Army.

1951,	Jan	Service in the Korean War, initially as chief of staff of the 47th Army
1953		Identified as deputy commander of the 47th Army
1954		Training at the Military Academy of the PLA
1963		Identified as commander of the 47th Army
1965,	Oct	Identified as chief of staff of Guangzhou Military Region
1967		Disappears during the Cultural Revolution
1973,	May	First appearance after the Cultural Revolution: Identified as military leader in Guangzhou Military Region
1974,	May	Identified as deputy commander of Guangzhou Military Region

Yan Deyi (Yen Te-yi)   阎德义

Posts held

NPC
Member of the Standing Committee of the 5th NPC
Deputy for Liaoning Province to the 5th NPC

Yan was born in 1928. He is a model worker and became known for manufacturing more than 20 kinds of welding guns.

1978,	Feb	Elected deputy for Liaoning Province to the 5th NPC
	Mar	Elected member of the Standing Committee of the 5th NPC

Yan Dunshi (Yen Tun-shih)   阎敦实

Posts held

Government
Vice-minister of petroleum industry

Yan was born circa 1935. He graduated from college after 1949 and later became vice-president of the Academy for Planning Oil Prospecting and Exploitation. He developed a geological theory that anciently submerged mountains contain oil deposits as well as a theory on the geological structure of Eastern China, a major contribution to prospecting and discovering oil fields in Northern China.

1978,	Aug	Identified as vice-minister of petroleum industry

Yan Jici (Yen Chi-tz'u, Ny Tze-ze)   尹济慈

Posts held

NPC
Member of the Standing Committee of the 5th NPC
Deputy for Liaoning Province to the 5th NPC

Others
Secretary of the Science and Technology Association

Vice-president of the Academy of Sciences

Director of the Technology Department of the Academy of Sciences

Vice-chairman of the Central Committee, Jiusan (Chiu-san) Society

Honorary president of the Optical Society

Yan Jici, better known under the name of Ny Tze-ze, was born in 1900 in Dongyang, Zhejiang Province. He studied at the National Southeast University until 1923 and then continued his studies in France where he was awarded a Ph.D. degree by Paris University in 1927. After his return to China he first lectured at the National Central University in Nanjing and was shortly afterwards appointed professor of Datong University in Shanghai. In 1930 he was made director of the Physics Research Institute of the Academia Sinica in Beijing. In 1944 he was elected a Central Committee member of the newly established Jiusan Society. In May 1949 Yan was elected a member of the Standing Committee of the Youth Congress. Four months later he represented scientists as a delegate at the CPPCC.

1949,	Nov	Appointed director of the General Office of the newly established Academy of Sciences; identified as director of the Physics Society and as member of the Peace Council
1950,	Aug	Appointed secretary-general of the newly established Federation of Scientific Societies (federation abolished in Sep 1958)
1952,	Nov	Appointed chairman of the newly set up Northeast China Branch of the Academy of Sciences; identified as member of the Standing Committee, Jiusan Society
1953,	Jan	Appointed member of Northeast China Administrative Council (until Sep 1954)
1954,	Sep	Elected deputy for Shenyang Municipality to the 1st NPC (until Mar 1959)
1955,	May	Appointed director of the Department of Technical Sciences, Academy of Sciences
1956		Identified as member of the Scientific Planning Commission
1957		Elected council member of the Sino-Soviet Friendship Association
1958,	Dec	Elected vice-chairman of the Jiusan Society; elected deputy for Liaoning Province to the 2nd NPC
1961,	Apr	Appointed vice-chancellor of the University of Science and Technology in Beijing
1963		Identified as alternate member, Secretariat of the Science and Technology Association
1965,	Jan	Elected member of the Standing Committee of the 3rd NPC
	Dec	Head of a delegation of scientists to Romania, Poland, and Czechoslovakia
1967		Yan survives the Cultural Revolution without loss of influence
1975,	Jan	Reelected member of the Standing Committee by the 4th NPC (confirmed in Mar 1978 by the 5th NPC)
	Apr	Identified as secretary of the Science and Technology Association
	Nov	Head of a delegation of scientists to Japan
1978,	Feb	Elected deputy for Liaoning Province to the 5th NPC

	Mar	Appointed vice-president of the Academy of Sciences
	Oct	Member of a government delegation led by Fang Yi to the Federal Republic of Germany and France
1979,	Jan	Identified as director of the Technology Department of the Academy of Sciences
	Jun	Vice-chairman of the Committee to Examine Proposals at the 2nd Session of the 5th NPC
	Oct	Elected vice-chairman of the Central Committee of the Jiusan Society
	Dec	Elected honorary president of the Optical Society

Yan Jimin (Yen Chi-min) 阎济民

Posts held

Provincial Administration
Vice-governor of Henan Province

1975,	Dec	Identified as vice-minister of the 6th Ministry of Machine Building (until 1978)
1979,	Sep	Elected vice-governor of Henan Province

Yan Jinsheng (Yen Chin-sheng) 严金生

Posts held

NPC
Deputy for the PLA to the 5th NPC

Military
Major-general
Deputy director, General Political Department of the PLA

In 1942 Yan commanded a regiment of the 120th Division, 8th Route Army. In 1947 he was political commissar of the 3rd Division, Northwest Field Army. He was appointed deputy political commissar of the 1st Army, 1st Field Army, in 1949.

1952		Identified as political commissar of the 1st Army
	Dec	Service in the Korean War (until 1958) with the 1st Army
1955,	Sep	Appointed major-general
1958		Based in Henan after return from Korea
1964,	Dec	Identified as deputy director of the Political Department of Wuhan Military Region
1965,	Apr	Appointed vice-minister of culture and director of the Political Department, Ministry of Culture (until 1967)
1967,	Apr	Accused by Red Guards as a counterrevolutionary revisionist and disappears
1973,	Jul	First appearance after the Cultural Revolution: Identified as member of the Standing Committee of Shaanxi Province CP (until 1975)
1976,	Jan	Identified as deputy political commissar of Xinjiang Military Region (until Aug 1977)
1977,	Oct	Identified as deputy director, General Political Department of the PLA
1978,	Feb	Elected deputy for the PLA to the 5th NPC

Yan Kelun (Yen K'e-lun)　　严克伦

<u>Posts held</u>

CCP
Secretary of Shaanxi Province CP

1954,	Dec	Identified as secretary-general of Shaanxi Province CP
1957,	Jun	Identified as member of the Standing Committee of Shaanxi Province CP
1958,	Aug	Identified as alternate secretary of Shaanxi Province CP
1963,	Oct	Identified as secretary of Shaanxi Province CP
1964,	Sep	Elected vice-governor of Shaanxi Province and deputy for this province to the 3rd NPC
1966,	Nov	Attacked by Red Guards and disappears
1978,	Apr	First appearance after the Cultural Revolution: Identified as secretary of Shaanxi Province CP

Yan Kuiyao (Yen K'uei-yao)　　阎揆要

<u>Posts held</u>

Military
Lieutenant-general

Others
Member of the Standing Committee of the 5th CPPCC

Yan was born in 1908 in Jia County, Shaanxi Province. He is a graduate of the 2nd Graduating Class of Whampoa Military Academy and later took part in the Eastern Expedition of the Nationalist Revolutionary Army. Before he joined the Communists in 1945 he had served as commander of the Special 2nd Regiment under the Xi'an Pacification Office. In 1946 he commanded the Shaanxi-Gansu Border Region Garrison Command. In the following year he was a commander of the 120th Division of Shanxi-Suiyuan PLA. In spring 1949 he was appointed chief of staff of the 1st Field Army (until September 1950).

1949,	Dec	Identified as member of the Northwest Military and Administrative Council
1950,	Sep	Identified as director of the Northwest Railway Trunk Lines Engineering Bureau (until Aug 1951)
1954,	Aug	Elected deputy for Shandong Province to the 1st NPC
1955,	Sep	Awarded the orders "Independence and Freedom" and "Liberation," both 1st class
1958,	Oct	Identified as lieutenant-general and as deputy commander of Jinan Military Region
1963,	Oct	Identified as a cadre of the PLA General Staff
1966,	Mar	Identified as deputy commandant of the PLA Senior Military Academy
1968,	Feb	Identified as 2nd political commissar of Jinan Military Region
1969-1977		Military leader in unknown position in Beijing
1978,	Mar	Elected member of the Standing Committee of the 5th CPPCC

Yan Wuhong (Yen Wu-hung)　　阎武宏

<u>Posts held</u>

Provincial Administration
Vice-governor of Shanxi Province

1979,	Dec	Elected vice-governor of Shanxi Province

Yan Xinmin (Yen Hsin-min)　　严仗民

<u>Posts held</u>

NPC
Deputy for Shaanxi Province to the 5th NPC

Others
Member of the Standing Committee of the 5th CPPCC
Vice-chairman of the Central Committee, China Peasants and Workers Democratic Party

Yan was born in 1902 in Shaanxi Province. He studied economics at the Universities of Frankfurt, Germany, and Vienna. In 1924 he returned to China and initially served in the Control Yuan of the Nationalist Government. In 1938 he was editor of the <u>People's Times</u>, a leftist magazine in Chongqing. In 1946 he served as editior of <u>China Review</u>, an organ of the Shanghai Chinese Peasants and Workers Democratic Party, of which he became director of the Propaganda Department in 1947. He joined the Communists in 1949 and in September of that year took part in the session of the 1st CPPCC.

1949,	Oct	Appointed counselor of the Government Adminstration Council
1951		Identified as member of the Central Executive Bureau, Chinese Peasants and Workers Democratic Party
1954,	Aug	Elected deputy for Xi'an Municipality to the 1st NPC
1957,	May	Identified as vice-president of the (Central?) Nationalities Institute
1958,	Sep	Elected deputy for Shaanxi Province to the 2nd NPC (reelected in 1964 to the 3rd NPC)
	Dec	Elected member of the Central Committee, Chinese Peasants and Workers Democratic Party
1964,	Dec	Appointed member of the Nationalities Affairs Commission under the State Council
1967		Disappears during the Cultural Revolution
1973,	Nov	First appearance after the Cultural Revolution
1978,	Feb	Elected deputy for Shaanxi Province to the 5th NPC
	Mar	Elected member of the Standing Committee of the 5th CPPCC
	Aug	Identified as member of the Central Presidium, China Peasants and Workers Democratic Party
1979,	Oct	Elected vice-chairman of the Central Committee of the China Peasants and Workers Democratic Party

Yan Youmin (Yen Yu-min)　严佑民

Posts held

CCP
Secretary of Shanghai Municipality CP

NPC
Deputy for Shanghai Municipality to the 5th NPC

Provincial Administration
Chairman of the People's Congress of Shanghai Municipality

Yan was born in 1918 in Shaanxi Province.

1964,	Oct	Appointed vice-minister of public security (until Aug 1965)
1965,	Aug	Appointed deputy director of the Staff Office of Civil Affairs under the State Council
1968,	Mar	Accused by Red Guards as being a follower of Luo Ruiqing; subsequently disappears
1975,	Sep	First appearance after the Cultural Revolution
1977,	Jan	Identified as secretary of the CP, and as vice-chairman of the Revolutionary Committee of Shanghai Municipality (until Dec 1979)
1978,	Sep	Deputy head of a municipal administration delegation to the U.S.A.
1979,	Jun	Member of the Credentials Committee at the 2nd Session of the 5th NPC
	Oct	Identified as head of the Shanghai Municipal Air Defense Leading Group
	Dec	Elected chairman of the People's Congress of Shanghai Municipality

Yan Zhixiang (Yen Chih-hsiang)　阎志祥

Posts held

Government
Deputy director-general of the General Administration of Civil Aviation

1973,	Nov	Identified as deputy director-general of the General Administration of Civil Aviation; head of a friendship delegation to Paris on the extension of Air France services to Beijing
1978,	Jan	Head of an aviation delegation to Yugoslavia and Switzerland

Yang Bo (Yang Po)　杨波

Posts held

Government
Vice-chairman of the State Planning Commission

1977,	Dec	Elected vice-chairman of the Revolutionary Committee of Shandong Province (until Jan 1979)

1978,	May	Member of a government delegation led by Gu Mu to France, Switzerland, Belgium, Denmark, and the Federal Republic of Germany
1979,	Sep	Identified as vice-minister of the State Planning Commission

Yang Chao (Yang Ch'ao)　杨超

Posts held

CCP
Secretary of Sichuan Province CP

NPC
Deputy for Sichuan Province to the 5th NPC

Yang was born in 1911 in Sichuan Province.

1961,	Aug	Identified as secretary of Sichuan Province CP (until Cultural Revolution)
1964,	Nov	Identified as vice-governor of Sichuan Province (until Cultural Revolution)
1967		Disappears during the Cultural Revolution
1975,	Feb	First appearance after the Cultural Revolution: Identified as secretary of Sichuan Province CP
1978,	Feb	Elected deputy for Sichuan Province to the 5th NPC
	Oct	Member of a government delegation led by Fang Yi to the Federal Republic of Germany and France

Yang Chengwu (Yang Ch'eng-wu)　杨成武

Posts held

CCP
Member of the CCP 11th Central Committee
1st secretary of the Party Committee, Fuzhou Military Region

NPC
Deputy for the PLA to the 5th NPC

Military
Colonel-general
Commander of Fuzhou Military Region

Yang was born in 1912 in Yangting, Fujian Province. In 1929 he took part in the West Fujian Uprising. He was political commissar of a regiment of the 5th Red Army in 1932 and two years later of a regiment of the 1st Front Army; this latter unit took part in the famous occupation of the Luding Bridge in May 1939 which during the Long March opened the entry into Northern Sichuan Province. In 1936 Yang attended a course at the Red Worker-Peasant Academy in Yan'an. After the outbreak of the Anti-Japanese War in 1937 he was made commander of an independent regiment under the 115th Division, 8th Route Army, which took part in the Battle of Pingxing Guan. During the following years he served under Nie Rongzhen as commander of guerrilla units in various parts of North China. In 1941 he was appointed commander of the 5th Region of West Hebei Military District. His units, which by the time of the Japanese capitulation had grown to 30,000 men, were incorporated as the 2nd Combat Unit into the Shanxi-Chahar-Hebei Border Area commanded by Nie Rongzhen in late 1945. During the Civil War the troops commanded by Yang took part in numerous battles in North China. Yang was appointed deputy commander of Beijing-Tianjin Military Region and commander of Tianjin Garrison following the occupation of Beijing in early 1949. At this time he served concurrently as chief of staff of North China Military Region. In May 1949 he was elected a member of the National Committee of the Democratic Youth Federation, and in September of that year member of the CPPCC.

1950,	Jan	Appointed member of the People's Government Council of Tianjin and commander of Beijing-Tianjin Military Region
1951,	Oct	Appointed member of the North China Administrative Council
1951		Commander of the 66th, 67th, and 68th Armies of the Chinese People's Volunteers in the Korean War
1953,	Jan	Identified as chief of staff of North China Military Region
1954,	Sep	Elected deputy for Tianjin Municipality to the 1st NPC (until Mar 1959)
	Oct	Appointed member of the National Defense Council (until Cultural Revolution)
1955,	Sep	Promoted to rank of colonel-general, conferred the orders "Independence and Freedom" and "Liberation," both 1st class
1956,	Jan	Appointed commander, Air Defense of the PLA
	Sep	Elected alternate member of the CCP Central Committee by the 8th Party Congress (until Cultural Revolution)
1957		Conferred the order "1st August"
1958		Yang temporarily serves as a common soldier in a company
1959,	Apr	Identified as deputy chief of PLA General Staff; member of a military delegation to Indonesia
1961,	Dec	Member of a military delegation to North Vietnam
1966,	Aug	Appointed acting chief of PLA General Staff
1967,	Jan	Appointed deputy head of the PLA Cultural Revolutionary Group
	Nov	Identified as vice-chairman, Military Council of the CCP Central Committee
1968,	Mar	Accused of opposition against Mao Zedong and Lin Biao; relieved of all posts
1974,	Jul	First appearance after the Cultural Revolution
	Dec	Identified as deputy chief of PLA General Staff (until 1977)
1977,	Mar	Head of a military delegation to Pakistan
	Aug	Elected member of the CCP Central Committee by the 11th Party Congress
	Sep	Head of a military delegation to France and Romania
1978,	Jan	Identified as commander of Fuzhou Military Region
	Feb	Elected deputy for the PLA to the 5th NPC
	Oct	Identified as member of the Standing Committee, CP Secretariat of Fuzhou Military Region
1979,	Sep	Identified as 1st secretary of the Party Committee of Fuzhou Military Region

Yang Chengzhong (Yang Ch'eng-chung)

杨澄中

Posts held

Others
Deputy director of the Modern Physics Institute of the Academy of Sciences in Lanzhou

1958,	Dec	Elected deputy for Gansu Province to the 2nd NPC (reelected in 1964 to the 3rd NPC)
1976,	Sep	Identified as deputy director of the Modern Physics Institute of the Academy of Sciences in Lanzhou; head of a delegation to the European Conference of Heavy Ion Nuclear Physics
1978,	Feb	Elected deputy for Gansu Province to the 5th NPC
	Jun	Head of a plasma nuclear physics delegation to the U.S.A.

Yang Chengzong (Yang Ch'eng-tsung)

杨承宗

Posts held

NPC
Deputy for Anhui Province to the 5th NPC

Provincial Administration
Vice-chairman of the People's Congress of Anhui Province

Others
Professor of modern chemistry, University of Science and Technology

Yang once worked at the Madame Curie Laboratory in France.

1964,	Oct	Elected deputy for Anhui Province to the 3rd NPC
1978,	Feb	Elected deputy for Anhui Province to the 5th NPC
	Mar	Identified as professor of modern chemistry at the University of Science and Technology
1979,	Dec	Elected vice-chairman of the People's Congress of Anhui Province

Yang Chun (Yang Ch'un) (f)

杨纯

Posts held

Government
Member of the State Nationalities Affairs Commission

Others
Vice-president of the Red Cross Society

1950,	Mar	Identified as member of the Land Reform Committee of East China Military and Administrative Council (until Jun 1954)
1952,	Sep	Identified as deputy director of the Textile Industry Administration, East China Military and Administrative Council
1953,	Apr	Elected member of the Standing Committee of the Democratic Women's Federation (until 1957)

1954,	Aug	Elected deputy for Shandong Province to the 1st NPC
1958,	Dec	Elected deputy for Henan Province to the 2nd NPC (reelected in 1964 to the 3rd NPC)
1961,	Feb	Identified as secretary of the CP of Beijing Medical College
1964,	Jan	Member of a solidarity delegation led by Liu Ningyi to North Vietnam
1966,	Mar	Appointed vice-chairman of the State Commission for Cultural Relations with Foreign Countries
	Apr	Elected vice-president of the Association for Cultural Relations and Friendship with Foreign Countries; subsequently disappears
1978,	Jun	First appearance after the Cultural Revolution
	Dec	Identified as vice-president of the Red Cross Society
1979,	May	Appointed member of the State Nationalities Affairs Commission
	Oct	Representative to the Red Cross Societies meeting in Geneva

Yang Dayi (Yang Ta-yi)   杨大易

Posts held

CCP
Alternate member of the CCP 11th Central Committee
Member of the Standing Commitee of Liaoning Province CP

Military
Major-general
Commander of Liaoning Military District

Yang's career started in the 1st Front Army. In 1946 he served as regiment commander in the Northeast China Joint Democratic Army. In the following year he was deputy commander of a division of the Northeast Field Army. In January 1949 he took part in the Battle of Tianjin.

1950		Identified as commander of the 112th Division, 4th Field Army
	Oct	Posted to the Korean War
1951,	Oct	Identified as chief of staff of the 38th Army
1954		Identified as deputy commander of the 38th Army
1955,	Sep	Promoted to rank of major-general; subsequently undergoes training at the Military Academy of the PLA in Nanjing
1964		Identified as commandant of the Infantry School in Guilin
1968,	Mar	Identified as deputy commander of Hunan Military District (until Mar 1969)
	Apr	Elected vice-chairman of the newly established Revolutionary Committee of Hunan Province (until 1975)
1969,	Mar	Identified as commander of Hunan Military District (until 1975)
1970,	Dec	Elected deputy secretary of Hunan Province CP (until Aug 1973)

1973,	Aug	Elected to first term as alternate member of the CCP Central Committee by the 10th Party Congress; identified as secretary of Hunan Province CP (until 1975)
1976,	Jul	Identified as commander of Liaoning Military District
1977,	Dec	Identified as member of the Standing Committee of Liaoning Province CP

Yang Dezhi (Yang Te-chih)   杨得志

Posts held

CCP
Member of the CCP 11th Central Committee
Member of the Standing Committee, Military Council under the CCP Central Committee
Member of the Secretariat under the CCP Central Committee

NPC
Deputy for the PLA to the 5th NPC

Military
Colonel-general
Chief of the PLA General Staff

Yang was born in 1910 in Zhuzhou, Hunan Province, as the son of a poor blacksmith. After his mother died, when he was eleven years old, he entered the service of a landlord as a shepherd. In 1924 he temporarily worked in the coal mines of Anyuan but soon proved physically unfit for this work and had to return to service as a farm laborer. In the summer of 1926 he was employed as a railway construction laborer in Hengyang. When the Communist forces passed this area after the failed Nanchang Uprising of autumn 1927 he joined the troops as a messenger. In 1928 he became a member of the CCP. By 1934 he was commander of a regiment of the 1st Front Army. During the Long March his unit took an important part in the battles to open the crossing of the River Dadu in May 1935. At the beginning of the Anti-Japanese War Yang was made commander of the 685th Regiment of the 115th Division. During the following years he served as troop commander in Hebei-Shandong-Henan Border Region. In 1947 the units under his command were reorganized to form the 19th Army Corps. In September 1949 his troops occupied Yinchuan in Ningxia; Yang was subsequently appointed chairman of the Yinchuan Military Control Commission and commander of Ningxia Military Region.

1950,	Jan	Appointed member of the Northwest China Military and Administrative Council and member of the Provincial People's Government of Shaanxi (until 1951)
1951,	Feb	Yang is transferred with the 19th Corps to Korea and concurrently becomes deputy commander of the Chinese People's Volunteers (until Oct 1954)
1954,	Oct	Appointed commander of the People's Volunteers; appointed member of the National Defense Council (until Cultural Revolution)
1955,	Mar	Recalled from Korea; training at Nanjing Military Academy (until 1958)

	Sep	Promoted to rank of lieutenant-general
1956,	Sep	Elected alternate member of the CCP Central Committee by the 8th Party Congress (until Oct 1967)
1958,	Sep?	Appointed commander of Jinan Military Region (until 1973) and 2nd secretary of Shandong Province CP; promoted to rank of colonel-general
	Nov	Elected deputy for Shandong Province to the 2nd NPC (reelected in 1954 to the 3rd NPC)
1959,	Apr–Jun	Member of a military delegation led by Peng Dehuai to the countries of Eastern Europe and to the People's Republic of Mongolia
1967,	May	Identified as vice-chairman of the Revolutionary Committee of Shandong Province (until May 1971)
	Sep	Head of a military delegation to North Korea
	Oct	Identified as member of the CCP Central Committee
1969,	Apr	Confirmed as member of the CCP Central Committee by the 9th Party Congress (again confirmed in this post in 1973 and 1977 by the 10th and 11th Congresses)
1971,	Apr	Elected 1st secretary of Shandong Province CP (until Dec 1973)
	May	Identified as chairman of the Revolutionary Committee of Shandong Province (until Dec 1973)
1974,	Jan	Identified as commander of Wuhan Military Region (until Dec 1978)
1976,	Jul	Identified as 1st secretary, CP Secretariat of Wuhan Military Region (until Dec 1978)
1978,	Feb	Elected deputy for the PLA to the 5th NPC
	Aug	Deputy head of a military delegation led by Su Yu to North Korea; awarded the Korean order "Freedom and Independence," 1st class
1979,	Feb	Identified as commander, and as 1st secretary of the CP Secretariat, of Kunming Military Region (both posts until Jan 1980)
1980,	Feb	Identified as Member of the Standing Committee, Military Council under the CCP Central Committee; elected member of the Secretariat under the CCP Central Committee by its 5th Plenum
	Mar	Identified as chief of the PLA General Staff

Yang Dongsheng (Yang Tung-sheng) 杨东生

Posts held

Government
Vice-minister of the Nationalities Affairs Commission

Others
Member of the Standing Committee of the 5th CPPCC

Yang belongs to the Tibetan minority.

1956,	Apr	Appointed deputy director of the Civil Affairs Office, Preparatory Committee

		for the Establishment of Tibet Autonomous Region
1965,	Sep	Identified as secretary of Tibet Autonomous Region CP (until 1967)
1966,	Jun	Head of a friendship delegation to Nepal
1968,	Sep	Elected vice-chairman of the Revolutionary Committee of Tibet Autonomous Region (last mention in this post in 1977)
1971,	Aug	Elected secretary of Tibet Autonomous Region CP (until 1977)
1978,	Mar	Elected member of the Standing Committee of the 5th CPPCC
1979,	May	Identified as vice-minister of the State Nationalities Affairs Commission

Yang Fangzhi (Yang Fang-chih) 杨放之

Posts held

Government
Director of the Bureau of Foreign Experts Affairs

Yang was born in 1906 in Henan Province. He studied at Sun Yat-sen University in Moscow in 1925. After his return to China in 1927 he worked in the Administrative Office of the CCP Central Committee. He was imprisoned from 1935 to 1937.

1950,	May	Identified as secretary-general of the Propaganda Department, North China Bureau of the CCP Central Committee, and deputy secretary-general of the Financial and Economic Commission of the Government Administration Council
1954,	Oct	Appointed deputy secretary-general of the State Council (until Cultural Revolution)
	Nov	Identified as director of the Foreign Experts Work Bureau under the State Council
1956,	May	Appointed director of the Bureau of Foreign Experts Administration (until Oct 1964)
1959,	Sep	Appointed director of the Secretaries Office under the State Council
1967,	Jun	Branded as a renegade and purged
1979,	Jul	First appearance after the Cultural Revolution: Identified as director of the Bureau of Foreign Experts

Yang Fuzhen (Yang Fu-chen) (f) 杨富珍

Posts held

CCP
Alternate member of the CCP 11th Central Committee
Member of the Standing Committee of Shanghai Municipality CP

Mass Organization
Vice-chairman of the Trade Union of Shanghai

Yang is the daughter of poor peasants and received no school education. At the age of fourteen, having served a landlord for some time, she went to Shanghai on her own where she joined the CCP in 1949.

1950		Weaver at the state operated Cotton Mill No.1 in Shanghai
from 1953		In the course of the 1st Five Year Plan (1953-1957) Yang is repeatedly ahead of her production quota and is named outstanding worker and model worker
1956,	Apr	Elected Shanghai delegate to the National Congress of Young Activists for Socialist Construction
1959,	Mar	Elected deputy for Shanghai Municipality to the 2nd NPC (reelected in 1964 to the 3rd NPC)
1966,	Jul	Named as activist in the study of Mao Zedong works
	Nov	Article in the local press: "The Philosophy of Weaving"
1968,	May	Identified as member of the Revolutionary Committee of Shanghai (until May 1970)
1969,	Apr	Elected member of the Central Committee by the 9th Party Congress (until Aug 1973)
1970,	May	Identified as vice-chairman of the Revolutionary Committee of Shanghai (until Mar 1979?)
1973,	Apr	Elected vice-chairman of the Trade Union of Shanghai
	Aug	Demoted from member to alternate member of the Central Committee by the 10th Party Congress (confirmed in 1977 by the 11th Congress)
1977,	Jan	Identified as member of the Standing Committee of Shanghai Municipality CP
1978,	Aug	Head of a friendship delegation to Romania

Yang Gongsu (Yang Kung-su) 杨公素

Posts held

Government
Ambassador to Vietnam

1949		Identified as deputy director of the Office for Foreign Residents of Tianjin Municipal People's Government
1956,	Aug	Member of a government delegation to Nepal
1958,	Sep	Identified as director of the Department of Foreign Affairs of the Preparatory Committee for the establishment of Tibet Autonomous Region (until about Oct 1963)
1960,	Aug	Head of a delegation discussing border problems in New Delhi
1963,	Oct	Appointed deputy director of the 1st Asia Department of the Ministry of Foreign Affairs (until Jan 1966)
1964,	Jun	Deputy head of a delegation, Chinese Section of the Sino-Afghan Border Delimitation Committee
1966,	Jan	Appointed ambassador to Nepal (until 1967)
1970,	Jun	Identified as a cadre of the Asia Department of the Ministry of Foreign Affairs
1971,	Oct	Identified as a cadre of the Administrative Bureau for Travel and Tourism (until 1978)
1974,	May	Head of a delegation of tourists to Iran

| 1978, | Dec | Appointed ambassador to Vietnam |
| 1979, | Jul | Appointed deputy head of the Chinese delegation to the Sino-Vietnamese negotiations |

Yang Guofu (Yang Kuo-fu) 杨国夫

Posts held

Military
Lieutenant-general

Others
Member of the Standing Committee of the 5th CPPCC

In 1943 Yang served as deputy commander of the 3rd Brigade, Shandong Column, and concurrently commander of Bohai Military District. In 1945 he commanded the 7th Division of the Northeast Democratic Joint Army. He was appointed deputy commander of the 14th Army Group, 4th Field Army, in 1949.

1949,	Nov	Identified as deputy commander of Jiangxi Military District
1950,	Mar	Identified as council member, People's Government of Jiangxi Province
1955		Identified as deputy commander of Jinan Military Region (probably still in 1978)
1958		Identified as lieutenant-general
1964,	Dec	Elected member of the 4th CPPCC
1968,	Apr	Elected member of the Standing Committee, Revolutionary Committee of Shandong Province (no later mention in this post)
1978,	Mar	Elected member of the Standing Committee of the 5th CPPCC

Yang Guoyu (Yang Kuo-yü) 杨国宇

Posts held

NPC
Deputy for the PLA to the 5th NPC

Military
Deputy commander of the PLA Navy

1966		Identified as chief of staff, Lüda (Lüshun-Dalian) Naval Command
1976,	Nov	Identified as chief of staff of the Navy Headquarters
1977,	Oct	Member of a military delegation to Tunisia
1978,	Feb	Elected deputy for the PLA to the 5th NPC
	Dec	Identified as deputy commander of the PLA Navy

Yang Hansheng (Yang Han-sheng) 阳翰笙

Posts held

Others
Member of the Standing Committee of the 5th CPPCC
Vice-chairman of the Federation of Literary and Art Circles

Yang was born in 1902 in Gao County, Sichuan Province. He graduated from the Social Science Department of Shanghai University. During his studies he joined the CCP in 1925. In 1927 he took part in the Nanchang Uprising, after the failure of which he went to Shanghai to publish the journal Earth and Spring under the pseudonym of Hua Han. From 1933 to 1935 he wrote a number of film scripts. In January 1935 he was arrested together with Tian Han because of subversive activities related to the Left-Wing Writers League. He was released in 1936, and in 1938 became chief secretary of the 3rd Bureau (director: Guo Moruo) of the Political Department under the Military Affairs Commission of the Nationalist Central Government. During the Anti-Japanese War Yang published a number of plays. In 1945 he returned to Shanghai to work in the field of literature and propaganda. In September 1949 he took part in the 1st CPPCC as a delegate representing the Federation of Literary and Art Circles.

1949,	Oct	Appointed deputy secretary-general of the Cultural and Educational Commission, Government Administration Council (until Sep 1954)
1950,	Feb	Identified as member of the Standing Committee, China Folk Literature Society
1951,	Oct	Identified as executive secretary of the Sino-Soviet Friendship Association (until Dec 1954)
1953,	Sep	Elected secretary-general of the Federation of Literary and Art Circles (until 1966)
	Oct	Identified as council member of the Union of Chinese Writers
1954,	Apr	Member of a friendship delegation to the USSR
	May	Elected vice-chairman of the Association for Cultural Relations with Foreign Countries (until Sep 1966)
	Jun	Member of a cultural delegation to Poland
	Aug	Elected deputy for Sichuan Province to the 1st NPC (reelected in 1958 and 1964 to the 2nd and 3rd NPCs)
1955,	Jul	Elected council member of the Sino-Indonesian Friendship Association
1956,	Feb	Elected member of the China-Asian Solidarity Committee (until 1958)
	Apr	Identified as council member of the Union of Stage Artists (until 1966)
1957,	Oct	Member of a friendship delegation to the USSR
1958,	Mar	Appointed member of the Association for Cultural Relations with Foreign Countries (until 1966)
	Jul	Identified as member of the Standing Committee of the Committee for World Peace, and as member of the National Committee of the China-Afro-Asian Solidarity Committee (until 1966)
1960,	Aug	Identified as vice-chairman of the Federation of Literary and Art Circles (until 1966)
1966,	Sep	Branded as a capitalist-roader
1967,	May	Undergoes "struggle" together with Tian Han
1979,	Jan	First appearance after the Cultural Revolution
	May	Identified as vice-chairman of the Federation of Literary and Art Circles
	Jul	By-elected member of the Standing Committee of the 5th CPPCC

Publications

Novel	Earth and Spring
Film scipts	Iron Board and Red Tears
	A Sad Song of Life
	The Roaring Tide of the China Sea
	The Peasants of North China
	One-Heartedness in Life and Death
Stage plays	Tianguo Chunqiu (The Annals of Tai Ping Heavenly Kingdom)
	Li Xiucheng Zhi Si (The Death of Li Xiucheng)
	The Heroes Among the Masses
	A Double Faced Man
	The Native Village in the White Clouds
	Lights from Ten Thousand Households
	The Volunteers

Yang Ji (Yang Chi)

Posts held

Others
Vice-chairman of the Association for Friendship with Foreign Countries

1961,	Oct	Identified as deputy secretary-general of the China-Afro-Asian Solidarity Committee
	Nov	Member of a delegation to Algeria
1964,	Feb	Member of a delegation of the Afro-Asian Solidarity Committee to Japan
	Aug	Member of a delegation of the Afro-Asian Solidarity Committee to Congo
1965,	Jun	Elected secretary of the Afro-Asian Solidarity Committee and vice-chairman of the Committee for World Peace
1972,	Jun	Identified as vice-chairman of the Association for Friendship with Foreign Countries
1975,	Jun	Head of a friendship delegation to Congo, Zaire, Sierra Leone, Mauritania, and Egypt
1977,	Jan	Head of a friendship delegation to Tanzania
1978,	Dec	Deputy head of a friendship delegation to Laos

Yang Jiarui (Yang Chia-jui)

Posts held

Military
Major-general
Deputy commander of Lanzhou Military District

Provincial Administration
Vice-chairman of the People's Congress of Gansu Province

Yang was born in 1908 in Shaanxi Province. In 1930 he served in a Communist unit in Hubei Province. He commanded a battalion in 1931, and in 1935 **a regiment** of the 6th Division, 2nd Front Army. In 1937 he was made commander of a battalion of the 716th Regiment, 358th Brigade, 120th Division, 8th Route Army. In 1939 he was sent to Moscow to study at the Red Army Academy. He was appointed commander of the 1st Military Subdistrict in Northwest Shanxi Military District in 1943. In 1945 he commanded a regiment and in 1949 a brigade of the 120th Division. In 1949 he was appointed commander of the 19th Division, 7th Army, 1st Field Army.

1953,	Jan	Identified as deputy commander of Shaanxi Military District (until 1964)
1955,	Sep	Promoted to rank of major-general
1958,	Mar	Identified as commander of Shaanxi Military District
1959,	Mar	Elected deputy for the PLA to the 2nd NPC (reelected in Sep 1964 to the 3rd NPC)
1964,	May	Identified as deputy commander of Lanzhou Military District
1968,	Jan	Elected member of the Revolutionary Committee of Gansu Province; subsequently disappears
1976,	Apr	Identified as military leader of Lanzhou Military District
1979,	Jun	Again referred to as deputy commander of Lanzhou Military District
	Dec	Elected vice-chairman of the People's Congress of Gansu Province

Yang Jiaxiang (Yang Chia-hsiang) 杨家祥

Posts held

Government
Deputy director and secretary-general of XNA

Yang was born in 1920.

1978,	Mar	Identified as secretary-general of XNA
	Aug	Identified as deputy director of XNA
	Oct	Head of a group of XNA technicians to Japan

Yang Jie (Yang Chieh)  杨 杰

Posts held

Military
Deputy political commissar of the PLA Capital Construction Engineering Corps

1968,	May	Identified as a cadre of the State Council
1971,	Feb	Identified as minister of communications (until Dec 1974); head of a government delegation to Pakistan
	Sep	Head of a communications delegation to Poland
	Dec	Official PRC representative at the celebrations of Independence Day in Burundi and subsequently Tanzania
1972,	Jan	Head of a government delegation to Zambia
	Apr	Head of a government delegation to Vietnam

1976,	Jan	Identified as vice-minister of posts and telecommunications (until 1978)
1979,	Apr	Identified as deputy political commissar of the PLA Capital Construction Engineering Corps

Yang Jike (Yang Chi-k'e) 杨纪珂

Posts held

Provincial Administration
Vice-governor of Anhui Province

1979,	Dec	Elected vice-governor of Anhui Province

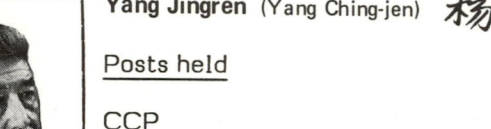

Yang Jingren (Yang Ching-jen) 杨静仁

Posts held

CCP
Member of the CCP 11th Central Committee
Deputy director, United Front Work Department of the CCP Central Committee

Government
Minister of the Nationalities Affairs Commission

NPC
Deputy for Ningxia Autonomous Region to the 5th NPC

Others
Vice-chairman of the 5th CPPCC

Yang belongs to the Hui minority; he was born in 1917 in Gansu Province. In 1941 he was appointed chief of staff of the Muslim Cavalry Brigade by the Communists. He was later head of the Minorities Department, Northwest China Bureau of the CCP Central Committee, and member of the Minorities Affairs Committee of the Shaanxi-Gansu-Ningxia Border Region Government. In April 1949 Yang was elected a member of the Central Committee of the New Democratic Youth League and one month later member of the National Committee of the newly established Federation of Democratic Youth (until June 1953). In September of that year he took part in the CPPCC as a delegate representing the minorities.

1949,	Oct	Appointed member of the Minorities Commission, Government Administration Council (until Oct 1954); appointed member of the Committee for the Reform of the Written Language (until Feb 1952)
1951,	Jan	Appointed member of the Northwest China Military and Administrative Council (until Jan 1953)
	Mar	Appointed member of the Minorities Committee of Northwest China Military and Administrative Council (until Jan 1953)
1953,	Jan	Appointed member of the Northwest China People's Council and member of its Minorities Committee (until Oct 1954)
	May	Elected vice-chairman of the Islamic Society

1954,	Aug	Elected deputy for Gansu Province to the 1st NPC (until Dec 1964)
	Oct	Appointed vice-chairman of the Minorities Commission (until Dec 1960)
1957,	Sep	Elected vice-chairman of the newly established Sino-Syrian Friendship Association (until Feb 1958)
1958,	Feb	Elected vice-chairman of the newly established Sino-United Arab Republic Friendship Association
	Apr	Elected vice-chairman of the Federation of Democratic Youth (probably until 1960)
1960,	Sep	Identified as chairman of Ningxia Autonomous Region
1961,	Feb	Identified as 1st secretary of Ningxia Autonomous Region CP
1964,	Apr	Identified as political commissar of Ningxia Autonomous Region
	Oct	Elected deputy for Ningxia Autonomous Region to the 3rd NPC
1965,	Mar	Identified as secretary, Northwest China Bureau of the CCP Central Committee
1967,	Aug	Branded as a capitalist-roader and disappears
1977,	Aug	First appearance after the Cultural Revolution: Elected member of the CCP Central Committee by the 11th Party Congress
1978,	Feb	Elected deputy for Ningxia Autonomous Region to the 5th NPC
	Mar	Elected vice-chairman of the 5th CPPCC; appointed minister of the Nationalities Affairs Commission
	Aug	Head of a friendship delegation to North Korea
	Dec	Identified as deputy director, United Front Work Department of the CCP Central Committee
1979,	Jun	Vice-chairman of the Credentials Committee at the 2nd Session of the 5th NPC
	Dec	Head of a CPPCC delegation to Romania

Yang Jue (Yang Chüeh)　　杨　珏

Posts held

Government
Vice-minister of forestry

1949,	Dec	Identified as director, Organization Department of Pingyuan Province CP (until 1953)
1953,	May	Identified as member of the Executive Committee of the Federation of Trade Unions (until Dec 1957)
	Oct	Identified as deputy secretary of Henan Province CP (until Oct 1956)
1955,	Oct	Identified as chairman of the Trade Unions of Henan Province (until Jun 1958)
1956,	Dec	Identified as secretary of Henan Province CP (until Jun 1958)
1958,	Jun	Branded as a rightist and purged
1964,	Jan	Identified in his former post as secretary of Henan Province CP (until Oct 1965)
1965,	Nov	Appointed vice-chairman of the State Economic Commission
1966		Yang disappears again

1975,	Sep	First appearance after the Cultural Revolution
1977,	Jul	Identified as responsible person of the North China Coordination Region Preparatory Group
1978,	Aug	Identified as deputy director of the State General Forestry Bureau
1979,	Mar	Head of a forestry delegation to the Federal Republic of Germany
	Jul	Identified as vice-minister of forestry

Yang Junsheng (Yang Chün-sheng) 杨俊生

Posts held

CCP
Alternate member of the CCP 11th Central Committee

Military
Major-general
Political commissar of Beijing Garrison

Yang is a native of Jiangsu Province. He took part in the Long March, serving in the 1st Front Army. In September 1937 he took part in the Battle of Pingxing Guan as a company leader of the 115th Division. In 1939 he served under Yang Yong as battalion and later regiment commander in West Shandong. In 1945 he commanded a regiment of the 1st Column, Hebei-Shandong-Hunan Military Region, and two years later a brigade of the Central Plains Field Army. In 1949 he was made commander of a division of the 2nd Field Army.

1952		Service in the Korean War as deputy commander of the 16th Army
1954?		Military training at a (Soviet?) artillery school
1955,	Sep	Promoted to rank of major-general
1958		Appointed commander of the Artillery Forces, Chinese People's Volunteers in Korea
1959-1962		Further training at the Military Academy of the PLA
1963		Identified as commander of the 16th Army based in Jilin Province
1968,	Jun	Identified as responsible cadre of Beijing Garrison
1969,	Apr	Elected alternate member of the CCP Central Committee by the 9th Party Congress (confirmed in 1973 and 1977 by the 10th and 11th Congresses)
	Jun	Identified as vice-chairman of the Revolutionary Committee of Beijing (until about 1973)
1971,	Mar	Elected secretary of Beijing Municipality CP (until about 1974)
1973,	Sep	Member of a friendship delegtion to North Korea; identified as political commissar of Beijing Garrison

Yang Kai (Yang K'ai)　　杨　恺

Posts held

Provincial Administration
Vice-mayor of Shanghai Municipality

1977,   Dec   Elected vice-chairman of the Revolution-
               ary Committee of Shanghai (until
               Dec 1979)
1978,   Jun   Identified as director of the Shanghai
               Education and Public Health Office
         Sep   Identified as president of the Shanghai
               Red Cross Society
1979,   Jul   Appointed member of the National Games
               Organizing Committee
         Dec   Elected vice-mayor of Shanghai Munici-
               pality

Yang Kanghua (Yang K'ang-hua) 杨康华

Posts held

Provincial Administration
Vice-governor of Guangdong Province

In 1947 Yang served as director of the Political Department of East River Column and two years later as
director of the Political Department of Guangdong-
Guangxi Column.

1950   Identified as council member of the Peo-
               ple's Government of Guangzhou
         Oct   Identified as deputy secretary, CP of Zhu
               Jiang District, and as director of the
               Political Department of Guangdong Mili-
               tary District
1951,   Nov   Identified as political commissar of the
               5th Public Security Division of the Cen-
               tral-South Military Region
1953   Identified as 3rd secretary of Central
               Guangdong District CP
1954,   Oct   Identified as vice-chairman of the Cultur-
               al and Educational Committee of Guang-
               dong People's Government
1957,   Apr   Identified as director of the Cultural and
               Educational Department of Guangdong
               Province CP (until 1961)
1958,   Nov   Member of a delegation led by Liu Ningyi
               to the anniversary celebrations of the
               October Revolution in the USSR
1961,   Feb   Head of a Guangzhou Opera troupe vis-
               iting Vietnam
         Nov   Identified as vice-governor of Guangdong
               Province (until Cultural Revolution)
         Dec   Identified as director of the United Front
               Work Department of Guangdong Prov-
               ince CP
1964,   Jun   Identified as president of the Jinan Uni-
               versity in Guangzhou (until Cultural Revo-
               lution)
         Sep   Elected deputy for Guangdong Province to
               the 3rd NPC
1967,   Jan   Branded as a capitalist-roader and purged
1972,   Nov   First appearance after the Cultural Revo-
               lution
1977,   Dec   Elected vice-chairman of the Revolution-
               ary Committee of Guangdong Province
               (until Dec 1979)
1979,   Jul   Appointed member of the National Games
               Organizing Committee
         Dec   Elected vice-governor of Guangdong Prov-
               ince

Yang Kecheng (Yang K'e-ch'eng) 杨克成

Posts held

Provincial Administration
Vice-governor of Yunnan Province

Yang belongs to the Bai minority.

1979,   Dec   Elected vice-governor of Yunnan Province

Yang Keming (Yang K'e-ming)   杨克明

Posts held

Government
Ambassador to Kenya

Yang was born in 1930 in Shanxi Province.

1960   Counselor at the embassy in the German
               Democratic Republic
1974,   Sep   Appointed ambassador to Ghana (until
               Feb 1979)
1979,   May   Appointed ambassador to Kenya

Yang is married to Ma Bingjing.

Yang Keng (Yang K'eng)   杨 铿

Posts held

Government
Vice-minister of the 1st Ministry of Machine Building

Yang was born in 1920 in Hebei Province.

1973,   Nov   Identified as vice-minister of the 1st Min-
               istry of Machine Building
1978,   Apr   Head of a motor vehicle industry study
               group visiting the Federal Republic of
               Germany

Yang Ligong (Yang Li-kung)   杨立功

Posts held

Government
Minister of agricultural machinery

NPC
Deputy for Shandong Province to the
5th NPC

1955,   May   Identified as 1st deputy director of the
               Tractor Factory No.1 in Luoyang
1959,   Nov   Identified as director of Tractor Factory
               No.1 in Luoyang
1962,   Oct   Appointed vice-minister of agricultural
               machinery (until Jan 1965)
1965,   Jan   The Ministry of Agricultural Machinery is
               reorganized into the 8th Ministry of
               Machine Building; Yang is appointed vice-
               minister of this new ministry
1967   Disappears during the Cultural Revolution
1970,   Sep   The Ministries of Agriculture and Forestry
               are merged to form the Ministry of

Agriculture and Forestry; Yang is appointed vice-minister (until Feb 1978)

1973,   Sep   Head of a scientific and technical delegation to Bulgaria

1974,   Sep   Head of the Chinese Section, Sino-Bulgarian Commission for Scientific and Technical Cooperation

1975,   Sep   Head of a scientific and technical delegation to Bulgaria

         Nov   Head of the Chinese delegation to the Food and Agriculture Organization Conference in Rome

1976,   Mar   Head of an agricultural delegation to the Philippines

1978,   Mar   Appointed minister of agriculture and forestry (until Feb 1979)

1979,   Feb   Appointed minister of the newly established Ministry of Agricultural Machinery

         May   Head of an agricultural machinery delegation to the International Agricultural Fair at Novi Sad, Yugoslavia

Yang Mo (Yang Mo) (f)   杨　沫

Posts held

NPC
Member of the Standing Committee of the 5th NPC
Deputy for Beijing Municipality to the 5th NPC

Yang, born in 1914, is a well-known novelist. She is the author of the best-seller Qingchun Zhi Ge (Song of the Youth).

1964,   Oct   Elected deputy for Sichuan Province to the 3rd NPC

1978,   Jan   Member of a delegation of writers to Pakistan

         Feb   Elected deputy for Beijing Municipality to the 5th NPC

         Mar   Elected member of the Standing Committee of the 5th NPC

Yang Qiaoling (Yang Ch'iao-ling) (f)

Posts held   杨愀玲

Others
Member of the Standing Committee of the 5th CPPCC

1978,   Mar   Elected member of the Standing Committee of the 5th CPPCC

         May   Officially rehabilitated, having been persecuted by Jiang Qing during the Cultural Revolution as a member of the Beijing Opera ensemble

Yang Qiliang (Yang Ch'i-liang)   杨瑛良

Posts held

Government
Ambassador to Portugal

During the final phase of the Revolutionary War Yang served as deputy political commissar of a PLA division.

1950,   Dec   Identified as counselor at the embassy in Poland (until 1960)

1961,   Jul   Appointed ambassador to Morocco (until about 1967)

         Oct   Yang visits Tunisia

1969,   Jul   Identified as ambassador to Algeria (until May 1971)

1971,   Jul   Appointed ambassador to Nigeria (until about Sep 1973)

1974,   Apr   Identified as director of the Political Department, Ministry of Foreign Affairs (until 1976)

1976,   Jan   Yang disappears

1979,   Aug   Reactivated as ambassador to Portugal

Yang Rudai (Yang Ju-tai)   杨汝岱

Posts held

CCP
Member of the Standing Committee of Sichuan Province CP

Provincial Administration
Vice-governor of Sichuan Province

1977,   Dec   Elected vice-chairman of the Revolutionary Committee of Sichuan Province (until Dec 1979)

1979,   Jan   Elected member of the Standing Committee of Sichuan Province CP

         Dec   Elected vice-governor of Sichuan Province

Yang Shangkui (Yang Shang-k'uei)   杨尚奎

Posts held

CCP
Secretary of Jiangxi Province CP

NPC
Member of the Standing Committee of the 5th NPC
Deputy for Jiangxi Province to the 5th NPC

Provincial Administration
Chairman of the People's Congress of Jiangxi Province

Yang was born in 1903 in Xingguo, Jiangxi Province. When the main Communist forces began the Long March from Jiangxi Province in autumn 1934, Yang was ordered to remain behind and conduct guerrilla operations in the Jiangxi-Guangdong Border Region. In late 1934 Yang was appointed deputy secretary of the CCP Special Committee for Jiangxi-Guangdong Border Region. In 1938 the troops under his command were incorporated into the New 4th Army. When Jiangxi Province had been occupied by the Communist forces Yang was appointed 2nd deputy secretary of Jiangxi Province CP (until July 1952).

1952,   Jul   Appointed 2nd deputy secretary of Jiangxi Province CP (until Oct 1953)

1953,	Oct	Appointed secretary of Jiangxi Province CP (until Sep 1956); appointed political commissar of Jiangxi Military District
1955,	Jan	Appointed chairman of the Jiangxi Section, CPPCC
1956,	Sep	Appointed 1st secretary of Jiangxi Province CP (until Cultural Revolution)
1965,	Mar	Identified as secretary, East China Bureau of the CCP Central Committee (until Cultural Revolution)
1967		Yang is accused of having boycotted the Cultural Revolution; relieved of all posts
1972,	Dec	First appearance after the Cultural Revolution
1973,	Apr	Identified as vice-chairman of the Revolutionary Committee of Jiangxi Province (until Dec 1979)
1975,	Mar	Identified as secretary of Jiangxi Province CP
1978,	Feb	Elected deputy for Jiangxi Province to the 5th NPC
	Mar	Elected member of the Standing Committee of the 5th NPC
1979,	Dec	Elected chairman of the People's Congress of Jiangxi Province

Yang Shangkun (Yang Shang-k'un) 杨尚昆

Posts held

CCP
Member of the CCP 11th Central Committee
2nd secretary of Guangdong Province CP
1st secretary of Guangzhou Municipality CP

Provincial Administration
Vice-governor of Guangdong Province
Chairman of the Revolutionary Committee of Guangzhou Municipality

Others
Member of the Standing Committee of the 5th CPPCC

Yang was born in 1904 in Tongnan, Sichuan Province. In 1925 he was a student at Shanghai University and in the same year joined the CCP. He was subsequently sent to Moscow to study at the Sun Yat-sen University. In 1928 he served as secretary to Chen Shaoyu during the 6th Congress of the Communist International. In 1931 he returned together with Chen and others (the so-called group of 28 Bolsheviks) to China and married the playwright Li Bozhao. In 1932 Yang was elected a member of the Central Executive Committee by the 2nd Congress of the Jiangxi Soviet Government. At this time he was also appointed director of the Political Department of the 1st Red Army. During the Anti-Japanese War he was head of a drama troupe performing propaganda plays for the Communist forces. In 1943 he was appointed secretary, North China Bureau of the CCP Central Committee, and director of the United Front Department of that bureau. In 1945 he became head of the General Office of the CCP Central Committee (until Cultural Revolution).

| 1951, | Dec | Elected council member of the Sino-Soviet Friendship Association (until 1954) |

1956,	Sep	Elected member of the CCP Central Committee by the 8th Party Congress and alternate member of the CCP Secretariat
1957,	Oct	Member of a delegation to the 40th anniversary of the October Revolution in Moscow
1960,	Nov	Member of a CCP delegation to Moscow
1963,	Jul	Member of a CCP delegation for ideological discussion in Moscow
1964,	Oct	Elected deputy for Sichuan Province to the 3rd NPC
1965,	Jan	Elected member of the Standing Committee of the NPC
1966,	Aug	Branded as a counterrevolutionary revisionist
	Dec	Together with Peng Zhen, Luo Ruiqing, and Lu Dingyi, Yang undergoes a struggle session at a Beijing mass rally
1978,	Dec	First appearance after the Cultural Revolution
1979,	Jan	Identified as 2nd Party secretary and vice-chairman of Guangdong Provincial Revolutionary Committee (until Dec 1979)
	Apr	Identified as 1st secretary of Guangzhou Municipality CP and as chairman of the Guangzhou Revolutionary Committee; head of a Guangzhou friendship delegation to Japan
	Jul	By-elected member of the Standing Committee of the 5th CPPCC
	Sep	By-elected member of the CCP 11th Central Committee
	Dec	Elected vice-governor of Guangdong Province

Yang Shifa (Yang Shih-fa) 杨士法

Posts held

CCP
Deputy secretary of Shanghai Municipality CP

Provincial Administration
Vice-mayor of Shanghai Municipality

Others
Chairman of the Shanghai Scientific and Technical Committee

1953		Identified as director of the Industry Department of Shanghai Municipality CP (until 1961)
1958,	Feb	Identified as 1st secretary of Yangpu District CP
1959,	Apr	Identified as member of the Standing Committee of Shanghai Municipality CP (until Cultural Revolution)
1964,	Oct	Identified as director of the Organization Department of Shanghai Municipality CP
1967,	Jan	Attacked as a revisionist and purged
1978,	Jun	First appearance after the Cultural Revolution: Identified as vice-chairman of the Revolutionary Committee of Shanghai Municipality (until Dec 1979)
	Sep	Identified as chairman of the Shanghai Scientific and Technical Commission

1979,   May   Identified as deputy secretary of Shanghai Municipality CP
        Jun   Deputy head of a Shanghai delegation, led by Peng Chong, to the Federal Republic of Germany, Spain, and Italy
        Dec   Elected vice-mayor of Shanghai Municipality

Yang Shijie (Yang Shih-chieh)   杨士杰

Posts held

Others
Member of the Standing Committee of the 5th CPPCC

1954,   Aug   Elected deputy for Anshan Municipality to the 1st NPC
1957,   Oct   Identified as 1st secretary of Anshan Municipality CP (until 1961?)
1978,   Mar   Elected member of the Standing Committee of the 5th CPPCC

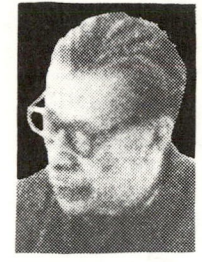

Yang Shixian (Yang Shih-hsien)   杨石先

Posts held

NPC
Deputy for Tianjin Municipality to the 5th NPC

Others
Member of the Standing Committee of the 5th CPPCC
President of Nankai University

Yang was born in 1896 in Huaining, Anhui Province. He studied chemistry in the United States where he received a doctorate from Yale University in 1931. Having returned to China he held the following posts successively: dean of the Science School of Nankai University; director of the Chemistry Department of Southwest Associated University, and visiting professor of the University of Indiana, U.S.A. In September 1949 he took part in the founding session of the 1st CPPCC.

1950,   Aug   Identified as member of the People's Government of Tianjin Municipality; chairman of the University Affairs Committee of Nankai University
1951,   Aug   Identified as member of the Standing Committee of the Chemistry Society
1953,   Jan   Identified as chairman of the Association for Promoting Democracy, Tianjin Branch (until 1963)
        Nov   Identified as vice-chairman of the Sino-Soviet Friendship Association, Tianjin Branch
1954,   Aug   Elected deputy for Tianjin Municipality to the 1st NPC
1955,   Jun   Appointed member of the Standing Committee, Department of Physics, Mathematics, and Chemistry of the Academy of Sciences (until Cultural Revolution)
1956,   Aug   Identified as president of the Chemistry Society; elected member of the Standing Committee, Association for Promoting Democracy

1957,   May   Identified as member of the State Scientific Planning Commission
        Aug   Identified as president of Nankai University (until Cultural Revolution); member of a NPC delegation to Finland
        Nov   Member of a scientific and technical delegation to the USSR
1958,   Oct   Elected deputy for Hebei Province to the 2nd NPC (reelected in 1964 to the 3rd NPC)
1961,   Feb   Identified as chairman of the Hebei Branch, Academy of Sciences
1963,   Dec   Identified as director of the Institute of Organic Elementary Chemistry, Nankai University
1964   Disappears
1977,   Dec   First appearance after the Cultural Revolution: Identified as a chemist of Nankai University
1978,   Feb   Elected deputy for Tianjin Municipality to the 5th NPC
        Mar   Elected member of the Standing Committee of the 5th CPPCC
1979,   Oct   Identified as president of Nankai University

Yang Shoushan (Yang Shou-shan)   杨寿山

Posts held

Government
Vice-minister of public health

During the final phase of the Revolutionary Period Yang served as deputy director of the Logistics Department of the 2nd Field Army.

1950,   Aug   Appointed member of the South Sichuan Administrative Office (until Aug 1952)
        Dec   Identified as vice-chairman of the Financial and Economic Committee of South Sichuan Administrative Office
1957,   Jun   Appointed assistant minister of the Ministry of Electric Industry (until Feb 1958 when the ministry was incorporated into the 1st Ministry of Machine Building)
1960,   Sep   Appointed vice-minister of the 1st Ministry of Machine Building (until Cultural Revolution)
1964,   Sep   Head of the Chinese Section, Sino-Czechoslovakian Commission for Scientific and Technical Cooperation
1971,   Jun   Identified as member of the Standing Committee of Beijing Municipality CP (until May 1978)
1973,   Oct   Identified as vice-chairman of the Revolutionary Committee of Beijing Municipality (until May 1978)
1978,   Jul   Identified as vice-minister of public health

Yang Shouzheng (Yang Shou-cheng)   杨守正

Posts held

Government
Ambassador to the USSR

1964,	Sep	Appointed ambassador to Somalia (until about 1967)
1970,	Apr	Appointed ambassador to Sudan (until Aug 1974)
	Aug	Yang accompanies the president of Sudan on his visit to China
	Nov	Yang conducts negotiations in Ethiopia for the establishment of diplomatic relations with the PRC
1974,	Dec	Appointed ambassador to Ethiopia (until Aug 1977)
1977,	Oct	Appointed ambassador to Mozambique (until Jan 1980)
1978,	May	Yang accompanies the president of Mozambique on his visit to China
1980,	Apr	Appointed ambassador to the USSR

Yang is married to Gong Runbing.

Yang Shu (Yang Shu)   杨 述

Yang was born in 1910 in Beijing. He is a graduate of Beijing China University. He joined the CCP as a student. In 1936 he made important contributions to the publication of several journals, including The Road to Emancipation, Our Army, and Our Life. From 1937 he served as deputy director of the Youth Department, North China Bureau of the CCP Central Committee. In 1945 he was concurrently secretary of the Communist Youth League, North China Committee. He was elected a member of the Executive Council of the New Democratic Youth League in April 1949 and represented that league as a delegate at the 1st CPPCC in September.

1952		Identified as alternate secretary of the New Democratic Youth League
1953,	Apr	Identified as director of the China Youth Press
	Nov	Identified as member of the Standing Committee of Beijing Municipality CP as well as director of the Propaganda Department of Beijing CP (until 1966)
1955,	Oct	Identified as 2nd secretary, Higher Party School of Beijing CP
1956,	Nov	Member of a delegation from Beijing to the USSR and European socialist countries (until Jan 1957)
1959,	Apr	Identified as vice-president of the Sino-Soviet Friendship Association, Beijing Branch
1960,	Sep	Identified as chairman of the Foreign Literature Commission of the Writers Association; deputy head of a friendship delegation to the USSR
1961,	May	Identified as director of the Cultural and Educational Office, North China Bureau of the CCP Central Committee
1962,	Feb	Member of a delegation to the Congress of Afro-Asian Writers in Cairo
1963,	Jul	Identified as deputy director of the Propaganda Department, North China Bureau of the CCP Central Committee
1965,	Dec	Identified as deputy director of the Department of Philosophy and Social Sciences, Academy of Sciences
1966,	Jun	Yang is accused as a member of the "Three Family Village" and purged
1979,	Jul	The verdict on Yang as a traitor is officially repealed

Yang Ti (Yang T'i)   杨 提

Posts held

Provincial Administration
Deputy mayor of Shanghai Municipality

1979,	Dec	Elected deputy mayor of Shanghai Municipality

Yang Tianfang (Yang T'ien-fang)   杨天放

Posts held

Government
Vice-minister of forestry

1950,	Mar	Identified as director of the Personnel Department of the Ministry of Heavy Industry
1959,	Aug	Identified as vice-mayor of Shenyang Municipality
1963,	Mar	Appointed vice-minister of forestry
1966		Yang disappears
1979,	Nov	First appearance after the Cultural Revolution: Identified as vice-minister of forestry; head of a forestry machinery study mission visiting Sweden and Finland

Yang Tingbao (Yang T'ing-pao)   杨廷宝

Posts held

NPC
Deputy for Jiangsu Province to the 5th NPC

Provincial Administration
Vice-governor of Jiangsu Province

Others
Vice-president of the Architecture Society

1961,	Jul	Delegate to the Meeting of the International Architecture Association in London; elected its vice-president; identified as vice-president of the Chinese Architecture Society
1964,	Sep	Elected deputy for Jiangsu Province to the 3rd NPC
1973,	Jun	First appearance after the Cultural Revolution: Identified in his former post as vice-president of the Architecture Society
1977,	Nov	Head of an educational delegation to the U.S.A.; identified as vice-chairman of the Revolutionary Committee of the Nanjing Engineering Institute
1978,	Feb	Elected deputy for Jiangsu Province to the 5th NPC
1979,	Dec	Elected vice-governor of Jiangsu Province

Yang Wanxuan (Yang Wan-hsüan)   杨万选

Posts held

CCP
Secretary of Sichuan Province CP

In 1949 Yang served as deputy secretary of Lishi District CP, Shanxi Province. In September of that year he took part in the 1st CPPCC as a delegate representing the peasants.

1950,	Oct	Elected secretary-general of Xikang Province CP and council member of the People's Government of Xikang Province
1954,	Jan	Identified as director of the Rural Work Department of Xikang CP
1955,	Jul	After Xikang Province is abolished as an administrative unit, Yang is identified as deputy director fo the Rural Work Department of Sichuan Province CP
1959,	Dec	Appointed director of the Rural Work Department of Sichuan Province CP
1963,	Aug	Elected vice-governor of Sichuan Province
1964,	Oct	Elected deputy for Sichuan Province to the 3rd NPC
1965,	Aug	Identified as secretary of Sichuan Province CP
1967		Disappears during the Cultural Revolution
1975,	Dec	First appearance after the Cultural Revolution: Identified as a cadre in Sichuan
1977,	Oct	Identified as vice-chairman of the Revolutionary Committee of Sichuan Province (until Dec 1977)
1978,	Jul	Identified as member of the Standing Committee of Sichuan Province CP (until Jan 1979)
1979,	Jan	Elected secretary of Sichuan Province CP

Yang Weiping (Yang Wei-p'ing) 杨蔚屏

Posts held

CCP
Secretary of Anhui Province CP

Provincial Administration
Vice-governor of Anhui Province

1954,	Oct	Identified as deputy secretary of Henan Province CP
1955,	Feb	Identified as member of the People's Government of Henan Province
1957,	Mar	Identified as secretary of Henan Province CP (until Cultural Revolution)
1958,	Oct	Identified as vice-president of the Shandong Branch of the Academy of Sciences
1967,	May	Branded as a revisionist and purged
1978,	Jan	First appearance after the Cultural Revolution: Elected vice-chairman of the Revolutionary Committee of Anhui Province (until Dec 1979)
	Jun	Identified as secretary of Anhui Province CP
1979,	Dec	Elected vice-governor of Anhui-Province

Yang Xiandong (Yang Hsien-tung) 杨显东

Posts held

Government
Vice-minister of agriculture

Others
Vice-president of the Academy of Agricultural Sciences
President of the Society of Agriculture

Yang was born in 1908. He was awarded a doctorate from Cornell University in 1937. From the mid-1940s he served as dean of the College of Agriculture, Wuhan University. In September 1949 he took part in the session of the 1st CPPCC.

1949,	Oct	Appointed vice-minister of agriculture (until Cultural Revolution) and council member of the Sino-Soviet Friendship Association (until 1954)
1952,	Mar	Identified as member of the Preparatory Committee for the Society of Agriculture
	Jun	Identified as member of the Federation of Scientific Societies
1953,	Sep	Delegate to the 3rd Congress of the World Federation of Scientific Workers in Budapest
1954,	Aug	Elected deputy for Henan Province to the 1st NPC (reelected in 1958 and 1964 to the 2nd and 3rd NPCs)
	Nov	Member of a delegation led by Li Xiannian to Albania
1955,	Mar	Member of a CCP delegation led by Deng Zihui to Hungary
1956,	Mar	Identified as member of the Academic Committee of the Academy of Agricultural Sciences
	May	Identified as member of the State Scientific Planning Commission
	Nov	Member of a scientific and technical delegation to the USSR
1958,	Jul	Head of an agricultural delegation to the German Democratic Republic and Czechoslovakia
	Dec	Identified as member of the Association of Science and Technology
1960,	Feb	Identified as council member of the Sino-Czechoslovakian Friendship Association
1967		Disappears during the Cultural Revolution
1972,	Dec	First appearance after the Culutral Revolution: Present at mourning ceremonies for Deng Zihui
1978,	Jan	Identified as president of the Society of Agriculture
	Jun	Identified as advisor to the Ministry of Agriculture and Forestry
	Jul	Identified as vice-president of the Academy of Agricultural Sciences
	Sep	Advisor to an agricultural delegation to Japan
1979,	Sep	Identified as vice-minister of agriculture

Yang Xianzhen (Yang Hsien-chen) 杨献珍

Posts held

CCP
Advisor to the Party School under the CCP Central Committee

Others
Member of the Standing Committee of the 5th CPPCC

Yang was born in 1899 in Xun, Hubei Province. After attending elementary school he studied at Beijing Normal University. He continued his studies after graduation in Moscow and later in Germany. During the years until the Communist victory in China he worked as a translator at the Moscow Far East Bureau.

1949,	Nov?	Appointed deputy director of the Institute of Marxism-Leninism of the CCP (until Apr 1955)
1954,	Mar	Identified as deputy director of the Sub-department for Theoretical Education, Propaganda Department of the CCP Central Committee
	Aug	Elected deputy for Hubei Province to the 1st NPC (until Sep 1964)
1955,	Apr	Appointed director of the Institute of Marxism-Leninism (until Sep 1955)
	Jun	Appointed member of the Department of Philosophy and Social Sciences, Academy of Sciences
	Sep	Appointed director of the Higher Party School of the CCP Central Committee, the successor of the Institute of Marxism-Leninism (until Dec 1961)
1956,	Sep	Elected alternate member of the CCP Central Committee by the 8th Party Congress (until May 1958)
1958,	May	Promoted to member of the CCP Central Committee
1964,	Dec	Confirmed as member of the CPPCC
1966,	Jun	Criticized as a rightist deviationist during the Cultural Revolution
1978,	Dec	First appearance after the Cultural Revolution
1979,	Jun	Identified as advisor to the Party School under the CCP Central Committee
	Jul	By-elected member of the Standing Committee of the 5th CPPCC
	Aug	A report in RMRB of 21st August says that the attack on the philosopher Yang and his comrades 15 years ago was a political frame-up

Yang Xiguang (Yang Hsi-kuang)　　杨西光

Posts held

Others
Editor-in-chief of GMRB

1950,	Nov	Identified as deputy director of the Propaganda Department of Fujian Province CP
1954,	Aug	Identified as chairman of the Culture and Education Department, People's Council of Fujian Province
1957,	May	Appointed vice-president of Fudan University
1958,	Oct	Identified as chief editor of Jiefang Ribao (Liberation Daily) (until Apr 1959)
1959,	May	Identified as director of the Department of Education and Public Health of Shanghai Municipality CP
1963,	Feb	Identified as member of the Standing Committee of Shanghai Municipality CP (until Apr 1965)

1965,	Apr	Identified as alternate member, Secretariat of Shanghai Municipality CP (until 1967)
1967,	Dec	Branded as a revisionist and disappears
1976,	May	First appearance after the Cultural Revolution: Identified as vice-chairman of the Revolutionary Committee of Shanghai (until May 1978)
1978,	Jul	Identified as editor-in-chief of GMRB

Yang Xinpei (Yang Hsin-p'ei)　　杨心培

Posts held

CCP
Member of the Commission for Inspecting Discipline under the CCP Central Committee
Member of the Standing Committee of Shanghai Municipality CP

NPC
Deputy for Shanghai Municipality to the 5th NPC

1978,	Feb	Elected deputy for Shanghai Municipality to the 5th NPC
	Sep	Identified as vice-chairman of the Revolutionary Committee of Shanghai (until Dec 1979)
	Dec	Appointed member of the Commission for Inspecting Discipline under the CCP Central Committee
1979,	May	Identified as member of the Standing Committee of Shanghai Municipality CP

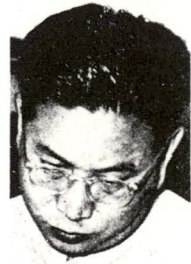

Yang Xiufeng (Yang Hsiu-feng)　　杨秀峰

Posts held

NPC
Member of the Standing Committee of the 5th NPC
Vice-chairman of the Legal Commission under the 5th NPC
Deputy for Tianjin Municipality to the 5th NPC

Others
Honorary president of the Education Society

Yang was born in 1897 in Qian'an, Hebei Province. After graduating from Beijing Normal School he continued his studies in France in 1929. After his return to China he became a lecturer at the Female Teachers College in Hebei. Circa 1934 he was appointed director of the Education Department of Hebei Provincial Government. After the outbreak of the Anti-Japanese War Yang commanded guerrilla units in the area of Baoding which were recruited from students of Beijing and Tianjin Universities. In 1938 he became commander of the guerrilla units of West Hebei and chairman of the Administrative Office of South Hebei. In the winter of 1940-41 the guerrilla units commanded by Yang had increased to 200,000 men and were operating behind the Japanese lines. With the establishment of Shanxi-Chahar-

Hebei Border Region, Yang was appointed chairman. His appointment as 3rd vice-chairman of the People's Government of North China followed in September 1948. In September 1949 the CPPCC elected him a member of its Standing Committee.

1949,	Nov?	Appointed chairman of the People's Government of Hebei
1952,	Nov	Appointed vice-minister of higher education (probably until Oct 1954)
1954,	Sep	Elected deputy for Hebei Province to the 1st NPC
	Oct?	Appointed minister of higher education (until Feb 1958)
1956,	Sep	Elected member of the CCP Central Committee by the 8th Party Congress
1958,	Feb	The Ministries of Education and Higher Education are joined to form the Ministry of Education with Yang as minister (until Jul 1964)
	Feb-Mar	Head of an educational delegation to Poland, East Germany, and the USSR
	Oct	Appointed chairman of the Sino-Vietnamese Friendship Association
1959,	Sep	Appointed deputy director of the Staff Office of Culture and Education (until Jul 1965)
	Dec	Head of a friendship delegation to North Vietnam
1962,	Aug	Head of a friendship delegation to North Vietnam
1963,	Sep	Head of an educational delegation to Albania
1964,	Mar-Apr	Head of an educational delegation to the United Arab Republic, Algeria, and Zanzibar
	Jul	After the Ministry of Education is divided into the Ministries of Education and of Higher Education, Yang is appointed minister of the latter (until Dec 1964)
1965,	Jan	Appointed president of the Supreme People's Court (until Cultural Revolution)
1966,	Sep	Branded as a black gangster
1967,	Jan	Yang attempts to commit suicide
	May	Displayed at a mass rally and disappears
1974,	Sep	First appearance after the Cultural Revolution
1975,	Mar	Identified as deputy to the 4th NPC
1978,	Feb	Elected deputy for Tianjin Municipality to the 5th NPC
	Mar	Elected member of the Standing Committee of the 5th NPC
1979,	Feb	Appointed vice-chairman of the Legal Commission under the NPC
	Apr	Elected honorary president of the Education Society
	Jun	Vice-chairman of the Draft Laws Committee at the 2nd Session of the 5th NPC

Yang Yan (Yang Yen)　杨岩

Posts held

CCP
Secretary of Qinghai Province CP

1973,	Jun	Identified as deputy secretary of Qinghai Province CP
1977,	Oct	Identified as secretary of Qinghai Province CP

Yang Yansen (Yang Yen-sen)　杨延森

Posts held

Government
Vice-minister of forestry

1974,	Oct	Identified as director of the Forestry Bureau, Ministry of Agriculture and Forestry
1978,	Aug	Identified as deputy director of the Forestry Administration Bureau, Ministry of Agriculture and Forestry
1979,	May	Identified as vice-minister of forestry

Yang Yepeng (Yang Yeh-p'eng)　杨叶澎

Posts held

Government
Vice-minister of chemical industry

1949,	Oct	Identified as deputy commander of Suiyuan Military District
	Dec	Identified as council member of the People's Government of Suiyuan Province
1955,	Apr	Identified as member of the People's Government of Inner Mongolia Autonomous Region
1961,	Mar	Identified as secretary, CP of the Nanjing Chemical Industrial Corporation
1966,	Jan	Disappears during the Cultural Revolution
1978,	Jun	First appearance after the Cultural Revolution: Identified as vice-minister of chemical industry

Yang Yibang (Yang Yi-pang)　杨义邦

Posts held

Government
Vice-minister of chemical industry

1975,	Jan	Identified as a cadre of the State Council
1976,	Nov	Identified as vice-minister of petroleum and chemical industry
1978,	Jun	Identified as vice-minister of chemical industry
	Oct	Identified as secretary, CP of Beijing Petrochemical Works

Yang Yichen (Yang Yi-ch'en)　杨易辰

Posts held

CCP
Member of the CCP 11th Central Committee
1st secretary of Heilongjiang Province CP

NPC
Deputy for Heilongjiang Province to the 5th NPC

Military
1st political commissar of Heilongjiang Military District

Yang was born in 1914 in Liaoning Province.

1951		Appointed governor of Liaoxi Province (until 1954)
1954,	Aug	Identified as vice-governor (until Cultural Revolution), and deputy secretary of the CP, of Heilongjiang Province
1956,	Jul	Identified as secretary of Heilongjiang Province CP (until Cultural Revolution)
1964,	Oct	Elected deputy for Heilongjiang Province to the 3rd NPC
1967		During the Cultural Revolution Yang is criticized as a deviationist; subsequently disappears
1973,	May	First appearance after the Cultural Revolution: Identified as secretary of Heilongjiang Province CP (until Dec 1977)
1974,	Jul	Identified as vice-chairman of the Revolutionary Committee of Heilongjiang Province (until Dec 1977)
1977,	Aug	Elected member of the CCP Central Committee by the 11th Party Congress
	Dec	Identified as 1st secretary of the CP, and chairman of the Revolutionary Committee, of Heilongjiang Province (until Dec 1979)
1978,	Feb	Elected deputy for Heilongjiang Province to the 5th NPC
	Jul	Head of an agricultural delegation to the U.S.A.
1979,	Aug	Identified as 1st political commissar of Heilongjiang Military District

Yang Yong (Yang Yung)   杨 勇

Posts held

CCP
Member of the CCP 11th Central Committee
Member of the Standing Committee, Military Council under the CCP Central Committee

Government
Vice-chairman of the Patriotic Health Campaign Committee

Military
Colonel-general
Deputy chief of PLA General Staff

NPC
Member of the Standing Committee of the 5th NPC
Deputy for the PLA to the 5th NPC

Yang was born in 1906 in Liuyang County, Hunan Province. During the Nanchang Uprising he joined a guerrilla unit commanded by Peng Dehuai. In 1933 he graduated from a training course of the Red Army University. In the summer of 1934 he became political commissar of the 10th Regiment, 4th Division. At the beginning of the Anti-Japanese War Yang served as commander of the 686th Regiment of the 115th Division (commanded by Lin Biao), 8th Route Army. In 1937-38 he was noted for distinguished service in several battles in Shanxi Province. He was wounded in September 1937 in the Battle of Pingxing Guan as political commissar of a regiment of the 115th Division commanded by Lin Biao. In summer 1938 Yang's regiment was reorganized to form the 1st Brigade of an independent corps under the command of Xu Xiangqian which fought the Japanese in the south of Hebei Province. In March 1939 Yang's brigade was incorporated into the units commanded by Yang Dezhi of which Yang Yong was appointed deputy commander. During the Civil War Yang took part in several battles in Shandong and Henan. In June 1948 he was appointed commander of the 5th Corps, 2nd Field Army, and took part in the Battle of Huaihai in Jiangsu clearing the crossing of the Chang Jiang. In late 1949 the units under Yang were operating in Southwest China.

1950,	Oct	Identified as member of the Southwest China Military and Administrative Council; chairman of the People's Government of Guizhou and member of the Military Control Commission of Guiyang
1952		Identified as commander of the Air Force of Southwest China Military Region (until 1954)
1954,	Sep	Appointed 2nd deputy commander of the Chinese People's Volunteers in Korea and member of the National Defense Council (until Cultural Revolution)
1955,	Mar	Appointed commander of the People's Volunteers in Korea (until Oct 1958)
1956,	Sep	Elected alternate member of the CCP Central Committee by the 8th Party Congress (until Cultural Revolution)
1958		Returns from Korea
1960,	May	Identified as commander of Beijing Military Region
	Oct	Member of a government delegation led by He Long to North Korea
1962,	May	Identified as deputy chief of PLA General Staff (until Cultural Revolution)
1964,	Nov	Head of a military delegation to Algeria
1965,	Oct	Head of a delegation to the 15th anniversary of the Chinese People's Volunteers' entry into the Korean War
1966		Yang is accused of having planned a coup d'état together with Luo Ruiqing and Peng Zhen and is relieved of all posts
1972,	Jul	First appearance after the Cultural Revolution
1973,	Jul	Identified as 2nd secretary of the CP, and vice-chairman of the Revolutionary Committee, of Xinjiang Autonomous Region; identified as commander of Xinjiang Military Region (until Aug 1977)
	Aug	Elected to first term as member of the CCP Central Committee by the 10th Party Congress
1975,	Feb	Head of a military delegation to Vietnam
1977,	May	Head of a military delegation to North Korea
	Jun	Conferred the Korean order "Freedom and Independence," 1st class
	Oct	Identified as deputy chief of PLA General Staff
1978,	Feb	Elected deputy for the PLA to the 5th NPC

	Mar	Elected member of the Standing Committee of the 5th NPC	1960,	Apr
	Apr	Appointed vice-chairman of the Patriotic Health Campaign Committee		Nov
	Jun	Head of a military delegation to Yugoslavia		

Mar Elected member of the Standing Committee of the 5th NPC

Apr Appointed vice-chairman of the Patriotic Health Campaign Committee

Jun Head of a military delegation to Yugoslavia

1979, Jul Head of a military delegation to Great Britain

Yang is married to Lin Bin.

Yang Yongliang (Yang Yung-liang) 杨永良

Posts held

CCP
Alternate member of the CCP 11th Central Committee

1977, Aug Elected alternate member of the CCP Central Committee by the 11th Party Congress

Yang Yunyu (Yang Yün-yü) (f) 杨蕴玉

Posts held

Government
Vice-minister of education
Vice-chairman of the National Committee of the PRC for UN Educational, Scientific and Cultural Organization (UNESCO)

Others
Member of the Executive Council of UNESCO

Yang was born of 1914 in Henan Province. In 1948 she was identified as a member, and one year later as vice-chairman, of the Democratic Women's Federation of North China.

1950 Identified as vice-chairman of the Democratic Women's Federation, Beijing Branch

1951, Apr Member of a friendship delegation to the May Day celebrations in Moscow

1952, Mar Appointed judge of the Beijing People's Court

1954, Jan Delegate to the Executive Committee Meeting of the International Democratic Women's Federation; elected secretary

Aug Elected deputy for Henan Province to the 1st NPC

1955, Jun Delegate to the World Mothers Conference in Lausanne, Switzerland

1957, Sep Elected secretary of the Democratic Women's Federation

1958, Feb Member of a delegation to the Afro-Asian Women's Conference in Colombo; identified as council member of the Sino-United Arab Republic Friendship Association

Sep Identified as member of the Sino-Albanian Friendship Asociation

Nov Elected deputy for Shandong Province to the 2nd NPC (reelected in 1964 to the 3rd NPC)

1959, Sep Appointed member of the State Physical Culture and Sports Commission

1960, Apr Appointed member of the Sino-African Society

Nov Head of a delegation to the Conference of the International Democratic Women's Federation in Warsaw

1961, Jan Head of a delegation to the Afro-Asian Women's Conference in Cairo

Sep Head of a delegation to the Conference of the International Women's Federation in Budapest

Oct Head of a women's delegation to the 5th Congress of the Albania Women's Delegation in Tirana

1962, Jan Head of a delegation to the Executive Council Session of the International Democratic Women's Federation in Bamako

Mar Head of a delegation to the World Women's Conference on Disarmament in Vienna

May Head of a delegation to the Session of the International Democratic Women's Federation in Prague

Nov Head of a delegation to the Conference of the International Women's Federation in East Berlin

Dec Delegate to the 3rd Conference of the Tunisian Democratic Women's Federation in Tunis

1963, Jan Delegate to the Conference of the International Women's Federation in East Berlin

Jun Head of a delegation to the Conference of the International Democratic Women's Federation in Moscow

1964, Jun Head of a women's delegation to Japan

Oct Head of a delegation to the Conference of the International Women's Federation in Sofia

Nov Member of a delegation to the International Conference for Resisting the United States and Aiding Vietnam in Hanoi

1965, Jan Elected member of the Standing Committee of the 3rd NPC

Jun Elected vice-chairman of the Committee for World Peace

1966, Dec Head of a women's delegation to Japan

1967 Disappears during the Cultural Revolution

1976, Oct First appearance after the Cultural Revolution: Identified as a cadre in the Bureau of Overseas Chinese Affairs of the Ministry of Education; deputy head of a delegation to the 19th UNESCO Conference in Nairobi

1977, Apr Delegate to the 102nd UNESCO Conference in Paris; elected member of the UNESCO Executive Council

1978, Apr Identified as director of the Foreign Affairs Department, Ministry of Education; delegate to the 104th UNESCO Conference in Paris

Oct Deputy head of a delegation to the 20th Meeting of the UNESCO General Conference in Paris

1979, Jan Appointed vice-chairman and secretary-general of the National Commission of the PRC for UNESCO

Apr Identified as vice-minister of education

Yang Zhantao (Yang Chan-t'ao) 杨战韬

Posts held

CCP
Member of the Standing Committee of Jilin Province CP

Provincial Administration
Vice-chairman of the Revolutionary Committee of Jilin Province

1949,	Nov	Identified as council member of the People's Government of Jilin Province and as director of its Civil Affairs Department
1956,	Jan	Identified as member of the Standing Committee of Jilin Province CP
1957,	Oct	Identified as vice-governor of Jilin Province (until Cultural Revolution)
1961,	May	Identified as 1st secretary of Tonghua Local Committee CP
1967		Disappears during the Cultural Revolution
1977,	Dec	First appearance after the Cultural Revolution: Elected vice-chairman of the Revolutionary Committee of Jilin
1979,	Sep	Identified as member of the Standing Committee of Jilin Province CP

Yang Zhen (Yang Chen) 阳 震

Posts held

Military
Deputy commandant, Military Academy of the PLA

1967,	Nov	Identified as military cadre of Guangzhou Garrison
1968,	Feb	Elected 1st vice-chairman of the Revolutionary Committee of Guangzhou
	Mar	Identified as commander of Guangzhou Garrison
1971,	Sep	Identified as deputy commandant of the PLA Military and Political Academy
1973,	Aug	Deputy head of a PLA vacation group to Romania
1978,	Jan	Identified as deputy commandant of the PLA Military Academy

Yang Zhengmin (Yang Cheng-min) 杨拯民

Posts held

Others
Member of the Standing Committee of the 5th CPPCC

Yang was born in 1909 in Pucheng, Shaanxi Province. He studied in the USSR. In 1949 he commanded the 4th Army, 2nd Army Group, 1st Field Army. In September of that year he took part in the inaugural session of the 1st CPPCC.

1949,	Dec	Identified as commander of the PLA Dali Military Subdistrict in Shaanxi Province
1954,	May	Identified as secretary, CP of Yumen Oil Field
	Dec	Identified as director of the Yumen Mineral Admintrative Bureau; elected member of the 2nd CPPCC (reelected in 1959

and 1964 to the 3rd and 4th CPPCCs)

1958,	Aug	Identified as vice-governor of Shaanxi Province (until Aug 1963)
1961,	Feb	Identified as secretary of Shaanxi Province CP (until Aug 1963)
1963,	Dec	Identified as deputy mayor of Tianjin Municipality (until Cultural Revolution)
1967		Disappears during the Cultural Revolution
1978,	Mar	First appearance after the Cultural Revolution: Elected member of the Standing Committee of the 5th CPPCC

Yang Zhilin (Yang Chih-lin) 杨植霖

Posts held

CCP
Secretary of Gansu Province CP

Yang was born in 1907 in Tumd Banner, Suiyuan Province. He was given primary and normal school education. Suspected of being a Communist in 1931, he was sentenced to two years in prison. Between 1933 and 1937 he organized guerrilla bands in Tumd Banner. In 1938 he met He Long and was ordered to reorganize his guerrillas to form a cavalry brigade of 300 men and join Li Jingquan's forces. In 1946 Yang was deputy director of the Administrative Office, Suiyuan-Mongolia Border Region. In 1948 he was appointed governor of Suiyuan Province.

1949,	Dec	Identified as vice-governor of Suiyuan Province
1950,	Feb	Identified as a member of the Suiyuan Military and Administrative Council (until 1952)
1952,	Aug	Elected vice-chairman of Inner Mongolia Autonomous Region People's Government (until 1962)
	Nov	Identified as secretary of Inner Mongolia Autonomous Region CP
1954		Identified as a member of the Committee for Removing the Remains of Jenghiz Khan to a New Tomb
1955,	Dec	Identified as 2nd secretary of Inner Mongolia Autonomous Region CP
1957,	Nov	Head of an Inner Mongolian delegation to the USSR
1962,	Apr	Identified as 1st secretary of Qinghai Province CP
1965,	Mar	Identified as secretary of the Northwest Bureau, CCP Central Committee
	Jul	Identified as 1st political commissar, Qinghai Military District
1967,	Feb	Denounced as a follower of Liu Shaoqi and Deng Xiaoping and purged
1979,	Jul	First appearance after the Cultural Revolution: Appointed member of the National Games Organizing Committee
	Aug	Identified as secretary of Gansu Province CP

Yang Zhong (Yang Chung) 杨 钟

Posts held

Provincial Administration
Vice-governor of Sichuan Province

1979,	Dec	Elected vice-governor of Sichuan Province

Yang Zongxin (Yang Tsung-hsin) 杨宗欣

Posts held

CCP
Member of the Standing Committee of Tibet Autonomous Region CP

Provincial Administration
Vice-chairman of Tibet Autonomous Regional People's Government

1965, May Identified as director of the Foreign Affairs Department of Tibet Autonomous Region
1975, Jan Identified as member of the Standing Committee of Tibet CP
       Sep Identified as vice-chairman, Revolutionary Committee of Tibet; reelected in December 1977 (until Aug 1979)
1979, Aug Elected vice-chairman of Tibet Autonomous Regional People's Government

Yangling Duoji (Yang'ling To'chi) 杨岭多吉

Posts held

Provincial Administration
Vice-governor of Sichuan Province

Yangling belongs to the Tibetan minority.

1979, Dec Elected vice-governor of Sichuan Province

Yao Guang (Yao Kuang) 姚广

Posts held

Government
Ambassador to Egypt and to Djibouti

1954, Dec Identified as director of the Foreign Affairs Office of Hubei Province People's Government
1956, May Identified as deputy director of the Western Europe and Africa Department of the Ministry of Foreign Affairs
1957, Nov Appointed counselor at the embassy in Poland (until Oct 1963)
1964, Apr Identified as deputy director of the 2nd Asia Department of the Ministry of Foreign Affairs (until Aug 1964)
       Aug Identified as director of the 2nd Asia Department in the Ministry of Foreign Affairs (until 1969)
1970, Aug Appointed ambassador to Poland (until Dec 1971)
1972, Mar Appointed ambassador to Canada (until Sep 1973)
1973, Sep Appointed ambassador to Mexico (until May 1977)
1974, Sep Yao accompanies a Mexican agricultural delegation to China
1977, Jul Appointed ambassador to Egypt
1979, Nov Appointed ambassador to Djibouti

Yao Jin (Yao Chin) 姚进

Posts held

Government
Vice-minister of finance

1976, Jan Identified as a cadre of the State Council
1977, Jul Identified as a cadre of the Ministry of Finance
1978, Sep Identified as vice-minister of finance

Yao Maoqi (Yao Mao-ch'i) 姚茂启

Posts held

NPC
Deputy for Anhui Province to the 5th NPC
Member of the Standing Committee of the 5th NPC

1978, Feb Elected deputy for Anhui Province to the 5th NPC
       Mar Elected member of the Standing Committee of the 5th NPC

Yao Shichang (Yao Shih-ch'ang) 姚士昌

Posts held

NPC
Member of the Standing Committee of the 5th NPC
Deputy for Shandong Province to the 5th NPC

Yao is a model peasant and a peanut specialist.

1975, Jan Elected member of the Standing Committee of the 4th NPC (confirmed in Mar 1978 by the 5th NPC)
1977, Sep Identified as vice-chairman of the Revolutionary Committee of Shandong Province (reelected in Dec 1978, until Dec 1979)
1978, Feb Elected deputy for Shandong Province to the 5th NPC

Yao Yilin (Yao Yi-lin) 姚依林

Posts held

CCP
Member of the CCP 11th Central Committee
Deputy secretary-general of the CCP Central Committee
Member of the Secretariat of the CCP Central Committee
Director of the General Office of the CCP Central Committee

Government
Vice-premier
Secretary-general of the State Financial and Economic Commission

Yao was born in 1917 in Guichi County, Anhui Province where he later attended a teachers college. He became known as one of the initiators of anti-Japanese demonstrations in Beijing on 9 December 1935, when a student at Qinghua University. During the Anti-Japanese War he served as secretary-general, North China Bureau of the CCP Central Committee, as secretary of Tianjin Municipality CP and as director of the Propaganda Department of the Hebei Province CP. He later took part in the armed uprising in eastern Hebei Province and served as director of the Propaganda Department of the Hebei-Rehe-Chahar Region CP and as secretary-general of the Shanxi-Chahar-Hebei Subbureau and the Shanxi-Chahar-Hebei Bureau of the Central Committee. In January 1949 he was appointed a member of the Committee of Finance and Commerce and director of the Commerce Department of the People's Government of North China, the predecessor of the PRC founded in October 1949 and until then based in Shijiazhuang, Hebei Province.

1949,	Oct	Appointed vice-minister of commerce (until Apr 1962)
1950,	Oct	Identified as head of the Central School for Commerce Cadres
1951,	Feb	Yao signs the Sino-Hungarian Trade Agreement in Beijing
	Jun	Signs the Sino-Soviet Trade Agreement in Moscow and the Sino-Polish Trade Agreement in Beijing
1954,	Aug	Elected deputy for Jiangxi Province to the 1st NPC (until Mar 1959)
1958,	May	Elected alternate member of the CCP Central Committee
1959,	Sep	Appointed deputy director, Bureau of Finance and Commerce under the State Council; identified as deputy director of the Department of Finance and Commerce of the CCP Central Committee
1962,	Apr	Appointed minister of commerce (until Cultural Revolution)
1964,	Mar	Head of a trade delegation to North Vietnam
	Jun	Identified as director of the Political Department, Department of Finance and Commerce of the CCP Central Committee
1967,	Feb	Criticized as a "three-anti element" of the Peng Zhen clique; reactivated after the Cultural Revolution in 1973
1973,	Aug	Elected alternate member of the CCP Central Committee by the 10th Party Congress (until Aug 1977)
	Dec	Identified as vice-minister of foreign trade (until Aug 1978)
1974,	Jan	Head of a trade delegation to North Korea
1975,	Sep	Acting minister of foreign trade during the absence of Minister of Foreign Trade Li Qiang
1977,	Apr	Identified as 1st deputy minister of foreign trade; head of a trade delegation to Austria and Holland
	Aug	Elected member of the CCP Central Committee by the 11th Party Congress
1978,	Aug	Appointed minister of commerce (until Feb 1979)
1979,	Jul	Appointed vice-premier and secretary-general of the State Financial and Economic Commission
	Aug	Identified as deputy secretary-general of the CCP Central Committee
1980,	Feb	Elected member of the Secretariat of the CCP 11th Central Committee by its 5th Plenum; identified as director of the General Office of the CCP Central Committee

Yao Zhongming (Yao Chung-ming) 姚仲明

Posts held

Government
Vice-minister of culture
Vice-chairman of the National Commission of PRC for UN Education, Scientific and Cultural Organization (UNESCO)

Yao was born in 1912 in Wei County, Shandong Province. He joined the CCP in 1931. At this time he was also a leading member of the student movement in Shandong. In 1937 he was temporarily imprisoned by the local authorities. When Shandong was attacked by the Japanese Yao organized anti-Japanese guerrilla units which were to be the nucleus of the later Communist Shandong Column. In 1938 he studied at the Lu Xun Art Academy and published the musical play National Flag Fluttering as well as the stage play Comrade, You Have Gone a Wrong Path (co-authored with Chen Boer). In 1939 he returned to his native province where he served as director of the United Front Work Department, Political Department of Shandong Column. Around 1941 he served as chief of staff of the 359th Brigade, 120th Division, 8th Route Army. In 1945 he was commander of the Yantai Military Subdistrict of East Shandong Military District and concurrently commander of the 25th Brigade of the 9th Column. During the peace negotiations with the Nationalist Government he served as CCP representative of the Qingdao Armistice Group of the Military Mediation Executive Commission. In 1947 he was appointed mayor of Yantai, in the following year mayor of Weifang in Shandong Province, and in 1949 deputy mayor of Jinan.

1950,	Jun	Appointed ambassador to Burma (until Mar 1958)
1958,	Aug	Identified as secretary of the Political Science and Law Society
1959,	Jan	Identified as member of the Maritime Arbitration Committee, Council for Promotion of International Trade
1960,	Jan	Identified as director of the Treaties and Law Department of the Ministry of Foreign Affairs (until 1961)
	Apr	Appointed member of the Standing Committee of the Sino-African Friendship Association
	Jun	Member of the Chinese delegation to the border negotiations in Rangoon
1961,	Jan	Conferred the Burmese "Heroic Honor Medal," 2nd class
	Jul	Appointed ambassador to Indonesia (until Apr 1966)
1963,	Jan	Yao accompanies the Indonesian minister of Foreign Affairs Subandrio on his visit to China
1967		Disappears during the Cultural Revolution

| 1978, | Jul | First appearance after the Cultural Revolution: Identified as vice-minister of culture |
| 1979, | Feb | Elected vice-chairman of the National Commission of the PRC for UNESCO |

Ye Chengzhang (Yeh Ch'eng-chang) 叶成章

Posts held

Government
Ambassador to Malaysia

1962,	Oct	Identified as counselor at the embassy in India (until about 1964)
1971,	Nov	Identified as a cadre of the Ministry of Foreign Affairs
1972,	Mar	Identified as deputy director of the Asia Department of the Ministry of Foreign Affairs
1973,	May	Member of a government delegation to Sri Lanka
	Jul	Appointed ambassador to Burma (until Oct 1977)
1977,	Apr	Ye accompanies the Burmese president Ne Win on his visit to China
	Dec	Appointed ambassador to Malaysia

Ye Daoying (Yeh Tao-ying) 叶道英

Posts held

Others
Member of the Standing Committee of the 5th CPPCC

| 1978, | Mar | Elected member of the Standing Committee of the 5th CPPCC |

Ye Fei (Yeh Fei) 叶飞

Posts held

CCP
Member of the CCP 11th Central Committee

Military
Colonel-general
Commander of the PLA Navy
1st secretary of the Party Committee of the PLA Navy

Ye was born in 1914 in Nan'an (Fuan?), Fujian Province. He joined the CCP in 1932. Shortly afterwards he attended a training course conducted by the Red Army in Jiangxi Province. Until the Anti-Japanese War Ye served with guerrilla units operating in his native province which were later incorporated as the 6th and 7th Regiment into the New 4th Army together with the units under Zhang Dingcheng. After the "New 4th Army Incident" of January 1941 and its subsequent reorganization, Ye was appointed commander of the 1st Division. Following the Japanese capitulation the units commanded by Ye took part in the East China People's Liberation Campaign in Fujian and Jiangsu Provinces.

1949		Identified as member of the Fuzhou Military Control Commission; commander of the 15th Corps, 3rd Field Army; member of the East China Military and Political Council; member of the Overseas Chinese Affairs Commission under the Central People's Government; and as 1st vice-chairman of the People's Government of Fujian Province (all posts until circa 1952)
1952		Appointed member of the East China Adminstrative Council (until 1954)
1954,	Oct	Appointed member of the National Defense Council (until Cultural Revolution)
1955,	Apr	Elected governor of Fujian Province (until 1959) and secretary of Fujian Province CP (until May 1958)
	Sep	Promoted to rank of colonel-general
1956,	Jun	By-elected deputy of Fujian Province to the 1st NPC (until Apr 1959)
	Sep	Elected alternate member of the CCP Central Committee by the 8th Party Congress (until Cultural Revolution)
1958,	May	Appointed 1st secretary of Fujian Province CP (until Cultural Revolution)
1960,	Feb	Appointed vice-chairman of the Commission for Receiving and Resettling Overseas Chinese
1961,	May	Identified as member of the Committee for Publication of the Party History of Fujian Province CP; identified as commander of Fuzhou Military Region (until Cultural Revolution)
1962,	Oct	Identified as chairman of the Fujian Section, CPPCC (until Cultural Revolution)
1963,	Sep	Identified as vice-governor of Fujian Province (until Sep 1964)
	Nov	Identified as member of the Secretariat, East China Bureau of the CCP Central Committee (until Cultural Revolution)
1964,	Jul	Identified as political commissar of Fuzhou Military Region (until Cultural Revolution)
1966,	Nov?	Ye is condemned as an "agent of the Liu-Deng clique"
1967,	Jan	Publicly condemned as a counterrevolutionary by Red Guards in Fuzhou and relieved of all posts; subsequently disappears
1973,	Aug	First appearance after the Cultural Revolution: Elected alternate member of the CCP Central Committee by the 10th Party Congress (until Aug 1977)
1975,	Jan	Appointed minister of communications (until Feb 1979)
	Jun	Head of a government delegation attending the independence celebrations of Mozambique
	Sep	Head of a government delegation to North Korea
1977,	May	Head of a communications delegation to Sweden, Finland, Norway, Denmark
	Aug	Elected member of the CCP Central Committee by the 11th Party Congress
	Oct	Head of a government delegation to North and South Yemen; conferred the order of "14 October" of the People's Democratic Republic of Yemen
1978,	Nov	Head of a communications delegation to

the Netherlands, Belgium, Federal Republic of Germany

1979,   Mar   Identified as 1st political commissar of the PLA Navy (until Feb 1980) and as 1st secretary of the Party Committee of the PLA Navy

1980,   Feb   Identified as commander of the PLA Navy

Ye Jianmin (Yeh Chien-min)   叶健民

Posts held

NPC
Deputy for the PLA to the 5th NPC

Military
Major-general
Deputy commander of Guangzhou Military Region

1959,   Apr   Identified as major-general and military leader of Guangzhou Military Region

1969,   Oct   Identified as military leader of Guangzhou Military Region

1974,   Sep   Identified as deputy commander of Guangzhou Military Region

1978,   Feb   Elected deputy for the PLA to the 5th NPC

Ye Jianying (Yeh Chien-ying)   叶剑英

Posts held

CCP
Vice-chairman of the CCP 11th Central Committee
Member of the Standing Committee of the CCP Politburo
Member of the Politburo of the CCP 11th Central Committee
Member of the CCP 11th Central Committee
Vice-chairman of the Military Council of the 11th CCP Central Committee

NPC
Chairman of the Standing Committee of the 5th NPC
Deputy for the PLA to the 5th NPC

Military
Marshal

Ye was born on 14 May 1897 as the son of a wealthy merchant belonging to the Hakka minority in Mei County, Guangdong Province. He spent part of his youth in Singapore and Hanoi. He is a graduate of the 16th course of Yunnan Military Academy, subsequently served as instructor at Whampoa Military Academy and commanded the 21st Division during the Northern Expedition. After the KMT-CCP rift in 1927 he joined the Communist Party and in December of that year took part in the Guangzhou Uprising. From 1928 to 1931 Ye studied military sciences in Moscow and subsequently joined the Jiangxi Soviet. Tnere he served initially as chief of staff of the Revolutionary Military Council and later as head of the Red Army School. He played a decisive roll in the planning

of the Long March during which he supported Zhang Guotao in his rivalry with Mao Zedong. During the Anti-Japanese War Ye was chief of staff of the 8th Route Army and later liaison officer in the Joint Headquarters of the KMT, the Communists, and the U.S. Armed Forces. During the Civil War he held the post of deputy chief of general staff of the Communist Armed Forces. After the occupation of Beijing in January 1949 Ye became chairman of the Military Control Commission of Beijing and mayor of the capital city. During the final phase of the Civil War he was appointed 1st secretary of South China Subbureau, Central-South China Bureau of the CCP Central Committee, as well as chairman of Guangdong People's Government and mayor of Guangzhou, commander of Guangdong Military Region and chairman of Guangzhou Military Control Commission.

1949,   Dec   Appointed member of the Central Government Council, member of the Overseas Chinese Affairs Commission, council member of the Sino-Soviet Friendship Association, member of the Revolutionary Military Council, and vice-chairman of Central-South China Military and Administrative Council (all posts until Sep 1954)

1954,   Aug   Elected deputy for the PLA to the 1st NPC (reelected in 1958 and 1964 to the 2nd and 3rd NPCs)

        Sep   Elected member of the Standing Committee by the 1st NPC (confirmed in this post in Apr 1959 and Jan 1965)

        Oct   Appointed vice-chairman of the National Defense Council (until Cultural Revolution) and director of the Department for Supervising Combat Strength of the PLA (until about 1960)

1955,   Sep   Promoted to rank of marshal; conferred the orders of "1st August," "Independence and Freedom," and "Liberation," all 1st class

1956,   Sep   Reelected as member of the CCP Central Committee

        Dec   Head of a military delegation to Burma

1958,   Mar   Appointed commandant of the Academy of Military Sciences of the PLA (until?)

        Oct   Head of a military delegation to Poland

1960,   Sep   Deputy head of a CCP delegation to North Vietnam

1963,   Sep   Member of a government delegation led by Liu Shaoqi to North Korea

1965,   Jan   Elected vice-chairman of the CPPCC (until 1975)

1966,   Aug   Elected member of the CCP Politburo

1967,   Jan   Appointed vice-chairman, Military Council of the CCP Central Committee

1969,   Apr   Confirmed as member of the Central Committee and of the CCP Politburo by the 9th Party Congress

        Sep   Member of a CCP and government delegation led by Zhou Enlai to Hanoi to attend the mourning ceremonies for Ho Chi-minh

1971,   Mar   Deputy head of a CCP and government delegation to Vietnam

1973,   Aug   Reelected member of the CCP Central Committee and of the Politburo by the 10th Party Congress; in addition elected vice-chairman of the CCP Central Committee and member of the Standing Committee, Politburo of the CCP (confirmed in all posts by the 11th Party Congress in 1977)

1975, Jan Appointed minister of national defense (until Feb 1978)

1978, Feb Elected deputy for the PLA to the 5th NPC

       Mar Elected chairman of the Standing Committee of the 5th NPC

Ye is married to Zeng Xianzhi.

Ye Lin (Yeh Lin)

Posts held

CCP
Secretary of Beijing Municipality CP

Provincial Administration
Vice-mayor of Beijing Municipality

Others
Director in the Board of Directors, China International Trust and Investment Corporation

Ye was born in 1912 in Jiangsu Province.

1954, Oct Appointed member of the State Planning Commission (until Dec 1956)

1956, Dec Appointed vice-chairman of the State Economic Commission (until Cultural Revolution)

1963, Oct Identified as director of the Supervisory Board, Federation of Handicraft Industries Cooperatives (until Cultural Revolution)

1966, Jun Head of a work team sent to Qinghua University by Liu Shaoqi

1967, Apr Engaged in anti-Red Guard acitivities at Qinghua University during which three persons were killed. This provoked severe counterattacks against Ye. He disappears.

1977, Dec First appearance after the Cultural Revolution: Identified as vice-chairman of the Revolutionary Committee of Beijing Municipality (until Dec 1979)

1978, May Member of a government delegation to France, Switzerland, Belgium, Denmark, and the Federal Republic of Germany (head: Gu Mu)

1979, Mar Identified as secretary of Beijing Municipality CP

       Oct Appointed director in the Board of Directors, China International Trust and Investment Corporation

       Dec Elected vice-mayor of Beijing Municipality

Ye Shengtao (Yeh Sheng-t'ao)

Posts held

NPC
Member of the Standing Committee of the 5th NPC
Deputy for Jiangsu Province to the 5th NPC

Others
Member of the Standing Committee of the 5th CPPCC
Vice-chairman of the Central Committee, China Association for Promoting Democracy

Ye was born in 1893 (1894?) in Jiangsu Province. After attending middle school he worked as a teacher. In 1922 he founded the journal Xiaoshuo Yuebao (Literary Monthly) together with a group of friends. In 1925 he founded "Poetry Reciting Society" together with Zheng Zhentuo. During the Anti-Japanese War he was professor of Sichuan University. He spent 1948 in Hong Kong. In March 1949 he served as chairman of the Textbook Editing Committee of the Education Department, North China People's Government. In July of that year he was elected a member of the Federation of Literary and Art Circles which he represented as a delegate at the 1st CPPCC.

1949, Oct Appointed deputy director of the General Publications Office of the Government Administration Council (until 1954)

1952, Feb Identified as member of the Committee for Reforming the Chinese Written Language

1953, Oct Identified as council member of the Union of Chinese Writers

1954, Aug Elected deputy for Jiangsu Province to the 1st NPC (reelected in 1958 and 1964 to the 2nd and 3rd NPCs)

       Oct Appointed vice-minister of education (until Cultural Revolution)

1956, Feb Identified as member of the Committee for Popularizing the Common Spoken Language

       Dec Member of a delegation of writers to the Asian Writers Conference in New Delhi

1958, Mar Identified as director of the People's Education Press

1967   Disappears during the Cultural Revolution

1973, Mar First appearance after the Cultural Revolution

1977, Oct Identified as a cadre in the field of education

1978, Feb Elected deputy for Jiangsu Province to the 5th NPC

       Mar Elected member of the Standing Committee of the 5th NPC and of the 5th CPPCC

1979, Oct Elected vice-chairman of the Central Committee of the China Association for Promoting Democracy

Publications

Collection of Writings

1922	Gemo	(Barrier)
1923	Huozai	(Huozai)
1925	Xian Xia	(Below the Horizon)
1926	Cheng Zhong	(In Town)
1928	Weiyan Ji	(Undefeated)
1936	Sisan Ji	(Written at the Age of 43)

Autobiographical Novel

1928	Ni Huanzhi	(Schoolmaster Ni Huanzhi)

Others
Straw Man
Wen Hsin
Stone Statue of an Ancient Hero
General Talks on Writing
Misunderstanding
A Conflagration
Firing Line

Ye Shuhua (Yeh Shu-hua) (f) 叶叔华

Posts held

Others
Director of the Shanghai Observatory,
Academy of Sciences
Vice-president of the Society of Astronomy

1963   Ye and her assistants set up China's independent high precision universal time

1978,   Sep   Identified as director of the Shanghai Observatory under the Academy of Sciences and identified as vice-president of the Society of Astronomy; head and of an astronomy and geodynamics delegation visiting France

Ye Zhiqiang (Yeh Chih-ch'iang) 叶志强

Posts held

Government
Vice-minister of metallurgical industry

NPC
Deputy for Tianjin Municipality to the 5th NPC

Others
President of the Metals Society

1959,   Oct   Identified as director of the Bureau of Metallurgy of Hebei Province People's Council

1965,   Mar   Appointed vice-minister of metallurgical industry

1973,   Oct   Head of metallurgical delegation to Albania

1977,   Sep   Identified as chairman of the Metals Society

        Oct   Head of a metallurgical delegation to Japan

1978,   Feb   Elected deputy for Tianjin Municipality to the 5th NPC

        Dec   Identified as director-general in charge of the Baoshan Steel Project to be built by Japan

Ye Zhuquan (Yeh Chu-ch'üan) 叶桔泉

Posts held

Others
Member of the Standing Committee of the 5th CPPCC

1978,   Mar   Elected member of the Standing Committee of the 5th CPPCC

Yi Lirong (Yi Li-jung) 易礼容

Posts held

Others
Member of the Standing Committee of the 5th CPPCC

Yi was born in 1898 in Xiangxiang, Hunan Province. He joined the New People's Society founded by Mao Zedong already in 1918. He subsequently worked under Chen Duxiu, then secretary-general of the CCP. In 1922 he represented laborers of Hunan Province as a delegate at the 1st Labor Conference in Guangzhou. He was then together with Li Shaoqi and Li Lisan responsible for the organization of workers of Anyuan Coal Mine. From 1924 to 1927 he was chairman of the Hunan Peasants Association. In the face of KMT persecution of the Communists he fled to Japan in late 1927. He returned to China circa 1931 to join the KMT and worked for their Labor Association. In 1943 he was made secretary-general of the All-China Federation of Labor. In 1946 he was accused of corruption by the KMT Government. He was elected a member of the Executive Council of the Communist-oriented Federation of Trade Unions in August 1948 and in addition served as director of the Department for Labor Insurance and Welfare (until 1951). As a trade union representative he took part in the 1st CPPCC in September 1949.

1949,   Dec   Identified as member of the Political and Legal Committee of the Government Administration Council

1951   Identified as director of the Labor Protection Department of the Federation of Trade Unions

1954,   Aug   Elected deputy for Hunan Province to the 1st NPC (reelected in 1958 and 1964 to the 2nd and 3rd NPCs)

        Dec   Elected deputy secretary-general of the CPPCC (until Cultural Revolution)

1957,   Dec   Elected deputy secretary-general of the Federation of Trade Unions (until Cultural Revolution)

1966   Disappears during the Cultural Revolution

1979,   Jul   First appearance after the Cultural Revolution: By-elected member of the Standing Committee of the 5th CPPCC

Yi Meihou (Yi Mei-hou) 蚁美厚

Posts held

NPC
Deputy for Guangdong Province to the 5th NPC

Provincial Administration
Vice-chairman of the People's Congress of Guangdong Province

Others
Vice-chairman of the Federation of Returned Overseas Chinese
Vice-chairman of the Board of Directors, Jinan University

Yi was born in 1910 in Chenghai County, Guangdong Province. In 1945 he was president of the Association for Relief of Overseas Chinese in Thailand, vice-chairman of the Chinese Overseas Welfare Society in Thailand, and member of the China General Chamber of Commerce, also in Thailand. In September 1949 he took part in the 1st CPPCC as a delegate representing the overseas Chinese.

1949,	Oct	Appointed member of the State Overseas Chinese Affairs Commission
1950,	May	Elected member of the Relief Administration
1952,	Jul	Elected member of the Preparatory Committee, Federation of Industry and Commerce
1953,	Oct	Identified as chairman of the Guangzhou Federation of Returned Overseas Chinese
	Nov	Identified as member of the Executive Council, Federation of Industry and Commerce
1954,	Jul	Elected deputy for Guangdong Province to the 1st NPC (reelected in 1958 and 1964 to the 2nd and 3rd NPCs)
1956,	Oct	Appointed vice-chairman of the Federation of Returned Overseas Chinese
1958,	May	Head of a trade delegation to Hong Kong
1962,	Jan	Identified as chairman of the Federation of Returned Overseas Chinese, Guangdong Province
1965,	Jun	Identified as member of the Afro-Asian Solidarity Committee
1967		Disappears during the Cultural Revolution
1972,	Feb	First appearance after the Cultural Revolution
1978,	Feb	Identified as chairman of the Federation for Returned Overseas Chinese, Guangdong Branch; elected deputy for Guangdong Province to the 5th NPC
	Oct	Identified as vice-chairman of the Board of Directors, Jinan University
	Dec	Elected vice-chairman of the Federation of Returned Overseas Chinese
1979,	Jun	Member of the Budget Committee, 5th NPC
	Dec	Elected vice-chairman of the People's Congress of Guangdong Province

Yi-min-nuo-fu Ha-mi-ti (Yi-min-no-fu Ha-mi-t'i)

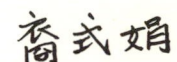

Posts held

Provincial Administration
Vice-chairman of the Xinjiang Autonomous Regional People's Government

Yi-min-nuo-fu belongs to the Uighur minority. He studied in the USSR.

1954,	Jul	Identified as 4th secretary of the CCP South Xinjiang District Committee
	Aug	Identified as director of the South Xinjiang Administrative Office; elected deputy for Xinjiang Province to the 1st NPC (reelected in 1958 and 1964 to the 2nd and 3rd NPCs)
1955,	Sep	Awarded the orders of "1st August," "Independence and Freedom," and "Liberation," all 1st class
	Oct	Elected vice-chairman of the Xinjiang Autonomous Region (until Sep 1968)
1956,	Jun	Identified as vice-president of the Sino-Pakistan Friendship Association
1958,	May	Accused of advocating localism and ousted from membership to the Xinjiang Province CP
1960,	May	Yi-min-nuo-fu heads a Muslim delegation to Mecca, Somalia, Egypt, and Yemen (until Sep)
1968,	Sep	Denounced as a follower of Liu Shaoqi and purged
1979,	Sep	First appearance after the Cultural Revolution: Elected vice-chairman of the Xinjiang Autonomous Regional People's Government

Yi Shijuan (Yi Shih-chüan) (f)

喬式娟

Posts held

NPC
Member of the Standing Committee of the 5th NPC
Deputy for Shanghai Municipality to the 5th NPC

Yi was born circa 1925. She became known as an outstanding textile worker in the 1950s.

1958,	Nov	Elected deputy for Shanghai Municipality to the 2nd NPC (reelected in 1964 to the 3rd NPC)
1961,	Mar	Identified as a worker at Shanghai No.2 Textile Mill
1975,	Jan	Elected deputy for Shanghai Municipality to the 4th NPC
1978,	Feb	Elected deputy for Shanghai Municipality to the 5th NPC
	Mar	Elected member of the Standing Committee of the 5th NPC; identified as a member of the CP Committee of Shanghai No.2 Textile Mill
1979,	Jun	Member of the Budget Committee at the 2nd Session of the 5th NPC

Yin Linping (Yin Lin-p'ing)

Posts held

NPC
Deputy for Guangdong Province to the 5th NPC

Military
Major-general

Others
Member of the Standing Committee of the 5th CPPCC

Yin was born in Xingguo, Jiangxi Province, as the son of a peasant. From 1934 to 1936 he supervised guerrilla activities in Fujian Province. He subsequently served in

Guangdong Province, from 1943 as political commissar of the East River Column and as secretary of Guangdong Province CP. In 1945 he went to Hong Kong for medical treatment after being wounded. In 1946 he was CCP representative with the rank of major-general in the Guangdong Military Mediation Department. In 1949 he commanded Communist forces in Guangdong Province.

1949,	Dec	Identified as member of the People's Government of Guangdong and as member of the Central-South China Military and Administrative Council (until Jan 1953)
1950,	Jul	Identified as deputy political commissar of Guangdong Military District
1954,	Aug	Elected deputy for Guangdong Province to the 1st NPC
1955,	Feb	Identified as vice-governor of Guangdong Province (until Sep 1958)
1957,	Mar	Identified as alternate member of Guangdong Province CP (until Feb 1961)
1958,	Oct	Identified as director of the Organization Department of Guangdong Province CP
1961,	Feb	Identified as secretary of Guangdong Province CP
1967,	Jun	Branded as a "three-anti element" and purged
1978,	Feb	First appearance after the Cultural Revolution: Elected deputy for Guangdong Province to the 5th NPC
	Mar	Elected member of the Standing Committee of the 5th CPPCC

Yin Zanxun (Yin Tsan-hsün)

Posts held

NPC
Deputy for Hebei Province to the 5th NPC

Others
Director of the Department of Earth Sciences, Academy of Sciences
President of the Palaeontological Society

Yin was born in 1903 in Pingxiang, Hebei Province. After receiving a doctorate in France from Lyons University in 1931 he studied palaeontology under Professor Depelret. In 1932 he returned to China to work initially at the Institute of Geological Survey of the Ministry of Industry, and later as researcher of the Institute of Geology of the Academy of Sciences. From 1934 to 1936 he conducted geological research in Yunnan Province. He subsequently held the post of director of the Institute of Ancient Biology.

1950,	Aug	Identified as member of the Association for Dissemination of Scientific and Technical Knowledge
	Sep	Identified as director of the Palaeontological Research Section of the Nanjing Institute of Geological Survey
1953,	Jan	Identified as vice-president of the Beijing Geological Institute (until Feb 1963)
1955		Identified as chairman of the Palaeontology Society
1956,	Mar	Appointed member of the State Scientific Planning Commission
1959,	Nov	Identified as deputy director of the Ter-

restrial Stratification Society and as director of the Department of Earth Sciences of the Academy of Sciences

1962		Identified as president of the Palaeontology Society
1964,	Oct	Elected deputy for Henan Province to the 3rd NPC
1966		Disappears during the Cultural Revolution
1973,	Mar	First appearance after the Cultural Revolution
1978,	Feb	Elected deputy for Hebei Province to the 5th NPC
1979,	Apr	Reelected president of the Palaeontological Society; identified as director of the Department of Earth Sciences, Academy of Sciences

Publications

The Annonites of the Latter Part of the Ancient Age in China
The Volcanos of the 4th Age in Shansi
Formation and Development of Geology
Progress of the Study of Ancient Biology in China

Yin Zhe (Yin Che)

Posts held

CCP
Secretary of Hebei Province CP

1959,	Nov	Identified as secretary-general of Hebei Province CP
1974,	Nov	Identified as a cadre in Hebei Province
1975,	Oct	Identified as a member of the Standing Committee, Hebei Province CP
1979,	Jul	Appointed member of the National Games Organizing Committee
	Aug	Identified as secretary of Hebei Province CP

Yin Zhongwei (Yin Chung-wei)

Posts held

Government
Vice-minister of the Physical Culture and Sports Commission

1969,	Oct	Identified as a cadre of the State Council
1976,	Jan	Identified as a sports cadre
1978,	Jul	Identified as vice-minister of the Physical Culture and Sports Commission
	Nov	Head of a sports delegation to Spain
1979,	Jul	Appointed member of the National Games Organizing Committee

Yin Ziming (Yin Tzu-ming)

Posts held

CCP
Member of the Standing Committee of Hunan Province CP

Provincial Administration
Vice-chairman of the People's Congress of
Hunan Province

1977,   Sep   Identified as member of the Standing
Committee of Hunan Province CP
Dec   Elected vice-chairman of the Revolution-
ary Committee of Hunan Province (until
Dec 1979)
1979,   Dec   Elected vice-chairman of the People's
Congress of Hunan Province

Yin Zuozhen (Yin Tso-chen)   尹佐珍

Posts held

Government
Deputy director, Foreign Affairs Bureau
of the Ministry of National Defense

Yin was born in 1919 in Shanxi Province.

1971,   Sep   Identified as deputy director of the Foreign Affairs Bureau of the Ministry of
National Defense
1974,   Jan   Member of a military delegation to Pakistan
1977,   Feb   Member of a military delegation to
Sri Lanka

Yong Wentao (Yung Wen-t'ao)   雍文涛

Posts held

Government
Vice-minister of forestry

NPC
Deputy for Guangdong Province to the
5th NPC

Yong is a native of Guizhou Province. In 1949 he was
identified as director of the General Office, Economic
Planning Commission of Northeast China People's Government.

1950,   May   Appointed member of the Standing Committee, Economic Planning Commission of
Northeast China People's Government
1952,   Aug   Identified as director of the Forestry
Department of Northeast China People's
Government
1953,   Jan   Appointed member of the Northeast China
Administrative Council
Sep   Appointed vice-minister of forestry (until
Oct 1956)
1956,   Oct   Appointed vice-minister of timber indus-
try (until Feb 1958)
1958,   Dec   Appointed vice-minister of forestry (until
Cultural Revolution)
1961,   Oct   Identified as secretary-general, Central-
South China Bureau of the CCP Central
Committee (until Cultural Revolution)
1963,   Sep   Identified as member of the Standing
Committee, Central-South China Bureau
of the CCP Central Committee (until
Cultural Revolution)

1965,   Mar   Identified as secretary of Guangdong
Province CP (until Cultural Revolution)
Jun   Identified as 1st secretary of Guangzhou
Municipality CP (until Cultural Revolution)
1966,   Aug   Appointed deputy director, Propaganda
Department of the CCP Central Commit-
tee
1967,   Jan   Criticized as a follower of Tao Zhu and
relieved of all posts
1972,   Nov   First appearance after the Cultural Revolution
1973,   Feb   Identified as vice-chairman of the Revolutionary Committee of Guangdong Prov-
ince (until 1976)
1974,   Jan   Identified as member of the Standing
Committee of Guangdong Province CP
1976,   Jan   Identified as secretary of Guangdong
Province CP (until 1976)
1977,   Apr   Identified as vice-minister of education
(until 1978)
1978,   Feb   Elected deputy for Guangdong Province to
the 5th NPC
Oct   Head of an educational delegation to
Japan and Canada
1979,   Oct   Identified as vice-minister of forestry

You Taizhong (Yu T'ai-chung)   尤太忠

Posts held

CCP
Member of the CCP 11th Central Committee

NPC
Deputy for Inner Mongolia Autonomous
Region to the 5th NPC

Military
Major-general
Commander of Chengdu Military Region

You is a native of Sichuan Province. He took part in the
Long March of 1934-35 as battalion commander of the
4th Front Army. In 1937 he attended a course at the
Anti-Japan Military and Political Academy. He then
served in the 129th Division of the 8th Route Army,
reaching the post of regiment commander in 1946. In 1947
he was appointed deputy brigade commander, and shortly
afterwards brigade commander, of the Shanxi-Hebei-
Shandong-Henan Field Army commanded by Liu Bocheng.
In late 1948 he took part in the Battle of Huaihai. In
early 1949 he was made commander of a division of the
2nd Field Army. In autumn of that year his division took
part in the battles of Chongqing.

1951,   Mar   Service in the Korean War as commander
of the 12th Army
1953   Return to China
1954   Identified as deputy commander of the
12th Army
1955,   Sep   Promoted to rank of major-general
1961   Identified as commander of the 27th Army
based in Wushi
1968,   Mar   Elected chairman of the Revolutionary
Committee of Wushi Municipality

480

1969, Apr Elected alternate member of the CCP Central Committee by the 9th Party Congress (until Aug 1973)

1970, Dec Identified as military leader in Beijing Military Region

1971, May Elected 1st secretary of Inner Mongolia Autonomous Region CP (until Oct 1978)

1973, Aug Elected to first term as member of the CCP Central Committee by the 10th Party Congress; identified as commander of Inner Mongolia Military District (until 1978)

1974, Feb Identified as chairman of the Revolutionary Committee of Inner Mongolia Autonomous Region (until Nov 1978)

1975, Nov Identified as deputy commander of Beijing Military Region (until Dec 1979)

1977, Aug Article in HQ: "Mao Zedong Thought Illuminates Inner Mongolia Autonomous Region"

Oct Appointed director of the Party School of Inner Mongolia CP (until Oct 1978)

1978, Feb Elected deputy for Inner Mongolia Autonomous Region to the 5th NPC

1980, Jan Identified as commander of Chengdu Military Region

Yu Aifeng (Yü Ai-feng) (f)　俞霭峯

Posts held

NPC
Member of the Standing Committee of the 5th NPC
Deputy for Tianjin Municipality to the 5th NPC

1950 Identified as head of the Obstetrics Department, Tianjin General Hospital

1951, Sep Identified as council member of the People's Government of Tianjin Municipality

1953, Apr Elected member of the Executive Council of the Democratic Women's Federation

1954, Aug Elected deputy for Tianjin Municipality to the 1st NPC

1955, Jan Identified as member of the People's Council of Tianjin

Aug Elected vice-chairman of the Tianjin Branch, Democratic Women's Federation

1957, Sep Elected member of the Executive Council of the Women's Federation

1959, Mar Elected deputy for Hebei Province to the 2nd NPC (reelected in 1964 to the 4th NPC)

1965, Jan Elected member of the Standing Committee by the 3rd NPC

1967 Disappears during the Cultural Revolution

1974, Mar First appearance after the Cultural Revolution: Again referred to as head of the Gynecology and Obstetrics Department of the hospital affiliated with the Tianjin Medical College

1975, Jan Confirmed as member of the Standing Committee by the 4th NPC (again confirmed in Mar 1978 by the 5th NPC)

1978, Feb Elected deputy for Tianjin Municipality to the 5th NPC

Yu Buxue (Yü Pu-hsüeh)　于步血

Posts held

Government
Vice-minister of the Physical Culture and Sports Commission

Others
President of the Aviation Sports Federation

1971, Nov Identified as a cadre of the Physical Culture and Sports Commission

1972, May Identified as vice-minister of the Physical Culture and Sports Commission

1977, Nov Head of a friendship delegation to Somalia and Benin

1978, Oct Head of a sports delegation to Japan

Dec Deputy head of a sports delegation to the 8th Asian Games in Bangkok

1979, May Identified as president of the Aviation Sports Federation

Jul Appointed member of the National Games Organizing Committee

Yu Dafu (Yü Ta-fu)　余大绂

Posts held

Others
Member of the Standing Committee of the 5th CPPCC

Yu was born in Shaoxing, Zhejiang Province. After graduating from Nanjing University he studied biology at the University of Iowa in the United States.

1953, Feb Identified as vice-chairman of the Society of Plant Pathology

1955, Jan Identified as professor, Department of Plant Protection of the Agricultural University in Beijing

May Identified as member of the Department of Biology and Geography of the Academy of Sciences

1956, Jan Elected member of the National Committee of the 2nd CPPCC (reelected in 1959 and 1964)

1957 Elected corresponding member of the Lenin Academy of Agro-sciences in the USSR

1967 Disappears during the Cultural Revolution

1973, Oct First appearance after the Cultural Revolution: Identified as member of the Standing Committee of the CPPCC (confirmed in Mar 1978 by the 5th CPPCC)

Yu Guangmao (Yü Kuang-mao)　余光茂

Posts held

CCP
Member of the Standing Committee of Anhui Province CP
Secretary of Anhui Military District Party Committee

NPC
Deputy for the PLA to the 5th NPC

Military
Major-general
Commander of Anhui Military District

In 1946 Yu was commander of a division in the East China Field Army.

1950		Identified as commander of a division of the 3rd Field Army
1958,	Oct	Identified as major-general
1966,	Nov	Identified as deputy commander of Shanghai Garrison
1972,	Jun	Identified as 1st deputy commander of Anhui Military District
1976,	Apr	Identified as commander of Anhui Military District
1977,	Feb	Identified as deputy secretary of Anhui Province CP (until Aug 1978)
1978,	Feb	Elected deputy for the PLA to the 5th NPC
	Sep	Identified as member of the Standing Committee of Anhui Province CP
1979,	Dec	Identified as secretary of Anhui Military District Party Committee

Yu Guangyuan (Yü Kuang-yüan) 于光远

Posts held

Government
Vice-minister of the State Scientific and Technical Commission

NPC
Deputy for Shanghai Municipality to the 5th NPC

Others
Vice-president of the Academy of Social Sciences
Advisor to the Society for the Study of the Future
Director of the Marxism-Leninism-Mao Zedong Thought Research Institute

Yu was born circa 1915. He became politicly active in 1935 with the December 9 Student Movement. He was subsequently engaged primarily in Communist youth work.

1950,	Sep	Identified as member of the Financial and Economic Committee of Wuhan People's Government
1955,	Jan	Identified as member of the Standing Committee of the Physics Society
	Feb	Identified as responsible person for the Organization Committee of a forum on atomic energy knowledge popularization
	Jun	Identified as member of the Department of Philosophy and Social Sciences of the Academy of Sciences (until Cultural Revolution)
1956,	Mar	Identified as deputy secretary-general of the State Scientific Planning Commission
	Sep	Identified as deputy director of the State Foreign Experts Bureau (until 1959) and as chief of the Scientific Section under the Propaganda Department of the CCP Central Committee

1957,	Sep	Yu criticizes Zhang Bojun and Luo Longji as rightists during the Anti-Rightist Campaign
	Nov	Member of a delegation of scientists to the USSR
1960,	Apr	Yu attends a discussion meeting of the magazine Peace and Problems of Socialism in Prague, Czechoslovakia
	Nov	Member of a delegation to the 6th Conference of International Scientists in Moscow
1962,	Sep	Identified as professor of philosophy at Beijing University
1964,	Jul	Appointed vice-chairman of the State Scientific and Technological Commission (until Cultural Revolution)
	Sep	Elected deputy for Hubei Province to the 3rd NPC
	Oct	Member of a CCP delegation to the 15th anniversary celebrations in the German Democratic Republic
1966,	Apr	Elected vice-chairman of the Association for Cultural Relations and Friendship with Foreign Countries
1967,	Mar	Branded as a counterrevolutionary revisionist
1975,	Sep	First appearance after the Cultural Revolution
1977,	Dec	Identified as vice-minister of the State Scientific and Technical Commission
1978,	Feb	Elected deputy for Shanghai Municipality to the 5th NPC; identified as vice-president of the Academy of Social Sciences
	Mar	Deputy head of a CCP workers delegation to Yugoslavia and Romania
1979,	Mar	Appointed advisor to the Society for the Study of the Future; head of a delegation of the Academy of Social Sciences to Japan
	Jun	Member of the Budget Committee at the 2nd Session of the 5th NPC
	Jul	Identified as director of the Marxism-Leninism-Mao Zedong Thought Research Institute

Publications

1950	Why Should the Polite Bourgeois Class Reform Its Thoughts?
	Problems of Methods for Beginners to Study Political Economy
	Ideology of Socialist Thought
	Several Fundamental Problems of Land Rent
1951	Fundamental Rules for the Development of a Community
	Primitive Society
	On the Fundamental Knowledge of Social Science
	Community with Slave-Possessing System
	Society of Capitalism
1964	Summing-up of Victory
	Combination of the Interest of the Laboring Individual and Communal Benefit
1955	To Master the Struggle against Hidden Counterrevolutionaries
1956	Further Strengthening the Party's Guidance in Scientific Work
1957	Two Roads to Develop our Country's

| 1959 | | Scientific Enterprises
Pricing Rules and the Regularity of Pricing Decision under a Socialist System
Discussion of Problems of Commodities under a Socialist System to Obtain the Highest Value of Utility with the Least Consumption of Labor |
| Later | | Discussions on Socialist Public Ownership and Distribution According to Work
On Economic Results of Socialist Production |

Yu Hongliang (Yü Hung-liang) 于洪亮

Posts held

CCP
Member of the CCP 11th Central Committee
Secretary of Heilongjiang Province CP

1973,	Jul	Elected chairman of the Trade Union of Heilongjiang Province
	Aug	Elected member of the Central Committee by the 10th Party Congress (confirmed in Aug 1977 by the 11th Congress)
	Sep	Identified as secretary of Heilongjiang Province CP
1977,	Dec	Elected vice-chairman of the Revolutionary Committee of Heilongjiang Province
1978,	Feb	Yu disappears; probably purged

Yu Hongliang (Yü Hung-liang) 于洪亮

Posts held

Government
Director of the USSR and Eastern Europe Department of the Ministry of Foreign Affairs

1973,	Mar	Identified as deputy director of the USSR and Eastern Europe Department of the Ministry of Foreign Affairs
1974,	Aug	Member of a Party and government delegation to Romania
1978,	Jun	Identified as director of the USSR and Eastern Europe Department of the Ministry of Foreign Affairs

Yu Jianting (Yü Chien-t'ing) 余建亭

Posts held

Government
Vice-minister of light industry

1978,	May	Identified as vice-minister of light industry
	Oct	Identified as vice-president of the Light Industry Society (until Nov 1979)
	Dec	Head of a scientific and technical delegation to Czechoslovakia
1979,	Apr	Deputy head of a light industry delegation to Japan

Yu Jie (Yü Chieh) 喻杰

Posts held

Others
Member of the Standing Committee of the 5th CPPCC

Yu studied for seven years in the USSR.

1950,	Mar	Identified as member of the Financial and Economic Committee of Northwest Military and Administrative Council
1953,	Jan	Identified as director of the Trade Bureau, Northwest Administrative Council (until Dec 1953)
1954,	Nov	Identified as vice-minister of food (until May 1955)
1962,	Jun	Appointed vice-minister of commerce (until Nov 1963)
1964,	Sep	Elected deputy for Hunan Province to the 3rd NPC; subsequently disappears
1978,	Mar	Elected member of the Standing Committee of the 5th CPPCC

Yu Ke (Yü K'e) 于克

Posts held

CCP
Secretary of Jilin Province CP

NPC
Deputy for Jilin Province to the 5th NPC

Provincial Administration
Vice-chairman of the Revolutionary Committee of Jilin Province

Yu was born in 1910 in Jilin Province. He studied at Sun Yat-sen University in Moscow. From 1936 he was a member of the Shaanxi-Gansu-Ningxia Border Region Government, political cadre of an army division, and instructor at the Central Party School. In 1946 he was made director of the Political Department of Jilin-Liaoning Military District.

1950		Identified as vice-governor of Jilin Province (until Cultural Revolution) and as director of the Department of Public Security of Jilin People's Government (until Cultural Revolution)
1951,	Oct	Identified as deputy chief procurator, Northeast Branch of the Supreme People's Procuracy (until 1953)
1957,	Sep	Identified as member of the Standing Committee of Jilin Province CP
1961,	Jun	Identified as alternate secretary of Jilin Province CP (until Cultural Revolution)
1967		Disappears during the Cultural Revolution
1977,	Oct	First appearance after the Cultural Revolution: Identified as deputy secretary of Jilin Province CP (until Dec 1979)
	Dec	Elected vice-chairman of the Revolutionary Committee of Jilin Province
1978,	Feb	Elected deputy for Jilin Province to the 5th NPC
1979,	Jun	Member of the Budget Committee at the 2nd Session of the 5th NPC
1980,	Jan	Identified as secretary of Jilin Province CP

Yu Ming (Yü Ming)   于 明

Posts held

Government
Vice-minister of the 1st Ministry of Machine Building

1978,   Apr   Identified as vice-minister of the 1st Ministry of Machine Building; deputy head of an agricultural machinery study group visiting Italy, France, Great Britain, and Denmark

Yu Mingtao (Yü Ming-t'ao)   于 明 涛

Posts held

CCP
Member of the CCP 11th Central Committee
Secretary of Shaanxi Province CP

NPC
Deputy for Shaanxi Province to the 5th NPC

Provincial Administration
Governor of Shaanxi Province

1952   Identified as a cadre of Lingling Special District, Hunan Province
1957,   May   Identified as director of the Industry Department of Hunan Province CP
1959,   Oct   Identified as secretary of Hunan Province CP
1963,   Sep   Identified as member of the Standing Committee, Central-South China Bureau of the CCP Central Committee
1967   During the Cultural Revolution, Yu is criticized as an anti-Party element and disappears
1971,   Dec   First appearance after the Cultural Revolution: Identified as vice-chairman of the Revolutionary Committee of Hunan
1972,   Feb   Identified as member of the Standing Committee of Hunan Province CP (until Aug 1973)
1973,   Jul   Identified as 1st secretary of Changsha Municipality CP (until Aug 1977)
        Aug   Identified as secretary of Hunan Province CP (until Aug 1977)
1977,   Aug   Elected member of the CCP Central Committee by the 11th Party Congress
        Oct   Identified as vice-chairman of the Revolutionary Committee of Shaanxi (until May 1979)
        Nov   Identified as secretary of Shaanxi Province CP
1978,   Feb   Elected deputy for Shaanxi Province to the 5th NPC
1979,   May   Identified as chairman of the Revolutionary Committee of Shaanxi Province (until Dec 1979); advisor of an agricultural delegation, led by Wang Feng, to the U.S.A.
        Jun   Member of the Credentials Committee at the 2nd Session of the 5th NPC
        Dec   Elected governor of Shaanxi Province

Yu is married to Wang Rongying.

Yu Peiwen (Yü P'ei-wen)   俞 沛 文

Posts held

Government
Permanent representative of the PRC to the Geneva Office of the United Nations

1950   Identified as deputy director, Foreign Office of the People's Council of Shanghai
1951,   Dec   Elected council member of the Shanghai Branch, Sino-Soviet Friendship Association
1954   Acting director of the Foreign Office of Shanghai
1955,   Jul   Elected member of the Institute of Foreign Affairs
1958,   Apr   Appointed director of the Protocol Department of the Ministry of Foreign Affairs
1961,   May   Advisor to the Chinese delegation led by Minister of Foreign Affairs Chen Yi to the Laos Conference in Geneva
        Jul   Member of a government delegation to Moscow
1963,   Apr- Yu accompanies the Chinese president Liu Shaoqi on several journeys to Indonesia, Burma, Cambodia, North Vietnam, and North Korea
        Sep
        Dec- Member of a delegation led by Premier Zhou Enlai to the United Arab Republic, Algeria, Morocco, Albania, Tunisia, Ghana, Mali, Guinea, Sudan, Ethiopia, Somalia, Burma, Pakistan, Ceylon
1964,   Feb
1966,   Jan   Appointed ambassador to Sudan (until about 1967)
1971,   May   Appointed ambassador to Ethiopia (until Jul 1974)
        Oct   Yu accompanies Emperor Haile Selassie of Ethiopia on his visit to China
1974,   Sep   Appointed ambassador to Austria (until Feb 1980)
1975,   Jan   Head of the Chinese delegation to the Vienna session of the United Nations Industrial Development Board
1978,   Feb   Head of the Chinese delegation to the United Nations Industrial Development Organization (UNIDO) Conference in New York
1979,   Apr   Head of the Chinese delegation to the UNIDO Conference in Vienna
1980,   Feb   Identified as permanent representative of the PRC to the Geneva Office of the United Nations

Yu Ping (Yü P'ing)   喻 屏

Posts held

Others
Deputy chief procurator of the Supreme People's Procuratorate

In the 1940s Yu served as director of the Department of Organization, West Tianjin-Pukou Railway District CP.

1954,   Nov   Identified as deputy secretary of Liaoning Province CP
1958,   May   Identified as secretary of Liaoning Province CP

Dec Elected deputy for Liaoning Province to the 2nd NPC

1961, Jan Identified as alternate secretary of the Northeast Bureau, CCP Central Committee

1964, Sep Elected deputy for Jilin Province to the 3rd NPC

1966, Nov Denounced as Liu Shaoqi's agent in Liaoning and purged

1979, May First appearance after the Cultural Revolution: Appointed deputy chief procurator of the Supreme People's Procuratorate

Sep Head of a Supreme People's Procuratorate delegation to Romania

Yu Qiuli (Yü Ch'iu-li) 余秋里

Posts held

CCP
Member of the Politburo of the CCP 11th Central Committee
Member of the CCP 11th Central Committee
Member of the Secretariat of the CCP Central Committee

Government
Vice-premier
Chairman of the State Planning Commission
Member of the State Financial and Economic Commission

NPC
Deputy for Jiangxi Province to the 5th NPC

Military
Lieutenant-general

Yu was born in 1914 in Ji'an County, Sichuan Province. He joined the CCP in 1931. In 1934 he served as adjutant to Ren Bishi, who was a corps commander at the time. He took part in the Long March in the 2nd Front Army. He then served as company, later as battalion, commander in the 120th Division, 8th Route Army, and later as a regimental political commissar, regimental commander, and political commissar of the 358th Brigade, mainly operating in Hebei Province. In 1947 he took part in all major campaigns in defense of Yan'an, the then headquarters of the CCP. In early 1949 he was deputy political commissar of the 7th Army, 1st Field Army.

1949-1955 Yu serves successively as deputy political commissar of the South-west China Military and Political Academy, commandant and political commissar of the 2nd Advanced Infantry Academy, and as director of the Logistics Department of the Southwest China Military Region

1955, Sep Promoted to rank of lieutenant-general; conferred the order "Liberation," 1st class

1956, Aug Identified as director of the General Finance Department of the Military Commission of the CCP Central Committee

1957, Nov Appointed political commissar of the General Logistics Department of the PLA (until Feb 1958)

1958, Feb Appointed minister of petroleum industry (until 1972)

Jul Elected deputy for Sichuan Province to the 2nd NPC (reelected in 1964 to the 3rd NPC)

1965, Nov Appointed vice-chairman of the State Planning Commission

1967 Though severely attacked by Red Guards during the Cultural Revolution, Yu survives the Cultural Revolution without loss of influence thanks to protection from Zhou Enlai

1969, Apr Elected member of the CCP Central Committee by the 9th Party Congress (confirmed in this post in 1973 by the 10th Congress)

1972, Oct Identified as chairman of the State Planning Commission

1975, Jan Appointed vice-premier

1977, Aug Elected member of the CCP Politburo by the 11th Party Congress

1978, Feb Elected deputy for Jiangxi Province to the 5th NPC

Nov Deputy head of a Party and government delegation led by Wang Dongxing to Kampuchea

1979, Jul Appointed member of the State Financial and Economic Commission

Oct Member of a government delegation, led by Hua Guofeng, to France, the Federal Republic of Germany, Great Britain and Italy

1980, Feb Elected member of the Secretariat of the CCP Central Committee by its 5th Plenum

Yu Sang (Yü Sang) 于桑

Posts held

CCP
Member of the CCP 11th Central Committee

Government
Vice-minister of public security

1955, Dec Member of a delegation to the German Democratic Republic to attend the 80th birthday of president Pieck

1961, Aug Identified as member of the Sino-Latin American Friendship Asociation

1964, Oct Appointed vice-minister of public security

1969, Apr Elected member of the CCP Central Committee by the 9th Party Congress (confirmed in 1973 and 1977 by the 10th and 11th Congress)

Yu Shude (Yü Shu-te) 于树德

Posts held

Others
Member of the Standing Committee of the 5th CPPCC

Yu was born circa 1895 in Fengrun County, Hebei Province. After graduating from Law College in Tianjin he continued his studies in the field of economics at Kyoto University. He joined the CCP in 1922. In 1924 he was one of the responsible cadres of the Beijing Branch of the KMT Central Executive Committee. In 1926 he served as political instructor at the Whampoa Military Academy. After the KMT-CCP rift in 1927, Yu renounced his Communist Party membership.

1949,	Oct	Appointed deputy director of the Central Administration Bureau of Cooperatives under the Financial and Economic Commission of the Government Administration Council
1950,	Aug	Appointed council member of the Federation of Cooperatives
1954,	Jul	Appointed vice-chairman of the Federation of Supply and Marketing Cooperatives (until 1965)
	Dec	Elected member of the 2nd CPPCC (reelected in 1959 and 1964 to the 3rd and 4th CPPCC)
1967		Disappears during the Cultural Revolution
1973,	Mar	First appearance after the Cultural Revolution: Identified as member of the Standing Committee of the CPPCC (confirmed in Mar 1978 by the 5th CPPCC)

Yu Wen (Yü Wen)   郁 文

Posts held

Others
Secretary-general of the Academy of Sciences

1958,	Mar	Identified as secretary, CP of Beijing Scientific and Technical University
	Aug	Identified as secretary, CP of the Academy of Sciences
1959,	Sep	Identified as deputy secretary-general of the Academy of Sciences
1967		Disappears during the Cultural Revolution
1973,	Oct	First appearance after the Cultural Revolution: Identified as deputy secretary-general of the Academy of Sciences
1978,	Jul	Identified as secretary-general of the Academy of Sciences

Yu Yichuan (Yü Yi-ch'uan)   于一川

Posts held

CCP
Deputy secretary of Henan Province CP

Provincial Administration
Vice-governor of Henan Province

Yu was born in Yunnan Province. He graduated from the CCP Party School. In 1949 he was deputy director of the Political Department of the 4th Army Corps, 2nd Field Army.

1949,	Nov	Identified as director of the Political Department of Yunnan Military District

1951,	Apr	Identified as deputy secretary of Yunnan Province CP
	Jul	Identified as director of the Propaganda Department, Yunnan Province CP
1955,	May	Identified as 2nd secretary of Yunnan Province CP (until Mar 1957)
1957,	Mar	Identified as secretary of Yunnan Province CP (until 1968)
1958,	Mar	Elected governor of Yunnan Province (until Jan 1964)
	Nov	Elected deputy for Yunnan Province to the 2nd NPC (reelected in 1964 to the 3rd NPC)
1964,	Sep	Yu disappears
1979,	Sep	First appearance after the Cultural Revolution: Elected vice-governor of Henan Province
	Oct	Identified as deputy secretary of Henan Province CP

Yu is married to Wang Jing.

Yu Yifu (Yü Yi-fu)   于毅夫

Posts held

Others
Member of the Standing Committee of the 5th CPPCC

Yu was born in 1901 in Baiquan, Heilongjiang Province. He studied at Qinghua University. After the Shenyang Incident he was principal of Manchukuo Higher School. He subsequently worked under General Zhang Xueliang. Following the Xi'an Incident he organized the Northeast National Salvation Association. In 1938 he edited the bimonthly magazine Counterattack in Wuhan. He then worked for Chongqing CP. Towards the end of the Anti-Japanese War he worked underground in the Japanese occupied areas. From 1945 to 1949 he served as governor of Nenjiang Province.

1949,	Oct	Appointed member of the Northeast People's Government; elected council member of the Sino-Soviet Friendship Association
1950,	Sep	Identified as governor of Heilongjiang Province (until Nov 1952)
1953,	May	Identified as director of the United Front Work Department, Northeast Bureau of the CCP Central Committee (until 1958)
1954,	Aug	Elected deputy for Harbin Municipality to the 1st NPC
1960,	Jun	Identified as secretary of Jilin Province CP
1962,	Aug	Identified as member of the Jilin People's Council
1965,	Jun	Elected member of the Standing Committee of the 4th CPPCC; subsequently disappears until 1978
1978,	Feb	First appearance after the Cultural Revolution
	Mar	Elected member of the Standing Committee of the 5th CPPCC
	Jun	Identified as a cadre of Jilin Province

Publications

1946	Which Road Should the Northeast People Follow?

1962   To Inherit and Give Play to the Excellent
            Tradition of the Communist Party

Yu is married to Du Guifu.

Yu Zhan (Yü Chan)   余　湛

Posts held

Government
Vice-minister of foreign affairs

1955,   Jan   Appointed counselor at the embassy in
                Poland (until Mar 1957)
1957,   Mar   Appointed deputy director of the Socialist
                Countries Department, Ministry of For-
                eign Affairs (until Dec 1958)
1958,   Oct   Appointed deputy director of the USSR
                and Socialist Countries Department of the
                Ministry of Foreign Affairs (until
                Sep 1964)
1963,   Sep   Identified as acting director of the USSR
                and Socialist Countries Department of the
                Ministry of Foreign Affairs
1964,   Sep   Identified as director of the USSR and
                Socialist Countries Department of the
                Ministry of Foreign Affairs
1972,   May   Identified as vice-minister of foreign af-
                fairs
1974,   Aug   Deputy head of a Party and government
                delegation to Romania to attend the
                30th anniversary of Liberation
         Nov   Member of a Party and government dele-
                gation to Albania
         Dec   Member of a Party and government dele-
                gation to Yugoslavia, traveling overland
                from Albania
1978,   Aug   Member of a Party and government dele-
                gation led by Hua Guofeng to Romania,
                Yugoslavia, and Iran

Yu is married to Zuo Yi.

Yuan Baohua (Yüan Pao-hua)   袁宝华

Posts held

CCP
Alternate member of the CCP 11th Central Committee

Government
Vice-minister of the State Economy Commission

Others
President of the Enterprise Management
Association

Yuan was born in 1916 in Henan Province.

1950,   Aug   Identified as secretary-general of the
                People's Government of Pingyuan Prov-
                ince and as member of its Finance and
                Commerce Committee

1957,   Jun   Identified as assistant minister of the
                Ministry of Metallurgical Industry
1959,   Sep   Appointed vice-minister of metallurgical
                industry (until Nov 1960)
1960,   Sep   Appointed vice-chairman of the Economy
                Commission
1963,   Sep   Appointed director of the General Bureau
                for State Material Control (abolished in
                Nov 1964)
1964,   Sep   Elected deputy for Henan Province to the
                3rd NPC
         Nov   Appointed minister of the newly estab-
                lished Ministry of Material Allocation
                (until Cultural Revolution)
1974,   Apr   Identified as vice-chairman of the State
                Planning Commission (until Aug 1978)
1977,   Aug   Elected alternate member of the CCP
                Central Committee by the 11th Party
                Congress
         Nov   Deputy head of a trade delegation to
                Great Britain and France
1978,   Sep   Identified as vice-minister of the State
                Economy Commission
         Oct   Head of an economic delegation to Japan
1979,   Mar   Elected president of the Enterprise Man-
                agement Association
         Nov   Head of a delegation to the U.S.A. to
                study industrial management and business
                administration

Yuan Fanglie (Yüan Fang-lieh)   袁芳烈

Posts held

CCP
Member of the Standing Committee of the
Zhejiang Province CP

Provincial Administration
Vice-governor of Zhejiang Province

1977,   Dec   Elected vice-chairman of the Revolution-
                ary Committee of Zhejiang Province (until
                Dec 1979)
1978,   May   Elected member of the Standing Commit-
                tee of Zhejiang Province CP
1979,   Dec   Elected vice-governor of Zhejiang Prov-
                ince

Yuan Kefu (Yüan K'e-fu)   袁克服

Posts held

Others
Member of the Standing Committee of the
5th CPPCC

1958,   Aug   Identified as political commissar of
                Shaanxi Military District (until 1970)
1970,   Oct   Identified as member of the Core Group
                for the Shaanxi Revolutionary Committee
1973,   Jun   Identified as member of the Standing
                Committee of Shaanxi Province CP (un-
                til 1976?)
1978,   Mar   Elected member of the Standing Commit-
                tee of the 5th CPPCC

Yuan Lulin (Yüan Lu-lin) 袁鲁林

Posts held

Government
Ambassador to Oman

1963,	Feb	Identified as counselor at the embassy in Denmark
1965,	May	Identified as commercial representative in Austria
1969,	Sep	Identified as deputy director of the Information Department of the Ministry of Foreign Affairs
1971,	Sep	Identified as counselor at the embassy in Switzerland (until 1974)
1975,	Nov	Identified as chargé d'affaires ad interim in the Federal Republic of Germany (until 1977)
1978,	Jun	Identified as PRC representative to the Council of the International Civil Aviation Organization (ICAO)
1979,	Apr	Appointed ambassador to Oman

Yuan Renyuan (Yüan Jen-yüan) 袁任远

Posts held

CCP
Deputy secretary of the Commission for Inspecting Discipline under the CCP Central Committee

NPC
Member of the Standing Committee of the 5th NPC
Deputy for Shanxi Province to the 5th NPC

Yuan was born in 1905 in Liuyang, Hunan Province. After attending middle school he joined the CCP. In 1928 he was one of the organizers of the Shimen Uprising in Hunan and subsequently served in the 7th Red Army. In 1934-35 he took part in the Long March. After receiving training at the Anti-Japan Military and Political Academy he became director of the Political Department, 359th Brigade, 120th Division, 8th Route Army, in 1938. During the following years he served as political commissar in North China and as cease-fire negotiator with KMT representatives. In August 1949 he was appointed vice-chairman of the Provisional People's Government of Hunan Province.

1950,	Mar	Appointed vice-chairman of the People's Government of Hunan (until 1953)
1953,	Dec	Appointed vice-minister of civil affairs (until May 1958)
1958,	Jun	Identified as secretary of Qinghai Province CP (until 1962)
	Jul	Identified as governor of Qinghai Province (until 1962); elected deputy for Qinghai Province to the 2nd NPC
1962,	Sep	Identified as member of the Control Commission of the CCP Central Committee (until Cultural Revolution)
1965,	Jan	Elected member of the Standing Committee of the CPPCC (until Feb 1978)
1978,	Feb	Elected deputy for Shanxi Province to the 5th NPC

	Mar	Elected member of the Standing Committee of the 5th NPC
	Dec	Appointed deputy secretary of the Commission for Inspecting Discipline under the CCP Central Committee

Yuan Shengping (Yüan Sheng-p'ing) 袁升平

Posts held

Military
Lieutenant-general
Political commissar of Beijing Military Region

Yuan started his career in the 1st Front Army and probably took part in the Long March in that unit. In 1937 he was political commissar of the 1st Battalion, Independent Regiment, 115th Division under the 8th Route Army. Two years later he was identified as political commissar of the 3rd Regiment, operating in the 1st Subdistrict of the Shanxi-Chahar-Hebei Military Region. In 1945 he was political commissar of the 3rd Division, Shandong Liberation Army, and in 1949 political commissar of the 40th Army under the 4th Field Army.

1950,	Jun	Identified as a member of the Hainan Military and Administrative Council
	Oct	Yuan takes part in the Korean War
1952		Identified as deputy director of the Cadres' Department of the Chinese People's Volunteers in Korea
1955,	Sep	Appointed lieutenant-general; awarded the order of "Liberation," 1st class
	Oct	Identified as director of the Political Department of Beijing Military Region
1959,	Nov	Identified as commander of Beijing Garrison
1960,	Jan	Identified as a member of the People's Government of Shandong Province
	Dec	Identified as vice-governor of Shandong Province
1961,	Dec	Identified as deputy political commissar of Jinan Military Region
1964,	Sep	Elected deputy for the PLA to the 3rd NPC
1967,	Feb	Elected member of the Standing Committee, Shandong Revolutionary Committee
1968,	Feb	Identified as political commissar of the Jinan Military Region (until 1973)
1969,	Apr	Elected member of the CCP 9th Central Committee (until 1973)
1971,	Apr	Elected 2nd secretary of Shandong Province CP (until 1973)
	May	Identified as vice-chairman of the Revolutionary Committee of Shandong Province (until 1973)
1973,	Jun	Yuan disappears
1978,	Aug	First reappearance after five years
1979,	Feb	Bai Rubing, 1st secretary of Shandong Province CP, declares the charges that Yuan had been a follower of Lin Biao to be false
1980,	Jan	Identified as political commissar of Beijing Military Region

Yuan Xuefen (Yüan Hsüeh-fen) (f) 袁雪芬

Posts held

NPC
Member of the Standing Committee of the 5th NPC
Deputy for Shanghai Municipality to the 5th NPC

Yuan was born in 1922 in Sheng County, Zhejiang Province. As a young girl she studied Yue Opera and became famous for her rendering of "Sister-in-law Xianglin," based on Lu Xun's novel Blessing. In 1946 she was elected "Queen of Yue Opera." She joined the Communists in early 1949 and in July of that year became a member of the Federation of Literary and Art Circles (until Cultural Revolution). In September 1949 she took part in the inaugural session of the CPPCC.

1950,	Oct	Member of a delegation led by Guo Moruo to the 2nd World Peace Conference in Warsaw
1952,	Dec	Identified as deputy director of the East China Opera and Drama Institute and as director of the East China Yue Opera Experimental Troupe
1953,	Mar	Elected member of the Executive Committee, Federation of Democratic Women
1954,	May	Identified as member of the Association for Cultural Relations with Foreign Countries
	Aug	Elected deputy for Shanghai Municipality to the 1st NPC (reelected in 1958 and 1964 to the 2nd and 3rd NPCs)
	Nov	Head of a Yue Opera troupe visiting the USSR
1955,	Mar	Identified as member of the Standing Committee of the Dramatists' Association
1957,	Aug	Identified as director of the Shanghai Institute of Yue Opera
1965,	Jun	Elected member of the Chinese People's Committee for Defense of World Peace
1967		Disappears during the Cultural Revolution
1978,	Feb	First appearance after the Cultural Revolution: Elected deputy for Shanghai Municipality to the 5th NPC
	Mar	Elected member of the Standing Comittee by the 5th NPC
1979,	Apr	Member of an NPC delegation led by Deng Yingchao to Japan

Yuan Zhen (Yüan Chen) 袁振

Posts held

CCP
Member of the Standing Committee of Anhui Province CP

1951	Mar	Identified as director, Propaganda Department of Hubei Province CP
1952,	Jan	Identified as deputy director of the Industrial Department, Central-South Bureau of the CCP Central Committee
1954,	May	Identified as deputy director of the Urban Work Department, Central-South Bureau of the CCP Central Committee

1955,	Dec	Identified as 2nd secretary of Anshan Municipalitiy CP and as manager of the Anshan Iron and Steel Company
1959,	Feb	Identified as 1st secretary, CP of Anshan Iron and Steel Company
1960,	Jun	Identified as secretary of Anshan Municipality CP and of Shanxi Province CP (until Jan 1967) as well as 1st secretary of Taiyuan Municipality CP (until Jan 1967)
1967,	Apr	Elected vice-chairman of the Revolutionary Committee of Shanxi Province; subsequently disappears
1979,	Jul	First appearance after the Cultural Revolution: Identified as member of the Standing Committee of Anhui Province CP and as vice-chairman of the Revolutionary Committee of Anhui Province (until Dec 1979)

Yue Daiheng (Yüeh Tai-heng) 岳岱衡

Posts held

Government
Deputy manager-general of the International Travel Service
Deputy director-general of the General Administration for Travel and Tourism in China

1960,	Oct	Deputy head of a delegation to the International Fair in Tunisia
1962,	Jan	Identified as 1st secretary of the Economic and Cultural Mission in Khang Khay, Laos
1964,	Apr	Identified a chargé d'affaires ad interim in Laos (until 1970)
1973,	Jun	Head of a friendship delegation to Australia
1975,	Jan	Identified as a cadre of the International Travel Service
1978,	Mar	Deputy head of a delegation of the International Travel Service to the United States
	May	Identified as deputy manager-general of the International Travel Service
	Aug	Identified as deputy director-general of the General Administration for Travel and Tourism in China

Yue Liang (Yüeh Liang) 岳良

Posts held

Government
Ambassador to Rwanda

1958,	Jul	Identified as deuty director of the General Office, Ministry of Foreign Affairs
1970,	May	Identified as a cadre of a department of the Ministry of Foreign Affairs
1971,	Feb	Appointed ambassador to Denmark (until Jul 1977)
1977,	Sep	Appointed ambassador to Rwanda

Yue Meizhong (Yüeh Mei-chung) 岳美中

<u>Posts held</u>

NPC
Member of the Standing Committee of the 5th NPC
Deputy for Shanghai Municipality to the 5th NPC

Others
Candidate chief physician at the Institute of Traditional Medicine

1963,	Feb	Member of a public health delegation to Indonesia
1978,	Feb	Elected deputy for Shanghai to the 5th NPC
	Mar	Elected member of the Standing Committee of the 5th NPC
	Jun	Identified as vice-chairman of the Preparatory Committee for the Society of Traditional Medicine
	Aug	Identified as candidate chief physician at the Institute of Traditional Medicine

Yue Weifan (Yüeh Wei-fan) 岳维藩

<u>Posts held</u>

Provincial Administration
Vice-governor of Shanxi Province

1950,	Jun	Identified as special commissioner of Yuncheng Administative District, Shanxi Province
1954,	Apr	Identified as deputy mayor of Taiyuan Municipality
1955,	Aug	Identified as mayor of Taiyuan Municipality
1958,	Dec	Elected deputy for Shanxi Province to the 2nd NPC (reelected in 1964 to the 3rd NPC)
1959,	Dec	Identified as secretary of Taiyuan Municipality CP
1965,	Sep	Identified as mayor of Nanjing Municipality
	Nov	Identified as secretary of Nanjing Municipality CP
1967,	May	Denounced as a counterrevolutionary revisionist and purged
1979,	Dec	First appearance after the Cultural Revolution: Elected vice-governor of Shanxi Province

Yue Xiaoxia (Yüeh Hsiao-hsia) 岳肖峡

<u>Posts held</u>

Provincial Administration
Vice-governor of Henan Province

| 1974, | Oct | Identified as a member of the Standing Committee of Yunnan Province CP (until 1978) |
| 1976, | Nov | Identified as director of the Office for Industry and Communications, Revolution- |

ary Committee of Yunnan Province

| 1979, | Sep | Elected vice-governor of Henan Province |

Yue Xin (Yüeh Hsin) 岳欣

<u>Posts held</u>

Government
Ambassador to Togo

1961,	May	Advisor to the Chinese delegation at the Laos Conference in Geneva
1963,	Apr-May	Member of a Chinese government delegation to Indonesia, Cambodia, and North Vietnam
1965,	Feb	Identified as deputy director of the Western Europe Department of the Ministry of Foreign Affairs (until Aug 1965)
	Aug	Appointed ambassador to Finland (until 1966)
1974,	Jul	Appointed ambassador to Togo

Yue Zhijian (Yüeh Chih-chien) 岳志坚

<u>Posts held</u>

Government
Vice-minister of the State Economic Commission
Director of the State Bureau of Standardization
Vice-president of the Recommendation and Examination Committee in charge of Classifying Inventions under the State Scientific and Technical Commission

Others
President of the Standardization Society
President of the Association of Quality Control

Yue was elected an alternate member of the Central Committee of the New Democratic Youth League in April 1949.

1964,	Apr	Identified as director of the State Bureau for Scientific and Technical Cadres
	Oct	Appointed vice-chairman of the State Scientific and Technological Commission (until Cultural Revolution)
1967,	Feb	Accused as a revisionist
1969,	Oct	Present at National Day celebration in Beijing
1970,	Sep	Head of a delegation of the Academy of Sciences to Albania
1971,	Apr	Head of a delegation of the Academy of Sciences to North Korea
1973,	Mar	Identified as acting secretary-general of the Academy of Sciences
	Apr	Head of a delegation of scientists to Romania
	Nov	Head of a delegation of scientists to Vietnam
1975,	Mar	Head of a delegation of the Academy of Sciences to Albania
1978,	Jun	Identified as a cadre of the National Bureau of Standards and Metrology

Aug Identified as president of the Standardization Society

Oct Identified as director of the State Bureau of Standardization (probably identical with the National Bureau of Standards and Metrology)

1979, Apr Appointed vice-president of the Recommendation and Examination Committee in charge of Classifying Inventions under the State Scientific and Technical Commission

Jun Identified as vice-minister of the State Economic Commission

Aug Elected president of the Association of Quality Control

Sep Head of a delegation to the 11th General Assembly of the International Organization for Standardization in Geneva

Yue Zongtai (Yüeh Tsung-t'ai) 岳宗泰

Posts held

Provincial Administration
Vice-governor of Hebei Province

1960, May Elected vice-governor of Shanxi Province (until 1961)

1965, Aug Identified as a cadre of the Industrial and Communications Department, North China Bureau of the CCP Central Committee

1977, Dec Elected vice-chairman of the Revolutionary Committee of Hebei Province (until Jan 1980)

1980, Feb Elected vice-governor of Hebei Province

Yun Beifeng (Yün Pei-feng) 云北峰

Posts held

Government
Member of the State Nationalities Affairs Commission

NPC
Director of the Office of the NPC Nationalities Committee

Others
Director of the Nationalities Institute, Academy of Social Sciences

Yun belongs to the Mongolian minority.

1978, Sep Identified as director of the Nationalities Institute of the Academy of Social Sciences

1979, May Appointed member of the State Nationalities Affairs Commission

Oct Identified as director of the Office of the NPC Nationalities Committee

Yun Shiying (Yün Shih-ying) 云世英

Posts held

CCP
Secretary of Inner Mongolia Autonomous Region CP

Provincial Administration
Vice-chairman of the People's Government of Inner Mongolia Autonomous Region

Yun belongs to the Mongolian minority.

1961, Sep Identified as deputy mayor of Baotou, Inner Mongolia Autonomous Region

1977, Dec Elected vice-chairman of the Revolutionary Committee of Inner Mongolia Autonomous Region (until Dec 1979)

1978, Sep Identified as director of the Public Security Bureau of Inner Mongolia Autonomous Region

Nov Identified as secretary of Inner Mongolia Autonomous Region CP

1979, Dec Elected vice-chairman of the People's Government of Inner Mongolia Autonomous Region

Zang Boping (Tsang Po-p'ing) 藏伯平

Posts held

Government
Vice-minister of education

1949,	Oct	Identified as deputy mayor of Shijiazhuang
1958,	Sep	Identified as 2nd secretary of the CP Committee, Beijing Aviation College
1964,	Jul	Identified as vice-president of Nankai University (until Cultural Revolution)
1979,	Dec	First appearance after the Cultural Revolution: Identified as vice-minister of education

Zeng Chengkui (Tseng Ch'eng-k'uei) 曾呈奎

Posts held

NPC
Deputy for Shandong Province to the 5th NPC

Others
Director of the Oceanographic Institute, Academy of Sciences

1964,	Sep	Elected deputy for Shandong Province to the 3rd NPC; identified as deputy director of the Institute of Marine Biology, Academy of Sciences
1966		Zeng disappears
1974,	Feb	First appearance after the Cultural Revolution
1975,	Sep	Identified as vice-chairman of the Revolutionary Committee, Oceanographic Institute of the Academy of Sciences
1977,	Feb	Identified as deputy director of the Oceanographic Institute, Academy of Sciences
1978,	Feb	Elected deputy for Shandong Province to the 5th NPC
	Mar	Head of a study group on oceanographic research ships to Japan and the U.S.A.
1979,	Jan	Identified as deputy director of the Oceanographic Institute, Academy of Sciences

Zeng Chuanliu (Tseng Ch'uan-liu) 曾传六

Posts held

Others
Member of the Standing Committee of the 5th CPPCC

Zeng was born in Hubei Province. In 1943 he was political commissar of the 31st Army, 4th Field Army.

| 1950, | Mar | Identified as member of the Financial and Economic Committee of the Central-South Military and Administrative Council |
| 1951, | Nov | Identified as director of the Trade Department, Central-South Military and Administrative Council |

1952,	Apr	Identified as vice-chairman of the Financial and Economic Committee, Central-South Military and Administrative Council
1953,	Oct	Identified as member of the Standing Committee of the Federation of Industry and Commerce
1954,	Aug	Elected deputy for Henan Province to the 1st NPC (reelected in 1958 and 1964 to the 2nd and 3rd NPC)
	Oct	Appointed vice-minister of commerce (until Feb 1958)
1958,	Feb	Appointed vice-minister of the 1st Ministry of Commerce (until Sep 1958)
	Sep	Appointed vice-minister of commerce (until Nov 1963)
1967		Disappears during the Cultural Revolution
1974,	Sep	First appearance after the Cultural Revolution
1978,	Mar	Elected member of the Standing Committee of the 5th CPPCC

Zeng Delin (Tseng Te-lin) 曾德林

Posts held

Government
Vice-minister of education

NPC
Deputy for Sichuan Province to the 5th NPC

1957,	May	Identified as a member of the Central Committee, Communist Youth League
1960,	Mar	Identified as an alternate member of the Secretariat of the Communist Youth League (until Jul 1964)
1964,	Jul	Zeng disappears
1978,	Feb	First appearance after the Cultural Revolution: Elected deputy for Sichuan Province to the 5th NPC
1979,	Nov	Identified as vice-minister of education

Zeng Dingshi (Tseng Ting-shih) 曾定石

Posts held

NPC
Deputy for Guangdong Province to the 5th NPC

Provincial Administration
Vice-governor of Guangdong Province

Others
Director of the Board of Directors, China International Trust and Investment Corporation

1960,	Dec	Identified as member of the People's Council of Guangdong Province
1964,	Sep	Identified as vice-chairman of the Planning Committee of Guangdong Province
1967		Disappears during the Cultural Revolution
1978,	Feb	First appearance after the Cultural Revolution: Elected deputy for Guangdong Province to the 5th NPC

1979, Jan Identified as vice-chairman of the Revolutionary Committee of Guangdong Province

Oct Appointed director of the Board of Directors of the China International Trust and Investment Corporation

Nov Deputy head of a Guangdong Provincial delegation, led by Xi Zhongxun, to Australia

Dec Elected vice-governor of Guangdong Province

Zeng Hanzhou (Tseng Han-chou) 曾汉周

Posts held

Others
Vice-president of the Supreme People's Court

1950, Apr Identified as director, Administration Office of the Supreme People's Court

1954, Jun Identified as deputy secretary-general of the Supreme People's Court

Nov Appointed chief judge, 1st Criminal Court of the Supreme People's Court (until 1960)

1955, Feb Appointed member of the Judicial Committee of the Supreme People's Court (until 1960)

1963 Identified as 1st chief judge, Court of Criminal Cases of the Supreme People's Court

1966, Mar Appointed vice-president of the Supreme People's Court

1967 Disappears during the Cultural Revolution

1972, Mar First appearance after the Cultural Revolution

Jul Identified in his former post as vice-president of the Supreme People's Court (confirmed in Mar 1978)

Zeng San (Tseng San) 曾三

Posts held

CCP
Deputy director of the General Office, CCP Central Committee
Member of the Commission for Inspecting Discipline, CCP Central Committee

Zeng is a native of Hunan Province. In 1931 he was the operator of the Red Army's broadcasting station in Jiangxi Province.

1950, Jun Identified as deputy director of the Administrative Office of the CCP Central Committee

1951, Apr Identified as director of the Party History Materials Office under the CCP Central Committee

1954, Aug Elected deputy for Hebei Province to the 1st NPC

Nov Appointed director of the State Archives Bureau (until Jan 1967)

1956, Sep Identified as deputy director of the General Office, CCP Central Committee (until Jan 1967)

1958, Sep Identified as council member of the Sino-Albanian Friendship Association; member of a friendship delegation to Albania

1959, Oct Appointed director of the Central Archives Library (until Jan 1967)

1965, Sep Head of an archives delegation to Albania

1967, Jan Denounced as anti-Party element and purged

1978, Dec First appearance after the Cultural Revolution: Appointed member of the Commission for Inspecting Discipline, CCP Central Committee

1979, Aug Identified as deputy director of the General Office, CCP Central Committee

Zeng Shaoshan (Tseng Shao-shan) 曾绍山

Posts held

CCP
Member of the CCP 11th Central Committee

NPC
Deputy for Liaoning Province to the 5th NPC

Military
Lieutenant-general
Political commissar of Shenyang Military Region
2nd secretary, CP Secretariat of Shenyang Military Region

Zeng was born in 1910 (1912?) in Sichuan (Hunan?) Province. He is a graduate of the Red Army Military School in Jiangxi. In 1934-35 he took part in the Long March. He then began a career in the army, reaching in 1938 the post of chief of staff of a regiment in the 129th Division, 8th Route Army. In 1941 he commanded the 2nd Military Subdistrict in Taihang Military District. He was deputy commander of the 3rd Column of Shanxi-Hebei-Shandong Military District in 1948, and in spring 1949 he became commander of the 19th Army, 2nd Field Army, which fought successfully to gain a crossing of the Chang Jiang.

1950, Aug Identified as member of the People's Council of East Sichuan (until 1951) and as deputy commander of East Sichuan Military District

1951 Appointed commander of the 12th Army serving in Korea

1953 Identified as deputy commander of the 3rd Army Group

1955 Identified as commander of Lüshun-Dalian Garrison and as member of the Joint Sino-Soviet Military Commission in Lüshun-Dalian preparing the transfer of the city to Chinese administration

Sep Appointed lieutenant-general

1959 Identified as deputy commander of Shenyang Military Region (until 1968)

1968, Mar Identified as political commissar of Shenyang Military Region

1969,	Apr	Elected member of the CCP Central Committee by the 9th Party Congress (confirmed in 1973 and 1977 by the 10th and 11th Congresses)
1971,	Jan	Elected 2nd secretary of Liaoning Province CP (until Sep 1975)
1973,	Jan	Identified as vice-chairman of the Revolutionary Committee of Liaoning Province (until Sep 1975)
1975,	Jun	Head of PLA friendship delegation to Romania
	Sep	Identified as 1st secretary of the CP, and as chairman of the Revolutionary Committee, of Liaoning Province (both posts until Sep 1978)
1977,	Jun	Identified as 2nd secretary, CP Secretariat of Shenyang Military Region
1978,	Feb	Elected deputy for Liaoning Province to the 5th NPC

Zeng Sheng (Tseng Sheng)   曾　生

Posts held

Government
Minister of communications

NPC
Member of the Standing Committee of the 5th NPC
Deputy for Guangdong Province to the 5th NPC

Military
Rear admiral

Others
President of the Marine Navigation Society

Zeng, formerly known as Zeng Zhensheng, is married to Ruan Qunying. He was born in 1910 in Huiyang, Guangdong Province, and attended school in Hong Kong. After school he went to Australia with his father to live in Sydney for six years. After his return to China he studied at Zhongshan University in Guangzhou. In 1935 he was a leading member of the student movement in Guangzhou propagating the "December 9 Movement" initiated by the Communists. In order to escape arrest for Communist activities he fled to Hong Kong where he signed on as a seaman on the "Queen Mary." During his period in Hong Kong he was also head of the Organization Department of the Hong Kong Seamen's Association. When Guangdong was occupied by the Japanese in 1938, Zeng organized seamen and students to form a guerrilla unit to operate in the Huiyang-Danshui Area. In 1939 this unit was integrated as the New Brigade of the 3rd Guerrilla Corps, 4th War Zone, into the Guangdong Guerrilla Headquarters of the Nationalist Government. In March 1940 Zeng revolted with this unit against the Nationalist Government. On instruction from Mao Zedong he then joined a Communist guerrilla unit operating in the area of the Guangzhou-Kowloon (Jiulong) Railway. In late 1943 he became commander of this unit. In 1946, after the beginning of negotiations between the CCP and the KMT, Zeng was appointed vice-chancellor of the Military and Political University in Shandong. He returned as commander to his old guerrilla unit in Guangdong in 1947 where he played an important part in numerous battles, particularly the battle of Huaihai.

1950,	Jan	Appointed council member of the People's Government of Guangdong Province
	Jul	Appointed deputy commander of Guangdong Military Region and commander of the Zhu Jiang (Pearl River) Military Subregion
	later	Appointed member of the South China Bureau of the CCP Central Committee
1954,	Aug	Elected deputy for Guangdong Province to the 1st NPC
1957,	Aug	Appointed rear-admiral
1960,	Dec	Elected vice-governor of Guangdong Province and mayor of Guangzhou (until Cultural Revolution)
1961,	Mar	Appointed secretary of Guangzhou Municipality CP (until Cultural Revolution)
1963,	Mar	Identified as member of the Standing Committee of Guangdong Province CP (until Cultural Revolution)
1964,	May	Member of the Chinese delegation attending a test flight of Pakistan International Airlines; member of the Chinese delegation to Cambodia for the opening of a direct air link between the two countries; acting chairman of the Spring Fair in Guangzhou
	Jun	Head of a delegation of Guangzhou Municipal Administration to Albania
	Nov	Identified as chairman of the Guangzhou Section, Sino-Soviet Friendship Association (until Cultural Revolution)
1965,	Mar	Identified as 3rd secretary of Guangzhou Municipality CP (until Cultural Revolution)
1967		At the height of the Cultural Revolution, Zeng is heavily attacked and eventually disappears in March
1974,	Sep	First appearance after the Cultural Revolution
1975,	Jan	Elected member of the Standing Committee by the 4th NPC (confirmed in Mar 1978 by the 5th NPC)
	Oct	Identified as vice-minister of communications (until Feb 1979)
	Nov	Head of a communications delegation to Great Britain
1978,	Feb	Elected deputy for Guangdong Province to the 5th NPC
1979,	Feb	Appointed minister of communications
	Mar	Zeng heads a government marine shipping delegation to Thailand
	Apr	Elected president of the Marine Navigation Society
	Sep	Head of a communications delegation to France and Italy
	Dec	Head of a communications delegation to the Philippines

Zeng Siyu (Tseng Szu-yü)   曾思玉

Posts held

CCP
Member of the CCP 11th Central Committee

NPC
Deputy for the PLA to the 5th NPC

Military
Lieutenant-general

Zeng was born in 1907 in Sichuan Province. Before the Long March he served in the 1st Front Army reaching the rank of regiment commander. In 1937-38 he was head of the Political Department of a regiment of the 115th Division, 8th Route Army. In 1941 he was political commissar of the 8th Military Subdistrict in West Shandong Military District, as well as political commissar of a unit of the New 4th Army. In 1949 he was appointed commander of the 64th Army, 1st Field Army.

1951		Service in the Korean War as commander of the 64th Army (until 1953)
1954		Identified as deputy commander of the 19th Army
1955,	Sep	Promoted to the rank of lieutenant-general; identified as deputy commander of Shenyang Military Region (until 1967)
1963,	Oct	Member of a Party and military delegation to North Korea
1964,	Sep	Elected deputy for the PLA in Shenyang to the 3rd NPC
1967,	Aug	Identified as commander of Wuhan Military Region (until Dec 1973)
1968,	Feb	With the establishment of the Revolutionary Committee of Hubei Province, Zeng is elected chairman (until Dec 1973)
1969,	Apr	Elected to first term as member of the CCP Central Committee by the 9th Party Congress
1971,	Mar	Elected 1st secretary of Hubei Province CP (until Dec 1973)
1974,	Jan	Identified as commander of Jinan Military Region (until Jan 1980)
1976,	Oct	Identified as 1st secretary, CP Secretariat of Jinan Military Region (until Jan 1980)
1978,	Feb	Elected deputy for the PLA to the 5th NPC

Zeng Tao (Tseng T'ao) 曾 涛

Posts held

Government
Director of XNA
Member of the Patriotic Health Campaign Committee

NPC
Deputy secretary-general of the NPC Standing Committee

Zeng was born in 1914 in Jiangsu Province.

1951		Identified as deputy secretary of the Work Committee of Zhenjiang CP in Jiangsu Province
1956,	Sep	Identified as secretary-general, People's Council of Shanghai Municipality (until 1960)
1960,	Mar	Elected council member of the Sino-Latin-American Friendship Association
	May	Identified as head of the Havana Bureau of XNA (until Mar 1961)
1961,	May	Advisor to the Chinese delegation at the Geneva Laos Conference

	Aug	Secretary-general of the Foreign Affairs Office in the State Council (until Nov 1962)
1962,	Nov	Appointed ambassador to Algeria (until about 1967)
1970,	Aug	Appointed ambassador to Yugoslavia (until Apr 1973)
1973,	May	Appointed ambassador to France (until Feb 1977)
1977,	Apr	Identified as deputy director of XNA
	Nov	Head of a delegation of journalists to Denmark, Great Britain, Italy
	Dec	Identified as director of XNA
1978,	Apr	Appointed member of the Patriotic Health Campaign Committee
	Aug	Head of a delegation of journalists to the U.S.A. and Canada; head of a delegation of XNA to Yugoslavia and Romania
	Nov	Appointed deputy secretary-general of the NPC Standing Committee

Zeng Xianzhi (Tseng Hsien-chih) (f) 曾宪植

Posts held

Mass Organization
Vice-president of the Women's Federation

Others
Member of the Standing Committee of the 5th CPPCC

Zeng is the wife of Ye Jianying. She was born in Xiangxiang, Hunan Province, and spent her childhood in Changsha. As a young woman she studied in Japan, probably at Waseda University. In spring 1949 she was elected deputy secretary-general, and alternate member of the Central Committee, of the Democratic Women's Federation.

1952,	Sep	Identified as director of the Administration Department, Democratic Women's Federation
1953,	Apr	Elected member of the Standing Committee, Democratic Women's Federation
1954,	Aug	Elected deputy for Hunan Province to the 1st NPC
1957,	Sep	Elected member of the Executive Council of the Women's Federation (successor organization of the Democratic Women's Federation)
1959,	Apr	Elected member of the 3rd CPPCC
1965,	Jan	Elected member of the Standing Committee of the 4th CPPCC (confirmed in Mar 1978 by the 5th CPPCC)
1978,	Sep	Elected vice-president of the Women's Federation

Zeng Yongquan (Tseng Yung-ch'üan) 曾湧泉

Posts held

Others
Member of the Standing Committee of the 5th CPPCC

Zeng was born in 1906 in Hunan Province. In 1949 he was vice-president of the North China Military and Political College.

1950,	Feb	Appointed counselor at the embassy in Moscow
1952,	Aug	Appointed ambassador to Poland (until Jan 1955)
1955,	Jan	Appointed ambassador to the German Democratic Republic (until Jun 1957)
1957,	Jun	Appointed vice-minister of foreign affairs (until March 1966)
1961,	Oct	Member of a Party and government delegation to the German Democratic Republic
1966,	Jan	Appointed ambassador to Romania (until 1969)
1972,	Apr	First appearance after the Cultural Revolution: Present at mourning ceremonies for Li Dequan; subsequently disappears again until Jan 1976
1976,	Jan	Present at mourning ceremonies for Zhou Enlai
1978,	Mar	Elected member of the Standing Committee of the 5th CPPCC

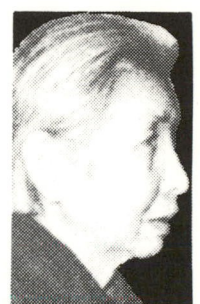

Zeng Zhi (Tseng Chih) (f)　　曾　志

Posts held

Government
Vice-minister of communications

NPC
Member of the Standing Committee of the 5th NPC
Deputy for Jiangxi Province to the 5th NPC

Zeng, the widow of Tao Zhu, was born in Yizhang, Hunan Province. She joined the CCP in 1933. During the final phase of the Revolutionary Period she temporarily served as deputy director of the Industry Department of Central Plains Provisional People's Government.

1950,	Mar	Identified as deputy director of the Industry Department, Central-South China Military and Administrative Council (until Jan 1951)
1951,	Jan	Identified as director of the Industry Department, Central-South China Military and Administrative Council
1954,	Aug	Elected deputy for Guangzhou Municipality to the 1st NPC
1955,	Jul	Identified as deputy secretary of Guangzhou Municipality CP (until Jul 1958)
1956,	Nov	Elected member of the People's Council of Guangzhou Municipality
1958,	Jul	Identified as secretary of Guangzhou Municipality CP
	Sep	Elected deputy for Guangdong to the 2nd NPC (reelected in 1964 to the 3rd NPC)
1963,	Jul	Identified as alternate member of Guangdong Province CP
1965,	Jan	Elected member of the Standing Committee by the 3rd NPC

1967		At the height of the Cultural Revolution, Zeng is criticized together with her husband and disappears
1973,	May	First appearance after the Cultural Revolution: Named in her former post as member of the Standing Committee of the NPC
1975,	Jan	Confirmed by the 4th NPC as member of the Standing Committee (again confirmed in Mar 1978 by the 5th NPC)
1978,	Feb	Elected deputy for Jiangxi Province to the 5th NPC
	Sep	Identified as deputy director, Organization Department of the CCP Central Committee (until Aug 1979?)
1979,	Jun	Member of the Committee to Examine Proposals at the 2nd Session of the 5th NPC
	Sep	Identified as vice-minister of communications

Zha Yusheng (Cha Yü-sheng)　　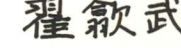

Posts held

NPC
Deputy for the PLA to the 5th NPC

Military
Deputy Commander of Kunming Military Region

1949		Identified as commander of the 41st Division, 14th Army Corps of the 2nd Field Army
1952		Identified as chief of staff, 14th Army Corps
1962		Identified as commander, 14th Army Corps
1965		Identified as deputy chief of staff of Kunming Military Region, which post Zha retained through the Cultural Revolution
1972,	Nov	Identified as deputy commander of the Kunming Military Region
1978,	Feb	Elected deputy for the PLA to the 5th NPC

Zhai Xiwu (Chai Hsi-wu)　　翟歆武

Posts held

CCP
Member of the Standing Committee of Zhejiang Province CP

Provincial Administration
Vice-governor of Zhejiang Province

1960,	Dec	Identified as director of the Office of Light Industry of Chekiang Province
1978,	Feb	Identified as vice-chairman of the Revolutionary Committee of Zhejiang Province (until Dec 1979)
	Sep	Identified as member of the Standing Committee of Zhejiang Province CP
1979,	Dec	Elected vice-governor of Zhejiang Province

Zhan Caifang (Chan Ts'ai-fang)

Posts held

NPC
Member of the Standing Committee, 5th NPC
Deputy for the PLA to the 5th NPC

Military
Lieutenant-general
Deputy commander, Guangzhou Military Region

Zhan is a native of Hubei Province. In early 1934 he was deputy commander of the 9th Army, 4th Front Army. It was probably in this unit that he took part in the Long March. During the Anti-Japanese War Zhan was deputy commander of the 3rd Military Subdistrict of West Hebei Military District in the Shanxi-Hebei Military Border Region. In November 1945 he served as deputy commander in Hebei-Rehe-Liaoning Military Region, and in July 1946 as commander of East Hebei Military District. Until the establishment of the People's Republic, Zhan commanded the 46th Brigade, 1st Army Corps of the 4th Field Army. In 1948 he was given the command of the 9th Army Corps, 4th Field Army, and one year later of the 46th Army Corps of the same army.

1950,	Mar	Identified as council member, Hunan Provincial Government
	Winter	Zhan takes part in the Korean War
1951,	Jul	Member of the Central-South China Military and Administrative Council
1952		Identified as commander, Public Security Forces, Central-South China Military Region
	Sep	Promoted to the rank of lieutenant-general
1955		Identified as deputy commander of Guangzhou Military Region and as commander of the Public Security Forces of Central-South China Military Region (?)
1958,	Jul	Elected deputy for the PLA to the 2nd NPC (reelected Sep 1964)
1959,	Apr	Elected member, National Defense Council; reelected Jan 1965 (the Defense Council was abolished during the Cultural Revolution)
1967,	Feb	Elected member, Standing Committee, Revolutionary Committee of Guangdong Province (subsequently not referred to in this post)
1978,	Feb	Elected deputy for the PLA to the 5th NPC
	Mar	Elected member of the Standing Committee, 5th NPC

Zhan Danan (Chan Ta-nan)

Posts held

Military
Major-general
Deputy commander of Nanjing Military Region

Zhan is a native of Shanxi Province. In 1935 he commanded a battalion, and in 1938 a regiment, of the Bingxi

Vanguard Army. In 1947 he was promoted to the post of commander, 5th Heavy Weapons Brigade.

1952		Identified as deputy commander of the 27th Corps, 3rd Field Army
1961		Identified as commander of the 28th Army
1965,	Nov	Identified as major-general and deputy commander of Lanzhou Military Region
1972,	Nov	Identified as deputy commander of Nanjing Military Region

Zhan Wu (Chan Wu)

Posts held

Others
Director of the Agricultural Economics Research Institute, Academy of Sciences

| 1957, | Sep | Identified as assistant manager-general of the Bank of China |
| 1979, | Mar | Identified as director of the Agricultural Economics Research Institute, Acacemy of Sciences; deputy head of an Academy of Social Sciences delegation to Australia |

Zhang Aiping (Chang Ai-p'ing) 张爱萍

Posts held

CCP
Member of the CCP 11th Central Committee

Government
Chairman, Scientific and Technological Commission for National Defense

NPC
Member of the Standing Committee, 5th NPC
Deputy for the PLA to the 5th NPC

Military
Colonel-general
Deputy chief, PLA General Staff

Zhang was born in 1908 in Sichuan Province. In 1927 he took part in an uprising in Hunan Province which had been organized by Peng Dehuai, and then served in the 5th Red Army commanded by Peng. From 1929 onward he led a unit of the 1st Division, 14th Red Army, operating in Jiangsu Province. In 1931 he headed the Organization Department of the Young Pioneers Corps in the Jiangxi Soviet. After the Long March, in which he probably took part, he was political commissar of the Cavalry Corps of the Workers' and Peasants' Red Army in North Shaanxi. Also in North Shaanxi he attended a course at the CCP Military Academy in 1936. In 1939, as commander of a regiment, he set up a guerrilla base in Anhui, and in the following year was made commander of the Huaibei Corps, New 4th Army. In January 1941 this unit joined with three others to form the New 4th Army's 3rd Division of which Zhang became deputy commander. This division operated in Jiangsu. In 1948 Zhang was identified as chief-of-staff of the 3rd Field Army (until 1954) and of the East China Military Region.

1952,	Jan	Identified as commander, 7th Army Corps, 3rd Field Army (until Jan 1954)

1952, Jan Identified as commander, 7th Army Corps, 3rd Field Army (until Jan 1954)

Sep Member of the East China Military and Administrative Council (until Jan 1953)

1953, Jan Member of the East China Administrative Council (until Aug 1954)

1954, Sep Appointed member of the National Defense Council; appointed deputy chief of PLA general staff

1955, Sep Made lieutenant-general, awarded orders of "1st August," "Independence and Freedom," and "Liberation"

1958, Jan Member of a military delegation to India; identified as colonel-general

1958, May Elected alternate member of the 8th CCP Central Committee by its 2nd Plenary Session

1960, Dec Head of a military delegation as part of the friendship delegation to Burma headed by Zhou Enlai

1967 During the Cultural Revolution accused as counterrevolutionary and relieved of all posts

1973, Oct First appearance after the Cultural Revolution

1975, Dec Identified as chairman, Scientific and Technological Commission for National Defense

1977, Aug Elected member of the CCP Central Committee by the 11th Party Congress

Oct Identified as deputy chief of PLA general staff

1978, Feb Elected deputy for the PLA to the 5th NPC

Mar Elected member of the Standing Committee, 5th NPC

Jun Head of a military goodwill delegation to Sweden and Italy

Zhang is married to Li Yulan.

Zhang Baifa (Chang Pai-fa)　张百发

Posts held

Government
Vice-minister of the State Capital Construction Commission

Zhang is a former construction worker.

1959 Zhang is head of the youth shock brigade that takes part in building the Great Hall of the People

Apr Elected deputy for Beijing Municipality to the 2nd NPC (confirmed in 1964 by the 3rd NPC)

1974, Sep Identified as a State Council cadre

1975, Apr Identified as vice-president of the Society of Architecture; head of a delegation of architects to Algeria

1976, Mar Identified as vice-minister of the State Capital Construction Commission

1977, Apr Appointed deputy secretary-general of the National Dazhai Conference

1978, Aug Member of a government delegation led by Chen Muhua to Somalia, Gabon, and Cameroon

Zhang Bangying (Chang Pang-ying)　张邦英

Posts held

Others
Member of the Standing Committee of the 5th CPPCC

Zhang was born in 1907 in Yao County, Shaanxi Province. He joined the Communists when they entered his native area after the Long March. Until 1949 he served in various offices mainly as a cadre of organization departments.

1949, Dec Identified as vice chairman of the People's Government of Shaanxi Province (until Jan 1953)

1950, Mar Identified as director of the Public Security Department of the Shaanxi People's Government

1951, Oct Identified as 3rd secretary, Xinjiang Subbureau in the CCP Central Committee (until 1958)

1953, Jan Identified as member of the Northwest China Administrative Council (until Nov 1954)

Dec Identified as director of the Political Department of Xinjiang Military Region

1954, Aug Elected deputy for Xinjiang Province to the 1st NPC

1957, Aug Member of an NPC delegation to Finland

1958, May Identified as deputy director of the Communications Work Department in the CCP Central Committee (until Cultural Revolution)

1959, Apr Elected member of the Standing Committee of the 3rd CPPCC (reelected in 1965 and 1978 to the 4th and 5th CPPCCs)

1960, Jan Appointed member of the Sparetime Education Committee under the State Council (until Cultural Revolution)

1963, Jul Identified as alternate secretary of the North China Bureau in the CCP Central Committee (until Cultural Revolution)

1967 Disappears during the Cultural Revolution

1973, May First appearance after the Cultural Revolution: Again referred to in his previous post as a member of the Standing Committee of the CPPCC (confirmed by the 5th CPPCC in 1978)

Zhang Bin (Chang Pin)　张彬

Posts held

Government
Vice-minister of power industry

1949, Oct Appointed deputy director of the North China General Electric Administrative Bureau under the Ministry of Fuel Industry

1954, Aug Elected delegate to the 1st Wuhan Municipality Congress (reelected in 1961)

1964, Jun Appointed vice-minister of water conservancy and electric power (until Feb 1979). Apart from a short absence, Zhang continues in this post throughout the Cultural Revolution

1971, Oct Head of a government delegation to Albania to inaugurate the Vau i Dejes Power Plant built with Chinese aid

1977, Dec Head of an electric power mission to Romania and

1978, Feb the Federal Republic of Germany and France

1979, Sep Identified as vice-minister of power industry

Zhang Binggui (Chang Ping-kuei) 张秉贵

Posts held

NPC
Member of the Standing Committee of the 5th NPC
Deputy for Beijing Municipality to the 5th NPC

Zhang was born in 1918. He won praise as a model worker in the candy section of the Beijing Department Store.

1978, Feb Elected deputy for Beijing Municipality to the 5th NPC

Mar Elected member of the Standing Committee of the 5th NPC; identified as a sales clerk at the Beijing Department Store

Zhang Bingyu (Chang Ping-yü) 张秉玉

Posts held

Government
Deputy director of the Foreign Affairs Bureau in the Ministry of National Defense

Chang was born in 1917.

1955, Oct Identified as military attaché at the embassy in Hungary

1956, Aug Identified as military attaché at the embassy in Bulgaria

1958, Jun Identified as deputy director of the Foreign Affairs Bureau in the Ministry of National Defense

1960, Oct Identified as senior-colonel of the PLA

1965, Jul Identified as military attaché at the embassy in Paris (until Cultural Revolution)

1966 Disappears during the Cultural Revolution

1975, Oct First appearance after the Cultural Revolution: Identified as deputy director of the Foreign Affairs Bureau in the Ministry of National Defense; member of a friendship delegation to North Korea

1977, Sep Member of a military delegation to France and Romania

1978, Jun Member of a military goodwill delegation to Sweden and Italy (head: Zhang Aiping)

Sep Zhang accompanies Zhang Caiqian to Mexico

Zhang Bochuan (Chang Po-ch'uan) 张勃川

Posts held

Government
Ambassador to Uganda

Zhang belongs to the Hui minority. In 1948 he was vice-president of the East China University.

1951 Identified as deputy director of the Department of Higher Education, Ministry of Education

1953, Feb Member of a scientific delegation to the USSR

1954, Jun Identified as vice-president of Wuhan University

1962, Jun Appointed ambassador to Finland (until Jul 1965)

1965, Jul Zhang disappears

1980, Jan First appearance after the Cultural Revolution: Appointed ambassador to Uganda

Zhang Caiqian (Chang Ts'ai-ch'ien) 张才千

Posts held

CCP
Member, CCP 11th Central Committee

Military
Lieutenant-general
Commander of Wuhan Military Region

Zhang was born in 1912 in Anhui Province. In the early 1940s he served in the 5th Division of the New 4th Army. In 1945 he commanded a brigade of the 1st Corps, Central Plains Military Region, and was concurrently commander of 4th Military District South Hubei. In 1946 he led guerrilla units in West Henan.

1950, Mar Identified as council member, People's Government of Hupei Province and as chief of staff of Hubei Military District

1951 Identified as commander of the 44th Army Corps

1952 After the reorganization of the 44th Army Corps, Zhang took part in the Korean War as chief of staff, 13th Army Chinese People's Volunteers

1955, Sep Promoted to rank of lieutenant-general and appointed chief of staff of Nanjing Military Region

1958, Apr Identified as deputy commander of Nanjing Military Region (until 1970)

1969, Apr Elected member of the CCP Central Committee by the 9th Party Congress (confirmed in 1973 and 1977 by the 10th and 11th Congresses)

1971, Jun Identified as deputy chief of PLA General Staff (until Jan 1980)

1974, Jan Leader of a military delegation to Pakistan

Oct Leader of a military goodwill delegation to Zambia

1978, Sep Leader of a military delegation to Japan and Mexico

1979, Feb Leader of a military delegation to Bangladesh

Oct   Leader of a military friendship delegation to Pakistan
1980,   Feb   Identified as commander of Wuhan Military Region

Zhang is married to Po Tao.

Zhang Canming (Chang Ts'an-ming) 张 灿 明

Posts held

Government
Vice-minister of foreign affairs

Zhang was born in Sichuan Province in 1914.

1952,   Feb(?)   Appointed deputy director of the East China Branch, Federation of Trade Unions (until Oct 1955)
         Jul   Appointed member of the Standing Committee, East China Branch, Chinese Peace Council (until Oct 1955)
         Oct   Appointed member of the Political and Legal Committee and deputy director of the Labor Department, East China Administrative Council (until Oct 1955)
1953,   Apr   Member of the Chinese Trade Union delegation to May Day celebrations in Moscow
1955,   Oct   Appointed director of the Consular Affairs Department, Ministry of Foreign Affairs (until Mar 1957)
1957,   May   Appointed ambassador to Ceylon (until Aug 1962)
1963,   Sep   Appointed ambassador to Mongolian People's Republic (until about 1966)
1971,   Oct   Reactivated after the Cultural Revolution
1973,   Feb   Appointed ambassador to Yemen (until Jul 1975)
1975,   Sep   Appointed ambassador to Finland (until Nov 1978)
1979,   Mar   Identified as vice-minister of foreign affairs; accompanies Zhen Muhua to Fiji

Zhang Ce (Chang Ts'e) 张 策

Posts held

CCP
Deputy secretary, Commission for Inspecting Discipline, CCP Central Committee
Secretary of Shaanxi Province CP

Government
Member of the Birth Planning Leading Group under the State Council

Others
Member of the Standing Committee of the 5th CPPCC

Zhang was born around 1919 in Mishui, Shaanxi Province. He joined the CCP as a youth and infiltrated into KMT service, becoming a member of the Treaty Committee of the Ministry of Foreign Affairs in 1937. In 1945 he belonged to Gao Gang's team posted to Manchuria. In 1948 he was appointed vice-governor of Xing'an Province.

1949,   Oct   Appointed secretary of Songjiang Province CP (until Sep 1952)
1952,   Nov   Appointed vice-minister of communications (until Oct 1954)
1953   Involved in purge of Gao Gang, but pardoned after self-criticism
1954,   Nov   Appointed deputy secretary-general of the State Council (until Apr 1958)
1958,   May   Identified as secretary of Shaanxi Province CP (until May 1968)
         Aug   Identified as 1st secretary, Xi'an Municipality CP
1967   Disappears during Cultural Revolution
1973,   Sep   First appearance after Cultural Revolution: Identified as vice-chairman of the Revolutionary Committee of Shaanxi Province (until Dec 1979) and as member of the Standing Committee, Shaanxi Province CP
1977,   Nov   Identified as secretary of Shaanxi Province CP
1978,   Mar   Elected member of the Standing Committee, 5th CPPCC
         Jul   Identified as member of the Birth Planning Leading Group under the State Council
         Dec   Elected Deputy Secretary of the Commission for Inspecting Discipline under the Central Committee of the CCP

Zhang Chengxian (Chang Ch'eng-hsien)

张 承 先

Posts held

CCP
Member of the Commission for Inspecting Discipline under the CCP Central Committee

Government
Vice-minister of education

Zhang was born in Shandong Province. From 1947 he served in the Mass Movement Department of Hebei-Shandong Military District. In 1949 he became director of the Propaganda Department of Pingyuan Province CP.

1953   Identified as member of the North China Administrative Council
1954,   May   Identified as deputy secretary of Hebei Province CP (until Jul 1957)
1955,   Sep   Identified as vice-governor of Hebei Province (until Apr 1958)
1957,   Jul   Elected secretary of Hebei Province CP (until May 1966)
1966,   Jun   Zhang heads a work team to Beijing University to take over the Beijing University CP Committee
         Jul   Identified as secretary, Beijing Municipality CP; disappears
1977,   Jul   First appearance after the Cultural Revolution; identified as vice-chairman of the Revolutionary Committee of Hebei Province CP (until Feb 1979)
         Nov   Identified as a member of the Standing Committee of Hebei Province CP

1978,   Dec   Appointed member of the Commission for Inspecting Discipline under the CCP Central Committee

1979,   May   Identified as vice-minister of education

         Jun   Head of an educational delegation to North Korea

Zhang Chengzong (Chang Ch'eng-tsung) 张承宗

Posts held

CCP
Director of the United Front Work Department, Shanghai Municipality CP

Provincial Administration
Vice-chairman of the Standing Committee of the People's Congress, Shanghai Municipality

Others
Vice-chairman of the CPPCC, Shanghai Branch

1950,   Sep   Identified as deputy director of the Organization Department of Shanghai Municipality CP

1952,   Sep   Identified as deputy director of the East China Textile Bureau under the Ministry of Textile Industry

1955,   Oct   Identified as director of the East China Textile Bureau under the Ministry of Textile Industry

1959,   Jun   Identified as director of the Bureau of Textile Industry, People's Government of Shanghai Municipality (until 1962)

1962,   Jul   Identified as vice-mayor of Shanghai (until Jan 1967)

1965,   Feb   Head of a Shanghai friendship delegation to the USSR

1967,   Jan   Denounced as a counterrevolutionary and paraded in Shanghai

1978,   Mar   Identified as director of the United Front Work Department of Shanghai Municipality CP

1979,   May   Identified as vice-chairman of the Revolutionary Committee of Shanghai Municipality (until Dec 1979), and identified as vice-chairman of the CPPCC, Shanghai Branch

         Dec   Identified as vice-chairman of the Standing Committee of the People's Congress, Shanghai Municipality

Zhang Chong (Chang Ch'ung) 张冲

Posts held

NPC
Deputy for Yunnan Province to the 5th NPC

Provincial Administration
Vice-chairman, People's Congress of Yunnan Province

Others
Vice-president, 5th CPPCC

Zhang belongs to the Yi minority. He was born in 1900 in Luxi, Yunnan Province. He was educated at the Bijie Officers' School in Guizhou. As a young man he had joined a group of bandits after having killed the murderer of his father. In 1917 he surrendered to the Yunnan Army. Serving in this and later in the 38th Army he rose to the rank of division commander by 1927. In 1931 he was made brigade commander, in 1938 commander of the New 3rd Army, and in 1940 commander of the 2nd Route Army. In 1946 he was elected delegate to the Constitutional Assembly. In 1947 he changed over to the Communists and became vice-governor of Xinjiang Province. In September 1949 he took part as delegate for the Yi minority in the 1st CPPCC.

1950,   Mar   Appointed vice-governor, Yunnan Province

         Jul   Appointed member, Southwest China Military and Administrative Council (until Jan 1953)

1953,   Jan   Appointed member, Southwest China Military and Administrative Council (until 1954)

1954,   Aug   Elected deputy for Yunnan Province to the 1st NPC (reelected in 1959 and 1964 to 2nd and 3rd NPCs)

1967   Disappears during the Cultural Revolution

1975,   May   First appearance after Cultural Revolution

         Sep   Identified as vice-chairman of the Revolutionary Committee of Yunnan Province (reelected Dec 1977; until Dec 1979)

1978,   Feb   Elected deputy for Yunnan Province to the NPC

         Mar   Elected vice-president of the 5th CPPCC

1979,   Dec   Elected vice-chairman, People's Congress of Yunnan Province

Zhang Dequn (Chang Te-ch'ün) 张德群

Posts held

Government
Ambassador to Brazil

1960,   Aug   Appointed counselor, embassy in the USSR

1970,   Dec   Appointed ambassador to Cuba (until Feb 1975)

1975,   Apr   Appointed ambassador to Brazil

Zhang Dingcheng (Chang Ting-ch'eng) 张鼎丞

Posts held

CCP
Member of the CCP 11th Central Committee

NPC
Vice-chairman, Standing Committee of the 5th NPC
Deputy for Fujian Province

Zhang was born in 1897 as the son of poor peasants in Yongding County, Fujian Province. After teaching at the primary school in his native village he attended in 1922 a course at the Guangdong Peasants' Seminar in Guangzhou which was supervised by Mao Zedong. Impressed with the communist ideas he was there introduced to, he probably returned home then and began organizing peasants' associations. During 1927-28 he set up Communist guerrilla units in Fujian and was temporarily chairman of the West Fujian Soviet Government. Zhang was first identified as CCP Central Committee member in 1928. In 1933 he commanded a guerrilla unit which called itself 21st Army. During the Long March he led guerrilla activities in Fujian-Jiangxi Border Region. After he joined the guerrilla forces of Deng Zihui and Tan Zhenlin in 1935, he established the Southwest Fujian Military and Administrative Council of which he became chairman. At the beginning of the Anti-Japanese War his troops were integrated into the New 4th Army commanded by Ye Ting, to form its 2nd Detachment. After the Southern Anhui incident of January 1941, when the New 4th Army was virtually destroyed by the KMT allies, Zhang became commander of the reorganized 4th Army under Chen Yi's command. After the end of the Anti-Japanese War Zhang became involved in the Red Army's training program. In 1949 he was elected to the National Committee of the 1st CPPCC.

1950,	Oct	Appointed member of the Overseas Chinese Affairs Commission, Government Administration Council; member of the East China Military and Administrative Council; chairman, People's Government of Fujian Province; political commissar of Fujian Military Region, and CP secretary of Fujian Province
1952,	Oct	Appointed chairman of the Political and Legal Committee, East China Military and Administrative Council. Following reorganization of this Council
1953,	Jan	Appointed vice-chairman of the Political and Legal Committee, East China Administrative Council (until Jul 1954)
1954,	Oct	Elected deputy for Fujian Province to the 1st NPC (confirmed in 1959 by the 2nd NPC) and vice-procurator of the Supreme People's Procuratorate (until Apr 1959)
1956,	Sep	Elected member of the CCP Central Committee by the 8th Party Congress
1959,	Apr	Appointed chief procurator of the Supreme People's Procuratorate (this office was abolished after the Cultural Revolution)
1975,	Jan	Elected vice-chairman of the 4th NPC Standing Committee (reelected to the same post for the 5th NPC)
1977,	Sep	Article in RMRB of 20 September: "The Rectification Campaign at the Party School of the CCP Central Committee in Yan'an"
1978,	Feb	Elected deputy to the 5th NPC for Fujian Province

Zhang Fengyun (Chang Feng-yün) (f)

Posts held

NPC
Member of the Standing Committee of the 5th NPC
Deputy for the PLA to the 5th NPC

Military
Deputy commander of an air force squadron

1978,	Feb	Elected deputy for the PLA to the 5th NPC
	Mar	Elected member of the Standing Committee of the 5th NPC
	May	Identified as deputy commander of an air force squadron

Zhang Fucai (Chang Fu-ts'ai)   张福财

Posts held

NPC
Member of the Standing Committee of the 5th NPC
Deputy for Hunan Province to the 5th NPC

1975,	Jan	Elected member of the Standing Committee of the 4th NPC (confirmed in 1978 by the 5th NPC)
1978,	Feb	Elected deputy for Hunan Province to the 5th NPC
	Jul	Identified as deputy director of the Coking Plant, Xiangtan Iron and Steel Works, Hunan Province

Zhang Fugui (Chang Fu-kuei)   张富贵

Posts held

CCP
Member, 11th CCP Central Committee

NPC
Deputy for Shandong Province to the 5th NPC

Provincial Administration
Vice-chairman of the People's Congress of Shandong Province

Mass Organization
Chairman, Peasants' Federation of Shandong Province

Others
Chairman, Dong Fang Hong Production Brigade, Gaocun People's Commune, Wendong County, Shandong Province

Zhang was born in 1919 in Wendong, Shandong Province.

1949		Declared model agricultural worker in his native village
1950		Made model agricultural worker of Shandong Province
1960-1962		In a number of publications Zhang criticizes Liu Shaoqi as an advocate of private plots for peasants
1964,	Sep	Elected deputy for Shandong Province to the 3rd NPC
1967,	Mar	Elected Standing Committee member of the Shandong Province Revolutionary Committee (until May 1969)

1969,	Apr	Elected to first term as CCP Central Committee member by the 9th Party Congress
	May	Identified as vice-chairman of Shandong Province Revolutionary Committee (not later referred to in this post)
1975,	May	Identified as chairman of the Shandong Province Peasants' Federation
1976,	Oct	Identified as vice-chairman of Shandong Province Revolutionary Committee (re-elected Dec 1977) (until Dec 1979)
1979,	Dec	Elected vice-chairman of the People's Congress of Shandong Province

Zhang Fuheng (Chang Fu-heng) 张富恒

Posts held

CCP
Member, CCP 11th Central Committee
Member, Standing Committee of Tianjin CP

Others
Vice-chairman, Revolutionary Committee, Tianjin No. 1 Machine Tool Factory

1969,	Apr	Elected to first term as member of the CCP Central Committee by the 9th Party Congress
1972,	Jul	Member of a workers' delegation to Romania; identified as Standing Committee member of Tianjin Municipality CP, as vice-chairman of the Tianjin Revolutionary Committee (until Dec 1977), and as vice-chairman of the Revolutionary Committee of Tianjin No. 1 Machine Tool Factory
1973,	May	Elected chairman of the Tianjin Trade Union (until 1976?)

Zhang Gensheng (Chang Ken-sheng) 张根生

Posts held

Government
Vice-minister of agriculture

1951,	Mar	Identified as secretary, CP of Zhujiang County, Guangdong Province
1952,	Feb	Identified as secretary, Beijiang District, Guangdong Province
1955,	Sep	Identified as secretary, CP of North Guangdong District
1958,	Feb	Identified as secretary-general of Guangdong Province CP
1961,	Mar	Elected member of the Standing Committee of Guangdong Province CP
1962,	Oct	Identified as alternate member of the Secretariat of Guangdong Province CP
1967,	Nov	Denounced as a supporter of Tao Zhu and purged
1972,	Aug	First appearance after the Cultural Revolution
1973,	Apr	Identified as vice-chairman of the Revolutionary Committee of Guangdong Province (until 1977)

	Dec	Identified as member of the Standing Committee of Guangdong Province CP (until Jul 1975)
1974,	Oct	Identified as deputy director of Guangzhou Canton Foreign Trade Fair (until 1977)
1975,	Jul	Identified as secretary of Guangdong Province CP (until 1977)
1978,	Mar	Identified as vice-minister of agriculture and forestry (until Feb 1979)
	May	Member of a government delegation led by Gu Mu to France, Switzerland, Belgium, Denmark, and the Federal Republic of Germany
1979,	Apr	Identified as vice-minister of agriculture
	May	Deputy head of an agricultural delegation to the U.S.A. (head: Wang Feng)

Zhang Gexin (Chang Ke-hsin) 张格心

Posts held

CCP
Director of the Propaganda Department of Fujian Province CP

Provincial Administration
Vice-governor of Fujian Province

1959,	Aug	Identified as deputy director of the Propaganda Department of Fujian Province CP
1977,	Nov	Identified as director of the Propaganda Department of Fujian Province CP
1978,	Jan	Elected vice-chairman of the Revolutionary Committee of Fujian Province (until Dec 1979)
1979,	Jul	Appointed member of the National Games Organizing Committee
	Dec	Elected vice-governor of Fujian Province

Zhang Guangdou (Chang Kuang-tou) 张光斗

Posts held

Others
Vice-president of Qinghua University

| 1959, | Mar | Identified as director of the Import and Export Society for Transport Machinery |
| 1964, | May | Identified as director of the Import and Export Society for Chemical Products |

Zhang had been deputy head of trade delegations to Finland (1959) and the German Democratic Republic (1962) as well as head of a delegation to Mexico (1963). In 1964 he was head of an exhibition in Chile.

| 1971, | Aug | Head of a trade delegation to Mexico; identified as director of the Import and Export Society for Chemical Products and as member of the Council for the Promotion of International Trade |

1973,   Jun   Identified as council member of the Hydraulic Engineering Society
1978,   Jun   Identified as professor of Qinghua University
        Aug   Identified as vice-president of Qinghua University

Zhang Guizhen (Chang Kuei-chen) (f)

张桂珍

Posts held

NPC
Member of the Standing Committee of the 5th NPC
Deputy for Tianjin Municipality to the 5th NPC

1973,   Apr   Elected deputy secretary of the Communist Youth League in Tianjin
1975,   Jan   Elected member of the Standing Committee of the 4th NPC (confirmed in 1978 by the 5th NPC)
1978,   Feb   Elected deputy for Tianjin Municipality to the 5th NPC

Zhang Guoji (Chang Kuo-chi)

张国基

Posts held

NPC
Deputy for Beijing Municipality to the 5th NPC

Others
Deputy director of the Research Institute of Literature and History

Zhang was born in 1898.

1958   Return from Indonesia; identified as deputy for the overseas Chinese to the 1st NPC (reelected in 1959 and 1964 to the 2nd and 3rd NPCs)
1959   Identified as head of a school for returned overseas Chinese
1975,   Mar   Identified as deputy to the 4th NPC
1978,   Feb   Elected deputy for Beijing Municipality to the 5th NPC
        May   Identified as deputy director of the Research Institute of Literature and History

Zhang Guoqing (Chang Kuo-ch'ing) (f)

张国清

Posts held

NPC
Member of the Standing Committee of the 5th NPC
Deputy for Hunan Province to the 5th NPC

1973,   Sep   Identified as vice chairman of the Women's Federation of Hunan (no later mention in this post)

1975,   Jan   Elected member of the Standing Committee of the 4th NPC (confirmed in this post in Mar 1978 by the 5th NPC)
1978,   Feb   Elected deputy for Hunan Province to the 5th NPC

Zhang Guosheng (Chang Kuo-sheng)

张国声

Posts held

CCP
Secretary of Qinghai Province CP

Provincial Administration
Governor of Qinghai Province

1959,   Aug   Identified as secretary of Qinghai Province CP
1960   Zhang disappears for unknown reasons
1979,   Apr   Identified as secretary of Qinghai Province CP and as chairman of the Revolutionary Committee of Qinghai (until Aug 1979)
        Sep   Elected governor of Qinghai Province

Zhang Guozhen (Chang Kuo-chen)

张国震

Posts held

Provincial Administration
Vice-governor of Jiangxi Province

1979,   Dec   Elected vice-governor of Jiangxi Province

Zhang Haifeng (Chang Hai-feng)

张海峰

Posts held

Government
Vice-minister of foreign affairs

Zhang was born about 1920.

1952,   Feb   Identified as secretary of Hebei Province CP
1953,   Aug   Elected secretary-general, People's Government of Wuhan Municipality
1957   Identified as deputy secretary, CP of Sanmenxia Construction Bureau
1958,   Nov   Identified as 1st secretary, CP of Sanmenxia Municipality
1959,   Oct   Identified as secretary of Guizhou Province CP
1964,   Feb   Appointed ambassador to the German Democratic Republic (until 1967)
1969,   Jun   Appointed ambassador to Romania (until May 1973)
1973,   Aug   Appointed ambassador to Yugoslavia (until Apr 1978)
1974,   Oct   Zhang accompanies a Yugoslav military delegation to China
1978,   Jun   Identified as vice-minister of foreign affairs

Zhang Haitang (Chang Hai-t'ang) 张海棠

Posts held

CCP
Member, Standing Committee of Yunnan Province CP

Military
Major-general
Deputy commander of Kunming Military Region
Commander of Yunnan Military District

Provincial Administration
Vice-chairman of the People's Congress of Yunnan Province

1955,	Feb	Appointed member of Liaoning People's Provincial Council
1956,	Jul	Identified as political commissar, 120th Division, 40th Army Corps
1959,	Oct	Identified as major-general and chief of staff of Liaoning Military District
1960,	Mar	Identified as deputy commander of Liaoning Military District (until 1971)
1971,	Jul	Identified as vice-chairman, Liaoning Province Revolutionary Committee (until 1975)
	Dec	Identified as commander of Liaoning Military District and member of the Standing Committee, Liaoning CP (until 1975)
1972,	Oct	Member of a delegation of Party members on vacation in North Korea
1975,	Nov	Identified as commander of Yunnan Military District
1977,	Feb	Identified as vice-chairman of the Revolutionary Committee (until Dec 1979) and member of the Standing Committee of Yunnan CP
1979,	Mar	Identified as deputy commander of Kunming Military Region
	Dec	Elected vice-chairman of the People's Congress of Yunnan Province

Zhang Hanying (Chang Han-ying) 张含英

Posts held

Others
Member of the Standing Committee of the 5th CPPCC
President of the Society of Water Conservancy and Power

Zhang was born in 1900 in Heze, Shandong Province. After studying at Fudan and Peking Universities he went to the University of Illinois from 1924 to 1925 and then graduated from Cornell University in civil engineering. After his return to China he lectured successively at the National Qingdao University and Beiyang University. From 1928 to 1930 he was chief engineer of the Shandong Provincial River Conservancy Commission, then until 1932 chief engineer of the Huludao Harbor Development Project (Gulf of Liaodung). From 1933 to 1936 he was chief engineer of the North China Water Conservancy Commission. He served as acting chairman of the Chang Jiang Conservancy Commission from 1940 to 1941, and then until 1943 as chairman of the Huang He Conser-

vancy Commission. He became a member of the National Water Conservancy Commission in 1943 (until 1949).

1950,	Jan	Identified as vice-minister of water conservancy (until Feb 1958)
	Aug	Identified as member of the Committee of the Federation of Scientific Societies (until Sep 1958)
1953,	Sep	Member of a delegation to the 3rd General Assembly of the World Federation of Scientific Workers in Budapest
1954,	Aug	Elected deputy for Shandong Province to the 1st NPC (reelected to the 2nd and 3rd NPCs)
1957,	Apr	Elected president of the Water Conservancy Society (until Cultural Revolution)
1958,	Mar	Appointed vice-minister of water conservancy and electric power (until Cultural Revolution)
1967		Disappears during the Cultural Revolution
1973,	Mar	First appearance after the Cultural Revolution
1975,	May	Identified as deputy director of the Bureau of Agriculture in the Ministry of Agriculture and Forestry (until 1977?)
1978,	Mar	Elected member of the Standing Committee of the 5th NPC
1979,	Jan	Identified as president of the Society of Water Conservancy and Power

Zhang Huailian (Chang Huai-lien) 张怀连

Posts held

CCP
Alternate member of the CCP 11th Central Committee

Military
Commander of the 1st Flight Division, PLA Air Force

Before joining the PLA, Zhang was a shepherd.

1964,	Nov	As flight lieutenant of an airborne division Zhang shoots down an unmanned U.S. reconnaissance aircraft over Guangxi Autonomous Region
1965,	Jan	After having shot down another unmanned reconnaissance aircraft, Zhang is made a PLA captain
1973,	Aug	Elected to first term as alternate member of the CCP Central Committee by the 10th Party Congress
1976,	Sep	Identified as a cadre in Liaoning
1978,	Oct	Identified as commander of the 1st Flight Division, PLA Air Force

Zhang Huaisan (Chang Huai-san) 张淮三

Posts held

CCP
Secretary of Tianjin Municipality CP

1953	Identified as director of the Public Utility Bureau of the Tianjin People's Government

1958, Jul Identified as secretary of Tianjin Municipality CP

1967, Feb Branded as a counterrevolutionary revisionist and purged

1979, Feb First appearance after the Cultural Revolution

       Mar Identified as secretary of the CP, and vice-chairman of the Revolutionary Committee, of Tianjin Municipality (latter post until Mar 1980)

Zhang Huaizhong (Chang Huai-chung)

张怀忠

Posts held

Government
Vice-minister of the 1st Ministry of Machine Building

1975, Dec Identified as a government cadre
1978, May Identified as vice-minister of the 1st Ministry of Machine Building

Zhang Jiafu (Chang Chia-fu)   张稼夫

Posts held

NPC
Deputy for Shanxi Province to the 5th NPC

Others
Member of the Standing Committee of the 5th Chinese People's Political Consultative Conference
Adviser of the Academy of Sciences

Zhang was born in 1900 in Shanxi Province. He studied at Shanxi University and joined the Institute of Social Sciences of the Academy of Sciences in 1927. Together with Chen Hansheng he published "The Deviation of the Mou." In 1948 he was director of the Propaganda Department of the Shanxi-Suiyuan District CP.

1949, Nov Identified as member of the Northwest China Military and Administrative Council (until Jan 1953)

1950, Mar Identified as vice-chairman of the Cultural and Educational Committee in the Northwest China Military and Administrative Council (until Jan 1953)

1953, Jan Appointed vice-president of the Academy of Sciences (until 1958)

       Feb Member of a delegation of scientists to the USSR

1954, Apr Identified as deputy director of the Department of Philosophy and Social Sciences of the Academy of Sciences (until 1955)

       Sep Elected deputy for Shanxi Province to the 1st National People's Congress

1956, Mar Identified as deputy secretary-general of the State Scientific Planning Commission (until 1957)

1958, Jun Elected deputy for Inner Mongolia to the 2nd NPC (confirmed in this post in 1964 by the 3rd NPC)

1959, Sep Identified as deputy director of the Office of Culture and Education in the State Council (until Cultural Revolution)

1967, Jan Criticized as a power holder of the capitalist road and disappears

1973, May First appearance after the Cultural Revolution

1978, Feb Elected deputy for Shanxi Province to the 5th NPC

       Mar Elected member of the Standing Committee of the 5th CPPCC

1979, Apr Identified as adviser of the Academy of Sciences

       Jun Member of the Draft Laws Committee at the 2nd Session of the 5th NPC

Zhang Jiahua (Chang Chia-hua)   张家骅

Posts held

Others
President of the Society of Nuclear Science and Technology
President of the Shanghai Municipal Nuclear Society
Member of the Shanghai Nuclear Research Institute, Academy of Sciences

1963   Identified as deputy director of the Institute of Atomic Physics, Academy of Sciences

1978, Jun Identified as president of the Society of Nuclear Science and Technology

1979, Nov Identified as president of the Shanghai Municipal Nuclear Society and as member of the Shanghai Nuclear Research Institute, Academy of Sciences

Zhang Jian'gang (Chang Chien-kang)

张建纲

Posts held

Provincial Administration
Vice-governor of Gansu Province

1958, Mar Identified as deputy director of the Rural Work Department, Gansu Province CP

1979, Dec Elected vice-governor of Gansu Province

Zhang Jianmin (Chang Chien-min) 张健民

Posts held

Provincial Administration
Vice-governor of Shanxi Province

1958, Apr Identified as director of the Organization Department of Guizhou Province CP

1966, Sep Identified as secretary of Guizhou Province CP

1967, Jan Dismissed from all posts

1973, Dec First appearance after the Cultural Revolution

1975, Mar Identified as a member of the Standing Committee of the Revolutionary Committee of Guizhou Province and as member of the Standing Committee of Guizhou Province CP

May Identified as vice-chairman of the Revolutionary Committee of Guizhou Province

1977, Sep Zhang disappears

1979, Dec Elected vice-governor of Shanxi Province

Zhang Jie (Chang Chieh, Hadj Mohammed Ali)

张 杰

Posts held

Government
Member of the State Nationalities Affairs Commission

NPC
Deputy for Hebei Province to the 5th NPC

Others
Vice chairman of the Moslem League

Zhang is a native of Shandong Province. He belongs to the Hui minority.

1950 Cadre in various offices of the Anshan City Administration, Liaoning Province

1956, May Elected council member of the Sino-Pakistan Friendship Association

Dec Elected vice-chairman of the Islamic Society

1958, Feb Elected vice-chairman of the Sino-United Arab Republic Friendship Association

Mar Identified as deputy director of the Institute of Islamic Theology

1959, Sep Appointed member of the State Council Commission of Nationality Affairs

1960, Apr Elected council member of the Sino-African Friendship Association

1964, Apr Head of a Chinese group of pilgrims to Mecca

Sep Elected deputy for Henan Province to the 3rd NPC

1965, Feb Deputy head of a delegation to the Asian-Islamic Conference in Bandung

Jun Elected vice-chairman of the Afro-Asian Solidarity Committee

1966, Mar Deputy head of a friendship delegation to the United Arab Republic, Syria, Lebanon, Kuweit, Sudan, and Pakistan (until Apr 1966)

1972, Sep Reactivated after the Cultural Revolution as a "cadre of the Islamic Society"

1978, Feb Elected deputy for Hebei Province to the 5th NPC

Oct Identified as vice-chairman of the Moslem League

1979, May Head of an Islamic delegation to Libya; appointed member of the State Nationalities Affairs Commission

Oct Head of Chinese moslems pilgrimage to Mecca

Zhang Jiecheng (Chang Chieh-ch'eng)

张竭诚

Posts held

Military
Major-general
Deputy Commander of Xinjiang Military Region
Commander of the Xinjiang Production and Construction Corps

Zhang served in 1938 in the 689th Regiment of the 8th Route Army. In 1949 he commanded a brigade of the Northeast Field Army which took part in the capture of Tianjin.

1950, Nov Commander of a 4th Field Army division

1952, Oct Deputy commander and chief of staff of the 39th Army

1955, Sep Appointed major-general

1963, May Identified as commander of the 39th Army

1966, Sep Identified as deputy commander of Shenyang Military Region (until 1968)

1968, Nov Appointed commander of the Xinjiang Production and Construction Corps and deputy commander of Xinjiang Military Region

1978, Feb Elected vice-chairman of the Revolutionary Committee of Xinjiang Autonomous Region (until Aug 1979)

Zhang Jihui (Chang Chi-hui)

张积慧

Posts held

CCP
Alternate member of the CCP 11th Central Committee

Military
Deputy Air Force Commander of the PLA

Zhang was born in 1927 in Yongzheng, Shandong Province, as son of a poor peasant. In 1945 he joined the CCP; in 1948 he underwent training at the Shenyang Air Force Academy.

1949, Oct Pilot in the 12th Squadron, 4th Air Force Division

1951 Took part in the Korean War

Sep Promoted to squadron leader

1952, Feb Shot down well-known U.S. fighter pilot A. Davis; conferred merit "Combat Hero, 1st Class"

Nov Promoted commander of a 4th Air Force Division fleet; awarded the North Korean order of "Freedom and Independence"

1954 Zhang returns with his unit to Manchuria

1955, Sep Promoted to the rank of lieutenant-colonel and commander of the 12th Squadron, 4th Air Force Division

Subsequent. Training in the USSR (until 1956)

1958 Identified as commander of the 1st Air Battalion, 1st Air Force Division

1965 Identified as colonel and commander, 1st Air Division, PLA Air Force

1969, Apr Elected to first term as alternate member of the CCP Central Committee by the 9th Party Congress (reelected by 10th and 11th Congresses, 1973 and 1977)

1970,	Oct	Member of a friendship delegation to North Korea commemorating the 20th anniversary of the entry of the "Chinese People's Volunteers" into the Korean War. Awarded the order "National Flag," 1st class, by the North Korean Government
1972,	Jun	Identified as high-ranking officer in Jilin (until 1974)
1973		Identified as commander of the 1st Air Division, PLA Air Force (?)
1974,	Oct	Identified as deputy commander of the PLA Air Force
1977,	Mar	Member of a military delegation to Pakistan
1978,	Jun	Member of a military delegation led by Yang Yong to Yugoslavia

Zhang Jinbang (Chang Chin-pang) 张金榜

Posts held

NPC
Member of the Standing Committee of the 5th NPC
Deputy for Gansu Province to the 5th NPC

1978,	Feb	Elected deputy for Gansu Province to the 5th NPC
	Mar	Elected member of the Standing Committee of the 5th NPC

Zhang Jingfu (Chang Ching-fu) 张劲夫

Posts held

CCP
Member of the CCP 11th Central Committee
Provincial Administration
Governor of Anhui Province

Zhang was born in 1909 in Anhui Province. He graduated from a Chinese university. In 1938 he was co-author of a "Primary School Teachers' Handbook." From May to August 1949 he was deputy mayor of Hangzhou. In August 1949 he was appointed vice-chairman of the Zhejiang Province Financial and Economic Committee (until 1951) and director of the Industry Department of the Zhejiang People's Government (until 1952).

1950,	Mar	Appointed member, Financial and Economic Committee in the East China Military and Administrative Council (until Jan 1953)
1953,	Jan	Appointed vice-chairman of the Financial and Economic Committee, East China Administrative Council (until Jun 1954)
1954,	Oct	Appointed vice-minister of local industries (until May 1956)
1956,	Mar	Appointed vice-chairman, State Planning Commission (until May 1957)
	Oct	Identified as vice-president of the Academy of Sciences
1958,	May	Elected alternate member of the CCP 8th Central Committee
1960,	Feb	Appointed member of the Spare-time Edu-

		cation Committee (until Cultural Revolution)
1962,	Nov	Appointed vice-chairman of the Scientific and Technological Committee (until Cultural Revolution)
1963,	May	Head of an Academy of Sciences delegation to North Korea
1965,	Jan	Elected member of the Standing Committee of the CPPCC
1967,	Aug	Zhang is accused of following the "capitalist road"
1974,	Sep	Rehabilitation after the Cultural Revolution
1975,	Jan	Appointed minister of finance (until Sep 1979)
1977,	Aug	Elected member of the CCP Central Committee by the the 11th Party Congress
1978,	Sep	Head of an economic study group to Yugoslavia and Romania
1979,	Jul	Appointed member of the State Financial and Economic Commission (until Dec 1979)
	Sep	Appointed deputy secretary-general of the State Financial and Economic Commission (until Dec 1979)
	Dec	Elected governor of Anhui Province

Zhang is married to Hu Xiaofeng.

Zhang Jingli (Chang Ching-li) 张敬礼

Posts held

Others
Director of the Board of Directors, China International Trust and Investment Corporation
Vice-chairman of the Executive Committee, Federation of Industrialists and Businessmen
Vice-chairman of the 5th CPPCC, Jiangsu Province Branch

Zhang formerly was manager of the Dasheng Textile Company in Nantong, Jiangsu Province.

1959,	Feb	Elected deputy for Jiangsu Province to the 2nd NPC (reelected in 1964 to the 3rd NPC)
1972,	Sep	First appearance after the Cultural Revolution
1979,	Oct	Appointed director of the Board of Directors, China International Trust and Investment Corporation; elected vice-chairman of the Executive Committee, Federation of Industrialists and Businessmen; identified as vice-chairman of the 5th CPPCC, Jiangsu Province Branch

Zhang Jingtao (Chang Ching-t'ao) 张敬寿

Posts held

Provincial Administration
Vice-governor of Shandong Province

1979,	Dec	Elected vice-governor of Shandong Province

Zhang Jinong (Chang Chi-nung) 张季农

Posts held

Government
Vice-minister of water conservancy

1976,	Jan	Identified as a State Council cadre
	Dec	Identified as vice-minister of water conservancy and electric power (until Feb 1979)
1978,	Aug	Identified as head of the survey for Chang Jiang water diversion to North China
1979,	Apr	Identified as vice-minister of water conservancy
	Aug	Head of a government delegation to Tunisia
	Sep	Member of a government delegation to Yugoslavia, Denmark, the Netherlands and Belgium (head: Wang Renzhong)

Zhang Jinxian (Chang Chin-hsien) 张进先

Posts held

CCP
Member of the Standing Committee, Hubei Province CP

Provincial Administration
Vice-governor of Hubei Province

1976,	Sep	Identified as member of the Standing Committee, Hubei Province CP
1977,	Jun	Identified as deputy director of Hubei Province Industrial Office
1979,	Aug	Identified as vice-chairman of the Revolutionary Committee, Hubei Province (until Dec 1979)
1980,	Jan	Elected vice-governor of Hubei Province

Zhang Junhua (Chang Chün-hua) 张俊华

Posts held

Government
Ambassador to Benin

1973,	Mar	Identified as counselor, embassy in Tanzania (until Aug 1977)
1978,	Jan	Appointed ambassador to Benin

Zhang Kaifan (Chang K'ai-fan) 张恺帆

Posts held

CCP
Secretary of Anhui Province CP
2nd secretary of the Committee for Inspecting Discipline, Anhui Province CP

Zhang is a native of Anhui Province.

1951,	Aug	Identified as member of the North Anhui People's Administrative Office
1952,	Jun	Identified as deputy director, United Front Work Department of Anhui Province CP
1954,	Aug	Identified as vice-governor of Anhui Province (until Cultural Revolution)
1956,	Jul	Identified as deputy secretary of Anhui Province CP
	Sep	Identified as secretary of Anhui Province CP (until Cultural Revolution)
1959		Zhang is accused as "rightist opportunist" (rehabilitated from this charge in Jan 1979)
1964,	Oct	Elected deputy for Anhui Province to the 3rd NPC
1967,	Jan	Accused as follower of Peng Dehuai and relieved of all posts
1977,	Feb	First appearance after the Cultural Revolution: Identified as vice-chairman of the Anhui Section, CPPCC
1979,	Feb	Identified as 2nd secretary of the Committee for Inspecting Discipline, Anhui Province CP
	Mar	Identified as secretary of the CP, and vice-chairman of the Revolutionary Committee, Anhui Province (until Dec 1979)

Zhang Kerang (Chang K'e-jang) 张克壤

Posts held

CCP
Member of the Standing Committee of Hebei Province CP

Provincial Administration
Vice-governor of Hebei Province

1979,	Sep	Identified as member of the Standing Committee of Hebei Province CP; identified as vice-chairman of the Revolutionary Committee, Hebei Province (until Jan 1980)
1980,	Feb	Elected vice-governor of Hebei Province

Zhang Kexia (Chang K'e-hsia) 张克侠

Posts held

Others
Member of the Standing Committee of the 5th CPPCC

Zhang was born in 1901 in Tong County, Hebei Province. He studied at Baoding Military Academy. After further military training in the USSR he served as chief of staff of the 33rd Army of the Nationalist Government forces. During the Anti-Japanese War he was at first deputy chief of staff in General Feng Yuxiang's army. As deputy commander of the KMT 3rd Pacification Area and concurrently commander of Xuzhou Garrison Headquarters, he changed over to the Communists with a force of 23,000 men in November 1948. He was then made commander of the 33rd Army, 3rd Field Army, which in May took part in the occupation of Shanghai.

1949,	Dec	Identified as chief of staff of Shanghai Garrison
1950,	Mar	Identified as member of the East China Military and Administrative Council and as deputy director of its Forestry Department
1954,	Oct	Appointed vice-minister of forestry (until Cultural Revolution)

1955,	Sep	Conferred the order of "Liberation," 1st class
1959,	Aug	Identified as president of the Forestry Society (until Cultural Revolution)
1960,	Feb	Head of a forestry delegation to the USSR
1966		Disappears during the Cultural Revolution
1972,	Apr	First appearance after the Cultural Revolution
1975,	Mar	Identified as deputy to the 4th NPC
1978,	Mar	Elected member of the Standing Committee of the CPPCC

Zhang Linchi (Chang Lin-ch'ih) 张林池

Posts held

CCP
Alternate member, CCP 11th Central Committee

In 1948 Zhang was deputy director of the Agricultural Department in the North China People's Government.

1949,	Dec	Appointed director, Staff Office in the Ministry of Agriculture
1951,	Oct	Appointed vice-minister of agriculture (until Oct 1956)
1952,	May	Head of a peasants' delegation to the USSR
1956,	Oct	Appointed vice-minister of state farms and land reclamation
1960,	Jun	Posted to Hejiang Region, Heilongjiang Province (apparently in connection with the discovery of Daqing oil field) as 1st CP secretary until at least 1964
1966,	Jul	Identified as secretary of Heilongjiang Province CP
1971,	Aug	Reelected as secretary after reorganization of Heilongjiang Province CP (until 1978)
	Oct	Identified as vice chairman of Heilongjiang Province Revolutionary Committee (until Dec 1977)
1973,	Aug	Elected to first term as alternate member of the CCP Central Committee by the 10th Party Congress

Zhang Lingbin (Chang Ling-pin) 张令彬

Posts held

CCP
Alternate member, CCP 11th Central Committee

Military
Lieutenant-general
Deputy director, Logistics Department of the PLA

Zhang served until 1936 in the 1st Front Army. From 1946 to 1948 he was engaged in logistics work in Shanxi-Rehe-Hebei Military Region.

1949,	Oct	Identified as deputy director of the PLA Rear Services Department and as director of its Transport Subdepartment (until Sep 1954)

1954,	Sep	After reorganization of the PLA Rear Services Department to form the PLA Logistics Department Zhang retains office of deputy director
1955,	Sep	Promoted to rank of lieutenant-general; awarded order of "Liberation," 1st class
1958,	Jul	Elected deputy for the PLA to the 2nd NPC (reelected Oct 1964 to the 3rd NPC)
1969,	Apr	Elected to first term as alternate member of the CCP Central Committee by the 9th Party Congress

Zhang Lixian (Chang Li-hsien) 张立宪

Posts held

CCP
Member, CCP 11th Central Committee; Secretary of Hunan Province CP

Military
2nd political commissar of Hunan Military District

1970,	May	Identified as political commissar of Hunan Military District (until Jul 1977)
	Sep	Identified as vice-chairman, Hunan Province Revolutionary Committee (until Dec 1979)
1971,	Dec	Identified as member of the Standing Committee of Hunan Province CP (until Sep 1973)
1973,	Sep	Identified as secretary of Hunan Province CP
1977,	Aug	Elected member of the CCP Central Committee by the 11th Party Congress
	Sep	Identified as 2nd political commissar of Hunan Military District

Zhang Longxiang (Chang Lung-hsiang) 张龙翔

Posts held

Others
Vice-president of Beijing University
Vice-president of the Society of Biochemistry

Zhang studied at the University of Toronto as a postgraduate in the early 1940s.

1978,	Jun	Identified as professor of Beijing University
	Aug	Identified as vice-president of Beijing University
	Oct	Head of a delegation of scientists to Belgium
1979,	May	Identified as vice-president of the Society of Biochemistry

Zhang Nansheng (Chang Nan-sheng) 张南生

Posts held

Military
Lieutenant-general

Others
Member of the Standing Committee of the
5th CPPCC

Zhang was born in 1908 in Fujian Province. He is a
graduate of Xiamen University. While taking part in the
Long March of 1934-35 he was first political commissar of
the Regiment of Political Security under the Bureau of
Political Security in the CCP Central Committee.
After the Zunyi Conference of January 1935 he became
political commissar of the 37th Regiment in the 5th Army
Corps. In 1949 Zhang served in the 2nd Field Army which
he represented in September 1949 as delegate at the
CPPCC.

1951,	Jun	Deputy commander of the 20th Army in the Korean War
1953,	Jul	Appointed 1st deputy commander of the Chinese People's Volunteers in North Korea (?)
	Oct	Conferred the North Korean order "National Flag," 1st class; identified as deputy director of the Political Department of the Chinese People's Volunteers in North Korea
1955,	Sep	Made lieutenant-general
1956		Identified as director of the Political Department of the Chinese People's Volunteers in North Korea (until 1957)
1957,	May	Identified as deputy political commissar of Beijing Military Region
1964,	Sep	Elected deputy for the PLA to the 3rd NPC
1976,	Apr	Article in China Reconstructs: "After the Zunyi Meeting"
1978,	Mar	Elected member of the Standing Committee of the 5th CPPCC

Zhang Panshi (Chang P'an-shih)　张磐石

Posts held

Others
Member of the Standing Committee of the
5th CPPCC

Zhang is a native of Shanxi Province. He was arrested and
imprisoned in 1931. In September 1949 he represented the
Preparatory Committee for the Journalists Association as
a delegate at the 1st CPPCC.

1950,	Nov	Identified as director of the Propaganda Department, North China Bureau of the CCP Central Committee, and as director of the Culture and Education Department, North China Department of the Government Administration Council (until Apr 1952)
1952,	Apr	Appointed council member of the North China Administrative Council (until Sep 1954)
1953,	Apr	Elected vice-chairman of the North China Section, Sino-Soviet Friendship Association (until Sep 1954)
1954,	Mar	Identified as 4th secretary, North China Bureau of the CCP Central Committee (until Sep 1954)
	Sep	Elected member of the CPPCC (until Apr 1959)

1960,	May	Identified as deputy director, Propaganda Department of the CCP Central Committee (until 1966)
1966		Zhang disappears
1979,	Jun	First appearance after the Cultural Revolution: By-elected a member of the 5th CPPCC
	Jul	By-elected a member of the Standing Committee of the 5th CPPCC

Zhang Peng (Chang P'eng)　张彭

Posts held

Provincial Administration
Deputy mayor of Beijing Municipality
Director of the Economic Commission,
Beijing Municipality

Others
Chairman of the Business Management
Association

1979,	Sep	Elected chairman, Business Management Association
	Dec	Elected vice-mayor of Beijing Municipality; identified as director of the Economic Commission, Beijing Municipality

Zhang Pengtu (Chang P'eng-t'u)　张鹏图

Posts held

CCP
Deputy secretary of Inner Mongolia Autonomous Region CP

1950,	Feb	Identified as director of the Civil Administration Department of Hubei People's Government
1957,	Apr	Identified as assistant minister in the Ministry of Supervision (until this Ministry was abolished in Jun 1958)
1958,	Sep	Identified as vice-governor of Gansu Province (until 1962)
1959,	Aug	Identified as secretary of Gansu Province CP (until 1962)
1966,	Oct	Identified as a cadre in Inner Mongolia
1967		Disappears during the Cultural Revolution
1978,	Jan	First appearance after the Cultural Revolution: Elected vice-chairman of the Revolutionary Committee of Inner Mongolia Autonomous Region (until Dec 1979)
	Nov	Identified as deputy secretary of Inner Mongolia Autonomous Region CP

Zhang Pinghua (Chang P'ing-hua)　张平化

Posts held

CCP
Member of the CCP 11th Central Committee

Government
1st vice-minister of the State Agricultural
Commission

NPC
Member of the Standing Committee
Deputy for Beijing Municipality to the 5th NPC

Zhang was born in 1906 in Hunan Province. During the Long March he served in the 2nd Front Army. In 1936 he was deputy director of the Political Department, 120th Division, 8th Route Army, and in 1940 deputy director of the Political Department in Shanxi-Suiyuan Military Region. In 1942 Zhang commanded the 105th Regiment of the 1st Division (?);in 1947 he became director of the Political Department in Shanxi-Suiyuan Military Region. Zhang was identified as CP secretary of Wuhan Municipality in May 1949.

1950,	Mar	Appointed member of Central-South China Military and Administrative Council (until Mar 1953); member of that Council's Finance and Trade Committee, and of Wuhan People's Government (until Jul 1955)
1951,	Jul	Appointed member, Finance and Trade Committee of Wuhan People's Government (Jul 1955) and chief procurator of Wuhan Municipality (until Dec 1951)
	Dec	Self-criticism at the 4th CP Wuhan Congress in connection with the Song Ying case
1952,	Feb	Demoted to post of deputy secretary, Wuhan CP
1953,	Mar	Identified as 2nd secretary, Wuhan CP
1954,	Mar	Identified as 1st secretary, Wuhan CP
1955,	Mar	Elected chairman of Wuhan Political and Consultative Conference
	Jul	Identified as 3rd secretary of Hubei CP
1956		Identified as 2nd secretary of Hubei CP
1958,	May	Elected alternate CC member of the Central Committee by the 8th Party Congress
1959,	Oct	Identified as 1st secretary of Hunan Province CP
1960,	Apr	Identified as political commissar of Hunan Military District
1960,	Dec	Elected member of Hunan People's Council
1962		Identified a secretary of the Central-South China Bureau in the CCP Central Committee
1963,	Jan	Member of a CCP delegation to the Socialist Unity Party of Germany (SED) Congress in East Berlin
1964,	Sep	Elected deputy for Hunan Province to the 3rd NPC
1966,	Jul	Identified as deputy director, General Affairs, Propaganda Department of the CCP Central Committee
1967,	Jan	Criticized in connection with Tao Zhu as a "counterrevolutionary double of Liu Shaoqi and Deng Xiaoping"
1971,	Apr	Elected secretary of Shanxi Province CP (until Apr 1973)
1972,	Feb	Identified as vice-chairman, Revolutionary Committee of Shanxi (until Oct 1973)
	Nov	Identified as political commissar of Guangzhou Military Region (until Nov 1977)
	Dec	Elected chairman of Hunan Peasants' Federation
1975,	Oct	Head of a friendship delegation to Romania
1977,	Nov	Identified as director of the Propaganda Department in the CCP Central Committee (until Dec 1978)
1978,	Feb	Elected deputy for Beijing Municipality to the 5th NPC
	Mar	Elected member of the 5th NPC's Standing Committee
	Dec	Zhang publishes an article in HQ: "Restore and Carry Forward the Three Great Work Styles Initiated by Chairman Mao Zedong - Commemorating the 85th Anniversary of Chairman Mao's Birth"
1979,	Jun	Member of the Committee to Examine Proposals at the Second Session of the 5th NPC
	Jul	Identified as 1st vice-minister of the State Agricultural Commission; adviser of an agricultural delegation headed by Huo Shilian to Great Britain and the Federal Republic of Germany

Zhang is married to T'ang Mu-lan.

Zhang Qilong (Chang Ch'i-lung)   张启龙

Posts held

CCP
Deputy secretary of the Commission for Inspecting Discipline under the CCP Central Committee

NPC
Member of the Standing Committee of the 5th NPC
Deputy for Jiangsu Province to the 5th NPC

Zhang was born in 1900 in Liuyang County, Hunan Province. After attending Changsha Normal School, he became a teacher and in 1924 joined the CCP. Following the Changsha Incident of 21 May 1927 which cost the lives of a number of Communist Party cadres, he withdrew to Liuyang to set up a Communist guerrilla unit. During the following years he was first vice-chairman of the Hunan-Jiangxi Soviet and commander of Hunan-Jiangxi Military Region. In 1933 the Communists sentenced Zhang to 14 months imprisonment for assisting in the escape of captured KMT general Zhang Chao and supporting the counterrevolutionary Liu Renwu.

1950		Identified as secretary of Liaodong Province CP
	Aug	Appointed a board member of the Federation of Cooperatives of Liaodong Province
1951,	Oct	Appointed member of the Northeast China Administrative Council (until Jan 1953)
	Nov	Appointed vice chairman of the Federation of Supply and Marketing Cooperatives
1954,	Dec	Elected member of the National Committee, Chinese People's Political Consultative Conference (probably until 1959)
1956,	Sep	Elected alternate member of the CCP Central Committee by the 8th Party Congress
1957,	Jul	Head of a Supply and Marketing Cooperatives' delegation to the USSR

	Dec	Delegate at the 4th Congress of Hungarian Consumer Cooperatives in Budapest
1958,	Jul	Elected deputy for Hunan Province to the 2nd NPC (until Sep 1964)
1959,	Apr	Elected member of the Standing Committee of the 2nd NPC
1960,	Jan	Appointed member of the Spare-time Education Committee
	Nov	Appointed deputy director of the Organization Department of the CCP Central Committee
1964,	Sep	Elected deputy for Heilongjiang Province to the 3rd NPC
1967		Zhang is relieved of all posts
1977,	Oct	First appearance after the Cultural Revolution
1978,	Feb	Elected deputy for Jiangsu Province to the 5th NPC
	Mar	Elected member of the Standing Committee of the 5th NPC
	Dec	Appointed deputy secretary of the Commission for Inspecting Discipline under the CCP Central Committee
1979,	Jun	Chairman of the Committee to Examine Proposals of the 2nd Session of the 5th NPC

Zhang Qingji (Chang Ch'ing-chi)   张青季

Posts held

Others
Vice-president of the Sports Federation

1956,	Oct	Identified as council member of the Athletic Federation (until 1964)
1958,	Mar	Identified as deputy director of the Propaganda Department, Beijing Municipality CP
1959,	Sep	Identified as member of the Physical Culture and Sports Commission
1963,	Jun	Identified as chairman of the Physical Culture and Sports Commission of Beijing Municipality
	Aug	Head of a sports delegation to the USSR and the German Democratic Republic
1964,	Feb	Identified as vice-chairman of the Athletic Federation (until Jul 1966)
	Nov	Head of a gymnastics delegation to the USSR, Hungary, and France
1965,	Mar	Identified as director of the Health and Physical Culture Department of Beijing Municipality CP
	Apr	Identified as president of the Basketball Association
	Jul	Branded as a black gangster and purged
1979,	Mar	First appearance after the Cultural Revolution: Elected vice-president of the Sports Federation
	Jul	Appointed member of the National Games Organizing Committee

Zhang Rongsen (Chang Jung-sen)   张荣森

Posts held

Military
Deputy commander of Kunming Military Region

1971,	May	Elected secretary of Guizhou Province CP (until Mar 1978)
1977,	Mar	Identified as vice-chairman, Guizhou Province Revolutionary Committee (until Dec 1977)
	Dec	Identified as deputy commander of Kunming Military Region

Zhang Ruguang (Chang Ju-kuang)   张汝光

Posts held

Government
Member of the Birth Planning Leading Group under the State Council

Military
Major-general
Deputy director of the PLA Logistics Department

During the revolution, Zhang worked together with the Canadian doctor Norman Bethune. This seems to indicate that in the Logistics Department Zhang is primarily responsible for field medical services.

1960,	Oct	Identified as major-general
1961,	Nov	Identified as deputy director, Health Department, PLA Logistics Department
1973,	Oct	Identified as deputy director, PLA Logistics Department
1975,	Nov	Identified as director, Health Department, PLA Logistics Department (until Oct 1978); leader of a delegation of PLA surgeons to Romania
1978,	Jul	Identified as member of the Birth Planning Leading Group under the State Council
	Dec	Zhang heads a military medical services delegation to France and the Federal Republic of Germany
1979,	Dec	Head of a military surgeons delegation to the Federal Republic of Germany

Zhang Ruiai (Chang Jui-ai)   张瑞霭

Posts held

Government
Deputy director of the General Administration of Civil Aviation

1974,	Sep	Identified as deputy director of the General Administration of Civil Aviation
	Nov	Deputy head of a goodwill delegation to France (inauguration of the direct air link)
1977,	May	Head of a civil aviation delegation to Senegal and Ethiopia

Jun Head of a civil aviation delegation to Pakistan

1978, Mar Head of a friendship delegation to Ethiopia (inauguration of the direct air link)

Jun Head of a civil aviation delegation to Laos

Nov Head of a civil aviation delegation to the Netherlands

1979, May Head of a civil aviation delegation to the Philippines

Zhang Ruihua (Chang Jui-hua) (f) 张瑞华

Posts held

CCP
Member of the Commission for Inspecting Discipline under the CCP Central Committee

Others
Member of the Standing Committee of the 5th CPPCC

1964, Sep Elected deputy for Henan Province to the 3rd NPC

1978, Mar Elected member of the Standing Committee of the 5th CPPCC

Dec Appointed member of the Commission for Inspecting Discipline under the CCP Central Committee

Zhang is the wife of Nie Rongzhen.

Zhang Ruiqing (Chang Jui-ch'ing) 张瑞清

Posts held

Government
Vice-minister of finance

1978, Sep Identified as vice-minister of finance

Zhang Ruiying (Chang Jui-ying) (f) 张瑞英

Posts held

NPC
Member of the Standing Committee of the 5th NPC
Deputy for Jiangsu Province to the 5th NPC

Mass Organization
Vice-chairman of the Federation of Trade Unions

1971, Aug Identified as member of the Standing Committee, Revolutionary Committee of Jiangsu Province

1973, Jul Elected vice-chairman of the Trade Union of Jiangsu Province

1977, Jun Identified as chairman of the Trade Union of Jiangsu Province (until Sep 1978)

1978, Jan Elected vice-chairman of the Revolutionary Committee of Jiangsu Province (until Feb 1979)

Feb Elected deputy for Jiangsu Province to the 5th NPC

Mar Elected member of the Standing Committee of the 5th NPC

Oct Elected vice-chairman of the Federation of Trade Unions

Zhang Shigong (Chang Shih-kung) 张世功

Posts held

CCP
Secretary, CP of Xinjiang Autonomous Region

1959, Aug Identified as 1st secretary, Yining Autonomous Region of the Kazakhs in Xinjiang and as political commissar of this region

1972, Sep Identified as secretary, CP of Xinjiang Autonomous Region

1978, Feb Elected vice-chairman, Xinjiang Branch of the CPPCC

1979, Elected chairman, Xinjiang branch of the CPPCC

Zhang Shijie (Chang Shih-chieh) 张士杰

Posts held

Government
Former ambassador to Somalia

1955, Aug Identified as counselor, embassy in Afghanistan

1956, May Identified as counselor, embassy in Hungary (until Jun 1957)

1957, Apr Identified as deputy director, Protocol Department, Ministry of Foreign Affairs (until Feb 1960)

1960, Feb Identified as deputy director, 1st Asian Affairs Department, Ministry of Foreign Affairs (until Jul 1960)

Aug Appointed ambassador to Nepal (until Cultural Revolution)

1972, Nov Reactivated after Cultural Revolution

1975, Mar Appointed ambassador to Somalia (until Apr 1979)

Zhang Shijun (Chang Shih-chün) 张世军

Posts held

Government
Vice-minister of forestry

Zhang was born in 1915 in Anhui Province.

1950, Sep Identified as director of the Agriculture and Forestry Bureau of the People's Government of Heilongjiang

1958, Sep Identified as director of the Forestry Department of Heilongjiang Province CP

1964, Oct Elected deputy for Heilongjiang Province to the 3rd NPC

1965, Apr Identified as vice-minister of forestry

1967		Disappears during the Cultural Revolution
1977,	Dec	First appearance after the Cultural Revolution: Elected vice-chairman of the Revolutionary Committee of Heilongjiang Province (until Dec 1979)
1978,	Sep	Identified as member of the Standing Committee of Heilongjiang Province CP (until Dec 1979)
1980,	Jan	Identified as vice-minister of forestry

Zhang Shiying (Chang Shih-ying) 张士英

Posts held

CCP
Secretary of Jilin Province CP

Provincial Administration
Vice-chairman of the Revolutionary Committee of Jilin Province

Zhang was born in 1918 in Shanxi Province.

1951		Identified as head of the Staff Office of Heilongjiang Province CP
	Oct	Identified as council member of the People's Government of Heilongjiang
1953,	Jun	Identified as deputy secretary of Heilongjiang Province CP
1955,	Jul	Identified as director of the Rural Work Department of Heilongjiang Province CP
1957,	Nov	Deputy head of a friendship delegation of Jilin Province to the 40th anniversary celebration of the October Revolution in Vladivostok
1961,	Jul	Identified as vice-governor of Jilin Province (until Mar 1968)
1964,	Feb	Identified as alternate secretary of Jilin Province CP (until Cultural Revolution)
1968,	Mar	Elected member of the Standing Committee, Revolutionary Committee of Jilin Province
1970,	Aug	Zhang disappears
1974,	Aug	First appearance: Identified as a cadre in Jilin
1977,	Oct	Identified as deputy secretary of Jilin Province CP (until Aug 1979)
	Dec	Elected vice-chairman of the Revolutionary Committee of Jilin Province
1979,	Sep	Identified as secretary of Jilin Province CP

Zhang Shude (Chang Shu-te) 张树德

Posts held

CCP
Secretary of Henan Province CP

1957,	Jul	Identified as secretary, CP of Harbin Municipality
1965,	Aug	Identified as deputy secretary-general, Northeast Bureau in the CCP Central Committee
1967		Disappears during Cultural Revolution

1973,	Jun	First appearance after the Cultural Revolution: Identified as member of the Standing Committee, Liaoning CP (until Oct 1977)
	Sep	Identified as vice-chairman, Liaoning Revolutionary Committee (until Nov 1977)
1977,	Oct	Identified as secretary of Liaoning Province CP (until Jan 1980)
1979	Jul	Appointed member of the National Games Organizing Committee
1980,	Feb	Identified as secretary of Henan Province CP

Zhang Siming (Chang Szu-ming) 张思明

Posts held

Provincial Administration
Vice-chairman of Xinjiang Autonomous Region People's Government

1965,		Identified as 2nd political commissar of Xinjiang Military Region (no later mention in this post)
1978,	Feb	Elected vice-chairman of the Revolutionary Committee of Xinjiang (until Aug 1979)
	May	Identified as chairman of the Xinjiang Planning Commission
1979,	Sep	Elected vice-chairman of the Xinjiang People's Government

Zhang Su (Chang Su) 张苏

Posts held

Others
Member of the Standing Committee of the 5th CPPCC
Deputy chief procurator of the Supreme People's Procuracy

Zhang was born in 1909 in Hebei Province and joined the CCP as a youth. In 1933 he served under the "Christian general" Feng Yuxiang who in that year mobilized the Chahar-Suiyuan Army to fight the Japanese. After the outbreak of the Anti-Japanese War in 1937 he served in Chahar Province. In 1944 he was appointed director of the Communist Administration Bureau for Hebei. In 1946 the Communists appointed him chairman of Chahar Province (until May 1952). In May 1948 Zhang was appointed director of the Administrative Bureau for Beiyue District following the establishment of the North China People's Government. He took part in the CPPCC in September 1949 representing the "Liberated Areas of North China."

1949,	Oct	Appointed council member of the Sino-Soviet Friendship Association
1952,	May	Appointed vice-chairman and secretary-general of the North China Government Administration Council
	Jun?	Appointed chairman of the North China Supreme People's Court (until Apr 1954)
1953,	Apr	Member of the presidium at the founding session of the Committee of Political and Legal Affairs

1954,	Oct	Appointed vice-president of the Supreme People's Court; elected deputy for Hebei Province to the 1st NPC
1956,	Aug	Member of a delegation under Song Qingling to Indonesia
1958,	May	Elected alternate member of the CCP Central Committee
1959,	Apr	Elected member of the Standing Committee of the NPC; member of a friendship delegation to Outer Mongolia
1961,	Feb	Member of a friendship delegation to the USSR
1962,	Apr	Member of an NPC delegation to North Korea
	Sep	Appointed deputy chief procurator. Member of an NPC delegation to North Vietnam
1963,	Jan	Chairman of the Legislative Committee of the NPC
1964,	Sep	Head of a friendship delegation to North Korea
	Oct	Elected vice-chairman of the Committee of Political and Legal Affairs
1967,	May	Branded as a counterrevolutionary revisionist
1978,	Feb	First appearance after the Cultural Revolution
	Mar	Elected member of the Standing Committee of the 5th CPPCC
	May	Appointed deputy chief procurator of the Supreme People's Procuracy

Zhang Tianfang (Chang T'ien-fang) 张天放

Posts held

NPC
Deputy for Yunnan Province to the 5th NPC

Provincial Administration
Vice-chairman of the Standing Committee, People's Congress of Yunnan Province

Zhang once served as manager of a silk-cotton company in Kunming.

1950,	Aug	Identified as a member of the Economic and Financial Committee, Southwest Military and Administrative Council, and as a council member of the People's Government, Yunnan Province
	Nov	Identified as a member of the 1st Central Committee of the KMT Revolutionary Committee (reelected until the 4th Central Committee in 1958)
1951,	May	Identified as a member of the Economic and Financial Committee, Yunnan Province, and concurrently director of its Bureau of Agriculture and Forestry
1958,	Nov	Elected deputy for Yunnan Province to the 2nd NPC (reelected in 1964 to the 3rd NPC)
1960,	Nov	Identified as chairman of the KMT Revolutionary Committee, Yunnan Branch
1964,	Jan	Identified as vice-governor of Yunnan Province
1968		Zhang disappears

1978,	Feb	First appearance after the Cultural Revolution: Elected deputy for Yunnan Province to the 5th NPC
1979,	Dec	Elected vice-chairman of the Standing Committee, People's Congress of Yunnan Province

Zhang Tianyi (Chang T'ien-yi) 张天乙

Posts held

Provincial Administration
Vice-governor of Shanxi Province

1950		Identified as special commissioner of the Zhangyi Office, Shanxi Province
1952,	Aug	Identified as director of the Federation of Cooperatives, Shanxi Province
1956,	Apr	Elected vice-governor of Shanxi Province (until 1961)
1963,	Oct	Identified as a member of the Board of Directors, Federation of Handicraft Cooperatives (until Cultural Revolution)
1979,	Dec	First appearance after the Cultural Revolution: Elected vice-governor of Shanxi Province

Zhang Tingfa (Chang T'ing-fa) 张廷发

Posts held

CCP
Member, Politburo of the CCP 11th Central Committee
Member, CCP Central Committee
1st secretary, CP Secretariat, PLA Air Force

NPC
Deputy for the PLA to the 5th NPC

Military
Major-general
Commander, PLA Air Force

Zhang joined the Red Army in 1928.

1955,	Sep	Awarded the order of "Liberation," 1st class
1956,	Oct	Identified as deputy chief of staff of the PLA Air Force
1958,	May	Identified as major-general of the Air Force
1964,	Feb	Identified as deputy commander of the PLA Air Force
1967		Disappears during the Cultural Revolution
1973,	Oct	First appearance after the Cultural Revolution
1975,	Jul	Identified as deputy commander of the Air Force
1976,	Oct	Identified as political commissar of the Air Force
1977,	Apr	Identified as commander of the Air Force
	Jun	Identified as 1st secretary, CP Secretariat of the Air Force
	Aug	Elected member of the CCP Central Committee by the 11th Party Congress; elected Politburo member, Central Committee of the CCP

1978,   Feb Elected deputy for the PLA to the 5th NPC
1979,   Mar Head of an air force delegation to Pakistan

Zhang Tong (Chang T'ung) 张彤

Posts held

Government
Ambassador to the Federal Republic of Germany

Military
Colonel

Zhang was born in 1919.

1956,   Sep Identified as military attaché in India (until about 1960)
1961,   Jul Identified as charge d'affairs ad interim in Congo (Stanleyville)
         Aug Presents letter of accreditation to Gizenga
         Sep Returns to China after embassy has been closed down
1962,   May Identified as deputy director, 1st Asian Affairs Department, Ministry of Foreign Affairs (until about Sep 1964)
         Nov Accompanies vice-minister of foreign affairs Huang Zhen to Burma, Indonesia, and Ceylon (until December)
1963,   Nov Accompanies the chairman of the Physical Culture and Sports Commission, He Long, to Games of New Emerging Forces in Indonesia
1964,   Sep Director of the 1st Asian Affairs Department, Ministry of Foreign Affairs (until about 1967)
1965,   Mar Accompanies foreign minister Chen Yi to Afghanistan, Pakistan, and Nepal
1966,   Mar Accompanies president Liu Shaoqi to Pakistan, Afghanistan and Burma (until Apr 1966)
1969,   Jun Appointed ambassador to Pakistan (until Aug 1974)
         Jul Accompanies Pakistani goodwill delegation to the PRC
1970,   May Accompanies the commander of the Pakistani Air Force to the PRC
1971,   Oct During Guo Moruo's illness leader of the Chinese delegation to the 2500th anniversary celebrations in Iran
1974,   Sep Appointed ambassador to Egypt (until May 1977)
1977,   Aug Appointed ambassador to the Federal Republic of Germany

Zhang is married to Fang Yanzhuan.

Zhang Tongyu (Chang T'ung-yü) 张同钰

Posts held

Government
Vice-minister of geology
Deputy director of the State Bureau for Geology

1949,   May Identified as deputy director of the Jiujiang Military Control Commission
1956,   Oct Appointed assistant minister of geology (until Jan 1960)
1959,   May Identified as director of the General Office, Ministry of Geology
1964,   Oct Elected deputy for Hebei Province to the 3rd NPC
1966   Zhang disappears
1977,   Jul First appearance after the Cultural Revolution: Identified as deputy director of the State Bureau for Geology
1979,   Oct Identified as vice-minister of geology

Zhang Wanfu (Chang Wan-fu) 张万福

Posts held

NPC
Member of the Standing Committee of the 5th NPC
Deputy for Shanxi Province to the 5th NPC

1964,   Sep Elected deputy for Shanxi Province to the 4th NPC; then disappears until 1978
1978,   Feb Elected deputy for Shanxi Province to the 5th NPC
         Mar Elected member of the Standing Committee of the 5th NPC

Zhang Wei (Chang Wei) 张维

Posts held

Others
Vice-president, Qinghua University
Vice-president of the Mechanics Society

Zhang was born in 1913 in Beijing. He studied at Berlin (?) University.

1953,   Apr Identified as dean of the Engineering Sciences Department at Qinghua University
1955,   Feb Member of the group of technical advisors for the construction of the Chang Jiang bridge at Wuhan
         May Appointed member of the Standing Committee, Department of Technical Sciences at the Academy of Sciences
1956,   Dec Appointed vice-chancellor of Qinghua University
1957,   Oct Elected vice-chairman of the Civil Engineering Society (until Sep 1962)
1960,   Mar Elected secretary-general of the Sino-Latin American Friendship Association
         Jun Identified as professor of dynamics
1961,   Nov Zhang represents Beijing and Qinghua Universities at the inauguration of the University of Ghana and the "Kwame Nkrumah" University of Science and Technology
1962,   Sep Delegate at the International Seminar on Higher Education, Moscow, and the 7th Congress of the World Federation of Scientific workers of which he is elected honorary secretary

1963,	Sep	With foundation of the Beijing Center of the World Federation of Scientific Workers, Zhang is elected director
1964,	Sep	Elected deputy for Jilin Province to the 3rd NPC
	Dec	Member of a delegation to Havana headed by Liu Shuzhou to the 6th anniversary celebrations of the Liberation of Cuba
1965,	Nov	Head of a delegation of educators to Cambodia
1972,	Oct	Identified as vice-chairman of the Revolutionary Committee of Qinghua University. Deputy head of the Chinese delegation to the 17th UN Educational Scientific and Cultural Organization (UNESCO) Conference in Paris
1973,	May	Head of the Chinese delegation to the 92nd session of the UNESCO Executive Committee in Paris
1975,	Jun	Identified as secretary of the Scientific and Technical Association
1976,	Sep	Head of the Chinese delegation to the 100th session of the UNESCO Executive Committee in Paris
	Oct	Delegate to the 19th UNESCO session in Nairobi
1977,	Nov	Deputy head of an educational delegation to the U.S.A.
1978,	Jan	Zhang heads a Qinghua University delegation to Sweden
	Jul	Identified as vice-president of Qinghua University
1979,	Jul	Identified as vice-president of the Mechanics Society

Zhang Weicheng (Chang Wei-ch'eng) 张维城

Posts held

Others
Vice-president of the Academy of Agricultural Sciences

1950,	Aug	Identified as secretary-general of the Rural Reform Committee, East China Military and Administrative Council
1957,	Mar	Identified as deputy director of Nanjing Agricultural College
1963,	Sep	Identified as vice-president of the Academy of Agricultural Sciences
1966		Disappears during the Cultural Revolution
1978,	Jul	First appearance after the Cultural Revolution: Identified on his former post as vice-president of the Academy of Agricultural Sciences

Zhang Weilie (Chang Wei-lieh) 张伟烈

Posts held

Government
Ambassador to Thailand
Permanent representative of the PRC to the Economic and Social Commission for Asia and the Pacific (ESCAP)

1955,	Apr	Identified as 2nd CP secretary of Hainan Island, Guangdong Province
1956,	Oct	Counselor at the embassy in the USSR (until about 1959)
1960,	Sep	Ambassador to Iraq (until 1965)
1970,	Jul	Vice-chairman of the Sino-Cuban Friendship Association. Head of a friendship delegation to Cuba
1971,	Feb	Ambassador to Morocco (until Jul 1974)
1974,	Oct	Ambassador to the PR Mongolia (until Apr 1978)
1978,	Jul	Ambassador to Thailand
1979,	Feb	Identified as permanent representative of the PRC to ESCAP

Zhang Weizhen (Chang Wei-chen) 张维桢

Posts held

Others
Member of the Standing Committee of the 5th CPPCC

Zhang is a native of Hunan Province. As a worker at Hunan No. 1 Textile Mill he was engaged in revolutionary activities in 1922. Working at Jardine Textile Mill in Shanghai in 1925 he organized a strike in connection with the "May 30th Movement." After having been imprisoned twice he was one of the organizers of the Japanese textile mill strikes in Shanghai in 1935. In 1937 he organized trade unions in his native province of Hunan. In 1948 he was a member of the Preparatory Committee for the 6th All-China Labor Congress. At this time he was also chairman of the Harbin Workers Federation. The Congress elected him a member of the Executive Council of the Federation of Labor. In the following year he became president of the Northeast Political University for Workers. In September 1949 he took part in the 1st CPPCC.

1949,	Nov	Appointed council member of the Northeast People's Government (until Jan 1953)
1952,	Sep	Identified as director of the Labor Department, Northeast People's Government (until Sep 1954)
1953,	Jan	Appointed member of the Northeast China Administrative Council (until Sep 1954)
	May	Member of a trade union delegation to the USSR
	Oct	Elected member of the General Council of the World Federation of Trade Unions (until about 1963)
1954,	Aug	Elected deputy for Benxi Municipality, Liaoning Province, to the 1st NPC
1955,	Apr	Head of a trade union delegation to PR Mongolia
	Aug	Elected council member of the Sino-Indian Friendship Association (until Cultural Revolution)
1957,	Dec	Elected secretary and member of the Executive Council of the Trade Union (until Cultural Revolution)
1958,	Nov	Elected deputy for Shanghai Municipality to the 2nd NPC (confirmed in 1964 by the 3rd NPC)
1967		Disappears during the Cultural Revolution
1977,	Oct	First appearance after the Cultural Revolution

1978,	Mar	Elected a member of the Standing Committee of the 5th CPPCC
	Apr	Identified as secretary of the Federation of Trade Unions (not confirmed in this post by the Trade Union Congress in Oct 1978)
1979,	Feb	Identified as adviser of the Federation of Trade Unions

Zhang Wenbin (Chang Wen-pin) 张文彬

Posts held

Government
Vice-minister of petroleum industry

Others
General manager of the China National Petroleum Corporation

1955,	Feb	Identified as member of the People's Council of Jilin Province
1957,	Oct	Identified as director of the Xinjiang Oil Administration Bureau under the Ministry of Petroleum Industry
1965,	Feb	Appointed vice-minister of petroleum industry
1972,	May	Head of a petroleum study group visiting Iran. Identified as director of the Petroleum Research and Exploitation Society
1973,	Oct	Identified as vice-minister of fuel and chemical industries (until Sep 1975)
1975,	Sep	Identified as vice-minister of petroleum and chemical industry; head of a petroleum delegation to Norway
1978,	Mar	Identified as vice-minister of petroleum industry
	Aug	Identified as general manager of the China National Petroleum Corporation

Zhang Wenguang (Chang Wen-kuang)

张文光

Posts held

CCP
Member of the Standing Committee of Hunan Province CP

Provincial Administration
Vice-governor of Hunan Province

1979,	Sep	Identified as a member of the Standing Committee of Hunan Province CP
	Dec	Elected vice-governor of Hunan Province

Zhang Wenjin (Chang Wen-chin) 章文晋

Posts held

Government
Vice-minister of foreign affairs

Zhang was born in Beijing in 1914. He studied at the Yanjing (Yenching) University in Beijing, at the Sun Yat-sen University in Moscow, and in Germany.

1952		Identified as director of the Overseas Chinese Office, Tianjin Municipal People's Government
1954,	Apr	Member of the delegation to the Geneva Indochina Conference headed by Premier Zhou Enlai
	Jun	Member of a delegation headed by Zhou Enlai to India and Burma
	Dec	Appointed deputy director of the Asian Affairs Department in the Ministry of Foreign Affairs (until Jul 1957)
1956,	Mar	Member of a government delegation to Pakistan
1957,	Jul	Director of the Asian Affairs Department, Ministry of Foreign Affairs (until Dec 1958)
1958,	Dec	Director of the 1st Asian Affairs Department in the Ministry of Foreign Affairs (until Sep? 1964)
1960,	Apr	Member of a government delegation to Burma, India, and Nepal
	Aug	Member of the Chinese delegation to the Sino-Indian border negotiations in New Delhi (until Oct 1960)
	Nov	Member of the Chinese delegation to the Sino-Burman border negotiations in Rangoon (until Dec 1960)
1963,	Apr	Member of a government delegation to Indonesia and Burma
1964,	Feb	Member of a government delegation to Burma
	Apr	Member of the Chinese delegation to the preparatory meeting of the 2nd Afro-Asian Solidarity Conference in Jakarta
	Dec	Member of a government delegation to Burma
1965,	Apr	Member of a government delegation to celebrations of the 10th anniversary of the Bandung Conference in Jakarta
	Jun	Adviser to the Chinese delegation to the planned 2nd Afro-Asian Solidarity Conference in Algiers
1965,	Aug	Member of a government delegation to Indonesia
1966,	Jul	Ambassador to Pakistan (until 1967)
1969,	Oct	Member at the Chinese section at the Sino-Soviet border negotiations in Beijing
1971,	Oct	Present at the talks between Zhou Enlai and Henry Kissinger
	Dec	Identified as director of the Western Europe, America, and Australia Department in the Ministry of Foreign Affairs
1972,	Feb	Present during the negotiations between Zhou Enlai and U.S. President Richard Nixon
	May	Appointed assistant minister, Ministry of Foreign Affairs
1973,	Feb	Member of the Chinese delegation to the Vietnam Conference in Paris
	Sep	Appointed ambassador to Canada (until May 1976)
1977,	May	Member of a delegation to the UN Law of the Sea Conference
1978,	Jan	Identified as vice-minister of foreign affairs
1979,	Jan	Member of a government delegation to U.S.A. (head: Deng Xiaoping)

Jul Head of the Chinese delegation to the International Conference on Indochinese Refugees in Geneva

Oct Member of the Chinese government delegation headed by Hua Guofeng to France, the Federal Republic of Germany, Great Britain, and Italy

Zhang Wenyu (Chang Wen-yü) 张文裕

Posts held

NPC
Member of the Standing Committee of the 5th NPC
Deputy for Shanghai Municipality to the 5th NPC

Others
Director of the Institute of High Energy Physics, Academy of Sciences
Council Member of the Physics Society
Director, Geological Research Institute
Chinese chairman of the PRC-U.S.A. Joint Committee on High Energy Physics

Zhang was born in 1910. He received his Ph.D. in physics from Cambridge University in 1938. He then taught physics at Princeton University where the later Nobel Prize winner Yang Zhenning was one of his students. In the course of 7 years at Princeton he was the author of numerous reports on his research in nuclear physics.

1956		Returns to China
1957,	May	Appointed member of the Standing Committee, Department of Physics, Mathematics, and Chemistry at the Academy of Sciences
1957-1960		Zhang worked at the Joint Nuclear Research Institute of the Socialist Countries in Dubna primarily in the field of neutron physics including experiments with the then newly developed electrostatic generator
1958,	Dec	Elected deputy for Liaoning Province to the NPC (confirmed in 1964)
1959,	Jul	Identified as vice-chairman, Editorial Board of the Academy of Sciences publication Kexue Tongbao (Science Bulletin)
1961		Identified as vice-chairman, Editorial Board of the journal Zhongguo Kexue (Scientia Sinica)
1971,	Aug	Present at Zhou Enlai's reception for American-Chinese Nobel Prize winner Yang Zhenning
1972,	Oct	Member of a delegation of scientists to Great Britain
1973,	May	Head of a delegation of physicists to the U.S.A. Identified as deputy director of the Institute of Atomic Energy at the Academy of Sciences. Identified as council member of the Physics Society
1975,	Jan	Elected member of the Standing Committee by the 4th NPC (confirmed by the 5th NPC in 1978)
1977,	Jul	Identified as director of the Institute of High Energy Physics, Academy of Sciences; head of a delegation of physicists to Japan

1978,	Mar	Identified as director of the Geological Research Institute; elected deputy for Shanghai to the 5th NPC
	Aug	Accepted for membership of the CCP
	Sep	Identified as adviser of the Popular Science Writers' Society
1979,	Jan	Identified as member of the Department for Mathematics, Physics and Chemistry, Academy of Sciences
	Mar	Elected vice-chairman of the Structural Geological Committee, Geological Society
	Jun	Identified as Chinese chairman of the PRC-U.S.A. Joint Committee of High Energy Physics
Note		According to unconfirmed reports Zhang is head of the Laboratory for Cosmic Radiation which is associated with the Institute of Atomic Energy.

Zhang Wenzhi (Chang Wen-chih) 张文治

Posts held

NPC
Deputy for Tianjin Municipality to the 5th NPC

Others
Deputy director of the Beijing Iron and Steel Institute
Vice-president of the Metallurgical Society

1954,	Aug	Elected deputy for Sichuan Province to the 1st NPC (confirmed in 1959 and 1964 for the 2nd and 3rd NPCs)
1962		Identified as chairman of the Shipbuilding Society
1978,	Feb	Elected deputy for Tianjin Municipality to the 5th NPC
	Oct	Identified as deputy director of the Beijing Iron and Steel Institute
1979,	Jan	Elected vice-president of the Metallurgical Society

Zhang Wenzhou (Chang Wen-chou) 张文舟

Posts held

Military
Deputy commander of the PLA Armored Forces

1951		Identified as chief of staff of the Chinese People's Volunteers in Korea
1965,	Oct	Identified as deputy commander of the PLA Armored Forces
1967		Disappears during the Cultural Revolution
1974,	Sep	First appearance after the Cultural Revolution
1978,	Nov	Identified as deputy commander of the PLA Armored Forces

Zhang Xiangshan (Chang Hsiang-shan)

张香山

Posts held

CCP
Deputy Director, Propaganda Department of the CCP Central Committee

Government
Director, Central Broadcasting Administration

Others
Member of the Standing Committee, 5th CPPCC

Zhang was born in 1914 in Zhejiang Province. He received part of his education in Japan. Around 1937 he was director of the Propaganda Department, Political Department of 129th Division, 8th Route Army. From 1946 to 1947 he was head of the Information Bureau, CCP section of the joint KMT CCP Military Subcommittee of the Political Consultative Conference.

1950		Identified as director, Institute of Marxism-Leninism in Beijing
1959,	Feb	Identified as a cadre of a department in the CCP Central Committee
1961,	Mar	Observer at the Conference for Afro-Asian Solidarity in Cairo
1962,	Apr	Elected council member of the Sino-African Society
1963,	Jan	Secretary-general of the Chinese delegation to the 3rd Conference for Afro-Asian Solidarity in Tanganyika
	Oct	Elected council member of the Sino-Japanese Friendship Association
1964,	Jul	Member of the Chinese delegation to the 10th World Conference Against Atomic and Hydrogen Bombs in Japan
	Nov	Member of Chinese delegation headed by Peng Zhen to the CP Japan 9th Party Congress, delegation is refused entry permit
1965,	Jun	Elected vice-chairman, Committee for Afro-Asian Solidarity
	Jul	Member of the Chinese delegation to the 11th World Conference Against Atomic and Hydrogen Bombs in Japan
1971,	May	Identified as cadre in the International Liaison Department, CCP Central Committee
1973,	Apr	Identified as vice-chairman of the Sino-Japanese Friendship Association (until 1976); deputy head of a friendship delegation to Japan
	Aug	Identified as deputy director, International Liaison Department of the CCP Central Committee (until 1976)
1977,	Mar	Identified as director of the Central Broadcasting Administration
	Oct	Head of a delegation of journalists to Japan
	Dec	Identified as deputy director of the Propaganda Department, CCP Central Committee
1978,	Mar	Elected member of the Standing Committee, 5th CPPCC
1979,	Oct	Head of a radio and television delegation to U.S.A.

Zhang Xiangtong (Chang Hsiang-t'ung)

张香桐

Posts held

NPC
Deputy for Shanghai Municipality to the 5th NPC

Others
Director of the Brain Research Laboratory of the Shanghai Institute of Physiology, Academy of Sciences

1959,	Apr	Elected deputy for Hebei Province to the 2nd NPC (confirmed in 1964 to the 3rd NPC)
1961,	Mar	Identified as a physiologist in the Biology Department of the Academy of Sciences (famed for his acupuncture analgesia theories)
1965,	Feb	Identified as a research scientist at the Institute of Physiology, Academy of Sciences; attends a medical conference in Cuba
1978,	Feb	Elected deputy for Shanghai Municipality to the 5th NPC
	Jun	Identified as director of the Brain Research Laboratory of the Shanghai Institute of Physiology, Academy of Sciences

Zhang Xianwu (Chang Hsien-wu) 张贤务

Posts held

Government
Deputy director of a department in the Ministry of Economic Relations with Foreign Countries

1972,	Sep	Deputy representative of the Chinese delegation to the 27th UN General Assembly
1973,	Jun	Deputy representative of the Chinese delegation to the UN Economic and Social Council Session in Geneva
1974,	Apr	Representative to the 8th UN Industrial Development Organization (UNIDO) Session in Vienna
	Sep	Member of the Chinese delegation to the 29th UN General Assembly
1975,	Jan	Deputy representative of the delegation to the UN Industrial Development Program (UNIDEP) Session in New York
	Aug	Appointed alternate representative of the PRC Mission to the UN (until 1976)
1976,	Jun	Head of a delegation to the 22nd Session of the Governing Council of the UN in Geneva
	Dec	Identified as deputy director of a department in the Ministry of Economic Relations with Foreign Countries
	Oct	Deputy head of a delegation to the 4th Session of the Intergovernmental Committee of UNIDO in Vienna
1977,	Apr	Representative of the Chinese delegation to the UNIDO Conference in Vienna
1978,	Aug	Deputy head of a delegation to the UN Technical Cooperation Conference of Developing Countries

Zhang Xianyue (Chang Hsien-yüeh) 张贤约

Posts held

Military
Lieutenant-general
Deputy director, PLA Logistics Department

In 1937 Zhang was brigade commander in the 120th Division, 8th Route Army. In 1949 he served in the Logistics Department, Northwestern Field Army.

1955,	Feb	Identified as director of the Logistics Department of Lanzhou Military Region
	Sep	Appointed lieutenant-general; conferred order of "Liberation," 1st class
1964,	May	Appointed deputy director, PLA Logistics Department
1978,	Oct	Head of a delegation of war veterans to Yugoslavia

Zhang Xiaoqian (Chang Hsiao-ch'ien)

张孝骞

Posts held

Others
Member of the Standing Committee of the 5th CPPCC

Zhang studied at first at Xiaoya Medical College (until 1923?) and from 1926 to 1927 at Johns Hopkins University, U.S.A. From 1933 to 1934 he worked at Stanford University, U.S.A.

1953,	Dec	Identified as a professor of the Internal Medicine Department of the China Medical University
1955,	May	Identified as a member of the Department of Biology, Geography, and Geology at the Academy of Sciences (until Cultural Revolution)
1957,	Nov	Adviser to a scientific and technical delegation to the USSR
1958,	Sep	Appointed member of the Scientific and Technological Association (until Cultural Revolution)
1959,	Apr	Elected member of the 3rd CPPCC (confirmed in 1964 and 1978 to the 4th and 5th CPPCC)
1960,	Apr	Appointed director of the Internal Medicine Department of the Institute of Medicine (until Cultural Revolution)
1962,	Apr	Appointed vice-president of the China Medical University (until Cultural Revolution)
1965,	Jan	Elected member of the Standing Committee of the CPPCC
1967		Disappears during the Cultural Revolution
1973,	May	First appearance after the Cultural Revolution; referred to in his previous post as member of the Standing Committee of the CPPCC
1978,	Mar	Confirmed as member of the Standing Committee by the 5th CPPCC

Zhang Xiaozeng (Chang Hsiao-tseng) 张效增

Posts held

Government
Vice-minister of the 1st Ministry of Machine Building

1955,	Mar	Identified as deputy director of the Government Offices Administration under the State Council (until May 1957); then disappears until 1978
1978,	Apr	Identified as vice-minister of the 1st Ministry of Machine Building

Zhang Xiqin (Chang Hsi-ch'in) 张希钦

Posts held

NPC
Deputy for the PLA to the 5th NPC

Military
Major-general
Deputy commander of Nanjing Military Region

Zhang was born in 1916. Around 1936 he served as deputy commander of the 2nd Subdistrict, Northwestern Shanxi Military District. In 1949 he was chief of staff of the 2nd Corps, 1st Field Army.

1949,	Dec	Identified as chief of staff of Xinjiang Military Region and as commander of Ürümqi Garrison
1955		Identified as major-general and deputy commander of Xinjiang Military Region
1970,	May	Identified as commander of Xinjiang Production and Construction Corps
1975,	Oct	Identified as deputy commander of Nanjing Military Region
1978,	Feb	Elected deputy for the PLA to the 5th NPC

Zhang Xiulong (Chang Hsiu-lung) 张秀龙

Posts held

CCP
Member of the Standing Committee, Hubei Province CP

NPC
Deputy for Hubei Province to the 5th NPC

Military
Major-general
Deputy commander, Wuhan Military Region
Commander of Hubei Military District

Provincial Administration
Vice-chairman of the People's Congress, Hubei Province

Zhang began his military career as a youth in the 2nd Front Army in 1934. The battalion in which he served had only three guns, the rest being equipped with red-tasseled spears. Wounded in action (in 1937?) and later served in a guerrilla unit. 1946 deputy commander of Central Plains Military District, 1947 commander of the 9th Division, East China Field Army. This unit was shortly afterward reorganized into the 66th Division, 3rd Field Army.

1957,	Mar	Identified as major-general in Zhejiang Military District
1959		Training at a military college
1963,	Oct	Identified as deputy commander of Zhejiang Military District
1965,	Dec	Identified as commander of Zhejiang Military District
1967,	Jul	Purged for anti-Mao activities
1974,	Jan	First appearance after Cultural Revolution
1976,	Apr	Identified as commander of Hubei Military District
1977,	Aug	Identified as member, Standing Committee of Hubei Province CP
1978,	Jan	Elected vice-chairman of Hubei Province Revolutionary Committee (until Dec 1979)
	Feb	Elected deputy for Hubei Province to the 5th NPC
	Sep	Identified as deputy commander of Wuhan Military Region
1980,	Jan	Elected vice-chairman of the People's Congress of Hubei Province

Zhang Xiushu (Chang Hsiu-shu) 张秀熟

Posts held

NPC
Deputy for Sichuan Province to the 5th NPC

Provincial Administration
Vice-chairman of the People's Congress of Sichuan Province

Others
Member of the Standing Committee of the 5th CPPCC
Vice-chairman of the Shanghai branch of the CPPCC

Zhang was born in Sichuan Province and studied at Chengdu Higher School. He joined the Communists after the May 4th Movement.

1950,	Jul	Identified as director of the Department of Culture and Education in the West Sichuan People's Administration Office
1952,	Aug	Identified as deputy director of the Cultural and Educational Office in the Sichuan People's Council
1954,	Aug	Elected deputy for Sichuan Province to the 1st NPC) confirmed by the 2nd and 3rd NPCs)
1958,	Jul	Elected vice-governor of Sichuan Province (until Cultural Revolution)
1966		Disappears during the Cultural Revolution
1978,	Feb	First appearance after the Cultural Revolution; elected deputy for Sichuan Province to the 5th NPC
	Mar	Elected member of the Standing Committee of the 5th CPPCC

| | Aug | Identified as vice-chairman of the Sichuan branch of the CPPCC |
| 1979, | Dec | Elected vice-chairman of the People's Congress of Sichuan Province |

Zhang Xiuzhu (Chang Hsiu-chu) 张修竹

Posts held

Government
Vice-minister of state farms and land reclamation

1949,	Nov	Identified as chairman of the Trade Union of Harbin Municipality
1952,	Apr	Identified as deputy director of the Culture and Education Department of the Federation of Trade Unions
	Oct	Member of a workers delegation to North Korea
1953,	May	Elected secretary of the Federation of Trade Unions (until 1962) and director of the Propaganda Department of the Federation of Trade Unions
1955,	Sep	Member of a trade union delegation to Yugoslavia
1957,	Dec	Elected member of the Executive Council of the Federation of Trade Unions (until 1962)
1958,	Apr	Head of a trade union delegation to Poland
1960,	Jan	Appointed member of the Spare-Time Educational Committee under the State Council
	Aug	Head of a trade union delegation to Indonesia
1961,	Apr	Head of a trade union delegation to the May Day celebrations in the USSR
1962,	Nov	Identified as director of the State Office of Agriculture and Forestry (until Cultural Revolution)
1967		Branded as a counterrevolutionary revisionist and disappears
1972,	Apr	First appearance after the Cultural Revolution followed by renewed disappearance until 1978
1978,	Apr	Identified as secretary of the Federation of Trade Unions (until Oct 1978)
1980,	Jan	Identified as vice-minister of state farms and land reclamation

Zhang Yan (Chang Yen) 张衍

Posts held

Government
Vice-minister of the State Planning Commission

1974,	Sep	Identified as a government cadre
1976,	Nov	Deputy head of a friendship delegation to North Korea
1978,	Apr	Identified as vice-minister of the Planning Commission
	Oct	Advisor to an educational delegation to Japan and Canada

Zhang Yaoci (Chang Yao-tz'u)   张耀祠

Posts held

CCP
Alternate member, CCP 11th Central Committee
Deputy director, General Office, CCP Central Committee

1969,   Apr   Member of the presidium of the 9th CCP Congress
1976,   Sep   At mourning ceremony for Mao Zedong Zhang is mentioned as heading the team of doctors who had treated Mao
1977,   Aug   Elected alternate member of the CCP Central Committee by the 11th Party Congress
1978,   May   Identified as deputy director of the General Office of the CCP Central Committee, member of a Party and government delegation to North Korea (leader: Hua Guofeng)
         Aug   Member of a Party and government delegation to Romania, Yugoslavia, and Iran (leader: Hua Guofeng)

Zhang Yi (Chang Yi)   张遗

Posts held

Provincial Administration
Vice-governor of Fujian Province

Others
Director of the Board of Directors, China International Trust and Investment Corporation

1979,   Oct   Appointed vice-chairman of the Revolutionary Committee of Fujian Province (until Dec 1979); identified as director of the Board of Directors, China International Trust and Investment Corporation
         Dec   Elected vice-governor of Fujian Province

Zhang Yijun (Chang Yi-chün)   张毅君

Posts held

Government
Deputy director of the Western Europe Department in the Ministry of Foreign Affairs

1973,   Jun   Member of a government delegation led by Ji Pengfei to Great Britain, France, and Iran
1974,   Sep   Identified as deputy director of the Western Europe Department in the Ministry of Foreign Affairs

Zhang Yimin (Chang Yi-min)   张益民

Posts held

Government
Vice-minister of metallurgical industry

1977,   Dec   Identified as vice-minister of metallurgical industry

Zhang Yixiang (Chang Yi-hsiang)   张翼翔

Posts held

Military
Lieutenant-general

In 1929 Zhang led a column in the 3rd Army Corps. Around 1932 he commanded a battalion belonging to the same unit. During the Long March he was engaged in guerrilla activities in Fujian Province. He was made commander of a New 4th Army battalion in 1937, of a regiment in 1939, and of a brigade around 1944. At the beginning of 1949 Zhang was deputy commander of the 20th Army. After the occupation of Shanghai in May of that year he became commander of the 20th Army.

1950,   Oct   Appointed deputy commander of the 9th Army Corps, which fought in Korea
1952   Training at Nanjing Military Academy
1955,   Sep   Promoted to rank of lieutenant-general
1957,   Jul   Identified as deputy commander of Nanjing Military Region
1958,   Jun   Identified as deputy commander of Fuzhou Military Region
1964,   Aug   Identified as deputy director of the Training Department, general staff of the PLA
1968,   Jun   Appointed commander of the PLA Railway Corps (until 1975?)
1969,   Apr   Elected to first term as member of the CCP Central Committee by the 9th Party Congress (until Aug 1977)

Zhang Yongli (Chang Yung-li)   张永励

Posts held

Government
Vice-minister of commerce

Zhang joined the CCP at a young age. From 1946 to 1949 he was director of the Salt Administration Bureau in Shaanxi-Gansu-Ningxia Border Region.

1950-1952   Zhang holds various administrative offices in the Central-South China Military and Administrative Council
1953   Identified as South China Commissioner in the Ministry of Foreign Trade
1954,   Aug   Elected deputy for Guangdong Province to the 1st NPC
1956   Appointed vice-chairman of the Federation of Supply and Marketing Cooperatives
1957,   Mar   Appointed vice-minister of urban services
1958,   Feb   The Ministry of Urban Services is reorganized to form the 2nd Ministry of Commerce; Zhang continues as vice-minister
         Sep   The 2nd Ministry of Commerce is merged with the 1st Ministry of Commerce; Zhang remains vice-minister
1967   Disappears during the Cultural Revolution
1975,   Jun   First appearance after the Cultural Revolution
         Jul   Identified as vice-minister of commerce

Zhang Youxuan (Chang Yu-hsüan) 张友萱

<u>Posts held</u>

Government
Vice-minister of the 6th Ministry of Machine Building

Others
General manager of the Chinese Ship-building Corporation
President of the Society of Shipbuilding Engineers

Before the foundation of the PRC Zhang lectured in mechanical engineering at Qinghua University.

1952,	Jun	Identified as director of the Bureau of Machinery Administration, Industrial Department in the Northeast People's Government
1954,	Oct	Identified as member of the State Planning Commission (until Apr 1957)
1957,	Jan	Identified as vice-chairman of the State Technology Commission (until Nov 1958)
1958,	Nov	Appointed vice-chairman of the State Scientific and Technological Commission (until Jan 1967)
1959,	Sep	Advisor to the Chinese delegation attending the 6th Conference of the World Federation of Scientific Workers in Warsaw
1961,	Nov	Member of a cultural delegation to Japan
1967,	Jan	Branded as a capitalist-roader and purged
1976,	Jan	First appearance after the Cultural Revolution; attending the mourning ceremonies for Zhou Enlai
1978,	Sep	Identified as vice-minister of the 6th Ministry of Machine Building
	Nov	Identified as president of the Society of Shipbuilding Engineers and as general manager of the Chinese Shipbuilding Corporation; head of a shipbuilding study group to Japan

Zhang Youyu (Chang Yu-yü) 张友渔

<u>Posts held</u>

Others
Member of the Standing Committee, 5th CPPCC

Zhang was born in 1899 in Lingshi, Shanxi Province. After graduating from the Beijing University of Political Science and Law he worked as a journalist for the Shanghai evening newspaper <u>Zhongmei</u>. Later he continued his studies at the Tokyo Institute of Political Science and Law. In 1931 he lectured as a professor at the Law Institute of Beijing University, at the National Institute, and at the Sino-French University. Concurrently he served as chief editor with the Beijing newspaper <u>World News</u>. In 1945 Zhang was manager of <u>Xinhua</u> (New China), the paper of the Communist Party in Chongqing. At the same time he served as deputy secretary of Sichuan Province CP and as director of the Propaganda Department of Sichuan CP. In January 1946 he was an advisor to the CCP delegation at the Nationalist Government's Political Consultative Conference. After the failure of cease-fire negotiations between the CCP and the KMT he left for

the Communist occupied areas of North China. In December 1947 he was identified as vice-chairman and as secretary-general of the Shanxi-Hebei-Shandong-Henan Border Region Government. In September 1949 he was elected a member of the CPPCC. From January to September of that year he was in addition deputy mayor of Tianjin.

1949,	Nov	Appointed deputy mayor of Beijing Municipality (until Aug 1958)
	Dec	Appointed chairman of the Finance and Commerce Committee and director of the Labor Bureau of Beijing People's Government
1950,	Mar	Appointed chairman of the Organization Committee of Beijing People's Government
	Apr	Appointed vice-chairman of the Urban Planning Committee of Beijing People's Government
1952,	Dec	Identified as member of the Standing Committee of Beijing Municipality CP
1953,	Jan	Appointed member of the North China Administrative Council (until Sep 1954)
1954,	Aug	Elected deputy for Beijing Municipality to the 1st NPC
1956,	Feb	Identified as deputy secretary of Beijing Municipality CP
1957,	Jan	Member of a Beijing City Council delegation led by Peng Zhen to the USSR and several East European countries
1958,	Jun	Identified as secretary of Beijing Municipality CP
	Aug	Elected vice-chairman of the Committee of Political and Legal Affairs
1959,	Apr	Identified as director of the Institute of Legal Research of the Academy of Sciences
	Nov	Elected chairman of the Sino-Burmese Friendship Association
1960,	Oct	Head of the Chinese delegation to the 7th Congress of the World Federation of Democratic Jurists in Sofia
	Dec	Identified as deputy director of the Department of Philosophy and Social Sciences, Academy of Sciences
1961,	Jun	Member of a delegation of scientists under Wu Youxun to conclude an agreement on scientific cooperation between the Academies of Sciences in Moscow
	Aug	Member of a delegation led by Guo Moruo to Indonesia and Burma
1962,	Apr	Appointed council member of the newly established Asian-African Society
	Aug	Publication of an article in HQ No. 13/62, "The Farce of Bourgeois Parlamentary Democracy"
	Oct	Head of the Chinese delegation to the 2nd Afro-Asian Conference in Guinea
1963,	Nov	Head of a group of scientists visiting Japan
1964,	Aug	Vice-chairman of the Chinese delegation at the Symposium of Scientific Workers in Beijing
1965,	Jan	Elected member of the Standing Committee of the 4th CPPCC
	Sep	Head of a friendship delegation to North Vietnam

1967,	Jan	Branded as a capitalist revisionist and purged
1979,	Feb	First appearance after the Cultural Revolution
	Jun	By-elelcted member of the Standing Committee of the 5th CPPCC at its 4th Plenum

Zhang Yu (Chang Yü) 张 雨

Posts held

Others
Deputy general manager of the China International Travel Service

1972,	Apr	Identified as deputy director of the Travel and Tourism Administrative Bureau
1975,	Oct	Head of a travel service delegation to Japan
1976,	Jan	Identified as deputy director of the China International Travel Service
1977,	Sep	Head of a travel service delegation to Japan
1978,	Aug	Identified as deputy general manager of the China International Travel Service

Zhang Yuanpei (Chang Yüan-p'ei) 张元培

Posts held

NPC
Deputy for the PLA to the 5th NPC

Military
Rear-admiral
Deputy director, Logistics Department of the PLA

1960,	Sep	Member of a military delegation to Egypt; identified as rear-admiral
1964,	Aug	Identified as a military officer in Qingdao
1975,	Sep	First appearance after the Cultural Revolution
	Dec	Identified as deputy director of the PLA Logistics Department
1978,	Feb	Elected deputy for the PLA to the 5th NPC

Zhang Yue (Chang Yüeh) 张 越

Posts held

Government
Ambassador to Italy

1952		Identified as deputy director, Western European and African Affairs Department in the Ministry of Foreign Affairs (until 1956)
1955,	Jul	Identified as council member of the Institute of Foreign Affairs
1956,	Feb	Identified as deputy head, Office of the Chinese Trade Representative in Cairo (until Jul 1956)

	Jul	Identified as counselor, embassy in Yemen (until Apr 1961)
1961,	Jun	Appointed ambassador to Somalia (until Sep 1964)
1974,	Sep	Appointed ambassador to Sudan (until Dec 1978)
1977,	Jun	Zhang accompanies President Numeri to the PRC
1979,	Feb	Appointed ambassador for Italy

Zhang Yuhua (Chang Yü-hua) 张玉华

Posts held

CCP
Member of the CCP 11th Central Committee
Secretary of Hubei Province CP

Military
Deputy Political Commissar of Wuhan Military Region

1959,	Feb	Identified as chief of staff, Artillery Forces, Shenyang Military Region
1967,	Sep	Identified as deputy political commissar of Wuhan Military Region
1971,	Mar	Elected secretary of Hubei Province CP following the reorganization of the Secretariat
1977,	Jun	Identified as member of the Standing Committee of the CP Secretariat, Wuhan Military Region
	Aug	Elected member of the CCP Central Committee by the 11th Party Congress

Zhang Yuhuan (Chang Yü-huan) 张玉环

Posts held

CCP
Member of the Standing Committee, Guizhou Province CP

Provincial Administration
Vice-governor of Guizhou Province

1973,	Dec	Identified as a Guizhou cadre
1974,	Feb	Identified as a member of the Standing Committee, Guizhou Province CP
1980,	Jan	Elected vice-governor of Guizhou Province

Zhang Yun (Chang Yün) 章 蕴

Posts held

CCP
Member of the Standing Committee, Yunnan Province CP

Provincial Administration
Vice-governor of Yunnan Province

Zhang is a native of Taiyuan, Shanxi Province.

| 1952, | Apr | Identified as secretary, CP of Central Guangdong District |

Sep Identified as director of the Organization Department, CP of West Guangdong District

1955, Jul Identified as secretary, CP of West Guangdong District

1956, Sep Identified as 1st secretary of Hainan District CP (until Jul 1958)

1959, Mar Identified as director of the Industry Department of Guangdong Province CP

1962, Feb Identified as alternate secretary of Guangdong Province CP (until Feb 1967)

1967, Feb Branded as a capitalist-roader and purged

1977, Dec First appearance after the Cultural Revolution: Elected vice-chairman of the Revolutionary Committee of Yunnan Province (until Dec 1979)

1979, Jan Identified as member of the Standing Committee, Yunnan Province CP

Dec Elected vice-governor of Yunnan Province

Zhang Yun (Chang Yün) (f) 张 云

Posts held

CCP
Deputy secretary of the Commission for Inspecting Discipline under the CCP Central Committee

Others
Member of the Standing Committee of the 5th CPPCC

Zhang was born in Wusi, Jiangsu Province. She studied at Fudan University in Shanghai. After the occupation of North China by Communist forces she took part in the founding session of the Democratic Women's Federation in April 1949 which elected her a member of its Executive Council.

1949, Dec Appointed member of the East China Military and Administrative Council (until Jan 1953)

1950, Mar Appointed member of the Rural Reform Committee in the East China Military and Administrative Council (until Jun 1954)

1952 Identified as director of the Women's Work Department in the East China Bureau of the CCP Central Committee; elected chairman of the Shanghai Section, Democratic Women's Federation

Dec Elected secretary-general of the Women's Federation

1953, Apr Elected vice-chairman and member of the Standing Committee of the Democratic Women's Federation

Jun Deputy head of a Chinese delegation attending the Congress of the International Democratic Women's Federation in Copenhagen

1954, Sep Elected deputy for Anhui Province to the 1st NPC (reelected in 1958 and 1964 to the 2nd and 3rd NPCs)

1955, Apr Elected secretary of the Democratic Women's Federation (until Sep 1957)

1956, Sep Elected alternate member of the CCP Central Committee

1957, Jun Identified as 3rd secretary of the Women's Work Department in the CCP Central Committee

Sep Reelected vice-chairman of the Women's Federation (hitherto Democratic Women's Federation)

1958, May Head of a delegation attending the 4th Congress of the International Democratic Women's Federation

1959, Apr Elected member of the CPPCC

1965, Jan Elected member of the Standing Committee of the CPPCC

1966 Disappears during the Cultural Revolution

1975, Sep First appearance after the Cultural Revolution

1978, Mar Elected member of the Standing Committee of the 5th CPPCC

Apr Identified as vice-chairman of the Women's Federation (not confirmed in this post by the October 1978 Congress of the federation)

Dec Appointed deputy secretary of the Commission for Inspecting Discipline under the CCP Central Committee

Zhang Yuqin (Chang Yü-ch'in) (f) 张玉芹

Posts held

Provincial Administration
Vice-governor of Guizhou Province

1977, Nov Elected vice-chairman of the Revolutionary Committee of Guizhou Province (until Dec 1979)

1979, Jul Appointed member of the National Games Organizing Committee

1980, Jan Elected vice-governor of Guizhou Province

Zhang Yuzhe (Chang Yü-che) 张钰哲

Posts held

NPC
Deputy for Jiangsu Province to the 5th NPC

Others
Chairman, Astronomy Society
Director, Zijinshan Observatory

Zhang was born in 1902.

1957 Identified as director of the Zijinshan Observatory, Nanjing

1964, Oct Elected deputy for Jiangsu Province to the 3rd NPC

1973, Jun Identified as chairman of the Astronomy Society

Oct Identified as member of the Zijinshan Observatory, Academy of Sciences

1977, Sep Identified as director of the Zijinshan Observatory

1978, Feb Elected deputy to the 5th NPC for Jiangsu Province

Zhang Zengwen (Chang Tseng-wen) 张曾文

Posts held

Provincial Administration
Vice-chairman of the Tibet Autonomous
Regional People's Government

1979,   Aug   Elected vice-chairman of the Tibet
                Autonomous Regional People's Govern-
                ment

Zhang Zhanwu (Chang Chan-wu) 张占武

Posts held

Government
Ambassador to Western Samoa

Zhang was born in 1924 in Shanxi Province.

1962,   Apr   Identified as 1st secretary at the embassy
                in Poland
1965,   Jul   Identified as deputy director, General
                Department of the Ministry of Foreign
                Affairs (until Cultural Revolution)
1975,   Apr   Reactivated after the Cultural Revolu-
                tion: Identified as deputy director, Gener-
                al Department of the Ministry of Foreign
                Affairs; member of a goodwill delegation
                to Switzerland
1978,   Oct   Appointed ambassador to Western Samoa

Zhang Zhao (Chang Chao) 张昭

Posts held

Government
Vice-minister of coal industry

Zhang is believed to have studied forestry sciences in
Great Britain.

1950,   Dec   Identified as member of the Institute of
                Forestry and Pedology, Academy of Sci-
                ences, and as director of the Department
                of Afforestation in the Ministry of For-
                estry and Reclamation (until 1952)
1955,   Mar   Director of the Bureau of Afforestation in
                the Ministry of Forestry (until Oct 1958)
1956,   Jul   Identified as assistant minister of forestry
                (until Sep 1959)
1957,   Nov   Member of a technical delegation to the
                USSR
1958,   Nov   Identified as vice-chairman of the For-
                estry Society (until Cultural Revolution)
1960,   May   Identified as vice-minister of forestry
                (until Cultural Revolution)
1975,   Sep   First appearance after the Cultural Revo-
                lution
1978,   Feb   Identified as vice-minister of coal indus-
                try

Zhang Zhen (Chang Chen) 张珍

Posts held

Government
Minister, 5th Ministry of Machine Building
Deputy director, National Administration
for Building Materials Industry

1954,   Aug   Appointed director, Chemical Industry
                Administrative Bureau, Ministry of Heavy
                Industry
1956   Elected vice-chairman, Chemical Industry
                Society
1957,   Mar   Appointed vice-minister of chemical in-
                dustry (until 1965)
1964,   Dec   Head of an Economic and Technical Ob-
                serving Team visiting Romania
1965,   Oct   Head of a scientific and technical delega-
                tion to North Korea
1967   Disappears during the Cultural Revolution
1974,   Sep   First appearance after the Cultural Revo-
                lution
1975,   Nov   Identified as vice-minister of petroleum
                and chemical industries (until Feb 1978)
1978,   Mar   Appointed minister of the 5th Ministry of
                Machine Building
         Sep   Identified as deputy director of the Na-
                tional Administration for Building Materi-
                als Industry

Zhang Zhen (Chang Chen) 张震

Posts held

CCP
Alternate member, CCP 11th Central
Committee

NPC
Deputy for the PLA to the 5th NPC

Military
Lieutenant-general
Director, Logistics Department of the
PLA

Zhang was born in 1907. In 1935 he underwent military
training in the USSR. In 1945 he commanded the 6th Column, Central China Military Region. In 1947 he was chief
of staff of an army corps and concurrently commander of
the 9th Military District of Jiangsu-Shandong Military
Region. Shortly afterward he was given the additional post
of deputy chief of staff, East China Field Army. At the
beginning of 1949 he was deputy chief of staff of the
3rd Field Army.

1949,   Oct   Appointed chief of staff, 3rd Field Army
1952   Identified as head of Department G-3,
                General Staff of the PLA
1955   Promoted to rank of lieutenant-general
1957   Identified as deputy commandant, Military
                Academy of the PLA in Nanjing
1963,   Jul   Identified as commandant, Military Acad-
                emy in Nanjing
1973   Identified as deputy commander, Wuhan
                Military Region; leader of a PLA group on
                vacation in Romania
1977,   Mar   Identified as deputy director, Logistics
                Department of the PLA (until Mar 1978)

Aug Elected alternate member of the CCP Central Committee by the 11th Party Congress

1978, Feb Elected deputy for the PLA to the 5th NPC

Apr Identified as director, Logistics Department of the PLA

1979, May Head of a government and military delegation to the 10th anniversary of the 25th May Revolution in Sudan

Zhang Zhengtao (Chang Cheng-t'ao) 张正桃

Posts held

NPC
Member of the Standing Committee of the 5th NPC
Deputy for Sichuan Province to the 5th NPC

1978, Feb Elected deputy for Sichuan Province to the 5th NPC

Mar Elected member of the Standing Committee of the 5th NPC

Zhang Zhidi (Chang Chih-ti) 张植弟

Posts held

CCP
Alternate member, CCP 11th Central Committee

1973, Dec Elected vice-chairman of the Hubei Province Peasants' Federation (until 1976?)

1977, Aug Elected alternate member of the CCP Central Committee

Zhang Zhiguo (Chang Chih-kuo) 张治国

Posts held

CCP
Secretary of Henan Province CP

1968, May Elected vice-chairman of the Revolutionary Committee, Liaoning Province, subsequently disappears until 1973

1973, Mar Identified as a cadre in Liaoning Province (until Sep 1977, when he disappears again)

1979, Aug Identified as secretary of Henan Province CP

Zhang Zhihuai (Chang Chih-huai) 张之槐

Posts held

Others
President of the Volleyball Association
Member of the International Volleyball Federation Council
2nd vice-president of the Asian Volleyball Federation

1962, Nov Identified as chairman of the Volleyball Association (until Cultural Revolution); head of a sports delegation to the USSR

1964, May Identified as vice-chairman of the Football Association (until Cultural Revolution)

1965, Jul Identified as director of the Ballgames Department in the Physical Culture and Sports Commission

Sep Head of a sports delegation to the USSR

Nov Head of a sports delegation to Cuba

1966, May Head of a sports delegation to Albania, then disappears

1978, May First appearance after the Cultural Revolution: Identified as president of the Volleyball Association. In this capacity, Zhang heads the Tournament Organizing Committee of the International Volleyball Tournament in Beijing

Sep Elected a member of the International Volleyball Federation Council

Dec Deputy head of a sports delegation to the 8th Asian Games in Bangkok

1979, Mar Identified as 2nd vice-president of the Asian Volleyball Federation

Jul Appointed member and secretary-general of the National Games Organizing Committee

Zhang Zhixiang (Chang Chih-hsiang) 张致祥

Posts held

CCP
Deputy director of the International Liaison Department in the CCP Central Committee

Zhang was first noted in the summer of 1949 as a member of the Standing Committee of the Federation of Literary and Art Circles.

1952, Aug Identified as deputy director of the Political Department of North China Military Region

1954, Oct Identified as vice-minister of culture (until Mar 1958)

1955, May Head of a theater group attending the International Theater Festival in Paris, followed by visits to Belgium and Czechoslovakia

Oct Attends World Conference of Capital Mayors in Florence on behalf of Peng Zhen

1957, Mar Head of a cultural delegation to PR Mongolia

1958, Mar Appointed vice-chairman of the Commission for Cultural Relations with Foreign Countries (until Cultural Revolution); head of a delegation led by Guo Moro to the Conference on Disarmament and International Cooperation in Stockholm

Sep Elected chairman of the Sino-Mongolian Friendship Association (until 1961)

1959, Apr Elected vice-chairman of the Association for Cultural Relations with Foreign Countries (until Cultural Revolution)

	May	Head of a delegation led by Guo Moro to attend the World Peace Council Session in Stockholm
	Nov	Head of a cultural delegation to Bulgaria
1960,	Mar	Elected member of the Standing Committee of the Sino-Latin American Friendship Association (until Cultural Revolution)
	Apr	Elected member of the Sino-African Friendship Association (until Cultural Revolution)
	May	Head of a cultural delegation to Greece
	Oct	Identified as acting secretary-general of the Sino-Soviet Friendship Association (until Cultural Revolution)
	Dec	Member of a friendship delegation headed by Zhou Enlai to Burma
1961,	Jul	Head of a friendship delegation to the PR Mongolia
	Sep	Identified as acting chairman of the State Commission for Cultural Relations with Foreign Countries
1962,	Apr	Head of a cultural delegation to North Korea
	Dec	Head of a cultural delegation to North Vietnam; identified as vice-president of the Sino-Cuban Friendship Association
1963,	Dec	Head of a friendship delegation to Cuba
1967,	Jul	Branded as a counterrevolutionary revisionist and purged
1978,	Apr	First appearance after the Cultural Revolution; identified as deputy director of the International Liaison Department in the CCP Central Committee
	Sep	Head of a delegation of Party workers to Romania
1979,	Nov	Member of a CCP delegation to Romania (head: Ulanhu)

Zhang Zhixiu (Chang Chih-hsiu)　张钰秀

Posts held

CCP
Member of the CCP 11th Central Committee

Military
Major-general
Commander of Kunming Military Region

Provincial Administration
Vice-chairman of the People's Congress of Yunnan Province

1957,	Nov	Identified as major-general and commander of the PLA units stationed in Yantai (Zhifu)
1968,	May	Participates in the May Day celebrations in Beijing
1970,	Jul	Identified as high-ranking officer in Jinan Military Region
1971,	Feb	Identified as deputy commander of Jinan Military Region (until Oct 1975)
		Identified as vice-chairman of the Revolutionary Committee of Shandong Province

	Apr	On election of new CP Secretariat for Shandong Province after Cultural Revolution, Zhang is elected deputy secretary (until Oct 1975)
1975,	Dec	Identified as deputy commander of Kunming Military Region (until Jan 1980)
1977,	Feb	Identified as deputy secretary of Yunnan Province CP (until Sep 1977) and as vice-chairman of the Revolutionary Committee of Yunnan Province (until Dec 1979)
	Aug	Elected member of the CCP Central Committee by the 11th Party Congress
	Sep	Identified as secretary of Yunnan Province CP (until Aug 1979)
1979,	Dec	Elected vice-chairman of the People's Congress of Yunnan Province
1980,	Feb	Identified as commander of Kunming Military Region

Zhang Zhiyi (Chang Chih-yi)　张执一

Posts held

Others
Member of the Standing Committee of the 5th CPPCC

Zhang was born in 1905 in Hanyang, Hubei Province. In 1929 he left his family to avoid a marriage contracted by his family. He studied at Wuchang Arts Institute and Hubei Rural Normal College. In 1932 he was imprisoned by the KMT. About 1938 he served as director of the Political Department of the 15th Brigade, 5th Division, under the New 4th Army. In 1942 he was again imprisoned in Xinjiang (until 1946). In 1947 he was made deputy director of the United Front Work Department of the CCP Central Plains Bureau.

1949,	Dec	Identified as secretary-general of the Central-South Military and Administrative Council and as vice-mayor of Hanyang
1950,	Jul	Identified as director of the United Front Work Department of the Central-South Bureau under the CCP Central Committee
1951,	Oct	Identified as vice-chairman of the Nationalities Affairs Committee under the Government Administrative Council (until 1954)
1954,	Aug	Elected deputy for Hubei Province to the 1st NPC
1955,	Apr	Identified as deputy director of the United Front Work Department under the CCP Central Committee (until Cultural Revolution)
	Jun	Appointed deputy director of the 8th Office of the State Council
1957,	Oct	Identified as deputy secretary-general of the 2nd CPPCC (reelected in 1959 to the 3rd CPPCC)
1959,	Apr	Elected member of the Standing Committee of the 3rd CPPCC
1967,	May	Denounced as a renegade and purged
1978,	Dec	First appearance after the Cultural Revolution
1979,	Jul	By-elected member of the Standing Committee of the 5th CPPCC

Zhang Zhiyuan (Chang Chih-yüan) 张知远

Posts held

Provincial Administration
Vice-governor of Liaoning Province

1966,	Jan	Identified as vice-chairman of the trade union of Henan Province
1978,	Jan	Elected vice-chairman of the Revolutionary Committee of Liaoning Province (until Jan 1980)
1979,	Sep	Identified as chairman of the Liaoning Provincial Scientific and Technical Commission
1980,	Jan	Elected vice-governor of Liaoning Province

Zhang Zhong (Chang Chung) 张中

Posts held

CCP
Member, Standing Committee of Kueichou Province CP

NPC
Deputy for the PLA to the 5th NPC

Military
Commander of Guizhou Military District

Zhang was first noted as a member of the 1st Front Army in which he probably took part in the Long March. In 1937 he commanded a company of the 686th Regiment, 343rd Brigade, 115th Division, 8th Route Army. In 1947 he was made a regiment commander in the Central Plains Field Army. In 1949 he became deputy commander of the 52nd Division.

1950		Identified as commander of the 54th Division, 18th Army. In this post in charge of the construction of the Xikang-Tibet Road
1959		Identified as deputy commander of Gansu Military District (until 1969)
1968,	Jan	Elected vice-chairman of the newly established Revolutionary Committee of Gansu Province
1970,	Sep	Identified as commander of Gansu Military District (until 1975)
1971,	Feb	After reorganization of the Gansu Province CP Secretariat, elected member of its Standing Committee (until May 1973)
1973,	Jun	Identified as secretary of Gansu Province CP (until 1975)
1976,	Oct	Identified as commander of Guizhou Military District
1978,	Feb	Elected deputy for the PLA to the 5th NPC
	Aug	Identified as member of the Standing Committee, Guizhou Province CP

Zhang Zhong (Chang Chung) 张忠

Posts held

CCP
Member of the Commission for Inspecting Discipline, CCP Central Committee

Government
Director of the State Archives Bureau

1950,	Mar	Identified as deputy director of the Livestock Raising Department, Northwest China Military and Administrative Council
1953,	Dec	Identified as director of the Administrative Office of the Northwest Bureau, CCP Central Committee (until 1954)
1955,	Mar	Identified as deputy director of the State Archives Bureau (until Cultural Revolution)
1966		Zhang disappears
1978,	Dec	First appearance after the Cultural Revolution: Appointed member of the Commission for Inspecting Discipline, CCP Central Committee
1979,	Aug	Identified as director of the State Archives Bureau

Zhang Zhongliang (Chang Chung-liang) 张仲良

Posts held

CCP
Secretary of Jiangsu Province CP

NPC
Deputy for Jiangsu Province to the 5th NPC

Provincial Administration
Vice-chairman of the People's Congress of Jiangsu Province

Zhang was born in 1912 in Yao, Shaanxi Province. In 1928 he joined the peasants movement. He served a jail sentence for communist activity. After military training at the Anti-Japan Military and Political Academy of the Red Army in Yan'an he was from 1937 to 1947 successively deputy commander of the 3rd Garrison Brigade, Defense Forces of the Shaanxi-Gansu-Ningxia-Shanxi-Suiyuan Area, political commissar of the 1st Garrison Brigade, special commissar of Guancho (?) District in the Shanxi-Gansu-Ningxia Border Area, and commander of the Peace Keeping Corps. In 1947 Zhang was appointed deputy political commissar of the Defense Forces' Headquarters, member of Shaanxi Province CP Committee, and commander of Longdung (?) Military Region. He was appointed political commissar of the 1st Field Army and secretary of Qinghai Province CP in September 1949 (until 1954).

1949,	Oct	Appointed vice-chairman, People's Government of Qinghai Province (until Nov 1952)
	Nov	Appointed member of the newly established Northeast China Military and Administrative Council (until Jan 1953)
1950,	Mar	Identified as political commissar of Qinghai Military Region (until Sep 1954)
1952,	Nov	Appointed chairman of Qinghai People's Government (until Sep 1954)
1953,	Jan	Appointed member of the Northeast China Administrative Council (abolished in Sep 1954)
1954,	Jul	Elected deputy for Gansu Province to the 1st NPC (until Mar 1959)
	Aug	Appointed acting secretary of Gansu Province CP

1956,	Feb	Appointed 1st secretary of Gansu Province CP (probably until Sep 1961)
1958,	May	Elected alternate member of the CCP Central Committee
1961		Zhang disappears for unknown reasons
1966,	Jan	Identified as secretary of Jiangsu Province CP, followed by another disappearance
1977,	Dec	First appearance after the Cultural Revolution; elected vice-chairman of the Revolutionary Committee of Jiangsu Province (until Dec 1979)
1978,	Feb	Elected deputy for Jiangsu Province to the 5th NPC
1979,	Jun	Identified as secretary of Jiangsu Province CP
	Dec	Elected vice-chairman of the People's Congress of Jiangsu Province

Zhang Ziyi (Chang Tzu-yi)　　张子意

Posts held

Others
Member of the Standing Committee of the 5th CPPCC

Zhang was born in 1906 in Liling, Hunan Province. In 1925 he joined the CCP and took part in guerrilla activities in the Jinggangshan Area. In 1930 he headed the Organization Department in the Hunan-Jiangxi Soviet District as well as the Political Department of Hunan-Jiangxi Military District. In 1934-35 he took part in the Long March. In 1936 he commanded a regiment of the 6th Red Army. In 1937 he went to the USSR to receive medical treatment. He returned to China in 1940 and was posted to Xinjiang where he was arrested in 1942. In 1946 he was released by Governor Zhang Zhizhong and went to Yan'an. He became deputy director of the Political Department of Southwest China Military Region in 1949.

1950,	Jun	Identified as member of the Southwest China Military and Administrative Council and as vice-chairman of its Cultural and Educational Committee (until Jan 1953)
1953,	Jan	Appointed member of the Southwest China Administrative Council
	Jun	Identified as director of the Propaganda Department in the Southwest China Bureau of the CCP Central Committee (until 1958)
1958,	Dec	Identified as deputy director of the Propaganda Department in the CCP Central Committee (until Jan 1967)
1959,	Apr	Elected member of the Standing Committee of the 3rd CPPCC (confirmed in 1965 by the 4th CPPCC)
1967,	Jan	Branded as a member of the "Tao Zhu Gang" and purged
1975,	May	First appearance after the Cultural Revolution
	Sep	Renewed mention in his previous post as a member of the Standing Committee of the CPPCC
1978,	Mar	Elected member of the Standing Committee of the 5th CPPCC

Zhang Zizhai (Chang Tzu-chai)　　张子斋

Posts held

Provincial Administration
Vice-chairman of the People's Congress of Yunnan Province

Zhang belongs to the Bai minority.

| 1979, | Apr | Identified as vice-chairman of the Revolutionary Committee of Yunnan Province (until Dec 1979) |
| | Dec | Elected vice-chairman of the People's Congress of Yunnan Province |

Zhang Zuoyin (Chang Tso-yin)　　张柞荫

Posts held

NPC
Deputy for Anhui Province to the 5th NPC

Provincial Administration
Vice-chairman of the People's Congress of Anhui Province

1951,	Jul	Identified as deputy director of the Agriculture and Forestry Department, North Anhui Administrative Office
1958,	Oct	Identified as director of the Department of Water Conservancy and Electric Power, Anhui People's Government
1960,	May	Elected vice-governor of Anhui Province (until Jan 1967)
1967,	Jan	Branded as a revisionist and relieved of all posts
1978,	Jan	First appearance after the Cultural Revolution: Elected vice-chairman of the Revolutionary Committee of Anhui Province (until Dec 1979)
	Feb	Elected deputy for Anhui Province to the 5th NPC
1979,	Dec	Elected vice-chairman of the People's Congress of Anhui Province

Zhao Beike (Chao Pei-k'e)　　赵北克

Posts held

Others
Deputy secretary-general of the Academy of Sciences

1958,	Jan	Identified as director of an ironworks in Anshan
1964,	Dec	Appointed member of the State Economic Commission
1965,	May	Identified as vice-chairman of the State Capital Construction Commission (until Cultural Revolution)
1967		Disappears during the Cultural Revolution
1978,	Sep	First appearance after the Cultural Revolution: Identified as deputy secretary-general of the Academy of Sciences
	Oct	Deputy head of a scientific delegation led by Hua Luogeng to North Korea

Zhao Benxi (Chao Pen-hsi)

Posts held

Others
President of the Association of Nuclear Energy

1978, Oct   Identified as president of the Association of Nuclear Energy

Zhao Boping (Chao Po-p'ing)   赵伯平

Zhao Boping was born in 1909 in Shaanxi Province. In May 1944 he was identified as a member of the Drama Committee of the Yan'an Literary and Art Association. In April 1946 he became deputy commissar for education in the Government of Shaanxi-Gansu-Ningxia Border Region.

1949,   Oct   Appointed deputy secretary, CP of Xian Municipality (until Jun 1951)
       Dec   Appointed member of the People's Government of Shaanxi Province (until Jan 1955) and director of the Work Department, Northwest China Military and Administrative Council
1950,   Oct   Appointed director of the Finance and Commerce Committee of Xian Municipality
1951,   Jun   Elected secretary, CP of Xian Municipality (until May 1954)
1953,   Jan   Identified as member of the Northwest China Administrative Council (until Nov 1954)
       May   Identified as director of the Propaganda Department, Northwest China Bureau of the CCP Central Committee (until Aug 1954)
1954,   May   Appointed 1st secretary, CP of Xian Municipality (until Dec 1956)
       Aug   Elected deputy for Shaanxi Province to the 1st NPC
1955,   Jan   Elected vice-governor of Shaanxi Province (until Oct 1959)
       May   Identified as 2nd secretary of Shaanxi Province CP (until Dec 1956)
1956,   Dec   Identified as secretary of Shaanxi Province CP (probably until Jan 1963)
1958,   May   Elected alternate member of the CCP Central Committee
       Jul   Elected council member of the Peace Council
1959,   Oct   Appointed governor of Shaanxi Province (until about Oct 1963)
1963,   Jan   Appointed deputy secretary-general, Standing Committee of the NPC
       Oct   Zhao accompanies the parliamentary spokesman of Tanganyika, Adam Sapi Mkwawa, on a tour of China
1967   Disappears during the Cultural Revolution
1978,   Dec   First appearance after the Cultural Revolution

Zhao Cangbi (Chao Ts'ang-pi)   赵苍壁

Posts held

CCP
Member of the CCP 11th Central Committee

Government
Minister for public security

Zhao was born in 1912 in Shaanxi Province. He was active as a cadre in the public security field from about 1939 to 1948 in the Shaanxi-Gansu-Ningxia Border Region. In early 1949 he was deputy director of the Bureau of Public Security of Nanjing Municipality and shortly afterward served in the 2nd Field Army.

1950,   Jul   Identified as deputy director of the Public Security Department in the Southwest China Military and Administrative Council
1953,   Jan   Zhao holds the same position in the Southwest China Administrative Council
1956   Identified as director of the Public Security Department in Sichuan Province
       Jul   Elected member of the Standing Committee of Sichuan Province CP
1958,   Jul   Elected vice-governor of Sichuan Province
1959,   Dec   Identified as secretary of Sichuan Province CP
1964,   Oct   Elected deputy for Sichuan Province to the 3rd NPC
1967   Disappears during the Cultural Revolution
1975,   Dec   First appearance after the Cultural Revolution
1976,   Jan   Identified as secretary of Sichuan Province CP until 1977)
1977,   Aug   Elected member of the CCP Central Committee by the 11th Party Congress
1978,   Mar   Appointed minister for public security
       Oct   Identified as deputy head of the Central Political and Judical Group
1979,   Aug   Article in HQ: "Strengthen the Concept of the Legal System and Act Strictly According to Law."

Zhao Changchun (Chao Ch'ang-ch'un)   赵长春

Posts held

Government
Vice-minister of foreign trade

1959,   Oct   Identified as director of the Organization Department of Wuhan CP
1965,   May   Identified as deputy director of the Political Department in the Ministry of Foreign Trade
1977,   Dec   Identified as director of the General Office of the Ministry of Foreign Trade
1978,   Nov   Identified as vice-minister of foreign trade
1979,   Jan   Head of a trade delegation to Japan
       Apr   Head of a trade delegation to Liberia, Senegal, and to the 28th Casablanca International Fair

Zhao Chunzheng (Chao Ch'un-cheng)

赵春正

Posts held

Government
Deputy director of the Foreign Affairs Department in the Ministry of National Defense

1964,	Aug	Member of a delegation to Congo (Brazzaville)
1971,	Feb	Identified as deputy director of the Foreign Affairs Department in the Ministry of National Defense
	May	Member of a military delegation to Guinea and Mali
1972,	May	Member of a government delegation to Sudan
1974,	Jan	Member of a government delegation to Tanzania
1975,	Jun	Member of a government delegation to Mozambique
1977,	Oct	Member of a military delegation to Tunisia

Zhao Chuqi (Chao Ch'u-ch'i)   赵虚琪

Posts held

CCP
Secretary of Gansu Province CP

1977,	May	Identified as member of the Standing Committee of Hunan Province CP (until Oct 1977) and as director of the Organization Department of Hunan Province CP
	Oct	Elected secretary of Hunan Province CP (until Feb 1978)
	Nov	Identified as member of the Standing Committee, Revolutionary Committee of Hunan Province (until Feb 1978)
1978,	Jul	Identified as secretary of Gansu Province CP

Zhao Dezun (Chao Te-tsun)   赵德尊

Posts held

CCP
Secretary of Heilongjiang Province CP

Provincial Administration
Chairman of the People's Congress of Heilongjiang Province

1979,	Aug	Identified as vice-chairman of the Revolutionary Committee (until Dec 1979), and as secretary of the CP, Heilongjiang Province
	Dec	Elected chairman of the People's Congress of Heilongjiang Province

Zhao Dexian (Chao Te-hsien)   赵得贤

Posts held

Others
Member of the Standing Committee of the 5th CPPCC

Zhao belongs to the Korean minority.

1964,	Oct	Elected deputy for Jilin Province to the 3rd NPC
1978,	Feb	Delegate at the 5th CPPCC as a member of the literary and art circles
	Mar	Elected member of the Standing Committee of the 5th CPPCC

Zhao Dongwan (Chao Tung-wan) 赵东苑

Posts held

Government
Vice-minister of the Science and Technology Commission

Others
Director of the Commission for the Promotion of International Measurements
Chinese chairman of the PRC-U.S.A. Joint Committee on High Energy Physics

Zhao was born in 1925 in Henan Province.

1977,	Nov	Identified as vice-minister of the Science and Technology Commission
1978,	Oct	Member of a government delegation led by Fang Yi to the Federal Republic of Germany and France
1979,	Mar	Appointed director of the Committee for the Promotion of International Measurements
	Jun	Identified as Chinese chairman of the PRC-U.S.A. Joint Committee on High Energy Physics

Zhao Fan (Chao Fan)   赵凡

Posts held

Government
Vice-minister of state farms and land reclamation
Director of the State Agricultural Reclamation Administration Bureau

1953,	Dec	Identified as deputy director of the Beijing Municipality Committee for National Sales Board
1955,	Dec	Identified as director-general of the Miyun Reservoir Construction Project near Beijing
1964,	Aug	Identified as member of the Standing Committee, CP of Beijing Municipality (until Apr 1965)
	Oct	Identified as deputy mayor of Beijing (until Cultural Revolution)
1965,	Apr	Elected secretary, CP of Beijing Municipality (until Cultural Revolution)

1967,   Jun   Branded as a renegade and follower of Peng Zhen
1978,   Mar   First appearance after the Cultural Revolution: Identified as vice-minister of agriculture and forestry (until Feb 1979)
         Apr   Identified as director of the State Agricultural Reclamation Administration Bureau
         Aug   Head of an agricultural delegation to Canada
1979,   Jun   Identified as vice-minister of state farms and land reclamation; head of a state farms delegation to Yugoslavia

Zhao is married to Guo Shun.

Zhao Fasheng (Chao Fa-sheng)   赵发生

Posts held

Government
Vice-minister of commerce
Member of the Birth Planning Leading Group under the State Council

NPC
Deputy for Jiangxi Province to the 5th NPC

1950,   Identified as member of the Financial and Economic Committee and as director of the Industry and Commerce Department, People's Government of Jiangxi Province
1954,   Jul   Appointed board member of the Federation of Supply and Marketing Cooperatives
1955,   Sep   Appointed assistant to the minister for purchase of agricultural products (until the ministry is abolished at the end of 1956)
1957,   Feb   Elected vice-chairman, Federation of Supply and Marketing Cooperatives
1959,   Sep   Appointed vice-minister of food (out of office for 2 years during the Cultural Revolution until approximately 1970 while the ministry was temporarily dissolved)
1972,   Dec   Identified as vice-minister of commerce
1978,   Feb   Elected deputy for Jiangxi Province to the 5th NPC
         Jul   Appointed member of the Birth Planning Leading Group under the State Council

Zhao Haifeng (Chao Hai-feng)   赵海峯

Posts held

CCP
Deputy secretary of Qinghai Province CP

Provincial Administration
Vice-governor of Qinghai Province

1977,   Dec   Elected vice-chairman of the Revolutionary Committee of Qinghai Province (until Aug 1978)
1978,   Jan   Identified as member of the Standing Committee of Qinghai Province CP (until May 1978)

         May   Identified as deputy secretary of Qinghai Province CP
1979,   Sep   Elected vice-governor of Qinghai Province

Zhao Jianmin (Chao Chien-min)   赵健民

Posts held

Zhao is a native of Shandong Province.

1949,   Nov   Identified as vice-chairman of the Gueiyang Military Control Commission
1951   Appointed director of the Communication Department, Southwest China Military and Political Council (until 1952)
1952   Appointed member of the Finance and Commerce Committee, Southwest China Administrative Council; appointed vice-minister of Railways (until Dec 1957)
1955   Appointed governor of Shandong Province (until about Nov 1958) and secretary of Shandong Province CP (until about 1960)
1956,   Jun   Reelected deputy for Shandong Province to NPC (until Mar 1959)
         Sep   Elected alternate member of the CCP Central Committee
1963,   Jun   Identified as secretary of Yunnan Province CP
1968,   Jul   Branded as a renegade and purged
1978,   Dec   First appearance after the Cultural Revolution

Zhao Jin (Chao Chin)   赵禁

Posts held

Government
Former ambassador of Yemen Arab Republic

1960,   Aug   Identified as counselor, embassy in the People's Republic of Mongolia (until 1964)
1971,   Mar   Appointed ambassador to Bulgaria (until Jul 1975)
1975,   Sep   Appointed ambassador to Yemen Arab Republic (until Dec 1979)

Zhao Jun (Chao Chün)   赵军

Posts held

Provincial Administration
Vice-chairman of the Revolutionary Committee of Tianjin Municipality

1959,   May   Identified as 1st CP secretary of the Southeast Shanxi District
1978,   Jan   Elected vice-chairman of the Revolutionary Committee of Inner Mongolia Autonomous Region
1979,   Nov   Identified as vice-chairman of the Revolutionary Committee of Tianjin Municipality

Zhao Jun (Chao Chün)   赵 军

Posts held

Provincial Administration
Vice-governor of Shanxi Province

| 1959, | May | Identified as 1st secretary of the Southeast Shanxi District CP |
| 1979, | Dec | Elected vice-governor of Shanxi Province |

Zhao Junmai (Chao Chün-mai)   赵君迈

Posts held

Others
Member of the Standing Committee of the
5th CPPCC

| 1979, | Jul | By-elected a member of the Standing Committee of the 5th CPPCC |

Zhao Lin (Chao Lin)   赵 林

Posts held

CCP
Secretary of Shandong Province CP

Provincial Administration
Chairman of the People's Congress of
Shandong Province

In 1937 Zhao was secretary of the CP of Taiyuan Municipality. Serving in the 1st Field Army, Zhao was posted to Sichuan at the end of 1949.

1950,	Jul	Identified as deputy secretary of North Sichuan District CP (until Dec 1952) and as member of the Southwest China Military and Administrative Council
1953,	Jan	Appointed member of the Southwest Administrative Committee (until Aug 1954)
1954,	Nov	Identified as deputy secretary of Sichuan Province CP
1956,	Oct	Identified as secretary of Jilin Province CP
1960,	Nov	Identified as 2nd secretary of Jilin Province CP
1966,	Jul	Identified as acting 1st secretary of Jilin Province CP
1967,	Feb	Branded as an anti-Party element and purged
1978,	Dec	First appearance after the Cultural Revolution: Identified as secretary of Shandong Province CP
1979,	Mar	Identified as vice-chairman of Shandong Provincial CP (until Dec 1979)
	Dec	Elected chairman of the People's Congress of Shandong Province

Zhao Lizhi (Chao Li-chih)   赵力之

Posts held

NPC
Deputy for Shanxi Province to the
5th NPC

Provincial Administration
Vice-governor of Shanxi Province

1958,	Mar	Identified as director of the Industry and Communications Department, CP of Taiyuan Municipality
1960,	Jul	Identified as secretary, CP of Taiyuan Municipality (until 1967)
1967		Disappears during the Cultural Revolution
1977,	Dec	First appearance after the Cultural Revolution: Elected vice-chairman of the Revolutionary Committee of Shanxi Province (until Dec 1979)
1978,	Feb	Elected deputy for Shanxi Province to the 5th NPC
1979,	Dec	Elected vice-governor of Shanxi Province

Zhao Pengfei (Chao P'eng-fei)   赵鹏飞

Posts held

Provincial Administration
Chairman of the People's Congress of
Beijing Municipality

NPC
Deputy for Beijing Municipality to the
5th NPC

Zhao was born in 1920 in Shanxi Province. In 1939 he served in the North China Bureau of the CCP Central Committee, in 1942 in the Administrative Office of the Shanxi-Chahar-Hebei-Border Area. In 1946 he became director of the Industry Department in the People's Government of Chahar Province.

1949,	Dec	Appointed deputy director of the Beijing Construction Bureau (until 1952)
1954,	Apr	Identified as procurator, Supreme People's Procuracy
1956		Identified as deputy director, General Office of the 1st NPC
1958,	Aug	Identified as member of the Beijing Municipal People's Council
1960,	Jul	Elected deputy mayor of Beijing (until Nov 1964)
1962,	Dec	Appointed director of the State Housing Administrative Bureau
1963,	Oct	Appointed deputy secretary-general of the State Council
1964,	Oct	Elected deputy for Hebei Province to the 3rd NPC
1967,	May	Denounced by Red Guards as a counter-revolutionary revisionist
1977,	Oct	First appearance after the Cultural Revolution
	Dec	Elected vice-chairman of the Beijing Revolutionary Committee (until Dec 1979)
1978,	Feb	Elected deputy of Beijing Municipality to the 5th NPC
	Sep	Leader of a municipality administration delegation to U.S.A.
1979,	Jun	Member of the Draft Laws Committee, 2nd Session of the 5th NPC
	Dec	Elected chairman of the People's Congress of Beijing Municipality

Zhao Puchu (Chao P'u-ch'u) 赵朴初

Posts held

NPC
Deputy for Anhui Province to the 5th NPC

Others
Member of the Standing Committee of the 5th CPPCC
Acting president of the Chinese Buddhist League
Vice-chairman of the Sino-Japanese Friendship Association
Vice-chairman of the China Association for Promoting Democracy
Vice-President of the Red Cross Society

Zhao was born about 1906 in Taihu, Anhui Province. Prior to his career as a cadre in various organizations he was a director of the Huatung Transportation Corporation in Shanghai. In September 1949 he was elected member of the Political Consultative Conference's National Committee as a Buddhist representative.

1949,	Oct	Identified as a council member of the Peace Council
1950,	Mar	Elected deputy director of the Civil Affairs Department in the East China Military and Administrative Council (until Mar 1951)
	Apr	Appointed council member of the Association for Promoting Democracy
1951,	May	Appointed deputy director, Personnel Department, East China Military and Administrative Council (until Dec 1952)
1952,	Oct	Elected board member, Shanghai section of the Sino-Soviet Friendship Association
	Nov	Elected chairman of the preparatory committee for the foundation of the Buddhist Association
1953,	Jun	Elected vice-chairman and secretary-general of the Buddhist Association
1954,	May	Elected council member of the Association for Cultural Relations with Foreign Countries
	Aug	Elected deputy for Anhui Province to the 1st NPC
1955,	Apr	Member of a delegation of Buddhists visiting Burma
	Jul	Elected council member of the Sino-Indian Friendship Association; member of the delegation attending the 1st World Conference Against the Use of Atomic Bombs in Tokyo
	Oct	Member of a delegation of Buddhists escorting a Buddha tooth relic to Burma
1956,	Feb	Identified as member of the Asian Solidarity Committee
1957,	Dec	Member of a delegation to the Afro-Asian Solidarity Conference in Cairo
1958,	Jul	Member of the delegation participating in the Conference on Disarmament and International Cooperation in Stockholm
1959,	May	Member of the delegation to the Special Conference of the World Peace Council in Stockholm
	Nov	Elected vice-chairman of the Sino-Burmese Friendship Association

1960,	Jan	Deputy head of a cultural and friendship delegation visiting Burma
	Aug	Member of the delegation attending the 6th World Conference Against the Use of Atomic Bombs in Tokyo
	Dec	Deputy head of a delegation of Buddhists visiting Burma
1961,	Mar	Member of the delegation taking part in the New Delhi World Peace Council session
	Jun	Deputy head of a delegation of Buddhists escorting a Buddha tooth relic to Ceylon
	Jul	Head of a delegation to the World Conference of Believers in Religion in Tokyo
	Aug	Deputy head of the delegation to the 7th World Conference Against the Use of Atomic Bombs in Tokyo
	Oct	Elected vice-chairman of the Red Cross Society
	Nov	Deputy head of a delegation attending the 6th World Conference of Buddhists in Cambodia
1963,	Apr	Head of a delegation of Buddhists to Japan
	May	Elected chairman of the preparatory committee for the commemoration of the 1200th anniversary of the death of the monk Jian Zhen
	Aug	Head of a delegation to the 9th World Conference Against the Use of Atomic Bombs in Tokyo
	Oct	Elected vice-chairman of the Sino-Japanese Friendship Association at its foundation
	Nov	Identified as member of the executive council of the Red Cross Society
1964,	Jul	Deputy head of the delegation to the 10th World Conference Against the Use of Atomic Bombs in Japan
1965,	Jan	Elected member of the Standing Committee of the 4th CPPCC
	Mar	Head of a delegation of Buddhists to Indonesia
	Jun	Elected vice-chairman of the Peace Council
1966,	Apr	Appointed vice-chairman of the Federation for Cultural Relations and Friendship with Foreign Countries
1972,	Jun	Reactivated after the Cultural Revolution; identified as a cadre in the Buddhist League
	Sep	Referred to as member of the Standing Committee of the CPPCC
1975,	Jan	Member of the presidium of the 4th NPC
1978,	Feb	Elected deputy for Anhui Province to the 5th NPC
	Apr	Zhao leads a Buddhists' delegation to Japan
	Aug	Identified as vice-chairman of the China Association for Promoting Democracy (re-elected Oct 1979)
1979,	Feb	Elected vice-president of the Red Cross Society
	Apr	Member of a NPC delegation headed by Deng Yingchao to Japan
	Jun	Member of the Committee to Examine Proposals, 2nd Session of the 5th NPC

Jul Acting president of the Chinese Buddhist League

Aug Head of a delegation drawn from Chinese religious circles to the World Conference on Religion and Peace in Princeton, U.S.A.

Zhao Qi (Chao Ch'i)   赵 奇

Posts held

Provincial Administration
Vice-governor of Liaoning Province

1958, Feb Identified as deputy director of the Rural Work Department of Liaoning Province CP

1977, Dec Elected vice-chairman of the Revolutionary Committee of Liaoning Province (until Jan 1980)

1980, Jan Elected vice-governor of Liaoning Province

Zhao Shouyi (Chao Shou-yi)   赵 守 一

Posts held

CCP
Secretary of Anhui Province CP
Director of Anhui CP Party School

NPC
Deputy for Anhui Province to the 5th NPC

1958, Nov Identified as a judge in Anqing District, Anhui Province

1968, May Purged as capitalist-roader

1977, Jun Zhao is sent by special directive of Hua Guofeng and the CCP Central Committee to Anhui to deal with difficulties within the local leadership

1978, Jan Elected vice-chairman of Anhui Revolutionary Committee (until Dec 1979)

Feb Elected deputy for Anhui Province to the 5th NPC; identified as director of the Anhui CP Party School

Zhao Wenfu (Chao Wen-fu)   赵 文 甫

Posts held

CCP
Secretary of Henan Province CP

1950 Identified as deputy director, Organization Department of Henan Province CP

1952, Jan Identified as director of the Personnel Department of Henan People's Government

1954, Aug Elected deputy for Henan Province to the 1st NPC (reelected in 1958 and 1964 to the 2nd and 3rd NPCs)

1955, Feb Elected vice-governor of Henan (until Cultural Revolution)

1956, Oct Identified as secretary of Henan Province CP (until Cultural Revolution)

1967, Nov Branded as a capitalist-roader and purged

1978, Dec First appearance after the Cultural Revolution: Identified as member of the Standing Committee of Henan Province CP

1979, Mar Identified as secretary of Henan Province CP

May Identified as vice-chairman of the Revolutionary Committee of Henan Province (until Aug 1979)

Oct Identified as chairman of the CPPCC, Henan Province

Zhao Wenjin (Chao Wen-chin)   赵 文 进

Posts held

Military
Deputy commander of Chengdu Military Region
Commander of Sichuan Military District

NPC
Deputy for the PLA to the 5th NPC

Provincial Administration
Member of the Revolutionary Committee of Sichuan Province

Zhao was born in 1914 in Guangxi Province. In 1938 he commanded a battalion in the 28th Army. He was deputy commander of a regiment of the Western Beijing Vanguard Army commanded by Xiao Ke in 1940. In 1944 he was made regiment commander in the Shanxi-Chahar-Hebei Training Corps. In 1947 he commanded a division in the Northeast China Liberation Army. In 1949 he was commander of a division in the 4th Field Army.

1952 Zhao leads his unit in the Korean War

1953 Identified as deputy commander of the 54th Army

1954 Dispatched to Tibet

1962, Aug Identified as deputy commander of Tibet Military Region (until 1975)

1975, May Zhao disappears for unknown reasons until 1977

1977, Dec Elected member of the Revolutionary Committee of Sichuan Province

1978, Feb Elected deputy for the PLA to the 5th NPC

Sep Identified as commander of Sichuan Military District and as deputy commander of Chengdu Military Region

Zhao Wenpu (Chao Wen-p'u)   赵 文 普

Posts held

Government
Vice-minister of railways

1960, Jul Identified as secretary, CP of the Beijing Railway Office

1978, Jul Identified as vice-minister of railways

Zhao Wucheng (Chao Wu-ch'eng) 赵武成

Posts held

CCP
Alternate member of the CCP 11th Central Committee
3rd secretary, CP of Tianjin Municipality

Provincial Administration
Vice-chairman of the Revolutionary Committee of Tianjin Municipality

1950,	Aug	Identified as deputy secretary, CP of Zhengzhou Municipality
1955,	Mar	Identified as 2nd secretary, CP of Guangzhou Municipality
1957,	Feb	Identified as secretary, CP of Guangzhou Municipality
1960,	Aug	Identified as 2nd secretary, CP of Guangzhou Municipality
1961,	Oct	Identified as acting 1st secretary, CP of Guangzhou Municipality (until Mar 1962)
1963,	Mar	Identified as 2nd secretary, CP of Guangzhou Municipality
1964,	Jun	Identified as secretary of Hebei Province CP and as 2nd secretary, CP of Tianjin Municipality (until approximately 1966)
1970,	Jun	Identified as vice-chairman of the Revolutionary Committee of Tianjin (until Nov 1977)
1974,	Apr	Head of a Tianjin friendship delegation to Japan
1975,	Aug	Identified as secretary, CP of Tianjin Municipality (until Sep 1977)
1977,	Aug	Elected alternate member of the CCP Central Committee by the 11th Party Congress
	Sep	Identified as 2nd secretary, CP of Tianjin Municipality (until Dec 1977)
	Nov	Identified as 1st vice-chairman of the Revolutionary Committee of Tianjin Municipality (until Dec 1977)
	Dec	Identified as 3rd secretary, CP of Tianjin Municipality, and as vice-chairman of Tianjin Revolutionary Committee

Zhao Xianshun (Chao Hsien-shun)
赵先顺

Posts held

NPC
Deputy for the PLA to the 5th NPC

Military
Commander of Heilongjiang Military District

1974,	Mar	Identified as deputy commander of Heilongjiang Military District
1976,	Dec	Identified as commander of Heilongjiang Military District
1978,	Feb	Elected deputy for the PLA to the 5th NPC

Zhao Xinchu (Chao Hsin-ch'u) 赵辛初

Posts held

CCP
Member of the CCP 11th Central Committee

Government
Vice-minister of the State Planning Commission

NPC
Deputy for Hubei Province to the 5th NPC

Zhao was born in 1915 in Hubei Province.

1952,	Apr	Identified as CP secretary of Huanggang District, Hubei Province
1957,	May	Identified as secretary of Hubei Province CP (until Apr 1965)
1958,	Dec	Elected vice-governor of Hubei Province (until Sep 1964)
1965,	Apr	Appointed vice-minister of culture (until about 1966)
1967		Though not referred to by name, Zhao is denounced as a counterrevolutionary together with the minister of culture Lu Dingyi and all vice-ministers of culture during the Cultural Revolution
1973,	Jul	1st appearance after the Cultural Revolution: Identified as secretary of Hubei Province CP (until Apr 1975)
	Aug	Elected alternate member of the CCP Central Committee by the 10th Party Congress (until Aug 1977)
1974,	Jan	Identified as vice-chairman of the Revolutionary Committee of Hubei Province (until Apr 1975)
1975,	Jan	Member of the presidium of the 4th NPC
	May	Identified as 1st secretary of Hubei Province CP (until Sep 1978); identified as chairman of the Revolutionary Committee of Hubei Province (until Sep 1978)
	Jul	Identified as 1st political commissar of Hubei Military District (until Sep 1978)
1977,	Aug	Elected member of the CCP Central Committee by the 11th Party Congress
1978,	Feb	Elected deputy for Hubei Province to the 5th NPC
	Oct	Identified as vice-minister of the State Planning Commission

Zhao Xingyuan (Chao Hsing-yüan) 赵兴元

Posts held

CCP
Alternate member, CCP 11th Central Committee
Member, Standing Committee of Heilongjiang CP

Military
Political commissar of Heilongjiang Military District

Zhao was born in 1926. In 1942, at the age of only 16, he joined the 5th Brigade, Shandong Column, of the PLA. Soon he became known as the "little hero" or "hero with the golden face" because of his bravery. After 1954 he served in PLA units in Manchuria. After receiving various decorations he was conferred the title of "War Hero" and was appointed deputy commander of the 353rd Regiment, 118th Division, 40th Army of the 4th Field Army.

1950,	Dec	Zhao visits the USSR
1951,	Feb	He participates in the Korea War (until 1953)
1953,	Apr	Identified as regiment commander
1954,	Jan	Zhao takes part in a PLA congress of the Northeast China Military Region. He attends Nanking Military Academy.
1955,	Sep	Promoted to the rank of lieutenant-colonel
1958		Identified as commander 353rd Regiment of the 118th Division
1959,	Mar	Elected deputy for the PLA units of Shenyang Military Region to the 2nd NPC (confirmed in this post in September 1964 by the 3rd NPC)
1962		Identified as chief of staff of the 118th Division
1965		Identified as deputy commander of the 118th Division
1967		Identified as commander of the 118th Division
1969,	Apr	Elected to first term as alternate member of the CCP Central Committee by the 9th Party Congress
1976,	Apr	Identified as political commissar of Heilongjiang Military District
1978,	Sep	Identified as member of the Standing Committee, Heilongjiang CP

Zhao Xingzhi (Chao Hsing-chih)　趙行志

Posts held

CCP
Secretary of Shanghai Municipality CP

NPC
Deputy for Shanghai Municipality to the 5th NPC

Provincial Administration
Vice-mayor of Shanghai Municipality

1963,	Apr	Identified as consul-general in Geneva (until Oct 1966)
1971,	Aug	Appointed ambassador to Cameroon (until May 1974)
1974,	Aug	Appointed ambassador to Iraq (until Nov 1976)
1977,	Feb	Identified as vice-chairman of the Revolutionary Committee of Shanghai (until Dec 1979) and as member of the Standing Committee, Shanghai CP
1978,	Feb	Elected deputy for Shanghai Municipality to the 5th NPC
1979,	May	Identified as secretary of Shanghai Municipality CP
	Dec	Elected vice-mayor of Shanghai Municipality

Zhao Xinran (Chao Hsin-jan)　趙欣然

Posts held

CCP
Member of the Standing Committee, Guangxi Autonomous Region CP

Military
Commander of Guangxi Military District

1963		Identified as a representative of the PLA in Tanzania
1970,	Aug	Identified as a leading military figure in Guangxi Autonomous Region
	Dec	Identified as vice-chairman of Guangxi Autonomous Region (until Mar 1979?)
1971,	Jun	Identified as commander of Guangxi Military District
		Identified as member of the Standing Committee of Guangxi CP

Zhao Xiu (Chao Hsiu)　趙修

Posts held

Government
Vice-minister of agriculture

1958,	Nov	Identified as 1st secretary of Xiangyang District CP, Hubei Province
1964,	Sep	Elected vice-governor of Hubei Province (until Cultural Revolution)
1966,	Aug	Zhao disappears
1973,	Jan	First appearance after the Cultural Revolution: Elected secretary of Hubei Province CP (until 1977)
1979,	Apr	Identified as director of the Animal Husbandry Bureau under the Ministry of Agriculture
	Aug	Identified as vice-minister of agriculture

Zhao Xuequan (Chao Hsüeh-ch'üan)　趙学全

Posts held

CCP
Alternate member, CCP 11th Central Committee
Member, Standing Committee, Yunnan Province CP

Mass Organization
Chairman of the Trade Union of Yunnan Province

1973,	Jun	Identified as vice-chairman of the Trade Union of Yunnan Province (until Oct 1978)
1977,	Aug	Elected alternate member of the CCP Central Committee by the 11th Party Congress
1978,	Jan	Identified as member of the Standing Committee of Yunnan CP
	Oct	Elected chairman of the Trade Union of Yunnan Province

Zhao Yimin (Chao Yi-min)   赵毅敏

Posts held

Others
Member of the 5th CPPCC

Zhao was born in 1905 (1903?) in Hebei Province. He is a graduate of the Senior Teachers College in Wuchang. In 1929 he joined the CCP. During the Anti-Japanese War he served temporarily as director of the "Lu Xun Art Institute" in Yan'an and as vice-chancellor of the Yan'an University.

1949,	Dec	Identified as director of the Propaganda Department, and as secretary of the Youth Work Committee, Central-South China Bureau of the CCP Central Committee (abolished in mid-1954)
1950,	Mar	Identified as member and director of the Culture Department, Central-South China Military and Administrative Council (until Jan 1953)
1951,	Apr	Identified as chairman of the Culture and Education Committee, Central-South China Military and Administrative Council (until Nov 1954)
1953,	Nov	Elected vice-chairman of the Sino-Soviet Friendship Association, Central-South China Section
1954,	Jul	Head of a cultural delegation to Chile
	Dec	Delegate representing the CCP at the CPPCC which elects him a council member
1955,	Mar	Identified as vice-chairman of the Association for Cultural Relations with Foreign Countries (until Apr 1959)
1956,	Feb	Identified as council member of the Asian Solidarity Committee (until May 1958)
1958,	May	Elected alternate member of the CCP Central Committee; identified as council member of the Afro-Asian Solidarity Committee
	Jun	Member of a CCP guest delegation attending the 2nd Congress of the CP Czechoslovakia; identified as council member of the Peace Council
1959,	Jan	Identified as council member of the World Peace Council
	Apr	Identified as council member of the Association for Cultural Relations with Foreign Countries
1960,	May	Identified as member of the Standing Committee of Hebei Province CP (until about 1961)
	Jun	Member of a CCP delegation to the funeral of Harry Pollitt, chairman of CP Great Britain, in London
1961,	Mar	CCP guest delegate to the 27th Congress of CP Great Britain
1962,	Nov	CCP guest delegate to the 10th Congress of CP Italy
1963,	Jun	Identified as deputy director, International Liaison Department of the CCP Central Committee
1964,	Sep	Elected deputy for Henan Province to the 3rd NPC
	Oct	Member of a Party and government delegation to Algeria

	Nov	Member of a Peace Council delegation to Italy
1965,	Jan	Elected member of the Standing Committee of the NPC
	Mar	Member of a Party and government delegation to the mourning ceremonies for Gheorghiu-Dej in Bucharest; subsequent visits to Albania and Algeria
	Apr	Member of a government delegation to the United Arab Republic, Pakistan, and Burma
	Jun	Elected vice-chairman of the Peace Council
	Jul	Head of the Chinese delegation to the World Peace Council session in Helsinki
1966,	Apr	Appointed vice-chairman of the Association for Cultural Relations and Friendship with Foreign Countries
	Jun	Member of a Party and government delegation led by Zhou Enlai to Romania and Albania
1967,	Sep	Zhao disappears
1979,	Jun	First appearance after the Cultural Revolution: By-elected member of the 5th CPPCC

Zhao Yuan (Chao Yüan)   赵源

Posts held

Government
Ambassador to Mauritania

1967,	Jun	Identified as deputy director of the West Asia and Africa Department in the Ministry of Foreign Affairs (until 1973)
1973,	Apr	Identified as director of the Africa Department in the Ministry of Foreign Affairs (until 1975)
1975,	Jun	Appointed councelor at the embassy in Mozambique (until 1977)
1978,	May	Appointed ambassador to Mauritania

Zhao Yuting (Chao Yü-t'ing)   赵雨亭

Posts held

CCP
Secretary of Shanxi Province CP

NPC
Deputy for Shanxi Province to the 5th NPC

1960,	Feb	Identified as 1st secretary, CP of Jinnan District, South Shanxi
1977,	Dec	Elected vice-chairman of the Revolutionary Committee of Shanxi Province (until Dec 1979)
1978,	Feb	Elected deputy for Shanxi Province to the 5th NPC
	May	Identified as member of the Standing Committee of Shanxi Province CP
1979,	Oct	Identified as secretary of Shanxi Province CP

Zhao Zengyi (Chao Tseng-yi) 赵增益

Posts held

CCP
Secretary of Yunnan Province CP

NPC
Deputy for Yunnan Province to the 5th NPC

Military
Deputy political commissar of the Kunming Military Region

Provincial Administration
Vice-governor of Yunnan Province

1956,	Jan	Identified as deputy secretary, CP of Kunming Municipality
1957,	Aug	Identified as 1st secretary, CP of Kunming Municipality
1966,	Aug	Identified as member of the Standing Committee of Yunnan Province CP
1967		Disappears during the Cultural Revolution
1977,	Dec	First appearance after the Cultural Revolution: Identified as deputy secretary of Yunnan Province CP (until Aug 1979)
1978,	Feb	Elected deputy for Yunnan Province to the 5th NPC
1979,	Jan	Identified as vice-chairman of the Revolutionary Committee of Yunnan Province (until Dec 1979) and as deputy political commissar of the Kunming Military Region
	Sep	Elected secretary of Yunnan Province CP
	Dec	Elected vice-governor of Yunnan Province

Zhao Zhengyi (Chao Cheng-yi) 赵政一

Posts held

Government
Ambassador to Botswana

1953,	Jun	Identified as 2nd secretary at the embassy in Romania
1959,	Aug	Identified as counselor, embassy in Indonesia (until 1964)
1965,	May	Identified as deputy secretary-general of the Institute of Foreign Affairs (until Cultural Revolution)
1970,	Aug	Identified as chargé d'affaires in Pakistan (until 1971)
1972,	Mar	Appointed ambassador to Sierra Leone (until Jun 1975)
1975,	Aug	Appointed ambassador to Botswana

Zhao Zhenqing (Chao Chen-ch'ing) 赵振清

Posts held

CCP
Deputy director of the Organization Department, CCP Central Committee

1978,	Jun	Identified as a member of the Standing Committee of the Shanghai Municipal CP

and as director of its Organization Department

	Dec	Identified as a cadre of the CCP Central Committee
1979,	Nov	Identified as deputy director of the Organization Department under the CCP Central Committee

Zhao Zhijian (Chao Chih-chien) 赵志坚

Posts held

CCP
Member of the CCP 11th Central Committee
Member of the Standing Committee, Kiangsi Province CP

Mass Organization
Vice-chairman of the Trade Union of Jiangxi Province

1973,	Aug	Identified as vice-chairman of the Trade Union of Jiangxi Province
1977,	May	Head of a friendship delegation to Romania
	Aug	Elected member of the CCP Central Committee by the 11th Party Congress
	Sep	Identified as member of the Standing Committee of Jiangxi Province CP
1978,	Feb	Elected vice-chairman of the Revolutionary Committee, Jiangxi Province (until Mar 1979?)

Zhao Zhongyao (Chao Chung-yao) 赵忠尧

Posts held

NPC
Member of the Standing Committee of the 5th NPC
Deputy for Shanghai Municipality to the 5th NPC

Others
Deputy director of the Institute of High Energy Physics, Academy of Sciences

Zhao was born in 1902. He studied Physics at the universities of Cambridge (England) and Halle (Germany) and eventually at the California Institute of Technology where in 1930 he received a doctorate in a subject in nuclear physics. All in all Zhao spent 24 years in the U.S. devoting himself to nuclear research and particularly the study of gamma-radiation. He was an official observer at American atomic bomb tests.

1950,	Sep	Zhao leaves the U.S.A. to return to the PRC; he is detained by American authorities in Yokohama
	Oct	Handed over to the Chinese Nationalist Government in Taiwan
	Nov	Deported to Guangzhou
1951,	Feb	Member of the Chinese delegation to the World Peace Council Session in East Berlin
1952,	Oct	Delegate at the Peace Conference of Asia and Pacific Regions in Beijing

1954,	Aug	Elected deputy for Zhejiang Province to the 1st NPC (reelected 1958 and 1964 to the 2nd and 3rd NPC)
1955,	Jun	Appointed member of the Department of Mathematics, Physics, and Chemistry, Academy of Sciences
1956-1961		Zhao joins the Soviet nuclear research center in Dubna
1957		Appointed deputy director, Institute of Nuclear Physics at the Academy of Sciences
1965,	Jan	Elected member of the Standing Committee, 3rd NPC
1972,	Mar	First official appearance after the Cultural Revolution
1975,	Jan	Reelected member of the Standing Committee, 4th NPC (again reelected by the 5th NPC in 1978)
1978,	Feb	Elected deputy for Shanghai Municipality to the 5th NPC
	Dec	Identified as deputy director of the High Energy Physics Institute, Academy of Sciences

Zhao Zishang (Chao Tzu-shang) 赵子尚

Posts held

Government
Vice-minister of coal industry

1949,	Dec	Identified as director of the Finance Bureau, People's Government of Beijing
1952		Identified as director of the Management Department, Ministry of Coal Industry (until 1959)
1956,	Dec	Identified as member of the State Construction Commission (until Feb 1958)
1958,	Feb	Identified as director of the Finance Department, Ministry of Coal Industry
1960,	Jan	Appointed vice-minister of coal industry (until approximately 1962)
1979,	Jun	Identified as vice-minister of coal industry

Zhao Ziyang (Chao Tzu-yang) 赵紫阳

Posts held

CCP
Member of the Standing Committee of the Politburo of the CCP 11th Central Committee
Member of the Politburo of the CCP 11th Central Committee

NPC
Deputy for Sichuan Province to the 5th NPC

Others
Vice-president of the 5th CPPCC

Zhao was born in 1918 under the name of Zhao Xiusheng in Hua County, Henan Province. His father was a landlord and owned facilities for grain storage. Between 1928 and 1936 he received his elementary education in his native town and subsequently attended middle schools in Kaifeng and Wuhan until 1937. In 1932 he joined the Communist Youth League and in 1938 the CCP. In 1940 he held the post of CP secretary of the 3rd Special District in the Hebei-Shandong Border Region. During 1945-46 he was engaged in rural reform work in the Hebei-Shandong-Henan Border Region. From 1948 to 1949 he served as CP secretary of Luoyang District in his home province.

1950		Identified as member of the Standing Committee, South-China Subbureau in the Central-South China Bureau of the CCP Central Committee
1952,	Aug	Identified as secretary-general in the same subbureau (until Oct 1954)
1953,	Sep	Identified as director of the Rural Work Department in the same subbureau (until Sep 1955)
1954,	Oct	Appointed 3rd secretary in the same subbureau (until Sep 1955)
1955,	Feb	Elected member of the People's Council of Guangdong Province
	Jul	Identified as deputy secretary of Guangdong Province CP (until Nov 1956)
1957,	Apr	Identified as secretary of Guangdong Province CP (probably until Dec 1961)
1961,	Dec	Identified as 2nd secretary of Guangdong Province CP (until Apr 1965)
1964,	Jan	Identified as political commissar of Guangdong Military District
	Jul	Identified as secretary of the Central-South China Bureau of the CCP Central Committee
1965,	Apr	Identified as 1st secretary of Guangdong Province CP
1967		In the course of the Cultural Revolution Zhao is sharply attacked as an agent of Tao Zhu and Liu Shaoqi and denounced as a counterrevolutionary revisionist and a stinking element of the landowning class, and is paraded with a fool's cap through the streets of Guangzhou: On 16th October 1967 he is publicly denounced together with Tao Zhu
1971,	May	First appearance after the Cultural Revolution: Identified as CP secretary of the Inner Mongolian Autonomous Region (until Apr 1972)
1972,	Jan	Identified as chairman of the Inner Mongolian Autonomous Region (until Apr 1972)
1972,	Apr	Identified as vice-chairman of the Revolutionary Committee of Guangdong Province (until Apr 1974)
1973,	Jan	Identified as secretary of Guangdong Province CP (until Apr 1974)
	Aug	Elected to first term as member of the CCP Central Committee by the 10th Party Congress
1974,	Apr	Identified as 1st secretary of Guangdong Province CP (until Oct 1975); identified as chairman of the Revolutionary Committee of Guangdong Province (until Oct 1975)
1975,	Jan	Member of the presidium of the 4th NPC
	Sep	Identified as political commissar of Guangzhou Military Region (until Dec 1975)

1976,	Jan	Identified as 1st secretary of Sichuan Province CP, as chairman of Sichuan Revolutionary Committee, and as 1st political commissar of Chengdu Military Region (the first and third post until Feb 1980, the second until Dec 1979)
1977,	Aug	Elected alternate member of the Politburo by the CCP 11th Congress (until Sep 1979)
1978,	Feb	Elected deputy for Sichuan Province to the 5th NPC
	Mar	Elected vice-president of the 5th CPPCC
	Aug	Member of a Party and government delegation, led by Hua Guofeng, to Romania, Yugoslavia, and Iran
1979,	Jun	Head of a Sichuan Province delegation to Great Britain, Switzerland, and France
	Sep	By-elected member of the Politburo by the 4th Plenary Session of the CCP 11th Central Committee
1980,	Jan	Article in HQ 80/1: "Study the New Situation and Fully Implement the Principle of Readjustment"
	Feb	Elected member of the Standing Committee of the Politburo, CCP 11th Central Committee, by its 5th Plenum

Zhao is married to Liang Boqi.

Zhao Zongyu (Chao Tsung-yü)　赵宗焕

Posts held

Others
Member of the Standing Committee of the 5th CPPCC

Chief engineer, Research Institute of Petrochemical Engineering

Zhao was born in Sichuan Province in 1904. From 1935 until 1939 he studied at Berlin University, where he received his doctor's degree, majoring in comprehensive utilization of combustible minerals.

1959,	Apr	Delegate of the Scientific and Technical Association to the 3rd CPPCC
1965,	Jan	Elected member of the Standing Committee of the 4th CPPCC
1967		Disappears during the Cultural Revolution
1973,	May	First appearance after the Cultural Revolution
1978,	Mar	Elected member of the Standing Committee of the 5th CPPCC
1979,	Apr	Identified as chief engineer of the Research Institute of Petrochemical Engineering
	May	Member of a government delegation headed by Rong Yiren to the Federal Republic of Germany

Zhao Zukang (Chao Tsu-k'ang)　赵祖康

Posts held

NPC
Deputy for Shanghai Municipality to the 5th NPC

Provincial Administration
Vice-mayor of Shanghai

Zhao was born in 1900 in Songjiang, Jiangsu Province. He graduated from the Tangshan Engineering College and later studied at Cornell University, U.S.A. After his return he served successively as director of the Wuzhou Municipal Bureau of Public Works, as director of the Highway Department, National Economic Affairs Commission, as director of the Highway Department, Transport Control Bureau under the Military Affairs Council, and as member of the Central Planning Bureau. In 1932 Zhao supervised the construction of highways in Xi'an, Lanzhou and Luoshan. In 1938 he was sent to the U.S.A. to negotiate the "Tong Oil Loan." In 1945 he was appointed director of the Shanghai Municipal Bureau of Public Works. When the Communists conquered Shanghai he went over to them.

1950,	Jun	Identified as director of the Public Works Bureau, Shanghai Municipal People's Government
	Aug	Elected member of the Federation of Natural Science Societies (until 1958)
1954,	Aug	Elected deputy for Shanghai to the 1st NPC (reelected 1958 and 1964 to the 2nd and 3rd NPCs)
1955,	Aug	Elected vice-chairman of the Shanghai Branch, KMT Revolutionary Committee
1956,	Feb	Elected member of the Central Committee, KMT Revolutionary Committee
1957,	Jan	Identified as vice-mayor of Shanghai (until Cultural Revolution)
1958,	Apr	Identified as vice-president of the Civil Engineering Society
	Sep	Identified as chairman of the Shanghai Branch, KMT Revolutionary Society
1959,	Aug	Identified as vice-chairman of the Administrative Committee for Sea and River Dike Construction, Shanghai Municipal People's Government
1967		Zhao disappears
1972,	Nov	First appearance after the Cultural Revolution
1978,	Feb	Elected deputy for Shanghai to the 5th NPC
1979,	Jun	Member of the Committee to Examine Proposals at the 2nd Session of the 5th NPC
	Dec	Elected vice-mayor of Shanghai

Zhaxi Wangqug (Cha·hsi·wang·hsü)　扎喜旺徐

Posts held

CCP
Secretary of Qinghai Province CP

Government
Member of the State Nationalities Affairs Commission

Others
Chairman of the Qinghai Branch of the CPPCC

Zhaxi Wangqug belongs to the Tibetan minority (his Tibetan name: Drashi Wongshi). He was born in Qinghai Province and studied in 1937 at the Yan'an Nationalities Institute.

1950		Identified as member of the Nationalities Committee, Northwest China Military and Administrative Council
1951,	Feb	Identified as a council member of the People's Government of Qinghai Province
1953,	Dec	Identified as chairman of the Guoluo Tibetan Autonomous Zhou in Qinghai Province
1954,	Aug	Elected deputy for Qinghai Province to the 1st NPC (reelected 1958, 1964, and 1975 to the 2nd, 3rd and 4th NPC)
	Dec	Identified as vice-governor of Qinghai Province (until Dec 1963)
1956,	Apr	Identified as a member of the State Nationalities Affairs Commission
1957,	May	Identified as secretary of Qinghai Province CP (until Cultural Revolution)
1967		Zhaxi Wangqug disappears
1975,	Mar	First appearance after the Cultural Revolution: Identified as deputy to the 5th NPC
1979,	May	Appointed member of the State Nationalities Affairs Commission
	Aug	Identified as secretary of Qinghai Province CP
1980,	Feb	Identified as chairman of the Qinghai Branch of the 5th CPPCC

Zheng Dongguo (Cheng Tung-kuo) 郑洞国

Posts held

Others
Member of the Standing Committee of the 5th CPPCC
Vice-chairman of the Central Committee, Revolutionary Committee of the Chinese KMT

Zheng was born in 1902 in Shimen County, Hunan Province. In 1924 he took a course at the Whampoa Military Academy. He subsequently served in the Nationalist Army in which he rose from the post of battalion commander (1925) to commander of the 1st Army Group (1948). In 1944 he was among other things deputy commander of the Chinese Expeditionary Forces which fought the Japanese in Burma. In October 1948 he joined the Communists.

1954,	Sep	Appointed member of the National Defense Council (abolished in 1975)
1959,	Apr	Specially invited delegate to the 3rd CPPCC (again in Dec 1964 to the 4th CPPCC)
1967		Disappears during the Cultural Revolution
1972,	Feb	First appearance after the Cultural Revolution during the visit of U.S. president Richard Nixon
1978,	Mar	Elected member of the Standing Committee of the 5th CPPCC
1979,	Oct	Elected vice-chairman of the Central Committee, Revolutionary Committee of the Chinese KMT

Zheng Guozhong (Cheng Kuo-chung) 郑国仲

Posts held

NPC
Deputy for the PLA to the 5th NPC

Military
Rear-admiral
Commander of the East China Sea Fleet

1964,	Aug	Identified as rear-admiral in Northeast China. Subsequently no public appearance until
1975,	Sep	Identified as a military officer in Beijing
1977,	Jun	Identified as commander of the East China Sea Fleet
1978,	Feb	Elected deputy for the PLA to the 5th NPC

Zheng Hantao (Cheng Han-t'ao) 郑汉涛

Posts held

Government
Deputy director of the National Defense Industry Office

1951		Identified as deputy director of the Ordnance Bureau in the Ministry of Heavy Industry (until 1954)
1955,	Feb	Identified as assistant minister in the 2nd Ministry of Machine Building (until Feb 1958)
1960,	Oct	Appointed vice-minister in the 2nd Ministry of Machine Building (until Apr 1962)
1967,	Jan	Criticized as a follower of Luo Ruiqing and purged
1978,	Aug	First appearance after the Cultural Revolution attending the mourning ceremony for Luo Ruiqing
	Sep	Identified as deputy director of the National Defense Industry Office

Zheng Jiqiao (Cheng Chi-ch'iao) 郑香翘

Posts held

NPC
Deputy secretary-general of the 5th NPC

1955,	Oct	Identified as deputy director of the Propaganda Department, CP of Tianjin Municipality
1958		Identified as secretary-general of Tianjin Municipality CP
1963,	Dec	Identified as alternate member of the Secretariat of Tianjin Municipality CP
1966,	Aug	The 6 August issue of RMRB carries an article by Zheng titled "Liquidate Without Compromise the Crimes Committed by Zhou Yang Against the Party and Socialism"
1967		During the Cultural Revolution Zheng is criticized as a "three-anti element" but is not purged thanks to the intercession of Kang Sheng

1968,	Mar	Elected vice-chairman of the newly established Revolutionary Committee of Jilin Province (until 1974)
1971,	Mar	Elected CP secretary of the newly established Party Secretariat in Jilin Province (until 1974)
1975,	Jan	Zheng disappears for unknown reasons until 1978
1978,	May	Appointed deputy secretary-general of the 5th NPC

Zheng Minzhi (Cheng Min-chih) (f) 郑敏之

Posts held

Others
Member of the Standing Committee of the 5th CPPCC

1978,	Mar	Elected member of the Standing Committee of the 5th CPPCC

Zheng Sansheng (Cheng San-sheng) 郑三生

Posts held

CCP
Alternate member of the CCP 11th Central Committee

Military
Deputy commander of Xinjiang Military Region

Zheng was born in 1923. He began his career as a member of the guards of Peng Dehuai, formally commander of the 1st Front Army and later minister for national defense. In 1948 he commanded a regiment.

Approx. 1952		Commander of the 199th Division of the 67th Army
1966		At the beginning of the Cultural Revolution Zheng is noted as a zealous activist
1967,	Feb	Identified as commander of Tianjin Garrison (until about 1970)
	Dec	At the establishment of the Revolutionary Committee of Tianjin Municipality Zheng is elected one of its vice-chairmen (until 1970)
1968,	Jun	Identified as high-ranking officer in Beijing Military Region
1969,	Apr	Elected to first term as alternate member of the CCP Central Committee by the 9th Party Congress
1971,	May	Elected 2nd secretary of Hebei Province CP; identified as 1st vice-chairman of the Revolutionary Committee of Hebei Province (until Feb 1976)
1973,	Jul	Identified as deputy commander of Beijing Military Region (until Feb 1976)
1976,	Feb	Identified as deputy commander of Xinjiang Military Region; head of a military delegation to Pakistan

Zheng Shaowen (Cheng Shao-wen) 郑绍文

Posts held

Others
Vice-president of the Supreme People's Court
Member of the Standing Committee of the 5th CPPCC

Zheng was born in 1910 in Sichuan Province. In 1940 he served in the 5th Division of the New 4th Army. In early 1949 he was political commissar of Hubei Military District. In September of that year he took part in the 1st CPPCC.

1950,	Mar	Identified as member of the Central-South Military and Administrative Council, as director of the Civil Affairs Department (until Jan 1953), and as member of the Political and Legal Committee of that council
1953,	Jan	Appointed member of the Central-South China Administrative Council (until Nov 1954)
1954,	Aug	Elected deputy for Wuhan Municipality to the 1st NPC
	Sep	Identified as president of the Central-South Branch of the Supreme People's Court (until Oct 1954)
	Oct	Appointed vice-minister of justice (until Apr 1959)
1958,	Jul	Elected deputy for Sichuan Province to the 2nd NPC
1959,	Apr	Zheng disappears for unknown reasons
1979,	Feb	First reappearance: Appointed vice-president of the Supreme People's Court
	Jul	By-elected member of the Standing Committee of the 5th CPPCC

Zheng Siyuan (Cheng Szu-yüan) 郑思远

Posts held

Government
Deputy secretary-general of the State Council

Others
Member of the Standing Committee of the 5th CPPCC

Zheng is a former member of the KMT Legislative Executive Yuan.

1951		Council member, Fujian Section of the Sino-Soviet Friendship Association
1960,	Sep	Identified as CP secretary of the Bureau of Government Office Administration under the State Council
1965,	Apr	Appointed deputy secretary-general of the State Council
1967		Disappears during the Cultural Revolution
1972,	Feb	First appearance after the Cultural Revolution attending a reception given for U.S. president Richard Nixon
1978,	Mar	Elected member of the Standing Committee of the 5th CPPCC

1979,   Mar   Identified as deputy secretary-general of the State Council
         Jul   Appointed member of the National Games Organizing Committee

Zheng Tianxiang (Cheng T'ien-hisang)

郑 天 翔

Posts held

NPC
Deputy for Beijing Municipality to the 5th NPC

Government
Minister of the 7th Ministry of Machine Building

1950,   Feb   Identified as mayor of Baotou
1955,   Feb   Identified as deputy secretary of Beijing Municipality CP
1957,   May   Identified as secretary of Beijing Municipality CP (until Jun 1966)
1966,   Jun   Together with Peng Zhen, relieved of all offices and disappears
1975,   Sep   First appearance after the Cultural Revolution
1977,   Aug   Identified as vice-chairman of the Revolutionary Committee of Beijing Municipality (until Feb 1979)
1978,   Feb   Identified as secretary of Beijing Municipality CP (until Feb 1979); elected deputy for Beijing to the 5th NPC
1978,   Feb   Appointed minister of the 7th Ministry of Machine Building
         Jun   Member of the Credentials Committee, 2nd Session of the 5th NPC

Zheng Tuobin (Cheng T'o-pin) 郑 拓 彬

Posts held

Government
Vice-minister of foreign trade

1960,   Apr   Identified as trade counselor at the embassy in Moscow (until 1964)
1972,   Apr   First appearance after the Cultural Revolution; identified as deputy director of a department in the Ministry of Foreign Trade
1973,   Jul   Identified as director of the 3rd Department in the Ministry of Foreign Trade (until 1977)
1975,   Feb   Head of a trade delegation to Canada
         May   Member of a government delegation to France headed by Deng Xiaoping
         Jun   Head of a trade delegation to Norway, Denmark, and Italy
1976,   May   Head of a trade delegation to the Benelux Countries and Sweden
1977,   May   Head of a trade delegation to Australia and New Zealand
1978,   Jan   Identified as vice-minister of foreign trade
         Apr   Zheng heads a trade delegation to North Korea

Zheng Wanjun (Cheng Wan-chün) 郑 万 钧

Posts held

Others
President, Academy of Forestry Sciences

1959,   Jun   Identified as deputy director of the Nanjing Forestry Institute (until 1962)
1963   Identified as vice-president of the Forestry Society
1964,   Sep   Elected deputy for Jilin Province to the 3rd NPC
1973,   Oct   First appreparance after the Cultural Revolution
1979,   Sep   Identified as president of the Academy of Forestry Sciences

Zheng Weizhi (Cheng Wei-chih) 郑 为 之

Posts held

Government
Ambassador to Venezuela

Zheng was born about 1912 in Guangdong Province. In 1946 he was head of the Political Department of 9th Brigade in the United Anti-Japanese Army. Later he held the post of deputy political commissar of a division with the rank of regiment commander.

1951,   Jun   Counselor, embassy in Pakistan (until 1955)
1956,   Jun   Appointed ambassador to Denmark (until May 1961)
1961,   Aug   Appointed director of the America and Australia Department in the Ministry of Foreign Affairs (until 1964)
1962,   Dec   Elected council member of the Sino-Cuban Friendship Association
1964,   Sep   Identified as council member of Institute of Foreign Affairs
1972,   Sep   Appointed ambassador to Argentina (until Oct 1977)
1978,   May   Appointed ambassador to Venezuela

Zheng Xiaoxian (Cheng Hsiao-hsien)

郑 校 先

Posts held

CCP
Member of the Standing Committee of Qinghai Province CP

Provincial Administration
Vice governor of Qinghai Province

1977,   Dec   Elected vice-chairman of the Revolutionary Committee of Qinghai Province (until Aug 1979)
1978,   Aug   Identified as member of the Standing Committee of Qinghai Province CP
1979,   Sep   Elected vice-governor of Qinghai Province

Zheng Yishan (Cheng Yi-shan) 郑义山

Posts held

Government
Vice-minister of foreign trade

1970,	Jul	Identified as a cadre of the State Council
1974,	Nov	PRC representative at the UN Conference on Trade and Development (UNCTAD) in Geneva
1977,	Apr	Identified as vice-minister of foreign trade
1979,	Aug	Head of a trade delegation to the Mongolian People's Republic

Zheng Yonghe (Cheng Yung-ho) 郑永和

Posts held

CCP
Deputy secretary of Henan Province CP

Government
Member of the Birth Planning Leading Group under the State Council

Zheng was born in 1922 in Henan Province.

1977,	Dec	Elected vice-chairman of the Revolutionary Committee of Henan Province (until Aug 1979)
1978,	Apr	Identified as deputy secretary of Henan Province CP
	Jul	Appointed member of the Birth Planning Leading Group under the State Council

Zheng Zhiping (Cheng Chih-p'ing) 程之平

Posts held

Government
Ambassador to Malta

1977,	Jul	Appointed ambassador to Malta

Zheng Zhong (Cheng Chung)

Posts held

Government
Vice-minister of agriculture

1975,	Jan	Identified as director of a department in the Ministry of Agriculture and Forestry
1979,	Dec	Identified as vice-minister of agriculture

Zhong Fuxiang (Chung Fu-hsiang)

锺夫翔

Posts held

CCP
Alternate member of the CCP 11th Central Committee

Zhong was born in Guangxi Province. During 1934-35 he took part in the Long March. When the Bureau of Telecommunications was established in the CCP Military Council in May 1949, Zhong was appointed deputy director.

1950,	Sep	Head of the Central-South China Bureau of Post and Telecommunications (until 1953)
1953,	Sep	Appointed vice-minister of post and telecommunications (until Jan 1957)
1955,	Aug	Head of a delegation to the 16th International Fair in Plovdiv, Bulgaria
	Sep	Head of a delegation to an international exhibition of postage stamps in Prague
	Nov	Identified as director of the College of Post and Telecommunications in Beijing (until Sep 1957)
1957,	May	Appointed vice-minister of the 2nd Ministry of Machine Building (until Feb 1958)
1958,	Sep	Appointed vice-minister of the 1st Ministry of Machine Building (until Sep 1960)
1960,	Sep	Appointed vice-minister of the newly established 3rd Ministry of Machine Building (until Oct 1962)
1962,	Oct	Appointed vice-minister of post and telecommunications (until Jul 1973)
1964,	Sep	Elected deputy for Guangxi Autonomous Region to the 3rd NPC
1965,	May	Head of a postal delegation to Romania
1971,	Aug	Head of a telecommunications delegation to Chile and Great Britain
	Sep	Head of a telecommunications delegation to Switzerland and France
1972,	Oct	Identified as director of the Telecommunications Bureau in the State Council (until Jul 1973)
1973,	Mar	Head of a telecommunications delegation to Japan
	Aug	Identified as minister of post and telecommunications (until Jun 1978)
1975,	May	Head of a postal delegation to Romania
	Oct	Head of a post and telecommunications delegation to Algeria
1977,	Aug	Elected alternate member of the CCP Central Committee by the 11th Party Congress
	Sep	Head of a postal delegation to North Korea
	Oct	Head of a postal delegation to Albania and Italy
1978,	Jun	Zhong disappears; probably purged

Zhong is married to Bai Ge.

Zhong Guochu (Chung Kuo-ch'u)

Posts held 钟国楚

CCP
Secretary of Jiangsu Province CP

NPC
Deputy for the PLA to the 5th NPC

Military
Major-general
2nd political commissar of Jiangsu Military District

Provincial Administration
Vice-chairman of the People's Congress of
Jiangsu Province

1958,	Apr	Identified as major-general in North Korea
1963,	Aug	Identified as military officer in Shanghai
1965,	Oct	Identified as deputy commander of Anhui Military District
1967		Disappears during the Cultural Revolution
1977,	May	First appearance after the Cultural Revolution: Identified as member of the Standing Committee of Jiangsu Province CP (until 1977) and as 2nd political commissar of Jiangsu Military District
	Dec	Elected secretary of Jiangsu Province CP
1978,	Feb	Elected deputy for the PLA to the 5th NPC
1979,	Aug	Identified as deputy head of the Jiangsu Provincial Leading Group for Air Defense
	Oct	Identified as chairman of the People's Armed Forces Committee, Jiangsu Province CP
	Dec	Elected vice-chairman of the People's Congress of Jiangsu Province

Zhong Hanhua (Chung Han-hua) 钟汉华

Posts held

Military
Lieutenant-general
Political commissar of Chengdu Military
Region

Zhong was born in 1913. In 1939 he served in a vanguard
unit of the 129th Division, 8th Route Army.

1950		Identified as director of the Political Department in East Sichuan Military District
1952,	Oct	Identified as 2nd political commissar in Sichuan Military District
1955,	Sep	Appointed lieutenant-general; conferred the order "Liberation," 1st class
1957,	Apr	Identified as judge of the Supreme People's Court (until 1961)
1961,	Jun	Identified as deputy political commissar of Wuhan Military Region (until 1966)
1964,	Sep	Elected deputy for the PLA to the 3rd NPC
1966,	Sep	Identified as political commissar of Wuhan Military Region (until Aug 1967)
1967,	Jul	Zhong is involved in the "Wuhan Incident"
	Aug	Placed under arrest and purged
1973,	Oct	First appearance after the Cultural Revolution: Identified as deputy political commissar of Guangzhou Military Region (until 1977)
1978,	May	Identified as political commissar of the PLA Armored Forces (until Dec 1978)
1979,	Jan	Identified as political commissar of Chengdu Military Region

Zhong Huilan (Chung Hui-lan) 钟惠兰

Posts held

Others
Member of the Standing Committee of the
5th CPPCC
Vice-president of the Medical Association
President of the Society of Internal Medicine
Director of the Institute of Tropical Medicine

Zhong is a former member of the Chinese Peasants' and
Workers' Democratic Party.

1953,	Feb	Member of a medical delegation to Lahore, Pakistan
	Apr	Identified as member of the Planning Committee for Health Propaganda of the Science and Technology Dissemination Association
1954,	May	Identified as superintendent of Beijing Central People's Hospital
1955,	Jun	Identified as member of the Biology Department of the Academy of Sciences
	Nov	Identified as member of the Standing Committee of the Medical Association
1956,	Feb	Self-criticism at the 2nd Plenary Session, 2nd CPPCC
	May	Elected council member of the Sino-Pakistani Friendship Association
	Aug	Identified as vice-president of the Medical Association
1957,	Mar	Speech before the 3rd Plenary Session of the 2nd CPPCC: "Birth Control Must Be Planned"
1959,	Apr	Elected member of the Standing Committee of the 3rd CPPCC (confirmed in Jan 1965 by the 4th CPPCC)
1967		Disappears during the Cultural Revolution
1973,	Mar	First appearance after the Cultural Revolution: Named in his previous post as member of the Standing Committee of the CPPCC
1978,	Mar	Elected member of the Standing Committee of the 5th CPPCC
1979,	Jan	Zhong attends the World Health Organization Conference in Manila; identified as president of the Society of Internal Medicine; as vice-president of the Medical Association; and as director of the Institute of Tropical Medicine

Zhong Qiguang (Chung Ch'i-kuang) 钟期光

Posts held

Military
Colonel-general

Others
Member of the Standing Committee of the
5th CPPCC

Zhong was born in 1909 in Pingjiang, Hunan Province.
From 1938 to 1945 he was director of the Political

Department of the New 4th Army. He was later appointed political commissar of the New 4th Army.

1955		Identified as director of the Political Department, East China Naval Headquarters
	Sep	Promoted to rank of colonel-general and conferred an order of merit
1956		Identified as deputy director (until Nov 1957), and probably in addition deputy political commissar, of the PLA Military Academy (until Nov 1957)
	Sep	Elected alternate member of the CCP Central Committee by the 8th Party Congress
1957,	Nov	Appointed political commissar of the PLA Military Academy (until Cultural Revolution)
1967		Disappears during the Cultural Revolution
1974,	Sep	First appearance after the Cultural Revolution
1978,	Mar	Elected member of the Standing Committee of the 5th CPPCC

Zhong Qingfa (Chung Ch'ing-fa) 钟庆发

Posts held

Others
Vice-chairman of the Federation of Returned Overseas Chinese

1959,	Apr	Elected deputy for the Overseas Chinese to the 2nd NPC (reelected in 1964 to the 3rd NPC)
1960,	Feb	Identified as director of the General Office, State Overseas Chinese Commission
1961,	Mar	Member of a government delegation to Indonesia
	Jul	Identified as vice-chairman of the Sino-Indonesian Friendship Association (until 1965)
1963,	Feb	Head of a friendship delegation to Indonesia
1966		Disappears during the Cultural Revolution
1979,	Jun	Identified as vice-chairman of the Federation of Returned Overseas Chinese

Zhong Shitong (Chung Shih-t'ung)

Posts held
钟师统

Others
Member of the Standing Committee of the 5th CPPCC
President of the Sports Federation
President of the Chinese Olympic Committee
Vice-chairman of the Athletic Federation
Director of the Beijing Physical Culture Institute
Chairman of the Weight Lifting Association

In 1946 Zhong was a member of the Communist section of the KMT-CCP Military Committee in Shanxi Province.

1955,	Feb	Appointed director of the Central Physical Culture Institute in Beijing
1956,	Oct	Elected member of the Standing Committee of the Athletic Federation
1957,	Sep	Elected council member of the Sino-Syrian Friendship Association (until Cultural Revolution)
1958,	Feb	Elected council member of the China-United Arab Republic Friendship Association (until Cultural Revolution)
	Jun	Identified as director of the Beijing Physical Culture Institute (until Cultural Revolution)
	Apr	Head of a sports delegation to the German Democratic Republic
1959,	Sep	Identified as member of the State Council Commission for Physical Culture and Sports (until Cultural Revolution)
1964,	Feb	Elected vice-chairman of the Athletic Federation
	Sep	Elected deputy for Shanxi Province to the 3rd NPC
	Oct	Deputy head of a sports delegation to North Vietnam
1974,	Apr	Head of a ping-pong delegation to North Vietnam
1975,	Apr	Identified as chairman of the Weight Lifting Association
1978,	Mar	Elected member of the Standing Committee of the 5th CPPCC
	Jun	Identified as holding his former post as director of the Beijing Physical Culture Institute
1979,	Mar	Elected president of the Sports Federation; identified as president of the Chinese Olympic Committee

Zhong Xidong (Chung Hsi-tung) 仲曦东

Posts held

Government
Vice-minister of foreign affairs

In 1945 Zhong was political commissar of the Communist Yantai Army in Shandong Province. As secretary of the Yantai Joint Action Committee Zhong conducted negotiations with the commander of U.S. Navy Pacific Fleet units operating in the Yellow Sea in October 1945. He rejected the U.S. commander's request to allow the crews of five warships ashore. In 1948 he served in the East China Field Army. In spring 1949 he was identified as director of the Political Department, 27th Army, 3rd Field Army.

1955,	Sep	Zhong is made a major-general
1961,	Jun	Appointed ambassador to the CSSR (until 1967)
1969,	Jun	Appointed ambassador to Tanzania (until Mar 1972)
1971,	Nov	Zhong conducts the negotiations in Rwanda leading to the establishment of diplomatic relations with the PRC
1972,	May	Appointed vice-minister of foreign affairs
1978,	Aug	Head of a government delegation to Vietnam to hold negotiations on border disputes

Zhong is married to Liu Jinlin.

Zhong Ziyun (Chung Tzu-yün) 钟子云

Posts held

Government
Vice-minister of coal industry

NPC
Deputy for Tianjin Municipality to the 5th NPC

Zhong is a native of Shandong Province. After Harbin was occupied by Communist units in 1946 he became political commissar of Harbin Garrison and in 1948 mayor of this city.

1951,	Oct	Identified as director of Fuxin Mining Bureau, Liaoxi Province (until 1953)
1955,	Aug	Assistant minister in the Ministry of Coal Industry (until Apr 1957)
1957,	Apr	Vice-minister of coal industry
1958,	Sep	Head of a scientific and technical delegation to Poland
1960,	Nov	Head of a scientific and technical delegation to Poland
1962,	Jun	Head of a scientific and technical delegation to Poland attending among others the 31st Poznam Fair
1964,	Sep	Elected deputy for Heilongjiang Province to the 3rd NPC
1967,	Apr	Zhong is denounced as a counterrevolutionary revisionist and disappears
1975,	Apr	First appearance after the Cultural Revolution
1976,	Nov	Identified as holding his previous post as vice-minister of coal industry
1978,	Feb	Elected deputy for Tianjin Municipality to the 5th NPC

Zhou Aqing (Chou Ah-ch'ing) 周阿庆

Posts held

CCP
Alternate member of the CCP 11th Central Committee

Mass Organization
Vice-chairman, Trade Union of Jiangsu Province

Zhou, a worker of the Nanjing Radio Factory, came into national prominence. He has brought in 500 technical innovations.

1973,	Jul	Elected vice-chairman of the Trade Union of Jiangsu Province (reelected Oct 1977)
1977,	Apr	Zhou takes part in the Daqing Conference in Daqing
	Aug	Elected member of the CCP Central Committee by the 11th Party Congress

Zhou Baofen (Chou Pao-fen) 周宝芬

Posts held

Others
Director of the Board of Directors, China International Trust and Investment Corporation

Vice-chairman of the Guangzhou Federation of Industrialists and Businessmen

Zhou was born in Guangdong Province in 1923.

1979,	Apr	Member of a government trade delegation led by Rong Yiren to the Federal Republic of Germany
	Oct	Appointed director of the Board of Directors, China International Trust and Investment Corporation; vice-chairman of the Guangzhou Federation of Industrialists and Businessmen

Zhou Beifeng (Chou Pei-feng) 周北峰

Posts held

NPC
Deputy for the Inner Mongolia Autonomous Region to the 5th NPC

Provincial Administration
Vice-chairman of the Inner Mongolia Autonomous Region People's Government

Zhou was born as a Mongol in Shanxi (Shaanxi?) Province.

1958,	Jun	Elected deputy for the Inner Mongolia Autonomous Region to the 2nd NPC (reelected in 1964 to the 3rd NPC)
1978,	Feb	First appearance after the Cultural Revolution: Elected deputy for the Inner Mongolia Autonomous Region to the 5th NPC
1979,	Jun	Member of the Budget Committee at the 2nd Session of the 5th NPC
	Dec	Elected vice-chairman of the Inner Mongolia Autonomous Region People's Government

Zhou Boping (Chou Po-p'ing) 周伯萍

Posts held

Government
Ambassador to Zaire

1967,	Jun	Counselor at the embassy in Tanzania (until 1971)
1973,	Mar	Appointed ambassador to Greece (until Jun 1975)
1975,	Aug	Appointed ambassador to Algeria (until May 1978)
1978,	Aug	Appointed ambassador to Zaire

Zhou Chunlin (Chou Ch'un-lin) 周纯麟

Posts held

CCP
Member of the CCP 11th Central Committee

Military
Major-general
Deputy commander of Nanjing Military Region

In 1944 Zhou commanded the Cavalry Regiment in the 4th Division of the New 4th Army.

1958,	Jan	Identified as major-general in Nanjing Military Region
1970,	Jul	Identified as commander of Shanghai Garrison (until May 1978)
	Aug	Identified as vice-chairman, Revolutionary Committee of Shanghai Municipality (reelected in Dec 1977) (until mid-1978)
1971,	Jan	Elected secretary, CP of Shanghai Municipality (until mid-1978)
1973,	Aug	Elected to first term as member of the CCP Central Committee by the 10th Party Congress
1978,	Aug	Identified as military leader of Nanjing Military Region
1979,	Oct	Identified as deputy commander of Nanjing Military Region

Zhou Chunquan (Chou Ch'un-ch'üan)

Posts held

Military
Colonel-general

Others
Member of the Standing Committee of the 5th CPPCC

Zhou was born in 1904 in Hubei Province. In 1931 he was a member of the Hubei-Henan-Anhui Border Region Government.

1949,	Dec	Identified as director of the Logistics Department of the 4th Field Army and as member of the Central-South China Military and Administrative Council (until 1951)
1952,	Feb	Identified as deputy director of the General Logistics Department of the People's Revolutionary Military Council (until 1954)
1954,	Aug	Elected deputy for the PLA to the 1st NPC (confirmed in 1959 and 1964 by the 2nd and 3rd NPCs)
	Sep	Appointed member of the National Defense Council (abolished in 1975)
1955,	Mar	Identified as deputy director of the General Logistics Department of the PLA
	Sep	Appointed lieutenant-general; awarded the orders of "August 1st" and "Liberation," both 1st class
1959,	Apr	Elected member of the Standing Committee by the 2nd NPC (confirmed in 1965 by the 3rd NPC)
1964,	Jun	Identified as colonel-general
1974,	Sep	Zhou disappears, having survived the Cultural Revolution unharmed, until Mar 1978
1978,	Mar	Elected member of the Standing Committee of the 5th CPPCC

Zhou Erfu (Chou Erh-fu)

周而復

Posts held

Government
Vice-minister of culture

Others
Deputy secretary-general of the 5th CPPCC

Zhou was born in 1914 in Nanjing. He attended the Nanjing YMCA Middle School. In 1933 he graduated from the Department of Foreign Languages of the Shanghai Guanghua University. During his studies he was editor of Literary Miscellany and the monthly Novelist. From 1938 he was in Yan'an and worked primarily as a press cadre in North and eventually Northeast China. From 1947 to 1949 he was editor-in-chief of the Hong Kong journal Northern Literature. In July 1949 he was elected an alternate member of the Association of Literary and Art Circles.

1949,	Oct	Identified as secretary of the United Front Work Department, East China Bureau of the CCP Central Committee
1950,	Mar	Identified as member of the Culture and Education Committee in the East China Military and Administrative Council
1951		Identified as secretary-general of the United Front Work Department, East China Bureau of the CCP Central Committee
1953,	Jul	Appointed member of the Culture and Education Committee of Shanghai People's Government; identified as deputy director of the United Front Work Department of Shanghai CP
	Sep	Elected council member of the Union of Chinese Writers
1954,	Nov	Deputy head of a cultural delegation to India and Burma
1955,	Jun	Deputy head of a cultural delegation to Indonesia; elected council member of the Sino-Indonesion Friendship Association
1956,	Apr	Elected council member of the Sino-Indian Friendship Association
1958,	Mar	Identified as deputy director of the Propaganda Department, CP of Shanghai Municipality
1959,	Apr	Elected council member and secretary-general of the Association for Cultural Relations with Foreign Countries
	Sep	Appointed member of the Commission for Cultural Relations with Foreign Countries
1960,	Jan	Elected member of the Peace Council
	Mar	Elected vice-chairman of the Sino-Latin-American Friendship Association
	Apr	Elected council member of the Sino-African Friendship Association
1961,	Feb	Head of the Chinese guest delegation attending the Latin-American Conference in Mexico
	Mar	Head of a cultural delegation to Cuba
	Jul	Elected vice-chairman of the Association for Cultural Relations with Foreign Countries (renamed Association for Cultural Relations and Friendship with Foreign Countries in Apr 1966)

1962,	Dec	Elected council member of the Sino-Cuban Friendship Association
1963,	May	Head of a cultural delegation to Japan
	Oct	Elected vice-chairman of the Sino-Japanese Friendship Association
1966,	Apr	Elected vice-chairman of the Association for Cultural Relations and Friendship with Foreign Countries
1967,	Jun	Branded as a capitalist-roader and purged
1978,	May	First appearance after the Cultural Revolution
	Aug	Identified as deputy secretary-general of the 5th CPPCC
	Dec	Identified as vice-minister of culture
1979,	May	Deputy head of a cultural delegation to Japan (head: Huang Zhen)
	Oct	Deputy head of a cultural delegation to Romania, Yugoslavia Turkey, Syria, Jordan, and Tunisia (head: Huang Zhen)

Publications

Morning in Shanghai (translated into English, Japanese, and Vietnamese)
The Story of Dr. Bethune (translated into Japanese)
Swallow Cliffs (translated into Japanese)
Children of Xiliushui (translated into Russian)
Spring in the Valley
People's Soldiers
When Niu Yongguei Was Wounded
Touring the Shanxi-Chahar-Hebei Region (translated into Japanese)
A New Starting Point (a collection of essays)

| 1979 | | Zhou published the third volume of his novel Mourning in Shanghai |

Zhou Guangchun (Chou Kuang-ch'un)

周光春

Posts held

CCP
Secretary of Guangxi Autonomous Region CP

Provincial Administration
Vice-chairman of the People's Government of Guangxi Autonomous Region

Zhou was born in Shandong Province. In spring 1949 he was appointed council member of Shandong People's Government.

1950,	Mar	Identified as director of the Finance Department of Shandong People's Government
1952,	Oct	Identified as director of the Finance Department in the East China Military and Administrative Council (until 1954)
1954,	Nov	Identified as director of the 4th Staff Office under the State Council (until Sep 1959)
1957,	May	Identified as member of the State Scientific Planning Commission (until 1958)
1958,	Jun	Appointed vice-chairman of the State Economic Commission (until Sep 1959)

1964,	Apr	Identified as director of the Guangzhou Nitrogenous Fertilizer Factory
1966,	Aug	Identified as member of the Central-South China Bureau of the CCP Central Committee
1968,	Feb	Branded as a bourgeois reactionary and follower of Tao Zhu
1978,	May	First appearance after the Cultural Revolution: Identified as vice-chairman of the Revolutionary Committee of Guangxi Autonomous Region (until Dec 1979)
1979,	Jan	Identified as secretary of Guangxi Autonomous Region CP
	Dec	Elected vice-chairman of the People's Government of Guangxi Autonomous Region

Zhou Guanwu (Chou Kuan-wu) 周贯五

Posts held

Government
Vice-minister of metallurgical industry

Military
Lieutenant-general

Others
General-manager of Beijing Iron and Steel Company

Zhou was born in 1915. In 1939 he served as political commissar in the 6th Brigade, 115th Division, 8th Route Army. In 1945 he was political commissar in Bohai Military District, and two years later political commissar of the East China 10th Column.

1955,	Jul	Identified as deputy political commissar of Zhejiang Military District
1957,	Jan	Identified as lieutenant-general
1958,	Nov	Member of a delegation attending the October ceremonies in the USSR
1963,	Feb	Identified as commander of Zhejiang Military District (until 1967)
1964,	Oct	Elected deputy for the PLA to the 3rd NPC
1968,	Feb	Identified as deputy political commissar of Nanjing Military Region (until 1975?)
1975,	Oct	Zhou disappears for unknown reasons until 1977
1977,	Feb	Present at mourning ceremonies for Liang Jiqing in Hefei
1978,	Aug	Identified as vice-minister of metallurgical industry
	Sep	Identified as general manager of the Beijing Iron and Steel Company

Zhou Gucheng (Chou Ku-Ch'eng) 周谷城

Posts held

NPC
Deputy for Shanghai Municipality to the 5th NPC

Provincial Administration
Vice-chairman of the Shanghai People's Congress

Others
Vice-chairman of the China Peasants' and Workers' Democratic Party

Zhou was born in 1910 in Yiyang, Hunan Province. He graduated from Beijing Normal University, majoring in English literature. From 1934 onward he served successively as a professor and director of the Sociology Department, Sun Yat-sen University in Guangzhou, as professor of history at the Jinan University in Shandong, and as professor of history at the Shanghai Fudan University. In September 1949 he was a delegate to the 1st CPPCC.

1950,	Mar	Identified as a member of the Cultural and Educational Committee, East China Military and Administrative Council
1951,	Oct	Elected member of the Central Committee, Chinese Peasants' and Workers' Democratic Party (until Cultural Revolution)
1954,	Aug	Elected deputy for Hunan Province to the 1st NPC (reelected in 1958 and 1964 to the 2nd and 3rd NPCs)
1961,	Feb	Elected chairman of the Shanghai Society of History
	Jun	Elected chairman of the Shanghai Branch of the China Peasants' and Workers' Democratic Party
1962,	Apr	Elected council member of the China Afro-Asian Society
	Jul	Identified as vice-chairman of the Shanghai Branch of the CPPCC
1966,	Jun	Denounced as a counterrevolutionary revisionist
1978,	Feb	First appearance after the Cultural Revolution: Elected deputy for Shanghai to the 5th NPC
1979,	Jun	Member of the Committee to Examine Proposals at the 2nd Session of the 5th NPC
	Oct	Elected vice-chairman of the China Peasants' and Workers' Democratic Party
	Dec	Elected vice-chairman of the Shanghai People's Congress

Publications

History of China
Social Structure of China
Political History of China
Evolution of Chinese Historical Studies
Changes of the Chinese Society
History of Chinese Education
Life System
Experimental Logic
The Current Situation of the Chinese Society
History of the Western World
Historical Significance of Art Creation

Zhou Huamin (Chou Hua-min)

Posts held

Government
Vice-minister of foreign trade

In August 1949 Zhou was appointed council member of the People's Government of Shanxi Province, member of its Financial and Economic Affairs Committee as well as director of its Commerce Department (until 1955).

1955		Identified as manager of the Chinese Metal and Electrotechnical Import Corporation (until 1960)
1958,	May	Member of a trade delegation to GDR
1960,	Aug	Identified as assistant minister in the Ministry of Foreign Trade (until Apr 1964)
1961,	Mar	Deputy head of a trade delegation to the USSR
1963,	Apr	Deputy head of a trade delegation to the USSR
1964,	Jan	Deputy head of a trade delegation to the USSR
	Apr	Appointed vice-minister of foreign trade
1968,	May	Head of a trade delegation to Guinea and GDR
1969,	Oct	Deputy head of a government and military delegation to Algeria
1970,	Mar	Head of a trade delegation to North Korea and the United Arab Republic
	Jun	Head of a trade delegation to GDR
	Aug	Head of a trade delegation to Syria attending the Damascus trade fair
	Sep	Head of a trade delegation to Algeria attending the Algiers trade fair
1971,	Jan	Head of a trade delegation to Guinea
	Apr	Head of a trade delegation to Chile and Peru
	May	Head of a trade delegation to Hungary, CSSR, and Poland
	Jun	Head of a trade delegation to PR Mongolia
	Aug	Head of a trade delegation to the USSR and Guyana
	Sep	Head of a trade delegation to Finland, Sweden, and Norway
	Oct	Head of a trade delegation to Denmark
1972,	Feb	Head of a trade delegation to Cuba
	Apr	Head of the Chinese delegation attending the UN Conference on Trade and Development (UNCTAD) in Santiago
	Sep	Head of a trade delegation to Italy
1973,	Mar	Head of a trade delegation to CSSR, GDR (Leipzig Trade Fair), and Hungary
1974,	Feb	Head of a trade delegation to Tunisia and Algeria
1976,	May	Head of a delegation attending the UNCTAD Conference in Nairobi
1979,	Jan	Head of a trade delegation to Guinea
	Apr	Head of a survey team on port administration to Romania

Zhou Huan (Chou Huan)

Zhou was born in 1904 in Liaoning Province. In the early 1930s he was identified as a political officer in the 3rd Army Corps of the Red Army. He took part in the Long March of 1934-35 as a member of the Main Force to which Mao Zedong also belonged. In 1938 he was made a political officer in the 18th Army Group. In 1945 he was one of the leading cadres who were posted to Manchuria together with Lin Biao. In June 1948 Zhou was identified as deputy director of the Political Department of Northeast China Military Region. In September 1949 he took part in the CPPCC as a delegate representing the Liberated Northeast Areas.

1949,	Dec	Appointed council member of the Northeast China People's Government (until Jan 1953) and director of the Political Department of Northeast China Military Region
1952		Identified as deputy political commissar of Northeast China Military Region (until Sep 1954)
1953,	Jan	Appointed member of the Northeast China Administrative Council (until Sep 1954)
1954,	Aug	Elected deputy for the PLA to the 1st NPC (until Mar 1959)
1955,	Sep	Appointed colonel-general
1956,	Sep	Elected alternate member of the CCP Central Committee by the 8th Party Congress
1958,	Feb	Identified as commander of Shenyang Garrison
	Dec	Appointed political commissar of Shenyang Military Region (until 1959)
1960,	Dec	Appointed secretary of Liaoning Province CP
1968,	May	Branded as a capitalist-roader and purged
1978,	Dec	First appearance after the Cultural Revolution

Zhou Hui (Chou Hui)   周 惠

Posts held

CCP
Member of the CCP 11th Central Committee
1st secretary, CP of Inner Mongolia Autonomous Region

Military
1st political commissar of Inner Mongolia Military District

1955,	Feb	Identified as member of the People's Government of Hunan Province
1956,	Mar	Identified as deputy secretary of Hunan Province CP
1957,	Dec	Identified as secretary of Hunan Province CP
1967		Disappears during the Cultural Revolution
1977,	Oct	First appearance after the Cultural Revolution: Identified as vice-minister of communications
1978,	Aug	Member of a scientific delegation under Gu Mu to England and France
	Oct	Identified as 1st secretary of the CP, and vice-chairman of the Revolutionary Committee, of Inner Mongolia Autonomous Region (latter post until Dec 1979)
	Dec	By-elected member of the CCP 11th Central Committee at its 3rd Plenum
1979,	Jun	Identified as 1st political commissar of Inner Mongolia Military District

Zhou Jiannan (Chou Chien-nan)   周 建 南

Posts held

Government
Vice-minister of the 1st Ministry of Machine Building
Vice-minister of the State Commission for Regulating Foreign Investments

Others
Vice-president of the Society of Mechanical Engineering

1954,	Sep	Identified as director of the Electric Instrument Administration Bureau of the 1st Ministry of Machine Building
1956,	Apr	Identified as assistant minister in the 1st Ministry of Machine Building (until Apr 1957)
1957,	Jun	Identified as assistant minister in the Ministry of Electrical Equipment Industry
1961,	Apr	Appointed deputy director of the Bureau for Economic Relations with Foreign Countries under the State Council (until 1964)
	Oct	Appointed vice-minister of the 1st Ministry of Machine Building (until Cultural Revolution)
1963		Identified as member of the Electrical Engineering Society (until Cultural Revolution)
1967		Disappears during the Cultural Revolution)
1978,	Apr	First appearance after the Cultural Revolution: Identified as vice-minister of the 1st Ministry of Machine Building
	Oct	Identified as vice-president of the Mechanical Engineering Society; head of a machine building delegation to Japan
1979,	Oct	Identified as vice-minister of the State Commission for Regulating Foreign Investments

Zhou Jianren (Chou Chien-jen)   周 建 人

Posts held

CCP
Member of the CCP 11th Central Committee

NPC
Vice-chairman of the 5th NPC
Deputy for Beijing Municipality to the 5th NPC

Others
Vice-chairman of the 5th CPPCC
Chairman of the Association for Promoting Democracy
Advisor to the Lu Xun Studies Society

Zhou is a younger brother of the best-known Chinese writer of this century, Lu Xun (Zhou Shuren). He was born in 1887 in the family of a wealthy landlord. Although the family fortune was lost in 1894, the three sons received a university education. Zhou Jianren at first lectured as professor of biology at various universities, finally in Shanghai, where he worked concurrently as editor for the

Commercial Press, China's largest publishing house. He remained in Shanghai during the Japanese occupation 1937-1945 and then went to Hong Kong. In 1947 he translated Darwin's <u>Origin of Species</u> (not published until 1955). His <u>On Eugenics and Racial Discrimination</u> was published in 1948. In that year he moved to Communist controlled North China and was given editorial work in the North China People's Government's Education Department. In September 1949 he was a delegate at the 1st CPPCC. He then belonged to the small group of outstanding scientists headed by Tong Biwu and entrusted with the drafting of a new constitution.

1949, Oct Appointed deputy director of the Publications Administration (until Oct 1954); appointed vice-chairman of the People's Government of Zhejiang Province (until 1955) and council member of the Sino-Soviet Friendship Association (until Dec 1954)

1950, Apr Elected member of the Association for Promotion of Democracy

1954, Sep Elected deputy for Zhejiang Province to the 1st NPC

       Oct Elected member of the Standing Committee of the NPC; appointed vice-minister for higher education (probably until Jan 1958)

1955, Jun Elected vice-chairman of the Chinese Association for Promoting Democracy

1956, Sep Elected chairman of the newly established Sino-Nepalese Friendship Association

1958, Jan Elected governor of Zhejiang Province (until Cultural Revolution)

       Jun Identified as director of the Hangzhou Branch of the Academy of Sciences

1962, May Identified as secretary of Zhejiang Province CP (until Cultural Revolution)

1965, Jan Elected vice-chairman of the Standing Committee, 3rd NPC

       Aug Identified as political commissar of Zhejiang Military Region (until Cultural Revolution)

1969, Apr Elected to first term as member of the CCP Central Committee by the 9th Party Congress

1975, Jan Reelected vice-chairman of the Standing Committee by the 4th NPC (reelected in 1978 to the 5th NPC)

1978, Feb Elected deputy for Beijing Municipality to the 5th NPC

       Mar Elected vice-chairman of the 5th CPPCC

1979, Jan Identified as acting chairman of the Chinese Association for Promoting Democracy (until Oct 1979)

       Oct Elected chairman of the Chinese Association for Promoting Democracy

       Dec Elected advisor to the Lu Xun Studies Society

Zhou Jue (Chou Chüeh)   周 觉

Posts held

Government
Director of the West Asia and North Africa Department in the Ministry of Foreign Affairs

1970, Nov Identified as director of a section in the West Asia and North Africa Department of the Ministry of Foreign Affairs (until May 1971); member of a government delegation to Mauritania to celebrate the 10th Independence Anniversary

1971, May Identified as deputy director of the West Asia and North Africa Department in the Ministry of Foreign Affairs

1972, Jun Member of a government and military delegation to Algeria

1974, Sep Member of the Chinese delegation attending the 29th UN General Assembly

       Dec Identified as acting director of the West Asia and North Africa Department, Ministry of Foreign Affairs

1977, Dec Zhou accompanies Deng Yingchao to Iran

1978, Nov Member of a government delegation, headed by Ulanhu, to Sudan and Turkey

1979, Nov Identified as director of the West Asia and North Africa Department in the Ministry of Foreign Affairs

Zhou Li (Chou Li)   周 里

Posts held

CCP
Secretary of Hunan Province CP

NPC
Member of the Standing Committee of the 5th NPC
Deputy for Hunan Province to the 5th NPC

Others
Chairman of Hunan Province CPPCC

Zhou was born in 1907 in Ling County, Hunan Province. He graduated from the 3rd Hunan Provincial Normal School. During the Long March he belonged to a guerrilla unit which operated in the area of the former Jiangxi Soviet. From 1936 he did underground work in his native province.

1949, Oct Identified as director of the Organization Department of Hunan Province CP

1950, Mar Identified as a member of the Hunan People's Government

1952, Jan Identified as director of the Personnel Department, Hunan People's Government

1954, Aug Elected deputy for Hunan Province to the 1st NPC (confirmed in 1958 and 1964 by the 2nd and 3rd NPCs)

1955, Jan Identified as deputy secretary of Hunan Province CP

1958, Jul Identified as vice-governor of Hunan Province (until Aug 1964)

1960, Apr Identified as secretary of Hunan Province CP (until 1964)

1962, Mar Elected vice-chairman of the CPPCC in Hunan

1965, Jan Elected member of the Standing Committee of the 3rd NPC

1967   Disappears during the Cultural Revolution

1977, Nov First appearance after the Cultural Revolution

1978, Feb Elected deputy for Hunan Province to the 5th NPC

Mar Elected member of the Standing Committee of the 5th NPC

1979,   Apr   Identified as secretary of Hunan Province CP; elected chairman of Hunan Province CPPCC

Jun   Member of the Committee to Examine Proposals, 2nd Session of the 5th NPC

Zhou Lin (Chou Lin) 周　林

Posts held

CCP
Secretary, Beijing University CP

Government
Vice-minister of education

NPC
Deputy for Beijing Municipality to the 5th NPC

Zhou was born in Guizhou Province. He was a graduate of Guizhou University. At the end of 1948 he was mayor of Xuzhou Municipality, Jiangsu Province. In early 1949 he was identified as secretary-general of the People's Government of Shanghai.

1951,   Oct   Identified as vice-chairman of Guizhou Province (until 1955) and as member of the Southwest Military and Administrative Council (until 1953)

1953,   Feb   Identified as member of the Southwest Administrative Council (until 1954)

1955,   Feb   Elected governor of Guizhou Province (until Cultural Revolution); identified as secretary of Guizhou Province CP (until Aug 1956)

1956,   Jun   Elected deputy for Guizhou Province to the 1st NPC in a by-election (reelected in 1958 and 1964 to the 2nd and 3rd NPCs)

Sep   Elected 1st secretary of Guizhou Province CP (until Jan 1965)

1958,   Aug   Identified as political commissar of Guizhou Military District

1960,   Apr   Identified as council member of the Sino-African People's Friendship Association

1968,   Feb   Branded as a counterrevolutionary revisionist and purged

1975,   Oct   First appearance after the Cultural Revolution

1977,   Dec   Identified as vice-minister of education

1978,   Feb   Elected deputy Beijing Peking Municipality to the 5th NPC

Sep   Identified as secretary, Beijing University CP

Zhou Min (Chou Min) 周　敏

Posts held

Government
Ambassador to Upper Volta

1961,   Apr   Appointed counselor at the embassy in Yugoslavia (until Jun 1964)

1964,   Nov   Identified as deputy director, Protocol Department of the Ministry of Foreign Affairs (until about 1969)

1973,   Jun   Identified as counselor at the embassy in Spain (until 1978)

1979,   May   Appointed ambassador to Upper Volta

Zhou Mingqi (Chou Ming-ch'i) 周 明 埜

Posts held

Government
Deputy director of the Africa Department in the Ministry of Foreign Affairs

1974,   Mar   Identified as deputy director of the Africa Department in the Ministry of Foreign Affairs

Zhou Peiyuan (Chou P'ei-yüan) 周 培 源

Posts held

Government
Deputy director of the Institute of Foreign Affairs

NPC
Member of the Standing Committee of the 5th NPC
Deputy for Beijing Municipality to the 5th NPC

Others
Vice-president of the Academy of Sciences
President of Beijing University
Chairman of the Scientific and Technical Association
President of the Physics Society
Vice-chairman of the Jiusan (Chiu-san) Society

Zhou was born in 1902 in Yixing, Jiangsu Province, in the family of a rich landlord. In 1924 he graduated in physics from Qinghua University in Beijing. In 1925 he went to the United States where he obtained a master's degree from the University of Chicago in 1927 and a doctorate from the California Institute of Technology in 1928. After his return to China in 1928 he assumed a professorship in physics at Qinghua University. From 1935 to 1936 he worked at the Institute for Advanced Studies in Princeton, New Jersey, and took part in the seminar on relativity under Einstein's direction. He then rejoined the faculty of Qinghua University which had been moved during the war to Kunming, Yunnan Province, and incorporated together with Beijing and Nankai Universities into the National United Southwest University. His third stay in the United States lasted from 1943 to 1947. In early 1949 he was engaged in research projects for the U.S. Navy dealing among others with the launching of torpedoes from aircraft. In spring 1947 he returned to Qinghua University which had been moved back to Beijing. In 1948 he was appointed chairman of the Physics Society. In late 1949 Zhou participated in an international conference on dynamics in London.

1950,   Aug   Appointed council member of the Federation of Scientific Societies

        Oct   Member of a friendship delegation to England

        Nov   Member of a delegation under Guo Moruo to the 2nd World Peace Congress in Warsaw

1952   Zhou submits to an "inquiry" in which he confesses to an earlier suspicion that the PRC would not tolerate free scientific research and that he had been persuaded to visit the U.S.A. for a third time by U.S. government special agents. He is then not only confirmed in his post as chairman of the Physics Society but also as director of the Organization Department of the Federation of Scientific Societies

1953,   Sep   Elected member of the Jiusan Central Committee; Zhou leaves Qinghua for Beijing University; member of the delegation to the 3rd World Peace Congress in Budapest

1954,   Sep   Elected deputy for Jiangsu Province to the 1st NPC (reelected to 2nd to 5th NPCs)

1955,   May   With the establishment of the four major departments of the Academy of Sciences, Zhou is appointed member of the Mathematics, Physics, and Chemistry Department

        Jun   Zhou takes part in the celebrations of the 200th anniversary of Moscow University

        Sep   Member of the Chinese delegation to a session of the World Federation of Scientific Workers in East Berlin

1956,   Mar   Elected council member of the World Federation of Scientific Workers

        Apr   Elected honorary secretary of the World Federation of Scientific Workers

        Sep   Addresses the 9th International Conference on Applied Mechanics in Brussels

1957,   Feb   Appointed council member of the newly established Dynamics Society

        Jun   Appointed member of the Scientific Planning Commission under the State Council (until 1958)

        Jul   Zhou takes part in the 1st "Pugwash Conference" in Canada (named after the native town of its initiator, the American industrialist Cyrus Eaton, who brought together outstanding scientists from both western and socialist countries in these conferences)

        Aug   Member of the Chinese delegation to a session of the World Federation of Scientific Workers in Helsinki

        Nov   Member of a delegation of scientists, headed by Guo Moruo, to Moscow, which first took part in the 40th anniversary of the October Revolution and during the following weeks negotiated various scientific and technical agreements in Moscow

1958,   Feb   Identified as vice-chairman of the Dynamics Society (this society is incorporated together with all other technical societies, including the Physics Society, into the Scientific and Technical Association in September 1958)

        Mar   Zhou takes part in the 2nd Pugwash Conference in Canada

        Jul   Elected member of the World Peace Council (until about 1965)

        Sep   Zhou is appointed secretary of the newly established Scientific and Technical Association

        Dec   Elected vice-chairman of the Jiusan Society

1959,   Jan   Zhou joins the CCP

        Apr   Elected member of the Standing Committee of the CPPCC representing the Jiusan Society (until Feb 1978)

        Sep   Secretary-general of the Chinese delegation to the Warsaw Congress of the World Federation of Scientific Workers

1960,   Jan   Zhou takes part in a scientific congress in New Delhi

        Mar   Elected member of the Executive Council of the newly established Sino-African Friendship Association

        Oct   Member of the Chinese delegation to the Budapest session of the World Federation of Scientific Workers

        Nov   Zhou takes part in the 6th Pugwash Conference in Moscow

1961,   Mar   Member of the Chinese delegation to the World Peace Council Session in New Delhi

        Apr   Member of the Chinese delegation to the Sofia session of the World Federation of Scientific Workers

        Aug   Head of the Chinese delegation to the World Conference against Atomic Bombs in Tokyo

        Sep   Member of the Chinese delegation to the Geneva session of the World Federation of Scientific Workers

1962,   Sep   Head of the Chinese delegation to the 7th Congress of the World Federation of Scientific Workers in Moscow; elected vice-chairman by the congress

        Nov   Head of an Academy of Sciences delegation to Albania

1963,   Sep   Identified as vice-chairman of the Scientific and Technical Association (until Dec 1977)

1964,   Aug   Head of the Chinese delegation to the International Science Forum in Beijing

        Oct   Head of an Academy of Sciences delegation attending the celebrations of the 100th anniversary of Bucharest University

1965,   Jun   Head of the Chinese delegation to the 8th Congress of the World Federation of Scientific Workers in Budapest

1970,   Oct   First appearance after the Cultural Revolution: Member of a friendship delegation to North Korea; awarded Korean order "National Flag," 2nd class; identified as vice-chairman of the Revolutionary Committee of Beijing University

1971,   Jun   Again identified after the Cultural Revolution as a member of the Standing Committee of the CPPCC

1972,   Apr   Identified as deputy director of the Institute of Foreign Affairs

1973,   Mar   Again identified after the Cultural Revolution as vice-chairman of the Scientific and Technical Association

1974,	May	Head of a delegation of scientists to the Federal Republic of Germany
	Jul	Head of a delegation of scientists to France
1975,	Sep	Head of a delegation of scientists to the U.S.A.
1977,	Sep	Article in HQ of 1977, No. 9: "Bear in Mind Chairman Mao's Concern for and Teaching on Education in Science and Technology"
1977,	Dec	Identified as chairman of the Scientific and Technical Association
1978,	Feb	Elected deputy for Beijing Municipality to the 5th NPC
	Mar	Elected member of the Standing Committee of the 5th NPC; appointed vice-president of the Academy of Sciences
	Jun	Identified as president of Beijing University
	Sep	Head of a delegation of the Academy of Sciences to Japan
	Oct	Head of an educational delegation to the U.S.A.
	Dec	Identified as president of the Physics Society
1979,	Jan	Identified as member of the Department of Mathematics, Physics and Chemistry, Academy of Sciences
	Mar	Appointed deputy director of the Committee for the Promotion of International Measurement; Zhou heads a delegation of the Academy of Sciences to Italy
	Oct	Elected vice-chairman of the Central Committee of the Jiusan Society

Zhou is married to Wang Dicheng.

Zhou Pengcheng (Chou P'eng-ch'eng)

周鵬程

Posts held

Others
Secretary of the Communist Youth League
Vice-chairman of the Youth Federation

1964,	Jul	Elected alternate secretary of the Communist Youth League; subsequently disappears
1978,	Oct	First appearance after the Cultural Revolution: Elected secretary of the Communist Youth League
1979,	May	Elected vice-chairman of the Youth Federation
	Oct	Head of a youth delegation to Iraq, Syria, and Tunisia

Zhou Qiuye (Chou Ch'iu-yeh)

周秋野

Posts held

Government
Ambassador to Yugoslavia

1955,	Apr	Identified as counselor at the embassy in Yugoslavia (until May 1961)

1961,	Jul	Identified as director of the 2nd Asian Affairs Department in the Ministry of Foreign Affairs (until May 1964) Member of a government delegation to Cambodia and North Vietnam
1964,	May	Appointed ambassador to Congo (Brazzaville) (until Cultural Revolution)
1971,	Sep	Identified as secretary-general of the Institute of Foreign Affairs Head of a dancing and theatrical troop visiting Albania
	Nov	Head of a dancing and theatrical troop visiting Yugoslavia
1974,	Oct	Identified as deputy director of the Institute of Foreign Affairs (an association with the Ministry of Foreign Affairs) (until Aug 1976)
1976,	Aug	Appointed ambassador to Australia (until Mar 1978)
1978,	Jul	Appointed ambassador to Yugoslavia

Zhou Renshan (Chou Jen-shan)

周仁山

Posts held

CCP
2nd secretary, Xinjiang Autonomous Region CP

Zhou was born in Qinghai Province.

1949,	Nov	Identified as director of the Organization Department of Qinghai Province CP
	Dec	Identified as council member of Qinghai People's Government (until 1954)
1951,	May	Identified as a member of the Nationalities Affairs Committee in the Northwest Military and Administrative Council (until 1953)
1952,	Sep	Identified as director of the United Front Work Department of Qinghai Province CP
1953,	Jan	Appointed member of the Nationalities Affairs Committee in the Northwest Administrative Council
1954,	Aug	Elected deputy for Qinghai Province to the 1st NPC
	Sep	Elected member of the Nationalities Committee of the 1st NPC (confirmed by the 2nd and 3rd NPCs)
1955,	Feb	Identified as deputy secretary of Qinghai Province CP (until Oct 1956)
1956,	Oct	Identified as secretary of Qinghai Province CP (until May 1957)
1957,	May	Identified as deputy secretary of the CCP Tibet Working Committee (until Aug 1965)
1959,	Mar	Elected deputy for Tibet to the 2nd NPC (confirmed in 1964 by 3rd NPC)
1961,	Sep	Appointed vice-chairman of the Preparatory Committee for Tibet Autonomous Region (until Sep 1965)
	Nov	Zhou accompanies the Panchen Lama to Xinjiang
1965,	Sep	Elected CP secretary, and vice-chairman, of Tibet Autonomous Region
1968,	Sep	Branded as an agent of the Chinese Khrushchev in Tibet and disappears
1978,	Jun	First appearance after the Cultural Revolution

	Jul	Identified as secretary, Xinjiang Autonomous Region CP
1979,	Jun	Identified as 2nd secretary, Xinjiang Autonomous Region CP

Zhou Shiguan (Chou Shih-kuan) 周士观

Posts held

Others
Member of the Standing Committee of the 5th CPPCC
Vice-chairman of the China Democratic National Construction Association

In 1945 Zhou was a member of the Standing Committee of the China Democratic National Construction Association. In September 1949 he was invited by the Communists to attend the 1st CPPCC.

1952		Identified as a member of the Peace Committee
1954,	Dec	Delegate representing the China Democratic National Construction Association at the 2nd CPPCC (again in 1959 and 1964 at the 3rd and 4th CPPCCs)
1955,	Apr	Identified as member of the Standing Committee, China Democratic National Construction Association
1959,	Feb	Identified as member of the Federation of Industry and Commerce
1962,	Oct	Identified as deputy secretary-general of the China Democratic National Construction Association
1965,	Jan	Elected member of the Standing Committee of the 5th CPPCC
1967		Disappears during the Cultural Revolution
1973,	Mar	First appearance after the Cultural Revolution
1978,	Mar	Elected member of the Standing Committee of the 5th CPPCC
1979,	Oct	Elected vice-chairman of the Central Committee, China Democratic National Construction Association

Zhou Shizhong (Chou Shih-chung) 周世忠

Posts held

Military
Major-general
Deputy commander of Wuhan Military Region
Member of the Standing Committee, CP Secretariat of Wuhan Military Region

1960,	Feb	Identified as a military cadre in Fuzhou Military Region
1963,	Jul	Identified as chief of staff of Fuzhou Military Region
1964,	Jan	Identified as major-general
1967		Unidentified post in the Central Military Leadership (until 1974)
1976,	Sep	Identified as a military cadre in Hubei
1977,	Jun	Identified as member of the Standing Committee, CP Secretariat of Wuhan Military Region

1978,	Mar	litary Region Identified as deputy commander of Wuhan Military Region

Zhou Shutao (Chou Shu-t'ao) 周叔弢

Posts held

NPC
Member of the Standing Committee of the 5th NPC
Deputy for Tianjian Municipality to the 5th NPC

Others
Vice-chairman of the Executive Committee, Federation of Industrialists and Businessmen

Zhou was born in 1900 in Zhide, Anhui Province. As one of China's leading industrialists and director-general of the Jixiu Cement Factory in Tianjin, he was invited by the Communists in September 1949 to take part in the 1st CPPCC, which elected him a member.

1949,	Oct	Appointed member of the Committee of Financial and Economic Affairs in the Government Administration Council (until Sep 1954)
1950,	Jan	Elected deputy mayor of Tianjin Municipality (until Cultural Revolution)
1953,	Feb	Identified as member of the North China Administration Council (until Aug 1954)
	Nov	Identified as member of the Standing Committee of the Federation of Industry and Commerce (until Cultural Revolution)
1954,	Aug	Elected deputy for Tianjin Municipality to the 1st NPC (until Apr 1959); member of the Budget Committee of the 1st NPC (reelected in 1959 for the 2nd NPC)
	Dec	Elected member of the Standing Committee of the 2nd CPPCC (until Apr 1959)
1956,	Jun	Elected member of the Standing Committee of the 1st NPC in by-election (reelected to 2nd to 5th NPCs)
	Nov	Member of an NPC delegation to the USSR and to Eastern Europe
1957,	Dec	Member of the Chinese delegation to the 1st Conference of Afro-Asian Solidarity in Cairo
1958,	Oct	Elected deputy for Hebei Province to the 2nd NPC
1965,	Jan	Reelected NPC deputy for Hebei and member of the Standing Committee of the NPC
1975,	Jan	Reelected member of the Standing Committee of the NPC (first appearance after the Cultural Revolution)
1978,	Feb	Elected deputy for Tianjin Municipality to the 5th NPC
1979,	Jun	Member of the Budget Committee, 2nd Session of the 5th NPC
	Oct	Elected vice-chairman of the Executive Committee, Federation of Industrialists and Businessmen

Zhou is, or has been, married to Zuo Daoyu.

Zhou Weishi (Chou Wei-shih)　周巍峙

Posts held

Government
Vice-minister of culture

Others
Member of the Executive Committee of the Welfare Institute

1960,	Jun	Identified as vice-chairman of the Dancers' Union (until Cultural Revolution)
	Nov	Identified as deputy director of the Art Bureau in the Ministry of Culture (until Cultural Revolution)
1964,	Sep	Elected deputy for Jiangxi Province to the 3rd NPC
1967		Disappears during the Cultural Revolution
1975,	Sep	First appearance after the Cultural Revolution
1978,	Jan	Identified as vice-minister for culture
	Jun	Appointed member of the Executive Committee of the Welfare Institute
1979,	Jul	Appointed member of the National Games Organizing Committee

Zhou Xinwu (Chou Hsin-wu)　周新武

Posts held

Government
Deputy director of the Central Broadcasting Administration

In 1944 Zhou served as director of the Shanghai People's Broadcasting Station and as well as director of the East China People's Broadcasting Station.

1950		Identified as deputy director of the Press Bureau, East China Military and Administrative Council
1955,	Mar	Appointed deputy director of the State Broadcasting Affairs Bureau (until 1964)
1962,	Dec	Identified as council member of the Sino-Cuban Friendship Association
1963,	Nov	Appointed director of the Beijing Broadcasting College
1966		Zhou disappears
1979,	Jan	First appearance after the Cultural Revolution
	May	Identified as deputy director of the Central Broadcasting Administration

Zhou Yang (Chou Yang)　周扬

Posts held

CCP
Member of the CCP 11th Central Committee

Others
Vice-president of the Academy of Social Sciences
Member of the Standing Committee of the 5th CPPCC

Vice-chairman of the Federation of Literary and Art Circles
Vice-chairman of the Union of Chinese Writers
Vice-president of the Folk Literature and Art Society
Chairman of the Federation of Literary and Art Circles
Advisor to the Lu Xun Studies Society

Zhou was born in 1907 under the name of Zhou Qiying in Yiyang County, Hunan Province. After graduating from middle school in his native province he enrolled at Shanghai University and later continued his studies in Japan. In 1930 he returned to Shanghai, at first as secretary in the Communist-inspired Cultural Federation and one year later also as secretary of the League of Left-Wing Writers. About 1932 he joined the CCP. In response to the Japanese threat, Communist cultural policy shifted in 1936 from "proletarian literature" to "literature of national defense." This led to a sharp controversy, and eventually a rift, among the Communist writers. Zhou took up a position against Ba Jin, Hu Feng and Feng Xuefeng and rejected some of Lu Xun's theses. After the outbreak of the Anti-Japanese War Zhou went to Yan'an. In the course of the following years he held various positions in Yan'an, including director of the Education Department in the Government of the Shaanxi-Gansi-Ningxia Border Region, editor-in-chief of the journal <u>Wenyi Chendi</u> (Literary Front), and director of the Lu Xun Art Institute. In 1946 he became vice-president of the North China Associated University and shortly afterwards followed an invitation from left-wing American cultural circles to the United States where he remained until 1948. In 1949 he was appointed director of the Propaganda Department in the North China Bureau of the CCP Central Committee (until 1954) as well as deputy director of the Propaganda Department of the CCP Central Committee. Concurrently, he was editor of the <u>Wen Xue Bao</u> (Literary Journal). In July of the same year he was elected member of the Standing Committee of the Association of Literary Workers and vice-chairman of the Federation of Literary and Art Circles. In September the CPPCC elected Zhou a member of its National Committee.

1949,	Oct	Appointed member of the Committee for Cultural and Educational Affairs of the Government Administration Council; vice-minister of culture and director of the Art Bureau in this Ministry (all posts held until Oct 1954); council member of the Association for Reforming the Chinese Written Language; council member of the Sino-Soviet Friendship Association (until Dec 1954); and council member of the Peace Council (until Jul 1958)
1953,	Sep	Elected vice-chairman of the Union of Chinese Writers
1954,	May	Appointed council member of the Association for Cultural Relations with Foreign Countries
	Aug	Elected deputy for Guangdong Province to the 1st NPC
	Dec	Head of a delegation attending the 2nd Congress of Soviet Writers in Moscow
1955,	Jun	Appointed member of the Philosophy and Social Science Department of the Academy of Sciences (during this year Zhou was a leading participant in the campaign

against Hu Feng who was purged as a counterrevolutionary)

1956, Feb Appointed member of the Work Committee for Popularization of the Standard Spoken Language

Mar Appointed member of the Scientific Planning Commission

Sep Elected alternate member of the CCP Central Committee by the 8th Party Congress

Dec Deputy head of a delegation of writers to the Conference of Asian Writers in New Delhi

1958 Jun Professorship at the Central Theatrical Institute

Oct Deputy head of the Chinese delegation to the 1st Afro-Asian Writers' Conference in Tashkent

1959, Apr Elected member of the Standing Committee of the CPPCC

1962, Apr Appointed chairman of the Asian-African Society

Dec Head of a cultural delegation to Cuba; identified as council member of the Sino-Cuban Friendship Association

1966, Jul Branded as "three-anti element"

Dec At the Workers' Stadium in Beijing, Zhou is publicly denounced together with Lu Dingyi and others and subsequently disappears

1977, Sep First appearance after the Cultural Revolution

1978, Feb Identified as advisor to the Academy of Social Sciences

Mar Elected member of the Standing Committee of the 5th CPPCC

Jun Identified as vice-chairman of the Association of Literary and Art Circles

Sep Identified as vice-chairman of the Union of Chinese Writers

Oct Identified as director of the Postgraduate Institute of the Academy of Social Sciences and as vice-president of the Academy of Social Sciences

1979, Jan Identified as director of the Cultural Group of the CPPCC National Committee

May Head of a writers delegation to Japan

Sep By-elected member of the CCP 11th Central Committee at its 4th Plenum

Oct Elected vice-president of the Folk Literature and Art Society

Nov Elected chairman of the Federation of Literary and Art Circles

Dec Elected advisor to the Lu Xun Studies Society

Zhou Ze (Chou Tse) 周 泽

Posts held

CCP
Secretary of Jiangsu Province CP

Provincial Administration
Vice-governor of Jiangsu Province

1963, Dec Identified as chairman of the Trade Union

of Jiangsu Province (until Cultural Revolution)

1963, Jan Identified as council member of the Sino-Latin American Friendship Association (until Cultural Revolution)

1970, Oct Identified as member of the Standing Committee, Revolutionary Committee of Jiangsu Province

Zhou disappears for the following seven years for unknown reasons.

1977, May Identified as vice-chairman of the Revolutionary Committee (until Dec 1979) and as member of the Standing Committee of Jiangsu Province CP

Dec Elected secretary of Jiangsu Province CP

1979, Dec Elected vice-governor of Jiangsu Province

Zhou Zhan'ao (Chou Chan-ao) 周占鳌

Posts held

CCP
Deputy secretary, CP of Daqing Oil Field

NPC
Member of the Standing Committee of the 5th NPC
Deputy for Heilongjiang Province to the 5th NPC

Zhou was formerly head of a drilling brigade in Daqing Oil Field.

1973, Jul Elected vice-chairman of the Trade Union of Heilongjiang Province (no later mention in this post)

1976, Nov Identified as deputy for Heilongjiang Province to the 4th NPC (confirmed in Feb 1978 by the 5th NPC); member of an NPC delegation to Iran and Kuwait

1978, Mar Elected member of the Standing Committee of the 5th NPC

Apr Identified as deputy secretary, CP of Daqing Oil Field

1979, Jun Member of the Credentials Committee of the 2nd Session of the 5th NPC

Zhou Zheng (Chou Cheng) 周 政

Posts held

Provincial Administration
Vice-governor of Hunan Province

1960, May Identified as 1st secretary of Xiangtan Municipality, Hunan Province

1979, Dec Elected vice-governor of Hunan Province

Zhou Zhijun (Chou Chih-chün) 周志俊

Posts held

Provincial Administration
Vice-chairman of the People's Congress of Shandong Province

Others
Director of the Board of Directors, China International Trust and Investment Corporation
Member of the Leading Group, Shandong Provincial Federation of Industrialists and Businessmen

1979, Oct Appointed director of the Board of Directors, China International Trust and Investment Corporation; identified as member of the Leading Group, Shandong Provincial Federation of Industrialists and Businessmen

Dec Elected vice-chairman of the People's Congress of Shandong Province

Zhou Zhitong (Chou Chih-t'ung) 周之同

Posts held

Military
Deputy director of the Cultural Department, General Political Department of the People's Liberation Army

Others
President of the Handball Association

1962, Oct Identified as PLA senior colonel
1965, Jul Identified as a cadre of the Cultural Department, PLA General Political Department
1978, Jun Identified as deputy secretary-general of the All-Army Physical Culture Guidance Committee
Oct Identified as deputy director of the PLA Physical Culture and Sports Commission; head of a PLA basketball team to the International Basketball Tournament, sponsored by the International Military Sports Council in Bangkok
1979, Jun Identified as president of the Handball Association
Jul Identified as deputy director of the Cultural Department, PLA General Political Department

Zhou Zijian (Chou Tzu-chien) 周子健

Posts held

CCP
Alternate member of the CCP 11th Central Committee

Government
Minister of the 1st Ministry of Machine Building

Zhou was born in 1914 in Anhui Province. During the Anti-Japanese War he was at one time identified as director of the 8th Route Army, Xi'an Office. In mid-1949 he was identified as head of the Secretariat of the United Front Work Department in the CCP Central Committee.

1949, Dec Appointed deputy head of the Secretariat and director of the General Office in the Government Administration Council

1950, Dec Identified as deputy director of the Bureau of Government Offices and Government Administration Council (until Oct 1956)
1956, Oct Appointed assistant minister in the 1st Ministry of Machine Building (until Sep 1959)
1959, Oct Identified as director of the 3rd Bureau in the 1st Ministry of Machine Building
1960, Sep Appointed vice-minister of the 1st Ministry of Machine Building
1967, Mar Identified as 1st deputy secretary, CP Committee of the 1st Ministry of Machine Building. During this period Zhou is attacked by Red Guards as a "person having extremely serious problems," without, however, suffering any setback.
1970, Oct First mention after the Cultural Revolution as a vice-minister of the 1st Ministry of Machine Building (until Oct 1977)
1973, Aug Head of a government delegation to Denmark
1977, Aug Elected alternate member of the CCP Central Committee by the 11th Party Congress
Oct Identified as minister of the 1st Ministry of Machine Building
1978, Oct Head of a machine building delegation to Romania, Yugoslavia, Italy, Switzerland, and Federal Republic of Germany

Zhu Benzheng (Chu Pen-cheng) 宋本正

Posts held

NPC
Deputy for Shandong Province to the 5th NPC

Provincial Administration
Vice-chairman of the People's Congress of Shandong Province

1977, Dec Elected vice-chairman of the Revolutionary Committee of Shandong Province (until Dec 1979)
1978, Feb Elected deputy for Shandong Province to the 5th NPC
1979, Dec Elected vice-chairman of the People's Congress of Shandong Province

Zhu Chunhe (Chu Ch'un-ho) 宋春和

Posts held

Government
Vice-minister of posts and telecommunications

1971, Aug Identified as a cadre in the State Council
1972, Nov Identified as director general of Postal Service in the Ministry of Communication
1973, Sep Identified as vice-minister of posts and telecommunications
1974, May Head of a delegation to the 17th Congress of the Universal Postal Union (UPU)

1979,   Jun   Identified as head of the Preparatory Group of the Posts and Telecommunications Trade Union; identified as deputy secretary of the Party Group, Ministry of Posts and Telecommunications
         Oct   Head of a delegation to the 18th Congress of the Universal Postal Union in Rio de Janeiro

Zhu Guangya (Chu Kuang-ya) 朱光亚

Posts held

CCP
Member of the CCP 11th Central Committee

NPC
Deputy for the PLA to the 5th NPC

Others
Cadre in the Scientific and Technical Commission for National Defense

Zhu was born about 1913 in Hubei Province. In 1940 he was a professor in the Technical Faculty of Beijing University. In 1950 he obtained a doctorate at the University of Michigan. After his return to China he lectured in nuclear physics at the Northeast People's University and later at Beijing University.

1953,   Jun   Elected member of the Youth League Central Committee
1964,   Sep   Elected deputy for Hubei Province to the 3rd NPC
1969,   Apr   Elected to first term as alternate member of the CCP Central Committee by the 9th Party Congress (until Aug 1977)
         Oct   Zhu publishes an article "Based on Mao Zedong Thought, Reach the Heights of Science and Technology" in the ideological journal HQ
1975   Jul   Identified as a cadre in the Scientific and Technical Commission for National Defense
1977,   Aug   Elected member of the CCP Central Committee by the 11th Party Congress
1978,   Feb   Elected deputy for the PLA to the 5th NPC

Zhu Hanming (Chu Han-ming) 朱汉明

Posts held

Government
Deputy secretary-general of the Institute of Foreign Affairs

Zhu was born in 1918 in Jiangsu Province.

1959,   Jan   Appointed counselor at the embassy in Pakistan (until Apr 1965)
1978,   Jul   Identified as deputy secretary-general of the Institute of Foreign Affairs

Zhu Hongyuan (Chu Hung-yüan) 朱洪元

Posts held

Others
Deputy director of the Institute of High Energy Physics, Academy of Sciences

Zhu is China's leading elementary particle physicist.

1964,   Sep   Elected deputy for Shandong Province to the 3rd NPC
1966,   Jul   Member of a Beijing science forum; subsequently disappears
1978,   Jul   First appearance after the Cultural Revolution
         Sep   Head of a high energy physics delegation to Japan
1979,   Jun   Identified as deputy director of the Institute of High Energy Physics, Academy of Sciences

Zhu Liangcai (Chu Liang-ts'ai) 朱良才

Posts held

NPC
Member of the Standing Committee of the 5th NPC
Deputy for the PLA to the 5th NPC

Military
Colonel-general

Zhu was born in 1911 in Hunan Province. In 1934 he was political commissar of the 114th Division, 1st Front Army. In autumn 1936 Zhu belonged to a unit of the 4th Front Army, which retreated westward from Shaanxi Province and suffered heavy casualties when engaged with KMT forces in Gansu Province. During the Anti-Japanese War Zhu was temporarily political commissar of the Shanxi-Chahar-Hebei Military Region. In September 1949 he was delegate for the North China Military Region to the CPPCC which elected him a member of its National Committee.

1949,   Oct   Appointed member of the People's Supreme Court (until Dec 1954)
1950,   Identified as political commissar, Headquarters of the Beijing-Tianjin Garrison (probably until 1957)
         Oct   Identified as director of the Political Department of North China Military Region (probably until Oct 1954)
1954,   Aug   Elected deputy for the PLA to the 1st NPC
1955,   Sep   Made colonel-general, awarded the orders of "1st August," "Independence and Freedom," and "Liberation," all 1st class
1957,   May   Identified as political commissar of Beijing Garrison (probably until Mar 1958)
1958,   Mar   Identified as political commissar of Beijing Military Region (until Cultural Revolution)
1959,   Apr   Elected member of the Standing Committee of the NPC (confirmed in 1964 and 1978)

1962,	Sep	Elected member of the Central Control Commission of the CCP Central Committee (until Cultural Revolution)
1968-1974		Zhu survives the Cultural Revolution and later appears on many occasions, usually as a member of the Standing Committee of the NPC
1975,	Jan	The 4th NPC confirms Zhu as member of its Standing Committee (again confirmed by the 5th NPC in 1978)
1978,	Feb	Elected deputy for the PLA to the 5th NPC

Zhu Muzhi (Chu Mu-chih)　　朱穆之

Posts held

CCP
Member of the CCP 11th Central Committee
Deputy director of the Propaganda Department in the CCP Central Committee
Member of the Commission for Inspecting Discipline in the CCP Central Committee

Others
Member of the Standing Committee of the 5th CPPCC

1952		Identified as secretary of the Sino-Soviet Friendship Association (until 1954)
	Dec	Appointed deputy director of the New China News Agency (until Oct 1972)
1958,	Sep	Identified as council member of the China-Iraq Friendship Association
	Oct	Elected deputy for Jiangsu Province to the 2nd NPC (reelected by the 3rd NPC in 1964)
1960,	Mar	Identified as vice-chairman of the Journalists' Association (this association has not been reactivated after the Cultural Revolution)
	Apr	Elected member of the Standing Committee of the Sino-African Friendship Association (until Cultural Revolution)
	Sep	Head of a delegation of journalists to Chile, Bolivia, Uruguay, and Brazil
1962,	Dec	Identified as vice-chairman of the Sino-Cuban Friendship Association
1972,	Oct	First appearance after the Cultural Revolution: Identified as director of the New China News Agency (until Dec 1977)
1973,	May	Identified as a cadre in a department of the CCP Central Committee; head of a delegation of journalists to the United States
	Aug	Elected to first term as member of the CCP Central Committee by the 10th Party Congress
1975,	May	Head of a delegation of journalists to Japan
1977,	May	Head of a delegation of journalists to North Korea
	Dec	Identified as deputy director of the Propaganda Department in the CCP Central Committee
1978,	Mar	Elected member of the Standing Committee of the 5th CPPCC
	Dec	Appointed member of the Commission for Inspecting Discipline of the CCP Central Committee

Zhu Qizhen (Chu Ch'i-chen)　　宋启祯

Posts held

Government
Deputy director of the America and Oceania Department in the Ministry of Foreign Affairs

1971,	Oct	Identified as section chief in the West Asia and Africa Department in the Ministry of Foreign Affairs; member of a government delegation to Somalia
1973,	Feb	Identified as counselor at the embassy in Australia (until 1976)
	Sep	Zhu conducts negotiations in Papua New Guinea for the establishment of diplomatic relations
1977,	Jun	Identified as deputy director of the America and Oceania Department in the Ministry of Foreign Affairs

Zhu Rong (Chu Jung)　　朱　荣

Posts held

Government
Vice-minister of agriculture

Others
Advisor to the Agronomy Society
President of the Engineering Society

1951,	Jan	Identified as member of the Executive Committee of the Hong Kong-Kowloon Shipyard and Wharves Carpenters Union
1952,	Apr	Chief-judge to handle "three-anti" bases in Guangzhou
	Nov	Identified as deputy director of the Civil Affairs Department, People's Government of Guangdong Province (until 1954)
1953,	Jan	Director of the Census Office of Guangdong People's Government
1954,	Jun	Identified as director of the Civil Affairs Department, Guangdong Province People's Government
	Jul	Elected deputy for North Guangdong to the 1st NPC
1956,	Feb	Identified as deputy director of the Organization Department of Guangdong Province CP
1960,	May	Identified as president of Guangdong Agricultural Academy
1961,	Oct	Identified as director of the Agricultural Office of Guangdong Province (until 1964)
1962,	Dec	Identified as secretary of Guangzhou Municipality CP (until 1964)
1964,	Jul	Appointed vice-minister of agriculture (until Cultural Revolution)
1966,	May	Member of an agricultural delegation to Albania

1968,	Apr	Branded as a capitalist-roader
1978,	Apr	First appearance after the Cultural Revolution: Identified as vice-minister of agriculture and forestry (until Feb 1979)
	May	Identified as advisor to the Agronomy Society; head of an agricultural delegation to Japan
1979,	Jun	Identified as vice-minister of agriculture
1979,	Nov	Elected president of the Engineering Society

Zhu Shaoqing (Chu Shao-ch'ing) 朱绍清

Posts held

CCP
Alternate member of the CCP 11th Central Committee

Military
Major-general
Deputy commander of Fuzhou Military Region
Member of the Standing Committee, CP Secretariat of Fuzhou Military Region

Zhu was born about 1910. In late 1927 he took part in the Autumn Harvest Uprising in Huarong, Hunan Province. Since 1929 he served in the Workers and Peasants Red Army which was later incorporated as the 25th Regiment to the 3rd Front Army. In 1946 he was regiment commander in the 6th Division of the New 4th Army, and in 1948 he was appointed commander of the 28th Division of the East China Field Army. In the following year he was given the command of the 28th Corps, 10th Army, 3rd Field Army.

1949,	Oct	In the attempted occupation of Jinmen (Quemoy) Island in the Taiwan Straits, five regiments commanded by Zhu are destroyed near Gulintou
1955,	Sep	Promoted to rank of major-general
1956		Identified as commander of the 31st Corps
1957		Appointed commander of Xiamen Garrison
1960,	Nov	Identified as troop commander in Fuzhou Military Region
1964,	Sep	Elected deputy for the PLA to the 3rd NPC
1971,	Apr	With the reestablishment of the CP Secretariat for Fujian Province after the Cultural Revolution, Zhu is elected secretary (until 1975?)
1976,	Jul	Identified as deputy commander of Fuzhou Military Region
1977,	Jun	Identified as member of the Standing Committee, CP Secretariat of Fuzhou Military Region
	Aug	Elected alternate member of the CCP Central Committee by the 11th Party Congress

Zhu Wuhua (Chu Wu-hua) 朱物华

Posts held

Others
President of the Shanghai Jiaotong University

1961,	Jul	Identified as vice-president of Harbin Technical University
	Oct	Appointed vice-president of Shanghai Jiaotong University
1963		Identified as vice-president of the Electronics Society
1964,	Sep	Elected deputy for Shanghai Municipality to the 3rd NPC
1967		Zhu disappears
1978,	Nov	First appearance after the Cultural Revolution: Identified as president of the Shanghai Jiaotong University

Zhu Xuefan (Chu Hsüeh-fan) 朱学范

Posts held

NPC
Member of the Standing Committee of the 5th NPC
Deputy for Shandong Province to the 5th NPC

Mass Organizations
Vice-president of the Federation of Trade Unions

Others
Vice-chairman of the Revolutionary Committee of the Chinese KMT

Zhu was born in 1905 in Jiashan, Zhejiang Province. He studied at the Shanghai Institute of Law. As an employee of the Shanghai Post Office he joined the Union of Postal Workers. After the persecution of left-wing unionists by the KMT in spring 1927 he worked closely with Lu Jingshi, a leader of the KMT labor movement. When Lu later left the trade union movement Zhu took over his post as head of the Arbitration Department of the trade unions and as chairman of the Trade Union of Postal Workers. During the Anti-Japanese War Zhu lived in Chongqing. In September 1945 he took part in the Congress of the World Federation of Trade Unions in Paris. Though he had publicly opposed the left-wing trade unions until 1947, he eventually moved to the Communist side in 1948 after another visit to Europe. As a result, he was elected vice-chairman of the 6th Workers' Congress meeting in Harbin in April 1948. Shortly afterward he became head of the Union of Postal Workers.

1949,	Oct	Appointed minister of Post and Telecommunications (until Cultural Revolution) and member of the Committee of Financial and Economic Affairs of the Government Administration Council; elected council member of the Sino-Soviet Friendship Association
1950		Identified as a member of the Red Cross Society
	Dec	Elected member of the Standing Committee of the KMT Revolutionary Committee
1954,	Sep	Elected deputy for Guangdong Province to the 1st NPC
	Dec	Elected member of the Standing Committee of the CPPCC
1960,	Jun	Identified as member of the General Council, World Federation of Trade Unions

1961,	Oct	Elected member of the Executive Council of the Red Cross Society
1964,	Jun	Head of a postal delegation to North Vietnam
1967		Disappears during the Cultural Revolution
1978,	Feb	First appearance after the Cultural Revolution: Elected deputy for Shandong Province to the 5th NPC
	Mar	Elected member of the Standing Committee of the 5th NPC
	Oct	Elected vice-president of the Federation of Trade Unions
1979,	Apr	Member of a NPC delegation, led by Deng Xiaoping, to Japan
	Oct	Elected vice-chairman of the Central Committee, Revolutionary Committee of the Chinese KMT

Zhu Yaohua (Chu Yao-hua) 朱耀华

Posts held

CCP
Member of the Standing Committee, Party Committee of Fuzhou Military Region

Military
Major-general
Deputy commander of Fuzhou Military Region

Zhu was commander of a regiment in the New 4th Army in 1946 and two years later of the 27th Division of the East China Field Army. In 1949 he commanded the 83rd Division, 28th Corps, 3rd Field Army.

1952		Identified as chief of staff of the 28th Corps
1955,	Sep	Promoted to rank of major-general; identified as deputy commander of the 28th Corps
1957		Made commander of the 28th Corps
1963		Identified as commander of Fujian Military District (until 1976?)
1968,	Aug	With establishment of the Revolutionary Committee for Fujian Province, Zhu is elected vice-chairman (until about 1971)
1973,	Jul	Identified as member of the Standing Committee of Fujian Province CP (until 1975?)
	Dec	Identified as a leading military officer in Fuzhou Military Region
1977,	Jun	Identified as member of the Standing Committee, Party Committee of Fuzhou Military Region
	Aug	Identified as deputy commander of Fuzhou Military Region

Zhu Yunqian (Chu Yün-ch'ien) 朱云谦

Posts held

CCP
Member of the Commission for Inspecting Discipline under the CCP Central Committee

Military
Major-general
Deputy director of the General Political Department of the PLA

1952,	Apr	Identified as commander of the 85th Division of the 29th Army
1958,	Aug	Identified as major-general of the Air Force in Guangzhou Military Region
1964,	Sep	Identified as deputy commandant of the PLA Air Force Academy
1967		Disappears during the Cultural Revolution
1974,	Mar	First appearance after the Cultural Revolution
1975,	Oct	Identified as political commissar of the Air Force in Guangzhou Military Region
1978,	Oct	Identified as deputy director of the General Political Department of the PLA
	Dec	Appointed member of the Commission for Inspecting Discipline under the CCP Central Committee

Zhu Yunshan (Chu Yün-shan) 朱蕴山

Posts held

NPC
Vice-chairman of the Standing Committee of the 5th NPC
Deputy for Anhui Province to the 5th NPC

Others
Vice-president of the 5th CPPCC
Chairman of the Revolutionary Committee of the KMT

Zhu was born in 1887 in Anhui Province. He joined the "Tong Meng Hui" (the Chinese Revolutionary League) led by Dr. Sun Yat-sen and was a veteran of the 1911 revolution. He took part in the Nanchang uprising on 1st August, 1927. During the Anti-Japanese war, he cooperated with the CCP and did a great deal of work to expand the revolutionary united front. He opposed Chiang Kai-shek's launching of the civil war and supported the democratic movement during the liberation war. He joined in founding the Revolutionary Committee of the KMT in Hong Kong in 1947. In September 1949 he took part as delegate for the KMT Revolutionary Committee in the 1st CPPCC which elected him a member.

1949,	Oct	Appointed member of the Supervisory Committee in the Government Administration Council; elected member of the 2nd Central Committee and member of the Standing Committee as well as director of the Organization Department of the Revolutionary Committee of the KMT (reelected to these posts in 1954 and 1958)
1951,	Oct	Elected council member of the Sino-Soviet Friendship Association (until 1954)
1954,	Aug	Elected deputy for Anhui Province to the 1st NPC (reelected for Anhui Province to the 2nd NPC in 1958 and to the 3rd NPC in 1965)
	Dec	Elected member of the Standing Committee of the 2nd CPPCC (reelected in 1959 to the 3rd and in 1965 to the 4th CPPCC)

1975,   Jan   Elected by the 4th NPC as member of its Standing Committee (confirmed by 5th NPC in 1978)
1978,   Feb   Elected deputy for Anhui Province to the 5th NPC
        Mar   Elected vice-president of the 5th CPPCC
1979,   Jul   By-elected vice-chairman of the Standing Committee of the 5th NPC
        Oct   Elected chairman of the Revolutionary Committee of the Chinese KMT

Zhuang Mingli (Chuang Ming-li) 庄明理

Posts held

NPC
Deputy for Tianjin Municipality to the 5th NPC

Others
Vice-president of the Federation of Returned Overseas Chinese

Zhuang was born in 1910 in Jinjiang, Fujian Province. After middle school he left for Penang in Malaya to join his brother in the management of Hsieh Cheng Company. Following the September 18th Incident in Machuria of 1931, he was made a member of the Penang Chinese War Relief Association's Executive Committee. In 1938 he was one of the cofounders of Penang's Modern Daily. He fled before the Japanese invasion to China in order to work for the KMT in Chongqing. After World War II. he returned to Malaya. He accompanied Chen Jiageng (Tan Kah-kee) to China in 1949. In September of that year he was a delegate representing the overseas Chinese at the 1st CPPCC.

1949,   Oct   Identified as member of the Overseas Affairs Commission, Government Administration Council
        Dec   Identified as vice-chairman of the Overseas Affairs Commission
1953,   Oct   Identified as member of the Executive Committee, Federation of Industry and Commerce
1954,   Aug   Elected deputy for overseas Chinese to the 1st NPC (reelected in 1958 and 1964 to the 2nd and 3rd NPCs)
1956,   Oct   Elected vice-chairman of the Federation of Returned Overseas Chinese (until Cultural Revolution); appointed vice-chairman of the State Overseas Chinese Affairs Commission (until Cultural Revolution)
1958,   Jul   Elected member of the China-Afro-Asian Solidarity Committee
1961,   Mar   Identified as vice-chairman of the Construction Committee, Overseas Chinese University at Quanzhou, Fujian Province
1967   Disappeared during the Cultural Revolution
1972,   Sep   First appearance after the Cultural Revolution
1975,   Jan   Elected deputy for Tianjin Municipality to the 4th NPC (reelected in 1978 to the 5th NPC)
1978,   May   Identified as vice-chairman of the Federation of Returned Overseas Chinese

1979,   Jan   Identified as vice-chairman, Board of Directors of the Quanzhou Overseas Chinese University

Zhuang Tian (Chuang T'ien) 庄田

Posts held

Military
Lieutenant-general

Provincial Administration
Vice-chairman of the People's Congress of Guangdong Province

Others
Member of the Standing Committee of the 5th CPPCC

Zhuang was born in 1908 in Guangdong Province. As a young man he joined the Merchant Navy and later became a laborer. In 1926 he took part in the Northern Expedition. After studying at the Moscow Red Army College he was given the command of a Red Army regiment in the Jiangxi Soviet. During the Long March he suffered the loss of a leg. He was sent to the USSR for medical treatment and returned in 1940 with a Russian wife. He subsequently organized guerrilla units on Hainan Island together with Feng Baiju. Until 1946 he was active in guerrilla operations in the south of Guangdong Province. In 1948 he joined his units with those of Zhu Jiabi to form the Yunnan-Guizhou-Guangxi Border Region Column of which he became commander.

1950,   Jul   Identified as deputy commander of Yunnan Military District and as member of the Southwest China Military and Administrative Council
1951   Deputy commander of the 3rd Army Group in the Korean War
1958,   Sep   Identified as political commissar of Nanjing Advanced Infantry School
1961,   Sep   Identified as lieutenant-general and as deputy commander of Guangzhou Military Region
1965,   Dec   Elected vice-governor of Guangdong Province
1967   Disappears during the Cultural Revolution
1977,   Jan   First appearance after the Cultural Revolution
        May   Identified as leading person of Guangzhou Military Region
1978,   Mar   Elected member of the Standing Committee of the 5th CPPCC
1979,   Dec   Elected vice-chairman of the People's Congress of Guangdong Province

Zhuang Xiquan (Chuang Hsi-ch'üan) 庄希泉

Posts held

NPC
Member of the Standing Committee of the 5th NPC
Deputy for Tianjin Municipality to the 5th NPC

Government
Vice-minister of the State Overseas Chinese Affairs Commission

Others
Vice-president of the 5th CPPCC
Chairman of the Federation of Returned Overseas Chinese

Zhuang was born in 1897 in Xiamen, Fujian Province. In the 1920s Zhuang was a cofounder of the Nanyang Girls High School in Singapore. Later he edited a Chinese newspaper in the Philippines. Having returned to China in 1937 he headed the Fujian Province Branch of the National Salvation Association and later joined the Democratic League.

1949,	Oct	Appointed vice-chairman of the Overseas Chinese Affairs Commission in the Central People's Government
1954,	Aug	Elected deputy for the overseas Chinese to the 1st NPC (reelected to 2nd and 3rd NPC in 1958 and 1964)
	Sep	Elected member of the Credentials Committee of the 1st NPC (reelected in 1959 and 1965)
1956,	Oct	Appointed vice-chairman of the Returned Overseas Chinese Federation
1959,	Sep	Appointed member of the State Council Physical Culture and Sports Commission (until Cultural Revolution)
1961,	Mar	Identified as chairman of the Construction Committee of the University for Returned Overseas Chinese in Quanzhou, Fujian Province (until Cultural Revolution)
	Aug	Following the death of Chen Jiageng identified as acting chairman of the Returned Overseas Chinese Federation (until Cultural Revolution)
1965,	Jan	Elected member of the Standing Committee of the 3rd NPC (confirmed by the 4th and 5th NPCs in 1975 and 1978)
1967		Zhuang survives the Cultural Revolution and later appears frequently as member of the Standing Committee of the NPC
1978,	Feb	Elected deputy for Tianjin Municipality to the 5th NPC
	Mar	Elected vice-president of the 5th CPPCC
	Dec	Elected as chairman of the Federation of Returned Overseas Chinese
1979	Jan	Identified as chairman of the Board of Directors Quanzhou Overseas Chinese University
	Jun	Member of the Credentials Committee and the Draft Laws Committee, 2nd Session of the 5th NPC
1980,	Jan	Identified as vice-minister of the State Overseas Chinese Affairs Commission

Zhuang Yan (Chuang Yen)　　庄 焰

Posts held

Government
Ambassador to Iran

Zhuang was born in October 1918 in Fujian Province.

1953,	Apr	Identified as deputy director of the De-

partment of International Relations in the Federation of Trade Unions

	Sep	Member of the Chinese delegation to the 3rd Conference of the World Federation of Trade Unions in Vienna
1957,	Jun	Appointed counselor at the Diplomatic Mission of the PRC in Great Britain (until about 1963)
1972,	Jul	Identified as deputy permanent representative of the PRC at the UN (until 1975)
1973,	Mar	Head of the Chinese delegation to the 2nd Subcommittee Meeting of the UN Committee on the Peaceful Use of the Seabeds and Ocean Floors outside areas of national jurisdiction
1974,	Jun	Zhuang signs the communiqué on the establishment of diplomatic relations between the PRC and Trinidad/Tobago
1975,	Jan	Head of the Chinese delegation to the UN Industrial Development Program (UNIDEP) Conference in New York
1976,	Apr	Appointed ambassador to Bangladesh (until Nov 1979)
1977,	Jan	Zhuang accompanies the president of Bangladesh to China
1980,	Apr	Appointed ambassador to Iran

Zhuang is married to Min Cijiang (born in 1921 in Hubei).

Zhuo Xiong (Cho Hsiung)　　卓 雄

Posts held

Government
Vice-minister of civil affairs

Zhuo was born in 1916 in Manchuria. In 1937 he was identified as a member of the CCP. In that year he belonged to the Contingent of Workers for the Self-Defense of Taiyuan, provincial capital of Shanxi, which was later renamed Workers Brigade for Self-Defense and then integrated into the 8th Route Army in 1939. In 1946 he belonged to the Northeast Democratic Allied Army. In 1948 he was deputy political commissar of the 5th Army Corps, 4th Field Army.

1949,	Oct	Appointed director of the Bureau of Public Security and Administration in the Ministry of Public Security (until Apr 1955)
1955,	Apr	Appointed vice-minister of geology (until Cultural Revolution)
1970,	May	Identified as vice-chairman of the Revolutionary Committee of Fujian Province
1971,	Apr	Elected secretary of Fujian Province CP
1974,	Feb	Zhuo disappears for unknown reasons until Dec 1978
1978,	Dec	Identified as vice-minister of civil affairs

Zi Yaohua (Tzu Yao-hua)　　次耀华

Posts held

Others
Director of the Board of Directors, China International Trust and Investment Corporation

Deputy secretary-general of the Central Standing Committee, China Democratic National Construction Association

1979,   Oct   Appointed director of the Board of Directors, China International Trust and Investment Corporation; elected deputy secretary-general of the Central Standing Committee, China Democratic National Construction Association

Zong Kewen (Tsung K'e-wen)   宗克文

Posts held

Government
Ambassador to Senegal

1964,   Jul   Identified as counselor at the embassy in Hungary (until about 1967)
1971,   May   Identified as chargé d'affaires ad interim in Czechoslovakia
         Jun   Appointed ambassador to Czechoslovakia (until Mar 1975)
1975,   Jul   Appointed ambassador to Sierra Leone (until Jul 1978)
1977,   Feb   Head of a goodwill delegation to Liberia
1978,   Sep   Appointed ambassador to Senegal

Zong Xiyun (Tsung Hsi-yün)   宗希云

Posts held

CCP
Member of the CCP 11th Central Committee
Member of the Standing Committee of Jilin Province CP

Mass Organization
Chairman of the Trade Union of Jilin Province

Zong was born in the winter of 1928 under a bridge in Qingdao, Shandong Province, where his parents and sister had fled during a famine catastrophe in the province. His mother died one year later in Manchuria. As a young man, Zong worked as a laborer in a coal mine.

1956,   Mar   Delegate at a national conference of model workers representing model workers in the coal industry
1959,   Mar   Elected deputy for Jilin Province to the 2nd NPC (reelected in 1964 to the 3rd NPC)
         Oct   As leader of a mining group at Jiaohe Coal Mine in Jilin Province, Zong again represents coal miners a a national conference of model work groups
1969,   Apr   Elected member of the CCP Central Committee by the 9th Party Congress (confirmed in 1973 and 1977 by the 10th and 11th Congresses)
1973,   Jun   Elected chairman of the Trade Union of Jilin Province

1974,   Oct   Identified as vice-chairman of the Revolutionary Committee of Jilin Province (reelected in Dec 1977)
         Nov   Head of a delegation of workers to Albania

Zou Jiahua (Tsou Chia-hua)   邹家华

Posts held

CCP
Alternate member of the CCP 11th Central Committee

Government
Deputy director of the State Office of National Defense Industry

Military
Cadre of the PLA Science and Technology Commission for National Defense

1974,   Sep   Identified as a cadre of the PLA Science and Technology Commission for National Defense
1977,   Aug   Elected alternate member of the CCP Central Committee by the 11th Party Congress
1978,   Jun   Member of a military goodwill delegation led by Zhang Aiping to Sweden and Italy
1979,   Feb   Identified as deputy director of the State Office of National Defense Industry

Zou Jiayou (Tsou Chia-yu)   邹家尤

Posts held

Others
President of the Academy of Geological Sciences

1978,   Jul   Identified as a cadre of the National General Geological Bureau and as president of the Academy of Geological Sciences
1979,   Apr   Deputy head of a delegation of geologists to the U.S.A. and Canada

Zou Tong (Tsou T'ung)   邹 桐

Posts held

Government
Vice-minister of coal industry

1966,   Mar   Appointed vice-minister of fuel and chemical industry (until 1974)
1975,   Jul   Identified as vice-minister of coal industry
1978,   Sep   Head of a coal study group visiting the U.S.A. and Japan

Zou Yu (Tsou Yü)   邹 瑜

Posts held

Government
Director of the State Seismological Bureau

1978,   Oct   Identified as director of the State Seismological Bureau

Zuo Chongyi (Tso Ch'ung-yi)   左崇义

Posts held

CCP
Alternate member of the CCP 11th Central Committee

Zuo is a hero-soldier.

1977,   Aug   Elected alternate member of the CCP Central Committee by the 11th Party Congress

Zuo Moye (Tso Mo-yeh)   左漠野

Posts held

Government
Deputy director of the Central Broadcasting Administration

1959,   Sep   Identified as deputy director of the Broadcasting Administrative Bureau
1963,   Aug   Head of a television delegation to the 2nd International Television Festival in Cairo
         Sep   Head of a television delegation to Afghanistan
1964,   Jun   Head of a broadcasting delegation to Cuba
1965,   May   Head of a broadcasting delegation to the German Democratic Republic; after this Zuo disappears
1979,   Sep   First appearance after the Cultural Revolution: Identified as deputy director of the Central Broadcasting Administration
         Oct   Head of a broadcasting delegation to Great Britain

中华人民
共和国
人名录

Biographies

of important deceased

and purged cadres

Chen Xilian (Ch'en Hsi-lien)

陈锡联

Chen was born of a poor family in 1913 in Huangan, Hubei Province. As a child he tended livestock for other families. During the Communist Autumn Harvest Uprising of 1926 in East Hubei he was member of a young arsonist group. Because of his boldness and cheerfulness during this episode he attracted the attention of Zheng Weisan, a leading military figure during the revolution and a member of the 7th and 8th CCP Central Committees from 1945 until the Cultural Revolution, who died on 27th July 1975. On Zheng's recommendation Chen became a member of the CCP. In 1930, at the age of 17, he joined a local Communist group which called itself "Peasant Self-Defense Army" and was later integrated into the Communist forces of the 4th Front Army. In autumn 1931 Chen joined the base of the Communist armed forces in Ruijin where he was first made group leader in the training regiment commanded by Lin Biao. He then attended a course at the Red Army Military School. Following this, he became political instructor in the 30th Regiment, 10th Division, 4th Front Army. During this period he was given the nickname "Little Steel Cannon" because of his massive build and his zeal. In 1933 Chen was made political commissar of the 263rd Regiment of the 4th Front Army and shortly afterwards became commander of the 88th Division at the age of only 20. At this time his unit belonged to the forces under Zhang Guotao which had separated themselves from the main forces commanded by Mao Zedong. In 1936 he eventually joined the main Communist forces in Shaanxi. Here he underwent further military training at the Anti-Japanese Military and Political Academy supervised by Lin Biao. After the Nationalist and the Communist forces had joined in their resistance against the Japanese invaders in 1937, Chen became commander of the 769th Regiment, 129th Division of the 8th Route Army. In 1940 he was given the command of the 385th Brigade taking part in August of that year in the "Battle of the 100 Regiments," the major military confrontation between the Chinese Communist forces and the Japanese in which 400,000 Communist soldiers fought 200,000 Japanese in 5 provinces. Nothing is known about Chen's activities during the remaining years of the Anti-Japanese War. This suggests that he may have received military training in the USSR during that period. From 1946 to 1949 Chen served in the 2nd Field Army commanded by Liu Bocheng. In 1946 he commanded the 3rd Column, Shanxi-Hebei-Shandong-Henan Military Region, and in October of that year became commander of the West Anhui Military Region. In October 1948 Chen commanded the Army Group West in the battle of Xuzhou-Pangbu. In February 1949 Chen was made commander of the 3rd Army Corps, 2nd Field Army, which in November of that year liberated Chongqing.

1949,	Dec	Appointed mayor of Chongqing and commander of East-Sichuan Military District
1950,	Jan	Appointed member of the Southwest China Military and Administrative Council

1951,	Oct	Appointed commander of the artillery forces of the PLA (until 1959)
1944,	Sep	Appointed deputy for the PLA to the 1st NPC; appointed member of the National Defense Council (until approximately 1967)
1955,	Sep	Made colonel-general; awarded the order of "1st August," "Independance and Freedom," and "Liberation," all 1st class
1956,	Sep	Elected alternate member of the CCP Central Committee by the 8th Party Congress (until 1969)
1957,	Nov	Member of the Chinese delegation led by Mao Zedong to attend the celebrations of the 40th anniversary of the October Revolution
1959,	Oct	Appointed commander of Shenyang Military Region (until Dec 1973)
1960,	Oct	Member of a military delegation to North Korea headed by Marshal He Long
1963,	Jun	Identified as secretary of the Northeast China Bureau of the CCP Central Committee (until Cultural Revolution)
1968,	May	With the foundation of the Revolutionary Committee for Liaoning Province, Chen is elected chairman (until Dec 1973)
1969,	Apr	Elected member of the CCP Central Committee and of the Politburo by the 9th Party Congress
1971,	Jan	With the reestablishment of the Party Secretariat of Liaoning Province, Chen is elected 1st secretary (until Dec 1973)
1972,	Apr	Head of a military delegation to North Korea
1973,	Aug	Confirmed as member of the CCP Central Committee and Politburo by the 10th CCP Congress
1974,	Jan	Identified as commander of Beijing Military Region (until Jan 1980)
1975,	Jan	Elected vice-premier by the 4th NPC (confirmed in 1978 by the 5th NPC)
	Feb	Head of the Chinese delegation to the crowning ceremonies for King Birendra of Nepal
	Aug	Head of a Party and government delegation to Hanoi to attend the 30th anniversary of the Democratic Republic of Vietnam
	Sep	Head of a delegation of the Chinese Central Government to attend the 20th anniversary of Xinjiang Autonomous Region
1977,	Jul	Identified as member of the Standing Committee of the Military Council, CCP Central Committee
1978,	Feb	Elected deputy for the PLA to the 5th NPC
	Nov	Identified as deputy leader of the National People's Air Defense Leading Group
1979,	Jul	Appointed chairman of the National Games Organizing Committee
	Oct	Identified as 1st secretary of the CCP Central Committee, Beijing Military Region (until Jan 1980)
1980,	Feb	Removed from all Party and state posts at the 5th Plenum of the CCP 11th Central Committee

Chen is married to Wang Xuanmei.

Dong Biwu (Tung Pi-wu)

董必武

Dong was born in 1886 as the son of a landlord in Hong'an (Huang'an) County, Hubei Province. His family provided him with a classical education which enabled him to pass the first state examination (xiucai) in 1901. He then attended the middle school in Wuchang for another five years. He obtained a teaching position in 1911 which he soon resigned after the fall of the Qing dynasty in order to take a subordinate post in the new military government. At this time he also joined the Revolutionary Society (Tongmenghui). After the failure of the so-called 2nd Revolution in 1913 he, like many other members of the Tongmenghui, had to escape to Japan where he began to study law and joined the KMT. The Society recalled him to China in 1915 in order to organize resistance against Yuan Shikai in his home province. After a short period of revolutionary activity he was arrested and only released after the death of Yuan Shikai in the summer of 1916. He then went back to Japan to complete his law studies. In 1917 he returned to China and subsequently held a number of administrative posts in his native province. During this period he was first introduced to the group of Communist intellectuals around Li Hanjun. In 1920 Dong founded a middle school in Wuhan. He was one of the founding members of the CCP in 1921 and subsequently set up a Party branch in Hubei Province. Until 1927 his political activities remained closer to the KMT than to the CCP. Only after the rift between the two Parties did he commit himself finally to the CCP. After a short period of underground activities and a renewed stay in Japan Dong eventually went to the USSR in 1928 where he studied at the Lenin School until 1931. Having returned to China in 1932 he joined the Jiangxi Soviet, which appointed him first head of the CCP Party School. The 5th Plenum of the 6th Central Committee elected Dong an alternate member of the Central Committee in January 1934. He took part in the Long March of 1934-35 after the end of which he returned to his post as head of the Party School. From late 1936 throughout the following decade Dong served as the leading liaison officer between the CCP and the KMT. In this capacity he was elected a member of the People's Political Council of the Nationalist Government in 1938. One year later the CCP Central Committee elected him a member of its Politburo. After the New 4th Army Incident in 1941 Dong remained in Chongqing as chief CCP representative of the Nationalist Government. In 1945 he was the only Communist among ten delegates led by Minister of Foreign Affairs Song Ziwen (T.V. Soong) to the founding session of the United Nations in San Francisco. Dong is the only leading cadre who visited the U.S.A. between the end of World War II and 1978. Still in 1945, he was elected a member of the CCP Central Committee by the 7th Party Congress. From 1946 to 1947 he served as adjutant to Zhou Enlai on the Communist delegation attempting to negotiate a peace settlement with the KMT. After the failure of these negotiations he returned to Yan'an. In August 1948 he was elected chairman of the newly established People's Government of North China. In September of the following year he represented the CCP as delegate to the CPPCC in Beijing.

1949,	Oct	Elected member of the Central Government Council; vice-premier; and chairman of the Political and Legal Affairs Council (until Sep 1954)
1953		Elected chairman of the Committee of Political and Legal Affairs (until Oct 1964)
1954,	Oct	Elected deputy for Hubei Province to the 1st NPC and president of the Supreme People's Court (until Apr 1959)
1955,	Mar	Elected secretary (head), Central Control Commission of the CCP Central Committee
	Sep	Delegate representing the Central Government at the celebrations marking autonomy for Xinjiang in Ürümqi
1956,	Sep	Elected member of the Politburo by the 8th CCP Congress (confirmed by the 9th and 10th Party Congresses)
1958,	May-Jul	Head of a CCP delegation to the Party Congresses in Bulgaria, Czechoslovakia, and East Germany
1959,	Apr	Elected vice-president of PRC (until Jan 1975)
1964,	Oct	Elected honorary chairman of the Committee of Political and Legal Affairs
1973,	Aug	Elected member of the Standing Committee of the Politburo by the 10th Party Congress
1975,	Jan	Elected vice-chairman, Standing Committee of the 4th NPC

Dong Biwu died on 2 April 1975.

Guo Moruo (Kuo Mo-jo)

郭 沫若

Guo was born in 1892 in Leshan, a small town in the southwest of Sichuan Province. He was the fifth child of a family of merchants and landlords. As a child he received private tutoring in classical literature, and in 1906-07 he attended the last form of a modern school. At the end of 1907 he was enrolled at a modern middle school where he started studying Japanese and English in preparation for later studies in Japan. A severe illness during this period resulted in defective hearing. From 1910 he attended high school in Chengdu, capital of Sichuan Province. His involvement in various strikes until 1911 had twice led to his dismissal from school which, however, were only temporary, thanks to the influence of his family. At the age of nineteen he was forced by his family to marry but left his wife after just one week in order to continue his studies in Chengdu. After graduating in 1913 he went to Japan to study medicine from 1914 to 1923. From 1915 he also continued to study English and in addition took up German and Latin. From 1916 to 1918 he lived with the Japanese nurse Sato Tomiko. During this period he became interested in literary studies. He was particularly impressed by the Indian poet Rabindranath Tagore and German poets. In 1917 he translated a number of poems by

Tagore. His own literary career began with his first narrative written in 1918. In 1920 Guo went for a short period to Shanghai where he worked for a publishing company and prepared for publication a collection of his own literary works under the title of Nüshen (The Goddesses) which immediately secured him wide recognition. After receiving an M.D. degree from the Imperial Kyushu University in March 1923 Guo again went to Shanghai where he for the first time became seriously interested in politics. His first attempts at editing new journals together with literary friends quickly failed. It was eventually the "May 4th Movement" which led Guo to political-literary activity in 1925. The newly established fortnightly Hongshui (The Flood) published a number of Guo's Marxist-orientated articles. At this time he also developed his first contacts with prominent leaders of the CCP. At the end of 1925 he joined the KMT, then the leading revolutionary movement in China which actively opposed the reactionary Beijing Government and the warlords in North China. In early 1926 he was appointed dean of Sun Yat-sen University in Guangzhou. There he first met Mao Zedong, then head of the Peasant's Movement Training Institute in Guangzhou, at which Guo also lectured. During the KMT Northern Expedition started in July 1926, Guo was at first head of the Propaganda Section in the Political Department of General Deng Yanda's forces. Shortly afterwards he was recalled to the KMT Headquarters in order to organize a political department there. However, after KMT Generalissimo Chiang Kai-shek had staged a coup against the only recently allied Communists in April 1927, Guo went over to the Communist side though without taking part in their military activities. After the failure of the Communist Nanchang Uprising he fled to Hong Kong and from there to Shanghai. In early 1928 he traveled to Japan where he remained for ten years.

Until the outbreak of the Anti-Japanese War in 1937 when Guo eventually returned to China, leaving his Japanese family behind, his most important works were written. They had found their way to China because Guo had succeeded in maintaining contacts with his Shanghai literary colleagues and publishers. After his return to China, Guo again supported the KMT with propaganda work against the Japanese aggressors. Together with Shen Yanbing (Mao Dun) and forty other literary colleagues, he founded the Resistance Society of Art and Literary Workers in 1938. During the following years Guo served on the Committee for Cultural Work in Chongqing, capital city of the Nationalist Government. His influence was gradually reduced owing to the increasing antagonism between the KMT and the Communists. Thus he spent the following years primarily with his own literary work. An essay by Guo, published in 1944 by the Communist paper Xinhua Ribao (New China), was praised by Mao Zedong as a valuable contribution.

From June to August 1945 Guo visited the USSR. After the Japanese capitulation he advocated a settlement between the KMT and the CCP. In late 1947 Guo went to Hong Kong to escape increasing persecution of leftist intellectuals as a result of the growing tension between the two parties. In November 1948, at an early stage of the Communist offensive from Manchuria, Guo went to Northern China. He arrived in Beijing in February 1949 a few days after the occupation of that city by the Communists. In March he was appointed by the Communists to head a delegation of 44 representatives to the 1st Session of the World Peace Council in Prague. In

September 1949 he was elected vice-chairman of the 1st CPPCC.

1949,	Oct	Appointed member of the Central People's Government Council; vice-premier and chairman of the Culture and Education Committee (all posts until Sep 1954)
	Nov	Appointed president of the newly established Academy of Sciences
	Dec	Elected vice-chairman of the CPPCC (until Dec 1954); chairman of the Federation of Literary and Art Circles and vice-chairman of the Sino-Soviet Friendship Association (until Cultural Revolution)
1950		Identified as chairman of the Peace Council (until Cultural Revolution)
1953,	Apr	Member of the Chinese delegation to the funeral ceremonies for Stalin
1954,	Aug	Elected deputy for Sichuan Province to the 1st NPC
	Oct	Elected vice-chairman of the Standing Committee of the 1st NPC (reelected by the 2nd to 5th NPCs)
1955,	Jun (?)	Elected vice-chairman of the World Peace Council (until about 1963)
1956		Identified as vice-chairman of the Afro-Asian Solidarity Committee and as vice-chairman of the Scientific Planning Commission (until Sep 1959)
1957,	Sep	Appointed honorary member of the Romanian Academy of Sciences
	Oct	Member of a delegation led by Mao Zedong to the celebrations of the 40th anniversary of the October Revolution in Moscow
1958,	Jun	Appointed member of the Soviet Academy of Sciences
	Sep	Appointed president of the University of Science and Technology (until Sep 1964)
	Dec	Member of the CCP
1960,	Apr	Appointed corresponding member of the Czechoslovakian Academy of Sciences
	Dec	Head of a friendship delegation to Cuba
1961,	Jan	Member of a friendship delegation to Burma
	May	Appointed member of the Academy of Sciences of Outer Mongolia
	Aug	Head of a NPC delegation to Indonesia and Burma
	Oct	Awarded honorary doctorate by the Humboldt University in East Berlin
1962,	Apr	Appointed council member of the Asian-African Society (until Cultural Revolution)
	Jun	First performance of Guo Moruo's drama Wu Zetian
1963,	Oct	Elected honorary chairman of the Sino-Japanese Friendship Association
1964,	Jul	Head of a Peace Council delegation to North Vietnam to attend the 10th anniversary of the Geneva Indochina Agreement
1966,	Jun	Head of the Chinese delegation to the Conference of Afro-Asian Writers in Beijing
1967		Guo retracts all his publications which "in comparison to the work of Mao Zedong may as well have remained unwritten"
1969,	Apr	Elected to first term as member of the

CCP Central Committee by the 9th Party Congress

1970, Feb Head of a government delegation to the wedding of Nepalese crown prince Birendra

Mar Head of a government delegation to Pakistan

Sep Head of a government delegation to the funeral ceremonies for Egyptian head of state Nasser

1971, Oct Head of a government delegation to the 2500 imperial anniversary in Iran. Guo does not take part in the celebrations due to illness

1978, Mar Elected vice-chairman of the 5th CPPCC

Guo Moruo died on 12 June 1978.

Publications by Kuo Mo-jo

The following is a selection of the most important works:

1918	Nüshen	(The Goddesses)
1922	Canchun	(Late Spring)
1926	Ganlan	(The Olive)
1926	Ta	(The Pagoda)
1928	Luo Ye	(Fallen Leaves)
1929	Wode Tongnian	(My Youth)
	Before and after the Revolution
1930	Zhongguo Gudai Shehui Yanjiu (Studies on Ancient Chinese Society)
1930	Hei Mao	(The Black Cat)
1931	Investigations on Oracle-Bone Inscriptions
1942	Gao Jianli	(Gao Jianli; a drama)
1942	Qu Yuan	(Qu Yuan; a drama)
1945	The Bronze Age

Translations by Guo Moruo

Tolstoi	War and Peace (partial translation)
Goethe	The Sorrows of Young Werthers
	Faust (partial translation)
Nietzsche	Thus Spoke Zarathustra
Hajime	Social Organization and Social Revolution
Turgenev	Virgin Soil
Hauptmann	The Heretic of Soana
Galsworthy	Strife

Guo was married to You Liqun.

Ji Dengkui (Chi Teng-k'uei)

纪登奎

1959, Nov Identified as 1st secretary, CP of Luoyang Municipality, Henan Province

1966, Jul Identified as alternate member, Secretariat of Henan Province CP

1967 Ji plays a leading role in the power struggles during the Cultural Revolution in Henan Province. Having been severely attacked for four months he is, however, rated a "leading revolutionary cadre" fol-

lowing the visit of Mao Zedong to Henan in the summer of this year.

1968, Jan With the establishment of a Revolutionary Committee for Henan, Ji is elected one of its vice-chairmen (until about 1973).

1969, Apr At the 9th CCP Congress Ji is a delegate but not a member of the Presidium. He is nevertheless elected not only a member of the Central Committee but also an alternate member of the Politburo of the CCP (until Aug 1973)

1971, Mar With the establishment of the new Party Secretariat for Henan Province, Ji is elected one of its secretaries (until about 1973)

1973, Aug The 10th CCP Congress promotes Ji from alternate member to member of the CCP Politburo

1974, Jan Identified as 1st political commissar of Beijing Military Region (until Aug 1978)

1975, Jan Elected vice-premier by the 4th NPC (confirmed by the 5th NPC in Mar 1978)

1978, Feb Elected deputy for Beijing Municipality to the 5th NPC

Aug Ji accompanies Hua Guofeng to Romania, Yugoslavia, and Iran

1980, Feb Removed from all Party and state posts at the 5th Plenum of the CCP 11th Central Committee

Jiang Qing (Chiang Ch'ing) (f)

江青

Jiang was born in 1913 under the name of Li Yunhe in Jiucheng, Shandong Province. Her parents separated when she was still a young child. Her mother then moved together with Jiang and her eldest sister to Jinan, capital of Shandong. In 1929, after elementary school, Jiang enrolled in an acting school in Taian (50 km from Jinan). In return for free instruction, the pupils of the school agreed to work for an unspecified period of time for the theatrical experimentation group of the school. After Jiang had an affair with the head of the acting school, Zhao Taimou, they went to Qingdao in 1930 where Zhao became a lecturer at the newly established university. Zhao quickly reached the position of dean of the university. He became involved with Yun San who was then one of the best known young actresses of both the classical Chinese and modern western theater. Jiang herself turned to Yu San's brother, Qiwei, who worked underground for the Communists under the assumed name of Huang Jing. It was probably on his recommendation that Jiang became a member of the CCP in 1931. This liaison, too, was of short duration. Jiang returned to Jinan where she met the film critic Ma Jiliang, also known as Tang Na. She and Ma, simultaneous with three other couples who were all involved in the film industry, married in 1934. Until 1937 Jiang acted under the assumed name of Lan Ping in several films produced in Shanghai. It is known from accounts by her then colleagues that these were, to her distress, minor rolls and that she could not afford the bus ride to the studio. An affair with a film director called Zhang Min led in 1937 to a divorce from Tang Na, which was widely publicized in the Shanghai press (Tang went to Zhongqing where he worked for the British among others; in 1947 he went to the United States; and in 1966 he owned a Chinese restaurant in Paris). At the beginning of the Anti-Japanese War, Jiang left together with Huang Jing for Yan'an, the Communist base after the Long March, where she arrived in 1938. Huang was sent to the Party School for further training, while Jiang joined the Lu Xun Art Institute. There she first met Mao Zedong. Within less than a year they decided to marry. Their plan met with some resistance, however, because at that time Mao was still married to He Zizhen, who had shared with him the period from Jinggangshan through the Long March. Although the old Party cadres, among them Mao's former teacher, Xu Teli, took He Zizhen's side, Mao insisted on a divorce from He and marriage with Jiang. Eventually a compromise was found under which Mao was permitted to marry Jiang under the condition that she should restrict herself to the role of housewife and not become active in politics.

There are two daughters from the marriage between Mao and Jiang: Li Na, born in 1941, who studied geophysics at Beijing University in 1963, and Mao Mao, who was born a few years later. Until the foundation of the PRC Jiang generally acted as personal secretary to Mao Zedong.

1950		Identified as a member of the Cinema Department in the Ministry of Culture (abolished in 1954)
1962		Jiang embarks on the ambitious task of reforming the Beijing Opera (giving it a revolutionary content while retaining its classical form) in which she is encouraged by Mao but not by the leading cultural cadres. She is supported by 1st secretary Ke Qingshi of the Shanghai CP. In Shanghai she meets Zhang Chunqiao and Yao Wenyuan.
1965,	Sep	Elected deputy for Shandong Province to the NPC
1965,	Nov	Jiang assures Yao Wenyuan of her support in attacking the drama Hai Rui Ba Guan (The Dismissal of Hai Rui) by the leading writer and cultural cadre Wu Han (in which Hai Rui stands for the former minister of National Defense Peng Dehuai who was purged in 1959). This attack is directed against Wu Han's superior Peng Zhen, a member of the Politburo and newly appointed head of the Cultural Revolutionary Group
1966,	Feb	Under the pseudonym of Gao Zhu, Jiang attacks the Beijing Party leadership in an article in the Beijing newspaper RMRB
	May	The previous Cultural Revolutionary Group under Peng Zhen is abolished and replaced by a new one under Chen Boda. In this group Jiang assumes the role of advisor
	Nov	Identified as cultural advisor to the PLA. From now on Jiang belongs to the leading advocates of the Cultural Revolution
1967		Frequent appearances during the first half of the year and official praise for her contribution to literature and art. Her

encouragement of the Red Guards to "Attack when justified but defend with force" leads to excesses in July and August for which she is held responsible. Some members of the Cultural Revolutionary Group, which is practically run by Jiang, are dismissed and in September she is forced to recall publicly the Red Guards to their studies. Jiang then withdraws from public life

1968,	Feb	Jiang again meets the Red Guards who are storming Beijing from all parts of China
1968,	Mar	The purge of several military leaders seems to announce a new radical phase and allows Jiang a return to activity
	Aug	The Red Guards are disbanded, thus ending the influential position Jiang had gained during the Cultural Revolution
1969,	Apr	Elected member of the Politburo and the Central Committee by the 9th CCP Congress (confimed in this post by the 10th Congress in 1973)
1970-1971		The purge of Chen Boda, head of the Cultural Revolutionary Group during the Cultural Revolution, and of Lin Biao, together with articles in the press against the policy "Left in appearance but right in reality," lead to doubts concerning the political future of the radical group headed by Jiang. A letter to Mao, written in 1966 but published only at this point, serves to indicate her previous doubts about the credibility of Lin Biao and to dissociate her from the fallen idols of the Cultural Revolution
1972-1973		Jiang Qing takes part in all important Party and government functions and is, in addition, mainly seen attending Chinese theater performances and performances by visiting foreign artists. Following the 10th Party Congress in August 1973, Jiang gains an additional role in the field of foreign policy by accompanying high ranking foreign visitors to nontheatrical functions
1974-1975		Jiang continues her activities, but with an emphasis on foreign policy from 1975 onward. This is also the case with her protégé, Wang Hongwen
1976,	Oct	Jiang is purged together with Wang Hongwen, Zhang Chunqiao and Yao Wenyuan, since that time officially called the "Gang of Four"

Lin Biao (Lin Piao)

林 彪

Lin was born in 1907 in Huihongshan, Hubei Province, as the son of a small factory owner who went out of business as the result of high taxation. After graduating from middle school in Wuchang, where he was first introduced to revolutionary ideology, he enrolled at the 4th training course of Whampoa Military Academy when he was not yet twenty years old. He joined the CCP in 1925. After graduating with outstanding examination results he first took part in the Northern Expedition with the rank of army captain. During this expedition he temporarily served as adjutant to the "Iron General" Zhang Fakui, commander of the 4th Nationalist Army. At the age of twenty Lin Biao was promoted to the rank of colonel. In August 1927, following the Nanchang Uprising, Lin joined the 20th Army under He Long and Ye Ting with his regiment. He subsequently took part in the organization of peasant uprisings in Hunan Province under Zhu De. When he arrived with Zhu De at the Communist base set up by Mao Zedong on Jinggangshan in 1928, he had already gained an outstanding military reputation in a number of battles with KMT troops. Owing to these successes he soon became one of the leading military officers of the Communist forces, as well as commandant of the Red Army Academy. In 1932 he was made commander of the 1st Red Army Corps, a unit of 20,000 men which soon developed into the main force of the Red Army. All attempts by the at times far greater KMT forces to destroy this corps ended in failure. During the Long March Lin Biao commanded vanguard troops under the supreme command of Peng Dehuai. In Shaanxi, the final destination of the Long March, Lin immediately returned to his duties as head of the Military Academy. At the beginning of the Anti-Japanese War he was commander of the 115th Division of the 8th Route Army. His military fame increased when his units won the first victory against the Japanese by defeating their advancing forces in the Battle of Pingxing Guan in September 1937. He was wounded shortly afterwards and sent to the USSR for medical treatment. He also used this stay abroad for further training in modern warfare. During the final phase of the Anti-Japanese War Lin Biao was a member of the Communist delegation negotiating with the Nationalist Government in Chongqing. At the time of the Japanese capitulation he was commander of Shandong Military Region and was immediately afterwards sent to Manchuria to set up the Northeast China Democratic Joint Army. This army was equipped with weapons from the Japanese army of 600,000 men and cooperated closely with the Soviet occupation forces. Later in the same year he was elected a member of the CCP Central Committee by the 7th Party Congress. When the KMT forces attempted to gain control of Manchuria, Lin's army was well enough established to limit KMT occupation to urban areas. Eventually, Lin Biao's forces decisively turned the balance in the ensuing civil war by driving the KMT forces out of Manchuria in November 1948. After this success Lin's troops were reorganized to form the famous 4th Field Army. The major developments during the following years leading to the eventual expulsion of the KMT forces from the mainland are closely linked to the name of Lin Biao.

1949,   Oct   Appointed vice-chairman of the Revolutionary Military Council and chairman of the Central-South Military and Political Council; identified as member of the Politburo and as secretary, Central-South China Bureau of the CCP Central Committee

1950,   Oct   The Chinese People's Volunteers Army, drafted largely from units of the 4th Field Army, enters the Korean War under the command of Lin Biao (until 1951)

1951,   Oct   Elected member of the Sino-Soviet Friendship Association (until Dec 1954)

1954,   Sep   Appointed vice-premier and vice-chairman of the National Defense Council; elected deputy for the PLA to the 1st NPC

         Dec   Elected vice-chairman of the Sino-Soviet Friendship Association

1955,   Sep   Appointed marshal; conferred the orders "1st August," "Independence and Freedom," and "Liberation," all 1st class

1958,   May   Elected member of the Standing Committee of the Politburo and vice-chairman of the CCP Central Committee by the 2nd Plenum of the 8th CCP Central Committee (confirmed by the 9th Party Congress in 1969)

1959,   Sep   Appointed minister of national defense (until 1971)

1971,   Sep   According to unofficial statements, Lin attempts a coup d'état with the aim of succeeding Mao Zedong as leader of the CCP. After the failure of this coup, the aircraft in which Lin allegedly attempted to flee to the USSR was shot down over the People's Republic of Mongolia. There are serious doubts about this theory of Lin's attempted coup. Rather, it may be assumed that Mao Zedong consented in the purge of Lin Biao by Mao's wife, Jiang Qing, in an attempt to secure her own succession to the Party leadership.

Lin Liming (Lin Li-ming)

林李明

Lin was a native of Guangdong Province.

1955,   Jan   Elected vice-chairman of the Guangdong Province Branch, CPPCC (until Feb 1959)

         Mar   Identified as deputy secretary, South China Bureau of the CCP Central Committee (until about 1962)

         Aug   Identified as deputy secretary of Guangdong Province CP (until Nov 1956)

         Dec   Elected vice-governor of Guangdong Province

1958,   Jul   Identified as 1st secretary of Hainan Island District CP

1960,   Feb   Appointed vice-chairman of the Guangdong Province Committee for Receiving and Resettling Returned Overseas Chinese (set up for the reception of Chinese returning from Indonesia)

1963,   Jul   Head of a friendship delegation to North Vietnam

1964,   Sep   Elected deputy for Guangdong Province to the 3rd NPC

1965,	Jun	Elected vice-chairman of the Federation of Poor and Lower-Middle Peasants of Guangdong Province (until Cultural Revolution)
1966		Attacked by Red Guards at the beginning of the Cultural Revolution
1968,	Feb	Elected member of the Standing Committee of the newly established Revolutionary Committee of Guangdong Province (until Jan 1970)
1970,	Jan	Identified as vice-chairman of the Revolutionary Committee of Guangdong Province
1973,	Jan	Identified as secretary of Guangdong Province CP
	Apr	Deputy director of the Spring Fair in Guangzhou
	Aug	Elected alternate member of the CCP Central Committee by the 10th Party Congress (until Aug 1977)
	Oct	Deputy director of the Autumn Fair in Guangzhou
1974-1976		Director of the Chinese Foreign Trade Fairs in Guangzhou
1977,	Aug	Lin Liming died one day after his election as member of the CCP Central Committee by the 11th Party Congress

Lin Liming died on 19 August 1977.

Liu Shaoqi (Liu Shao-ch'i)

刘少奇

Liu Shaoqi was born in 1898 in Yinshan, Ningxiang County, Hunan Province, as the son of a small landowner. From 1916 he attended the Teachers College in Changsha where Mao Zedong had also studied between 1913 and 1918. He began to study French with a view to going to France as a worker-student, but he was turned down in 1919. In the following year he went to Shanghai where he joined the Socialist Youth League and a Russian language course taught by Comintern agent Woitinsky. In late 1920 he was sent by Woitinsky with a group of young Chinese for further training to Moscow, where he arrived after a three months journey. In Moscow, he joined the CCP shortly after its foundation. In spring 1922 he returned to China and first worked under Zhang Guotao in the Chinese Workers Syndicate in Shanghai. Later he was sent into the area of Pingxiang Coal Mine in Jiangxi-Hunan to set up labor organizations. Thanks to his organizing skills, the Pingxiang coal district soon developed into the center of the workers movement. His achievements were acknowledged by his election as vice-chairman of the Chinese Federation of Trade Unions in May 1925. Two years later he was elected a member of the CCP Central Committee by the 5th Party Congress. After the KMT-CCP rift, Liu spent the following years organizing underground work. He is believed to have been involved in the organization of railway workers in Harbin in 1928. In the following year he was head of the Hebei Section of the CCP in Beijing.

During the years 1930 to 1932 he headed the National Workers Federation from Shanghai. He fled to the Jiangxi Soviet in autumn 1932. From about this time he was also a member of the CCP Politburo. At the beginning of the Long March in 1934 Liu remained behind in order to organize guerrilla units. He emerged in Beijing in 1935 as head of the North China Bureau of the CCP Central Committee. In this capacity he was mainly involved in the organization of students, many of whom he persuaded to join the Communists who by now had arrived in North China. Having taken part in the purge of the anti-Mao-group in North China in the same year, he spent the following years with renewed underground activity in Beijing and Tianjin. In 1937 he returned to Yan'an and supported Mao Zedong in the purge of Zhang Guotao. During the Anti-Japanese War Liu was in charge of Party work in the Japanese-occupied areas. In 1941 he was given the post of secretary, Central China Bureau of the CCP Central Committee. He played an important role in the reorganization of the New 4th Army, of which he became political commissar, after the defeat of the Communist forces in Anhui Province that year. In 1943 Liu Shaoqi was appointed secretary of the CCP Central Committee Secretariat and vice-chairman of the Military Council of the CCP Central Committee. He was elected vice-chairman of the Politburo by the 7th CCP Congress in 1945. When in the same year Mao Zedong traveled to Chongqing for several weeks of negotiations with the Nationalist Government, Liu acted for the first time as Mao's deputy. In August 1948 he was elected honorary chairman of the Federation of Trade Unions (until December 1957). He was elected vice-chairman of the Federation of Trade Unions in June 1949 (until October 1953). In September 1949 he was elected a member of the Standing Committee of the CPPCC.

1949,	Oct	Appointed vice-chairman of the Central People's Government and vice-chairman of the Revolutionary Military Council
	Nov	Mao Zedong's deputy during his absence until Febrary 1950 for negotiations in Moscow
	Dec	Elected chairman of the Sino-Soviet Friendship Association (until 1954)
1952,	Oct	Head of a CCP delegation to the 19th CPSU Congress in Moscow
1954,	Oct	Member of a delegation to Moscow; elected deputy and chairman of the Standing Committee of the 1st NPC (until Mar 1959)
1956,	Sep	Elected member of the Standing Committee of the Politburo
1959,	Apr	Elected president of the PRC (ex officio chairman of the National Defense Council)
1960,	Nov	Head of a CCP delegation to attend the 43rd anniversary of the October Revolution in Moscow
1963,	Apr	Head of a government delegation to Indonesia and Burma
	May	Head of a government delegation to Cambodia and North Vietnam
	Sep	Head of a Party and government delegation to North Korea
1966,	Mar-Apr	Head of a government delegation to Pakistan, Afghanistan, and Burma
1967		Branded as a renegade, traitor, lackey of imperialism, and as China's Khrushchev

1969   Liu dies in prison on 12 November

Publications
1939   How to Be a Good Communist
1941   On Inner-Party Struggle
            On the Class Character of Man
1943   Liquidate the Menshevik Ideas in the Party
1945   On the Party
1948   Internationalism and Nationalism

Luo Ruiqing (Lo Jui-ch'ing)

罗瑞卿

Luo was born in 1906 in Nanchong, Sichuan Province, as the son of a landlord. After a school education in his native area he attended the 5th training course at Whampoa Military Academy from February 1926, and already in the summer of that year joined the Northern Expedition. On 1 August 1927 Luo took part in the Nanchang Uprising which in the PRC is considered to mark the beginning of the PLA. In 1928 he served in the 4th Front Army on Jinggangshan. In 1930 he was political commissar of the 11th Division in the 4th Front Army commanded by Lin Biao. In spring 1932 Luo was severely wounded in a battle with KMT units. According to unconfirmed reports he subsequently spent three years in the USSR where he received training in security and intelligence work. In early 1934 he was elected a member of the Executive Council, Central Soviet of the CCP. During the Long March Luo served initially as director of the Security Bureau and later as director of a department of the 1st Front Army. After the Long March he attended a course of the Red Army University and in 1936 was appointed head of the Education Department of that university. In the following year he was made deputy head of the Anti-Japan Military and Political Academy, and head of that institute in 1940. Shortly afterwards he was appointed director of the Political Department of the 8th Route Army as well as member of the North China Bureau of the CCP Central Committee. In 1944 he headed the Political Department of the 18th Army Corps and in 1945 was elected alternate member of the CCP Central Committee by the 7th Party Congress. During the Civil War he served in various posts in the PLA, but throughout as political commissar or head of political departments in North China. In September 1949 he was elected a member of the CPPCC.

1949,   Oct   Appointed member of the Government Administration Council; minister of public security (until Sep 1959); member of the Committee of Political and Legal Affairs; as well as member of the Revolutionary Military Council and of the Supreme People's Procuracy
1950   Appointed member of the People's Government Council of Beijing and director of its Bureau of Public Security

        Jan   Appointed commander of the Public Security Forces (until 1959)
1954,   Apr   Appointed member of the National Defense Council
        Oct   Elected deputy for Hebei Province to the 1st NPC (until Mar 1959); appointed director of the 1st Staff Office (Public Security) under the State Council (until Sep 1959)
1955,   Sep   Appointed army general; awarded the orders "1st August," "Independence and Freedom," and "Liberation," all 1st class
1956,   Nov   Appointed director of the Institute of Public Security (until Jan 1959)
1958,   Jul   Elected deputy for Sichuan Province to the 2nd NPC (until Dec 1964)
1959,   Apr   Appointed vice-premier (until Cultural Revolution)
        Sep   Appointed vice-minister of national defense and chief of PLA General Staff (until Cultural Revolution)
1960   Deputy head of a military delegation to North Korea
1961,   Jan   Member of a government delegation to Burma. Identified as secretary-general, Military Council of the CCP Central Committee (until Cultural Revolution)
1962,   Sep   Elected member of the CCP Central Committee Secretariat (until Cultural Revolution)
1964,   Sep   Elected deputy for the PLA to the 3rd NPC
1965,   Jan   Appointed vice-chairman of the National Defense Council (until Cultural Revolution)
        Dec   Luo has to appear at a criticism conference in Shanghai at which he rejects all charges
1966,   Mar   Luo again has to answer criticism under the supervision of the CCP Central Committee. During one of these criticism sessions on 18 March Luo jumps from the top floor of the building where the investigation is being held. Prior to his attempted suicide he had prepared a testament in which he revoked all extorted confessions of guilt. Having survived the fall, he was handed over still in his bandages to an enraged public. The charges against Luo were:
              1. Hostility and opposition to Mao Zedong Thought
              2. Bourgeois military thinking
              3. Lack of organization and discipline and the undermining of centralized Party democracy
              4. Faulty and insufficient quality, adherence to the point of view of the exploiting class
              5. Urgent appeals to Lin Biao to step down in favor of the "better man," by which he was supposed to have meant himself
              Luo disappears following this criticism.
1975,   Jul   First appearance after the Cultural Revolution
        Sep   Referred to as military leader
1977,   Aug   Elected member of the CCP Central Committee by the 11th Party Congress

Sep   Identified as member of the Military Council of the CCP Central Committee

Oct   Article in RMRB: "A Serious Two-Line Struggle on the Road of the Long March - in Memory of the 1st Anniversary of Chairman Mao's Death"

Luo Ruiqing died on 3 August 1978.

Ma Li (Ma Li)

马 力

1950,	Jul	Appointed member of the Financial and Economic Committee of the People's Government of Chongqing Municipality
1953,	Apr	Identified as director of the Finance Department of Hebei Province
1955,	Feb	Elected member of the People's Council of Hebei Province
1957		Identified as vice-governor of Hebei Province (until 1960)
1958,	Jul	Identified as member of the Standing Committee of Hebei Province CP
1960,	Jun	Identified as 1st secretary of Tangshan District CP in Hebei Province
1966,	Jul	After the old CP Secretariat of Beijing is dissolved, Ma is recalled to Beijing as new secretary
	Nov	Disappears during the Cultural Revolution
1971,	May	Reactivated after the Cultural Revolution: Identified as deputy secretary of Hebei Province CP (until Feb 1977)
1972,	Aug	Identified as vice-chairman of the Revolutionary Committee of Hebei Province (until Feb 1977)
1977,	Mar	Identified as 1st secretary of the CP, and as chairman of the Revolutionary Committee, of Guizhou Province, as well as 1st political commissar of Guizhou Military District
	Aug	Elected member of the CCP Central Committee by the 11th Party Congress
1978,	Feb	Elected deputy for Guizhou Province to the 5th NPC
	May	Article by Ma in HQ on commune democracy

Ma Li died on 25 September 1979.

Mao Zedong (Mao Tse-tung)

毛泽东

Mao Zedong was born in 1893 in the village of Shaoshan, Xiangtan County, Hunan Province, as the son of a poor peasant. Thanks to his savings from prolonged military service and a small shop opened subsequently, his father became moderately wealthy. Between the ages of eight and thirteen Mao was instructed by a private teacher in reading and writing. During the following three years he worked on his father's land, did his father's accounts, and read the classic Chinese novels.

In 1907 a marriage was arranged for him by his parents with a girl four years his junior, a marriage Mao refused to acknowledge.

In 1910 he attended elementary school for one year in Xiangxiang, a small town in which his mother was born. There he read a great deal about such Chinese and Western national heroes as Kang Youwei, Liang Qichao, Napoleon, Washington, and Peter the Great and developed a strong sense of patriotism. His teacher in this school was Xu Teli who until his death in November 1968 was a member of the CCP Central Committee. In 1911 Mao passed the entrance examination for Changsha Middle School, just at the time when the Qing dynasty was brought to an end. Sharing the revolutionary spirit of the period, Mao Zedong joined the army under General Zhao Hengtian in which he remained as a soldier until February 1912. He continued his education at a school of commerce and at the 1st Middle School of Hunan, but was soon dissatisfied. In early 1913 he was admitted to the 4th Teachers Training College, which was shortly afterwards reorganized into the 1st Teachers Training College. According to Mao this college laid the foundation of his education until autumn 1918. His favorite subjects were history, geography, and philosophy, while he showed less interest in natural sciences, mathematics, and languages. Mao was described as quiet, eager to help and always prepared to speak up for those suffering an injustice. It was this latter quality which nearly caused his expulsion from the college if it had not been for the intervention of some of his teachers, among them again Xu Teli. One of the books which particularly impressed Mao during his studies was Friedrich Paulsen's Ethics, which had been translated into Chinese. The teacher who probably had the strongest influence on Mao was Yang Changji. Yang had studied for six years in Japan and four years in England and lectured at Changsha in ethics, logic, psychology, pedagogics, and philosophy and was influenced by the pragmatism of Wang Fuzhi and the writings of Kant, Spencer, and Rousseau.

From the beginning of his studies Mao was active in the Student Society, in which he served for two years as secretary and, from autumn 1917 until his graduation in spring 1918, as chairman.

In September 1918 Mao went to Beijing, where Professor Li Dazhao, whom he had met earlier, helped him to find work as an assistant at the library of Beijing University. He did not join the group of his friends from Changsha who traveled to France as worker-students at this time, although he had planned to do so for some time. Thus he soon dropped his recent efforts to learn French and English.

During his first period in Beijing Mao was particularly attracted by the Russian writers Kropotkin, Bakunin, and Tolstoi who laid the foundation for his radical and anarchist views.

In spring 1919 Mao returned to Changsha to teach at elementary school. His political activities, which had received new impetus in Beijing, were in Changsha initially directed at the "Xinmin Xuehui" (New People's Study Society), of which he had became a cofounder one year earlier. In the wake of the May 4th Movement Mao initiated the weekly journal Xiang Jiang Pinglun (Xiang River Review) which, however, was banned after the fifth issue. This journal carried in three installments the first important essay by Mao, "The Great Unification of the People," in which he drew conclusions from the Russian October Revolution for the organization required for popular unification.

Following the ban on his weekly journal, Mao continued to publish articles in another weekly, Xin Hunan (New Hunan). In addition, he organized the "Wenti Yanjin Hui" (Problem Discussion Group). When Mao returned to Beijing in 1920 he studied Communist writings for the first time with which he had hitherto been only acquainted through articles by Chen Duxiu. At this time he read the Communist Manifesto, Kirkupp's History of Socialism, Kautsky's Class Struggle, and Engels' Socialism.

In July 1920 Mao returned to Changsha to become head of the Elementary Education Department at the 1st Teachers Training College, a post he held until late 1920. At the same time he increased his revolutionary activities. He founded a bookstore which sold Communist literature and after a short while owned seven branches in other cities of Hunan. This enterprise served primarily for fund-raising for political activities. At the same time, Mao founded together with other young intellectuals a study group on problems of Marxism. At the end of the year Mao set up a socialist youth corps in Changsha. He was one of the twelve founding members of the CCP on 1 July 1921 in Shanghai and acted as secretary during its 1st Congress. After the congress he returned to Changsha to set up the CCP Hunan Branch, of which he became secretary.

The following period Mao devoted mainly to the organization of workers in the coal mines of Anyuan in West Jiangxi, where he first met Liu Shaoqi. In the winter of 1921 he married Yang Kaihui, the daughter of his revered teacher Yang Changji. From this marriage, which was celebrated by the young intellectuals in Hunan as a romance, there was one son, Mao Anying, and a daughter. Yang Kaihui was executed in 1930 together with the sister of Mao, Mao Zehong, by order of the governor of Hunan Province, He Jian.

After an arrest warrant had been issued against Mao in early 1923 he fled to Shanghai where he served in the Party Center throughout the year. From there he joined the 3rd CCP Congress convened in Guangzhou in June. At this congress, which elected Mao for the first time as a member of its Central Committee, Mao was one of the advocates of a united front policy with the KMT in accordance with the directives of the Comintern.

When the united front was established the KMT elected a Central Executive Committee in January 1924 comprising 24 members (3 Communists) and 16 alternate members (6). Mao belonged to the latter group and served concurrently as secretary of the Propaganda Department. He is not, however, thought to have exerted great influence on this organization. Dissatisfied with this situation, Mao withdrew to Hunan in late 1924 where he remained until the summer of 1925. At this time he began to turn seriously towards the problems of peasant organization, which had not been adequately considered by either the CCP or the KMT. His preoccupation with this question can be gauged from the fact that he took part neither in the 4th CCP Congress in January 1925, nor in the organization of the May 30 Movement.

Only a new arrest warrant issued by the governor of Hunan persuaded Mao to leave his native province, this time for Guangzhou, where he lectured at a training school for cadres in the peasant movement.

In late 1925 he moved to Shanghai in order to organize the resistance against the governor of Hunan, General Zhao Hengti, who had brutally suppressed a strike by the workers in Anyuan. For this reason he also missed the 2nd KMT National Congress in January 1926, which was largely dominated by its left wing.

After Chiang Kai-shek had come to power in the KMT in spring of that year, he quickly moved to purge a number of Communist cadres. In this process Mao Zedong also lost his post in the Propaganda Department of the KMT. Instead, he became head of the newly established Peasants Department of the CCP. Immediately after the purge of Governor Zhao Hengti in the course of the Northern Expedition led by Chiang Kai-shek, Mao returned to Hunan in the summer of 1926. Until April 1927 he first proved his organizational talents in mobilizing peasants with great success.

In April 1927 Mao took part in the 5th CCP Congress and shortly afterwards was elected chairman of the Chinese Peasants Federation. After the collapse of the KMT-CCP united front and the failure of the Nanchang Uprising, Mao was a participant in the historic CCP Conference held in Jiujiang in August. The conference entrusted Mao with the leadership of the Autumn Harvest Uprising in Hunan and Jiangxi which in September also ended in failure. With the remainder of the units involved in this uprising Mao soon set up the first armed Communist base on Jinggangshan. In early 1928 he was joined by Zhu De, Chen Yi, and Lin Biao who combined their forces at this base to form the Red Army with Zhu as commander and Mao as political commissar. In 1929 the army moved its base to Ruijin in Jiangxi. At about this time (possibly as late as 1930) Mao Zedong was married to the teacher He Zizhen.

From this time until the beginning of the Long March Mao succeeded in consolidating his position in the recently established Ruijin Soviet, while he did not exert great influence within the CCP, which was at the time dominated by the "Moscow Group." Immediately before the Long March he also lost his leading position in the Soviet Government. At the time Zhou Enlai was one of the most determined opponents of Mao.

After the Communist units in Ruijin had failed four times to fight back attacks by the KMT forces, they were eventually forced to retreat from the crushing superiority of their opponents in October 1934. This marked the beginning of the Long March. In January 1935 a conference of the CCP Politburo took part in Zunyi and firmly placed the Party leadership in the hands of Mao. The true circumstances of this conference are still not clear; in particular Mao's sudden success remains unexplained after he had started from a position of virtually no influence at the beginning of the Long March. He was elected chairman of the Politburo, a new post in the leadership to which the secretary-general was subordinated. It may be assumed that the reason for this change of leadership was the recognition of Mao's concept of mobile warfare by the majority of the Politburo members. Mao's victory was, from an inner-Party point of view, a victory for the theory of revolution led by the peasant masses over the previously dominating theory of the leadership by the urban industrial proletariat.

The Long March, which has justly been called one of the

greatest military feats in world history, ended in October 1935 in the only remaining Chinese Soviet, in Shaanxi Province. During the following years Mao was primarily involved in determining the ideological course of the Party. A number of his writings contributed to this end: Strategic Problems of the Chinese Revolutionary War (December 1936); On Delaying Action (March 1938); Strategic Problems of the Anti-Japanese War and of Delaying Actions (May 1938); Problems of War Strategy (November 1938); On the New Democracy (January 1940).

After separation from his second wife He Zizhen Mao was married to Jiang Qing (Lan Ping) in 1939.

The by now unchallenged leadership of Mao Zedong was confirmed in 1945 by his reelection as chairman of the Politburo and of the Central Committee by the 7th CCP Congress. During that year his essay On Coalition Government was published.

After the defeat of the Japanese Mao for the first time met with Chiang Kai-shek who was taking part in the peace negotiations in Chongqing in August 1945. Before the Communist victory over the KMT, Mao's On Democratic People's Dictatorship appeared in July 1949. In September of that year he was elected chairman of the Standing Committee of the CPPCC.

1949,	Oct	Elected chairman of the Central People's Government (Head of State) and chairman of the Revolutionary People's Military Council (until Dec 1958)
	Dec	On his first visit abroad, Mao conducts negotiations in Moscow
1950		Mao's eldest son, Mao Anying, is killed in the Korean War where he was serving as a division commander
1954,	Sep	Following the reorganization of the People's Government Mao is confirmed as chairman of the Government and of the Military Council (until Dec 1958); elected deputy for Beijing Municipality to the 1st NPC
	Dec	Elected honorary chairman of the CPPCC
1955,	Jul	Mao reports "On Cooperation in Agriculture" and initiates measures for an accelerated collectivization
1956,	Sep	Elected member of the Standing Committee, Politburo of the CCP Central Committee
1957,	Oct	Head of the Chinese delegation to the 40th anniversary of the October Revolution in Moscow
1958,	Dec	Mao steps down as Head of State in favor of Liu Shaoqi

During the following period Mao's influence in the Party began to diminish. The failure of his "Great Leap Forward Campaign," devised to propel China's economy to enormous achievements within a short period of time, is particularly held against him. In 1961 he virtually disappeared under the political shadow of Liu Shaoqi and Deng Xiaoping. Dissatisfied with his new role as idolized figurehead, he worked to secure the support of the military by winning over its leader, Lin Biao. With the assurance of military support he initiated the Cultural Revolution in late 1965. Mao's primary aim was to regain his decisive position within the Party. He succeeded by giving the young "Red Guards" an opportunity to question all kinds of authority, an unheard of idea in China. His

wife, Jiang Qing, who since their marriage in 1939 had remained in the background, actively encouraged the fanatic young during the Cultural Revolution and began to develop political ambitions, including the eventual succession of Mao Zedong. With the help of Jiang Qing and Lin Biao the established power structure was destroyed. At the top of the hierarchy alone, two thirds of the leading cadres were attacked and humiliated and sent to labor camps, among them many prominent military leaders of the revolutionary period. Eventually only the military was able to restore order among the vandalizing Red Guards. In 1969 the 9th CCP Central Committee was elected, the first after the Cultural Revolution. Mao had regained absolute control over this leading Party organ in which Lin Biao and Jiang Qing also played prominent roles. Lin Biao disappeared in 1971 following an alleged attempt to stage a coup d'état. According to a more probable version, Mao consented to allow his wife to purge her most serious rival for the succession. The 10th Central Committee elected in 1973 in fact shifted to balance in favor of the Jiang Qing faction supported by Mao.

Mao Zedong died on 9 September 1976. One month later his widow was purged together with her three major supporters who have since become known as the "Gang of Four." His second return to power in July 1977 gave Deng Xiaoping an opportunity to gradually eliminate the Jiang Qing faction promoted by Mao. This process was largely completed by the end of 1978.

While seeking legitimization by citing the will of Mao Zedong, the new Chinese leadership has since his death removed Mao from his pedestal, paying little more than lip service to his works.

Peng Dehuai (P'eng Te-huai)

彭德怀

Peng Dehuai was born in 1901 in a peasant family in Xiangtan, Hunan Province. He probably received no school education as a child. As a young boy he ran away from his native village and a tyrannical stepmother. Until the age of sixteen, when he returned to Xiangtan, he had worked as a herdsman, miner, cobbler, and construction worker. He again left his native village in 1918 during a catastrophic famine in Hunan to become a soldier. One year later, when he already held the rank of lieutenant, he was involved in an unsuccessful attempt to assassinate the governor-general of Hunan, Fu Liangzuo, and was arrested shortly afterwards. No details are known about his sentence and term of imprisonment. At the time of the Northern Expedition in 1926 he joined the KMT with the rank of major. In 1927 he commanded a brigade under He Jian. In the same year, or possibly in 1928, he joined the CCP and took an active part in the organization of peasants federations. In 1928 he participated in the Pingjiang Uprising and subsequently founded the Hunan Soviet. Soon after he joined Mao Zedong and Zhu De, who had established a guerrilla base on Jinggangshan. Before finally committing himself to Mao, Peng Dehuai successfully attacked Changsha as part of the then CCP policy of striking against the cities, but was forced to retreat after ten days under the pressure of He Jian's superior forces. In June 1930 Peng reorganized his 5th Red Army into the 3rd Red Army Corps and two months later joined forces with the Red Army under Zhu De. During the Long March he commanded the vanguard units and distinguished himself in countless battles with the KMT forces. At the beginning of the Anti-Japanese War Peng was appointed deputy commander of the 8th Route Army and organized effective guerrilla units in East and South Shanxi. Until the foundation of the PRC in 1949 little is known about Peng Dehuai, although he had held the post of deputy commander-in-chief of the PLA and commander of the 1st Field Army at the end of the Anti-Japanese War.

1950		Appointed member of the Central Government Administration Council and vice-chairman of the Northwest China Revolutionary Military and Administrative Council
1951		Appointed commander of the Chinese People's Volunteers in Korea
1953,	31 Jul	Decorated by the North Korean Government for distinguished service
1954,	Sep	Recalled from Korea; appointed marshal as well as minister of national defense (until Sep 1959) and vice-chairman of the National Defense Council; elected deputy for the PLA to the 1st NPC (until Dec 1964)
	Oct	Member of a government delegation to Moscow
1955,	Feb	Head of a Chinese delegation to see the Soviet troops off at Lüshun and Dalien (Port Arthur)
	May	Head of a military delegation to the German Democratic Republic and to Poland and the USSR
1957,	Nov	Member of a CCP delegation led by Mao Zedong to the 40th anniversary celebrations of the October Revolution in Moscow
1959,	Apr-Jun	Head of a military delegation visiting the countries of the Warsaw Pact and Outer Mongolia
	Sep	Peng is purged
1974,	Nov	Peng dies on 29 November
1978,	Dec	Peng is officially rehabilitated

Peng Shaohui (P'eng Shao-hui)

彭绍辉

Peng was born in 1910 in Hunan Province. In 1928 he took part in a Communist uprising in his native province and subsequently joined the 5th Red Army commanded by Peng Dehuai. He was severely wounded during a guerrilla mission in 1929 and again in 1933 as commander of the 1st Division of the 3rd Army Corps. In August 1937 he was appointed commander of the 358th Brigade, 120th Division, 8th Route Army. In 1943 he served concurrently as head of the East Shaanxi Branch of the Anti-Japan Military and Political Academy. In 1947 Peng was made commander of the 7th Column of the Shanxi-Suiyuan Field Army. In February 1949 he was appointed deputy chief of staff of the 1st Field Army.

1952		Appointed chief of staff of Northwest China Military Region and of the 1st Field Army (until Sep 1954)
1953,	Jan	Appointed member of the Northwest Administrative Council (until Sep 1954)
1954,	Apr	Appointed deputy commander of Northwest China Military Region (until Sep 1954)
	Oct	Appointed deputy chief of PLA General Staff and member of the National Defense Council
1955,	Sep	Appointed lieutenant-general; conferred the orders "1st August," "Independence and Freedom," and "Liberation," all 1st class
1958,	Mar	Identified as colonel-general
1959,	Mar	Elected deputy for the PLA to the 2nd NPC
	Apr	Elected member of the Standing Committee of the 2nd NPC (reelected in 1965 to the 3rd NPC)
1961,	Feb	Head of a military sports group visiting Poland
1963,	Sep	Head of a military delegation to Sweden
1966,	Oct	Member of a CCP delegation to the 5th Congress of the Workers Party of Albania
1969,	Apr	Elected to first term as member of the CCP Central Commmittee by the 9th Party Congress
1972,	Apr	Member of a military delegation led by Chen Xilian to North Korea
1975,	Jan	Reelected member of the Standing Committee by the 4th NPC (confirmed in 1978 by the 5th NPC)

Peng Shaohui died on 25 April 1978.

Peng was married to Zhang Wei.

Su Zhenhua (Su Chen-hua)

苏振华

Su was born in 1911 in Hunan Province. In 1928 he took part in the Pingjiang Uprising and subsequently served in a unit commanded by Peng Dehuai on his way to join the guerrilla base established by Mao Zedong on Jinggangshan. In 1930 he was political commissar of a battalion, in 1933 political commissar of the 13th Regiment, 3rd Front Army, commanded by Huang Zhen. In 1934-35 he took part in the Long March and subsequently attended the 1st training course of the Anti-Japanese Military and Political Academy. In 1937 he was made political commissar of the 343rd Brigade, 115th Division, 8th Route Army and contributed to the victory of Lin Biao over the

Japanese in Pingxing Guan (Shanxi). Two years later he was political commissar of the Training Regiment of the 115th Division. He then served as political commissar of Shanxi-Chahar-Hebei Military District. In 1949 he was political commissar of an army corps of the 2nd Field Army.

1949,	Nov	Identified as political commissar of Guizhou Military District and as secretary of Guizhou Province CP (until Feb 1953)
	Dec	Identified as council member of the People's Government of Guizhou Province and as chairman of its Financial and Economic Council (until 1953)
1950,	Jul	Identified as member of the Southwest China Military and Administrative Council (until 1953)
1953,	Feb	Identified as deputy political commissar of the PLA Navy (until Aug 1957)
1954,	Sep	Appointed member of the National Defense Council (until Cultural Revolution)
1955,	Sep	Appointed admiral; conferred the orders of "Independence and Freedom" and "Liberation," all 1st class
1956,	Sep	Elected alternate member of the CCP Central Committee by the 8th Party Congress (until Cultural Revolution)
1957,	Aug	Identified as political commissar of the PLA Navy
1958		Su commands the naval units of the PLA in the Strait of Taiwan in a conflict with the Nationalist Government
1959-1964		Su introduces a tactic of close combat into the Navy which involves attacks at a distance of 200 meters
1967,	Jan	Accused of having planned a coup d'état together with He Long and subsequently disappears
1972,	Mar	First appearance after the Cultural Revolution
	Oct	Identified as deputy commander of the PLA Navy
1973,	Aug	Elected alternate member of the Politburo (until Aug 1977) and member of the Central Committee by the 10th Party Congress
1976,	Nov	Appointed 1st secretary of the CP, and chairman of the Revolutionary Commitee, of Shanghai Municipality
	Dec	Appointed chairman of the Revolutionary Committee of Shanghai Municipality
1977,	Aug	Elected member of the Politburo by the 11th CCP Congress
	Dec	Identified as 1st political commissar of the PLA Navy
1978,	Feb	Elected deputy for Shanghai Municipality to the 5th NPC
	Jul	Identified as 1st secretary of the PLA Navy Party Committee

Su Zhenhua died on 7 February 1979.

Tao Zhu (T'ao Chu)

Tao was born circa 1906 in Hunan Province. He was a member of the National Revolutionary Army during the Northern Expedition in 1926. In 1930 he freed eighteen arrested CCP cadres in a raid in Xiamen. Shortly afterwards he was identified as a cadre of the CCP Fujian Committee. During the following years he led guerrilla units in Hubei Province. In 1948 he joined these units with the forces under Li Xiannian to form the 5th Division of the 4th Army. In 1948 Tao was identified as deputy director of Shenyang Military Control Commission, and in the following year as deputy director of the Political Department of the 4th Field Army and of Central-South China Military Region.

1949,	Dec	Appointed chairman of Wuhan Military Control Commission
1950		Appointed member of Central-South China Military and Political Council; member of its Committee of Finance and Commerce; political commissar of Guangxi Military Region; and 2nd political commissar of South China Military Region under the CCP Central Committee
1952		Appointed member of Central-South China Administrative Council and 4th secretary, Central-South China Bureau of the CCP Central Committee
1953,	Jun	Elected vice-chairman of the People's Government of Guangdong Province (until 1955)
1955		Appointed governor (until Aug 1957), and secretary of the CP (until Aug 1957), of Guangdong Province
1956,	Sep	Elected member of the CCP Central Committee by the 8th Party Congress; identified as 1st secretary of Guangdong Province CP (until Mar 1957)
1960,	Mar	Appointed vice-chairman of the Commission for Receiving and Resettling Returned Overseas Chinese under the State Council
1961,	Oct	Member of the Party delegation attending the 22nd CPSU Congress
	Nov	Identified as 1st secretary, Central-South China Bureau of the CCP Central Committee
1962,	Mar	Identified as political commissar of Guangzhou Military Region
1964,	Sep	Elected deputy for Guangdong Province to the 3rd NPC
1965,	Jan	Appointed vice-premier (until Jan 1967)
1966,	Mar	Identified as advisor to the Cultural Revolution Group under the CCP Central Committee
	Jul	Identified as secretary of the CCP Central Committee Secretariat and as director, Propaganda Department of the CCP Central Committee

Aug Elected member of the Politburo of the 8th CCP Central Committee

1967, Sep Branded as a counterrevolutionary revisionist and purged

Tao Zhu died on 30 November 1969.

Wang Dongxing (Wang Tung-hsing)

王东兴

Wang was born in 1916 in Jiangxi Province. As a youth he joined the Jiangxi Soviet where he served in a guard unit in 1933. After the Long March he belonged at first to the bodyguard of Mao Zedong. In 1937 he became instructor in the 1st Battalion of the Central Guard Regiment. During a Communist withdrawal in 1947 Wang commanded Mao's bodyguard. A close association between both men dated from this period. In 1949 Wang was head of the Security Department, Staff Office of the CCP Central Committee.

1949, Oct Appointed deputy director, Secretariat of the Government Administration Council (until 1953) and director of the Security Office of this secretariat

Dec Wang accompanies Mao to Moscow, probably again as bodyguard; appointed deputy director of the 8th Bureau, Ministry of Public Security

1955, Dec Appointed vice-minister of public security (until Jan 1959)

1958, Jun Appointed vice-governor of Jiangxi Province (until Dec 1960)

1960, Jan Again appointed vice-minister of public security

1961, Jan Article in Gongzuo Tongxun (Work Bulletin) No 1: "Report by Comrade Wang Dongxing on the Ideological Situation in the Central Security Corps"

1964, Jun Wang is present at receptions given by Mao Zedong for delegations of the Security Forces, the Political College, and the Central Political Cadres School

Oct Elected deputy for Jiangxi Province to the 3rd NPC

1966, Mar Member of the delegation led by President Liu Shaoqi to Pakistan, Afghanistan, and Burma

later Wang takes a prominent part in demonstrations at the beginning of the Cultural Revolution

1967, Jul Identified as director of the General Office of the CCP Central Committee

1969, Apr Elected member of the Central Committee and alternate member of the Politburo by the 9th Party Congress

1973, Aug Confirmed as member of the CCP Central Committee by the 10th Party Congress and promoted to member of the Politburo

1976, Aug Confirmed in all previous Party offices by the 11th CCP Congress and in addition elected vice-chairman of the CCP Central Committee and member of the Standing Committee, Politburo of the CCP Central Committee

Oct As commander of the Security Forces for the Politburo members living in Beijing, Wang plays a key role in the purge of the "Gang of Four"

1977, Oct Appointed 1st vice-president of the Party School under the CCP Central Committee

1978, Feb Elected deputy for Beijing Municipality to the 5th NPC

Nov Head of a Party and government delegation to Kampuchea

1980, Feb Removed from all Party and state posts at the 5th Plenum of the CCP 11th Central Committee

Wang Hongwen (Wang Hung-wen)

王洪文

Wang was born in 1932 in Jilin (Liaoning?) Province in a family of poor peasants. His ancestors had been peasants for some generations. As a young man he joined the PLA in which he served initially as a "little red soldier," a term usually referring to fourteen-to-fifteen-year-old boys serving as messengers and orderlies.

1950-1953 Service in the Korean War (no details known about type of service or unit)

1953, end Identified as a worker at Cotton Mill No.17 in Shanghai in which he is soon appointed a cadre of the Security Department

1966, Jun 12 Wang publishes a wall poster together with six others which attacks the "capitalist management" of his factory. This wall poster is later praised by Mao Zedong as the "first significant wall poster of the Great Proletarian Cultural Revolution"

until The 1st secretary of Shanghai Municipali-
Sep ty CP, Chen Pixian, sends a work group to Cotton Mill No.17 in order to prevent "counterrevolutionary activities by rebelling workers." Wang subsequently sets up a "struggle group" with 30 other workers against the suppression of rebel groups. During a visit to Beijing he accuses the Shanghai Party leadership to this effect. He receives the support of the Cultural Revolution Group led by Jiang Qing and is received by Mao Zedong and Lin Biao.

Oct With Wang Xiuzhen Wang organizes several thousand workers on 9 October to besiege the Shanghai Party building in Kangping Road and call upon the Party leadership to offer criticism. Chen Pixian rejects the five demands presented. Two days later a "petition group" numbering 10,000 and organized by Wang travels to Beijing by rail in order to present their accusations against Chen. The Shanghai Party leadership attempts to stop the train in Anting, 30 km west of Shanghai. In spite of the ensuing violence they do not succeed in stopping the train.

Nov   Zhang Chunqiao is posted to Shanghai in order to mediate between the rival factions. Wang and his demonstrators return from Beijing only after Zhang's arrival. At a mass demonstration organized by Wang on 13 November Zhang Chunqiao declares the "Revolutionary Rebel Headquarters of the Shanghai Workers" a "legal" revolutionary organization.

until Thanks to the support of Cultural Revolu-
Dec   tion groups in Beijing Wang is able to eliminate other rebel groups and succeeds in isolating the old Party leadership of Shanghai

1967, Jan   On 3 January Wang has the building occupied in which Wenhui Bao (Literature Journal) is published. In its issue of 5 January the "Revolutionary Rebels Headquarters of the Shanghai Workers" led by Wang publish together with eleven other workers' organizations a declaration addressed to all citizens of Shanghai in which the Municipal CCP Committee are accused as capitalist-roaders. At a mass demonstration organized by Wang on 6 January Chen Pixian and Cao Diqiu are called upon to confess their crimes. On 16 January Wang issues a statement to all citizens of Shanghai urging them to observe work discipline.

Feb   Headed by Zhang Chunqiao, revolutionary rebels take over the leadership of Shanghai. On 5 February the "Provisional Committee of the Shanghai People's Commune" is founded based on the model of the Paris Commune. It comprises five labor representatives, two peasants and soldiers respectively, and one "revolutionary cadre" (a member of the former establishment) and one "Red Guard representative" each. Wang is one of the five labor representatives.

Mar   On official instruction from Beijing the Shanghai People's Commune is replaced by the "Shanghai Revolutionary Committee" on 24 February. Zhang Chunqiao is made chairman of the Revolutionary Committee with Wang as vice-chairman. Shortly afterwards Wang is in addition identified as chairman of the Revolutionary Committee of Cotton Mill No.17 in Shanghai.

1969, Apr   Elected member of the CCP Central Committee by the 9th Party Congress (confirmed in this post by the 10th Party Congress in 1973)

1970   Head of a delegation of workers to Albania

1971, Jan   Elected secretary of the new CP Secretariat of Shanghai Municipality after the Cultural Revolution (1st CP secretary: Zhang Chunqiao; 2nd CP secretary: Yao Wenyuan). Owing to this new Party

position Wang is virtually the Party leader of Shanghai, since Zhang and Yao have by now moved to Beijing.

1972, Apr   Identified as political commissar of Shanghai Garrison (no later mention in this post)

Sep   Wang is recalled to Beijing to take up duties within the Central Leadership

1973, Apr   Elected chairman of the Shanghai Trade Union (no later mention in this post)

Aug   During the 10th CCP Congress Wang acts as vice-chairman of the Presidium. He is elected a member of the Politburo and vice-chairman of the CCP Central Committee by the Congress. At the Congress Wang reads the report on the revision of the Party constitution.

1976, Oct   Wang is arrested together with Jiang Qing, Zhang Chunqiao, and Yao Wenyuan and expelled from the CCP.

Wang Zheng (Wang Cheng)

王　净

Before joining the Jiangxi Soviet around 1929, Wang had served in the Chinese Nationalist Army. He was appointed head of the newly organized Red Army Radio Service in 1931. After the Long March Wang was made head of the 3rd Communications Bureau, Military Council of the CCP Central Committee, and training supervisor of the Communications School of the 8th Route Army. Together with Michael Lindsay he set up the Broadcasting Station Xinhua during this period. In September 1949 Wang represented the PLA as delegate at the 1st CPPCC which elected him a member of its National Committee (until December 1954).

1949, Oct   Appointed vice-minister of posts and telecommunications (until Oct 1954)

Dec   Identified as director, Communications Bureau of the Revolutionary Military Council

1952, Aug   Advisor of a government delegation led by Zhou Enlai to the USSR

1954, Aug   Elected deputy for Liaoning Province to the 1st NPC (until Mar 1959)

1955   Identified as head of the Communications Department, Logistics Department of the PLA

Sep   Appointed lieutenant-general; conferred the orders "1st August" and "Liberation," both 1st class

1957, Jun   Appointed member of the Scientific Planning Commission (until Nov 1964)

1958, Jul   Elected deputy for the PLA to the 2nd NPC (until Dec 1964)

1959, Apr   Identified as commander, Signal Corps of the PLA (until 1963)

1960, Feb   Appointed vice-chairman of the Commission for Receiving and Resettling Returned Overseas Chinese

1963, May Appointed minister of the 4th Ministry of Machine Building
1964, Sep Elected deputy for Heilongjiang Province to the 3rd NPC
1965, Jan Appointed member of the National Defense Council (until Cultural Revolution)
Feb Head of a delegation to the spring fair in Leipzig
1967 Disappears during the Cultural Revolution
1972, Mar First appearance after the Cultural Revolution
1973, Aug Elected to first term as member of the CCP Central Committee by the 10th Party Congress
1975, Jan Appointed minister of the 4th Ministry of Machine Building by the 4th NPC

Wang Zhen died on 13 August 1978.

Wu De (Wu Te)

吴　德

Wu was born in 1909 in Tangshan, Hebei Province. He joined the CCP as a student at China University in Beijing. In 1931 he organized youths in his home province for guerrilla activities. In 1932 he was engaged in Communist propaganda work at Kailuan Coal Mine. He took a leading part in the great labor strike at Tangshan in 1935. During the year of 1940 he spent a short period of time in Yan'an where he probably received training in intelligence work. He was subsequently responsible for labor organization in the provinces of Hebei, Chahar, Rehe, and Liaoning. In 1942 he became political commissar of a regiment. About 1945 he served as secretary general of the Political Department of Shaanxi-Chahar-Hebei Military District. In August 1948 the Federation of Trade Unions elected Wu a member of its Executive Committee and deputy director of its North China Administrative Office. Two months later he was posted to his native town of Tangshan as secretary of the CP.

1949, Oct Appointed vice-minister of fuel industry (until 1950)
1950 Identified as secretary of the CP, and member of the People's Government of Pingyuan Province (abolished in Nov 1952)
1952, Aug Identified as deputy secretary (until Sep 1956), and deputy mayor (until Jun 1953), of Tianjin
Oct Identified as president of Tianjin University
1953, Jan Appointed member of the North China Administrative Council (probably until 1955)
Jun Appointed mayor of Tianjin (until Jan 1955)
1954, Aug Elected deputy for Tianjin Municipality to the 1st NPC
1955, Mar Identified as secretary of Jilin Province CP

1956, Sep Elected alternate member of the CCP Central Committee by the 8th Party Congress (until Apr 1969); identified as 1st secretary of Jilin Province CP (until Jun 1966)
1960, Feb Identified as political commissar of Jilin Military District (until Jun 1966)
1963, Oct Identified as secretary, Northeast China Bureau of the CCP Central Committee (until Jun 1966); member of a delegation representing this bureau to North Korea
Dec Identified as 1st political commissar of Jilin Military District
1966, Jun Following the purge of the Beijing CP Committee, Wu is appointed 2nd secretary of Beijing Municipality CP
Jul Identified as acting mayor of Beijing
1967, Apr Elected vice-chairman of the newly established Revolutionary Committee of Beijing
1968, Apr Identified as 1st political commissar of Beijing Garrison (no later mention in this post)
Nov Member of a Party and government delegation to Albania
1969, Apr Elected member of the CCP Central Committee by the 9th Party Congress
1971, Mar Elected secretary of Beijing Municipality CP
Aug Identified as member of the Cultural Group under the State Council (until Dec 1974)
1972, Jun Identified as chairman of the Revolutionary Committee of Beijing (until Oct 1978)
1973, Mar Identified as 1st secretary of Beijing Municipality CP (until Oct 1978)
Aug Confirmed by the 10th Party Congress as member of the Central Committee and in addition elected member of the Politburo
1974, Jan Identified as 2nd political commissar of Beijing Military Region (until Apr 1976)
1975, Jan Elected vice-chairman of the 4th NPC (confirmed in Mar 1978 by the 5th NPC)
1978, Feb Elected deputy for Beijing Municipality to the 5th NPC
1980, Feb Removed from all Party and state posts at the 5th Plenum of the CCP 11th Central Committee

Wu Han (Wu Han)

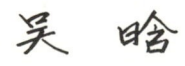

吴　晗

Wu was born in 1909 in a poor family in Yiwu, Zhejiang Province. As a worker-student he graduated from Qinghua University in Beijing in 1934. Only one year later he was appointed professor of that university. In 1938 he lectured in history at Yunnan University in Kunming. During the Anti-Japanese War he was a lecturer at the Joint Southwest University in Kunming which consisted of the evacuated universities of Beijing, Qinghua, and Nankai. In autumn 1945 he returned to Qinghua University. He moved to the Communist-occupied areas of North China in autumn 1948 and in early 1949 returned with the Communists to Beijing. His appointments as dean of the Art Institute of Qinghua University and as director of the History Department of the same university followed immediately. In May he was appointed secretary-general of the Federation of Democratic Youth (until April 1958); in November he took part in the CPPCC which elected him a member of its Standing Committee (until December 1964).

1950,	Oct	Appointed member of the Culture and Education Commission of the Government Administration Council (until Sep 1954); elected council member of the Sino-Soviet Friendship Association
	Nov	Sent to Moscow as delegate at the anniversary celebrations of the October Revolution
	Dec	Elected member of the Standing Committee of the Democratic League; appointed deputy mayor of Beijing
1953,	Jan	Appointed chairman of the Peace Council of Beijing; elected chairman of the Democratic League of Beijing
	Jun	Elected vice-chairman of the Federation of Democratic Youth (until Apr 1958)
1954,	Sep	Elected deputy for Beijing Municipality to the 1st NPC
1955,	Jun	Appointed member of the Department of Philosophy and Social Sciences, Academy of Sciences
1956,	Feb	Head of a cultural delegation to India
	Apr	Elected council member of the Sino-Indian Friendship Association
1957,	Dec	Member of a delegation to the 1st Afro-Asian Solidarity Conference in Cairo
1958,	Apr	Head of a troupe of artists visiting France
	Jul	Elected council member of the World Peace Council
1960,	Dec	Member of a goodwill delegation to Cuba
1961,	Jul	Identified as vice-chairman of the Sino-Nepalese Friendship Association
1962,	Apr	Elected vice-chairman of the China-Afro-Asian Society
	Oct	Head of a friendship delegation to Nepal
1964,	Sep	Identified as president of Beijing Television University
1965,	Jun	Elected vice-chairman of the Peace Council
	Nov	Wu Han's play Hai Rui Dismissed from Office is criticized by Yao Wenyuan in Wenhui Bao (Literature Journal), an event marking the beginning of the Cultural Revolution
1966,	May	Subjected to "struggle" for the first time
	Dec	Dismissed from all posts and purged
1978,	Dec	Wu's play Hai Rui Dismissed from Office is rehabilitated by a forum of writers in Beijing

Wu Han died on 11 October 1969.

Publications

The Career of Hu Yingling
A Study of the Mother of the Emperor Cheng Zu of the Ming Dynasty
The Jing Nan Incident of the Ming Dynasty and the Moving of the Country's Capital to the North
China and the South Sea Islands Before the 16th Century
The Collapse of the Yuan Empire and the Founding of the Ming Dynasty
The Career of Shen Gua
The Biography of Zhu Yuanzhang
Mirror of History
Notes from Reading History
Collections under the Lamp
Hai Rui Dismissed from Office

Xie Zhengrong (Hsieh Cheng-jung)

谢正荣

1951,	Sep	Appointed commander of the 191st Division of the 64th Corps
1958,	May	Appointed commander of Jilin City Garrison; identified as major-general
1968,	Jan	Appointed commander of Jilin Military District
1971,	Aug	Elected secretary of Sichuan Province CP
1973,	Apr	Identified as vice-chairman of the Revolutionary Committee of Sichuan Province; identified as deputy commander of Chengdu Military Region
1974,	Sep	Identified as commander of Sichuan Military District (until Jun 1976)
1977,	Aug	Elected alternate member of the CCP Central Committee by the 11th Party Congress

Xie Zhengrong died on 4 December 1977 at the age of 59.

Yao Wenyuan (Yao Wen-yüan)

姚文元

Yao was born in 1931 in Shaoxing, Zhejiang Province. His father, Yao Benzi, had been a well-known leftist writer during the thirties.

1951	Identified as a cadre of the Shanghai Section, New Democratic Youth League
1952	Beginning of Yao's literary career as correspondent for the Wenhui Bao (Literature Journal)
1955	During the mid-fifties Yao begins to advocate an orthodox literary line, adhering closely to Mao Zedong Thought, in opposition to the then generally liberal tendency in literature. His article "Hu Feng's Three Methods of Falsifying Marxism" was a significant cause of the purge of Hu.
1957	During the "One Hundred Flowers Campaign" Yao actively participates in the criticism of "rightist deviationist" writers. In the meantime he has become a protégé of Zhang Chunqiao.
1958, Apr	Elected member of the National Committee of the Youth Federation (reelected in 1962)

1960,	Feb	Yao takes part in a congress of the Shanghai Branch, Union of Chinese Writers
	later	In the course of the "anti-revisionist movement" within literary circles Yao turns against Wang Renshu (pen name Ba Ren) and Qian Gurong
1963,	Nov	Yao delivers a speech at the enlarged session of members of the Department of Philosophy and Social Sciences, Academy of Sciences. Before this speech Yao had criticized the composer Debussy as bourgeois in an article in Wenhui Bao. His close association with Jiang Qing, and later Mao Zedong, dates from about this time when both turned to Shanghai as a result of opposition in Beijing.
1965,	Nov	Article in Wenhui Bao: "Notes on the New Historical Drama 'Hai Rui Dismissed from Office'" which marked the beginning of the Cultural Revolution. This drama, written by the well-known historian and propaganda cadre Wu Han, is an allegory in defense of the former Minister of National Defense, Peng Dehuai, who had been dismissed in 1959. Publications circulated during the Cultural Revolution indicate that Yao's article had been written "at the suggestion of Mao and under the direct supervision of Jiang Qing and with the support of Zhang Chunqiao."
1966,	Aug	Yao for the first time takes part in a demonstration in Beijing in support of the Cultural Revolution
	Oct	Identified as member of the Cultural Revolution Group of the CCP Central Committee
1967,	Feb	Appointed 2nd secretary of Shanghai People's Commune, which is renamed Revolutionary Committee of Shanghai a few days later, as well as vice-chairman of the Revolutionary Committee (no later official reference to Yao in this post)
	Jun	Head of a Red Guard delegation to Albania
	Nov	Yao is listed in place 10 of the Beijing Party hierarchy
1968,	Jan	Zhang Chunqiao and his protégé Yao become members of the "Group for the Rectification and Renewal of the Party" headed by Kang Sheng
1969		Beginning: According to rumors believed to have originated in Moscow, Yao is married to Xiao Li, one of the two daughters of Mao and Jiang Qing
	Apr	Elected member of the CCP Central Committee and of the Politburo by the 9th Party Congress
1971,	Jan	Elected 2nd secretary of Shanghai Municipality CP (no later official reference in this post)
1973,	Aug	Confirmed as member of the CCP Central Committee and of the Politburo by the 10th Party Congress
1974,	Nov	Head of a Party and government delegation to Albania
1975,	Jan	Member of the Presidium of the 4th NPC
1976,	Oct	On 6 October Yao is purged together with

Jiang Qing, Zhang Chunqiao, and Wang Hongwen. They have since become known as the "Gang of Four".

Zhang Chunqiao (Chang Ch'un-ch'iao)

张春桥

Zhang was born in about 1915. In 1936 Zhang was a member of the left-wing Shanghai Society of Writers. During 1942-43 he joined CCP guerrilla units operating behind the Japanese front in North and East China.

1950,	Mar	Appointed deputy director, Information and Publication Bureau, East China Military and Administrative Council, and deputy director, East China Branch, NCNA
1954,	Jan	Member of a delegation of journalists headed by Deng Tuo (editor-in-chief of RMRB) to the USSR
	Apr	Appointed managing director of the PLA daily Jiefangjun Bao based in Shanghai
1955,	Apr	Identified as vice-chairman of the Shanghai branch of the Journalists' Association
	Oct	Identified as acting secretary of the Literary and Art Work Committee, Shanghai CP
1958,	Jun	Elected member of the CP secretariat in Shanghai
1959,	Apr	Elected member of the Standing Committee of Shanghai CP
	Sep	Identified as vice-chairman of the Shanghai Branch of the Association for Cultural Relations with Foreign Countries
1960,	Mar	Identified as board member of the Sino-Latin American Friendship Association
1963,	Apr	Identified as director of the Propaganda Department, Shanghai CP
1964,	Feb	Identified as alternate member of the CP secretariat, Shanghai (until Mar 1965)
1965,	Mar	Elected secretary, Shanghai CP
1966,	Oct	Deputy head of the cultural revolutionary group in the CCP Central Committee; appointed secretary of the East China Bureau in the CCP Central Committee
1967,	Jan	Zhang is one of the initiators of a demonstration by Revolutionary Rebels
	5 Feb	On establishment of the Shanghai People's Commune, Zhang is made chairman and 1st CP secretary (until 24 Feb 1967)
	24 Feb	Shanghai People's Commune is renamed Shanghai Revolutionary Committee and Zhang becomes chairman
	Apr	Zhang takes part as delegate from the Shanghai Revolutionary Committee in the establishment of the Beijing Revolutionary Committee
	May	Zhang conducts a celebration in Shanghai of the 25th anniversary of the publication of Mao Zedong's "Yan'an Talks on Literature and Art"

Identified as 1st Political Commissar of Shanghai Garrison and of Nanjing Military Region

1969,	Apr	Elected member of the CCP Central Committee and of the Politburo by 9th CCP Congress (confirmed in both offices by the 10th Party Congress in 1973)
1971,	Jan	Elected 1st secretary after reorganization of the Shanghai CP secretariat
1973,	Aug	Elected member of the Politburo Standing Committee by the 10th CCP Congress
1975,	Jan	Appointed vice-premier
	Sep	Leader of a Party delegation to North Korea
	Oct	Identified as director of the General Political Department of the PLA
1976,	Oct	Purge of the "Gang of Four," including Zhang

Zhou Enlai (Chou En-lai)

周恩来

Zhou Enlai was born in 1898 in an upper middle class family in Shaoxing, Zhejiang Province. His father, who passed the state examinations in the same year, never held an official position. Zhou spent his early years in the house of this grandfather, a high-ranking state official, in Huaian, Jiangsu Province. There he studied the classics in preparation for the state examinations. At the age of twelve Zhou moved to his father's elder brother's home in Shenyang. In 1913 he was enrolled at Nankai Middle School in Tianjin and soon played a leading part in the student movement. After graduation from middle school in 1917, Zhou Enlai went to Japan to study for two years at Waseda University and at Japan University. In 1919 he continued his studies at the American missionary Nankai University in Tianjin. Zhou's leading participation in student demonstrations during the May 4th Movement led to his arrest and six months imprisonment. Shortly after his release he joined a group of young intellectuals going to France as worker-students. There he founded the Chinese Communist Youth League together with Li Lisan, Wang Ruofei, and Zhao Shiyan. He remained in France initially for two years, then went to Great Britain for several months, returned to France, and eventually studied for one year in Germany. In 1924 Zhou returned to China and immediately took a leading part in the Chinese Communist movement. Still in the same year, the second of the KMT-CCP united front, Zhou was appointed director of the Political Department of the Whampoa Military Academy headed by Chiang Kai-shek. At this academy he established a strong Communist base under the particular encouragement of Soviet advisor Galen (Marshal Blücher). In 1925 Zhou organized workers' uprisings in Shanghai. During the Northern Expedition he was political commissar of the 1st Nationalist Army. Zhou Enlai barely escaped alive from the events following the rift between KMT and CCP in 1927. Having managed initially to flee to Wuhan he took part in the Nanchang Uprising of 1 August; after its failure he escaped via

Shantou to Guangzhou in order to help organize the Guangzhou Commune. In that year he was elected a member of the CCP Politburo in which he served continuously, and for many years as its most senior cadre, until his death. In July 1928 Zhou Enlai attended the 6th CCP Congress meeting in Moscow. In 1931 he joined the Jiangxi Soviet. He held a variety of posts during the years until the Long March. This period was also the beginning of Zhou's rivalry with Mao Zedong whom he replaced as political commissar of the Red Army shortly before the Long March. After the Long March and a settlement between Zhou and Mao, Zhou continued to hold leading Party positions. Following the Xi'an Incident he negotiated with Chiang Kai-shek in December 1936, thus creating the precondition for a new united front period between the KMT and the CCP. In 1939 Zhou took part with Zhu De as an observer at a session of the Supreme Soviet in Moscow. During the united front period Zhou Enlai served primarily as liaison officer for the Communists with the Nationalist Government in Chongqing. There he held among others several senior posts as director of the Nationalist Government's Political School, vice-chairman of the Nationalist Government Political Council, deputy director of the Political Council in the Military Council, member of the Military Council's Standing Committee, and member of the National Defense Council. The 7th CCP Congress in Yan'an confirmed Zhou as a member and elected him vice-chairman of the Politburo and vice-chairman of the Revolutionary Military Council in 1945. Until early 1947 Zhou again represented the Communists at the negotiations under General Marshall. After the failure of these negotiations he returned to Yan'an in March 1947.

1949,	Oct	Appointed premier of the Government Administration Council; minister of foreign affairs; member of the Central People's Government Council; vice-chairman of the Revolutionary People's Military Council; honorary president of the Institute of Foreign Affairs
1950,	Feb	In Moscow, Zhou signs the Friendship and Assistance Pact, the Agreement on the Return of the Manchurian Railways, Lüshun (Port Arthur) and Dalian, and a Soviet loan agreement for the PRC
1952,	Aug	Head of a delegation to renewed negotiations in Moscow
1954		Head of the delegation to the Geneva Indochina Conference. During the same year head of delegations to India and Burma
1955,	Apr	Head of the delegation to the Bandung Conference
1958,	Feb	Head of a government delegation to North Korea
1959,	Jan	Head of a CCP delegation to the CPSU Congress
1960,	Apr	Head of a government delegation to India and Burma
	May	Head of government delegations to North Vietnam, Cambodia, and Outer Mongolia
1961,	Jan	Head of a friendship delegation comprising 400 members to Burma
	Oct	Head of a CCP delegation to the CPSU Congress
1963,	Dec-	Head of a government delegation to the
1964,	Jan	United Arab Republic, Algeria, Morocco,

Albania, Tunisia, Somalia, Ghana, Mali, Guinea, Ethiopia, Sudan

1964,	Feb	Head of a government delegation to Burma, Pakistan, Indonesia, Ceylon
	Jul	Head of a government delegation to Burma
1965,	Mar	Head of a government delegation to Romania, Albania, Algeria, Pakistan
	Apr	Head of a government delegation to United Arab Republic, Burma, Indonesia, Pakistan
	Jun	Head of a government delegation to Tanzania and United Arab Republic
1966,	Jun	Head of a government and Party delegation to Romania, Albania, Pakistan (en route stopover in Afghanistan)
1969,	Apr	Elected member, Standing Committee of the Politburo, by the 9th CCP Congress
	Sep	Head of a Party delegation to Vietnam to attend mourning for Ho Chi-minh
1970,	Apr	Head of a Party and government delegation to North Korea
1971,	Mar	Head of a Party and government delegation to North Vietnam

Zhou Enlai died on 8 January 1976.

Zhu De (Chu Te)

朱　德

Zhu De was born in 1886 in the village of Linglongcai, Yilong County, Sichuan Province, as the son of poor peasants. After attending elementary school and the private sunday school of a landlord from 1892 he moved to his uncle's household in Dawan in 1902 where he was enrolled at the Xiping'an School. He passed the state examinations in autumn of 1906 in Yilong and was awarded the title of xiucai. After this examination he enrolled at the Sports School in Chengdu. In 1907 he returned to Yilong as a sports teacher at a new school. In 1909 Zhu joined the Military Academy of Yunnan Province in Kunming (Yunnan-fu) in order to study under brigadier Cai E. He was thus one of the first Chinese to receive modern military training. At the same time he became a member of the Tongmenghui, a revolutionary society led by Sun Yat-sen, and a member of the Gelaohui. In July 1911 he passed the final examination of his military studies and was appointed sub-lieutenant. In October of that year Zhu joined the Revolutionary Expeditionary Corps under Cai E; at the time of the proclamation of the Republic of China he served as captain. In May 1912 he was promoted to the rank of major and appointed lecturer at the Military Academy of Kunming.

In autumn of that year Zhu De was married to Xiao Jiufen and during this period also became a member of the KMT. During 1913 and 1914 he commanded border forces in the Indochinese Border Area. In 1915 he was appointed colonel and commander of the 10th Yunnan Regiment with which he joined the units under Cai E to oppose the Yuan Shikai regime. After the successful completion of this campaign

Zhu De was promoted to the rank of brigadier in 1916 at the age of 40. His wife died in that year while he was based with a unit of the Garrison Forces of Yunnan in Luzhou. In 1917 Zhu was married to Zhen Youzhen. During the following years he reportedly led a dissolute life and took to opium smoking. He eventually underwent treatment for this addiction at a French hospital in Shanghai in August 1922. At this time Zhu first met Sun Yat-sen and submitted his first application for CCP membership which was, however, rejected. In September of that year he traveled to Europe where he met Zhou Enlai in Berlin in October. He joined the CCP shortly afterwards. In 1923 Zhu began to study political science at Göttingen University. In 1924 he organized a KMT branch in Berlin. He worked closely with German Communists during this period and was arrested by the German police in June 1926. Having returned to China after his release he was appointed director of the Military School and concurrently political commissar of Nanchang District in early 1927. In August 1927 Zhu played an important role in the Nanchang Uprising organized by Zhou Enlai. After its failure Zhu went with 900 soldiers to Fujian Province and reorganized his forces into the 9th Revolutionary Army. Constantly harassed by KMT troops, his unit was forced to cross large parts of Jiangxi Province. At this point Zhu De was asked by his fellow student and sworn brother, Fan Shisheng, who commanded the 16th KMT Army in Sichuan, to join his forces. Zhu did so on the advice of his political commissar, the later minister of foreign affairs Chen Yi. Having arrived in Sichuan, a change in the political situation forced him to move on to South Hunan. There he was called upon by Mao Zedong to move his troops to Jinggangshan where Mao had organized a strong Communist base. Zhu De arrived in 1928, significantly adding to the base's military strengh. The combined forces were reorganized into the 4th Army with Zhu as commander and Mao Zedong as political commissar. During the following years until the beginning of the Long March Zhu De on many occasions proved his strategic abilities in the war against the KMT forces (in 1929 his third wife, Wu Youlan, was arrested and executed by the government). Still in the same year he married Kang Keqing.

In 1930 Zhu was elected to his first term on the CCP Central Committee as well as chairman of its Military Council. During the Long March Zhu De showed outstanding strategic ability and unfailing energy. In the inner-Party struggles going on during the Long March, Zhu De completely committed himself to Mao Zedong. After the Communist forces and the KMT had formed a joint front against the Japanese in 1937, Zhu De was made commander-in-chief of the 8th Route Army, the former 4th Communist Army. In 1939 Zhu De took part as observer together with Zhou Enlai at the session of the Supreme Soviet in Moscow. The events during the following years until the Japanese capitulation and eventually the expulsion of the KMT from the mainland were to a large extent determined by the military achievements of Zhu De as commander-in-chief of the PLA.

1949,	Oct	Appointed vice-chairman of the Central People's Government Council
1954,	Aug	Elected deputy for Sichuan Province to the 1st NPC
	Sep	Elected vice-president of the PRC (until Mar 1959); appointed vice-chairman of the National Defense Council (until Mar 1959)

Winter		The post of PLA commander-in-chief is abolished; since then Zhu De holds no military posts	1956,	Sep	Elected member of the Standing Committee of the Politburo by the 8th CCP Congress
1955,	Aug	Head of a government delegation to North Korea	1959,	Mar	Head of a CCP delegation to Poland
	Dec	Head of a Chinese delegation to the German Democratic Republic on the 80th birthday of Wilhelm Pieck. Stopovers in Czechoslovakia, Hungary, Romania, Poland, USSR, and Outer Mongolia		May	Elected chairman of the Standing Committee of the 3rd NPC (reelected in 1975 to the 4th NPC)

Zhu De died on 6 July 1976.

Appendix
The organization of the People's Republic of China

Note to the Appendix

In addition to the abbreviations listed on page xii, the following abbreviations occur in the Appendix:
CC   Central Committee
CCm   Member of the Central Committee
CCa   Alternate member of the Central Committee
PBm   Member of the Politburo
PBa   Alternate member of the Politburo.

Numbers following a name indicate the year and month when the cadre was appointed or elected to the post or first identified as holding it.

I. BACKGROUND TABLES

**The Members and Alternate Members of the
7th - 11th CCP Central Committees**

The 7th CC was elected in 1945, four years before the foundation of the People's Republic of China. Comprised almost exclusively of proven military and political officers of the revolutionary period, it determined the course of the People's Republic during its first years. The 8th CC in 1956 had not only a significantly larger number of members and alternate members, again increased in a by-election during the 2nd plenum in 1958, but also a new composition. The previous military preponderance gave way to a new class of Party cadres modeled after the Soviet Russian example. This bureaucratization of a party previously sustained by revolutionary spirit was one of the causes of the Cultural Revolution beginning in 1966, which consequently first turned against these Party cadres. Thus the 9th CC was again dominated by the military with the support of the Red Guards who emerged during the Cultural Revolution. The purge of Lin Biao in 1971 automatically reduced the military influence in the 9th CC. However, the 10th CC elected in 1973 was by no means a "purged guard" of Cultural Revolutionary cadres. By then a process of rehabilitating the cadres purged during the Cultural Revolution had begun. The membership of the 10th CC was deeply divided into two factions. Along with the main activists of the Cultural Revolution, their supporters were largely removed from power one month after the death of Mao Zedong. As a result, the 11th CC elected in 1977 contains only a remnant of cadres whose influence derives entirely from the Cultural Revolution. In addition, further cadres purged during that period were restored to their former positions. All members by-elected by the 11th CC 4th Plenum in September 1979 are cadres who held high positions before the Cultural Revolution.

The table of the 7th — 11th CC lists 651 cadres of whom 66 are, or were, concurrently cadres of the Politburo. The CC is responsible for the implementation and supervision of the policies determined by the Politburo. In other words, during the 30 years since the foundation of PR China, 651 cadres have sufficed to govern a population now grown to almost a billion.

The Members and Alternate Members of the 7th - 11th CCP Central Committees

No.	Name	7th CC 1945 PB-M	PB-A	CC-M	CC-A	8th CC 1956 PB-M	PB-A	CC-M	CC-A	9th CC 1969 PB-M	PB-A	CC-M	CC-A	10th CC 1973 PB-M	PB-A	CC-M	CC-A	11th CC 1977 PB-M	PB-A	CC-M	CC-A	POST HELD ON JANUARY 1, 1980 / REMARKS
1	An Pingsheng															X				X		First secretary, Yunnan CP
2	An Ziwen							X												X		Vice-chairman, Legal Commission, 5th NPC
3	Bai Dongcai																			X		Secretary, Jiangxi CP
4	Bai Rubing															X				X		First secretary, Shandong CP
5	Bao-ri-luo-tai f.											X				X				X		Secretary, Nei Monggol CP
6	Basang f											X				X				X		Secretary, Tibet CP
7	Bo Yibo			X		X		X														Vice-premier
8	Bu Guxiang																X				X	Worker in Hunan
9	Cai Chang f			X				X				X				X						Honorary president, Women's Federation
10	Cai Fenglan f																				X	Vice-chairman, Qinghai People's Congress
11	Cai Shufan							X														Died October 17, 1958
12	Cai Shumei f											X				X						Disappeared May 1977
13	Cai Xiao															X				X		Deputy secretary-general, 5th CPPCC
14	Cai Xiebin											X				X						Disappeared December 1976
15	Cao Lihuai											X								X		Deputy commander, PLA Air Force
16	Cao Siming																			X		Deputy political commissar, PLA Logistics Department
17	Cao Yiou f											X				X						Disappeared March 1978
18	Cen Guorong												X			X				X		Chairman, Guangxi Trade Unions
19	Chen Aie f																				X	Textile worker in Hubei
20	Chen Boda				X			X		X												Purged in 1970
21	Chen Daifu																X					Disappeared September 1976
22	Chen Fuhan																				X	Vice-chairman, Railway Workers' Trade Union
23	Chen Ganfeng												X									Disappeared June 1971
24	Chen Gang												X			X						Disappeared May 1977
25	Chen Geng				X			X														Died March 16, 1961
26	Chen Guodong																				X	Minister of food
27	Chen Hefa											X				X						Disappeared October 1975
28	Chen Huatang												X									Disappeared May 1973
29	Chen Jiazhong																X					Disappeared October 1976
30	Chen Liyun											X										Disappeared January 1970
31	Chen Manyuan								X													Military cadre in Beijing
32	Chen Muhua f															X			X	X		Minister, Min. of Economic Relations w. Foreign Countries
33	Chen Peizhen f																X					Disappeared April 1976
34	Chen Pixian							X												X		First secretary Hubei CP
35	Chen Puru																			X		Secretary, Liaoning CP
36	Chen Qihan							X				X				X				X		Disappeared August 1978
37	Chen Renfu																				X	Worker-engineer in Shanghai
38	Chen Renqi											X										Disappeared March 1972
39	Chen Shaomin f				X				X													Died December 14, 1977
40	Chen Shaoyu			X				X														Died March 25, 1974
41	Chen Shiqu											X				X						Disappeared January 1976
42	Chen Tanqiu			X																		Died September 23, 1943
43	Chen Weida																			X		First secretary Tianjin CP
44	Chen Xianrui											X				X				X		Political commissar, Chengdu Military Region
45	Chen Xilian									X		X		X		X		X		X		Commander, Beijing Military Region
46	Chen Yi			X		X		X		X		X										Died January 6, 1972
47	Chen Yonggui											X		X		X		X		X		Vice-premier
48	Chen Yonglin																			X		Disappeared May 1979
49	Chen Yu				X			X				X				X						Died March 21, 1974
50	Chen Yubao															X					X	Cadre, Fujian Province
51	Chen Yun	X		X		X		X				X				X		X		X		Vice-premier
52	Chen Zaidao							X												X		Commander, PLA Railway Corps
53	Chen Zhengren								X													Died April 6, 1972
54	Chen Zuolin																			X		Secretary, Zhejiang CP
55	Cheng Shiqing											X										Disappeared February 1972
56	Cheng Yitai																			X		Vice-chairman, Liaoning Revolutionary Committee
57	Cheng Zihua				X			X												X		Minister of civil affairs
58	Chi Biqing																			X		2nd secretary Guizhou CP
59	Chu Jiang																			X		Secretary Jiangsu CP
60	Cui Hailong											X				X						Disappeared May 1977

Column key: Each Central Committee (CC) is divided into Politburo (**P B**) and Central Committee (**C C**) sections, each with **Member** (M) and **Alternate Member** (A) sub-columns.

#	Name	7 PB M	7 PB A	7 CC M	7 CC A	8 PB M	8 PB A	8 CC M	8 CC A	9 PB M	9 PB A	9 CC M	9 CC A	10 PB M	10 PB A	10 CC M	10 CC A	11 PB M	11 PB A	11 CC M	11 CC A	POST HELD ON JANUARY 1, 1980 / REMARKS
61	Cui Xiufan											X				X						Disappeared September 1976
62	Da Le											X				X						Disappeared October 1976
63	Dai Guangqian																				X	Worker in Guangdong
64	Dai Suli																				X	Vice-governor, Henan Province
65	Deng Haiqing											X										Disappeared October 1977
66	Deng Hua							X				X										?
67	Deng Xiaoping			X		X		X						X		X		X		X		Vice-premier
68	Deng Yingchao (f)							X				X				X		X		X		Vice-chairman, 5th NPC
69	Deng Zihui			X				X				X										Died December 10, 1972
70	Ding Changhua (f)																				X	Peasant in Jiangxi
71	Ding Guoyu															X				X		Chairman, Beijing CPPCC
72	Ding Keze															X				X		Chairman, Jiangsu Trade Unions
73	Ding Sheng											X				X						Disappeared October 1976
74	Dong Biwu	X		X		X		X		X		X		X								Died April 2, 1975
75	Dong Minghui											X										Disappeared September 1976
76	Du Ping																				X	Political commissar, Nanjing Military Region
77	Du Xueran																				X	Henan miner
78	Du Yide																				X	Commander, Lanzhou Military Region
79	Duan Junyi											X				X						First secretary, Henan CP
80	Fan Deling								X			X				X						Member, Standing Committee, 5th NPC
81	Fan Wenlan							X				X										Died July 29, 1969
82	Fan Xiaoju (f)											X					X					Disappeared September 1976
83	Fang Ming											X										Disappeared August 1974
84	Fang Yi								X							X		X		X		Vice-premier
85	Feng Baiju							X														Died July 19, 1973
86	Feng Pinde																X				X	Disappeared October 1977
87	Feng Xuan												X				X					Deputy director, Internat. Liaison Dept., CCP CC
88	Feng Zhanwu											X				X						Disappeared September 1977
89	Fu Chuanzuo											X				X						Disappeared September 1976
90	Gan Siqi							X														Died February 5, 1964
91	Gao Gang	X		X																		Died 1954 after purge
92	Gao Houliang																				X	Political commissar, PLA Air Force
93	Gao Kelin							X														Vice-chairman, Legal Commission, 5th NPC
94	Gao Shulan (f)																X					Disappeared October 1977
95	Gao Weisong											X										Disappeared October 1976
76	Geng Biao											X				X		X		X		Vice-premier
97	Geng Qichang											X				X						Disappeared August 1977
98	Gu Dacun				X			X														Died November 4, 1966
99	Gu Mu															X						Vice-premier
100	Gu Xiulian (f)																				X	Vice-minister, Planning Commission
101	Guan Xiangying			X																		Died July 21, 1946
102	Guan Zehai																				X	Cadre in Yunnan
103	Guang Rennong											X										Disappeared August 1978
104	Guo Fenglian (f)																				X	Chairman, Dazhai Production Brigade
105	Guo Hongjie											X				X						Disappeared June 1977
106	Guo Moruo											X								X		Died June 12, 1978
107	Guo Yaoqing																X				X	Secretary, Nanning CP
108	Guo Yufeng											X				X					X	Disappeared October 1977
109	Han Guang								X								X					Vice-minister, Capital Construction Commission
110	Han Xianchu								X			X				X				X		Commander, Lanzhou Military Region
111	Han Ying											X				X						First secretary, Communist Youth League
112	Hao Jianxiu (f)																			X		Vice-president, Women's Federation
113	He Cheng																				X	Deputy director, PLA General Logistics Department
114	He Jinnian																				X	Deputy commander, PLA Armored Forces
115	He Long			X		X		X														Died June 9, 1969
116	Hong Xuezhi								X													Director, 2nd Office of National Defense
117	Hu Jindi (f)																X				X	Disappeared December 1978
118	Hu Jizong											X				X						Died July 4, 1974
119	Hu Lijiao																				X	Second secretary, Henan CP
120	Hu Qiaomu								X											X		President, Academy of Social Sciences

No.	Name	7th PB M	7th PB AM	7th CC M	7th CC AM	8th PB M	8th PB AM	8th CC M	8th CC AM	9th PB M	9th PB AM	9th CC M	9th CC AM	10th PB M	10th PB AM	10th CC M	10th CC AM	11th PB M	11th PB AM	11th CC M	11th CC AM	POST HELD ON JANUARY 1, 1980 / REMARKS
121	Hu Song																				X	Peasant on Hainan Island
122	Hu Wei											X				X						Disappeared December 1976
123	Hu Yaobang								X									X		X		Director, Propaganda Department, CCP Central Committee
124	Hua Guofeng											X		X		X		X		X		Chairman, CCP
125	Hua Linsen											X				X						Purged September 1976
126	Huang Bingxiu f.											X				X						Disappeared September 1977
127	Huang Chenglian											X										Disappeared September 1976
128	Huang Hua															X				X		Minister of foreign affairs
129	Huang Huoqing								X											X		Chief Procurator, Supreme People's Procuratorate
130	Huang Jing							X														Died February 10, 1958
131	Huang Kecheng			X				X												X		Permanent secr., CCP Committee for Inspecting Discipline
132	Huang Oudong								X													Second secretary, Liaoning CP
133	Huang Ronghai											X				X					X	Deputy commander, Guangzhou Military Region
134	Huang Wenming											X				X						Disappeared May 1977
135	Huang Xinting																				X	Commander, PLA Armored Forces
136	Huang Yongsheng								X	X		X										Disappeared June 1971
137	Huang Zhen											X				X				X		Minister of culture
138	Huang Zhiyong											X										Disappeared March 1972
139	Huang Zhizhen															X				X		Secretary, Hubei CP
140	Huang Zuozhen											X				X						Disappeared February 1979
141	Huo Shilian																				X	Minister of agriculture
142	Ismail Amat																X			X		Chairman, Xinjiang People's Government
143	Janabil																X				X	Vice-chairman, Xinjiang People's Government
144	Ji Dengkui											X		X		X		X		X		Vice-premier
145	Ji Guixin																				X	?
146	Ji Pengfei															X				X		Vice-premier
147	Ji Yinglin																			X		?
148	Jia Tofu							X														Died May 7, 1967
149	Jiang Baodi f.											X				X				X		?
150	Jiang Hua								X							X				X		President, Supreme People's Court
151	Jiang Liyin											X				X				X		Disappeared April 1978
152	Jiang Nanxiang								X											X		Minister of education
153	Jiang Qing f.									X		X		X		X						Purged October 1976
154	Jiang Weiqing								X							X				X		First secretary, Jiangxi CP
155	Jiang Xieyuan											X				X					X	Deputy commander, Guangzhou Military Region
156	Jiang Yonghui											X				X					X	Deputy commander, Shenyang Military Region
157	Jin Minghan																				X	Member, Standing Committee, Jilin CP
158	Jin Zumin											X				X						Disappeared January 1976
159	Kang Jianmin											X										Died January 18, 1977
160	Kang Keqing f.																			X		Vice-president, Women's Federation
161	Kang Lin											X				X				X		Deputy commander, Beijing Military Region
162	Kang Sheng	X		X			X	X		X		X		X		X						Died December 16, 1975
163	Kang Shien																				X	Vice-premier
164	Ke Qingshi					X		X														Died April 9, 1965
165	Kong Shiquan											X				X				X		Disappeared January 1979
166	Kong Yuan								X											X		Deputy secretary-general, 5th NPC
167	Kong Zhaonian															X				X		Deputy commander, PLA Navy
168	Kuibi								X													Chairman, Nei Monggol CPPCC
169	Lai Jifa											X										Disappeared March 1978
170	Lai Ruoyu							X														Died May 20, 1958
171	Lan Rongyu												X									Disappeared January 1978
172	Lan Yinong												X									Disappeared May 1971
173	Li Baohua				X			X												X		President, People's Bank
174	Li Chang								X											X		Vice-president, Academy of Sciences
175	Li Chang'an																				X	?
176	Li Chengfang																				X	First political commissar, Wuhan Military Region
177	Li Da															X				X		Deputy chief of staff, PLA
178	Li Dazhang							X				X				X						Died May 3, 1976
179	Li Desheng										X	X		X		X		X		X		Commander, Shenyang Military Region
180	Li Dingshan											X				X						Disappeared May 1977

#	Name	7 PB M	7 PB A	7 CC M	7 CC A	8 PB M	8 PB A	8 CC M	8 CC A	9 PB M	9 PB A	9 CC M	9 CC A	10 PB M	10 PB A	10 CC M	10 CC A	11 PB M	11 PB A	11 CC M	11 CC A	POST HELD ON JANUARY 1, 1980 / REMARKS
181	Li Fuchun			X		X		X				X				X						Died January 9, 1975
182	Li Huamin											X				X					X	Deputy commander, Shenyang Military Region
183	Li Jianzhen f								X												X	Secretary, Guangdong CP
184	Li Jiebo								X													Disappeared April 1978
185	Li Jiliang																				X	Cadre, Maoming oilfield
186	Li Jingquan					X		X								X				X		Vice-chairman, 5th NPC
187	Li Kenong							X														Died February 9, 1962
188	Li Li											X										Member, Standing Committee, 5th CPPCC
189	Li Lisan			X																		Died June 22, 1967
190	Li Qiang											X				X				X		Minister of foreign trade
191	Li Qiaoyun f																			X		Disappeared March 1979
192	Li Qiming																			X		Secretary, Yunnan CP
193	Li Renzhi																X					First secretary, Wuhan CP
194	Li Rinai																X				X	Disappeared Dec 1978
195	Li Ruishan											X				X					X	Vice-minister, Agricultural Commission
196	Li Shijun																				X	Cadre, Shaanxi Province
197	Li Shoulin												X			X				X		Disappeared August 1977
198	Li Shuiqing											X				X				X		Vice-minister of communications
199	Li Shumao											X										Disappeared March 1977
200	Li Shunda											X				X						Disappeared February 1977
201	Li Siguang											X										Died April 29, 1971
202	Li Suwen f											X				X						Disappeared May 1977
203	Li Tao								X													Disappeared October 1967
204	Li Tianyu											X										Died September 27, 1970
205	Li Weihan							X														Vice-chairman, 5th CPPCC
206	Li Yaosong												X			X						Disappeared September 1976
207	Li Yaowen																				X	Political commissar, National Defense Commission
208	Li Yu				X																	Disappeared 1959
209	Li Yuan											X				X					X	Deputy director, PLA Capital Construction Engin. Corps
210	Li Xiannian			X		X		X		X		X		X		X		X		X		Vice-premier
211	Li Xuefeng							X			X											Disappeared 1970
212	Li Xuezhi																				X	First secretary, Ningxia CP
213	Li Zaihan											X										Disappeared July 1969
214	Li Zhen											X				X						Disappeared October 1977
215	Li Zhimin								X							X					X	Political commissar, Fuzhou Military Region
216	Li Ziyuan																				X	Secretary, Sichuan CP
217	Li Zuopeng									X		X										Disappeared September 1971
218	Li Zugen																X				X	Vice-chairman, Jiangxi Trade Unions
219	Liang Biye																				X	Deputy director, PLA General Political Department
220	Liang Jintang												X			X						Disappeared January 1977
221	Liang Xingchu											X										Disappeared October 1971
222	Liao Chengzhi				X			X								X					X	Vice-chairman, 5th NPC
223	Liao Hansheng								X												X	First political commissar, Nanjing Military Region
224	Liao Luyan							X														Died between 1969 and 1972
225	Liao Zhigao								X								X				X	First secretary, Fujian CP
226	Lin Biao			X		X		X		X		X										Disappeared September 1971
227	Lin Boqu			X				X														Died May 29, 1960
228	Lin Feng				X			X														Died September 29, 1977
229	Lin Hujia																				X	First secretary, Beijing CP
230	Lin Liming															X						Died August 19, 1977
231	Lin Liyun f															X					X	Vice-president, Women's Federation
232	Lin Tie							X														Member, Standing Committee, 5th NPC
233	Liu Bocheng			X		X		X		X		X		X		X		X		X		Vice-chairman, 5th NPC
234	Liu Changsheng								X													Died January 28, 1967
235	Liu Chonggui																				X	2nd secretary, Guangxi CP
236	Liu Chunqiao															X						Vice-chairman, Hunan People's Congress
237	Liu Daosheng																				X	First deputy commander, PLA Navy
238	Liu Feng											X										Disappeared July 1971
239	Liu Geping								X			X										Disappeared May 1969
240	Liu Guangtao															X				X		Disappeared December 1977

#	Name	7PB M	7PB A	7CC M	7CC A	8PB M	8PB A	8CC M	8CC A	9PB M	9PB A	9CC M	9CC A	10PB M	10PB A	10CC M	10CC A	11PB M	11PB A	11CC M	11CC A	Post held on January 1, 1980 / Remarks
241	Liu Haotian												X									Disappeared April 1971
242	Liu Jianxun								X			X				X				X		Disappeared April 1978
243	Liu Jieting											X										Disappeared May 1970
244	Liu Junyi											X				X						Disappeared October 1976
245	Liu Lanbo								X												X	Minister of power industry
246	Liu Lantao			X				X													X	Vice-chairman, 5th CPPCC
247	Liu Minghui																				X	Secretary, Yunnan CP
248	Liu Ningyi								X													Deputy secretary-general, 5th CPPCC
249	Liu Ren								X													Died October 26, 1973
250	Liu Ruiqing																				X	Miner in Guangdong
251	Liu Shaoqi	X		X		X		X														Died November 12, 1969
252	Liu Shengtian											X				X						Disappeared February 1977
253	Liu Wei												X			X						Minister, 2nd Ministry of Machine Building
254	Liu Weiming												X				X					Secretary, Communist Youth League
255	Liu Xiangping f																X					Disappeared October 1976
256	Liu Xianquan											X				X						Disappeared September 1976
257	Liu Xiao				X				X													Member, Standing Committee, 5th CPPCC
258	Liu Xichang											X				X					X	Disappeared December 1978
259	Liu Xingyuan											X				X					X	Disappeared August 1977
260	Liu Xiyao												X			X					X	Vice-governor, Sichuan Province
261	Liu Yalou								X													Died May 7, 1965
262	Liu Zhen								X												X	Disappeared February 1979
263	Liu Zhenhua											X				X					X	Vice-minister of foreign affairs
264	Liu Zhijian											X										First political commissar, Kunming Military Region
265	Liu Zhiqiang																X					Model worker in Hunan Province
266	Liu Zihou								X			X				X				X		First secretary, Hebei CP
267	Liu Zijiu				X																	Reactivated December 1978
268	Long Guangqian											X				X						Disappeared October 1977
269	Long Shujin											X										Disappeared February 1972
270	Lu Dadong															X					X	Governor, Sichuan Province
271	Lu Dingyi			X			X	X														Vice-chairman, 5th CPPCC
272	Lu Jinlong															X					X	Disappeared December 1977
273	Lu Ruilin											X				X					X	Disappeared February 1978
274	Lu Tianji											X				X					X	Disappeared December 1978
275	Lu Zhongyang											X					X				X	Disappeared December 1978
276	Luo Chundi f												X				X				X	Disappeared February 1978
277	Luo Guibo							X														Second secretary, Shanxi CP
278	Luo Qingchang															X					X	Deputy secretary-general, 5th NPC
279	Luo Ronghuan			X		X		X														Died December 16, 1963
280	Luo Ruiqing				X			X													X	Died August 3, 1978
281	Luo Xikang												X			X						Disappeared June 1977
282	Luo Yuanfa												X				X					Disappeared May 1978
283	Lü Cunjie f												X				X				X	Disappeared December 1978
284	Lü He																X				X	Disappeared December 1978
285	Lü Xuguo																				X	?
286	Lü Yulan f											X				X					X	Secretary, Hebei CP
287	Lü Zhengcao			X				X													X	Political commissar, PLA Railway Corps
288	Ma Fuquan											X										Disappeared April 1976
289	Ma Hui																				X	Commander, Hebei Military District
290	Ma Jinhua f																X				X	Peasant in Ningxia Province
291	Ma Li																				X	Died September 25, 1979
292	Ma Lixin																X					Disappeared September 1976
293	Ma Ming																				X	Disappeared December 1978
294	Ma Mingfang			X				X														Died August 13, 1974
295	Ma Ning															X						Disappeared September 1976
296	Ma Sizhong																				X	Vice-chairman, Ningxia Revolutionary Committee
297	Ma Tianshui											X				X						Purged October 1976
298	Ma Wenrui								X												X	First secretary, Shaanxi Province CP
299	Ma Xiaoliu																X					Disappeared May 1977
300	Ma Xingyuan																			X		Secretary, Fujian Province CP

Column key — each congress is divided into Politburo (PB) and Central Committee (CC), and each of those into Member (M) and Alternate Member (A):

No.	Name	7PB M	7PB A	7CC M	7CC A	8PB M	8PB A	8CC M	8CC A	9PB M	9PB A	9CC M	9CC A	10PB M	10PB A	10CC M	10CC A	11PB M	11PB A	11CC M	11CC A	POST HELD ON JANUARY 1, 1980 / REMARKS
301	Mao Xinxian f																				X	Shanghai textile worker
302	Mao Zedong	X		X		X		X		X		X		X		X						Died September 9, 1976
303	Mao Zhiyong																			X		First secretary, Hunan CP
304	Mei Songlin												X									Member of "Hard-Bones" 6th Company
305	Mo Xianyao											X				X						Disappeared March 1977
306	Nan Ping											X										Disappeared January 1972
307	Ni Zhifu												X			X			X	X		President, Federation of Trade Unions
308	Nian Jirong															X						Disappeared May 1977
309	Nie Fengzhi																			X		Commander, Nanjing Military Region
310	Nie Rongzhen			X		X		X		X		X		X				X				Vice-chairman, Standing Committee, 5th NPC
311	Nie Yuanzu f											X										Disappeared October 1970
312	Ou Mengjue f								X													Vice-chairman, Guangdong People's Congress
313	Ouyang Qin								X													Died May 15, 1978
314	Pan Fusheng								X			X										Disappeared December 1970
315	Pan Meiying f															X						Disappeared August 1977
316	Pan Shigao											X				X						Disappeared September 1976
317	Pan Shixing																				X	Peasant in Guangxi
318	Pan Zili								X													Died May 22, 1972
319	Pei Zhouyu												X			X						Disappeared December 1977
320	Peng Chong											X		X		X		X				First secretary, Shanghai CP
321	Peng Dehuai	X		X		X		X														Died November 29, 1974
322	Peng Guihe											X				X						Disappeared January 1977
323	Peng Shaohui											X				X						Died April 25, 1978
324	Peng Tao								X													Died November 14, 1961
325	Peng Zhen	X		X		X		X										X		X		Chairman, Legal Commission, 5th NPC
326	Pi Dingjun											X				X						Died July 7, 1976
327	Qian Junrui								X													Director, Inst.of World Economics, Acad.of Social Sciences
328	Qian Xuesen											X				X				X		Vice-chairman, Science and Technol.Comm.f.Nat.Defense
329	Qian Ying f								X													Disappeared November 1966
330	Qian Zhengying f															X				X		Minister of water conservancy
331	Qian Zhiguang											X				X						Minister of textile industry
332	Qiao Guanhua											X				X						Disappeared November 1976
333	Qiao Linyi																			X		First secretary, Guangzhou CP
334	Qiao Xiaoguang											X				X				X		First secretary, Guangxi CP
335	Qilin Wandan												X							X		Disappeared December 1977
336	Qin Jiwei												X							X		Commander, Beijing Military Region
337	Qin Bangxian			X																		Died April 8, 1946
338	Qin Yingji																			X		Secretary, Guangxi CP
339	Qiu Chuangcheng											X										Disappeared May 1973
340	Qiu Guoguang												X									Disappeared August 1978
341	Qiu Huizo								X			X										Disappeared May 1971
342	Raidi																				X	Secretary, Tibet CP
343	Ran Guiying f																				X	Peasant in Gansu
344	Rao Shushi			X																		Purged 1954
345	Rao Xingli												X			X				X		Member, Standing Committee, Hubei CP
346	Ren Bishi	X																				Died October 27, 1950
347	Ren Rong														X					X		First secretary, Tibet CP
348	Ren Sizhong											X				X						Deputy political commissar, Jinan Military Region
349	Ren Zhibin																				X	Secretary-general, Anhui CP
350	Ren Zhongyi																			X		First secretary, Liaoning CP
351	Rigdzin Wanggyal												X							X		Disappeared December 1978
352	Ruan Bosheng												X				X			X		Chairman, Shanxi People's Congress
353	Ruzi Turdi												X									Disappeared August 1977
354	Seypidin							X				X		X		X		X		X		Vice-chairman, 5th NPC
355	Shao Shiping							X														Died March 24, 1965
356	She Jide															X						Military cadre, Fuzhou Military Region
357	Shen Chuyun f																				X	Hangzhou textile worker
358	Shen Maogong											X									X	Disappeared December 1978
359	Shi Shaohua												X			X						Disappeared October 1977
360	Shu Jicheng											X				X						Disappeared May 1973

Column key: For each Central Committee — PB = Politburo (Member / Alternate Member), CC = Central Committee (Member / Alternate Member).

No.	Name	7th CC 1945 PB M	PB Alt	CC M	CC Alt	8th CC 1956 PB M	PB Alt	CC M	CC Alt	9th CC 1969 PB M	PB Alt	CC M	CC Alt	10th CC 1973 PB M	PB Alt	CC M	CC Alt	11th CC 1977 PB M	PB Alt	CC M	CC Alt	Post held on January 1, 1980 / Remarks
361	Shu Tong			X																		Member, Standing Committee, 5th CPPCC
362	Shuai Mengqi f							X														Member, Standing Committee, 5th CPPCC
363	Song Peizhang															X						Disappeared June 1977
364	Song Ping																			X		First secretary, Gansu CP
365	Song Qingyou															X				X		Disappeared December 1978
366	Song Renqiong			X		X		X												X		Director, Organization Department, CCP Central Committee
367	Song Shilun											X				X				X		President, PLA Academy of Military Science
368	Song Shuanglai												X			X						Disappeared October 1976
369	Su Jing											X				X				X		Vice-minister, State Planning Commission
370	Su Yiran																			X		Secretary, Shandong CP
371	Su Yu			X				X				X				X						Vice-minister of national defence
372	Su Zhenhua							X						X				X				Died February 7, 1979
373	Sun Jian											X										Disappeared June 1977
374	Sun Xuemei f																			X		?
375	Sun Yuguo															X						Disappeared January 1977
376	Sun Zhiyuan							X														Died October 11, 1966
377	Tan Furen											X										Died December 18, 1970
378	Tan Qilong							X				X				X						2nd secretary, Sichuan CP
379	Tan Shanhe																			X		Commander, PLA Engineering Corps
380	Tan Wenzhen f												X									Cadre in Hunan
381	Tan Zhenlin				X	X		X						X						X		Vice-chairman, 5th NPC
382	Tan Zheng			X			X	X														Vice-chairman, Legal Commission, 5th NPC
383	Tang Ke																			X		Minister of metallurgical industry
384	Tang Kebi f															X				X		Member, Standing Committee, Sichuan CP
385	Tang Liang								X				X							X		Central military cadre
386	Tang Qishan											X				X						Disappeared September 1976
387	Tang Wensheng f																			X		Disappeared February 1979
388	Tang Zhongfu											X				X						Disappeared September 1976
389	Tao Lujia								X							X						Disappeared September 1976
390	Tao Zhu					X		X														Died November 30, 1969
391	Teng Daiyuan			X								X				X						Died December 1, 1974
392	Tian Bao								X			X				X				X		Secretary, Tibet CP
393	Tian Huagui											X				X						Disappeared November 1977
394	Tian Weixin															X						Disappeared December 1976
395	Tie Ying															X				X		First secretary, Zhejiang CP
396	Ulanhu			X		X		X						X						X		Dir., United Front Work Dept, CCP Central Committee
397	Wan Da																			X		Second secretary, Hunan CP
398	Wan Li																			X		First secretary, Anhui CP
399	Wan Yi				X				X													Member, Standing Committee, 5th CPPCC
400	Wang Baidan											X										Disappeared December 1969
401	Wang Baide																X					Disappeared September 1976
402	Wang Bicheng															X				X		Commander, Wuhan Military Region
403	Wang Bingzhang											X										Disappeared May 1971
404	Wang Chaozhu											X				X				X		?
405	Wang Congwu				X			X														Member, Standing Committee, 5th CPPCC
406	Wang Deshan																X					Disappeared September 1976
407	Wang Dongxing										X	X		X				X				First vice-president, Party School, CCP Central Committee
408	Wang Enmao							X				X								X		First secretary, Jilin CP
409	Wang Feng							X												X		First secretary, Xinjiang CP
410	Wang Fuzhi																				X	Commander, Shanxi Military District
411	Wang Guanglin												X			X						Disappeared September 1976
412	Wang Guangyu																			X		Secretary, Anhui CP
413	Wang Guofan												X			X						Disappeared August 1977
414	Wang Heshou							X												X		Deputy secretary, Comm. for Inspecting Discipline, CCP CC
415	Wang Hongkun											X				X						Disappeared May 1977
416	Wang Hongwen											X		X								Purged October 1976
417	Wang Huaixiang											X				X						Disappeared November 1977
418	Wang Huiqiu											X				X						Disappeared November 1978
419	Wang Jiadao											X				X						Disappeared September 1977
420	Wang Jiaxiang			X				X								X						Died January 25, 1974

#	Name		7th CC 1945 PB Member	7th PB Alt Member	7th CC Member	7th CC Alt Member	8th CC 1956 PB Member	8th PB Alt Member	8th CC Member	8th CC Alt Member	9th CC 1969 PB Member	9th PB Alt Member	9th CC Member	9th CC Alt Member	10th CC 1973 PB Member	10th PB Alt Member	10th CC Member	10th CC Alt Member	11th CC 1977 PB Member	11th PB Alt Member	11th CC Member	11th CC Alt Member	POST HELD ON JANUARY 1, 1980 / REMARKS
421	Wang Jingsheng																	X					Disappeared October 1975
422	Wang Jinling	f																				X	?
423	Wang Jinshan																					X	Secretary, Hebei CP
424	Wang Jinxi													X									Died November 15, 1970
425	Wang Jinyou																					X	Member, Standing Committee, Zhejiang CP
426	Wang Junshao																					X	Anshan worker
427	Wang Linhe																				X		Disappeared April 1978
428	Wang Liusheng												X					X					Disappeared February 1979
429	Wang Maoquan																				X		Disappeared December 1978
430	Wang Meiji	f																X					Disappeared September 1976
431	Wang Meng																				X		Minister, Physical Culture and Sports Commission
432	Wang Minzhang																				X		Secretary, Shanghai Communist Youth League
433	Wang Ping																				X		Political commissar, PLA Logistics Department
434	Wang Qian																	X			X		First secretary, Shanxi CP
435	Wang Renzhong								X														Minister, State Agricultural Commission
436	Wang Ruofei				X																		Died April 8, 1946
437	Wang Shangrong								X												X		Deputy chief of staff, PLA
438	Wang Shitai																					X	Chairman, Gansu People's Congress
439	Wang Shoudao				X				X				X				X				X		Vice-chairman, Legal Commission, 5th NPC
440	Wang Shusheng								X				X				X						Died January 7, 1974
441	Wang Shuzhen	f																X					Disappeared December 1977
442	Wang Ti												X										Disappeared October 1976
443	Wang Weiguo												X										Disappeared February 1971
444	Wang Weizhou				X				X														Died January 10, 1970
445	Wang Xiangjun	f																X					Disappeared October 1976
446	Wang Xiaoyu												X										Disappeared October 1969
447	Wang Xin													X									Disappeared May 1973
448	Wang Xinting												X										Disappeared December 1978
449	Wang Xiuxiu	f																X					Disappeared October 1977
450	Wang Xiuzhen	f											X				X						Disappeared October 1976
451	Wang Yiping																				X		Secretary, Shanghai CP
452	Wang Zhen				X				X				X		X		X				X		Vice-premier
453	Wang Zheng								X														Died August 13, 1978
454	Wang Zhiqiang												X										Disappeared January 1977
455	Wei Bingkui												X										Disappeared January 1977
456	Wei Fengying	f											X				X				X		Disappeared July 1978
457	Wei Guoqing								X				X		X		X		X				Director, PLA General Political Department
458	Wei Xingzheng																				X		Worker in Heilongjiang
459	Wei Zuzhen													X									Disappeared February 1973
460	Wen Xianglan	f																X				X	Member, Standing Committee, Henan CP
461	Wen Yucheng												X										Disappeared June 1970
462	Wu Chunren												X										Cadre, Fuzhou Military Region
463	Wu Congshu																X						Disappeared May 1977
464	Wu Dasheng												X				X						Disappeared October 1976
465	Wu De								X				X		X				X				Vice-chairman, 5th NPC
466	Wu Faxian										X												Disappeared August 1971
467	Wu Guixian	f											X			X	X				X		Disappeared September 1977
468	Wu Huojin																					X	Peasant in Jiangsu
469	Wu Jinquan													X				X					Cadre in Sichuan
470	Wu Kehua																				X		Commander, Xinjiang Military Region
471	Wu Lengxi																				X		Member, Standing Committee, 5th NPC
472	Wu Quanqing																					X	Chairman, Daqing Oilfield Revolutionary Committee
473	Wu Ruilin												X										Disappeared April 1972
474	Wu Tao												X				X						Disappeared September 1977
475	Wu Xiangbi																	X			X		Secretary, Guizhou CP
476	Wu Xiuquan								X												X		Deputy chief of staff, PLA
477	Wu Yude																X						Disappeared February 1977
478	Wu Yuzhang				X				X														Died December 12, 1966
479	Wu Zhifu								X								X						Died (date unknown)
480	Wu Zhong													X				X				X	Deputy commander, Guangzhou Military Region

Legend: Each congress block is divided into P B (Politburo) and C C (Central Committee); each is divided into Member (M) and Alternate Member (A).

No.	Name	7 PB M	7 PB A	7 CC M	7 CC A	8 PB M	8 PB A	8 CC M	8 CC A	9 PB M	9 PB A	9 CC M	9 CC A	10 PB M	10 PB A	10 CC M	10 CC A	11 PB M	11 PB A	11 CC M	11 CC A	POST HELD ON JANUARY 1, 1980 / REMARKS
481	Xi-he-ba																				X	Vice-governor, Anhui Province
482	Xi Zhongxun			X				X												X		First secretary, Guangdong CP
483	Xia Bangyin											X				X						Disappeared May 1976
484	Xian Henghan											X				X						Disappeared June 1977
485	Xiang Zhonghua															X					X	Political commissar, Guangzhou Military Region
486	Xiao Han																				X	Minister of coal industry
487	Xiao Hua							X														First political commissar, Lanzhou Military Region
488	Xiao Jingguang			X				X				X				X				X		Commander, PLA Navy
489	Xiao Ke							X								X				X		Commandant, PLA Military Academy
490	Xiao Wangdong																				X	Political commissar, Jinan Military Region
491	Xie Fuzhi							X		X		X										Died March 26, 1972
492	Xie Jiatang											X				X						Disappeared October 1976
493	Xie Jiaxiang											X				X						Member, Standing Committee, Fuzhou Mil.Reg.,CCP Comte.
494	Xie Jingyi f															X						Disappeared September 1976
495	Xie Juezai							X														Died June 19, 1971
496	Xie Xuegong											X				X				X		Disappeared May 1978
497	Xie Zhengrong															X						Died December 4, 1977
498	Xie Zhenhua															X						Disappeared August 1978
499	Xing Yanzi f																X				X	Disappeared June 1978
500	Xu Biaojun																				X	?
501	Xu Bing							X														Died as a result of persecution (during Cultural Revolution?)
502	Xu Chi											X				X					X	Vice-minister of metallurgical industry
503	Xu Guangda							X														Died (date unknown)
504	Xu Haidong							X				X										Died March 25, 1970
505	Xu Jiatun																			X		First secretary, Jiangsu CP
506	Xu Jingxian											X				X						Disappeared October 1976
507	Xu Liqing																				X	Deputy director, PLA General Political Department
508	Xu Shiyou								X	X		X		X		X		X		X		Commander, Guangzhou Military Region
509	Xu Teli			X				X														Died November 28, 1968
510	Xu Xiangqian			X		X		X		X		X		X		X		X		X		Minister of national defense
511	Xu Zirong							X														Died (between 1969 and 1972)
512	Xue Jinda																			X		?
513	Xue Jinlian f																X				X	Disappeared December 1978
514	Xue Wangchun f											X				X						Disappeared November 1976
515	Yan Hongyan							X														Died January 8, 1967
516	Yan Zhongchuan											X										Disappeared September 1971
517	Yang Bolan f															X						Disappeared September 1976
518	Yang Chengwu							X											X	X		Commander, Fuzhou Military Region
519	Yang Chunfu											X				X						Disappeared October 1976
520	Yang Dayi																X				X	Commander, Liaoning Military District
521	Yang Dezhi							X				X				X				X		Commander, Kunming Military Region
522	Yang Fuzhen f											X				X						Disappeared March 1979
523	Yang Gui											X										Disappeared May 1977
524	Yang Huanmin											X										Commander, Air Force,Nanjing Military Region
525	Yang Jingren																			X		Minister, Commission of Nationalities Affairs
526	Yang Junsheng											X				X					X	Disappeared February 1979
527	Yang Shangkun							X														First secretary, Guangzhou CP
528	Yang Xianzhen							X														Member, Standing Committee, 5th CPPCC
529	Yang Xiufeng							X														Member, Standing Committee, 5th NPC
530	Yang Yichen											X								X		First secretary, Heilongjiang CP
531	Yang Yong							X								X				X		Deputy chief of staff, PLA
532	Yang Yongliang																				X	?
533	Yang Zong f											X				X						Disappeared October 1977
534	Yao Lianwei											X				X						Disappeared May 1977
535	Yao Wenyuan									X		X		X		X						Purged October 1976
536	Yao Yilin							X												X		Vice-premier
537	Ye Fei							X								X				X		First political commissar, PLA Navy
538	Ye Jianying			X		X		X		X		X		X		X		X		X		Chairman, 5th NPC
539	Ye Jizhuang							X														Died June 27, 1967
540	Ye Qun f									X		X										Disappeared May 1971

No.	Name	7PB M	7PB AM	7CC M	7CC AM	8PB M	8PB AM	8CC M	8CC AM	9PB M	9PB AM	9CC M	9CC AM	10PB M	10PB AM	10CC M	10CC AM	11PB M	11PB AM	11CC M	11CC AM	POST HELD ON JANUARY 1, 1980 / REMARKS
541	Yi Yaocao												X									Disappeared May 1970
542	You Taizhong												X				X				X	Commander, Chengdu Military Region
543	Yu Hongliang												X								X	Disappeared February 1978
544	Yu Huiyong																X					Purged October 1976
545	Yu Mingtao																				X	Governor, Shaanxi Province
546	Yu Qiuli											X				X						Vice-premier
547	Yu Sang												X									Vice-minister of public security
548	Yuan Baohua																				X	Vice-minister, State Economic Commission
549	Yuan Shengping												X									Political commissar, Beijing Military Region
550	Zeng Guohua												X									Disappeared May 1971
551	Zeng Jingbing				X																	Disappeared January 1955
552	Zeng Shan			X				X					X									Died April 16, 1972
553	Zeng Shaoshan												X				X				X	Disappeared December 1978
554	Zeng Siyu											X				X				X		Commander, Jinan Military Region
555	Zeng Xisheng							X														Died July 15, 1978
556	Zeng Yongya											X										Disappeared July 1978
557	Zhang Aiping								X											X		Deputy chief of staff, PLA
558	Zhang Caiqian												X				X			X		Deputy chief of staff, PLA
559	Zhang Chiming												X									Disappeared October 1977
560	Zhang Chunqiao								X	X				X								Purged October 1976
561	Zhang Dazhi											X				X						Disappeared October 1977
562	Zhang Desheng																					Died March 4, 1965
563	Zhang Dingcheng			X				X				X				X				X		Vice-chairman, 5th NPC
564	Zhang Fugui												X				X				X	Vice-chairman, Shandong People's Congress
565	Zhang Fuheng												X				X			X		?
566	Zhang Guohua								X			X										Died February 21, 1972
567	Zhang Guoquan																X					Disappeared January 1976
568	Zhang Hanfu							X														Died January 1, 1972
569	Zhang Hengyun												X				X					Disappeared November 1976
570	Zhang Hongchi												X									Purged October 1976
571	Zhang Huailian																X			X		Commander, 1st Flight Division, PLA Air Force
572	Zhang Jianglin												X				X					Disappeared February 1977
573	Zhang Jichun				X			X														Died during cultural Revolution
574	Zhang Jihui												X				X			X		Disappeared June 1978
575	Zhang Jingfu								X											X		Governor, Anhui Province
576	Zhang Jingwu							X														Died as a result of persecution during Cultural Revolution
577	Zhang Linchi																X			X		Disappeared February 1979
578	Zhang Lingbin															X				X		Deputy director, PLA Logistics Department
579	Zhang Linzhi											X										Died as a result of persecution during Cultural Revolution
580	Zhang Lixian																				X	Secretary, Hunan CP
581	Zhang Pinghua								X							X				X		First vice-minister, State Agricultural Commission
582	Zhang Qilong								X													Member, Standing Committee, 5th NPC
583	Zhang Riqing												X									Military cadre, Wuhan Military Region
584	Zhang Shizhong												X				X					Disappeared May 1977
585	Zhang Shuzhi															X						Disappeared June 1977
586	Zhang Sizhou												X									Disappeared May 1975
587	Zhang Su								X													Deputy chief procurator, Supreme People's Procuratorate
588	Zhang Tianyun											X										?
589	Zhang Tingfa															X		X				Commander, PLA Air Force
590	Zhang Tixue												X				X					Died September ?, 1973
591	Zhang Weimin												X									Disappeared September 1976
592	Zhang Wentian	X		X			X	X														Died July 1, 1976
593	Zhang Xi								X													Died January 8, 1959
594	Zhang Xiting f												X									Disappeared May 1970
595	Zhang Xiuchuan												X									Disappeared May 1971
596	Zhang Yancheng												X				X					Disappeared October 1976
597	Zhang Yaoci																				X	Deputy director, General Office, CCP Central Committee
598	Zhang Yingcai												X				X					Disappeared May 1976
599	Zhang Yixiang											X				X						Disappeared December 1978
600	Zhang Yuhua																				X	Secretary, Hubei CP

Columns are grouped by Central Committee (7th CC 1945, 8th CC 1956, 9th CC 1969, 10th CC 1973, 11th CC 1977). Within each: **P B** (Member / Alternate Member) and **C C** (Member / Alternate Member).

No.	Name	7 PB M	7 PB A	7 CC M	7 CC A	8 PB M	8 PB A	8 CC M	8 CC A	9 PB M	9 PB A	9 CC M	9 CC A	10 PB M	10 PB A	10 CC M	10 CC A	11 PB M	11 PB A	11 CC M	11 CC A	POST HELD ON JANUARY 1, 1980 / REMARKS
601	Zhang Yun								X													Vice-president, Women's Federation
602	Zhang Yunyi			X				X				X				X						Died November 19, 1974
603	Zhang Zhen																				X	Director, PLA Logistics Department
604	Zhang Zhidi																					?
605	Zhang Zhixiu																X					Deputy commander, Kunming Military Region
606	Zhang Zhongliang							X														Secretary, Jiangsu CP
607	Zheng Zongxun			X				X								X						Disappeared February 1977
608	Zhao Boping							X														Reactivated December 1978
609	Zhao Cangbi																X					Minister of public security
610	Zhao Erlu							X														Died February 2, 1967
611	Zhao Feng											X				X						Vice-chairman, Shandong People's Congress
612	Zhao Jianmin							X														Reactivated December 1978
613	Zhao Qimin											X										Disappeared January 1972
614	Zhao Wucheng																				X	Third secretary, Tianjin CP
615	Zhao Xinchu																X			X		Vice-minister, State Planning Commission
616	Zhao Xingyuan																X				X	Political commissar, Heilongjiang Military District
617	Zhao Xuechuan																				X	Chairman, Yunnan Trade Unions
618	Zhao Yimin							X														Member, Standing Committee, 5th CPPCC
619	Zhao Zhijian																				X	Disappeared March 1979
620	Zhao Ziyang															X			X	X		First secretary, Sichuan CP
621	Zheng Sansheng											X									X	Deputy commander, Xinjiang Military Region
622	Zheng Weisan			X				X														Died July 27, 1975
623	Zheng Weishan											X										Disappeared December 1970
624	Zhong Fuxiang																				X	Disappeared June 1978
625	Zhong Qiguang							X														Member, Standing Committee, 5th CPPCC
626	Zhou Aqing																				X	Labor hero of Nanjing Radio Factory
627	Zhou Baozhong							X														Died February 22, 1964
628	Zhou Chiping											X										Disappeared May 1971
629	Zhou Chunlin																X					Deputy commander, Nanjing Military Region
630	Zhou Enlai	X		X		X		X		X		X		X		X						Died January 8, 1976
631	Zhou Hongbao																X					Disappeared October 1976
632	Zhou Huan							X														Reactivated December 1978
633	Zhou Hui																X					First secretary, Inner Mongolia CP
634	Zhou Jianren											X				X				X		Vice-president, 5th CPPCC
635	Zhou Liqin f																X					Disappeared September 1977
636	Zhou Xiaozhou							X														Died December 26, 1966
637	Zhou Xing											X				X						Died October 3, 1975
638	Zhou Yang							X													X	Vice-president, Academy of Social Sciences
639	Zhou Zijian																				X	Minister, 1st Ministry of Machine Building
640	Zhu De	X		X		X		X		X		X		X		X						Died July 6, 1976
641	Zhu Dehai							X														Died September 1972
642	Zhu Guangya												X				X				X	Cadre, Science and Technol. Comm. for National Defense
643	Zhu Huifen f																X					Disappeared November 1976
644	Zhu Jiayao																X					Disappeared January 1976
645	Zhu Kejia																X					Purged June 1977
646	Zhu Muzhi															X					X	Deputy director, Propaganda Dept.,CCP Central Committee
647	Zhu Shaoqing																				X	Deputy commander, Fuzhou Military Region
648	Zhuang Zedong											X				X						Disappeared October 1976
649	Zong Xiyun											X				X					X	Vice-chairman, Jilin Revolutionary Committee
650	Zou Jiahua																				X	Cadre, National Defense Industry ?
651	Zuo Chongyi																				X	Hero-soldier

In the above tables two cadres are missing: Hu Liangcai, alternate member of the 9th, 10th and 11th Central Committee, and Xie Wangchun (f), alternate member of the 9th and 10th Central Committee. Three further cadres have been misspelled, namely Chen Gang, Deng Haiqing and Qiao Linyi. The correct transcription should be Chen Kang, Teng Haiqing and Jiao Linyi.

The Members and Alternate Members
of the Politburo, 7th-11th
Party Congresses, Fifth Plenum

The Members and Alternate Members of the Politburo
7th through 11th Party Congresses, 5th Plenum

#		Name	Deceased	Purged
1	7th CC 1945/6	Chen Yun		
2		Dong Biwu	1975, Apr 2	
3		Gao Gang		1955
4		Kang Sheng	1975, Dec 12	
5		Lin Boqu	1960, May 29	
6		Liu Shaoqi	1969, Nov 12	1967
7		Mao Zedong	1976, Sep 9	
8		Peng Dehuai	1974, Nov 24	1959
9		Ren Bishi	1950, Oct 27	
10		Zhang Wentian	1976, Jul 1	1961
11		Zhou Enlai	1976, Jan 8	
12		Zhu De	1976, Jul 6	
13	1950/7	Lin Biao		1971
14	1951/10	Peng Zhen		
15	1955/4	Deng Xiaoping		
16	8th CC 1956/9	Bo Yibo		(1966)
17		Chen Boda		1970
18		Chen Yi	1972, Jan 6	
19		He Long	1969, Jun 9	1966
20		Li Fuchun		
21		Li Xiannian		
22		Lu Dingyi		(1968)
23		Liu Bocheng		
24		Luo Ronghuan	1963, Dec 16	
25		Ulanhu		
26	1958/2	Ke Qingshi	1965, Apr 9	
27		Li Jingquan		(1967)
28		Tan Zhenlin		(1967)
29	1966/8	Xie Fuzhi	1972, Mar 26	
30	1966/10	Tao Zhu	1969, Nov 30	1967
31	1967/1	Nie Rongzhi		
32		Song Renqiong		(1967)
33		Xu Xiangqian		
34		Ye Jianying		

#	Group / Date	Name		Date
35	9th CC 1969/4	Chen Xilian		1980
36		Huang Yongsheng		1971
37		Ji Dengkui		1980
38		Jiang Qing	f	1976
39		Li Desheng		
40		Li Xuefeng		1970
41		Li Zuopeng		1971
42		Qiu Huizuo		1971
43		Wang Dongxing		1980
44		Wu Faxian		1971
45		Xu Shiyou		
46		Yao Wenyuan		1976
47		Ye Qun	f	1971
48		Zhang Chunqiao		1976
49	10th CC 1973/8	Chen Yonggui		
50		Hua Guofeng		
51		Ni Zhifu		
52		Seypidin		
53		Su Zhenhua		1979, Feb 7
54		Wang Hongwen		1976
55		Wei Guoqing		
56		Wu De		1980
57		Wu Guixian	f	1977
58	11th CC 1977/8	Chen Muhua	f	
59		Fang Yi		
60		Geng Biao		
61		Peng Chong		
62		Yu Qiuli		
63		Zhang Tingfa		
64		Zhao Ziyang		1978/12
65		Deng Yingchao	f	
66		Wang Zhen		1980/2
67		Hu Yaobang		

Legend:
⊠ Member
✕ Alternate Member

The First Party Secretaries of the Provinces
1949-June 1980

Positions held in June 1980 / Remarks

Province	Dates	Name	Positions held in June 1980 / Remarks
Anhui	1952-1962	Zeng Xisheng	Died 1978, July 15
	1963-1967	Li Baohua	President, People's Bank
	1971-1975	Li Desheng	Commander, Shenyang Military Region
	1975-1977	Song Peizhang	Disappeared 1977, June
	1977-1980	Wan Li	Member, Secretariat, CCP Central Committee
	1980-	Zhang Jingfu	
Beijing	1949-1966	Peng Zhen	Chairman, Legal Commission under 5th NPC
	1966-1970?	Li Xuefeng	Disappeared 1970
	1971-1972	Xie Fuzhi	Died 1972, March 26
	1973-1978	Wu De	Member, CCP Central Committee
	1978-	Lin Huijia	
Fujian	1949-1954	Zhang Dingcheng	Vice-chairman, 5th NPC
	1955-1968	Ye Fei	Commander, PLA Navy
	1971-1973	Han Xianchu	Member, Stand. Committee, CCP Military Commission
	1975-	Liao Zhigao	
Gansu	1949-1954	Zhang Desheng	Died 1965, March 4
	1954-1961	Zhang Zhongliang	Secretary, Jiangsu CP
	1961-1967	Wang Feng	1st secretary, Xinjiang CP
	1971-1977	Xian Henghan	Disappeared 1977, June
	1977-	Song Ping	
Guangdong	1951-1955	Ye Jianying	Vice-chairman, CCP Central Committee
	1955-1965	Tao Zhu	Died 1969, November 30
	1965-1967	Zhao Ziyang	Member, Stand. Committee, CCP Politburo
	1971-1972	Li Desheng	Commander, Shenyang Military Region
	1972-1973	Ding Sheng	Disappeared 1976, October
	1974-1975	Zhao Ziyang	Member, Stand. Committee, CCP Politburo
	1975-1978	Wei Guoqing	Vice-chairman, Stand. Committee, 5th NPC
	1978-	Xi Zhongxun	
Guangxi	1949-1955	Zhang Yunyi	Died 1974, November 19
	1955-1957	Chen Manyuan	Leading military figure in Beijing
	1957-1961	Liu Jianxun	Disappeared 1978, April
	1961-1975	Wei Guoqing	Vice-chairman, Stand. Committee, 5th NPC
	1975-1976	An Pingsheng	1st secretary, Yunnan CP
	1977-	Qiao Xiaoguang	

Province	Dates	Name	Positions held in June 1980 / Remarks
Liaoning	1954-1958	Huang Oudong	2nd secretary, Liaoning CP
	1958-1968	Huang Huoqing	Chief procurator, Supreme People's Procuratorate
	1971-1973	Chen Xilian	Member, CCP Central Committee
	1975-1978	Zeng Shaoshan	?
	1978-	Ren Zhongyi	
Nei Monggol	1949-1966	Ulanhu	Vice-chairman, Stand. Committee, 5th NPC
	1971-1978	You Taizhong	Commander, Chengdu Military Region
	1978-	Zhou Hui	
Ningxia	1949-1951	Pan Zili	Died 1971, May 22
	1953-1956?	Zhu Min	?
	1958-1961	Wang Feng	1st secretary, Xinjiang CP
	1961-1967	Yang Jingren	Minister, Nationalities Affairs Commission
	1971-1977	Kang Jianmin	Died 1977, January 18
	1977-1978	Huo Shilian	Minister of Agriculture
	1979-	Li Xuezhi	
Qinghai	1949-1954	Zhang Zhongliang	Secretary, Jiangsu CP
	1954-1960	Gao Feng	Disappeared 1961, April
	1961-1962	Wang Zhao (acting)	Died 1970, Feb 12
	1962-1966	Yang Zhilin	Disappeared 1966, October
	1971-1976	Liu Xianquan	Disappeared 1976, September
	1977-1979	Tan Qilong	1st secretary, Sichuan CP
	1980-	Liang Buting	
Shaanxi	1949-1952	Ma Mingfang	Died 1974, August 13
	1952-1954	Pan Zili	Died 1972, May 22
	1955-1965	Zhang Desheng	Died 1965, March 4
	1965-1965	Hu Yaobang (acting)	Member, Stand. Committee, CCP Central Committee
	1965-1968	Huo Shilian	Minister of agriculture
	1971-1978	Li Ruishan	Vice-minister, State Agricultural Commission
	1979-	Ma Wenrui	
Shandong	1949-1955	Kang Sheng	Died 1975, December 16
	1955-1960	Shu Tong	Member, Stand. Committee, 5th CPPCC
	1960-1961	Zeng Xisheng	Died 1978, July 15
	1961-1967	Tan Qilong	1st secretary, Sichuan CP
	1971-1973	Yang Dezhi	Chief, PLA General Staff
	1975-	Bai Rubing	

Province	Name	Years	Notes
Guizhou	Su Zhenhua	1949-1954	Died 1979, February 7
	Zhou Lin	1955-1965	Vice-minister of education
	Li Dazhang	1965-1965	Died 1976, May 3
	Jia Qiyun	1965-1967	Disappeared 1977, January
	Lan Yinong	1971-1971	Disappeared 1971, May
	Lu Ruilin	1974-1976	Disappeared 1977, February
	Ma Li	1977-1979	Died 1979, September 25
Hebei	Lin Tie	1949-1966	Member, Stand.Committee, 5th NPC
	Liu Zihou	1971-1979	?
	Jin Ming	1980-	
Heilongjiang	Zhang Qilong	1949-1950	Member, Stand.Committee, 5th NPC
	Zhao Decun	1950-1954	Secretary, Heilongjiang CP
	Ouyang Qin	1955-1967	Died 1978, May 15
	Wang Jiadao	1971-1976	Disappeared 1977, September
	Liu Guangtao	1977-1977	Disappeared 1977, December
	Yang Yichen	1977-	
Henan	Zhang Xi	1949-1952	Died 1959, January 8
	Pan Fusheng	1953-1958	Disappeared 1970, December
	Wu Zhifu	1958-1961	Died (during Cultural Revolution?)
	Liu Jianxun	1961-1978	Disappeared 1978, April
	Duan Junyi	1978-	
Hubei	Li Xiannian	1949-1954	Vice-premier
	Wang Renzhong	1954-1967	Minister, State Agricultural Commission
	Zeng Siyu	1971-1973	?
	Zhao Xinchu	1975-1978	Minister of food
	Chen Pixian	1978-	
Hunan	Huang Kecheng	1949-1952	Permanent secr., Discipline Inspecting Comm., CCP CC
	Jin Ming	1952-1953	1st secretary, Hebei CP
	Zhou Xiaozhou	1953-1959	Died 1966, Dec 26
	Zhang Pinghua	1959-1966	1st vice-minister, State Agricultural Commission
	Hua Guofeng	1970-1973?	Chairman, CCP Central Committee
	Mao Zhiyong	1977-	
Jiangsu	Ke Qingshi	1952-1955	Died 1965, April 9
	Jiang Weiqing	1956-1968	1st secretary, Jiangxi CP
	Xu Shiyou	1970-1973	Member, Stand.Committee, CCP Military Commission
	Peng Chong	1975-1976	Member, Secretariat, CCP Central Committee
	Xu Jiatun	1977-	
Jiangxi	Chen Zhengren	1949-1952?	Died 1972, April 6
	Yang Shangkui	1956-1967	Secretary, Jiangxi CP
	Cheng Shiqing	1970-1972	Disappeared 1972, February
	Jiang Weiqing	1975-	
Jilin	Li Xiwu	1950-1952	?
	Wu De	1956-1966	Member, CCP Central Committee
	Wang Huaixiang	1971-1977	Disappeared 1977, November
	Wang Enmao	1977-	
Shanghai	Rao Shushi	1949-1952	Purged 1955
	Chen Yi	1952-1954	Died 1971, January 6
	Ke Qingshi	1955-1965	Died 1965, April 9
	Chen Pixian	1965-1967	1st secretary, Hubei CP
	Zhang Chunqiao	1971-1976	Purged October 1976
	Su Zhenhua	1976-1978	Died 1979, February 7
	Peng Chong	1979-1980	Member, Secretariat, CCP Central Committee
	Chen Guodong	1980-	
Shanxi	Cheng Zihua	1949-1951	Minister of Civil Affairs
	Lai Ruoyu	1951-1951	Died 1958, May 20
	Gao Kelin	1952-1953	Disappeared 1966, July
	Tao Lujia	1953-1965	Disappeared 1976, September
	Wei Heng	1965-1967	Disappeared 1968, August
	Xie Zhenhua	1971-1974?	Deputy commander, Shenyang Military Region
	Wang Qian	1975-	
Sichuan	Li Jingquan	1952-1965	Vice-chairman, Stand.Committee, 5th NPC
	Liao Zhigao	1965-1968	1st secretary, Fujian CP
	Zhang Guohua	1971-1972	Died 1972, December
	Liu Xingyuan	1973-1975	Disappeared 1977, August
	Zhao Ziyang	1976-1980	Member, Stand.Committee, CCP Politburo
	Tan Qilong	1980-	
Tianjin	Xie Xuegong	1971-1978	Disappeared 1978, May
	Lin Hujia	1978-1978	1st secretary, Beijing CP
	Chen Weida	1978-	
Tibet	Zhang Jingwu	1956-1965	Died 1971
	Zhang Kuohua	1965-1968	Died 1972, February 21
	Ren Rong	1971-1980	?
	Yin Fatang (acting)	1980-	
Xinjiang	Wang Zhen	1949-1952	Vice-premier
	Wang Enmao	1952-1968	1st secretary, Jilin CP
	Long Shujin	1971-1972	Disappeared 1972, February
	Seypidin	1973-1977	Vice-chairman, Stand.Committee, 5th NPC
Yunnan	Song Renqiong	1951-1953	Member, Secretariat, CCP Central Committee
	Xie Fuzhi	1953-1959	Died 1972, March 26
	Yan Hongyan	1959-1967	Died 1967, January 8
	Zhou Xing	1971-1975	Died 1975, October 3
	Jia Qiyun	1975-1977	Disappeared 1977, January
	An Pingsheng	1977-	
Zhejiang	Tan Zhenlin	1949-1952	Vice-chairman, 5th NPC
	Tan Qilong	1952-1955	1st secretary, Sichuan CP
	Jiang Hua	1955-1968	President, Supreme People's Court
	Nan Ping	1971-1972	Disappeared 1972, January
	Tan Qilong	1973-1977	1st secretary, Sichuan CP
	Tie Ying	1977-	

The Ministers of the PRC
1949- June 1980

The following list contains - in alphabetic order - the ministries and their ministers, past and present. Some ministries existed only for a few years; some others were dissolved, divided and reunited after some time. The interested reader will find clues to a ministry's fate in the column containing the years. The abbreviation CR means Cultural Revolution.

Ministry	Years	Minister	Posts held in June 1980 / Remarks
Agriculture	1949-1954	Li Shucheng	Died 1965, Aug 26
	1954- CR	Liao Luyan	Died (between 1969 and 1972)
	1979-	Huo Shilian	
Agriculture and Forestry	1970-1977	Sha Feng	Disappeared 1978, August
Agricultural Machinery	1959-1965	Chen Zhengren	Died 1972, Apr 6
	1979-	Yang Ligong	
Agricultural Supplies, Purchase of	1955-1956	Yang Yichen	1st secretary, Heilongjiang CP
Allocation of Materials	1964-1965	Yuan Baohua	Vice-minister, State Economic Commission
Aquatic Products	1956- CR	Xu Deheng	Vice-chairman, Stand. Committee, 5th NPC
Building Construction	1952-1954	Chen Zhengren	Died 1972, Apr 6
	1954-1964	Liu Xiufeng	Disappeared 1964
	1964-1965	Li Renjun	Vice-chairman, State Planning Commission
	1965- CR	Liu Yumin	Died (during Cultural Revolution?)
Building Materials	1956-1958	Lai Jifa	Member, Stand. Committee, 5th CPPCC
	1965-1974	Lai Jifa	Member, Stand. Committee, 5th CPPCC
	1979-	Song Yangchu	
Chemical Industry	1956-1961	Peng Tao	Died 1961, Nov 14
	1962- CR	Gao Yang	Minister of State Farms and Land Reclamation
	1978-	Sun Jingwen	
Civil Affairs	1979-	Cheng Zihua	
Coal Industry	1955-1957	Chen Yu	Died 1974, Mar 21
	1957- CR	Zhang Linzhi	Died (during Cultural Revolution?)
	1975-1976	Xu Jinqiang	Died 1976, Jul 21
	1977-1980	Xiao Han	Vice-minister, State Economic Commission
	1980-	Gao Yangwen	
Commerce	1952-1956	Zeng Shan	Died 1972, Apr 16
	1956-1958	Chen Yun	Vice-chairman, CCP Central Committee
	1958-1960	Cheng Zihua	Minister of Civil Affairs
	1960- CR	Yao Yilin	Vice-premier
	1972-1977	Fan Ziyu	Deputy director, PLA General Logistics Dept.
	1978-1979	Yao Yilin	Vice-premier
	1979-	Wang Lei	
Communications	1949-1958	Zhang Bojun	Disappeared 1964
	1958-1964	Wang Shoudao	Vice-president, 5th CPPCC
	1964- CR	Sun Daguang	Minister of Geology
	1971-1974	Yang Jie	Vice-minister, Post and Telecommunication
	1975-1979	Ye Fei	Commander, PLA Navy
	1979-	Zeng Sheng	
Culture	1949-1965	Shen Yanbing	Chairman, Writers' Union
	1965- CR	Lu Dingyi	Vice-chairman, 5th CPPCC
	1975-1976	Yu Huiyong	Purged 1976, October
	1977-	Huang Zhen	

			Posts held in June 1980 / Remarks
Economic Relations with	1971-1976	Fang Yi	Vice-premier
Foreign Countries	1977-	Chen Muhua f	
Education	1949-1952	Ma Xulun	Died 1970, May 4
	1952-1958	Zhang Xiruo	Died 1973, July 18
	1958-1964	Yang Xiufeng	Member, Stand.Committee, 5th NPC
	1964- CR	He Wei	Died 1973, March 9
	1975-1976	Zhou Rongxin	Disappeared 1976, January
	1977-1979	Liu Xiyao	Vice-governor, Sichuan Province
	1979-	Jiang Nanxiang	
Electric Power Industry	1955-1958	Liu Lanbo	Minister of Power Industry
Finance	1949-1953	Bo Yibo	Minister, Machine Building Industry Commission
	1953-1954	Deng Xiaoping	Vice-premier
	1954-1975?	Li Xiannian	Vice-premier
	1975-1979	Zhang Jingfu	1st secretary, Anhui Province CP
	1979-	Wu Bo	
Food	1952-1958	Zhang Naiqi	Died 1977, May 13
	1958-1965?	Sha Qianli	Member, Stand.Committee, 5th NPC
	1979-1980	Chen Guodong	1st secretary, Shanghai CP
	1980-	Zhao Xinchu	
Food Industry	1949-1950	Yang Lisan	Died 1954, Nov 28
	1956-1958	Li Zhuchen	Died 1970?
Foreign Affairs	1949-1958	Zhou Enlai	Died 1976, Jan 8
	1958-1972	Chen Yi	Died 1972, Jan 6
	1972-1974	Ji Pengfei	Dir., Internat.Liaison Dept., CCP Central Committee
	1974-1976	Qiao Guanhua	Disappeared 1976, November
	1976-	Huang Hua	
Foreign Trade	1952-1970	Ye Jizhuang	Died 1967, June 27
	1970-1973	Bai Xiangguo	Dpty.political commissar, PLA Logistics Dept.
	1973-	Li Qiang	
Forestry	1949-1958	Liang Xi	Died 1958, Dec 10
	1959- CR	Liu Wenhui	Died 1976, Jun 24
	1979-	Lo Yuchuan	
Fuel and Chemical Industry	1971-1974	-	
Fuel Industry	1949-1955	Chen Yu	Died 1974, March 21
Geology	1952- CR	Li Siguang	Died 1971, April 20
	1979-	Sun Daguang	
Heavy Industry	1949-1950	Chen Yun	Vice-chairman, CCP Central Committee
	1950-1952	Li Fuchun	Died 1975, Jan 9
	1952-1956	Wang Heshou	Dpty.secretary, Com. for Inspecting Discipline, CCP CC
Higher Education	1952-1954	Ma Xulun	Died 1970, May 4
	1954-1958	Yang Xiufeng	Member, Stand.Committee, 5th NPC
	1964-1965	Yang Xiufeng	Member, Stand.Committee, 5th NPC
	1965- CR	Jiang Nanxiang	Minister of education
Internal Affairs	1949-1959	Xie Juezai	Died 1971, June 19
	1959-1960	Qian Ying	?
	1960-1969	Zeng Shan	Died 1972, April 16
Justice	1949-1959	Shi Liang f	Member, Stand.Committee, 5th NPC
	1979-	Wei Wenbo	
Labor	1949-1954	Li Lisan	Died 1967, Jun 22
	1954- CR	Ma Wenrui	1st secretary, Shaanxi Province CP

			Posts held in June 1980 / Remarks
Light Industry	1949-1954	Huang Yanpei	Died 1965, Dec 21
	1954-1956	Jia Tuofu	Died 1967, May 7
	1956-1958	Sha Qianli	Member, Stand.Committee, 5th NPC
	1958- CR	Li Zhuchen	Died (1970 ?)
	1970-1978	Qian Zhiguang	Minister of Textile Industry
	1978-	Liang Lingguang	
Light Industry, First	1965-1970		
Light Industry, Second	1965- CR	Xu Yunbei	?
Local Industry	1954-1956	Sha Qianli	Member, Stand.Committee, 5th NPC
Machine Building, First	1952-1958	Huang Jing	Died 1958, Feb 10
	1958-1960	Zhao Erlu	Died 1967, Feb 2
	1960- CR	Duan Junyi	1st secretary, Henan CP
	1971-1976	Li Shuiqing	Vice-minister of Communications
	1977-	Zhou Zijian	
Machine Building, Second	1952-1958	Zhao Erlu	Died 1967, Feb 2
	1958-1960	Song Renqiong	Dir., Organization Dept., CCP Central Committee
	1960- CR	Liu Jie	Governor of Henan Province
	1975-1976	Liu Xiyao	Vice-governor of Sichuan Province
	1978-	Liu Wei	
Machine Building, Third	1955-1956	Zhang Linzhi	Died (during Cultural Revolution?)
	1956-1958	Song Renqiong	Director, Organization Dept., CCP Central Committee
	1960-1961	Zhang Liankui	Died 1978, April 22
	1961-1966	Sun Zhiyuan	Died 1966, Oct 11
	1975-1977	Li Jitai	Disappeared 1977, September
	1978-	Lü Dong	
Machine Building, Fourth	1963- CR	Wang Zheng	Died 1978, Aug 13
	1975-1978	Wang Zheng	Died 1978, Aug 13
	1978-	Qian Min	
Machine Building, Fifth	1963- CR	Qiu Chuancheng	Disappeared 1973, May
	1975-1977	Li Chengfang	1st political commissar, Wuhan Military Region
	1978-	Zhang Zhen	
Machine Building, Sixth	1963- CR	Fang Qiang	Disappeared 1977, May
	1975-1977	Bian Jiang	Disappeared 1977, October
	1978-	Chai Shufan	
Machine Building, Seventh	1965- CR	Wang Bingzhang	Disappeared 1971, May
	1975-1978	Wang Yang	Dpty.commander, Beijing Military Region
	1978-1978	Song Renqiong	Dir., Organization Dept., CCP Central Committee
	1979-	Zheng Tianxiang	
Machine Building, Eighth	1965- CR	Chen Zhengren	Died 1972, April 6
	1979-	Jiao Ruoyu	
Metallurgical Industry	1956-1964	Wang Heshou	Dpty.secretary, Com.for Inspecting Discipline, CCP CC
	1964- CR	Lü Dong	Minister, Third Ministry of Machine Building
	1971-1976	Chen Shaokun	Disappeared 1976, September
	1977-	Tang Ke	
National Defense	1954-1959	Peng Dehuai	Died 1974, Nov 29
	1959-1971	Lin Biao	Died 1971
	1975-1978	Ye Jianying	Vice-chairman, CCP Central Committee
	1978-	Xu Xiangqian	
North China Affairs	1950-1953	Liu Lantao	Vice-chairman, 5th CPPCC
Personnel	1950-1954	An Ziwen	Vice-chairman, Legal Commission, 5th NPC
Petroleum and Chemical Industry	1975-1978	Kang Shien	Vice-premier

			Posts held in June 1980 / Remarks
Petroleum Industry	1955-1958	Li Jikui	Member, Stand.Committee, 5th NPC
	1958-1971?	Yu Quili	Vice-premier
	1978-	Song Zhenming	
Post and Telecommunications	1949- CR	Zhu Xuefan	Vice-president, Trade Unions
	1973-1978	Zhong Fuxiang	Disappeared 1978, June
	1978-	Wang Zigang	
Power Equipment Industry	1956-1958	Zhang Linzhi	Died (during Cultural Revolution?)
Power Industry	1979-	Liu Lanbo	
Public Health	1949-1965	Le Tequan f	Died 1972, April 23
	1965-1966	Qian Xinzhong	Minister of Public Health
	1973-1976	Liu Xiangping f	Disappeared 1976, October
	1977-1979	Jiang Yizhen	2nd secretary, Hebei CP
	1979-	Qian Xinzhong	
Public Security	1949-1959	Luo Ruiqing	Died 1978, Aug 3
	1959-1972	Xie Fuzhi	Died 1972, March 26
	1972-1974	Li Zhen	Disappeared 1978, August
	1975-1977?	Hua Guofeng	Chairman, CCP
	1978	Zhao Cangbi	
Railways	1949-1965	Teng Daiyuan	Died 1974, Dec 1
	1965- CR	Lü Zhengcao	1st political commissar, PLA Railway Corps
	1975-1976	Wan Li	Vice-premier
	1977-1978	Duan Junyi	1st secretary, Henan CP
	1978-	Guo Weicheng	
State Farms and Land Reclamation	1956- CR	Wang Zhen	Vice-premier
	1979-	Gao Yang	
Supervision	1954-1959	Qian Ying	?
Textile Industry	1949-1952	Zeng Shan	Died 1972, April 16
	1952-1967	Jiang Guangnai	Died 1967, June 8
	1978-	Qian Zhiguang	
Timber Industry	1 956-1958	Luo Zhongji	?
Trade	1949-1952	Ye Jizhuang	Died 1967, June 27
Urban Construction	1956-1958	Wan Li	Vice-premier
Urban Services	1956-1958	Yang Yichen	1st secretary, Heilongjiang CP
Water Conservancy	1949-1958	Fu Zuoyi	Died 1974, April 19
	1979-	Qian Zhengying f	
Water Conservancy and Electric Power	1958-1974	Fu Zuoyi	Died 1974, April 19
	1975-1978	Qian Zhengying f	Minister of Water Conservancy

The Commanders of the Military Regions
1954-June 1980

			Posts held in June 1980 / Remarks
Beijing	1955-1959	Yang Chengwu	Commander, Fuzhou Military Region
	1959-1966	Yang Yong	Deputy chief, PLA General Staff
	1968-1970	Zheng Weishan	Disappeared December 1970
	1974-1979	Chen Xilian	Member, CCP 11th Central Committee
	1980-	Qin Jiwei	
Chengdu	1954-1960	Ho Bingyan	Died 1960, July 1
	1960-1967	Huang Xinting	Commander, PLA Armored Forces
	1967-1971	Liang Xingchu	Disappeared October 1971
	1974-1975	Qin Jiwei	Commander, Beijing Military Region
	1976-1977	Liu Xingyuan	Disappeared August 1977
	1977-1979	Wu Kehua	Commander, Guangzhou Military Region
	1980-	You Taizhong	
Fuzhou	1957-1960	Ye Fei	Commander, PLA Navy
	1960-1973	Han Xianchu	Member, Stand.Comte., CCP Military Commission
	1974-1976	Pi Dingjun	Died 1976, July 7
	1978-	Yang Chengwu	
Guangzhou	1954-1958	Huang Yongsheng	Purged 1971
	1958-1960	Li Tianyou	Died 1970, September 27
	1960-1966	Wen Niansheng	Rehabilitated 1978, September
	1966-1968	Huang Yongsheng	Purged 1971
	1970-1973	Ding Sheng	Disappeared 1976, October
	1974-1980	Xu Shiyou	Member, Stand.Comte., CCP Military Commission
	1980-	Wu Kehua	
Jinan	1957-1958	Wang Xinting	Member, Stand.Committee, 5th CPPCC
	1958-1973	Yang Dezhi	Chief, PLA General Staff
	1974-1980	Zeng Siyu	?
	1980-	Rao Shoukun	
Kunming	1954-1958	Xie Fuchi	Died 1972, March 26
	1958-1963	Qin Jiwei	Commander, Beijing Military Region
	1972-1978	Wang Bicheng	?
	1979-1980	Yang Dezhi	Chief, PLA General Staff
	1980-	Zhang Zhixiu	
Lanzhou	1954-1968	Zhang Dazhi	Disappeared October 1977
	1970-1973	Pi Dingjun	Died 1976, July 7
	1974-1980	Han Xianchu	Member, Stand.Comte., CCP Military Commission
	1980-	Du Yide	
Nanjing	1957-1973	Xu Shiyou	Member, Stand.Comte., CCP Military Commission
	1974-1978	Ding Sheng	Disappeared October 1976
	1977-	Nie Fengzhi	
Shenyang	1955-1959	Deng Hua	Alternate member, CCP 11th Central Committee
	1959-1973	Chen Yilian	Member, CCP 11th Central Committee
	1974-	Li Desheng	
Wuhan	1954-1967	Chen Zaidao	Commander, PLA Railway Corps
	1967-1967	Yu Lijin	Died 1978, December 2
	1967-1973	Zeng Sixu	?
	1974-1979	Yang Dezhi	Chief, PLA General Staff
	1979-1980	Wang Bicheng	?
	1980-	Zhang Caiqian	
Xinjiang	1956-1968	Wang Enmao	1st secretary, Jilin Provincial CP
	1968-1972	Long Shujin	Disappeared 1972, February
	1973-1977	Yang Yong	Deputy chief, PLA General Staff
	1977-1979	Liu Zhen	?
	1979-1980	Wu Kehua	Commander, Guangzhou Military Region
	1980-	Xiao Quanfu	
Nei Monggol [1]	1952-1966	Ulanhu	Vice-chairman, Stand.Committee, 5th NPC
Tibet (Xizang) [1]	1951-1968	Zhang Guohua	Died 1972, February 21
	1969-1970	Zeng Yongya	Disappeared July 1978
	1971-1974	Chen Mingyi	Deputy commander, Chengdu Military Region

[1] Demoted to Military Districts

China's Diplomatic Relations and Ambassadors
1949- June 1980

Country	Diplomatic Relations since	Ambassador	Term of Office
Afghanistan	1955, Jan 1	Ding Guoyu	1955-1958
		Hao Ting	1958-1965
		Chen Feng	1965-1967
		Xie Bangzhi	1969-1973
		Gan Yetao	1973-1977
		Huang Mingda	1977-
Albania	1949, Nov 23	Xu Yixin	1954-1957
		Luo Shigao	1957-1964
		Xu Jianguo	1964-1966
		Liu Xiao	1967-
		Geng Biao	1969-1970
		Liu Zhenhua	1971-1976
		Liu Xinquan	1976-1977?
		Wen Ning	1979-
Algeria	1962, August	Zeng Tao	1962-1966
		Yang Qiliang	1969-1971
		Lin Zhong	1971-
		Zhou Boping	1975-1978
		Xu Ming	1978
Argentina	1972, Feb 19	Cheng Weizhi	1972-1977
		Xu Zhongfu	1978-
Australia	1972, Dec 22	Wang Guoquan	1973-1976
		Zhou Qiuye	1976-1978
		Lin Ping	1978-
Austria	1971, May 28	Wang Yueyi	1971-1974
		Yu Peiwen	1974-1980
Bangladesh	1975, Oct 4	Zhuang Yan	1976-1979
Barbados	1977, May 30	Wang Tao	1979-
Belgium	1971, Oct 25	Li Lianbi	1972-1976
		Huan Xiang	1976-1978
		Kang Maozhao	1978-
Benin	1964, Nov 21	Li Yunchuan	1965-1966
		Gu Xiaobo	1973-1977
		Zhang Junhua	1978-
Botswana	1975, Jan 1	Zhao Zhengyi	1975-
Brazil	1974, Aug 15	Zhang Dequn	1974-
Bulgaria	1949, Oct 4	Cao Xiangren	1950-1954
		Zhou Zhu'an	1954-1957
		Zhu Qiwen	1957-1962
		Xie Bangzhi	1962-1966?
		Zhao Jin	1971-1975
		Meng Yue	1975-

Country	Diplomatic Relations since	Ambassador	Term of Office
Burma	1950, Jun 8	Yao Zhongming	1950-1958
		Li Yimeng	1958-1963
		Geng Biao	1963-1966?
		Chen Zhaoyuan	1971-1973
		Ye Chengzhang	1973-1977
		Mo Yanzhong	1977-
Burundi	1963, Dec 23 severed	Liu Yufeng	1964-1965
	1965, Jan 30 resumed	Chen Feng	1972-1977
	1971, Oct 13	Shi Ziming	1978-
Cameroon	1971, Mar 26	Zhao Xingzhi	1970-1974
		Wei Baoshan	1974-
Canada	1970, Oct 13	Huang Hua	1971-1971
		Yao Guang	1972-1973
		Zhang Wenjin	1973-1976
		Wang Dong	1977-
Cape Verde	1976, Apr 15	Jia Huaiji	1976-1979
Central African Republic	1964, Sep 29	Meng Ying	1964-1966
		Li Shi	1976-
Chad	1972, Nov 28	Wang Rensan	1973-1977
		Miao Jiurui	1977-
Chile	1970, Dec 15	Lin Ping	1971-1973
		Xu Zhongfu	1973-1977
		Hu Chengfang	1978-
Colombia	1980, Feb 7		
Comoros	1975, Nov 13	He Gongkai	1980-
Congo, People's Republic	1964, Feb 18	Zhou Qiuye	1964-1966?
		Wang Yutian	1969-1972
		Lü Zhixian	1973-1976
		Li Lianbi	1976-
Cuba	1960, Sep 28	Shen Jian	1960-1964
		Wang Youping	1964-1966?
		Zhang Dequn	1970-1975
		Li Shanyi	1975-1979
		Wang Zhanyuan	1979-
Cyprus	1971, Dec 14	Dai Lu	1972-1977
		Cao Chi	1978-

CZECHOSLOVAKIA next page

Country	Diplomatic Relations since	Ambassador	Term of Office
Czechoslovakia	1949, Oct 8	Tan Xilin	1950-1954
		Cao Ying	1954-1961
		Zhong Xidong	1961-1966?
		Zong Kewen	1971-1975
		Li Enqiu	1975-1978
		Li Tingquan	1979-
Denmark	1950, May 11	Geng Biao	1950-1955
		Chai Zhengwen	1955-1956
		Zhen Weizhi	1956-1961
		Wang Sen	1961-1963
		Ke Bonian	1963-1967
		Yue Liang	1971-1977
		Qin Jialin	1977-
Ecuador	1980, Jan 2		
Egypt	1956, June 30	Chen Jiakang	1956-1965
		Huang Hua	1966-1970
		Chai Zemin	1970-1974
		Zhang Tong	1974-1977
		Yao Guang	1977-1980
		Liu Chun	1980-
Equatorial Guinea	1970, Oct 15	Chen Tan	1971-1974
		Hu Jingrui	1974-1979
		Lin Song	1980-
Ethiopia	1970, Nov 24	Yu Peiwen	1971-1974
		Yang Shouzheng	1974-1977
		Wang Jinchuan	1977-
European Community	1975, Sep 16	Li Lianbi	1975-1976
		Huan Xiang	1976-1978
		Kang Maozhao	1978-
Fiji	1975, Nov 5	Mi Guojun	1977-
Finland	1950, Sep 14	Geng Biao	1950-1954
		Chen Xinren	1954-1959
		Gan Yetao	1959-1962
		Zhang Boquan	1962-1965
		Yue Xin	1965-1967
		Shi Ziming	1970-1975
		Zhang Canming	1975-1978
		Xie Bangzhi	1979-1980
France	1964, Jan 27	Huang Zhen	1964-1973
		Zeng Tao	1973-1977
		Han Kehua	1977-1980
		Yao Guang	1980-
Gabon	1974, Apr 20	Liu Yingxian	1974-1979
		Liu Yufeng	1980-
Gambia	1974, Dec 14	Lei Yang	1975-1979
German Democratic Republic	1949, Oct 27	Ji Pengfei	1950-1955
		Zeng Yongquan	1955-1957
		Wang Guoquan	1957-1964
		Zhang Haifeng	1964-1966?
		Song Zhiguang	1970-1972
		Peng Guangwei	1972-1977
		Chen Dong	1978-

Country	Diplomatic Relations since	Ambassador	Term of Office
Germany, Federal Republic	1972, Oct 11	Wang Yutian	1973-1974
		Wang Shu	1974-1976
		Zhang Tong	1977-
Ghana	1960, Jul 6 severed	Huang Hua	1960-1965
	1960, Oct resumed	Chen Chu	1966-1966
	1972, Feb 29	Ke Hua	1972-1974
		Yang Keming	1974-1979
		Jia Huaiji	1980-
Great Britain	1954, Jun 17	Huan Xiang*)	1954-1962
*) Chargé d'affaires		Xiong Xiangfu*)	1962-1967
		Ma Jiajun*)	1969-1970
		Song Zhiguang	1972-1977
		Ke Hua	1978-
Greece	1972, June 5	Zhou Boping	1973-1975
		He Yang	1975-
Guinea	1959, Oct 4	Ke Hua	1960-1964
		Chai Zemin	1964-1966?
		Han Kehua	1969-1974
		Qian Jizhen	1974-1976
		Peng Hua	1977-
Guinea-Bissau	1974, Mar 15	Qian Jizhen	1974-1975
		Jia Huaiji	1976-1979
		Liu Yingxian	1980-
Guyana	1972, Jun 27	Wang Zhanyuan	1973-1979
		Wang Yanchang	1979-
Hungary	1949, Oct 6	Huang Zhen	1950-1954
		Hao Deqing	1954-1961
		Chai Zemin	1961-1964
		Han Kehua	1964-1966?
		Lü Zhixian	1970-1973
		Li Zewang	1973-1976
		Liu Tiesheng	1977-1979
		Feng Yujiu	1979-
Iceland	1971, Dec 8	Chen Dong	1972-1977
		Chen Feng	1978-
India	1950, Jan 4	Yuan Zhongxian	1950-1956
		Pan Zili	1956-1962
	No ambassador until		
		Chen Zhaoyuan	1976-1979?
		Shen Jian	1980-
Iran	1971, Aug 16	Chen Xinren	1972-1974
		Hao Deqing	1974-1977
		Jiao Ruoyu	1977-1979
		Zhuang Yan	1980-
Iraq	1958, Aug 31	Chen Zhifang	1958-1960
		Zhang Weilie	1960-1965
		Cao Chi	1966-?
		Gong Dafei	1970-1973
		Hu Chengfang	1973-1974
		Zhao Xingzhi	1974-1976
		Hou Yefeng	1977-
Ireland	1979, Jun 22		

Country	Diplomatic Relations since	Ambassador	Term of Office		Country	Diplomatic Relations since	Ambassador	Term of Office
Italy	1970, Nov 6	Shen Ping	1971-1974		**Mali**	1961, January	Lai Yali	1961-1965
		Han Kehua	1974-1977				Ma Ziqing	1965-1967?
		Wang Guoquan	1977-1978				Meng Yue	1970-1975
		Zhang Yue	1979-				Fan Zuokai	1975-1978
							Du Yi	1979-
Jamaica	1972, Nov 21	Li Chao	1973-1976					
		Wang Chongli	1977-		**Malta**	1972, Jan 31	Liu Fu	1972-1977
							Cheng Zhiping	1977-
Japan	1972, Sep 29	Chen Chu	1973-1976					
		Fu Hao	1977-		**Mauritania**	1965, Jul 19	Lü Zhixian	1965-1966
							Feng Yujiu	1969-1973
Jibouti	1979, Jan 8	Yao Guang	1979-				Wang Peng	1973-1974
							Kang Maozhao	1975-1978
Jordan	1977, Apr 14	Gu Xiaobo	1977-				Zhao Yuan	1978-
Kampuchea	1958, Jul 23	Wang Youping	1958-1962		**Mauritius**	1972, Apr 15	Wang Ze	1972-1977
		Chen Shuliang	1962-1966				Wang Ruojie	1977-
		Kang Maozhao	1969-1974					
		Sun Hao	1974-		**Mexico**	1972, Feb 14	Yao Guang	1973-1977
							Liu Fu	1977-
Kenya	1963, Dec 14	Wang Yutian	1964-1967					
		No ambassador until			**Mongolia, PR**	1949, Oct 16	Ji Yatai	1950-1954
		Wang Yueyi	1974-1979				He Ying	1954-1958
		Yang Keming	1979-				Xie Fusheng	1958-1963
							Zhang Canming	1963-1966?
Kiribati	1980, Jun 25						Xu Wenyi	1971-1974
							Zhang Weilie	1974-1978
Korea, DPR	1949, Oct 6	Ni Zhiliang	1950-1954				Meng Ying	1978-
		Pan Zili	1954-1956					
		Qiao Xiaoguang	1956-1961		**Morocco**	1958, Nov 1	Bai Ren	1959-1961
		Hao Deqing	1961-1965				Yang Qiliang	1961-1967
		Jiao Ruoyu	1965-1966				Zhang Weilie	1971-1974
		Li Yunchuan	1970-1976				Song Hanyi	1974-1979
		Lü Zhixian	1976-				Mi Yong	1979-
					Mozambique	1975, Jun 25	Yang Shouzheng	1977-1980
Kuwait	1971, Mar 29	Sun Shengwei	1971-1977					
		Ding Hao	1977-		**Nepal**	1955, Aug 1	Yuan Zhongxian	1955-1956
							Pan Zili	1956-1960
Laos	1962, Sep 7	Li Chun	1962-1967				Zhang Shijie	1960-1965
		No ambassador until					Yang Gongsu	1966-1967?
		Guo Ying	1974-1977				Wang Ze	1969-1972
		Xu Huang	1977-				Cao Chi	1972-1977
							Peng Guangwei	1978-
Lebanon	1971, Nov 9	Xu Ming	1972-1978		**Netherlands**	1954, Nov 19	Xie Li*)	1955-1963
		Xu Wenyi	1979-				Li Enqiu	1963-1966
					*) Charged'affaires		Hao Deqing	1972-1974
Liberia	1977, Feb 17	Wang Rensan	1977-				Chen Xinren	1975-1978
							Ding Xuesong	1979-
Libya	1978, Aug 9	Pei Jianzhang	1979-					
					New Zealand	1972, Dec 22	Pei Jianzhang	1973-1979
Luxembourg	1972, Nov 16	Li Lianbi	1973-1976				Qin Lizhen	1979-
		Huan Xiang	1976-1978					
		Kang Maozhao	1978-		**Niger**	1974, Jul 20	Xie Kexi	1975-1979
							Wang Chuanbin	1979-
Madagascar	1972, Nov 6	Tian Zhidong	1974-1979					
		Gan Yetao	1979-		**Nigeria**	1971, Feb 10	Yang Qiliang	1971-1973
							Feng Yujiu	1973-1979
Malaysia	1974, May 31	Wang Youping	1975-1977				Lei Yang	1980-
		Ye Chengzhang	1977-					
					Norway	1954, Oct 5	Wang Youping	1954-1958
Maldives	1972, Nov 16	Huang Mingda	1973-1977				Xu Yixin	1958-1962

Country	Diplomatic Relations since	Ambassador	Term of Office	Country	Diplomatic Relations since	Ambassador	Term of Office
NORWAY (continued)		Qin Lizhen	1962-1965	Somalia	1960, Dec 27	Zhang Yue	1961-1964
		Feng Yujiu	1965-1966			Yang Shouzheng	1964-1966?
		Hao Deqing	1971-1972			Fan Zuokai	1970-1975
		Cao Chungeng	1972-1976			Zhang Shijie	1975-1979
		Liu Shuqing	1977-1980			Li Yuchi	1979-
Oman	1978, May 25	Yuan Lulin	1979-	Soviet Union	1949, Oct 3	Wang Jiayiang	1949-1951
Pakistan	1951, May 21	Han Nianlong	1951-1956			Zhang Wentian	1951-1955
		Geng Biao	1956-1959			Liu Xiao	1955-1962
		Ding Guoyu	1959-1966			Pan Zili	1962-1966?
		Zhang Wenjin	1966-?			Liu Xinquan	1970-1976
		Zhang Tong	1969-1974			Wang Youping	1977-1979
		Lu Weizhao	1974-1979			Yang Shouzheng	1980-
		Xu Yixin	1979-	Spain	1973, Mar 9	Chen Zhaoyuan	1973-1976
PLO	1965, Mar 22	No ambassador yet				Ma Muming	1976-1980
Papua New Guinea	1976, Oct 12	Pei Jianzhang	1977-1979	Sri Lanka	1957, Feb 7	Zhang Canming	1957-1962
		Lin Ping	1980-			Xie Kexi	1962-1963
Peru	1971, Nov 2	Jiao Ruoyu	1971-1976			Ma Ziqing	1970-1973
		Wang Ze	1977-			Huang Mingda	1973-1977
Philippines	1975, Jun 9	Ke Hua	1975-1978			Sun Shengwei	1977-
		Chen Xinren	1978-	Sudan	1959, Jun 2	Wang Yutian	1959-1962
Poland	1949, Oct 7	Peng Mingzhi	1950-1952			Gu Xiaopo	1962-1965
		Zeng Yongquan	1952-1955			Yu Peiwen	1966?
		Wang Bingnan	1955-1964			Yang Shousheng	1970-1974
		Wang Guoquan	1964-1966?			Zhang Yue	1974-1978
		Yao Guang	1970-1971			Song Hanyi	1979-
		Li Shuijing	1972-1977	Surinam	1976, May 28	Li Chao	1977-
		Li Zewang	1977-	Sweden	1950, May 5	Geng Biao	1950-1956
Portugal	1979, Feb 8	Yang Qiliang	1979-			Han Nianlong	1956-1958
Romania	1949, Oct 5	Wang Youping	1950-1954			Dong Yueqian	1958-1964
		Ke Bonian	1954-1959			Yang Bozhen	1964-1967
		Xu Jianguo	1959-1964			Wang Dong	1969-1971
		Liu Fang	1964-1965			Wang Luming	1972-1974
		Zeng Yongquan	1966-?			Qin Lizhen	1974-1979
		Zhang Haifeng	1969-1973			Cao Keqiang	1979-
		Li Dingquan	1973-1978	Switzerland	1950, Sep 14	Feng Xuan	1950-1959
		Chen Shuliang	1979-			Li Jingquan	1959-1966
Rwanda	1971, Nov 12	Huang Shixie	1972-1977			Chen Zhifang	1970-1975
		Yue Liang	1977-			Li Yunchuan	1976-
San Marino	1971, May 6	Wang Chuanbin (consul-general)	1973-1979	Syria	1956, Aug 10	Chen Zhifang	1956-1958
Sao Tome & Principe	1975, Jul 12	Liu Yingxian	1976-1979			Xu Yixin	1962-1965
		Liu Yufeng	1980-			Chen Tan	1966-?
Senegal	1971, Dec 7	Wang Jinchuan	1972-1977			Qin Jialin	1969-1974
		Zong Kewen	1978-			Cao Keqiang	1974-1979
Seychelles	1976, Jun 30	Liu Chun	1978-1979			Lu Weizhao	1979-
		He Gongkai	1980-	Tanzania	1961, Dec 9	He Ying	1962-1967
Sierra Leone	1971, Jul 29	Zhao Zhengyi	1972-1975			Zhong Xidong	1969-1972
		Zong Kewen	1975-1978			Li Yaowen	1972-1976
		Tian Ping	1978-			Liu Chun	1976-1979
						He Gongkai	1980-
				Thailand	1975, Jul 1	Chai Zemin	1976-1978
						Zhang Weilie	1978-
				Togo	1972, Jul 19	Wei Baoshan	1973-1974
						Yue Xin	1974-

Country	Diplomatic Relations since	Ambassador	Term of Office
Trinidad & Tobago	1974, Jun 20	Wang Zhanyuan	1975-1979
		Wang Yanchang	1979-
Tunisia	1964, Jan 11	Yao Nian	1964-1967
	embassy closed 1967, Jan	Hou Yefeng	1972-1977
	embassy reopened 1971, Oct	Cui Jian	1977-
Turkey	1971, Aug 4	Liu Chun	1972-1976
		Wei Yongqing	1976-1978
		Wang Yueyi	1979-
Uganda	1962, Oct 8	He Ying	1963-1964
		Chen Zhifang	1964-1966?
		Ge Buhai	1972-1977?
		Dai Lu	1978-1979
		Zhang Bochuan	1980-
U.N.O.	1971, Nov 2	Huang Hua	1971-1976
		Chen Chu	1977-
Upper Volta	1973, Sep 7	Xie Bangzhi	1973-1978
		Zhou Min	1979-
U.S.A.	1979, Jan 1	Chai Zemin	1979-
Venezuela	1974, Jun 28	Ling Qing	1975-1978
		Zheng Weizhi	1978-
Vietnam	1950, Jan 10	Luo Guibo	1954-1957
		He Wei	1957-1962
		Zhu Qiwen	1962-1966?
		Wang Youping	1969-1974
		Fu Hao	1974-1977
		Chen Zhifang	1977-1978?
		Yang Gongsu	1978-
Western Samoa	1975, Nov 6	Zhang Zhanwu	1978-
Yemen, Arab Republic	1956, Jun 24	Chen Jiakang	1957-1964
		Wang Ruojie	1964-1972
		Zhang Canming	1973-1975
		Zhao Jin	1975-1979
		Zhong Hanjiu	1980-

Country	Diplomatic Relations since	Ambassador	Term of Office
Yemen, PDR	1968, Feb 2	Li Qiangfen	1970-1972
		Cui Jian	1972-1977
		Huang Shixie	1977-
Yugoslavia	1955, Jan 10	Wu Xiuquan	1955-1958
		No ambassador	1958-1970
		Zeng Tao	1970-1973
		Zhang Haifeng	1973-1978
		Zhou Qiuye	1978-
Zaire	1972, Nov 24	Gong Dafei	1973-1978
		Zhou Boping	1978-
Zambia	1964, Oct 29	Qin Lizhen	1965-1966?
		Li Qiangfen	1972-1977
		Ge Buhai	1978-
Zimbabwe	1980, April		

Diplomatic Relations Formerly Existing with

Country	Diplomatic Relations since	Ambassador	Term of Office
Congo (Stanleyville)	1961, Feb 20		
	severed 1961, September		
Indonesia	1950, Jun 9	Wang Renshu	1950-1954
		Huang Zhen	1954-1961
		Yao Zhongming	1961-1966
	severed 1967		
South Vietnamese Liberation Front (united with North Vietnam in 1977)	1969, June	Wang Ruojie	1973-1976
Zanzibar (united with Tanganyika in 1964)	1963, Dec 11	Meng Ying	1964-1964

THE PARTY ORGANIZATION OF THE PRC

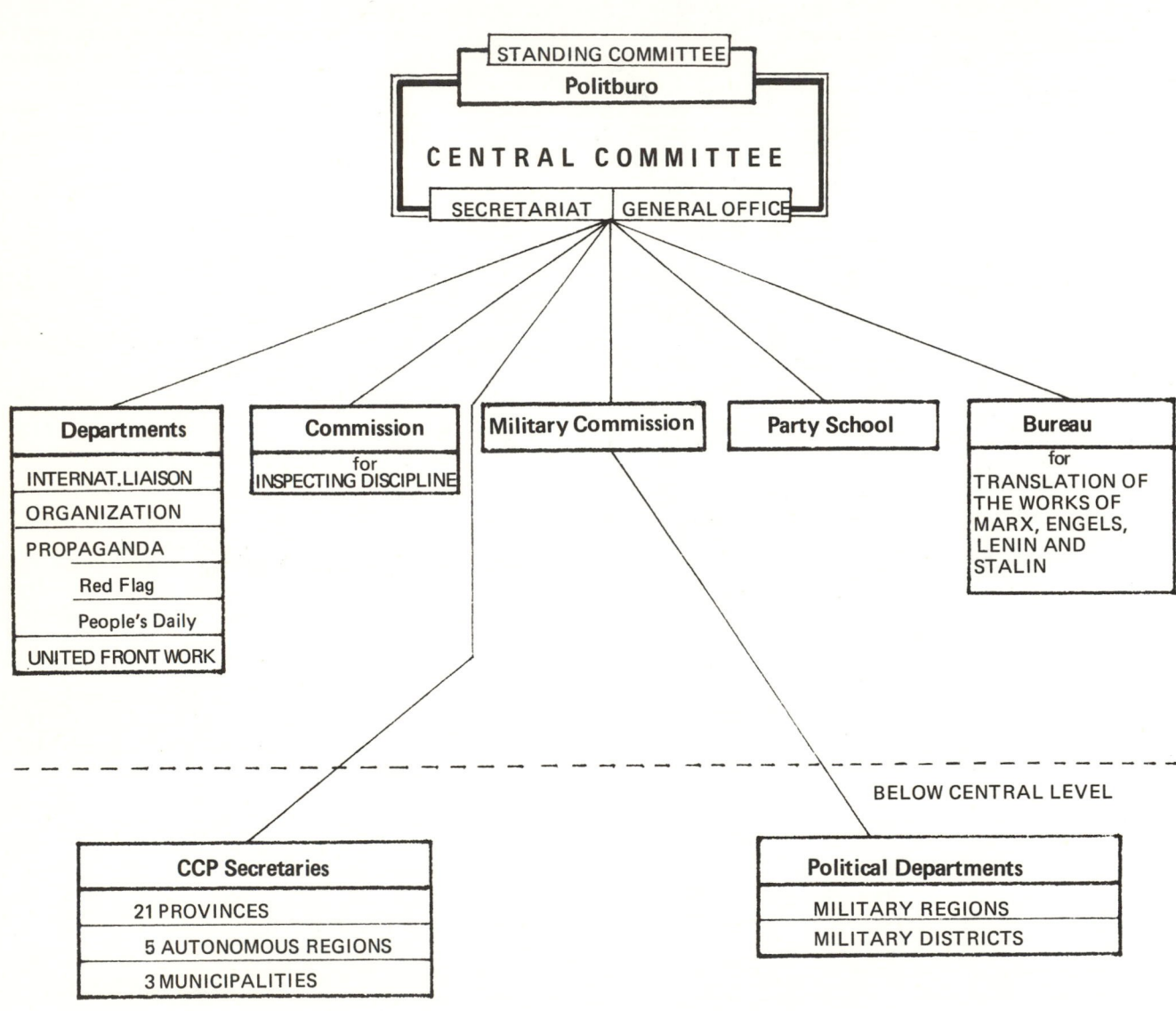

POLITBURO

Standing Committee, Members:

Chen Yun	78/12
Deng Xiaoping	77/ 7
Hu Yaobang	80/ 2
Hua Guofeng	76/10
Li Xiannian	77/ 8
Ye Jianying	73/ 8
Zhao Ziyang	80/ 2

Members:

Chen Yonggui		73/ 8
Deng Yingchao	f	78/12
Fang Yi		77/ 8
Geng Biao		77/ 8
Li Desheng		73/ 8
Liu Bosheng		69/ 4
Ni Zhifu		77/ 8
Nie Rongzhen		77/ 8
Peng Chong		77/ 8
Peng Zhen		79/ 9
Ulanhu		77/ 8
Wang Zhen		78/12
Wei Guoqing		73/ 8
Xu Shiyou		69/ 4

Xu Xiangqian	77/ 8
Yu Qiuli	77/ 8
Zhang Tingfa	77/ 8

Alternate Members:

Chen Muhua	f	77/ 8
Seypidin		73/ 8

SECRETARIAT

Secretary-general:

Hu Yaobang	PBm CCm 78/12

Members:

Fang Yi	PBm CCm 80/ 2
Gu Mu	CCm 80/ 2
Hu Qiaomu	CCm 79/ 9
Peng Chong	PBm CCm 80/ 2
Song Renqiong	CCm 80/ 2
Wan Li	CCm 80/ 2
Wang Renzhong	CCm 80/ 2
Yang Dezhi	CCm 80/ 2
Yao Yilin	CCm 78/ 8
Yu Qiuli	PBm CCm 80/ 2

Some Data of the Politburo Cadres

		Born in		Main Positions held in				
		Year	Province	Party	Government	NPC	Military	Former Military Rank
Members, Stand.Committee	Chen Yun	1905	Shanghai		X	X		
	Deng Xiaoping	1904	Sichuan		X			
	Hu Yaobang	1915	Hunan	X				
	Hua Guofeng	1921	Shanxi	X	X			
	Li Xiannian	1905	Hubei		X			Army general
	Ye Jianying	1897	Guangdong			X		Marshal
	Zhao Ziyang	1918	Henan		X			
Members	Chen Yonggui	1913	Shanxi		X			
	Deng Yingchao f	1904	Henan			X		
	Fang Yi	1916	Fujian	X				
	Geng Biao	1909	Hunan	X				Major-general
	Li Desheng	1916	Hubei				X	Major-general
	Liu Bosheng	1892	Sichuan			X		Marshal
	Ni Zhifu	1932	Shanghai					
	Nie Rongzhen	1899	Sichuan			X		Marshal
	Peng Chong	1915	Fujian	X				
	Peng Zhen	1902	Shanxi			X		
	Ulanhu	1904	Suiyuan					Colonel-general
	Wang Zhen	1908	Hunan	X				Colonel-general
	Wei Guoqing	1906	Guangxi			X	X	
	Xu Shiyou	1906	Henan				X	Colonel-general
	Xu Xiangqian	1902	Shanxi	X			X	Marshal
	Yu Qiuli	1914	Sichuan		X			Lieutenant-general
	Zhang Tingfu	1915 ?					X	Major-general
Alternate Members	Chen Muhua f	1926 ?	?		X			
	Seypidin	1916	Xinjiang			X		

Posts held by the Politburo Members
in June 1980

This organogramme shows the almighty grip of the Politburo members over all essential organs of the PR China. It gives an idea of the function of a body of two dozen governing the fate of one billion people.

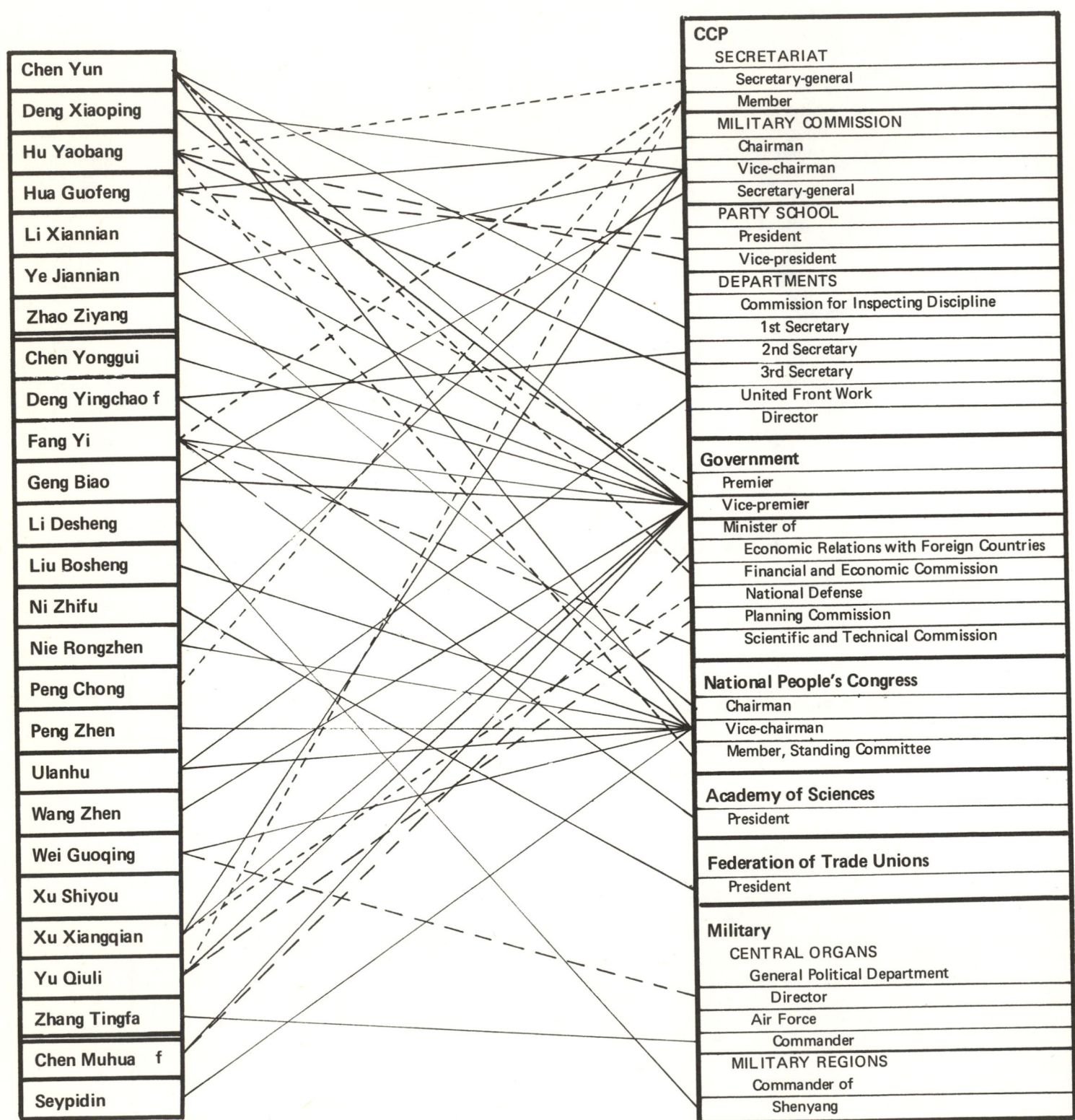

The Central Committee

CCP

11th Central Committee
after the 5th Plenum

The Members

as of April 15, 1980

Legend:

Military Regions

Ch	Chengdu
Fu	Fujian
Gu	Guangzhou
Ji	Jinan
Ku	Kunming
La	Lanzhou
Na	Nanjing
Pe	Peking
Sh	Shenyang
Wu	Wuhan
Xi	Xinjiang

Abbreviations

Af	Airforce
CC	Central Committee
CPPCC	Chinese People's Political Consultative Conference
Log	Logistics
NPC	National People's Congress
Nv	Navy
Pol	Political
Rw	Railway Corps

Government

Commissions

1 Agricultural
2 Capital Construction
3 Economic
4 Financial and Economic
5 Foreign Investment
6 Machine Building Industry
7 Nationalities Affairs
8 Physical Culture and Sports
9 Planning
10 Scientific and Technical

Ministries

11 Agriculture
12 Civil Affairs
13 Communications
14 Culture
15 Econ. Relations with Foreign Countries
16 Education
17 Food
18 Foreign Affairs
19 Foreign Trade
20 Machine Building II
21 Metallurgical Industry
22 National Defense
23 Power Industry
24 Public Security
25 Textile Industry
26 Water Conservancy

Provinces

1 Anhui
2 Beijing
3 Fujian
4 Gansu
5 Guangdong
6 Guangxi
7 Guizhou
8 Hebei
9 Heilongjiang
10 Henan
11 Hubei
12 Hunan
13 Jiangsu
14 Jiangxi
15 Jilin
16 Liaoning
17 Nei Monggol
18 Ningxia
19 Qinghai
20 Shaanxi
21 Shandong
22 Shanghai
23 Shanxi
24 Sichuan
25 Tianjin
26 Tibet
27 Xinjiang
28 Yunnan
29 Zhejiang

Excluding the deceased

Guo Moruo	1978, Jun 6
Lin Liming	1977, Aug 19
Luo Ruiqing	1978, Aug 3
Ma Li	1979, Sep 25
Peng Shaohui	1978, Apr 25
Su Zhenhua	1979, Feb 7
Wang Zheng	1978, Aug 13
Chen Xilian	1980, Feb
Ji Dengkui (purged)	1980, Feb
Wang Dongxing	1980, Feb
Wu De	1980, Feb

No	Name	Last Appearance	Others
1	An Pingsheng	80/4	
2	An Ziwen	80/3	Vice-pres., Party School, CCP Central Comte.
3	Basang	79/8	
4	Bai Dongcai	80/4	
5	Bai Rubing	80/3	
6	Baerlitai	79/12	
7	Bo yibo	80/4	
8	Cai Chang	79/6	Honorary pres., Women's Federation
9	Cai Xiao	79/10	Dpty. secretary-general, 5th CPPCC
10	Cao Lihuai	80/1	
11	Cao Yiou	78/7	Widow of Kang Sheng; probably purged
12	Chen Fuhan	79/6	Vice-chairman, Railwayworkers' Trade Union
13	Chen Guodong	80/4	
14	Chen Muhua	80/3	
15	Chen Pixian	80/3	
16	Chen Puru	80/3	
17	Chen Qihan	78/8	
18	Chen Weida	80/3	
19	Chen Yonggui	80/3	
20	Chen Yun	80/2	
21	Chen Zaidao	80/1	

#	Name	Date	Position/Notes
22	Cheng Zihua	80/4	
23	Chi Biqing	80/2	
24	Chu Jiang	80/4	1st secretary, Nanjing CP
25	Dai Guangqian	79/12	Cadre in Guangdong Province
26	Deng Xiaoping	80/4	
27	Deng Yingchao	80/4	Honorary president, Women's Federation
28	Ding Guoyu	79/2	
29	Ding Keze	80/3	
30	Du Yide	80/4	
31	Duan Junyi	80/3	
32	Fan Deling	79/12	
33	Fang Yi	80/4	President, Academy of Sciences
34	Feng Xuan	80/2	Dpty dir., Dpt. of Internat'l Liaison, CCP CC
35	Geng Biao	80/4	
36	Geng Qichang	77/8	Probably purged
37	Gu Mu	80/4	
38	Guo Yufeng	77/10	Probably purged
39	Han Guang	80/2	
40	Han Xianchu	80/3	
41	Han ying	80/4	1st secretary, Communist Youth League
42	Hao jianxiu	79/10	Vice-president, Women's Federation
43	He Cheng	79/2	
44	Hong Xuezhi	80/4	
45	Hu Lijiao	80/3	
46	Hu Qiaomu	80/3	President, Academy of Social Sciences
47	Hu Yaobang	80/4	
48	Hua Guofeng	80/4	
49	Huang Hua	80/4	
50	Huang Huoqing	80/4	Chief procurator, Supreme People's Procuratorate
51	Huang Kecheng	80/3	Permanent sec...Com'f. Inspect Discipline, CCP CC
52	Huang Oudong	80/2	
53	Huang Zhen	80/4	
54	Huang Zhizhen	80/3	
55	Huo Shilian	80/4	
56	Ismail Amat	80/4	
57	Ji Pengfei	80/4	Dir. Internat'l Liaison Dpt. CCP Central Comte.
58	Jiang Hua	80/4	President, Supreme People's Court
59	Jiang Nanxiang	80/4	Probably purged
60	Jiang Liyin		
61	Jiang Weiqing	80/4	
62	Jiang yonghui	80/3	
63	Jiao Linyi	80/3	
64	Kang Keqing	80/4	Widow of Zhu De; vice-pres., Women's Federation
65	Kang Shien	80/3	
66	Kong Shiquan	79/1	
67	Kong Yuann	79/6	Deputy secretary-general, 5th NPC
68	Kong Zhaonian	79/10	
69	Li Baohua	80/1	President, People's Bank
70	Li Chang	80/3	Vice-president, Academy of Sciences
71	Li Da	80/3	
72	Li Desheng	80/4	
73	Li Jingquan	80/1	
74	Li Qiang	80/4	
75	Li Qiming	80/3	1st secretary, Wuhan CP
76	Li Renzhi	80/3	
77	Li Ruishan	79/6	
78	Li Shijun	78/12	
79	Li Shuiqing	79/10	
80	Li Xiannian	80/4	Cadre, in Shaanxi Province
81	Li Zhimin	80/2	
82	Li Ziyuan	80/4	
83	Liang Biye	79/2	
84	Liao Chengzhi	80/3	
85	Liao Hansheng	80/2	
86	Lin Zhigao	80/4	
87	Lin Hujia	80/3	
88	Lin Liyun	80/3	Vice-president, Women's Federation
89	Liu Bocheng	79/9	
90	Liu Chunqiao	79/12	

No	Name	Last Appearance	Others
91	Liu Guangtao	77/12	Probably purged
92	Liu Jianxun	78/4	Probably purged
93	Liu Lanbo	79/9	1st dpty.dir., United Front Work Dpt., CCP CC
94	Liu Lantao	80/4	
95	Liu wei	80/3	
96	Liu Xichang	79/12	Probably purged
97	Liu Xingyuan	77/8	Probably purged
98	Liu Zhen	79/2	Probably purged
99	Liu Zihou	79/11	
100	Lu Dadong	80/4	
101	Lu Dingyi	79/9	Vice-chairman, 5th CPPCC
102	Lu Tianji	78/12	Probably purged
103	Luo Qingchang	80/3	
104	Lü yulan	79/9	
105	Lü Zhengcao	80/3	1st polit.commissar, PLA Railway Corps
106	Ma Hui	80/4	
107	Ma Wenrui	80/4	
108	Ma Xingyuan	80/3	
109	Mao Zhiyong	80/3	
110	Ni Zhifu	80/4	
111	Nie Fengzhi	80/2	President, Federation of Trade Unions
112	Nie Rongzhen	79/12	
113	Peng Chong	80/3	
114	Peng Zhen	79/6	Chairman, Legal Commission, 5th NPC
115	Qian Zhengying	80/3	
116	Qian Zhiguang	80/3	
117	Qiao Xiaoguang	80/3	
118	Qin Jiwei	80/2	
119	Rao Xingli	80/4	
120	Ren Rong	80/4	
121	Ren Zhongyi	80/4	
122	Ren Sizhong	79/7	
123	Ruan Bosheng	80/3	
124	Seypidin	80/2	
125	Song Ping	80/3	Dir., Organisation Dpt., CCP Central Comte.
126	Song Renqiong	80/3	Commandant, PLA Academy of Mil. Science
127	Song Shilun	80/1	
128	Su Jing	79/2	
129	Su Yiran	80/1	
130	Su Yu	80/3	
131	Tan Qilong	80/3	
132	Tan Yingji	80/3	
133	Tan Zhenlin	80/4	
134	Tang Ke	80/2	
135	Tian Bao	80/3	
136	Tie ying	80/4	
137	Ulanhu	80/4	Dir., United Front Work Dpt., CCP Central Comte.
138	Wan Da	80/3	
139	Wan Li	80/4	
140	Wang Bicheng	80/1	
141	Wang Enmao	80/2	
142	Wang Chaozhu	80/3	
143	Wang Feng	80/4	
144	Wang Guangyu	80/2	

Dates (column headers, top): 77/8, 80/1, 78/4, 78/12, 80/3, 80/3, 80/4, 80/2, 80/3, 80/2, 80/3, 77/7, 80/4, 80/3, 80/3, 77/10, 78/12, 80/2, 80/3, 80/4, 80/2, 80/4, 80/3, 78/5, 79/8, 80/4, 80/2, 80/3, 80/1, 78/12, 80/3, 80/4, 80/4, 80/4, 80/4, 80/2, 80/4, 78/2, 80/4, 79/2, 78/12, 80/1, 80/3, 80/3, 79/6, 79/12, 80/4, 80/3, 80/2, 80/3, 80/3, 80/1, 80/2, 80/4, 80/3, 80/3, 80/4, 79/6, 80/4, 80/1

Annotations:

- Probably purged
- Dpty. sec., Commission (Insp. Discipline, CCP CC
- Sec., Shanghai Communist Youth League
- Political commissar, PLA Logistics Department
- Dir., Propaganda Dpt, CCP Central Comte.
- Vice-chm., Legal Commission, 5th NPC
- Probably purged
- Chairman, Daqing Oilfield Rev. Comte.
- Commandant, PLA Military Academy
- Probably purged
- 1st secretary, Guangzhou CP
- Probably purged
- Probably purged
- Vice-president, Academy of Social Sciences
- Vice-president, Nuclear Society
- Dpty. dir., Propaganda Dpt., CCP CC

Names:

145	Wang Guofan
146	Wang Heshou
147	Wang Linhe
148	Wang Maoquan
149	Wang Meng
150	Wang Mingzhang
151	Wang Ping
152	Wang Qian
153	Wang Renzhong
154	Wang Shitai
155	Wang Shoudao
156	Wang Xiuxiu
157	Wang Yiping
158	Wang Zhen
159	Wei Guoqing
160	Wu Guixian
161	Wu Quanqing
162	Wu Xiuquan
163	Xi-hou-ba
164	Xi Zhongxun
165	Xiao Hua
166	Xiao Jingguang
167	Xiao Ke
168	Xie Xuegong
169	Xing Yanzi
170	Xu Jiatun
171	Xu Shiyou
172	Xu Xiangqian
173	Xue Jinda
174	Yang Chengwu
175	Yang Dezhi
176	Yang Jingren
177	Yang Shangkun
178	Yang Yichen
179	Yang Yong
180	Yao Yilin
181	Ye Fei
182	Ye Jianying
183	You Taizhong
184	Yu Hongliang
185	Yu Mingtao
186	Yu Qiuli
187	Yu Sang
188	Zeng Shaoshan
189	Zeng Siyu
190	Zhang Aiping
191	Zhang Caiqian
192	Zhang Dingcheng
193	Zhang Fugui
194	Zhang Fukeng
195	Zhang Jingfu
196	Zhang Lixian
197	Zhang Pinghua
198	Zhang Tingfa
199	Zhang Yuhua
200	Zhang Zhixiu
201	Zhao Cangbi
202	Zhao Xinchu
203	Zhao Zhijian
204	Zhao Ziyang
205	Zhou Chunlin
206	Zhou Hui
207	Zhou Jianren
208	Zhou Yang
209	Zhu Guangya
210	Zhu Muzhi
211	Zong Xiyun

CCP

11th Central Committee
after the 5th Plenum

The Alternate Members

Excluding the deceased Xie Zhengrong (1977, Dec 4)

as of May 1, 1980

Legend:

Mil. Regions
1 Beijing
2 Chengdu
3 Fuzhou
4 Guangzhou
5 Jinan
6 Kunming
7 Lanzhou
8 Nanjing
9 Shenyang
10 Wuhan
11 Xinjiang

Government

Commissions
1 Capital Construction
2 Economic
3 Planning
4 Science and Technology for National Defense

Ministries
5 Machine Building I
6 Metallurgical Industry

PLA Services
Af Airforce
Am Armored Forces
CEn Capital Construction Engineering Corps
En Engineering Corps
Nv Navy

Provinces
1 Anhui
2 Beijing
3 Fujian
4 Gansu
5 Guangdong
6 Guangxi
7 Guizhou
8 Hebei
9 Heilongjiang
10 Henan
11 Hubei
12 Hunan
13 Jiangsu
14 Jiangxi
15 Jilin
16 Liaoning
17 Nei Monggol
18 Ningxia
19 Qinghai
20 Shaanxi
21 Shandong
22 Shanghai
23 Shanxi
24 Sichuan
25 Tianjin
26 Tibet
27 Xinjiang
28 Yunnan
29 Zhejiang

Posts held in

No. | **Name**

Central Committee: 8th / 9th / 10th — Alternate member, Member, Alternate member, Member, Alternate member, Member

Military:
- Central Level: Gvmt., NPC
  - Gvmt: Minister, Vice-minister, Member, Stand. Committee
  - Log. Dpt.: Deputy chief of staff, Deputy director, Deputy polit. commissar
  - Services: Commander, Deputy commander, Political commissar
  - Mil. Region: Commander, Deputy commander, 1st polit. commissar, 2nd polit. commissar, Political commissar
  - Mil. Distr.: Commander, Political commissar
  - Rank: Colonel-general, Lieutenant-general, Major-general, Senior-colonel

Provinces:
- CCP: 1st secretary, 2nd secretary, Secretary, Deputy secretary, Member, Stand. Committee
- People's Govmt. / People's Congr.: Governor, Vice-governor, Chairman, Vice-chairman

Others / Remarks

Last Appearance

633

#	Name	Position / Notes	Date
1	Bu Guxiang	of Hunan Province	78/12
2	Cai Fenglan (F)		80/4
3	Cao Siming	Chairman, Guangxi Trade Unions	80/3
4	Cen Guorong	Hubei textile worker	80/2
5	Chen Aie (F)	of Shanghai Inst. of Computing Technology	79/9
6	Chen Renfu		79/3
7	Chen Xianrui		78/10
8	Chen Yonglin	of Gansu Province	79/5
9	Chen Yubao	of Fujian Province	78/12
10	Chen Zuolin		80/4
11	Cheng Yitai	of Liaoning Province	78/12
12	Chilin Wandan	probably purged	77/12
13	Dai Suli		80/3
14	Deng Hua		79/10
15	Ding Changhua (F)	of Jiangxi Province	79/6
16	Du Ping		80/4
17	Du Xueran	Henan miner	77/10
18	Feng Pinde	of Shanghai Municipality	77/10
19	Feng Zhanwu	probably purged	77/8
20	Gao Houliang		80/4
21	Gu Xiulian (F)	of Yunnan Province	79/6
22	Guan Zehai	Secretary, Dazhai Brigade CP	78/12
23	Guo Fenglian (F)		79/6
24	Guo Yaoqing	Secretary, Nanning Municipality CP	78/12
25	He Jinnian		78/12
26	Hu Jindi (F)		78/12
27	Hu Liangcai		79/12
28	Hu Song	probably purged	79/12
29	Huang Ronghai	of Guangdong Province	80/3
30	Huang Xinting		79/4
31	Huang Zuozhen		79/2
32	Ji Guixin		77/8
33	Ji Yinglin		78/12
34	Janabil		79/9
35	Jiang Baodi (F)		79/7
36	Jiang Xieyuan		80/3
37	Jin Minghan		80/1
38	Kang Lin		79/9
39	Li Chang'an		79/2
40	Li Chengfang	of Beijing Municipality	80/2
41	Li Huamin		80/3
42	Li Jianzhen (F)		80/4
43	Li Jiliang	of Maoming Petroleum Corp.	77/8
44	Li Qiaoyun (F)	of Beijing Municipality	79/3
45	Li Rinai	probably purged	78/12
46	Li Shoulin	probably purged	77/8
47	Li Xuezhi		80/2
48	Li Yaowen	Polit.com., Nat'l Defense and Technological Com.	79/2
49	Li Yuan	Dpty.dir., Capital Constr. Engineering Corps, PLA	79/4
50	Li Zugen	Vice-chm., Jiangxi Trade Unions	80/2

No.	Name	Military / Province posts (selected)	Others / Remarks	Last Appearance
51	Liu Chonggui	CCP 2nd secretary 6; Mil. Distr. Political commissar 6; Central Level Services Deputy commander Nv		80/3
52	Liu Daosheng			79/7
53	Liu Minghui			80/2
54	Liu Ruiqing		Guangdong miner	78/12
55	Liu Weiming		Secretary, Communist Youth League	80/1
56	Liu Xiyao	Governor 28; CCP Secretary 28		80/3
57	Liu Zhenhua	Vice-governor 24; Mil. Region 1st polit. commissar Ku; 2nd polit. commissar Sh; Rank Lieutenant-general		80/3
58	Liu Zhijian		Hunan worker	80/4
59	Liu Zhiqiang		probably purged	78/12
60	Lü Jinlong			77/12
61	Lü Zhongyang	CCP Member Stand. Committee 10	Qinghai peasant	78/12
62	Lü Cunjie		Heilongjiang peasant	78/12
63	Lü He			78/12
64	Lü Xuguo			78/12
65	Ma Jinhua		Ningxia peasant	78/12
66	Ma Ming		Hebei worker	79/2
67	Ma Sizhong			80/2
68	Mao Xinxian	CCP Member Stand. Committee 18	Shanghai textile worker	78/10
69	Mei Songling		of "Hard Bones 6th Company"	77/8
70	Pan Meiying		Guangxi worker	77/9
71	Pan Shixing		Guangxi peasant	78/12
72	Qian Xuesen		Vice-pres., Assn. f. Science and Technology	80/3
73	Raidi	People's Congr. Vice-chairman 26; CCP Deputy secretary 26		80/1
74	Ran Guiying	CCP Member Stand. Committee 1	Gansu peasant	78/12
75	Ren Zhibin			79/2
76	Rigdzin Wanggyal		Tibet cadre	78/12
77	Ruzi Turdi		Xinjiang peasant; probably purged	77/12
78	Shen Chuyun		Zhejiang textile worker	77/8
79	Shen Maogong		purged	78/12
80	Song Qingyou	CCP Member Stand. Committee 21		79/12
81	Sun Xuemei			78/12
82	Tan Shanhe	Rank Major-general		80/1
83	Tan Wenzhen	Log. Dpt. Commander En	Hunan cadre	78/12

635

#	Name	Sex	Description	Date
84	Tang Kebi			79/6
85	Tang Liang	F	Military cadre	79/2
86	Tang Wensheng	F	Dpty.dir., America Dpt., Foreign Ministry	79/2
87	Wang Fuzhi			79/11
88	Wang Jinling	F		79/2
89	Wang Jinshan			79/11
90	Wang Jinyou			79/6
91	Wang Jurshao		Anshan worker	78/12
92	Wang Liusheng			79/2
93	Wang Shangrong			79/11
94	Wei Fengying	F	Liaoning worker	78/7
95	Wei Xingzheng		Heilongjiang worker	78/12
96	Wen Xianglan	F	Jiangsu peasant	80/3
97	Wu Huojin			79/1
98	Wu Jinquan			78/12
99	Wu Kehua			80/4
100	Wu Lengxi			79/6
101	Wu Xiangbi			79/2
102	Wu Zhong			79/4
103	Xiang Zhonghua			79/10
104	Xiao Han			80/3
105	Xiao Wangdong			80/4
106	Xu Biaojun			78/12
107	Xu Chi			79/8
108	Xu Liqing		of Nei Monggol	80/4
109	Xue Jinlian	F		78/12
110	Yang Dayi			80/4
111	Yang Fuzhen	F		80/3
112	Yang Junsheng			80/2
113	Yang Yongliang			77/9
114	Yuan Baohua		Commander, PLA Airforce 1st Flight Division	80/3
115	Zhang Huailian			79/9
116	Zhang Jihui			78/6
117	Zhang Linchi			79/2
118	Zhang Lingbin			78/12
119	Zhang Yaoci			78/12
120	Zhang Zhen			80/4
121	Zhang Zhidi		Hubei cadre	79/9
122	Zhao Wucheng			80/4
123	Zhao Xingyuan			80/2
124	Zhao Xuequan			79/12
125	Zheng Sansheng			79/8
126	Zhong Fuxiang		Jiangsu worker	78/6
127	Zhou Aqing			79/2
128	Zhou Zijian			80/4
129	Zhu Shaoqing			80/2
130	Zou Jiahua		Dpty.dir., State Office of Nat'l. Defense Ind.	80/1
131	Zuo Chongyi		Hero-soldier	78/12

ORGANS UNDER THE CENTRAL COMMITTEE

General Office
Director	Yao Yilin	CCm 80/ 2
Deputy Directors		
	Feng Wenbin	79/ 8
	Li Zhizhong	79/ 5
	Zeng San	79/ 8
	Zhang Yaoci	CCa 77/10

Commission for Inspecting Discipline
1st Secretary	Chen Yun	PBm CCm	78/12
2nd Secretary	Deng Yingchao f	PBm CCm	78/12
3rd Secretary	Hu Yaobang	PBm CCm	78/12
Permanent Secretary			
	Huang Kecheng	CCm	78/12
Deputy Secretaries			
	Guo Shushen		78/12
	Li Yimeng		78/12
	Liu Shunyuan		78/12
	Ma Guorui		78/12
	Wang Heshou	CCm	78/12
	Wang Congwu		78/12
	Wei Wenbo		78/12
	Yuan Renyuan		78/12
	Zhang Ce		78/12
	Zhang Qilong		78/12
	Zhang Yun f		78/12
Members	An Jianbing		78/12
	Bing Jiesan		78/12
	Chen Lin		78/12
	Dobyal Ceyyang		78/12
	Duan Yun		78/12
	Fan Rusheng		78/12
	Hamdinnyas		78/12
	He Dongchang		78/12
	He Shanyuan		78/12
	He Tingyi		78/12
	Hu Dehua f		78/12
	Huang Ganying f		78/12
	Huang Minwei		78/12
	Huang Rong		78/12
	Jian Xianren f		78/12
	Jie-er-ge-le		78/12
	Li Huasheng		78/12
	Li Ligong		78/12
	Li Zhen		78/12
	Li Zhenghai		78/12
	Li Zhilian		78/12
	Liu Jingzhi		78/12
	Liu Liying		78/12
	Liu Mingjiu		78/12
	Liu Ying		78/12
	Liu Renzan		78/12
	Ma Duo		78/12
	Ma Xin		78/12
	Peng Ru		78/12
	Pu Anxiu f		78/12
	Rao Zhengxi		78/12
	Song Cheng		78/12
	Wang Dazhong		78/12
	Wang Ruoshui		78/12
	Wang Sumin		78/12
	Wang Wenfeng		78/12

Wang Wenxuan		78/ 2
Wang Zhaowen		78/ 2
Wang Zhengyi		78/ 2
Wang Zhizhe		78/ 2
Wu Bo		78/ 2
Xu Shaofu		78/ 2
Xu Shenji		78/ 2
Yan Dongsheng		78/ 2
Yan Xiufeng		80/ 4
Yang Changchun		78/ 2
Yang Xinbei		78/ 2
Yang Xiushan		78/ 2
Yin Jichang		78/ 2
Zeng San		78/ 2
Zhang Chengxian		78/ 2
Zhang Kai		78/ 2
Zhang Qi		78/ 2
Zhang Ruihua		78/ 2
Zhang Zhaomei		78/ 2
Zhang Zhong		78/ 2
Zheng Aiping		78/ 2
Zhou Fengming		78/ 2
Zhou Taihe		78/ 2
Zhu Muzhi	CCm	78/ 2
Zhu Yunqian		78/ 2

Military Commission
Chairman			
Hua Guofeng		PBm CCm	77/ 5
Vice-chairmen			
Deng Xiaoping		PBm CCm	77/ 7
Nie Rongzhen	Marshal	PBm CCm	61/ 3
Xu Xiangqian	Marshal	PBm CCm	66/11
Ye Jianying	Marshal	PBm CCm	67/ 3
Member, Standing Committee			
Han Xianchu	Colonel-general	CCm	80/ 2
Su Yu	Army General	CCm	75/ 6
Wang Ping	Colonel-general	CCm	80/ 2
Xu Shiyou	Colonel-general	PBm CCm	80/ 4
Yang Dezhi	Colonel-general	CCm	80/ 2
Yang Yong	Colonel-general	CCm	80/ 2
Secretary-general			
Geng Biao	Major-general	PBm CCm	80/ 3
Member			
Xiao Hua	Colonel-general	CCm	79/ 9
Adviser			
Li Da	Colonel-general	CCm	80/ 3
Leading Cadre			
Wang Zhen	Colonel-general	PBm CCm	80/ 3

International Liaison Department
Director	Ji Pengfei	CCm	79/ 3
Deputy Directors			
	Feng Xuan	CCm	73/11
	Jiao Shi		78/ 3
	Li Yimeng		75/10
	Liu Xinquan		79/ 6
	Ou Tangliang f		78/ 3
	Sun Ping		79/ 9
	Wu Xueqian f		78/ 5
	Zhang Zhixiang		78/ 4

Organization Department

Director	Song Renqiong	CCm	79/ 1
Deputy Directors			
	Chen Yeping		78/ 8
	Li Buxin		78/11
	Zhao Zhenqing		79/11
Secretary-general			
	Wang Zhaohua		79/ 5

Propaganda Department

Director	Wang Renzhong	CCm	80/ 3
1st Deputy Director			
	Huang Zhen	CCm	79/ 9
Deputy Directors			
	Liao Jingdan		77/12
	Zhang Xiangshan		77/12
	Zhou Yang	CCm	80/ 4
	Zhu Muzhi	CCm	77/12
Secretary-general			
	Li Shubin		78/ 8
General office			
Director	Wang Zhongfang		79/ 7

Hong Qi

Chief editor	Xiang Fu		78/10
Deputy editor-in-chief			
	Liu Zongzhuo		77/ 5

Renmin Ribao

Chief Editor	Hu Jiwei		77/ 4
Deputy editors-in-chief			
	An Gang		76/ 5
	Li Zhuang		77/ 4
	Pan Fei		77/ 4
	Qin Chuan		78/ 4
	Wang Ruoshui		78/ 7
Secretary-general			
	Guo Wei		77/ 4

United Front Work Department

Director	Ulanhu	PBm CCm	77/ 7
1st deputy director			
	Liu Lantao	CCm	79/ 3

Deputy Directors			
	Fang Zhida		79/ 4
	Li Gui		77/11
	Liu Ningyi		80/ 2
	Ping Jiesan		79/ 1
	Tong Xiaopeng		77/11
	Xiong Xianghui		79/ 1
	Xue Zizheng		79/10
	Yang Jingren	CCm	78/12
	Zhang Zhiyi		80/ 4
Secretary-general			
	Peng Youjin		78/ 6
General office			
Dpty. director	Yun Li-wen	f	78/10

Bureau for the Translation of the Works of Marx, Engels, Lenin and Stalin

Director	Wang Huide		78/10

Political and Judicial Leadership Group

Deputy Head	Zhang Cangbi	CCm	78/10

Schistosomiasis Prevention Leadership Group

Head	Peng Chong	PBm CCm	78/10
Deputy Head	Qian Xinzhong		78/10
Member	Wang Zhiguo		78/10

Party School

President	Hua Guofeng	PBm CCm	77/10
Vice-presidents			
	An Ziwen	CCm	79/ 5
	Feng Wenbin		79/ 5
	Hu Yaobang	PBm CCm	77/10
Deputy Secretary			
	An Ziwen	CCm	79/ 5
Political Department			
Director	Li Yifei		78/ 8
Dean of education			
	Song Zhenting		79/ 7
Associate dean of academic affairs			
	Feng Wenbin		78/ 8
Adviser	Yang Xianzhen		79/ 6

THE STANDING COMMITTEE OF THE 5th NATIONAL PEOPLE'S CONGRESS after Its 3rd Session in September 1980

Left section — National People's Congresses

No.	Name	Politburo Member	Politburo Alt. Member	CC Member	CC Alt. Member
1	Ye Jianying	X		X	
2	Bainquen Erdeni				
3	Chen Yun	X		X	
4	Deng Yingchao (f)	X		X	
5	Hu Juewen				
6	Ji Pengfei			X	
7	Li Jingquan			X	
8	Liao Chengzhi			X	
9	Ngapoi Ngawang Jigmi			X	
10	Peng Zhen	X		X	
11	Peng Chong	X		X	
12	Seypidin			X	
13	Shi Liang (f)				
14	Song Qingling (f)				
15	Su Yu			X	
16	Tan Zhenlin			X	
17	Ulanhu	X		X	
18	Wei Guoqing	X		X	
19	Xi Zhongxun			X	
20	Xiao Jingguang			X	
21	Xu Deheng				
22	Yang Shangkun		X	X	
23	Zhu Yunshan				
24	Ba Jin				
25	Basang (f)			X	
26	Ba Yikai				
27	Bai Shouyi				
28	Barritai				
29	Bei Shizhang				
30	Bi-ken				
31	Cai-dan Zhuo-ma (f)				
32	Cao Juru			X	
33	Cao Yiou (f)				
34	Cao Yu				
35	Chen Cisheng				
36	Chen Xiaoshun				
37	Chen Yisong				
38	Chen Yongxiang				
39	Chen Yuniang (f)				
40	Chen Zaidao			X	
41	Cheng Shicai				

Right section — National People's Congresses

No.	Name	CC Member	CC Alt. Member	Politburo Member	Politburo Alt. Member
98	Liu Danian				
99	Liu Fei				
100	Lu Shenghe				
101	Luo Qingchang	X			
102	Luo Shuzhang (f)				
103	Lü Ji				
104	Lü Shuxiang	X			
105	Lü Yulan (f)				
106	Ma Haoqian				
107	Ma Hengchang				
108	Ma Yinchu				
109	Mao Diqiu				
110	Mao Yisheng				
111	Miao Yuntai				
112	Na-mu-la				
113	Ni Guyin (f)				
114	Ou Tangliang (f)				
115	Pak Chun Za (f)				
116	Pei Changhui				
117	Peng Mingzhi				
118	Puncog Wangje				
119	Qi Zisheng				
120	Qian Xinzhong				
121	Ren Xinmin				
122	Rong Yiren				
123	Rui Ban				
124	Sha Qianli				
125	Shan Huaxiang				
126	Shao Rongbin				
127	Shen Hong				
128	Sheng Wan (f)				
129	Shi Laihe				
130	Shi Zhongqin (f)				
131	Su Buqing				
132	Tan Zheng				
133	Tang Tianji				
134	Tao Zhiyue				
135	Tomur Dawamat				
136	Wang Ganchang				
137	Wang Guanlan				
138	Wang Jian'an				

139	Wang Kunlun	
140	Wang Ping	
141	Wang Yaohua	f
142	Wang Yeqiu	
143	Wang Yongxing	
144	Wang Yuexia	f
145	Wang Yugui	
146	Wu Chengqing	
147	Wu Lengxi	
148	Wu Xianfeng	
149	Wu Xinyu	
150	Wu Yubu	
151	Xia Juhua	f
152	Xiang Layu	f
153	Xie Tieli	
154	Xu Dixin	
155	Xu Jie	
156	Yan Deyi	
157	Yan Jici	
158	Yang Mo	f
159	Yang Shangkui	
160	Yang Xiufeng	
161	Yang Yong	f
162	Yao Maoqi	
163	Yao Shichang	
164	Ye Shengtao	
165	Yi Shijuan	f
166	Yu Aifeng	f
167	Yuan Renquan	
168	Yuan Xuefen	f
169	Yue Meizhong	
170	Zeng Sheng	
171	Zeng Zhi	f
172	Zhan Caifang	
173	Zhang Aiping	
174	Zhang Binggui	
175	Zhang Fengyun	f
176	Zhang Fucai	f
177	Zhang Guizhen	f
178	Zhang Guoqing	f
179	Zhang Jinbang	
180	Zhang Pinghua	
181	Zhang Qilong	
182	Zhang Ruiying	f
183	Zhang Wanfu	
184	Zhang Wenyu	
185	Zhang Zhengtao	
186	Zhao Zhongyao	
187	Zhou Li	
188	Zhou Peiyuan	
189	Zhou Shutao	
190	Zhao Zhan'ao	
191	Zhu Liangcai	f
192	Zhu Xuefan	
193	Zhuang Xiquan	

42	Chu Tunan	
43	Deng Zhaoxiang	
44	Deng Chumin	
45	Deng Diantao	
46	Dong Qiwu	
47	Dong Tianzhen	
48	Fan Deling	
49	Fan Zhongzhi	
50	Fang Zhichun	
51	Fei Yimin	
52	Fu Qiutao	
53	Fu Zhong	
54	Gan Zuchang	
55	Gao Kelin	
56	Gu Kangluo	
57	Guo Fenglian	f
58	Guo Huaruo	
59	Guo Shushen	
60	Guo Yingfu	
61	Hai Yuzhen	
62	Hao Deqing	
63	Hong Xuezhi	
64	Hu Qiaomu	
65	Hu Sheng	
66	Hu Yaobang	
67	Hu Yuzhi	
68	Hu Ziang	
69	Hua Luogeng	
70	Huang Bingwei	
71	Huang Juxiang	f
72	Huang Rongchang	
73	Huang Zuoqin	
74	Ismail Amat	
75	Ji Changshan	
76	Ji Fang	
77	Jiang Liyin	
78	Jiang Nanxiang	
79	Jin Guixiang	f
80	Kang Keqing	f
81	Ke-you-mu Mai-ti-ni-ya-zi	
82	Kui Bi	
83	Kwok Tseng Kai	
84	Li Chang	
85	Li Fenglan	f
86	Li Fuzhong	
87	Li Jukui	
88	Li Ruihuan	
89	Li Yanlu	
90	Li Zhen	f
91	Liang Biye	
92	Liang Jiquan	
93	Lin Liyun	f
94	Lin Qiaozhi	f
95	Lin Tie	
96	Lin Yiping	
97	Lin Yishan	

Former members of the Standing Committee of the 5th National People's Congress

deceased or ousted as of June 1980

deceased	Guo Moruo	1978, Jun 12
	Luo Ruiqing	1978, Aug 3
	Ma Chungu	1979, Mar 16
	Meng Jimao	1980, Jan 24
	Ouyang Qin	1978, May 15
	Tan Yubao	1980, Jan 10
	Tong Dizhou	1979, Mar 30
	Wu Yaozong	1979, Sep 17
	Yang Dongchun	1979, Sep 25
	Zhou Shidi	1979, Jun 30
ousted	Wu De	1980, Feb

THE NATIONAL PEOPLE'S CONGRESS

Secretariat
Acting secretary-general

	Peng Zhen	PBm CCm 79/11

Dpty. secretary-generals

	Gao Dengbang	79/11
	Kong Yuan	CCm 79/ 2
	Luo Qingchang	CCm 73/ 8
	Xing Yimin	78/ 5
	Zeng Tao	79/11
	Zhang Jialuo	78/ 5
	Zheng Jiqiao	78/ 5

Legal Commission
under the NPC Stand. Comte.

Chairman	Peng Zhen	PBm CCm 79/ 2
Vice-chairman	An Ziwen	CCm 79/ 2
	Gao Kelin	79/ 2
	Gu Ming	80/ 4
	Hu Qiaomu	CCm 79/ 2
	Liu Fuzhi	80/ 4
	Sha Qianli	79/ 2
	Shi Liang f	79/ 2
	Tan Zheng	79/ 2
	Tao Xijin	79/ 2
	Wang Hanbin	80/ 4
	Wang Shoudao	CCm 79/ 2

	Wu Xinyu	79/ 2
	Yang Xiufeng	79/ 2
	Zhang Youyu	80/ 4
Secr.-general	Wang Hanbin	80/ 4

Dpty. secretary-generals

	Xiang Chunyi	80/ 4
	Zou Yu	80/ 4
Members	Chen Shouyi	79/11
	Chen Zhuo	80/ 4
	Gao Xijiang	80/ 4
	Gu Angran	80/ 4
	Jui Mu	79/11
	Li Pu	80/ 4
	Liu Jingxi	79/11
	Qin Chuan	80/ 4
	Shi Lei	80/ 4
	Xiang Chunyi	80/ 4
	Zou Yu	80/ 4

Nationalities Committee

Vice-chairman	Amudong Niyazi	79/10
	Bai Shouyi	79/10
	Jie-er-ge-le	79/10
	Li Gui	79/10
	Wu Yunchang	79/10

THE STATE COUNCIL

Premier
Vice-Premiers

| General Office | Counselors' Office |

Commissions of

- Agriculture
- Capital Construction
- Economy
- Finance and Economy
- Foreign Investment
- Nationalities Affairs
- Overseas Chinese
- Physical Culture and Sports
- Planning
- Science and Technology
- Trade
- Finance
- Food
- Foreign Affairs
- Foreign Trade
- Forestry
- Geology
- Justice
- Light Industry
- Machine Building I
- Machine Building II
- Machine Building III
- Machine Building IV
- Machine Building V
- Machine Building VI

Ministries of

- Agriculture
- Agricultural Machinery
- Building Materials
- Chemical Industry
- Civil Affairs
- Coal Industry
- Commerce
- Communications
- Culture
- Economic Relations with Foreign Countries
- Education
- Machine Building VII
- Machine Building VIII
- Metallurgical Industry
- National Defense
- Petroleum Industry
- Posts and Telecommunications
- Power Industry
- Public Health
- Public Security
- Railways
- State Farms and Land Reclamation
- Textile Industry
- Water Conservancy

Other State Organs

- Agricultural Bank
- Agricultural Mechanization Service Corp.
- Archives Bureau
- Aquatic Products Bureau
- Bank of China
- Birth Planning Leading Group
- Birth Planning Office
- Broadcasting Administration
- Building Materials Bureau
- Building Materials Industry, National Administration
- Chinese Written Language Reform Committee
- Civil Aviation, Administration
- Commodity Prices, Administrative Bureau
- Construction Company
- Customs Administration
- Defense Industry Office, National
- Earthquake Bureau
- Educated Youth Settled in the Countryside, Leading Group
- Environment Protection Office
- Exchange Control, Administration
- Farmland Capital Construction, Office
- Film Production Company, Chinese Joint
- Foreign Affairs, Institute
- Foreign Experts Affairs, Bureau
- Forestry Bureau
- Geological Bureau
- Government Offices' Administration
- Health Campaign Committee, Central Patriotic
- Insurance Company

- International Measurement, Committee for Promotion of
- International Trust and Investment Corp.
- Labor, State Bureau
- Land Reclamation, Bureau
- Machinery and Equipment, Bureau
- Maritime Arbitrage Commission
- Material Supply Administration
- Medicine, Adminstration Bureau
- Meteorological Bureau
- Metrology, Bureau
- Mining Committee
- Municipal Construction, Administration of
- Museums and Archaeological Data, Administrative Bureau

- Natural Agricultural Resources
- Surveying and Agricultural Zoning, Committee
- Oceanographical Bureau
- Overseas Chinese Affairs, Office
- People's Bank
- Pharmaceutical Administration
- Planned Parenthood Leading Group
- Population Group
- Promotion of International Trade, Council for
- Publication Administration Bureau
- Publication Center
- Publications Import Corporation
- Religious Affairs, Bureau

- Scientific and Technological Cadres, Bureau
- Seismological Bureau
- Sports Service Company
- Standardization, Bureau
- Statistics Bureau
- Supplies, Bureau
- Supply and Marketing Co-operatives, Federation
- Surveying and Cartography, Bureau
- Translation and Publishing Corporation
- Travel and Tourism, Administration Bureau
- Weights and Measures, Bureau
- Xinhua News Agency

THE ORGANIZATION OF THE GOVERNMENT OF THE PRC

STATE COUNCIL

Premier

Hua Guofeng	PBm CCm	76/ 4

Vice-premiers

Bo Yibo	CCm	79/ 7
Chen Muhua f	PBa CCm	78/ 3
Chen Yonggui	PBm CCm	75/ 1
Chen Yun	PBm CCm	79/ 7
Deng Xiaoping	PBm CCm	77/ 7
Fang Yi	PBm CCm	78/ 3
Geng Biao	PBm CCm	78/ 3
Gu Mu	CCm	75/ 1
Ji Pengfei	CCm	79/ 9
Kang Shien	CCm	78/ 3
Li Xiannian	PBm CCm	54/ 9
Wan Li	CCm	80/ 4
Wang Renzhong	CCm	78/12
Wang Zhen	PBm CCm	75/ 1
Xu Xiangqian	PBm CCm	78/ 3
Yao Yilin	CCm	79/ 7
Yu Qiuli	PBm CCm	75/ 1
Zhao Ziyang	PBm CCm	80/ 4

Secretary-general

Ji Pengfei	CCm	80/ 2

Deputy Secretary-generals

Wu Qingtong		79/ 4
Zheng Siyuan		79/ 5

General Office

Director	Wu Qingtong	77/ 7
Deputy Directors		
	Li Liyin	78/10
	Li Mengfu	78/ 7
	Lin Xiude	80/ 2
	Lin Yixin	80/ 2
	Liu Yi	78/ 9
	Wang Fulin	77/11
	Zhu Liquan	79/ 1

Counselor's Office

Director	Liu Yi	78/11
Deputy Director		
	Bai Guangtao	79/ 1
Counselor	Han Quanhua f	78/11

Commissions

Agriculture

Minister	Wang Renzhong	CCm 79/ 2
1st Vice-minister		
	Zhang Pinghua	CCm 79/ 9
Vice-ministers		
	Du Runsheng	79/ 9
	He Kang	79/ 6
	Li Ruishan	CCm 79/ 4

Capital Construction

Minister	Gu Mu	CCm 65/ 3

Vice-ministers

Bai Xiangyin		77/ 7
Han Guang	CCm	78/ 4
Li Chaobo		78/ 8
Li Jingzhao		78/ 4
Li Renlin		78/ 6
Lü Kebai		78/ 5
Peng Min		75/12
Ren Puzhai		78/ 5
Xie Beiyi		65/ 4
Zhang Baifa		76/ 3
Zhao Wucheng	CCa	80/ 4
Adviser Miao Shusen		78/10

Economy

Minister	Kang Shien	CCm 78/ 3
Vice-ministers		
	Guo Hongtao	78/10
	Ma Yi	78/ 8
	Qiu Chunfu	78/12
	Xiao Han	80/ 3
	Xu Liangtu	78/10
	Xue Renzong	78/ 7
	Yuan Baohua	CCa 78/ 9
	Yue Zhijian	79/ 6

Finance and Economy

Chairman	Chen Yun	PBm CCm	79/ 7
Vice-chairman	Li Xiannian	PBm CCm	79/ 7
Secretary-general			
	Yao Yilin	CCm	79/ 7
Members	Bo Yibo	CCm	79/ 7
	Fang Yi	PBm CCm	79/ 7
	Gu Mu	CCm	79/ 7
	Kang Shien	CCm	79/ 7
	Wang Renzhong	CCm	79/ 7
	Wang Zhen	PBm CCm	79/ 7
	Yu Qiuli	PBm CCm	79/ 7

Foreign Investment Control

Minister	Gu Mu	CCm 79/ 7
Vice-ministers		
	Gu Ming	80/ 2
	Ma Bin	79/ 7
	Wang Daohan	79/ 7
	Zhou Jiannan	79/ 7

Machine Building Industry

Minister	Bo Yibo	CCm 80/ 2
Vice-minister	Shen Hong	80/ 3

Nationalities Affairs

Minister	Yang Jingren	CCm 78/ 3
Vice-ministers		
	Bu He	79/ 5
	Hu Jiabin	79/ 4
	Jiang Ping	79/ 5
	Tomur Dawamat	79/ 5
	Wu Jinghua	79/ 5
	Xie Hechou	79/ 5
	Yang Dongsheng	79/ 5

Overseas Chinese Affairs
Vice-minister   Zhuang Xiquan   80/ 1

Physical Culture and Sports
Minister   Wang Meng   CCm 77/ 3
1st Vice-minister
                Xu Yinsheng   77/ 3
Vice-ministers
                Chen Peimin   77/ 3
                Huang Zhong   78/ 7
                Li Jingchuan   77/ 8
                Li Menghua   78/ 7
                Lu Jindong   78/ 6
                Rong Gaotang   79/ 8
                Yin Zhongwei   78/ 7
                Yu Buxue   72/ 5

Planning
Minister   Yu Qiuli   PBm CCm 72/10
Vice-ministers
                Duan Yun   73/10
                Fang Weizhong   78/ 3
                Gan Ziyu   78/11
                Gu Xiulian   f   CCa 73/10
                Gu Ming   72/ 5
                Jin Xiying   78/ 1
                Kang Yonghe   80/ 3
                Li Renjun   74/11
                Su Jing   CCm 75/ 9
                Yang Bo   79/ 9
                Zhang Yan   78/ 4
                Zhao Xinchu   CCm 78/10
Adviser   Xue Muqiao   79/ 3
Economics Institute,
   Director   He Jianzhang   80/ 5

Science and Technology
Minister   Fang Yi   PBm CCm 78/ 2
Vice-ministers Jiang Ming   78/ 6
                Jiang Nanxiang   CCm 77/12
                Liu Huaqing   78/11
                Tong Dalin   78/ 3
                Wu Heng   78/ 3
                Yu Guangyuan   77/12
                Zhao Dongwan   77/11
2nd Bureau, Director
                Lin Hua   79/ 7
Planning Bureau
   Director   Yang Leisi   79/ 3
Award Committee for Natural Science
   Director   Wu Heng   80/ 5
   Depty. directors
                Huang Xinbai   80/ 5
                Qian Sanqiang   80/ 5
   Members   Bei Shizhang   80/ 5
                Hua Luogeng   80/ 5
                Huang Kun   80/ 5
                Jin Shanbao   80/5
                Mao Yisheng   80/ 5
                Qian Xuesen   CCa 80/ 5
                Su Buqing   80/ 5
                Tang Aoqing   80/ 5
                Wang Ganchang   80/ 5
                Wang Huzhen   80/ 5
                Zhang Wenyu   80/ 5
                Zhang Yuzhe   80/ 5
                Zhao Zongao   80/ 5
                Zheng Wanjun   80/ 5
                Zhou Peiyuan   80/ 5

Recommendation and Examination Committee in
   Charge of Classifying Inventions
                Director   Wu Heng   79/ 4
                Deputy Directors
                            He Kang   79/ 4
                            Huang Jiasi   79/ 4
                            Yue Zhijian   79/ 4
Scientific Research Attainments Bureau
   Deputy Director
                            Song Yonglin   80/ 2
Specialized Academic Section for Measuring and
   Testing Techniques, Apparatus and Meters
   Director   Sun Youyu   79/12
Specialized Automation Section
   Director   Cao Weilian   79/12

Trade
Minister   Gu Mu   CCm 79/ 7

Ministries

Agriculture
Minister: Huo Shilian   CCm 79/ 2
Vice-ministers Cai Ziwei   79/ 9
                Hao Zhongshi   73/11
                Li Youjiu   79/ 7
                Liu Xigeng   79/ 5
                Xing Chongzhi   79/ 9
                Yang Xiandong   79/ 7
                Zhang Gensheng   79/ 4
                Zhao Xiu   79/ 8
                Zheng Zhong   79/12
                Zhu Rong   79/12
Foreign Affairs Bureau
   Director   Kong Candong   79/ 8
Animal Husbandry Bureau
   Director   Zhao Xiu   79/ 4
   Deputy Directors
                Han Yijun   79/10
                Li Yifang   78/10
Science and Technology Committee
   Director   Jin Shanbao   79/ 5
Technical and Science Bureau
   Director   Zang Chengyao   79/ 8
Water and Soil Conservation Bureau

Agricultural Machinery
Minister   Yang Ligong   79/ 2
Vice-ministers Liu Ang   f   79/ 9
                Wu Shaowen   79/10
                Xiang Nan   79/ 6
                Yuan Chenglong   80/ 4
Advisers   Erwin Engst   79/10
                Joan Hinton   79/10

Building Materials
Minister   Song Yangchu   79/ 4
Vice-minister   Du Chunyong   79/ 4
Cement Bureau
   Director   Ding Hong   79/ 9

Chemical Industry
Minister   Sun Jingwen   78/ 3
Vice-ministers Feng Bohua   78/ 6
                Jia Qingli   80/ 1
                Li Guocai   79/ 1
                Li Yilin   78/ 9
                Qin Zhongda   78/ 7

	Tao Tao	f	78/ 6
	Yang Yepeng		78/ 6
	Yang Yibang		78/ 6

Science and Technology Department
Director	Chen Zixin		78/ 4

Civil Affairs
Minister	Cheng Zihua	CCm	78/ 3
Vice-ministers	Liu Jingfan		78/10
	Shi Huaibi		80/ 2
	Wang Guoquan		80/ 4
	Zhuo Xiong		78/12

Coal Industry
Minister	Gao Yangwen		80/ 2
Vice-ministers	He Bingzhang		78/ 2
	Jia Huisheng		78/ 2
	Li Kuisheng		78/ 7
	Ren Zhiheng		78/ 5
	Wang Xinsan		79/ 4
	Xu Zailian		75/11
	Zhang Zhao		78/ 2
	Zhao Zishang		79/ 6
	Zhong Ziyun		76/11
	Zou Tong		75/ 7

Foreign Affairs Bureau
Director	Xu Nan		77/10

Commerce
Minister	Wang Lei		79/ 2
Vice-ministers	An Fajian		76/ 5
	Gao Xiu		64/ 4
	Ren Quansheng		73/11
	Zhang Yongli		75/ 7
	Zhao Fasheng		72/12
Adviser	Wei Jinfei		78/ 6

Foreign Affairs Bureau
Director	Lin Boqing		78/ 4

Communications
Minister	Zeng Sheng		79/ 2
Vice-ministers	Cheng Wang		78/11
	Guo Jian	f	77/11
	He Chongsheng		80/ 2
	Li Qing		79/11
	Li Shuiqing	CCm	79/10
	Pan Qi		76/ 1
	Peng Deqing		75/10
	Tao Qi		65/ 4
	Wang Xiping		79/ 3
	Zeng Zhi	f	79/ 9

Foreign Affairs Bureau
Director	Dong Huamin		78/ 9

Foreign Aid Office
Director	Wang Jinjian		77/10

Water Transport Bureau
Harbors Engineering Company
General manager			
	Li Haoran		80/ 5

Culture
Minister	Huang Zhen	CCm	77/12
Vice-ministers	He Jingzhih		78/ 1
	Lin Mohan		78/ 1
	Liu Fuzhi		78/11
	Situ Huimin		78/ 8
	Wang Lanxi		78/ 1
	Yao Zhongming		78/ 7

	Zhou Erfu		78/12
	Zhou Weizhi		78/ 1
Counselor	Zhou Heng		79/ 6
Adviser	Xia Yan		79/ 1

Foreign Affairs Department
Cadre	Lu Yaowu		78/ 5

Art and Education Administrative Bureau
Director	Wang Zicheng		80/ 3

Cinema Bureau
Director	Chen Bo		79/ 8
Deputy Director			
	Zhang Junxiang		79/ 3

Cultural Relations with Foreign Countries
Director	Zhu Ming		78/ 8

Film Department
Performing Arts Bureau
Director	Zhang Dongchuan		80/ 4

Party School
President	Huang Zhen	CCm	80/ 5

Economic Relations with Foreign Countries
Minister	Chen Muhua	f	PBa	CCm	77/ 1
Vice-ministers	Cheng Fei				77/ 2
	Li Ke				73/ 5
	Shi Lin				73/ 5
	Wang Daohan				78/ 9
	Wei Yuming				77/ 2

Education
Minister	Jiang Nanxiang	CCm	79/ 2
Vice-ministers	Dong Chuncai		79/ 4
	Gao Yi		77/12
	Huang Xinbai		79/ 7
	Li Qi		77/10
	Li Qitao		77/10
	Liu Xuechu		78/12
	Liu Yangqiao		79/ 5
	Liu Zhonghou		77/11
	Pu Tongxiu		78/ 1
	Xiao Yan		78/ 6
	Yang Yunyu	f	79/ 4
	Zang Boping		79/12
	Zeng Delin		79/11
	Zhang Chengxian		79/ 5
	Zhou Lin		77/12

Foreign Affairs Department
Director	Yang Yunyi		78/ 4
Deputy Director			
	Li Jiong		78/ 6

Finance
Minister	Wu Bo		79/ 9
Vice-ministers	Chen Rulong		79/ 5
	Chen Xiyu		73/ 6
	Li Peng		80/ 5
	Lü Peijian		78/ 9
	Wang Pingqian		73/ 6
	Xie Ming		79/ 6
	Xin Yuanxi		78/ 9
	Yao Jin		78/ 9
	Zhang Ruiqing		78/ 9

Taxation Department
Director	Ren Ziliang		78/ 6

Food
Minister	Zhao Xinchu	CCm	80/ 2
Vice-minister	Li Yanshou		80/ 3

Foreign Affairs

Minister	Huang Hua	CCm	76/12
Vice-ministers	Gong Dafei		79/12
	Han Kehua		80/ 3
	Han Nianlong		64/ 4
	He Ying		72/ 5
	Pu Shouchang		80/ 4
	Wang Hairong	f	74/ 9
	Wang Shu		78/ 6
	Wang Youping		79/ 9
	Yu Zhan		72/ 5
	Zhang Canming		79/12
	Zhang Haifeng		78/ 6
	Zhang Wenjin		78/ 1
	Zhong Xidong		72/ 5

Assistant Ministers

Fan Zuokai		79/ 8
Lin Zhong		78/ 5
Song Zhiguang		78/ 1

Africa Department
Deputy Directors

Dai Peizhen		78/ 5
Xu Hanbing	f	74/ 6
Zhou Mingqi		74/ 3

America and Oceania Department

Director	Han Xu		79/ 3
Dpty.directors			
	Shen Zhiwie		75/10
	Tang Wensheng	f CCa	74/11
	Zhu Jizhen		77/ 6

Asia Department

Director	Shen Ping		75/ 8
Depty.directors			
	Liu Junpei		80/ 1
	Qiu Lixing		76/ 6
	Xiao Xiangqian		78/11

Soviet Union and Eastern Europe Department

Director	Yu Hongliang		78/ 6
Dpty.directors			
	Liu Jinlin	f	74/ 9
	Xiang Zhongfu		73/ 8

West Asia and North Africa Department

Director	Zhou Jue	79/11
Dpts.directors		
	Chen Yuanxing	74/ 9
	Wen Yezhan	76/11

Western Europe Department
Depty.directors

Qi Zonghua	f	75/ 4
Zhang Yijun		74/ 9
Zhu Liqing		78/ 9

Consular Department

Dpty.director	Nie Gongcheng	80/ 4

Information Department

Director	Qian Qizhen		77/ 1
Dpty.director			
	Wang Zhen	f	73/ 4

International Organizations and Conferences, Agreements and Law, Department of

Director	Ling Qing		78/ 8
Dpty.directors			
	Bi Jilong		74/ 8
	He Liliang	f	77/ 8
	Ji Chaozhu		79/ 1

Protocol Department

Director	Wei Yongqing	78/10

Dpty.directors

Dai Ping		78/ 7
Gao Jianzhong		72/ 7

Foreign Affairs, Institute of

Director	Hao Deqing	77/ 3
Dpty.directors		
	Ke Bonian	73/ 6
	Xiong Xianghui	78/11
	Zhou Peiyuan	72/ 4
Secr.-general		
	Xie Li	78/11
Dpty. secr.-general		
	Li Dehua	78/ 8
	Zhu Hanming	78/ 7

Foreign Trade

Minister	Li Qiang	CCm	73/10
Vice-ministers	Chen Jie		71/ 9
	Cui Qun		77/12
	Jia Shih		77/ 4
	Liu Xiwen		77/ 5
	Wang Runsheng		77/ 4
	Zhao Changchun		78/11
	Zheng Tuobin		78/ 1
	Zheng Yishan		77/ 4
	Zhou Huamin		64/ 4

Assistant Minister

Du Yuyun		72/11

General Office

Export Bureau

Director	Zou Siyi	80/ 3

Aeronautic Technological Import and Export Corporation, China National

Arts and Crafts Import and Export Corporation, China National
General Manager

Gao Zuojie		78/ 8

Chartering Corporation, China National
General Manager

Pang Zhijiang		78/ 5
Deputy General Manager		
Gao Zhufeng		78/ 5

Cereals, Oils and Foodstuffs Import and Export Corporation, China National

Chemicals Import and Export Corporation, China National
Deputy General Managers

Du Daoyou		79/11
Zhang Yupu		79/ 5

Complete Plant Export Corporation, China National
Deputy General Manager

Yan Peide		78/ 4

Electronic Supply Industrial General Company, China

Electronic Technology Import and Export Corporation, China National
Chairman, Board of Directors

Liu Yin		80/ 3

Foreign Trade Transportation Corporation, China National
General Manager

Pang Zhijiang		78/ 5
Deputy General Managers		
Gao Zhufeng		78/ 5
Liu Ruoming		78/ 9

Land Reclamation Import and Export
  Corporation, China
Light Industrial Products Import and
  Export Corporation, China National
    Deputy General Manager
            Shi Heng   78/ 5
Machinery Import and Export Corporation,
  China National
    Deputy General Manager
            Wei Huajun   78/ 4
Machinery and Equipment Import and Export
  Corporation, China National
    Deputy Managing Director
            Lei Weizong   80/ 3
Metals and Minerals Import and Export
  Corporation, China National
    General Manager
            Tian Guangdao   73/ 3
    Deputy General Manager
            Wang Boyun   78/ 8
Native Produce and Animal By-products Im-
  port and Export Corp., China National
    Adviser   Gu Gengyu   79/ 1
Ocean Shipping Company, China National
    Dpty. Managing Director
            Yuan Zhiping   77/11
Oil and Gas Exploration Development
  Corporation, China National
    Dpty. General Manager
            Li Qingxin   79/ 1
Petroleum Corporation, China National
    General Manager
            Zhang Wenbin   78/ 8
    Dpty. General Managers
            Li Tianxiang   78/11
            Qin Wencai   80/ 5
Ship-Chartering Corporation, China National
Technical Import Corporation, China Nat.
    General Manager
            Peng Runmin   78/ 7
    Dpty. General Managers
            Chen Yang   78/ 5
            Yang Yude   78/ 5
Textiles Import and Export Corporation,
  China National
    General Manager
            Wang Mingjun   80/ 1

Forestry
    Minister   Luo Yuchuan   79/ 2
    Vice-ministers Liang Changwu   79/ 9
            Liu Kun   79/ 6
            Wang Bin   79/11
            Yang Jue   79/ 7
            Yang Tianfang   79/11
            Yang Yansen   79/ 5
            Yong Wentao   79/10
            Zhang Shijun   80/ 1

Geology
    Minister   Sun Daguang   79/ 9
    Vice-minister Zhang Tongyu   79/11

Justice
    Minister   Wei Wenbo   79/ 9

Light Industry
    Minister   Liang Lingguang   78/ 3

Vice-ministers Du Ziduan   77/ 9
            Han Peixin   78/ 6
            He Zhihua   79/ 9
            Li Jianping   79/ 4
            Song Jiwen   78/ 1
            Xia Zhixu   f   71/10
            Yu Jianting   78/ 5
    Foreign Affairs Department
      Dpty.Director
            Zhang Shouping   78/ 4
    Workers' Wages Department
      Dpty.Director
            Zhang Shuding   78/10
    Scientific Research Institute
      Director   Ge Chunlin   80/ 3

Machine Building I
    Minister   Zhou Zijian   CCa 77/10
    Vice-ministers Cao Weilian   79/12
            Liu Hekong   79/ 9
            Qi Tian   78/ 4
            Rao Bin   78/ 6
            Shen Hong   61/12
            Sun Youyu   73/ 3
            Wang Ziyi   78/ 4
            Xu Binzhou   72/ 2
            Yang Geng   73/11
            Yu Ming   78/ 4
            Zhang Huaizhong   78/ 5
            Zhang Xiaozeng   78/ 4
    Adviser   Jiang Zemin   78/10

Machine Building II
    Minister   Liu Wei   CCm 78/ 3
    Vice-ministers Jiang Shengjie   80/ 2
            Wang Ganchang   79/ 6

Machine Building III
    Minister   Lü Dong   78/ 3
    Vice-ministers Chen Shaozhong   79/ 2
            Duan Zijun   79/ 1
            Mo Wenxiang   79/ 8
            Xu Changyu   79/ 3
    Research Institute,
      Deputy Chief Engineer
            Rong Ke   79/ 6

Machine Building IV
    Minister   Qian Min   78/ 8
    Vice-ministers Gao Yun   80/ 5
            Li Yuanru   78/ 8
            Li Zhaoji   78/ 5
            Liu Peirong   78/12
            Liu Yin   75/ 4
            Shen Zhongyi   78/12
            Sun Junren   78/12
            Wang Shiguang   78/12
            Wang Zongjin   78/ 7
    International Liaison Department
      Director   Deng Guojun   78/ 8
    General Broadcasting and Television
      Industry Bureau
      Director   Li Yuanru   78/ 8

Machine Building V
    Minister   Zhang Zhen   78/ 3
    Vice-ministers Li Yutang   78/10
            Wang Chuan   78/ 4
            Wang Li   77/ 3

Research Intitute,			
Chief Engineer			
	Zhang Xianglin		79/ 6
Machine Building VI			
Minister	Chai Shufan		78/ 3
Vice-ministers	Fan Muhan		79/ 7
	Lin Yi		79/10
	Liu Fang		79/ 6
	Zhang Youxuan		78/ 9
Machine Building VII			
Minister	Zheng Tianxiang		79/ 2
Vice-minister	Lu Ping		79/12
Machine Building VIII			
Minister	Jiao Ruoyu		79/ 9
General Bureau			
Director	Liu Bingyan		79/ 2
Metallurgical Industry			
Minister	Tang Ke	CCm	77/ 7
Vice-ministers	Li Dongye		79/ 7
	Li Feiping		78/ 8
	Li Hua		79/ 1
	Lin Zesheng		59/ 9
	Liu Xuexin		77/12
	Lu Da		78/ 4
	Mao Lin		79/ 5
	Qian Chuanjun		78/ 7
	Wang Yuqing		78/11
	Xu Chi	CCa	78/ 4
	Ye Zhiqiang		72/11
	Zhang Yimin		77/12
	Zhou Guanwu		78/ 8
Automation Research Institute			
Iron and Steel Research Institute,			
Physics Department			
Director	Chen Qi		78/ 4
Precious Metals Research Institute			
National Defense			
Minister	Xu Xiangqian	PBm CCm	78/ 3
Vice-ministers	Su Yu	CCm	59
	Xiao Jingguang	CCm	59
	Xiao Ke	CCm	80/ 3
	Yang Dezhi	CCm	80/ 5
Foreign Affairs Bureau			
Director	Zhai Chengwen		70/ 8
Deputy Directors			
	Xi Yi		78/ 8
	Yin Zuozhen		71/ 9
	Zhang Bingyu		75/10
	Zhao Chunzheng		71/ 2
Defense Research Institute			
Petroleum Industry			
Minister	Song Zhenming		78/ 3
Vice-ministers	Chen Liemin		78/ 3
	Di Ququ		79/ 2
	Hou Xianglin		78/ 6
	Huang Kai		78/ 7
	Jiao Liren		78/ 7
	Li Jing		79/10
	Li Tianxiang		78/ 9
	Min Yu		78/ 7
	Qin Wencai		79/ 3
	Sun Xiaofeng		78/ 6

	Yan Dunshi		78/ 7
	Zhang Wenbin		78/ 3
Pipelines Bureau			
Director	Zhu Hongchang		78/ 6
Posts and Telecommunications			
Minister	Wang Zigang		78/11
1st Vice-minster			
	Li Yiqing		78/10
Vice-ministers	Hou Deyuan		79/ 9
	Li Linchuan		79/ 9
	Li Yukui		73/10
	Luo Shuzhen		76/ 1
	Shen Guang		56/ 4
	Yan Xiaofeng		80/ 5
	Zhu Chunhe		73/10
Directorate-general of Posts			
Acting Director			
	Song Xingmin		77/11
Deputy Director			
	Yan Ding		78/ 5
Power Industry			
Minister	Liu Lanbo	CCm	79/ 2
Vice-ministers	Li Daigeng		79/ 6
	Li Eding		79/ 5
	Li Peng		80/ 4
	Li Rui		79/ 5
	Li Ximing		79/ 6
	Wang Lin		80/ 5
	Zhang Bin		79/ 9
Public Health			
Minister	Qian Xinzhong		79/ 4
Vice-ministers	Cui Yueli		78/ 7
	Guo Ziheng		79/ 6
	Hu Zhaoheng		79/ 2
	Huang Shuze		73/ 5
	Ji Zongquan		79/ 2
	Tan Yunhe		78/ 3
	Wang Wei		78/ 3
	Yang Shoushan		78/ 7
Advisers	Ke Lin		78/ 6
	Ma Haide		80/ 2
Foreign Affairs Bureau			
Director	Xue Gongzhuo		73/11
Medical Education Department			
Director	Zhu Chao		79/11
Traditional Medicine Department			
Director	Lü Bingkui		79/ 9
Public Security			
Minister	Zhao Cangbi	CCm	78/ 3
Vice-ministers	Gao Wenli		78/10
	Li Guangxiang		80/ 5
	Ling Yun		79/ 5
	Lü Jianguang		79/ 2
	Xi Guoguang		78/ 6
	Yu Sang		64/10
Guards Bureau			
Director	Yang Dezhong		79/10
Railways			
Minister	Guo Weicheng		78/11
Vice-ministers	Deng Cunlun		80/ 4
	Li Guang		78/ 6
	Li Xiebo		78/ 7
	Liao Shiquan		78/ 8
	Liu Baitao		78/ 9

	Liu Jianzhang		75/ 4
	Wang Xiaobin		78/ 6
	Wu Yeshan		78/ 5
	Zhao Wenpu		78/ 7

Foreign Affairs Bureau
Director Han Libing   78/10
2nd Engineering Bureau
  Political Department
    Deputy Director
      Wu Chengqing   78/ 5
Machinery Design Institute No.1

State Farms and Land Reclamation

Minister	Gao Yang		79/ 6
Vice-ministers	Lü Qing		79/ 9
	Zhang Xiuzhu		80/ 1
	Zhao Fan		79/ 6

Textile Industry

Minister	Qian Zhiguang		CCm	78/ 3
Vice-ministers	Chen Weiji			78/ 4
	Hao Jianxiu	f	CCm	78/ 3
	Hu Ming			78/ 5
	Jiao Shanmin			78/ 5
	Li Tao			79/ 4
	Li Zhengguang			78/ 7
	Wang Ruiting			79/ 7
	Xie Hongsheng			79/ 2

Water Conservancy

Minister	Qian Zhengying	f	CCm	79/ 2
Vice-ministers	Li Boning			79/ 5
	Liu Xiangsan			79/ 5
	Shi Xiangsheng			80/ 3
	Zhang Jinong			79/ 4

OTHER GOVERNMENT ORGANIZATIONS

Agricultural Bank

Agricultural Mechanization Service Corp.
Manager	Wu Shaowen	79/10

Aquatic Products Bureau, State
Director	Xiao Peng	78/ 8
Dpty. director	Xiao Feng	80/ 5

Archives Bureau, State
Director	Zhang Zhong	79/ 8

Bank of China
President	Bu Ming	79/10
Vice-presidents		
	Chang Yanqing	79/10
	Chen Xiyu	78/10
	Cui Yanxu	79/10
	Wang Weicai	79/ 9
	Xiang Kefang	79/11
General manager		
	Bu Ming	77/12
Acting general manager		
	Feng Tianshun	78/12

Dpty. general managers
	Lin Jixin	71/12
	Wang Youcheng	78/ 6
	Zhao Bingde	78/ 6

Managing directors
	Chen Kedong	79/ 7
	Cui Yanxu	79/ 3
	Li Pinzhou	79/ 7
	Luo Fuqing	79/ 5
	Rong Yiren	79/ 4
	Sun Xiaocun	79/10
	Xiang Kefang	79/ 5
	Zhang Yanqing	79/ 7

Board of Directors
  Honorary chairman

	Qiao Peixin	79/ 7
Chairman	Bu Ming	79/10
Vice-chairmen		
	Cui Ping	79/10
	Cui Yanxu	80/ 5
	Fang Gao	77/11
	Geng Daoming	76/ 3
	Wang Weicai	80/ 5
	Xiang Kefang	79/10
Chief inspector		
	Li Fei	79/ 7
Inspectors	Li Shizhang	79/ 7
	Zhuang Ming	79/ 7

Branch Offices
  Hong Kong
  London
Director	Wang Weicai	79/11

  Luxembourg
Director	Li Yumin	79/ 2

  Manchester
  Singapore
    General manager
	Xue Wenlin	80/ 3

Birth Planning Leading Group under the State Council

Director	Chen Muhua	f	PBm	CCm	78/ 7
Dpty. directors					
	Jiang Yizhen				78/ 7
	Li Xiuzhen	f			78/ 4
	Su Jing			CCm	78/ 7
	Wang Shoudao				78/ 7
Members	Chou Youwen				78/ 7
	Du Xinyuan				78/ 7
	Hu Zhaoheng				78/ 7
	Hu Hong				78/ 7
	Huang Zhizhen			CCm	78/ 7
	Jiang Dongping				78/ 7
	Jin Guixiang	f			78/ 7
	Jin Zhuan				78/ 7
	Li Ligong				78/ 7
	Li Qiming			CCm	78/ 7
	Li Qin	f			78/ 7
	Li Rinai			CCa	78/ 7
	Li Xian				78/ 7
	Lin Jiamei	f			78/ 7
	Liu Fuzhi				78/ 7
	Lu Jianguang				78/ 7
	Lü Yulan	f		CCm	78/ 7
	Tao Dao	f			78/ 7
	Tian Xiuzhuan	f			78/ 7
	Wang Pingfan				78/ 7
	Wang Yiping			CCm	78/ 7

	Wu Heng		78/ 7
	Zhang Ce		78/ 7
	Zhang Fuyuan		78/ 7
	Zhang Kai		78/ 7
	Zhang Ruguang		78/ 7
	Zhao Fasheng		78/ 7
	Zheng Yonghe		78/ 7

Birth Planning, Office of
Director	Li Xiuzhen	f	78/ 4
Dpty. director	Lin Jiamei	f	78/ 4

Broadcasting Administration, Central
Director	Zhang Xiangshan		77/ 3
Dpty. directors			
	Jin Zhao		73/ 3
	Li Lianqing		77/ 3
	Zhou Xinwu		79/ 5
	Zuo Moye		79/ 9

Building Materials Bureau, State
Director	Bai Xiangyin	78/11

Building Materials Industry, National Administration of
Director	Xiao Tong	79/10
Dpty. director	Zhang Zhen	78/ 9

Children's Book Publishing House
Director	Chen Mo	80/ 4

Chinese Written Language Reform Committee
Chairman	Dong Shuncai	80/ 5
Vice-chairmen	Hu Yuzhi	80/ 5
	Lü Shuxiang	80/ 5
	Wang Li	80/ 5
	Ye Laishi	80/ 5
	Zhang Youyu	80/ 5
Members	Chen Hanbo	80/ 5
	Ma Dayou	80/ 5
	Ni Haishu	80/ 5
	Qian Weichang	80/ 5
	Wang Zhuxi	80/ 5
	Zeng Shiying	80/ 5
	Zhang Zhigong	80/ 5
	Zhou Youguang	80/ 5
	Zhu Dexi	80/ 5

Civil Aviation, General Administration of
Director-general		
	Shen Tu	78/ 1
Dpty. director-generals		
	Li Ming	78/ 4
	Lin Zheng	79/12
	Lu Zhengzhe	79/ 5
	Yan Zhixiang	73/11
	Zhang Ruiai	74/ 9
Dpty. political commissars		
	Chi Long	78/ 6
	Wang Wen	78/ 6
Scientific Institute		
Dpty. director		
	Hua Fengxiang	79/ 2

Commodity Prices, State Administrative Bureau for
Director	Liu Zhuofu	79/10

Computers, State Bureau of
Director	Li Rui	80/ 4

Computer Industry, State Administration of
Manager, Technical Service Comp.		
	Xu Zhen	80/ 6

Construction Engineering Corp., China
Dpty. managing director		
	Zhang Enshu	80/ 5

Customs Administration
Dpty. director	Wang Douguang	78/ 7

Defense Industry Office, National
Director		
Dpty. directors		
	Ye Zhengda	80/ 3
	Zheng Hantao	78/ 6
	Zhou Jiahua	79/ 2
2nd Office		
Director	Hong Xuezhi	79/ 2

Earthquake Bureau, National

Educated Youth Settled in the Countryside, Leading Group of
Head	Wang Renzhong	CCm	79/ 8
1st dpty. head	Kang Yonghe		79/ 1

Environment Protection Office, State
Director	Li Chaobo	78/ 7
Dpty. director	Qu Geping	79/ 4

Exchange Control, General Administration of
Dpty. general director		
	Wang Weicai	80/ 5

Exhibition Corporation, China
Manager	Chen Dayuan	80/ 3

Farmland Capital Construction, Office of
Responsible Person			
	Qian Zhengying f	CCm	79/ 2

Film Production Company, Chinese Joint
Manager	Zhao Wei	79/12

Fine Arts Publishing House, Shanghai People's
Editor-in-chief		
	Li Huaizhi	80/ 5

Foreign Experts Affairs, Bureau of
Director	Yang Fangzhi	79/ 7

Foreign Language Publishing and Distribution Administration
Director	Luo Jun	80/ 3

Forestry Bureau, State General
Director	Luo Yuchuan	78/ 8
Dpty. directors		
	Liang Changwu	78/10
	Wang Bang	78/10
	Yang Jue	78/ 8

Geological Bureau, National General
Director	Sun Daguang	75/12

```
Dpty. directors
          Li Xuan                          78/ 5
          Xu Jie                           79/ 4
          Zhang Guoyu                      78/ 5
          Zhang Tongyu                     77/ 7
```

Geological Knowledge, National Committee for the Dissemination of
```
Chairman        Gao Zhenxi                 80/ 5
```

Government Offices' Administration, Bureau of
```
Dpty. director Gao Fuyou                   79/ 1
```

Health Campaign Committee, Central Patriotic
```
Chairman        Li Xiannian      PBm CCm   78/ 4
Vice-chairmen   Chen Muhua     f PBa CCm   78/ 4
                Gu Mu                CCm   78/ 4
                Jiang Yizhen               78/ 4
                Kang Keqing    f     CCm   78/ 4
                Kang Shien           CCm   78/ 4
                Yang Yong            CCm   78/ 4
                Zhang Ruguang              78/ 4
Members         An Wenyi                   78/ 4
                Cheng Hongyi               78/ 4
                Cheng Zihua          CCm   78/ 4
                Gu Wenhua                  78/ 4
                Guo Jian       f           78/ 4
                He Kang                    78/ 4
                Huang Shuze                78/ 4
                Huang Zuozhen        CCa   78/ 4
                Li Guisheng                78/ 4
                Liu Fuzhi                  78/ 4
                Liu Jianzhang              78/ 4
                Lü Jianguang               78/ 4
                Qian Xinzhong              78/ 4
                Ren Quansheng              78/ 4
                Sun Xiaofeng               78/ 4
                Tao Tao        f           78/ 4
                Wang Meng            CCm   78/ 4
                Xia Zhixu      f           78/ 4
                Yang Jingren         CCm   78/ 4
                Zeng Tao                   78/ 4
                Zhang Jinong               78/ 4
```

Insurance Company
```
General manager
                Feng Tianshun              75/11
Dpty. general manager
                Lin Zhenfeng               73/11
```

International Measurement, Committee for Promotion of
```
Director        Zhao Dongwan               79/ 3
Dpty. directors
                Mao Yisheng                79/ 3
                Qian Sanqiang              79/ 3
                Qian Xuesen          CCa   79/ 3
                Zhou Peiyuan               79/ 3
```

International Trust and Investment Corp., China
```
Board of Directors
Chairman        Rong Yiren                 79/10
  Vice-chairman
                Lei Renmin                 79/10
  Executive directors
                Chen Shuzi                 79/10
                Wang Jianshi               79/10
                Wu Zhichao                 79/10
```

Financing Department
```
  Leading member
                Min Yimin                  80/ 4
Directors       Chang Yanqing              79/10
                Chen Xizhong               79/10
                Du Xinbo                   79/10
                Duan Yun                   79/10
                Gu Gengyu                  79/10
                Guo Dihuo                  79/10
                He Haoju                   79/10
                He Xian                    79/10
                Hu Ziying                  79/10
                Hua Yuqing                 79/10
                Huo Yingdong               79/10
                Jing Shuping               79/10
                Li Jiacheng                79/10
                Li Wenjie                  79/10
                Liu Jingji                 79/10
                Liu Xiwen                  79/10
                Ma Wanqi                   79/10
                Mao Yisheng                79/10
                Miao Yuntai                79/10
                Pei Xianbai                79/10
                Qian Changzhao             79/10
                Qiu Zhunfu                 79/10
                Rui Mu                     79/10
                Sun Fuling                 79/10
                Sun Xiaocun                79/10
                Tang Yuanbing              79/10
                Tong Shaosheng             79/10
                Wang Guangying             79/10
                Wang Jiyuan                79/10
                Wang Kuancheng             79/10
                Wang Shaoyan               79/10
                Xiao Tong                  79/10
                Ye Lin                     79/10
                Zeng Dingshi               79/10
                Zhang Jingli               79/10
                Zhang Yi                   79/10
                Zhou Baofen                79/10
                Zhou Zhijun                79/10
                Zi Yaohua                  79/10
```

Labor, State Bureau of
```
Director        Kang Yonghe                77/11
```

Machinery and Equipment, State Bureau of

Maritime Arbitrage Commission under the Council for Promotion of International Trade
```
Chairman        Wang Wenlin                78/12
```

Material Supply Administration, General

Medicine, General Administration Bureau of

Meteorological Bureau, Central
```
Director        Rao Xing                   79/ 9
Dpty. director Wu Xueyi                    79/ 4
```

Metrology, State Bureau of
```
Director        Li Leshan                  80/ 5
```

Mining Committee, China National
```
Director        Xu Zailian                 78/ 7
Dpty. secretary-
  general       Bo Xingji                  78/ 9
```

Weight and Measures, Bureau of
Director   Li Zhengting   79/ 4
Dpty.director Li Luoshan   79/ 5

Xinhua News Agency
Director   Zeng Tao   77/12
Dpty.directors Li Pu   78/ 6
              Liu Jingzhi   78/ 8
              Mu Qing   72/10
              Yang Jiaxing   78/ 8

Dpty.editor-in-chief
              Li Qin   f   79/10
Secr.-general Yang Jiaxiang   77/ 9

Xinhua News Agency, Hong Kong Branch
First director Wang Guang   78/ 7
2nd director Li Jusheng   78/ 7
Dpty.Directors Ji Feng   78/ 8
              Li Jixin   78/ 7
              Luo Keming   78/ 7
              Zhu Yi   78/ 8

THE SUPREME PEOPLE'S COURT

President   Jiang Hua   CCm 75/ 1
Vice-presidents He Lanjie   73/ 4
                Wang Weigang   78/ 3
                Zeng Hanzhou   72/ 7
                Zheng Shaowen   79/ 2

Judicial Committee
  Members   He Lanjie   79/11
                Jiang Hua   CCm 79/11

Li Rongdi   f   79/11
Li Yuebo   79/11
Lu Mingjian   79/11
Wang Huaian   79/11
Wang Weigang   79/11
Wang Zhanping   79/11
Yang Hua'nan   79/11
Zeng Hanzhou   79/11
Zheng Shaowen   79/11

THE SUPREME PEOPLE'S PROCURATORATE

Chief Procurator Huang Huoqing   CCm 78/ 3
Dpty.chief procurators
              Chen Yangshan   79/ 2
              Guan Shanfu   80/ 2
              Li Shiying   78/12

Wang Fu   78/12
Xi Zhanyuan   79/ 9
Yu Ping   78/ 5
Zhang Su   78/ 5
Secretary Gen. Yang Ziqian 80/ 2

THE CENTRAL MILITARY LEADERSHIP

General Staff

Commission
  Science and Technology Commission for National
    Defense

Departments
  Armament
  Communications
  Intelligence
  Logistics, General
  Military Training
  Political, General

Services
  Air Force
  Armored Forces
  Artillery
  2nd Artillery
  Capital Construction Corps
  Engineering Corps
  Navy
  Railway Corps

Schools
  Academies
    Air Force Engineering Academy
    Art Academy
    Communications and Engineering Academy
    Military Academy
    Military Science Academy
    Political Academy
    Railway Corps Academy
  Schools
    Aviation School
    Navy 1st Surface Ships School
    Wired Signalling Technical School
  Institutes
    Artillery Institute
    Electronics Engineering Institute
    International Strategic Studies, Institute for
    Logistics Institute
    Medical Aviation Research Institute
    Radar Institute
  Colleges
    4th Military Medical College
    Naval College

THE MILITARY ORGANIZATION OF THE PRC

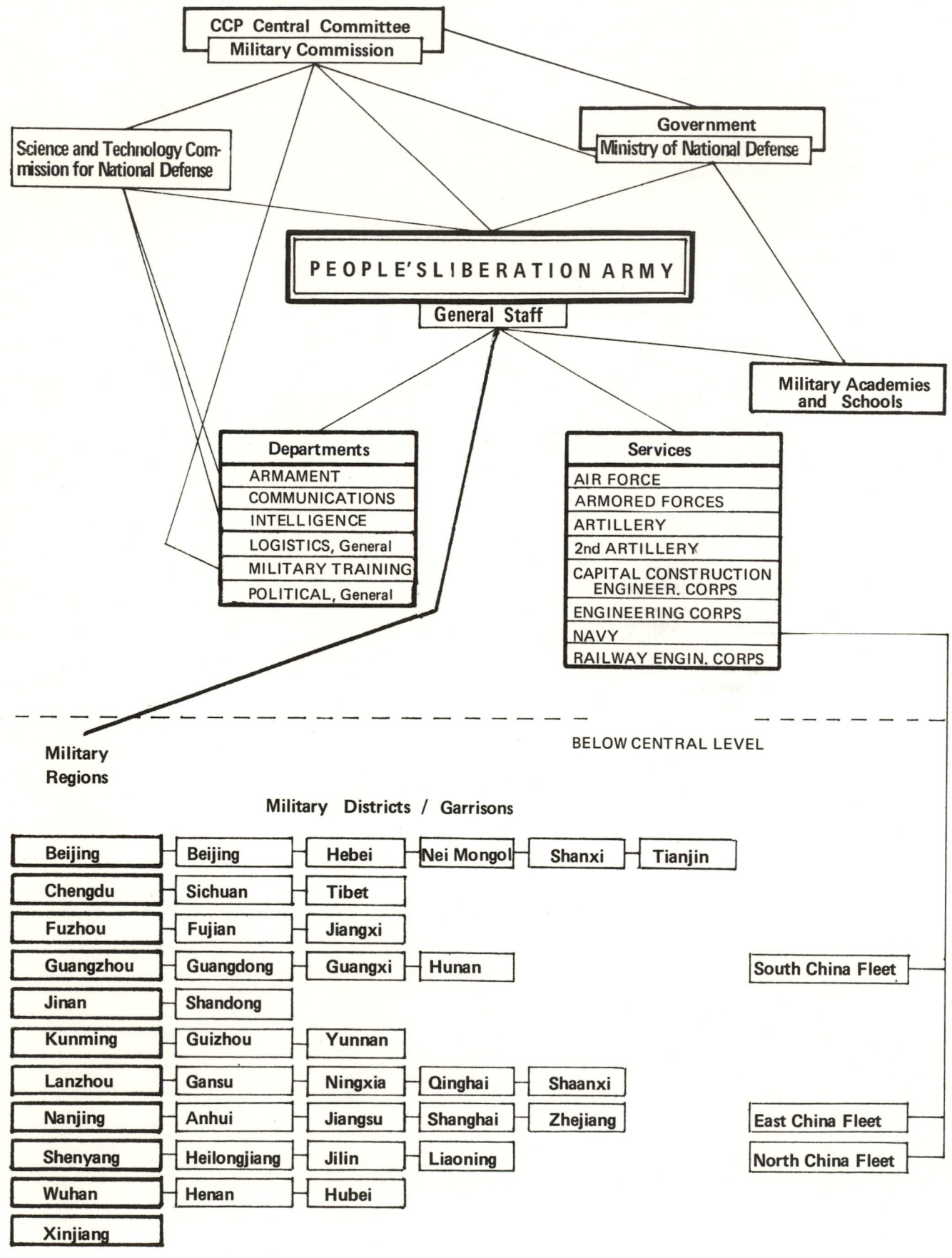

THE CENTRAL MILITARY LEADERSHIP

General Staff

Chief	Yang Dezhi	CCm	80/ 2
Dpty. chiefs	Chi Haotian		77/11
	He Zhengwen		74/12
	Li Da	CCm	72/11
	Liu Huaqing		80/ 3
	Wang Shangrong	CCa	74/12
	Wu Xiuquan	CCm	75/ 5
	Yang Yong	CCm	77/10
	Zhang Aiping	CCm	77/10
	Zhang Zhen	CCa	80/ 4
Assistant chief			
	Liu Kai		79/ 4
Adviser	Kong Yuan		80/ 6

Science and Technology Commission for National Defense

Chairman	Zhang Aiping	CCm	75/12
Vice-chairmen	Qian Xuesen	CCa	69
	Zhang Zhenhuan		77/10
Political commissar			
	Li Yaowen	CCa	77/10

Departments of
Armament
Dpty. director
	Wang Letian		77/ 2

Communications
Director	Jiang Wen		79/ 5

Intelligence
Dpty. director
	Huang Zhengji		80/ 5

Logistics, General
Director	Hong Xuezhi		80/ 3
Dpty. directors			
	Chen Lei		80/ 5
	Fan Ziyu		78/ 6
	Feng Yongshun		71/ 6
	He Biao		78/10
	He Cheng	CCm	77/ 8
	Li Yuan		77/ 2
	Rao Zhengxi		78/ 4
	Sun Hongzhen		73/ 9
	Zhang Lingbin	CCa	64
	Zhang Ruguang		73/10
	Zhang Xianyue		64
	Zhang Yuanpei		75/12
Political commissar			
	Wang Ping	CCm	78/ 4
Dpty. political commissars			
	Bai Xiangguo		77/ 2
	Cao Siming	CCa	76/12
	Li Zhen		75/12
Health Division			
Director	He Biao		78/10
Dpty. director			
	Zhang Xiang		79/11

Military Training
Dpty. director
	Han Fudong		79/ 9

Political, General
Director	Wei Guoqing	PBm	CCm	77/ 9
Dpty. directors				
	Fu Zhong			77/ 7
	Gan Weihan			80/ 4
	Hua Nan			80/ 4
	Huang Yukun			75/ 9
	Liang Biye		CCm	75/ 1
	Yan Jinsheng			77/10
	Zhu Yunqian			78/10
Dpty. polit. commissar				
	Li Yue			79/10
Dpty. secretary-general				
	Li Wei			76/ 6

Culture Section
Director	Liu Baiyu		77/11
Dpty. directors			
	Zhang Shaoting		78/ 5
	Zhou Zhitong		79/ 7
Dpty. secretary-general			
	Yao Kang		79/ 7

Liaison Department
Director	Yang Side		77/ 7

Mass Work Department
Director	Lu Cunfu		75/ 6

Propaganda Department
Dpty. secretary-general
	Hua Nan		73/11

Services
Air Force
Commander	Zhang Tingfa	PBm	CCm	77/ 4
Dpty. commanders				
	Cao Lihuai		CCm	56/10
	Cheng Jun			65/10
	He Tingyu			76/ 5
	Zhang Jihui		CCa	74/10

Logistics Department
Dpty. director
	Duan Shikai		78/ 5

Political Department
Dpty. director
	Gao Texiang		78/ 5

Training Department
Director	You Zhenwu		78/10
Polit. commissar			
	Gao Houliang	CCa	78/ 5
Dpty. polit. commissars			
	Huang Liqing		77/ 5
	Liu Shichang		78/ 6

Chief of staff
    Wang Dinglie   76/ 4
Dpty. chiefs of staff
    Ma Zhanmin   78/10
    Zeng Youzheng   78/ 5
    Zhang Zhong   77/ 8
CP Committee
  1st secretary
    Zhang Tingfa   PBm CCm 77/ 6
  2nd secretary
    Gao Houliang   CCa 77/ 6
  3rd secretary
    Cao Lihuai   CCm 77/ 6

Armored Forces
Commander Huang Xinting CCa 75/ 9
Dpty. commanders
    Cheng Shicai   78/ 6
    Deng Jiatai   78/ 8
    He Jinnian   CCa 75/10
    Lin Bin   65/10
    Zhang Wenzhou   78/11
Chief of staff
    Yan Zhenheng   77/11

Artillery
Commander Song Chengzhi   78/ 6
Dpty. commanders
    Gao Zunxin   78/ 8
    Kong Congzhou   78/ 5
    Li Maozhi   77/ 9
Polit. commissar
    Jin Rubo   78/ 6
Dpty. polit. commissars
    Ouyang Yi   78/ 6
    Yang Yinsheng   78/ 7

2nd Artillery
Commander Liao Chengmei   77/ 9
Dpty. commander
    Sheng Zhihua   80/ 2
    Yan Jiaan   77/ 9
Dpty. polit. commissar
    Liu Lifeng   80/ 2

Capital Construction Engineering Corps
Director   Li Renlin   79/ 4
Dpty. director
    Li Yuan   CCa 79/ 4
Polit. commissar
    Gu Mu   CCm 79/ 4
Dpty. polit. commissar
    Yang Jie   79/ 4

Capital Construction Engineering Corps

Engineering Corps
Commander Tan Shanhe   CCa 78/ 5
Dpty. commander
    Xu Guoxian   78/ 7

Navy
Commander Ye Fei   CCm 80/ 2
1st dpty. commander
    Li Daosheng   CCa
Dpty. commanders
    Fang Qiang   79/10
    Kong Zhaonian   CCm 80/ 2

    Mei Jiasheng   76/12
    Wang Wanlin   74/ 1
    Yang Guoyu   78/12
CP Committee
  2nd secretary
    Ye Fei   CCm 79/ 3

East China Fleet
Commander Zheng Guozhong   77/ 6
Dpty. commanders
    Chen Dexue   78/ 4
    Gao Xizeng   76/ 6
    Wang Xueqing   79/ 4
    Xie Zhenghao   75/12
Polit. commissar
    Fang Zhenping   79/10
Dpty. chief of staff
    Huang Shengdian   78/ 4

North China Fleet
Dpty. commander
    Deng Zhaoxiang   78/10
Polit. commissars
    Du Xishu   79/ 1
    Kang Zhiqiang   79/ 1

South China Fleet
Commander Tan Zhigeng   78/11
Polit. commissar
    Duan Dezhang   65/ 8

Railway Engineering Corps
Commander Chen Zaidao CCm 78/ 7
Dpty. commander
    Lan Tinghui   75/ 8
1st polit. commissar
    Lü Zhengcao   CCm 79/ 2
2nd polit. commissar
    Kuang Fuzhao   78/ 7

Military Academies and Schools
Academies
Air Force Engineering Academy (in Xi'an)
  President Qi Kun   79/10
  Polit. commissar
    Zhang Huchen   79/10

Art Academy
  Commandant Wei Chuantong 79/ 9
  Dpty. commandant
    Le Meng   80/ 4

Communications and Engineering Academy
  (in Nanjing)

Military Academy
  Commandant Xiao Ke CCm 78/ 1
  Dpty. commandants
    He Changgong   78/10
    Jia Ruoyu   79/11
    Tao Hanzhang   79/ 9
    Yang Zhen   78/ 1
  1st polit. commissar
    Xiao Ke   CCm 79/10

Military Science Academy
  Commandant Song Shilun   CCm 73/ 9
  Dpty. commandants
          Gao Rui   78/ 8
          Guo Huaruo   78/ 2
          Shu Dong   79/ 1

Political Academy
  Commandant Lin Hao   79/ 7
  Dpty. polit. commissar
          Xie Ming   78/ 9

Railway Corps Academy (in Changsha)
  Dpty. commandant
          He Bing   78/ 9

Schools
  Aviation School (in Shijiazhuang)
  Commandant Wang Tao   79/10

  Navy 1st Surface Ships School
  Polit. commissar
          He Mingzhi   80/ 3

  Wired Signaling Technical School

Institutes
  Artillery Institute (in Anhui)

  Electronics Engineering Institute (in Anhui)

  International Strategic Studies, Institute for
  Director   Wu Xuquan   CCm 80/ 6

Logistics Institute
  Instructor in politics
          Shao Weizheng   80/ 3

Medical Aviation Research Institute

Radar Institute of the Air Force
  Director   Li Nengjing   80/ 3

Colleges
  4th Military Medical College

  Naval College
  Polit.com. Zuo Ai   78/10

Others

  Air Defense Leading Group, National People's
  Dpty.leader Chen Xilian   CCm 78/11

  Physical Culture Guidance Comte., All-Army
  Director   Li Da   CCm 78/ 6
  Dpty.dir.   Fu Zhong   78/ 6
               Wang Ping   CCm 78/ 6
  Secretary-general
               Li Wei   78/ 6
  Dpty. secretary-generals
               Han Fudong   78/ 6
               Zhang Zhongjie   78/ 6
               Zhou Zhitong   78/ 6

  Military Procuratorate

MASS ORGANIZATIONS, PARTIES, ASSOCIATIONS, SOCIETIES

Chinese People's Political Consultative Conference

Chairman	Deng Xiaoping	PBm	CCm	78/ 3
Vice-chairmen	Banqen Erdeni Qoigyi			
	Gyancan			79/ 7
	Hu Yuzhi			79/ 7
	Hu Ziang			78/ 3
	Ji Fang			78/ 3
	Kang Keqing f		CCm	78/ 3
	Li Weihan			79/ 7
	Liu Lantao		CCm	79/ 7
	Lu Dingyi		CCm	79/ 7
	Pagbalha Geleg Namgyai			59/ 4
	Peng Chong	PBm	CCm	78/ 3
	Rong Yiren			78/ 3
	Shen Yanbing			75/ 1
	Shi Liang f			78/ 3
	Song Renqiong		CCm	75/ 1
	Ulanhu	PBm	CCm	78/ 3
	Xu Deheng			75/ 1
	Wang Kunlun			79/ 7
	Wang Shoudao		CCm	78/ 3
	Wei Guoqing	PBm	CCm	75/ 1
	Yang Jingren		CCm	78/ 3
	Zhang Chong			78/ 3
	Zhao Ziyang	PBm	CCm	78/ 3
	Zhou Jianren		CCm	78/ 3
	Zhu Yunshan			78/ 3
	Zhuang Xiquan			78/ 3

Literary and Historical Materials Research Committee

Chairman	Wang Shoudao	CCm	78/ 6

Parties

China Democratic League

Chairman	Shi Liang f	79/10
Vice-chairmen	Chu Tunan	79/ 1
	Deng Chumin	79/10
	Fei Xiaotong	79/10
	Hu Yuzhi	79/10
	Hua Luogeng	79/10
	Li Wenyi f	79/10
	Peng Dixian	79/10
	Sa Kongliao	79/10
	Su Buqing	79/10

All-China Federation of Industrialists and Businessmen

Executive Committee			
Chairman	Hu Ziang		79/10
Vice-chairmen	Gu Gengyu		79/10
	Hu Ziying f		79/10
	Hua Yuqing		79/10
	Huang Changshui		79/10
	Jiang Peilu		79/10

Liang Shangli		79/10
Liu Jingji		79/10
Liu Nianzhi		79/10
Luo Shuzhang f		79/10
Rong Yiren		79/10
Sha Qianli		79/10
Sun Qimeng		79/10
Wu Xuezhi		79/10
Xiong Yingdong		79/10
Zhang Jingli		79/10
Zhou Shutao		79/10

Jiu-san Society

Chairman	Xu Deheng	79/10
Vice-chairmen	Jin Shanbao	79/10
	Ke Zhao	79/10
	Lu Yudao	79/10
	Mao Yisheng	79/10
	Pan Shu	79/10
	Shui Xiheng	79/10
	Sun Chengpei	79/10
	Wang Zhuxi	79/10
	Yen Jici	79/10
	Zhou Peiyuan	79/10

Revolutionary Committee of the Chinese Kuomintang

Chairman	Zhu Yunshan	79/10
Vice-chairmen	Chen Cisheng	79/10
	Jia Yibin	79/10
	Gan Cisen	79/10
	Li Shizhang	79/10
	Liu Fei	79/10
	Pei Changhui	79/10
	Qian Changzhao	79/10
	Qu Wu	79/10
	Wang Kunlun	79/10
	Wu Maosun	79/10
	Zheng Dongguo	79/10
	Zhu Xuefan	79/10

China Democratic National Construction Association

Chairman	Hu Juewen		79/10
Vice-chairmen	Guo Dihuo		79/10
	Hu Dixin		79/10
	Hu Ziang		79/ 1
	Pu Jiexiu	f	79/10
	Sun Qimeng		79/10
	Sun Xiaocun		79/10
	Tang Yuanbing		79/10
	Tong Shaosheng		79/10
	Wang Guangying		79/10
	Wu Zhichao		79/10
	Zhou Shiguan		79/10
Central Committee			
Member	Li Wenjie		79/10

China Peasants and Workers Democratic Party

Chairman	Ji Fang	79/10
Vice-chairmen	Liu Shuxun	79/10
	Shen Qizhen	79/10
	Xu Binju	79/10

	Yan Xinmin		79/10
	Ye Jiequan		79/10
	Zhou Gucheng		79/10

China Association for Promoting Democracy

Chairman	Zhou Jianren		79/10
Vice-chairmen	Lei Jieqiong	f	79/10
	Wu Ruoan	f	79/10
	Wu Yifang	f	79/10
	Xie Bingxin	f	79/10
	Xu Boxin		78/ 8
	Ye Shengtao		79/10
	Zhao Puchu		78/ 8

Taiwan Democratic Self-government League

Council of the General Office

Chairman	Cai Xiao	CCm	79/10
Vice-chairmen	Li Chunqing		79/10
	Su Ziheng		79/10
	Tian Fuda		79/10
Council member	Chen Wenbin		80/ 1

Zhi Gong Dang

Chairman	Huang Dingchen		79/10
Vice-chairmen	Wu Chan		79/10
	Wu Juetian		79/10

Political Organizations

Communist Youth League

1st secretary	Han Ying	CCm	78/10
Secretaries	Gao Zhanxiang		78/10
	Hu Dehua	f	78/10
	Li Haifeng	f	78/10
	Li Ruihuan		80/ 1
	Liu Weiming	CCa	78/10
	Wang Minsheng		78/10
	Zhou Pengcheng		78/10

Friendship with Foreign Countries, Association for

Chairman	Wang Bingnan		75/ 8
Vice-chairmen	Chu Tu'nan		78/ 9
	Hou Tong		79/ 2
	Lin Lin		73/ 6
	Luo Shigao		78/ 8
	Xia Yan		78/ 4
	Xie Bangding		78/ 9
	Yang Ji		72/ 6
Secr.general	Wang Zhifan		78/ 5

Dpty. secr. general

	Guo Dongjun		72/10

Member, Stand.Comte.

	Lu Zui		78/ 5
	Ma Peijiang		78/ 8
	Wen Pengjiu		78/ 9
	Zhang Shuyuan		78/ 4
	Zhu Ziji		78/ 5

Council members

	Chen Dayuan		77/ 7
	Fan Ruguang		78/ 8
	Hou Tian		78/ 2
	Li Maozhai		78/ 8

	Tang Jiaxuan		78/ 8
	Wei Jianye		77/11
	Wu Qing		78/ 4

Returned Overseas Chinese, Federation of

Honorary chairman

	Liao Chengzhi	CCm	78/12
Chairman	Zhuang Xiquan		78/12
Vice-chairmen	Chen Zongji		80/ 2
	Guo Ruiren		80/ 2
	Hong Sisi		79/ 9
	Lian Guan		79/ 1
	Zhong Qingfa		79/ 6
	Zhuang Mingli		78/ 5

Dpty. secr.-general

	Hong Sisi		78/ 5

Memeber, Stand.Comte

	Qiu Ji		78/ 5

Students Federation

Chairman	Wu Shaozu		79/ 1
Vice-chairmen	Ai-er-ken Si-di-ke		79/ 5
	Cui Li	f	79/ 5
	Du Songyan		79/ 5
	Guo Ruyan		79/ 5
	Han Jianmin	f	79/ 5
	Hu Shuxiang		79/ 5
	Huang Mingfen		79/ 5
	Luo Zhihao		79/ 5
	Qi Baolin		79/ 5
	Wang Jichuan		79/ 5
	Wang Shengheng		79/ 5
	Wu Xuefan		79/ 5
	Xu Weiyang		79/ 5
	Yu Guilin		79/ 5
	Yuan Zhunqing		79/ 5

Trade Unions, All China Federation of

President	Ni Zhifu	PBm CCm	78/10

Vice-presidents

	Chen Yu		78/10
	Gu Dachun		79/11
	Han Ronghua		78/10
	Huang Minwei		78/10
	Jin Zhifu		79/11
	Kang Yonghe		78/ 4
	Liu Yue	f	78/10
	Song Kanfu		78/10
	Wang Chonglun		78/10
	Zhang Ruiying	f	78/10
	Zhu Xuefan		78/10
Secretary	Li Wanghua		79/ 2

Alternate secretaries

	Han Xiya		79/ 7
	Qi Ping		80/ 3

Production Department

Director	Wang Chonglun		79/ 4

Cadre School

President	Ni Zhifu	PBm CCm	78/11

9th Executive Committee

Standing members

	Chen Yongwen		79/11
	Gu Dachun		79/11
	Jiang Yi		79/11
	Li Wanghuai		79/11

Education Workers' Trade Union

Vice-chairman

	Fang Ming		79/ 1

Railway Workers' Union, All-China
Chairman	Wang Shijie		78/11
Vice-chairmen			
	Bi Siyun		78/11
	Chen Fuhan	CCm	78/11
	Li Zhengang		78/11
	Lin Yi	f	78/11
	Wu Jinzhu		78/11
	You Zhujie		78/11
	Zai Lianxing		78/11
	Zhang Jie		78/11
	Zheng Xikun		78/11

Seamen's Trade Union
Vice-chairman		
	Qiu Jin	80/ 4

Women's Federation, National
Honorary chairmen			
	Cai Chang	CCm	78/ 9
	Deng Yingchao	PBm CCm	78/ 9
	Song Qingling		78/ 9
Chairman	Kang Keqing	CCm	78/ 9
Vice-chairmen	Guan Jian		78/ 9
	Hao Jianxiu	CCm	78/ 9
	Huang Ganying		78/ 9
	Lei Jieqiong		78/ 9
	Li Baoguang		78/ 9
	Lin Liyun	CCm	78/ 9
	Lin Qiaozhi		78/ 9
	Luo Qiong		78/ 9
	Mayenur		78/ 9
	Nyapoi Cedan Zhoigar		78/ 9
	Shi Liang		78/ 9
	Wu Yifang		78/ 9
	Zeng Xianzhi		78/ 9
1st secretary	Luo Qiong		78/ 9
Secretaries	Dong Bian		78/ 9
	Huang Ganying		78/ 9
	Li Baoguang		78/ 9
	Li Qin		78/ 9
	Li Shuzheng		78/ 9
	Tian Xiuquan		78/ 9
	Wu Quanheng		78/ 9
	Guo Liwen		80/ 5
Standing Committee			
Members	Hu Naijiu		78/10
	Lu Cui		79/ 6
Internat'l. Liaison Dpt.			
Director	Zhang Jiexun		80/ 4

Youth Federation
Vice-chairmen	Du Jinfang	f	79/ 5
	Gao Zhanxiang		79/ 5
	Jia-mu-yang Luo-zang-jiu-ruo		
	Tu-dan Que-ji-ni-ma		79/ 5
	Li Haifeng	f	79/ 5
	Li Shoubao		79/ 5
	Liu Hanliang		80/ 5
	Liu Houming		79/ 3
	Liu Weiming	CCa	79/ 5
	Qu Qingyue		79/ 5
	Rong Hongren		80/ 5
	Wu Shaozu		79/ 5
	Xu Yinsheng		79/ 5
	Yang Luo		79/ 5
Secretary-general			
	Yin Minglian		79/ 5

Dpty.sec.-generals			
	Hu Huanzhang		79/ 5
	Li Yi		79/ 5
	Wang Jide		79/ 5
	Zhu Shanqing		79/ 5
Standing Committee			
Members	A-gu-la		79/ 5
	Bi Wenming		79/ 5
	Cai Detai		79/ 5
	Chen Dabin		79/ 5
	Chen Guoji		79/ 5
	Chen Jiaqi		79/ 5
	Chen Yuzhong		79/ 5
	Cui Yi		79/ 5
	Fu Tingdong		79/ 5
	He Guangyue		79/ 5
	Hu Songhua		79/ 5
	Jiang Baiju		79/ 5
	Jin Zhuhua	f	79/ 5
	Kang Beisheng	f	79/ 5
	Li Shulan	f	79/ 5
	Liu Chunpu		79/ 5
	Liu Hanliang		79/ 5
	Liu Xinwu		79/ 5
	Ma Ji		79/ 5
	Mao Baoyu		79/ 5
	Mu-ha-mai-ti Zu-nong		79/ 5
	Pan Jingli	f	79/ 5
	Qi Lieyun		79/ 5
	Rong Hongren		79/ 5
	Sun Jiachang		79/ 5
	Tao Siliang	f	79/ 5
	Wang-dui Zhu-miao		79/ 5
	Wang Erzhong		79/ 5
	Wu Jin		79/ 5
	Wu Yingfu		79/ 5
	Yan Honghua		79/ 5
	Ye Yonglie		79/ 5
	Yin Minglian		79/ 5
	Zhang Shuxun		79/ 5
	Zheng Dazhen	f	79/ 5
	Zhong Peizhang		79/ 5
	Zhu Shanqing		79/ 5
	Fan Zeng		80/ 5
	Han Meiling		80/ 5
	Wang Hua	f	80/ 5

Social Organizations

Blind and Deaf-mutes Association
Honorary chairman			
	Cheng Zihua	CCm	80/ 4
Chairman	Wu Qian	f	80/ 4
Vice-chairmen	Huang Nai		80/ 4
	Li Shihan		80/ 4
	Li Zheng		80/ 4

Defense of Children, Chinese People's National
Committee for
Chairman	Song Qingling	f		80/ 5
Vice-chairmen	Deng Yingchao	f	PBm CCm	80/ 4
	Cui Yueli			79/ 4
	Yang Yunyu	f		80/ 1

Zhu Futang				80/ 1
Kang Keqing	f		CCm	80/ 4

Dpty.sec.-general

Zhang Shuyi	f		78/11

Nursery and Child Welfare Work Leading Group

Head	Chen Muhua	f	PBa CCm	80/ 1
Dpty. heads	Dong Chuncai			80/ 1
	Su Xiuzhen			80/ 1
	Wu Quanheng	f		80/ 1
	Wang Chengyuan			80/ 1

Red Cross, Chinese

President	Xu Hui		79/10
Vice-presidents			
	Gu Jinxin	f	78/11
	Liu Pengfei		79/ 2
	Shen Qizhen		79/ 2
	Wang Yi		78/12
	Yang Chun		78/12
	Zhao Puchu		79/ 2

Welfare Institute
Executive Committee

Members	Ba Jin			78/ 6
	He Jiuzheng			78/ 6
	Kang Keqing	f	CCm	78/ 6
	Li Taizheng			78/ 6
	Liu Fang			78/ 6
	Peng Chong		PBm CCm	78/ 6
	Qi Yanming			78/ 6
	Shen Cuizhen	f		78/ 6
	Wang Mingzhang		CCm	78/ 6
	Wang Yiping		CCm	78/ 6
	Wu Yaozong			78/ 6
	Zhang Suping			78/ 6
	Zhe Wenyi			78/ 6
	Zhou Weizhi			78/ 6

Sports Organizations

Sports Federation, All-China

President	Zhong Shitong	79/ 3
Vice-presidents		
	Chen Xian	79/11
	Du Qian	79/ 3
	Han Fudong	79/ 9
	Huang Zhong	78/ 9
	Li Menghua	78/10
	Liu Jianzhang	79/ 9
	Lu Jindong	79/ 3
	Rong Gaotang	79/ 3
	Xia Xiang	79/ 6
	Zhang Qingji	79/ 3
Secretary-general		
	Song Zhong	73/ 2

Athletic Association

President	Li Wenyao		79/10
Vice-presidents			
	Jiao Yulian		79/10
	Zheng Fengrong	f	80/ 5

Aviation Sports Federation

President	Yu Buxue	79/ 5
Vice-president	Han Mingyang	78/ 2
Secretary-general		
	Han Mingyang	78/ 5

Badminton Federation

President	Zhu Ze	77/ 9
Vice-president	Wang Wenjiao	78/10

Baseball and Softball Association

Basketball Association

President	Mou Zuoyun	78/ 7
Secretary-general		
	Zhang Changlu	78/11

Fencing Association
Dpty.sec.-general

Lin Houru	78/ 6

Football Association

President	Li Fenglou	79/ 7
Secretary-general		
	Chen Jialiang	76/ 5

Gymnastics Association

Handball Association

President	Zhou Zhitong	79/ 6

Kite-flying Association

President	Zhang E	80/ 5
Vice-president	Li Bingsheng	80/ 5

Marksmanship Association

Vice-president	Jian Jinfu	78/ 4

Mountaineering Association

President	Qiuo Jiajin	80/ 5
Vice-president	Shi Zhanchun	80/ 3
Secretary-general		
	Wang Fuzhou	80/ 3
Cadre	Han Fudong	78/ 4

Olympic Committee, Chinese

President	Zhong Shitong	79/ 3
Vice-president	Li Menghua	80/ 1
Secretary-general		
	Song Zhong	79/ 3
Dpty.sec.-general		
	He Zhenliang	79/ 8

School Sports Association

Shooting Association

President	Liu Junchen	80/ 1

Swimming Association

President	Zhang Xirang	80/ 3

Table Tennis Association

President	Xu Yinsheng	79/ 4
Vice-presidents		
	Liang Zhuohui	80/ 3
	Zhang Chunhan	78/ 9

Tennis Association
```
     President     Lu Zhengzao          79/ 3
     Vice-president Mou Zuyun            80/ 4
```

Track and Field Association
```
     Vice-president Zheng Fengrong  f    80/ 6
```

Volleyball Association
```
     President     Zhang Zhihuai        78/ 5
     Vice-presidents
                   Ma Jiwei             79/ 9
                   Zhao Bin             79/ 5
     Secretary-general
                   Qian Jiaxiang        78/10
```

Weiji Chess Association
```
     Honorary president
                   Fang Yi      PBm CCm 78/ 8
     President     Li Menghua           78/ 8
     Vice-president Sun Luoyi            78/ 6
```

Weight Lifting Association

Winter Sports Association

Wrestling Association

Professional Organizations

Armymen's, Chinese
```
     President     Wu Xiuquan       CCm 79/ 6
     Vice-presidents
                   Kong Yuan            80/ 4
                   Sun Yi               79/11
```

Artists' Association
```
     President     Jiang Feng           79/11
     Vice-presidents
                   Hua Junwu            80/ 3
                   Liu Kaiqu            79/ 8
                   Wu Zuoren            79/ 7
```

Cinema Workers Union
```
     Cadre         Yuan Wenshu          79/ 1
```

Dancers' Union
```
     Chairman      Wu Xiaobang          79/11
     Vice-chairmen Chen Jinqing         78/10
                   Dai Ailian      f    78/11
```

Dramatists' Union
```
     President     Cao Yu               79/11
     Vice-presidents
                   Chang Xiangyu   f    80/ 6
                   Huang Zuolin         80/ 2
                   Zhang Geng           80/ 2
                   Zhao Xun             80/ 4
```

Film Artists Association
```
     Chairman      Xia Yan              79/11
     Vice-chairman Yuan Wenshu          80/ 5
        Council member
                   Te Wei               80/ 4
```

```
     Secretary-general
                   Meng Guangjun        80/ 5
```

Fine Artists Association

Industrialists and Businessmen Federation
```
     Vice-chairman  Rong Yiren          79/ 7
     Secretary-general
                   Hu Ziying            79/10
     Dpty.sec.-general
                   Jing Shuping         79/10
```

Musicians Association
```
     President     Lü Ji                78/ 6
     Vice-presidents
                   He Lüting            79/10
                   Le Meng              80/ 4
                   Li Huanzhi           80/ 6
                   Li Lin               80/ 6
                   Zhao Feng            79/11
```

Nurses' Society
```
     President     Lin Juying      f    80/ 3
```

Physicians and Pharmacists Practicing Traditional
Chinese Medicine, Society of
```
     President     Cui Yueli            79/ 5
     Vice-presidents
                   Tao Fu               79/ 5
                   Zhang Bingnan        79/ 5
                   Zhou Yunxiang        79/ 5
```

Publishers' Association
```
     Honorary chairman
                   Hu Yuzhi             79/12
     Chairman      Chen Hanbo           79/12
        Council member
                   Wei Junyi            80/ 5
```

Shipbuilding Engineers
```
     President     Zhang Yuxuan         78/11
     Vice-presidents
                   Liu Fang             77/10
                   Wu Runding           77/10
                   Yang You             77/10
        Council member
                   Cheng Wang           77/10
```

Sports Press Association
```
     Acting chairman
                   Xu Cai               79/ 5
     Secretary-general
                   Gu Bingfu            79/ 5
```

Stage Artists Association

Writers' Union
```
     Chairman      Mao Dun              78/ 5
     1st vice-chairman
                   Ba Jin               79/11
     Vice-chairmen Ai Qing              80/ 3
                   Chen Huangmei        79/12
                   Ding Ling       f    80/ 2
                   Feng Mu              80/ 4
                   Feng Zhi             80/ 4
                   He Jingzhi           80/ 2
                   Liu Baiyu            78/ 6
                   Zhou Yang        CCm 78/ 9
```

Scientific and Technical Associations and Societies

Abacus Association
Honorary president
Dong Chuncai 80/ 4
Vice-president Yin Changsheng 80/ 3

Accounting Society
Honorary president
Duan Yun 80/ 1
President Wang Bingqian 80/ 1

Acoustics Society
President Wang Dezhao 79/ 6

Acupuncture Society

Aeronautics and Astronautics Society
President Shen Yuan 79/ 6

Aesthetics Society
Honorary president
Zhou Yang CCm 80/ 6
President Zhu Guangqian 80/ 6

African History Society
Honorary presidents
Liu Simu 80/ 3
Zhang Yong 80/ 3
President Na Zhong 80/ 3

Agricultural Crops Society
Vice-president Yang Shouren 78/ 9

Agricultural Economics Society

Agricultural Machinery Society
Vice-presidents
Xiang Nan 78/ 4
Zeng Dezhao 78/ 6

Agronomy Society
President Yang Xiandong 78/ 1
Vice-presidents
Cheng Shaojiong 78/ 8
He Kang 80/ 3
Jin Shanbao 76/ 6
Shen Qiyi 73/ 9
Dpty.sec.-general
Ma Ling 78/ 6
Adviser Zhu Rong 78/ 5
Council member Zhang Qirui 77/ 6

American Literature, Society for the Study of
President Wu Fuheng 79/11
Vice-presidents
Chen Jia 79/11
Yang Qishen 79/11
Yang Zhouhan 79/11

Anti-Tuberculosis Association
President Huang Dingchen 78/ 6

Aquatic Products Society

Archaeology Society
Director-general
Xia Nai 79/ 4
Dpty.dir.-generals
Pei Wenzhong 79/ 4
Su Bingqi 79/ 4
Yin Da 79/ 4

Architecture Society
Acting president
He Guangqian 74/ 6
Vice-presidents
Dai Nianzi 74/ 6
Lin Kemin 80/ 3
Qiao Xingbei 78/ 7
Xiao Tong 78/ 1
Yang Tingbao 73/ 6

Astronomy Society
President Zhang Yuzhe 73/ 6
Vice-presidents
Dai Wensai 78/10
Gong Shumo 78/10
Li Heng 78/10
Wang Shouguan 78/10
Ye Shuhua f 78/10
Zheng Maolan 78/10

Application of Atomic Energy in Agronomy, Society for the
President Xu Guanren 79/ 4
Vice-presidents
Chen Ziyuan 79/ 6
Ren Zhi 79/ 4
Xiao Lun 79/ 6

Automation Society
President Song Jian 80/ 5
Vice-president Lü Qiang 78/ 4
Council member Yang Jiachi 78/ 5

Aviation Society
Vice-chairman Han Minyang 78/ 5

Beekeeping Society
President Ma Defeng 79/ 7

Biochemistry Society
President Wang Yinglai 79/ 5
Vice-presidents
Cao Tianqin 79/ 5
Liang Zhiquan 79/ 5
Zhang Longxiang 79/ 5
Zou Chenglu 79/ 5

Biophysics Society
President Bei Shizhang 80/ 5
Vice-presidents
Cheng Jiji 80/ 5
Lin Kechun 80/ 5
Xu Jinghua 80/ 5
Secretary-general
Shen Shumin 80/ 5

Botany Society
President Tang Peisong 78/11
Vice-president Wu Zhengyi 78/11

Business Management Association
Chairman	Zhang Peng	79/ 9
Vice-chairmen	Liu Yuanneng	79/ 9
	Xu Weili	79/ 9
Secretary-general		
	Zhang Yanning	80/ 3

Cardio-vascular Diseases Society

Central Asian Culture Society
| President | Chen Hansheng | 79/11 |

Chemistry Society

Chemical Engineering Society

Chemical Industry Society
| Board of Directors, | | |
| Chairman | Tao Dao (f) | 78/12 |

Chinese Literature Research Society, Contemporary
| President | Feng Mu | 79/11 |

Cinema Society, World
| Director general | | |
| | Meng Guangjun | 80/ 3 |

Civil Engineering Society
| President | Mao Yisheng | 62/ 9 |
| Vice-president | Li Guohao | 79/10 |

Coal Mining Society
President	He Bingzhang	75/11
Council member	Zhao Zhuanfu	77/ 9
Adviser	Zou Tong	78/ 9

Contemporary Chinese History Society
Honorary president		
	Lu Dingyi	CCm 80/ 6
President	Li Shu	80/ 6

Contemporary World History, Study of

Cotton Society
| President | Xi Yuanling | 79/ 5 |

Destruction-free Testing Society

Du Fu, Society for the Study of the Tang Dynasty Poet
Honorary president		
	Zhang Xiushu	80/ 6
President	Miao Yue	80/ 6
Vice-president	Qu Shouyuan	80/ 6

Distribution of Means of Production, Society for the Study of
Honorary president		
	Yuan Baohua	CCa 80/ 3
President	Yu Xiaogu	80/ 3
Vice-presidents		
	Hua Luogeng	80/ 2
	Ma Hong	80/ 2
Advisers	Hua Luogeng	80/ 3
	Sun Yefang	80/ 3
	Xue Muqiao	80/ 3
	Yu Guangyuan	80/ 3

Ecology Society
| President | Ma Shijun | 79/12 |

Economy of Oceania, Research into
| President | Luo Yuanzheng | 80/ 4 |
| Vice-president | Teng Yuancao | 80/ 4 |

Electrical Engineering Society
| Acting president | | |
| | Li Daigeng | 78/ 7 |

Education Society
Honorary presidents		
	Chen Heqin	79/ 4
	Cheng Fangwu	79/ 4
	Yang Xiufeng	79/ 4
President	Dong Chuncai	79/ 4
Vice-presidents		
	Chen Dao	79/ 4
	Dai Botao	79/ 4
	Li Qi	78/10
	Liu Funian	79/ 4
	Zhang Jian	79/ 4

Electronics Society
President	Liu Yin	79/ 9
Vice-presidents		
	Ma Dayou	62
	Sun Junren	78/ 5
Secretary-general		
	Luo Peilin	78/12
Dpty.sec.-general		
	Deng Guojun	75/11
Council member	Li Zhaoji	76/11

Engineering Society
| President | Zhu Rong | 79/11 |

Enterprise Management Association
President	Yuan Baohua	CCa 79/ 3
Vice-presidents		
	Hua Luogeng	80/ 2
	Ma Hong	80/ 2
Secretary-general		
	Zhan Yan	80/ 2

Environment Society
| President | Li Chaobo | 79/ 3 |
| Council member | Qu Geping | 79/ 9 |

Esperanto League
Chairman	Hu Yuzhi	79/ 9
Standing Committee		
Members	Ye Junjian	79/ 9
	Zhang Qicheng	78/ 7

Ethics Society
Honorary president		
	Huang Zhen	CCm 80/ 6
President	Li Qi	80/ 6

Family Planning Association
| President | Wang Shoudao | CCm 80/ 5 |

Finance Society
Honorary president		
	Bo Yibo	CCm 80/ 1
President	Rong Zihe	80/ 1

Fishery Association			
Chairman	Xiao Peng		77/ 5
Vice-chairman	Ma Ling		77/ 6

Foreign Economic Theories Society

Honorary president			
	Xu Dixin		79/11
President	Chen Daisun		79/11

Foreign Literature Society

Secretary	Zhou Luoqun	79/ 5

Forestry Society

Vice-president	Chen Luqi	80/ 3

Future, Society for the Study of the

Director-general			
	Du Dagong		79/ 3
Secretary-general			
	Qin Linzheng		80/ 6
Advisers	Mao Yisheng		80/ 6
	Qian Junrui		79/ 3
	Qian Xuesen	CCa	79/ 3
	Tong Dalin		80/ 6
	Yu Guangyuan		79/ 3

Genetics Society

Geography Society

President	Huang Bingwei	80/ 1
Vice-president	Hou Renzhi	79/ 6

Geology Society

President	Huang Jiqing	79/ 3
Vice-president	Xu Jie	79/10
Council member	Song Shuhe	78/ 4
Structural Geology Committee		
Chairman	Huang Jiqing	79/ 3
Vice-chairman		
	Zhang Wenyu	79/ 3

Geophysics Society

President	Gu Gongxu	77/12

Glaciology and Cryopedology Society

President	Shi Yafeng	80/ 3

Grasslands Society

Honorary president		
	Sun Zhongyi	80/ 1
President	Jia Shenxiu	80/ 1
1st vice-president		
	Ren Jizhou	80/ 1

Historical Figures of the CCP, Society on the

President	He Changgong	79/12
Vice-presidents		
	Hu Hua	79/12
	Li Xin	79/12

History Society

Presidium members		
	Bai Shouyi	80/ 4
	Deng Guangmin	80/ 4
	Liu Danian	80/ 4
	Zheng Tianting	80/ 4
	Zhou Gucheng	80/ 4

Hydraulic Engineering Society

President	Qian Zhengying f	CCm	73/12
Vice-president	Li Boning		80/ 3
Sedimentation Committee			
Vice-chairman			
	Qian Ning		80/ 3

Instruments and Meters Society

President	Wang Dezhao	79/ 4

Insurance Society

Honorary president		
	Xu Dixin	79/12

International Law Society

President	Huan Xiang		80/ 2
Vice-presidents			
	Chen Tiqiang		80/ 2
	Ren Jianxin		80/ 2
	Rui Shu		80/ 3
	Shao Tianren		80/ 2
	Wang Daohan		80/ 2
	Wang Tieya		80/ 2
	Xu Hegao		80/ 2
	Zhang Huiwen f		80/ 2

Japanese Literature, Society for the Study of

President	Lin Lin	79/11

Journalism Society, Beijing

Honorary chairman			
	Hu Qiaomu	CCm	80/ 2
Chairman	Hu Jiwei		80/ 2
Vice-chairmen	An Gang		80/ 2
	Dai Bang		80/ 2
	Jin Zhao		80/ 2
	Li Pu		80/ 2
	Wang Yi		80/ 2
	Xiong Fu		80/ 2
Advisers	Chen Kehan		80/ 2
	Fan Jin f		80/ 2
	Ge Baoquan		80/ 2
	Gu Zhizhong		80/ 2
	Hu Yuzhi		80/ 2
	Liao Gailong		80/ 2
	Liao Mosha		80/ 2
	Liu Zunqi		80/ 2
	Mei Yi		80/ 2
	Sa-kong-liao		80/ 2
	Shi Shaohua		80/ 2
	Shi Ximin		80/ 2
	Wang Yunsheng		80/ 2
	Wen Jize		80/ 2
	Wu Kejian		80/ 2
	Wu Xileng		80/ 2
	Xia Yan		80/ 2
	Xu Maijin		80/ 2
	Zhang Youyu		80/ 2
	Zhu Muzhi	CCm	80/ 2

Laser Society, National

Law History Society

President	Xie Tieguang	79/ 9
Vice-presidents		
	Li Guangcan	79/ 9
	Xiao Yongqing	79/ 9

Libraries Society
    President   Liu Jiping   79/ 8

Light Industry Society
    President   Liang Lingguang   79/12
    Vice-presidents
                Cai Zuquan   79/12
                Ge Chunlin   79/12
                Han Peixin   79/12
                Ma Jilin   79/12
                Zhang Ruyan   79/12
                Zhu Baoyong   79/12
    Secretary-general
                Huang Yiqi   79/12

Logic Society

Lu Xun Studies Society
    Honorary President
                Song Qingling f   79/12
    President   Mao Dun   79/12
    Advisers   Hu Qiaomu   CCm 79/12
                Zhou Jianren   79/12
                Zhou Yang   CCm 79/12

Marine Navigation Society
    President   Zeng Sheng   79/ 4

Mathematics Society
    President   Hua Luogeng   53/
    Vice-pres.   Jiang Zehan   78/ 4
                Su Buqing   87/ 4

Mechanics Society
    President   Qian Xuesen   CCa 80/ 3
    Vice-president Zhang Wei   79/ 7

Mechanical Engineering Society
    President   Wang Daohan   78/ 9
    Vice-presidents Jiang Zemin   78/ 9
                Liu Ding   78/ 9
                Shen Hong   78/ 9
                Zhou Jiannan   78/10
    Secr.-general Tao Hengxian   78/ 9

Mechanics and Automation Society
    President   Qian Xuesen   CCa 78/11

Medical Association, Chinese
    President   Qian Xinzhong   78/ 4
    Vice-presidents
                Chen Zhiming   78/ 6
                Guo Ziheng   78/ 7
                Huang Jiasi   78/ 6
                Lin Qiaozhi   f   78/ 6
                Lu Zhijun   78/ 6
                Wu Jieping   78/ 6
                Zhong Huilan   79/ 1
                Zhu Zhanggeng   78/ 2
    Secr.-general Chen Zhiming   78/11

Medicine, Internal, Association of
    President   Zhong Huilan   79/ 1

Metallurgical Society
    President   Ye Zhiqiang   77/ 9
    Vice-presidents
                Hong Ge   79/ 1

                Huang Peiyun   79/ 1
                Li Hua   79/ 1
                Li Xun   79/ 1
                Liu Kegang   79/ 1
                Liu Xuexin   78/ 8
                Lu Da   78/ 4
                Ma Bin   79/ 1
                Wang Yuqing   78/11
                Xu Chi   CCa 78/ 7
                Zhang Wenzhi   79/ 1
    Council member Wang Chundu   78/ 6

Meteorology Society
    Vice-presidents
                Cheng Jishu   79/ 5
                Xie Yibing   79/ 2
                Zou Jingmeng   75/10
    Council member Lu Dongming   79/ 5

Metrology and Instrumentation Society
    Vice-president Ma Lin   79/ 5

Micropalaeontology Society
    President   Chen Xu   79/ 3

Modern Foreign Philosophy, Society of the Study of

Mongolian History Society
    President   Weng Dujian   79/ 8
    Vice-presidents
                Gewa   79/ 8
                Han Rulin   79/ 8
                Huang Jingtao   79/ 8
                Te-bu-xin   79/ 8
    Secr.-general Lu Minghai   79/ 8

Mongolian Literature Society
    President   Zolen   79/12

Nationality Research Society
    President   Ya Hanzhang   79/ 5
    Vice-presidents
                Fu Maoji   79/ 5
                Weng Dujian   79/ 5
                Zhang Yangwu   79/ 5

Naval Architecture and Marine Engineering Society
    President   Zhang Youxuan   79/ 3
    Vice-presidents
                Shen Yuerui   79/ 3
                Yang You   79/ 3

Navigation Society
    Vice-president Deng Zhaoxiang   80/ 3

Nuclear Society
    Honorary president
                Qian Sanqiang   80/ 2
    President   Wang Ganchang   80/ 2
    Vice-presidents
                Jiang Shengjie   80/ 2
                Jin Shiqu   80/ 2
                Li Jue   80/ 2
                Zhang Wenyu   80/ 2
                Zhang Zhenhuan   80/ 2
                Zhao Zhongyao   80/ 2
                Zhu Guangya   CCm 80/ 2

Nuclear Science and Technology Society		
President	Zhang Jiahua	78/ 6

Nursing Science Society

Occupational Disease Prevention Society		
President	Wu Zhizhong	79/10
Vice-presidents		
	Gu Xueji	79/10
	Jin Cui	79/10
	Liu Shishu	79/10

Oceanography Society		
President	Luo Yuru	79/ 8
Council member	Wang Dezhao	75/ 3

Operations Research Society		
President	Hua Luogeng	80/ 5
Vice-presidents		
	Xu Guozhi	80/ 5
	Yu Qianxiu	80/ 5
	Yue Minyi	80/ 5

Optical Society		
Honorary president		
	Yan Jici	79/12
President	Wang Daheng	79/12

Otolaryngology Society		
President	Zhang Qingsong	80/ 3

Palaeontology Society		
President	Yin Canxun	79/ 4
Vice-presidents		
	Lu Yanhao	79/ 4
	Zhou Mingzhen	80/ 5
Secr.-general	Zhou Mingzhen	79/ 4

Palynology Society		
President	Xu Ren	79/ 3

Pedology Society		
President	Li Qingkui	78/ 6

Petroleum Society		
President	Hou Xianglin	78/12
Dpty. director-general		
	Min Yu	79/ 9

Pharmacy Society		
Vice-president	Wang Xu	78/ 6

Photography Society		
President	Xu Xiaobing	79/11
Vice-presidents		
	Chen Fuli	79/11
	Sun Jian	80/ 2

Physics Society		
President	Zhou Peiyuan	78/12
Vice-presidents		
	Qian Sanqiang	78/ 8
	Shi Ruwei	78/ 8
	Xie Xide f	78/ 8

Plant Association

Popularization of Science and Technology and Inventions, Association for		
Honorary presidents		
	Gao Shiqi	79/ 8
	Mao Yisheng	79/ 8
President	Dong Chuncai	79/ 8
Vice-presidents		
	Bei Zuzhang	79/ 8
	Fang Zongxi	79/ 8
	Gu Junzheng	79/ 8
	Wang Wenda	79/ 8
	Wen Jize	79/ 8
	Ye Zhishan	79/ 8

Precision Machinery Society

Pre-school Education, Society for the Study of		
Honorary president		
	Chen Heqin	79/11

Printing Technology Association

Psychology Society		
President	Pan Shu	78/ 7

Pulp and Paper Engineering Society		
Vice-president	Xue Lingshan	78/10

Qigong Society		
President	Liu Jianhua	80/ 5

Quality Control Association			
President	Yue Zhijian		78/ 8
Vice-presidents			
	Cao Weilian		79/ 8
	Hao Jianxiu f	CCm	79/ 8
	Liu Yuanzhang		79/ 8
	Song Ligang		79/ 8
	Yang Jizhi		79/ 8

Quantitative Economics Society

Quaternary Research Society		
Secr.-general	Liu Dongsheng	79/ 7

Radiation Protection Society		
President	Li Zhenping	80/ 3
Vice-president	Li Deping	80/ 3

Railways Society		
Board of Directors, Director	Liu Jianzhang	79/11

Reform of Chinese Script Association		
President	H.K. Yuan	80/ 3
Vice-presidents		
	Lo Shui-yin	80/ 3
	John B. Tsu (vice-president San Francisco Univ.)	80/ 3

Refrigeration Association

Religion, Society for the Study of		
Honorary President		
	Zhao Puchu	79/ 2
President	Ren Jiyu	79/ 2

Science Film Society

Science and Technology Association
President	Zhou Peiyuan		80/ 3
Vice-presidents			
	Hua Luogeng		80/ 3
	Huang Jiasi		80/ 3
	Liu Shuzhou		78/ 6
	Mao Yisheng		78/ 2
	Pei Lisheng		78/ 4
	Qian Xuesen	CCa	80/ 3
	Wang Shuntong		80/ 5
	Yan Jici		80/ 5
Secretaries	Wang Shuntong		79/ 2
	Yan Jici		75/ 4
	Zhang Wei		75/ 6

Scientific and Technological Information,
Association for

Seismology Society
President	Gu Gongxu	79/11

Silicate Research Society
Vice-president Liu Songjiu	78/ 9

Sociology Society
President	Fei Xiaotong	79/ 3
Vice-president Lei Jieqiong		80/ 3

Solar Energy Society
President	Wang Buxuan	79/ 9

South Asian Study Society

Soviet Literature, Society for the Study of
Honorary presidents		
	Cao Jinghua	80/ 3
	Jiang Chunfang	80/ 3
President	Ye Shuifu	80/ 3

Space Flight Society
President	Ren Xinmin	78/ 8

Spanish, Portugese and Latin American
Literature, Society for the Study of

Standardization Society
President	Yue Zhijian	78/ 8
Vice-presidents		
	Xu Haofeng	80/ 4
	Zheng Zhuanhui	78/ 8

Statistical Society
President	Xue Muqiao	79/11

Stratigraphy Society
Vice-president Wu Heng	79/11

Surveying and Cartography Society
President	Li Tingzan	79/ 7

Taiping Heavenly Kingdom, Society for the Study
of
Vice-president Wang Qingcheng	80/ 3

Technical Economics Society

Textile Engineering Society
President	Chen Weiji	78/ 7

Tibetan Buddhism, Society for the Study of
President	Ren Jiyu	79/ 4
Vice-presidents		
	Dongga	79/ 4
	Fa Cun	79/ 4
	Luozang Jinlie	79/ 4
	Ya Hanzhang	79/ 4
	Yu Daquan	79/ 4

Traditional Chinese Medicine Society
Preparatory Committee		
Chairman	Lü Bingkui	78/ 6
Vice-chairmen		
	Hu Ximing	78/ 6
	Lu Zhijun	78/ 6
	Wang Wending	78/ 6
	Wei Longxiang	78/ 6
	Yue Meizhong	78/ 6
	Zhao Bingnan	78/ 6
	Zhao Xiwu	78/ 6

Tropical Crops Society
President	Liang Wenqi	79/ 1

Tuberculosis, Association for Prevention and
Treatment

Vacuum Society
Honorary president		
	Lu Ping	79/12
President	Jin Jianzhong	79/12

Veterinary Society
President	Cheng Shaohui	79/ 8

Water Conservancy and Power Society
President	Zhang Hanying	79/ 1

West European Economy, Society for the Study of

World Economics Society
President	Qian Junrui		80/ 4
Vice-presidents			
	Chou Qihua		80/ 4
	Guan Mengjue		80/ 4
	Pu Shan		80/ 4
	Song Zexing		80/ 4
	Tao Darong		80/ 4
	Teng Weizao		80/ 4
	Wu Jixian		80/ 4
	Wu Dakun		80/ 4
	Yu Kaixiang		80/ 4
Advisers	Chen Hansheng		80/ 4
	Chen Daisun		80/ 4
	Xu Dixin		80/ 4
	Hu Qiaomu	CCm	80/ 4
	Huan Xiang		80/ 4
	Wang Daohan		80/ 4
	Yu Guangyuan		80/ 4
	Sol Adler		80/ 4
	Frank Coe		80/ 4

World Nationalities Studies, Society of
Honorary president		
	Fei Xiaotong	80/ 6

Young People, Society for the Study of
President	Wang Mingzhang	80/ 4

Young Pioneers Work, Society for
Chairman	Hu Dehua	f	79/ 8
Vice-chairmen	Chen Mo		79/ 8
	Jiang Jingwen		79/ 8
	Liu Yuanzhang		79/ 8
	Zhang Junfa		79/ 8

Yugoslav Economy, Society for the Study of
Adviser	Qian Junrui	80/ 1

Zoology Society

Arts Societies

Arts and Crafts Society

Film Association
Vice-chairmen	Yu Lin	80/ 2
Secretary-general		
	Meng Guangjun	80/ 3

Folk Art and Literature Society
Chairman	Zhou Yang	CCm	79/19
Vice-chairmen	Jia Zhi		79/11
	Zhong Jingwen		79/11

Graphic Art Association
Chairman	Li Hua	80/ 4
Vice-chairmen	Lai Shaoqi	80/ 4
	Li Qun	80/ 4

Literary and Art Circles Federation
Honorary Chairman			
	Mao Dun		79/11
Chairman	Zhou Yang	CCm	79/11
Vice-chairmen	Ba Jin		79/11
	Fu Zhong		79/11
	Ganbaerhan		79/11
	He Lüding		79/11
	Lin Mohan		79/11
	Tao Dun		79/11
	Wu Zuoren		79/11
	Xia Yan		79/11
	Xie Bingxin	f	79/11
	Yang Hansheng		79/11
	Yu Zhenfei		79/11

Pen Center, Chinese
President	Ba Jin	80/ 4
Vice-presidents		
	Ai Qing	80/ 4
	Chen Huangmei	80/ 4
	Ding Ling	f	80/ 4
	Feng Zhi	80/ 4
	Mao Dun	80/ 4
	Xia Yan	80/ 4
	Ye Junjian	80/ 4

Religious Associations

Atheism Society

Buddhist Association
President	Zhao Puchu	79/ 8
Secretary-general		
	Zheng Guo	78/10

Catholic Association, China Patriotic
Chairman	Zong Huaide	80/ 5
Vice-chairmen	Cao Daosheng	80/ 5
	Fu Tieshan	80/ 5
	Li Depei	80/ 5
	Tang Ludao	80/ 5
	Tu Shihua	80/ 5
	Wang Liangzuo	80/ 5
	Yang Gaojian	80/ 5
	Zhang Jiashu	80/ 5
Mem.,Stand.Comte.		
	Zong Huaide	80/ 5

Catholic Church, National Administrative Commission of the Chinese
Director	Zhang Jiashu	80/ 6
Dpty.directors	Chang Shouyi	80/ 6
	Duan Yinming	80/ 6
	Fu Tieshan	80/ 6
	Guo Zhong	80/ 6
	Li Depei	80/ 6
	Lin Puan	80/ 6
	Lu Weidu	80/ 6
	Tu Shihua	80/ 6
	Wang Xueming	80/ 6
	Xu Zhenjiang	80/ 6
	Yang Gaojian	80/ 6
	Zong Huaide	80/ 6

Catholic Bishops' College, Chinese
Director	Zhang Jiashu	80/ 6
Dpty.directors	Dong Guangqing	80/ 6
	Fu Tieshan	80/ 6
	Qian Yurong	80/ 6
	Tu Shihua	80/ 6
	Wang Xueming	80/ 6
	Yang Gaojian	80/ 6
	Zong Huaide	80/ 6

Islamic Association
Honorary chairman		
	Burhan Xahidi	80/ 4
Chairman	Zhang Jie	80/ 4
Vice-chairmen	An Shiwei	80/ 4
	Bai Shouyi	80/ 4
	Ma Songting	80/ 4
	Shen Xiaxi	79/11
	Yemliha	80/ 4

Protestant Churches of China, Three-Self Patriotic Movement Comt.

Taoist Association
Chairman	Li Yuhang	80/ 5
Vice-chairmen	Chen Lishi	80/ 5
	Wang Jiaohua	80/ 5
Secretary-general		
	Wang Weiye	80/ 5

THE MAIN PRESS ORGANS

Beijing Review			
Chief editor	Wang Xi	f	80/ 5
Broadcasting Station, Chinese People's			
Dpt.director	Luo Qing		78/10
China Pictorial			
Chief editor	Cai Shangxiong		80/ 6
China Reconstructs			
Chief editor	Li Bodi		78/ 5
China Youth			
Chief editor	Guan Zhihao		79/11
Chinese Literature			
Chief editor	Mao Dun		80/ 1
Da Gong Bao			
President	Fei Yimin		79/ 6
Guangming Ribao			
Chief editor	Yang Xiguang		79/ 7
Dpty.chief editors	Du Yuekai		77/ 4
	Hu Sha		79/ 4
	Yin San		78/ 5
Secretary-general	Sha Xuguang		79/ 4

Liberation Army		
Director	Hua Nan	75/10
Newsreel and Documentary Film Studio, Central		
Chief editor	Qian Xiaozhang	77/ 4
Television Station, Central		
Director	Li Lianqing	79/ 8
Dpty.directors	Dai Linfeng	78/ 6
	Meng Qiqu	78/ 1
	Wang Feng	75/ 9
Wen Yi Bao		
Chief editor	Feng Mu	78/ 7
Workers' Daily		
Chief editor	Xing Fangqun	79/ 7

(<u>Hongqi</u> and <u>Renmin Ribao</u> see under CCP Central Committee)

THE SCIENTIFIC APPARATUS

The material in this section relies on the Chinese press as published since 1977. This means that only the organs stemming from the post-Mao period have been included. As the reorganization of the scientific apparatus is still in progress, the material can by no means be regarded as complete. It should be noted that the data for the higher organs are usually more complete than the data for the lower ones. Thus, the Academy of Sciences with its institutes, branches and leading personnel may be considered fairly complete, as far as the observer of the Chinese scene has been able to gather from the Chinese press up to June 1980. The lowest organs in the scientific apparatus are the colleges, and here it is evident that only part of the ones existing have been identified from notes in the press. Nevertheless, in accordance with our goal to publish all available material, even the few colleges identified have been included in the lists.

On the whole it is believed that the material gives at least an impression of the diversity of the scientific apparatus which has started to bloom after a decade of repression during the Cultural Revolution which completely neglected the sciences.

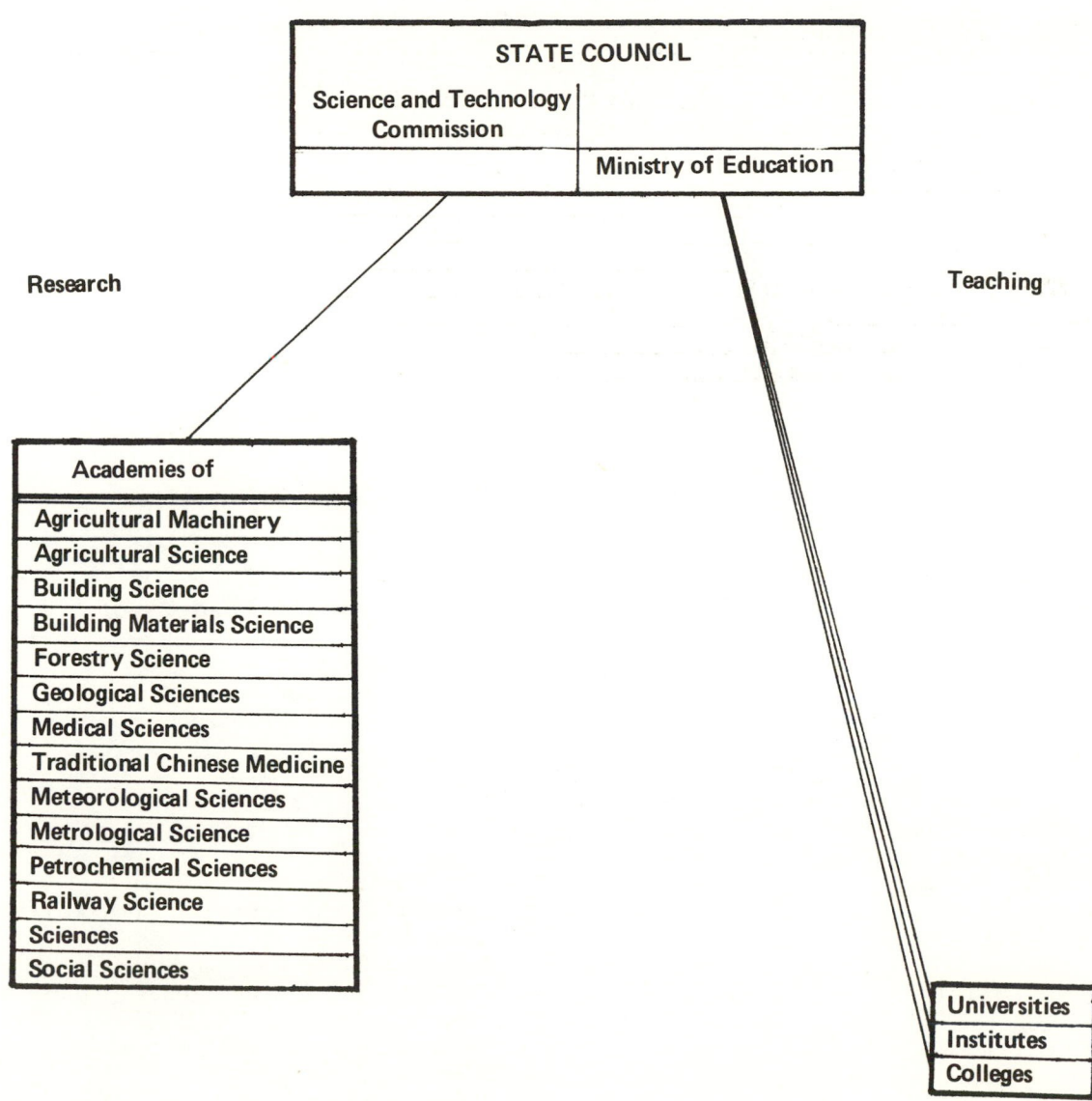

(The organization of the scientific apparatus has been nowhere defined so far.
This diagram therefore is based on the assumptions of the author.)

ACADEMIES

Agricultural Machinery, Academy of
President   Guo Suncai   79/ 1

Agricultural Science, Academy of
President   Jin Shanbao   79/ 9
Vice-presidents
                   Cheng Shaojiong   78/ 8
                   He Guangwen   78/ 8
                   Shi Xiangsheng   78/ 8
                   Yang Xiandong   78/ 8
                   Zhang Weizheng   78/ 8
Dpt. of Scientific Research
Director   Ren Zhi   77/ 9

Institutes
Application of Atomic Energy to Agriculture

Cereal Crops
Director   Li Jizhen   78/ 9

Crop Resources and Strains
Dpty.direct.   Xu Yuntian   80/ 6

Pedology and Fertilzers

Plant Protection (Jilin)

Sericulture

Soil Science and Fertilizers

Vegetable Research

Provincial Academies

Gansu Provincial Academy

Guangdong Provincial Academy
    Food Crops Institute

Hunan Provincial Academy

Jiangsu Provincial Academy (in Nanjing)
    Vice-pres.   Chen Yongkang   78/ 5
                   Jiang Feng   78/ 5
                   Lu Liangshu   79/ 8

Jilin Provincial Academy

Qinghai Provincial Academy

Shaanxi Provincial Academy

Shandong Provincial Academy

Shanghai Municipal Academy

Sichuan Provincial Academy

Building Science, Academy of
    Chief Architect
                   Dai Nianzi   79/ 6

Building Materials Science, Academy of

Institute
    Cement

Forestry Science, Academy of
President   Zheng Wanjun   79/ 9
Vice-president   Wu Zhonglun   80/ 4

Institutes
    Forestry (Beijing)

    Forest Chemical Industry

    Forest Economics and Information

    Forest Machinery

    Shellac

    Subtropical Forestry

    Timber Industry

    Tropical Forestry

Geological Sciences, Academy of
President   Zou Jiayou   78/ 7
Vice-presidents
                   Cheng Yuqi   79/10
                   Wang Zejiu   79/ 8

Institute
    Geology and Mineral Deposits

Medical Sciences, Academy of
President   Huang Jiasi   74/ 5
Vice-presidents
                   Deng Jiadong   80/ 5
                   Gu Fangzhou   78/ 9
                   Huang Hu   78/ 6
                   Qi Tao   78/11
                   Shen Qizhen   78/10
                   Wu Jieping   78/ 7

Academic Committee
It consists of the specialized committees for:
    Basic Medicine
    Clinical Medicine
    Combination of Traditional Chinese and Western
        Medicine
    Information and Publications
    Nursing
    Pharmaceutics
    Preventive Medicine

Institutes
    Biological Medicine

Cancer (Beijing)
```
    Director       Wu Huanxing                    78/ 5
    Dpty.Direct. Xu Guangwei                      78/ 7
```

Information of Medical Sciences
```
    Dpty.Direct. Richard Frey                     80/ 2
```

Medical Science, Basic

Oncology
```
    Director       Wu Huanxing                    78/ 8
```

Parasitic Diseases
```
    Director       Mao Kebai                      79/12
```

Pediatrics

Pharmacology

Radioactive Medicine
```
    Dpty.direct. Wang Shizhen                     80/ 2
```

Tumor Prevention and Treatment (Beijing)

Tumor Hospital (Beijing)
```
    Director       Wu Huanxing                    78/ 5
```

Virology (Beijing)

Meteorological Sciences, Academy of
under the Central Meteorological Bureau

Metrological Science, Academy of

Petrochemical Sciences, Academy of

Railway Science, Academy of
```
President       Mao Yisheng                       76/ 9
```

Academy of Sciences
```
President       Fang Yi          PBm CCm 79/ 7
Vice-presidents
                Hu Keshih                 78/ 3
                Hua Luogeng               78/ 3
                Li Chang                  78/ 3
                Qian Sanqiang             78/ 3
                Yan Jici                  78/ 3
                Zhou Peiyuan              78/ 3
Secretary-general
                Yu Wen                    78/ 7
Dpty.sec.-generals
                Dai Sugen                 79/ 1
                Gan Zhongdou              77/12
                Gao Dengbang              78/ 9
                Li Su                     78/ 6
                Liu Chun                  78/ 9
                Zhao Beke                 78/ 9
                Zhang Wensong             80/ 2
Foreign Affairs Bureau
    Director       Hao Ting              76/ 4
    Dpty.direct. Zhu Yongxing            74/ 5
```

Departments of
```
  Biology
    Members        Bei Shizhang          79/ 1
                   Chen Shixiang         79/ 1
                   Li Lianjie            79/ 1

  Geology and Geography
    Director       Yin Canxun            79/ 4
    Members        Huang Jiqing          79/ 1
                   Wu Heng               79/ 1
                   Zhang Wenyu           79/ 1

  Mathematics, Physics and Chemistry
    Members        Hua Luogeng           79/ 1
                   Jiang Zehan           79/ 1
                   Qian Sanqiang         79/ 1
                   Qian Xuesen      CCa  79/ 1
                   Wu Xuezhou            79/ 1
                   Zhang Wenyu           79/ 1
                   Zhou Peiyuan          79/ 1

  Technology
    Director       Yan Jici              79/ 1
    Members        Hou Xianglin          79/ 1
                   Huang Wenzhao         79/ 1
                   Li Wencai             79/ 1
                   Wang Zhixi            79/ 1
```

INSTITUTES OF THE ACADEMY OF SCIENCES

				Locality	Province/Municipality
Acoustics				Beijing	Beijing
Director	Wang Dezhao	79/ 4			
Dpty.directors	Ma Dayou	79/ 3			
	Yin Chongfu	79/ 8			
Agricultural Modernization					Hebei
Agricultural Modernization					Heilongjiang
Agricultural Modernization				Taoyuan	Hunan
Atomic Energy				Beijing	Beijing
Director	Wang Ganchang	78/10			
Dpty.directors	Jiang Shengjie	72/11			
	Li Shounan	78/ 5			
	Wang Dexi	80/ 2			
Automation				Beijing	Beijing
Automation				Shenyang	Liaoning
Biochemistry				Shanghai	Shanghai
Director	Wang Yinglai	61			
Dtpy.directors	Cao Tianqin	78/ 3			
	Gao Kewu	78/10			
Biology				Chengdu	Sichuan
Biology, Pedology and Sand Deserts					Xinjiang
Biophysics				Beijing	Beijing
Director	Bei Shizhang	61/ 4			
Dpty.directors	Yang Fuyu	78/ 5			
	Zuo Chenglu	79/ 1			
Botanics				Beijing	Beijing
Botanics				Kunming	Yunnan
Director	Wu Chengyi	79/ 3			
Botanics				Guangzhou	Guangdong
Botanics				Wuhan	Hubei
Cells Biology				Shanghai	Shanghai
Chemical Metallurgy				Beijing	Beijing
Chemical Physics				Dalian	Liaoning
Chemical Physics				Lanzhou	Gansu
Chemistry				Beijing	Beijing
Director	Liu Dagang	60			
Dpty.directors	Qian Renyuan	79/ 3			
	Wang Baoren	80/ 5			
Chemistry				Guangzhou	Guangdong
Chemistry					Xinjiang

Chemistry, Applied		Changchun	Jilin
Chemistry, Organic		Chengdu	Sichuan
Chemistry, Organic Dpty.director Wang Yaozeng	80/ 6	Shanghai	Shanghai
Chemistry, Photographic		Beijing	Beijing
Coal and Chemistry		Taiyuan	Shanxi
Computer Technology Dpty.director Wu Jikang	79/ 6	Beijing	Beijing
Computer Technology		Shenyang	Liaoning
Cosmic Rays		Kunming	Yunnan
Desert Research		Lanzhou	Gansu
Electrical Engineering		Beijing	Beijing
Electronic Techniques		Guangzhou	Guangdong

Electronics
   Director   Liu Yin
   Dpty.directors Lü Baowei
               Sun Junren
	79/ 7
	78/ 9
	79/ 7
		Beijing	Beijing

Energy Research		Guangzhou	Guangdong
Entomology		Shanghai	Shanghai
Environment Chemistry		Beijing	Beijing
Forestry and Pedology		Shenyang	Liaoning
Genetics Director Hu Han	77/12	Beijing	Beijing
Geochemistry		Guiyang	Guizhou
Geodesy and Geophysics		Wuhan	Hubei
Geography Director Huang Bingwei	74/11	Beijing	Beijing
Geography		Changchun	Jilin
Geography		Chengdu	Sichuan
Geography			Xinjiang
Geology		Beijing	Beijing
Geology		Lanzhou	Gansu

Geology and Palaeontology
   Dpty.directors Lu Yanhao
               Mu Enzhih
	79/ 5
	79/ 5
		Nanjing	Jiangsu

Geology and Palaeontology		Wuhan	Hubei
Geophysics Dpty.director Gu Gongxu	78/ 4	Beijing	Beijing
Geotectonics		Changsha	Hunan
Glaciology and Cryopedology		Lanzhou	Gansu

Hydrobiology			Wuhan	Hubei
Materia Medica			Shanghai	Shanghai
Mathematics			Beijing	Beijing
Director	Hua Luogeng	63		
Dpty.director	Tian Fangzeng	79/ 8		
Mechanics			Beijing	Beijing
Director	Liu Huixian	80/ 4		
Dpty.director	Wu Chonghua	79/11		
Metallurgical			Shanghai	Shanghai
Metals Research			Shenyang	Liaoning
Dpty.director	Guo Kexin	80/ 2		
Microbiology			Beijing	Beijing
Dpty.director	Xue Yugu	78/11		
Natural Resources, Researches of			Beijing	Beijing
Natural Sciences, History of			Beijing	Beijing
Nuclear Research			Shanghai	Shanghai
Oceanography			Guangzhou	Guangdong
Oceanography			Qingdao	Shandong
Director	Zeng Chengkui	79/ 1		
Optical and Precision Machinery			Changchun	Jilin
Director	Wang Daheng	78/11		
Optical and Precision Machinery			Hefei	Anhui
Optical and Precision Equipment			Shanghai	Shanghai
Director	Gan Fuxi	80/ 5		
Optical and Precision Machinery			Xi'an	Shaanxi
Director	Gong Zudong	78/ 9		
Optics and Electronics			Chengdu	Sichuan
Pedology			Nanjing	Jiangsu
Director	Xiong Yi	79/12		
Pharmacology			Shanghai	Shanghai
Photo-sensitivity				Beijing?
Physics			Beijing	Beijing
Director	Shi Ruwei	72/ 6		
Dpty.director	Guan Weiyan	78/ 9		
Physics			Changchun	Jilin
Physics			Wuhan	Hubei
Physics				Xinjiang
Physics, Atmospheric			Beijing	Beijing
Physics, High Energy			Beijing	Beijing
Director	Zhang Wenyu	77/7		
Dpty.directors	He Cehui f	78/ 3		
	Meng Gefei	78/5		
	Zhao Zhongyao	78/12		
	Zhu Hongyuan	79/ 6		

Physics, Modern				Lanzhou	Gansu
Director	Jin Jianzhong		79/12		
Dpty.director	Yang Chengzhong		78/ 6		
Physics, Plateau Atmospheric				Lanzhou	Gansu
Physics, Technical				Shanghai	Shanghai
Dpty.director	Xie Xide	f	78/ 9		
Physics, Theoretical				Beijing	Beijing
Physiology				Shanghai	Shanghai
Director	Feng Depei		78/ 7		
Plant Physiology				Shanghai	Shanghai
Plasmaphysics				Hefei	Anhui
Precision Instruments				Harbin	Heilongjiang
Psychology				Beijing	Beijing
Salt Lake Research					Qinghai
Dpty.director	Zhang Congzhun	f	78/ 9		
Semi-conductors				Beijing	Beijing
Director	Huang Kun		77/12		
Dpty.directors	Lin Lanying	f	77/12		
	Wang Shouwu		78/ 7		
Silicate Chemistry Technology				Shanghai	Shanghai
Director	Yan Dongsheng		80/ 6		
Space Technology				Xi'an	Shaanxi
Director	Ren Xinmin		78/ 7		
Structure of Material				Fuzhou	Fujian
Director	Lu Jiaxi		78/ 3		
Systems Science				Beijing?	Beijing?
Director	Guan Zhaozhi		80/ 3		
Tropical Plant Research				Guangzhou	Guangdong
Dpty.director	Huang Zongdao		78/10		
Tropical Plant Research				Kunming	Yunnan
Vertebrate Palaeontology and Palaeoanthropology				Beijing	Beijing
Dpty.directors	Sun Ailing	f	77/12		
	Zhou Mingzhen		80/ 5		
Viruses Research				Wuhan	Hubei
Zoology				Beijing	Beijing
Dpty.directors	Cai Banghua		78/10		
	Ma Shijun		79/12		
	Zhu Hongfu				
Zoology				Kunming	Yunnan
Observatory				Beijing	Beijing
Dpty.director	Wang Shouguan		78/10		
Observatory, Zijinshan				Nanjing	Jiangsu
Director	Zhang Yuzhe		77/ 9		
Observatory				Shanghai	Shanghai
Director	Ye Shuhua	f	78/ 9		

Observatory
  Dpty.director Zhang Borong   80/ 2   Kunming   Yunnan

Plant for Astronomical Instruments   Nanjing   Jiangsu

Plant for Scientific Instruments   Beijing   Beijing
  Director   Wu Zuoli   78/ 6

Plant for Scientific Instruments   Shenyang   Liaoning

Plant for Scientific Instruments   Wuhan   Hubei

Plant for Semi-conductor Equipment   Xinxiang   Henan

Office for Applied Mathematics   Beijing   Beijing

Comprehensive Exploration of Natural Resources,   Beijing   Beijing
Committee for

Branches of the Academy of Sciences

Locality	Province		
Changchun	Jilin		
Chengdu	Sichuan		
Guangzhou	Guangdong		
Hefei	Anhui		
Kunming	Yunnan		
Lanzhou	Gansu		
President	Dong Jie		79/ 3
Shanghai	Shanghai		
President	Wang Yinglai		78/ 6
Vice-president	Feng Depei		78/ 3
Shenyang	Liaoning		
Wuhan	Hubei		
Xi'an	Shaanxi		
President	Zhang Ze		80/ 2
Xinjiang	Xinjiang		
Vice-presidents			
	Chen Shanming		80/ 6
	Peng Jiamu		79/12

Social Sciences, Academy of

President	Hu Qiaomu	CCm 78/ 3
Vice-presidents		
	Deng Liqun	78/ 2
	Huan Xiang	78/ 9
	Ma Hong	79/ 7
	Song Yiping	79/11
	Wu Guang	80/ 2
	Xu Dixin	78/11

	Yu Guangyuan		78/ 2
	Zhang Youyu		80/ 2
	Zhou Yang	CCm	78/10
Secretary-general			
	Song Yiping		79/ 6
Dpty.sec.-generals			
	Du Ganquan		79/ 6
	Mei Yi		79/ 4
	Wang Zhongfang		79/ 7
Foreign Affairs Bureau			
Director	Wang Guangmei	f	79/ 8
Planning Bureau			
Director	Mei Yi		79/ 2

Institutes
  Archeology
    Director   Xia Nai   72/ 9

  Economics
    Director   Xu Dixin   78/ 6
    Dpty.directors
                Dong Fureng   79/ 3
                Sun Shangqing   79/ 9
    Adviser   Sun Yefang   78/ 8

  Economics, Agricultural
    Director   Zhan Wu   79/ 3

  Economics, Industrial

  Economics, Technological

  Economics, World
    Director   Qian Junrui   79/ 1
    Dpty.director
                Luo Yuanzheng   78/10

  Ethnology
    Dpty.director
                Fei Xiaotong   79/ 2

Finance, Commerce, Commodities and Economics

History
  Dpty.director
                Lin Ganquan   79/ 9

History, Modern
  Director   Li Xin   79/11
  Dpty.directors
                Li Shu   78/10
                Liang Hanbin   79/ 4
                Yang Xianggui   79/ 4

History, World
  Director   Liu Simu   80/ 3

Journalism
  Director   An Gang   79/ 7

Journalism and Information

Law
  Director   Wang Zhongfang   79/ 7
  Dpty.directors
                Han Yutong   f   78/ 2
                Rui Shu   80/ 3
                Xie Tieyuan   78/ 6

Linguistics
  Director   Lü Shuxiang   78/ 5

Literature
  Dpty.director
                Chen Huangmei   79/10

Literature, Foreign
  Director   Feng Zhi   78/ 3

Marxism-Leninism-Mao Zedong Thought
  Director   Yu Guangyuan   79/ 7

Nationalities
  Director   Yun Beifeng   78/ 9
  Dpty.director
                Fu Maoji   78/ 9

Philosophy

Philosophy
  Dpty.directors
                Jin Yuelin   80/ 3
                Ru Xin   79/ 6
                Sun Gengfu   79/ 6
                Xing Bensi   79/ 9

Postgraduate
  Director   Zhou Yang   CCm 78/10

South Asian Studies
  Director   Ji Xianlin   80/ 6

World Religions
  Director   Ren Jiyu   79/ 2
  Dpty.directors
                Huang Xingchuan   79/ 4
                Zhao Fusan   79/ 4

Branches
  Nei Monggol
    Vice-president
                Doran Tibo   79/ 9

  Shanghai

  Xinjiang

Traditional Medicine, Academy of
  President   Ji Zhongpu   78/ 3
  Vice-president Li Yongchun   78/ 6

Institutes
  Acupuncture

  Traditional Chinese Pharmacology

UNIVERSITIES

General Universities

Anhui

Beijing
  Honorary president
                Ma Yinchu   79/ 9
  President   Zhou Peiyuan   78/ 6
  Vice-presidents
                Feng Ding   79/ 1
                Gao Tie   78/ 9
                Ji Xianlin   78/ 9
                Shen Keji   78/ 8
                Wang Lubin   80/ 4
                Wang Zhuqi   78/ 8
                Zhang Longxiang   78/ 8
  Faculties
  Archaeology
  Biology
  Chinese Language and Literature
    Dean   Ji Zhenhuai   80/ 6
    Vice-dean   Xiang Jingjie   80/ 6
  Geophysics
    Director   Xie Yibing   79/ 2
  Law
    Director   Chen Shouyi   79/ 5
  Mathematics
    Director   Duan Xuefu   78/ 8
  Philososphy

Chengdu (Sichuan Province)

Chongqing (Sichuan Province)

Fudan (Shanghai)
  President   Su Buqing   78/ 6

Vice-presidents

Sheng Hua		80/ 1
Tan Jiazhen		78/ 6
Xie Xide	f	78/ 9

Fujian

Hangzhou (Zhejiang Province)

Harbin (Heilongjiang Province)

Jiaotong (Xi'an, Shaanxi Province)
Vice-president Zhuang Liting   79/ 3

Jiaotong (Shanghai)
President   Fan Xuji   80/ 5
Vice-presidents

Zhang Zhou	79/ 7
Zhu Yaxuan	80/ 5

Jichu (Xi'an, Shaanxi Province)

Jilin
President   Fang Aoqing   79/ 8
Vice-president Zhang Dexing   79/ 6

Jinan (Guangdong Province)
Board of Directors
   Vice-chairmen

Fei Yimin	78/10
He Yin	78/10
Ke Lin	78/10
Tang Pingda	78/10
Wang Guanzheng	78/10
Yi Meihou	78/10

Jishou (Hunan Province)

Lanzhou (Gansu Province)
President   Liu Bing   80/ 1

Liaoning
Vice-president Song Zexing   80/ 1

Nanjing (Jiangsu Province)
President   Kuang Yaming   78/ 5

Nankai (Tianjin Municipality)
President   Yang Shixian   79/10
Vice-presidents

Hu Guoding	80/ 4
Teng Weizao	80/ 4
Wu Daren	80/ 4
Zheng Tianting	80/ 4

Nei Monggol (in Baotou)

Northwest (Shaanxi Province)

People's, Chinese (Beijing)
President   Cheng Fangwu   79/ 1
Vice-presidents

Sun Liyu	79/11
Zhang Zengxiao	80/ 2

Qinghua (Beijing)
President   Liu Da   78/ 9

Vice-presidents

Gao Jingde	80/ 5
He Dongchang	79/ 5
Zhang Guangdou	78/ 8
Zhang Wei	78/ 7
Zhao Fangxiong	80/ 5

Shandong
President   Wu Fuheng   80/ 1

Shanxi

Sichuan
Vice-president Ke Zhao   78/ 7

Tianjin

Tongji (Shanghai)
President   Li Guohao   79/ 4

Wuhan (Hubei Province)
President   Zhuang Guo   80/ 2

Xiamen (Fujian Province)

Xiangtan (Hunan Province)
President   Zhang Yong

Xinjiang

Yunnan
President   Liu Biyun   78/ 4

Zhejiang
President   Qian Sanqiang   79/ 2

Zhengzhou (Henan Province)

Zhongshan (Guangdong Province)

Agricultural Universities

Beijing

Lanzhou (Gansu Province)
Vice-president Ren Jizhou   80/ 1

Shanxi

Zhejiang

North China
Vice-president Shen Qiyi   79/ 1

Communications Universities

Shanghai

Xi'an (Shaanxi Province)

Industrial Universities

Harbin (Heilongjiang Province)

Hefei (Anhui Province)

Jilin
Vice-president Wu Cunya — 79/ 9

Northwest

Shanghai

Labor Universities

Anhui

Jiangxi

Medical Universities

China (Beijing?)

Bethune (Jilin Province)

Harbin (Heilongjiang Province)

Wuhan (Hubei Province)

Zhongshan (Guangdong Province)

Overseas Chinese Universities

Guangzhou (Guangdong Province)

Quanzhou (Fujian Province)
President   Liao Chengzhi — CCm 79/ 1
Board of Directors
Chairman   Zhuang Xiquan — 79/ 1
Lian Guan — 79/ 1
Lin Yixin — 79/ 1
Zhuang Mingli — 79/ 1

Science and Technology Universities

Beijing
1st vice-president
Li Chang — 78/ 4

Chengdu (Sichuan Province)

Harbin (Heilongjiang Province)

Hefei (Anhui Province)
President   Yan Jici — 80/ 6

Shanghai
Vice-president Yan Dongsheng — 80/ 6

Teachers' Universities

Beijing
Vice-president Nie Zhusun — 79/ 5

Shaanxi

Shanghai
President   Liu Funian — 79/12
Vice-presidents
Yuan Yunkai — 79/12
Zhou Yuanping — 79/ 8

Xinjiang

Television Universities

Central (Beijing?)

Hubei

Hunan

Jiangxi

Shanghai

Sichuan

Broadcasting and Television Universities

Fujian

Gansu

Guangdong

Heilongjiang

Nei Monggol

Qinghai

Shandong

Xinjiang

Other Universities

Land Reclamation University (in Tarim, Xinjiang)

National Defense Science and Technology
Vice-presidents
Cao Hesun	80/ 1
Ci Yungui	80/ 1

Normal University (in Beijing)

Normal University (in Shanghai)

Shipbuilding Industrial University (in Shanghai)

Spare-time Engineering University (in Shanghai)

INSTITUTES

Province	Locality

Agriculture and Forestry

Agricultural Science
Anhui		
Beijing		
Guangdong		
Guangxi		
Director	Sun Zhongyi	80/ 1
Hebei	Luancheng County	
Heilongjiang	Hailun County	
Hunan	Taoyuan County	
Jiangsu	Nanjing	
Liaoning	Jinzhou	
	Lüda	
	Shenyang	
North China	?	
Nortwest China	Yangling, Shaanxi	
Shaanxi		
Shanghai		
Sichuan	Mianyang	
	Xichang	
Tibet		
Xinjiang		
Yunnan	Yuxi	

Agriculture and Animal Husbandry
Tibet

Agriculture and Animal Husbandry Mechanization
Nei Monggol

Agriculture and Forestry
Gansu
Qinghai

Animal Husbandry
Guangdong

Animal Husbandry and Veterinary Sciences
Heilongjiang	Hulun Buir League
Henan	Zhengzhou

Aquatic Products
Guangdong	Zhu River

Beekeeping
Dpty.director	Ma Defang	79/ 7

Dairy Industry
Heilongjiang

Field Crops

Fishery

Food
Henan	Zhengzhou

Forestry
Heilongjiang
Guangxi
Sichuan

Forestry and Pedology

Grain Crop
Gansu

Horticulture
Heilongjiang

Maize
Guangxi

Marine Products
Liaoning	Lüda
Shandong	

Milch Cow
Shanghai

Rice
Liaoning	Yingu

Sericulture
Liaoning

Sugarcane and Hemp
Fujian

Subtropical Plants
Fujian

Tropical Plants
Guangdong	Baoding

Medicine

Medicine
Heilongjiang	Mudanjiang
	Qiqihar
Hubei	Kaifeng
Jiangsu	Luoyang
	Yangzhou
Liaoning	Shenyang
Nei Monggol	Jerim League
Shaanxi	Yan'an
Shandong?	Heze
Tianjin	
Tibet	

Medicine, Chinese
Guangdong   Guangzhou
Jiangsu   Nanjing
Shandong
Sichuan   Chengdu
                   Chongqing

Biological Products
(under the Ministry of Public Health)
Beijing

Cardiovascular Diseases on the Plateau
Qinghai
Honorary president
                   Wu Yingkai   79/ 8

Immunology
Shanghai
Director   Ni He   79/ 5

Liver Cancer
Jiangsu   Qidong County
Assist.director   Zhu Yuanrong   79/10

Metallurgical Medicine
Zhejiang?   Huashan

Pharmaceutical Industry
Shanghai
Dpty.director   Lei Shenghan   79/12

Schistosomiasis
Beijing?
Director   Mao Kebai   79/12
Dpty.directors   Lei Shenghan   79/12
                   Xi Shoutai   79/12

Traumatology and Orthopedics
Shanghai

Tropical Medicine
Director   Zhong Huilan   79/ 1

Tuberculosis
Beijing

Tumor
Tianjin

Tumor Prevention and Treatment
Beijing

Medicine, Traditional Chinese

Anhui
Beijing
Guangdong   Guangzhou
Shanghai
Director   Huang Wendong   79/ 6
Dpty.director   Liu Dao   78/11

Research in Tibetan Medicine
Tibet   Lhasa

Medicine, Veterinary

Heilongjiang   Harbin

Traditional Chinese Veterinary Medicine

Nationalities

Central (Beijing)
Director   Ya Hanzhang   80/ 6
Dpty.director   Zong Qun   80/ 6
Central South (Wuhan)
Northwest (Lanzhou)
Southwest (Chengdu)
Guangxi
Tibet   (Lhasa)

Sciences

Sciences
Shanghai

Science and Technology, Advanced
Tianjin

Aeronautics and Astronautics
Beijing

Biology
Jilin
Qinghai
Sichuan

Biological Preparations
Jilin   Changchun

Biological Products
Shanghai

Biology, Experimental

Biology and Soil Science for Water and Soil
Conservation
Shaanxi   Yanglin

Chemistry, Applied
Jilin

Chemistry, Oceanographic
Liaoning

Chemistry and Physics
Gansu   Lanzhou

Cytology and Biology
Shanghai

Desert Research
Nei Monggol   Yih Ju League

Electrical Science
(under the Ministry of Water Conservancy)

Energy
  Liaoning

Financial Sciences
(under the Ministry of Finance)

Food Sciences

Forestry Economics

Geology
  Fujian   Fuzhou
  Guangxi   Guilin
  (under the Ministry of Metallurgical Industry)
  Hubei   Wuhan
  Jilin   Changchun
  Qinghai
  Shaanxi   Xi'an
  Sichuan   Chengdu

Geology and Ore
(under the State Geological Bureau)
  Tianjin

Geophysics
(under the State Seismological Bureau)
  ?
  Heilongjiang   Harbin

Geothermal Sources Exploitation

Gold
  Liaoning   Shenyang

Hydrology
  Jiangsu   Nanjing
    Dpty.director   Hua Shiqian   79/ 9

Laser Research
  Henan   Jianzuo

Laterite
  Jiangxi

Mathematics, Applied

Metallurgy
  Nei Monggol   Baotou

Metallurgical Economics
  Zhejiang

Metallurgical Safety Technology
  Hubei   Wuhan

Meteorolgy
  Beijing (under the Central Meteorological
            Bureau)
  Jiangsu   Nanjing
  Jilin   Changchun
  Sichuan   Chengdu

Metrology
  National (Beijing?)
    Director   Ju Kangjie   78/ 6

  Heilongjiang
  Liaoning

Metrological Measurement
  Jilin

Microbiology
  Liaoning

Microelectronics
  Shaanxi   Lintong

Natural Resources
  Heilongjiang   Harbin

Oceanography
(under the State Oceanography Bureau)
  First (Shandong)
  Second

Oils and Fats Science

Osteopathy
    Director   Shang Tianyu   79/10
    Dpty.director   Feng Tianyou   79/10

Petrochemistry
  Northeast (Heilongjiang)

Photoelectricity
  Sichuan

Physics
  Beijing
  Southwest
  Xinjiang

Radio Research
  Zhejiang   Hangzhou

Scientific and Technical Information
  Heilongjiang
  Yunnan

Soil Science
  Jiangsu   Nanjing

Solar Energy
  Jiangsu   Haian County

Technology and Physics
  Shanghai

Utilization of Rejected and Old Materials

Utilization of Wild Plants

Water Conservancy
  East China   Nanjing
    Director   Yan Ai   78/10

Weights and Measures

Zoology
  Shaanxi

Zoological Specialties
  Jilin

Social Sciences

Social Science
Chinese (Beijing?)
Guangxi
Liaoning
Shaanxi
Zhejiang

Economics
(under the State Planning Commission)
    Director   He Jianzhang   80/ 5

Environment Protection
Beijing

Financial and Economic Management
Liaoning

Foreign Languages
Beijing
    Dpty.director   Liu Ke   80/ 4
Shanghai
No.2

History
Yunnan

International Relations

International Trade
(under the Ministry of Foreign Trade)
    Director   Shu Ziqing   79/ 5

Journalism

Languages
Beijing
    Dpty.director   Qin Ji   78/ 5

Literature
Beijing
Heilongjiang

Literature and Art
(under the Ministry of Culture)
Beijing

Literature and History
    Dpty.director   Zhang Guoji   78/ 5

Literature, Minority
Gansu   Lanzhou

Management Modernization

Mercantile Marine
Liaoning   Dalian

Ocean Navigation History
Fujian   Quanzhou

Philosophy and Social Sciences

Political Science and Law
Beijing
East China
Shaanxi   Xi'an
Shanghai
Southwest   Chongqing

Radio Propagation
    Director   Jin Fengrong

Teachers'

Teachers
Anhui	Fuyang
	Hanshan
	Hefei
	Qingyang
	Wuhu
Fujian	Hetian
	Jianyang
	Ningde
	Putian
	Xiamen
Gansu	Lanzhou
	Zhangye
Guangdong	Huiyang
	Leizhou
	Shaoguan
Guangxi	Hechi
	Nanning
	Yulin
Guizhou	Tongren
	Xingyi
	Zunyi
Hebei	Baoding
	Chengde
	Hengshui
	Tangshan
Heilongjiang	Baoshan
	Harbin
	Jiamusi
	Suihua
	Yichun
Henan	Anyang
	Luoyang
	Nanyang
	Xuchang
	Zhengzhou
Hubei	Enshi
	Huanggang
	Xiangyang
	Yichang
Hunan	Chenzhou
	Yueyang
Jiangsu	Huaiyin
	Nantong
	Taizhou
	Yancheng
	Zhenjiang
Jiangxi	Jiujiang
	Shangrao
Jilin	Tonghua

Liaoning	Anshan
	Beizhen
	Dandong
	Jinzhou
	Lüda
Ningxiang	Guyuan
Qinghai	
Shaanxi	Hanzhong
	Weinan
	Xianyang
Shandong	Changwei
	Dezhou
	Heze
	Jining
Shanxi	Jindongnan
	Jinzhong
	Taiyuan
Sichuan	Aba
	Jiangjin
	Mianyang
	Neijiang
	Xichang
	Yibin
	Yunyang
Tianjin	
Yunnan	Menzi
	Qujing
	Simao
	Xiaguan
	Zhaotong
Zhejiang	Jiaxing
	Lin'an
	Lishui
	Ningbo
	Wenzhou

Teachers' Advanced Studies
| Zhejiang | Hangzhou |

Teachers of Nationalities
Guizhou	Qiannan
	Qiandongnan
Tibet	Xigaze
Liaoning	Ju Ud League

Technical

Aeronautical Engineering
Beijing		
Director	Xu Changyu	80/ 6
Dpty.director	Shen Yuan	79/ 3

| Jiangxi | Nanchang |
| Liaoning | Shenyang |

Aeronautical Industrial Management
| Henan | Zhengzhou |

Agricultural Machinery
Anhui	
Heilongjiang	
Jilin	

Agricultural Mechanization
| Heilongjiang | |
| Liaoning | Jinzhou |

Architectural Engineering
| Fujian | |

Automatic Meter Research
| Sichuan | Chongqing |

Automation
Beijing?
(under the Ministry of Metallurgy)
| Zhejiang | Hangzhou |

Broadcasting
Beijing?

Building Materials Industry
| Shanghai | |

Building Research
(under the State Capital Construction Commission)
| Dpty.director | He Guangjian | 78/10 |

Ceramic Industrial Science
| Jiangxi | Jingdezhen |

Chemical Engineering
Beijing	
Liaoning	Shenyang
Shanghai	
Sichuan	

Chemical Fibers
| Beijing | |

Chemical Industry
| Guangdong | |
| Zhejiang | Ningbo |

Cine-film Research
| Liaoning | Dalian |

Civil Engineering
| Shanghai | | |
| Director | Chen Zhi | 78/12 |

Clock and Watch
(under the Ministry of Light Industry)

Coal
| Hunan | Xiangtan |
| Yunnan | Kunming |

Coal and Chemistry
| Shanxi | |

Coal, Comprehensive Utilization
| Shanxi | |

Communications Engineering
| Director | Li Zhaoji | 78/ 4 |
| Dpty.director | Lei Hong | 78/ 4 |

Computer Research
| Liaoning | |

Computing Technology
    Shanghai
    Tianjin
    Zhejiang

Cotton, Linen and Tobacco Processing

Construction and Engineering
    Shandong

Construction Materials
    Yunnan

Designing
(under the 1st Ministry of Machine Building)
    Sichuan   Chongqing

Design and Research
    Jilin

Electric Computer
    Jilin

Electric Furnace Engineering
    Shaanxi   Xi'an

Electric Industry
    Beijing

Electric Power
    Shanghai

Electric Power Construction
    Beijing?

Electric Power Engineering
    Northeast (Jilin)

Electric Power Experiment
    Anhui

Electrical Engineering
(under the 1st Ministry of Machine Building)
    Beijing

Electronic Calculation
    Zhejiang

Electronics
    Heilongjiang
    Liaoning   Yingkou

Electronics, Scientific
    Anhui

Engineering
    Beijing
        Director   Su Qianyi   80/ 6
        Dpty.director   Zhou Faqi   80/ 2
    Central China   Wuhan?
    Hunan   Changsha
    Jiangsu   Nanjing
    Jilin
    Liaoning   Dalian
    Northeast
    Shandong
    Shanghai
    South China (Guangdong)

Engineering and Machinery
    Tianjin

Farm Machinery
    Heilongjiang
    Hunan
    Jilin

Farm Mechanization

Heat Treatment
(under the Association of Mechanical Engineering)

Heavy Machinery
    Northeast (Heilongjiang)
    Shaanxi   Xi'an

Heavy Machinery Designing
    Shaanxi   Taiyuan

Hydraulic Sciences
    Jiangsu   Nanjing
    Shaanxi   Yanglin

Hydraulic and Electric Engineering
    Hubei   Wuhan

Hydraulic Power Engineering
    Dpty.director   Huang Yuanzhen   78/11

Industrial
    Guizhou
    Jiangsu   Nantong
                        Yancheng
    Liaoning   Jinzhou
    Shaanxi   Xi'an

Instruments and Meters
    Shandong   Qingdao

Instruments in Electrical Engineering
    Shanghai

Iron and Steel
(under the Ministry of Metallurgical Industry)
    Beijing
        Dpty.director   Zhang Wenzhi   78/10

    Liaoning   Anshan
    (under the Anshan Iron and Steel Company)
    Shanghai

Laser Technology
    Jilin
    Shanghai
    Tianjin

Light Industry
    Hubei
    Jilin
    Liaoning
    Shandong
    Shanghai
    Yunnan

Machine-tool
    Beijing

Machinery
   Liaoning   Shenyang
      Director   Li Xin   79/ 2

   Xinjiang

Machinery Automation
(under the 1st Ministry of Machine Building)

Machinery Design
   Jilin

Material Research
   Shanghai

Measurement Science

Mechanical Engineering
   Shanghai

Mechanics
   Beijing
   Xinjiang

Mechanical and Electrical Engineering
(under the 1st Ministry of Machine Building)

Metals, Nonferrous
   Beijing

Metallurgy
   Liaoning   Shenyang
   Shanghai
   Xinjiang

Metallurgy, Thermal
   Liaoning   Anshan

Metallurgical and Geological Research
   Guangxi   Guilin

Metallurgical and Mechanical Engineering
   Liaoning   Shenyang

Metallurgical Building

Metallurgical, Mechanical and Electrical
Engineering
   Shanghai

Metallurgical Materials
   Tianjin

Mining
   Central South
      Dpty.director   Chen Xinmin   79/ 6

Mining and Metallurgy
   Cent.China(Hunan)   Changsha

Naval Engineering
      Director   Shao Zhen   78/11

Navigation
   Fujian   Jimei

Navigation Engineering
   Jiangsu   Nanjing

Oceanographic Instruments
   Tianjin

Optical Machinery
   Shanghai

Optical Research
   Anhui?

Paper-processing
   Tianjin

Petrochemical Industry
   Beijing

Petroleum
   Liaoning   Fushun

Posts and Telecommunications
   Beijing

Powder Industry Design
   East China

Powder Metallurgy
   Beijing

Printing Technology
   Yunnan

Quality Testing
   Yunnan

Radio Engineering
   Sichuan   Chengdu

Railway
   Shanghai

Refractory Material
   Henan   Luoyang

River Navigation
   Hubei   Wuhan

Semi-conductor Equipment
   Gansu   Pingliang

Silicates
   Tianjin

Sparkless Dynamo
   Heilongjiang   Jiamusi

Stereoscopic Technology
   Zhejiang   Ningbo

Steel
   Sichuan   Panzhihua

Supersonic Electronics
   Guangdong   Shantou
      Director   Yao Jinzhong   78/ 3

Supply, Marketing and Storing Machinery

Tea and Silk Processing

Technical Equipment
(under The PLA General Logistics Department)

Technology
  Liaoning

Textile Engineering
  Shandong

Textile Industry
  Shanghai
  Tianjin

Thermal Energy
  Jilin

Tobacco and Beet Industry
  Henan

Tools Research
  Sichuan   Chengdu

Water Conservancy
  East China   Nanjing
  (Jiangsu)
    Director   Yan Kai

Water Control and Electric Power
  Hubei   Wuhan

Miscellaneous

Banking
(under the People's Bank of China)

International Issues
  Beijing

International Relations for Training Cadres
    Director   Chen Zhongjing   80/ 1

Physical Culture
  Beijing
    Director   Zhong Shitong

Satellite Observation and Control Center
  Shaanxi   Xi'an

COLLEGES

Province	Locality

Agricultural
  Beijing
  Central China
  Heilongjiang
  Hunan   Changsha
  Jiangsu

Province	Locality
Jilin	Yanbian
Liaoning	Shenyang
Ningxia	
Shaanxi	
Shandong	Laiyang
Sichuan	
Xinjiang	
Xinjiang	
August 1	Ürümqi
Zhejiang	
North China	
Dpty.director	Shen Qiyi 78/ 6
Northeast	Harbin
Northwest	Shaanxi
South China	Guangzhou
Southwest	

Agricultural and Animal Husbandry
  Tibet

Agricultural Machinery
  Anhui
  Beijing

Agricultural Mechanization
  Jilin

Animal Husbandry and Veterinary Sciences
  Jilin   Jirem League
  Qinghai
  Sichuan

Aquatic Products
  Liaoning   Dalian

Architectural Engineering
  Fujian   Xibei
  Hebei
  Heilongjiang   Harbin
  Jilin

Aviation
  Jiangsu   Nanjing

Building Materials Industry
  Shandong

Chemical Engineering
  Beijing
  Jilin

Chemical Engineering and Power
  Jiangsu   Nanjing

Chemistry and Mineral
  Jiangsu   Lianyungang

Coal Chemical Engineering
  Shanxi   Taiyuan

Coalmining
  Hebei

Commerce
  Beijing
  Jiangsu

Province	Locality
Communications	
Hunan	Changsha
Sichuan	Chongqing
Economics	
Beijing	
Shandong	
Education	
Beijing	
Electrical Engineering	
Jiangsu	Nanjing
Engineering	
Henan	Zhengzhou
Jiangsu	Nanjing
Jilin	
Liaoning	Dalian
Dpty.director	Qian Lingxi
Ningxia	
Shanghai	
Zhejiang	
Central China	
Northeast	
Finance and Economics	
Guizhou	
Hubei	
Hunan	
Jiangxi	
Shanghai	
Sichuan	
Finance and Credit	
Central	
Finance and Trade	
Anhui	
Beijing	
Hebei	
Jilin	
Forestry	
Beijing	
Jilin	
Nei Monggol	
Yunnan	
Zhejiang	
Northeast	
Forest Products	
Jiangsu	Nanjing
Geology	
Anhui	Hefei
Hubei	Wuhan
Jilin	Changchun
Herbal Medicine, Chinese	
Jiangsu	Nanjing
Industry	
Liaoning	Shenyang
Shanghai	

Province	Locality		
International Relations			
Iron and Steel			
Beijing			
Nei Monggol	Baotou		
Law and Political Science			
Beijing			
Light Industry			
Beijing			
Machine Industry			
Guangxi			
Mechanical and Electrical Engineering			
Anhui			
Mechanical Engineering			
Guangdong			
Shanghai			
Medicine			
Beijing			
Dpty.directors	Feng Chuanhan	80/ 5	
	Peng Ruicong	80/ 5	
Guangdong	Zhongshan University		
	Zhanjiang		
Guizhou	Zunyi		
Hebei			
Heilongjiang	Harbin		
Dpty.director	Yu Weihan	79/ 6	
Henan			
Hubei	Wuhan		
Jiangsu	Nanjing		
	Suzhou		
	Xuzhou		
	Zhenjiang		
Jilin	Changchun		
	Yanbian		
Liaoning	Dalian		
	Shenyang		
Nei Monggol	Baotou		
Shaanxi	Xi'an		
Director	Hou Zonglian	79/ 6	
Shandong	Qingdao		
Shanghai, No.1			
No.2			
Sichuan			
Tianjin			
Tibet			
Xinjiang	Shihezi		
Yunnan	Dali		
Zhejiang, No.1	Hangzhou		
Medicine, Chinese			
Fujian			
Gansu			
Hebei			
Jiangsu	Nanjing		
Tianjin			
Medicine, Nationality			
Guangxi	Yujiang		
Nei Monggol			

Province	Locality

Medicine, Traditional Chinese

Jiangsu	Nanjing
Sichuan	Chengdu

Medicine and Pharmacy

Guangdong	

Metallurgical Industry

Shandong	

Metallurgy and Geology

Guangxi	Guilin

Meteorology

Jiangsu	Nanjing
Sichuan	Chengdu

Mining

Heilongjiang	Jixi

Mining and Metallurgy

Anhui?	

Petrochemical Industry

Guangxi	

Pharmacy

Jiangsu	Nanjing

Physical Culture and Sports

Fujian	
Heilongjiang	Harbin
Shandong	
Shanghai	

Political Science and Law

Beijing	
Shanghai	Huadong
Northwest	

Posts and Telecommunications

Jiangsu	Nanjing
Jilin	Changchun

Printing

Beijing	

Radio and Television

Qinghai	

Science and Technology

Beijing?	

Shipbuilding

Jiangsu	Zhenjiang

Teachers'

Beijing	
Guangdong	Guangzhou
Guangxi	
Heilongjiang	Harbin
Henan	Xinyang
Hubei	Huangshi
Hunan	
Jiangsu	Nanjing
	Xuzhou

Province	Locality
Liaoning	Shenyang
Nei Monggol	
Shaanxi	Baoji
Shanghai	
Sichuan	
Tianjin	
Tibet	
Xinjiang	Kashi
Yunnan	Kunming
Zhejiang	Hangzhou
Central China	

Teachers, Coalmine

Anhui	Huaibei

Teachers, Nationality

Nei Monggol	
Qinghai	
Yunnan	

Teachers, Railway

Jiangsu	Suzhou

Teachers, Sports

Beijing	

Textile Engineering

Fujian	Xibei
Hubei	Wuhan

THE ARTS

Academies

Dance

Beijing			
President		Chen Jinqing	78/10

Drama

Central	
Shanghai	

Fine Arts

Central			
President		Wu Zuoren	79/ 7
Vice-president		Ai Zhongxin	80/ 7
Sichuan			
Zhejiang			

Industrial Arts

Central	

Traditional Chinese Painting

Shanghai			
Vice-president		Wang Geyi	79/12

Institutes

Art
  Hubei
  Jiangsu   Nanjing
  Shanxi

Arts and Crafts
  Central
    President   Zhang Ting   79/ 5

  Yunnan

Chinese Painting
  Jiangsu   Nanjing

Fine Arts
  Guangdong   Guangzhou
  Sichuan

Fine Arts, Lu Xun

Literature
  Beijing

Literature and Art
(under the Ministry of Culture)

Music
  Liaoning   Shenyang
  Sichuan

Music, National
(under the Ministry of Culture)

Opera
(under the Ministry of Culture)

Colleges

Art
  Central
  (under the Ministry of Culture)
  Jilin
  Shandong
  Yunnan

Cinema
  Beijing

Dance
  Beijing

Opera, Chinese

Painting and Calligraphy
  Anhui

Theater
  Central
  (under the Ministry of Culture)

Conservatories of Music

Central
  President   Zhao Feng   79/ 6

Shanghai
  President   He Luding   79/11
  Vice-president   Li Shande   79/10

Schools of Art

Jilin   Yanbian
Nei Mongol

School of Traditional Operas

Henan
  Director   Chang Xiangyu   f   80/ 6

Film Studio

Beijing
  Director   Yu Lan   f   79/ 8
  Dpty.director   Wang Renmei   80/ 3

THE PROVINCIAL LEADERSHIP
as of June 1980

The following lists contain the leading cadres of the CCP, the administration and the military districts in the 29 Provinces, Autonomous Regions and Municipalities with provincial status. This mode of representation, which combines the three fields of activities, enables the reader to get an impression of the real hierarchical structure.

The additional column "Posts in Central CP" shows the cadres truly in power who have been delegated from the CCP Central Committee to the provinces and who are responsible for the implementation of all its directives.

(Instead of governor read mayor in the municipalities
and chairman in the autonomous regions)

Provincial Leadership — Anhui

CCP: 1st Secretary	2nd Secretary	3rd Secretary	Secretary	Deputy Secretary	Member, Stand. Comte.	Secretary-General	Dir. Dept. Organization	Propaganda	United Front Work	Director, Party School	Admin: Governor	Vice-Governor	People's Congr. Chairman	Vice-Chairman	MD: Commander	Deputy Commander	1st Political Commissar	2nd Political Commissar	Political Commissar	Deputy Political Comm.	CP Comte. 1st Secretary	2nd Secretary	Secretary	Member, Stand. Comte.	Name	Politburo Member	Alt. Member	CC Member	Alt. Member
					X								X		X										Cheng Guanghua				
					X									X	X										Cheng Yetang				
			X											X											Gu Zhuoxin				
												X													Guo Tixiang				
														X											Hou Yong				
														X											Hu Kaiming				
																									Huang Yan				
												X													Huang Yu				
																									Li Fanfu				
			X											X											Li Shinong				
					X	X								X											Liu Lianmin				
														X											Liu Rulin				
																				X				X	Liu Yaozong				
														X											Ma Changyan				
												X													Meng Fulin				
																									Meng Jiaqin				
					X		X																		Ren Zhibin				X
				X																					Su Yu				
					X																				Wang Guangyu			X	
				X														X						X	Wang Wenmo				
									X																Wei Jianzhang				
																									Wei Xinyi				
														X											Yang Chengzong				
																									Yang Jike				
														X											Yang Ming				
				X																					Yang Weiping				
														X											Ying Yiquan f				
					X							X											X		Yu Guangmao				
																									Yuan Zhen				
X											X														Zhang Jingfu			X	
				X																					Zhang Kaifan				
										X				X											Zhang Zuoyin				
				X																				X	Zhao Shouyi				

Beijing Municipality

	CCP											Administration				Military District										Name	Posts in Central CP			
	1st Secretary	2nd Secretary	3rd Secretary	Secretary	Deputy Secretary	Member, Stand. Comte.	Secretary-General	Organization	Propaganda	United Front Work	Director, Party School	Governor	Vice-Governor	Chairman	Vice-Chairman	Commander	Deputy Commander	1st Political Commissar	2nd Political Commissar	Political Commissar	Deputy Political Comm.	1st Secretary	2nd Secretary	Secretary	Member, Stand. Comte.		Politburo Member	Politburo Alt. Member	CC Member	CC Alt. Member
An Zhaojun															X															
Bai Jiefu						X							X		X															
Cai Xu															X															
Chen Kehan				X																										
Chen Peng															X															
Chen Xitong															X															
Fang Jin f														X																
Guo Xianrui															X															
Hou Jingru																														
Huang Zuozhen				X											X															X
Jia Tingsan					X									X																
Lei Jieqiong f															X															
Li Ligong				X																										
Li Zhongqi																	X													
Li Zhongxuan																														
Lin Hujia	X											X																	X	
Liu Daosheng						X		X					X																	
Liu Jianfu						X																								
Liu Xichang						X							X																X	
Liu Zuchun													X																	
Lu Yu																														
Ma Yaoji					X										X															
Mao Lianjue																														
Pan Yan														X	X															
Pu Jiexiu f																	X													
Qiu Weigao													X																	
Su Zhan					X										X															
Wang Chun															X															
Wang Feiran					X										X															
Wang Xian						X							X																	
Wang Xiaoyi															X															
Wen Jiasi																														
Wu Lie																				X										
Yang Chunmao																														
Yang Junsheng																				X										X
Ye Gongshao																														
Ye Lin					X								X																	
Ye Zilong													X																	
Zhang Peng																														
Zhao Pengfei															X															

Provincial Leadership
Fujian

																										Name				
Bi Jichang													X																	
Cai Li															X															
Cai Liangcheng															X															
Chen Xizhong																X														
Cong Dezhi															X															
Fu Baicui																														
Guo Chao				X									X																	
Guo Ruiren																														
He Minxue															X															
He Ruoren						X																								
Hou Linzhou															X															
Hu Weizhi					X																									
Jia Jiumin															X															
Jiang Runguang																					X									
Jin Zhaodian				X									X																	

	CCP											Administration				Military District										Name	Posts in Central CP			
	1st Secretary	2nd Secretary	3rd Secretary	Secretary	Deputy Secretary	Member, Stand. Comte.	Secretary-General	Organization	Propaganda	United Front Work	Director, Party School	Governor	Vice-Governor	Chairman	Vice-Chairman	Commander	Deputy Commander	1st Political Commissar	2nd Political Commissar	Political Commissar	Deputy Political Comm.	1st Secretary	2nd Secretary	Secretary	Member, Stand. Comte.		Politburo Member	Politburo Alternate Member	CC Member	CC Alternate Member

Fujian (continued)

1st Sec	2nd	3rd	Sec	Dep Sec	Stand	Sec-Gen	Org	Prop	UFW	PSch	Gov	V-Gov	Chair	V-Chair	Cmdr	DCmdr	1PolC	2PolC	PolC	DPolC	1Sec	2Sec	Sec	Stand	Name	PMbr	PAlt	CCMbr	CCAlt
														X											Lan Rongyu				
																									Li Wenren				
			X																						Li Zhengting				
X			X										X				X								Liao Zhigao			X	
														X											Liu Yongsheng				
																									Lu Jiaxi				
			X								X			X											Ma Xingyuan			X	
														X											Ren Manjun f				
												X													Wang Yan				
														X											Wang Zhi				
												X													Wen Fushan				
				X								X													Wu Hongxiang				
												X													Xu Ya				
					X				X																Yuan Gai				
												X													Zhang Gexin				
												X													Zhang Yi				

Provincial Leadership

Gansu

1st Sec	2nd	3rd	Sec	Dep Sec	Stand	Sec-Gen	Org	Prop	UFW	PSch	Gov	V-Gov	Chair	V-Chair	Cmdr	DCmdr	1PolC	2PolC	PolC	DPolC	1Sec	2Sec	Sec	Stand	Name	PMbr	PAlt	CCMbr	CCAlt
				X																					Bai Ming				
																									Cao Youmin				
			X								X			X											Feng Jixin				
																									Gao Jinchun				
				X								X													Ge Shiying				
																									Huang Zhengqing				
			X											X											Li Dengying				
														X											Li Keru				
														X											Li Peifu				
												X													Li Qiyang f				
														X											Li Shenghua				
																				X					Liang Renjie				
																									Liu Bing				
														X											Liu Haisheng				
																									Meng Dingjun				
												X													Nian Dexiang				
														X											Qiang Zixiu				
X														X			X								Song Ping			X	
																									Sun Renhua				
								X																	Wang Bingxiang				
												X	X												Wang Shijie				
												X													Wang Shitai			X	
												X													Wang Zhibang				
														X											Wu Hongbin				
																									Wu Junyang				
																									Wu Zhiguo				
																				X					Xiao Binggong				
			X																						Xiao Hua			X	
												X													Xiao Jianguang				
																									Xu Feiqing				
														X											Yang Jiarui				
			X																						Yang Zhilin				
																									Zhang Jian'gang				
			X																						Zhao Chuqi				

Provincial Leadership

Guangdong

1st Sec	2nd	3rd	Sec	Dep Sec	Stand	Sec-Gen	Org	Prop	UFW	PSch	Gov	V-Gov	Chair	V-Chair	Cmdr	DCmdr	1PolC	2PolC	PolC	DPolC	1Sec	2Sec	Sec	Stand	Name	PMbr	PAlt	CCMbr	CCAlt
								X																	Chen Yueping				
																				X					Deng Xiufang				
													X												Du Changtian				
											X														Fan Xixian				
			X																						Gong Zirong				

Column groups: **CCP** (1st Secretary … Director, Party School) · **Administration** — People's (Govt.: Governor, Vice-Governor; Congr.: Chairman, Vice-Chairman) · **Military District** (Commander … Deputy Political Comm.; CP Committee: 1st Secretary, 2nd Secretary, Secretary, Member, Stand. Comte.) · **Posts in Central CP** (Politburo: Member, Alternate Member; CC: Member, Alternate Member)

CCP 1st Sec	2nd Sec	3rd Sec	Sec	Dep Sec	Mem Stand Comte	Sec-Gen	Dir Organization	Dir Propaganda	Dir Utd Front Work	Dir Party School	Governor	Vice-Governor	Chairman	Vice-Chairman	Commander	Dep Commander	1st Pol Commissar	2nd Pol Commissar	Pol Commissar	Dep Pol Comm	CP 1st Sec	CP 2nd Sec	CP Sec	CP Mem St.Comte	Name	Pol Member	Pol Alt	CC Member	CC Alt
			X									X													Guo Dihuo				
												X													Guo Rongchang				
														X											Huang Jingbo				
																X									Huang Youmou				
																									Jiang Xianyu				
			X																						Jiao Linyi			X	
						X																			Kou Qingyan				
												X													Li Jian'an				
														X											Li Jianzhen f				X
																									Li Xuexian				
																									Liang Guang				
			X									X													Liang Weilin				
														X											Liu Tianfu				
																									Luo Ming				
														X											Luo Tian				
					X							X													Meng Xiande				
														X											Ou Mengjue f				
														X											Ouyang Shan				
																			X						Su Kezhi				
			X																						Wang De				
			X	X								X													Wang Ning				
			X	X																					Wang Quanguo				
			X											X											Wang Zuoyao				
																									Wu Nansheng				
X											X														Xi Zhongxun			X	
														X											Xiao Huanhui				
																									Xiao Junying				
														X						X					Xiong Fei				
					X																				Xue Guangjun				
					X							X													Yang Kanghua				
	X																								Yang Shangkun			X	
														X											Yi Meihou				
																									Yun Guangying				
												X		X											Zeng Dingshi				
														X											Zhong Ming				
																									Zhuang Tian				

Guangxi Autonomous Region

CCP 1st Sec	2nd Sec	3rd Sec	Sec	Dep Sec	Mem Stand Comte	Sec-Gen	Dir Organization	Dir Propaganda	Dir Utd Front Work	Dir Party School	Governor	Vice-Governor	Chairman	Vice-Chairman	Commander	Dep Commander	1st Pol Commissar	2nd Pol Commissar	Pol Commissar	Dep Pol Comm	CP 1st Sec	CP 2nd Sec	CP Sec	CP Mem St.Comte	Name	Pol Member	Pol Alt	CC Member	CC Alt
														X											Cai Yongwei				
																									Chen An				
																	X								Chen Kailu				
			X								X														Chin Yingji			X	
												X													Du Yi				
																									Gan Gu				
												X													Gan Huaiyi				
																									Guo Cheng				
																				X					Guo Zhifu				
																									Han Shifu				
												X													He Yiran				
												X													Huang Rong				
														X											Huang Yun				
																									Jin Baosheng				
																									Li Lin f				
														X											Li Yindan				
					X	X																			Liang Chengye				
												X		X											Liang Huaxin				
																									Liao Shengdong				

	CCP											Administration (People's)				Military District						CP Committee				Name	Posts in Central CP — Politburo		CC	
	1st Secretary	2nd Secretary	3rd Secretary	Secretary	Deputy Secretary	Member, Stand. Comte.	Secretary-General	Organization	Propaganda	United Front Work	Director, Party School	Governor	Vice-Governor	Chairman	Vice-Chairman	Commander	Deputy Commander	1st Political Commissar	2nd Political Commissar	Political Commissar	Deputy Political Comm.	1st Secretary	2nd Secretary	Secretary	Member, Stand. Comte.		Member	Alternate Member	Member	Alternate Member

Guangxi (continued)

Name	Marks
Lin Kewu	Vice-Chairman
Liu Chonggui	2nd Secretary; CC Alternate Member
Lu Di	Propaganda
Lu Rongshu	Vice-Chairman
Luo Libin	Vice-Governor
Mo Naiqun	Vice-Governor
Qiao Xiaoguang	1st Secretary; 1st Political Commissar; CC Member
Qin Zhenwu	Vice-Chairman
Ren Gengqing	
Ren Guozhang	Vice-Chairman
Shi Qingsheng	Vice-Chairman
Shi Zhaotang	
Xiao Han	Deputy Secretary; Vice-Chairman
Xu Qihai	
Ye Fusun	Vice-Chairman
Zhang Shengzhen	Secretary-General
Zhang Xudeng	
Zhao Maoxun	Deputy Secretary
Zhao Mingjian f	
Zhong Feng	Vice-Chairman
Zhou Guangchun	Deputy Secretary; Governor

Provincial Leadership Guizhou

Name	Marks
Bai Lin f	Vice-Chairman
Chen Tie	Governor
Chen Xinggang	3rd Secretary
Chi Biqing	1st Secretary; CC Member
Dai Xiaodong	Vice-Chairman
Duan Zhizhong	2nd Political Commissar
Geng Wanqing	
Hou Guoxiang	Vice-Chairman
Hui Shiru	Director, Party School
Jin Feng	
Li Tinggui	Member, Stand. Comte.
Long Xiangzhou	Deputy Secretary; Governor
Luo Dengyi	Vice-Chairman
Luo Ying	Vice-Chairman
Meng Ziming	Vice-Chairman
Miao Chunting	Deputy Secretary
Qin Tianzhen	Vice-Governor
Ran Yannong	Vice-Governor
Shen Yunpu	
Song Xiaopeng	
Su Gang	Secretary
Tian Junliang	Governor
Wang Bingyun	Vice-Chairman
Wang Zhaowen	Organization
Wang Zhenjiang	
Wu Su	Governor
Wu Xiangbi	Deputy Secretary; CC Alternate Member
Xu Jiansheng	Vice-Governor; Vice-Chairman
Ye Gulin	
Zeng Xian	Vice-Chairman
Zhang Liang	Deputy Commander
Zhang Yuhuan	
Zhang Yuqin f	
Zhang Zhong	Propaganda; Commander

Provincial Leadership — Hebei / Heilongjiang

1st Secretary	2nd Secretary	3rd Secretary	Secretary	Deputy Secretary	Member, Stand. Comte.	Secretary-General	Organization	Propaganda	United Front Work	Director, Party School	Governor	Vice-Governor	Chairman	Vice-Chairman	Commander	Deputy Commander	1st Political Commissar	2nd Political Commissar	Political Commissar	Deputy Political Comm.	1st Secretary (CP Comm.)	2nd Secretary (CP Comm.)	Secretary (CP Comm.)	Member, Stand. Comte. (CP Comm.)	Name	Politburo Member	Politburo Alternate Member	CC Member	CC Alternate Member
														X											Cao Yumin				
																									Ding Tingxin				
																			X						Ge Min				
														X											Ge Qi				
														X											Geng Changsuo				
																									Guo Fang				
			X									X													Guo Zhi				
												X													Han Qimin f				
																			X						He Ming				
														X											Hong Yi				
																									Hu Yi				
														X											Huang Hua				
X																									Jiang Yizhen				
																	X								Jin Ming				
																									Lan Kaimin				
			X								X														Li Erzhong				
																									Li Feng				
						X																			Liu Ying				
					X																				Lü Yulan f			X	
													X	X											Ma Hui				
														X											Niu Shucai				
														X											Pan Chengxiao				
														X											Peng Qing f				
														X											Quan Zhemin				
														X											Sun Yueqi				
																X									Wang Aixi				
												X													Wang Dongning				
			X																						Wang Jinshan				X
																									Wang Kedong				
														X											Wu Qingcheng				
												X													Xu Ruilin				
														X											Yang Ding'an				
												X													Yang Naijun				
																									Yang Yuan				
			X																						Yin Zhe				
												X													Yue Zongtai				
						X													X						Zeng Mei				
																									Zhang Da				
														X											Zhang Kerang				
						X																			Zhao Zhenzhong				
														X											Zhou Xueao				

Provincial Leadership — Heilongjiang

1st Secretary	2nd Secretary	3rd Secretary	Secretary	Deputy Secretary	Member, Stand. Comte.	Secretary-General	Organization	Propaganda	United Front Work	Director, Party School	Governor	Vice-Governor	Chairman	Vice-Chairman	Commander	Deputy Commander	1st Political Commissar	2nd Political Commissar	Political Commissar	Deputy Political Comm.	1st Secretary (CP Comm.)	2nd Secretary (CP Comm.)	Secretary (CP Comm.)	Member, Stand. Comte. (CP Comm.)	Name	Politburo Member	Politburo Alternate Member	CC Member	CC Alternate Member
														X											Bai Qing f				
	X											X													Chen Jianfei				
				X	X																				Chen Junsheng				
			X								X														Chen Lei				
																									Chen Liemin				
					X																				Chen Yuanzhi				
														X											Du Guoping				
				X	X																				Guan Zhou				
					X							X													Hou Jie				
																									Li Haifeng f				
				X																					Li Jianbai				
																									Li Li'an				
												X													Li Rui				
														X											Liu Huxian				

	CCP											Administration				Military District										Name	Posts in Central CP			
	1st Secretary	2nd Secretary	3rd Secretary	Secretary	Deputy Secretary	Member, Stand. Comte.	Secretary-General	Organization	Propaganda	United Front Work	Director, Party School	Governor	Vice-Governor	Chairman	Vice-Chairman	Commander	Deputy Commander	1st Political Commissar	2nd Political Commissar	Political Commissar	Deputy Political Comm.	1st Secretary	2nd Secretary	Secretary	Member, Stand. Comte.		Politburo Member	Politburo Alternate Member	CC Member	CC Alternate Member
Heilongjiang (continued)															X											Liu Qian				
						X																				Lu Guang				
															X											Ni Wei				
					X										X											Ruan Yongsheng				
															X											Sun Ziyuan				
													X													Wang Caoli				
													X													Wang Jinling				
				X																						Wang Jinzi				
													X													Wang Jun f				
															X											Wang Luming				
													X													Wang Pinian				
																	X									Wang Zhaozhi				
															X											Wang Zhengxin				
													X													Wei Zhimin				
				X																						Wen Minsheng				
																										Wu Cheng				
						X																				Xia Guangya				
																	X									Xie Changhua				
						X																				Xie Xuejing				
													X													Xie Yunping				
	X																X									Yang Yichen			X	
										X																Zhang Ruilin				
					X																					Zhang Xiuzhi f				
				X																						Zhao Decun				
																										Zhao Xianshun				
						X																		X		Zhao Xingyuan				X

Provincial Leadership
Henan

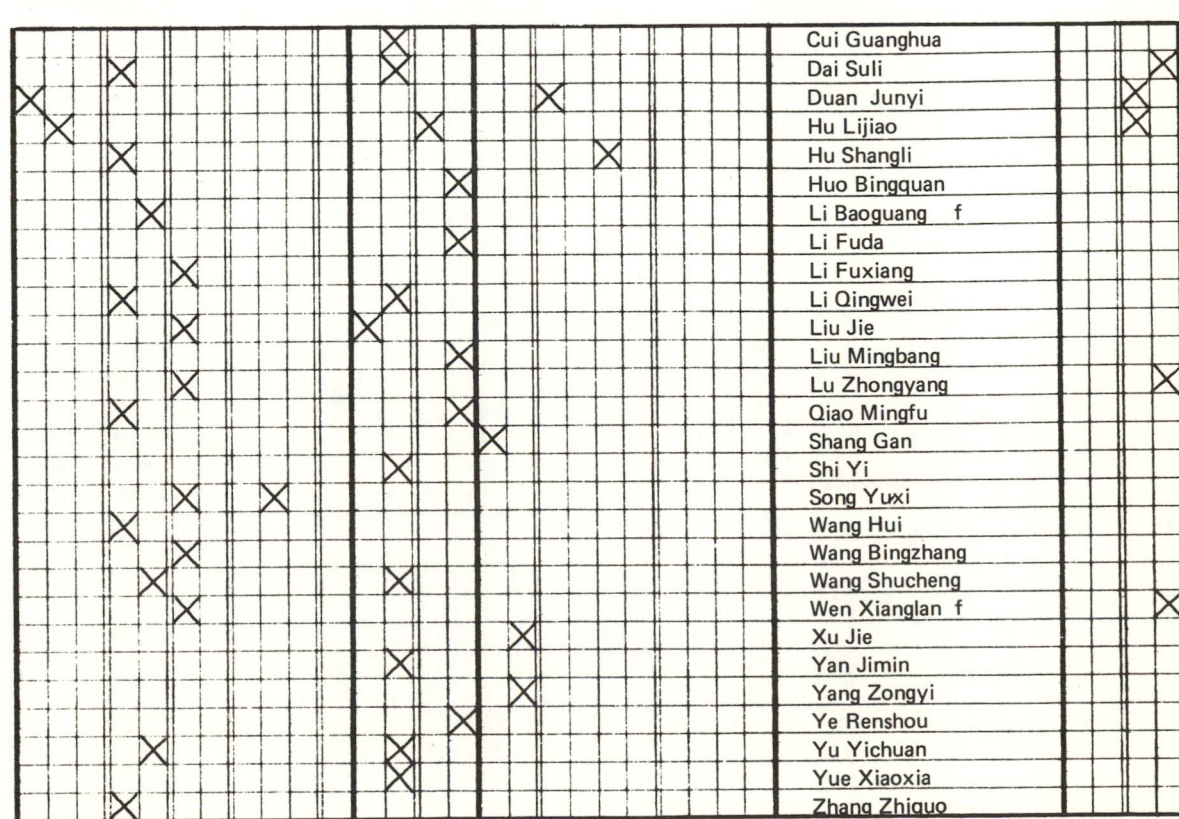

	CCP											Administration				Military District										Name	Posts in Central CP			
	1st Secretary	2nd Secretary	3rd Secretary	Secretary	Deputy Secretary	Member, Stand. Comte.	Secretary-General	Organization	Propaganda	United Front Work	Director, Party School	Governor	Vice-Governor	Chairman	Vice-Chairman	Commander	Deputy Commander	1st Political Commissar	2nd Political Commissar	Political Commissar	Deputy Political Comm.	1st Secretary	2nd Secretary	Secretary	Member, Stand. Comte.		Politburo Member	Politburo Alternate Member	CC Member	CC Alternate Member
													X													Cui Guanghua				
					X																					Dai Suli				X
	X															X										Duan Junyi			X	
		X															X									Hu Lijiao				
															X											Hu Shangli				
																										Huo Bingquan				
					X																					Li Baoguang f				
																										Li Fuda				
													X													Li Fuxiang				
					X																					Li Qingwei				
																										Liu Jie				
					X	X							X													Liu Mingbang				
																										Lu Zhongyang			X	
																	X									Qiao Mingfu				
															X											Shang Gan				
																										Shi Yi				
				X			X																			Song Yuxi				
																										Wang Hui				
					X																					Wang Bingzhang				
					X																					Wang Shucheng				
																										Wen Xianglan f				X
																X										Xu Jie				
																										Yan Jimin				
																X										Yang Zongyi				
																										Ye Renshou				
					X																					Yu Yichuan				
																										Yue Xiaoxia				
				X																						Zhang Zhiguo				

	CCP											Admin-istration				Military District										Name	Posts in Central CP			
								Director Dept. of				People's										CP Committee					Politburo		CC	
	1st Secretary	2nd Secretary	3rd Secretary	Secretary	Deputy Secretary	Member, Stand. Comte.	Secretary-General	Organization	Propaganda	United Front Work	Director, Party School	Governor	Vice-Governor	Chairman	Vice-Chairman	Commander	Deputy Commander	1st Political Commissar	2nd Political Commissar	Political Commissar	Deputy Political Comm.	1st Secretary	2nd Secretary	Secretary	Member, Stand. Comte.		Member	Alternate Member	Member	Alternate Member
Henan (continued)				X																						Zhao Wenfu				
															X											Zhao Wenjie				
					X																					Zheng Yonghe				
Provincial Leadership Hubei						X							X								X					Chen Jide				
	X												X								X					Chen Ming				
				X																						Chen Pixian			X	
																										Gu Dachun				
					X								X													Han Dongshan				
					X																					Han Ningfu				
								X																		Hu Jinkui				
					X								X													Hua Yuqing				
					X																					Huang Zhizhen			X	
																										Jiang Zhonghua f				
						X		X		X																Jiao Dexiu				
				X																						Li Fuquan				
																										Li Renzhi				
																										Li Wei				
																										Lin Musen				
													X													Lin Shaonan f				
																										Liu Hegeng				
					X																					Liu Huinong				
															X											Liu Jin				
																										Lü Wenyuan				
						X																				Ma Xueli				
					X																					Rao Xingli				X
																										Ren Zhonglin				
													X													Shi Chuan				
																										Tang Zhe				
															X											Tao Shuzeng				
													X													Tian Ying				
						X																				Wang Buqing				
															X											Wang Haishan				
													X													Wang Hanzhang				
																										Wang Qun				
																										Wu Xianwen				
																					X					Xia Shihou				
				X																						Xu Daoqi				
					X	X				X																Xue Dan				
																										Yan Jun				
													X													Zhang Hinxian				
															X											Zhang Wangwu				
					X	X																				Zhang Xiulong				
				X																						Zhang Yuhua				X
Provincial Leadership Hunan						X							X													Cao Wenju				?
														X												Chen Xinmin				
																	X									Cheng Qiwen				
																										Cheng Xingling				
				X																						Ding Weike				
																	X									Dong Zhiwen				
																										Gou Xianxue				
															X											Guo Sen				
																										Kong Anmin				
																										Lin Xiaxin				
					X																					Liu Chunqiao			X	

	CCP											Administration				Military District										Name	Posts in Central CP			
													People's									CP Committee						Politburo		CC	
	1st Secretary	2nd Secretary	3rd Secretary	Secretary	Deputy Secretary	Member,Stand.Comte.	Secretary-General	Organization	Propaganda	United Front Work	Director, Party School	Governor	Vice-Governor	Chairman	Vice-Chairman	Commander	Deputy Commander	1st Political Commissar	2nd Political Commissar	Political Commissar	Deputy Political Comm.	1st Secretary	2nd Secretary	Secretary	Member, Stand.Comte.		Member	Alternate Member	Member	Alternate Member
Hunan (continued)																														
			X									X								X						Liu Fusheng				
															X											Liu Shihong				
												X														Liu Ya'nan				
						X																				Liu Yu'e f				
																										Luo Qiuyue f				
X																	X									Mao Zhiyong			X	
																										Qi Shouliang				
														X												Shang Zijin				
					X																					Shi Bangzhi				
																										Shi Xinshan				
																										Shi Yuzhen f				
			X									X														Sun Guozhi				
																										Tao Zhiyue				
					X																					Tong Guogui				
	X													X												Wan Da			X	
																										Wang Hanfu				
																	X									Wang Youhua				
			X									X														Wang Zhiguo				
																	X	X								Wei Kaiqiang				
																										Wu Haijing				
				X	X																					Xu Tiangui				
												X														Yin Ziming				
			X													X										Zhang Lixian			X	
				X																						Zhang Wenguang				
			X																							Zhou Li				
												X														Zhou Zheng				
Provincial Leadership **Jiangsu**																														
			X																							Bao Houzhang				
															X											Chen Heqin				
																X										Chen Jin				
			X																							Chen Ketian				
													X													Chu Jiang			X	
							X																			Dai Weiran				
																X										Dai Runsheng				
				X	X																					Ding Keze			X	
													X													Gong Weizhen				
																										He Binghao				
																										Hong Peilin				
				X																						Hu Hong				
															X											Huang Zhaotian				
				X	X								X													Hui Yuyu				
													X													Jin Xun				
															X											Kuang Yaming				
																X										Li Guohou				
													X													Li Zhizhong				
															X											Liao Yunze				
																X										Lin Yousheng				
															X											Liu Lin				
																										Liu Shuxun				
				X	X																					Ma Guorui				
													X													Wang Bingshi				
																										Wang Haisu				
									X																	Wang Zhaoquan				
														X												Wu Yifang f				
															X											Xie Kedong				
																										Xie Zhongguang				

Column groups:

- **CCP**: 1st Secretary · 2nd Secretary · 3rd Secretary · Secretary · Deputy Secretary · Member, Stand. Comte. · Secretary-General · Organization (Director Dept. of) · Propaganda · United Front Work · Director, Party School
- **Administration**: Governor (People's Govt.) · Vice-Governor · Chairman (People's Congr.) · Vice-Chairman
- **Military District**: Commander · Deputy Commander · 1st Political Commissar · 2nd Political Commissar · Political Commissar · Deputy Political Comm. · 1st Secretary (CP Committee) · 2nd Secretary · Secretary · Member, Stand. Comte.
- **Posts in Central CP**: Politburo Member · Politburo Alternate Member · CC Member · CC Alternate Member

Jiangsu (continued)

Name	CCP posts	Administration posts	Military District posts	Central CP posts
Xin Shaobo	Member, Stand. Comte.; Organization	Vice-Chairman		
Xu Fangheng	1st Secretary; Director, Party School	Chairman	1st Political Commissar	
Xu Jiatun				CC Member
Yang Hanlin		Vice-Governor		
Yang Tingbao		Vice-Chairman		
Ye Xuchao		Vice-Chairman		
Zhang Zhongliang	Secretary; Deputy Secretary			
Zhong Guochu			2nd Political Commissar	
Zhou Ze		Vice-Chairman		

Provincial Leadership — Jiangxi

Name	CCP posts	Administration posts	Military District posts	Central CP posts
Bai Dongcai	Member, Stand. Comte.	Governor		CC Member
Chen Ting			Deputy Commander	
Chen Yi			Secretary	
Di Sheng	Deputy Secretary			
Fang Qian		Vice-Governor		
Fu Yutian	Secretary	Vice-Governor		
Gu Jiguang		Vice-Chairman		
Hu Dingqian			Deputy Commander	
Jiang Weiqing	1st Secretary	Governor		CC Member
Li Fangyuan		Vice-Chairman		
Li Shizhang		Vice-Governor		
Li Yizhang	Member, Stand. Comte.			
Liang Kaixuan	Member, Stand. Comte.			
Liu Junxiu			1st Political Commissar	
Lu Mingjing	United Front Work			
Luo Mengwen	Deputy Secretary			
Ma Jikong			Deputy Commander	
Shen Gan		Vice-Chairman		
Wang Shixian	Member, Stand. Comte.	Vice-Governor		
Wang Zhaorong	Deputy Secretary	Vice-Chairman		
Xie Xianghuang		Vice-Chairman	Commander	
Xin Junjie		Vice-Governor		
Xu Min f		Vice-Chairman		
Xu Qin	Secretary; Deputy Secretary			
Yang Shangkui		Vice-Governor		
Yang Shangkun			Deputy Political Comm.	
Ye Changgeng		Vice-Chairman		
Zhang Guozhen		Vice-Governor		
Zhang Lixiong	Deputy Secretary; Member, Stand. Comte.		2nd Political Commissar	
Zhang Yuqing	Deputy Secretary			
Zhao Zhijian	Deputy Secretary; Member, Stand. Comte.			CC Member
Zhou Linggui			Deputy Political Comm.	

Provincial Leadership — Jilin

Name	CCP posts	Administration posts	Military District posts	Central CP posts
Chen Hong	Member, Stand. Comte.; Secretary-General			
Chen Zhong		Vice-Chairman		
Cheng Shengsan		Vice-Governor		
Dong Xin				
Feng Yingkui	Deputy Secretary			
He Youfa			Commander	
Huang Yunchang				
Jin Minghan	Deputy Secretary			CC Alternate Member
Jin Tairan f				
Lan Ganting	Deputy Secretary; Member, Stand. Comte.			
Li Diping				
Li Mengling		Chairman		
Li Shuren		Governor		

Jilin (continued)

Provincial Leadership
Liaoning

	CCP							Director Dept. of				Administration (People's Govt. / Congr.)				Military District						CP Committee				Name	Posts in Central CP (Politburo)		CC	
	1st Secretary	2nd Secretary	3rd Secretary	Secretary	Deputy Secretary	Member, Stand. Comte.	Secretary-General	Organization	Propaganda	United Front Work	Director, Party School	Governor	Vice-Governor	Chairman	Vice-Chairman	Commander	Deputy Commander	1st Political Commissar	2nd Political Commissar	Political Commissar	Deputy Political Comm.	1st Secretary	2nd Secretary	Secretary	Member, Stand. Comte.		Member	Alternate Member	Member	Alternate Member
																										Li Youwen				
															X											Liu Cikai				
													X													Liu Yunzhao				
																										Luo Yuejia f				
																										Mao Cheng f				
					X								X													Mu Lin				
																										Ren-qin-zha-mu-su				
			X										X													Song Jiehan				
					X				X																	Song Renyuan				
																				X						Su Junlu				
			X																							Wang Daren				
X											X							X								Wang Enmao				X
													X													Wang Guanchao				
																										Wang Liping				
															X											Wu Tuo				
																										Wu Xuezhou				
																										Xiao Chun				
																										Xu Shouxuan				
						X																				Yang Zhantao				
				X								X														Yu Ke				
				X																						Yu Lin				
																										Yu Ruihuang				
					X																					Zhang Fensheng				
																										Zhang Kaijing				
													X													Zhang Shiying				
																										Zhao Nanqi				
															X											Zhao Tianye				
					X																					Zong Xiyun				X
			X										X													Bai Qian				
				X							X															Chen Beichen				
				X										X												Chen Puru			X	
														X												Deng Yu				
														X												Fu Zhonghai				
				X																						Gu Jingxin				
													X													Hu Yimin				
																X										Huang Guozhong				
				X									X													Huang Oudong			X	
				X																						Li Huang				
														X												Li Xun				
														X												Liu Duoquan				
																									Liu Wen f				
							X	X																	Liu Yuyun				
				X																						Lou Erkang				
																									Qiu Youwen				
X					X												X								Ren Zhongyi			X	
																									Shen Yue				
																									Tan Liren				
												X														Tang Hongguang				
					X								X													Wang Guangzhong				
																									Wang Jiyuan				
																									Wang Kuncheng				
														X												Xiao Zuohan				
											X															Xie Huangtian				

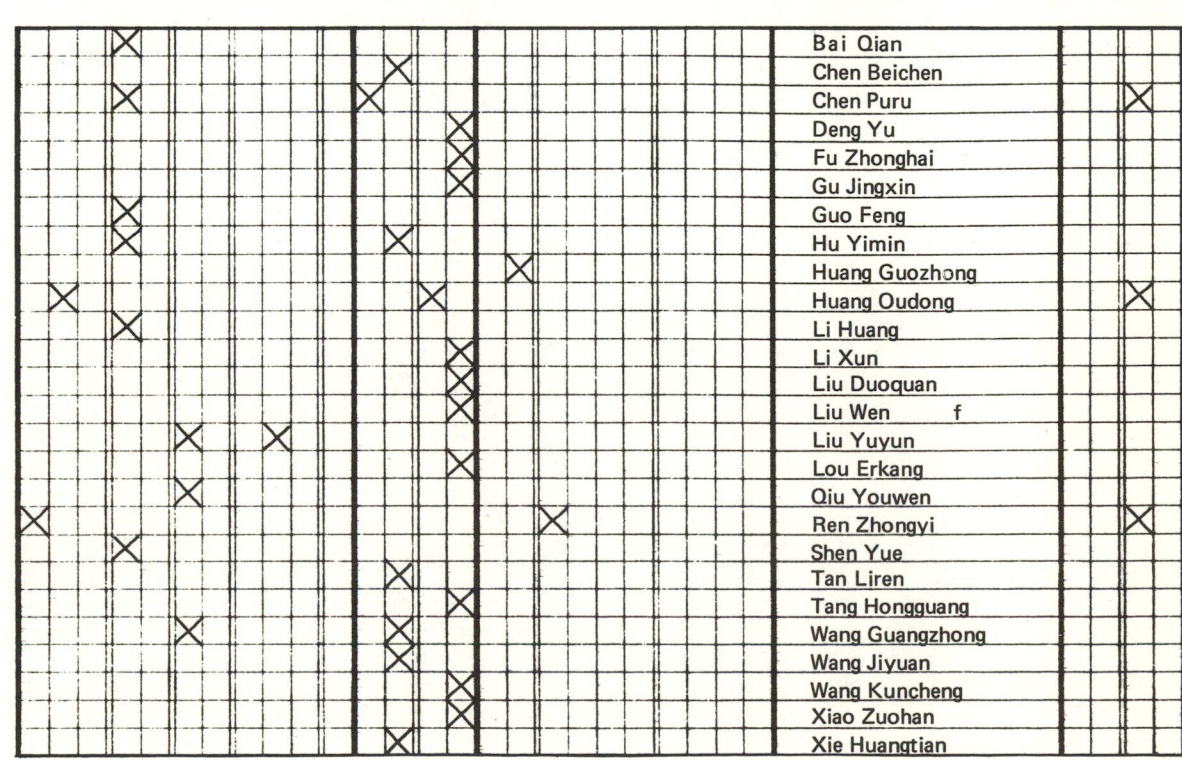

Column groups: **CCP** (1st Secretary, 2nd Secretary, 3rd Secretary, Secretary, Deputy Secretary, Member Stand. Comte., Secretary-General, Director Dept. of Organization, Propaganda, United Front Work, Director Party School) · **Administration** (Govt.: Governor, Vice-Governor; People's Congr.: Chairman, Vice-Chairman) · **Military District** (Commander, Deputy Commander, 1st Political Commissar, 2nd Political Commissar, Political Commissar, Deputy Political Comm., CP Committee: 1st Secretary, 2nd Secretary, Secretary, Member Stand. Comte.) · **Name** · **Posts in Central CP** (Politburo: Member, Alternate Member; CC: Member, Alternate Member)

1st Sec	2nd Sec	3rd Sec	Sec	Dep Sec	Mbr SC	Sec-Gen	Org	Prop	UFW	Dir PS	Gov	V-Gov	Chair	V-Chair	Cmdr	Dep Cmdr	1st PC	2nd PC	PC	Dep PC	CP 1st Sec	CP 2nd Sec	CP Sec	CP Mbr SC	Name	PB Mbr	PB Alt	CC Mbr	CC Alt

Liaoning (continued)

			X																						Xu Shaofu				
					X										X										Yang Dayi				X
														X											Yang Kebing				
																									Zhang Qingtai				
				X								X													Zhang Shude				
																									Zhang Tiejin				
				X																					Zhang Xincun				
									X																Zhang Yan f				
												X													Zhang Zhiyuan				
																									Zhang Ziheng				
												X													Zhao Qi				
																									Zhao Shi				
																									Zhou Chiheng				
												X													Zhou Ming'an				
																									Zhu Chuan				

Nei Monggol Autonomous Region

			X										X												Bariltai f			X	
				X																					Ba-tu-ba-gen				
												X													Bu He				
												X				X									Cai Ying				
												X													Chen Bingyu				
												X													Gao Zengpei				
																									Han Feng				
												X													Hao Xiushan				
																X									Huang Hou				
																									Jargal				
				X																					Ke Ligeng				
				X								X													Kong Fei				
																									Li Binsan				
																									Liu Chang				
																X									Liu Huaxiang				
				X																			X		Liu Jingping				
														X											Ochirhuyagt				
					X							X													Peng Mengyu				
																		X							Qi Junshan				
																			X						Sainbayar				
					X																				Shen Xinfa				
					X							X													Shi Guanghua				
																									Sun Lanfeng				
X					X															X					Teng Junqing				
				X								X					X								Ting Mao				
				X																					Wang Duo				
			X									X													Wang Xi				
			X	X																					Wang Yilun				
																									Yun Shiying				
				X																			X		Zhang Pengtu				
																			X						Zhang Rongzhen				
																									Zhang Rugang				
X																									Zhou Beifeng				
X																			X						Zhou Hui			X	

Ningxia Autonomous Region

													X												Cheng Hao				
				X										X											Ding Yimin				
															X										Huang Jingyao				
																									Huang Zhizhong				
												X													Kang Zhijie				

Column groups: **CCP** (1st Secretary; 2nd Secretary; 3rd Secretary; Secretary; Deputy Secretary; Member, Stand. Comte.; Secretary-General; Director Dept. of: Organization, Propaganda, United Front Work; Director, Party School) — **Administration** (People's Govt.: Governor, Vice-Governor; People's Congr.: Chairman, Vice-Chairman) — **Military District** (Commander; Deputy Commander; 1st Political Commissar; 2nd Political Commissar; Political Commissar; Deputy Political Comm.; CP Committee: 1st Secretary, 2nd Secretary, Secretary, Member, Stand. Comte.) — **Name** — **Posts in Central CP** (Politburo: Member, Alternate Member; CC: Member, Alternate Member)

Ningxia (continued)

1st Sec	2nd Sec	3rd Sec	Secretary	Dep. Sec.	Mbr.St.C.	Sec.-Gen.	Organiz.	Propag.	Utd.Front	Party School	Governor	Vice-Gov.	Chairman	Vice-Chair	Commander	Dep.Cmdr	1st Pol.Com	2nd Pol.Com	Pol.Com	Dep.Pol.Com	1st Sec(CP)	2nd Sec(CP)	Sec(CP)	Mbr.St.C.(CP)	Name	PB Mbr	PB Alt	CC Mbr	CC Alt
												X													Li Li				
														X											Li Shumin				
X																									Li Weidong				
					X																				Li Xuezhi				X
												X													Li Yunhe				
														X											Lu Ming				
					X																				Ma Qingnian				
																									Ma Sizhong				X
											X														Ma Teng'ai				
				X																					Ma Xin				
												X													Ma Yuhuai				
																									Ma Xizhong				
														X											Ma Youde				
																									Qi Anchang				
				X																					Shao Jingwa f				
					X																				Shi Yulin				
												X													Xia Siping				
					X																				Xue Hongfu				
														X											Zhang Junxian				

Provincial Leadership — Qinghai

1st Sec	2nd Sec	3rd Sec	Secretary	Dep. Sec.	Mbr.St.C.	Sec.-Gen.	Organiz.	Propag.	Utd.Front	Party School	Governor	Vice-Gov.	Chairman	Vice-Chair	Commander	Dep.Cmdr	1st Pol.Com	2nd Pol.Com	Pol.Com	Dep.Pol.Com	1st Sec(CP)	2nd Sec(CP)	Sec(CP)	Mbr.St.C.(CP)	Name	PB Mbr	PB Alt	CC Mbr	CC Alt
														X											Cai Fenglan f				X
														X											Guan-bao-jia				
									X					X											Guo Ruozhen				
														X											Han Ming				
					X															X					Ji Chunguang				
															X										Li Desheng				
					X				X																Li Sihai				
X																									Li Xingwang				
																									Liang Buting				
																									Liang Changhan				
				X																					Liu Chengyun				
																									Lu Zhian				
																									Ma Wanli				
																									Ma Wending				
					X																				Shang Zhitian				
					X							X													Shen Ling				
																									Song Lin				
																			X						Wang Wenying				
				X								X											X		Wu Shengrong				
																									Xi-hou-ba			X	
																									Xia-rong-ya-bu				
																									Xie Gaofeng				
					X							X													Xu Linfeng				
																									Ya-bu-long				
			X	X																					Yang Yan				
																									Zhaxi Wangqug				
												X													Zhang Guosheng				
																									Zhao Haifeng				
																									Zheng Wenqing				
					X																				Zheng Xiaoxian				
															X										Zhou Rong				

Provincial Leadership — Shaanxi

1st Sec	2nd Sec	3rd Sec	Secretary	Dep. Sec.	Mbr.St.C.	Sec.-Gen.	Organiz.	Propag.	Utd.Front	Party School	Governor	Vice-Gov.	Chairman	Vice-Chair	Commander	Dep.Cmdr	1st Pol.Com	2nd Pol.Com	Pol.Com	Dep.Pol.Com	1st Sec(CP)	2nd Sec(CP)	Sec(CP)	Mbr.St.C.(CP)	Name	PB Mbr	PB Alt	CC Mbr	CC Alt
					X							X													Bai Jinian				
			X											X											Chang Lifu				
												X													Chen Yuanfang				
																									Deng Guozhong				

	CCP											Administration				Military District										Name	Posts in Central CP			
								Director Dept. of				People's Govt.		People's Congr.						CP Committee							Politburo		CC	
	1st Secretary	2nd Secretary	3rd Secretary	Secretary	Deputy Secretary	Member,Stand.Comte.	Secretary-General	Organization	Propaganda	United Front Work	Director, Party School	Governor	Vice-Governor	Chairman	Vice-Chairman	Commander	Deputy Commander	1st Political Commissar	2nd Political Commissar	Political Commissar	Deputy Political Comm.	1st Secretary	2nd Secretary	Secretary	Member, Stand. Comte.		Member	Alternate Member	Member	Alternate Member
Shaanxi (continued)																														
						X									X											Dong Xueyuan				
						X							X													Fu Zihe				
															X											He Chenghua				
				X		X									X	X										Hou Zonglian				
																										Hu Bingyun				X
								X																		Hu Jindi f.				X
																										Huang Zhi				
				X											X											Hui Shigong				
																										Jiang Yi				
															X											Lin Yinru				
													X													Liu Geng				
																										Liu Haibin				
																										Liu Lizhen f.				
	X			X																						Lü Jianren				
				X											X											Ma Wenrui			X	
																										Shi Feng				
																										Shi Yizhi				
						X							X		X											Song Youtian				
													X													Sun Zuobin				
																										Tan Weizu				
					X																					Wang Lin				
																										Wang Tai				
																				X						Wu Hengsheng				
						X							X													Xie Huaide				
																X										Xiong Guangyan				
															X											Xiong Yingdong				
																X										Xu Lishu				
																										Yan Kelun				
				X																						Yang Wenhai				
				X								X			X											Yu Mingtao			X	
				X											X											Yuan Zhengting				
																										Zhang Ce				
															X											Zhang Hanwu				
																X										Zhang Tao				
																										Zhang Yizhen f				
Provincial Leadership **Shandong**	X																									Bai Rubing			X	
				X																X						Chen De			X	
				X									X													Chen Lei				
													X													Ding Fangming				
																										Gao Qiyun				
																			X							He Zhiyuan				
																										Li Rinai				X
															X											Li Yuang				
				X																						Li Zhen				
																										Li Zichao				
						X			X																	Lin Ping				
															X											Liu Binglin				
																										Liu Peng				
													X													Liu Xianzhi				
																										Liu Zhongqian				
				X		X																				Lu Tianji			X	
																										Qin Hezhen				
					X																					Song Qingyou				X
																										Song Yimin			X	
				X								X				X										Su Yiran			X	

	CCP											Administration (People's)				Military District						(CP Committee)					Posts in Central CP			
	1st Secretary	2nd Secretary	3rd Secretary	Secretary	Deputy Secretary	Member, Stand. Comte.	Secretary-General	Director Dept. of Organization	Propaganda	United Front Work	Director, Party School	Govt. Governor	Vice-Governor	Congr. Chairman	Vice-Chairman	Commander	Deputy Commander	1st Political Commissar	2nd Political Commissar	Political Commissar	Deputy Political Comm.	1st Secretary	2nd Secretary	Secretary	Member, Stand. Comte.	Name	Polit-buro Member	Alternate Member	CC Member	Alternate Member
Shandong (continued)																														
																				X						Tang Jianru				
															X											Wang Jiezhen				
						X							X													Wang Zhongyin				
				X																						Wu Kaizhang				
						X									X											Xu Jianchun f				
													X													Xu Leijian				
																										Yang Jieren				
																										Zeng Chengkui				
																										Zhang Fugui			X	
														X												Zhang Jingtao				
																										Zhang Ye				
															X											Zhang Zhusheng				
															X	X										Zhao Feng				
				X																						Zhao Lin				
																										Zheng Zijiu				
															X											Zhou Zhijun				
																										Zhu Benzheng				
													X													Zhu Qimin				
Shanghai Municipality						X																				Che Wenyi				
	X																									Chen Guodong			X	
						X					X															Chen Jinhua				
																										Chen Yi				
															X											Chen Zonglie				
																			X							Di Jingxiang				
																		X								Dong Changyun				
	X												X													Du Changde				
					X																					Han Zheyi				
					X																					He Yixiang				
																X			X						Jia Defa				
																										Li Baoqi				
																										Li Peinan				
																										Liang Guobin				
						X									X											Liu Jingji				
												X														Pei Xianbai				
																										Peng Chong	X		X	
															X											Su Buqing				
																		X								Sun Linrui				
				X		X							X													Wang Fuzhen f				X
					X																					Wang Jian				
																				X						Wang Mei				
					X																					Wang Mingzhang				X
															X											Wang Tao				
			X	X									X													Wang Yiping				X
			X			X																				Wu Ruoan				
							X								X											Xia Zhengnong				
													X		X											Yan Youmin				
						X																				Yang Di				
															X											Yang Kai				
						X																				Yang Shifa				
																										Yang Xinpei				
																	X									Yao Xiaocheng				
									X																	Zhang Chengzong				
						X																				Zhao Xingzhi				
															X											Zhao Zukang				

Table columns (left to right): **CCP** — 1st Secretary, 2nd Secretary, 3rd Secretary, Secretary, Deputy Secretary, Member Stand. Comte., Secretary-General, Director Dept. of Organization, Propaganda, United Front Work, Director Party School; **Administration** — People's Govt. (Governor, Vice-Governor), People's Congr. (Chairman, Vice-Chairman); **Military District** — Commander, Deputy Commander, 1st Political Commissar, 2nd Political Commissar, Political Commissar, Deputy Political Comm., CP Committee (1st Secretary, 2nd Secretary, Secretary, Member Stand. Comte.); **Name**; **Posts in Central CP** — Politburo (Member, Alternate Member), CC (Member, Alternate Member).

1st Sec	2nd Sec	3rd Sec	Secretary	Dep Sec	Mbr Std Cte	Sec-Gen	Organization	Propaganda	United Front	Dir Party School	Governor	Vice-Gov	Chairman	Vice-Chair	Commander	Dep Cmdr	1st Pol Com	2nd Pol Com	Pol Com	Dep Pol Com	CP 1st Sec	CP 2nd Sec	CP Sec	CP Mbr Std	Name	PB Mbr	PB Alt	CC Mbr	CC Alt
														X											**Shanghai (continued)** Zhong Min				
																X									Zhou Gucheng				
																				X					Zhu Wanguo				
																									Zuo Bingguang				
														X											**Provincial Leadership Shanxi** Cao Pu				
			X																						Chen Sigong				
														X											Chen Yonggui	X		X	
																									Feng Sutao				
												X													Guo Qi'nan				
							X																		Hu Xiaoqin				
			X																						Jia Chongzhi				
																									Jia Jun				
														X											Jiao Guonai				
																									Jiao Yunbiao				
																			X						Li Bude				
																									Liu Kaiji				
X											X														Luo Guibo				
																									Ma Guishu				
																									Pan Ruizheng				
																									Ren Yinglun				
														X											Ruan Bosheng			X	
																									Shi Jiyan				
												X													Wang Chongzhi				
				X											X										Wang Fuzhi				X
																									Wang Kewen				
												X													Wang Maolin				
X																		X							Wang Qian			X	
				X																					Wang Tingdong				
												X													Wei Fengqi				
												X													Wu Guangtang				
												X													Yan Wuhong				
																									Yue Weifan				
					X																				Zhang Jianmin				
																									Zhang Tianyi				
																X									Zhang Zhaoyuan				
																									Zhao Jun				
				X																					Zhao Lizhi				
																									Zhao Yuting				
				X																					Zheng Xiaofeng				
				X																					Zhu Weihua				
			X																						**Provincial Leadership Sichuan** Du Xingyuan				
														X											Du Xinyuan				
																									Gu Zhibiao				
												X													Guan Xuesi				
				X																					He Haoju				
																			X						Hu Yongchang				
																									Li Linzhi				
																									Li Zhongyi				
																									Li Ziyuan			X	
												X													Liu Haiquan				
																									Liu Xiyao				X
								X																	Liu Yinbo　f				
																									Liu Ziyi				
			X								X														Lu Dadong			X	

	CCP: 1st Secretary	2nd Secretary	3rd Secretary	Secretary	Deputy Secretary	Member, Stand.Comte.	Secretary-General	Organization	Propaganda	United Front Work	Director, Party School	Governor	Vice-Governor	Chairman	Vice-Chairman	Commander	Deputy Commander	1st Political Commissar	2nd Political Commissar	Political Commissar	Deputy Political Comm.	CP Cttee 1st Secretary	2nd Secretary	Secretary	Member, Stand.Comte.	Name	Politburo Member	Politburo Alt. Member	CC Member	CC Alt. Member
Sichuan (continued)															X											Ma Shitu				
													X													Meng Dongbo				
													X													Mou Haixiu				
															X											Pei Changhui				
													X													Peng Dixian				
																										Qiao Zhimin				
						X																				Qin Quanhou				
																										Ren Mingdao				
	X					X																				Tan Qilong			X	
						X																				Tang Kebi f				X
															X											Tong Shaosheng				
				X		X																				Wang Lizhi				
																										Wei Jie				
															X											Wu Jinghua				
													X													Wu Xihai				
						X																				Xu Mengxia				
																										Yang Chao				
													X													Yangling Puoji				
				X		X								X												Yang Rudai				
					X	X							X													Yang Wanxuan				
																										Yang Zhong				
						X																				Zhang Lixing				
				X																						Zhang Xiushu				
															X											Zhao Wenjin				
				X									X													Zhao Zengyi			X	
	X																									Zhao Ziyang	X		X	
Tianjin Municipality							X								X											Bai Hua				
															X											Cao Xikang				
																			X							Cao Zhongnan				
	X														X											Chen Weida			X	
				X									X													Du Xinbo				
						X							X													Fan Quan				
				X																						Fan Rusheng				
						X							X													Guo Chunyuan				
				X									X													Hao Tianyi				
	X												X													Hu Qili				
		X													X											Huang Zhigang				
													X													Li Huasheng				
													X		X											Li Zhongyuan				
						X									X											Liu Gang				
													X		X											Liu Jinfeng				
													X													Lu Da				
						X								X												Wang Enhui				
													X													Wang Guangying				
						X							X													Wang Peiren				
															X											Wang Yi				
																			X							Wang Yifu				
																										Wu Zhen				
					X																					Xing Yanzi f			X	
																			X							Xu Cheng				
																										Xu Ming f				
						X								X												Yan Dakai				
																										Yang Jianbai				
															X											Yu Fujing				
						X																				Zhang Fuheng				X

	CCP							Director Dept. of				Administration Govt.		People's Congr.		Military District						CP Committee				Name	Posts in Central CP Politburo		CC	
	1st Secretary	2nd Secretary	3rd Secretary	Secretary	Deputy Secretary	Member,Stand.Comte.	Secretary-General	Organization	Propaganda	United Front Work	Director, Party School	Governor	Vice-Governor	Chairman	Vice-Chairman	Commander	Deputy Commander	1st Political Commissar	2nd Political Commissar	Political Commissar	Deputy Political Comm.	1st Secretary	2nd Secretary	Secretary	Member, Stand.Comte.		Member	Alternate Member	Member	Alternate Member
Tianjin (continued)				X																						Zhang Huaisan				
													X													Zhao Jun				
														X												Zhou Shutao				
Tibet Autonomous Region													X													Basang f			X	
					X																					Chen Jingbo				
																										Chen Zhuo				
															X											Cirenlamu f				
																										Dege Gasang Wangdui				
				X																						Dobgyal Ceyyang				
													X													Guo Xilan				
																										Hou Jie				
															X											Hu Zonglin				
													X													Langdun Gonggawangqiu				
																					X					Li Benshan				
															X											Li Chuanen				
													X													Luozong Zucheng				
				X																						Miao Piyi				
													X													Ngapoi Ngawang Jigmi				
				X																						Niu Ruizhou				
														X												Pagbalha Geleg Namgyai				
																										Qiao Jiajin				
				X						X																Raidi				X
						X																				Ren Chang				
														X												Rigdzin Wanggyal				X
																				X						Senggen Losang Gyancan				
					X																					Song Kaiyuan				
																										Song Ziyuan				
				X																X						Sun Yushan				
				X																						Tian Bao			X	
														X												Wang Heting				
																										Wang Jingzhi				
																X										Wang Yunxiang				
					X																					Wang Zhuquan				
					X								X													Xi Jinwu				
	X																									Yang Zongxin				
																										Yin Fatang				
													X							X						Zhang Guisen				
																										Zhang Zengwen				
Xinjiang Autonomous Region					X									X												A-man-tu-er				
					X								X													Amudong Niyazi				
					X																					Ba Dai				
					X																					Bai Chengming				
																										Cao-da-nuo-fu				
				X																						Hu Liangcai				X
				X								X														Ismail Amat			X	
													X													Janabil				X
																										Li Jinyu				
													X													Liu Zimo				
															X											Lu Xuebin				
															X											Mayenur f				
																										Mai-he-su-de Tie-yi-bo-fu				
					X																					Mushayef				
																										Qi Guo				
												X														Si-ma-yi Ya-sheng-nuo-fu				

	CCP											Administration				Military District										Name	Posts in Central CP			
1st Secretary	2nd Secretary	3rd Secretary	Secretary	Deputy Secretary	Member, Stand. Comte.	Secretary-General	Director Dept. of Organization	Propaganda	United Front Work	Director, Party School	Governor	Vice-Governor	Chairman	Vice-Chairman	Commander	Deputy Commander	1st Political Commissar	2nd Political Commissar	Political Commissar	Deputy Political Comm.	1st Secretary	2nd Secretary	Secretary	Member, Stand. Comte.		Politburo Member	Politburo Alternate Member	CC Member	CC Alternate Member

Xinjiang (continued)

1st Sec	2nd Sec	3rd Sec	Sec	Dep Sec	Mbr SC	Sec-Gen	Org	Prop	UFW	Party Sch	Gov	V-Gov	Chmn	V-Chmn	Cmdr	Dep Cmdr	1st PC	2nd PC	PC	Dep PC	1st Sec	2nd Sec	Sec	Mbr SC	Name	PB	PB Alt	CC	CC Alt
			X									X													Song Zhihe				
														X											Tan Youlin				
												X													Tian Zhong				
				X									X												Tomur Dawamat				
																									Tu-er-xun A-ta-wu-la				
																									Tuo-hu-ti Sha-bi-er				X
X									X			X													Wang Feng				
																									Wang Heting				
														X											Wang Zhenwen				
																									Xie Gaozhong				
					X																				Yang Ke				
																									Yang Yiqing				
														X											Yi-er-ha-li				
														X											Yi-mi-nuo-fu Ha-mi-ti				
														X											Yu Zhanlin				
																									Zhang Fengqi				
				X																					Zhang Shigong				
												X													Zhang Siming				
														X											Zhao Yuzheng				
			X																						Zhou Renshan				

Provincial Leadership

Yunnan

1st Sec	2nd Sec	3rd Sec	Sec	Dep Sec	Mbr SC	Sec-Gen	Org	Prop	UFW	Party Sch	Gov	V-Gov	Chmn	V-Chmn	Cmdr	Dep Cmdr	1st PC	2nd PC	PC	Dep PC	1st Sec	2nd Sec	Sec	Mbr SC	Name	PB	PB Alt	CC	CC Alt
X					X							X					X								An Pingsheng			X	
												X													Dao Guodong				
																X									Ding Rongchang				
																	X								Gao Zhanjie				
																									Gao Zhiguo				
																									Li Hecai				
				X																					Li Qiming			X	
																									Li Yuan				
					X	X																			Liang Wenying				
					X			X																	Lin Chao				
	X											X													Liu Minghui				X
																									Ma Wendong				
																									Meng Qi				
																									Shao Feng				
				X	X									X											Sun Yuting				
																									Tang Xiaomin				
														X											Wang Shaoyan				
																	X								Wang Yinshan				
																									Wu Shengmin				
														X											Wu Zhiyuan				
																									Wu Zuomin				
																									Xi Congzhen				
				X																					Xue Tao				
												X													Yang Kecheng				
																									Yu Lanfu				
																									Zhang Enbu				
					X									X											Zhang Haitang				
																									Zhang Tianfang				
				X								X													Zhang Yun				
														X											Zhang Zhixiu			X	
																									Zhang Zhong				
																									Zhang Zihai				
																									Zhao Xuequan				X
						X																			Zhao Zengyi				
																X									Zhu Jiabi				

Provincial Leadership

Zhejiang

CCP											Administration				Military District										Name	Central CP			
1st Secretary	2nd Secretary	3rd Secretary	Secretary	Deputy Secretary	Member, Stand. Comte.	Secretary-General	Organization	Propaganda	United Front Work	Director, Party School	Governor	Vice-Governor	Chairman	Vice-Chairman	Commander	Deputy Commander	1st Political Commissar	2nd Political Commissar	Political Commissar	Deputy Political Comm.	1st Secretary	2nd Secretary	Secretary	Member, Stand. Comte.		Politburo Member	Alternate Member	CC Member	Alternate Member
					X						X														Chen Zuolin				X
					X										X										Feng Ke				
					X																				Guan Junting				
																			X						Jiang Baodai				X
			X								X														Li Bincheng				
																									Li Fengping				
					X							X													Li Kechang				
														X											Li Lanyan				
														X											Li Yuhua f				
														X											Lin Huishan				
												X													Liu Dan				
														X											Liu Yifu				
					X																				Liu Zizheng				
																			X						Mou Hanqing				
																				X					Sun Zhaoxu				
												X													Tang Yuanbing				
X													X				X				X				Tie Ying			X	
				X																					Wang Boping				
				X	X																				Wang Fang				
					X		X																		Wang Jiayang				
																									Wang Jinyou				X
					X			X																	Wang Qidong				
							X																		Wang Yaoting				
		X			X														X						Xia Qi				
		X																							Xue Ju				
					X						X														Yuan Fanglie				
					X																				Zhai Xiwu				
			X																						Zhang Jingtang				
																X									Zhong Xianwen				
														X											Zhu Zuxiang				

The Military Regions

THE MILITARY REGIONS

Beijing / Chengdu

Military Region / Name	Commander	Deputy Commander	1st Political Commissar	2nd Political Commissar	Political Commissar	Dpty. Political Comm.	Chief of Staff	Director	Deputy Director	1st Secretary	2nd Secretary	3rd Secretary	Colonel-General	Lieutenant-General	Major-General	Politburo Member	Politburo Alternate Member	CC Member	CC Alternate Member
Beijing																			
Fu Chongbi		X																	X
Kang Lin		X																	
Li Zhongxuan		X																X	
Lin Hujia			X															X	
Liu Haiqing						X								X					
Liu Zihou					X														
Luo Yinghuai		X																	
Ma Weihua						X													
Pan Yan											X								
Qin Jiwei	X																	X	
Wan Haifeng		X				X													
Wang Yang		X																	
Wang Zonghuai		X							X										
Wu Dai		X													X			X	
Wu Xianen		X												X					
Xiao Xuanjin					X									X					
Yuan Shengping					X									X				X	
Zheng Xiwen		X												X				X	
Chengdu																			
Chen Mingyi		X												X	X			X	
Chen Xianrui		X							X					X					X
Kong Shiquan		X																	
Lu Jiahan		X																	
Ru Fuyi		X																	
Wang Chenghan		X													X				
Wang Dongbao		X												X					
Wei Jie		X																X	
You Taizhong	X				X														X
Yu Shusheng		X				X													
Zhao Wenjin			X																
Zhao Ziyang																		X	
Zhong Hanhua					X														

Kunming (continued) / Lanzhou / Nanjing

Military Region / Name	Commander	Deputy Commander	1st Political Commissar	2nd Political Commissar	Political Commissar	Dpty. Political Comm.	Chief of Staff	Director	Deputy Director	1st Secretary	2nd Secretary	3rd Secretary	Colonel-General	Lieutenant-General	Major-General	Politburo Member	Politburo Alternate Member	CC Member	CC Alternate Member
Kunming (continued)																			
Xu Qixiao		X																	
Zha Yusheng		X																	
Zhang Haitang		X													X			X	
Zhang Rongsen															X				
Zhang Zhixiu																		X	
Zhao Zengyi																			
Lanzhou																			
Chen Kang		X												X					
Du Yide		X				X									X				
He Guangyu		X													X				
Hu Bingyun		X																	
Huang Jingyao								X											
Jiang Bo		X													X				
Kong Junbiao		X				X													
Liang Renjie																			
Liu Jinghai																			
Song Ping				X														X	
Wu Shengrong			X			X							X					X	
Xiao Hua																	X		
Nanjing																			
Yang Jiarui	X														X				X
Deng Yue					X									X					
Du Ping			X															X	
Guo Linxiang		X							X									X	
He Yixiang		X																	
Liao Rongbiao		X																	
Liu Xiyuan		X																	
Nie Fengzhi						X								X	X			X	
Peng Chong								X									X		
Sun Keji		X																X	X
Wang Zhan																			
Wu Shihong		X													X				
Xiang Shouzhi		X																	

Delegation name roster (voting/attendance matrix). Names by group:

[First group]
Xiong Zuofang, Zhan Danan, Zhang Xiqin, Zhou Chunlin, Fu Kuiqing, Gan Weihan, Jiang Yonghui, Li Desheng, Li Huamin, Li Shaoyuan, Liao Hansheng, Liu Yongyuan, Liu Zhenhua, Tang Zian, Wang Enmao, Xie Zhenhua, Zeng Shaoshan, Zhang Wu, Zou Yan

Shenyang
Chen Fahong, Chen Pixian, Kong Qingde, Li Chengfang, Li Guangjun, Lin Weixian, Ma Zhaokun, Min Xuesheng, Wu Lanting, Wu Ruishan, Xie Tangzhong, Yan Zheng, Zhang Caiqian, Zhang Xiulong, Zhang Yuhua, Zheng Zhishi, Zhou Shizhong, Zhou Zhigang

Xinjiang
Cao-da-nuo-fu, Ismail Amat, Li Changlin, Liu Faxiu, Ma Sen, Tan Youlin, Wang Feng, Wei Youzhu, Xiao Quanfu, Xing Yuanlin, Zhang Jiecheng, Zheng Sansheng

Fuzhou
Cao Punan, Jiang Weiqing, Li Zhimin, Liao Haiguang, Liao Zhigao, Long Feihu, Song Weishi, Wang Zhi, Yang Chengwu, Zhu Shaoqing, Zhu Yaohua

Guangzhou
Chen Qingshan, Chen Zhibin, Deng Yifan, Gu Jingsheng, Huang Ronghai, Jiang Lindong, Jiang Xieyuan, Liu Changyi, Ou Zhifu, Qiu Guoguang, Shan Yinzhang, Wang Chun, Wu Kehua, Wu Zhong, Xi Zhongxun, Xiang Zhonghua, Xiao Yuanli, Yan Teming, Yang Shugen, Ye Jianming, Zhan Caifang, Zhou Deli

Jinan
Bai Rubing, Fan Chaoli, Fang Zheng, Li Bo, Rao Shoukun, Ren Sizhong, Sun Jixian, Xiao Wangdong, Yin Fatang, Zuo Qi

Kunming
Hu Ronggui, Li Kezhong, Liu Yanquan, Liu Zhijian, Shi Jingban, Sun Ganqing

Wade-Giles/Pinyin conversion table

for the biographical entries

A

Ah·p'ei Ah-wang Chin-mei	Ngapoi Ngawang Jigmi
Ah·p'ei Ts'ai·t'an Cho·ke	Nyapoi Cedan Zhoigar
An Ch'i-yüan	An Qiyuan
An Chih-wen	An Zhiwen
An Chih-yüan	An Zhiyuan
An Fa-ch'ien	An Faqian
An Kang	An Gang
An P'ing-sheng	An Pingsheng
An Shih-wei	An Shiwei
An Tzu-wen	An Ziwen

B

Bi-k'en	Biken
Burhan Shahidi	Burhan Xahidi

C

Cha·hsi·wang·hsü	Zhaxi Wangqug
Cha Yü-sheng	Zha Yusheng
Ch'ai Ch'eng-wen	Chai Chengwen
Chai Hsi-wu	Zhai Xiwu
Ch'ai Shu-fen	Chai Shufan
Ch'ai Tse-min	Chai Zemin
Chan Ts'ai-fang	Zhan Caifang
Chan Wu	Zhan Wu
Chang Ai-p'ing	Zhang Aiping
Chang Chan-wu	Zhang Zhanwu
Chang Chao	Zhang Zhao
Chang Chen	Zhang Zhen
Chang Ch'eng-hsien	Zhang Chengxian
Chang Cheng-t'ao	Zhang Zhengtao
Chang Ch'eng-tsung	Zhang Chengzong
Chang Chi-hui	Zhang Jihui
Chang Ch'i-lung	Zhang Qilong
Chang Chi-nung	Zhang Jinong
Chang Chia-fu	Zhang Jiafu
Chang Chia-hua	Zhang Jiahua
Chang Chieh	Zhang Jie
Chang Chieh-ch'eng	Zhang Jiecheng
Chang Chien-kang	Zhang Jian'gang
Chang Chien-min	Zhang Jianmin
Chang Chih-hsiang	Zhang Zhixiang
Chang Chih-hsiu	Zhang Zhixiu
Chang Chih-huai	Zhang Zhihuai
Chang Chih-kuo	Zhang Zhiguo
Chang Chih-ti	Zhang Zhidi
Chang Chih-yi	Zhang Zhiyi
Chang Chih-yüan	Zhang Zhiyuan
Chang Chin-hsien	Zhang Jinxian
Chang Chin-pang	Zhang Jinbang
Chang Ch'ing-chi	Zhang Qingji
Chang Ching-fu	Zhang Jingfu
Chang Ching-li	Zhang Jingli
Chang Ching-t'ao	Zhang Jingtao
Chang Ch'un-ch'iao	Zhang Chunqiao
Chang Chung	Zhang Zhong
Chang Ch'ung	Zhang Chong
Chang Chung-liang	Zhang Zhongliang
Chang Chün-hua	Zhang Junhua
Chang Feng-yün	Zhang Fengyun
Chang Fu-heng	Zhang Fuheng
Chang Fu-kuei	Zhang Fugui
Chang Fu-ts'ai	Zhang Fucai
Chang Hai-feng	Zhang Haifeng
Chang Hai-t'ang	Zhang Haitang
Chang Han-ying	Zhang Hanying
Chang Hsi-ch'in	Zhang Xiqin
Chang Hsiang-shan	Zhang Xiangshan
Chang Hsiao-ch'ien	Zhang Xiaoqian
Chang Hsiao-tseng	Zhang Xiaozeng
Chang Hsien-wu	Zhang Xianwu
Chang Hsien-yüeh	Zhang Xianyue
Ch'ang Hsin-ts'un	Chang Xincun
Chang Hsiu-chu	Zhang Xiuzhu
Chang Hsiu-lung	Zhang Xiulong
Chang Hsiu-shu	Zhang Xiushu
Chang Huai-chung	Zhang Huaizhong
Chang Huai-lien	Zhang Huailian
Chang Huai-san	Zhang Huaisan
Chang Ju-kuang	Zhang Ruguang
Chang Jui-ai	Zhang Ruiai
Chang Jui-ch'ing	Zhang Ruiqing
Chang Jui-hua	Zhang Ruihua
Chang Jui-ying	Zhang Ruiying
Chang Jung-sen	Zhang Rongsen
Chang K'ai-fan	Zhang Kaifan
Chang K'e-hsia	Zhang Kexia
Chang Ke-hsin	Zhang Gexin
Chang K'e-jang	Zhang Kerang
Chang Ken-sheng	Zhang Gensheng
Chang Kuang-tou	Zhang Guangdou
Chang Kuei-chen	Zhang Guizhen
Chang Kuo-chen	Zhang Guozhen
Chang Kuo-chi	Zhang Guoji
Chang Kuo-ch'ing	Zhang Guoqing
Chang Kuo-sheng	Zhang Guosheng
Chang Li-hsien	Zhang Lixian
Chang Lin-ch'ih	Zhang Linchi
Chang Ling-pin	Zhang Lingbin
Chang Lung-hsiang	Zhang Longxiang
Chang Nan-sheng	Zhang Nansheng
Chang Pai-fa	Zhang Baifa
Chang P'an-shih	Zhang Panshi
Chang Pang-ying	Zhang Bangying
Chang P'eng	Zhang Peng
Chang P'eng-t'u	Zhang Pengtu
Chang Pin	Zhang Bin
Chang P'ing-hua	Zhang Pinghua
Chang Ping-kuei	Zhang Binggui
Chang Ping-yü	Zhang Bingyu
Chang Po-ch'uan	Zhang Bochuan
Chang Shih-chieh	Zhang Shijie
Chang Shih-chün	Zhang Shijun
Chang Shih-kung	Zhang Shigong
Chang Shih-ying	Zhang Shiying
Chang Shu-te	Zhang Shude
Chang Su	Zhang Su
Chang Szu-ming	Zhang Siming
Chang Te-ch'ün	Zhang Dequn
Chang T'ien-fang	Zhang Tianfang
Chang T'ien-yi	Zhang Tianyi
Chang Ting-ch'eng	Zhang Dingcheng
Chang T'ing-fa	Zhang Tingfa
Chang Ts'ai-ch'ien	Zhang Caiqian
Chang Ts'an-ming	Zhang Canming
Chang Ts'e	Zhang Ce
Chang Tseng-wen	Zhang Zengwen
Chang Tso-yin	Zhang Zuoyin
Chang T'ung	Zhang Tong
Chang T'ung-yü	Zhang Tongyu
Chang Tzu-hai	Zhang Zihai
Chang Tzu-yi	Zhang Ziyi
Chang Wan-fu	Zhang Wanfu
Chang Wei	Zhang Wei
Chang Wei-chen	Zhang Weizhen
Chang Wei-ch'eng	Zhang Weicheng
Chang Wei-lieh	Zhang Weilie
Chang Wen-chih	Zhang Wenzhi
Chang Wen-chin	Zhang Wenjin
Chang Wen-chou	Zhang Wenzhou
Chang Wen-kuang	Zhang Wenguang
Chang Wen-pin	Zhang Wenbin
Chang Wen-yü	Zhang Wenyu
Chang Yao-tz'u	Zhang Yaoci
Chang Yen	Zhang Yan
Ch'ang Yen-ch'ing	Chang Yanqing
Chang Yi	Zhang Yi
Chang Yi-chün	Zhang Yijun
Chang Yi-hsiang	Zhang Yixiang
Chang Yi-min	Zhang Yimin
Chang Yu-hsüan	Zhang Youxuan
Chang Yu-yü	Zhang Youyu
Chang Yung-li	Zhang Yongli
Chang Yü	Zhang Yu
Chang Yü-che	Zhang Yuzhe
Chang Yü-ch'in	Zhang Yuqin
Chang Yü-hua	Zhang Yuhua
Chang Yü-huan	Zhang Yuhuan
Chang Yüan-p'ei	Zhang Yuanpei
Chang Yüeh	Zhang Yue
Chang Yün	Zhang Yun
Chao Ch'ang-ch'un	Zhao Changchun
Chao Chen-ch'ing	Zhao Zhenqing
Chao Cheng-yi	Zhao Zhengyi
Chao Ch'i	Zhao Qi
Chao Chien-min	Zhao Jianmin
Chao Chih-chien	Zhao Zhijian
Chao Chin	Zhao Jin
Chao Ch'u-ch'i	Zhao Chuqi
Chao Ch'un-cheng	Zhao Chunzheng
Chao Chung-yao	Zhao Zhongyao
Chao Chün	Zhao Jun
Chao Chün-mai	Zhao Junmai
Chao Fa-sheng	Zhao Fasheng
Chao Fan	Zhao Fan
Chao Hai-feng	Zhao Haifeng
Chao Hsien-shun	Zhao Xianshun

720

Wade-Giles	Pinyin
Chao Hsin-ch'u	Zhao Xinchu
Chao Hsin-jan	Zhao Xinran
Chao Hsing-chih	Zhao Xingzhi
Chao Hsing-yüan	Zhao Xingyuan
Chao Hsiu	Zhao Xiu
Chao Hsüeh-ch'üan	Zhao Xuequan
Chao Li-chih	Zhao Lizhi
Chao Lin	Zhao Lin
Chao Pei-k'e	Zhao Beike
Chao Pen-hsi	Zhao Benxi
Chao P'eng-fei	Zhao Pengfei
Chao Po-p'ing	Zhao Boping
Chao P'u-ch'u	Zhao Puchu
Chao Shou-yi	Zhao Shouyi
Chao Te-hsien	Zhao Dexian
Chao Te-tsun	Zhao Dezun
Chao Ts'ang-pi	Zhao Cangbi
Chao Tseng-yi	Zhao Zengyi
Chao Tsu-k'ang	Zhao Zukang
Chao Tsung-yü	Zhao Zongyu
Chao Tung-wan	Zhao Dongwan
Chao Tzu-shang	Zhao Zishang
Chao Tzu-yang	Zhao Ziyang
Chao Wen-chin	Zhao Wenjin
Chao Wen-fu	Zhao Wenfu
Chao Wen-p'u	Zhao Wenpu
Chao Wu-ch'eng	Zhao Wucheng
Chao Yi-min	Zhao Yimin
Chao Yü-t'ing	Zhao Yuting
Chao Yüan	Zhao Yuan
Ch'en Ai-o	Chen Aie
Ch'en Chao-yüan	Chen Zhaoyuan
Ch'en Cheng-hsiang	Chen Zhengxiang
Ch'en Ch'i-han	Chen Qihan
Ch'en Chieh	Chen Jie
Ch'en Chien-fei	Chen Jianfei
Ch'en Chih-fang	Chen Zhifang
Ch'en Chin-hua	Chen Jinhua
Ch'en Ching-po	Chen Jingbo
Ch'en Ch'u	Chen Chu
Ch'en Fang-wu	Cheng Fangwu
Ch'en Feng	Chen Feng
Ch'en Fu-han	Chen Fuhan
Ch'en Han-po	Chen Hanbo
Ch'en Han-sheng	Chen Hansheng
Ch'en Hsi-chung	Chen Xizhong
Ch'en Hsi-lien	Chen Xilian
Ch'en Hsi-yü	Chen Xiyu
Ch'en Hsiao-shun	Chen Xiaoshun
Ch'en Hsien-jui	Chen Xianrui
Ch'en Hsin-jen	Chen Xinren
Ch'en Hsing-kang	Chen Xinggang
Ch'en Huang-mei	Chen Huangmei
Ch'en Jenfu	Chen Renfu
Ch'en Ju-lung	Chen Rulong
Ch'en Jui-t'ing	Chen Ruiting
Ch'en K'ang	Chen Kang
Ch'en K'e-han	Chen Kehan
Ch'en K'e-t'ien	Chen Ketian
Ch'en Kuang	Chen Guang
Ch'en K'un-ti	Chen Kunti
Ch'en Kuo-tung	Chen Guodong
Ch'en Lei	Chen Lei
Ch'en Lieh-min	Chen Liemin
Ch'en Man-yüan	Chen Manyuan
Ch'en Ming	Chen Ming
Ch'en Ming-yi	Chen Mingyi
Ch'en Mu-hua	Chen Muhua
Ch'en P'ei-min	Chen Peimin
Ch'en Peng	Chen Peng
Ch'en P'i-hsien	Chen Pixian
Ch'en Ping-yü	Chen Bingyu
Ch'en P'u-ju	Chen Puru
Ch'en Shao-chung	Chen Shaozhong
Ch'en Shu-liang	Chen Shuliang
Ch'en Shu-tzu	Chen Shuzi
Ch'en Tai-sun	Chen Daisun
Ch'en T'ieh	Chen Tie
Ch'en Tsai-tao	Chen Zaidao
Ch'en Tso-lin	Chen Zuolin
Ch'en Tsung-lieh	Chen Zonglie
Ch'en Tung	Chen Dong
Ch'en Tz'u-sheng	Chen Cisheng
Ch'en Wei-chi	Chen Weiji
Ch'en Wei-ta	Chen Weida
Ch'en Yang-shan	Chen Yangshan
Ch'en Yeh-p'ing	Chen Yeping
Ch'en Yi-sung	Chen Yisong
Ch'en Yung-hsiang	Chen Yongxiang
Ch'en Yung-kuei	Chen Yonggui
Ch'en Yung-lin	Chen Yonglin
Ch'en Yü	Chen Yu
Ch'en Yü-niang	Chen Yuniang
Ch'en Yü-pao	Chen Yubao
Ch'en Yüan-fang	Chen Yuanfang
Cheng Chi-ch'iao	Zheng Jiqiao
Cheng Chih-p'ing	Zheng Zhiping
Cheng Chung	Zheng Zhong
Ch'eng Chün	Cheng Jun
Ch'eng Fei	Cheng Fei
Cheng Han-t'ao	Zheng Hantao
Ch'eng Hao	Cheng Hao
Cheng Hsiao-hsien	Zheng Xiaoxian
Ch'eng Hsing-ling	Cheng Xingling
Ch'eng Kuang-hua	Cheng Guanghua
Cheng Kuo-chung	Zheng Guozhong
Cheng Min-chih	Zheng Minzhi
Cheng San-sheng	Zheng Sansheng
Ch'eng Shao-chiung	Cheng Shaojiong
Ch'eng Shao-hui	Cheng Shaohui
Cheng Shao-wen	Zheng Shaowen
Ch'eng Shih-ts'ai	Cheng Shicai
Cheng Szu-yüan	Zheng Siyuan
Ch'eng T'an	Cheng Tan
Cheng T'ien-hsiang	Zheng Tianxiang
Cheng T'o-pin	Zheng Tuobin
Cheng Tung-kuo	Zheng Dongguo
Ch'eng Tzu-hua	Cheng Zihua
Cheng Wan-chün	Zheng Wanjun
Ch'eng Wang	Cheng Wang
Cheng Wei-chih	Zheng Weizhi
Cheng Yi-shan	Zheng Yishan
Ch'eng Yi-t'ai	Cheng Yitai
Cheng Yung-ho	Zheng Yonghe
Ch'eng Yüan-hsing	Cheng Yuanxing
Chi Ch'ang-shan	Ji Changshan
Chi Ch'un-kuang	Ji Chunguang
Chi Chung-p'u	Ji Zhongpu
Chi Fang	Ji Fang
Chi Hsien-lin	Ji Xianlin
Chi Kuei-hsin	Ji Guixin
Chi P'eng-fei	Ji Pengfei
Ch'i Shou-liang	Qi Shouliang
Ch'i T'ao	Qi Tao
Chi Teng-k'uei	Ji Dengkui
Ch'i T'ien	Qi Tian
Chi Tsung-ch'üan	Ji Zongquan
Ch'i Tsung-hua	Qi Zonghua
Ch'i Tzu-sheng	Qi Zisheng
Ch'i-lin Wan-tan	Chilin Wandan
Chi Ying-lin	Ji Yinglin
Chia Ch'ung-chih	Jia Chongzhi
Chia Chün	Jia Jun
Chia Huai-chi	Jia Huaiji
Chia Hui-sheng	Jia Huisheng
Chia Jo-yü	Jia Ruoyu
Chia-na-pu-erh	Janabil
Chia Shih	Jia Shi
Chia T'ing-san	Jia Tingsan
Chia Yi-pin	Jia Yibin
Chia Yün-piao	Jia Yunbiao
Chiang Ch'ing	Jiang Qing
Chiang Ch'un-fang	Jiang Chunfang
Chiang Feng	Jiang Feng
Chiang Hsüeh-shan	Jiang Xueshan
Chiang Hsüeh-yüan	Jiang Xieyuan
Chiang Hua	Jiang Hua
Chiang Li-yin	Jiang Liyin
Chiang Ming	Jiang Ming
Chiang Nan-hsiang	Jiang Nanxiang
Chiang Pao-ti	Jiang Baodi
Chiang P'ing	Jiang Ping
Chiang Tse-han	Jiang Zehan
Chiang Tse-min	Jiang Zemin
Chiang Wei-ch'ing	Jiang Weiqing
Chiang Wen	Jiang Wen
Chiang Yi	Jiang Yi
Chiang Yi-chen	Jiang Yizhen
Chiang Ying	Jiang Ying
Chiang Yung-hui	Jiang Yonghui
Ch'iao Chia-hsin	Qiao Jiaxin
Ch'iao Chih-min	Qiao Zhimin
Ch'iao Hsiao-kuang	Qiao Xiaoguang
Chiao Jo-yü	Jiao Ruoyu
Chiao Li-jen	Jiao Liren
Chiao Lin-yi	Jiao Linyi
Ch'iao Ming-pu	Qiao Mingbu
Ch'iao P'ei-hsin	Qiao Peixin
Chiao Shan-min	Jiao Shanmin
Ch'iao Shih	Qiao Shi
Ch'ien Ch'ang-chao	Qian Changzhao
Ch'ien Cheng-ying	Qian Zhengying
Ch'ien Ch'i-ch'en	Qian Qichen
Ch'ien Chih-kuang	Qian Zhiguang
Ch'ien Ch'uan-chün	Qian Chuanjun
Ch'ien Chün-jui	Qian Junrui
Chien Hsien-jen	Jian Xianren
Ch'ien Hsin-chung	Qian Xinzhong
Ch'ien Hsüeh-sen	Qian Xuesen
Ch'ien Jen-yüan	Qian Renyuan
Ch'ien Li-jen	Qian Liren
Ch'ien Min	Qian Min
Ch'ien San-ch'iang	Qian Sanqiang
Ch'ien Wei-ch'ang	Qian Weichang
Ch'ih Hao-t'ien	Chi Haotian
Ch'ih Pi-ch'ing	Chi Biqing
Chin Chao	Jin Zhao
Chin Chao-tien	Jin Zhaodian
Ch'in Chi-wei	Qin Jiwei
Ch'in Chia-lin	Qin Jialin
Chin Ch'eng	Jin Cheng
Chin Chien-chung	Jin Jianzhong
Chin Chih-fu	Jin Zhifu
Ch'in Ch'uan	Qin Chuan
Ch'in Chung-ta	Qin Zhongda
Ch'in Ho-chen	Qin Hezhen
Chin Hsi-ying	Jin Xiying

Chin Hsün	Jin Xun
Chin Kuei-hsiang	Jin Guixiang
Ch'in Li-chen	Qin Lizhen
Ch'in Li-sheng	Qin Lisheng
Chin Ming	Jin Ming
Chin Ming-han	Jin Minghan
Chin Pao-sheng	Jin Baosheng
Chin Shan-pao	Jin Shanbao
Chin T'ai-jan	Jin Tairan
Ch'in T'ien-chen	Qin Tianzhen
Ch'in Wen-ts'ai	Qin Wencai
Ch'in Ying-chi	Qin Yingji
Ching Shu-p'ing	Jing Shuping
Ch'iu Ch'un-fu	Qiu Chunfu
Ch'iu Kuo-kuang	Qiu Guoguang
Cho Hsiung	Zhuo Xiong
Chou Ah-ch'ing	Zhou Aqing
Chou Chan-ao	Zhou Zhan'ao
Chou Cheng	Zhou Zheng
Chou Chien-jen	Zhou Jianren
Chou Chien-nan	Zhou Jiannan
Chou Chih-chün	Zhou Zhijun
Chou Chih-t'ung	Zhou Zhitong
Chou Ch'iu-yeh	Zhou Qiuye
Chou Ch'un-ch'üan	Zhou Chunquan
Chou Ch'un-lin	Zhou Chunlin
Chou Chüeh	Zhou Jue
Chou En-lai	Zhou Enlai
Chou Erh-fu	Zhou Erfu
Chou Hsin-wu	Zhou Xinwu
Chou Hua-min	Zhou Huamin
Chou Huan	Zhou Huan
Chou Hui	Zhou Hui
Chou Jen-shan	Zhou Renshan
Chou Ku-ch'eng	Zhou Gucheng
Chou Kuan-wu	Zhou Guanwu
Chou Kuang-ch'un	Zhou Guangchun
Chou Li	Zhou Li
Chou Lin	Zhou Lin
Chou Min	Zhou Min
Chou Ming-ch'i	Zhou Mingqi
Chou Pao-fen	Zhou Baofen
Chou Pei-feng	Zhou Beifeng
Chou P'ei-yüan	Zhou Peiyuan
Chou P'eng-ch'eng	Zhou Pengcheng
Chou Po-p'ing	Zhou Boping
Chou Shih-chung	Zhou Shizhong
Chou Shih-kuan	Zhou Shiguan
Chou Shu-t'ao	Zhou Shutao
Chou Tse	Zhou Ze
Chou Tzu-chien	Zhou Zijian
Chou Wei-shih	Zhou Weishi
Chou Yang	Zhou Yang
Ch'ou Yu-wen	Chou Youwen
Chu Ch'i-chen	Zhu Qizhen
Ch'u Chiang	Chu Jiang
Chu Ch'un-ho	Zhu Chunhe
Chu Han-min	Zhu Hanmin
Chu Hsüeh-fan	Zhu Xuefan
Chu Hung-yüan	Zhu Hongyuan
Chu Jung	Zhu Rong
Chu Kuang-ya	Zhu Guangya
Chu Liang-ts'ai	Zhu Liangcai
Chu Mu-chih	Zhu Muzhi
Chu Pen-cheng	Zhu Benzheng
Chu Shao-ch'ing	Zhu Shaoqing
Chu Te	Zhu De
Ch'u T'u-nan	Chu Tunan

Chu Wu-hua	Zhu Wuhua
Chu Yao-hua	Zhu Yaohua
Chu Yün-ch'ien	Zhu Yunqian
Chu Yün-shan	Zhu Yunshan
Chuang Hsi-ch'üan	Zhuang Xiquan
Chuang Ming-li	Zhuang Mingli
Chuang T'ien	Zhuang Tian
Chuang Yen	Zhuang Yan
Chung Ch'i-kuang	Zhong Qiguang
Chung Ch'ing-fa	Zhong Qingfa
Chung Fu-hsiang	Zhong Fuxiang
Chung Han-hua	Zhong Hanhua
Chung Hsi-tung	Zhong Xidong
Chung Hui-lan	Zhong Huilan
Chung Kuo-ch'u	Zhong Guochu
Chung Shih-t'ung	Zhong Shitong
Chung Tzu-yün	Zhong Ziyun
Ch'ü Ke-p'ing	Qu Geping
Ch'ü Wu	Qu Wu

F

Fan Ch'ao-li	Fan Chaoli
Fan Chin	Fan Jin
Fan Chung-chih	Fan Zhongzhi
Fan Hsi-hsien	Fan Xixian
Fan Ju-sheng	Fan Rusheng
Fan Mu-han	Fan Muhan
Fan Te-ling	Fan Deling
Fan Tso-k'ai	Fan Zuokai
Fan Tzu-yü	Fan Ziyu
Fang Ch'iang	Fang Qiang
Fang Ch'ien	Fang Qian
Fang Chih-ch'un	Fang Zhichun
Fang Chih-ta	Fang Zhida
Fang Chung-ju	Fang Zhongru
Fang Kao	Fang Gao
Fang Wei-chung	Fang Weizhong
Fang Yi	Fang Yi
Fei Hsiao-t'ung	Fei Xiaotong
Fei Yi-min	Fei Yimin
Feng Chan-wu	Feng Zhanwu
Feng Chi-hsin	Feng Jixin
Feng Chih	Feng Zhi
Fu Ch'ung-pi	Fu Chongbi
Feng Hsüan	Feng Xuan
Feng P'in-te	Feng Pinde
Feng Te-p'ei	Feng Depei
Feng T'ien-shun	Feng Tianshun
Feng Wen-pin	Feng Wenbin
Feng Yung-shun	Feng Yongshun
Feng Yü-chiu	Feng Yujiu
Feng Yün-ho	Feng Yunhe
Fu Ch'iu-t'ao	Fu Qiutao
Fu Chung	Fu Zhong
Fu Hao	Fu Hao
Fu Mao-chi	Fu Maoji
Fu Yü-t'ien	Fu Yutian

H

Hai Yü-chen	Hai Yuzhen
Hamdinnyas	Amudong Niyazi
Han Che-yi	Han Zheyi
Han Fu-tung	Han Fudong
Han Hsien-ch'u	Han Xianchu
Han Hsü	Han Xu
Han Jung-hua	Han Ronghua

Han K'e-hua	Han Kehua
Han Kuang	Han Guang
Han Lien-ch'eng	Han Liancheng
Han Nien-lung	Han Nianlong
Han Ning-fu	Han Ningfu
Han P'ei-hsin	Han Peixin
Han Tung-shan	Han Dongshan
Han Ying	Han Ying
Han Yü-t'ung	Han Yutong
Hao Chien-hsiu	Hao Jianxiu
Hao Chung-shih	Hao Zhongshi
Hao Hsiu-shan	Hao Xiushan
Hao Te-ch'ing	Hao Deqing
Hao T'ing	Hao Ting
Ho Ch'ang-kung	He Changgong
Ho Ch'eng	He Cheng
Ho Ch'eng-hua	He Chenghua
Ho Cheng-wen	He Zhengwen
Ho Ch'i-fang	He Qifang
Ho Chi-feng	He Jifeng
Ho Chih-hua	He Zhihua
Ho Chin-nien	He Jinnian
Ho Ch'ing-chi	He Qingji
Ho Ching-chih	He Jingzhi
Ho Chu-kuo	He Zhuguo
Ho Hao-chü	He Haoju
Ho Hsien	He Xian
Ho K'ang	He Kang
Ho Kuang-chien	He Guangjian
Ho Kuang-yü	He Guangyu
Ho Kuang-wen	He Guangwen
Ho Kung-k'ai	He Gongkai
Ho Lan-chieh	He Lanjie
Ho Li-liang	He Liliang
Ho Lü-t'ing	He Lüting
Ho Min-hsüeh	He Minxue
Ho Piao	He Biao
Ho Ping-chang	He Bingzhang
Ho T'ing-yi	He Tingyi
Ho Ts'e-hui	He Cehui
Ho Tung-ch'ang	He Dongchang
Ho Yi-hsiang	He Yixiang
Ho Yi-jan	He Yiran
Ho Ying	He Ying
Ho Yang	He Yang
Ho Yu-fa	He Youfa
Hou Chieh	Hou Jie
Hou Ching-ju	Hou Jingru
Hou Hsiang-lin	Hou Xianglin
Hou Te-feng	Hou Defeng
Hou Te-yüan	Hou Deyuan
Hou T'ung	Hou Tong
Hou Yeh-feng	Hou Yefeng
Hsi Chan-yüan	Xi Zhanyuan
Hsi Chin-wu	Xi Jinwu
Hsi Chung-hsün	Xi Zhongxun
Hsi Chü-hua	Xi Juhua
Hsi hou ba	Xi-hou-ba
Hsi Kuo-kuang	Xi Guoguang
Hsi Ye-sheng	Xi Yesheng
Hsi Yi	Xi Yi
Hsia Cheng-nung	Xia Zhengnong
Hsia Ch'i	Xia Qi
Hsia Chih-hsü	Xia Zhixu
Hsia Nai	Xia Nai
Hsia Shih-hou	Xia Shihou
Hsia Szu-p'ing	Xia Siping
Hsia Yen	Xia Yan

Hsiang Chao-tsung	Xiang Zhaozong	Hsü Kuan-jen	Xu Guanren	Huang Chi-ch'ing	Huang Jiqing
Hsiang Chung-hua	Xiang Zhonghua	Hsü Kuo-hsien	Xu Guoxian	Huang Chia-szu	Huang Jiasi
Hsiang K'e-fang	Xiang Kefang	Hsü Lei-chien	Xu Leijian	Huang Chih-chen	Huang Zhizhen
Hsiang La-yü	Xiang Layu	Hsü Li-ch'ing	Xu Liqing	Huang Chih-kang	Huang Zhigang
Hsiang Nan	Xiang Nan	Hsü Li-ch'ün	Xu Liqun	Huang Ching-po	Huang Jingbo
Hsiang Shou-shih	Xiang Shouzhi	Hsü Li-yi	Xu Liyi	Huang Chung	Huang Zhong
Hsiao Chien-kuang	Xiao Jianguang	Hsü Liang-t'u	Xu Liangtu	Huang Chü-hsiang	Huang Juxiang
Hsiao Ching-tuang	Xiao Jingguang	Hsü Mai-chin	Xu Maijin	Huang Hou	Huang Hou
Hsiao Ch'üan-fu	Xiao Quanfu	Hsü Meng-hsia	Xu Mengxia	Huang Hsin-pai	Huang Xinbai
Hsiao Fang-chou	Xiao Fangzhou	Hsü Ming	Xu Ming	Huang Hsin-t'ing	Huang Xinting
Hsiao Han	Xiao Han	Hsü Piao-chün	Xu Biaojun	Huang Hu	Huang Hu
Hsiao Hsien-fa	Xiao Xianfa	Hsü Pin-chou	Xu Binzhou	Huang Hua	Huang Hua
Hsiao Hua	Xiao Hua	Hsü Pin-ju	Xu Binru	Huang Huo-ch'ing	Huang Huoqing
Hsiao Huan-chin	Xiao Xuanjin	Hsü Po-hsin	Xu Boxin	Huang Jung	Huang Rong
Hsiao K'e	Xiao Ke	Hsü Shao-fu	Xu Shaofu	Huang Jung-ch'ang	Huang Rongchang
Hsiao P'eng	Xiao Peng	Hsü Shih-yu	Xu Shiyou	Huang Jung-hai	Huang Ronghai
Hsiao Szu-ming	Xiao Siming	Hsü Tao-ch'i	Xu Daoqi	Huang K'ai	Huang Kai
Hsiao T'ung	Xiao Tong	Hsü Te-heng	Xu Deheng	Huang Kan-ying	Huang Ganying
Hsiao Wang-tung	Xiao Wangdong	Hsü Ti-hsin	Xu Dixin	Huang K'e-ch'eng	Huang Kecheng
Hsiao Yen	Xiao Yan	Hsü Tsai-lien	Xu Zailian	Huang K'un	Huang Kun
Hsieh Chen-hua	Xie Zhenhua	Hsü Wen-yi	Xu Wenyi	Huang Min-wei	Huang Minwei
Hsieh Cheng-hao	Xie Zhenghao	Hsü Ya	Xu Ya	Huang Ming-ta	Huang Mingda
Hsieh Cheng-jung	Xie Zhengrong	Hsü Yi-ch'iao	Xu Yiqiao	Huang Ou-tung	Huang Oudong
Hsieh Ho-ch'ou	Xie Hechou	Hsü Yi-hsin	Xu Yixin	Huang Ping-wei	Huang Bingwei
Hsieh Hsi-te	Xie Xide	Hsü Yin-sheng	Xu Yinsheng	Huang Shih-hsieh	Huang Shixie
Hsieh Hsüeh-kung	Xie Xuegong	Hsüeh Chin-lien	Xue Jinlian	Huang Shu-tse	Huang Shuze
Hsieh Huai-te	Xie Huaide	Hsüeh Chin-ta	Xue Jinda	Huang Ting-ch'en	Huang Dingchen
Hsieh Huang-t'ien	Xie Huangtian	Hsüeh Hung-fu	Xue Hongfu	Huang Tso-chen	Huang Zuozhen
Hsieh Hung-sheng	Xie Hongsheng	Hsüeh Jen-tsung	Xue Renzong	Huang Tso-ch'in	Huang Zuoqin
Hsieh Kao-chung	Xie Gaozhong	Hsüeh Kuang-chün	Xue Guangjun	Huang Wei	Huang Wei
Hsieh K'e-hsi	Xie Kexi	Hsüeh Kung-cho	Xue Gongzhuo	Huang Yen	Huang Yan
Hsieh Li	Xie Li	Hsüeh Mu-ch'iao	Xue Muqiao	Huang Yü	Huang Yu
Hsieh Ming	Xie Ming	Hsüeh Tzu-cheng	Xue Zizheng	Huang Yü-k'un	Huang Yukun
Hsieh Pang-chih	Xie Bangzhi	Hu Chao-heng	Hu Zhaoheng	Huang Yün	Huang Yun
Hsieh Pang-ting	Xie Bangding	Hu Ch'eng-fang	Hu Chengfang	Hui Shi-kung	Hui Shigong
Hsieh Pei-yi	Xie Beiyi	Hu Ch'i-li	Hu Qili	Hui Yü-yü	Hui Yuyu
Hsieh Ping-hsin	Xie Bingxin	Hu Chi-wei	Hu Jiwei	Hung Hsüeh-chih	Hong Xuezhi
Hsieh T'ieh-kuang	Xie Tieguang	Hu Chia-pin	Hu Jiabin	Hung P'ei-lin	Hong Peilin
Hsieh T'ieh-li	Xie Tieli	Hu Ch'iao-mu	Hu Qiaomu	Hung Yi	Hong Yi
Hsieh Yün-ch'ing	Xie Yünqing	Hu Chin-ti	Hu Jindi	Huo Shi-lian	Huo Shilian
Hsin Chün-chieh	Xin Junjie	Hu Ching-jui	Hu Jingrui		
Hsin Yüan-hsi	Xin Yuanxi	Hu Chüeh-wen	Hu Juewen		
Hsing Ch'ung-chih	Xing Chongzhi	Hu Han	Hu Han	**J**	
Hsing Fang-ch'ün	Xing Fangqun	Hu Hung	Hu Hong		
Hsing Yen-tzu	Xing Yanzi	Hu K'e-shih	Hu Keshi	Jamyang Lozang	Jiamuxiang Luosang-
Hsing Yi-min	Xing Yimin	Hu Li-chiao	Hu Lijiao	Jigme Thubtan	jiumei Tudanque-
Hsing Yüan-lin	Xing Yuanlin	Hu Liang-ts'ai	Hu Liangcai	Chuji Nima	jinima
Hsiung Fu	Xiong Fu	Hu Ming	Hu Ming	Jan Kuli-ying	Ran Guiying
Hsiung Hsiang-hui	Xiong Xianghui	Hu Ping-yün	Hu Bingyun	Jan Yen-nung	Ran Yannong
Hsiung T'ien-ching	Xiong Tianjing	Hu Shang-li	Hu Shangli	Jao Cheng-hsi	Rao Zhengxi
Hsiung Tso-fang	Xiong Zuofang	Hu Sheng	Hu Sheng	Jao Hsing	Rao Xing
Hsiung Yi	Xiong Yi	Hu Sung	Hu Song	Jao Hsing-li	Rao Xingli
Hsü Chang-yü	Xu Changyu	Hu Te-hua	Hu Dehua	Jao Pin	Rao Bin
Hsü Ch'i-hai	Xu Qihai	Hu Ting-yi	Hu Dingyi	Jao Shou-k'un	Rao Shoukun
Hsü Ch'i-hsiao	Xu Qixiao	Hu Tzu-ang	Hu Ziang	Je-t'i	Raidi
Hsü Chia-t'un	Xu Jiatun	Hu Tzu-ying	Hu Ziying	Jen Chi-yü	Ren Jiyu
Hsü Chieh	Xu Jie	Hu Yao-pang	Hu Yaobang	Jen Chih-heng	Ren Zhiheng
Hsü Chien-ch'un	Xu Jianchun	Hu Yi-min	Hu Yimin	Jen Chih-pin	Ren Zhibin
Hsü Chien-sheng	Xu Jiansheng	Hu Yü-chih	Hu Yuzhi	Jen Chung-yi	Ren Zhongyi
Hsü Ch'ih	Xü Chi	Hua Kuo-feng	Hua Guofeng	Jen Ch'üan-sheng	Ren Quansheng
Hsü Ch'in	Xu Qin	Hua Lo-keng	Hua Luogeng	Jen Hsin-min	Ren Xinmin
Hsü Ch'u-p'o	Xu Chupo	Hua Ying-tung	Hua Yingdong	Jen Jung	Ren Rong
Hsü Chung-fu	Xu Zhongfu	Hua Yü-ch'ing	Hua Yuqing	Jen Keng-ch'ing	Ren Gengqing
Hsü Fei-ch'ing	Xu Feiqing	Huan Hsiang	Huan Xiang	Jen Ming-tao	Ren Mingdao
Hsü Hsiang-ch'ien	Xu Xiangqian	Huang Ch'ang-shui	Huang Changshui	Jen Pai-ke	Ren Baige
Hsü Hsiao-ping	Xu Xiaobing	Huang Chao-t'ien	Huang Zhaotian	Jen P'u-chai	Ren Puzhai
Hsü Huang	Xu Huang	Huang Chen	Huang Zhen	Jen Szu-chung	Ren Sizhong
Hsü Jen	Xu Ren	Huang Cheng-ch'ing	Huang Zhengqing	Ju Fu-yi	Ru Fuyi
				Jui Mu	Rui Mu

Jui Pan	Rui Ban	Kuan Tse-hai	Guan Zehai	Li Ch'iang	Li Qiang
Jung Kao-t'ang	Rong Gaotang	K'uang Ya-ming	Kuang Yaming	Li Ch'iao-yün	Li Qiaoyun
Jung Tzu-ho	Rong Zihe	K'uei Pi	Kui Bi	Li Chien-an	Li Jian'an
Jung Yi-jen	Rong Yiren	K'ung An-min	Kong Anmin	Li Chien-chen	Li Jianzhen
		K'ung Chao-nien	Kong Zhaonian	Li Chien-pai	Li Jianbai
		K'ung Ch'ing-te	Kong Qingde	Li Chien-p'ing	Li Jianping
K		K'ung Fei	Kong Fei	Li Chih-chung	Li Zhizhong
		K'ung Hsiang-chen	Kong Xiangzhen	Li Chih-min	Li Zhimin
Kan Ch'un-lei	Gan Chunlei	K'ung Hsiao	Kong Xiao	Li Ch'in	Li Qin
Kan Ku	Gan Gu	K'ung Shih-ch'üan	Kong Shiquan	Li Chin-te	Li Jinde
Kan Tsu-ch'ang	Gan Zuchang	Kung Ta-fei	Gong Dafei	Li Ching	Li Jing
Kan Tzu-sen	Gan Zisen	Kung T'ien-min	Gong Tianmin	Li Ch'ing	Li Qing
Kan Tzu-yü	Gan Ziyu	K'ung Ts'ung-chou	Kong Congzhou	Li Ching-chao	Li Jingzhao
Kan Wei-han	Gan Weihan	Kung Tzu-jung	Gong Zirong	Li Ching-ch'üan	Li Jingquan
Kan Yeh-t'ao	Gan Yetao	Kung Wei-chen	Gong Weizhen	Li Ch'ing-ch'üan	Li Qingquan
K'ang Chih-chieh	Kang Zhijie	K'ung Yüan	Kong Yuan	Li Ch'ing-k'uei	Lin Qingkui
K'ang K'e-ch'ing	Kang Keqing	Kuo Ch'ao	Guo Chao	Li Ching-lin	Li Jinglin
K'ang Lin	Kang Lin	Kuo Ch'eng	Guo Cheng	Li Ch'ing-wei	Li Qingwei
K'ang Mao-chao	Kang Maozhao	Kuo Ch'i-nan	Guo Qinan	Li Cho-jan	Li Zhuoran
Kang Shih-en	Kang Shien	Kuo Chien	Guo Jian	Li Ch'u-li	Li Chuli
K'ang Yung-ho	Kang Yonghe	Kuo Chih	Guo Zhi	Li Ch'uan	Li Chuan
Kao Chan-hsiang	Gao Zhanxiang	Kuo Feng-lien	Guo Fenglian	Li Chuang	Li Zhuang
Kao Ch'i-yün	Gao Qiyun	Kuo Hsi-lan	Guo Xilan	Li Ch'un-ch'ing	Li Chunqing
Kao Chien-chung	Gao Jianzhong	Kuo Hsien-jui	Guo Xianrui	Li Chung-hsüan	Li Zhongxuan
Kao Chih-kuo	Gao Zhiguo	Kuo Hua-jo	Guo Huaruo	Li Chung-yüan	Li Zhongyuan
Kao Fu-yu	Gao Fuyou	Kuo Hung-t'ao	Guo Hongtao	Li Chü-k'uei	Li Jukui
Kao Hou-liang	Gao Houliang	Kuo Jui-jen	Guo Ruiren	Li Ch'üan-chung	Li Quanzhong
Kao Hsiu	Gao Xiu	Kuo Jung-ch'ang	Guo Rongchang	Li En-ch'iu	Li Enqiu
Kao Jui	Gao Rui	Kuo Mo-jo	Guo Moruo	Li Erh-chung	Li Erzhong
Kao K'e-lin	Gao Kelin	Kuo Shu-shen	Guo Shushen	Li Fei-p'ing	Li Feiping
Kao Teng-pang	Gao Dengbang	Kuo T'i-hsiang	Guo Tixiang	Li Feng-lan	Li Fenglan
Kao T'ieh	Gao Tie	Kuo Ti-huo	Guo Dihuo	Li Feng-lou	Li Fenglou
Kao Wen-hua	Gao Wenhua	Ku Tzu-heng	Guo Ziheng	Li Feng-p'ing	Li Fengping
Kao Wen-li	Gao Wenli	Kuo Wei	Guo Wei	Li Fu-chung	Li Fuzhong
Kao Yang	Gao Yang	Kuo Wei-ch'eng	Guo Weicheng	Li Fu-ch'üan	Li Fuquan
Kao Yang-wen	Gao Yangwen	Kuo Yao-ch'ing	Guo Yaoqing	Li Fu-k'e	Li Fuke
Kao Yi	Gao Yi	Kuo Ying-ch'iu	Guo Yingqiu	Li Hai-feng	Li Haifeng
K'e Chao	Ke Zhao	Kuo Ying-fu	Guo Yingfu	Li Ho-lin	Li Helin
K'e Hua	Ke Hua	Kuo Yü-feng	Guo Yufeng	Li Hsi-ming	Li Ximing
K'e Li-keng	Ke Ligeng			Li Hsieh-po	Li Xiebo
K'e Po-nien	Ke Bonian	**L**		Li Hsien-nien	Li Xiannian
Ke Pu-hai	Ge Buhai			Li Hsüan	Li Xuan
Ke Shih-ying	Ge Shiying	Lai Chi-fa	Lai Jifa	Li Hsüeh-chih	Li Xuezhi
Keng Ch'ang-so	Geng Changsuo	Lai Ya-li	Lai Yali	Li Hua-min	Li Huamin
Keng Ch'i-ch'ang	Geng Qichang	Lai Yi	Lai Yi	Li Huang	Li Huang
Keng Piao	Geng Biao	Lan Jung-yü	Lan Rongyu	Li Jen-chih	Li Renzhi
Keng Tao-ming	Geng Daoming	Lan K'ai-min	Lan Kaimin	Li Jen-chün	Li Renjun
Kergen	Ke-li-gen	Lan Kan-t'ing	Lan Ganting	Li Jen-lin	Li Renlin
Keyum Matniyaz	Ke-you-mu-mai-ti	Lan T'ing-hui	Lan Tinghui	Li Jih-nai	Li Rinai
	Ni-ya-zi	Lei Chieh-ch'iung	Lei Jieqiong	Li Jui	Li Rui
K'ou Ch'ing-yen	Kou Qingyan	Lei Jen-min	Lei Renmin	Li Jui-huan	Li Ruihuan
Ku Chih-piao	Gu Zhibiao	Lei Yang	Lei Yang	Li Jui-shan	Li Ruishan
Ku Cho-hsin	Gu Zhuoxin	Li Ch'ang	Li Chang	Li K'ai-hsin	Li Kaixin
Ku Fang-chou	Gu Fangzhou	Li Ch'ang-an	Li Chang'an	Li K'e	Li Ke
Ku Hsiao-po	Gu Xiaobo	Li Ch'ang-lin	Li Changlin	Li K'e-ch'ang	Li Kechang
Ku Hsiu-lien	Gu Xiulian	Li Ch'ao	Li Chao	Li Kuang	Li Guang
Ku K'ang-lo	Gu Kangluo	Li Chao-chi	Li Zhaoji	Li Kuei	Li Gui
Ku Keng-yü	Gu Gengyu	Li Ch'ao-po	Li Chaobo	Li K'uei-sheng	Li Kuisheng
Ku Kung-hsü	Gu Gongxu	Li Chen	Li Zhen	Li Kuo-hao	Li Guohao
Ku Ming	Gu Ming	Li Ch'eng-fang	Li Chengfang	Li Kuo-ts'ai	Li Guocai
Ku Mu	Gu Mu	Li Cheng-kuang	Li Zhengguang	Li Li	Li Li
Ku Ta-ch'un	Gu Dachun	Li Zhengting	Li Cheng-t'ing	Li Li-an	Li Li'an
Ku Yün-t'ing	Gu Yunting	Li Ch'i	Li Qi	Li Li-kung	Li Ligong
Kuan Chien	Guan Jian	Li Chi-liang	Li Jiliang	Li Li-yin	Li Liyin
Kuan Chün-t'ing	Guan Junting	Li Ch'i-ming	Li Qiming	Li Lin	Li Lin
Kuan Hsüeh-szu	Guan Xuesi	Li Ch'i-t'ao	Li Qitao	Li Lien-ch'ing	Li Lianqing
Kuan Jui-wu	Guan Ruiwu	Li Ch'i-yang	Li Qiyang	Li Lien-pi	Li Lianbi
Kuan Shan-fu	Guan Shan-fu	Li Chia-ch'eng	Li Jiacheng	Li Lin-chih	Li Linzhi

Li Lin-ch'uan	Li Linchuan	
Li Mao-chih	Li Maozhi	
Li Meng-fu	Li Mengfu	
Li Meng-hua	Li Menghua	
Li Ming	Li Ming	
Li O-ting	Li Eding	
Li Pao-hua	Li Baohua	
Li Pao-kuang	Li Baoguang	
Li P'ei-fu	Li Peifu	
Li Pen-shan	Li Benshan	
Li Pin-san	Li Binsan	
Li Po-ning	Li Boning	
Li P'u	Li Pu	
Lu Pu-hsin	Li Buxin	
Li Shan-yi	Li Shanyi	
Li Shao-yü	Li Shaoyu	
Li Shih	Li Shi	
Li Shih-chang	Li Shizhang	
Li Shih-chi	Li Shiji	
Li Shih-chün	Li Shijun	
Li Shih-nung	Li Shinong	
Li Shih-ying	Li Shiying	
Li Shou-lin	Li Shoulin	
Li Shou-pao	Li Shoubao	
Li Shu	Li Shu	
Li Shu-cheng	Li Shuzheng	
Li Shu-pin	Li Shubin	
Li Shu-te	Li Shude	
Li Shu-ying	Li Shuying	
Li Shui-ch'ing	Li Shuiqing	
Li Su	Li Su	
Li Ta	Li Da	
Li Tai-keng	Li Daigeng	
Li T'ao	Li Tao	
Li T'ieh-cheng	Li Tiezheng	
Li T'ien-hsiang	Li Tianxiang	
Li T'ing-ch'üan	Li Tingquan	
Li T'ing-kuei	Li Tinggui	
Li T'ing-tsan	Li Tingzan	
Li Te-hua	Li Dehua	
Li Te-sheng	Li Desheng	
Li Teng-ying	Li Dengying	
Li Tse-wang	Li Zewang	
Li Tsu-ken	Li Zugen	
Li Tung-yeh	Li Dongye	
Li Tzu-ch'ao	Li Zichao	
Li Tzu-yüan	Li Ziyuan	
Li Wei-han	Li Weihan	
Li Wen-chieh	Li Wenjie	
Li Wen-ch'ing	Li Wenqing	
Li Wen-yao	Li Wenyao	
Li Wen-yi	Li Wenyi	
Li Yao-wen	Li Yaowen	
Li Yen-lu	Li Yanlu	
Li Yen-shou	Li Yanshou	
Li Yi-chang	Li Yizhang	
Li Yi-ch'ing	Li Yiqing	
Li Yi-lin	Li Yilin	
Li Yi-meng	Li Yimeng	
Li Yu-chiu	Li Youjiu	
Li Yu-wen	Li Youwen	
Li Yü-ch'ih	Li Yuchi	
Li Yü-k'uei	Li Yukui	
Li Yü-t'ang	Li Yutang	
Li Yüan	Li Yuan	
Li Yüan-ju	Li Yuanru	
Li Yün-ch'ang	Li Yunchang	
Li Yün-ch'üan	Li Yunquan	
Li Yün-ho	Li Yunhe	

Liang Ch'ang-wu	Liang Changwu
Liang Ch'eng-yeh	Liang Chengye
Liang Chi-ch'üan	Liang Jiquan
Liang Hsiang	Liang Xiang
Liang Hua-hsin	Liang Huaxin
Liang K'ai-hsüan	Liang Kaixuan
Liang Ling-kuang	Liang Lingguang
Liang Pi-yeh	Liang Biye
Liang Pu-t'ing	Liang Buting
Liang Shang-li	Liang Shangli
Liang Wei-lin	Liang Weilin
Liang Wen-ch'i	Liang Wenqi
Liang Wen-ying	Liang Wenying
Liao Ch'eng-chih	Liao Chengzhi
Liao Ch'eng-mei	Liao Chengmei
Liao Chih-kao	Liao Zhigao
Liao Ching-tan	Liao Jingdan
Liao Han-sheng	Liao Hansheng
Liao Jung-piao	Liao Rongbiao
Liao Mo-sha	Liao Mosha
Liao Sheng-tung	Liao Shengdong
Liao Shih-ch'üan	Liao Shiquan
Lien Kuan	Lian Guan
Lin Ch'ao	Lin Chao
Lin Chao-nan	Lin Zhaonan
Lin Chen-feng	Lin Zhenfeng
Lin Chi-hsin	Lin Jixin
Lin Ch'iao-chih	Lin Qiaozhi
Lin Ch'ing	Lin Qing
Lin Chung	Lin Zhong
Lin Hai-yün	Lin Haiyun
Lin Hao	Lin Hao
Lin Hsiu-te	Lin Xiude
Lin Hu-chia	Lin Hujia
Lin Lan-ying	Lin Lanying
Lin Li-ming	Lin Liming
Lin Li-yün	Lin Liyun
Lin Lin	Lin Lin
Lin Mo-han	Lin Mohan
Lin Piao	Lin Biao
Lin Pin	Lin Bin
Lin P'ing	Lin Ping
Lin Shao-nan	Lin Shaonan
Lin Sung	Lin Song
Lin T'ieh	Lin Tie
Lin Tse-sheng	Lin Zesheng
Lin Tsung-t'ang	Lin Zongtang
Lin Yi	Lin Yi
Lin Yi-hsin	Lin Yixin
Lin Yi-p'ing	Lin Yiping
Lin Yi-shan	Lin Yishan
Lin Yin-ju	Lin Yinru
Ling Yün	Ling Yun
Liu Ang	Liu Ang
Liu Ch'ang-yi	Liu Changyi
Liu Chen	Liu Zhen
Liu Chen-hua	Liu Zhenhua
Liu Chi-p'ing	Liu Jiping
Liu Chieh	Liu Jie
Liu Chien-chang	Liu Jianzhang
Liu Chien-fu	Liu Jianfu
Liu Chien-hsün	Liu Jianxun
Liu Chih-ch'iang	Liu Zhiqiang
Liu Chih-chien	Liu Zhijian
Liu Chih-p'ing	Liu Zhiping
Liu Chin-feng	Liu Jinfeng
Liu Ching-chi	Liu Jingji
Liu Ching-chih	Liu Jingzhi
Liu Ching-fan	Liu Jingfan

Liu Ch'ing-hai	Liu Qinghai
Liu Ching-p'ing	Liu Jingping
Liu Cho-fu	Liu Zhuofu
Liu Ch'un	Liu Chun
Liu Ch'un-ch'iao	Liu Chunqiao
Liu Chung-ch'ien	Liu Zhongqian
Liu Chung-hou	Liu Zhonghou
Liu Chung-jung	Liu Zhongrong
Liu Ch'ung-kuei	Liu Chonggui
Liu Chün-hsiu	Liu Junxiu
Liu Fa-hsiu	Liu Faxiu
Liu Fang	Liu Fang
Liu Fei	Liu Fei
Liu Fu	Liu Fu
Liu Fu-chih	Liu Fuzhi
Liu Fu-sheng	Liu Fusheng
Liu Hai-ch'ing	Liu Haiqing
Liu Hai-ch'üan	Liu Haiquan
Liu Ho-keng	Liu Hegeng
Liu Ho-k'ung	Liu Hekong
Liu Hou-ming	Liu Houming
Liu Hsi-ch'ang	Liu Xichang
Liu Hsi-keng	Liu Xigeng
Liu Hsi-wen	Liu Xiwen
Liu Hsi-yao	Liu Xiyao
Liu Hsiang-san	Liu Xiangsan
Liu Hsiao	Liu Xiao
Liu Hsin-ch'üan	Liu Xinquan
Liu Hsing	Liu Xing
Liu Hsing-yüan	Liu Xingyuan
Liu Hsüeh-ch'u	Liu Xuechu
Liu Hsüeh-hsin	Liu Xuexin
Liu Hua-ch'ing	Liu Huaqing
Liu Jui-ch'ing	Liu Ruiqing
Liu Jui-lung	Liu Ruilong
Liu Kang	Liu Gang
Liu Kuang-t'ao	Liu Guangtao
Liu K'un	Liu Kun
Liu Lan-po	Liu Lanbo
Liu Lan-t'ao	Liu Lantao
Liu Liang-mo	Liu Liangmo
Liu Lin	Liu Lin
Liu Ming-hui	Liu Minghui
Liu Ming-pang	Liu Mingbang
Liu Nien-chih	Liu Nianzhi
Liu Ning-yi	Liu Ningyi
Liu Pai-t'ao	Liu Baitao
Liu Pai-yü	Liu Baiyu
Liu P'ei-jung	Liu Peirong
Liu P'eng	Liu Peng
Liu Ping	Liu Bing
Liu Po-ch'eng	Liu Bocheng
Liu Shao-ch'i	Liu Shaoqi
Liu Shao-wen	Liu Shaowen
Liu Shih-hung	Liu Shihong
Liu Shu-ch'ing	Liu Shuqing
Liu Shu-chou	Liu Shuzhou
Liu Shun-yüan	Liu Shunyuan
Liu Ta-kang	Liu Dagang
Liu Ta-nien	Liu Danian
Liu Tao-sheng	Liu Daosheng
Liu T'ieh-sheng	Liu Tiesheng
Liu T'ien-fu	Liu Tianfu
Liu Ting	Liu Ding
Liu Tsung-cho	Liu Zongzhuo
Liu Tzu-hou	Liu Zihou
Liu Tzu-mo	Liu Zimo
Liu Wei	Liu Wei
Liu Wei-ming	Liu Weiming

Liu Ya-hsiung	Liu Yaxiong	Ma Hsin	Ma Xin	Niu Jui-chou	Niu Ruizhou
Liu Ya-nan	Liu Ya'nan	Ma Hsing-yüan	Ma Xingyuan	Niu P'ei-tsung	Niu Peizong
Liu Yang-ch'iao	Liu Yangqiao	Ma Hsiu-chung	Ma Xiuzhong	Niu Yin-kuan	Niu Yinguan
Liu Yi	Liu Yi	Ma Hui	Ma Hui		
Liu Yi-fu	Liu Yifu	Ma Hui-chih	Ma Huizhi	**O**	
Liu Yin	Liu Yin	Ma Hung	Ma Hong		
Liu Ying	Liu Ying	Ma Kuei-shu	Ma Guishu	Ou Chih-fu	Ou Zhifu
Liu Ying-hsien	Liu Yingxian	Ma Li	Ma Li	Ou Meng-chüeh	Ou Mengjue
Liu Yung-sheng	Liu Yongsheng	Ma Ming	Ma Ming	Ou T'ang-liang	Ou Tangliang
Liu Yung-yüan	Liu Yongyuan	Ma Mu-ming	Ma Muming		
Liu Yü-o	Liu Yu'e	Ma Pin	Ma Bin	**P**	
Lo Ch'ing-ch'ang	Luo Qingchang	Ma Szu-chung	Ma Sizhong		
Lo Ch'iu-yüeh	Luo Qiuyue	Ma Ta-yu	Ma Dayou	Pa Chin	Ba Jin
Lo Ch'iung	Luo Qiong	Ma T'eng-ai	Ma Teng'ai	Pa·sang	Basang
Lo Fan-ch'ün	Luo Fanqun	Ma Wan-ch'i	Ma Wanqi	Pa Tai	Ba Dai
Lo Jui-ch'ing	Luo Ruiqing	Ma Wan-li	Ma Wanli	Pa·t'u·pa·ken	Ba-tu-ba-gen
Lo Kuei-po	Luo Guibo	Ma Wei-hua	Ma Weihua	Pa Yi-k'ai	Ba Yikai
Lo Li-pin	Luo Libin	Ma Wen-jui	Ma Wenrui	Pai Ch'eng-ming	Bai Chengming
Lo·sang·tz'u·ch'eng	Luosangcucheng	Ma Wen-tung	Ma Wendong	Pai Chi-nien	Bai Jinian
Lo Shih-kao	Luo Shigao	Ma Yi	Ma Yi	Pai Chieh-fu	Bai Jiefu
Lo Shu-chang	Luo Shuzhang	Ma yi·nu·erh	Ma-yi-nu-er	Pai Ch'ien	Bai Qian
Lo Shu-chen	Luo Shuzhen	Ma Yin-ch'u	Ma Yinchu	Pai Chih-min	Bai Zhimin
Lo T'ien	Luo Tian	Ma Yü-huai	Ma Yuhuai	Pai Hsiang-kuo	Bai Xiangguo
Lo Yü-ch'uan	Luo Yuchuan	Ma Yün-han	Ma Yunhan	Pai Hsing-yin	Bai Xingyin
Lo Yü-ju	Luo Yuru	Mai·ho·su·te	Mahsut Teibov	Pai Hua	Bai Hua
Lu Chen-fan	Lu Zhenfan	T'ieh·yi·po·fu		Pai Ju-ping	Bai Rubing
Lu Chia-hsi	Lu Jiaxi	Mao Chi-yung	Mao Zhiyong	Pai Shou-yi	Bai Shouyi
Lu Chih-an	Lu Zhian	Mao Hsin-hsien	Mao Xinxian	Pai Tung-ts'ai	Bai Dongcai
Lu Chin-lung	Lu Jinlong	Mao Lien-chüeh	Mao Lianjue	Pak Chun Za	Bu Chunzi
Lu Chin-tung	Lu Jindong	Mao Lin	Mao Lin	P'an Chen-wu	Pan Zhenwu
Lu Chung-yang	Lu Zhongyang	Mao Ti-ch'iu	Mao Diqiu	P'an Ch'i	Pan Qi
Lu Hsü-chang	Lu Xuzhang	Mao Tse-tung	Mao Zedong	P'an Fei	Pan Fei
Lu Kuang	Lu Guang	Mao Yi-sheng	Mao Yisheng	P'an Jui-cheng	Pan Ruizheng
Lu Pei-chien	Lu Beijian	Mei Chia-sheng	Mei Jiasheng	P'an Mei-ying	Pan Meiying
Lu P'ing	Lu Ping	Mei Sung-lin	Mei Songlin	P'an Shih-hsing	Pan Shixing
Lu Sheng	Lu Sheng	Mei Yi	Mei Yi	P'an Shu	Pan Shu
Lu Sheng-ho	Lu Shenghe	Meng Ch'i	Meng Qi	P'an Yen	Pan Yan
Lu Ta	Lu Da	Meng Chi-mao	Meng Jimao	Panchen Erdeni	Banqen Erdeni
Lu Ta-tung	Lu Dadong	Meng Chia-ch'in	Meng Jiaqin	Chhoekyi-	Qoigyi Gyancan
Lu T'ien-chi	Lu Tianji	Meng Fu-lin	Meng Fulin	Gyaltsan	
Lu Ting-yi	Lu Dingyi	Meng Hsien-te	Meng Xiande	Pao Hou-ch'ang	Bao Houchang
Lu Wei	Lu Wei	Meng Tung-po	Meng Dongbo	Pao-jih lo t'ai	Bariltai
Lu Wei-chao	Lu Weizhao	Meng Ying	Meng Ying	Pebala Gelieh	Pagbalha Geleg
Lu Yü	Lu Yu	Meng Yüeh	Meng Yue	Namje	Namgyai
Lung Fei-hu	Long Feihu	Mi Kuo-chün	Mi Guojun	P'ei Ch'ang-hui	Pei Changhui
Lü Cheng-ts'ao	Lü Zhengcao	Mi Yung	Mi Yong	P'ei Chien-chang	Pei Jianzhang
Lü Chi	Lü Ji	Miao Chiu-jui	Miao Jiurui	P'ei Hsien-pai	Pei Xianbai
Lü Chien-jen	Lü Jianren	Miao P'i-yi	Miao Piyi	P'ei Li-sheng	Pei Losheng
Lü Chien-kuang	Lü Jianguang	Miao Yün-t'ai	Miao Yuntai	P'ei Shih-chang	Bei Shizhang
Lü Chih-hsien	Lü Zhixian	Min Hsüeh-sheng	Min Xuesheng	P'ei Wen-chung	Pei Wenzhong
Lü Ch'ing	Lü Qing	Min Yü	Min Yu	P'eng Chen	Peng Zhen
Lü Ho	Lü He	Mo Nai-ch'ün	Mo Naiqun	P'eng Ch'ung	Peng Chong
Lü Hsü-kuo	Lü Xuguo	Mo Wen-hsiang	Mo Wenxiang	P'eng Hua	Peng Hua
Lü K'e-pai	Lü Kebai	Mo Yen-chung	Mo Yanzhong	P'eng Kuang-wei	Peng Guangwei
Lü Shu-hsiang	Lü Shuxiang	Mou Hai-hsiu	Mou Hai-hsiu	P'eng Meng-yü	Peng Mengyu
Lü Ts'un-chieh	Lü Cunjie	Mu Ch'ing	Mu Qing	P'eng Min	Peng Min
Lü Tung	Lü Dong	Mu Lin	Mu Lin	P'eng Ming-chih	Peng Mingzhi
Lü Yü-lan	Lü Yulan	Mushayef	Mu-sha-ye-fu	Peng Shao-hui	Peng Shaohui
				P'eng Te-ching	Peng Deqing
M		**N**		Peng Te-huai	Peng Dehuai
				P'eng Ti-hsien	Peng Dixian
Ma Ch'ang-yen	Ma Changyan	Namdon Kunga	Langdun Gongga-	Pi Chi-ch'ang	Bi Jichang
Ma Chi-k'ung	Ma Jikong	Wongchug	wangqiu	Pi Chi-lung	Bi Jilong
Ma Chin-hua	Ma Jinhua	Na·mu·la	Na-mu-la	P'ing Chieh-san	Ping Jiesan
Ma Ch'ing-nien	Ma Qingnian	Ni Chih-fu	Ni Zhifu	Po Yi-po	Bo Yibo
Ma Hao-ch'ien	Ma Haoqian	Ni Ku-yin	Ni Guyin	Pu Ho	Bu He
Ma Heng-ch'ang	Ma Hengchang	Nieh Chen	Nie Zhen	Pu Ku-hsiang	Bu Guxiang
Ma Hsi-chung	Ma Xizhong	Nie Feng-chih	Nie Fengzhi	Pu Ming	Bu Ming
		Nieh Jung-chen	Nie Rongzhen		

Pu Tung-hsiu	Bu Tongxiu

R

Rigdzin Wanggyual	Renzeng Wangjie
Ruzi Turdi	Rouzi Tuerdi

S

Sa K'ung-liao	Sa K'ung-liao
Saifudin	Seypidin Äzizi
Se·yin·pa·ya·erh	Se yin ba ya er
Seng-ch'en Lo·sang Gyan ts'an	Sengqen Losang Gyancan
Sha Ch'ien-li	Sha Qianli
Shan Huai-hsiang	Shan Huaixiang
Shang Chih-t'ien	Shang Zhitian
Shang Kan	Shang Gan
Shang Tzu-chin	Shang Zijin
Shao Ching-wa	Shao Jingwa
Shao Feng	Shao Feng
Shao Jung-pin	Shao Rongbin
Shao Kung-wen	Shao Gongwen
Shen Chen-tung	Shen Zhendong
Shen Ch'i-chen	Shen Qizhen
Shen Chien	Shen Jian
Shen Chih-wei	Shen Zhiwei
Shen Ch'u-yün	Shen Chuyun
Shen Chung-yi	Shen Zhongyi
Shen Hsin-fa	Shen Xinfa
Shen Hung	Shen Hong
Shen Kuang	Shen Guang
Shen Ling	Shen Ling
Shen Mao-kung	Shen Maogong
Shen P'ing	Shen Ping
Shen T'u	Shen Tu
Shen Yen-ping	Shen Yanbing
Shen Yüan	Shen Yuan
Shen Yüeh	Shen Yue
Shen Yün-p'u	Shen Yunpu
Sheng Wan	Sheng Wan
Shih Ch'ing-sheng	Shi Qingsheng
Shi Ch'uan	Shi Chuan
Shih Chung-ch'in	Shi Zongqin
Shih Hsiang-sheng	Shi Xiangsheng
Shih Huai-pi	Shi Huaibi
Shih Ju-wei	Shi Ruwei
Shih-kuang-hua	Shi Guanghua
Shih Lai-ho	Shi Laihe
Shih Li-te	Shi Lide
Shih·Liang	Shi Liang
Shih Lin	Shi Lin
Shih Pang-chih	Shi Bangzhi
Shih Tzu-ming	Shi Ziming
Shih Yi	Shi Yi
Shih Yi-chih	Shi Yizhi
Shih Yü-lin	Shi Yulin
Shu T'ung	Shu Tong
Shuai Meng-ch'i	Shuai Mengqi
Su Chan	Su Zhan
Su Chen-hua	Su Zhenhua
Su Ching	Su Jing
Su Kang	Su Gang
Su Pu-ch'ing	Su Buqing
Su Tzu-heng	Su Ziheng
Su Yi-jan	Su Yiran

Su Yü	Su Yu
Sun Ch'eng-p'ei	Sun Chengpei
Sun Chi-hsien	Sun Jixian
Sun Ch'i-meng	Sun Qimeng
Sun Ching-wen	Sun Jingwen
Sun Chün-jen	Sun Junren
Sun Fu-ling	Sun Fuling
Sun Hao	Sun Hao
Sun Hsiao-feng	Sun Xiaofeng
Sun Hsiao-ts'un	Sun Xiaocun
Sun Hsüeh-mei	Sun Xuemei
Sun Hung-chen	Sun Hongzhen
Sun Kuo-chih	Sun Guozhi
Sun Lan-feng	Sun Lanfeng
Sun P'ing	Sun Ping
Sun P'ing-hua	Sun Pinghua
Sun Sheng-wei	Sun Shengwei
Sun So-ch'ang	Sun Suochang
Sun Ta-kuang	Sun Daguang
Sun Tzu-yüan	Sun Ziyuan
Sun Yeh-fang	Sun Yefang
Sun Yi	Sun Yi
Sun Yu-yü	Sun Youyu
Sun Yü-t'ing	Sun Yuting
Sung Chen-ming	Song Zhenming
Sung Chen-t'ing	Song Zhenting
Sung Ch'eng-chih	Song Chengzhi
Sung Chi-wen	Song Jiwen
Sung Chieh-han	Song Jiehan
Sung Chih-ho	Song Zhihe
Sung Chih-kuang	Song Zhiguang
Sung Ch'ing-ling	Song Qingling
Sung Ch'ing-yu	Song Qingyou
Sung Chung	Song Zhong
Sung Han-yi	Song Hanyi
Sung Hsi-lien	Song Xilian
Sung Hsiao-p'eng	Song Xiaopeng
Sung Jen-ch'iung	Song Renqiong
Sung Kan-fu	Song Kanfu
Sung Lin	Song Lin
Sung P'ing	Song Ping
Sung Shih-lun	Song Shilun
Sung Yang-ch'u	Song Yangchu
Sung Yi-min	Song Yimin
Sung Yi-p'ing	Song Yiping
Sung Yu-t'ien	Song Youtian
Szu ma yi Ai mai t'i	Ismail Amat
Szu·ma·yi Ya·sheng no·fu	Si-ma-yi Ya-sheng-nuo-fu
Szu-t'u Hui-min	Situ Huimin

T

Tai Kuang-ch'ien	Dai Guangqian
Tai P'ei-chen	Dai Peizhen
Tai P'ing	Dai Ping
Tai Su-li	Dai Suli
Tai Wei-jan	Dai Weiran
T'an Chen-lin	Tan Zhenlin
T'an Cheng	Tan Zheng
T'an Ch'i-lung	Tan Qilong
T'an Chia-chen	Tan Jiazhen
T'an Kuang-san	Tan Guansan
T'an Li-jen	Tan Liren
T'an Shan-ho	Tan Shanhe
T'an Wei-hsü	Tan Weixu
T'an Wen-chen	Tan Wenzhen
T'an Yü-pao	Tan Yubao

T'an Yün-ho	Tan Yunhe
T'ang Ao-ch'ing	Tang Aoqing
T'ang Hung-kuang	Tang Hongguang
T'ang K'e	Tang Ke
T'ang K'e-pi	Tang Kebi
T'ang Liang	Tang Liang
T'ang P'ei-sung	Tang Peisong
T'ang T'ien-chi	Tang Tianji
T'ang Tzu-an	Tang Zian
T'ang Wen-sheng	Tang Wensheng
T'ang Yüan-ping	Tang Yuanbing
T'ao Ch'i	Tao Qi
T'ao Chih-yüeh	Tao Zhiyue
T'ao Chu	Tao Zhu
T'ao Han-chang	Tao Hanzhang
T'ao Hsi-chin	Tao Xijin
Tao Kuo-tung	Dao Guodong
T'ao T'ao	Tao Tao
Tao Tung-t'ing	Dao Dongting
Teng Chao-hsiang	Deng Zhaoxiang
Teng Chia-t'ai	Deng Jiatai
Teng Chu-min	Deng Chumin
Teng Hsiao-p'ing	Deng Xiaoping
Teng Hua	Deng Hua
Teng Kuo-chung	Deng Guozhong
Teng Li-ch'ün	Deng Liqun
Teng Tien-t'ao	Deng Diantao
Teng Ying-ch'ao	Deng Yingchao
Teng Yüeh	Deng Yue
Ti Ching-hsiang	Di Jingxiang
Ti Ch'ü-ch'ü	Di Ququ
T'ieh·mu·erh Ta·wa·mai·t'i	Tomur Dawamat
T'ieh Ying	Tie Ying
T'ien Chih-tung	Tian Zhidong
T'ien Chung	Tian Zhong
T'ien Fu-ta	Tian Fuda
T'ien Hsiu-ch'üan	Tian Xiuquan
T'ien Pao	Tian Bao
T'ien P'ing	Tian Ping
T'ien Ying	Tian Ying
Ting Ch'ang-hua	Ding Changhua
Ting Hao	Ding Hao
Ting Hsüeh-sung	Ding Xuesong
Ting K'e-tse	Ding Keze
Ting Kuang-hsün	Ding Guangxun
Ting Kuo-yü	Ding Guoyu
Ting Ling	Ding Ling
T'ing Mao	Ting Mao
Ting Yi-min	Ding Yimin
T'o·hu·t'i Sha·pi·erh	Tuo-hu-ti Sha-bi-er
Ts'ai Ch'ang	Cai Chang
Ts'ai Feng-lan	Cai Fenglan
Ts'ai Hsiao	Cai Xiao
Ts'ai Pang-hua	Cai Banghua
Ts'ai·tan·Cho·ma	Caidan Zhuoma
Ts'ai Tsu-ch'üan	Cai Zuquan
Ts'ai Tzu-wei	Cai Ziwei
Tsang Po-p'ing	Zang Boping
Ts'ao Ch'ih	Cao Chi
Ts'ao Chü-ju	Cao Juru
Ts'ao Ke-ch'iang	Cao Keqiang
Ts'ao Kuang-hua	Cao Guanghua
Ts'ao Li-huai	Cao Lihuai
Ts'ao Szu-ming	Cao Siming
Ts'ao ta no fu	Cao-da-nuo-fu
Ts'ao Wei-lien	Cao Weilian
Ts'ao Wen-chü	Cao Wenju

Ts'ao Yi-ou	Cao Yiou
Ts'ao Yu-min	Cao Youmin
Ts'ao Yü	Cao Yu
Ts'en Kuo-jung	Cen Guorong
Tseng Ch'eng-k'uei	Zeng Chengkui
Tseng Chih	Zeng Zhi
Tseng Ch'uan-liu	Zeng Chuanliu
Tseng Han-chou	Zeng Hanzhou
Tseng Hsien-chih	Zeng Xianzhi
Tseng San	Zeng San
Tseng Shao-shan	Zeng Shaoshan
Tseng Sheng	Zeng Sheng
Tseng Szu-yü	Zeng Siyu
Tseng T'ao	Zeng Tao
Tseng Te-lin	Zeng Delin
Tseng Ting-shih	Zeng Dingshi
Tseng Yung-ch'üan	Zeng Yongquan
Tso Ch'ung-yi	Zuo Chongyi
Tso Mo-yeh	Zuo Moye
Tsou Chia-hua	Zou Jiahua
Tsou Chia-yu	Zou Jiayou
Tsou T'ung	Zou Tong
Tsou Yü	Zou Yu
Ts'ui Chien	Cui Jian
Ts'ui Ch'ün	Cui Qun
Ts'ui Kuang-hua	Cui Guanghua
Ts'ui P'ing	Cui Ping
Ts'ui Yen-hsü	Cui Yanxu
Ts'ui Yüeh-li	Cui Yueli
Tsung Hsi-yün	Zong Xiyun
Tsung K'e-wen	Zong Kewen
Tu Chin-fang	Du Jinfang
Tu Ch'un-yung	Du Chunyong
Tu Hsin-po	Du Xinbo
Tu Hsin-yüan	Du Xinyuan
Tu Hsing-yüan	Du Xingyuan
Tu Hsüeh-jan	Du Xueran
Tu Jun-sheng	Du Runsheng
Tu P'ing	Du Ping
Tu Tzu-tuan	Du Ziduan
Tu Yi	Du Yi
Tu Yi-te	Du Yide
Tu Yü-ming	Du Yuming
Tu Yü-yün	Du Yuyun
Tuan Chün-yi	Duan Junyi
Tuan Huan-ching	Duan Huanjing
Tuan Tzu-chün	Duan Zijun
Tuan Yün	Duan Yun
Tun Hsing-yün	Dun Xingyun
Tung Ch'i-wu	Dong Qiwu
Tung Chih-wen	Dong Zhiwen
Tung Ch'un-ts'ai	Dong Chuncai
T'ung Hsiao-p'eng	Tong Xiaopeng
T'ung Kuo-kuei	Tong Guogui
Tung Pi-wu	Dong Biwu
Tung Pien	Dong Bian
T'ung Shao-sheng	Tong Shaosheng
T'ung Ta-lin	Tong Dalin
Tung T'ien-chen	Dong Tianzhen
Tz'u jen la mu	Cirenlamu
Tzu Yao-hua	Zi Yaohua

U

Ulanfu	Ulanhu

W

Wachamuchi	Wa-zha-mu-ji
Wan Fu	Wan Fu
Wan Li	Wan Li
Wan Ta	Wan Da
Wan Yi	Wan Yi
Wang Chan-yüan	Wang Zhanyuan
Wang Ch'ao-chu	Wang Chaozhu
Wang Chao-hua	Wang Zhaohua
Wang Chao-jung	Wang Zhaorong
Wang Chao-wen	Wang Zhaowen
Wang Chen	Wang Zhen
Wang Chen-chiang	Wang Zhenjiang
Wang Chen-wen	Wang Zhenwen
Wang Cheng	Wang Zheng
Wang Ch'eng-han	Wang Ch'enghan
Wang Jiyuan	Wang Chi-yüan
Wang Chien	Wang Jian
Wang Ch'ien	Wang Qian
Wang Chien-an	Wang Jian'an
Wang Chien-shih	Wang Jianshi
Wang Chih-kuo	Wang Zhiguo
Wang Chih-pang	Wang Zhibang
Wang Chin-ch'uan	Wang Jinchuan
Wang Chin-hsiang	Wang Jinxiang
Wang Chin-ling	Wang Jinling
Wang Chin-shan	Wang Jinshan
Wang Chin-tzu	Wang Jinzi
Wang Chin-yu	Wang Jinyou
Wang Ching-chih	Wang Jingzhi
Wang Ching-jung	Wang Jingrong
Wang Chu-hsi	Wang Zhuxi
Wang Ch'uan	Wang Chuan
Wang Ch'uan-pin	Wang Chuanbin
Wang Ch'un	Wang Chun
Wang Chung	Wang Zhong
Wang Ch'ung-chih	Wang Chongzhi
Wang Ch'ung-li	Wang Chongli
Wang Ch'ung-lun	Wang Chonglun
Wang Chung-yin	Wang Zhongyin
Wang Ch'üan-kuo	Wang Quanguo
Wang Chün	Wang Jun
Wang Junchao	Wang Chün-shao
Wang En-hui	Wang Enhui
Wang En-mao	Wang Enmao
Wang Fang	Wang Fang
Wang Feng	Wang Feng
Wang Fu	Wang Fu
Wang Fu-chih	Wang Fuzhi
Wang Hai-jung	Wang Hairong
Wang Hai-su	Wang Haisu
Wang Han-chang	Wang Hanzhang
Wang Ho-shou	Wang Heshou
Wang Ho-t'ing	Wang Heting
Wang Hsi	Wang Xi
Wang Hsi-p'ing	Wang Xiping
Wang Hsiao-pin	Wang Xiaobin
Wang Hsiao-tz'u	Wang Xiaoci
Wang Hsiao-yi	Wang Xiaoyi
Wang Hsiao-yün	Wang Xiaoyun
Wang Hsien	Wang Xian
Wang Hsin-san	Wang Xinsan
Wang Hsiu-hsiu	Wang Xiuxiu
Wang Hsüeh-wen	Wang Xuewen
Wang Hsüeh-ying	Wang Xueying
Wang Hui	Wang Hui
Wang Hui-te	Wang Huide
Wang Hung-wen	Wang Hongwen
Wang Jen-chung	Wang Renzhong
Wang Jen-san	Wang Rensan
Wang Ruojie	Wang Jo-chieh
Wang Jo-shui	Wang Ruoshui
Wang Jui-t'ing	Wang Ruiting
Wang Jun-sheng	Wang Runsheng
Wang Kan-ch'ang	Wang Ganchang
Wang K'e-chün	Wang Kejun
Wang K'e-tung	Wang Kedong
Wang K'e-wen	Wang Kewen
Wang K'uan-ch'eng	Wang Kuancheng
Wang K'uang	Wang Kuang
Wang Kuang-chung	Wang Guangzhong
Wang Kuang-mei	Wang Guangmei
Wang Kuang-ying	Wang Guangqing
Wang Kuang-yü	Wang Guangyu
Wang K'un-lun	Wang Kunlun
Wang Kuo-ch'üan	Wang Guoquan
Wang Kuo-fan	Wang Guofan
Wang Lan-hsi	Wang Lanxi
Wang Lei	Wang Lei
Wang Li	Wang Li
Wang Li-chih	Wang Lizhi
Wang Lin	Wang Lin
Wang Lin-ho	Wang Linhe
Wang Liu-sheng	Wang Liusheng
Wang Lu-ming	Wang Luming
Wang Mao-ch'üan	Wang Maoquan
Wang Mao-lin	Wang Maolin
Wang Meng	Wang Meng
Wang Min-sheng	Wang Minsheng
Wang Ming-chang	Wang Mingzhang
Wang Ning	Wang Ning
Wang Pi-cheng	Wang Bicheng
Wang Pin	Wang Bin
Wang P'ing	Wang Ping
Wang Ping-ch'ien	Wang Bingqian
Wang Ping-hsiang	Wang Bingxiang
Wang Ping-nan	Wang Bingnan
Wang Ping-shih	Wang Bingshi
Wang Ping-yün	Wang Bingyun
Wang Po-p'ing	Wang Boping
Wang Shang-jung	Wang Shangrong
Wang Shao-yen	Wang Shaoyan
Wang Shih-hsien	Wang Shixian
Wang Shih-kuang	Wang Shiguang
Wang Shih-t'ai	Wang Shitai
Wang Shou-kuan	Wang Shouguan
Wang Shou-tao	Wang Shoudao
Wang Shu	Wang Shu
Wang Shu-sheng	Wang Shusheng
Wang Ta-heng	Wang Daheng
Wang Ta-jen	Wang Daren
Wang T'ao	Wang Tao
Wang Tao-han	Wang Daohan
Wang Te	Wang De
Wang Te-chao	Wang Dezhao
Wang Te-jun	Wang Derun
Wang T'ing-tung	Wang Tingdong
Wang To	Wang Duo
Wang Tou-kuang	Wang Douguang
Wang Tsai-t'ien	Wang Zaitian
Wang Ts'ao-li	Wang Caoli
Wang Tse	Wang Ze
Wang Tse-chiu	Wang Zejiu
Wang Tsung-chin	Wang Zongjin
Wang Ts'ung-wu	Wang Congwu

Wang Tung	Wang Dong
Wang Tung-hsing	Wang Dongxing
Wang Tung-pao	Wang Dongbao
Wang Tzu-kang	Wang Zigang
Wang Tzu-yeh	Wang Ziye
Wang Tzu-yi	Wang Ziyi
Wang Wan-lin	Wang Wanlin
Wang Wei	Wang Wei
Wang Wei-kang	Wang Weigang
Wang Wei-ts'ai	Wang Weicai
Wang Wen-lin	Wang Wenlin
Wang Yang	Wang Yang
Wang Yao-hua	Wang Yaohua
Wang Yao-t'ing	Wang Yaoting
Wang Yeh-ch'iu	Wang Yeqiu
Wang Yen	Wang Yan
Wang Yen-ch'ang	Wang Yanchang
Wang Yi	Wang Yi
Wang Yi-lun	Wang Yilun
Wang Yi-p'ing	Wang Yiping
Wang Ying-chung	Wang Yingzhong
Wang Ying-lai	Wang Yinglai
Wang Yu-p'ing	Wang Youping
Wang Yung-hsing	Wang Yongxing
Wang Yü-ch'ing	Wang Yuqing
Wang Yüeh-hsia	Wang Yuexia
Wang Yüeh-yi	Wang Yueyi
Wang Yün-sheng	Wang Yunsheng
Wei Chen-wu	Wei Zhenwu
Wei Ch'eng-yi	Wei Chengyi
Wei Chieh	Wei Jie
Wei Chih-min	Wei Zhimin
Wei Ch'uan-t'ung	Wei Chuantong
Wei Feng-ch'i	Wei Fengqi
Wei Feng-ying	Wei Fengying
Wei Hsin-yi	Wei Xinyi
Wei Hsing-cheng	Wei Xingzheng
Wei Kuo-ch'ing	Wei Guoqing
Wei Pao-shan	Wei Baoshan
Wei Wen-pao	Wei Wenbao
Wei Yongqing	Wei Yung-ch'ing
Wei Yü-ming	Wei Yuming
Wen Chia-szu	Wen Jiasi
Wen Fu-shan	Wen Fushan
Wen Hsiang-lan	Wen Xianglan
Wen Min-sheng	Wen Minsheng
Wen Ning	Wen Ning
Wen Yeh-chan	Wen Yezhan
Weng Tu-chien	Weng Dujian
Wu Ch'eng-ch'ing	Wu Chengqing
Wu Chieh-p'ing	Wu Jieping
Wu Chih-ch'ao	Wu Zhichao
Wu Chih-chung	Wu Zhizhong
Wu Chin-ch'üan	Wu Jinquan
Wu Ching-hua	Wu Jinghua
Wu Ch'ing-t'ung	Wu Qingtong
Wu Chung	Wu Zhong
Wu Ch'üan-ch'ing	Wu Quanqing
Wu Ch'üan-heng	Wu Quanheng
Wu Chüeh-nung	Wu Juenong
Wu Fu-shan	Wu Fushan
Wu Han	Wu Han
Wu Heng	Wu Heng
Wu Hsi-hai	Wu Xihai
Wu Hsiang-pi	Wu Xiangbi
Wu Hsiao-ta	Wu Xiaoda
Wu Hsien-en	Wu Xianen
Wu Hsien-feng	Wu Xianfeng
Wu Hsien-wen	Wu Xianwen

Wu Hsin-yü	Wu Xinyu
Wu Hsiu-ch'üan	Wu Xiuquan
Wu Hsüeh-ch'ien	Wu Xueqian
Wu Hsüeh-chih	Wu Xuezhi
Wu Hsüeh-yi	Wu Xueyi
Wu Huan-hsing	Wu Huanxing
Wu Hung-hsiang	Wu Hongxiang
Wu Hung-pin	Wu Hongbin
Wu Huo-chin	Wu Huojin
Wu Jui-shan	Wu Ruishan
Wu K'ai-chang	Wu Kaizhang
Wu K'e-hua	Wu Kehua
Wu Kuang-t'ang	Wu Guangtang
Wu Kuei-hsien	Wu Guixian
Wu Lan-t'ing	Wu Lanting
Wu Leng-hsi	Wu Lengxi
Wu Liang-p'ing	Wu Liangping
Wu Mao-sun	Wu Maosun
Wu Nan-sheng	Wu Nansheng
Wu Po	Wu Bo
Wu Shao-tsu	Wu Shaozu
Wu Shao-wen	Wu Shaowen
Wu Sheng-min	Wu Shengmin
Wu Shih-hung	Wu Shihong
Wu Su	Wu Su
Wu Tai	Wu Dai
Wu Tai-feng	Wu Daifeng
Wu Te	Wu De
Wu Tso-jen	Wu Zuoren
Wu Tso-min	Wu Zuomin
Wu Wen-chün	Wu Wenjun
Wu Yeh-shan	Wu Yeshan
Wu Yi-fang	Wu Yifang
Wu Ying-k'ai	Wu Yingkai
Wu Yü-pu	Wu Yubu

Y

Ya-pu-lung	Ya-bu-long
Yang Chan-t'ao	Yang Zhantao
Yang Ch'ao	Yang Chao
Yang Chen	Yang Zhen
Yang Ch'eng-chung	Yang Chengzhong
Yang Cheng-min	Yang Zhengmin
Yang Ch'eng-tsung	Yang Chengzong
Yang Ch'eng-wu	Yang Chengwu
Yang Chi	Yang Ji
Yang Chi-k'e	Yang Jike
Yang Ch'i-liang	Yang Qiliang
Yang Chia-hsiang	Yang Jiaxiang
Yang Chia-jui	Yang Jiarui
Yang Ch'iao-ling	Yang Qiaoling
Yang Chieh	Yang Jie
Yang Chih-lin	Yang Zhilin
Yang Ch'ing-jen	Yang Jingren
Yang Ch'un	Yang Chun
Yang Chung	Yang Zhong
Yang Chüeh	Yang Jue
Yang Chün-sheng	Yang Junsheng
Yang Fang-chih	Yang Fangzhi
Yang Fu-chen	Yang Fuzhen
Yang Han-sheng	Yang Hansheng
Yang Hsi-kuang	Yang Xiguang
Yang Hsien-chen	Yang Xianzhen
Yang Hsien-tung	Yang Xiandong
Yang Hsin-p'ei	Yang Xinpei
Yang Hsiu-feng	Yang Xiufeng
Yang Ju-tai	Yang Rudai

Yang K'ai	Yang Kai
Yang K'ang-hua	Yang Kanghua
Yang K'e-ch'eng	Yang Kecheng
Yang K'e-ming	Yang Keming
Yang K'eng	Yang Keng
Yang Kung-su	Yang Gongsu
Yang Kuo-fu	Yang Guofu
Yang Kuo-yü	Yang Guoyu
Yang Li-kung	Yang Ligong
Yang-ling P'o-chi	Yangling Puoji
Yang Mo	Yang Mo
Yang Po	Yang Bo
Yang Shang-k'uei	Yang Shangkui
Yang Shang-k'un	Yang Shangkun
Yang Shih-chieh	Yang Shijie
Yang Shih-fa	Yang Shifa
Yang Shih-hsien	Yang Shixian
Yang Shou-cheng	Yang Shouzheng
Yang Shou-shan	Yang Shoushan
Yang Shu	Yang Shu
Yang Ta-yi	Yang Dayi
Yang Te-chih	Yang Dezhi
Yang T'i	Yang Ti
Yang T'ien-fang	Yang Tianfang
Yang T'ing-pao	Yang Tingbao
Yang Tsung-hsin	Yang Zongxin
Yang Tung-sheng	Yang Dongsheng
Yang Wan-hsüan	Yang Wanxuan
Yang Wei-p'ing	Yang Weiping
Yang Yeh-p'eng	Yang Yepeng
Yang Yen	Yang Yan
Yang Yen-sen	Yang Yensen
Yang Yi-ch'en	Yang Yichen
Yang Yung	Yang Yong
Yang Yi-pang	Yang Yibang
Yang Yung-liang	Yang Yongliang
Yang Yün-yü	Yang Yunyu
Yao Chin	Yao Jin
Yao Chung-ming	Yao Zhongming
Yao Kuang	Yao Guang
Yao Mao-ch'i	Yao Maoqi
Yao Shih-ch'ang	Yao Shichang
Yao Wen-yüan	Yao Wenyuan
Yao Yi-lin	Yao Yilin
Yeh Ch'eng-chang	Ye Chengzhang
Yeh Chien-min	Ye Jianmin
Yeh Chien-ying	Ye Jianying
Yeh Chih-ch'iang	Ye Zhiqiang
Yeh Chu-ch'üan	Ye Zhuquan
Yeh Fei	Ye Fei
Yeh Lin	Ye Lin
Yeh Sheng-t'ao	Ye Shengtao
Yeh Shu-hua	Ye Shuhua
Yeh Tao-ying	Ye Daoying
Yen Chi-min	Yan Jimin
Yen Chi-tz'u	Yan Jici
Yen Chih-hsiang	Yan Zhixiang
Yen Chin-sheng	Yan Jinsheng
Yen Hsin-min	Yan Xinmin
Yen K'e-lun	Yan Kelun
Yen K'uei-yao	Yan Kuiyao
Yen Ta-k'ai	Yan Dakai
Yen Te-ming	Yan Deming
Yen Te-yi	Yan Deyi
Yen Tun-shih	Yan Dunshi
Yen Wu-hung	Yan Wuhong
Yen Yu-min	Yan Youmin
Yi Li-jung	Yi Lirong
Yi Mei-hou	Yi Meihou

Yi·mi·no·fu Ha·mi·t'i	Yi·min·nuo·fu Ha·mi·ti	Yü K'e	Yu Ke
Yi Shih-ch'üan	Yi Shiquan	Yü Kuang-mao	Yu Guangmao
Yin Che	Yin Zhe	Yü Kuang-yüan	Yu Guangyuan
Yin Chung-wei	Yin Zhongwei	Yü Ming	Yu Ming
Yin Linping	Yin Lin-p'ing	Yü Ming-t'ao	Yu Mingtao
Yin Tsan-hsün	Yin Zanxun	Yü P'ei-wen	Yu Peiwen
Yin Tso-chen	Yin Zuozhen	Yü P'ing	Yu Ping
Yin Tzu-ming	Yin Ziming	Yü Pu-hsüeh	Yu Buxue
Yu T'ai-chung	You Taizhong	Yü Sang	Yu Sang
Yung Wen-t'ao	Yong Wentao	Yü Shu-te	Yu Shude
Yü Ai-feng	Yu Aifeng	Yü Ta-fu	Yu Dafu
Yü Chan	Yu Zhan	Yü Wen	Yu Wen
Yü Chieh	Yu Jie	Yü Yi-ch'uan	Yu Yichuan
Yü Chien-t'ing	Yu Jianting	Yü Yi-fu	Yu Yifu
Yü Ch'iu-li	Yu Qiuli	Yüan Chen	Yuan Zhen
Yü Hung-liang	Yu Hongliang	Yüan Fang-lieh	Yuan Fanglie

Yüan Hsüeh-fen	Yuan Xuefen
Yüan Jen-yüan	Yuan Renyuan
Yüan K'e-fu	Yuan Kefu
Yüan Lu-lin	Yuan Lulin
Yüan Pao-hua	Yuan Baohua
Yüan Sheng-p'ing	Yuan Shengping
Yüeh Chih-chien	Yue Zhijian
Yüeh Hsiao-hsiao	Yue Xiaoxiao
Yüeh Hsin	Yue Xin
Yüeh Liang	Yue Liang
Yüeh Mei-chung	Yue Meizhong
Yüeh Tai-heng	Yue Daiheng
Yüeh Tsung-t'ai	Yue Zongtai
Yüeh Wei-fan	Yue Weifan
Yün Pei-feng	Yun Beifeng
Yün Shih-ying	Yun Shiying